Gun Digest 2019

Photo: Vista Outdoors

Edited by
JERRY LEE

Published by

Gun Digest® Books, an imprint of Caribou Media
Gun Digest Media, 5600 W. Grande Market Drive, Suite 100
Appleton, WI 54913
www.gundigest.com

To order books or other products call 920.471.4522 ext. 104
or visit us online at **www.gundigeststore.com**

CAUTION: Technical data presented here, particularly technical data on handloading and on firearms adjustment and alteration, inevitably reflects individual experience with particular equipment and components under specific circumstances the reader cannot duplicate exactly. Such data presentations therefore should be used for guidance only and with caution. Caribou Media accepts no responsibility for results obtained using these data.

ISBN 13: 978-1-946267-34-4
ISBN 10: 1-946267-34-1

Cover Design by Gregory S. Krueger
Interior Design by Dave Hauser & Jeromy Boutwell

Edited by Jerry Lee & Corey Graff

Printed in the United States of America

10 9 8 7 6 5 4 3 2 1

John T. Amber LITERARY AWARD

Phil Massaro

Phil's wife Suzanne often accompanies him on his hunting adventures, making safaris like this one a family affair.

The John T. Amber Literary Award is named for the editor of *Gun Digest* from 1950 to 1979, a period that could be called the heyday of gun and outdoor writing. Amber worked with many of the legends in the business during his almost 30 years with the book, including the great shooting and hunting writer, Townsend Whelen. In 1967, Amber instituted an award to honor each year an outstanding author of *Gun Digest*, which he named for Whelen. In 1982, three years after Amber's retirement, the award was renamed in his honor.

I am pleased to announce that this year's John T. Amber Literary Award goes to Phil Massaro. Each year, a contributor to the previous year's edition of *Gun Digest* is presented with the award in recognition of the author's knowledge of the subject matter, and for the ability to inform and entertain the reader. This year's award goes to Phil for his excellent story, "British Style, German Engineered," a review of the Heym 39B double rifle on safari in Africa.

Born and raised in New York's Hudson Valley, Phil Massaro has spent his life hunting, hiking and exploring the vast wildernesses the state has to offer. Massaro began his love affair with the outdoors as a young boy, accompanying his father on hunting and trapping excursions and being taught not only proper shooting techniques but firearms safety. Being raised in a hunting family, the spark was there early on, and backpack hunts into the Catskills and Adirondack Mountains fueled a strong desire to hunt abroad. He has made seven safaris to Africa, as well as having hunted Europe, Australia and numerous trips across North America. With a passion for big game, especially the large, dangerous species, he developed a love of larger centerfire rifles, and the wild places of the world.

Massaro is an avid handloader and, as president of Massaro Ballistics Laboratories, he creates custom ammunition for his clients. His love of handloading led to a working knowledge of internal, external and terminal ballistics as a science, with practical application to a variety of field conditions, from long-range target shooting to the pursuit of the largest animals on earth. He has written several books for Gun Digest Books, including *The Shooter's Guide to Reloading*, *Understanding Ballistics: Complete Guide to Bullet Selection*, and *Big Book of Ballistics*, as well as being a regular contributor to *Gun Digest the Magazine* and others. He is the Ammunition, Ballistics and Components editor for *Gun Digest*, as well as a regular contributor, and is a co-host of the *Modern Shooter* television show, in addition to frequently appearing on other hunting programs.

A Life Member of the NRA, he is passionate about the 2nd Amendment and individual firearms rights, as well as preserving the right to hunt for future generations. Phil still lives in Upstate New York, with his beautiful wife Suzanne.

Congratulations to the recipient of this year's John T. Amber award, the very talented, knowledgeable, and personable Phil Massaro!

– Jerry Lee, Editor

WELCOME

to the 2019 Gun Digest, the 73rd annual edition of the World's Greatest Gun Book!

by Jerry Lee

We've put together for your reading pleasure a collection of gun stories, technical articles, firearms history, shooting tests and field reports by some of the top shooting and outdoor writers. Whichever category in the gun world you enjoy, we hope you'll find in these pages a combination of entertainment and information on your favorite subject.

HIGHLIGHTS OF THIS EDITION

Some of the great old names in guns are featured this year — legendary brands such as Rigby, Westley-Richards, and Browning — and lesser-known but important guns in history like Baker and Fusil Daudeteau. Wayne van Zwoll writes about the Rigby Resurrection with a new rifle called the Highland Stalker and, as the name suggests, trekking in the hills of Scotland after red stag. (He had a good excuse as to why he was not successful.) Phil Massaro tells the story about bringing a German Gehwehr 8x57 Mauser back to life with a custom rifle chambered in .318 Westley-Richards, a great 100-year old cartridge. Our Browning article is a sad one, a eulogy by Patrick Sweeney to the Hi Power, the world's first high-capacity 9mm, which Browning has decided to put out to pasture after 83 years of service.

If older military rifles are your thing, you'll like Jeff John's story on the Baker rifles of the British 95th Rifles and their ability to apply violence "four times the range of rebuttal." He illustrates this with some great photography. By the way, we're glad to welcome Jeff to the pages of *Gun Digest*. He and I go back to our California days with *Guns & Ammo* and *Rifle Shooter*, and we each had a turn as editor of *Guns*. Paul Scarlata shares his list of favorite "strange" rifles he has known, George Layman profiles Russia's Mosin-Nagant of 1944, one of the last of the Cold War rifles that is still in service.

Harry Selby was a legend among professional hunters in Africa in the last century. Joe Coogan was a PH himself and a friend of Harry's. He writes a wonderful tribute to this great hunter who played a major role in the world of the African safari. We also want to welcome Joe to *Gun Digest*. The previous editor of *Petersen's Hunting*, he has hunted all over the world. Another warm personal story is Terry Wieland's tribute to his uncle and the importance of remembering members of the greatest generation and their guns. Terry is one of the best storytellers in the business and "A Private Valour" is a fine example. Another personal look at one's guns and what to do with them later in life is Tom Caceci's "Letting Go." It's about a time that we all are likely to face one day.

For handgunners, we have Nick Sisley's piece on the great .45 Colt, Bob Campbell's profile of the Smith & Wesson Combat Magnum, AKA Model 19. Jim Wilson looks at cop guns, then and now, and Patrick Sweeney tells all about his favorite 1911. Tom Tabor shares a story in the One Good Gun section about another 1911, his brother's GI .45. Also under the One Good Gun umbrella, our pal Rick Hacker presents his love and respect for Dirty Harry's favorite, the Model 29 Smith & Wesson, the .44 Magnum, "the most powerful handgun in the world."

Another welcome to *Gun Digest* goes out to Shane Jahn down in Texas. "Guns of the Brite Ranch Raid" gives us a piece of history, looking back at those times along the Texas/Mexico border 100 years ago when *bandidos* and cowboys were in what could be called a war zone.

Our catalog section provides a buyer's guide to virtually every gun currently on the market in the USA, and the updated ballistics tables provide data on every rifle, handgun and shotgun load you will find at your local gun store. This year we have added something new, a Report from the Field devoted to airguns, one of the fastest growing categories in the industry.

Since the last edition of *Gun Digest* went to press there have unfortunately been several more mass shooting incidents in the country. News coverage in the mainstream media has been focused more on the guns than on the shooters who pulled the trigger. Some of the usual suspects in the anti-gun movement are openly challenging the Second Amendment and whether it applies in today's world. How far this attack on gun owners and manufacturers will go is hard to predict.

A new approach against the industry involves tactics to try to stop financial institutions from doing business with the gun makers. This is an attempt to cripple or shut down some gun manufacturers or even the entire industry. Some banks and credit card companies have agreed to cut ties with the gun industry while others seem temporarily restrained from jumping on the politically correct bandwagon. Specifically, there is the recent case in which Wells Fargo refused to give in to threats from the American Federation of Teachers (AFT). The AFT warned Wells Fargo that it could have a mortgage market that included America's teachers or "continue to do business with the NRA and gun manufacturers. They can't do both."

Wells Fargo CEO Timothy Sloan told the teachers union, "We believe the best way to make progress on the complex issues concerning gun violence is through the political and legislative process in which all citizens have the opportunity to participate." (*Shooting Industry*, June 2018 "Industry Watch" – Russ Thurman.)

While we are hopeful other financial institutions take the same approach, Wells Fargo's response might not be the gun rights victory many believe. For one thing, what sort of "progress" does Sloan want to make on so-called "gun violence" and how does he define that term? It may not be friendly. If WF wanted to send a clear message, it could have simply said it supports the Second Amendment and will not be manipulated into blatant discrimination to help the anti-gun agenda achieve its aims. Not only that, but the bank doesn't exactly have a great track record in its dealings with gun owners.

"Vice President of Business Banking at Wells Fargo, called Friday Nov 2nd to alert Mr. Maddox, owner of BMADDOX

ENTERPRISES, that Wells Fargo would not extend business credit or loans to any firearms related business, period," reports bulletsfirst.com. ("Surprise, Anti-Gun Banks Rate Worst in Nation," August 4, 2016). "Your credit is impeccable, and your business model is sound, but our corporate legal department will not allow us to extend credit to any business related to firearms. We understand you are fully licensed under federal and state law, although…the corporate directive is still no."

Wells Fargo is not alone. There is also the case of Bank of America turning on its long-time customer of 12 years, McMillan Group, forcing the family business to change financial institutions. The backlash from gun owners was swift, but the "too big to fail" banks just keep on discriminating against legitimate businesses that work with guns.

It would be a good time for all of us to find out how our bank and credit card companies are responding to the strong-arm tactics that are being used against the firearms industry. And we would be wise to remember the words of John T. Amber, the longtime editor of this *Gun Digest*, who wrote in the 1952 6th Edition the following:

THE GUN DIGEST … is dedicated to America's No. 1 man … the man with a rifle. Our eyes turn toward him as he carries on our fight against the forces that would undermine and enslave all liberty-loving peoples. And we regard it as his duty to bear arms for his country.

But what about his right to bear arms, for his own pleasure, when he comes home? Will we fail to protect his rights while he is protecting ours?

This birthright is deep-rooted in the hearts of American citizens. A heritage handed down by the founders of our nation, it was guaranteed to us in the Constitution, as the second amendment of the Bill of Rights: "A well-regulated Militia, being necessary to the security of a free State, the right of the people to keep and bear Arms, shall not be infringed."

Too often we take this right for granted, as just one more of the individual freedoms we are entitled to in our democratic country. But this privilege would be regarded as exceptional — even unbelievable — by the unfortunate citizens of certain other countries, where private possession of firearms is a crime against the state.

Our forefathers guaranteed this prerogative to us. They realized that the backbone of national defense is a well-trained body of citizens, willing and able to bear arms. It is every American's duty. Let's not lose it as our right.

ACKNOWLEDGMENTS

The editor wants to thank Corey Graff for his hard work helping with the hands-on editing of this massive book and keeping us on schedule.

ABOUT THE COVER

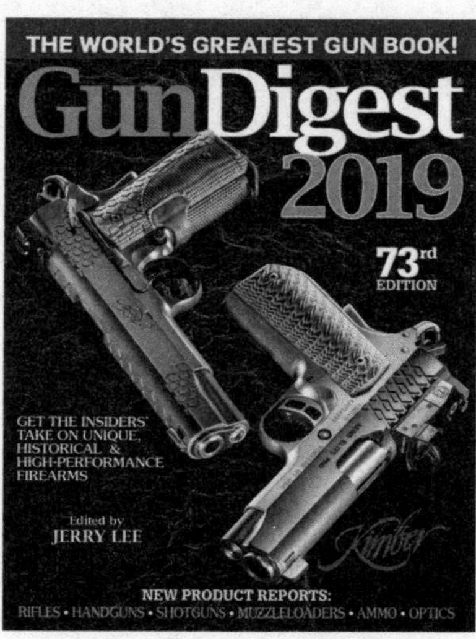

On the following page you'll find a detailed look at this edition's cover guns by photographer Yamil Sued — two stunning new 1911s from Kimber USA, the KHX Custom and Aegis Elite Pro. The KHX proves there is still much room left for makers to refine the 1911, with its Hogue laser-enhanced grip and match-grade barrel. Meanwhile, the Aegis represents the trend toward optics-ready defensive handguns and comes with a factory-installed Vortex Venom red-dot sight for lightning-fast target acquisition and speedy follow-up shots.

Kimber KHX Custom and Aegis Elite Pro (OI) Raise the Bar on Factory-Custom 1911s

BY **YAMIL SUED**

Kimber's KHX and Aegis 1911 lines bring affordable performance to shooters. The KHX (top) is ready to compete right from the box, while the Aegis Pro (OI) (bottom) might be Kimber's most capable concealed carry handgun yet.
All Photos: Yamil Sued

Since its introduction, the 1911 pistol has been a staple in military, law enforcement and civilian markets alike. All branches of the U.S. military used it until it was unceremoniously replaced in 1986 by the Beretta M9. Bullseye competition shooters loved the 1911 for its accuracy, reliability and ease of customization. But in 1976 the 1911 would see a revival with the emerging shooting sport of International Practical Shooting Competition (IPSC). IPSC shooters embraced the 1911 and made it the pistol to shoot in the new and fast-growing sport. IPSC not only breathed new life into the century-old design, but created a cottage industry for the design, creation and manufacturing of custom parts to accessorize and customize the timeless classic.

Prior to the mid–1990s, the only choice for a reliable, quality 1911 custom pistol was to purchase a Colt Government Model and send it to a big name gunsmith. Suddenly your Colt 1911 had quadrupled in price.

Kimber changed all that. The creative minds of Chip McCormick and Kimber joined together to release a factory pistol with all the features that everybody wanted on a custom 1911, only at a reasonable price. The Kimber Custom featured refinements like beavertail grip and extended thumb safeties, match trigger, low-profile rear sights, dovetail front sights, front and rear serrations and custom internal parts. The Kimber Custom was competition-ready right out of the box and it was a hit.

The legacy of great 1911's from Kimber continues. This year two new 1911 families have hit the market, the KHX and Aegis Elite. Two completely different pistol families for two completely different purposes, they come in Custom with a 5-inch barrel, Pro with a 4-inch tube and Ultra with a 3-inch barrel. Each share standard Kimber enhancements like lightweight aluminum trigger and commander-style hammer, beavertail grip safety, extended tactical magazine release and extended thumb safety. They're available in .45 ACP or 9mm, with the 9mm magazines holding 9 rounds, and the .45 ACP magazine holding 8 rounds.

The Aegis Pro OI has a tall, optics-ready rear sight that allows co-witnessing with the included Vortex Venom 6 MOA red-dot sight.

The Standard KHX features a green fiber-optic low mount rear sight.

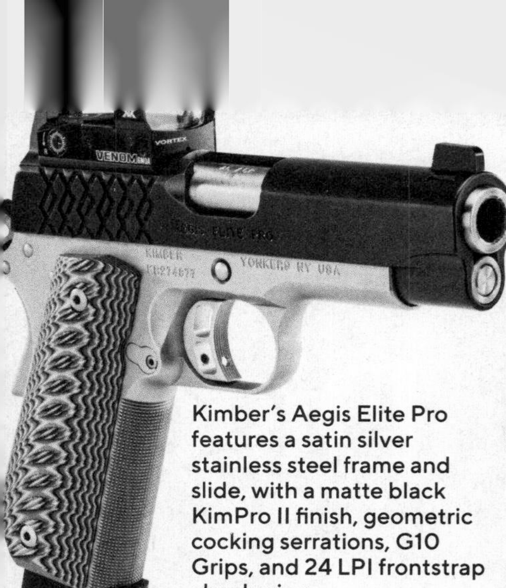

Kimber's Aegis Elite Pro features a satin silver stainless steel frame and slide, with a matte black KimPro II finish, geometric cocking serrations, G10 Grips, and 24 LPI frontstrap checkering.

The AEGIS Elite Pro has a 4-inch bull barrel to increase accuracy and tame the .45 ACP's stout recoil and muzzle flip.

Rounded grip heels and G10 grips make the Aegis Ultra Pro an ideal choice for concealed carry.

KIMBER AEGIS PRO (OI)

The Aegis series of pistols consists of five models with a satin silver stainless steel frame and slide and a matte black KimPro II finish. They sport geometric cocking serrations, G10 Grips and 24 LPI frontstrap checkering.

The Aegis Custom and Pro models have rounded grip heels and the Aegis Ultra model has a standard square grip. The OI models have tall dovetailed white dot front and optics-ready rear sights that allow co-witnessing with the included Vortex Venom 6 MOA red-dot optic. The standard models have a low mount green fiber-optic rear sight and red fiber-optic dovetail front sight.

KIMBER KXH

The KHX series of pistols consist of five models as well. They feature a stainless steel frame and slide with a matte black KimPro II finish. KHX slides have an octagonal pattern on the top of the slide.

The KHX frame has a Stiplex frontstrap stippling. The grips are Hogue G10 with laser enhancements on the basic models. Standard Hogue G10 MagGrips on the OR and Custom models are available with or without lasers, depending on the model.

The KHX Pro models have rounded heel grips — optimal for concealed carry — while the Custom and Ultra have the standard square grips. KHX OR models are optics-ready, with tall sights front and rear for either Leupold or Vortex optical sights, not included. Standard KHXs sport a green fiber-optic, low mount rear sight and a red fiber-optic dovetail front sight.

Kimber has taken the 1911 platform to new levels in the 21st century. By sticking to the foundation of a quality 1911, and adding competition-ready features like scopes, lasers, and aesthetic accents such as engraving, stippling, checkering and advanced finishes, the Kimber Aegis Elite and KHX series of pistols not only bring us the accuracy and reliability we expect from Kimber, but the performance we would expect from custom gunsmiths.

The KHX Custom's stainless steel frame and slide are finished with a matte black KimPro II treatment, Stiplex frontstrap stippling and octagonal pattern on the top of the slide and cocking serrations.

The KHX uses a similar trigger as the Aegis Elite, but both the frame and slide are of a matte black KimPro II finish.

Kimber's standard KHX has a red fiber-optic dovetail front sight. You can also see the octagonal pattern on the slide, which aids grip for slide manipulations.

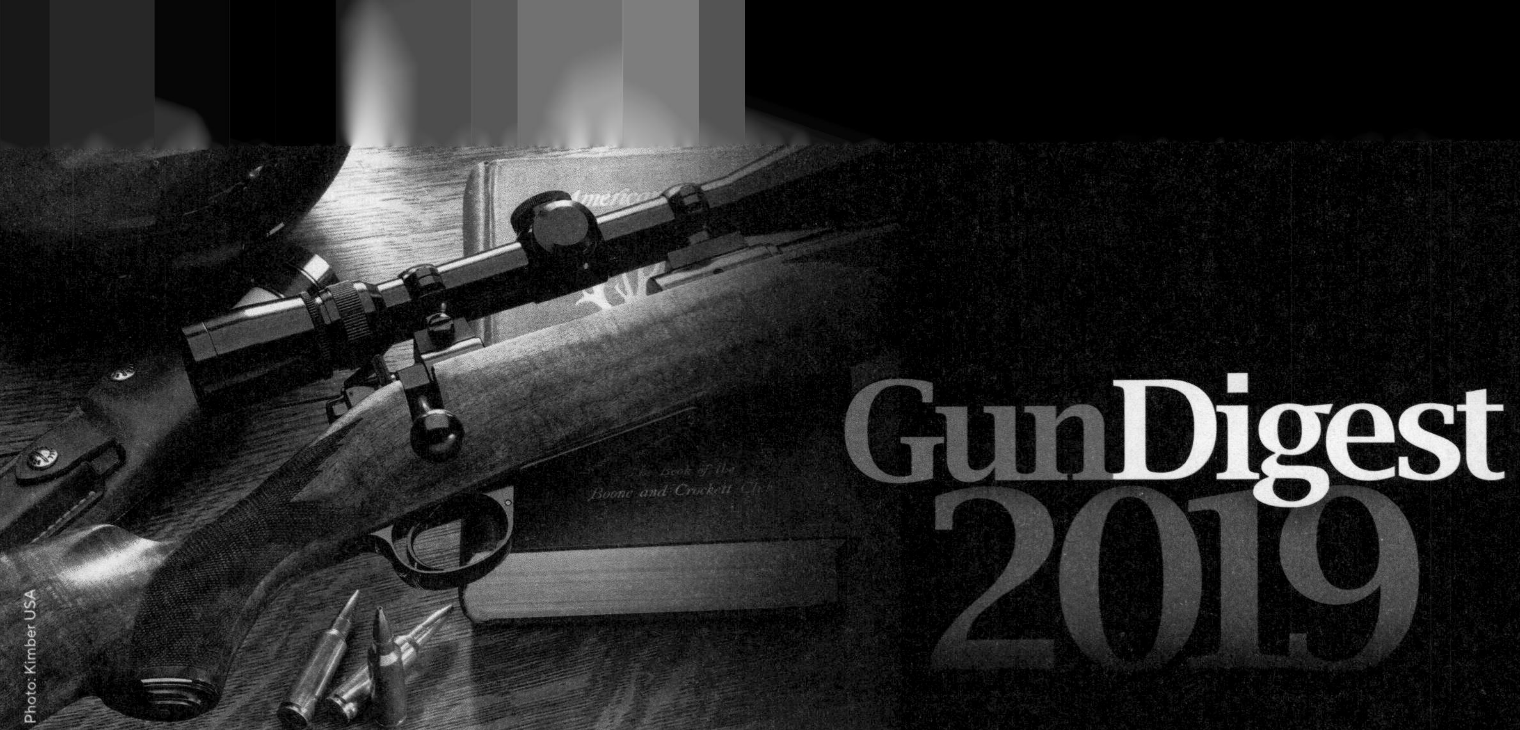
GunDigest
2019
Photo: Kimber USA

FEATURES

ONE GOOD GUN

TESTFIRES

REPORTS FROM THE FIELD

2019 FIREARMS CATALOG

BALLISTICS TABLES

HANDGUNS

RIFLES

SHOTGUNS

BLACKPOWDER

AIRGUNS

REFERENCES

Here in .275 Rigby, the Highland Stalker also comes in .270, .308, .30-06 and 9x3x62.

THE RESURRECTION OF RIGBY

Britain's Oldest Gunmaker Has New Fire in its Belly, and a Rifle Proven on Jungle Man-Eaters!

BY **WAYNE VAN ZWOLL**

Twenty years to the day before I was born, he met the tiger in a jungle pocket the size of a small garage. She was looking at him, eight feet away.

Eastern reaches of the Kumaon Division of the United Provinces held many of the great cats then. A few took to killing people. Her pug marks "showed the tigress to be a very old animal," wrote Corbett. Deeply rutted pads sandwiched a cleft across the right forefoot, "and the toes were elongated to a length I had never before seen in a tiger."

He first came upon those tracks at the hem of a field more than three years and three dozen victims after the Chowgarh tigers began preying on people. A trio of women cutting wheat that day were saved only when one of the cats was spotted stalking them and the alarm was raised. Retreating into the forest, the old female and her cub would soon try again.

By the late 1920s, Major (then Lieutenant Colonel) Jim Corbett had established himself as a superb hunter. A representative of the British government in the rugged Indian hills bordering Nepal, he'd killed several man-eating tigers and leopards, which were commonly named after the villages suffering the losses. The trail of the Chowgarh tigers led Corbett into a thicket, where he spied the protruding

Rigby's figured Turkish walnut is shaped, "papered" and finished to client specs by skilled stockers.

leg of a domestic cow. It jerked as the tigers tore into the carcass. "Dropping on hands and knees … I crawled through the bracken [to within 20 yards]." There he checked his rifle, eased to the top of a big rock, identified the light-colored tiger as the eldest, "aligned the sights very carefully on her and fired." She fell. The other cat dashed off.

To his chagrin, Corbett had shot the youngster. That error would "cost the district fifteen lives…."

Lists of extraordinary hunters include famous explorers — the likes of Sir Samuel Baker in Africa and Daniel Boone in North America — as well as those who followed to tap markets in ivory or meat and hides — Bell, Cody and many others. Sportsmen followed, from Theodore Roosevelt and other pioneers in conservation, to platoons of sportsmen obsessed with records-book recognition. I can think of just one hunter who used his exceptional instincts, skills and courage to shoot man-killing beasts. Corbett met the physical challenges and privations of wild India with unassuming grace. The risks he took exceeded those of any hunter on record.

By all accounts, Jim Corbett was less a firearms enthusiast than he was a naturalist. He carried a variety of guns on his missions to bring man-eaters to bag. Smoothbore with buckshot, heavy double rifle and flat-shooting bolt-action all had their application. He praised his Rigby Mauser in .275 Rigby (7x57) as "light to carry, accurate and sighted up to 300 yards" — a glowing defense for any rifle to be carried far and used at distance. Surely, Corbett trekked many miles in difficult terrain. But the .275's reach seems almost irrelevant in retro-

This Rigby-branded 2-15x42 scope made its first hunt in Scotland. Waterproof? Fog-proof? You bet!

John Rigby & Co. Managing Director Marc Newton examines a new Highland Stalker, patterned after Jim Corbett's rifle.

Are we in Scotland? Bagpipes welcomed the hunting party at trackside, and woke residents at 6 a.m.

"Best adjust reticle focus before you check zero." Despite open terrain, hunters zeroed at 100 yards.

spect, as it wore open sights, and many shots came at mere feet!

Corbett was loath to burden himself with extra ammunition. Typically, he carried only five rounds for his Rigby. On a beat (drive) for the Champawat man-eater, he loaded both barrels of his .500 double, pocketing a single cartridge for "an emergency." That tigress's tally had by then topped, by grim estimate, 400 people — half in Nepal, from which she had entered Kumaon. When he glimpsed the animal turn to the sound of a gunshot from the beaters, he "sent a despairing bullet after her." He'd just charged the empty barrel when the tigress broke cover at 30 yards. He fired both remaining cartridges. Hit hard, she escaped into cover. Corbett abandoned his rifle, dashed toward the converging beaters, grabbed a double shotgun and hurried along the cat's trail. He came upon her at 20 steps, "raised the gun and found to my horror [a 3/8-inch gap] between the barrels and the breech…." He triggered the decrepit smoothbore anyway, and missed. But by that time his previous bullets took effect, and the beast died.

Killing the Champawat tigress brought Jim Corbett many plaudits. Best known is the Rigby rifle presented to him in 1907 for that effort. A rifle enthusiast with no tigers on my resume, I'd read Corbett's books early on and had thrilled to his encounters with fearsome predators. What impressed me most were his frank, detailed narratives, his affinity for all things wild, and the understated commitment and courage marking his hunts. But the few photos in my books included none of that rifle.

Good glass — as in Leica Trinovids — is a requisite for spotting far-off stags on heather-cloaked steeps.

A couple of years ago it came to hand, courtesy Marc Newton, Managing Director of a recovering John Rigby & Company. Carefully, I cheeked that rifle. Slim, agile, its steel silvered by use and the stock all but devoid of finish, it balanced as if alive and pointed eagerly. Even without its matchless history, this rifle would have stirred the soul.

"That .275 *had* to come back to Rigby," said Marc, who'd pulled no stops to make it happen. "It's the archetypal Rigby rifle of its day. Now, a century later, we're building rifles like that again."

He was speaking of Rigby's then-new Big Game series on Magnum Mauser actions. The single-square-bridge versions (flat-topped bridge but round front ring, original flag safety) are designed for iron-sight shooting. A banded front sight pairs with a fixed V and two folding

(above) Hunters endure stiff, cold wind as they glass for herds of stags above the mouth of a glacial valley.

(right) Collapsible scopes steadied on walking sticks owe much to tradition. Rifles are carried in soft cases.

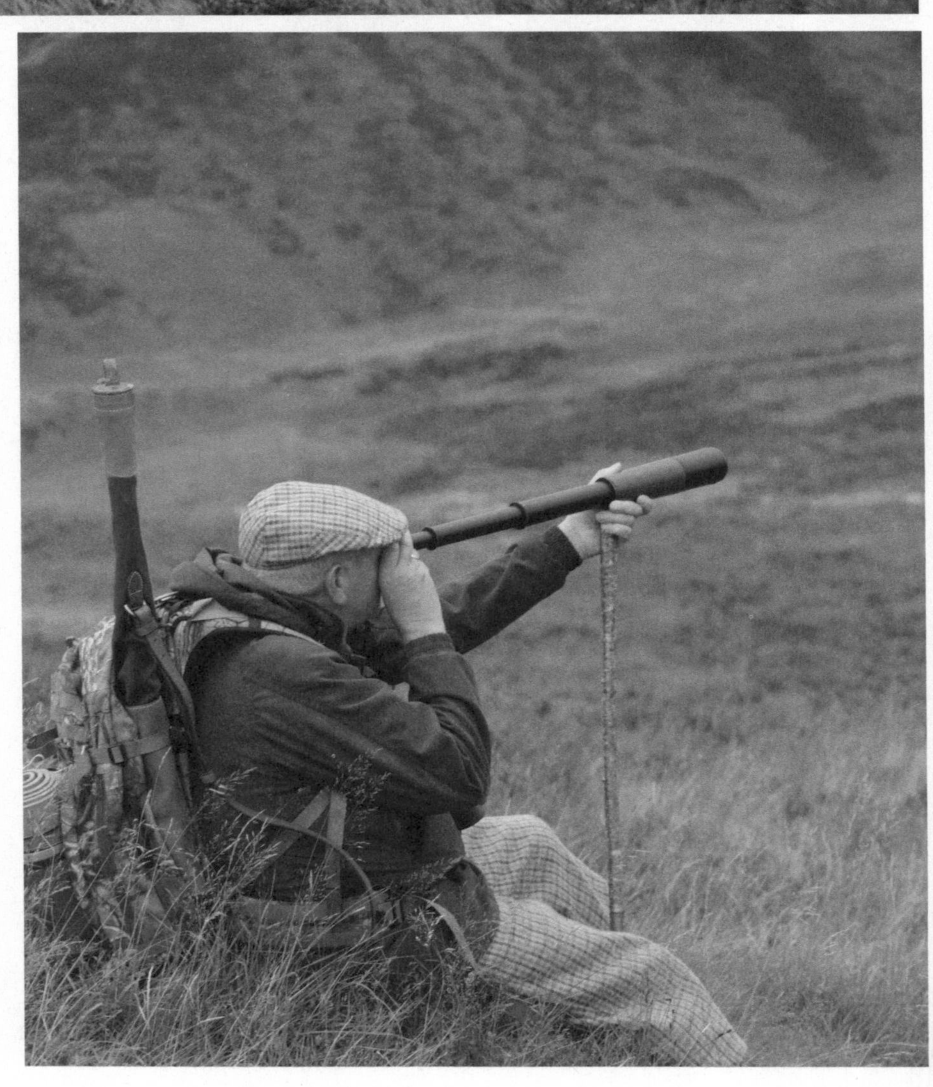

leaves inscribed for 65, 150 and 250 yards on a quarter-rib. A "lightweight" 24-inch barrel in .416 Rigby holds weight to 10 pounds. Add 8 ounces for the heavier, stepped 22-inch barrel in .416 or .450 Rigby. Double-square-bridge rifles are configured for scope use — though they have the same iron-sight setup: In .375 H&H and .416 Rigby, they come only with the slender barrel and a three-position wing safety. Big Game rifles boast Turkish walnut stocks with classic point-pattern checkering. Cosmetic touches distinguish "PH" and "Deluxe" versions.

My pick of this series: the "Vintage" single-square-bridge .416 with 24-inch barrel, a retractable cocking-piece aperture. Once common on fine rifles, the cocking-piece sight is all but gone. A shame! As practical as it is elegant, it perches close to your eye for quick aim and flies ahead with the striker. Any rear-mounted aperture blesses you with a long sight radius, for the best accuracy you can get with irons.

I had used such a rifle mere months before my introduction to Corbett's .275. As no man-eating predators prowl the Okanogan hills, I turned the .416 on black bullseyes. Cradled by the massive Mauser claw, the stogie-size cartridges slid home with a relaxed *clackety-thunk,* each characteristic bump of the bolt silky-smooth. The trigger obeyed my touch like a fragile icicle, sending 400-grain solids at 2,400 fps into knots tight enough to brain elephants many times as far away as elephants are shot.

Long after the first John Rigby was born in Ireland in 1758, British explorers were still compelled to get very close to kill Africa's biggest game. The ponderous black-powder rifles they carried required as much. A 4-bore George Gibbs built for 19-year-old Samuel Baker in 1840 used 16 drams (437 grains) of powder to drive a 4-ounce (1,750-grain) silk-patched lead ball through 2-groove rifling in a 36-inch barrel. The rifle weighed 21 pounds! Later, Baker would patronize the gun shop that tobacconist Harris Holland had started in 1837, then managed with his nephew Henry. The Hollands' fortunes followed Baker's celebrity.

The only way to deliver a stiffer punch in the early 19th century was to launch heavier bullets. Not until the advent of smokeless powder in the late 1880s would hunters hurl *faster* bullets. Years after ivory hunter William Finaughty sold his big-bore rifle in 1875, the fourth owner hung 3 pounds of lead up front to keep it down in recoil. The .450/400 Black Powder Express introduced in 1880 was gentler, but hardly a stopping round. Its 270-grain bullets at 1,650 fps had less punch than modern .45-70 loads.

A century earlier, in 1775, John Rigby had opened a gun shop in Dublin. His son William joined him to build dueling pistols, hunting rifles and shotguns. The Protestant Rigbys emerged from the short-lived Irish revolution in 1798 as landed militia, sanctioned by the victorious British. Eldest son William joined John in 1816. Two years later the elder Rigby died, and William invited his brother John Jason into the shop. It became, for a time, William and John Rigby, 24 Suffolk St., Dublin. John Jason died in 1845; but William Rigby lived until 1858, when *his* son John, then 29, assumed control of the company. In 1865 the enterprise put down roots in London as John Rigby & Co. at 72 James Street, to market "breech- and muzzle-loading guns, revolvers and ammunition." The Dublin facility would be shuttered in 1892.

Rigby's first double rifle appeared in 1879 using the Bissell patent, filed that

Sturdy "hill ponies" are bred and trained to walk with hunters, pack downed stags from tough places.

year. It described a vertical or "rising bite" lockup. The handwork required made this action expensive, but over the next 50 years rising-bite doubles from Rigby defined London's "best guns." Examples remain rare, as only about 1,000 were built between 1879 and 1932.

In 1887, the third-generation John Rigby was appointed Superintendent of the Royal Small Arms Factory at Enfield Lock, to oversee the black powder-to-smokeless transition in rifles and ammunition. There he worked on the .303 SMLE rifle that would serve British forces until 1957. Obliged to retire at age 65, he returned to the family shop, where he worked with the gunpowder firm of Curtis & Harvey on a powerful new cartridge for hinged-breech rifles. It appeared in 1898 as the .450 NE 3 1/4" — its 70 grains of Cordite accelerating 480-grain bullets to 2,200 fps, for 5,186 ft-lbs of energy. A pivotal development, the .450 3 1/4" sent to pasture the ponderous 4- and 8-bore muzzleloaders, long standard in Africa. It eclipsed in power and popularity Jeffery's .450/400 3-inch, developed in 1896 to wring 2,100 fps from 400-grain bullets. Rigby's long-hulled .450 would become a ballistic template for dozens of double-gun rounds that appeared in the years leading up to the Great War.

But Rigby saw early on the potential

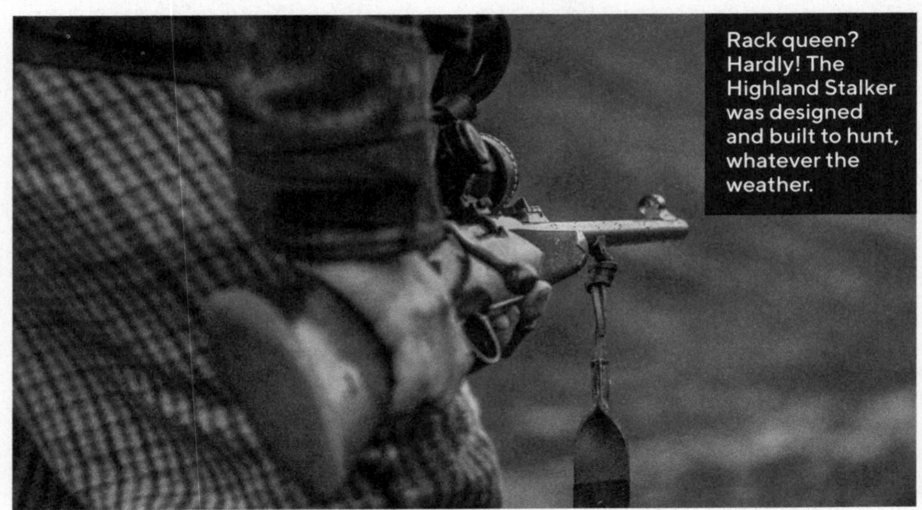

Rack queen? Hardly! The Highland Stalker was designed and built to hunt, whatever the weather.

Many stags are shot from prone, hunters easing through coulees to pop over a rise inside 200 yards.

(below) This lung-shot stag ran 50 yards after struck by a 140-grain Hornady from Rigby's Highland Stalker.

of powerful repeating rifles, and shortly after Paul Mauser's model of 1898 appeared, John secured in Germany a 12-year exclusive license to sell Mauser actions and rifles across the U.K. and its colonies. No bolt mechanism feeds more reliably than an original 98, largely because Paul Mauser tapered each box for a specific cartridge. Case shape and shoulder location influence follower design, too — taper, height, and slope, and the 61-degree step from top to bottom shelf. Its spring has clearance to shift under the stack as cartridges strip. Mauser's non-rotating, controlled-feed extractor, engineered to prevent double-loading jams in battle, was clearly as valuable on dangerous-game rifles.

In 1899, Rigby requested a bigger action for its new .400/350 NE, a rimmed round driving 310-grain bullets at 2,000 fps. Mauser responded with a magnum action. In 1908, the .350 No. 2 and rimless .350 Magnum upstaged the .400/350. Three years later, the rimless .416 Rigby appeared, a muscle-bound cartridge clearly fashioned to make the most of Mauser's magnum receiver. A 410-grain bullet driven by 71 grains of Cordite left the muzzle at 2,370 fps, hurling 5,100 ft-lbs. The .416 brought double-gun power to bolt actions. Hunters snapped it up. After a century, it remains among the most popular "safari" rounds, one of few pre–WWI rimless cartridges competing ably with modern .416 and .458 magnums.

The first .416 rifle shipped in 1912, as Rigby opened its shop at 43 Sackville St., London. John Rigby's passing in 1916 halted development of a .33-bore cartridge on the .416 hull. This project, and its target velocity of 3,000 fps with 250-grain bullets, would be revived in the 1980s. Lapua of Finland and the U.S. firm, Research Armament, collaborated to produce the .338 Lapua.

Early in the smokeless era, Rigby profited from Corbett's use of its rifles, and presentation of the .275 after Corbett killed the Champawat man-eater. But other notables of the day also carried Rigbys. Winston Churchill wielded a Rigby-Mauser pistol at the Battle of Omdurman in 1898. Theodore Roosevelt added a Rigby big-bore to his battery of rifles for his 1909 safari. W.D.M. Bell later ordered two Rigbys in .416, and owned one in .22 Savage High-Power — as well as six .275s.

Theo Rigby's death in 1951 ended family ownership in the company. Significant change came 17 years later when David

Marks bought John Rigby & Co. and engaged J. Roberts & Son, established in the 1950s, to build its firearms. Paul Roberts acquired the brand in 1984. He developed the .450 Rigby using .416 brass in 1995. Two years later, Neil Gibson had the firm and moved it to California. In 2010, a Dallas-based investor group bought John Rigby & Co., returned it to London and asked Paul Roberts to manage it. Within three years the L&O Group, which owns Mauser, Blaser and Sauer, had purchased Rigby. At 72, Roberts was due to retire. His search for a successor led to Marc Newton, who as a Rigby apprentice had shown uncommon enthusiasm and talent. Patty Pugh, recently at Rigby after 35 years in the British gun trade, came out of retirement to help.

With the blessing of L&O, Newton tapped the industry to build a strong gun-making team at 13-19 Pensbury Place in London, a short street in an unpretentious industrial district. By 2014, Rigby had set its roots. I visited soon after to find not a gaggle of groomed gents in tweed vests, but tattooed men in shop aprons colored by sanding dust and gun oil. "Our focus now is to build fine rifles," Newton explained, "not to sell a lifestyle." Within a year, the return of Corbett's rifle drew attention to the "new Rigby" — and to hunting traditions now blurred by boasts of 1,000-yard kills from bipods.

Admiring the clean, carnivorous lines of Big Game rifles, and harking to rumors of a lightweight, Corbett-inspired version, the Chowgarh tigress again came to mind. By April of 1930, she had killed at least 64 people. Her trail threaded cover, limiting vision to mere feet. Senses honed to an edge, Jim Corbett spied on the ground a pair of rare bird's eggs. He picked them up. Easing around a bend, he looked up "straight into the tigress's face" three steps away. The eggs, still in his left palm, checked his reflexive urge to cheek the rifle. That would have brought the tiger, he wrote later. Instead, with one hand Corbett eased the .275 slowly across his chest. "It appeared that my arm was paralyzed, and that the swing would never be completed…." He fired as soon as the muzzle covered the cat. The bullet minced her spine and heart.

Though not yet 30 at this writing, Marc Newton has keen interest in and appreciation for history. He knows that Rigby's past and products, and the customers whose orders fill a logbook dating back centuries, have a lot to do with how clients view Rigby now. "We haven't done anything clever with the brand," he says. "Our passion is to restore it! Rigby rifles aren't mere tools. They join art with history and superb craftsmanship. Clients expect shadow-tight wood-to-metal fit and flawless finish on agile, reliable rifles that function smoothly, shoot accurately and endure. They want the *best*. Our task is to deliver it."

Peerless quality doesn't tumble off conveyor belts. Each Rigby spends many hours at the bench, tended to by people who know the difference between serviceable and perfect. "Between 1912 and 1940," he tells me, "Rigby built only 189 .416 bolt rifles. Annual production of *all* rifles barely reached 70!"

Thanks to a growing team of craftsmen, and CNC machines that speed preliminary work, monthly output of bolt-actions has now reached that mark. A couple of years ago, Rigby revived the rising bite, building the first rifle of this type since 1932. Visiting the shop in August 2017, I saw barrels in .470 and .500 NE ready for fitting. "Actioner" and production chief Ed Workman labored seven years at Purdey and 34 at Holland & Holland before bringing his talents to Rigby. He told me a rising bite action requires 200 hours to finish. His off-hours relieve him of the demands of tight tolerances: he's a *tank* enthusiast! And during his long career, Workman confided, he has never fired a bolt rifle.

Olivier Leclerque, Rigby's factory foreman, learned his skills at the Liege School of Gunmaking, as did gun-crafter Brice Swieton and engraver Geoffrey Lignon. "The rising bite is my pet project too," says Leclerque. "It's a demanding mechanism to build, but beautiful in operation, and very strong."

Still, bolt-actions have broad appeal

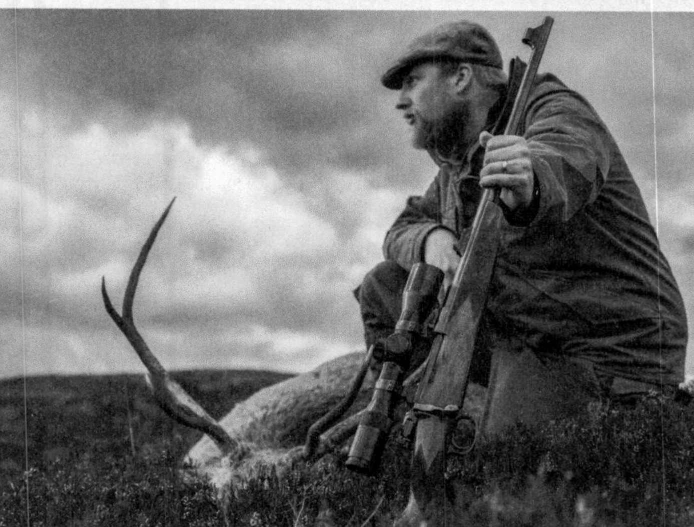

(above) Smaller than elk, red stags share their antler conformation. Ghillies manage herds on private estates.

(left) A hunter pauses after a kill. Note his Rigby traditional sights, checkering and Mauser 1898 action.

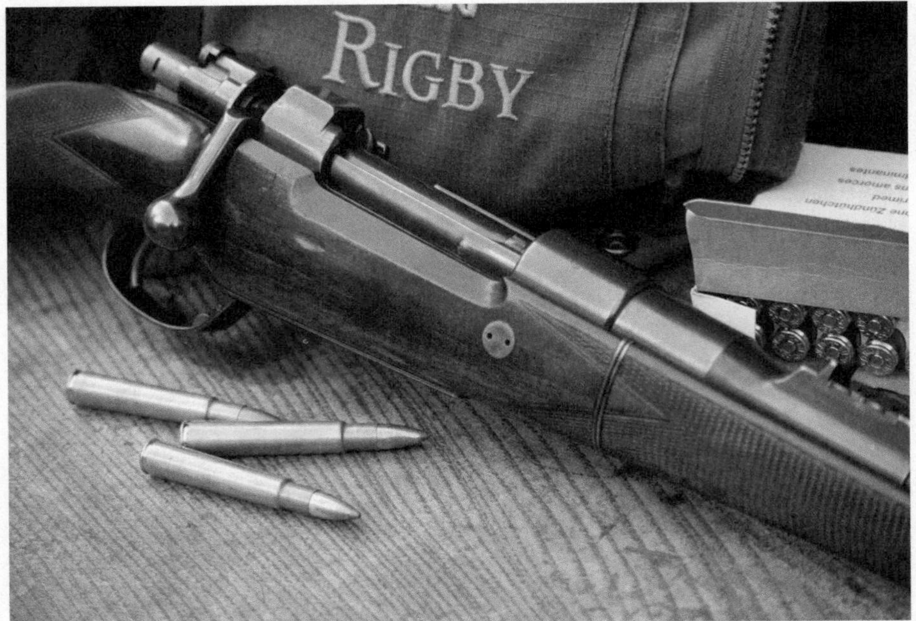

(above) This vintage single-square-bridge Rigby is a takedown rifle. The .350 Rigby cartridge dates to 1908.

(right) Rigby's magnum in .416 is predictably heavier and friskier in recoil than its svelte Highland Stalker.

(below) The author range-tested this lovely new vintage-model Rigby Magnum in .416 with cocking-piece sight.

and a much bigger client base than do doubles. And Rigby's commitment to Mauser actions has long blessed both companies. After WWII, Mauser signaled a new direction with a name change: "Werke" (works) replaced "Waffenfabrik" (arms factory). Targeting the U.S. hunting market, it engaged A.F. Stoeger, Inc., of New York as its sales agent. By the Depression's end, there were 20 configurations of Mauser actions in four lengths. Magnum and Kurz actions were designed specifically for the hunting market.

Surplus military Mausers sold at clearance prices after armistice, but sporters came dear. In 1939, a Model 70 Winchester retailed for $61.25, while Mauser listed sporters at $110 to $250. Square-bridge or magnum actions cost more. Left-hand versions commanded a $200 premium. Despite an affinity for Winchester 70s, gun guru and widely read columnist Jack O'Connor liked the Mauser. His first custom rifle was a .30-06 on a 98 action. Of the 1903 Springfield (the 98's military contemporary) he once wrote, "Various departures were made from the Mauser design, and in every instance the designers laid an egg."

Post-war efforts to keep the 98 alive resulted in rifles with commercial actions from FN (Fabrique Nationale) in Belgium. Browning's High Power series had FN actions, as did rifles for "big box" retailers like Sears. Subsequently, Mauser's label appeared on actions whose design differed starkly from the 98's.

When Marc Newton committed to restoring Rigby to its former glory, he knew bolt rifles would have to feature 98 Mauser actions. He got ready agreement from Bernhard Knobel, who oversees Mauser production for the L&O Group. Mauser, Blaser and Sauer share a campus in Isny, Germany, but operate as separate factories. Current Rigby Big Game and Highland Stalker rifles begin life as Model 98 actions at Isny. The rifles are built and proofed in London. Their

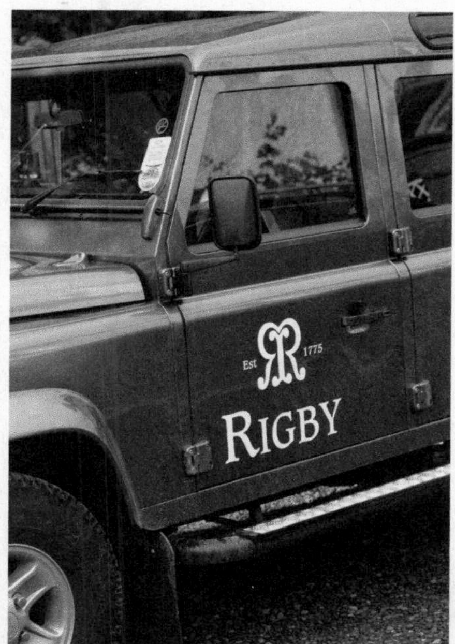

It's a Land Rover, of course. An obvious choice for Scottish mud — and hunters with Rigby rifles.

pre–war profiles, detailing, feel, and quality mark a purposeful return to what gave Rigby its status among seasoned hunters.

A bolt rifle's appeal owes much to stock design. Rigby woodworkers marry form to function and pride themselves in skin-tight fit of walnut to steel. Rifles are trim but exquisitely balanced, quick to hand, and steady on target. Mark Renmant, 30 years with Paul Roberts, checkers to client preferences. "Pointed or English flat diamonds. Our 24 line-per-inch spacing is popular, but 21 or 22 lpi makes more sense for hunting." Slovakian stock-maker Vladimir Tomascik brings his cabinet-making skills to the Rigby bench, explaining that first applications of linseed oil fill wood pores, then are papered (sanded) back. After up to 14 coats, the figured Turkish walnut has a deep, warm glow under a glass-smooth, high-luster sheen.

No rifle better displays traditional British stock design (including a properly sculpted round grip) than Rigby's latest rifle. A svelte version of the Big Game model, the 7 ¾-pound Highland Stalker all but mirrors the .275 carried by Jim Corbett and is properly scaled for that cartridge. It's also barreled to .270, .308, .30-06, 8x57 and 9.3x62. The rifle slips easily into the crook of your arm and cheeks like a grouse gun. Lean Turkish walnut joins deep-black steel as if the two grew together. The safety is scope-friendly. Like the trigger, it is crisp but compliant. The iron sights are attractive and functional.

With no chance to introduce this rifle on a tiger hunt, Rigby settled on what attendees will long remember as a trip back through time. Meeting in London, a small group of journalists from Europe and the U.S. gathered at a rail station, then boarded the Caledonia Sleeper, in whose small but comfortable compartments we slumbered to the rhythmic clack and lazy sway of the coach. The train carried us into rural Scotland. We were met at dawn, trackside, by a burly, kilted Scot blowing mightily and skillfully into pipes bristling above his broad shoulders. Lights flickered on in adjoining stone houses before he'd finished the welcome. We bundled our duffles into Land Rovers, leaving residents to brew the morning's tea in silence.

The next couple of days we paired up with Scottish *ghillies* to hike steep and gentle hills, in mild weather and into the teeth of an Atlantic storm, our aim to bag red stags with the new Rigby. Most of the hunters would succeed. My only chance came when, after climbing into horizontal rain, we got a break in the clouds and managed a mile-long sneak on a bachelor group of stags. True to tradition, our *ghillie* kept the rifle cased on his shoulder and peeked over the last ridge to select a proper specimen. But the animals were not so patient as he'd hoped.

Those who fired their rifles at stags were pleased with the results. Hornady loads, with 140-grain Interlock bullets clocking 2,680 fps, proved deadly. "Hill ponies" bred for the hunt dutifully carried stags off places too steep for the Argos. Even the few who didn't bring back game were rewarded, though, with topside views of great glacial valleys, the rush of mountain water against their boots, and a chance to fire Rigby double rifles and a .416 at a local range. A misstep the second day broke my ankle but didn't deny me a minute-of-angle group on paper, prone over a backpack.

Coming out of the hills in the Land Rovers, we had to agree with Newton that the Highland Stalker is indeed no rack queen. Despite drop-dead good looks, it's a *hunting* rifle, bred for the

Rigby's famous rising bite action is hand-filed and -fitted. "Each takes 200 man-hours to finish."

steeps — or jungle — and too lively in hand to leave in the gun room. As the Caledonia Sleeper rocked us back to London, the ghost of the Talla Des man-eater drifted through my coach. Days after flattening a .275 softnose on the great bulge of her shoulder, then tracking her into thick jungle, "within three yards of the bracken I saw movement…."

If your commute doesn't take you past 13-19 Pensbury Place, London, visit johnrigbyandco.com. And add to your reading list, *Rigby: A Grand Tradition*. (Rigby Press, 2012, Dallas TX).

The Hi Power is still an entirely suitable pistol for everyday carry, or EDC. However, you must want one for sentimental or historical reasons, because it will cost you more than a modern polymer handgun.

EULOGY TO THE HI POWER

It May Be Surpassed, But There's Nothing Like a Genuine Hi Power!

BY **PATRICK SWEENEY**

In the immortal words of the great Dr. Who, "There comes an end to everything. The last door you walk through. The last room you enter." To which I add: The last Browning Hi Power to be made. The question is, which one was last? What was its serial number? Where is it located today? I don't know, because, well, Fabrique Nationale just doesn't talk much about what goes on inside the walls of their plant. What happens in Liege, stays in Liege, I guess.

But you can hardly buy a brand new Hi Power any longer, and those who import them, or try, can't get them. How did this happen? To figure that out, we must go back to the beginning.

After the Great War, aka World War I, the smart military establishments planned and stockpiled for subsequent conflicts. However, governments and people were tired of paying for war and, as a result, budgets were tight. It took a while to get around to purchasing new handguns. When the French Army came looking, FN turned to the late, great John Browning as they had for so many previous firearms. He worked up a prototype and it was a doozy. Browning's creation was chambered in 9mm, held 17 rounds, and the slide portion of the firing mechanism could be removed as a complete assembly. It was, in that regard, just like the Savage pistols. Potentially, you could change the same pistol from a duty trigger to a target trigger and back again in a few seconds. The Browning Museum, in Ogden, Utah has the prototype on display.

Alas, before he could complete it, John Browning passed away. Work on the pistol then went to Dieudonné Saive, the FN designer who would later design the FN-49, the forerunner of the FAL.

Saive ironed out the details of a double-column magazine, which fed to a single feed point, for use in pistols. By the early 1930s, the French Army was ready to begin trials but, (and apologies here) being French, they just couldn't decide. After a few fruitless attempts at trying to satisfy the French, FN made the pistol its own as the P-35. (In the end, the French selected a single-stack .32-caliber pistol, which used a cartridge remarkably like the .30 Pedersen. It was designed and manufactured in France.)

The P-35 was hardly through its initial production run when the whole world came apart. In 1940 the Germans overran Belgium, and once the Nazis had cleared the dust and rubble from the machinery in Liege they had the plant up and running again for the Reich. Despite the quick advance, a few of the essential staff and designers managed to get out of Dodge, as it were. The Hi Power blueprints were spirited off to Canada, where John Inglis & Co. set up production for use by the Allies. Thus began the decades-long irony of both sides in a conflict using a pistol of the same design.

The Germans produced hundreds of thousands of the P-35, noted in inventory and marked as the "Pistole 640(b)." Pretty much everywhere they went, when the Germans took over they kept the production lines of whatever was being made going in their name. Those 640(b) pistols were, for the most part, shipped off to the Eastern Front where they were used, captured, picked up, and later stored in Soviet warehouses.

The Canadian model, the Inglis P-35, went to the armed forces in Commonwealth service, as American troops received 1911A1s and various Colt and Smith & Wesson revolvers, for use in the war.

My first introduction to the Hi Power came when I was working at The Gun Room, a gun store I called employer from 1978 to 1982 or so. One time, we had

The original Hi Power safety was hopeless. This is the one Ted Yost uses in his builds. It is beautiful, but you must have Ted build the gun to get the safety.

Stippling on Hi Powers is the most cost-effective. And let's be honest: checkering just doesn't fit the aesthetics of the pistol.

The Canadians and the British went through a dizzying number of "marks" in the Hi Power.

Collectors get excited over things like this. For a while, Canada used decals to mark property. To find a Hi Power with the decal still more-or-less intact is wondrous.

a weekend barbeque at the boss's house out in the country. This included shooting all the odd, rare, different or just loud firearms that we had in the shop or in our personal safes. When the rain began we retired into the walk-out basement and fired out of the sliding door, across the patio. (A brief aside: when firing a handgun chambered in 7.63 Tokarev from inside of a room, it is best to be wearing both earplugs and over-the-ears muffs.) I was handed a Hi Power to shoot. To give you the full flavor of the event, the pistol was a commercial-polished blue, pre-war, tangent-sight model, but with *Waffenampt* proofs. It was a pre-war commercial gun, cut for a shoulder stock as many back then were, that had been appropriated by the Germans while still in the FN vaults, stamped, and issued for use in the war effort. It was most likely shipped to a *Waffen SS* or *Fallschirmjaeger* unit.

I slapped in a 20-round magazine and began shooting. "Hmm, the recoil seems a bit sharp compared to the other handguns. It does hit to the sights. The grips are a bit blocky."

Just as I was finishing, my internal monologue was interrupted by the owner. "What are you *doing*?" Looking down, my reply was, "Bleeding, I think."

The sharp recoil was caused by the hammer biting the web of my hand, and the result was me bleeding all over the Browning. Sorry about that, Roger. Two valuable lessons learned that day: The P-35 bites if you use the then-new IPSC hand grip. And blood, when properly cleaned from blued steel and wooden grips, does not leave any lasting marks or stains.

During the war, we bombed and rained artillery down on the FN plant in Liege to deny its output to the Germans, and when they had to leave, they returned the favor. The place was a wreck by late 1944. The Belgians cleaned up the mess, rebuilt the plant, and began planning. You see, the war had changed many things, including the tools to be used in the next war. Nearly everyone took the lessons learned and began improving what they had. But not us. We pretty much stuck with what we had. Hey, we won the war, and what we used had won, so there wasn't much pressure to change or upgrade.

(above) A Hi Power taken into police service in 1946. The proof marks and inspectors' stamps tell an involved tale. Whole books have been written on marks alone.

When countries were still run by kings, the royal crest would be put on firearms for their respective kingdoms.

A lot of countries felt differently.

The rifle got the most focus. Once the U.S. Army had forced our allies to adopt a "new" rifle cartridge — the .308 Winchester — new rifles were needed for it. The .308, aka the 7.62 NATO, is essentially a .30-06 with a shorter case and ball powder, which takes up less volume for the same energy. The difference between them is essentially naught. In the U.S., the rifle change was to adopt the M14, which is pretty much an M1 Garand with a 20-round box magazine. Even the Italians rebuilt their Garands into the M14 configuration, calling them the BM-59.

The rest of Europe went a different route. Saive, still at the helm at FN, took the 10-shot box magazine-fed FN-49 rifle and changed the externals, which produced the FN-FAL — a 20-round box magazine-fed battle rifle of amazing durability, adaptability, and reliability. It was also almost four feet long, but in the 1950s that wasn't seen as that much of a problem. How, you ask, does the worldwide adoption of the FAL figure into the history of the P-35, the Hi Power? Simple: the same FN salesmen who were making sure the FAL earned the name "The Free World's Right Arm" were also busy

Think so-called hi-cap magazines are new? Here is a pair of 20-round Hi Power mags, complete with belt pouch, for use with a Hi Power.

The handmade prototype that John Moses Browning had developed before things changed.

Stocked pistols were all the rage in the early decades of the 20th century. Hence the rear sights marked to 500 or 1,000 yards.

pushing the P-35. And why not? If you are going to re-arm your military with top-of-the-line battle rifles complete with service, repair, upgrades, and warranty, why not do the same with the sidearm?

It didn't hurt that it used the ubiquitous 9mm Parabellum cartridge, and that it was used with great enthusiasm by all sides in World War II, and that it was made in the world-famous FN plant in Liege.

That's how the Hi Power ended up in service in pretty much every non-communist (and even some communist) countries. The Commonwealth countries were going to use the Hi Power once it was officially adopted by Great Britain. That meant Canada, New Zealand, Australia, and all the colonies. Even after they shrugged off the status of a colony, a lot of the new countries kept using the Hi Power. Once in service, it was treated to various modifications, improvements, markings, and tests. The sights were changed and finishes applied. Generally, since there were a million of them out there, the users (or rather, the using organizations) felt free to try their hand at improving it any way they thought possible.

There were other countries that were more interested in having the production of essential arms in-country, and they licensed the manufacture from FN. Argentina, for one, and Canada kept on using the ones built by Inglis and added more as they needed them. India, after becoming independent, began using the arsenals built by the British to manufacture firearms for their own use. The Indian government licensed the manufacture of the Hi Power from the Inglis company and began making them in Ishapore. One of the other places those pistols went was Nepal.

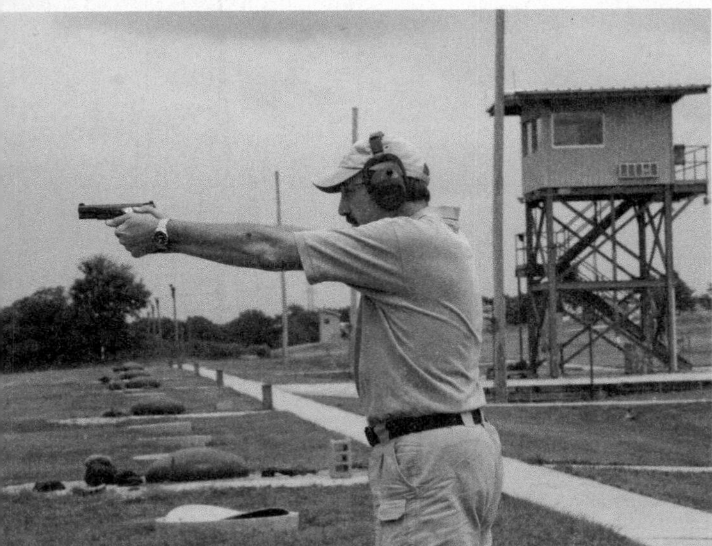

The author hard at work on 300-meter pop-ups, dropping them like bad habits with a Hi Power.

Later that day, at the entrance to the local army base, I saw a sergeant armed with a holstered Hi Power. It had to have been either a British pistol dating from WWII or an Indian-made Inglis-licensed copy, but it was a Hi Power.

Which brings us to the question. Why did the Hi Power remain in service for so long?

The size and shape, to start. The pistol held a useful amount of ammunition, 12 or 13 rounds of 9mm in the magazine. The grip, depending on the panels installed, ranges from comfortable to alluring. Its size is not burdensome to pack. It isn't a bundle, as even the smallest carbines of the day would have been. As lightweight and handy as the US M1 Carbine is, it is still a carbine with a stock. Yes, that's better than a handgun when you need to shoot, but until then a lot less handy, and a lot more of a hindrance than a holstered handgun.

Pistols smaller than the Hi Power often don't hold sufficient ammo or, if they do, it's of an undersized cartridge. A sidearm larger than the Hi Power starts to verge into M1 Carbine territory, more hassle. The recoil was not a big deal, as some shooters back then (and yet today) felt the .45 ACP presents. In many militaries and police departments worldwide, a handgun is a badge of office. In many places, the police are armed with the same rifle that the military uses because law enforcement is just the army dressed in blue instead of green. The guy in charge of the local group has a holstered handgun because it is his job to supervise the rifle-armed guys, not enforce the laws himself. The holster marks him as the head guy in charge. For that purpose, pretty much anything that fits the holster and fires a bullet will do the job.

Before the Hi Power, a British officer would likely have carried a revolver like this Webley in .455.

In my travels around the world, I keep an eye out for the local police and military (in some places one and the same) to see what they are using. In Nepal I saw a truly historic range of firearms. One museum had two Gurkha guards. One was armed with the utterly wretched Indian-made AK clone-compromise, the INSAS. It takes real work to make an AK-derived firearm that is unreliable, but trusted sources say the INSAS comes as close as any. The other Gurkha guard was armed with an Enfield three-band model 1853 rifled musket, complete with bayonet. I asked if I could take a photo and was given a smiling "No."

Two police pistols. On top, the author's Novak FBI Hostage Rescue Team clone. Below, a Belgian police lightweight BHP turn-in exchanged for something more "modern."

The Belgian gendarmerie inspector, acceptance, and inventory markings.

The panache of the Hi Power extended beyond issue handguns. It was apparently not uncommon to see someone in the Vietnam War, someone who just couldn't quite be placed as to what organization they were with, armed with the Hi Power. (That was true for non-GI rifles and submachine guns as well.) Then again, if your senior NCO didn't object, what was carried as personal gear in Vietnam seemed to be pretty much whatever you wanted. Some organizations were a lot more freeform than others.

The Hi Power was more than just a badge of rank. The frame was made from forged steel, with the magazine well, slide rails, and other openings machined from the forging. The barrel used the John Browning tilt-down method. The slide and frame were locked together for a short distance until a cammed face on the bottom lug of the barrel struck the cross-lug in the frame. This caused the barrel to cam down out of the path of the slide, as the slide continued rearward.

Once to the rear of its travel, the slide moved forward, propelled by the recoil spring underneath the barrel. The slide forced a round out of the magazine, collected the barrel, then cammed the barrel up to lock it. Once closed, it was ready to fire again.w

The locked-breech design allowed the Hi Power (and all other locked-breech pistols) to readily handle the recoil forces of the cartridge. Without some means of locking the slide and barrel together at the start of the cycle, the upper limit of force the pistol cartridge can generate is limited — limited by the weight of the slide and the force of its spring, and the ability or willingness of the shooter to fire it. For handguns chambered in anything larger than the .380 Auto cartridge, weight and required recoil spring forces become too great to make a handy pistol, or to find willing shooters.

The efficiency of the cam surfaces makes the Hi Power function with a relatively light slide and recoil spring. That means less weight to carry and less force needed to initially work the slide.

However, the design is not without its costs or drawbacks. One is the lack of a barrel bushing on the front of the slide. This makes barrel and slide manufacturing easier, as it eliminates several machining steps. But, the barrel can only be removed from the slide through the rear — unlike the 1911's barrel that can be removed out the front or rear once the bushing is unlocked from the frame. This became a stumbling block for pistolsmiths wishing to improve performance decades later.

Aluminum frame shaves 6 whole ounces from the weight of a comparable all-steel Browning Hi Power.

Fitting a replacement bushing in a 1911 allows for a more precise barrel fit and can improve accuracy. You can't do that with the Hi Power. When compensators or muzzle brakes became popular in IPSC competition, the Hi Power was left behind. On the P-35, once the brake or comp was attached the barrel could not be removed from the slide. This made cleaning a bit more difficult. On the 1911 it was easy to remove even with a comp or brake installed.

Another obstacle to pistolsmithing was the barrel lockup — specifically, the frame and what FN calls the "barrel seat." The 1911 cams up and down on the slide stop pin, a removable, replaceable, and easy-to-fit part. The timing can be adjusted by using different-sized barrel links. The Hi Power employs a cam that is pressed and staked into the frame. It cannot be serviced by anyone but the factory. The cam surfaces on the barrel are machined to a given dimension. Again, they are not serviceable by a pistolsmith, unless he or she obtains a barrel that has those surfaces over-sized and files and machines them to fit the frame and slide.

The trigger pull is a problem. When it's good, it's fine. When it isn't, it's hard to work on. The 1911 (the exemplar here) has a few parts that operate in a simple manner, and many, many replacements to be had. The Hi Power? The trigger pivots or cams against a lever, which likewise pivots, pressing down on the edge of the sear. Working on the Hi Power trigger requires the patience of Job and specialized skills.

Two .40 S&W Hi Powers. On top, the author's range rental score, and below, his Ted Yost custom. One is an off-the-rack, the other a bespoke suit.

If Ted Yost built it, you'll know it.

The thumb safety is worse. It is small, unusable as-is, and difficult to replace. You see, the thumb safety shaft is the hammer pivot shaft. Replacing a safety can adversely affect your trigger pull.

In a military setting those were not obstacles, they weren't even noticed. If a slide, frame, or barrel became unserviceable, it was simply exchanged for a replacement part. That the new part fit somewhat loosely was not a problem, the old one was often no better. Military organizations were interested in "minute of opponent" accuracy at just-outside-of-the-foxhole distances. And the standard carry method of a handgun in military service was with the hammer down, safety off, and chamber empty. Thumb safety shortcomings were not even noticed.

But, those were big deals to competition shooters and especially American users, who were interested in better ergonomics. Unlike most of the world, where the sidearm is a backup and often even just the badge of rank mentioned above, we Americans view the handgun as a fighting tool. Yes, you use it to fight your way back to the rifle or shotgun you should not have put down, but you fight with it. It isn't just a status symbol, and in many instances it is the only tool used.

In the early days of the now common but then radical competition known as IPSC, the Hi Power acquitted itself well. Today, IPSC is seen as a 9mm or .38 Super competition. Back then, it was a .45 competition. And yet, of the first four IPSC World championships, two were won with 9mm pistols, and one of those was a Hi Power.

Back in that era, the Hi Power was involved in one well-known conflict where both sides were armed not just with the same pistols, but the same rifles and machine guns as well. We won't go into the ownership of *Las Malvinas*, or The Falklands, but I do point out that the British and the Argentines used Hi Powers, FALs, and MAG-58 GPMGs all made by or under license from FN in Liege, Belgium. I've been to the islands a few times and it is interesting to note that pretty much every bar or restaurant, museum, or public office has a captured, welded-inoperative FAL on display, but there are no Hi Powers similarly shown.

Here in the U.S., one agency that showed a lot of interest in the Hi Power was the FBI, specifically for its Hostage Rescue Team. Although, that was back when the FBI allowed personal weapons for service and the Hi Power was on the approved list. They went to a great deal of effort in the mid-to-late-1980s to have Wayne Novak build up a batch of Hi Powers for them. The initial build was to install Novak sights on the pistols, but after various shipments, returns for repairs and overhaul, and requests for improvements, they were a buffet of 9mms with a host of custom features. The plain guns went to the field agents, and (no surprise) apparently the ones with the custom features went to supervisors, office heads, and the like.

What the FBI found out was what we IPSC shooters had learned some years before: the original Hi Power was not a heavy-duty pistol. The FBI did not feed its Hi Powers anything but a steady diet of standard-pressure 9mm ammunition, unlike the U.S. Army and its first problems with the M9 pistol. The M9 had issues in part because the idea of 9mm ammunition was new to the army. To the FBI, not at all. And despite using only standard pressure (not +P) ammunition, the FBI found, as the rest of us had, that the Hi Power couldn't take the volume of shooting IPSC required.

In the days of Bullseye competition, you'd be hard pressed to shoot more than 5,000 rounds a year. A match ran you 50 rounds of ammunition. If you shot a match every single weekend and practiced once in between, that came to 5,200 rounds a year. That was considered a lot of shooting. When I began IPSC competition I was shooting 10,000 rounds a year, and I was not keeping up with the Joneses. When I went to a Dillon loading press, I jumped up to 35,000 rounds a year and kept at it (or more) for the next 20 years. A 1911, even when firing .45 ACP +P, or 9mm +P or +P+ ammo, can do that for as long as the barrel's rifling holds up. Once you've worn out the bore, you can refit the slide to the frame, install a new barrel, and start over again.

I have several 1911s that have had 100,000 rounds or more through them, and you'd be hard-pressed to tell them from the lower mileage pistols. I am a slacker, as I know of people who have much more than that through their 1911s. The Hi Power? Tens of thousands in the old Mk II or earlier guns meant the end of service.

Browning was the importer of Hi Powers made by FN. When Browning wasn't bringing in as many as the market wanted, other importers shipped in pistols made in places other than Liege. Sometimes, especially once the patents expired, the manufacturer would see if an American importer wanted to buy a batch of "just like Liege" licensed Hi Powers. I have one like that, which was imported under the Charles Daly name, back when. These were Hungarian-made clones, and while I haven't tried to see

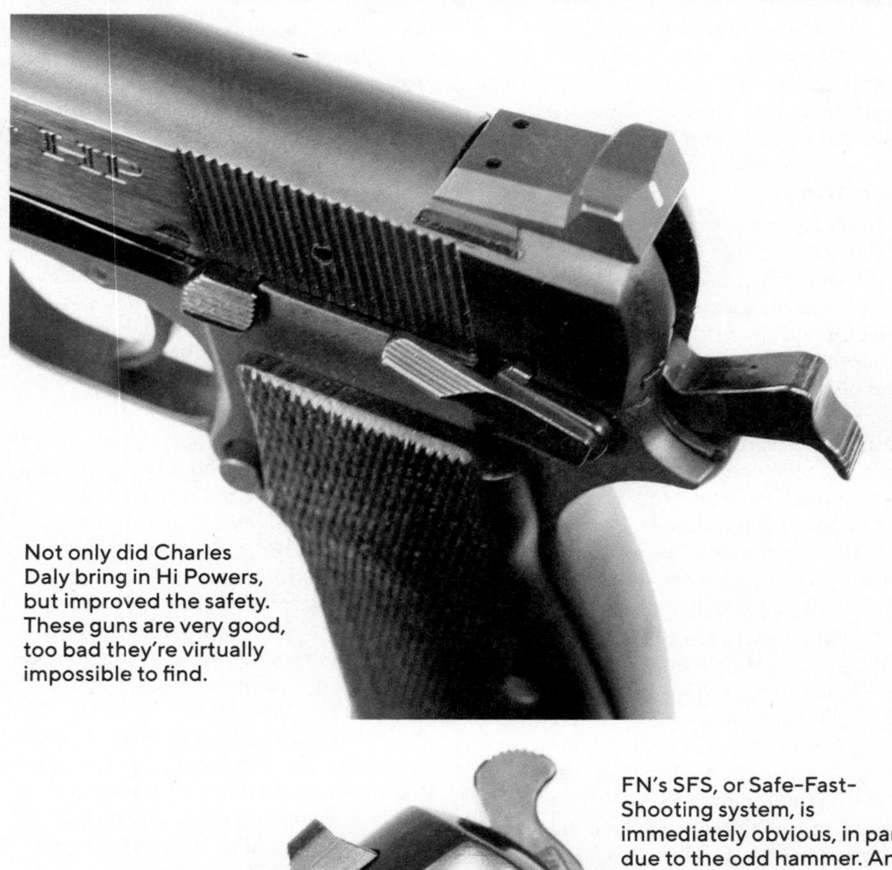

Not only did Charles Daly bring in Hi Powers, but improved the safety. These guns are very good, too bad they're virtually impossible to find.

FN's SFS, or Safe-Fast-Shooting system, is immediately obvious, in part due to the odd hammer. And the real clue: the hammer is "down" but the safety is on.

if small internal parts fit (none have shown signs they need to be replaced) magazines and grips fit just fine. Interesting tidbit of info: they were imported as parts, assembled and fitted here in the U.S. — hence the "Made in USA" markings they bear.

Don't get me wrong, the Hi Power will still be dependable even when heavily used. Our gun club's treasurer a couple of decades ago, who used to work for the city of Detroit, carried a brace of T-Series Hi Powers. This was during the bad old days when Detroit was aflame, and no one who needed a CPL back then could get one. He carried anyway. He used his so much that the recoil springs were more than a bit tired. I had a spring tester and the standard Hi Power recoil spring measured at 17 pounds. His two 9mms had springs worn down to 10 and 11 pounds. They still worked.

But when parts start breaking or falling off, it's time to move on. And move on we all did. So did the FBI HRT. One agency I still wonder about is the Hong Kong Airport Police. I encountered them while traveling to the 1999 IPSC World Shoot in the Philippines. We changed planes in Hong Kong and the police made us get off the plane and identify our bags, and inspected our firearms transport paperwork. They were bored, we were fascinated. We closely studied (all of us were gun geeks, there were 30-40 IPSC competitors for the match on that plane) the MP5s they carried, their handguns, holsters, etc. One thing we got tired of studying was their sloppy gun handling. When one supervisor had trouble reading the paperwork in the fading light (we were out of the plane, on the tarmac, with the other passengers peering out through the plane's windows at us), one of his subordinates lifted his MP5 over the boss's shoulder and clicked on the light on its handguard. Me, I looked around to see what I could hide behind should the inevitable accidental discharge happen. It didn't, thank goodness.

FN tried to keep up. One such change was the SFS. The Safe-Fast-Shooting system was an attempt to gain the benefits of a double-action (DA) pistol while retaining the upside of a single-action. The main benefit of the SFS was that the hammer was down. This made it appear to be a DA pistol and not one with a cocked hammer. Once you loaded the SFS, you pushed the hammer down with your thumb. When it clicked into place, the thumb safety popped up to engage the system. You now had a hammer-down pistol with a thumb safety. On the draw, you could thumb the safety down, which caused the hammer to automatically pop up, ready to go to work.

The one big change that made a difference was the introduction of the .40 S&W cartridge. When Jeff Cooper and others were experimenting with a cartridge that was called the .40 G&A, they used a Hi Power as their base pistol. They were happy with the results, but when the actual .40 came out in 1990 (their experiments had happened in the 1970s), things were different.

The prevailing wisdom of the time was that a .40 S&W pistol could be had simply by plugging a .40-caliber barrel into a 9mm model and installing a stiffer recoil spring. When the various pistol manufacturers did that, they found that the job was a lot tougher than they thought. It took a few years and a few model variants for everyone to work out the details. FN built some .40 prototypes on their Mk II frames and tested them. Those R&D guns died in an embarrassingly short time span. The word on the street was that they lasted about 2,500 rounds, and then were simply scrapped. The problem? The frames. A forged frame, one in which 85-90 percent of the steel is machined away, simply cannot be all that tough. So, FN went to cast frames for the Mk III. Since the machining needed is just for cleanup or to reach the final dimensions, they could make the frames of much, much tougher steel. I have one of these, and Wayne Novak built it into his top-end clone of the HRT gun. During testing for an article of the time, I put 23,000 rounds through it. I had two malfunctions in all that time. One was a low-powered lead bullet reload that had somehow gotten all the way to the chamber (but only partially into it) with a great big glob of bullet lube stuck to the case. The other was a seriously tired old 20-round magazine. The spring, when I extracted it, was a full inch shorter than the spring in a brand-new 20-round magazine. So, both malfunctions were blamed on things other than the pistol.

For those willing to indulge a Major League Baseball analogy, these were chalked up to errors on the part of the fielders, and so not hurting the Hi Power's ERA.

I have two other Mk IIIs, one a box-stock .40 that was a rental gun at Double Action range in Madison Heights, Michigan. They lost count of the ammo that had gone through it, but other than the usual handling and shop wear from going through a thousand hands, it looks, feels, and works fine. The other is a custom .40 built by Ted Yost. I managed to acquire it for less than the cost of the custom work Ted had done, so it's a keeper for sure. It is also a tack driver.

The rarest one I have is a lightweight Hi Power. These were made a few times, and only in short runs with aluminum frames, which pared a few ounces off the weight.

Just before Hi Power production ended, Nighthawk Custom imported a batch of FN Mk IIIs and built them into custom guns. The result was a hi-cap 9mm with more style than most people could handle but at the price of a custom 1911. They also solved the hammer bite

A "Made in the USA" Hi Power. Well, assembled in the USA from parts made in Hungary.

(top)The author's Novak BHP on a pile of brass and the stacks of ammo it chewed through during testing.

(above) From 10 to 20 rounds in a magazine, the BHP is easy to carry, simple to shoot, and brings envy in spades from jealous onlookers.

problem by welding on a tang to protect your hand. It was a love-it-or-hate-it proposition. If you must have the *ne plus ultra* of 9mm pistols, then track down a Nighthawk Hi Power. There will be no one who is not envious of you.

The Hi Power has a lot going for it — mystery, panache, style, grip-fit, and great looks to boot. So why has FN stopped making it? And why should you acquire one anyway? The word is that the tooling is worn out. Me, I don't buy it. Modern CNC machining uses slabs of steel called tombstones to hold the parts. The "tooling" consists of the cutters that are shaped to make the exact cut needed for a part or dimension. Cutting tools are purchased by the gross by big-time manufacturers.

No, the truth is much simpler: the polymer-framed, striker-fired pistols have won. The soul-less, industrial, common-as-dirt with no heart pistol has taken over. No one wants to pay what it would take to make a competitive Hi Power when you can literally buy a ready-to-go polymer handgun for half that amount.

Oh, FN could make a ready-to-go Hi Power, one with a nice trigger, no bite, durability, and a thumb safety you could use. It would cost as much as two Glock G17s or more, and it would still, at best, hold 15 rounds to the G17's 17+1.

Luckily, there are still makers of the Hi Power, but those that are not Liege-made will be rougher, and you may have to do some persuading to find a pistol-smith to tame them. My advice? Get a Liege-made one now, while you still can. The Hi Power, there's nothing like it.

HI POWER OR HIGH POWER: WHAT'S IN A NAME?

What do we call this pistol? Verbally it is no problem, because all the choices, save one, sound the same. But is it Hi Power? Hi-Power? High Power? Or High-Power? FN and Browning varied the spelling over the years and have even used a variant of these to describe the bolt-action rifles FN made and Browning imported. The editorial form is Hi-Power, but advertising over the decades has used all of them.

Then there are the acronyms. There's HP, GP, BHP, and P-35, the year of introduction. If you travel in Canada, you'll run into shooters there who call it the Inglis, and on an expedition to (of all places) the island of South Georgia, I ran into a former British serviceman who simply referred to it as "the Browning."

A pedant would scatter the spelling throughout a scholarly work according to the time, place, and origins of the model being discussed. While precise, it would be somewhere between annoying and maddening to read, and best to be avoided.

Me, I opt for the shorthand (BHP) where I can get away with it. Hi Power everywhere else unless it is a specific model like the Inglis. And "Browning"? In Britain, there may be only the one, but for the rest of us there are more than a dozen Browning guns worth considering. Make it Hi Power or BHP for me, then.

THE .318 WESTLEY RICHARDS RISES FROM THE ASHES

An Old Mauser Gew. 98 Breathes New Life Into the Iconic .318 Westley Richards

BY **PHIL MASSARO**

I have an undeniable attraction to classic cartridges, especially those used in Africa in the early part of the 20th century. This was an era of exploration, with the advent of the motor vehicle playing a role in how hunters reached the nooks and crannies of North America and Africa. It was also an era steeped in cartridge development. The huge black powder cartridges began to give way to smaller, smokeless powder cartridges, with higher pressures and jacketed bullets. Bore diameters became increasingly smaller, and hunters had to test the effectiveness of these new developments. In many cases they were in uncharted waters.

The first two decades of the 20th century saw the unveiling of what would become some of our most revered

The author's Ugly Duckling spent its first century as a World War I Amberg Arsenal Mauser Gew. 98.

cartridges, many of which are still at the top of their respective categories today thanks to the nostalgia of big game hunting. Some of the American developments made their way to Africa and Europe, and European innovations were accepted by American hunters, as well as playing a dominant role in European colonies around the world. This was the height of the British Empire, the high-water mark in British cartridge development. Gun makers with prestigious names — Rigby, Holland & Holland, Jeffery, and Gibbs — put a considerable amount of effort and research into perfecting the cartridges that would bear their names. Though the engineers have long gone to their reward, their creations live on. Each hunting season, across continent and country, those cartridges are loaded and carried afield for the purpose for which they were designed. The .416 Rigby, .375 Holland & Holland, .404 Jeffery, and the .505 Gibbs are all still viable big game cartridges, but there were others. The .350 Rigby Magnum, .275 H&H Magnum, and the .333 Jeffery all had their moment in the sun, as did one of my particular favorites: the .318 Westley Richards.

Westley Richards & Co, Ltd., was founded by William Westley Richards in Birmingham, England, in 1812. By the time the .318 Westley Richards Accelerated Express cartridge hit the market — sometime in 1909 by most accounts — Mr. Leslie B. Taylor was at the helm. While the Westley Richards name isn't rolling off hunters' tongues like it was a century ago, we all owe them a considerable debt of gratitude for the Anson & Deeley boxlock alone, a design still utilized to this day.

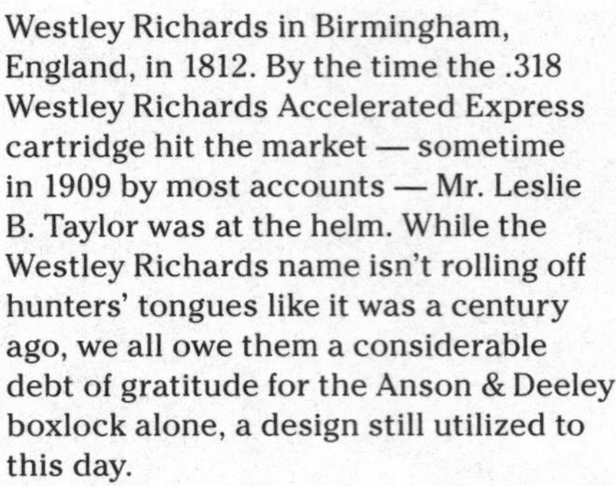

(right) An original Kynoch .318 Westley Richards cartridge with 250-grain solid.

(below) The .318 Westley Richards is also referred to as the .318 Nitro Express.

Westley Richards produced two prominent cartridges for their bolt-action rifles: the .318 and .425 Westley Richards. The .425 — with its severely rebated rim — required a magazine and feed ramp that were flawlessly balanced (and many were not), but that .318 became a darling of the connoisseurs of the smaller bore cartridges. Folks like W.D.M. 'Karamoja' Bell and Capt. Jimmy Sutherland used the cartridge with good effect on animals up to and including elephant. As a matter of fact, before the .375 Holland & Holland Magnum was considered the all-around worldwide cartridge, the .318 WR held that position. John "Pondoro" Taylor, in his excellent book, African Rifles and Cartridges, wrote extensively about the .318 Westley Richards, noting that it may not have been well-suited for elephants and other large, dangerous game in the thick bush, but that the cartridge could "certainly be recommended for African hunting."

The cartridge's recipe is rather simple. A rimless, bottlenecked case measuring 2.368 inches long, with a case head just a whisker smaller than the Mauser cartridges and the .30-06 Springfield, drove a .330-inch-diameter bullet of 250 grains to a muzzle velocity of 2,400 fps. That long, lean 250-grain bullet has a sectional density of 0.328, which translates to all sorts of excellent penetration. Combine that with the rather sedate muzzle velocity (have you ever noticed that all the classics run at a similar velocity?) and you'll see bullets that don't over-expand, yet have enough length to penetrate an animal from stem to stern. Westley Richards offered a lighter "L.T." 180-grain load at a muzzle velocity of 2,700 fps for lighter game, but it never really caught on. Perhaps it was the L.T. copper-capped bullet (which, by the way, was named after Leslie B. Taylor), or perhaps it was the fact that the penetration of the 250-grain load was damned-near unprecedented, but the fact remains that the .318 Westley Richards made its reputation with the heavier bullet.

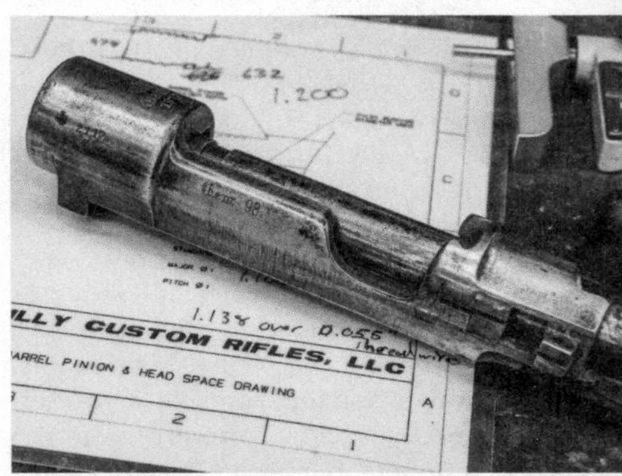

(top) The Gew. 98 action, disassembled and ready to start its new journey.

(above) The New England Custom Gun (NECG) barrel band front sight.

The concept of a heavy-for-caliber bullet propelled at 2,400 fps or so is more common than you'd think. The 6.5x54 Mannlicher-Schoenauer, 7x57 Mauser, .30-06 Springfield (with 220-grain slugs), and .416 Rigby all subscribe to this formula and have a stellar reputation. The .318 Westley Richards shares (or shared) that reputation, with the modern .338-06 A-Square mimicking the performance of the earlier cartridge. Delving through the older African hunting books, I began to see this common velocity/bullet weight thread, and the writings of my friend Dr. Kevin Robertson confirmed the idea. I'd handloaded ammunition for my .300 Winchester Magnum, loaded with 220-grain bullets, to a muzzle velocity of 2,425 fps and have taken whitetail deer and black bear with it, with great success. But, I still wanted a .318 Westley Richards of my own. I priced some used Westley Richards rifles and found that they were well out of my price range, so I decided to do the next best thing: I'd build one.

THE UGLY DUCKLING

One of the beauties of the .318 Westley Richards cartridge is that it can be housed in a trim, light rifle, and with a relatively narrow cartridge diameter, magazine capacity is no issue at all. Like many other British gun makers, Westley Richards utilized the German Gewehr 98 bolt-action receiver as the platform for their rifle. This classic model is very strong — over-designed some might say — and utterly reliable. Of course, Westley Richards would go on to bedeck the rifle in fine walnut, with their own stylistic appointments, including folding leaf sights for a variety of shooting distances (telescopic sights weren't anywhere near as popular or reliable before the First World War), and the result was a very handsome piece of kit.

It so happened that among the hunting gear I'd collected over the years was a 1916 Gew. 98, chambered in 8x57 Mauser from the Amberg Arsenal, with all matching serial numbers. I bought it from a childhood friend, though it had rested in the corner of a wet basement, muzzle down, for a number of years. The rifle was intact, if pitted and uncared for,

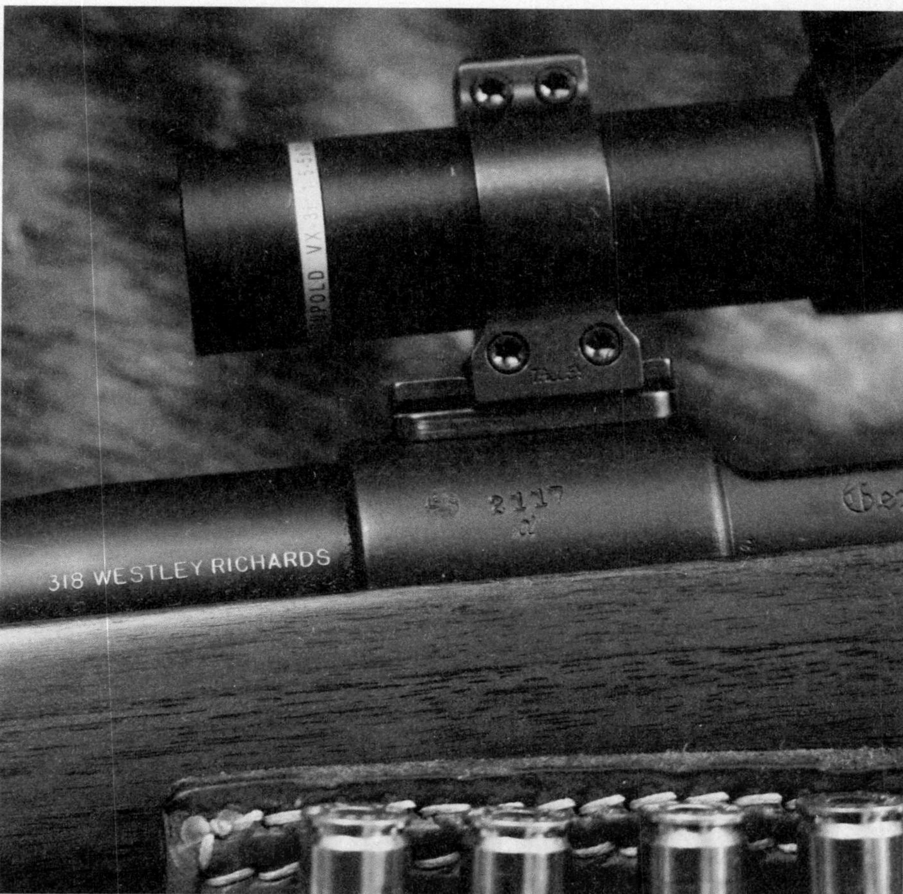

(top) The Gew. 98 had nearly every part marked with serial number 2117, and the author used the receiver, bolt, magazine, follower, and bottom metal for the rifle build.

(lbelow) A Timney trigger allows for accurate shot placement and is a pleasure to shoot.

(above) A NECG island rear sight, with fixed blade and flip-up sight for distant shots, being regulated before bluing.

(bottom) Matte bluing, Talley rings and bases, and a solid Leupold 1.5-5x20 scope made for a flexible hunting rifle.

with the 2117 serial number stamped on all the parts. I long thought about having a sporting stock put on it and using the 8x57 as a hunting round. The first three inches of the bore were beyond hope. Though I had it cut back, the rifle printed shotgun-like groups. Then the idea popped into my head: I'd use the century-old rifle as the platform for the build of the .318 I so desperately wanted.

It wouldn't be a difficult process. The bolt face could remain intact, and though the overall cartridge length wouldn't fit into the magazine box of the Mauser, I could easily seat the bullets just a bit deeper into the case without compromising case capacity or affecting performance. Cases for the .318 could easily be fashioned from .30-06 Springfield brass (more about that later) and component bullets are readily available from a few good sources. The traditional flag safety of the 98 Mauser would have to go, as it wouldn't allow for the use of a low-mounted scope. The military trigger — which was creepier than a clown in a windowless van — would also be replaced. Screw on a new barrel, swap out the military stock, drill and tap it for scope bases, and this thing should be underway. I'd never had a custom rifle built, and I was eager to embark on the journey.

My buddy Nathan Chesney, owner of Hillbilly Rifles in Newport, Vermont, was on the other end of the phone one day and we were discussing some load data for a new cartridge he was chambering in one of his rifles. I pitched him the idea of building a .318 for me, as outlined above, and he took the bait emphatically. "I love those old timers! Let's do this."

I sent him the rifle for disassembly, and we discussed the parts we'd need for the project. Nosing around the Interwebs, I found that Krieger made a .330-inch barrel. Their stuff has always shot well for me, and I had no issue using their barrel for my rifle. For a trigger, I knew I wanted a Timney. I personally love the clean, crisp feel of a well-tuned Timney trigger, and have used in them in more than a few of my rifles in the past. Brownells sells a three-position Model 70-style wing safety that would allow me to mount a scope nice and low to the bore, so that was put on the shopping list. For rings and bases, there was no real discussion. Talley Manufacturing makes what I consider to be the finest and most reliable set of detachable rings on the market. They have served me well on many different rifles, and always return to zero when the scope is removed to access the iron sights.

Now, regarding those iron sights, I'd wanted an island rear sight, with a wide 140° V-style leaf for up to 50 yards, and a flip-up secondary sight for 100 to 125 yards. New England Custom Guns would provide the answer to that issue, offering a barrel band front sight and neat island rear, both of which would work perfectly without cluttering the barrel. Bottom metal, including trigger guard and follower, would be brought over from the 1916 Mauser, pitting and all. The game was afoot.

(top left) Reaming the chamber in the Krieger barrel.

(bottom left) Go/No-Go gauges were provided by 4D Reamer Rentals.

(below) The author had an opportunity to get his hands dirty while reaming the chamber.

(top) Dave Simon did an excellent job reshaping the stock and adding little touches, like the bevel on the right side of the receiver.

(above) The Ugly Duckling at the bench during load development.

With the barrel attached to the receiver, Nathan fitted the Timney trigger and the three-position safety. The safety work was something well above my pay grade, and required some serious attention, yet I am happy to report that it works flawlessly when someone who knows how to work metal is at the helm. The iron sights were secured, and the receiver was drilled and tapped to accept the Talley mounts. Nathan replaced the perpendicular bolt handle of the military Mauser with a custom bent bolt, leaving room to clear a riflescope. Bluing work was handled by Dark Horse Gunsmithing in Massachusetts. I chose a matte finish for all the metal and they gave me a perfect, non-reflective surface on all parts.

I chose a Leupold VX-3i 1-5x20 scope, which is the classic dangerous game optic for this rifle. Almost all shooting would be within 250 yards. It's a clean, trim, and light scope that will stand up well to some terrible recoil. That left us with the problem of a stock.

I couldn't afford having a custom stock made, so I ordered one of those gray laminate jobs that come all nicely inletted. However, there was an issue with it; the bottom inlet didn't match the action and was off by nearly 1/8 inch, and things weren't lining up right. I got a bit lucky, finding a used stock on eBay that was set up for a Mauser action and had

Dave Simon thinned out the stock and added the thumb groove, which is normally used for loading stripper clips. It's just another cool little feature on the classic Mausers.

We'd need a chamber reamer, and for that we turned to 4D Reamer Rentals. They provided both the reamer and a set of Go/No-Go gauges to ensure things would work properly. My wife Suzie and I drove to Newport one late spring day to meet Nathan at his shop to begin work on the rifle. We began by cutting the proper threads on the barrel end. Next came the chamber reamer. During this process Nathan even let me work the lathe so I could claim a bit of responsibility. Once cut and reamed, the barrel was affixed to the front of the receiver, and I saw the first signs of life from my .318! We lopped the barrel off at an even 25 inches — a length to give what I felt would be good balance between weight and accuracy.

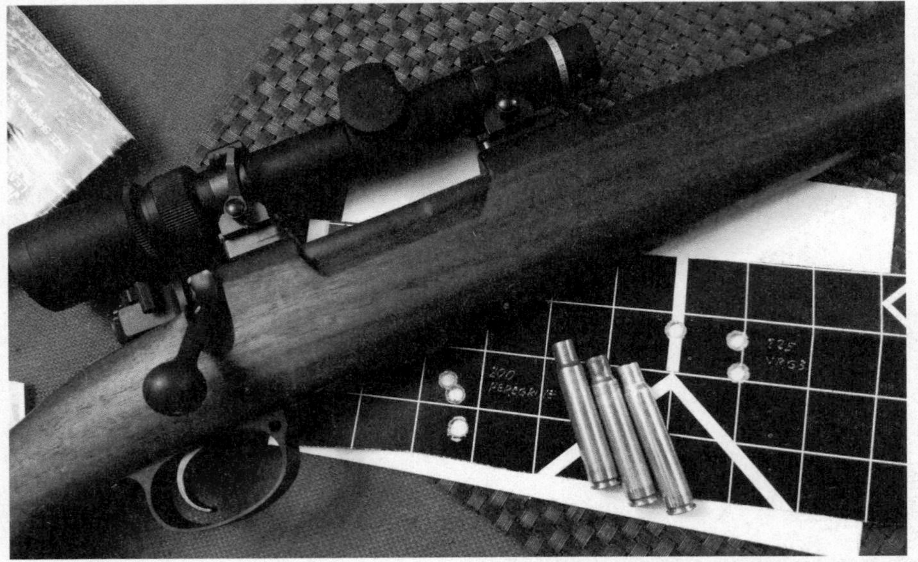

The monometal 200-grain Peregrine VRG3 (left-most group in the photo) makes an excellent choice for a hunting bullet, giving great accuracy and muzzle velocities. The 225-grain Peregrine VRG3 BushMaster (group on the right) gave excellent accuracy.

(below) The 250-grain Woodleigh Weldcore round-nose bullet delivers the ballistics for which the .318 Westley Richards is famous.

(bottom) South Africa's Peregrine bullets are well-made, being turned on a lathe. The monometal design uses a flat-nose brass plunger over a hollow cavity to initiate expansion. They give excellent terminal ballistics.

some decent figure to it. It set me back all of $115, and while it would need some love and attention, it was a good start.

I met with my pal Dave Simon, who is a fine woodworker, and showed him some changes I wanted. He'd cut out the thumb groove on the left side, bevel the stock for loading on the right side of the receiver, and shape the rest to give it some class. I used some photos of vintage Westley Richards rifles, along with my own Heym Express as a model for some of the refinements. Dave did a fantastic job. He's a meticulous carpenter who should really take up stock making. The pistol grip was opened up and thinned a bit to feel much better than it had, the nose of the stock was rounded and thinned, and the overall shape was evened out. Mr. Simon, stock making should be in your future.

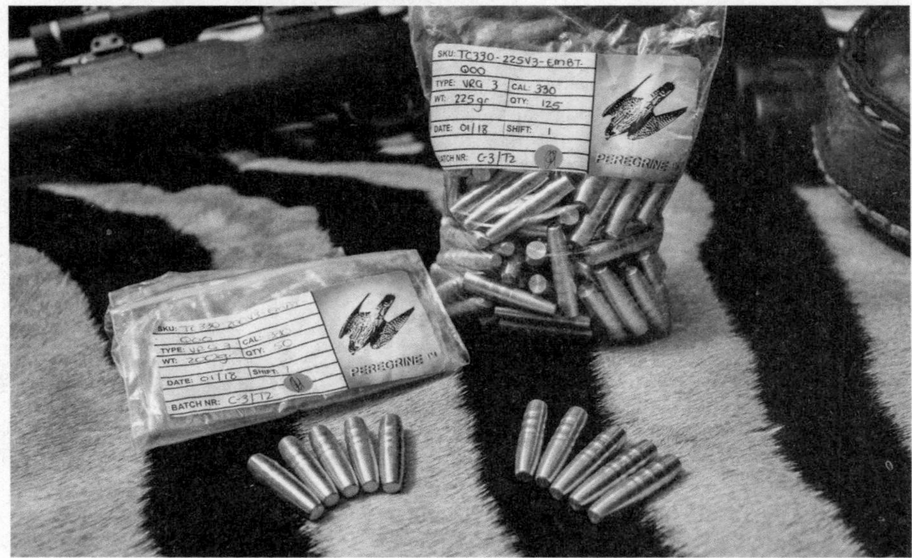

MODERN LOAD, CLASSIC CARTRIDGE

While modern rifles chambered in the .318 are still being manufactured, factory ammunition is a completely different story. Kynoch is the only manufacturer to my knowledge that still produces ammo, and that is at the average price of $10 per shot, which just won't do for my budget. So, I figured I could make my own ammunition and set out to do just that. I procured a set of reloading dies and some good .30-06 brass. It was a simple matter of trimming the brass down from 2.494 down to 2.370 inches, allowing for a bit of length when the shoulder got moved rearward, and running that brass through a full-length resizing die. A tapered expander ball and plenty of lubricant (Imperial Sizing Die

Wax for the case body and Imperial Dry Lube for stretching the necks) makes perfect brass with one pass through the die. A good chamfer and deburring makes for easy bullet seating, and load development had begun.

Load data for the .318 is not exactly abundant. Woodleigh provides good data, and their manual is a worthy investment, plus I wanted to use one of the new temperature insensitive powders, as I had big plans for this .318 in all sorts of climates. Between Nathan and I, we stumbled onto a load of Reloder 16, which we had to interpolate and work up from the bottom, that gave us exactly what we were after. Loading a 250-grain round-nosed Woodleigh Weldcore over an even 52.0 grains of RL-16 and sparking that load with a Federal GM210M primer showed a muzzle velocity of 2,475 fps, and my rifle put three of those bullets into a nice 1-inch group at 100 yards. Woodleigh isn't the only source of bullets available for the .318 WR. Hawk Bullets makes a sweet 200-grain round-nosed bullet, Hornady produces a 205-grain spitzer InterLock (for the 8x65R, but it's .330-inch diameter) and my pals at Peregrine Bullets in South Africa crank out a fantastic VRG3 BushMaster in 200, 225, and 250 grains.

The Hornady 205-grain bullet printed 1.25-inch groups at 100 yards at a velocity of 2,750 fps over a charge of Reloder 16. The Hawk bullet, while operating at safe pressures, didn't provide the greatest accuracy in my rifle, but the Peregrine BushMasters were a different story. Both the 200- and 225-grain BushMasters gave excellent accuracy from my rifle/scope combination, and based on my past experiences with these bullets on dangerous and plains game alike, this is a winning combination. Though there is little published data on modern powders for the .318 — save for the Woodleigh Manual, which gives good data for the 250s — the loads I've painstakingly developed here are a good guide, but realize that those I've published herein are near maximum and need to be reduced by 5 percent to start.

PROVING GROUNDS

I spent the following deer and bear seasons carrying that rifle up and down the Catskill Mountains and around my old haunts in the Hudson Valley. Not for any lack of effort, neither buck nor bear were in the cards, but one evening an old doe stepped out and paused just a bit too long. One 250-grain Woodleigh put her down as quickly as any cartridge I've ever used. The Ugly Duckling had spoken, and it was good. For some, the simple act of taking a doe for meat may seem like a rather routine process. But for me, using a rifle I had a hand in building, chambered in a cartridge I'd long dreamed of, was a moving experience. And it was only the beginning. This .318 will accompany me to Botswana next year, and many more adventures around the world.

(top) Hornady's 205-grain InterLock spitzer — though marketed for the 8x65R — is of proper diameter for the .318 Westley Richards cartridge.

(above) Hawk, Inc., from New Jersey makes custom bullets and the customer may choose from different jacket thicknesses. They offer a couple choices for the .318 Westley Richards. Here are the 200-grain bullets, with a jacket thickness of .035 inch.

From the top: the Snider-Enfield, a Langenhan (German) pistol, and the Starr carbine. The book is Sgt. Johnson's wartime log from his years in German prisoner of war camps.

A Private Valour AND THE IMPORTANCE OF REMEMBERING

BY **TERRY WIELAND**

By anyone's standards, my uncle, Marshall Angus Johnson of St. Thomas, Ontario, Canada, had an interesting life. He was one of the World War II generation — those men that Tom Brokaw termed in 1998 "the greatest generation that any society has ever produced." It's a broad generalization, to be sure, but terribly difficult to dispute. They were, indeed, great men.

Canada was in Hitler's war from the beginning — six long years, having declared war on Germany on September 10, 1939, just ten days after the mother country, Great Britain. At the time, Canada's armed forces were modest, to say the least. The regular army had 4,500 men, the air force had only 20 combat aircraft, and the navy consisted of a meager six destroyers.

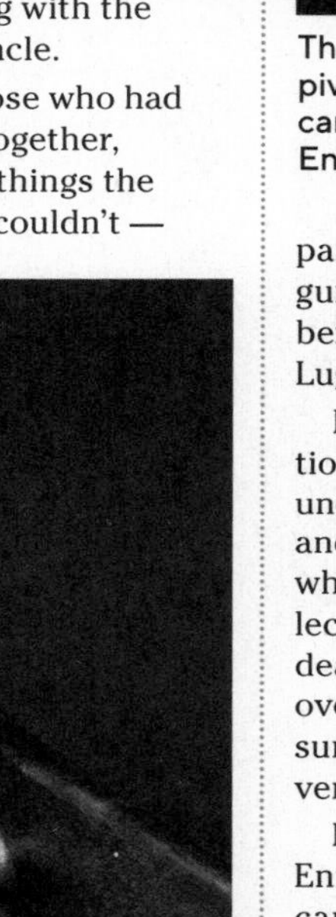
The Snider-Enfield is the 1853 Enfield muzzleloading rifle converted to breechloading, using a mechanism designed by Jacob Snider of Philadelphia.

When the call went out for volunteers, some boarded ships for England to sign on in the British Army, the Royal Navy or the Royal Air Force (RAF). Others enlisted in the Canadian armed forces. My uncle Marsh was one of the latter. He volunteered in the fall of 1939 at the age of 18, trained as an air gunner, and sailed for England in April, 1941, with the rank of sergeant in the Royal Canadian Air Force. He became a tail-gunner in a Wellington bomber, flying under Canadian colors as part of the RAF.

Even early in the war, tail-gunner in a bomber was not an occupation with a long life-expectancy, so taking the long view, one could say that Marsh Johnson was one of the lucky ones. After all, he did come back alive.

***

As a child, I loved visiting my uncle Marsh, but even at that age I knew something set him apart.

My mother had four sisters, so there were five brothers-in-law. Of the five, one was too old for the war, another too young and a third disabled. This left my father and uncle Marsh as the two war veterans, but they were not the only military members of the family. My mother served in the Canadian Army, which is where she met my father. He had enlisted immediately and went to England with the 1st Canadian Division. His sister married an Englishman who was stationed in Canada for flight training with the RAF — another military uncle.

At family gatherings, those who had been in the war often sat together, talking in low tones about things the rest of us wouldn't — and couldn't — understand. Even in this select group, however, Marsh was different. He was always pleasant to me, but he had a dark side and was known for lightning flashes of temper. A photograph from early in the war, in his air force uniform, shows a man resembling the young Paul Newman, but when I knew him his angular features had a slight tic. I learned much later that his mouth had an uneven cast as a result of having his face frozen to the ground — twice — while he was a guest of the Third Reich as a prisoner of war. It gave him a permanent sardonic expression.

It was the 1950s, and the idea of the "recreation room" had taken root in the suburbs. Marsh (he hated being called "uncle") had turned the basement of his house into a combination museum and gun room. The walls were hung with muskets, rifles, swords, bayonets and a pair of elaborate Gurkha kukris. Being a gun nut from as far back as I can remember (my first water pistol was a "German Luger"), I was endlessly fascinated.

The Snider conversion employed a pivoting breechblock. The .577 Snider cartridge was designed for the Snider-Enfield.

Marsh inherited much of this collection from a childless relative, a distant uncle who left half his guns to Marsh and the rest to a cousin. No one knows what was in the other part of the collection; apparently, the lucky recipient deactivated the guns and handed them over to his children to play with. Not surprisingly, all were reduced to junk very quickly.

Marsh's share included a Snider-Enfield, with bayonet; a Starr percussion carbine; a percussion over/under of the "side hammer" variety (apparently an obscure specialty of upstate New York gunsmiths); a Belgian-made 8-bore percussion shotgun; and a Middle Eastern flintlock of indeterminate age. These were arranged on one wall, interspersed with bayonets and other militaria. Locked away in a desk, I later learned, were two handguns — a revolver and a pistol. Needless to say, I adored the place.

***

Air/Gunnery Sergeant Marshall A. Johnson had just turned 20 when he sailed for England. His convoy skirted the Denmark Strait and put into port in Iceland for a few days. They didn't know it at the time, but they had dodged their first bullet: A month later, the German battleship Bismarck broke out through the Strait in search of convoys such as theirs, sank HMS Hood, and was herself sunk three days later by HMS Rodney. It was an exciting time in the North Atlantic.

A Crandell side-hammer double rifle, made by Marvin F. Crandell of Gowanda, New York. It is a .38-caliber (.357) muzzleloading percussion rifle. Such guns were something of a specialty for upstate New York gunsmiths in the 19th century. Crandell was listed as a gunmaker in Gowanda from 1860 to 1880.

The lockplate of the Crandell rifle has certainly seen some wear. The maker's name and address are only partially decipherable, but it was traced through old records and gun listings.

Having made it safely to England, Marsh was assigned to an operational training unit (OTU) in Oxfordshire, then to 214 Bomber Squadron at RAF Stradishall in Suffolk. There, he became the tail-gunner in a Vickers Wellington, a long-range medium bomber used for night bombing missions, captained by Pilot Officer Gordon Crampton. On July 14, 1941, the Wellington took off for its second night-bombing mission over Germany.

Somewhere near Bremen, the plane was attacked by a night fighter that dove on it from behind. P/O Crampton, in a letter to Marsh's mother after the war, described what happened.

"You know we were attacked by a night fighter," he wrote. "Well, although the German dived straight out of the blackness and opened fire almost before he could be seen (Marsh was the first to see him) your son said quite calmly down the phones 'There's a fighter attacking.' He might have been asking for the salt!

"Although shells were smashing through the top of his turret he carefully leveled his guns on the German and gave him a good long burst."

The "good long burst" crippled the Messerschmidt, which turned away, but the hard-hit Wellington went down in flames. Two of its six-man crew were killed, while the others bailed out and parachuted into a farmer's field. All that night and the next day, they "hid in ditches," but were soon captured.

In the early part of the war, fliers on both sides observed the "knights of the air" chivalry of 1914–18. There was a camaraderie among men sharing equal risks. This changed later, as the RAF responded to Luftwaffe bombing of English cities with massive carpet-bombing raids of its own. By 1944, downed aircrews in Germany could be lynched as "murderers and terrorists."

While Crampton and his surviving crew were being interrogated, they received a surprise visit from the pilot of the attacking fighter, who had managed to get out in one piece. For Oberleutnant Walter Nowotny, the Wellington was his seventh kill but the first time he'd been shot down himself. He wanted to make sure the crew was being well-treated and, Marsh wrote in his journal, "he congratulated me on my marksmanship."

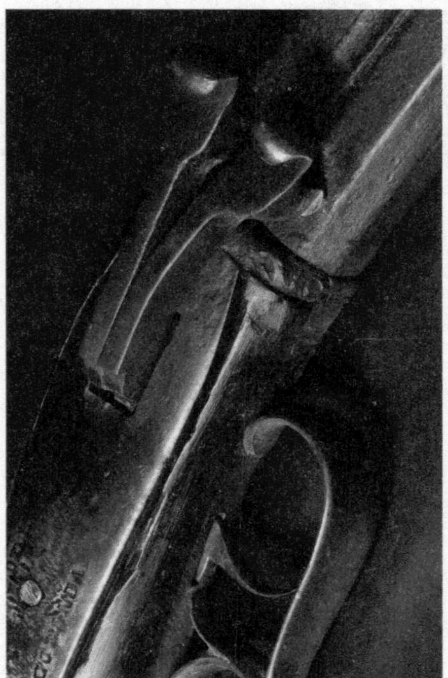

The side-hammers of the Crandell are powered by springs. Such designs are sometimes called "side-slappers."

As a Kriegie (short for Kriegsgefangener, or prisoner of war,) A/G Sgt. Johnson kept a journal almost from the beginning, including observations, poems and drawings. One section includes snippets from letters received by his fellow Kriegies. The first such, to a flier from his mother, read, "I am so glad you were shot down before flying became dangerous."

His journal also contains a clipping from a German newspaper in October, 1944, reporting the death in action of now-Hauptmann Walter Nowotny, holder of the Knight's Cross with Crossed Swords and Diamonds, described as the "7th soldier of Germany." He crashed while attempting his 258th air victory. Marsh described Nowotny as "upper class, not a Nazi."

"He was undoubtedly one of their best fighter pilots. I liked him."

Later accounts of Nowotny's unquestionably stellar career as a fighter pilot disagree with some of the above information, including the date and place of his first kill (given as July 19, 1941, on the Russian Front), but considering the destruction of records, secrecy, censorship and the problems of piecing together information after the war, A/G Sgt. Johnson's account, put together at the time as events were unfolding, rings true.

***

A/G Sgt. Marshall A. Johnson spent almost four years in prisoner of war camps spread across eastern Europe. "They moved us often," he wrote, to "discourage escape attempts." Altogether, he did time in seven different camps. On March 30, 1942, he was moved to Stalag Luft III in Sagan, Silesia (now part of Poland), later site of the "Great Escape." There he remained until June 25, 1943. The Great Escape, made famous in the movie of the same name, was the largest mass escape of the war, with 76 prisoners getting out under the wire through a tunnel. By the time the escape took place in March, 1944, Sgt. Johnson had been moved yet again, to Stalag Luft VI in Heydekrug, in what is now Lithuania. Stalag Luft VI was designated especially for British and Canadian Air Force NCOs. From there, he was transferred to another infamous camp, Stalag 357, in Poland. Like most POW camps, it was divided into sections. One section held Russian prisoners, of whom 10,000 starved to death. Stalag 357 was later shifted west and relocated in southern Saxony.

(top A/G Sgt. Marshall A. Johnson, on graduation from air-gunnery school in early 1941.

(above) Hauptmann Walter Nowotny in 1944. He was shot down attempting his 258th air victory. Marsh Johnson's Wellington bomber was his seventh kill, but Nowotny was shot down himself in the encounter. He later congratulated Marsh on his marksmanship.

By late 1944, with the Red Army advancing through Poland, the Germans began evacuating both prisoner of war and concentration camps, sending their inmates west, on foot, in a series of forced marches through the bitter winter of 1944–45. There were many such marches, some worse than others, but all dreadful, and thousands died of exposure, exhaustion, starvation or a bullet in the neck. These forced marches are known by several names. In his journal, Sgt. Johnson calls his simply "Death March." It began on April 8, 1945, and ended on May 2 when they reached British lines.

It was during this ordeal that Sgt. Johnson came across a German staff car by the side of the road. In it were two dead officers. He searched them for anything of interest — food, mainly, or cigarettes — and finally took a pistol which he tucked away. That pistol accompanied him from that time until he arrived back home in Canada in the summer of 1945. It was one of the handguns that remained locked away during my childhood visits.

***

Shortly after his return to Canada, Sgt. Johnson was informed that he had been promoted, retroactively, to the commissioned rank of pilot officer and, being the son of a former mayor of his hometown, he became something of a celebrity. Not surprisingly, however, he had trouble settling down.

Eventually, he married my aunt Shirley, who at 22 was one sexy chick. Marsh went to work for Canada Customs and set about assiduously keeping his promise that "I am never leaving home again." To the best of my knowledge, he never did. He eventually rose to the rank of inspector in the customs service, and during this time acquired the other handgun in the collection — a no-name double-action .32 revolver that had been fished out of the Detroit River. One can only speculate. All I know is, that revolver ain't talkin'.

After his experiences in Europe, P/O Johnson, RCAF (Ret'd), might have been forgiven for wanting nothing more to do with the military. Instead, he pursued it with serious interest. With his new commissioned rank, he was welcomed into the Elgin Regiment, the local army reserve unit that had converted during the war from infantry to armour. Marsh served with them for years, finally retiring for good as a major. I once saw a photo of him in his army uniform; he still looked like Paul Newman.

It was during this time that he acquired the gun collection that graced the walls of his den. He also collected the swords, bayonets, kukris, medals, insignia and even a deactivated hand grenade.

I may have found it all endlessly fascinating, but Marsh's two children, a son and a daughter, did not. In fact, they had no interest whatsoever, nor did their own children after Marsh became a grandfather. They also had little interest in Marsh's war experiences, his journals, the notes and memorabilia, the medals.

Sometime in the 1960s, thieves broke in and stole all the firearms. Police recovered them quite quickly, but Marsh was only able to get them all back (particularly the handguns) if he undertook to have them deactivated. Undoubtedly, his position as both an army officer and a Customs officer made this possible; had it been anyone else, all the guns would have disappeared into the fiery furnaces of the Stelco steel mill.

As a Kriegie (prisoner of war), Marsh kept a journal of his time in seven different camps across eastern Europe between July 1941 and May 1945.

In 2003, my uncle, Marshall Angus Johnson, died, having lived to the not-inconsiderable age of 82. Not to be flippant, but he would have been the first to agree that it was a damned admirable age for a Wellington tail-gunner.

As my darling aunt grew older, she began to worry about the fate of Marsh's extensive collection of guns and militaria. As the only person in our entire family with any interest in such things, she asked me if I would like to have them. A Snider-Enfield? A Starr carbine? Let me count the ways. By this time, I was living in the United States, and getting the whole collection across the border was an experience. Luckily, I drew a U.S. Customs officer with both an interest in old guns and a sense of humor, and the only delay was to allow him time to handle and admire each of the artifacts. Impatient cars piled up behind us as he asked about my uncle and his war experiences.

There were two conditions attached to the collection. One was that I should keep them all together should I ever decide to part with them. Such a promise cannot be kept beyond one's own lifetime, of course, but I readily agreed. For my part, I wanted my aunt's blessing to get them all shooting again, if that was possible. And so began the second part of this adventure.

***

Deactivated firearms are of little interest to me, since every gun I pick up I want to shoot, if only to see how difficult or easy it is, what obstacles the shooter had to overcome, and how it might or might not be a great gun in the field. Never before, however, had I started by having to deactivate the deactivation.

I soon found that, while Marsh might have told everyone the guns were deactivated, only some of them really were. My immediate interests, being a breechloading-rifle guy, were the Snider-Enfield and the Starr carbine.

SNIDER-ENFIELD

The Snider-Enfield is not a rare collector's item. In fact, it's one of the most commonly found and reasonably priced of all the original black powder, breechloading military rifles from the early cartridge era.

It was born out of the British War Office's need for a breechloading rifle with which to arm its troops around the world. As usual, the Exchequer, which controlled the purse strings, insisted on the most economical solution in the shortest period of time. Since the army had tens of thousands of 1853 Enfield muzzleloaders in storage, the War Office called for inventors to offer conversion designs. Out of 47 submitted, nine were given further testing, and the one chosen was that of Jacob Snider of Philadelphia. Hence, "Snider-Enfield."

Jacob Snider did not specify a cartridge, merely stating the rifle would need a cartridge "of some kind." He did include an extractor mechanism in his design.

The task of designing a cartridge and ignition system fell to Colonel Edward Mounier Boxer, an artillery officer and superintendent of the laboratory at the Royal Arsenal at Woolwich. The result was not only the .577 Snider, ancestor of every British cartridge that came after, but also the famous Boxer primer, in common use to this day.

Both the Snider-Enfield and the .577 Snider cartridge progressed through many models and iterations during their lifetimes. The cartridge began as a paper case built upon a steel washer, similar to a shotshell, then progressed through a coiled-brass and finally a drawn-brass case. Although it's now a bottlenecked cartridge, the chambers are actually straight. This is because Col. Boxer had to work with the existing Enfield .577 bore. Early chambers were large to accommodate paper cases, but later ammunition had to function in all the early chambers. Since brass is thinner, it was necked down to hold the bullet, which finally ended up as a 480-grain Minié ball.

The rifles also underwent some evolution, but nothing major. Mostly the changes had to do with locking the rotating breechblock closed. The Snider-Enfield was the British Army rifle for a very short time — 1866 to 1871, when it was replaced by the Martini-Henry — but it exists in enough variations that a collector could confine himself to just that rifle and cartridge and have more than enough variations to keep busy for a lifetime.

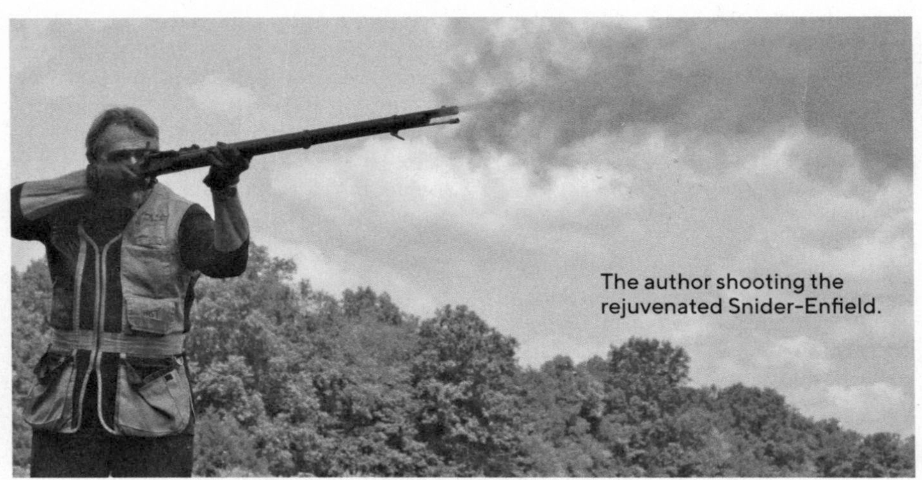
The author shooting the rejuvenated Snider-Enfield.

Marsh's Snider-Enfield is an 1862 Enfield, converted by the Birmingham Small Arms Co. (BSA) to a pattern II* model. It was missing its cleaning rod, but that was easily replaced. After a thorough cleaning and a trip to gunmaker Nick Tooth to dismantle the rifle and fit the rod (the threads were clogged), it was ready to shoot. For ammunition, I turned to Bob Hayley (Hayley's Custom Ammunition) in Texas, who fashioned brass. C-H offers large, 1-inch dies as a standard item. For these, you need a large press such as the Redding Ultramag. Usually, a 24-gauge case holder works.

After all this, the old girl was ready to return to action. The first time I pulled the trigger, filling the air with smoke and launching the 480-grain ball downrange, I felt like Dr. Frankenstein when his creation rose from the operating table and lurched out the door.

STARR CARBINE

The Starr was an early breechloader, designed by Ebenezer Starr. It vaguely resembles the Sharps, with a falling breechblock that pivots to the rear. It employs paper or linen cartridges, is .58 caliber with a 21-inch barrel, and was used mostly by Union cavalry during the American Civil War.

The Starr company was short-lived. Sample carbines were submitted to Washington in 1858, and several thousand were purchased and used during the war. In 1865, a redesigned version for brass cartridges was submitted, but not accepted, and the company closed its doors.

Marsh's Starr had obviously endured a long period when no one cared very much, but mechanically it seemed to be in good condition. Bob Hayley cast some bullets and assembled some paper cartridges. We loaded one in the chamber, closed our eyes (at least, I did) and pulled the trigger. It fired perfectly well — boom, smoke, the usual — except the percussion nipple blew out in the other direction, never to be seen again in the tall Brazos grass. Corrosion had weakened the threads holding it in place.

There followed a domino-like sequence of events that involved drilling out the threads, making an insert, tapping new threads and fitting a new nipple. The first nipple was too long, preventing the breechblock from pivoting far enough back to load, so a shorter one was found to replace it. During this, the cutting edge on the face of the breechblock was accidentally crushed in a vise, leaving

The Starr carbine employed a falling block that pivoted to the rear, allowing its paper cartridge to be inserted into the chamber. These rifles were used by Union cavalry during the American Civil War.

the old Starr hors de combat.

It's still in therapy, but I have a supply of ammunition and I'm looking forward to shooting it again — with my eyes open this time.

CRANDELL SIDE-HAMMER OVER/UNDER RIFLE

This rifle was a puzzle from the start. Until now, I had never even seen a photo of such a gun, much less handled one.

It's an odd percussion mechanism with two octagonal barrels, one atop the other. Ignition is by two hammers on the side, powered by springs, that slap the percussion caps (hence the nickname "side slapper" used by some collectors). The gun is heavy — 9 pounds, 10 ounces — which is good, because if it had any recoil at all the sharply curved buttplate could do you some damage.

The name and location of the maker was originally engraved on the lock plate, but time and abuse has erased all but a few letters. Firearms historian Garry James came to my rescue on this, deciphering enough to determine that the maker was Marvin F. Crandell of Gowanda, New York (just south of Buffalo). Bob Hayley had suggested earlier that it was from that area, since such guns, he knew, were something of a local specialty in upstate New York.

The upper "hammer" had a broken spring and flopped around like a broken wing, but Nick Tooth soon put that right. He cleaned the flash holes, worked on the trigger a little, and she was ready to go. Apparently, deactivation had been achieved by some white glue in the flash holes. The Crandell (as she is now known) is a .36 caliber. Rather remarkably, it has a single non-selective trigger. The only thing missing is its ramrod, but a piece of dowel serves admirably.

Again, Bob Hayley and I touched her off, with 150-grain .38-caliber hollow-base bullets he cast and using a .45 Colt case as a powder scoop. A little FFg black powder and some percussion caps, and it was back in operation.

Probably the most interesting thing about this gun, aside from its remarkable design, is its maker. Marvin F. Crandell was in business in Gowanda, New York, during the period 1860 to 1880, so this was a very late percussion gun and, by anyone's standards, more an example of folk art than great gunmaking. Still, it's a piece of history. Marvin Crandell apparently struck on this design and then made more guns exactly like it, because Garry James was able to find photos of some other examples. Some of these are more elaborate than others, but all have the same features: sculpted side hammers, single trigger, sharply curved buttplate and scrolled brass trigger guard.

It's difficult to use the word accuracy in the same sentence with the Crandell, but it is certainly fun to shoot.

BELGIAN 8-BORE PERCUSSION SHOTGUN

The big, single-barrel 8-bore gun was originally a very respectable piece with brass fittings. Mechanically, there is nothing wrong with the gun. Nick Tooth, who began his gunmaking career in the restoration shop at James Purdey in London, simply replaced the corroded nipple and pronounced it perfectly shootable. As yet, I have not found a need to fire it, but I do know that a percussion cap fires through the flash hole with gratifying force and regularity.

When a stray pterodactyl is sighted in the neighborhood, I'll know the 8-bore's time has come.

THE TUFEK

Initially, in my ignorance of the niceties of early muzzleloaders, I assumed the flintlock was a jezail, but Garry James set me right on that. In fact, it's a tufek, most probably made in Turkey around 1800. The lock is in the miquelet style, with an external hammer spring.

Garry James: "Another nice piece — not fancy but completely honest. It's a miquelet Ottoman Tufek. I'd date it circa 1800, perhaps a tad later. These were

Belgian 8-bore percussion shotgun. It needed a new nipple (the old one was corroded beyond use) but is now ready to shoot again, should a stray pterodactyl venture into the neighborhood.

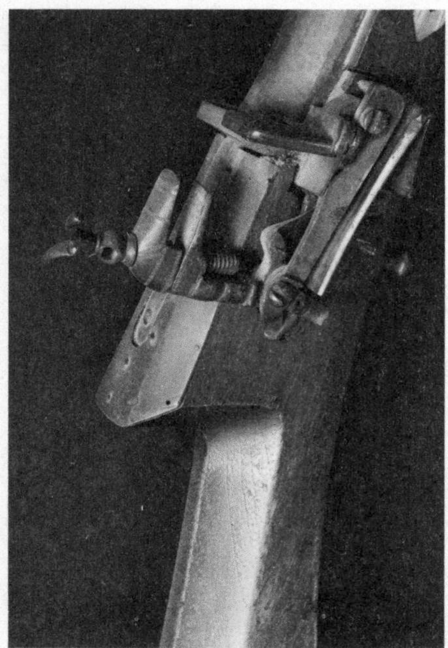
A Turkish tufek, with a miquelet lock, probably made around 1800.

made throughout the Ottoman Empire, first as matchlocks, then miquelets. There are various nuances depending on where they were constructed. This one looks Turkish — I don't believe it's Persian. These first appeared in the 16th century, though some were still being used in the hinterland well after the introduction of Martinis, Remington Rolling Blocks and Mausers.

"Most Turkish Tufeks were made in Bursa and Istanbul. Some were quite elaborate. It was not uncommon for miquelets to be fitted with older matchlock barrels, but I believe all the parts on your Tufek are of the same vintage."

As far as I can tell, there is no rifling in the bore, which measures .625 inch at the muzzle. To all appearances, nothing was done to deactivate the old beast, but following the advice of my two mentors on black powder, Garry James and Bob Hayley, I'm happy to let it hang on the wall among the African and Indian artifacts. Firing it could be an adventure just a little too far.

THE NO-NAME REVOLVER

Both of Marsh's handguns had been seriously deactivated, possibly irreversibly so. The no-name revolver, recovered from the Detroit River, is an old double-action with the striker integral to the hammer. This had been ground off. So far, attempts to weld a new one in place have not borne fruit, but hope springs eternal. Meanwhile, this true "Saturday Night Special" is maintaining a stubborn silence.

THE LANGENHAN PISTOL

Finally, there is the pistol my uncle took from the body of the dead German officer in 1945. It's a Langenhan Selbstlader (self-loader) in 7.65mm (.32 ACP). This was an emergency design dating from the Great War, when 50,000 were ordered for issue to the military and police. It was made in Zella-Mehlis, future home of Walther.

The Langenhan was made in two calibers, .32 and .25, and while it does not have the authority of a Luger or Mauser C96, it gained quite a good reputation for reliability. They remained in scattered use until the end of the Second World War. There seem to be quite a few of them in the stocks of companies that supply guns for motion pictures, because they show up quite often in the hands of movie detectives in 1930s Berlin.

Langenhan .32 ACP pistol. About 50,000 were ordered late in the Great War to supplement Lugers, which were in short supply. Langenhans were subsequently issued to police and the military.

Outwardly, the Langenhan resembles the early Colt semi-autos, but the barrel is underneath the return spring mechanism. Marsh deactivated the gun by putting a lag bolt into the muzzle and then pouring molten solder into the barrel, effectively plugging it. The threads were smaller than the bore and there was no damage done, but the molten lead filled both the threads and rifling and locked the bolt firmly in place. It's a clever way of doing it because, while it undoubtedly works and certainly looks permanent, a few minutes with a propane torch returned the gun to operational readiness.

Unfortunately, there is a threaded piece that holds the spring in the cylinder above the barrel. That part and the return spring are both missing, as are the spring and follower for the magazine. Until I find one, I'm afraid the Langenhan is out of commission.

***

Going through the jumbled box of notes and journals, newspaper clippings, letters, photos, medals and insignia, some his own, some that he collected, I learned things about my uncle I never suspected. I also had the twin feelings that A/G Sergeant Marshall Angus Johnson's war deserves to be remembered, but that it would not be. Like mountains receding in the rear-view mirror, shrinking in the distance until they become a low line on the horizon and finally slipping from sight, the significant events of yesterday become footnotes of tomorrow.

Today, there are many people — adult, educated people — with only the vaguest notion of who Adolf Hitler was, or the Russian Front, the blitz, or the bombing of Germany. Even Auschwitz and the Holocaust are becoming distant unrealities.

Marsh's generation may well have been the greatest any society has ever produced, facing an extraordinary threat and meeting it the way they did. Every single one of the men who fought in the Second World War deserves to be remembered in some way, or at least, to not be forgotten. Society owes them all a great debt, and the only way to repay that debt is to remember.

In a way, the men of that generation were like the guns in Marsh's collection: They had done a lot, but talked about it very little. It was a private valour.

BEYOND RANGE OF REBUTTAL

America and France Put British Officers in Their Sights, But Britain's New Rifle Corps — Armed with the .62-Caliber Baker — Enthusiastically Returned the Favor

BY **JEFF JOHN**

French Voltigeurs, like the British Rifles, were usually first in the fight and last off. Covering the army's retreat or movement, they had a similar mission of scouting and sniping, as did the British Rifles. The 95th Riflemen lived on the standard (usually bad) rations of bread or ships biscuit, dried peas and salt beef or pork — when they got it — and starvation was always a possibility. It was policy to buy when rations ran short, but the rapacious French lived off the land, often leaving starvation in their wake.

Hard-pressed by French cavalry during the retreat to Corunna near Astorga, Spain, 1809, Britain's 95th Rifles fought as part of the rearguard. Dashing back, General Sir Edward Paget offered his purse to the rifleman who could shoot French Cavalry General Auguste François-Marie de Colbert-Chabanais harrying the retreat. General Paget obligingly pointed out the General on his gray horse.

"[Thomas] Plunket immediately started from his company and, running about a hundred yards nearer to the enemy, threw himself on his back on the road, which was covered with snow, placing his foot in the sling of his rifle, and taking deliberate aim, shot General Colbert. His Trumpet-Major riding up to him shared the same fate, from Tom's unerring rifle … he had just time, by running in upon the rear-most sections, to escape some dozen troopers who made chase after him."

The actual range is lost to history, but it is a safe bet the shots were at least 200 yards away or more, since he was able to run back the 100 yards before French cavalry rallied to overtake him. Revolutionary France's hatred for royalty may have put the officer class in the sights of their marksman, but Britain's 95th Rifles

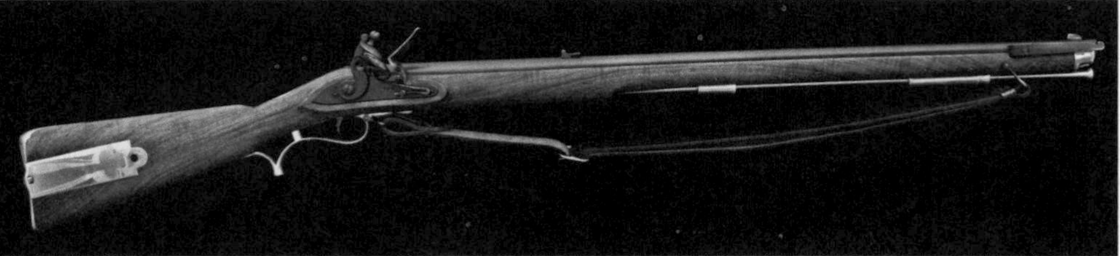

The sturdy, accurate Baker rifle proved itself in the hands of British soldiers and served from 1800 to the late 1830s.

could — and did — return the favor in spades.

Major George Simmons, then a lieutenant with the 95th in Portugal, relates a story from a dying French Captain: "I was sent out to skirmish against some of those in green — grasshoppers I call them; you call them Rifle Men. They were behind every bush and stone, and soon made sad havoc amongst my men, killing all the officers of my company, and wounding myself without [us] being able to do them any injury."

HARD LESSON LEARNED

Britain's use of rifles was discarded after the French and Indian War and the American Revolution. Indifferent, tea-sipping major generals excepted, serious men didn't ignore the lessons, and the third go-around proved eminently successful with the adoption of the Baker rifle and formation of a new Experimental Corps of Rifles.

The concepts weren't new, even to the British. The simple fact was, a rifleman could apply violence "four times the range of rebuttal." In the American Revolution, both sides successfully employed rifles with America's Morgan's Riflemen and Britain's Queen's Rangers just two of the better known and most successful units.

Targeting officers was something the British mostly eschewed, but not always! In a fit of pique at being stymied by Colonial Major General Friedrich Wilhelm von Steuben at a river crossing, Queen's Ranger Commander Lt. Col. John Simcoe brought up his 3-pounder gun to fire on the General and a group of American officers 400 yards away across the river, killing an aide's horse — certainly a unique form of long-range sniping. Simcoe's Rangers employed riflemen armed with the German-designed, Birmingham-made P1776 .62 caliber to lethal effect as well in a more conventional manner.

The rise of Britain's Rifles began after the American Revolution with the 1785 treatise on "Kleinen Krieg" (guerrilla war) by Hessian Jäger Captain Johann von Ewald who had served with the British against America. This — and works by other German military theorists — captured the interest of the Duke of York.

The Duke — Frederick Augustus of the House of Hanover (the German province where many Hessian Jäger regiments were raised) — was King George III's second son and had begun the reorganization of the British Army after suffering several embarrassing losses to France's mob-like Revolutionary army in the 1790s. Upon the rise of Napoleon, French skirmishers — Voltigeurs — stalked close to shoot officers and artillerymen.

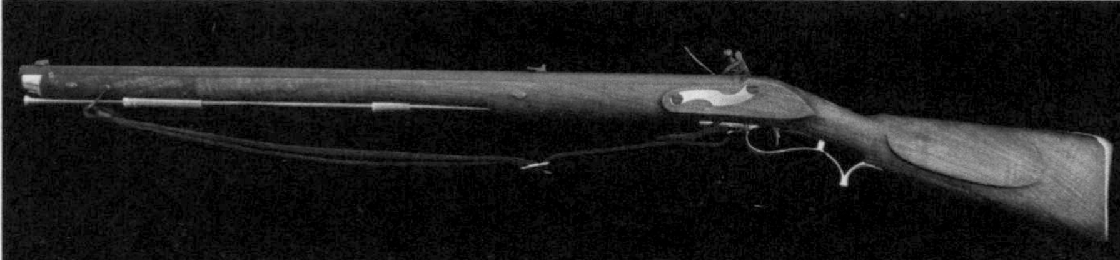

A cheekrest and easy takedown are among the Germanic influences found in the Baker rifle, along with the short, handy length and brass pistol grip forming a triggerguard.

This hold duplicates one shown on the frontispiece of the 1808 book *Scloppetaria*, written by Captain Henry Beaufroy of The Rifles. It offers a remarkably steady offhand hold. The service charge of 95 grains of "Fine Glazed" powder (FFFg used, since the actual definition of "FG" is lost to history) delivered 1,495 fps and 1,708 ft-lbs of energy.

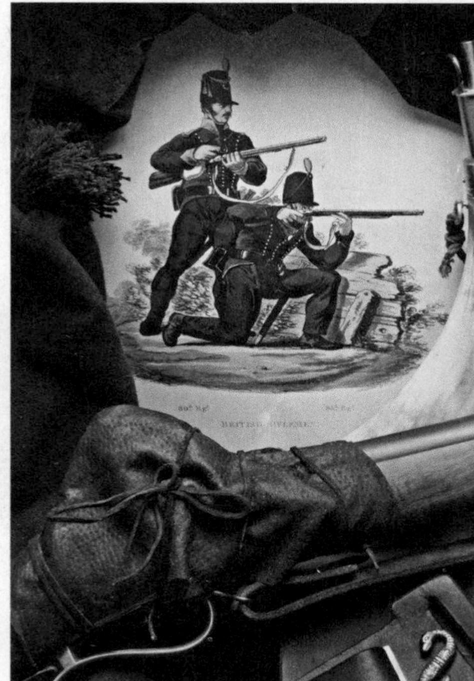

Standing in this print from 1812 is a Rifleman from the 60th Loyal American Regiment, a storied regiment going back to the French and Indian War. Their uniform was similar but slightly different in that they had red facings and blue trousers. Kneeling is a Rifleman from the 95th Rifles dressed in green. (Original in the British Army Museum, www.nam.ac.uk, prints available from www.kingandmcgaw.com.)

The Duke, full of these fresh ideas, began the transformation of the British Army into a professional fighting force, including giving merit weight in promotion rather than rank through patronage alone. Importantly (to this story at least), he authorized a new fast-moving light infantry featuring a Rifle Corps armed with what was then a state-of-the-art rifle.

In an era dominated by masses of men slugging it out shoulder-to-shoulder with ball and bayonet, the new light infantry mission was defined as "...a corps, which can disperse itself over an extensive tract of country, and unite in a body with rapidity and precision; a corps which, from the hedges and eminences gall and annoy the enemy in his march and act where it is impracticable to attack, either in line or column..."

General Sir John Moore shared the enthusiasm for the value of light infantry. He shepherded the formation of the "Experimental Corps of Rifles" based on a new, unique concept of a "thinking soldier." Col. Coote Manningham and Lt. Col. William Stewart had liberty organizing and developing the unique tactical doctrine codified in The Green Book for the 95th Rifles Corps. During the invasion scare of 1804, Moore was able to supervise and train this advanced light infantry with their innovative tactics at Shorncliffe barracks. This included several other newly formed light infantry regiments with rifle-armed companies, and included the 60th Loyal Americans, the 52nd and 43rd.

The 95th Rifles, whose symbols were the hunting horn and green uniform, were unique because they were the only regiment comprised solely of riflemen in the British Army. Other regiments had rifle-armed companies among their musket-armed companies and still wore the red coats. The 95th Rifles, and rifle companies within the 60th Loyal Americans and King's German Legion, were the only ones in the signature green jackets. Red or green, these men would be first in the fight and the last to leave the field. With them, the concept of the new "thinking soldier" was honed.

Their training included working as pairs, scouting and marksmanship. The 95th especially became famous in England, and their exploits and singular green jackets drew recruits like a magnet. The Rifles preferred to recruit among the Irish, who they believed hardier than Englishmen. Lt. Col. Stewart noted Irishmen were preferable "... perhaps from being less spoiled and more hardy than British soldiers, better calculated for active light troops." The Irish in the 95th were noted for "conspicuous and reckless gallantry."

The 95th is also singular because, as the only regiment of riflemen, they were the only one without colours. The other rifle-armed companies were part of musket-armed light infantry regiments, and those riflemen could rally to their regimental colours in a fight if need be.

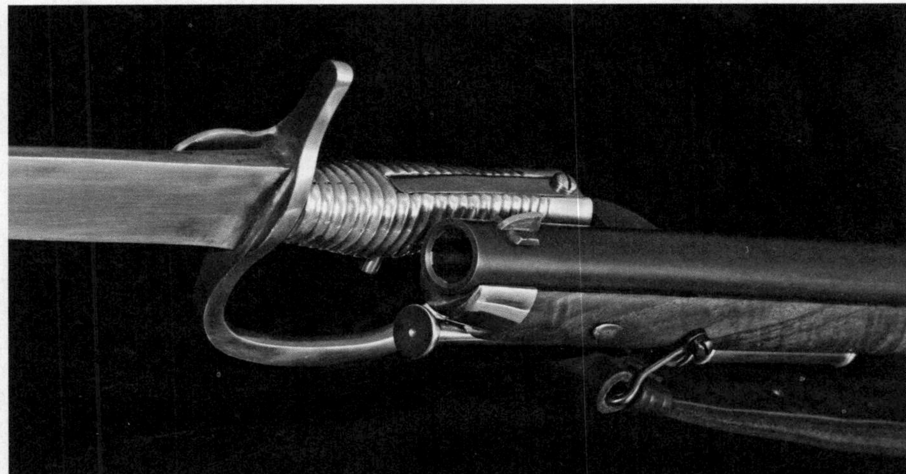

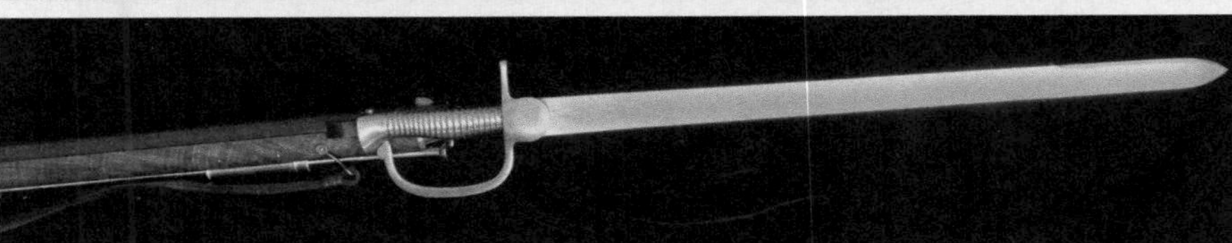

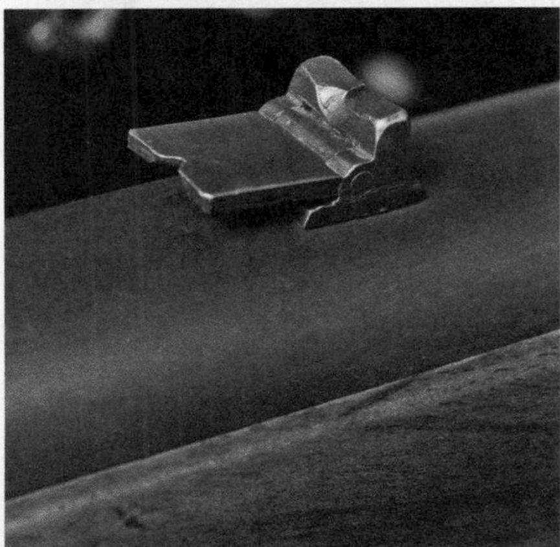

(top) The front sight is a simple brass blade dovetailed into the barrel. Via a slot in its handle, the sword bayonet attaches to a sturdy bar brazed onto the barrel.

(above)With its 71-inch reach, the Baker could fence with a musket, but a musket would be about 2 pounds lighter at the front end and quicker to parry and thrust. The last 5 inches of the Baker bayonet was sharpened on both sides, and could slash an opponent's hands, while musket bayonets were thrusting weapons alone.

(left) The rear sight has two leaves, and The Rifles practiced long-range shooting.

RIFLE TRIALS

This new, highly capable rifle was the culmination of a long, open design process involving top gunmakers worldwide. The barrel had to use the long-in-service .62-caliber carbine ball weighing approximately 344 grains, and the rifling style and twist chosen in a shoot-off, which was won by Ezekial Baker.

The Baker entered production in 1800, and roughly 2,500 1st Patterns were made. The Rifle Shoppe reproduction tested in this article (www.therifle-shoppe.com) is this early Pattern 1800 rather than the more common P1805. The Baker, with production of more than 32,000, would go on to serve for almost 40 years, and with other countries as well — perhaps most famously with Mexico at the Alamo.

The equally new Rifle Corps issued each P1800 rifle and its "stand of arms" (horn, cartridge box, bayonet and specialty tools) to an individual. It was his rifle, and he was responsible for it. Indifference had consequences, and specific rules for the rifle's maintenance laid out. No lock was to be removed "except by permitted men" or in the presence of an armorer, and action "lock covers" worn always with muzzle tompions in place.

Sluggards were not well tolerated. "As Riflemen are supposed to be Soldiers of the greatest attention towards arms, no

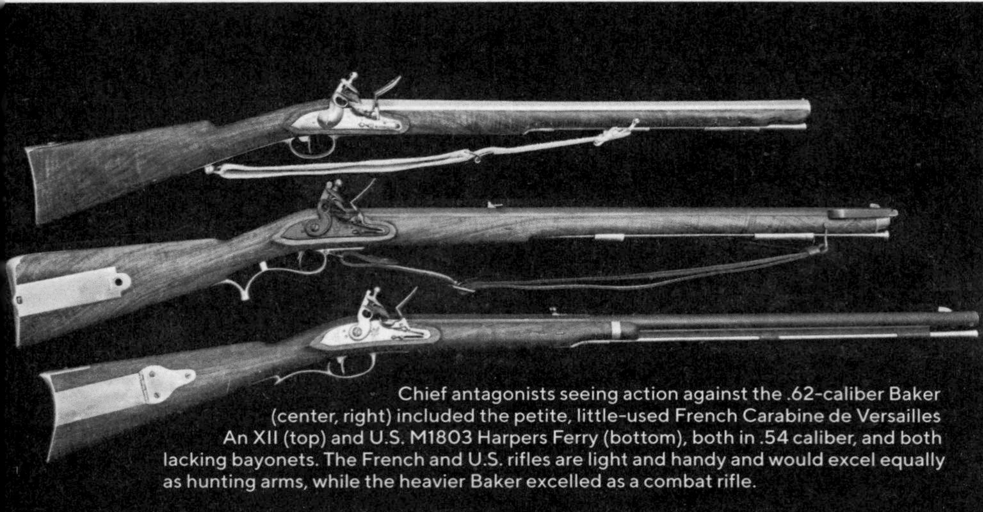
Chief antagonists seeing action against the .62-caliber Baker (center, right) included the petite, little-used French Carabine de Versailles An XII (top) and U.S. M1803 Harpers Ferry (bottom), both in .54 caliber, and both lacking bayonets. The French and U.S. rifles are light and handy and would excel equally as hunting arms, while the heavier Baker excelled as a combat rifle.

wood would be much sturdier if the barrel was held by bands — long used in French arms — instead of the expensive and fragile key system.

Still, wood was the weak link in all the era's small arms. At Le Haye Sainte, Waterloo, King's German Legion Rifleman Cpl. Friedrich Lindau notes, "…but then I found myself suddenly surrounded by the French. Now I used the butt of my rifle and hit out in all directions around me so that I soon had only the barrel in my hands…"

FIX SWORDS!

Other armies' riflemen relied on short swords or knives for final defense. Britain combined the two concepts, which required some thoughtful engineering

lenity will be shewn those who injure or spoil them … for' if a Soldier's lock cannot be trusted out of the sight of his Officer at all parades, he is totally unfit for the rifle service; so serious indeed is the trust which it is expected may be put in a Rifleman, that if any man be found, after fair trial and instruction, a dull, stupid, careless character, valuing not his arms, and never improving at the target, he will be applied for to be exchanged out of the corps."

PREMIUM CONSTRUCTION

The Baker rifle has many features found only in expensive sporting rifles and, unlike nearly all its contemporaries, is designed for durability and ease of maintenance. The rifle's lock is finely tuned, it's tumbler fitted with a fly allowing for an excellent trigger pull. The trigger itself is fitted to a metal trigger plate rather than pinned through the wood stock as nearly all its contemporaries. Thus, the trigger pull remains consistent as the wood swells, shrinks and wears.

The standing breech, providing a solid recoil plate for the removable barrel, is secured to the trigger plate by screws from the top and bottom. Both screws sandwich the wood between metal. Like a German Jäger, the triggerguard forms a pistol grip. The patchbox is inletted with separate compartments for the tools and greased linen patches. The left side of the stock features a large cheekpiece, ending in a solid brass buttplate.

The barrel, using a break-off breech, is held to the slender forestock by three keys or slides, which makes takedown for cleaning nearly a snap (oddly, you must remove the screw retaining the forward sling swivel, too). The fore-end

British Riflemen used every offense/defense resource known. Meandering across from the bayonet/short sword, a priming flask (1), carried in the jacket's pocket ensured the main charge was consistent whether paper cartridge or single load. As the enemy closed, rapidity of accurate fire was ensured by paper ammunition (2), shown in its wooden block removed from the cartridge box. Extra cartridges, wrapped in paper and tied with twine, or spare loose ball and patches were carried in tin boxes under the wooden cartridge block – a flexible system (3). A spare flint (4) peaks out from the pocket on the cartridge box. Beneath the cartridge box are three balls tied in linen patches (5) by the soldier, and "greased" (dipped in mutton tallow here). These were carried in the belt pouch (6) for loading when time permitted but was pressing, along with unpatched balls (7) when time permitted. These balls were larger in diameter than the ones used in cartridges – and round greased patches were stored in the rifle's patchbox along with tools. A powder horn (8) had a fixed measure for the service charge. A mallet started the ball in the barrel and its handle doubled as a short starter. A pick and brush (9) on a chain swept the priming pan of debris and cleared a clogged touch hole. Finally, a cork tompion (10) protected the barrel from weather. Soldiering with The Rifles was a complicated business and led (to their credit) the British to see their men as worthier than just "cannon fodder." Such changes in thinking led to the creation of a more powerful, thoroughly professional army.

(read: contraption). First, in the scabbard, the Baker's long, nearly 2-foot sword-like bayonet was an impediment to rapid movement and could entangle the legs. The bayonet weighs a whopping 2 pounds, 2 ounces, and attaches to a long, sturdy bar brazed to the barrel. The rifle with bayonet attached weighs more than 12 pounds — much of it forward. The command was changed from, "Fix bayonets!" to "Fix swords!" and remains so to this day for the British Rifles.

When fencing, men of The Rifles must have tired quickly. Roughly the last 5 inches of the Baker bayonet was sharpened, and it was devastatingly effective slashing at a foe's hand on the fore-end of his musket, since both edges — top and bottom — were sharp, compared to foes who only were able to wound by thrust.

After a peninsular action, Lt. Simmons relates Brigadier General "Black Bob" Craufurd saying, "That British troops should defeat a superior number of enemy is nothing new, but the action reflects honour … inasmuch that it was of a sort that Rifle Men of other Armies would shun. In other Armies the Rifle is considered ill calculated for close action with an enemy armed with Musket and Bayonet, but the 95th Regiment has proved that the Rifle in the hands of a British soldier is a fully efficient weapon to defeat the French in the closest fight in whatever manner they are armed."

These sword bayonets were not well tempered, it seems. At Le Haye Sainte, Cpl. Lindau notes, "I saw more Frenchmen on the wall. One of them jumped down on the stand but in that instant I ran him through with a bayonet. He collapsed on me and I flung him to one side, but my bayonet was bent, so I had to detach it."

By 1815, the British began modifying existing Baker rifles to take a more common musket-style socket bayonet. A difficult, time-consuming and expensive conversion, it involved removing the brazed-on bayonet bar and brazing a small stud under the barrel. Sensibly, a triangular-bladed bayonet was installed to the sword handle already fitting the existing bayonet bar and used to the end of the Baker's long service.

WATERLOO COINCIDENCE?

My Rifle Shoppe Baker arrived the day before the 200th Anniversary of the Battle of Waterloo, June 18, 1815. There, Riflemen of the King's German Legion held the farmhouse of Le Haye Sainte until running out of ammunition. My ammunition, on back order, arrived a day later. Chalk one up for the "Funny Coincidence Dept."

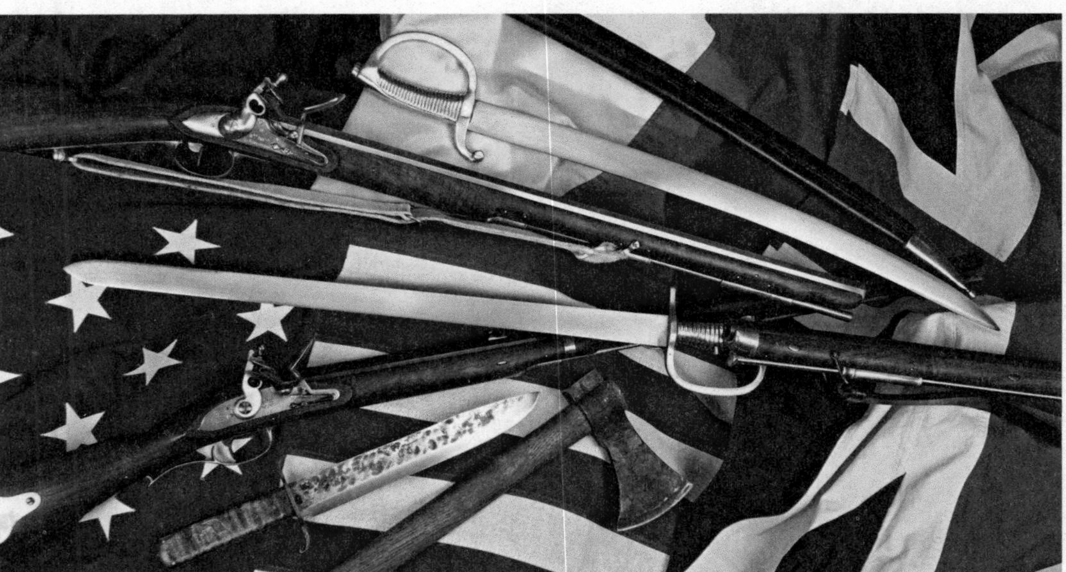

(above) The rifle would be part of all major battles by 1803. England's major combatant, France, issued Voltigeur officers and sergeants the Carbine de Versailles rifle (top left, albeit in very limited numbers) and a short sword for close defense. Soon-to-be-foe United States issued the M1803 rifle (bottom left). In lieu of a bayonet, American riflemen often carried a "rifleman's knife" such as this one by Matt Lesniewski, and perhaps a tomahawk — both very useful on the American frontier. British riflemen were issued a short sword doubling as a bayonet (center) affixed to a sturdy bar on the side of the barrel. Close quarters combat was a certainty, and — rifle or musket — battle eventually came down to butts and blades.

(left) The three men generally credited with the rise of The Rifles — and particularly the 95th — were Col. Coote Manningham (pictured in this 1808 grey-wash watercolor portrait by Henry Eldridge), Lt. Col. William Stewart who laid out the principals, training and tactics for the Rifle Corp., and General Sir John Moore, who honed the Light Infantry — which included other regiments such as line infantry — into a premium force. Manningham is shown in the 95th's officer's early, elaborate cavalry-style dress including Tarleton helmet, tall boots and spurs. Junior officers wore a shako (right), similar to the infantry one, sometimes pictured with more elaborate tassels and a feather rather than wool plume. Officers of The Rifles were adept with the use of pocket watch, map, compass and spyglass for reconnaissance. Print: allposters.com

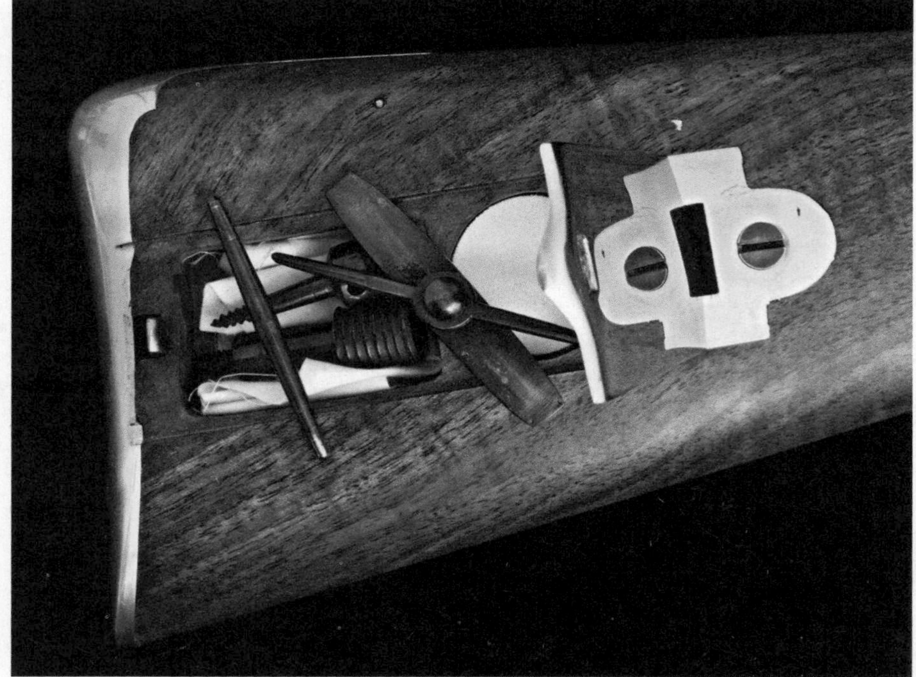

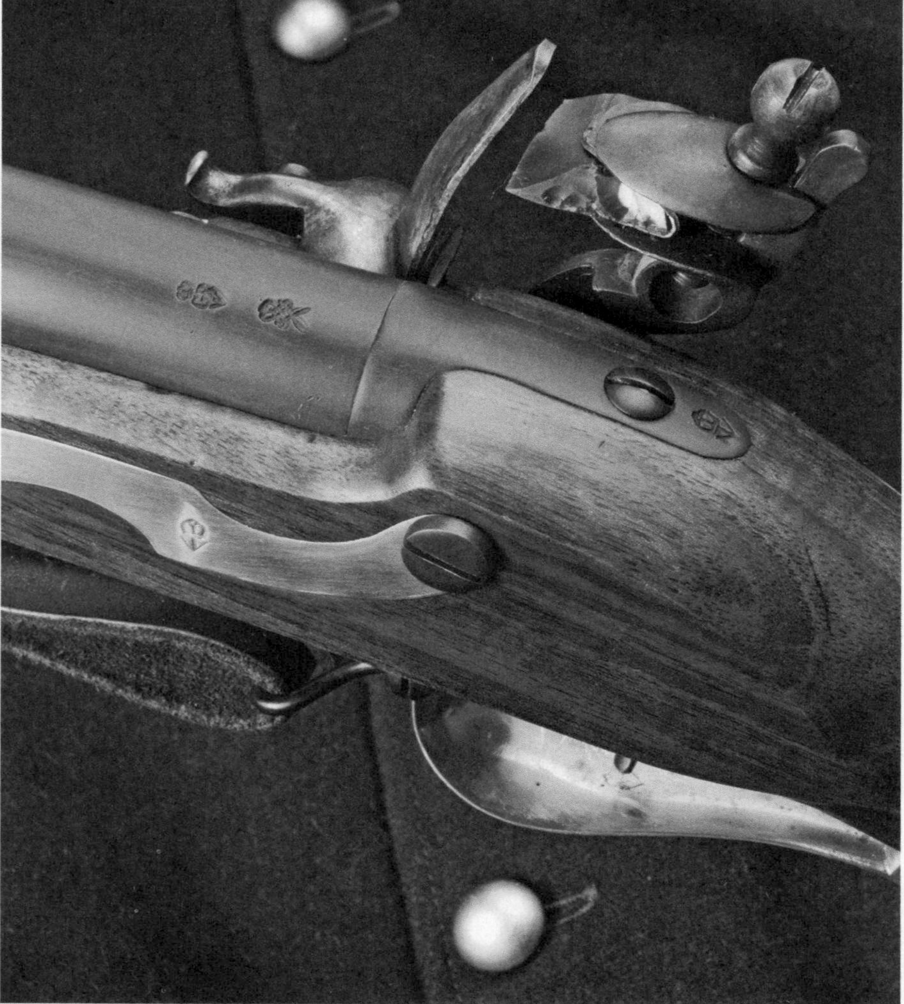

(left) The Pattern 1800 had a 2-compartment patchbox holding tools, including a multi-tool screwdriver, patch jag, ball draw, and a rod fitting a hole in the rammer so torque could be applied to the ball draw. The round, front compartment held greased patches.

(bottom) The barrel sports the "Crown GR" over broad-arrow proof and the crown-over-crossed-scepters proof. Many other parts, including the tang, sideplate and triggerguard, have the crown-over-broad-arrow acceptance proofs.

The Baker is a large, heavy gun with nearly neutral balance. The carry point is almost dead center. Unlike the graceful U.S. M1803 Harpers Ferry and light, handy French Carabine de Versailles An XII (both .54 caliber), the .62-caliber Baker handles pretty much like a truck — with manual steering. Nonetheless, it holds steady offhand without being too muzzle-heavy or muzzle-light. Of these combatants, the Baker certainly has better, more thoughtful design and construction; is more offensively versatile with its long, heavy bayonet; and its 344-grain ball — one-third more weight than the .54 — hits harder farther out. A 2-leaf backsight enhanced its ability to do so. Riflemen were issued special "fine glazed" powder, too, more refined than the coarse musket powder.

CAPABLE ACCURACY

Originally, both round bullseye and man-sized targets were used in practice, with the man target of stretched canvas on wood. "The colour of the figure and groundwork will always be different … In the exact center of the body will be described a circle or ring, similar to the inner circle of the bulls eye [sic] on the round target, viz 8 inches in diameter."

The best shots — 3rd-class Marksman — were capable of placing three shots out of six on this man-sized silhouette at 200 yards. A Rifleman had to accomplish this during two of three practice sessions for two consecutive months to enter the "3rd" or "Marksman class" and be awarded the small green cockade to wear above the black cockade of his shako. They were the only ones who regularly practiced at 300 yards.

Men placing two shots out of six on the man-sized target at 140 yards were called 2nd class, or ordinary Riflemen, and got a white cockade to prove it, while 1st class — also called the "awkward class" — generally shot at 90 and 140 yards.

Whether the cockades were ever given out is a mystery, but they appear in the original regulations.

The most common horn and lever spout (left) goes back to the American Revolution or before and was issued to artillery units well into the Napoleonic War. It was likely issued with the Baker early on. No official description of the Baker horn or flask remain. This reproduction horn (right) is based on one issued to a Baker-armed homeguard unit called the "Percy Tenantry." Serving only in England, some of their gear survived. There is a huge hole to the powder when the measure is in use or worse – lost. No doubt this design was the one known for "their constant liability to blow up in Action ..." Surviving flasks were leather covered, with a horn "window" so the powder level could be observed. A slightly modified Pedersoli "Derringer" flask serves yeoman duty for the author.

FAST IGNITION

The Rifle Shoppe Baker's touchhole is a large 3/32-inch — the size encountered in originals. The gun fires instantly, or as instantly as the flint system allows, but also allows powder to freely flow out. Target shooters of the day plugged the touchhole with a feather or a brass pin (Hobby Lobby or Michaels has feathers if you don't hunt), and I've replaced feathers with a more durable brass pin. Range safety requires the hammer be at rest and the frizzen open. But this brings up a question I haven't found any reference to, except about sporting guns.

The frizzen has a cutout underneath, so when closed, the touchhole is fully exposed to the pan. In tests — due precautions observed — I found pouring a charge down the barrel using powder as coarse as 1-1/2 Fg primed the pan if the frizzen was closed. This could significantly improve the rate of fire. Riflemen likely primed the pan first, since it was already long a part of doctrine. Either practice — "prime first" or "self-priming" — would get you thrown off a muzzleloading range today. Safety first!

Shooting commenced at 100 yards on a French Voltigeur consisting of a dark blue Birchwood Casey Splatter Target with white tape simulating crossbelts. Lt. Simmons, with the 95th in Portugal said of a night action, "... the moon for a few minutes shone brightly ... We profited by this circumstance, as their belts were white and over their greatcoats, so that where they crossed upon the breast ... gave a grand mark for our rifles."

After regulating the sights, I was gratified to find the first shot with patched ball from a cold, clean barrel consistently landed over the front sight at 100 yards. Starting with 85 grains, accuracy was quite good, and improved after working up to the service load of 95 grains. Recoil is tolerable.

My loads included Old Eynsford FFFg, FFg and 1-1/2 Fg, one Wonder Wad and a 0.010-inch patch and 0.610-inch roundball, lubed with Lehigh Valley Patch Lube. Lehigh Valley patches allow me to shoot all day without cleaning. Recoil was sharpest with the FFFg, but all grades delivered similar accuracy. Frankly, the rifle shoots better than I can hold a flintlock, and group size depended on how well I was holding on a given day.

Further exploration of ammo called for paper cartridges, and these were rolled in clean newsprint and tied with twine. Surprisingly, cartridge ammunition groups very well with caveats. From a cold, clean barrel, shot 1 was wide; 2, 3, and 4 grouped well; and 5 and 6 wild. Since using Lehigh Valley Lube is like cleaning the barrel each time a patched ball is loaded, the transition from patched ball to paper cartridges gave great accuracy — for 3 shots. The paper cartridges foul the barrel rapidly and, having a smaller ball to be easy to load, don't fit tightly enough to allow the powder to burn cleanly. Using the same amount of powder, the paper-wrapped balls travel some 100 fps slower than linen-patched balls.

Table 1

Baker .62 Patched Ball Performance

Bullet (brand/bullet weight/type)	Power Charge (brand/grains)	Group Velocity (fps)	Group Size (inches)
Three Rivers 344-gr. Roundball	Old Eynsford 2Fg 85 gr.	1,475	3.25
Lyman 344-gr. Roundball	Old Eynsford 2Fg 95 gr.	1,464	2
Three Rivers 344-gr. Roundball	Old Eynsford 3Fg 85 gr.	1,391	2.75
Track of the Wolf 344-gr. Roundball	Old Eynsford 3 Fg 95 gr.	1,495	2.50

Note: Ball size 0.610-inch (20 to the pound), 0.010-inch Ox-Yoke patch, over 1 Ox-Yoke Wonder Wad. Patch lubed with Lehigh Valley Patch Lube. Groups: 3 shots at 100 yards. Competition Electronics Pro Chrono chronograph set 15 feet from the muzzle.

Table 2

Baker .62 Paper Cartridge Performance

Bullet (brand/bullet weight/type)	Power Charge (brand/grains)	Group Velocity (fps)	Group Size (inches)
Three Rivers 318-gr. Roundball	Old Eynsford 1-1/2 Fg 95 gr.	1,292	2.50*
Lyman 318-gr. Roundball	Old Eynsford 3Fg 95 gr.	1,407	1.50**

Note: Ball size 0.595-inch (22 to the pound), wrapped in newsprint and tied with twine. *Group size: 3 shots at 50 yards (shots 2, 3 and 4). **Group size: 3 shots at 100 yards (shots 1, 2 and 3 after firing a patched ball). Chronograph set 15 feet from the muzzle.

P1800 Baker Rifle Specifications
Maker: The Rifle Shoppe, 870740 S Hwy 177, Wellston OK 74881, (405) 356-2583, www.therifleshoppe.com
Action type: Flintlock
Caliber: .62, square-grooved rifling
Capacity: 1
Barrel length: 30 inches, 1:66 twist (tested), 1:120 (original twist) now available
Overall length: 46.25 inches, 71 inches with bayonet attached
Weight: 9 pounds, 15 ounces, Weight with bayonet: 12 pounds, 1 ounce
Sights: 2-leaf rear, brass Patridge front
Finish: Brown
Stock: English walnut, oil finished
Bayonet length overall: 27.5 inches, Blade length: 22.75 inches
Price: $3,995

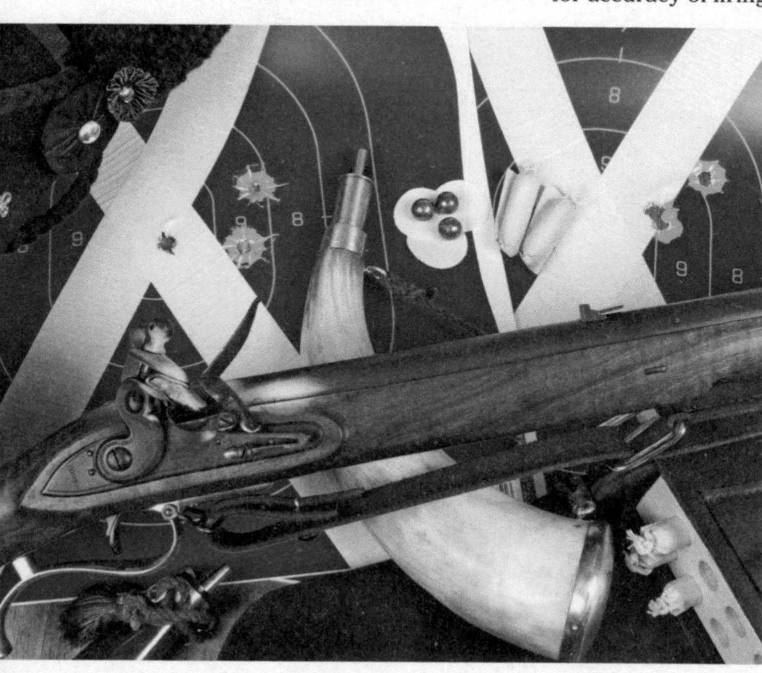

Shooting a patched roundball over a 95-grain service charge (left target) produced this three-shot 2.50-inch 100-yard group. The first shot from a cold, clean barrel went right into the "X" of the Birchwood Casey "Voltigeur" target. Paper cartridges proved very accurate, if only for three shots giving a group of 1.75 inches (right target). The author found fouling accrued rapidly, and the group exploded after five or six shots. The 95th Rifles Shako has the green cockade awarded the best shots.

EPITAPH

Pitched battle meant the Rifle Corps fired greater quantities of faster-to-load paper cartridges than loose ball and patch. After Waterloo, the Rifles began using paper cartridges and were no longer issued a powder horn, flask, loose ball and patches. Their unique ability to apply gunfire "four times the range of rebuttal" was diminished. Later, a fixed backsight replaced the 2-leaf sight.

To an 1826 request for an issue of powder horns and loose ball and patch from the Rifles, the Commander-in-Chief replied, "… it has appeared from the oldest practical soldiers in the Rifle Briga that the Copper Flasks were discontinued on service in the peninsular campaign in consequence of the Accidents, and the Personal injuries thereby sustained, from their constant liability to blow up in Action.

"… His Royal Highness is quite aware that the accuracy of Rifle firing is in some measure lost by Balls being made up in Cartridges which are much smaller than the Calibre of the Rifle — though He cannot concur in the notion generally and erroneously entertained, that in such a case, a Rifle is no more effective for accuracy of firing than a common musket!

"[R]educing the ball to Twenty-two to the pound, for the purposes of increasing the celerity of loading in Rank and File, has been most un-necessarily adopted …

"His Royal Highness will recommend … that all cartridge ammunition for the Rifle Brigade in future be made up in Paper with Bullets of Twenty to the Pound."

Thus, the British Rifle Corp's unique value (ameliorated somewhat by the larger ball size) and the utility of accurate long-range fire was no longer in the toolbox. Because these troops were trained to show initiative and independent thinking, I like to believe they loaded patched ball and practiced long-range shooting. No problem scrounging some greased patches. Piece of cake to break up a paper cartridge for powder and ball. After all, they were Rifle Men.

CONTACTS

GOEX, 6430 Vista Dr., Shawnee, KS 66218, (913) 362-9455, www.goexpowder.com

The Gun Works, 247 South 2nd St., Springfield, OR 97477, (541) 741-4118, www.thegunworks.com

Hussar Saddlery, 853 Brunstetter Road, Warren, OH 44481, (330) 360-8640, www.hussarsaddlery.com

Jim Keller's Historical Reenactment, 2205 Nature Trail Crescent, Orleans, Ontario, K1W 1E7, Canada www.jgkeller.ca

Lehigh Valley Patch Lube, 474 West 3rd Street South, Fulton, NY 13069, www.lehighvalleylube.com

UK Expo Int., P.O. Box 351, Sialkot - Pakistan, www.bagpipers.eu

Bibliography

Adventures of a Soldier; Being the Memoirs of Edward Costello, ©1852, Colburn And Co., London, Print On Demand book, www.abebooks.com

A British Rifleman Journals and Correspondence during the Peninsular War and the Campaign of Wellington by Major George Simmons, edited by Col. Willoughby Verner, ©1899, ©1986 Lionel Levinthal Ltd, Greenhill Books, ISBN: 0-947898-33-6, OP

Sir John Moore and the Universal Soldier, Vol. 1: The Man, the Commander and the Shorncliffe System of Training, ©2016 Stephen Summerfield and Susan Law, ISBN: 978-1-907417-71-9, Ken Trotman Publishing, www.kentrotman.com, www.shorncliffe-trust.org.uk

History & Campaigns of the Rifle Brigade Pt. I, Col. Willoughby Verner, ©2002, ISBN: 9781843422136, Naval & Military Press, www.naval-military-press.com

A Waterloo Hero, the Reminiscences of Frederich Lindau, by James Bogle and Andrew Uffindell, ©2009, Frontline Press, ISBN: 978-1-84832-539-5

British Military Flintlock Rifles: 1740-1840, by DeWitt Bailey, ©2002, ISBN: 1-931464-30-0, Mowbray Publishing, (800) 999-4697, www.gunandswordcollector.com

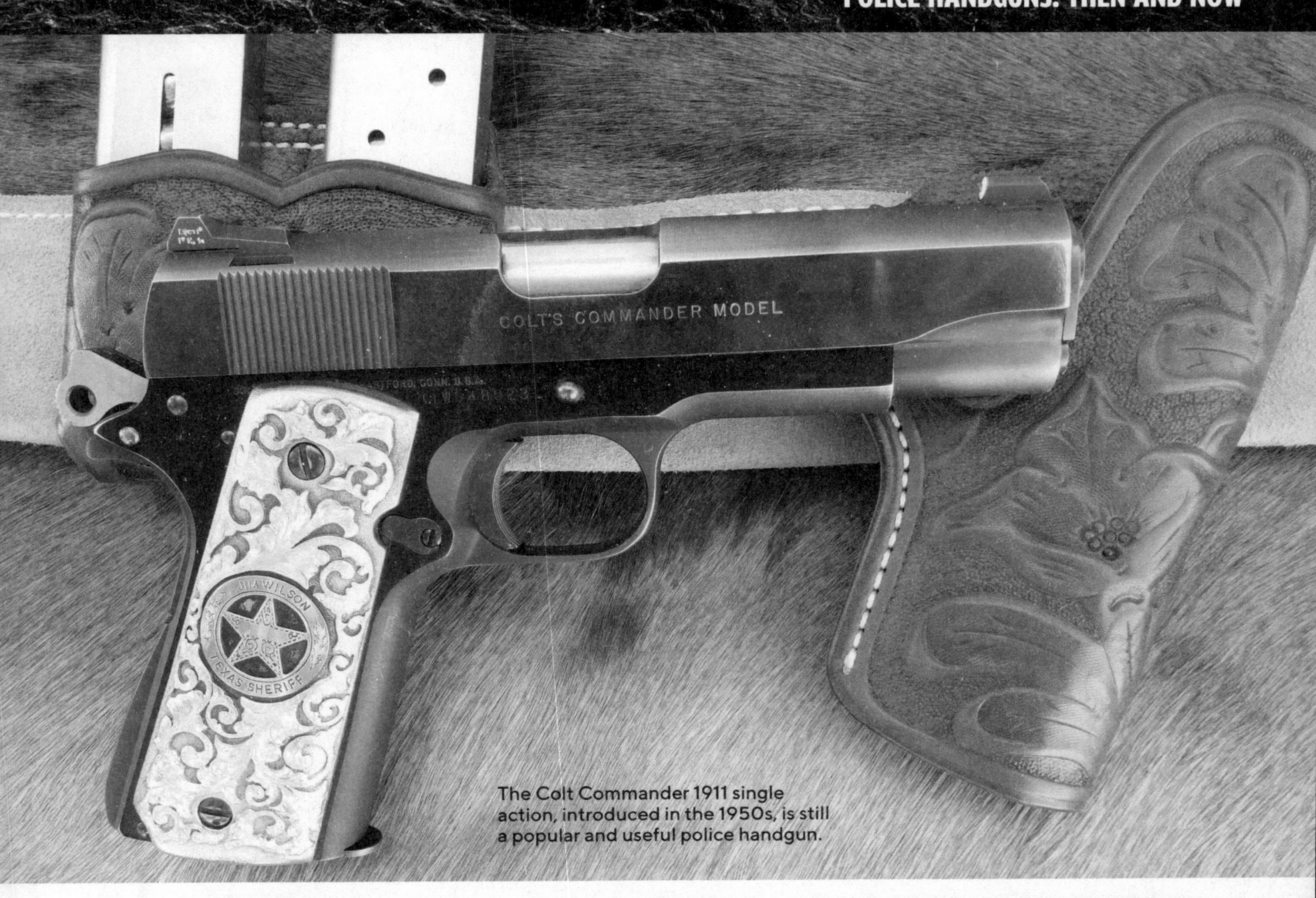

The Colt Commander 1911 single action, introduced in the 1950s, is still a popular and useful police handgun.

POLICE HANDGUNS: THEN AND NOW

For Many Long-Time Lawmen, Nothing Beats the Old Standbys

BY **JIM WILSON**

The evolution of the police handgun can be a very interesting study — not only for peace officers, but also armed citizens. It gives a clear indication of the broad variations in department policies and what police administrators considered suitable armament. As early as the 1880s, possibly even the 1870s, the Texas Rangers purchased .45-caliber Colt single actions for their men, with the cost being taken out of the individual's paycheck. In spite of this policy, Rangers were allowed to carry their own guns if they chose to do so, with some preferring the Colt in .44-40 or .38-40. And there is no doubt that some men passed on the Colt altogether and elected to pack a big-bore Smith & Wesson revolver.

The Colt 1911 still serves today, as it has for over 100 years.

Despite this early Ranger policy, most police agencies across the country expected their men to purchase their own guns and left the type and caliber up to the individual officer. These same agencies also expected their police applicants to already know how to shoot. As one can imagine, this opened the door to all sorts of handgun choices — choices that today seem rather odd. Some lawmen felt perfectly well armed with guns like the Colt Pocket Auto in .32 ACP or .380 ACP, while others liked Smith & Wesson or Colt revolvers in .32 caliber or .38 S&W.

However, a cursory study of history indicates that the real gunfighters who wore badges preferred big-bore handguns. Lawmen who had seen duty in World War I tended to prefer large-frame double-action revolvers. And, of course, this is the same era in which the Colt 1911 auto in .45 ACP began to gain popularity.

By the 1930s, Texas Ranger Captain Frank Hamer still wore a .45 Colt single action every day, but he had begun to supplement it with a 1911 in .38 Super when the going got tough. Jelly Bryce, who joined the FBI in 1934, preferred to carry an N-frame Smith & Wesson in .44 Special. Another FBI agent from that same era, Col. Walter Walsh, was known to carry a 3 1/2-inch S&W .357 Magnum on his hip and a Colt 1911 in a shoulder holster.

By the middle of the last century the double-action revolver in .38 Special was the most commonly found handgun in the holster of most lawmen. When I started my police career in the late 1960s, you could carry anything you wanted, provided it was a Colt or Smith & Wesson double action chambered for the .38 Special round. A real broad choice right there.

In the past 100 years, law enforcement has always been in search of better tools to do the job. The evolution from the Colt single action of yesteryear to the Smith & Wesson striker-fired M&P of today illustrates that ongoing search for the best tools.

I recall the Christmas that my patrol sergeant was given a Ruger Security Six revolver. It shot well and fit in his duty holster, so he started carrying it on duty. When it was discovered that he was packing this strange revolver, he was nearly fired. I remember that one administrator asked, “Ruger? Isn’t that the German outfit that used to make automatics?”

Another interesting dilemma from those days was the fact that many law enforcement agencies would not allow officers to use speedloaders. Now, for the cop on the street, being able to reload your revolver quickly seemed like a good idea. But the bosses, many of whom were not shooters and rarely had to face bad guys with guns, thought that speedloaders were some sort of new-fangled gizmo that couldn’t possibly be any good.

My department was one of those, and we were required to continue to load from the cartridge slides on our duty belts. The FBI and many other state and municipal agencies had the same prohibition. Then, as now, lawmen on the street were always looking for something that did a better job of protecting them, while the bosses tended to remain conservative and resist innovation.

For all that, the double-action revolver was not a bad police gun. The good guns — Colt, Smith & Wesson and Ruger — were sufficiently accurate for gunfighting. And, in addition, they could take a lot of abuse and neglect before they failed. In the 1960s, Lee Jurras came along with his Super Vel ammo and considerably improved the fight-stopping qualities of the .38 Special cartridge. And, other agencies allowed their officers to carry revolvers chambered for the .357 Magnum, .41 Magnum and even .44 Magnum, all of which would stop a fight when properly applied.

However, by the late 1960s and early 1970s, something was going on in California that would change the whole landscape regarding law enforcement handguns. Jeff Cooper, a retired Marine colonel, Ray Chapman, Thell Reed and others were beginning to make use of the 1911 pistol in .45 ACP as a fighting gun for police and defensive shooters. Through his writings and teachings, Col. Cooper became the primary advocate for the big auto pistol.

Many lawmen, especially in the Southwest, simply transitioned from one Colt to another.

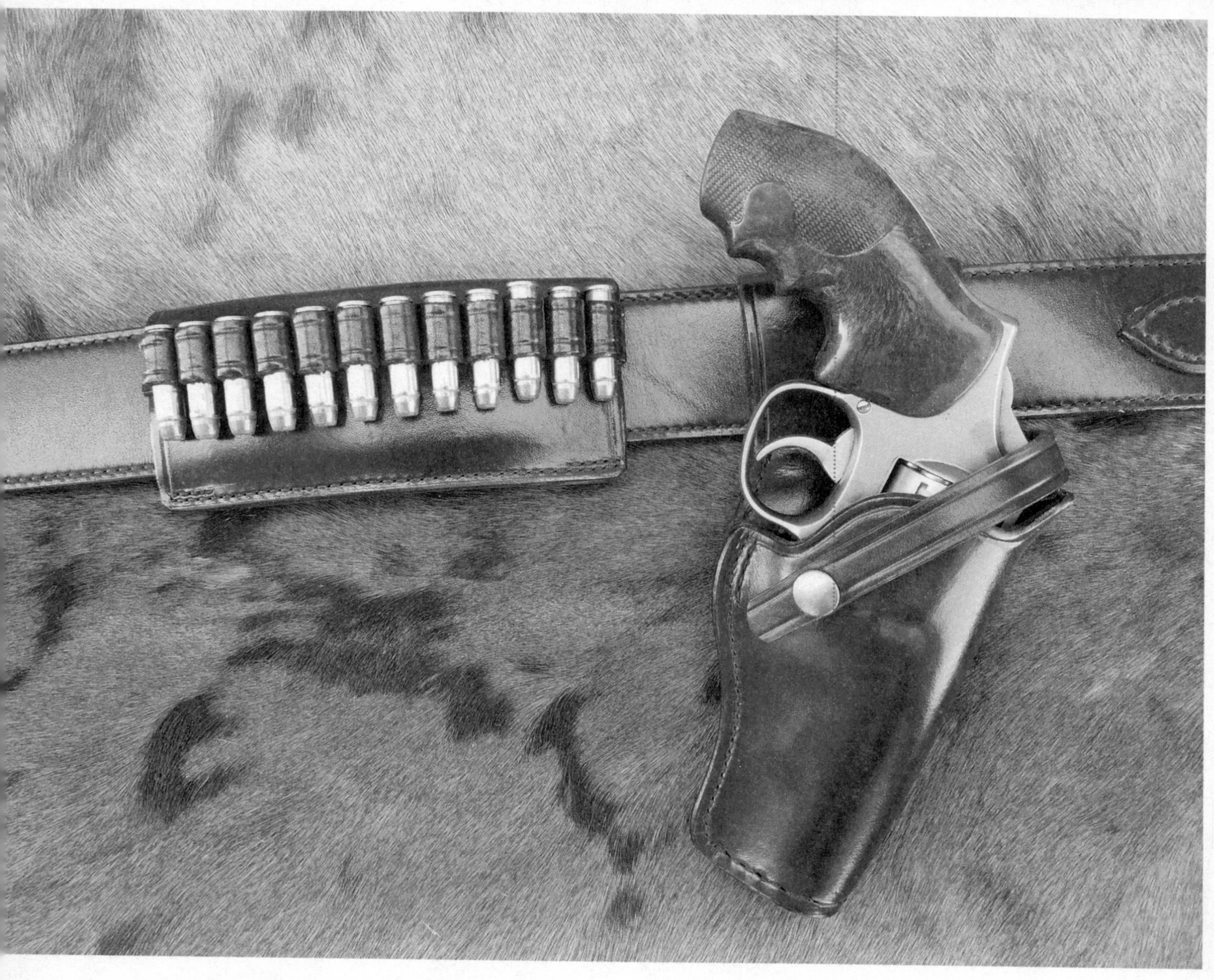

The Smith & Wesson Model 66, shown here with the Don Hume-Bill Jordan rig, was the mainstay of lawmen for many years.from Nighthawk Custom.

It's difficult today for most people to understand the impact that this advocacy of the 1911 had on America's lawmen. The pistol was almost as rugged as the DA revolver and its cartridge gave fight-stopping hits much more reliably than did the .38 Special. It was almost as effective as the .357 Magnum, without the felt recoil of the magnum. In addition, the single-action trigger was much easier to manage than the DA revolver where accurate fire was needed. To top it all off, the 1911 was much quicker to reload than the revolver and held two more rounds. Across the country, law enforcement officers began to put pressure on their bosses to allow them to carry the 1911.

When, as a detective sergeant, I was assigned to head up the newly formed narcotics unit in our department, I was allowed to carry an auto if I so desired. My immediate choice was the Colt 1911. At that point, I knew very little about Col. Cooper and his teachings. But I knew from prior experience that the .45 auto was the most powerful handgun that I could shoot quickly and accurately. And that is a position that I maintain to this day.

While American lawmen began to transition to the auto pistol, some police administrators had their doubts about the Colt 1911. After all, it was carried "cocked and locked," and that business of having the hammer back just didn't look very safe. In many cases, a compromise was reached in which the officers could carry autos but they had to be of the DA/SA variety, such as the Smith & Wesson Models 39 and 59, and the early SIG pistols.

Regardless of brand, the DA/SA auto was carried with the hammer down on a chambered round. This type of pistol is designed so that the first shot is fired with a long pull on the trigger much like the DA revolver. Once the action cycles from that first shot, the hammer stays back and subsequent shots are fired in single-action mode. Most models also had a decocking lever that would drop the hammer, without firing the gun, when the officer had finished shooting. Most of these guns were designed with

Two great single-action autos, the Hi Power and the 1911, these from Nighthawk Custom.

double-stack magazines that significantly increased the number of cartridges that they carried.

Critics of the DA/SA autos often pointed out that the guns were heavier and bulkier than many preferred. However, the biggest challenge with the DA/SA pistols came in trying to manage the triggers. The bulky, difficult trigger management is why they never appealed to me. The first shot, fired in DA mode, required something in the neighborhood of an 8-pound trigger pull. However, subsequent shots — which were fired single action — needed only a 4- to

GASTON GLOCK DESIGNED THE FIRST SUCCESSFUL HANDGUN THAT UTILIZED A POLYMER FRAME AND THE STRIKER-FIRE SYSTEM. HIS DESIGN HAS BECOME WILDLY POPULAR AND REMAINS SO TODAY EVEN THOUGH NUMEROUS MANUFACTURERS NOW OFFER VERSIONS OF THIS HANDGUN STYLE. THE STRIKER-FIRE SYSTEM IS NOTABLE FOR THE FACT THAT THE GUN IS PARTIALLY COCKED WHEN A ROUND IS CHAMBERED. WITH THE PRESS OF THE TRIGGER, THE COCKING FUNCTION IS COMPLETED, AND THE PISTOL IS FIRED. MANY STRIKER-FIRED PISTOLS, FROM VARIOUS MANUFACTURERS, DO NOT HAVE ANY EXTERNAL SAFETIES.

5-pound pull. This required the shooter to use the first joint of his trigger finger, much like the revolver shooter, for the first shot fired in DA mode. But then he would have to switch to the tip of his shooting finger to get the best results when shooting follow-up shots in SA mode. This was a challenge that could be overcome, but it took a good bit of training and practice to successfully master. As a result, manufacturers developed what they called a DA-only auto, which fired all of its shots with the long double-action trigger pull — an improvement, but not much of one.

Gaston Glock designed the first successful handgun that utilized a polymer frame and the striker-fire system. His design has become wildly popular and remains so today even though numerous manufacturers now offer versions of this handgun style. The striker-fire system is notable for the fact that the gun is partially cocked when a round is chambered. With the press of the trigger, the cocking function is completed, and the pistol is fired. Many striker-fired pistols, from various manufacturers, do not have any external safeties.

Striker-fired handguns caught on relatively quickly with law enforcement agencies across the country; they were simple to operate, were chambered for all the popular auto cartridges, were suitable for right- or left-handed shooters and generally cost less. As with the other autos mentioned, the striker-fired pistols are adequately accurate for police work.

The biggest problem with the striker-fired guns has to do with those that lack an external safety. Negligent discharges have increased among law enforcement and civilian shooters as a result of ignoring, or not understanding, how the pistol operates. Most generally, this is a result of having the finger on or near the trigger when it shouldn't be. Often these NDs (negligent discharges) occur while holstering.

During holstering, if the trigger finger is still in the trigger guard, it will impact the holster and then press the trigger with a resulting loud noise, and often some injury. It also happens when some part of the officer's clothing becomes tangled with the trigger, causing the pistol to discharge.

Not too long ago, a large police department decided to transition from the Beretta 92 DA/SA pistol to a striker-fired gun. They immediately experienced a marked increase in the number of negligent discharges. The reason was

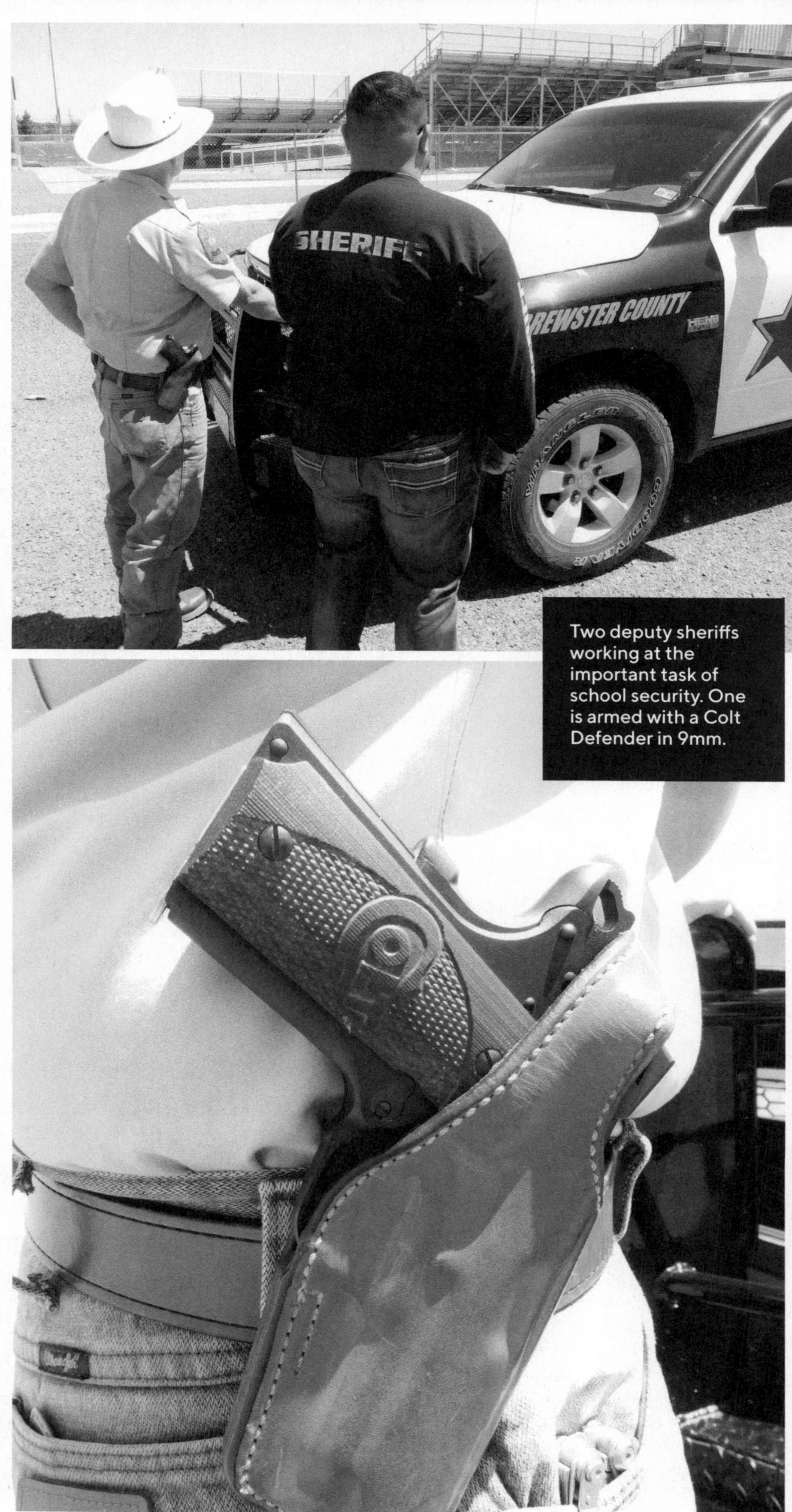

Two deputy sheriffs working at the important task of school security. One is armed with a Colt Defender in 9mm.

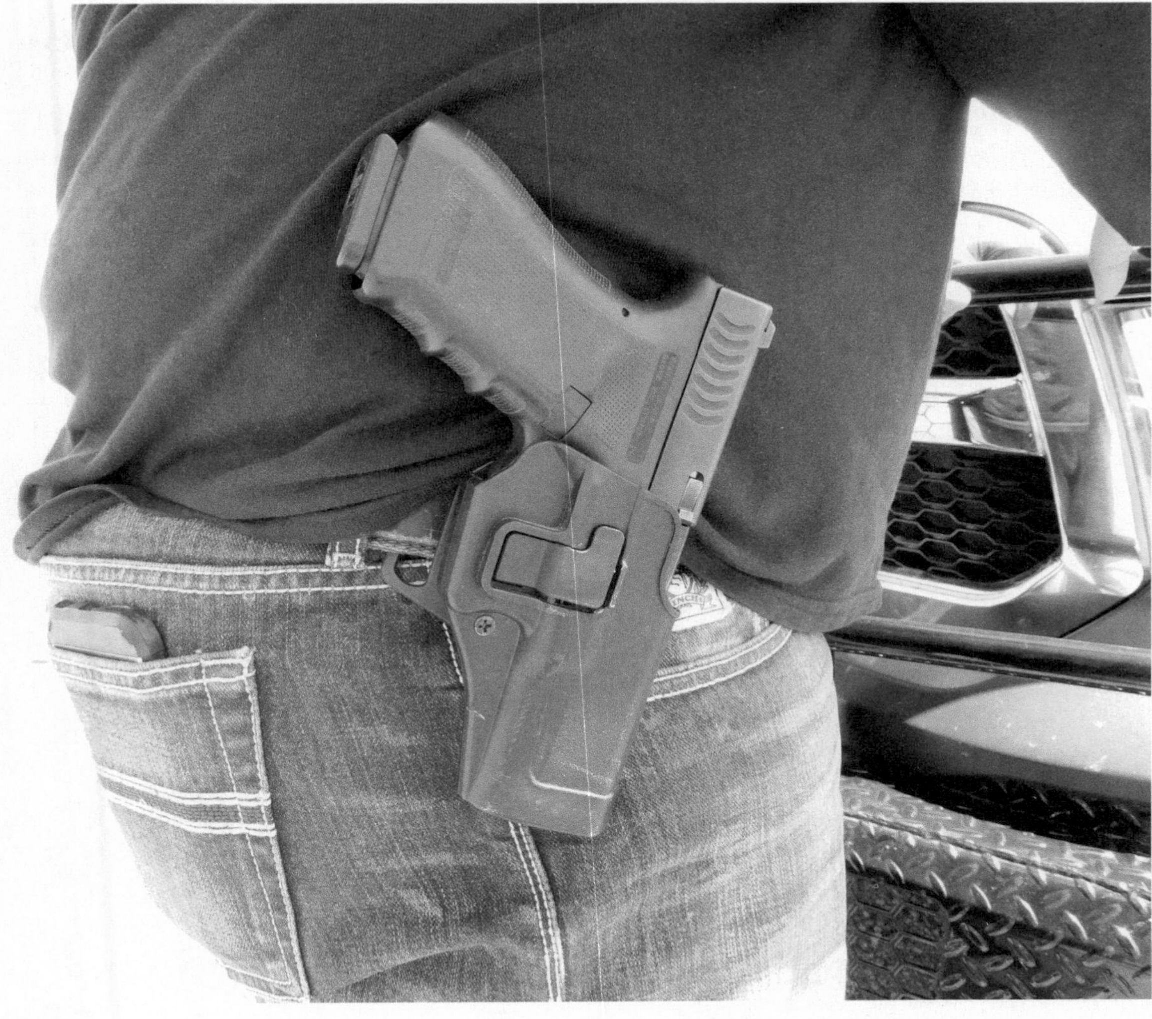

Another very popular police handgun is the striker-fired Glock 17 9mm.

that, with the Beretta's long double-action trigger pull, the department had not been enforcing the safety rule of keeping the trigger finger completely out of the trigger guard unless the gun was on target. This is important with all handguns, but it is especially important with striker-fired guns that lack an external safety.

Those who advocate one type of police handgun at the expense of others will often try to justify their choice by telling why the others are unreliable: The 1911, and other single-action autos, have that hammer cocked and a relatively light trigger, all of which makes them dangerous, they say, DA/SA guns are difficult to shoot well. Striker-fired guns will go off unexpectedly and, besides that, no one should expect a plastic gun to hold up to the rough use to which a law enforcement handgun is often subjected.

None of which are true.

Each of the different handgun styles has its own manual of arms. That is, there is a method of operation that the shooter must learn in order to operate the pistol effectively and safely. In addition, he or she must also learn the type and level of care that each type requires. For example, an auto pistol — any auto pistol — cannot be expected to function properly if it is run as dirty and dry as a DA revolver. The DA/SA auto has a difficult trigger system, but it can be learned. And the officer who carries a striker-fired pistol must be even more conscious of safety. It is up to the individual officer to learn a gun and run it accordingly.

Adequate training has a lot to do with helping the law enforcement officer find the type of gun that is best suited to the individual. Sadly, this is an area where many agencies are lacking. An armed citizen who successfully completes a week-long training class at Gunsite, Thunder Ranch or a few other schools is better trained in gunfighting techniques

IT IS QUITE PROBABLE THAT NOTHING I'VE SAID ABOUT THE TRENDS IN LAW ENFORCEMENT HANDGUNS WILL STOP THE DEBATES THAT RAGE AROUND THIS TOPIC. EACH TYPE OF GUN HAS ITS GOOD POINTS AND NOT-SO-GOOD POINTS. I'VE DESCRIBED WHY I PREFER SOME OVER OTHERS. WHEN I TALK TO A GROUP OF OFFICERS, I GENERALLY TELL THEM NOT TO WASTE TIME ARGUING ABOUT WHAT THEY CHOOSE TO CARRY. INSTEAD, I TELL THEM JUST SHOW ME WHAT YOU CAN DO WITH IT.

than many of today's police officers. Departments are notorious for skimping on training, or they fail to stay up with modern training techniques that will benefit their officers.

In addition, too many officers only shoot their guns in practice when they are required to do so. They reluctantly show up for qualification when the department mandates it and otherwise they don't mess with their guns. The officer who is intent on staying alive should take every opportunity to train and practice, entering practical matches whenever possible, and signing up for classes in the private sector. This is the only way for the individual to find out which type of police handgun works best, or learns how to really run the gun that the department says he or she must carry.

My personal preference in law enforcement handguns includes the single-action autos, the 1911 and Browning Hi Power, and double-action revolvers. Both types of handguns have been around long enough to give us a full understanding of how to make them work effectively. It's comforting for me to bet my life on gun systems that were successfully resolving armed encounters long before I was born. Years ago, I met an old retired Texas Ranger who still carried a Colt single-action revolver. At the time, I couldn't understand it, but then it dawned on me. It's very difficult to quit a gun that has saved your life. Call me old-fashioned if you will, but that is why I still cleave to the Colt 1911 and the Smith & Wesson Model 19.

It is quite probable that nothing I've said about the trends in law enforcement handguns will stop the debates that rage around this topic. Each type of gun has its good points and not-so-good points.

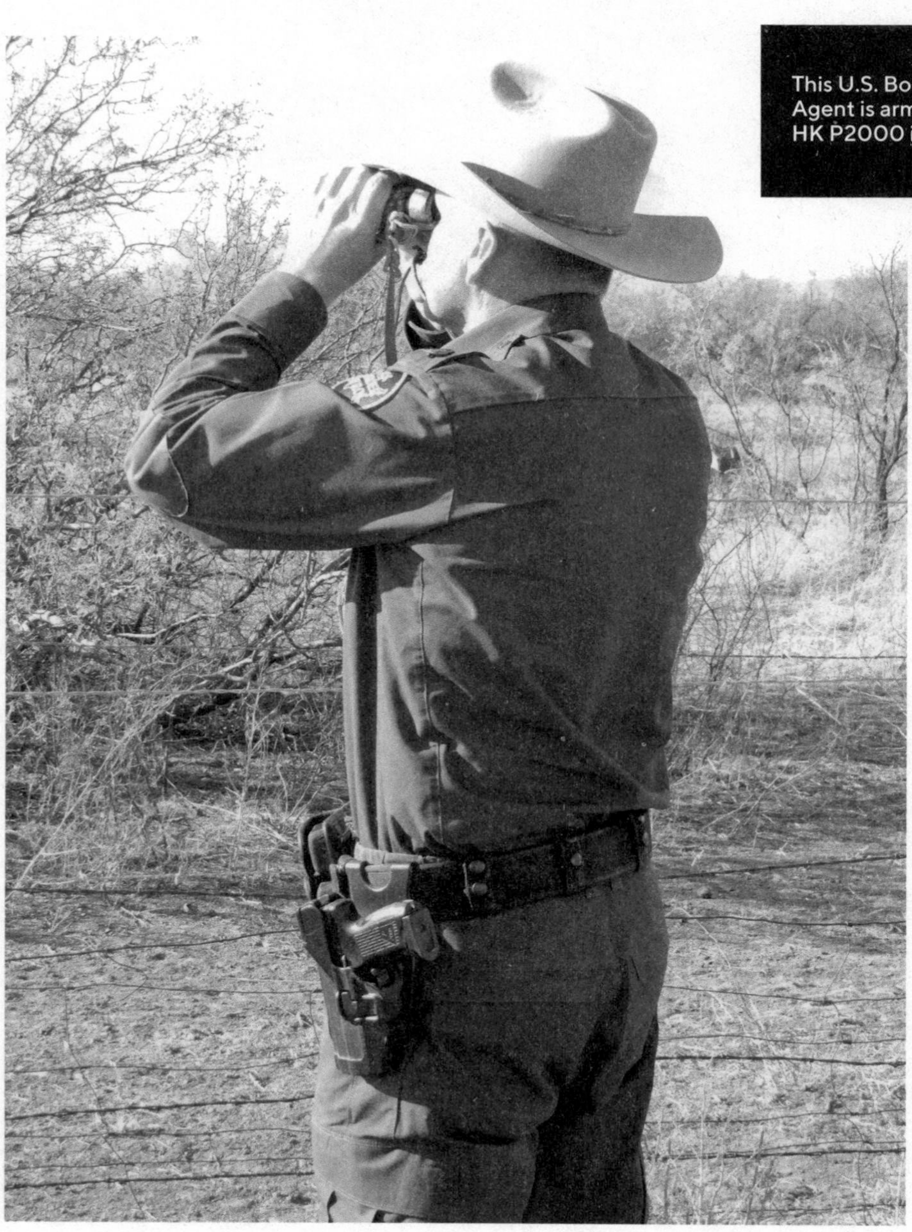

This U.S. Border Patrol Agent is armed with an HK P2000 in .40 S&W.

I've described why I prefer some over others. When I talk to a group of officers, I generally tell them not to waste time arguing about what they choose to carry. Instead, I tell them just show me what you can do with it.

In the end, that's what really matters.

For Most of My Hunting Needs, Make it a .25!

BY **STAN TRZONIEC**

THOSE GREAT QUARTER-BORES

When it comes to sporting cartridges, everyone has their favorite. I, for one, like the .22-caliber centerfires for my varmint duties. Working with commercial cartridges like the .223 or the .22-250 Remington, a nicely tuned, off-the-shelf rifle is a joy to use in the field. On the other hand, my wildcatting fantasies take me into the land of the .219 Donaldson Wasp, .22 Mashburn Bee, .22 K-Hornet or.220 Weatherby Rocket. Engineering a rifle from scratch to shoot these loads is yet another part of my fascination. Here, the Ruger No. 1 or a blueprinted bolt gun is a perfect match, as little or no modifications are necessary to utilize the full potential of these vintage cartridges.

Moving up, the .24 caliber offers a combination of a harder-hitting cartridge for larger varmints while still providing plenty of reloading opportunities in both the .243 Winchester and the 6mm Remington. On top of all that, working with a 6mm Remington case and necking it down to .22 caliber gives me the .224 TTH — a cartridge that will hit 4,000 fps+ for those chucks that always seem to get away at closer distances.

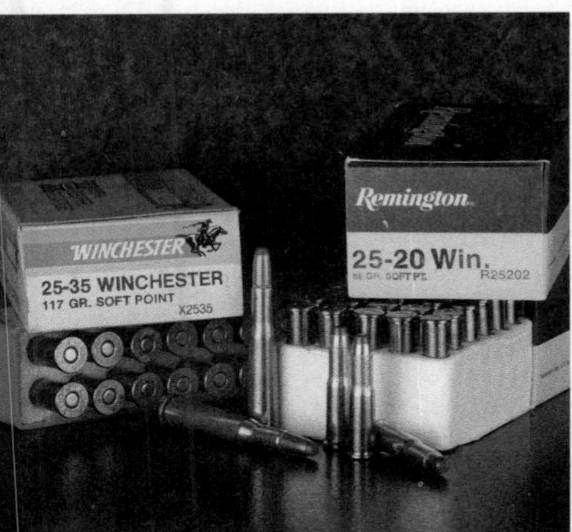

For shooters who like to dabble in vintage cartridges, both Winchester and Remington can help, with the factory .25-35 and .25-20 ammo.

For big game, the .270 Winchester and the .30 calibers are great for hunting in the western plains of the United States. Mule deer, caribou and black bear are easily taken with these, but if you are an astute reader, you are going to ask, why skip over the .25-caliber cartridges? You'll get no argument from me, for the quarter-bores fall right in line with my shooting requirements in the field and rate high on my list of all-time favorite cartridges.

While I lean toward the more modern .25s, history is an important part of the development of any cartridge. With some of these cartridges dating back to the late 1800s, it makes for fascinating reading on some of the more interesting .25 calibers — some of which are either obsolete, hard to find, or lack a rifle to use them in. This is the case for the lesser-known .25-20 Winchester, .256 Winchester or the recent .25 WSSM Winchester that I will detail later in the article.

THE .25-20 WINCHESTER

First up in our .25-caliber roundup is the .25-20 Winchester. It's interesting to note that this cartridge was specially designed and developed for the Winchester Model 1892 rifle, which was added to the company's lineup in 1895. Along with other short-action-type cartridges, the Model 1892 obtained a reasonable amount of popularity with this cartridge, having been made available for a time in the older .25-20 single-shot rifle. Looking back, the .25-20 WCF made its name as a popular varmint and small game cartridge, and with that reputation other manufacturers followed. Those included the Remington Model 25 and Marlin Model 27 slide-actions, and the Savage Model 23 bolt-action repeater. For those die-hard enthusiasts who enjoy vintage cartridges today, there are still rifles available on the used-gun market.

When it comes to the cartridge itself, even before the advent of the .22 Hornet

Getting ready for a western hunt back in the 1980s, the author wanted a new rifle to take along. He got his wish when Winchester reissued the Featherweight chambered for the nostalgic .257 Roberts. The rifle is still in the author's battery and ready for another hunt. Graceful fleur-de-lis checkering was standard back then.

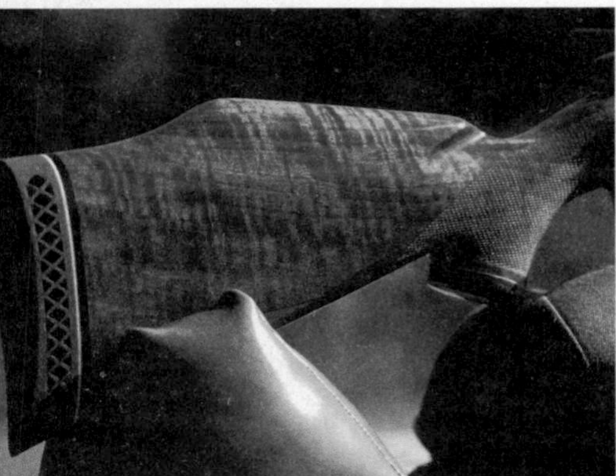

The author never met a Weatherby he didn't like. One reason is the nice wood on this .257 Deluxe rifle.

and .218 Bee, it was a spunky offering. Considered a rimmed, bottle-necked cartridge, it is based on the .32-20 Winchester — which in prior times was considered a popular varmint to small game cartridge — necked down to .25 caliber. Because of bullet designs from this era, ranges needed to be kept short. Even so, some accounts tell of hunters killing deer with it, no doubt at close range, with heavier bullets in the 86-grain class. Additionally, turkey hunters who are into vintage guns will find this cartridge fun to use on these birds (where legal), as it tends to ruin less meat than modern, high-powered rifles. Trappers also find favor with this cartridge, as the guns are light to carry on the back and factory ammunition is still available from several sources. Recently, cowboy action shooters have given the .25-20 some play with older-style rifles introduced in recent years by Marlin.

Handloading brings out the best in the .25-20 and loading data goes back many years. Brass cases are available and can be purchased for good prices at gun shows, as the .25-20 is not a big seller and dealers are happy to rid their tables of them. Primers are no problem; any small rifle primer is the key to consistent ignition. Bullets of 60 grains seem to be the norm and, for a compromise, Speer makes a 75-grain soft point, flat-nose bullet.

If you have deep pockets, the Custom Shop at Remington will be happy to accommodate any of your whims in stock work, engraving or chamberings. In .25-06 Remington, this example would be a nice addition to anyone's rifle battery.

Checking the 1941 edition of Phil Sharpe's reference, "Complete Book of Handloading," nothing major has changed in the way the .25-20 Winchester is loaded today. For example, Sharpe states that a 60-grain bullet with 12.7 grains of 4227 will get to around 2,195 fps. Looking at the Hornady manual, 12.0 grains of IMR 4227 will get it to 2,200 fps. Considering the state of chronographs in those days, I'd say he gets a cigar for his efforts. Cast bullets were another option with Sharpe, for a 60-grain lead bullet hitting 1,835 fps with a mild load of 5.4 grains of Unique is listed in his book.

Those seeking an enjoyable cartridge to shoot, and willing to keep distances short, will come to see that the .25-20 Winchester can be a lot of fun in the field.

THE .25-35 WINCHESTER

Moving upward, the next step in our .25-caliber review is the .25-35 Winchester cartridge. Along with the famous .30-30 Winchester, it was introduced in 1895 by parent Winchester, chambered in the Model 1894 lever-action rifle, both of which historically were the first of many to be loaded with the new smokeless powder. Not only was it considerably more powerful than the preceding .25-20 Winchester, it gave field hunters the advantage of being able to hunt deer-sized game at longer distances. Additionally, as if to add to the versatility of the cartridge, it was also available in the Winchester Model 1885 High Wall single-shot rifle.

As it relates to present-day factory ammunition, at one time Winchester offered two loads topped off with a 117-grain bullet. Today, one load is still offered, that being the 117-grain Power Point delivering 2,230 fps with a muzzle energy of 1,292 ft-lbs of energy. Handloaders will benefit greatly with commercial bullets and, depending on the bullet weight (60 or 117 grains), muzzle velocities can top 2,900 and 2,300 fps, respectively. Again, in Phil Sharpe's book, he moved the 60-grain hollowpoint up to 2,880 fps with a hardy dose of 20.1 grains of 2400 propellant. With the 117-grain soft point, he went to 4320 powder and, with 28.0 grains, hit very close to modern velocities with his version closing in on 2,300 fps. It's fun to see how the loads of almost 80 years ago compare with today's bullets and powders. Because the .30-30 Winchester stole most of the .25-35's thunder, it has lagged behind

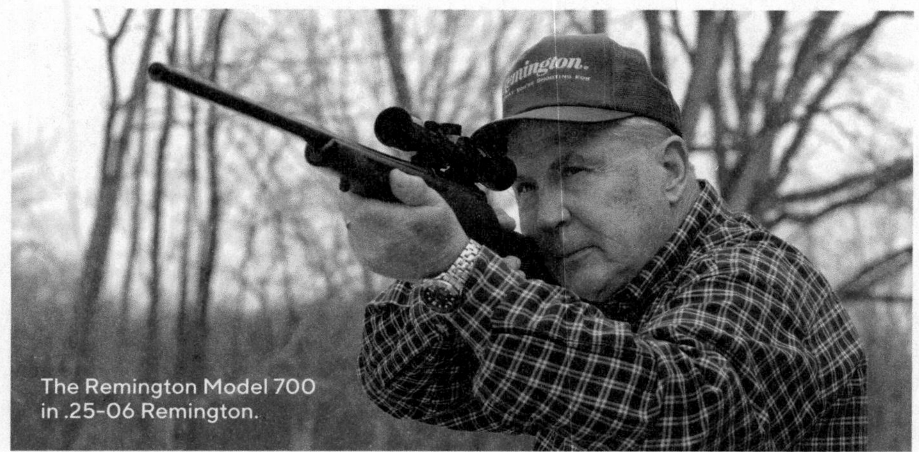

The Remington Model 700 in .25-06 Remington.

all these years simply because of lack of interest and a short supply of rifles.

Again, resourceful shooters will find rifles on the secondary market, and with the availability of modern reloading dies and powders, the .25-35 can be a hoot to shoot, especially for younger folks. To me, nothing compares with giving an up-and-coming hunter a lever-action gun. There seems to be a certain mystique about a lever gun and everyone takes to it like a duck to water. With lighter bullets, loads can be tailored to reduced levels, young people can have a blast with a big-time lever gun.

The last time Winchester chambered a gun in this caliber was around 2005. For deer hunters who like to pick their shots and stay within a moderate range, this is a great "old-time" cartridge ready for a reissue. Winchester has chambered a few of its guns this year in the .38-55 Winchester; perhaps the .25-35 is next. Then again, who knows? Perhaps Marlin will offer it as a special edition in its newly organized custom shop.

THE .250-3000 SAVAGE

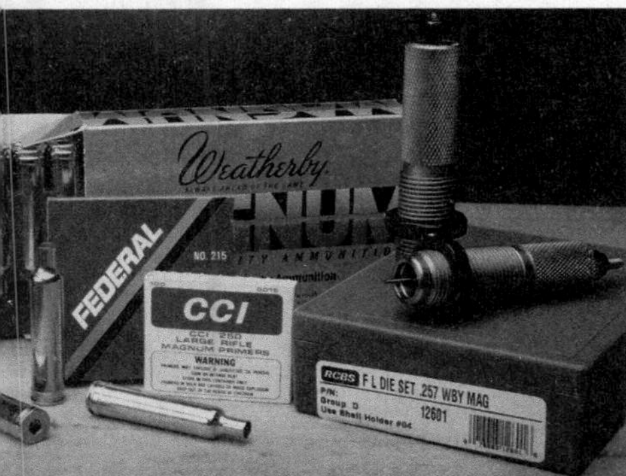

For the handloader who likes to squeeze the most out of their .25-caliber rifle, there are plenty of components available to make a life's work out of any cartridge.

Although I've never used the .250 Savage for any serious big game hunting, the cartridge and a gun so chambered have always had a spot on my rifle rack. I've toyed with the cartridge in the fields of New York State with lighter bullets after woodchucks with fine results, although after a short period of time the .22 centerfires were much better suited for the job. I have a friend who finds the .250 Savage a great plains rifle. He loves to stalk, and his trophy room has some fine examples of both pronghorn and mule deer gracing its walls. Chambered in a limited-run Classic Remington Model 700, he still finds both the gun and cartridge much to his favor.

The .250 Savage has plenty of romance about it, having been developed by Charles Newton and introduced by Savage in its more than famous Model 99. As with the history of any cartridge, I came across some interesting details about the .250 Savage that add to the depth of its history. For example, while Newton was credited with the development of the cartridge for Savage, there seems to be a gray area here. He started out with a .30-40 Krag, cutting it back to .30-30 Winchester length, then necking it down to .25 caliber. The problem was that, since the Krag had a rim much too large to fit into the chamber of the Model 99, the engineers at the plant dropped the idea, as retooling the 99 would be out of the question. Newton left in a huff, approaching Winchester, but they, too, were unresponsive, as they already had a .25-35 Winchester in the mix.

The plan lay inactive for a while, later revived by well-known ballistics expert Harvey Donaldson with information from his book, "Yours Truly." Apparently, Donaldson was in close with the engineers at Savage and, after much discussion over the dormant cartridge, and because of its interesting qualities, suggested they use a case with a smaller rim. Up came the .30-06 Springfield, cutting it back to function in the Model 99, necking it down to .25 caliber, and adding a slight taper. The only alterations needed on the rifle were to modify the extractor and headspace. Savage engineers really wanted to introduce the .250 Savage with a 100-grain bullet for serious hunting. They hit upon the idea of using a lighter bullet — perhaps around 87 grains — so they could reach the then unheard-of velocity of 3,000 fps! The .250-3000 Savage was born.

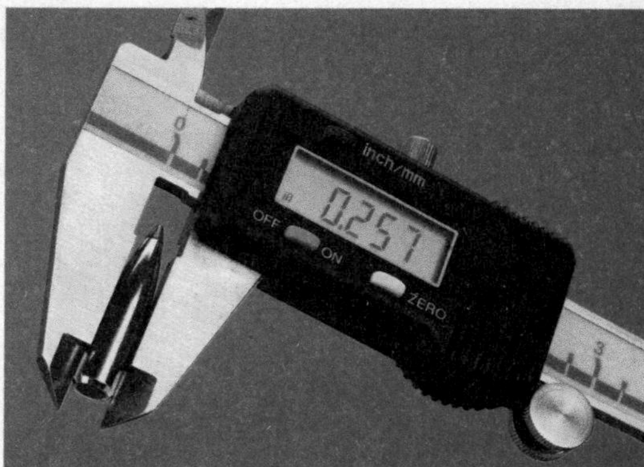

Measuring .257 inch in diameter, .25-caliber bullets are available in weights from 60 to 120 grains in a wide variety of designs from a host of manufacturers.

Over the years, my collection of rifles chambered for the .250 Savage came and went, with examples that ran from a Remington Classic refitted to a custom stock, to Rugers chambered in every cartridge under the sun, and some in between. While the .250 Savage does not seem to be on the all-time list when it comes to factory ammunition, this soft-spoken cartridge finds its niche within handloading circles. Both beginners and veterans marvel at its accuracy and, with a wide range of bullets from 75 to 120 grains, it's hard not to find that perfect load for the game at hand.

Regarding powders, I found AA 2520 and IMR-3031 much to my liking, especially with 87- and 100-grain bullets. With the Hornady 87-grain spire point over 36.5 grains of Accurate Arms 2520, groups averaged between an inch and an inch and a quarter at 3,100 fps. With the Remington 100-grain Core-Lokt and 32.0 grains of IMR-3031 (a favorite of the old masters), velocity went 2,734 fps with groups that circled three-eighths of an inch! With AA 2520 and 32.5 grains, velocity peaked at 2,748 fps with groups under an inch.

With its storied history and reputation, the .250 Savage is a classic cartridge that belongs in the modern hunter's battery of rifles. For deer or antelope at moderate ranges, this cartridge delivers the goods while still having a more than satisfactory recoil effect and excellent groups.

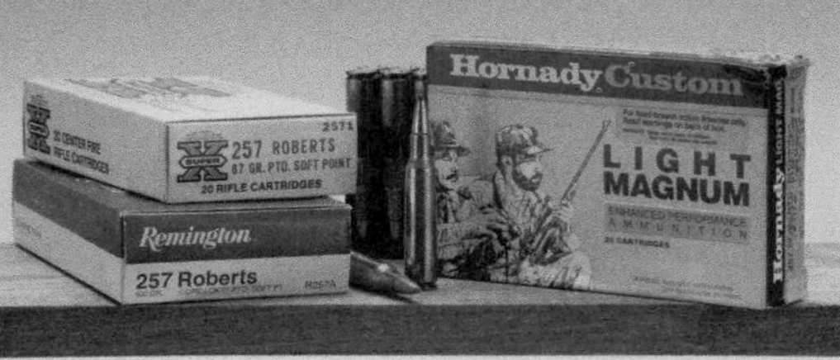

Even if you don't handload, and for those who like milder cartridges like the .250 Savage or .257 Roberts, there is still a wide variety of factory ammunition available from all the major players in the industry. For a comparison against his handloads, the author picked these three factory offerings for the .257 Roberts.

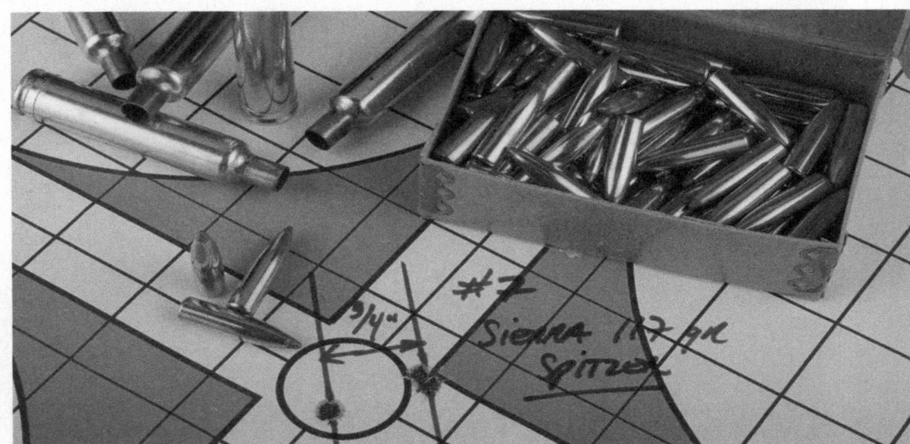

For hunting larger medium game like mule deer or antelope, the .257 Weatherby will deliver the goods. This example shows how the Sierra 117-grain spitzer performs at 100 yards with an outstanding 3/4-inch group.

THE .257 ROBERTS

My interest in the .257 Roberts began almost four decades ago. I had been interested in the cartridge for some time and, with a hunt coming up in Montana, I was looking for a new rifle to take along. A casual trip up to the flagship Orvis store in Vermont seemed to provide the answer in the form of a brochure laying on the counter in the sporting arms department. It contained Winchester's announcement of the introduction of the Model 70 in the Featherweight model. A call to the public relations department of the parent company netted me a new Model 70 in the .257 Roberts a short time later and in time for the hunt. Since then, I've been a big fan of the .257 Roberts.

Over time, Remington, Ruger and Winchester have supplied us with guns chambered for the Roberts and I've worked with all of them. Browning had a BLR for the .257, but I never shot a sample. Back around 1909, we find that F.W. Mann was interested in working up an efficient .25-caliber cartridge based on the .30-40 Krag — the same parent cartridge that led to the .250 Savage. About the same time, Ned Roberts was tinkering with the 7x57 Mauser case, which had similar powder capacity as the .30-40 Krag. Working in the company of F.J. Sage, Townsend Whelen, A.O. Niedner and L.C. Weldin of the Hercules Powder Company, a new star was born in the form of the .257 Roberts. It was based on the 7x57 case and necked to .25 caliber, complete with a 15-degree shoulder. In 1934, Remington Arms took an interest in the Roberts, commercialized it, changed the shoulder angle to 20 degrees and offered it in their Model 30 bolt-action rifle.

Winchester took it from there by chambering it in its Model 54 and Model 70, but today rifles chambered for the Roberts are few and far between. This baffles me, as the .257 Roberts has been highly touted by such luminaries as Elmer Keith, Jack O'Connor and Warren Page. Like the .250 Savage, it is easy to shoot and a pleasure to reload. And, while there's not much in the way of factory ammunition, there's enough to keep one interested (including the new +P loadings) even if you don't handload ammunition. To me, it not only makes an ideal deer load in rifles with shorter 22-inch barrels, but for the open plains the cartridge will get you back to basics by pushing you to stalk closer while keeping your aim true.

For those who want the most from the Roberts, handloading is the way to go. Unprimed and once-fired cases are available either at your local gun shop or at shows, and if by chance you can't find any, you can purchase some 7x57 Mauser brass and neck it down to .25 caliber. Common large rifle primers handle ignition. And although some of the loading manuals show how to up the ante with +P loads, for my use I never saw the need to "magnumize" the .257 Roberts just to gain another 100 fps or so. Still another way of obtaining a small increase in velocity would be to work with this cartridge as the .257 Roberts Improved.

For powders, Sharpe favored IMR-4064 with a 100-grain bullet. I tried that same combination, and while IMR-4064 fared much better accuracy-wise with an 87-grain bullet, IMR-4895 was the powder of choice for this bullet weight. When it came to the 75- and 100-grain bullets, W760 was the best choice; the heavier 117-grain Hornady loved H-4350 as a propellant. Seems like it was all in the family with factory loads, as the commercial version of the .257 Roberts under the Hornady brand with a 117-grain bullet was also one of the most accurate.

For the traditional shooter who might like to try something more comfortable on this side of the popular magnum loadings for medium game, I urge you to investigate the possibilities of using the .257 Roberts on your next trip. You may never look back!

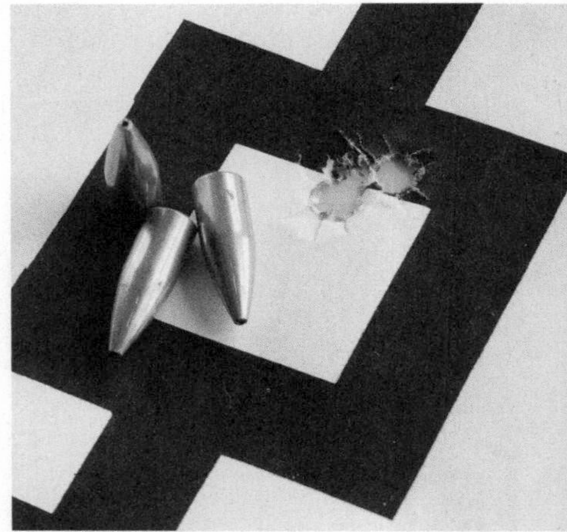

The .257 Roberts is good for small game, as demonstrated by this diminutive group coming in at .30-inch at 100 yards. This is a consistent load over the years for the author with a combination of 51.0 grains of Winchester 760 powder and a Remington large rifle primer for a mean velocity of 3,521 fps.

THE .25 WINCHESTER SUPER SHORT MAGNUM

Like many cartridges over the years, the .25 WSSM never seemed to gain much ground. For one, it was too close to the .257 Roberts Improved and the .25-06 Remington for most to even look at it. Another strike against it: Browning and Winchester were the only arms makers to chamber a rifle for it. That narrowed the choice even more, and at times it was just hard to order and receive a rifle to shoot it in. Based on an ad hoc .404 Jeffery case, it is short, stubby, and inferior to the other .25-caliber rounds that have already made their mark in the shooting sports.

Introduced in 2004, the .25 WSSM (along with other WSSM cartridges) tried to make inroads into the hunting fraternity with hard-hitting cartridges that overshadowed present-day entries. In form, it is a necked-up version of the .243 WSSM or, from a different perspective, a shortened .300 WSM (Winchester Short Magnum), all of which were designed to be more efficient due to their short, fat cases that were intended to be used in lighter rifles utilizing a short action. While called a "magnum," this is a misnomer. That's because the handle is only based on the case that it uses in order to achieve better accuracy through a more uniform burn rate of powder within the case.

At one time, Browning and Winchester had a couple dozen rifles chambered for .223, .243 and .25-caliber members of the WSSM family. Currently, the only references I find in the catalogs are those rifles chambered for the .270 Win., .300 Win. Mag. and the .325 WSM; noting that the .25 WSSM has indeed bitten the bullet and is out of favor with both Browning and Winchester. That is not to say that custom rifle builders will not offer the .25 WSSM as a choice, but in all honesty, a super short cartridge deserves a short action to benefit both the cartridge and shooter. The only thing that is keeping the .25 WSSM alive is factory ammunition being produced by Winchester on a very irregular basis, if at all. According to the web and catalog, they produce a 120-grain Super X loading launching at around 2,990 fps, depending upon the barrel length. Strangely enough, it matches the .25-06 in velocity (SAAMI specs) but my testing with a Remington Model 700 showed velocities over 3,020 fps with factory ammunition, which illustrates just how close the .25 WSSM actually is to its nearest competition.

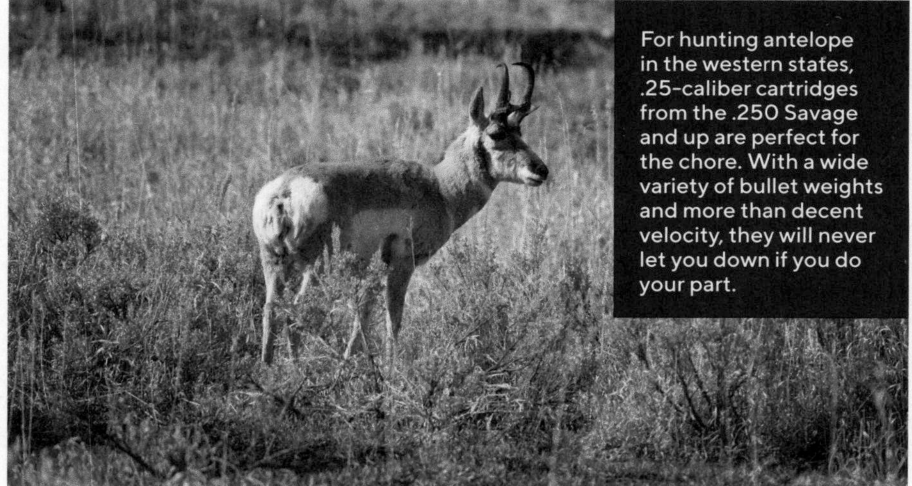

For hunting antelope in the western states, .25-caliber cartridges from the .250 Savage and up are perfect for the chore. With a wide variety of bullet weights and more than decent velocity, they will never let you down if you do your part.

Finally, consider this: The last time the .25 WSSM was chambered in a Browning A-Bolt was in 2007.

While the .25 WSSM sure is an interesting cartridge from an appearance and ballistics standpoint, with no rifles being produced at this time by any vendor, and the lack of factory ammunition leading to no brass, for my needs on plains game the .25-06 Remington or the .257 Weatherby will do just fine.

THE .25-06 REMINGTON

Checking my logbooks, I got interested in the .25-06 Remington back in the early part of 1977. A bit prior to that I had read a long article by friend Dean Grennell about the advantages of reloading this .25-caliber entry after having tested it in a Remington Model 700. Sadly, Dean passed away in 2004. He was a devoted handloader and I miss his articles in *Gun World* magazine.

Like others in the fold, I became obsessed with the .25-06 starting around the 1920s. Proponents of a wildcat initially known as the .25-06 Niedner often said it shot "reasonably well," but argued that because of its large powder capacity they would stick to the cartridge of the times, the .257 Roberts. At that time, it became painfully obvious that the right powder had yet to come along.

It was not until after World War II that the .25-06 started to move out on its own. IMR-4350 and slower powders emerged, making the .25-06 Remington a cartridge of interest, especially when it came to available components. For example, .30-06 Springfield cases were then in abundance, and by running the '06 case into the .25-06 die, you had the makings of the future .25-06 Remington. In fact, it has the same dimensions as the parent .30-06. Complete with a 17-degree, 30-minute shoulder, and with an overall

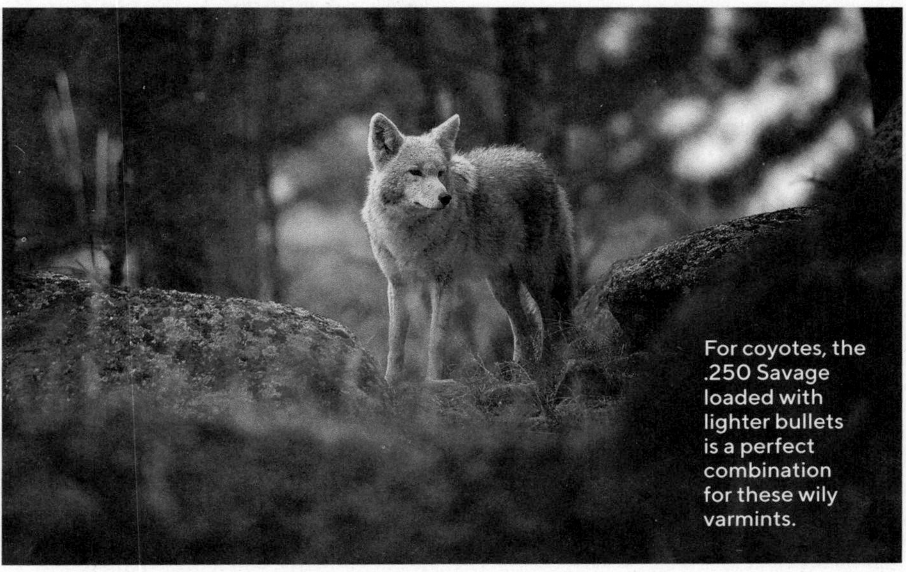

For coyotes, the .250 Savage loaded with lighter bullets is a perfect combination for these wily varmints.

length of 2.494 inches, it easily fit into long- action rifles with butter-smooth feeding of its streamlined profile. Experimenting in the field, I've taken eastern woodchucks out past 325 yards with it, using lighter 75-grain Sierra bullets over 56.0 grains of H-4350 for 3,616 fps.

Will all the good vibes the cartridge was sending out, Remington commercialized it in 1969. So now, just about every manufacturer worth its salt would chamber rifles in the .25-06 Remington. Back in 1977, I went to a local gun show and there was the Remington Custom Shop displaying its wares. On the right side of the table was a nice example of a Model 700 all decked out in semi-fancy wood and called the "C" Model. Placing an order with an emphasis on "nice" wood, the rifle was in my hands some nine months later. Testing handloads after a nominal barrel break-in, the 100-grain Hornady spire point over 51.2 grains of IMR-4831 placed three shots into a neat cluster that didn't then — and never has since — exceed an impressive 5/8-inch.

I loved that cartridge so much that, two years later, a Weatherby Vanguard on the rack in another store seemed to have my name on it. Straight from the factory, this fine .25-caliber rifle had a Weatherby Premier scope mounted in a set of Buehler rings. As par for the course with Weatherby, the rifle has nice wood on it, and I use the present tense, as the gun is still in my rack. With a Speer 87-grain spritzer and 50.6 grains of IMR-4350 in the tank, groups still peak under an inch no matter when I shoot it.

There is no doubt the popularity of the .25-06 Remington has been enhanced by the availability of commercial ammunition by everyone from Federal to Winchester, and with it, a ton of handloading components. Since the .30-06 Springfield is the parent of the Remington clone, there never seems to be a shortage of brass. But if you go the route of necking down military brass, make sure the internal capacity is close to the commercial cases. In some instances, the cartridge walls on military samples are a bit thicker, which could lead to higher pressures. With a case capacity of just over 65.0 grains of water (slightly more or less depending upon the manufacturer), powders in the slower category like H-4350, IMR-4831, RL-19 or 22 and IMR-7828 fill the case with aplomb, leading to excellent accuracy. Ignition is supplied by common large rifle primers. Never have I needed to install hot magnum primers in any of my loads.

For plains game, rifles chambered in .25-06 Remington have netted a fine array of mule deer and antelope in both Montana and Wyoming. While some lament how the .243 Winchester or 6mm Remington have stolen some of the .25-06's thunder, the .25 always seems to come back.

While the .25-06 is good for many things, the pronghorn antelope must be its forte. I've taken my share of mule deer and antelope and it has never let me down. Maybe it was the gun, the lighter recoil, or just me. Whatever it was, the .25-06 Remington did make the difference.

THE .257 WEATHERBY MAGNUM

Sticking my neck out again, I will say that out of all the .25-caliber offerings, the .257 Weatherby Magnum is my all-time favorite. I'll stand behind that by noting that in my gun rack are three rifles chambered for the cartridge, including a sharp-looking Mark V Deluxe, a Weatherby Custom Shop Vanguard with all the trimmings, and a readily available, off-the-shelf, Vanguard Deluxe with nice wood.

Over the past few years the .257 WM has turned out to be the "darling" of the Weatherby line. For example, in the current line of Mark V rifles there are 14 different models, 11 of which are chambered for the .257 WM. With the less expensive Vanguard, 19 models are listed in the catalog with 11 chambered for its .257. Out of 33 various models, 22 are available for the .257 WM — quite a margin even for .25-caliber guns, and a proprietary cartridge at that.

In 1944, the master of high velocity, Roy Weatherby, set out to make a niche for himself with his own line of high-performance cartridges. Introduced commercially by the company in 1945, the .257 WM was originally made and developed by using a close variant to the .300 H&H Magnum that was shortened a bit, blown out, and finally necked down to accept a .25-caliber bullet. Looking at the history of the cartridge, the .257 followed in the footsteps of the .270 Win. and 7mm and .300 Weatherby magnums, as it is based on the same case. In the early stages of Weatherby's thrust into the market, .257 WM ammunition was loaded in-house. Later, Weatherby contracted with Richard Speer to help. Finally, because of demand and space, Weatherby signed a contract with Norma Projektilfabrik in Sweden to manufacture his ammunition, a partnership still intact today. At one time, Remington made .257 Weatherby Magnum ammo with a 122-grain Extended Range bullet that traveled around 3,200 fps.

This lineup of .25-caliber cartridges includes (L to R), the .250 Savage, .257 Roberts, .25-06 Remington and three offerings for the .257 Weatherby Magnum.

The author loves the .257 Weatherby Magnum and had this Vanguard made in the Weatherby Custom Shop to his specifications. A synthetic stock and Teflon-coated action are highlights of this special rifle. Topped off with a Leupold 3-9x scope, it is ready for antelope hunting in the west.

From a ballistics standpoint, the .257 WM is an interesting cartridge, if not over bore capacity by a large margin. It has a case capacity of 84.0 grains of water, leading to hefty doses of slow-burning powder. All of the Weatherby cartridges feature a double-radius shoulder, which promotes the slower-burning propellants. In all accounts, the .257 WM is a very accurate and long-range cartridge and, if sighted in properly, allows the hunter a minimum holdover (if any) at longer distances up to 500 yards. In fact, looking up some of the numbers for long-range shooting, if comparing Remington and Weatherby ammunition using a 115-grain bullet, with both zeroed at 200 yards, the Remington brand will drop around 44 inches at 500 yards — the Weatherby 115-grain only 30 inches. Much of this is due to the fact that Weatherby .257 ammo is around 300 to 400 fps faster than the nearest competition.

I have used the .257 Weatherby with great success on plains game, and if one would pigeonhole this cartridge without any doubts, it just has to be the premier antelope, mountain goat or sheep cartridge. For varmints, if you must use the .257 WM, you will not be using it long, as muzzle blast, recoil and, if you use only factory ammunition, cost per round are all rather high. In the end, regardless of the game pursued, handloading is the way to go.

Checking my own records, using the Mark V and the Vanguard Custom, factory ammunition hovered around one inch at the customary 100 yards. With handloads, bullet weights from 75 to 120 grains from a variety of makers grouped from an abysmal 5 to 8 inches up to very respectable 1-inch groups with the Hornady 120-grain hollowpoint with 67.1 grains of IMR-7828 and a Federal #215 primer supplying the ignition.

In closing, I'd like to offer this quote in part from Ed Weatherby, "The .257 Weatherby Magnum was my father's all-time Weatherby cartridge. My father used this caliber extensively in Africa for plains game. I learned quickly that it wasn't only going to be my father's favorite, for it became mine as well. I love the light recoil and its versatility for a wide assortment of game animals."

The .25-caliber cartridges covered here have a place in one or more hunting situations. From the oldest to the most modern, today's shooter has a wide choice of rifles, ammunition and handloading supplies. While the twenty-five may be surrounded by some stiff competition, once sorted out and matched to the game at hand, you will never turn back.

I never did!

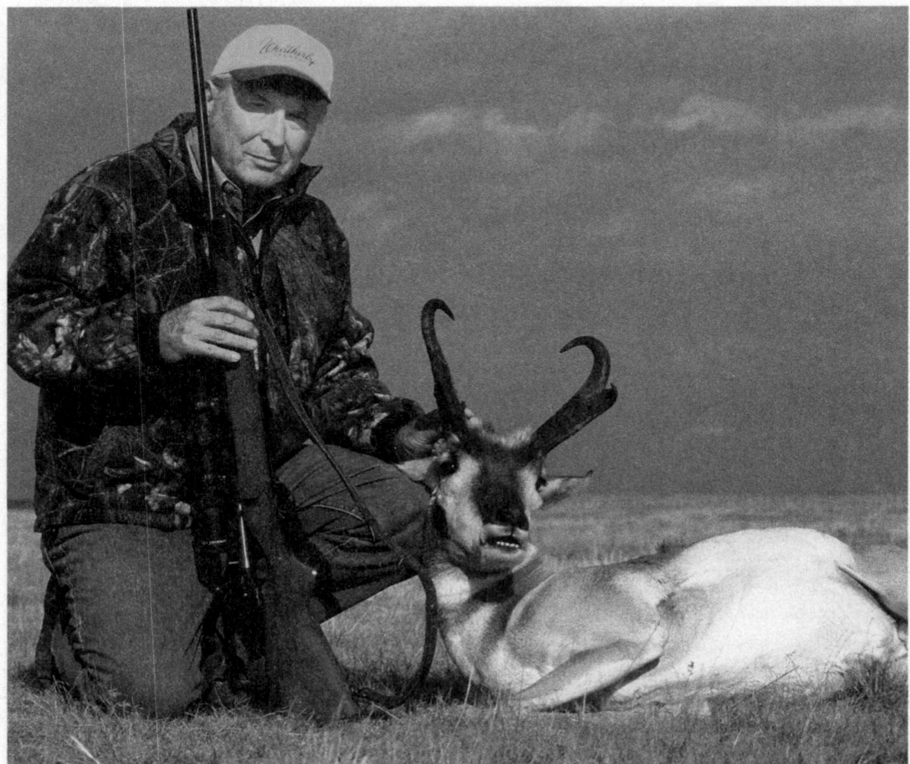

Proof that the right cartridge and gun will do the job in the field: The author took this nice pronghorn with a Weatherby Vanguard in .257 Weatherby.

KOLAR'S CLASSY OVER/UNDER SHOTGUNS

The Kolar Over/Under is Making Waves in Trap, Sporting Clays and Skeet

BY **NICK SISLEY**

The Kolar Max Skeet over/under is the epitome of classy sporting shotguns today.

A highly engraved Kolar receiver — beautiful and functional.

Kolar is a name in shotgunning that is not well-known to those outside the high stakes world of professional skeet shooting. But to those in the know, it's the sporting scattergun to have if you want to compete against the best in the business. Kolar guns are entirely made right here in America — in Racine, Wisconsin, to be exact. But how did the Kolar over/under come about?

Don Mainland is the man behind the Kolar concept. In the 1960s, '70s and beyond, Mainland was making parts for the auto and aero industries to tolerances of +/- .003-inches — unheard of at the time. Pioneer Products (one of three companies he owns) had more than 50 parts on various space shuttles.

2015 National Sporting Clays Champion Pat Lieske.

Mainland was shooting a lot of skeet in the early 1980s with Ed Scherer and Debra Raschella, both Skeet Hall of Famers. For those who don't know, skeet is a four-gauge game involving the 12-, 20-, 28- and .410-gauge shotgun. Leading up to the 1980s most competitors shot four-barrel sets with one 12-gauge receiver using interchangeable 12, 20, 28 and .410 over/under barrels, thus the term four-barrel set. But coming on strong by the early 1980s were "tube sets." These were light aluminum alloy full-length tubes precision fit to individual 12-gauge barrels. The tubes were tapped into place with a tight fit and had stainless-steel chambers (titanium chambers for lighter weight were later used).

It was Ed Scherer who suggested Mainland meet with Larry Kolar. During that time Kolar was making skeet tubes under his own name and was initially reluctant to sell. But after Mainland visited for several days Kolar decided to sell his sub-gauge tubes. Today these are called Kolar Max Lite AAA Sub-Gauge Tubes.

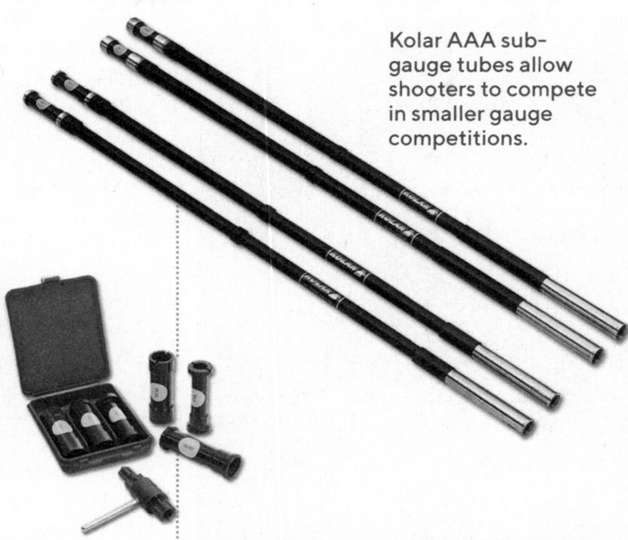

Kolar AAA sub-gauge tubes allow shooters to compete in smaller gauge competitions.

Sometime around 1990, Remington Arms had an idea for a single-barrel trap gun that was eventually called the 90-T. Don Mainland made ten of these trap guns under contract with Remington. After extensive testing, Remington gave Mainland a contract to manufacture the 90-T. So, all Remington Model 90-T trap guns were made by Don Mainland's company, not Remington.

Gun companies were very concerned about barrel blowups, which were often caused by overloads with reloaded shells. Mainland developed the technology to measure wall thickness the full length of the barrel. For the Remington 90-T, Mainland's company rejected any barrel that was out of tolerance by +/- .003-inch wall thickness down the full length of the barrel. He told me that Remington did extensive testing trying to blow up 90-T barrels, but they couldn't.

Remington was going through a sale of the company when it came time to renew the contract for more model 90-T trap guns. Perhaps because of the impending sale Remington did not want to renew the contract for additional 90-T single-barrel shotguns. So, what was Mainland to do with the tooling he had set up to make this Remington trap gun? He made a few starts trying to make over/under shotguns for at least one other manufacturer, but then he got the backing, in the way of orders, to come up with his own Kolar shotgun — the gun originally named the Kolar Competition — and the first orders came from Hal DuPont and Robert Paxton, both very well-known names in clay target competition. Later in this article Paxton gives more insight into how the Kolar gun got started.

In coming up with the design of the Kolar, Mainland already had the concept and technology to make barrels of consistent wall thickness, i.e. no thin areas. He also looked at areas that had failed in other competition shotguns, even if those failures took hundreds of thousands of rounds before occurring. Mainland redesigned these parts, made them stronger, removed sharp corners and more. He also beefed up the sides of his new receiver, adding more strength. As Mainland put it to me, "I overbuild everything."

The Kolar triggers went through three generations of design. Some of the trigger design changes were to ensure the gun wouldn't fan fire. The latest triggers were also designed so they could quickly be changed back and forth between pull and release. Release triggers are of great importance to trap shooters.

Mainland also designed the Kolar O/U so it would be easy to work on. No complicated tools were required by a gunsmith other than those virtually all gunsmiths had on hand. This is not true of many other shotgun receivers.

Enter John Ramagli, who came along during the early years of Kolar gun production. Ramagli was particularly interested in .410 patterns. He used Mainland's indoor range for seemingly endless experiments. Ramagli described those experiments. "In those years, used .410 Remington semi-auto 1100 barrels could be bought for as little as $50. I'd take them to Kolar's indoor patterning range and start cutting barrel muzzles back a small amount at a time, thus reducing the choke trying to see if I could improve .410 patterns. I also painstakingly polished chokes, thus polished away some more choke … to see if I could improve those .410 patterns. But my results were sketchy.

"Next, I started overboring those Remington 1100 .410 barrels from .410 to .412 to .415, to even .420. It was overboring that improved my .410 patterns. This was the technology that we began building

Inside the Elite Shotguns traveling mobile sales van, where many high-end Kolar shotguns are on display and for sale.

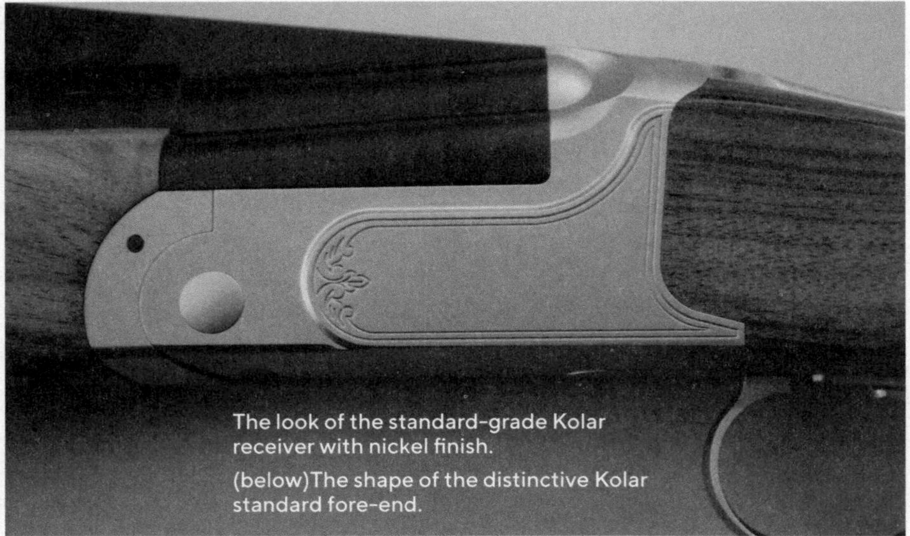

The look of the standard-grade Kolar receiver with nickel finish.

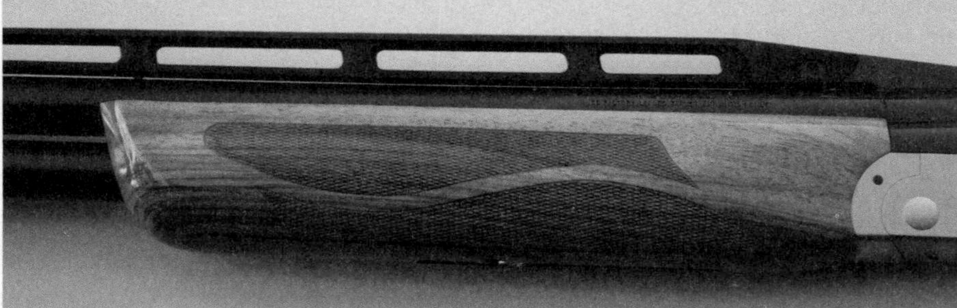

(below)The shape of the distinctive Kolar standard fore-end.

into our .410 sub-gauge tubes. Eventually, we overbored all our sub-gauge tubes."

Back to chokes. Another thing Ramagli discovered with his choke experiments was that a conical shape worked best in sub-gauge tubes. Most of us have always assumed that a parallel/taper was the best way to build a choke. After all, the latter way is more time-consuming and expensive, so it should be better. Not so according to Ramagli's experiments.

If discovering the benefits of overboring was the first bonus Ramagli brought to Kolar, it wasn't the last. He invested in the company and is now President of the company. As Don Mainland had been the guiding and shining light behind the Kolar gun concept, Ramagli was getting ready to take the gun to new heights.

"Shooters are going to see more innovation at Kolar in the next 10 years than they have in our previous 10 years," Ramagli said.

Kolar over/under sales started only with Hal DuPont and "K Guns" and Robert Paxton with Paxton Arms near Dallas, Texas. After a few years, Ramagli spread sales of the Kolar to several other high-end dealers, but his current financial plan has been to reduce the number of gun shops that sell it to a select few. Robert Paxton is still on, big time, as is Pat Lieske with the Bald Mountain and Island Lake Shooting Centers in Michigan, the Indiana Gun Club with Phil Baker and their mobile sales units manned by John Harden, and now the joint venture between Dan Lewis on the West Coast, Murry Gerber's Elite Shotguns in Pennsylvania, and mobile sales units manned by Aaron Willoughby.

What shot the Kolar over/under through the figurative roof in popularity is not only the company's financial plan, but also its shooters. And Kolar relies heavily on these shooters (as well as regular Kolar customers) for input on how to make the Kolar O/U better. In the skeet realm it has been mainly Paul Giambrone III. He not only shoots a Kolar and has for years, but also has provided suggestions for the current Kolar Max Lite Skeet model. Guys like Giambrone don't suggest major changes, but the little tweaks are what make great guns better. For close to 10 years, Giambrone has been just about unbeatable on skeet's biggest stages.

For trap input, Ramagli relied heavily on All-American Ricky Marshall (now

A typical Kolar with Monte Carlo-type step-down at the back of the stock.

(left) The typical high-quality checkering pattern on the Kolar Max.

an employee) and other All-American trap shooters. While the Max Trap is still available with an adjustable rib, with Marshall's input (and other trap shooters) the Kolar has recently reintroduced the fixed rib — both a standard and an elevated one. Other subtle changes have gone into the current Kolar trap model.

Similarly, Kolar has listened to their customers and professional team members to tweak the shotgun for sporting clays. One result: the Max Lite Sporter. This input came from shooters like Doug Fuller, who won the National Sporting Clays Championship in 2000; Pat Lieske, who won the National Sporting Clays Championship in 2015 and the National F.I.T.A.S.C. Championship in 2015; and Derrick Mein, who won the National Sporting Clays Championship in 2017 and the 2016 World F.I.T.A.S.C. Championship in Italy.

Murry Gerber of Elite Shotguns.

Another aspect that keeps the Kolar models ahead of the competition is the wood. "Dollar for dollar we put on the best walnut of any gun in the industry," Ramagli said. "We know our shooters love a great piece of wood on their gun, and we go overboard to produce for them. Great wood is not easy to find. I've spent two decades contacting the best wood producers."

In addition to superb wood stocks, the company is also putting more and more emphasis on engraved guns. The Standard model is engraved (with either a blued or nickeled receiver), but an increasing number wear significant engraving that pushes price tags to well over $100,000. These high-grade Kolars are selling about as fast as engravers can turn them out, according to Ramagli.

The lockup system of the Kolar is super strong, with two lugs protruding from the sides of the inside of the receiver that fit into two recesses milled into either side of the barrels upon closing the gun. Barrels pivot on trunnions. Receiver wall thickness is wider than most at .329 inch. When Ramagli started with Kolar he wanted a lighter receiver. Mainland was dead set against doing that. These days, Ramagli admits Mainland was right. Other over/under manufacturers have redesigned their receivers similarly.

"The receiver is the key to virtually everything about the Kolar," Ramagli explains. "Strength is only the beginning. The gun stays in balance whether we hang 30- or 32-inch barrels on that receiver. However, most importantly, it's how easy the receiver is to take apart, repair and put back together. That's Don Mainland's genius. Virtually every gun that comes in for service goes out the same or next day. They are that easy to take apart, that easy to service. And no special tools are needed to undress a Kolar receiver.

"Recently a very low serial number Kolar came in — I think #244. It was bought by a trap shooter in 1996. Reportedly, he had shot over two million rounds through the gun. It had never been to Racine for any service! That says a lot about how well these guns are built," he said.

"I'm so proud to have been a part of this Kolar story," he continued. "The success certainly has not been all my doing. The sales team that's now assembled with Robert Paxton, Pat Lieske, Phil Baker, Murry Gerber and Dan Lewis — we're going to be around for a long, long time."

To get more of the Kolar story, I next spoke with Jeff Mainland (Don's son) and Jeff's son, Sean.

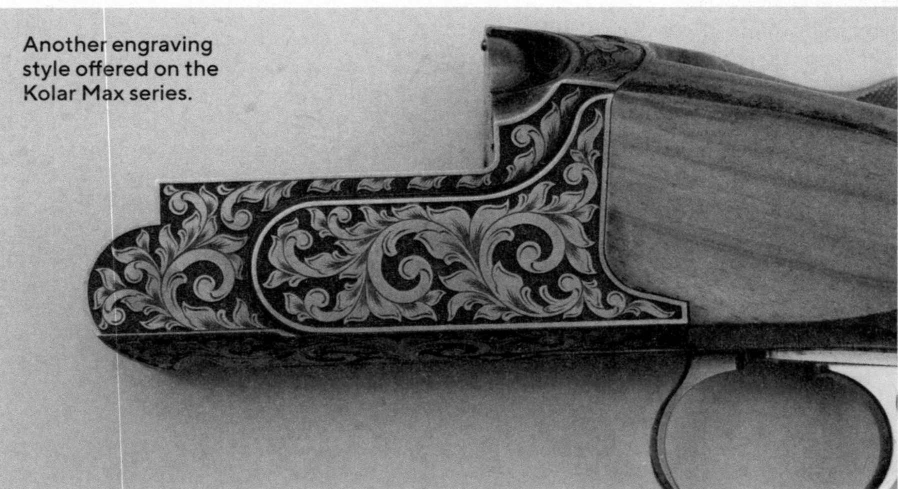
Another engraving style offered on the Kolar Max series.

Jeff Mainland, President of US Competition Arms, Inc. (the company is the affiliated entity that produces the Kolar), explained that Kolar barrels have gone through a few changes over the years. Input from shooters advised that original barrels were a bit heavy. Jeff attacked this issue first by overboring the barrels — first to .740 inner diameter, then to .750, then even more — to reduce weight. Those significant inner bore dimensions were abandoned when it became evident that .740 inch offered the best patterns. Jeff and others worked on the technology to machine metal from the outer diameter of the barrels instead. The result is an even greater weight loss compared to boring metal from inside the barrels. Recall earlier how Don Mainland developed the technology to measure barrel thickness every few inches to ensure uniform thickness. The net result of reducing the outer diameter of the barrels was the removal of 8 to 10 ounces of barrel weight. Now the new Kolar guns became even more lively.

The further result was the introduction of three new guns — the current Max Lite Skeet, Max Lite Sporter and Max Lite Trap. These three guns are the current state-of-the-art from Kolar, and are winning big in serious competition. When it comes to new skeet guns sold, 99 percent are shipped with 30-inch barrels as well as the Kolar Max AAA Sub-Gauge Tubes. Most are sold with a low-profile adjustable rib and comb (all Kolar guns now come with an adjustable comb — save the ones that are individually fitted to a customer). All three models are stocked with a 14.75-inch length of pull (LOP). As Jeff says, "Few shooters require a longer stock than that." If necessary, reducing LOP is easy. All stocks come with a Monte Carlo step-down at the rear (see photo). This stock configuration reduces felt recoil as the gun tends to come straight back — not up into the face.

Full-length view of the Max Lite Sporter.

Four different stock configurations are available in the skeet, sporting and trap models, and left-handed stocks are offered as well. All stocks are crafted in-house via close-tolerance CNC machinery. Jeff has become a master stock fitter, and with many of the Kolar guns sold customers come into Racine for his special fitting. This takes all day. After considerable work fitting a customer, he uses CNC machines to mill small segments of the stock — always leaving a bit of extra wood. Final stock dimensions are completed by hand.

According to Jeff Mainland, one customer from Utah asked for trap guns that printed patterns 80 percent above the point of aim, then ordered additional Kolars that shot 100 percent above point of aim. More and more Kolar trap guns are going out the door with these two configurations. The idea behind the very high shooting guns is that the rising trap target is still in view when the trigger is pulled. With patterns printing 50/50 the bird is usually covered by the barrels, thus not seen when the trigger is pulled. According to him, Kolar has 20 different stock/rib choices for trap shooters.

Jeff's son Sean came on at Kolar a few years ago. That makes three generations of Mainlands at the company. Sean is the one who attends many of the trap, sporting and skeet competitions. These events are attended to obtain shooter input that will make a great American-made competition gun even better.

What about the special distributors that sell Kolar competition guns? The first to come on board was the aforementioned Robert Paxton. Paxton is one of the most seasoned shotgunners to ever break clay. A many-time All-American and member of the Skeet Shooting Hall of Fame, Paxton's introduction to Don Mainland came via phone. Mainland had ordered a competition over/under with a set of sub-gauge tubes. A few weeks later, he ordered another gun and set of tubes, then a third, fourth — perhaps a fifth set — all within only a four-month period. Paxton was thinking, "This is my best customer!"

Shooting the Kolar is an experience that is tough to put into words. There's a reason why competition shooters are flocking to the brand.

Eventually, Paxton asked Mainland what he was doing with all those expensive guns and sub-gauge tube sets. Mainland was dissecting them, cutting them into small pieces trying to find out what made them tick, thus how to make his gun better. When Mainland bought Kolar Sub-Gauge Tubes, Paxton was the first on board to sell them.

Mainland made his first 12 prototype Kolar shotguns and gave them to a dozen serious shooters with the request they shoot them for two years and report back. Robert Paxton received #4 and, like the other field testers, shot that prototype for two years. Skeet-shooting legend Wayne Mayes also received one of the prototypes. From 1994 until his untimely death, Mayes shot the same Kolar O/U. In fact, Mayes was significantly involved with Mainland and Ramagli as an adviser.

"This is a great American story – not just a gun company story," Robert Paxton began. "When Mainland retired from bicycle competition he was looking for something new to do. His successful companies already employed hundreds, thus he began making a shotgun — not out of profit motive but of a genuine love for the shotgun game. You can see that by his creating twelve prototypes and giving them to serious shooters to shoot for two years. He wasn't about to rush into anything. He was taking his time!

"It has been great to work with not only an American gunmaking company, but to work with one of the finest companies anyone could work with. Kolar has always been about quality, not quantity."

Phil Baker, another Kolar distributor, heads up the Indiana Gun Club where only shotgun shooting takes place — trap, skeet and sporting clays. But this club also has an extensive gun room where all the popular competition guns are displayed and sold. "The Kolar guns outsell any of the other high-end shotguns," Baker said. "We sell mostly trap guns, but also sell our share of sporting and skeet guns."

Baker also has a mobile sales unit run by John Hardin. The vehicle is filled with all the competition guns Baker sells at the Indiana Gun Club, with a special concentration on Kolar models. The mobile unit stays on the road visiting the bigger shoots — especially trap shoots — showing shooters the guns inside often with the offer to test fire them for a round or two. This traveling truck has been a very successful way for Phil Baker to market more of his shotguns.

Pat Lieske has two gun ranges — Island Lake Shooting Range just north of Ann Arbor, and Bald Mountain Shooting Range near Detroit. His gun shop is in Bald Mountain. Both clubs offer sporting clays, trap, skeet, 5-stand and rifle and pistol ranges. Lieske is no stranger to

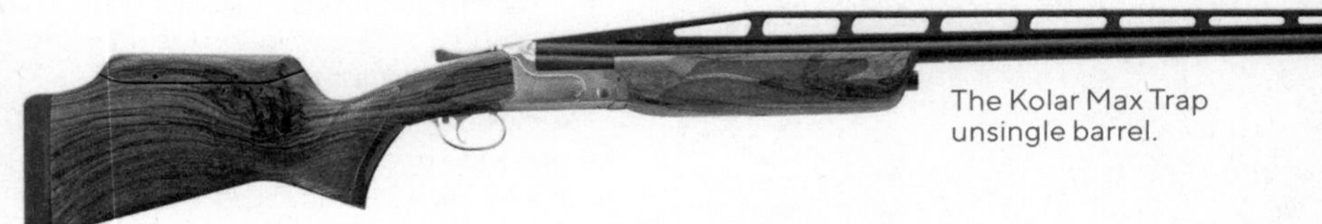

The Kolar Max Trap unsingle barrel.

Jerry Stillions' highly engraved Kolar Max Lite Skeet. Stillions spent a full day at the Racine, Wisconsin, factory to have Jeff Mainland do a custom gun fitting. When you order a Kolar, it will fit you like a glove.

KOLAR OVER/UNDER SHOTGUN MODELS

The Max Trap T/S is the unsingle trap — i.e. the barrel is at the bottom over/under receiver position. It has a 34-inch barrel.

There are three Max Trap over/under shotguns: a. with 30- or 32-inch barrels; b. with high rib; and c. the Combo - O/U and unsingle.

The Max Lite Skeet comes in two versions: Lite Contour barrels in 30 or 32 inches in either standard or "carrier" types. The latter is not for shooting 12-gauge shells, only for insertion and shooting with the sub-gauge Max Lite AAA Kolar Tubes. Also, a two-barrel set is available in this skeet category, one barrel for shooting 12-gauge shells, the other the "carrier" barrel to use only with sub-gauge tubes.

The Max Lite Sporter is offered like the Max Skeet — Lite Contour 30- or 32-inch barrels with titanium chokes, or a two-barrel set with regular and "carrier" barrels in 30- or 32-inch lengths.

KOLAR MAX LITE AAA SUB-GAUGE TUBES

Kolar Max Lite AAA Sub-Gauge Tubes are made of high-strength aircraft aluminum alloy with titanium chambers. Each tube is precision fit to your individual barrel. They're marked "top" and "bottom" and are not interchangeable, even between barrels of the same gun. The aluminum portion is anodized for hardness.

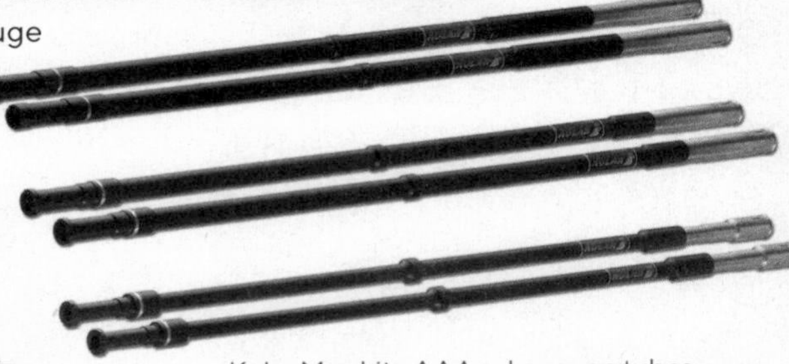

Kolar Max Lite AAA sub-gauge tubes.

clay target shooting. Previously a many-time skeet All-American and multiple skeet champion, Lieske found sporting clays some years ago and, evidently, has never looked back. Some of his wins have been highlighted previously. He negotiated with John Ramagli to become a Kolar dealer. No doubt winning the National Championship with a new Max Lite Sporter sealed that deal.

Actually, Lieske shot a Kolar years before when barrels were a bit heavier, but he told me the new Max Lite Sporter was a significant improvement. "The balance, dynamics and lack of recoil put this current Kolar Sporter in a class by itself," he said. Lieske hasn't been the first person I've talked with who is adamant about the Kolar's lack of recoil.

He now shoots a low gun at sporting clays unless the targets being presented suggest a mounted gun. "When shooting low gun, the balance and dynamics of a shotgun are even more important than when shooting a mounted gun. Here again the new Kolar shines."

He also told me that both he and his customers like dealing with a company that makes its guns right here in America. "Further, this is the only gun ever designed from the beginning to accommodate sub-gauge tubes. Small-gauge sporting competition is becoming more important, so the gun's design for 12-gauge and sub-gauges again set the Kolar apart."

Murry Gerber started Elite Shotguns, based north of Pittsburgh, five years ago. In a short time, he and his staff of only two have experienced a meteoric rise in shotgun sales, especially Kolars. When Gerber was starting his gun shop he had several choices for a high-end clay target over/under. He and his partners researched the possibilities and found Kolar was an American company. The fact that Kolar guns were made in America made the decision for them.

Kolar receivers are crafted on a CNC machine. Next comes additional finishing.

(top) A CNC milling machine is used to rough out the shape of all Kolar stocks prior to extensive handwork and application of the finish.

(middle) A Kolar employee checks for barrel straightness. And you can bet these barrels are straight!

(bottom) Kolar triggers are easily removable by the owner. Here an employee makes some final trigger adjustments.

But how to convince Kolar to have Elite become a distributor?

Gerber and partner Don Watt flew to Racine after they had set up a meeting with John Ramagli. In addition to promising to place a significant order with Kolar, Ramagli wanted more and Gerber wanted to give more. Elite was adamant about giving customers exceptional service. Elite also committed to support clay target tournaments.

Regarding those promised tournaments, Elite became a sponsor of what had been the Great Eastern Skeet Championships. The last two years the tournament has been called the Elite Classic, so this relatively new company has made the commitment to support competitive shooting. But Elite has gone further, supporting such events as the World Skeet Shooting Championships, National Sporting Clays Championships, and the U.S. Open Championships in both sporting and skeet.

Unique in the world of clay target shooting, Elite is the driving force behind their Pro Shooters Weekend. During this springtime event, Kolar pro shooters are invited to Western Pennsylvania for a three-day shoot. For a small entry fee, participants get lessons from these pros in trap, sporting and skeet, including shells and targets. "This is a prime way of giving back to our customers," said Gerber. "Once we sell them a great clay target gun we want them to use it most effectively."

Paul Giambrone III, longtime Kolar champion skeet shooter and advisor.

"This is clearly a world-class product," said Gerber. "More and more shooters are seeing the gun's advantages and switching to it. When customers come to us with a problem, Kolar has been so cooperative. Their customer service is exceptional, and customer service is a main reason our company was started."

Two years ago, Elite Shotguns teamed up with Dan Lewis, who is based in California. Lewis had become the top Kolar distributor in the Western U.S., and Elite was the leading sales shop in the East. Since then, the two have purchased space on Industry Row at the National Gun Club in San Antonio, another venue to sell their shotguns.

Louise Terry and her Dad Larry Kolar at the 2000 World Skeet Shooting Championships.

LOUISE TERRY AND KOLAR

Louise Terry is not only a great clay target shooter, she has given back so much to the clay shooting sports. She's a former president of the National Skeet Shooting Association as well as a member of the Skeet Shooting Hall of Fame. She's still shooting and has become a serious sporting clays contender.

But why a sidebar on Louise Terry? Before she met her husband, Bill Terry, she was Louise Kolar — yes, Larry Kolar's daughter. Her dad loved to shoot, and they shot together often from 1959 to 1966. In New York, Larry Kolar was the only shooter who ever won the High Over All in skeet, trap and live pigeon competition.

Along with her dad and husband, Terry started shooting competitively again in 1976. "My dad was a toolmaker all his life," she said. "He closely inspected the extractors of the original Purbaugh skeet tubes." Those extractors were separate and not permanently attached to the sub-gauge tubes.

"Dad called his company Target Arms, and he figured out a way to build the sub-gauge extractors right into the tubes themselves," Terry explained. "This was a big breakthrough. He called them Kolar Tubes.

"But my dad was having severe eye problems so was thinking of shutting down his sub-gauge tube business and machine shop. Ed Scherer found out about this and put Don Mainland in contact with my dad. Eventually a sale was made. All of the tube-making equipment was moved from New York to Wisconsin."

STRANGE RIFLES I HAVE KNOWN

I Like Odd Military Rifles — the More Unusual the Better!

(top) Members of the Michigan National Guard armed with Remington M1899 rifles.

(above) The M1895 Lee "Straight-Pull" rifle was the smallest caliber (6mm) used by American armed forces until the adoption of the M16 in the 1960s.

BY **PAUL SCARLATA**

PHOTOS BY **PAUL BUDDE, BECKY SCARLATA, JAMES WALTERS AND NATHAN REYNOLDS**

I have written about and test fired surplus military rifles that date from shortly after the end of the American Civil War (The War of Northern Aggression, as we in the South refer to it) to the Vietnam conflict. A question I am often asked is, "What is the strangest or oddest military rifle you have ever fired?" To which I answer, "Strange in what way? Place of manufacture, operating system, cartridge/caliber, age, scarcity, or who used it and where?" The list is rather lengthy. In this article I am going to discuss eight rifles that fit all of these categories — truly the strangest of the strange.

BELGIAN MODÉLE 1853/67/80 ALBINI

In the late 1860s and early 1870s, most armies were trying to find ways of converting the vast quantities of rifled muskets then in service to breechloading, cartridge-firing arms. Of the many systems used to accomplish this, one of the most common — and successful — is known as the "trapdoor." The trapdoor system consists of a breechblock, attached to the rear of a musket barrel, which is opened by a handle or catch, either to the side or toward the muzzle, allowing the insertion of a cartridge. It is a foolproof system that required very few modifications to existing muskets. And it was inexpensive! Within a few years, rifles using trapdoor-type breech systems appeared simultaneously in the U.S., France, Belgium, Switzerland, and Italy.

In 1865, Captain Augusto Albini presented a trapdoor-type rifle to the Italian Army and Navy, both of whom rejected it. Not the type to be dissuaded by mere failure, the good Captain arranged for a well-known Birmingham gun maker, Francis Augustus Braendlin, to manufacture his rifle and proceeded to offer it on the world market.

The Albini-Braendlin system consisted of a "... fronthinged, forward-lifting breech and action mechanism working together with a hammerstriker assembly to simultaneously lock and fire the rifle. The breechblock itself houses a longitudinal spring-loaded firing pin which is struck by a cylindrical striker, the back end of which is attached to the hammer via a screw through the hammer nose, and which passes through the rear of the receiver behind the firing pin. When fired, the striker moves into the back of the breechblock striking the firing pin and locking the block in place at ignition ... Pulling the hammer back withdraws the striker from the breechblock allowing it to be lifted on its pivot pin by means of a fixed knob on the right side of the block."

In 1867, after a series of trials, the Belgian Army adopted the Albini-Braendlin breech system and used it to produce rifles from a variety of obsolete muzzleloaders, namely the Fusils d'infanterie Modéle 1841/53/67, Modéle 1864/67, and Modéle 1777/67. Conversion was a fairly simple process. First the barrel was sleeved down to 11mm (.44 caliber) and the breech end cut off, threaded, and screwed into the breech unit that contained the hinged block. The stock was then relieved to accept the breech, and a new hammer with the striker was installed along with new sights. Most of the conversions were performed by the firms of Pirlot Freres et Cie and Dresse-Laloux et Cie, both of Liege.

The Mle. 67 is simple to operate. First the hammer is cocked, which withdraws the striker sufficiently to allow the breechblock to be swung up and forward by means of a handle with a bulb end. This activates a pivoting extractor, which pulls the spent cartridge case from the chamber and tips it out of the breech. A new cartridge is inserted and the breechblock snaps shut, where it is held closed by a small, spring-loaded stud on its rear face. The rifle can then be fired.

The Belgian Albini is chambered for the 11mm Cartouche Modéle 1867, a rimmed, bottle-necked Potet-type cartridge, consisting of a coiled brass foil body attached into a rimmed, drawn brass base containing a centerfire primer. The cartridge was 50mm in length containing a 386-grain paper-patched lead bullet with 75 grains of black powder propelled to 1,370 fps. Eight years later the 11mm Cartouche Modéle 1875, with a drawn brass case, was adopted.

By 1873, supplies of muskets suitable for conversion having dried up, manufacture of a purpose-built rifle, the Fusil d'infanterie Mle. 1873, began at government arsenals Fabrique d'Armes de l'Etat and Fabrique d'Armes Henri Pieper.

SPECIFICATIONS: FUSIL D'INFANTERIE MODÉLE 1873
Caliber: 11mm Cartouche Modéle 1867 et 1875 (11x50R Belgian Albini)
Overall length: 53 in.
Barrel length: 34.7 in.
Weight: 9.9 lbs.
Action: Single shot, breechloader
Sights: Front: Inverted V-blade
Rear: V-notch adj. by ramp and left from 200 to 1,100 meters
Bayonet: Socket-style with 17.7-in. blade

For use by gendarmes and military cadets, the Mosquetons de Gendarmerie Modéle 1777/1873 and Modéle 1873 were produced by Dresse-Laloux et Cie and Fabrique d'Armes Henri Pieper. They differed in having 26.7-inch barrels and were chambered for a shorter cartridge, the 11mm Cartouche Modéle 73, which used a rimmed Potet-type case (drawn brass cases were later substituted) 42mm in length, loaded with a 330-grain lead bullet and 54 grains of black powder.

In 1880, a new rear sight adjustable to 1,400 meters was adopted. A V-notch on an extension of the slider could be used with a stud on the middle barrel band for long-range volley fire from 1,500 to 2,100 meters. The Modéle 1853/67/80 was the standard arm of the Force Publique, a military/police force composed of European officers and native Askaris who policed the Belgian Congo. In 1891, the Belgians adopted Paul Mauser's bolt-action, small-bore, charger loaded, magazine rifle, the Fusil d'infanterie Modéle 1889, and most of the army's Albinis were sold off to surplus arms dealers.

A friend was kind enough to loan me a Modéle 1853/67/80 in what, considering its age, can only be described as excellent condition. A cartouche on the buttstock indicates that this rifle was converted by Pirlot Freres et Cie.

Test firing was conducted on my club's 75-yard range using custom-loaded 11mm Albini ammunition containing lead bullets and modest charges of Goex Clearshot. With its lowest sight setting of 200 meters, I had to fire several rounds to figure out how much Kentucky elevation and windage to use. After that, my best target had five rounds in a 4.5-inch group that, while well centered, was strung vertically. Considering the rifle was graced with a very heavy trigger pull, I felt this was more than satisfactory performance from this Vieille fille Belge (old Belgian girl).

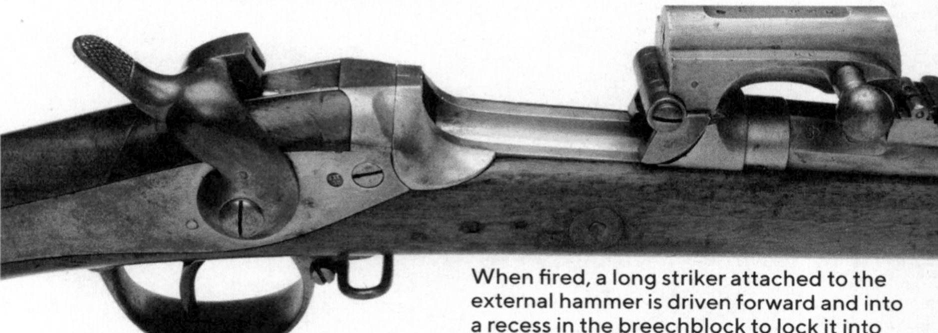

When fired, a long striker attached to the external hammer is driven forward and into a recess in the breechblock to lock it into place. It then strikes the firing pin.

PORTUGUESE ESPINGARDA MODELO 1886 KROPATSCHEK

Between 1870 and 1885, several successful military black powder repeating rifles were developed by Vetterli, Mauser, Kropatschek, Lee, and Mannlicher. In 1881, Swiss Army officer Major Eduard Rubin perfected a copper jacketed bullet that, despite the low velocities achieved with black powder, had on-target performance similar to larger caliber cartridges.

The Kingdom of Portugal possessed colonies in Africa, India, Asia, and the Pacific where European administrators, soldiers, and policemen — with some locally raised troops — were responsible for maintaining order over often less than cooperative native peoples. To keep their military and police forces well equipped for this arduous duty, the Portuguese took advantage of advances in small arms.

The Portuguese Modelo 1886 Mosqueton (Kropatschek) was one of the first small-bore repeating rifles adopted for service by any army.

In 1885, Portugal was the first nation to adopt a small-bore rifle, the Espingarda Modelo 1885 (also known as the Guedes-Castro). Made by Österreichische Waffenfabriks-Gesellschaft of Steyr, Austria, it was a single-shot, falling block rifle chambered for the Cartucho com bala 8mm m/85. This round consisted of a rimmed case 60mm in length loaded with a 248-grain round-nosed, full metal jacketed bullet, which 70 grains of compressed black powder pushed to a velocity of 1,755 fps.

In 1884, French chemist Paul Marie-Eugène Vieille produced the first successful smokeless powder. Two years later the French Army adopted a tubular magazine rifle, the Fusil d'Infanterie Modéle 1886 (the "Lebel"), chambered for a smokeless powder 8mm cartridge loaded with a jacketed bullet. The Lebel made the Modelo 1885 obsolete, so the Portuguese began a search for a repeating rifle. They found what they wanted in another Steyr product, the Kropatschek.

Designed by Alfred Ritter von Kropatschek (1838–1911), it utilized a bolt similar to the Mauser Infanteriegewehr M.71 and tubular magazine based on the Swiss Vetterli. To load the magazine, the bolt was pulled to the rear and rounds were slid forward into the magazine through the open receiver. Earlier the Portuguese Navy had purchased a number of Kropatscheks, the Espingarda Modelo 1878 Marinha, chambered for an 11mm cartridge.

In October of 1885, the Portuguese Army tested the Kropatscheks that were similar to the Modelo 1878 except they used a modified cartridge lifter and magazine cutoff and were chambered for the Guedes Cartucho cal. 8 com bala m/85. After field trials it was adopted as the Espingarda Modelo 1886, the Guedes order was canceled and replaced with a contract for 49,000 Kropatscheks.

The bolt was a three-piece affair with a separate bolt head that contained an extractor and was locked by the bolt rib-bearing on the front edge of the split-bridge receiver. As it was drawn to the rear it pulled the cartridge lifter up, positioning a round for chambering, at the same time activating the retainer to keep the next round in the magazine. When the bolt was closed it forced the lifter down, releasing the retainer so the next round could be pushed rearward onto the lifter. When moved upward, a cutoff lever on the right of the receiver deactivated the lifter, holding the contents of the magazine in reserve.

SPECIFICATIONS: ESPINGARDA MODELO 1886
Caliber: Cartucho com bala 8mm m/85
Length: 52 in.
Barrel length: 31.6 in.
Weight: 10.5 lbs.
Magazine: 8 rounds
Sights: Front: Inverted V-blade
Rear: 300-meter fixed V-notch, fold-up leaf adj. From 400 to 2,000 meters
Bayonet: Knife style w/10-in. blade

To equip mounted units, 4,000 Carabina were ordered from Steyr along with 4,800 Mosquetons (short rifles) for cavalry, artillery units, and the navy. The carbine had a 20.5-inch barrel and 5-round magazine, while the mosqueton's was 25.8 inches long and its magazine held six rounds.

In 1896, the smokeless Cartucho com bala 8mm m/96 was adopted, which increased muzzle velocity to 1,900 fps. Three years later the Cartucho com bala 8mm m/99 was fielded, which utilized a 56mm case with a 248-grain projectile moving at 2,265 fps. In 1904, the 6,5mm Espingarda Mod.1904 (see below) was accepted. By 1910, most European base units had been equipped with it, and the Kropatschek was relegated to the navy, colonial (native) troops, police units, and reservists. During World War I, Portuguese Askaris from Angola and Mozambique used them in action against the German forces in East Africa. When the Indian Army occupied the Portuguese enclave of Goa in 1961, some were issued to Portuguese reserve troops. Lastly, in the 1970s and 1980s some showed up during the National Liberation Wars in Portugal's African colonies.

For this article I tested a Mosqueton Modelo 1886 using handloads provided by the owner. It was manufactured by Steyr in 1889 and was in VG condition. Loading the magazine was time-consuming, but the cock-on-opening bolt made bolt manipulation easy. The trigger had a long, heavy pull, so to err on the side of caution I set my targets at a moderate 75 yards. With the lowest sight setting of 200 meters, it printed about 7 inches above point of aim, but it proved accurate enough with my best group measuring 2.8 inches.

I found the Espingarda Modelo 1886 a fitting example of the military rifle common to the late 19th century. It had the advantages of rapid firepower hindered by a slow-loading tubular magazine, and a small-bore cartridge with the added inconvenience of black powder propellant. One foot in the future, and one in the past.

UNITED STATES NAVY RIFLE, CALIBRE 6MM, MODEL OF 1895

Unlike the hidebound U.S. Army, the American Navy was an early proponent of repeating rifles. During the 1870s and 1880s, the navy adopted a series of bolt-action Remington-Lee, Remington-Keene, and Hotchkiss magazine rifles. While the U.S. Army adopted its first small-bore, smokeless powder rifle, the M1892 Krag-Jörgensen rifle, in 1894, the navy felt that the Krag's manually loaded magazine was incapable of providing the level of firepower they desired, while the .30 Army cartridge (.30-40 Krag) failed to produce the type of ballistics that Navy types insisted upon. Naval tacticians wanted a cartridge capable of penetrating the armor fitted to the new motor torpedo boats that were then coming into service and causing considerable consternation among "battleship sailors."

Trials in 1892 led to the decision that a smaller-caliber, ballistically impressive cartridge was needed and the Navy approached Winchester about designing one. The Navy found the resulting cartridge suitable and adopted it as the 6mm USN (a.k.a. 6mm Lee, .236 Navy). It used a semi-rimmed case 2.35 inches in length with a distinctively long bottleneck. Originally loaded with a long, round-nosed 112-grain projectile, it was propelled at a velocity of 2,560 fps by a smokeless powder known as Riflelite. The new bullet reduced chamber pressures and the 112-grain bullet gave an average barrel life of 10,000 rounds, as opposed to only 3,000 for the steel-jacketed load. From a tactical viewpoint, the 6mm's lighter weight, when compared to the .30 Army cartridge, enabled sailors and marines to carry more rounds of ammo for the same weight.

With the question of the cartridge settled, the Navy began casting about for a weapon to fire it from, which Winchester was happy to provide.

James Paris Lee was born in Scotland and immigrated to Canada with his family in 1831. He developed a fascination for firearms and, after moving to the United States in 1858, began experimenting in earnest. He received a patent for a bolt-action rifle with a detachable box magazine in 1877, which Remington Arms Company produced. In the early 1890s, Lee developed a straight-pull bolt-action in which the bolt was locked by a wedge-shaped lug on the bottom of the bolt body, engaging a recoil shoulder in the receiver. The bolt was opened and closed by means of a pivoting bolt handle that first cammed the bolt up, disengaging the lug, and then pulling it to the rear, ejecting the cartridge case. As the bolt was pushed forward it stripped the next round from the magazine and chambered it, cocking the firing mechanism as it cammed the bolt down against the recoil shoulder, locking it into battery. A gas escape hole on the top of the bolt allowed venting of powder gases from a ruptured case or pierced primer.

The rifle used a single-column magazine that was loaded with a special clip. As the clip was pushed into the magazine, a stud in the magazine well turned a small retaining catch on its rear face, allowing the follower to push the rounds up out of the clip so they could be picked up by the bolt. After the first few rounds had been chambered, the clip fell out of the open bottom of the magazine housing while the remaining cartridges were held in place by a catch. At the request of the Navy, Winchester made changes to the stock, fittings, and bayonet and the Lee was adopted as the United States Navy Rifle, Calibre 6mm, Model of 1895. Winchester received an order for 10,000 rifles and the first issues were made in October 1896.

The Lee proved capable of a very high rate of fire and was notably accurate. It was the smallest caliber military rifle of the era, the first clip-loaded rifle used by American troops, and the first time that the metric system was used by the U.S. armed forces.

SPECIFICATIONS: UNITED STATE S NAVY RIFLE, CALIBRE 6MM, MODEL OF 1895
Caliber: 6mm USN
Overall length: 47 in.
Barrel length: 28 in.
Weight: 8.75 lbs.
Magazine: 5 rounds, clip loaded
Sights: Front: Blade
Rear: V-notch adj. by ramp and leaf from 300 to 2,000 yards
Bayonet: Knife-style w/8.25-in. blade

With the outbreak of the Spanish-American War in 1898, the U.S. Navy ordered an additional 5,000 rifles. These second-contract rifles differed in the design of the safety lever, bolt release catch, firing pin, and sling swivels, and used a screw in the left receiver wall to better secure the extractor spring.

The Lee saw service in the Philippine Insurrection, Boxer Rebellion, and many U.S. military interventions in Latin America, the Pacific, and Asia. Its most famous moment came in China during the Boxer Rebellion (1900), where 58 U.S. Marines and sailors armed with M1895 Lee rifles helped to defend the foreign legations in Peking from Boxer terrorists. The Lee's accuracy in the hands of marine sharpshooters earned favorable comment from a number of foreign military officers on the scene.

While popular, the Lee was plagued with problems. The bolt was difficult to field strip and included small parts that were easily lost. The open magazine housing allowed the entry of dirt and debris into the action, and the use of a special clip made it impossible to top off a partially empty magazine. Its 112-grain bullet proved a poor "man stopper" unless a large bone or vital organ was hit. The bullet's effectiveness decreased significantly after 600-700 yards, while the 220-grain round-nosed bullet of the .30 Army was effective past 1,000 yards. Lastly, the hot-burning Rifleite powder and corrosive primers tended to erode the shallow Metford-style rifling, a condition that was exacerbated by the fact that the Navy never issued cleaning rods for the rifles.

Accordingly, a board made up of U.S. Army, Navy, and USMC officers recommended that the Krag-Jörgensen rifle be made standard issue for the armed forces. In 1899, the Navy began replacing their M1895s with Krags, although some ships and USMC contingents on remote stations continued to use them until 1902.

The magazine was loaded with a special 5-round charger/clip. The magazine housing had an open bottom to allow the clip to fall out.

I obtained a Second Contract M1895 Lee to test. I ran it through its paces at 100 yards by firing a series of five-shot groups with custom handloads from a rest. Loading the magazine with the clip was fast and fumble-free and recoil was extremely light.

The bolt worked smoothly, although it took a while to get the hang of its "up and back" manipulation. With the lowest sight setting of 300 yards, the rifle shot about 8 inches above point of aim, forcing me to use some Kentucky elevation to put rounds where I wanted them. I eventually produced some nice groups, all of which measured under 3 inches.

While the M1895 Lee only served as the Navy's issue rifle for five years, the 6mm USN cartridge pioneered the concept of the small-caliber military cartridge, which today is universally accepted by the world's armies.

FRENCH FUSIL DAUDETEAU MODÉLE B

Toward the end of the 19th century, the French high command realized that the Lebel, with its slow-loading tubular magazine and awkward rimmed cartridge, had been rendered obsolete by developments in other countries, which was just the opportunity a former French officer had been waiting for. Louis Daudeteau (1845–1926) served in the French Army during the Franco-Prussian War (1870–1871). He left the army and turned his inventive nature to the development of a repeating rifle and ammunition. In 1884 he presented what today is known as the Fusil Daudeteau Modéle B.

The basis of the rifle was a tubular, split-bridge receiver and a two-piece, cock-on-opening bolt with a separate bolt head containing dual locking lugs and the extractor. Its forward-mounted bolt handle, which turned down in front of the receiver bridge to provide emergency locking, had an odd forward angle to it. A hole in the front of the bolt would safely vent gas from a punctured primer out through a semi-circular cutout in the right receiver wall.

Its single-column, 5-round magazine was loaded by a unique and overly complicated charger/stripper clip that could only be introduced from one direction, thus the top was painted red to lessen the chances of confusion. The lip in the magazine functioned as an interrupter, holding down the second cartridge in the column to ensure smooth feeding of the first. As the bolt was closed, the base of the bolt handle pushed a catch on the right side of the receiver, retracting the lip and allowing the next round to move up into position to be loaded. With the bolt open, manually pushing the catch unloaded any unfired cartridges from the magazine.

The Modéle B had a straight-grip stock, thin forearm and a "pregnant guppy" bulge around the magazine housing. It featured a stacking rod on the muzzle band while a full-length, brass-tipped cleaning rod was carried in a groove on the left of the forearm. The rifle was chambered for a 6.5mm cartridge of Louis' design, the Cartouche Daudeteau No. 12. It consisted of a semi-rimmed, bottlenecked case 53.5mm in length with a 150-grain FMJ round-nosed bullet propelled to 2,400 fps.

The French Army tested Louis' rifle in 1895 and expressed guarded interest in it. Not having the means to produce his rifle, Louis sold his patents to the Compagnie des Forges et Acieries de la Marine et des Chemins de Fer a Saint-Chamond, who turned the project over to their subsidiary La Société Francais des Armes Portative a Saint-Denis. In 1896, the French Navy purchased a quantity of rifles for issue to French Marines in Indo-China for extended field trials. Because of this, Daudeteau's rifle is often referred to as the Fusil de Marine Modéle 1896 ("Navy Rifle Model 1896").

SPECIFICATIONS: FUSIL DAUDETEAU MODÉLE B
Caliber: 6,5mm Cartouche Daudeteau No. 12
Overall length: 50.65 in.
Barrel length: 32.5 in.
Weight: 8.7 lbs.
Magazine: 5 rounds, charger loaded
Sights: Front: Inverted V-blade
Rear: V-notch adj. by ramp & leaf from 200 to 2,000 meters
Bayonet: Epee w/20.5-in. cruciform blade

Saint-Denis also produced a Daudeteau mosqueton (short rifle) with a 24-inch barrel. Trial rifles were provided to Romania, Portugal, Chile, El Salvador, and Uruguay. While the French Army lost interest in the Daudeteau, Saint-Denis continued to promote it until 1902 when the stock of rifles was sold to Manufacture Francaise d'Armes et Cycles de Saint-Etienne (ManuFrance). Between 1905 and 1914, ManuFrance offered a sporting rifle known as the Rival, built on the Daudeteau action.

A fellow collector kindly lent me a Daudeteau Modéle B mosqueton in very nice condition. The left-front of receiver is marked "L.F.A.P. St. Denis," while the signature "L. Daudeteau" graces the rear. The receiver ring bears an S in a shield, serial number, and the manufacturer's symbol. Test firing was conducted at 75 yards from a rest using custom reloaded ammunition. While bolt manipulation

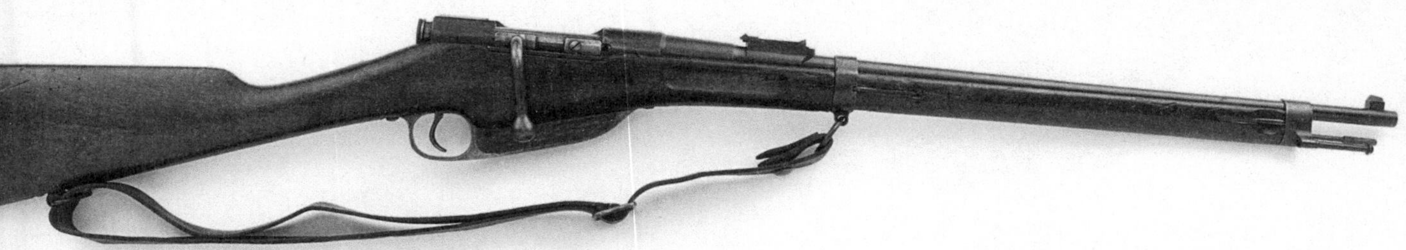

The Mosqueton Daudeteau Modéle B was a light, elegant rifle. Note the forward curved bolt handle, "pregnant guppy" stock and cleaning rod inletted into the left side of the forearm.

The Mod.1904 used a Mannlicher-style split-bridge receiver, charger-loaded Mauser-style magazine, and a simplified bolt designed by José Alberto Vergueiro.

In this view of the Modelo 1886's receiver you can see the bolt guide rib-bearing on the split bridge receiver and the magazine cutoff lever.

A Spanish-American War-era sailor armed with an M1895 Lee Rifle.

(right) The author's best group of the day shooting the M1895 produced five rounds in 2.8 inches at 100 yards.

was stiff, rounds fed smoothly and the sights provided a decent sight picture. But the rifle's heavy trigger pull caused several flyers, and my best effort had four rounds in 2.7 inches, with a flyer opening the group up to a disappointing 4.5 inches.

As did most European 6.5mm military cartridges, the 6.5mm Daudeteau No. 12 proved to be a quite accurate, low-recoiling round. Although my test firing was limited, I would have to say that the Modéle B appears to be a far more user-friendly arm than most of the bolt-action French military rifles I have fired.

REMINGTON LEE MILITARY SMALL BORE MAGAZINE RIFLE (MODEL 1899)

The French Army's adoption of the Fusil d'Infanterie Modéle 1886 created a situation similar to the U.S.-Soviet atomic weapons race of the post-WWII period, as the world's armies raced to develop rifles similar, and hopefully superior, to those of the French. The next 20 years would see engineers, ballisticians, and soldiers perfecting the smokeless small-bore cartridge and bolt-action rifle.

In 1875, the aforementioned James Paris Lee received a patent for a detachable, single-column box magazine for rifles. Four years later he patented a bolt-action rifle (using his magazine), which was produced by Remington, 1,000 of which were sold to the U.S. Navy as the Lee Magazine Navy Rifle, Model 1875. Over the next decade, the Navy purchased an additional 2,350 improved Lee Model 1879 and Remington-Lee Model 1885 rifles.

In the 1890s, Remington updated the Lee rifle to use the new small-bore smokeless powder cartridges, and in 1899 released it on the market as the Remington-Lee Military Small Bore Magazine Rifle (better known as the M1899 Remington-Lee) available in .30 Army, .303 British, 7x57, and 7.65x53 Mauser.

The basis of the new rifle was a two-piece, cock-on-closing bolt with dual lugs located on a detachable bolt head that locked directly into the receiver ring. Additional locking was provided by the bolt guide rib-bearing on the front of the receiver bridge, and a lug on the bolt body engaging a mortise in the left receiver wall. A spring-loaded ejector was located in the left receiver wall, while an interrupter in the right side of the receiver prevented double feeding of cartridges.

Its single-column, 5-round magazine located beneath the receiver had to be removed from the rifle for reloading. Remington declined to utilize a Mauser-style charger (stripper clip) loading system — instead it was intended that each rifle be issued with four spare magazines for quick reloading. When the magazine was removed, a plate pivoted out over the magazine well opening, allowing manual loading of single rounds.

SPECIFICATIONS: REMINGTON-LEE MILITARY SMALL BORE MAGAZINE RIFLE
Caliber: .30 Army
Overall length: 49.5 in.
Barrel length: 29 in.
Weight (unloaded): 8.5 lbs.
Magazine capacity: 5 rounds
Sights: Front: Inverted V-blade
Rear: V-notch and aperture adj. by ramp & leaf from 200 to 1,900 yards
Bayonet: Knife-style w/5.25-in. blade

Remington proceeded to market it in the United States and abroad with what can only be called dismal results.

The U.S. Army tested the Remington but declared the Krag superior. After testing it in 1900, the Navy issued a favorable report and purchased additional rifles for trials, but the government's insistence on the Navy adopting the Krag doomed the Remington's chances. The only significant sale inside the United States occurred in 1899. The Michigan National Guard (MNG), unable to obtain Krags from the U.S. government, placed an order with Remington for 2,000 Remington-Lee Small Bore rifles chambered for the .30 Army. Unfortunately for Remington, field service showed the rifle had several shortcomings. On December 14, 1900, the Quartermaster General of the MNG wrote the Navy Bureau of Ordnance that "... the .30 caliber Remington rifle in the hands of the Michigan National Guard has not proven satisfactory, and that requisition will not be made at present to supply the Mich. N.M. (Naval Militia) with same."

In 1904, the government of Cuba, then an American protectorate, purchased 2,600 M1899 carbines for issue to their Guardia Rurales and 400 rifles for the Artillery Corps and presidential guard. The carbines had a 20-inch barrel, short forearm, side-mounted sling swivels, and rear sights that were adjustable to 1,300 yards. The U.S. began supplying the new Cuban Army in 1912 with Krag-Jörgensen rifles and carbines, and the Guardia's remaining M1899s were returned to the Remington factory for refurbishing, after which they were put into storage.

When World War I erupted, Remington sold more than 1,100 ex-Cuban rifles and carbines to the French, who issued them as the Fusil et Carabine Lee Remington Modéle 1887 to second-line troops to release their Berthier carbines for issue to frontline units.

I obtained a factory refinished Cuban contract M1899 Remington-Lee rifle from a fellow collector to test. The cock-on-closing bolt operated with the typical Lee resistance and, while it was graced with a decent trigger, the 19th century-style sights provided a poor sight picture. I fired several five-shot groups with Winchester and Remington .30-40 Krag ammunition on my club's 100-yard range. While the rifle tended to print low, I produced some decent groups, my best being a presentable 2.5 inches. While I found the M1899 Remington-Lee to be a well-made and accurate rifle, I feel it was still inferior to many of its contemporaries. For this reason, it could not hope to compete with the Mauser rifles that were beginning to dominate the world market.

The Remington-Lee Small Bore Military Rifle (a.k.a. M1899) was Remington's attempt to make a small-bore, smokeless powder military rifle from the venerable Remington-Lee design.

PORTUGUESE ESPINGARDA PORTUGUEZA 6.5 MOD.1904

By the end of the 19th century, the Portuguese Army realized their Espingarda Modelo 1886 was obsolete. Between 1896 and 1903 they tested the Mauser Infanteriegewehr 98, Dutch M.95

The Espingarda Portugueza 6.5 Mod.1904 (a.k.a. Mauser-Verguiero) was the first "modern" military rifle adopted by Portugal.

and Romanian Md. 1893 Mannlichers, MannlicherSchönauer, and the French Daudeatau. While the Mannlicher-Schönauer came out on top, the Portuguese balked at the price tended by Steyr.

Into the midst of this indecision stepped a Portuguese Army Officer by the name of José Alberto Vergueiro, who combined an Infanteriegewehr 88-type receiver with a Mauser-style charger-loaded magazine, sights, stock, and fittings. His contribution was a greatly simplified bolt with dual frontal locking lugs, a separate bolt head containing the extractor and ejector, and a straight bolt handle that turned down in front of the receiver bridge. No bolt sleeve was provided, and the safety was fitted directly into the cocking piece and the bolt cocked halfway upon opening and halfway on closing.

As did many nations, the Portuguese wanted a rifle with "national character" and Vergueiro's rifle provided just that. After a series of trials it was adopted as the Espingarda Portugueza 6,5 Mod.1904, and 100,000 rifles were ordered from the Deutsche Waffenund Munitionsfabriken (DWM) of Berlin. The Mod.1904 featured a stock with a shallow pistol grip, spring-retained barrel, and muzzle bands. The staggered-column magazine was loaded via five-round chargers and the magazine floorplate could be released for quick and safe unloading.

SPECIFICATIONS: ESPINGARDA PORTUGUEZA 6,5 MOD.1904
Caliber: Cartucho cal. 6,5 com bala m/04
Overall length: 48.2 in.
Barrel length: 29 in.
Weight: 8.4 lbs.
Magazine: 5 round, charger loaded
Sights: Front: Inverted V-blade
Rear: V-notch adj. by tangent from 200 to 2,000 meters
Bayonet: Knife-style w/11-in. blade

The Cartucho cal. 6,5 com bala m/04 consisted of a rimless, bottlenecked case 58mm long with a 155-grain round-nosed, FMJ bullet that was propelled to 2,350 fps. The Portuguese never updated this round with a Spitzer bullet.

The Mod.1904 saw its most extensive service during World War I, with Portuguese troops in Mozambique and Angola who campaigned against German forces in East Africa while the Germans used captured Mod.1904s to arm their own Askaris. Numbers were sold to South Africans who used them to equip their commando units fighting the Germans in Southwest Africa.

In 1937, Portugal adopted a 98 Mauser short rifle, the Espingarda Modelo 937-A. To extend the service life of the Modelo 1904s, they shortened the barrels to 24 inches and re-chambered them for the 7.9x57 cartridge (Cartucho cal. 8 com bala m/37). Converted rifles were re-baptized the Espingarda Modelo 904/39. Numbers of both Modelo 1904 and 904/39s saw service with all sides during the "National Liberation" wars that ravaged Portugal's African colonies during the 1970s and 1980s.

I tested a Mod.1904 from a rest at 100 yards. The bolt worked very smoothly, the rifle had a crisp, two-stage trigger pull, and the long sighting radius provided a rather decent sight picture. Using custom ammunition I produced a series of groups, all under 3 inches.

To my way of thinking, the Espingarda Mod. 1904 typifies the military rifle of the late 19th and early 20th centuries. It was well made, fine handling, accurate and, as were many of its contemporaries, long-serving. We shall never see its like again.

FRENCH FUSIL AUTOMATIQUE MODÈLE 1917

In the late 1890s the French Army embarked upon a secret, long-term plan to equip their troops with a semi-automatic rifle firing a high-performance cartridge. According to Jean Huon's book, Proud Promise - French Autoloading Rifles 1898-1979, by 1894 several 6mm, 6.5mm and 7mm rimless cartridges had been developed.

Semi-auto rifle trials, heavily shrouded in secrecy, began in 1898 and continued until 1914, but none of the designs proved satisfactory. So, when the merde hit the fan in 1914, French soldiers were still encumbered with the Fusil d'Infanterie Modéle 1886 Lebel, supplemented with some clip-loading Berthier carbines and rifles. Trials continued despite wartime pressures, and in 1917 the French approved the issue of the Fusil Automatique Modèle 1917.

The Modèle 1917 was a gas-operated rifle chambered for the 8mm balle D cartridge and developed by Monsieurs Chauchat, Sutter, and Ribeyrolles, who also designed the Modèle 1916 CSRG "Chauchat" light machine gun.

The Modéle 1917's long, tubular upper receiver housed the bolt and had a slot for the bolt handle, which would prove to be a design fault as it allowed dirt and debris to enter the action of the rifle. The upper receiver was welded to the lower section, which contained a trigger unit and a rotating safety lever.

A gas cylinder under the barrel contained a piston and operating spring. The piston was attached to a flat operating rod, which was exposed on the right side of the receiver and was connected to the bolt handle. Upon firing, as the bullet passed a gas port near the front of the barrel, gas was bled off, pushing the piston/operating rod unit rearward, compressing the operating spring and moving the bolt to the rear.

The two-part bolt had six interrupted screw-locking lugs and a shaft at its rear with dual cams that were inserted into helical channels in the bolt carrier. As the bolt carrier moved rearward, these cams rotated the bolt head, unlocking and extracting the spent case from the chamber and ejecting it. The operating spring then pulled the bolt forward, stripping the next round out of the maga-

To load the Modèle 1917, the magazine housing was opened and a 5-round clip inserted.

zine, chambering it, rotating and locking the bolt as it went into battery.

The magazine housing contained a spring-loaded follower and was hinged to the bottom of the receiver. In operation, the rifle was held on its side and the magazine housing pulled down and forward, compressing the follower. A 5-round clip was inserted into the bottom of the receiver and the magazine housing closed, releasing the follower, which pushed rounds up to be picked up by the forward-moving bolt.

SPECIFICATIONS: FUSIL AUTOMATIQUE MODÈLE 1917
Caliber: 8mm balle D (a m)
Overall length: 52.3 in.
Barrel length: 31.5 in.
Weight: 11.45 lbs.
Magazine: 5 rounds, clip loaded
Sights: Front: Wide blade with groove
Rear: Square notch adj. by ramp and leaf from 250 to 2,400 meters
Bayonet: Epee w/16-in. cruciform blade

Production commenced in April, 1917, at several arsenals. Manufacture Nationale d'Armes Tulle (MAT) produced the receiver, barrel, and trigger guard; Manufacture National d'Armes de Châtellerault (MAC) made the trigger mechanism; Manufacture Nationale d'Armes de St-Etienne (MAS) was the source of the bolt, bolt carrier, piston, gas cylinder, stock, and barrels; and Manufacture d'Armes de Paris produced the bolt handle, magazine housing, and follower assembly. Using these components, all 85,333 Modèle 1917s produced were assembled at MAS.

The French Army intended to issue 16 rifles per company, with platoon leaders and selected marksmen receiving them. Because of the high level of maintenance and repairs that the rifles required, only those Poilus who displayed a "higher mental aptitude" received them.

Field service soon showed the Modèle 1917 was not quite up to the task. Besides its inordinate length and weight, debris entering the receiver caused continual functioning problems. The rimmed 8mm Balle D cartridge case was poorly suited for semi-automatic operation and frequently jammed while the primers often backed out of the cases, jamming the bolt; the clip proved fragile and prone to bending; lastly, the violent operation of the gas system tended to damage the stock and shake metal parts loose.

In 1918, the Mosqueton automatique Modèle 1918 was adopted. It was 10 inches shorter, a pound lighter and featured a rotating dust cover over the bolt handle slot. In addition to a catch to the bolt open when the magazine was empty, components of the bolt, gas system and magazine were strengthened, and it used the widely available Berthier clip.

Both Modéle 1917 and 1918s saw limited service after the war. According to Jean Huon, some Modèle 1918s were used by the Garde Mobile and special army assault units before the Fall of France in 1940 and by some French troops in Japanese occupied Indochina.

I was fortunate that one of my fellow collectors had a Modéle 1917 he was willing to loan me for testing. It bore MAT markings on the receiver and a cartouche on the buttstock indicating manufacture in 1918. While the exterior was a bit worse for wear, the bore was excellent and it had a very decent trigger. I test fired it from a rest with custom-loaded ammunition and was surprised from the get-go! Despite the rather

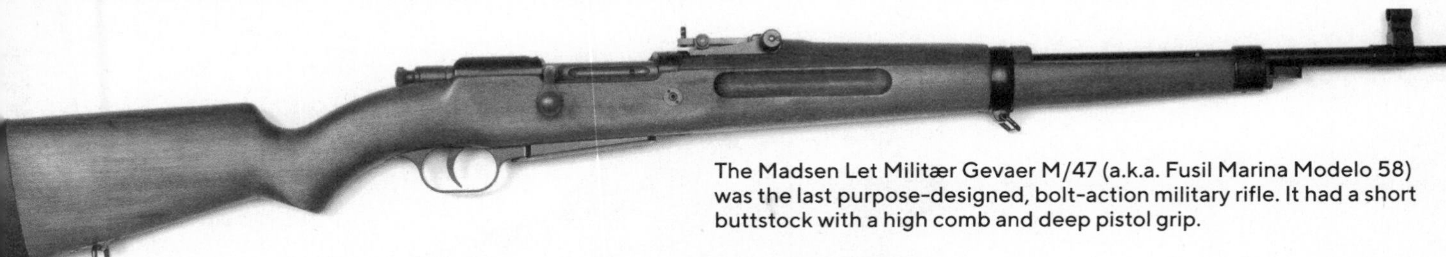

The Madsen Let Militær Gevaer M/47 (a.k.a. Fusil Marina Modelo 58) was the last purpose-designed, bolt-action military rifle. It had a short buttstock with a high comb and deep pistol grip.

crude sights, I was able to produce well-centered groups in the 3-inch range at 100 yards with regularity. Functioning was 100 percent although ejection of spent cases was somewhat violent.

While the Modèle 1917 was crude, the pressures to provide sufficient weaponry were enormous and the fact that this rifle was developed at all speaks volumes for the determination of the French Army and industry to provide its troops with the tools they needed.

DANISH LET MILITAER GEVAER M/47

In 1898, Vilhelm Madsen and Julius Rasmussen organized the Dansk Rekylriffel Syndikat A.S. to manufacture and market the world's first successful light machine gun — the Let Maskingevær Madsen (Madsen Light Machine Rifle), which was produced from 1902 until the 1960s. In the post-World War II years, with large numbers of surplus weapons available, sales of their light machine guns began to fall off and the company, renamed Dansk Industri Syndikat A.S. (a.k.a. Madsen), search for a new product to expand sales.

Madsen had always attempted to tailor their products toward the smaller armies of the world. Realizing that some of these armies could not afford the new breed of semi-auto rifles then coming on the market, they decided to develop a bolt-action rifle that was inexpensive to produce, simple to maintain, and with ergonomics suited to soldiers of small stature. The resulting weapon, the Let Militær Gevaer M/47 (Light Military Rifle Model 47), met these goals.

The M/47 used a tubular receiver and a one-piece bolt with dual locking lugs at the rear of the bolt body. The bolt handle turned down in front of a split-receiver bridge, while a half-length bolt rib prevented wobble and binding during manipulation. Its 5-round, charger-loaded magazine could be removed for cleaning or for installing an optional 10-round magazine.

The muzzle of the barrel had 36 ports to help reduce recoil. Its short stock had a high comb, deep pistol grip, and thick rubber recoil pad, intended to make the M/47 suitable for use by the small-stature soldiers common to many Third World armies. Madsen offered it chambered in 6.5x55, 7x57, 7.65x53, .30 M2 Ball, 7.9x57, and, in late production rifles, 7.62mm NATO.

The rear sight, a large aperture mounted on a tangent in front of the receiver, was adjustable from 100 to 900 meters and for windage by means of a knurled knob.

SPECIFICATIONS: MADSEN LET MILITAER GEVAER M/47
Caliber: .30 M2 Ball
Overall length: 43.3 in.
Barrel length: 23.4 in.
Weight: 8.5 lbs.
Magazine: 5- or 10-round charger loaded box
Sights: Front: Hooded post
Rear: Aperture adj. by tangent from 100 to 900 meters
Bayonet: Knife-style w/8.3-in. blade

The M/47's bolt handle turned down in front of the split-bridge receiver to provide extra locking.

Thirty-six ports on the M/47's muzzle vented gas outward to hold down muzzle flip.

While the M/47 was tested by several armies, the only sale was 5,000 rifles bought by Columbia in the mid 1950s. Chambered in .30 M2 Ball, they were issued to the Columbian Navy as the Fusil Marina Modelo 58. All Columbian Modelo 58s I have examined have been in excellent condition, which leads me to believe they were never issued or only used for ceremonial purposes. According to reports, only about 6,000 M/47 rifles were produced, the majority being for the Columbian order.

I fortunately obtained a Columbian Modelo 58 rifle to photograph and test. It was in excellent condition with a pristine bore, and all metal parts (with the exception of the bolt) were finished with a baked-on black enamel paint. Marking included "Madsen MG/A....2137-58 ... Cal. 30" on the left side of the receiver while the chamber area bore the legend "FUERZAS ARMADAS DE COLUMBIA" (Columbian Navy).

Accuracy testing consisted of firing a series of five-shot groups from a rest at 100 yards using surplus .30 M2 Ball. My 60-something-year-old eyes found the sights easy to use, allowing me to produce a series of nicely centered groups of about 3 inches. When firing the rifle offhand, I found that the ported barrel and thick recoil pad did indeed lessen felt recoil to a marked degree.

CONCLUSION

I want to assure my readers that I plan to continue to test and write about military surplus rifles for many years to come. And I have no doubt that I will continue to find more "strange" ones in the process. Indeed, when it comes to military firearm history, truth really is stranger than fiction!

The M1899's rear sight was adjustable from 200 to 1,900 yards.

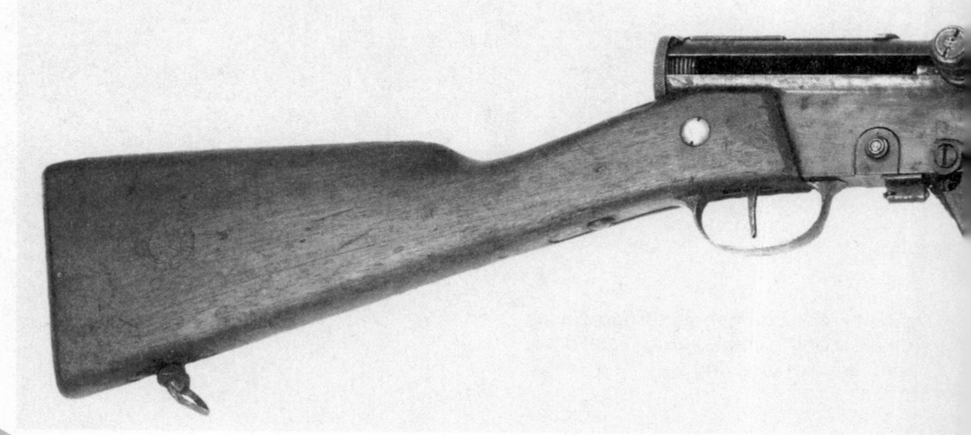

Test firing from a rest at 100 yards showed the M/47 to be a soft-recoiling, easy handling, and accurate rifle.

The Mosqueton automatique Modèle 1918 proved superior to the Modèle 1917 but was still plagued with reliability problems.

One of the Last and Greatest of the "Great White Hunters"

BY **JOE COOGAN**

HARRY SELBY
AN AFRICAN LEGEND

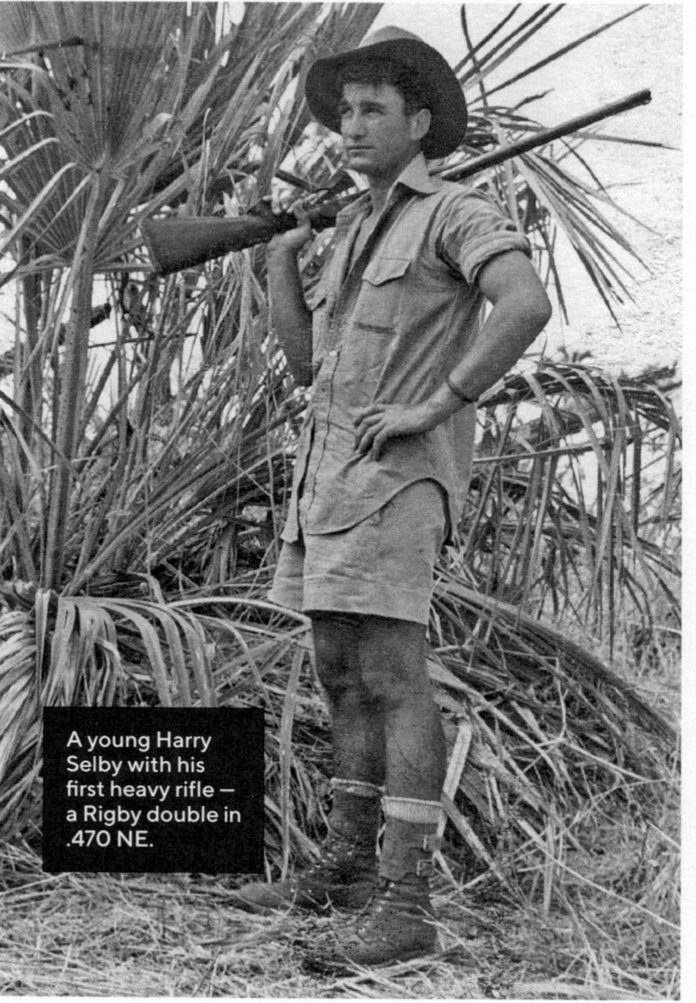
A young Harry Selby with his first heavy rifle – a Rigby double in .470 NE.

"Clients tend to see their white hunter as a father. They boast of him, when he is out of earshot, and, when he has returned, tell things around the campfire they might not tell their own father. He looms in their imagination. They are proud of him, and should he happen to visit them at their home in the northern hemisphere they will make sure that as many of their friends as possible meet him and see for themselves his invincibility." — John Hemingway, No Man's Land, 1983

Harry Selby might have been who Hemingway had in mind when he wrote the above quote. For most of his life, Selby walked among Africa's biggest game, slept in bush camps and was continually expanding his knowledge of the continent, people and animals he loved. He was a master at running an efficient and comfortable safari camp and his reputation was well established by the age of 25, with a steady stream of safari clientele booking five years in advance in order to hunt with him. Some of his clients included Prince Bernhard of the Netherlands, oil-family scion John Mecom Jr., baseball executive Walter O'Malley, opera singer Lauritz Melchior, the maharajah of Jaipur, Prince Stanislaw Radziwill of Poland and Miguel Alemán Valdés, a former president of Mexico.

Harry Selby was born in South Africa on July 22, 1925, the youngest of six children born to Arthur and Evelyn Selby. Shortly after World War I, many settler farmers and ranchers left South Africa seeking affordable land on which to raise cattle. The British government was offering land in Kenya to all British subjects who had served with the British forces during WWI. In 1928, Harry's father, encouraged by reports from relatives who'd already made the trip to East Africa, packed up his family and all their worldly belongings and moved to Kenya. The Selby family eventually acquired ranchland in the shadow of Mt. Kenya, where they built their homestead overlooking game-filled plains.

The farm was mostly wilderness, consisting of miles of grass-covered plains strewn with flat-topped acacia trees and punctuated by whistling thorn bush. Only the occasional rise

Harry Selby (right) and Warren Winkler with a big-maned Botswana lion taken in 1985. This is the lion that mauled Soren Lindstrom a month earlier when his client wounded it with a non-fatal gunshot.

of a brushy hill or deep-cut streambed interrupted the vast landscape. Harry's earliest memories of mealtime conversations were of his father and uncles discussing the troublesome herds of game, particularly buffalo and zebra, that competed with their cattle for grazing.

Growing up among such a rich diversity of wildlife fueled Selby's interest in nature, and in the constant presence of game he learned to stalk and shoot at an early age. During the war years, he spent much of his extra time hunting with native trackers to supply meat for the wartime effort. Following the end of the war in 1945, he embarked on an adventure that would change the direction of his life — an adventure that happened almost by accident.

SAFARI BEGINNINGS

During the Ethiopian campaign, Selby's brother-in-law, Peter Pedersen, a British Army officer, became friendly with J.F. Manley, a fellow officer in his regiment. Manley had managed a safari outfitting company before the war called African Guides, which included a roster of Kenya's top-rated white hunters including Philip Percival, Alan Black, Pat Ayre, Tom Murray-Smith and Bror Blixon. On Harry's behalf, Pederson asked Manley if he could use another hand on safari. In October 1945, Philip Percival was preparing for his first safari following the end of the war. Percival, considered the dean of East African white hunters, had been Ernest Hemingway's professional hunter (PH) during the Green Hills of Africa safari in 1932/33. It was widely known that Percival hated vehicles and needed someone with mechanical knowledge to maintain his safari car and equipment while on safari.

Based on Pedersen's recommendation, Manley signed on 20-year-old Harry Selby as Percival's field mechanic for that safari. Percival quickly recognized that Selby's talents extended well beyond his mechanical abilities, and not only arranged for the issue of a PH license, but also sponsored him for membership in the prestigious East African Professional Hunters Association. Harry's personable nature, considerable big game experience and skilled gun handling made his imminent transition to PH a smooth one.

Selby quickly earned second-hunter status under Percival and was constantly captivated by the senior hunter's campfire tales about Hemingway, George Eastman, Martin and Osa Johnson, and Carl Ackley. It seemed that Selby was always on the move and one of Percival's gunbearers christened him with the Swahili nickname "Haraka," meaning "man in a hurry," a name that would stick with him. Selby conducted many successful safaris through the late 1940s and his destiny to become one of Africa's best known and most-respected professional hunters was sealed by the age of 22.

The author (right) with a fine Botswana leopard that he collected with Harry Selby in the Okavango in 1997. The rifle Coogan used was a Lon Paul-enhanced BRNO ZKK600 in .243 caliber.

Good with his hands, Selby was not only a capable mechanic, but also took pride in his gunsmithing abilities. Considered something of a "gun nut," a label he embraced, he was interested and knowledgeable in every aspect of firearms, ammunition and ballistics — all crucial elements to his trade. In many cases, it was his gun handling expertise that kept his clients, trackers and him

Young Harry Selby glasses the surrounding countryside for elephants from a hill in Kenya's Northern Frontier District (NFD) in 1949. The NFD was Selby's favorite hunting grounds for trophy ivory. He guided many clients in that country, including Robert Ruark, who did his last Kenya safari there in 1962.

safe and injury free while pursuing dangerous game, often at close quarters in thick bush.

When Selby began his hunting career he, like many of his contemporaries, carried a double rifle. His was a particularly fine rifle by Rigby in .470 NE caliber. Owing to an unfortunate accident when a vehicle ran over the barrels of his Rigby and damaged them beyond repair, he needed to find another heavy rifle on short notice to use on his next safari. There were no doubles for sale in Nairobi at the time, but he was able to locate a Rigby bolt-action rifle in .416 Rigby caliber. It was a unique Rigby in that it was built on a standard commercial Mauser action — not a magnum action. With no other options, he bought the .416 Rigby for 100 pounds from the Nairobi gun dealer, May & Co.

Having grown up shooting bolt guns, Selby was familiar with the fit and feel of the Rigby bolt-action rifle. A finely balanced rifle, the Rigby felt comfortable in his hands and shooting it was not at all unpleasant. Although he was left-handed, early on he had adapted to shooting right-handed bolt guns. He was delighted to find the rifle inherently accurate from the first shot and quickly discovered that the .416 Rigby, pushing a 400-grain bullet, was effective out to 300 yards or more when finishing a wounded animal. For close work in thick bush on dangerous game, Selby found the .416 Rigby to be even more effective. The penetration of a solid .416 bullet through thick skin and heavy bones was impressive, indeed. Furthermore, he really appreciated the magazine capacity, which gave him four cartridges ready and waiting when needed.

After using the .416 Rigby for two safaris, Selby never looked back on his rifle preference — he had no intention of returning to a double gun. Even his Wakamba gunbearers developed a great affinity for his .416 Rigby, which they dubbed the "Skitini," having trouble saying "416." So began a lifelong love affair between Harry Selby, the .416 caliber and the Rigby rifle.

THE RUARK YEARS

In 1952, Selby took a newspaper columnist and his wife on a six-week hunting safari in Tanganyika (currently called Tanzania). That man was Robert Ruark, who, along with his wife, Virginia, so enjoyed his safari with Selby that it resulted in his writing a book, Horn of the Hunter — one of the most hailed and widely read books ever written about the safari experience.

Describing his thoughts in the book, Ruark wrote, "The hunter's horn sounds early for some, I thought, later for others. For some unfortunates prisoned by city sidewalks and sentenced to the cement jungle more horrifying than anything to be found in Tanganyika, the horn of the hunter never winds at all. But deep in the guts of most men is buried the involuntary response of the hunter's horn, a prickle of the nape hairs, an acceleration of the pulse, an atavistic memory of his fathers, who killed first with stone, and then with club, and then with spear, and then with bow, and then with gun, and finally with formulae. How meek the man is of no importance; somewhere in the pigeon chest of the clerk is still the vestigial remnant of the hunter's heart; somewhere in his nostrils the half-forgotten smell of blood."

Harry quickly gained Ruark's respect, who described him thusly, "Selby is an extraordinarily handsome young man, with the kind of curly black hair and dark eyes that bring out the mother in women. He also has wrists as thick as an ordinary man's ankles, and a hard mouth that turns down at the corners. In town, he looks like what the fagot writers call a 'pretty boy.' Taking him into the bush, among the blacks and the beasts, and he is called 'm'zee' by natives. M'zee means old man. It means respected, ancient sir.

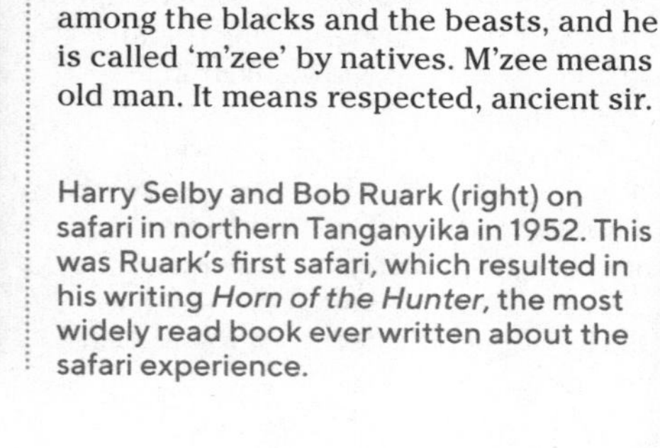

Harry Selby and Bob Ruark (right) on safari in northern Tanganyika in 1952. This was Ruark's first safari, which resulted in his writing *Horn of the Hunter*, the most widely read book ever written about the safari experience.

Harry Selby takes a break from tracking lion while on safari in the Okavango in 1984. Photo: Cliff Woerner

It means wisdom and courage and experience. At that particular moment I decided that I had met few people with so much to admire and so little to worry about."

Ruark wrote an article about Selby for the Reader's Digest series "My Most Unforgettable Character." Ruark described him in this way: "Harry Selby, a professional hunter of Kenya, British East Africa, is the most man I ever met. It is a rare thing to find a man who can combine gentleness with toughness, bravery with timidity, recklessness with caution, sophistication with naiveté, kindness with harshness, mechanics with poetry, adult judgment with juvenile foolishness. And, all the while, making every woman he meets want to mother him or marry him, and every man he meets respect him. I forgot honest. He invented it.

"I have seen Selby slap a lion in the face with his hat. I have seen him hide from a woman. I have seen him equally at home with Bernard Baruch and with a witch doctor in Tanganyika. His business is killing, yet he is gentler with animals than anybody I ever saw."

Ruark's profile generated a massive amount of fan mail for the normally shy PH.

Ruark returned to Africa many times during the 1950s and early 1960s, not only for hunting, but also on writing assignments covering the "winds of change" sweeping across Africa. Selby accompanied Ruark on trips to Somalia, Rhodesia, South Africa and even Ethiopia, where they once had an audience with the Emperor Haille Salassie. On two occasions, Selby guided Ruark to elephants in the hundred-pound (weight per tusk) class, one of which was filmed for a movie released in theaters in the late 1950s. Ruark's African Adventure can still occasionally be seen today on cable TV's Turner Movie Classics (TMC).

During the early 1950s, serious political unrest developed in Kenya, which heralded the beginning of the Mau Mau insurrection. The British colonial government dispatched a detail of hunters and game wardens to investigate the situation. During this assignment, the group camped at various locations throughout the dark rainforests of Mount Kenya and among the Aberdare mountains. In fact, Selby came straight from one of those surveillance camps in the Abadares to start Ruark's second safari — a hunt slated to take place in Kenya's Northern Frontier District (NFD).

Selby actually took Ruark back to the camp he had recently left so that Ruark could see for himself what was happening in the mountain forests. Little did Selby know the impact this experience would have on Ruark. The trip to the Aberdares, as well as extensive interviews with Selby and others involved in the Mau Mau Uprising, provided Ruark with the material he used in developing the characters and plot of the novel Something of Value. The book was adapted into a successful film starring Rock Hudson and Sidney Poitier. Seven years later, Ruark published Uhuru, not meant as a sequel to Something of Value, but along a continuing and similar theme. The follow-up novel portrays Kenya after its independence, and it is said that

Back in the 1970s, if there was unused quota available, Selby allowed the KDS PHs to take out a buffalo and elephant license for their own private hunts at the end of the season. In 1975, author Joe Coogan and Harry Selby with a buff that Harry himself collected in the Okavango Delta.

characters based on Selby's character and experience continued to appear in Ruark's fiction.

Ruark's books, *Horn of the Hunter*, *Something of Value* and *Uhuru*, as well as his magazine articles and syndicated newspaper column, brought East Africa into focus for a large number of international readers, especially in the United States. Many safaris certainly resulted from the attention and publicity that Ruark lavished upon Africa.

It was during this time in the mid-1950s that Harry Selby, Andrew Holmberg and a few other Ker & Downey hunters split from Ker & Downey Safaris and began a new safari company called Selby & Holmberg Safaris. The company was successful, operating safaris throughout East Africa through the 1950s and into the beginning of the 1960s.

BOTSWANA YEARS

In 1961, Selby returned to Ker & Downey Safaris and was appointed a director of the company, which was renamed Ker, Downey & Selby (KDS) Safaris. Around the same time, he began hearing about a British protectorate located in southern Africa called Bechuanaland, which was to later become Botswana. There it was reported that abundant game existed, and with East Africa's future uncertain and hunting pressures increasing, he decided to explore the possibilities in Bechuanaland.

Furthermore, Selby's wife Miki hailed from South Africa and the move would mean being that much closer to her family. KDS agreed to Selby's reconnaissance plans, accepting that it was complete speculation as to whether Bechuanaland would be viable for a commercial safari operation. In 1963, taking the risk together with his family, he moved south.

The move presented great challenges for the family as well as a unique opportunity for Harry Selby. He found Bechuanaland to be an incredible unspoiled country that time had seemingly forgotten. He was all the more incredulous that such a country could still exist into the latter part of the 20th century. The country was sparsely populated with little infrastructure — there were few if any roads or tracks, and no communications existed other than a meager telegram and erratic postal system.

"But the fact that the country was crawling with a variety of game species made all the inconveniences seem minor," Selby recalled. "It was like suddenly arriving on a new planet. Delightful as the unspoiled nature of the country was, it presented great challenges to the satisfactory operation of a modern safari company. Safari clients expected 20th-century efficiency, similar to that which had become routine in East Africa."

In spite of the challenging circumstance, Selby was able to adapt to difficult logistics and still provide the services and excellent big game hunting that safari clients had come to expect. Largely through his trailblazing efforts in the Okavango Delta and Kalahari Desert, it wasn't long before Botswana became an established and popular safari destination. Its reputation for producing huge lions, as well as outstanding buffalo, kudu, sable, lechwe, sitatunga and giant oryx, certainly put Botswana on the safari-hunting map. By the late 1970s, Kenya, in an ill-conceived effort to stop the escalating poaching of elephants and rhinos, had banned all safari hunting. This was a major policy shift, confirming that Harry's instincts — which had taken him to Botswana more than 10 years earlier — were correct.

I had the good fortune to meet Harry Selby back in December 1972, when I was introduced to him by Bill Ryan, one of the senior PHs for KDS Safaris, Kenya. Selby was at the KDS Safari headquarters in Nairobi to finalize some business at the end of the Botswana hunting season. My meeting with him was short and to the point, but eventful — he offered me a job, resulting in my relocating to Botswana and beginning my professional hunter's apprenticeship under his guidance. At the time, the future of hunting in Kenya was looking very bleak, so I was extremely pleased to have the chance to move to Botswana and work for such a prestigious safari company.

In 2007, Selby and the author meet up in a safari camp in Botswana, where they reminisced about the many days they shared on safari over the years.

In 1978, KDS Safaris (Botswana) amalgamated with Safari South (PTY) Ltd., making it the largest-operating safari company in Africa, with concession areas totaling more than 90,000 square miles. Selby remained with the new company as one of the directors, and the PH roster listed some of Africa's best-known professional hunters, including Lionel Palmer, Tony Henley, John Kingsley-Heath, Soren Lindstrom, Wally Johnson, Walter Johnson, Dougie Wright, Simon Paul, Mark Selby, Steve Liversedge, Willie Englebrecht, Daryl Dandridge, Chris Collins, Mark Kyriacou, Tom Friedkin, Hugh McNiel, Don Lindsay and Charles Williams. I was proud to be listed among that fine group of professionals.

During the next 20 years, I shared many campfires with Harry and listened carefully whenever he reflected on his incredible career. I once asked him which of the Big Five he liked hunting most — it seemed to me after hearing his stories about big ivory that it might be elephant. I remember the light of the campfire dancing in his eyes as he smiled, savoring the memories of past hunts.

"Hunting elephants for big ivory will always hold that special attraction like it did when I first hunted the NFD. But at a young age I rapidly found that I was excited by all kinds of hunting. And even today, I think one of the most exciting hunts, and most challenging, is leopard. Although you bait them, it's always a case of matching wits — yours against his. You do something and the leopard will respond to it and then you have to counter that with something else. It's as if he is trying to outsmart you.

"And I think that if I had to choose something for real fun, it's to creep up into a herd of buffalo and have them all around you — your senses are completely alive. That's probably one of the greatest feelings that big game provides. Now if you want real chilling stuff, it's tracking lion in thick bush — nothing can compare," he said.

Selby declared this with conviction, backed by his vast experience. His answer was thoughtful and clear with no words wasted. It bespoke a respect, even compassion, for the animals that he spent his life hunting. The scope of a safari-hunting career in Africa has always been limited because of the constant changes taking place on the continent. Harry proved particularly adept at adapting to the changes affecting the safari industry, most particularly in the early 1960s when he traded the well-worn paths of East Africa for the trackless bush of Bechuanaland Protectorate. He, along with other hunters, provided the guidance and direction that enabled Botswana to establish many of the rules and regulations that governed responsible safari hunting and ensured the foundation for future conservation policies through the ethical behavior of hunters.

Throughout his hunting career, Selby always abhorred cruelty to the African animals he respected so highly. Ruark quoted Selby in Horn of the Hunter, "I can understand killing something you want so badly that you are willing to go to weeks of trouble and great expense to collect it, so that you will have it and enjoy it and remember it all your life. But this wanton stuff gravels the devil out of me. I hate conscious cruelty."

Selby retired from safari hunting in 2000 after completing 55 seasons, but he continued to enjoy returning to the bush with close friends and family on private safaris. His long-running tenure as a career African PH unequivocally established him as one of Africa's most respected. In 2009, Harry Selby was awarded the Presidential Certificate of Honor in recognition of his long and faithful service to Botswana.

For those safari clients who were lucky enough to hunt with him, there were two guns that became synonymous with a "Selby Safari." They were his .416 Rigby, which he carried almost as an extension of his left arm, and a .22 Colt Woodsman that he carried for finishing off game. When his clients watched how Selby could handle and shoot his .416 Rigby, the big rifle became a comforting presence whenever they stalked dangerous game with him. As for the Woodsman, often during lunchtime breaks in the bush he would include a bit of target practice with the little .22, which his clients thoroughly enjoyed doing.

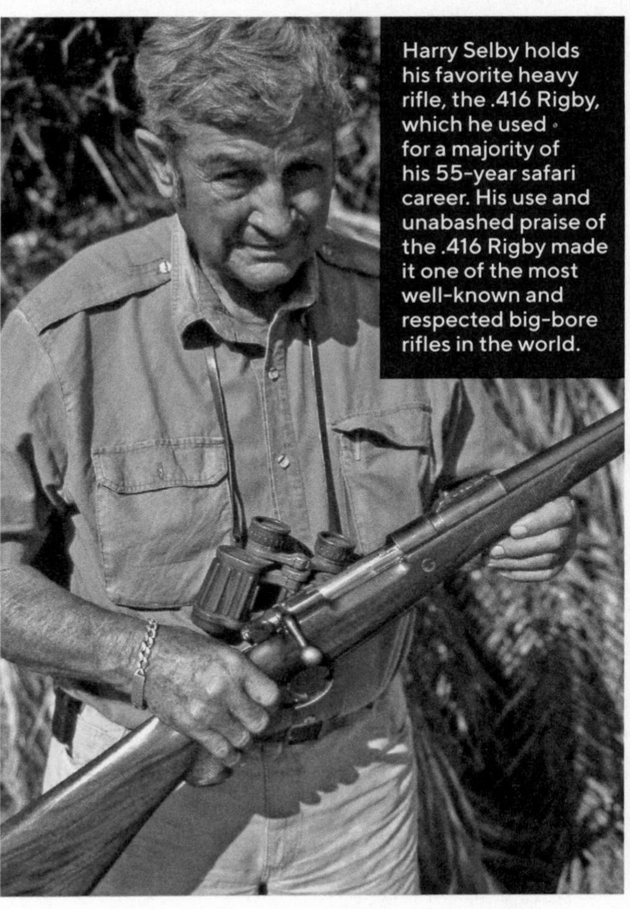

Harry Selby holds his favorite heavy rifle, the .416 Rigby, which he used for a majority of his 55-year safari career. His use and unabashed praise of the .416 Rigby made it one of the most well-known and respected big-bore rifles in the world.

In 2016, knowing how much I admired his Colt .22, and as a token of our long-standing friendship, Harry presented me with his Colt Woodsman. I was honored beyond words when he handed me the pistol, a truly special gun with a rich history of many years on safari in his hands.

My last visit with him was in August 2017, at his home in Maun. We sat on his back veranda with Miki and his daughter, Gail, and enjoyed a beer together watching the lazy flow of the Thamalakane River. The late afternoon African light turned the river golden as we reminisced about the memorable days we'd shared on safari. There is no doubt that Harry Selby experienced the best of what Africa offers. He lived his life at the absolute best of times and shared his love of Africa, its people and the wildlife with many wonderful people. He was truly a blessed man.

On January 20, 2018, John Henry (Harry) Selby, 92, died peacefully at his home in Maun. He is survived by Miki, his wife of 65 years, and his daughter, Gail, who both live in Maun, and three grandchildren, Reginah, Serena and Michael. His son, Mark, passed away in 2017.

IN SELBY'S OWN WORDS:

"I've read several versions by various writers describing how Bob Ruark came to hunt with me on his first safari. Most versions are incorrect, and the truth of the matter is rather anticlimactic. Here's how Bob came to hunt with me. Frank Bowman, an Australian who had lived in East Africa for many years and who hunted for Ker & Downey Safaris, decided to return to Australia. He had recently taken a client on safari, who was the kind of fellow who, when telling about his safari back home, minimized the role of the PH and gave the impression that he'd made all the decisions along with his gunbearer, Kidogo. Bob met this chap and asked for advice as to how to arrange a safari. He told Bob, amongst other things, to request the hunter with whom Kidogo, the gunbearer, was then employed. That happened to be me. Bob did this and that is how I happened to take him on safari the first time. So, in fact, Ruark came to hunt with Kidogo, which shows what nonsense is sometimes put out by those who pretend to have done it all by themselves."

– Harry Selby, Maun, Botswana

THIS SAPHIRE'S A GEM IN RIFLE TECHNOLOGY

Could the Sabatti Saphire Change What We Know About Bolt Guns? BY JON R. SUNDRA

As tested, the Sabatti Saphire .30-06 with a Bushnell Tactical Elite 4.5-18x50 scope in Warne QD lever rings weighed 9 3/4 lbs.

There's a new bolt-action rifle in town and it comes from, of all places, Italy. I say "of all places" because, let's face it, Italy is not the first country that comes to mind when the subject of bolt-action rifles — or any rifle, for that matter — comes up. Shotguns, yes, fantastic shotguns of all types — over/unders, side-by-sides, and semi-autos — but for some reason Italy is just not generally associated with rifle manufacturing.

That new rifle I mentioned is from Sabatti, and it's called the Saphire. Not a newcomer to the industry, the Sabatti family can trace its gunmaking roots back 344 years to 1674 when Ludovico Sabatti began making pistols in Gardone, the town that became the historical center of Italian firearms manufacturing.

The Saphire is not Sabatti's first centerfire rifle. For 21 years they've been producing a line of bolt actions called the Rover, based on a rather conventional twin-lug Mauser-type action. The family claims that, when the Rover was introduced in 1987, it was the first bolt-action centerfire rifle totally designed and manufactured in Italy (which bears out what we said about Italy not known for being a hotbed of rifle production).

The Rover line has grown into a surprisingly comprehensive one, comprised of wood- and synthetic-stocked hunting-type sporters in right- and left-handed versions, along with tactical, chassis, varmint, competition, scout and Battue models chambered in 19 calibers ranging from the .222 Rem. to .458 Win. Magnum. But again, it's a rather conventional rifle, much like a Remington 700 or Savage 100-series.

The new Saphire on the other hand, has several noteworthy as well as unique features, not the least of which is its Multi-Radial Rifling (MRR). But we'll get to that later. The Saphire belongs to the

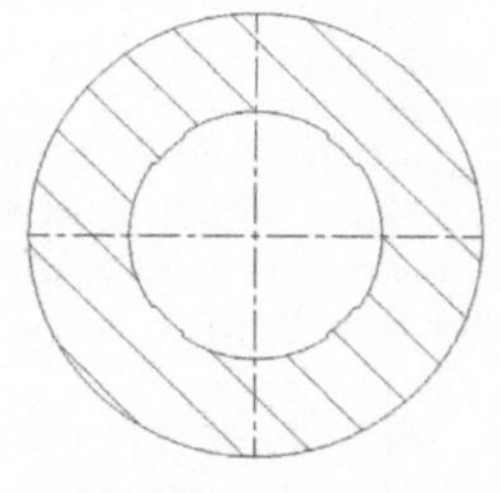

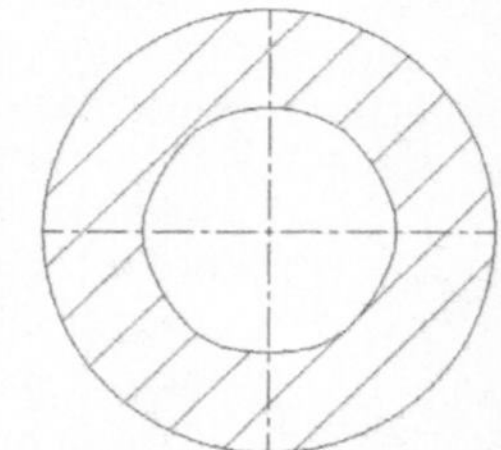

The line drawing in the catalog illustrating Multi-Radial Rifling is wildly exaggerated. To the naked eye (fig.3), it's obvious there are pronounced lands and grooves, but with a decided absence of sharp edges and corners.

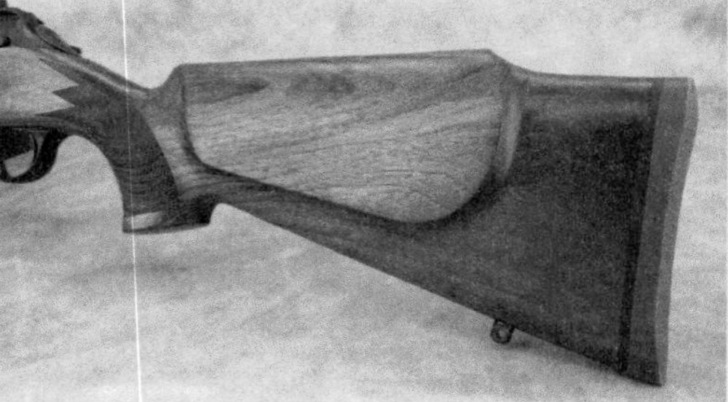

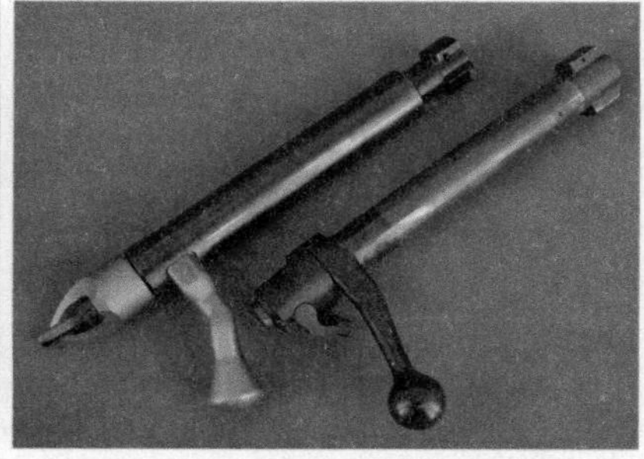

(left) The detachable magazine fits flush with the belly of the stock and looks very much like a hinged floorplate. (middle) The Turkish walnut stock is nicely done and styled to American taste. However, the Monte Carlo style is not as popular as it once was. (right) The difference between a fat bolt and conventional twin-lug action is clearly evident here.

growing fat-bolt, tri-lug family of bolt actions. I say "growing" because most bolt-action centerfire rifles introduced over the past few years belong to this genre. Domestically, we're talking guns like the Ruger American, Winchester XPR, Browning A-Bolt, Weatherby Mark V and Thompson-Center Venture and Dimension. And from overseas there's the Merkel 16, Sauer 100 and 202, Mauser M18, Lithgow 102, Roessler 3 and 6, Franchi Momentum and Steyr SM12. It should be noted that not all tri-lug actions are of the fat-bolt family — the Sako 85 and Browning X-Bolt being two exceptions.

So, that's 15 rifles all sharing the same two distinguishing design features: 1) All have bolt bodies that are about .150-inch larger in diameter than your typical Mauser-type bolt, allowing the locking lugs up front to be formed by machining metal from the bolt head. Having no lugs protruding beyond the body diameter, only a round hole is needed for the bolt's raceway in the receiver. 2) Instead of having two large, 180-degree opposed locking lugs, there are three (or multiples thereof) smaller lugs oriented on 120-degree centers requiring only a 60-degree handle lift to cycle the action. But there can also be two rows of three lugs as on the smaller Weatherby Mark V and Austrian Roessler 6, or three rows of three for a total of nine like on the Weatherby Mark V Magnum. The number of locking lugs doesn't change anything; all share the same basics.

Inherent with the design is that it can be produced more economically than

The three-lug Saphire bolt head is typical of most fat-bolt designs. There could be two rows of three lugs, or three rows of three, but that wouldn't change the fact they are of the same basic design.

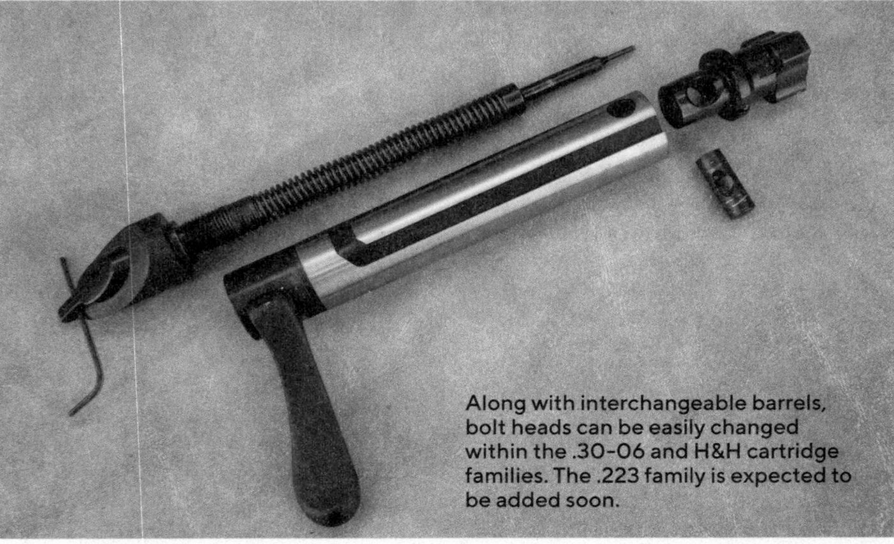

Along with interchangeable barrels, bolt heads can be easily changed within the .30-06 and H&H cartridge families. The .223 family is expected to be added soon.

Mauser-type actions, assuming that's the intent. If indeed economy is the goal — and with most of the aforementioned guns it is — receivers can be machined from bar or tube stock, which requires less machine time than is required for a casting or forging. If mated to an injection-molded stock, complete rifles can be marketed at surprisingly affordable prices. Ruger's American and Winchester's XRP are perfect examples, in that both carry almost budget-level price tags compared to their flagship siblings, the Hawkeye and Model 70, respectively. And it applies even more so with rifles coming out of Europe, because we're accustomed to seeing starting prices of $3,000 or more from the likes of Mauser, Steyr, Sauer and Merkel, yet recent entries from those companies into the fat-bolt tri-lug market all carry MSRPs under $800. Truly remarkable.

However, Sabatti chose not to compete in that highly competitive budget market with the Saphire. The price tag for the .30-06 sent to me for testing, with its deluxe grade walnut stock, is $1,695; the synthetic-stocked version goes for $1,395, and the synthetic thumbhole $1,495. Let's now see if those prices, which are essentially double those of competitors' guns, are justified.

The receiver is not just a simple tube, but rather it's machined from a solid billet of 7075-T6 aluminum, featuring a flat bedding surface, an integral 6-slot Weaver-type scope mount base, an integral recoil lug, and a split receiver ring that allows for barrel/caliber switching. It follows, then, that bolts (in this case, bolt heads) and magazines can also be swapped, meaning that calibers can be switched among cartridge families. With test guns being in such demand, however, I was sent only the Saphire — no accessory barrel, bolt head or magazine in another caliber was furnished.

At this point, you may be wondering how Sabatti is able to get away with using an aluminum receiver when no one else does. No one, that is, employing a bolt that locks up with abutments in the receiver ring, because aluminum isn't strong enough to handle the bolt thrust generating by 65,000 psi chamber pressure. They do it by having the bolt lock up with the barrel itself, thus reducing the receiver to a non-stressed component.

A split receiver is essentially a C-clamp that tightens around the smooth barrel shank by three transverse machine bolts. Loosen the bolts and the

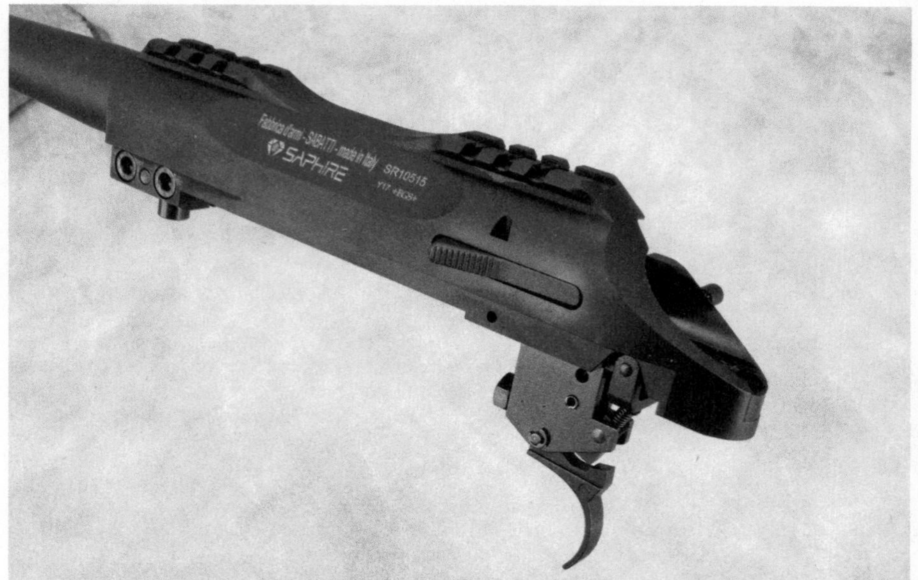

(top) The Sabatti Saphire's receiver is beautifully machined from a solid billet of 7075 T6 aluminum.

(above) The receiver ring is split at the bottom to act as a C-clamp. Loosening the three transverse machine bolts allows the barrel to be removed. A complete caliber switch of barrel, bolt head and magazine takes about five minutes.

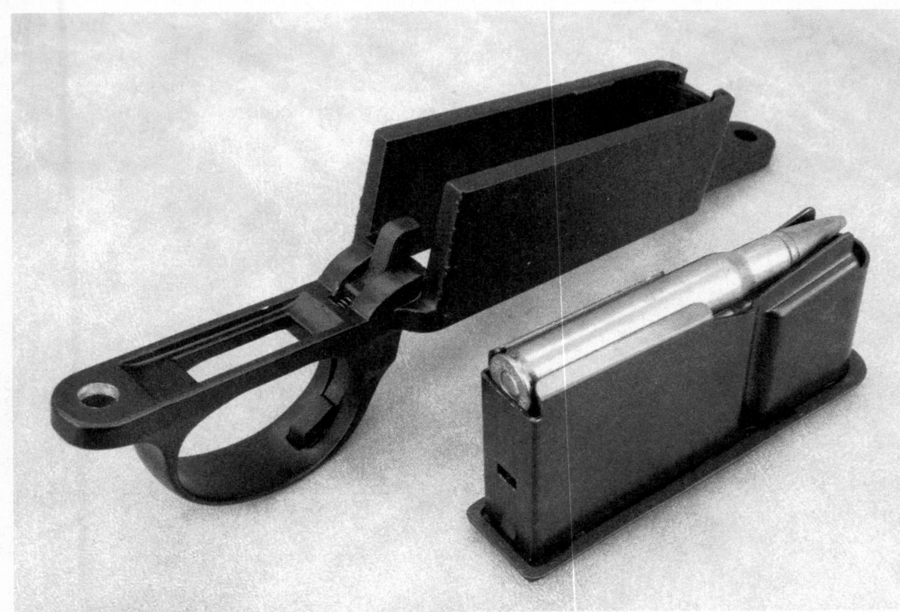

(above) The trigger guard and magazine well are one integrated unit, just like on the '98 Mauser. The detachable magazine is single-stack, central feed.

(below) The inletting was exceptional on the Saphire, so tight that a good tug was required to remove the barreled action. It was like it was glass bedded.

barrel can be slid free of the receiver. The bolt itself is exactly like that of the Savage 100-series in that the bolt head, complete with locking lugs, extractor and plunger ejector, is a separate component that's held captive by a transverse pin. By removing the striker assembly, this pin is simply pushed out and the bolt head detaches. There is a hole through the center of the pin that allows passage of the firing pin. The barrel, bolt head and magazine can be swapped in less than five minutes, so you can switch from, say, a .243 Win. to a .300 Win. Magnum.

The bolt glide on the test gun was exceptionally smooth, but then that's characteristic of fat-bolts because the design allows the tolerances between bolt and receiver to be extremely tight. It results in virtually no wobble, even when the bolt is fully withdrawn. And it also minimizes the tendency for the bolt to bind when cycling the action from the shoulder.

The fire control system is rather

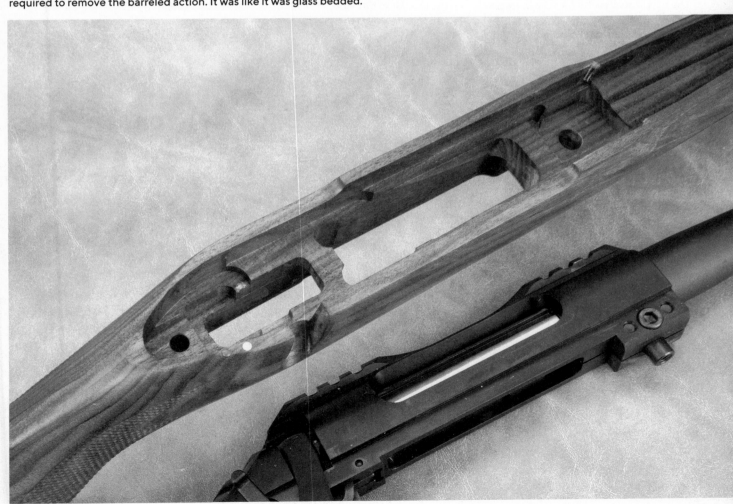

straightforward; it employs a two-position side safety that blocks trigger and sear movement and locks the action. The latter feature is seldom seen nowadays because the consensus has long been that it's better to be able to chamber and extract a round with the safety engaged. After all, that's when it's most needed. The catalog does state, however, that a three-position safety will soon replace the current one.

In removing the barreled action from the stock, it took such a tug to separate the two that I assumed the action was glass bedded. It was not. The quality of

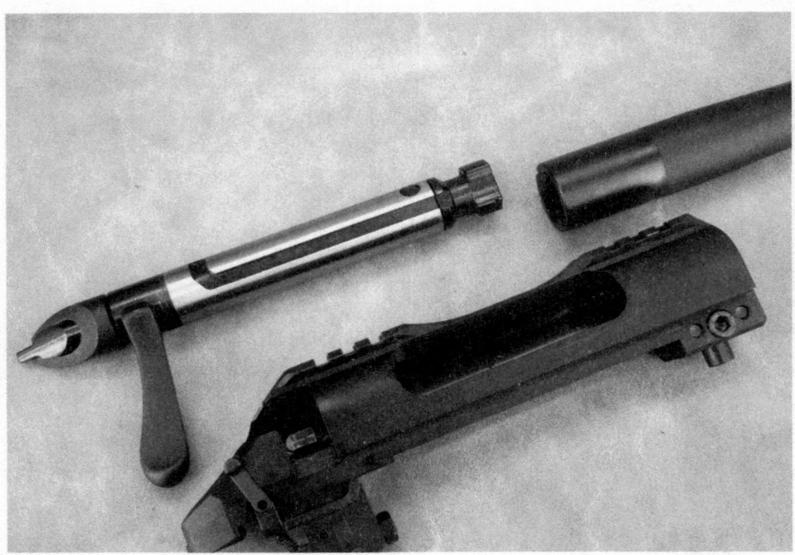

The bolt locks directly with the barrel, allowing the receiver to be made of aluminum.

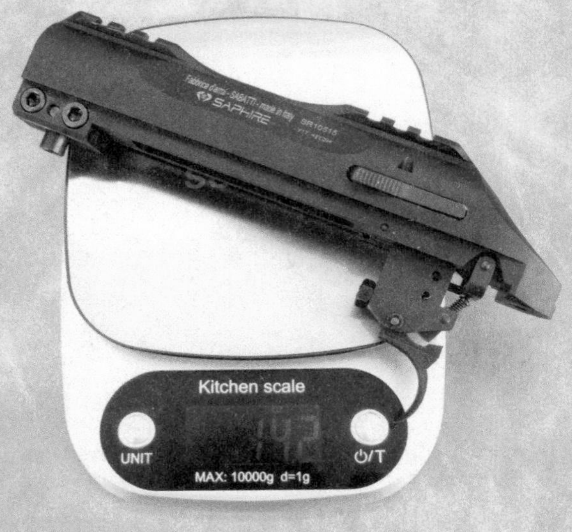

The entire receiver complete with the trigger/safety assembly weighs 14.2 oz., the bolt alone weighs 14.5 oz.!

The Sabatti Saphire is a handsome, quality rifle by any standard.

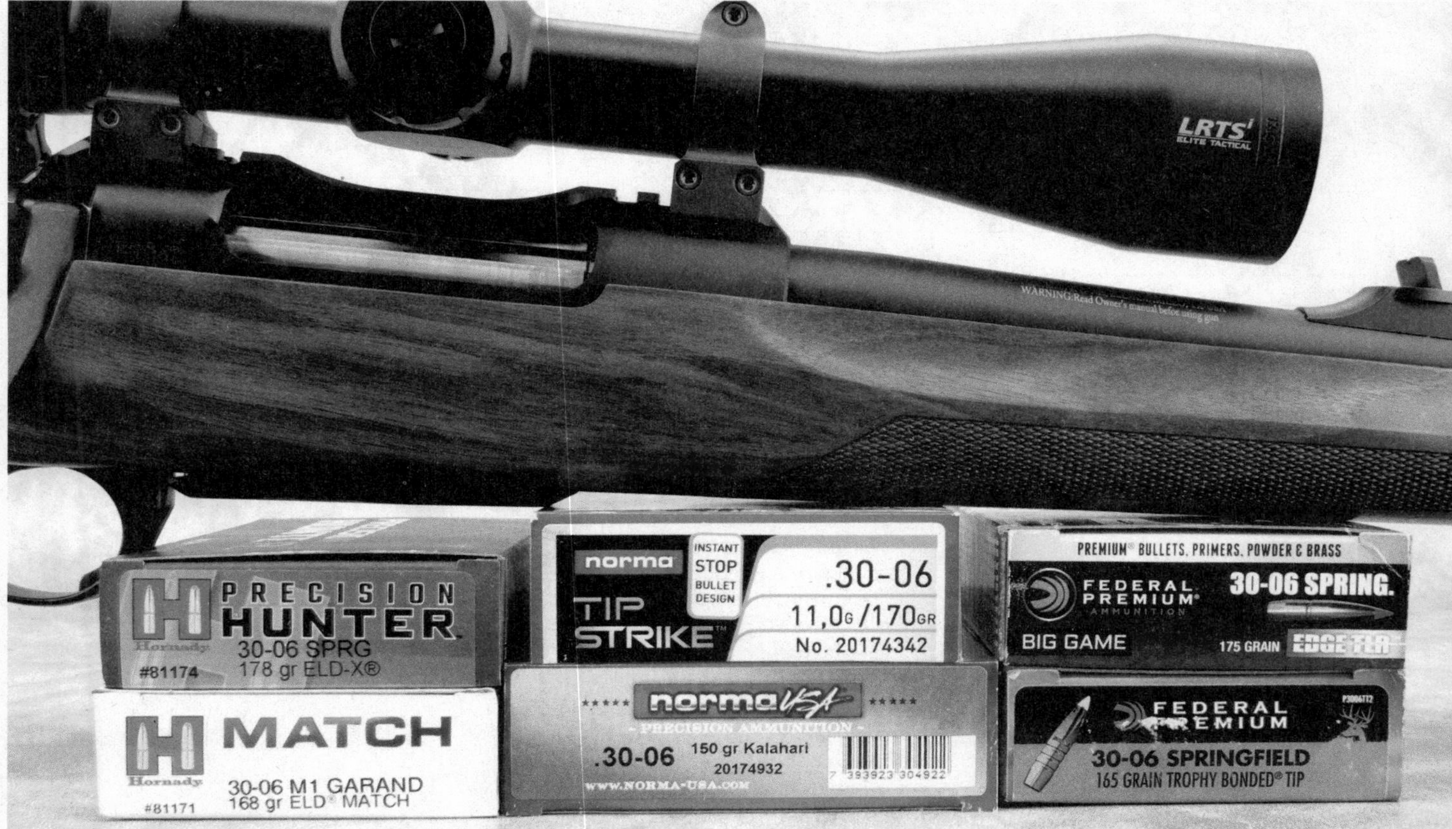

Four of the six loads used in testing exceeded nominal specs.

the inletting and wood-to-metal fit along the barrel and receiver was superb. What looks like a hinged floorplate is actually the bottom plate of a single-stack detachable magazine that fits flush with the belly of the stock. It's very well done. The detachable mag locked into place with a satisfying snap, and was released by pushing a lever located in the front wall of the trigger guard bow, just like the Remington 700.

We now come to that Multi-Radial Rifling I mentioned at the outset. Simply stated, radiused rifling does away with the sharp 90-degree inside corners formed at the land/groove juncture and replaces them with radii. The same with the sharp outer edges of the lands — they're radiused, too. Does it work? Well, let's look at the claims Sabatti makes for MRR:

- Higher velocity
- Tighter groups
- Fewer fliers
- Less copper deposit
- Less cleaning required
- Easier cleaning
- Less barrel wear

All the above claims are somewhat intuitive. Take the one about velocity, for example. With no sharp outer edges and inside corners, the bullet is deformed less, and less energy is needed for the engraving process. The result is less friction between bullet and bore, and obturation (gas sealing) is better because it's easier to seal rounded corners than sharp ones. It does seem logical then that, all other things being equal, velocity would increase. And because there's less bullet deformation, accuracy should also improve, though surely not dramatically enough to be discerned in the limited testing of one gun. Also, with no sharp corners to collect copper fouling and carbon deposits, bore cleaning should be easier and required less frequently. If all that's true, it would seem the accuracy life of a barrel should be extended as well.

It must be noted here that there has been one successful alternative to conventional rifling and it's called 5R. The salient feature that distinguishes 5R is that it employs an odd number of lands and grooves — normally five, but that's not chiseled in stone. With an odd number of lands and grooves, there's less bullet compression/deformation because each land is opposed by a groove, whereas with conventional even-numbered rifling the lands and grooves oppose one another. The other defining 5R feature is that the lands have sloping sides rather than being perpendicular to the surface of the land. In other words, the angle formed at the land/groove juncture is around 105 to 110 degrees instead of 90. That of course means less fouling and easier cleaning. Thompson-Center uses 5R rifling in its Venture and Dimension rifles, and Remington in its tactical models.

Now there is no way that shooting a hundred rounds or so through one gun is going to prove anything one way or another about Sabatti's claims of better accuracy, fewer fliers and longer accuracy life, intuitive though they may be. However, we might get a handle on the claims of higher velocity and less frequent and easier cleaning. In our experience, rarely does a factory load live up to, let alone exceed, nominal velocity, so Sabatti's claim of "higher bullet speed" was especially intriguing.

To ready the test gun for the range, I mounted one of Bushnell's excellent Elite Tactical LRTS scopes, this one the 4.5-18x50, using Warne's 30mm QD

ACCURACY AND VELOCITY RESULTS — SABATTI SAPHIRE .30-06		
Load/Factory Velocity (fps)	Measured Velocity (fps)	Group Average (inches)
Hornady 168-gr. ELD-Match — 2,710	2,620	1.30
Hornady 175-gr. ELD-X — 2,750	2,740	1.80
Norma 170-gr. Tip Strike — 2,790	2,835	1.10
Norma 150-gr. Kalahari — 2,985	2,950	1.25
Federal 165-gr. Nosler AccuBond — 2,800	2,850	1.85
Federal 175-gr. Edge TLR — 2,730	2,755	1.15

Note: The above are the results of firing five 3-shot groups from a benchrest at 100 yards as measured in inches. Velocities measured using an Oehler 35 chronograph 12 feet from the muzzle and rounded to nearest 5 fps.

lever rings. As it came from the box the Saphire weighed in at 7 lbs., 10 oz., with the Bushnell aboard, 9 3/4 lbs.

The accompanying data table shows the average 100-yard group size, plus the nominal velocities claimed for each factory load, and what I clocked using the Oehler 35P chronograph. With velocities for factory ammo being established in 24-inch test barrels — and the Saphire's spout also being 24 inches — the playing field was level. As the results show, three of the loads exceeded nominal velocities by an average of nearly 40 fps, and one came within 10 fps of matching it. Remember, too, that our velocities were taken 15 feet from the muzzle, so if you add another 10-15 fps to our figures (factory figures are based on actual velocities at the muzzle), four of the six loads exceeded nominal specs. Only one load, the Hornady Match, was significantly slower than claimed, but it is specifically loaded for the M1 Garand, so we really shouldn't have included it. Considering that the velocities claimed for factory ammo are always optimistic — sometimes decidedly so — the results are quite impressive.

As for the claims of better accuracy and fewer fliers, better and fewer than what? A single shooting session cannot tell you much, other than how one rifle, that rifle, performed with a small selection of factory loads under a specific set of range conditions. The group averages are not stellar, but well within the norm for a sporter-weight rifle and factory ammunition. The fact that two loads came close to the magic MOA for 15 shots shows the gun is certainly capable. Besides, range conditions were not the best, with gusts of 5-10 mph, which could have added 1/4 inch to group averages.

As for claims of less fouling and easier and less frequent cleaning, that seems to be borne out. Even though I cleaned after every 20 shots, it wasn't all that necessary. Just a couple of swipes with a bore brush and a few patches and the bore was squeaky clean. I also noticed less resistance as patches were run through with the cleaning rod. The claim for longer barrel life also seems plausible because there are no sharp edges to wear. With radiused rifling they're pre-worn, if you will.

On the range, the gun performed admirably and was a pleasure to shoot. The bolt glide was smooth as silk, and cartridges fed effortlessly, which is characteristic of single-stack mags where the feeding cartridge is perfectly aligned with the chamber. It also loads easily, something that can't be said for all detachable-mag guns. But alas, like most detachable magazines, this one can't be charged through the ejection port while in place. That, however, can be remedied with a pre-loaded spare. The trigger was crisp and free of creep, and it broke at 3 lbs. on the nose.

This is one well-designed and highly refined rifle, one that can hold its own among any in its price class … and then some. Current caliber offerings include .243, 7mm-08, 7mm Rem SAUM and .308 Win. in Group A. Group B consists of 6.5x55, .270, 7x57, 7x64, .30-06 and 8x57 JS. In Group C are the 7mm Rem. and .300 Win. magnums. The MSRP for a caliber switch ranges from $395 for the barrel only, to $575 for barrel, bolt head, bottom metal and magazine. I expect the .223 Rem. family to be added soon. For more information, visit www.sabatti.com

5R rifling shown here, compared to conventional rifling (right), is gaining adherents.

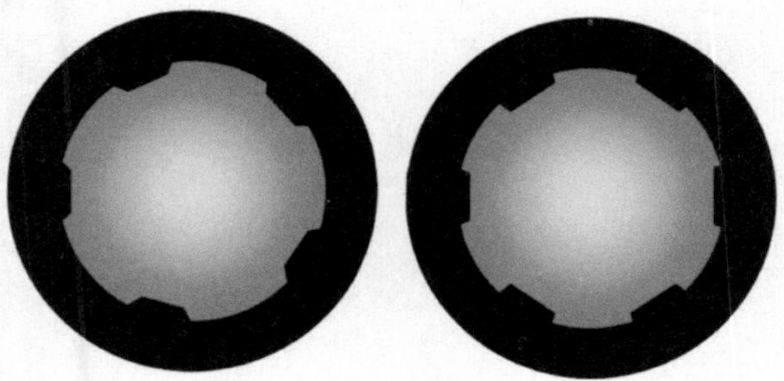

The author says Sabatti's claim of "higher bullet speed" may well be true, as four of the six loads tested exceeded nominal velocities, which are generally optimistic to begin with.

CUSTOM AND ENGRAVED GUNS

Our Annual Review of the Finest Examples of Beauty and Artistry in the World of the Custom Gun BY TOM TURPIN

Reto Buehler RUGER NO. 1s

A superb pair of No.1 Rugers crafted by Buehler in an unusual chambering combination. The full-length photo shows a No.1 chambered for the .404 Jeffery cartridge. The second rifle is chambered for the .303 cartridge. The factory Ruger actions were heavily modified, including removing the slotted screw in the action, adding new sliding safeties and a steel trigger and other cosmetic touches. He also fitted a set trigger to the smaller-caliber rifle. Both rifles feature PacNor barrels and are stocked in English walnut checkered with "flat-topped" patterns. The fore-ends are attached using the traditional wedge and escutcheons. Buehler installed a recoil reducer in the .404 buttstock, primarily to achieve a better balance due to the heavy .404 barrel. Photos by Brian Dierks

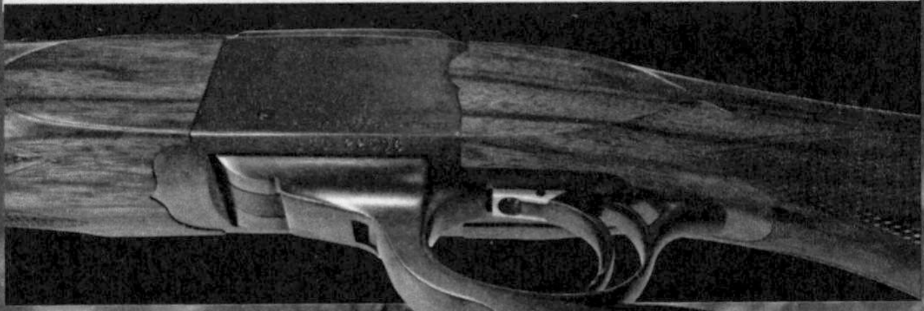

Swiss-born and educated, Reto Buehler is one of the new breed of custom gunmakers turning out very high-quality firearms. He and his contemporaries are the future of the custom gun trade. His work is impeccable and his talents seemingly endless, with many years left to further his chosen craft. Except for engraving, he is a one-man, one-stop shop in that he is equally adept at stockmaking and metalwork.

[CONTINUED ON PAGE 106]

Reto Buehler

CUSTOM .404 JEFFERY

This lovely rifle is built on a Granite Mountain Arms action and is typical of a Buehler Custom Sporting Arms "English Express" model. Chambered for the old but excellent .404 Jeffery cartridge, it features most all the "bells and whistles" one expects to see on such a rifle. Buehler used a PacNor 24-inch barrel, fitting it with a quarter rib, front sight ramp and sling swivel band. He mounted the Leupold straight tube scope in his own quick detachable cam-lever mount. He also installed a trap grip cap, which holds a peep sight that can be installed on the rear bridge when the scope is detached. Buehler crafted the stock from a spectacular stick of Turkish walnut, finishing it with many coats of hand-rubbed oil, and used a flat-topped checkering pattern with 20 LPI.

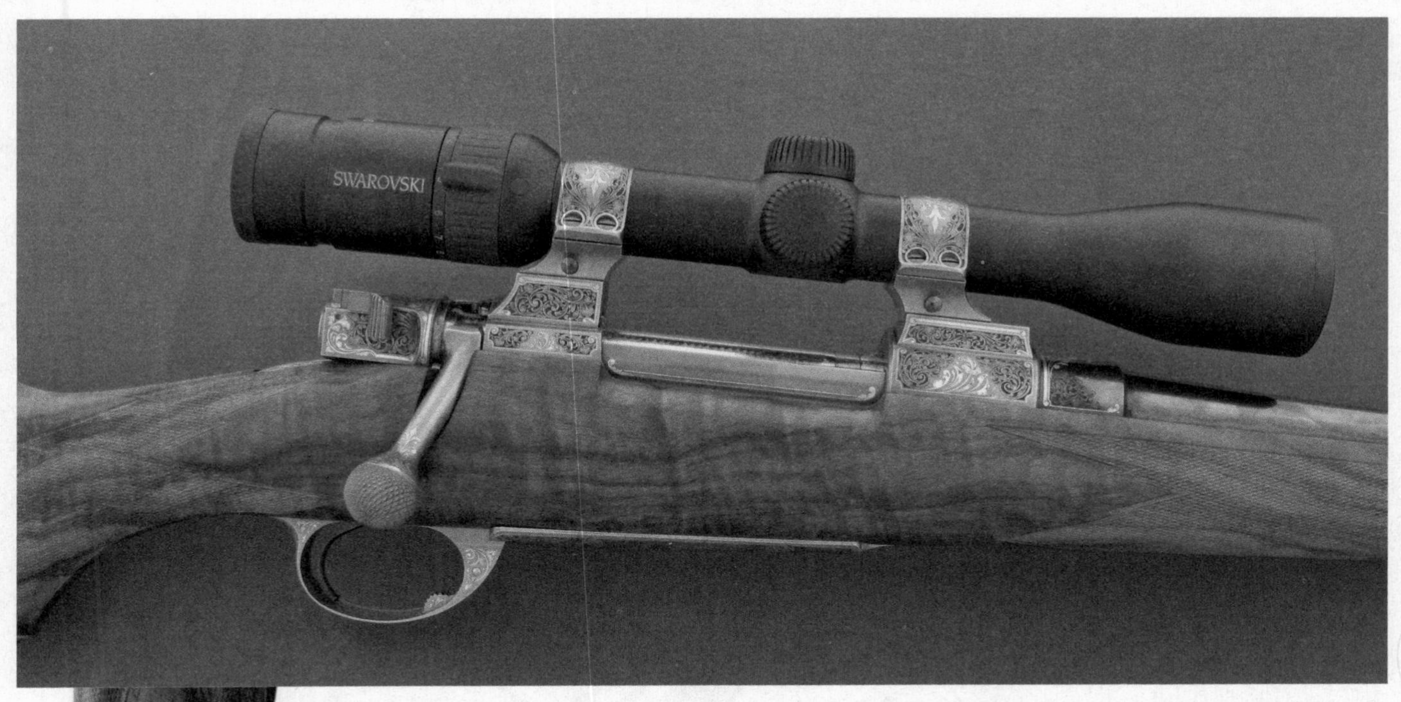

Bryan Hochstrat

"BEST ENGRAVED RIFLE" WINNER

Brian Hochstrat is one of the younger master engravers to have reached this level of artistic creative ability. His skills take a back seat to no one. The rifle shown here took the Best Engraved Rifle Award, and the Firearms Engravers Guild of America (FEGA) equivalent to Hollywood's best picture Oscar, the Engravers Choice Award. Photos by Sam Welch

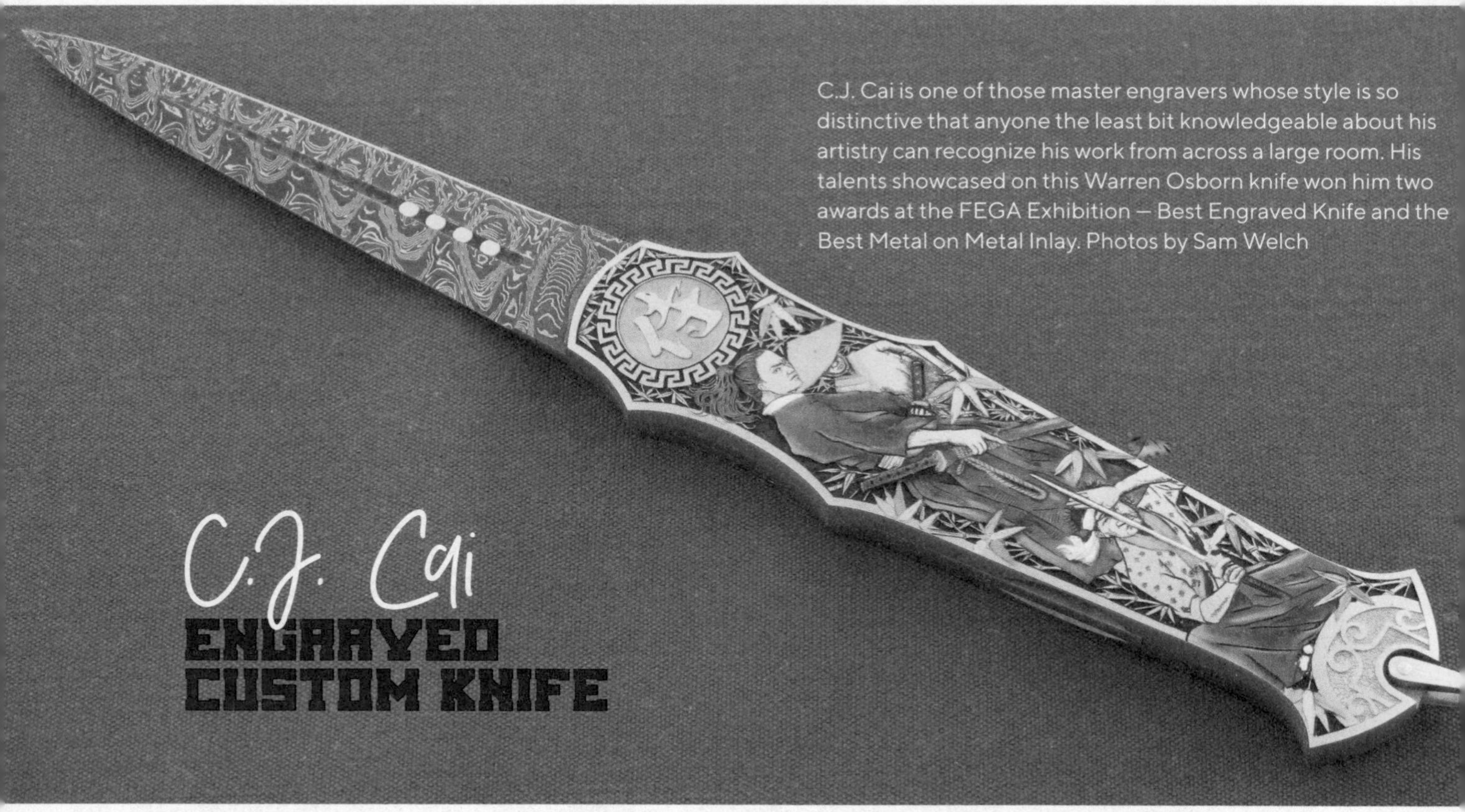

C.J. Cai
ENGRAVED CUSTOM KNIFE

C.J. Cai is one of those master engravers whose style is so distinctive that anyone the least bit knowledgeable about his artistry can recognize his work from across a large room. His talents showcased on this Warren Osborn knife won him two awards at the FEGA Exhibition – Best Engraved Knife and the Best Metal on Metal Inlay. Photos by Sam Welch

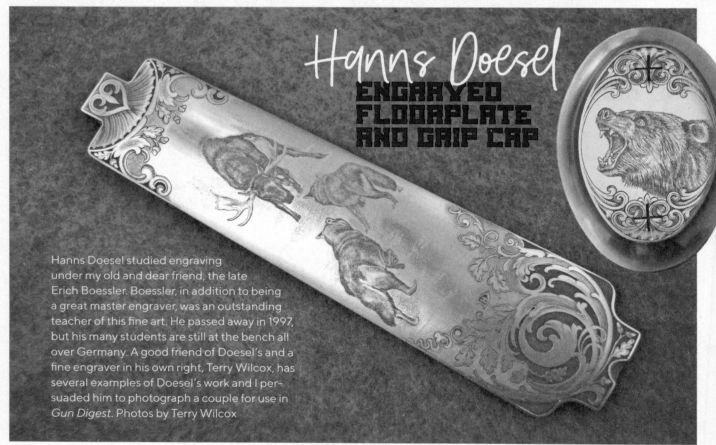

Hanns Doesel
ENGRAVED FLOORPLATE AND GRIP CAP

Hanns Doesel studied engraving under my old and dear friend, the late Erich Boessler. Boessler, in addition to being a great master engraver, was an outstanding teacher of this fine art. He passed away in 1997, but his many students are still at the bench all over Germany. A good friend of Doesel's and a fine engraver in his own right, Terry Wilcox, has several examples of Doesel's work and I persuaded him to photograph a couple for use in *Gun Digest*. Photos by Terry Wilcox

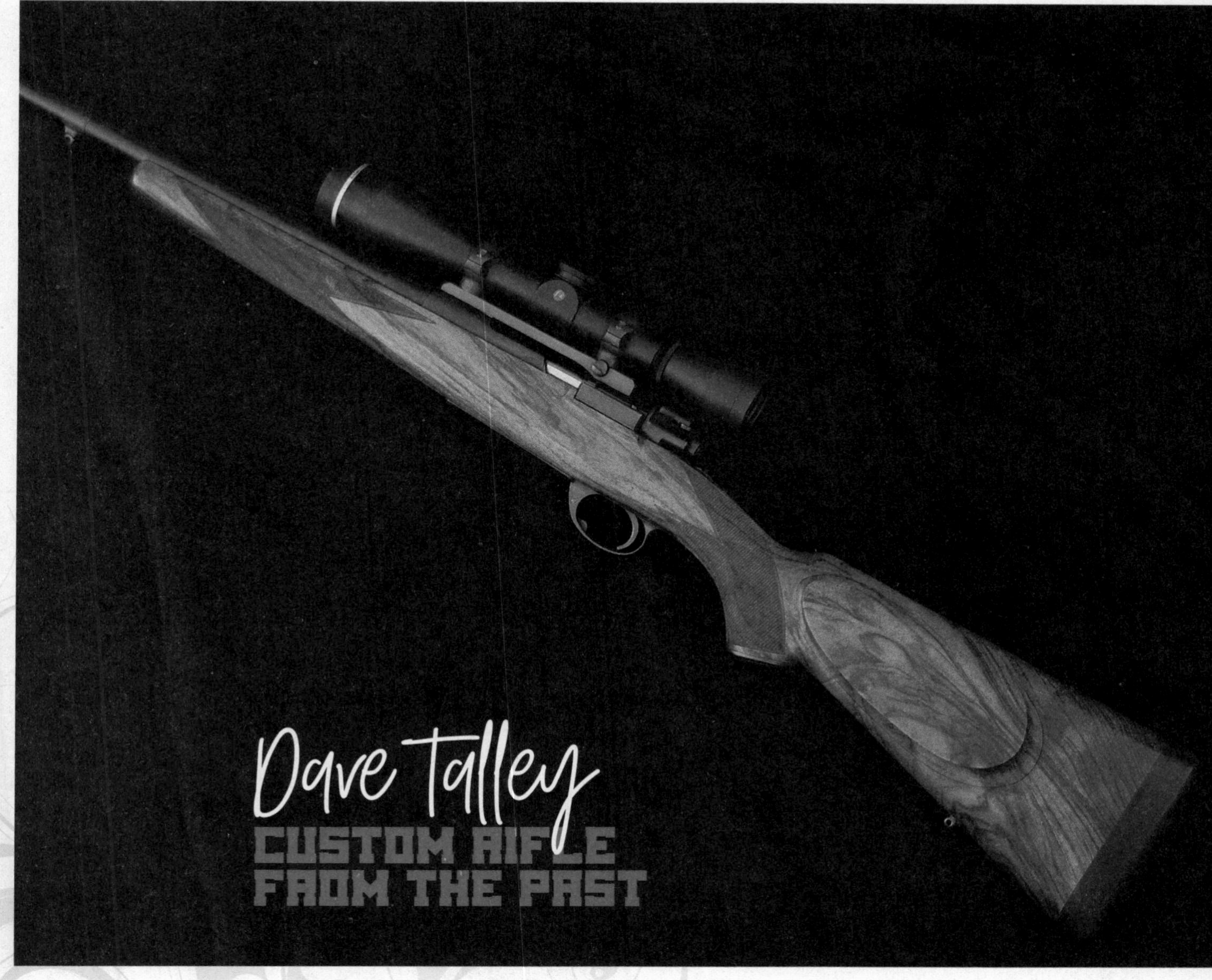

This rifle is not one that was made for me, but was crafted by a good friend of mine, Mr. Dave Talley, many years ago. He used a Mauser action, most likely of WWII Czech manufacture, and the .308-chambered barrel is probably from Douglas. I say probably, as I can't be certain, but I do know he used a lot of Czech actions and Douglas barrels in his work. The action is clearly marked as Talley's work on the recoil lug of the action. The stock is unmarked as to the maker. I suspect that it was crafted by Jere Eggleston, primarily due to the fact that they were both in South Carolina and used each other's talents frequently. I also showed the stock to a colleague and dear friend of Eggleston, Mr. Gary Goudy. He has seen a lot of Eggleston's work and told me that he thought it was an Eggleston stock, but couldn't be certain.

I came across an ad on a website listing the rifle for sale at a very attractive price. Further investigation revealed that the seller was also an Arizonan, living in the Phoenix area, making it an easy acquisition. The photo was taken of the rifle exactly as I bought it. I've since had it professionally cleaned up, swapped out the scope mounts for Talleys (what else!), had the recoil pad exchanged with a red Old English pad from Pachmayr, and had the checkering dressed up by Kathy Forster. Some work at the range revealed that the rifle loved Varget powder and, with its preferred load, gives sub-MOA groups with regularity. It's a neat little rifle that I'm proud to own and use. Photo by Tom Turpin

James Anderson
CUSTOM .22

One of our best custom gunmakers can be found most anytime in his South Dakota shop turning out exquisite custom rifles. In addition to being exceptionally talented, James Anderson is also one of our younger generation gunmakers in a craft whose superstars are mostly dominated by "mature" craftsmen.

One of his latest creations is this custom .22 rimfire, something not often seen in custom rifles. He started with a factory Remington 40X action, which he modified substantially. In addition to the normal honing and general cleanup, he made a new mag housing to accept Kimber magazines. He also made the floor metal unit and replaced the factory trigger with one made by Jewel.

He fit and match-chambered a Shilen hand-lapped barrel and crafted a set of custom scope mounts for a March 2.5-25X scope to the rifle. He then whittled out the stock from a nice stick of California English walnut and fitted an old Niedner-checkered steel buttplate. He then checkered the stock in a pleasing point pattern. To add a final touch, he took the rifle to his South Dakota neighbor, engraver Jesse Kaufman, who embellished the original factory markings.

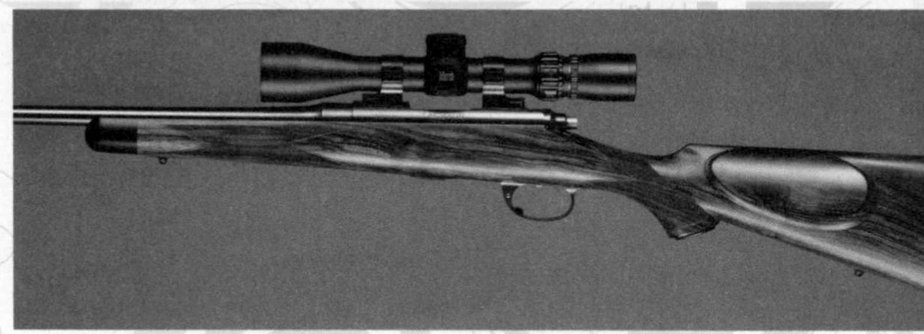

To sum up the project in one sentence, it just doesn't get any better than this. Photos by James Anderson

JOINT PROJECT SINGLE-SHOT FALLING BLOCK

Members of both the FEGA and the American Custom Gunmakers Guild (ACGG) joined together to craft this lovely single-shot falling block rifle. The metalwork was executed by Glenn Fewless, the stock by Doug Mann, and the outstanding engraving was by Bob Strosin. The modern version of a Daniel Fraser falling block action used in this project was machined by Steve Earl.

Photos by Sam Welch

Marty Rabeno
WINCHESTER MODEL 1876

Master engraver Marty Rabeno engraved this Winchester Model 1876 rifle. Rabeno excels at all styles of engraving, but he is at his absolute best when doing western motif scenes on period firearms. This Model 76 won runner-up Engravers Choice Award at the annual FEGA Exhibition this year. Photo by Mary Rabeno

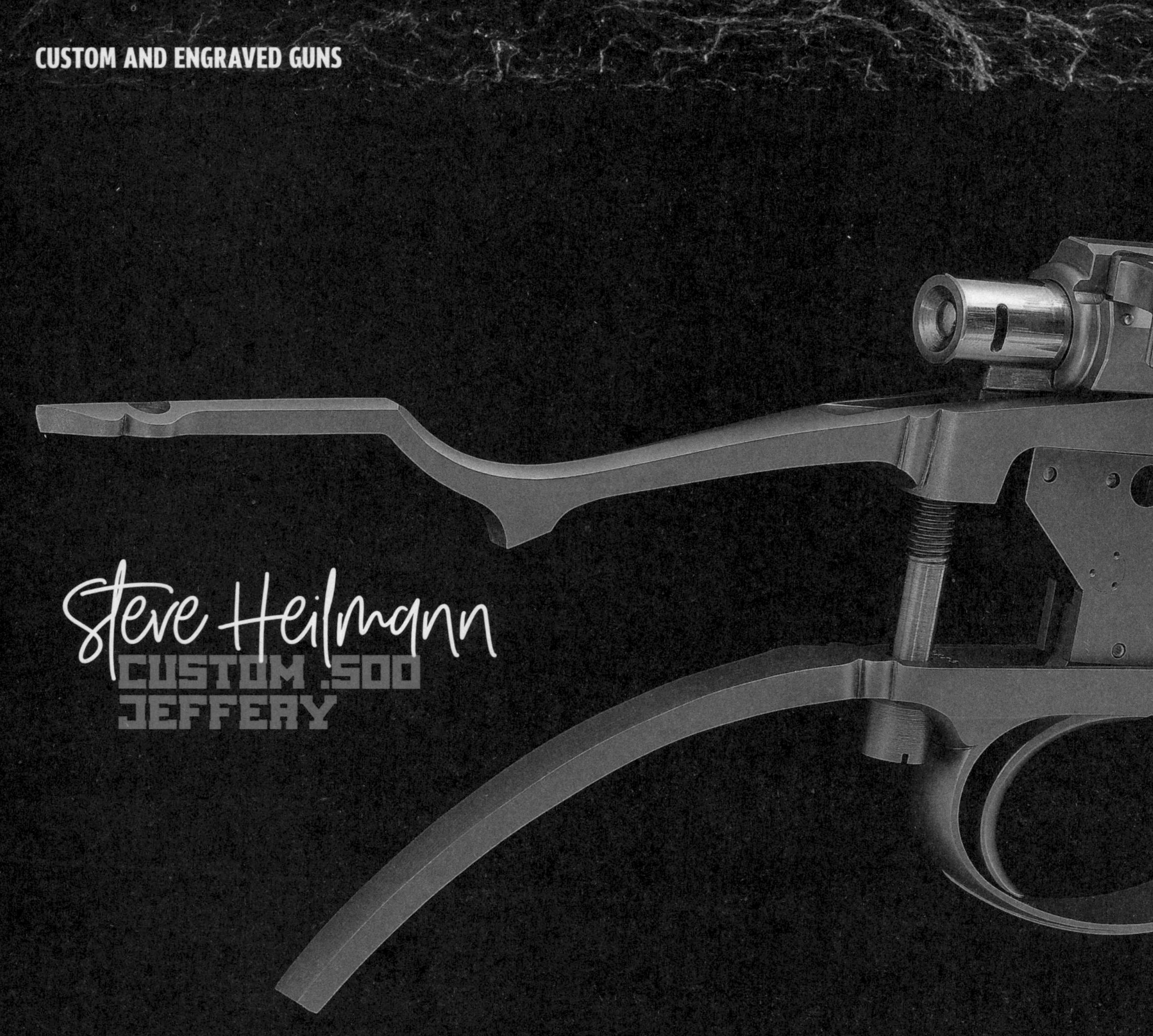

Steve is one of the very best custom gunmakers in the USA today. I would go so far as to expand that statement to encompass the globe. Some of the finest custom guns that I've ever had the pleasure of seeing and handling have come from his Grass Valley, California, shop. Like most superb craftsmen, his creations are always for his clientele and never for himself.

The old saw that the cobbler never makes new shoes for himself notwithstanding, pictured here is a creation that he's been working on for a while now, and believe it or not, it is for himself. He only works on it when he has a few spare hours, which isn't often, but he intends to finish this one as he wants it. So far, the metalwork is nearing completion.

Starting with a military '98 Mauser action, a Ted Blackburn bottom metal set and trigger, Model 70-type safety and shroud, and a .50-caliber 2-inch diameter Krieger barrel blank as raw material, Steve added over 350 hours of his precise metalsmithing. It is now as you see it in these photos.

The barrel has been chambered for the .500 Jeffery cartridge and milled octagonal in shape. The full-length rib, quarter-rib, front sight ramp, extra recoil lug and front sling swivel base are all milled integral with the barrel steel. The Mauser action has been extensively machined and has all the bells and whistles usually found and substantially more. Extended top and bottom tangs are but one example. The sculpted bolt has required more of Heilmann's time than some 'smiths devote to an entire action.

[CONTINUED ON PAGE 114]

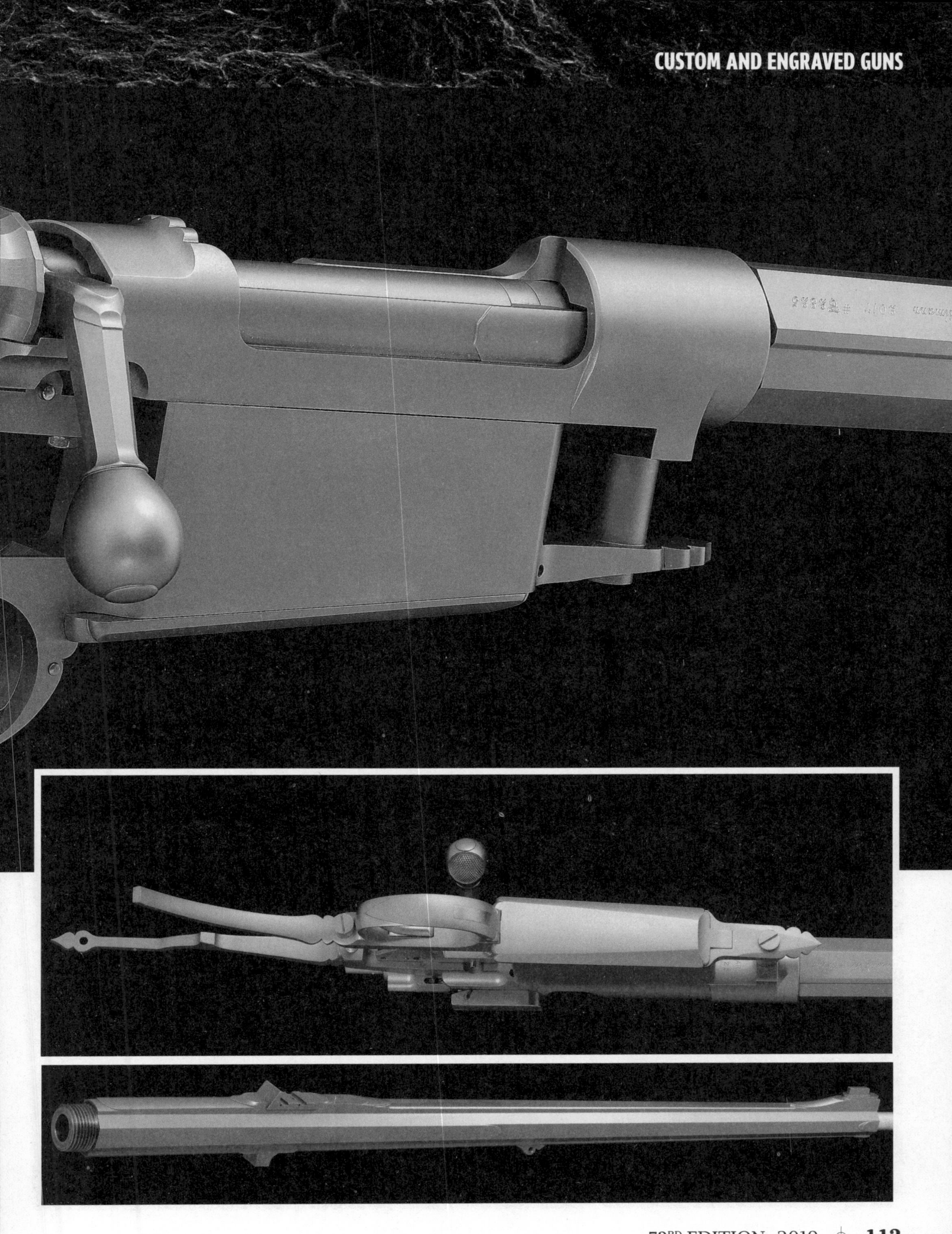

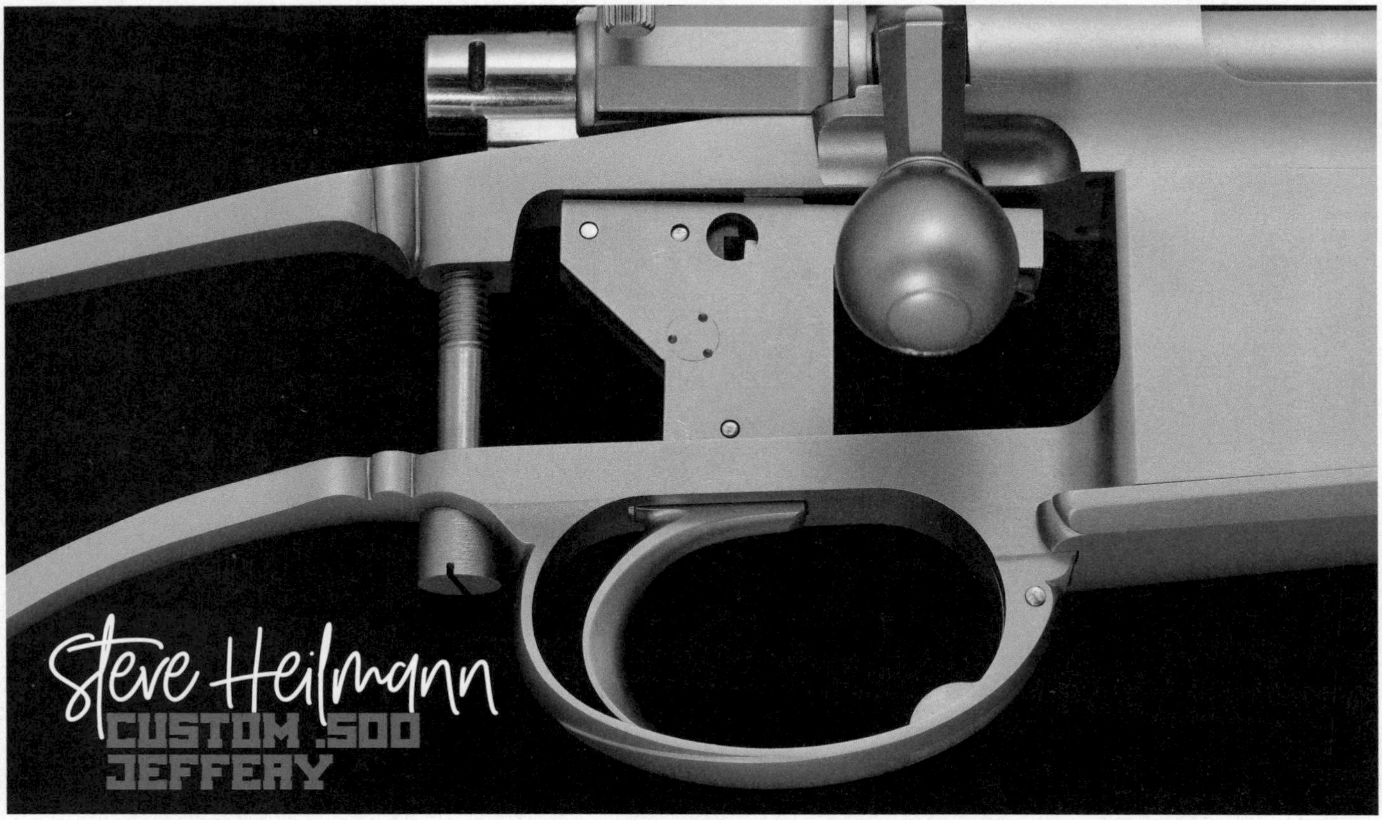

Steve Heilmann
CUSTOM .500 JEFFERY

Heilmann says he has set aside a spectacular Turkish walnut blank for this rifle from his substantial stash of impressive walnut blanks. Eventually, he will inlet, shape and mate the blank to the metal. Hopefully, I will remain above ground long enough to see its completion. If I don't, my successor for these pages will surely do so. It will be a sight to behold. All photos by Steve Heilmann

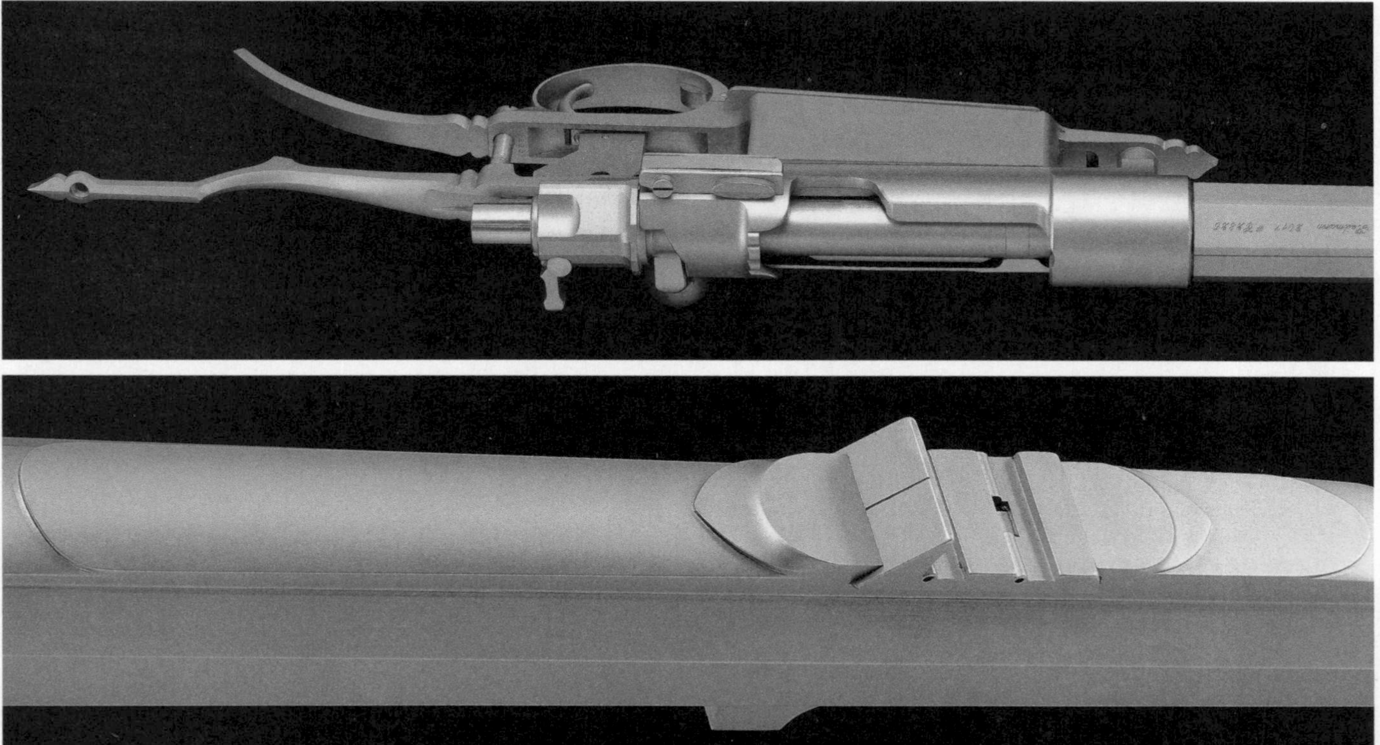

Lee Griffiths

HAGAN SINGLE SHOT AND CUSTOM 1911

Master Engraver Lee Griffiths is a fantastic engraver and is normally the recipient of several awards at the annual FEGA bash in Las Vegas. The 2018 show was no exception. His artistry on this Hagn-action single shot won him the Best Modern Firearm Award and the Model 1911 pistol won the Best Engraved Handgun Award. Photos by Sam Welch

THE CASE FOR **BOTTLENECK CARTRIDGES** IN REVOLVERS

Proprietary Bottleneck Cartridges From Gary Reeder Custom and Freedom Arms Produce Blistering Velocities and Tons of Fun!

BY **DICK WILLIAMS**

The Freedom Arms .224-32 revolver with a 7.5-inch barrel sports a Bushnell 2-6X variable scope. During its first Wyoming outing, the handgun and caliber played havoc with the prairie rats at ranges beyond 100 yards.

The shorter-barreled .224-32 with iron sights is a great field gun for varmint hunting, but the author's aging eyes required a little help from Decot glasses.

As an avid young handgunner in the early to mid-1960s, I spent a fair amount of time over a loading press refilling empty brass cases so I had some ammo to shoot. It was basic stuff, .38- and .44-caliber revolvers filled with the latest bargain-priced powder from Gene's Trading Post and lead bullets cast from whatever wheel weights I could scrounge at local tire stores. I was happy with my lifestyle, but like all young people, I had dreams — dreams fueled by reading gun magazines and loading manuals, of revolvers that could shoot bottleneck cartridges producing higher velocities and flatter trajectories. Written reviews on necked-down revolver cartridges were mixed, ranging from, "Setback of the case is so severe the cylinder locks up and the gun becomes unusable," to, "These cartridges work fine in a revolver if you keep chambers and cases dry and minimize the case taper." A tour of duty in Southeast Asia followed by an assignment in Washington, D.C., and the arrival of two daughters delayed my investigations and slowed the development of my recreational pursuits during the latter half of the sixties.

In the 1970s, I became hooked on handgun hunting, followed by metallic silhouette shooting. In the earlier days of my handgun hunting career, some states had rather strict rules for what handgun calibers (if any) could be used on big game. Specialized wildcat cartridges for which there was no factory ammo were not well-received by bureaucrats making hunting rules. Budding handgun hunters were steered toward the known magnums in revolvers and single-shot handguns shooting rifle-shaped cartridges. The same went for silhouette shooting. Revolvers had strict rules requiring them to be "production" guns and calibers. There were a lot of bottleneck cartridges on the firing line, but they were all chambered in single-shot handguns. The only true production revolver I can recall as chambered for a rifle-type cartridge was Smith & Wesson's Model 53 in the .22 Remington Jet, and it was long gone from the Smith inventory by the seventies. Even if you could find one on the used gun market and were willing to overlook its collectors' value and use it in matches, its .22-caliber 40-grain bullets would not reliably topple the steel targets.

Today, handgun hunters are still a relatively small contingent of the hunting community, and silhouette shooting isn't as popular as it once was. I'm still committed to hunting with handguns, mostly revolvers, but not with the same wild abandon as in my younger days. Likewise, the years have convinced me that manhood

(above) Utilizing Elmer Keith's classic field rest, Paul Pluff goes to work with the Ruger Single-Six rechambered by Reeder Custom Guns to the tried-and-true .218 Bee.

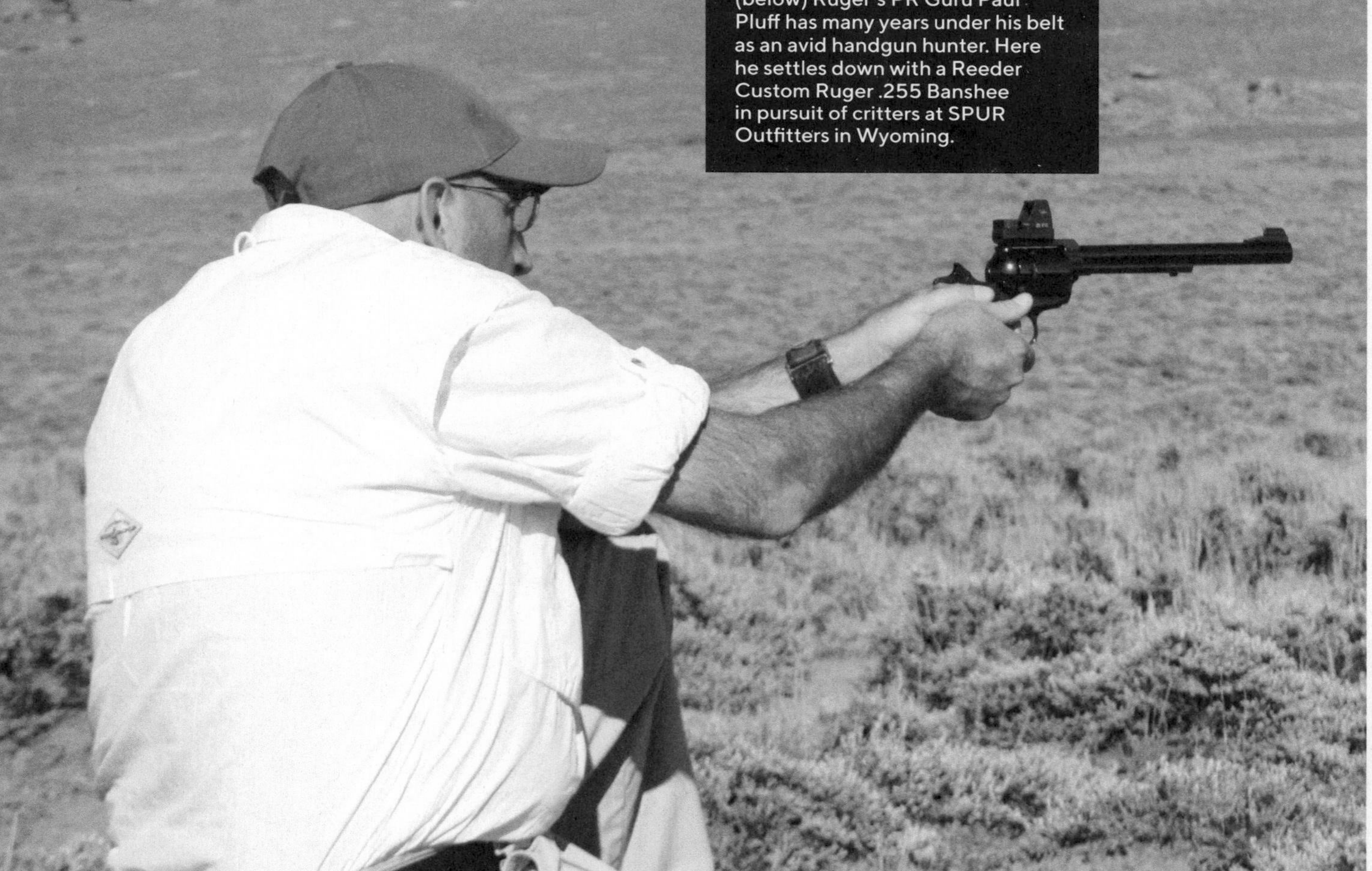

(below) Ruger's PR Guru Paul Pluff has many years under his belt as an avid handgun hunter. Here he settles down with a Reeder Custom Ruger .255 Banshee in pursuit of critters at SPUR Outfitters in Wyoming.

isn't best proved by repeated demonstrations of how much recoil one can absorb. I like shooting smaller calibers and packing lighter-weight revolvers on my hip, preferably without surrendering performance. Despite our lack of numbers, we handgun hunters have had a stroke of luck in the last few years, getting new models from manufacturers staffed with avid handgun hunters. Bob Baker of Freedom Arms is making his Model 97 (the small-framed single-action) in .224-32, while Gary Reeder of Reeder Custom Guns modifies existing wheelguns to accept bottleneck cartridges from .22 caliber to just about anything that will fit in the revolver's cylinder. Let's start with the smaller bores.

Freedom Arms is known worldwide for the quality and accuracy of its stainless-steel handguns. When first released in 1983, its flagship revolver, the large Model 83 chambered in .454 Casull, redefined the hunting handgun in terms of maximum power in an easily carried handgun. Fourteen years later, Freedom maintained those quality and accuracy standards in the smaller-framed Model 97. And while I had hunted with a variety of Freedom's revolvers chambered in straightwall cartridges, it was the introduction of the Model 97 chambered for a centerfire rifle cartridge that really got my attention. This new bottleneck cartridge is a "handload only" proposition that uses a .327 Magnum case necked down to .224, but since the case preparation involves one pass through a sizing die, making your own ammo couldn't be simpler.

The .327 Magnum case is designed for higher pressures (over 40,000 psi) than the original three handgun magnums, so greater velocities are possible from a given volume of powder. Freedom provides detailed loading instructions and explanations with each gun, including slight increases in powder charges after the case is initially fireformed. My first few loads with the suggested fireforming charge produced just over 2,000 fps, and that was from a 5.5-inch barrel. With R&D complete, we loaded 'em up and headed for Wyoming!

The first .224-32 I used on prairie rats sported a 7.5-inch barrel and was topped with a 2-6X Bushnell Elite scope. I hadn't used a scoped handgun for a while, so I wasn't the suave, competent pistolero of yesteryear. But, once I reacquainted myself with proper eye alignment and field of view vs. magnification settings, the little gun proved to be devastating at distances beyond 100 yards. On my next trip to Wyoming, I was accompanied by a .224-32 with a 5.5-inch barrel and topped with a Trijicon red-dot. I liked this setup better simply because we moved around during the varmint hunts and shot from different positions. Plus, I like storing a handgun in a belt holster when I'm not shooting it, and it's not difficult finding a scabbard these days that accommodates the small red-dot optics. I find the shorter 5.5-inch barrel works in a belt holster, while the longer 7.5-inch outfit would be better served with a chest rig. If you remain stationary on a shooting bench, the longer barrel and scope with higher power settings would probably be a better choice.

For many years, I thought that the .218

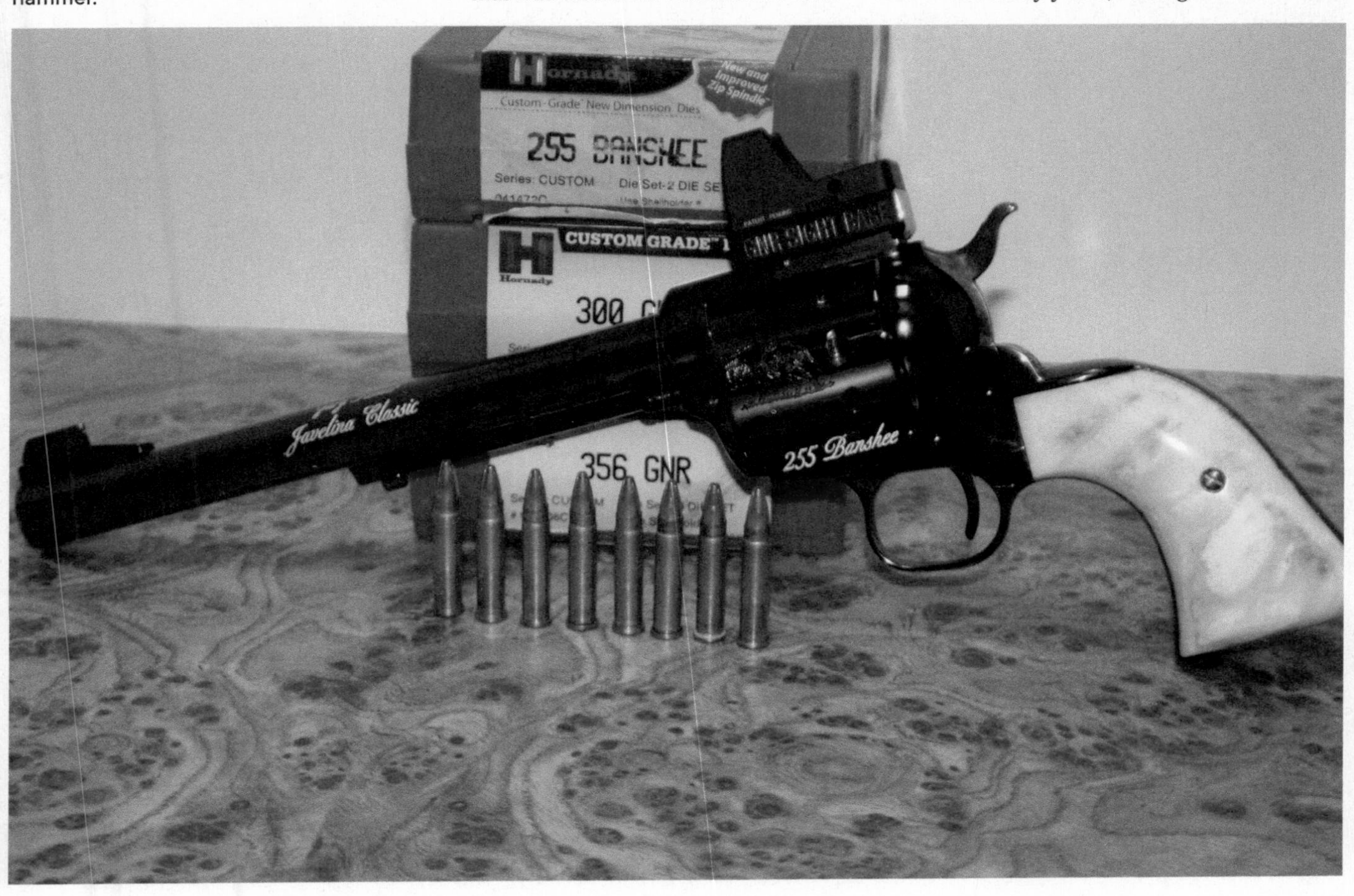

The .255 Banshee is equipped with a Trijicon red-dot and modified to hold eight rounds. Since this gun was built on a 3-screw Ruger with no transfer bar, prudence dictates carrying only seven rounds with an empty chamber under the hammer.

I'VE ALWAYS HAD A SOFT SPOT FOR THE RUGER SINGLE-SIX, PROBABLY BECAUSE I GOT MY FIRST RUGER HANDGUN AS A TEENAGER BACK IN ... WELL, NEVER MIND WHEN.

Bee would be a great revolver cartridge. Its overall length, at least when loaded with the lighter-weight and/or flat-nose bullets, is within the limits imposed by the revolver's cylinder. Case diameter is sufficiently larger than the .22 Hornet case to allow for some performance increase, while still allowing your wheelgun to carry a full complement of six rounds. The .218 case is a little tougher than the Hornet, so you're less likely to cause damage during the reloading process. But the real clincher is the availability of factory ammo and cases. That translates to no case- or fireforming. Load up and go hunting!

Reeder's .300 GNR (or mini .30 Herrett) required more time at the reloading bench than any cartridge in this article, but it brought back fond memories, recounts the author, of hunts and silhouette shoots with the original Herrett.

I've always had a soft spot for the Ruger Single-Six, probably because I got my first Ruger handgun as a teenager back in … well, never mind when. When I started this project, I had a Single-Six in the vault with both the .22 LR and .22 Mag cylinders, so I headed over to Reeder's Pistol Parlor in Flagstaff and asked Gary Reeder if he could wave his magic wand and turn my Ruger into a .218 Bee. Since it had two cylinders, he suggested making one a standard .218 Bee cylinder and the other a .218 Mashburn Bee. Naturally, I responded with the appropriate, "Duh, why didn't I think of that?"

It was quite a transformation. The barrel grew from 5.5 to 7 inches; the bluing became a highly polished blue/black finish; both cylinders and several smaller components acquired a highly polished stainless-steel appearance; the grip frame was rounded in the Reeder "Gunfighter" style and fitted with a handsome set of wood grips; and a 2X Leupold scope was mounted on the top strap. Like most artists, Reeder signs stuff, so he put his name and "Javelina Classic" on the barrel. I initially thought the finished gun with the longer barrel and Leupold scope might be a little too muzzle-heavy, but the balance point remains just in front of the trigger guard, which suits me perfectly for a semi-walkabout smallbore revolver with a 2X scope.

I chronographed some Hornady and Winchester .218 Bee factory loads in the converted Ruger and achieved consistent readings in the upper-1,700 fps range with 45- and 46-grain bullets. I clocked a few handholds consisting of 13 grains of 680 with 40-grain Speer and got slightly less than 1,700 fps. I'm not totally surprised at these velocity reductions since factory .218 Bee loads were clocked in rifles. I did not expect velocities to

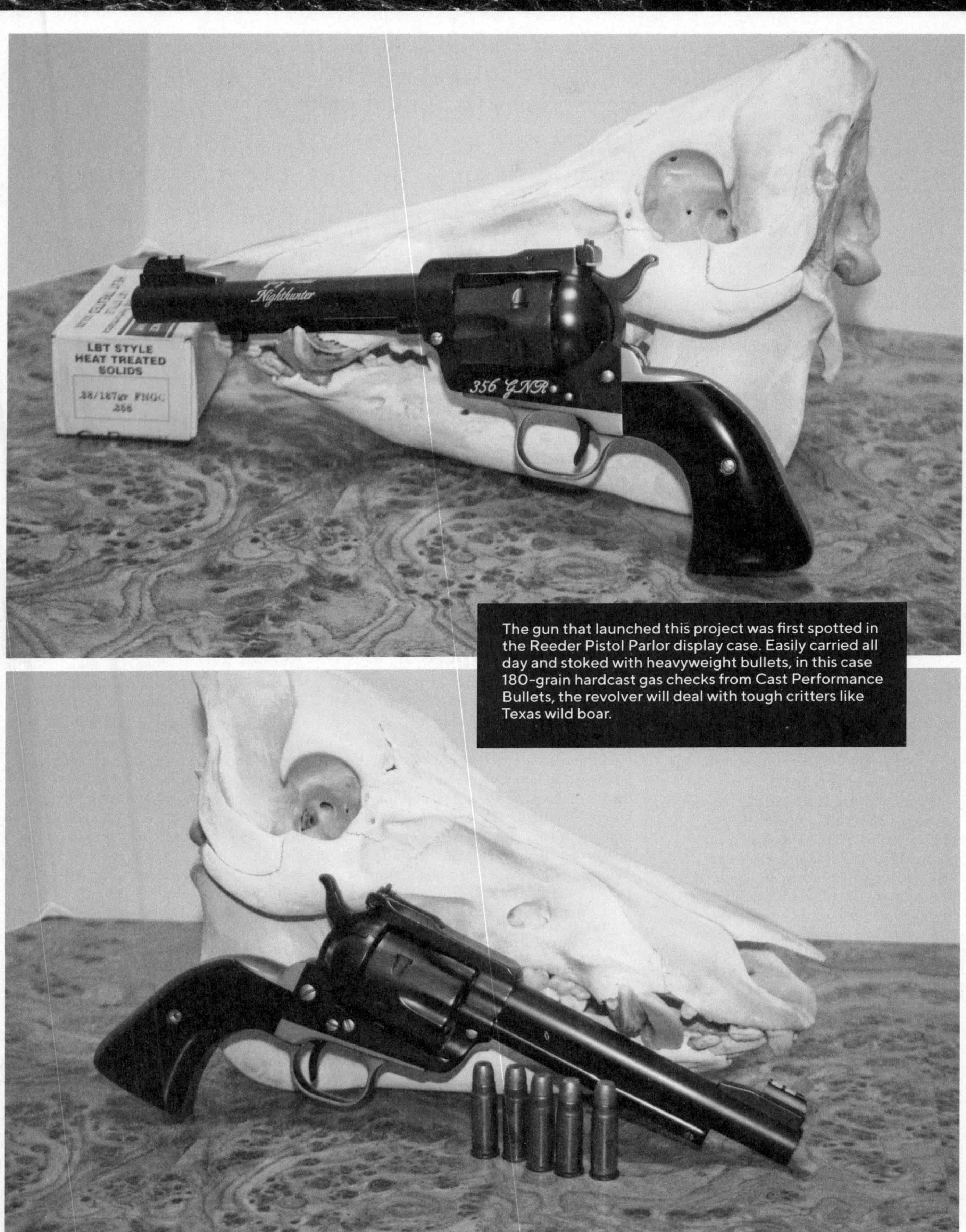

The gun that launched this project was first spotted in the Reeder Pistol Parlor display case. Easily carried all day and stoked with heavyweight bullets, in this case 180-grain hardcast gas checks from Cast Performance Bullets, the revolver will deal with tough critters like Texas wild boar.

be anywhere near 2,500 or 3,000 fps. Deadlines precluded me from a meaningful dialogue with factory ballisticians at this time, but I will be looking for some input regarding use of factory ammo in a revolver. And while it would be nice to use factory ammo, I'm OK with having to build my own loads, particularly since there are properly formed cases already available.

The next custom gun from Reeder was totally unplanned. During a visit, I noticed he had one of his .255 Banshee Rugers for sale in the display case. It had his highly polished blue/black finish and wore some striking synthetic ivory grips. It also had an 8-inch barrel and a cylinder 1.75 inches in length or 1/8-inch longer than the .218 Bee. In addition, it was built on the larger Blackhawk frame, meaning he had taken advantage of the larger cylinder window and made an extended-length, 8-shot cylinder for the conversion.

Having played with the .256 Winchester in a couple of single-shot pistols, I have an interest in the .25 caliber. The Reeder Banshee is a .22 Hornet case necked up to .25 caliber with the shoulder blown out to .22K Hornet shape. The desired goal was a pistol that would launch 60- to 75-grain bullets at 2,000 fps and be useful on game up to small-bodied deer. The Reeder reloading manual shows the caliber will do that with 12 grains of H110 topped by a 75-grain HP when loaded in a 12-inch-barrel Contender. When I loaded a 75-grain HP over 12 grains of 296, I saw 1,600 fps from the Ruger.

Loading for the .255 Banshee is a bit more involved than for the .218 Bee. First, .22 Hornet brass isn't as robust as the .218. I got rather careless and crushed a case mouth seating one of the bullets in my first box of brass. Second, initial loads have reduced powder charges until the Hornet case has been expanded to K Hornet dimensions. If you find an accurate fireforming load that produces less than your desired velocities, load up a batch and go small game hunting. I did not have an opportunity to do this with the Banshee, but I have a plan for future activities. When I return to the loading bench, I'll be using 60-grain flat-point bullets and trying for an extra 100 fps or better. I would expect a bit more killing power from the flat point than from a 75-grain HP, particularly at velocities under 2,000 fps.

Back in my handgun silhouette days, I spent some time at the reloading bench and on the range with the .30 Herrett. My interest in the caliber waned when I found some 7mm calibers that performed better and involved much less case prep work, but I always thought the .30 Herrett concept would be great in a revolver. Fortunately, Reeder's hunting experiences with the .30 Herrett lead him to modify the cartridge for a revolver. He shortened the overall case to 1.315 inches, shortened the neck by .100 inch, made a sharper shoulder, and slightly reduced case taper. You don't have to go through all those steps to make cases. Simply lube a new .30-30 case, run it through the cutoff die, and trim the brass flush with the die. Remove the shortened case, chamfer the case mouth, dry the case, and load.

This gun started life as a Ruger .30 Carbine with a 7-inch barrel. It had been sitting in my vault, rudely ignored, for more than 20 years. The caliber conversion itself didn't involve anything fancy — all six chambers were enlarged to handle the modified .30-30 cases. After that, it did get a little fancier, with the polished Reeder finish, a V-notch rear sight blade, green fiber optic front sight bead, and finally the simulated "ivory" grips. (Reeder assured me that no elephants were harmed during the manufacture of his handguns!) The gun wears the label, "300 GNR Coyote Classic." The reloading manual shows a 20-grain starting load with either H110 or 296 and 110-grain bullets. Using 21 grains of 296 topped by 110-grain Speer and Sierra JHPs, velocities clocked from 1,700 to 1,750 fps. The manual states that a maximum load of 23 grains H110/296 will produce in excess of 2,100 fps from a 7-inch-barreled custom Ruger Blackhawk. If I'm in the neighborhood of 2,000 fps, I'll be a happy dude.

Although reloading the .300 GNR isn't overly demanding, remember you are altering more than just the shape of the cartridge case. And since this is a bottleneck cartridge, it's more like loading a rifle round than a handgun cartridge. You're chambering the case mouth rather than belling it, so extra care must be taken as you seat the bullet. Don't get overly frugal. I tried some used .30-30 cases and had some difficulties. Chambering and ejecting .30-30 ammo through a lever-action carbine exposes the round to some harsh environments. Any deformations to the rim caused by the extractor, or from smacking rocks during ejection, may cause future chambering or extraction problems in your revolver.

Although I'm addressing it last, Reeder's .356 GNR is the gun that started this flurry of activity on bottleneck cartridges in revolvers. He calls his .356 GNR the "Nighthunter," and mine is built on an older Ruger 3-screw model Blackhawk, a model to which I'm rather partial. At first glance, it reminded me of the old .357 Bain & Davis, but instead of being a necked-down .44 Mag case, it's a necked-down .41 Magnum case with a straight body, sharper shoulder and shorter neck. This Nighthunter has a brushed silver finish on the grip frame with the barrel, cylinder, and frame finished in a flat black rather than the highly polished blue/black found on the other guns. The adjustable rear sight blade has a V-notch, while the front sight contains a green fiber optic. The barrel is 6 inches long and the back of the grip frame has been slightly rounded in the Gunfighter-style grip. All in all, it is an elegant but entirely workmanlike wheelgun. It's my kind of gun!

Cases are simple to make: one pass through a carbide die and you're done.

CASES ARE SIMPLE TO MAKE: ONE PASS THROUGH A CARBIDE DIE AND YOU'RE DONE. AS WITH OTHER BOTTLENECK ROUNDS, YOU LIGHTLY CHAMFER THE CASE MOUTH RATHER THAN BELLING IT AND LET THE SEATING DIE GUIDE THE BULLET INTO THE CASE. I DON'T KNOW HOW SMOOTHLY PLAIN BASE CAST BULLETS WILL LOAD BECAUSE I HAVEN'T TRIED ANY, BUT THE GAS-CHECKED 180-GRAIN CAST BULLETS WORK NICELY, AS DO JACKETED BULLETS.

As with other bottleneck rounds, you lightly chamfer the case mouth rather than belling it and let the seating die guide the bullet into the case. I don't know how smoothly plain base cast bullets will load because I haven't tried any, but the gas-checked 180-grain cast bullets work nicely, as do jacketed bullets. The Reeder Reloading Manual suggests 21 grains of H110/296 with 158-grain jacketed bullets. With that load using Hornady, Speer, and Sierra bullets, velocities ranged from 1,350 to 1,425 fps. The manual also says that the maximum load of 24 grains with these bullets should produce around 1,800 fps in an 8-inch-barreled Ruger. Since I only had once-fired .41 Mag brass available to start this project, I haven't visited max loads yet. Listed starting loads using 180-grain LBT cast bullets are 22 grains, and with that I got over 1,500 fps. With the max load of 24 grains H110/296, top velocities in an 8-inch-barreled revolver should be 1,700 fps. I expect to be somewhat slower than that, but I'll wait for new brass to find out.

Recoil experienced with loads tested to date is noticeable, but well below painful. I like the idea of the smaller gun with a 6-inch barrel simply because it will be carried in a belt holster for reasonably quick access. I hope to try the 180-grain load on a pending spring hog hunt in Texas. With a hardcast bullet having a reasonably sized meplat, it should be capable of full penetration through the gristle plate and chest cavity of a mature boar. Beyond that, I have no specific plans in terms of desired loads. The Nighthunter is definitely a hunting handgun that's meant to be carried, and the power level attainable is well above the standard 357. With loads tested to date, it's easier for me to shoot than a full-house .44 Magnum. I see a fun-filled future with the .356 GNR.

You might say this entire effort was a trip down memory lane. I had a chance to see some beautiful handguns and explore the old-time "mysteries" of shooting rifle-shaped cartridges in revolvers. My conclusion is that bottleneck rounds in revolvers do offer some advantages and can be quite reliable. The original caveats were correct — when building the gun, keep the cartridge walls as straight as possible, use minimal taper transitioning to the cartridge neck, and keep the neck no longer than necessary. When shooting the handgun, keep it and the cartridge cases clean and dry with special emphasis on dry chambers.

Although Freedom Arms revolvers are factory production guns, you can choose specific features like barrel length, sights, grip shape, barrel shape, and more. Reeder Custom Guns begin with the model of your choice — such as Smith & Wesson or Ruger in different frame sizes — and build features and accessories from there to meet your specifications. Both Freedom and Reeder offer reloading dies and data for the cartridges. Give the hot bottleneck cartridges a whirl in your revolvers. I bet you'll enjoy yourself as much as I have.

Bottleneck cartridges from left to right: Freedom Arms .224-32, standard .218 Bee, .218 Mashburn Bee, .255 Banshee, .300 GNR, and the .356 GNR. All fill a niche in the handgun hunting world.

Russia's Mosin-Nagant Model 1944 Carbine

Last of the Cold War Favorites that Continue to Serve

BY GEORGE LAYMAN

From the Korean and Vietnam Wars, to Syria, Angola and the jungles of South and Central America, the Russian Model 1944 Mosin-Nagant carbine in any of its variations or clones has seen steady service from WWII to the Cold War, and right up to the present.

What may be considered the final, full production variant of Russia's famed 7.62x54mm-caliber Mosin-Nagant family of bolt-action rifles, the Model 1944 was manufactured by at least four other countries, and even appears to have been assembled from parts kits by two others. In an age of automatic rifles, it's still in use by several militias and armed elements in former Soviet republics and the Third World.

Two years after the German invasion of the Soviet Union, Russia's military was about to introduce a replacement for the heavy, unwieldy 7.62x54mm Model 91/30 Vintovka Mosina, better known in the U.S. as the Mosin-Nagant rifle. The Model 1938 carbine was in issue at the time, its lack of being adapted for a bayonet was its major shortcoming, and was issued primarily to artillery, tank or machine gun crews. Following fierce house-to-house urban fighting in places such as Stalingrad, Soviet military leaders of the time decided a short, handier arm would be far better suited for the infantry in mass attacks. However, the bayonet was still a prerequisite of the Soviet order of battle. Keep in mind, the intention of such an arm was not geared to special troops or units, but for all soldiers in the field.

By late 1943, the Izhevsk arms factory simply took the pre-existing Model 1938 carbine and installed a sweated ring base behind the front sight area with a

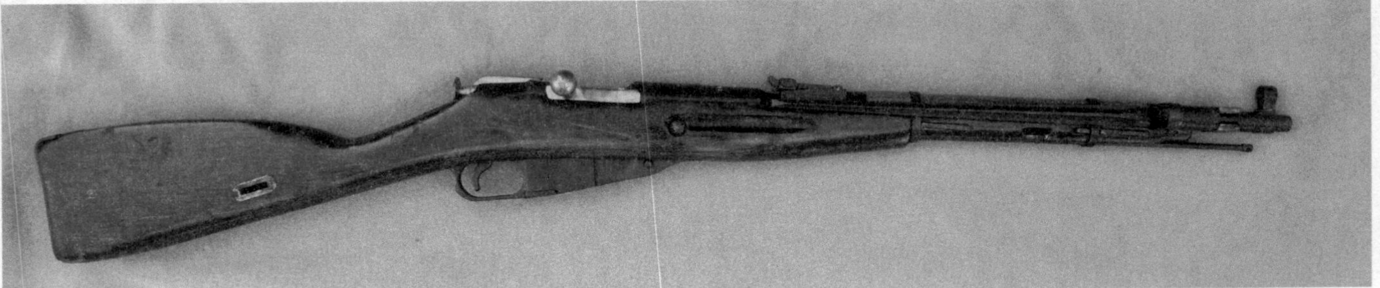

The Russian Mosin-Nagant Model 1944 carbine was developed in the middle of WWII by the Soviet Union as a replacement for the heavier Model 91/30 rifle. The entire concept of the M44 was to provide every field soldier with an infantry arm that could be handled quickly and efficiently for close-in fighting and house-to-house engagements. It was after WWII that the M1944 became one of the most widely issued bolt-action rifles of the Cold War.

cruciform folding bayonet assembly that was mounted to the right side of the barrel. Production of the older 91/30 rifles was halted about this time, and the new folding-bayonet carbine — christened the Model 1944 — was in full-scale production by January of that year. Since the Tula factory was moved 120 miles south of Moscow due to German advancements, the Izhevsk factory undertook most of the M44 production, though once the Nazis were driven back, machinery and equipment saw the Tula arsenal return to its original location. Because of its late war issue, it was difficult to rearm every soldier in the frontlines as they advanced so rapidly to the west — it was logistically impossible to catch up with the soldiers in the front. Few photographs or newsreels show the M44 in the hands of the victorious Red Army in Germany, but for those lucky enough to have received the lightweight M44, it was a relief after carrying the heavier 91/30 rifle through many an engagement. In addition, the permanently fastened folding bayonet of the new carbine prevented inadvertent loss or having to carry it in a separate scabbard.

There is, however, some archive newsreel of the feared Russian Narodnyy Komissariat Vnutrennikh Del (NKVD) blocking units or "file closers" carrying the Model 1944 carbine. These political officers' primary objective was to shoot Russian soldiers who hesitated to fight or attempted desertion in combat. Though manufactured and issued in fair numbers during late World War II, the M44 did not see its intended potential genuinely realized at the time. Close quarters combat requiring a high volume of fire on the road to Berlin saw an instantaneous change in tactics, with a critical priority placed on arming every forward-area soldier with a high-capacity PPSH 41 or PPS 43 submachine gun. By late 1945, the Soviet military was already getting set to field the new semi-automatic SKS rifle in a lighter-recoiling 7.62x39mm caliber, which would condemn the M44 to obsolescence in very short order.

It is believed that production of the M44 lasted through 1948, as by this time the SKS was practically at the point of standard issue to all Soviet first-line troops. A late-appearing but true veteran of Russia's Great Patriotic War, it was not during this time that the Model 1944 would carve its niche. It would not be until the coming Cold War that its full potential would be realized. At the end of World War II, Eastern Europe was securely in communist hands controlled by Soviet hegemony and along with the ideology came the distribution of approved ordnance. Though technologically obsolete, the M44 was to become a non-stop, worldwide key player from 1946 to the present. As was the norm with Soviet doctrine, first equipping those countries under the communist heel led to forced, in-country licensed production of certain weaponry for those having an industrial capability. It is believed that, as early as 1949, tooling for the Mosin-Nagant Model 1944 was in the process of being shipped to Poland's Lucznik Arms Factory in

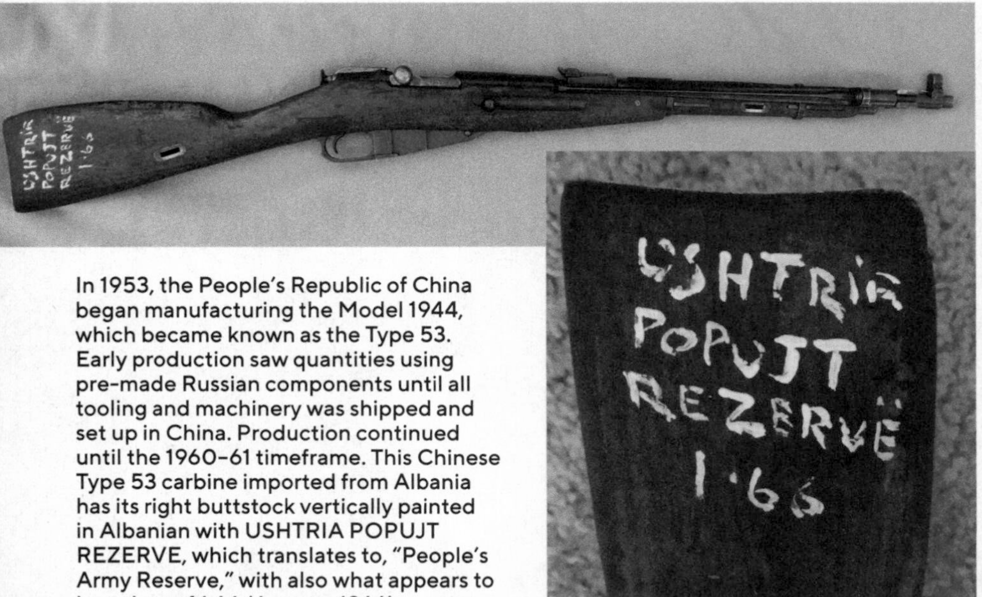

In 1953, the People's Republic of China began manufacturing the Model 1944, which became known as the Type 53. Early production saw quantities using pre-made Russian components until all tooling and machinery was shipped and set up in China. Production continued until the 1960–61 timeframe. This Chinese Type 53 carbine imported from Albania has its right buttstock vertically painted in Albanian with USHTRIA POPUJT REZERVE, which translates to, "People's Army Reserve," with also what appears to be a date of 1.66 (January 1966).

The upper chamber markings of a 1948-manufactured M44 carbine. This was the last year of production of the Mosin-Nagant at the Izhevsk factory in the Soviet Union. Gradually replaced in late 1945 by the semi-automatic SKS, a large number of these obsolescent, post-war, production Model 1944 carbines seem to have been unissued. Thousands of fresh, new, late production carbines, however, were supplied to North Korea from 1949 to 1951. This example appears unissued, unfired and practically new.

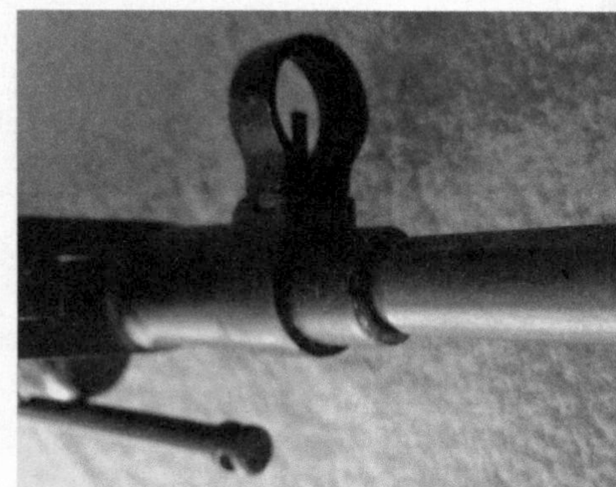

(above) The process of counterboring was primarily undertaken by the Soviet Union in the post-war era. Steel cleaning rods aren't the best for cleaning, and the wearing down of rifling at the crown is almost inevitable with barrels that are not chrome lined. It was found that counterboring was a less expensive procedure than re-barreling, and accuracy returned equally as well. Placing a loaded 7.62mm cartridge nose first into the muzzle as shown will indicate whether a barrel is counterbored. If it is, the cartridge neck will loosely drop to the shoulder. A normal crown would allow a bullet placed as such to grab the rifling and enter about ¼ inch.

Radom, known primarily by its warmly coded name, "Factory 11." It may be accurate to assume that Poland became one of the first countries to manufacture the Model 1944 outside the Soviet Union.

Overall distribution of the M44 was an economic method to spread political ideologies to those countries following the path of Lenin. The Russians were apparently in no hurry to supply nations such as Hungary, Romania, Czechoslovakia and others with their improved SKS or such highly advanced technology as the still-classified AK-47 series of rifles. Not yet at least. By 1953, Romania, Hungary and the People's Republic of China had already received tooling to manufacture the Model 1944, with the latter copping the lion's share of distribution worldwide over the next 40 years. East Germany never manufactured the M1944 but was issued the M44 carbine through Soviet war reserve stocks. Those used by East Germany can be identified by a number one inside a triangle stamped on the chamber, above the year of manufacture.

A comparison of muzzle crowns before and after counterboring. The counterbored Russian M1944 at left versus a standard 7.62mm muzzle at right. The results are obvious, with the larger bore measuring a diameter of .360 inch.

When communist North Korea invaded the South on June 25, 1950, many of the NK regulars were noted to have carried the M44, which were undoubtedly the Russian-made product. At the time, the USSR was the source of North Korea's ordnance pipeline, which shipped across the Tumen River where the North shares an 11-mile border with Russia. With well over 7.5 million Model 1944 carbines manufactured between 1943 and 1948, there were plenty available for everyone. Chinese production of the Model 1944 began in 1953, hence its nomenclature, the Type 53. Production terminated about 1960. China would later temporarily supply the North Koreans with the Type 53 up through the early 1960s. However, one of China's larger recipients was the People's Republic of North Vietnam.

This Model 1944 was imported by PW Arms of Redmond, Washington, sometime in the late 1990s to early 2000s. Note that it has an importation serial number. Most of the Russian-made Model 1944 surplus carbines that were imported and refurbished in the Ukraine were given a matching electro-penciled serial number on many parts. U.S. import law demands that the importer must sequentially issue a new die-stamped serial number to each surplus military rifle prior to release of such arms into the U.S. surplus market. Marked here on several components is an electro-penciled, Cyrillic, "ZN" and the number 813, which is also lightly marked on the bolt. Note the remarked number on the Russian M44 magazine floor plate.

Markings over the chamber of this Type 53 show it was produced at Arsenal 296, followed by Chinese characters that read "Type 53," with a production date of December 1954 over the serial number.

(left) The upper receiver of the Polish-manufactured variant of the Model 1944 have the Circle 11 of the Luczknik factory in Radom, Poland, followed by the year of manufacture and the serial number. Large numbers of the 1990s-era imported versions from Poland have been in arsenal fresh condition.

After a number of temporary duty missions to Vietnam in the early 1970s, while a member of a U.S. Army technical intelligence group, I can attest to viewing rows of mixed captured Chinese Type 53 and Russian-made Model 1944 carbines that were stacked like cordwood at a storage facility near Long Binh. Differences to the Russian variation are minimal, but include the Chinese markings over the chamber, plus the stocks are made from a different type of decay-resistant wood of the Manchurian catalpa tree known locally as Qiu. Its porosity is such that it does not deteriorate in jungle-like, high humidity conditions. Several friends of mine in Vietnam brought Type 53 carbines back to the states as war souvenirs, as they were on the GCA 68 (Gun Control Act of 1968) approved list. Such examples are highly prized by collectors only if they are accompanied by provenance, such as a DD Form 603 capture, and/or import papers. The Type 53 was also supplied by Chinese advisors or sold to several Third World nations in Africa and Latin America.

The Balkans is another area. While working for a government contractor in the 1990s and early 2000s, I was on temporary duty in the former Yugoslavia after the Kosovo crisis and observed numerous Chinese Type 53 carbines that were formerly Albanian communist state property and confiscated from the Kosovo Liberation Army. Since the U.S. ban on Chinese military arms imports in the mid-1990s, limited quantities of the Type 53 carbines have oddly surfaced, at least until the last few years. For unknown reasons, some 2,000 genuine Chinese-imported T-53s were believed held in storage by an importer in Arizona for more than 20 years until released in the late 2000s.

The fanatical Enver Hoxha's Stalinist Albanian government broke with the Soviet Union in 1962 and became closely allied with the People's Republic of China. Not long after, Albania received substantial military aid, which of course included quantities of the Type 53 carbine. As a result, a fair number of Type 53 carbines began being imported from Albania and a few other locations in the Balkan region. Occasional quantities arriving from Albania through Century International have yielded sporadic examples, with painted stock markings in the Albanian language such as "People's Reserve Army," with others having dates or unit numbers and/or other related markings. Most, however, are unmarked. The imported Albanian batches are, for the most part, in only "good" to "good-plus" condition at best, and appear to have experienced substantial use. In addition to receiving assistance from China, Albania in friendlier times is said to have obtained the Russian Model 1944 from the USSR in complete carbines, with parts kits assembled at their own arsenal at the Gramsh factory, some of which used older Mosin-Nagant 91/30 rifles as the basis for the receiver. This, however, has yet to be confirmed. A similar program was undertaken in Bulgaria, which at one time had limited industrial capability and, in turn, modified several thousand 91/30 Mosin-Nagant rifles into

Shown are the chamber markings of two Eastern European-made clones of the Russian Mosin-Nagant Model 1944. On the left is an East German Model 1944, which was not made in the German Democratic Republic. The Soviet Union provided the GDR with Russian-made 1944 carbines, and to distinguish them as such they were stamped with a "1" in a triangle just below the hammer and sickle. The Romanian copy of the Russian M1944 also had a rather short production run, from about 1953 to 1955, and was produced at Factory 21 within the Cugir Arsenal. The receiver markings have the crest of the People's Republic of Romania, or RPR, followed by the year of manufacture and the serial number. At bottom is an arrow inside a triangle.

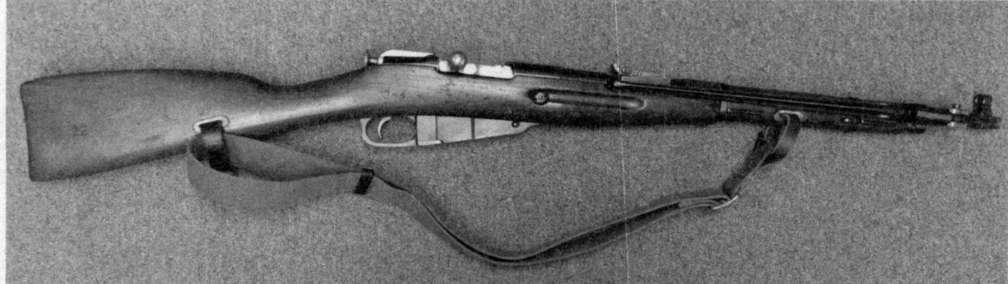

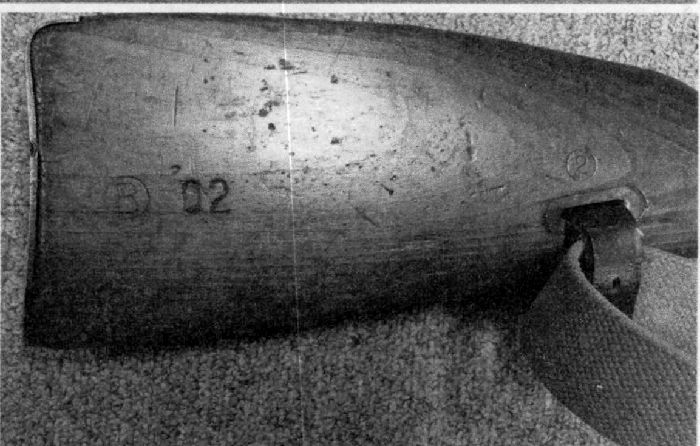

The Hungarian-made version of the Mosin-Nagant M1944, locally known as the Gyalogsagi Karabely M 48 Minta, or Model 1948 Infantry Carbine. The upper receiver is stamped "02" at chamber top, which is the Warsaw Pact country code, followed by the manufacturing date of 1953 with the communist Rakosi crest marked beneath it, followed by the serial number. Hungarian versions are also stamped with the 02 on the right side of the buttstock with a B. They were manufactured from 1952 to late 1953 with a grand total of 160,000 produced.

This photo shows a female Viet Cong guerilla carrying what appears to be a Chinese Type 53 carbine, of which many thousands were supplied by China to communist North Vietnam from the late 1950s on. A fair number of these were brought back to the U.S. by returning Vietnam veterans as trophies of war.

carbines that became known as the 91/59, as we shall later see.

In the late 1990s, the Eastern European copies of the Model 1944 from Poland, Hungary and Romania were imported into the United States with many in "very good" to "like new" condition. A large number of the Polish examples arrived in pristine condition and appear practically unissued. Aside from in the Hungarian Revolution of 1956, few of the Eastern European-made copies of the Model 1944 were used in action, with the exception of those sold to North Vietnam or other global areas of conflict such as Angola or Nicaragua during the 1970s. In 1988, members of my Army intelligence detachment and I had a rare chance to observe some of the captured crates of Model 1944 carbines, stored at Aberdeen Proving Grounds, that were taken during the Grenada operation of 1983. Examination revealed there were variants with Chinese, Polish and Russian markings. It's believed that the majority of those M44 carbines and clones clandestinely arrived in Grenada via Cuba, with many packed in cases marked Oficina Economica Cubana (Cuban Economic Office).

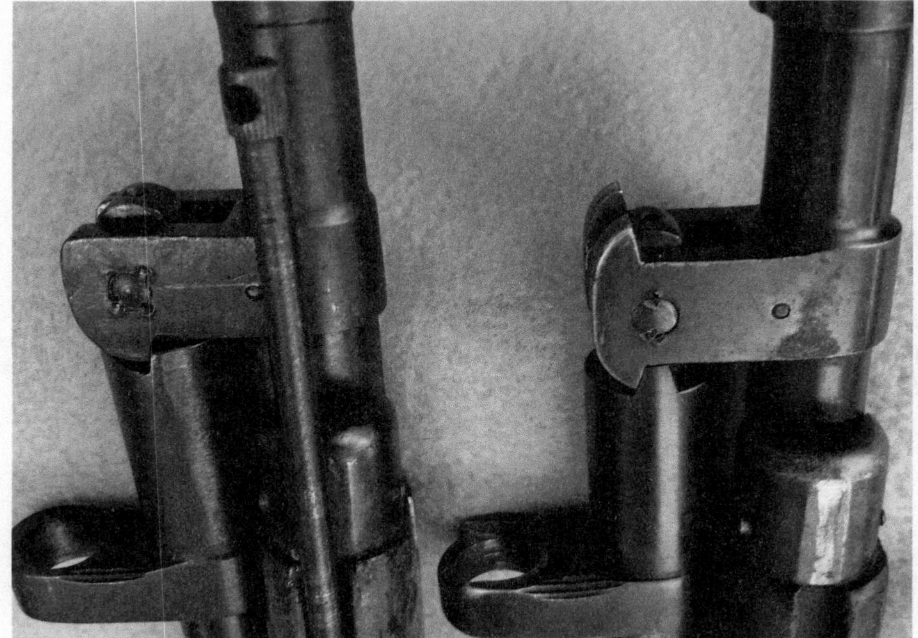

One of the post-war modifications made to latter-production Russian Model 1944 carbines and foreign offspring was the widening of the bayonet swivel flange. At left is the pre-1945 style, which shows the rear tip of the bayonet exposed. The improved mount has what appears to be a mushroom-shaped configuration that protects the rear tip when the bayonet is in the closed position. Close observation of the Chinese Type 53 at right shows the sides of the bayonet fastening ring were also lengthened.

Using the Albanian-marked Chinese Type 53 copy of the Russian Model 1944 carbine with TulAmmo brand ammunition, the upper five-shot group was fired at 65 yards offhand. Groups run from 3 to 7 inches. The open adjustable rear sight and hooded post front sight of these carbines are strictly intended for combat-size targets and not precision clusters. Using a rest position, the bottom target printed far tighter. However, consistent 1-inch groups were not the norm. All in all, despite its short sight radius, the author was satisfied with the results.

A feature common to Russian Mosin-Nagant M1944 carbines is that most arsenal reworked examples were counterbored at the crown of the muzzle. The reason stems from improper maintenance and lack of use of the muzzle protector/cap during cleaning. This accessory is supplied with the standard Mosin-Nagant cleaning kit and its main purpose is to keep the cleaning rod centered and away from the rifling at the tip of the muzzle. Frequent contact of the issued steel cleaning rod against the rifling at the crown eventually wears the lands down and affects accuracy over time. To remedy those afflicted carbines or rifles, the counterbored muzzle was reamed from one to three inches to a flat stop point, returning accuracy to normal. The bore above this point is, of course, nothing more than smooth, over-bored, dead space that merely allows a higher degree of unburnt powder to follow the bullet as it leaves the muzzle, increasing the muzzle flash. The easiest method to detect whether a rifle has been counterbored is to put a 7.62x54mm cartridge nose first into the muzzle. If the rifling does not grab the bullet, the oversize bore will allow the cartridge neck to slide down and stop at the shoulder. A quick way to measure how far a barrel has been counterbored is to simply place a cigarette into the muzzle and measure its stop point on the first flat step where the counterboring ends. Arms depots in the Ukraine were well known for performing this procedure primarily on M44 carbines of Russian make.

The immense fireball produced at the muzzle by unburnt powder coupled with the short carbine length is highly apparent for a microsecond. Recoil of the Model 1944 carbine is far more noticeable compared to the heavier 91/30 Mosin-Nagant rifle. Use of the sling is a great boon to accurate offhand shooting, not to mention helping the body to roll, consistent with the sharp recoil. Photo: Shawn Kelly

Regarding other modifications, it is important to note that there are two types of bayonet mounts. The earliest versions of the M44 did not have a protective lip on the swivel point of the bayonet mount to protect the exposed protrusion at the rear portion of the bayonet. Without this mushroom-like addition, the cruciform bayonet base could be bent by a violent drop, preventing it from swiveling to the right into the open position. An alteration was implemented during the post-war period on new production arms. From the 1960s until the early 1990s, the Model 1944 carbine in any of its variations was a difficult item to find. The only examples in circulation were, again, those that were brought home by veterans from both the Korean or Vietnam wars as combat souvenirs. Interestingly, many of the Type 53 or M44 carbines brought back from Vietnam were occasionally presented to departing officers or NCOs, many times with a mounted plaque and inscription from grateful, fellow unit members as a token of gratitude for faithful service.

Ironically, the Model 1944 carbine continues to see use in the world especially by various ad hoc insurgent organizations worldwide. Several decades ago, a Reuters photograph of captured arms from the Angolan Civil War showed dozens of well-used M1944 carbines in a sizeable cache of ordnance. The M44 is still commonly carried by some Somalian local militia organizations. In addition, AP news video of a Syrian rebel firing an M44 was aired in 2013. Furthermore, current intelligence summaries indicate this bolt-action carbine is still in use by such terrorist baddies as Al Qaeda, ISIS and other radical groups. Since importation began on and off in the 1990s to 2000s, all variants of the M44 have become highly popular with American collectors and its cartridge is an especially great favorite with shooters. There is, however, another Mosin-Nagant carbine of the Cold War era that deserves mention here.

THE MOSIN-NAGANT 1891/59 CARBINE

In the late 1950s, the Cold War was at a pinnacle. Several Warsaw Pact countries had the notion that an attack from the West was imminent, and of course the U-2 spy plane incident on May 1, 1960, didn't help matters. One communist country of Eastern Europe that was basically an agrarian economy was Bulgaria. Though having a limited industrial capability in the ordnance field, Bulgaria's old Artillery Arsenal under its communist government was renamed the Friedrich Engels Machine Works, among other names at various times. Located in central Bulgaria at Kazanlak, it was also code-named Factory 10, and in 1959 would take on a role in the refurbishment of converting over a million Mosin-Nagant 91/30 rifles into carbines. Since 1945, Bulgaria was normally armed with older, hand-me-down small arms, such as the World War II vintage non-communist caliber 8x56R in the Steyr 95 Stutzen carbine, which was issued to low-level security forces and prison guards and remained in service as late as the 1970s. It is now known that the aforementioned 91/30 rifles slated for overhaul were shipped to Bulgaria directly from the USSR.

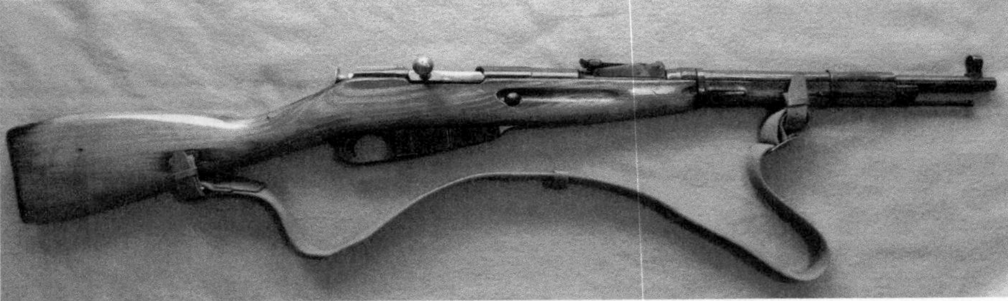

The Model 1891/59 Bulgarian conversion is one of the most intriguing carbines of the Mosin-Nagant family of military arms of the Cold War era. It retains the original Model 91/30 rifle rear sight versus the shorter Model 1938 or 1944-type carbine sight. The 91/59 was not intended for use with a bayonet, and all appear to have been superbly reconditioned, with most stocks taking on a blondish appearance.

This program and its entire concept is an enigma to this day. The million-plus converted rifles would become known as the Model 1891/59 Carbine. The oddity of it was the fact that there were countless millions of the Model 1944 carbine in the Soviet Union in reserve, as well as in various Warsaw Pact member countries, so the reasoning for refurbishing a seven-figure total of well-used rifles is truly vexing. The 91/59 carbines are, for the most part, reconfigured surplus World War II vintage Mosin-Nagant 1891/30 rifles with barrels shortened to 20 1/4 inches, with most of the refinished, birchwood stocks and handguards taking on a blondish appearance. These carbines also retain their old rifle sights. However, the 1,110- to 2,000-meter markings on the rear sight were ground off, leaving the sights adjustable from only 100 to 1,000 meters.

While doing research for my latest book, Handguns of the Communist Bloc, I was fortunate through the assistance of a Russian collector to have been able to contact a former employee of the current Bulgarian Arsenal AD who retired in 1993. One Mr. Dimitru M. had been a technician for the old Factory 10 during the communist era and was hired not long before 1960. In addition to questions on handguns, I was also anxious to query him regarding Bulgaria's role in the 91/59 conversion, simply because many American collectors have been skeptical of this. He explained that a project in late 1959 was indeed undertaken by the Bulgarian government at the behest of the Soviet Union to provide a million or more such carbines for both Bulgaria and, if needed, Czechoslovakia. Specifically, these carbines were produced for future contingency use by the Bulgarian People's Militia, with an undisclosed number of them to be returned and stored at the Balakleya Armory in the Ukraine.

The rework program lasted until 1963–64, he recollected, with most of the rifles from Russia received by ship at the Bulgarian port of Varna, then transported overland to Factory 10 at Kazanlak. He never learned exactly why the Soviet Union ordered more carbines to be converted, but was only told that they were to rework large numbers of older 91/30 rifles in dire need of repair into a carbine configuration. Ironically, Bulgaria wished to manufacture the Russian Makarov pistol about this time, and Mr. Dimitru strongly feels that the Soviets were testing the ability of the Bulgarians prior to licensing them, and providing the tooling to produce the Makarov, which they did beginning slowly in 1970. In any case, the Model 91/59 began to arrive in the United States from surplus importers in the late 2000s and were a previously unknown variation in the American market.

There is no provision to fix a standard Mosin-Nagant rifle bayonet on these 7 1/2-pound carbines, given their larger diameter at the muzzle. Practically all that have come into the U.S. appear unissued and are very serviceable conversions. They are the last modified variation of

THE CARE AND FEEDING OF SURPLUS AMMO FOR THE MOSIN-NAGANT

Using the commercially available Russian-made non-corrosive, TulAmmo in 7.62x54mm (left), I found its 122-grain bullet maintained a more satisfactory grouping on a per shot basis than some of the 1950s and '60s vintage Cold War-era surplus fodder. Beneath the 20-round TulAmmo box at left is a 15-round pack of Yugoslavian-made (now Serbia) Privi Partizan surplus ammunition with a headstamp date of 1985. I feel it is some of the highest-quality milsurp ammunition available, however stocks of it have dried up since the 1990s. The unmarked, 20-round box at top far right is Bulgarian 7.62x54mm Russian surplus dated 1960. Shown from left is TulAmmo's Berdan-primed steel-cased cartridge, which of course is non-reloadable. In the center is the 1960 vintage, Bulgarian, copper-cased 7.62 Russian cartridge produced at the Kazanlak Arsenal.

Supplies of this ammunition are still found rather commonly and are often sold in 20-round boxes, as shown, or can be purchased in the 440-round "spam can." Compared to the 1990's $88 to $100.00 price tag, much of this bulk ammo currently runs for prices in $150.00 to $200.00 range. At far right, the Yugoslavian PPU cartridge is one of the best surplus buys for the money. Still offered commercially today and made in Serbia, it can be seen that even in the communist days they nonetheless utilized high quality, annealed brass cases with consistent powder charges and practically no misfires.

After shooting Iron Curtain surplus corrosive fodder, I spray my barrels down while at the range with ammonia-based Windex to break up the mercuric priming salts, making standard bore maintenance at home an easier task. Left uncleaned for even a few hours – especially in humid weather – the corrosive potassium chlorate priming compound quickly attacks the bore, which can lead to severe pitting over time.

Though this one-time 91/30 Mosin-Nagant rifle was manufactured at the Izhevsk Mechanical Plant in 1942, those of its ilk were remarked during the Bulgarian conversion program at Factory 10 with 1891/59 cartouches, and appear to have been re-serial numbered, or rather, force numbered.

the Mosin-Nagant known in modern times. Whether any had been exported to communist-inclined Third World countries is unknown, although it is reported one collector observed a single example said to have been brought back from the Vietnam War. As with the Model 1944 family of carbines, the 91/59 is truly one of the most enigmatic Mosin-Nagant carbines of the Cold War era.

Of noteworthy mention is when Hungary was licensed to manufacture the Model 1944 at its FEG factory in Budapest, a mere 160,000 were produced from 1952 to 1953 at 80,000 per year. The Hungarian version is known as the Mosina Gyalogsagi Karabely 48 Minta, or rather the Mosin Model 1948 Infantry Carbine. These well-made clones had stocks of beech with a sheen-like finish and were marked with the Hungarian Warsaw Pact code of 02 throughout. The upper chamber is stamped with a date, serial number and the crest of Matyas Rakosi, whose brutal regime was deposed by Janos Kadar following the Hungarian Revolution of 1956. Period photographs show many of these M48 carbines in the hands of Hungarian freedom fighters who put them to good use against invading Soviet troops, which explains why many of those imported seem to show signs of heavy to moderate usage. Being of Hungarian ancestry myself, I also learned why almost all of those U.S.-imported M48 carbines do not have matching serial numbered bolts. Two of my uncles who were former Hungarian Army NCOs during the revolution explained that when the dust settled, all Mosin-Nagant M48 carbines and rifles were later rounded up by both Soviet and Hungarian troops and had had their bolts removed and thrown into crates separate from the rifles. All were later shipped to be stored in Romania and, interestingly, the majority of the surplus Hungarian rifles and carbines were imported to the U.S. from Romania during the surplus boom of the 1990s! It is perhaps for this reason that many Hungarian M48 carbines are often found with Romanian-made Model 1944 carbine bolts along with other mismatching components.

Introduced in 1891, the 7.62x54 Mosin-Nagant is without question the longest lasting military rifle system and cartridge ever devised, one that has been in continuous service throughout the world since its inception. From the Boxer Rebellion in 1900 to the more recent War of the Donbass in the Ukraine, not to mention the ongoing Syrian Civil War, it

has participated in more conflicts than can be counted. Even the U.S. used both rifle and cartridge during the Northern Russian troubles between the "reds and whites" in 1919. Availability-wise, the choice of both surplus and commercial ammunition is unlimited and can be located practically anywhere. It should be kept in mind that the 7.62 Russian cartridge has a moderately hefty recoil with even the longer Model 91/30 rifle. The M1944 carbine tips the scales at about 9 pounds and is rather weighty for an arm of its size. Using surplus ammunition of heavier bullet weights, recoil becomes noticeable on the pocket of the shoulder after about 20 or fewer rounds. Firing offhand with various types of surplus fodder at 100 yards, the M44 will holds its own with 5- to 6-inch groups on the average. However, bench-rested using commercial-made Tulammo 122-grain FMC ammunition will shrink

Left view of the receiver tells us this 91/59 carbine was originally a wartime production Mosin-Nagant given the rounded contour of the side of the frame. A wartime shortcut to speed up manufacture, those Mosin-Nagant rifles and carbines made from 1945 to end of production in 1948 returned to the earlier, original, scalloped-type receiver sides.

groups to 4 to 4-1/2 inches. Though never a tack-driver by any sense of the word, accuracy is nevertheless satisfactory within military standards.

It is interesting to note that the 7.62 Russian is also cataloged in Winchester's metric ammunition line. Many shooters, however, have found that installation of a recoil pad on the M44 will make the shooting day a noticeably more comfortable one. From the business end, in early evening or on an overcast day, the tremendous flash of unburnt powder from the muzzle of the short 20 1/2-inch barrel with different varieties of Eastern European surplus ball ammunition is very noticeable. The Russian-produced M44 carbines imported to the U.S. have, for the most, hailed from the Ukraine and were primarily leftovers stored there since the breakup of the Soviet Union. For the modern collector however, the Model 1944 carbine is great area in which to base a collecting theme, as there are plenty of variants available. Realistically speaking, an attempt to start collecting all Mosin-Nagant rifles and carbines would be a two-plus lifetime challenge, as several hundred variations that were manufactured from 1891 through the 1960s. With more than 37 to 50 million of all Mosin-Nagant military arms produced worldwide, such a venture would be a near impossibility. Thus, for those who wish to zero in specifically, the last mass-produced variant of Colonel Sergei Ivanovich Mosin's design would again do well to choose the M44 and/or its clones. It may be an obsolete, slower firing bolt action in semi-automatic rifle times, but rest assured, in hands both good and bad, it is still in service somewhere in the world, and is widely available and immensely popular in the United States.

During the Vietnam War, both Chinese Type 53 and Model 1944 Mosin-Nagant carbines were popular bring-back souvenirs, as they complied with the GCA of '68. In addition, enemy-captured examples were popular farewell gifts to military officers and NCOs returning to the States, and oftentimes were presented complete with a metal or brass plaque reflecting the individual's name and unit, as the examples shown. Such specimens complete with import/DD Form 603 capture papers greatly enhance values. Photos: Adrian Van Dyk Collection

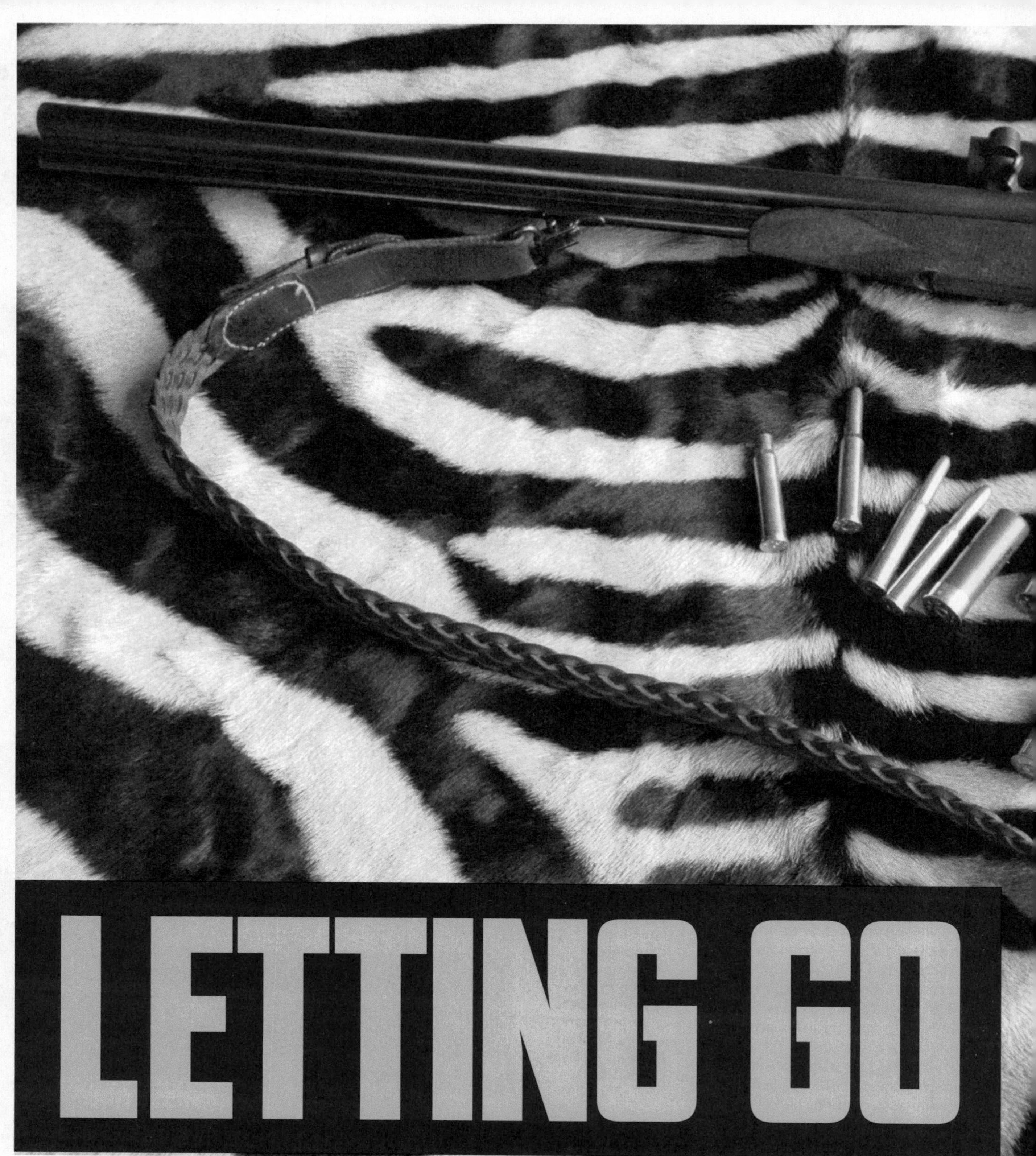

LETTING GO

Passing On the Guns You Cherish is the Best Way to Preserve Them

BY **TOM CACECI**

This beautiful ***Burgsmüller*** drilling was made in Germany in 1940. Like virtually all drillings of similar vintage, it came to the USA as a war souvenir brought home by some returning GI. The author hunted with it in the U.S. for a few seasons, taking deer and an enormous feral hog, then it went with him on his second Namibian safari, where he became convinced that it is truly an "all-around gun." It's earmarked for a close friend of his.

BY MEDICINE LIFE MAY BE PROLONG'D;
YET DEATH WILL SEIZE THE DOCTOR, TOO.
– WILLIAM SHAKESPEARE, CYMBELINE, ACT V, SCENE 5

It comes to all of us in time: the moment when we're compelled to admit our own mortality and think about what we should do with material objects, most especially those which have fascinated us, enriched our lives, and given us a means to pursue adventure. Humans tend to get attached to "things." Guns and hunting equipment, in particular, acquire a personal emotional significance that's hard to comprehend for those who don't shoot or hunt.

Nevertheless, it's a reality. Think about that first .22 rifle you found under a Christmas tree as a youngster, of the shotgun bequeathed to you by a revered grandparent or uncle, or a firearm you may own that's connected to some major event in history. These aren't just "things," they're symbols of personal achievement or markers of life's milestones. Since the gun will likely long outlast its owner, it isn't a trivial matter to consider what you'll do with yours when it's time to quit, and what should happen when you're no longer able to use or even keep it.

Ultimately, there are only two practical options: sell or give it away. The decision about which course of action is best is based on many considerations, not the least of which is just how to pass along not only the objects, but the values and tradition they represent.

SELLING GUNS

If you decide to sell your guns, recognize that you probably aren't going to make much, if any, money. It's certainly not impossible, but unless what you have to sell is something you bought many years ago with intrinsic appeal to collectors or shooters, or something with commercial value that has risen well beyond the inflation-adjusted price, you'll probably break even at best. A realistic attitude about the commercial value of the gun you want to sell is important. Many pricing guides are available, both in print and online — the Standard Catalog of Firearms is a must-have — and they're kept reasonably up to date, but in the end they're only guides. "Book value" is a fluid concept: any given firearm may sell for less or more than "book" depending on uncontrollable factors. The region of the country in which you live, the laws that apply to what you want to sell, the time of year, and most of all rarity and condition, all affect the price you'll get. No price guide can take all these factors into account in making estimates. It pays to use a guide but, as the saying goes, it's only worth what someone will pay, so it's advisable to follow sales of similar items at online auction sites and in shops. What you'll get is what someone thinks the gun is worth to him or her, not what it's worth to you.

As an early teen, the author convinced his father to buy him a .22 rifle, a Remington Nylon 11. One of the first production runs in 1962, the Nylon rifles are significant collector items today and command amazing prices, but this one has been delineated in his will to go to one of his young relatives. It's not for sale at any price.

LEGALITIES

One thing to keep in mind is that any transfer of a firearm must be done in strict compliance with both federal and state law. If a friend or relative wants to buy the gun and he or she is a resident of the same state as you, usually you can sell it directly. Federal laws generally don't apply to intrastate private party transfers and, while in most states no paperwork is required for a direct private party transfer, in some it is, so find out. Anything that crosses a state line must go to and through a Federal Firearms License (FFL) holder unless it's a legal "antique" as defined in the Gun Control Act of 1968 — and a few states even require paperwork on these.

THE MECHANICS OF A SALE

Most of us don't "invest" in guns. We buy them because we like them, without any real thought of making money. Over the course of an active life in the shooting sports, we tend to acquire a number that are "just guns," with no special personal significance. These are the easy ones, you sell them for what they can bring. There are several ways to do this. Perhaps the best option is to sell directly to a friend who's expressed admiration for one of them and is interested in buying it. If you belong to a shooting or hunting club, an offer sent to the general membership is another good way to find a buyer who'll be known to you as trustworthy and legally able to own the gun you want to sell.

Be very wary of using newspaper advertisements or "penny-saver" type newsletters. Regrettably, a lot of shady characters routinely scan these hoping to find a gun for sale with no paper trail and no questions asked. If you do decide to try such an ad, always demand identification and proof of residency and eligibility and check the validity of an address or phone number on publicly available databases. If you smell a rat, turn down the offer; the faintest whiff of illegality should send you running like a scared deer.

This caution also applies to some online sites. There's at least one such specifically dedicated to firearms sales which, in my experience, is frequently a source of problems. It tends to attract scammers and potentially illegal buyers. If you use any listing site that creates a direct contact between seller and buyer be very, very cautious

(top) The author bought this SMLE when he was in the U.S. Air Force long ago. It was made in 1923 at the Small Arms Factory in Lithgow, Australia, a year in which very few rifles were made. About 10 years ago, at the request of the Lithgow Museum, he donated it to complete the "rifle fan" that is the centerpiece of their collection of factory production.

(above) The Lithgow factory produced Lee-Enfield rifles for the Australian armed forces beginning in 1913. This massive display replicates the "Rising Sun" cap badge their soldiers wear, recreating it with rifles from every year of production. The SMLE the author donated is the eleventh one counting from the left side of the display. While it will never be fired again, as part of this historical exhibit it's safe from destruction, a source of considerable satisfaction.

with whom you deal, and absolutely insist on a face-to-face meeting. Never deal with an unknown buyer any other way. People can be and have been held liable for criminal acts committed with guns they sold without "due diligence," so it's far better and safer to deal with someone you know personally or to route the sale through a dealer who can take care of the legal niceties.

DEALER CONSIGNMENTS

If you haven't got a friend or acquaintance who's a potential buyer, consider a consignment or auction sale. Sometimes a dealer will offer to buy a gun outright and enter it into his shop's inventory, but consignments are a better deal for him because he doesn't have to invest anything in the gun up front.

Consignment sales via a local gun shop are pretty much hit-or-miss affairs. Sometimes the gun will sell immediately while other times it will languish for months or years before a buyer comes along. The larger the shop, the bigger its customer base and the better the chance of a quick sale. You'll have to pay the dealer a fee or commission to handle the sale for you. A dealer earns his money by providing safe storage and following all legally required steps for a transfer, including a background check. The risk that a consigned gun might end up in the hands of a prohibited person is minimized, and any potential liability risk is transferred to the dealer.

When you bring the gun to the dealer, you'll discuss the price you want to get, and the dealer considers their profit and marks it up from there. Ideally, they'll have a fairly good idea of the value of the gun in the local market and will be able to advise you about a realistic net amount to expect from the sale after expenses and commission are covered. Once a deal is struck, the dealer will log the gun into their "bound book," and upon selling it log it out again to the buyer. This not only ensures that the law is followed, it insulates you from a buyer who comes to regret his purchase later (it happens) and demands a refund.

An FFL dealer's commission can range from 10 to 25 percent, but sometimes the percentage can be negotiated. A large gun shop with a good client base will be likely to expose the gun to great numbers of possible buyers. If the shop owner attends gun shows, thousands of potential purchasers may get a chance to see and perhaps handle it. It's generally not a good idea to sell at a gun show by paying for a table and doing it directly. It's perfectly legal to do this, but it opens you up to a number of hazards, including direct liability for a sale to a prohibited person, not to mention the cost to rent the table.

This Savage 110 is a plain-vanilla rifle without much in the way of commercial value, but it has served the author well over the 20-odd years he's had it. He hunted with it in the U.S. for many deer seasons and took it to Africa on his first safari. It's taken a lot of large plains game. This is another one that won't ever be sold, but instead will go to a young friend and fellow hunter via provisions of his will.

Another very unfortunate risk is that plain-clothes police or ATF agents will cruise a show with the deliberate intention of entrapping an unwary private seller into a "straw man" purchase (meaning someone who is eligible to buy the gun purchases it and transfers it to someone who isn't) — highly illegal. One or two states allow private parties to use their background check system, but most don't. Since you likely won't know your buyer personally at a show, better to let a licensee handle such sales. If you get caught in the trap it will be very expensive and difficult to escape charges for an "illegal" sale. The complexities of firearms laws vary from state to state and the ins and outs of federal law are difficult for a non-licensee to navigate. Play it safe at gun shows.

One drawback to a dealer consignment is that if you later decide not to sell and to recover your gun (this possibility is always included as part of the agreement) you'll have to go through the background check and any other legal steps, just as if you were buying it for the first time. It seems absurd that you should have to jump through legal hoops to retrieve your own property, but that's the way the law is written. Nobody says it has to make sense.

AUCTION SALES

Another option is to sell at an auction, either live or online. Many local auctioneers specialize in firearms sales. Many of them participate in a nationwide Internet auction listing service by which people all over the country can place bids. All the very large well-established firms that typically handle high-dollar collectors' guns do this, but a lot of small houses do so as well. The online aspect of such auctions can potentially expose the gun to tens of thousands — perhaps hundreds of thousands — of likely buyers. Usually such auctions are conducted not just online, but simultaneously with a live auction for the same items. The real money is in the online bidding because so many more bidders can be accommodated. This is a good option if you're selling a very rare, fully provenanced gun with a connection to some famous person. Valuable collector guns should get as much exposure as possible to affluent bidders.

The big-name houses provide just that. If you're lucky enough to own such a firearm, one of the high-end houses is probably the best sales venue, while it wouldn't be for a plain-vanilla, run-of-the-mill mass-produced gun. If your grandfather brought home a mint-condition Luftwaffe-issue drilling with its original case and accessories from WWII, one of the "name" houses is your best bet. For most people and most guns, it isn't.

The drawbacks to any auction (especially for non-collector guns) are steep sales commissions that run 18-20 percent, and the fact that auction houses invariably charge an additional "buyer's premium," which may push the final price of the gun out of the reasonable range. It's one thing if you're selling a

This Thompson-Center New Englander is another one of those "special" guns the author will never sell but will pass along to someone who will appreciate it. He hunted with it for many years in the U.S. and took it to Namibia on his second safari, where he used it to take this trophy warthog. A firearm used in a memorable hunting expedition becomes more than "just a gun," it becomes woven into the fabric of the experience.

genuine Colt Model 1860 Army with iron-clad provenance (and preferably a factory letter of origin) that belonged to one of your ancestors who fought in the Civil War and whose use in a major battle can be proven. It's quite another matter if you're offering a modern mass-produced gun.

Let's say you have a RemChester autoloading shotgun that you feel is — and likely is — well worth $350.00. You consign it to a medium-sized auction house, which puts it into an upcoming sale with "no reserve," that is, a starting price of whatever the first bidder thinks is a good deal. The gun garners bids. If you take from that $350 the 18 percent you pay in sales commission, you'd actually net only $287 … but the buyer pays the auction house the $350, plus another 20 percent plus shipping to his local FFL holder, plus a fee for a background check. That $350 shotgun, from the buyer's viewpoint, is now a $420 shotgun, before shipping and FFL fees are added. Tack on another $50 to $100 and many potential buyers will simply pass.

There are other auction options. Several well-established online listing services are run on an auction basis. They're called "auction sites," but they aren't really, because they don't take the gun into possession and sell it for you as a surrogate. You retain it in your possession and list it on the site. When the online auction is completed, you ship the gun to a receiving FFL holder and they take it from there. These services are preferable to the direct-contact sites because normally a bidder must be registered with the site, some degree of credit checking has been done, and the mechanics of the actual transfer nearly always involve using a dealer to handle the final step.

Commissions at online listing sites are fairly low, ranging from 2.5 to 5 percent. Let's go back to that $350 shotgun. Assuming you pay the listing service 3 percent, you'll net about $340. You can legitimately ask the buyer to pay a reasonable shipping charge to send it to his Federal Firearms License holder for final transfer. One snag is that if you're not an FFL holder, when you go to ship it you may run into a stubborn licensee who simply won't accept a gun from a private party. Some insist it must come from another FFL holder — which is not required by federal law, though some states have this provision in their codes — so you get stuck with transfer and service fees on your end. Federal law clearly and specifically allows a dealer licensee to accept a firearm in interstate commerce from anyone, but some shop owners simply don't care what the law says and won't do it. It's always best to make a specific point in your ad that the buyer should assure that his chosen transfer agent is willing to accept the gun directly from a private party. Another problem is that if the buyer is dissatisfied (he is, after all, buying the gun sight unseen) and wants to return it, you'll have to go through all the rigmarole with a transfer at your end just to get it back.

When you reach the point of shipping to the dealer, be aware that unlicensed individuals can ship long guns via the U.S. postal system, but not handguns, which must go by common carrier. This is usually at a modest additional cost compared to the U.S. Postal Service (USPS), but private carriers typically have better tracking and notification than the USPS and in my opinion are worth what they cost.

The large online sites have high-volume sellers who work on a reasonable commission basis. Instead of listing a gun yourself, you ship it to one of these FFL dealers and have them sell it for you via the site. Such second-party sellers typically have a very high reputation among the site's users and will almost always get a higher final price than you would as a private seller, even if they put the gun up at a very low start price. If you decide to use a second-party seller, pick one who does a really good job with photography. Good pictures sell guns faster than any other factor in online auctions, and good gun photography is an art. Look over a site to get a feel for who the "best sellers" are and how they present consigned items. Second-party sellers charge a commission in the range of 10-18 percent depending on the final value, but they not only offer the same advantages of a local dealer, they have a larger reach thanks to the national coverage of the sites they use.

AMMUNITION

Disposing of ammunition is marginally simpler than firearms. You can include it in the price of the sale, which is usually a good idea if the gun fires some oddball caliber that's not easy to find. Most states have no laws against buying "mail order" ammunition, but a few do. In those cases, the stuff must go through a state-licensed dealer, which adds expense. Better to sell it or give it away locally if your buyer is in one of these states. The online gun auction sites will usually have a listing category specifically for ammunition. Alerting your club or relatives to its availability is also a good idea.

GIVING GUNS AWAY

I've sometimes regretted selling a gun, but I've given away quite a few and I've never regretted that. There are many reasons to give away a gun, not the least of which is that making it a gift really serves the shooting community. You don't get any money out of it, but it's a form of investment in the future of the shooting sports. It's a regrettable fact that in recent decades the number of active hunters and shooters has declined as the population has aged. Furthermore, the constant demonization of gun ownership by the press and broadcast media has become ever more ferocious as they campaign to make the shooting sports socially unacceptable. By passing a treasured firearm along to a new generation you help perpetuate time-honored activities. The recipient of the gift immediately becomes a vested, active participant in the fight to maintain the right to keep and bear arms, and to continue the traditions of hunting and field sports.

This Ruger Standard Autoloading Pistol was purchased by the author as a college student in the mid-1960s. It's been used for the past half-century as a plinker, to train new shooters and for small game hunting. It's another one of those guns with importance in his hunting and shooting life, one that will go to his younger brother.

WHO GETS WHAT?

In some ways, giving away a favorite firearm is like finding a new home for a pet you can no longer keep. You want to know it'll go to someone who'll cherish and care for it properly. It's likely you already know someone who'd be a good choice — a son, daughter, niece, nephew or grandchild. Perhaps you mentored him or her and feel the time is ripe. If you do, there's no better time than right now to make the gift. If you've had the thought that one of your younger relatives or friends would appreciate the gun, go ahead.

Even if you don't have a relative in mind there are other options. Perhaps you're actively involved with firearms or hunter training as a hunter education instructor, or you're a summer camp or high school rifle team coach, a scout troop merit badge counselor or a mentor for a 4H club. Organizations committed to training young people in shooting have active programs that will welcome donations of firearms and ammunition. They're especially appropriate recipients of donations of small-caliber rifles and simple shotguns for training. Such organizations are a fine contact point and a conduit to young shooters as well as an excellent way to encourage participation in the sport. Incidentally, a gift to groups like these safeguards you from the standpoint of personal liability.

Probably there's a chapter of the Friends of NRA not far from you. This non-profit group is specifically dedicated to encouraging youth shooting. There are other worthy hunting and conservation-based charities including Ducks Unlimited, Quail Unlimited, Rocky Mountain Elk Foundation, Izaak Walton League and many others with youth programs. Local chapters typically raise money through annual banquets with raffles and games. Donating a gun as a prize advances the cause directly and gives you as the donor a small tax deduction.

One of the best and most satisfying ways to pass on a firearm to those who will truly appreciate it is to give it to a museum, something that's especially appropriate when it has significant historic or collector value. I once owned a No. 1 Mark III Lee-Enfield rifle that was manufactured at the Small Arms Factory in Lithgow, Australia in 1923. Very few SMLE's were made in Lithgow that year.

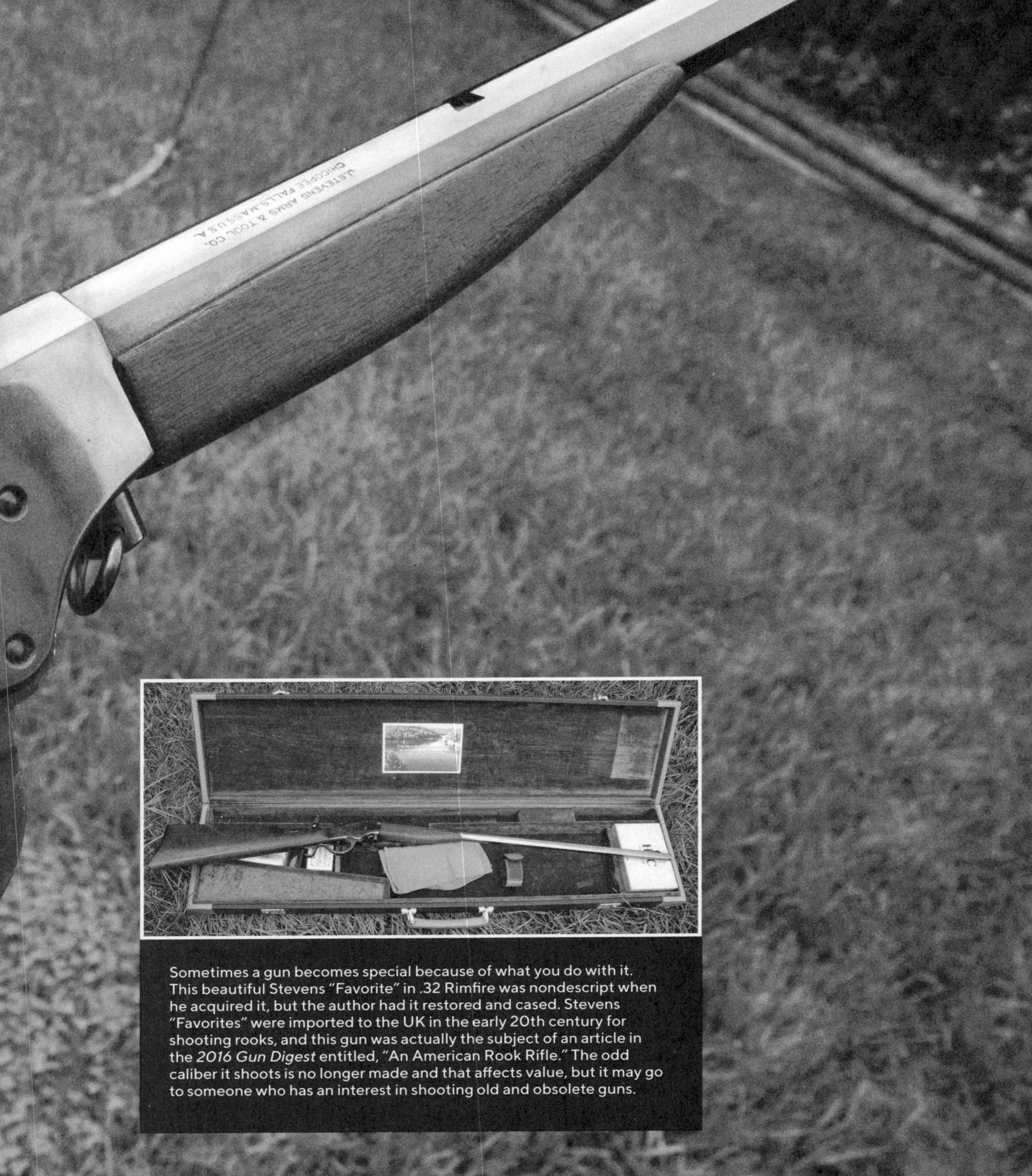

Sometimes a gun becomes special because of what you do with it. This beautiful Stevens "Favorite" in .32 Rimfire was nondescript when he acquired it, but the author had it restored and cased. Stevens "Favorites" were imported to the UK in the early 20th century for shooting rooks, and this gun was actually the subject of an article in the *2016 Gun Digest* entitled, "An American Rook Rifle." The odd caliber it shoots is no longer made and that affects value, but it may go to someone who has an interest in shooting old and obsolete guns.

Somehow, the Small Arms Factory Museum learned I owned it, tracked me down and asked if I would send it to them to complete an elaborate display that was to be the centerpiece of their collection, because even the factory didn't have a 1923 example. I was happy to do so and shipped it to them. I'm very satisfied because that little piece of history "went home" to the place where it was made and perhaps the Aussie soldier who carried it into battle may someday see it!

Some museums are specialized, with gun collections associated with various eras or events in our country's history. All of them will happily take donated guns. Museums dedicated to commemorating the Civil War or the Westward expansion are obvious places where guns of those eras would be welcome gifts should you own one. Other museums are less specialized, but very prestigious and professionally run. The National Firearms Museum in the suburbs of Washington, DC, has a vast collection open to the public. Most of the NFM's collection — only a part of which is on display — came to it via donation. I've sent them several guns, including one I inherited from my late father-in-law — a scarce Sauer und Sohn Behordenmodel pistol that he brought home as a war souvenir in 1945. I gave it to the NFM in honor of his service to the country and I could think of no more fitting place for it to be. That pistol is now part of their World War II display and I take considerable satisfaction in knowing that it's not only properly curated, but that it's also safe from those whose hatred for all guns would lead them to wantonly throw such artifacts into a smelter.

There isn't a better example of how a museum donation can save a historic artifact from destruction than the most famous hunting firearm ever: the Holland & Holland double rifle President Theodore Roosevelt used on his famous 1909 safari. It's now a prominent display item at the Frazier Museum of History in Louisville, Kentucky, a tangible connection between today's public, the life and legacy of a great man, and a long-gone era. It is preserved forever thanks to the generosity of its former owners.

CONCLUSION

Let's face facts, none of us are getting any younger, and our hobbies and interests won't last forever. It's imperative that we plan for the future, that we do whatever we can to save those things and those traditions we revere. We must leave a real legacy for the next generation, to ensure there is a next generation of shooters and hunters. Honest and serious contemplation of how best to let go of today's tangible possessions — one's cherished gun collection — is an essential part of protecting the intangible values we all share.

Editor's Note: For firearm values online, visit gunvalues.gundigest.com to search gun values by make and model.

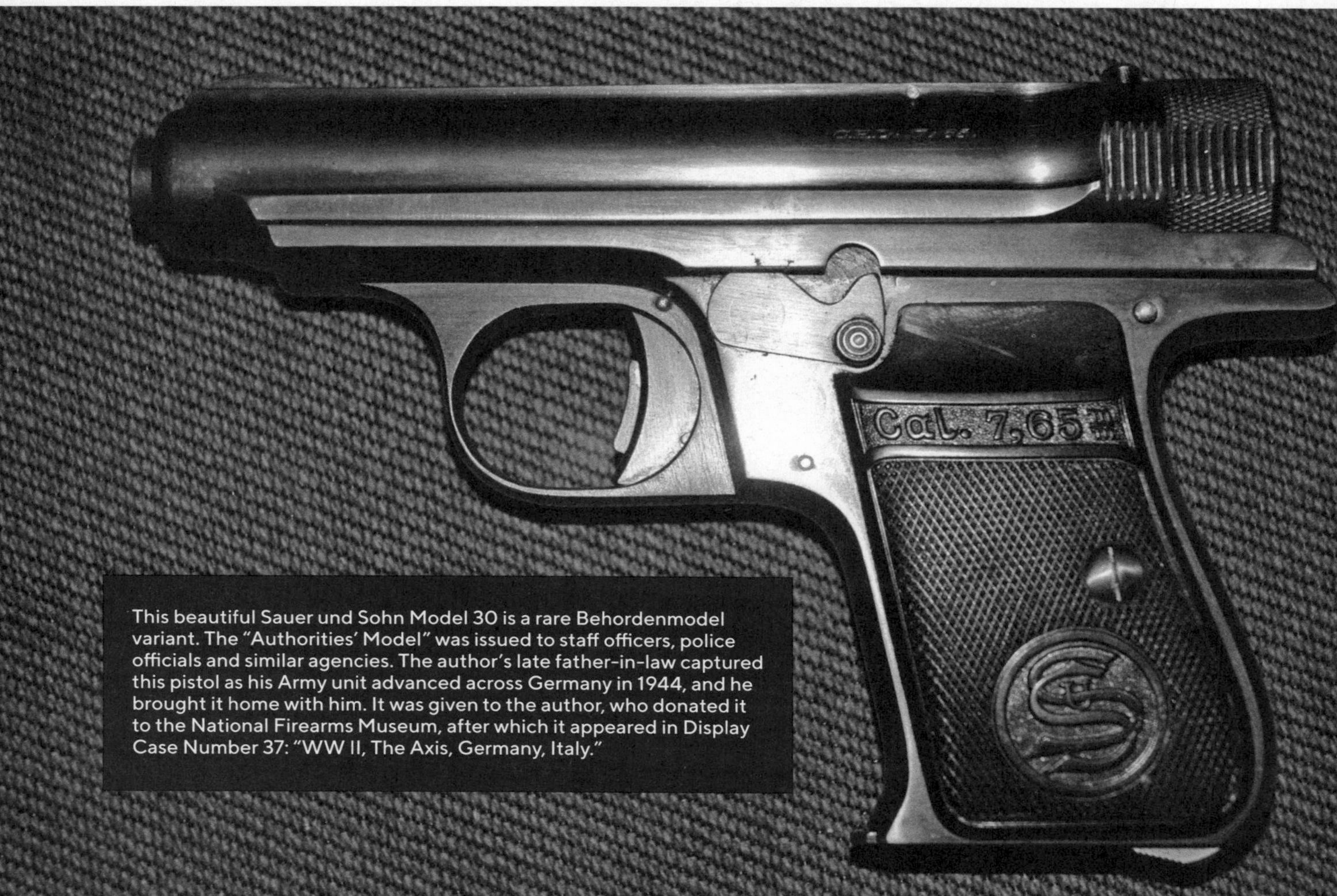

This beautiful Sauer und Sohn Model 30 is a rare Behordenmodel variant. The "Authorities' Model" was issued to staff officers, police officials and similar agencies. The author's late father-in-law captured this pistol as his Army unit advanced across Germany in 1944, and he brought it home with him. It was given to the author, who donated it to the National Firearms Museum, after which it appeared in Display Case Number 37: "WW II, The Axis, Germany, Italy."

Lessons From a Life-Long Handgunner on Choosing the Right Tool for the Job

BY **WALT HAMPTON**

This Harrington & Richardson Model 622 started the author down the merry road of all things handgun. It was also his first attempt at woodworking, for at age 12 he made the left-hand thumb rest grips out of American chestnut from a 200-year-old cabin.

50 YEARS A HANDGUN MAN

My first handgun was a Harrington & Richardson Model 622 revolver, bought for me by my father in 1966 as a training aid for my rabbit dog, a beagle named "Charlie." The 622 is an inexpensive .22 Long Rifle revolver, perfect for the trapline or tackle box. Simple, strong, and reliable, it was down near the bottom on the H&R catalog list. You did not get in a hurry with the 622. To reload the cylinder, you had to first pull the base pin, then the cylinder fell from the frame into your waiting hand. Ejection of the spent casings was accomplished by use of that base pin, one at a time, then the cylinder was reloaded, reinserted into the frame, and the pin replaced. As my father was fond of saying, "it will work just as fast as you can think," a slight jab at his inattentive son. Today, I still have that revolver, and I would give anything to go back and thank that old man for starting me down the road to all things handguns and the great outdoors.

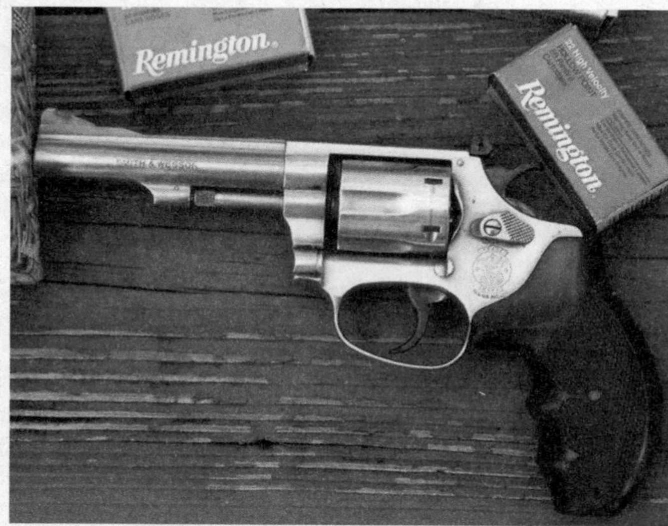

(left) For a double-action .22 revolver, you will have a hard time besting the Smith & Wesson Model 63.

(below) Two favorite revolvers from the author's stable, a Commemorative Ruger Blackhawk in .44 Magnum, and the Ruger Single-Six in .22 Magnum. Strength, quality, and reliability — the hallmarks of a dependable handgun.

(left) Handguns for concealed carry are a matter of personal preference. What's important is choosing a gun you will always carry and not leave behind. This Smith & Wesson Model 36 .38 Special with 3-inch barrel is comfortable and reliable.

Using the 622 for my introduction to handguns was brilliant on my father's part: not only did he start me with a revolver, but he introduced me to single-action shooting (the 622 is a double-action revolver, but I did not know that for at least a year after I received it). Its fixed sights made me think and figure out how to use them for accuracy, and the entire exercise was built around one accurate shot, not spraying the brush with lead. The lesson was that the handgun is a specialized tool for specialized work. That is as true today as it was 52 years ago.

I do not claim to be some grand guru of the handgun. I have owned and used handguns for over a half-century, and since 1978 there have been very few days when I did not have one either on my person or within reach. I carried a handgun as a Special State Game Warden with the Virginia Department of Game and Inland Fisheries, and have hunted with handguns all my adult life. As a writer, I have handled, shot, and tested handguns for the various manufacturers, and over a period of 28 years of outdoor and gun writing, that has amounted to dozens of different models, makes, and calibers. I have my favorites, as I am sure you have yours. This is a short essay on how I picked my handguns and why.

SELF-DEFENSE HANDGUNS

Let's get this over with first: If you intend to carry a handgun for self-defense, you need training, and I do not mean just range practice (which of course is very important). You need training to gain the understanding that shooting the handgun and fighting with the handgun are very different concepts. And if you are going to survive a violent encounter, you must learn the fighting mindset and how the handgun fits into it. This can only come from serious training from experienced instructors who understand the research on actual cases of armed self-defense. I shudder to think of all the folks who buy a handgun, spend a few hours on the range, and sally forth thinking they are "prepared" to stand between good and evil. The only saving grace is the fact that most criminals have no training whatsoever.

I have carried both revolvers and semi-autos at various times concealed. The argument over which is better is a waste of time. In the hands of a person with the "gunfight" mentality, either is fine. Since I was raised on revolvers, and because I have strong feelings about the reliability of the revolver, my usual carry

Short-barreled revolvers have always been popular for concealed carry and personal protection. The Smith & Wesson Model 36 .38 Special (top) and Colt Python .357 Magnum cover the size spectrum. Only you can decide which is more comfortable to carry concealed.

piece is a wheelgun. I'm not a tier-one terrorist-killer. I don't expect to be kicking down doors or executing warrants. I'm just a guy who knows that in 99 percent of encounters where a handgun is needed for self-defense, short range, one-on-one or two-on-one confrontations are the norm. In this regard, I want a handgun that I have faith will not let me down, a belief validated from spending hundreds of hours of shooting and training under simulated circumstances that cover the most likely scenarios.

The first rule of surviving a gunfight is, "DON'T GET IN A GUNFIGHT." If that's not an option, then "FIGHT" is the optimal word.

My first serious handgun was a .357 Magnum N-frame Smith & Wesson Model 28 Highway Patrolman with a 6-inch barrel, not exactly what one would call a concealable handgun. I bought it for hunting and it was my only handgun for several years. When I started working for the Virginia Game Department, we commissioned officers outside of the Law Enforcement Division (I was part of the Wildlife Division, with the other biologists) had to provide our own sidearms. I carried the Model 28 for two years and then bought a Smith & Wesson Model 59 9mm semi-auto for work carry.

At that time, wardens were making the switch from the Smith Model 10 .38

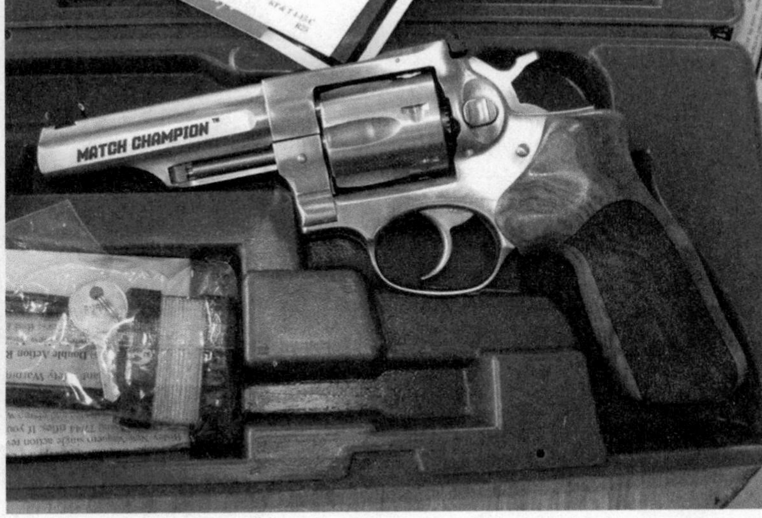

This Ruger Match Champion was donated by that great company to Special Operations Wounded Warriors (sowwcharity.com) for a wounded Special Forces veteran, SSgt. Bobby Dove (Ret). Bobby is shown getting familiar with the revolver on the range. He is testing it in a specialized High-Threat Concealment holster made for him that allows one-handed loading and unloading.

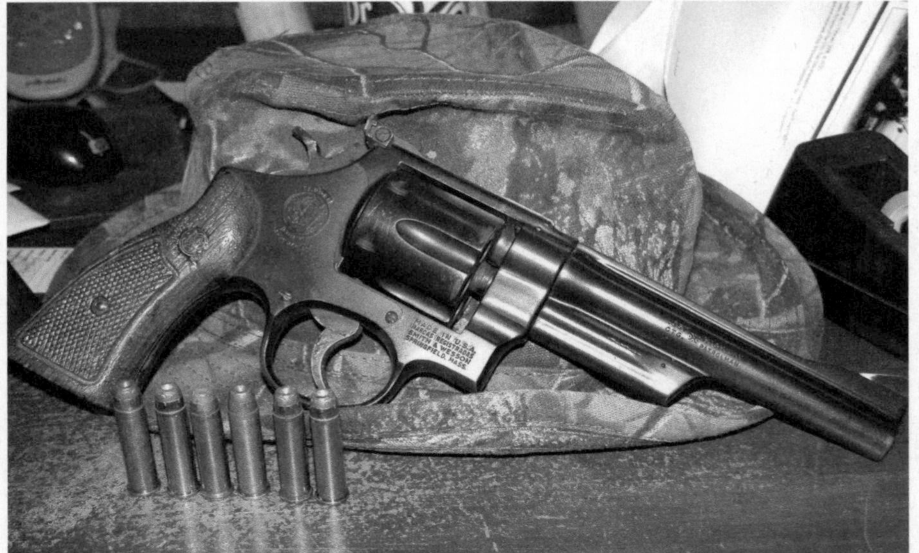

The author's first "serious" handgun was this Smith & Wesson Model 28 .357 Magnum, shown with some of his 158-grain handloads. For 40 years this handgun has never let him down.

Special revolver to the semi-auto, and I wanted to be prepared to meet the annual training and qualification requirements. Ammo was cheap (I handload) and I was shooting the 59 to the tune of about 100 rounds a week in practice. Both the Model 28 revolver and Model 59 semi-auto were very accurate handguns — the revolver more so of course because of its adjustable sights — but at short range the semi was very comfortable for me and I shot it well.

When I started to carry a handgun concealed, I bought a Smith & Wesson Model 60 with the 2-inch barrel and felt entirely comfortable with it in a pocket. Now I use a Smith Model 36 for carry on most occasions. The point is, I'm confident that I can shoot the gun accurately, that it will go bang every time I pull the trigger, and that, if need be, it can be as fast as I am able to be with a gun. Here is my advice: Buy the handgun that you will carry. If you don't carry it, it can't be of much help. Weight and size are very important. When I get ready to go out, I pick up the gun just as I do the keys, wallet and hat. The right concealed carry gun for you is the one you will never leave in the car or at home on the dresser.

Just as there is the never-ending argument between the revolver and the semi-auto folks, there is the battle over the best caliber for self-defense guns. My philosophy is simple: carry the caliber that is the largest you can shoot fast and accurately. For me, there are two that fit the bill — the 9mm and the .38 Special +P. I don't want to have to shoot anyone, but if I do, foremost I want the rounds to land where I intend them to land, and I want them to stop the threat. I am confident that these calibers will get the job done. Yes, the .45 Auto, the various .44 calibers, and the .45 Colt all carry more freight, and my handguns in those calibers are certainly adequate for man-stopping. But when it comes to handguns that I'm comfortable carrying concealed, and that I have confidence in using, the 9mm and .38 get the call.

THE HUNTING AND WORKING HANDGUN

I have been blessed to live most of my life in the Appalachian Mountain region in a very rural setting, and I carry a

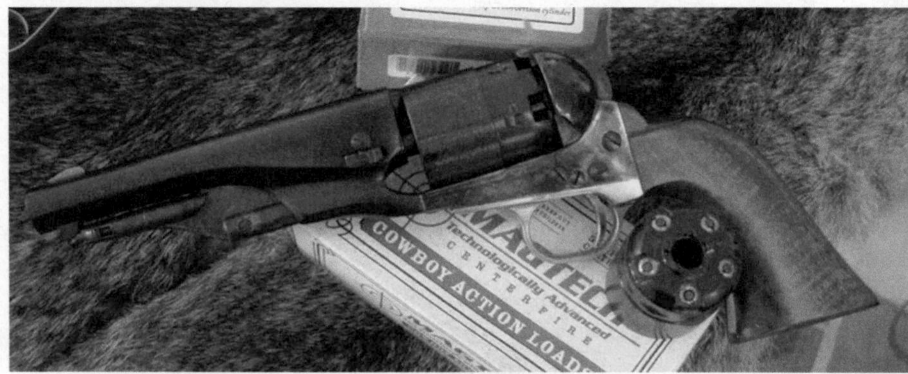

For hunting, the author favors single-action revolvers. The reproduction Colt 1860 with conversion cylinder (above) is chambered for .45 Colt, as is the Ruger Bisley Vaquero (left). The Super Blackhawk (below) is, of course, is .44 Magnum.

(top) What is it? This one started life as a Ruger 3-screw Blackhawk chambered in .30 Carbine, then received a Power Custom grip frame, Colt grips, and a refinish.

(above) The Colt Single Action Army is a classic. This is a nickel-plated .38-40 with a 7 ½-inch barrel.

For a .22 LR revolver in double-action, I don't think you can best the Smith & Wesson Model 63. The little J-frame Smith is just sweet. I don't know another adjective that better describes it. The double action is smooth as butter, and with the adjustable sights, it is as accurate a handgun as you can find. These now command premium prices on the used market, which makes me wish I'd bought two of them. That's because my youngest son commandeered mine for his trap line work!

We can debate the relative merits of the single- versus double-action revolver, but why waste time? There have been many instances where I've used both for a hurried first shot — and the single-action revolver, if you practice with it, can be just as fast as the double action. In the semi-auto, I've had good success with three different models: the ubiquitous Colt 1911 in .45 ACP, the Beretta 92 in 9mm and the Smith & Wesson Model 59 in .357 Magnum mentioned earlier. (The Colt is single action, the others are double action.) Do not believe that the 9mm round is inadequate for hunting, especially in a good handgun. If you respect your limitations on range and shot selection, and select the proper bullet, the 9mm will get the job done, and it is very pleasant to shoot, with little recoil

[CONTINUED ON 150]

handgun when I work the farm, whether I'm feeding the horses, checking my coyote traps, or the doing the hundred other chores that have to be done. If you are a "gun person," I do not see how you can get along without a .22-caliber handgun. For pure enjoyment, there is nothing like plinking with the .22, whether revolver or semi-automatic. My all-time favorite is the wonderful Ruger Single-Six and mine has been hard-used. I carry it with the .22 Magnum cylinder in place and it is accurate, fast, and very comfortable to shoot. The .22 Magnum rimfire round is far more capable than paper ballistics will have you believe, and I have used this outfit to dispatch hogs and cattle for the freezer, close-range head-shots that have always gotten the job done. The 40-grain solid load will penetrate an amazing amount of tissue and bone and, with the adjustable sights on the 6-inch barrel of the Ruger, this combination has even been responsible for a few limits of squirrels, grouse and rabbits, along with dispatching the various varmints found in country living. As a trapper of coyote and bobcat, the .22 revolver is my gun of choice on the trapline.

The Beretta 92 in 9mm (left) and the Colt 1911 in .45 ACP (right). The Colt is affectionately known as "Hard Candy." Every good gun deserves a name.

MADE IN U.S.A.
THE HIGH STANDARD MFG.CO
NEW HAVEN, CONN.
PATENT PENDING
22 CAL
LONG RIFLE

Semi-auto handguns come in many, many makes and models. For an accurate .22, the models from High Standard are hard to beat.

Two classic Colt revolvers. The Bisley is a .32-20 and the New Frontier is a .45 Colt.

and blast. No matter what you hunt, shot placement is far more important than caliber.

For most of my handgun hunting I carry either my Smith & Wesson Model 28 N-frame in .357 Magnum or the Ruger Blackhawk in .44 Magnum. My Ruger Blackhawk is the 50th Anniversary Commemorative model, not the Super Blackhawk, which is also a fine, strong revolver. Here we are talking about deer and hogs, with the possibility of a black bear at close range. I'm a great fan of the .357 Magnum as a deer revolver with the proper bullet and have extensive experience with it.

Once again, you must restrain yourself to close range (under 100 yards) and pick your shots. Elmer Keith once said that the true test of any handgun is in long-range shooting; I believe this, and have practiced many times out to 200 yards, but one should only take the shot on game with the highest confidence of a sure killing hit. In the .357 Magnum, I use exclusively 158-grain hollowpoints from Hornady for my deer load, and they have never let me down. In the .44 Magnum, I regularly use two loads, one the heavy .44 Special load of the 250-grain cast lead slug driven to about 900 fps, and the magnum load with the jacketed 240-grain Nosler or Hornady bullet to about 1,400 fps. I have killed both coyotes and deer to 100 yards with these loads.

I carry the Ruger in a "cross-belly" leather rig, out of the way yet still instantly accessible, and the Smith Model 28 in a stock Uncle Mike's shoulder holster. Both setups can be worn either inside or outside the hunting coat, and for me provide the most comfort.

For small game hunting that epitomizes fair chase, try using a handgun. Your big game handgun can be used here, with the right bullet and load. In my handguns, I always carry one or two rounds of reduced-power loads, in case the odd grouse or squirrel presents itself. In the .357 Mag., the cast 148-grain wadcutter at about 800 fps is perfect, and in the .44 Special the light load using a cast 250-grain bullet at about the same velocity will punch through and damage minimal meat. If you are feeling overconfident and want a good lesson in humility, take your .22 revolver or semi-auto handgun to the squirrel woods — it will certainly put the "hunt" back into hunting! If you want to be an accurate handgun shooter, the more you practice, the better you will get, and using the handgun under field conditions for small game is great practice. It forces you to slow down and take your time, a great lesson in our instant-gratification world.

FINDING THE RIGHT HANDGUN

American gun folk now have an astonishing array of handguns from which to choose. Just a peek into the back of this volume will show you dozens of pages of guns of every description and caliber. There's also a wonderful used gun market, and on various sites on the

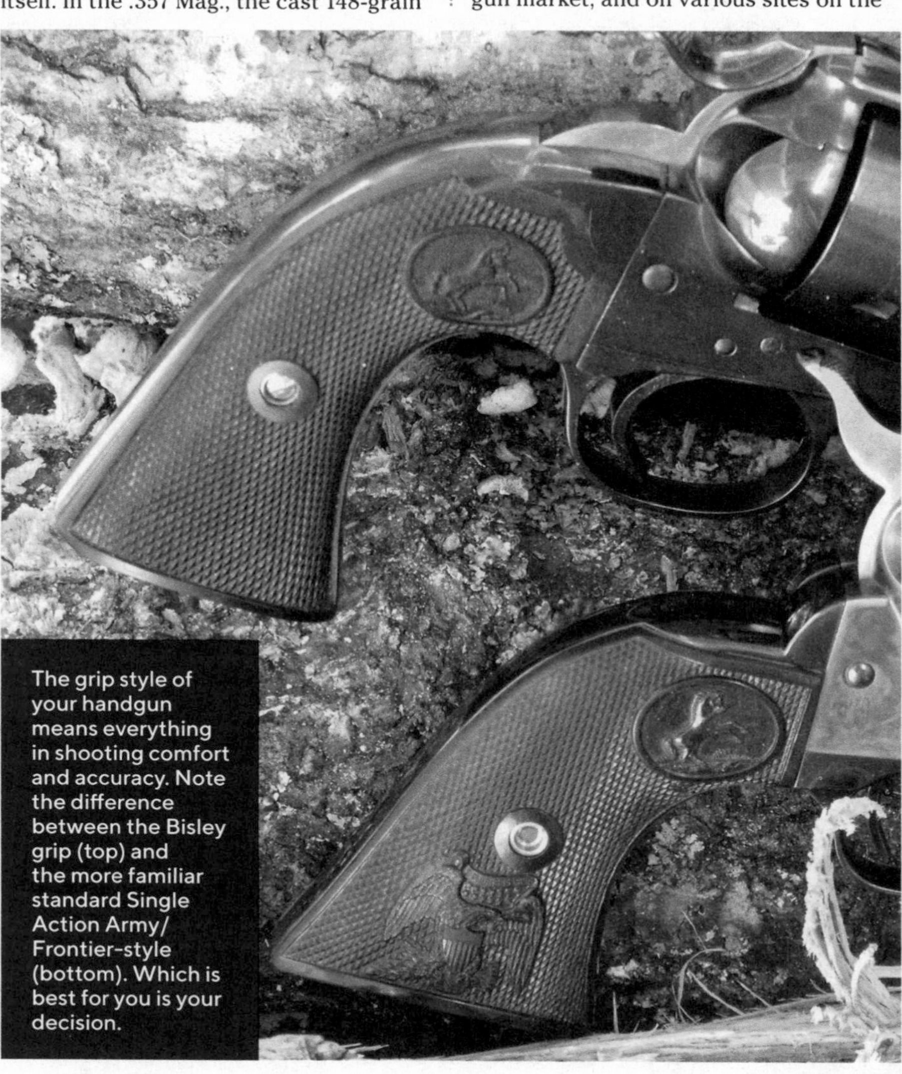

The grip style of your handgun means everything in shooting comfort and accuracy. Note the difference between the Bisley grip (top) and the more familiar standard Single Action Army/ Frontier-style (bottom). Which is best for you is your decision.

The Ruger 50th Anniversary Commemorative model .44 Magnum Blackhawk is the author's current favorite handgun. He could not tolerate plastic grips on such a fine gun, so made a replacement pair from black walnut, complete with an old monogrammed cuff-link.

Internet you can find just about every handgun that has ever been available. If you think you are going to be in the market for a handgun, my advice is to visit the local gun store and handle a few different makes and models. Do not look for a handgun that is all things, it does not exist. Some guns are more suitable for certain tasks (concealed carry, target, hunting and so forth) than others. Do your research on the guns. Which action type is better suited for your purposes? What barrel length, grip shape and sights meet your needs? And what caliber will you be comfortable with in practice?

My observation on spending has always been that you must expect to pay for top quality. It has also been my experience that quality and reliability go hand in hand, and it would not make any sense to skimp on a tool that you may have to rely upon to save your life or that of a loved one. Some handguns on the market today, in various styles, calibers or makes, have stood the test of time, so start your search with proven models. If a handgun has been around for a few decades and has a strong following today, there is a lesson there and attention should be paid. That is not to say that some of the new handguns are not wonderful, certainly some of them are. But you must determine that for yourself.

.44 MAGNUM RIFLES

A .44 Magnum Rifle is Well Suited for a Great Many Applications

BY **JAMES E. HOUSE**

A compact .44 Magnum carbine is a superb tool for hunting or roaming in remote areas.

The year 1873 was an auspicious one for the shooting sports, and the developments are still with us today. It was in that year that the .44-40 Winchester, .45 Colt and .45-70 Government cartridges were introduced. Although approaching a century and a half in age, all three are still popular.

The .44-40 Winchester became a very popular cartridge for use in rifles such as the Winchester 73, and revolvers like the Colt Single Action Army. The idea of having a common caliber for both rifle and handgun appealed to many shooters. It still does, but there are more popular and potent calibers than the .44-40 Winchester.

Introduced in 1956, the .44 Remington Magnum came about largely because of experiments by Elmer Keith and others to develop a magnum handgun for use in hunting. Maximum and overloaded .44 Special-loaded revolvers led the way, but numerous handguns in that caliber were not able to withstand the stress, so a new case that was about 1/8-inch longer was developed. The longer case would not fit into the shorter .44 Special cylinders. That's important because the .44 Magnum operates at about 35,000 psi, whereas the .44 Special develops slightly less than one-half that pressure, 15,500 psi. The earliest revolvers chambered for the .44 Magnum were the Ruger Super Blackhawk and the Smith & Wesson Model 29.

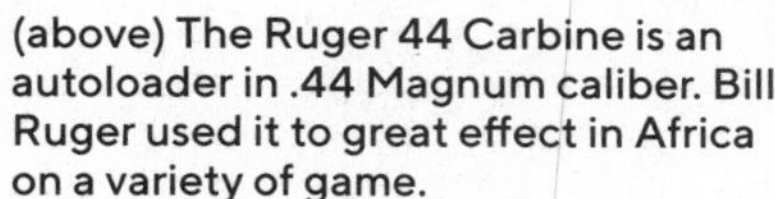

(above) The Ruger 44 Carbine is an autoloader in .44 Magnum caliber. Bill Ruger used it to great effect in Africa on a variety of game.

(left) These Hornady .44 Special and .44 Magnum (right) cartridges show the greater length of the magnum round.

It was not long after the .44 Magnum was introduced before gunsmiths began modifying rifles to handle the cartridge. One of them was the Winchester 92, a lever action that is of slightly smaller stature than the legendary Model 94. Ruger introduced a locked-breech, gas-operated autoloader in .44 Magnum. Known as the Ruger Carbine or Model 44, it utilized a tubular magazine that loaded from the bottom. The general profile was later followed in the Ruger 10/22 chambered for the .22 LR. Following a trend that Ruger has exploited in other cases, the next Ruger .44 Magnum rifle was the Model 96/44 lever action. Except for the lever in the grip area, the 96/44 followed the same profile as the 44 Carbine autoloader.

William B. Ruger tested the Ruger 44 Carbine on an extended safari in Africa during the spring of 1961. The story of that carbine in Africa was described in three publications by Pete Kuhlhoff. The first of these was in the August 1961 issue of *Argosy* and the second was in the September 1961 issue of *Guns & Ammo*. Kuhlhoff's analysis of the safari was also published as "The Ruger Carbine in Africa" in the 1963 edition of the *Gun Digest*, pp. 172-175. In the definitive work by R. L. Wilson, *Ruger and His Guns*, there is a quote (on p. 71) from a letter sent by Ruger to Jack O'Connor, the long-time gun editor of *Outdoor Life*, in which Ruger tells O'Connor about some of the species taken with the 44 Carbine. Leopard, topi, waterbuck, spotted hyena, kob, bushbuck, warthog and reedbuck were mentioned specifically. Ruger also gave high praise regarding the performance of the Remington .44 Magnum ammunition. It was stated that most game was shot at distances of 75-100 yards, ranges at which a .44 Magnum would be most effective.

Although it seems as if the developers of new cartridges would like for us to

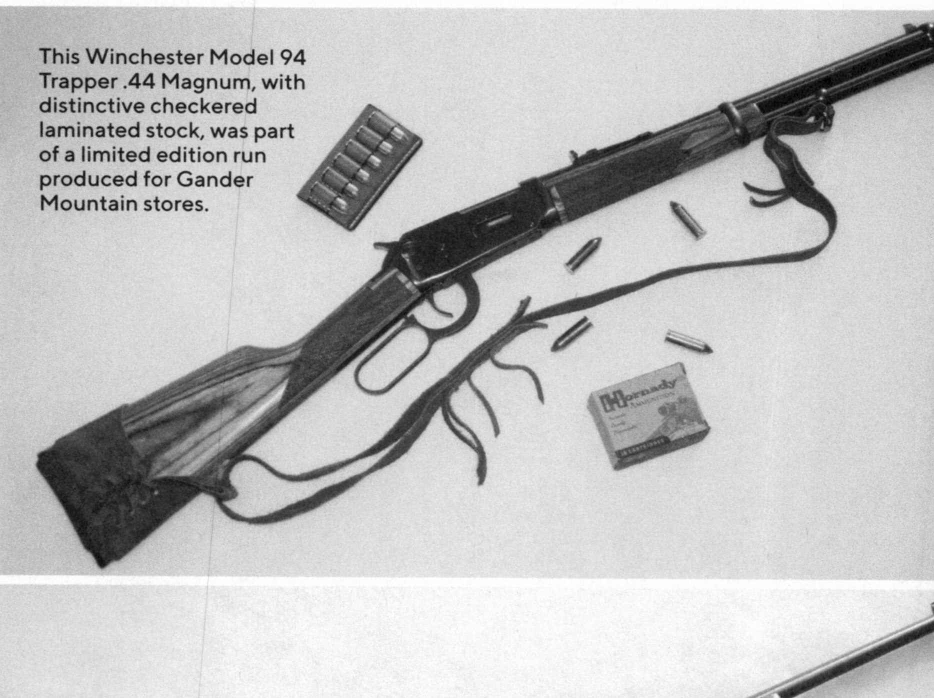

This Winchester Model 94 Trapper .44 Magnum, with distinctive checkered laminated stock, was part of a limited edition run produced for Gander Mountain stores.

With a compact scope like the 2-7X Leupold, the Ruger 77/44 is a versatile tool.

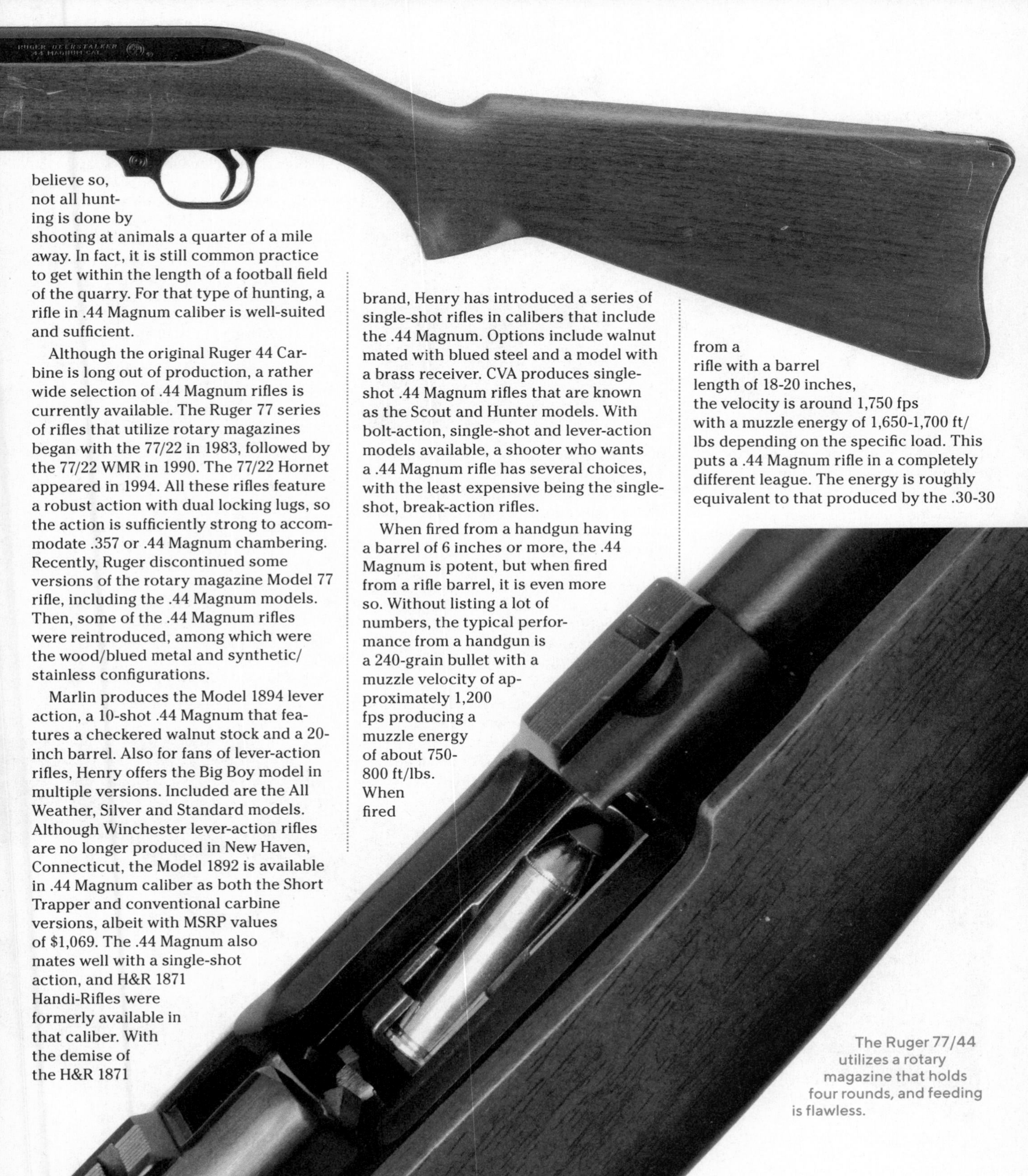

believe so, not all hunting is done by shooting at animals a quarter of a mile away. In fact, it is still common practice to get within the length of a football field of the quarry. For that type of hunting, a rifle in .44 Magnum caliber is well-suited and sufficient.

Although the original Ruger 44 Carbine is long out of production, a rather wide selection of .44 Magnum rifles is currently available. The Ruger 77 series of rifles that utilize rotary magazines began with the 77/22 in 1983, followed by the 77/22 WMR in 1990. The 77/22 Hornet appeared in 1994. All these rifles feature a robust action with dual locking lugs, so the action is sufficiently strong to accommodate .357 or .44 Magnum chambering. Recently, Ruger discontinued some versions of the rotary magazine Model 77 rifle, including the .44 Magnum models. Then, some of the .44 Magnum rifles were reintroduced, among which were the wood/blued metal and synthetic/stainless configurations.

Marlin produces the Model 1894 lever action, a 10-shot .44 Magnum that features a checkered walnut stock and a 20-inch barrel. Also for fans of lever-action rifles, Henry offers the Big Boy model in multiple versions. Included are the All Weather, Silver and Standard models. Although Winchester lever-action rifles are no longer produced in New Haven, Connecticut, the Model 1892 is available in .44 Magnum caliber as both the Short Trapper and conventional carbine versions, albeit with MSRP values of $1,069. The .44 Magnum also mates well with a single-shot action, and H&R 1871 Handi-Rifles were formerly available in that caliber. With the demise of the H&R 1871 brand, Henry has introduced a series of single-shot rifles in calibers that include the .44 Magnum. Options include walnut mated with blued steel and a model with a brass receiver. CVA produces single-shot .44 Magnum rifles that are known as the Scout and Hunter models. With bolt-action, single-shot and lever-action models available, a shooter who wants a .44 Magnum rifle has several choices, with the least expensive being the single-shot, break-action rifles.

When fired from a handgun having a barrel of 6 inches or more, the .44 Magnum is potent, but when fired from a rifle barrel, it is even more so. Without listing a lot of numbers, the typical performance from a handgun is a 240-grain bullet with a muzzle velocity of approximately 1,200 fps producing a muzzle energy of about 750-800 ft/lbs. When fired from a rifle with a barrel length of 18-20 inches, the velocity is around 1,750 fps with a muzzle energy of 1,650-1,700 ft/lbs depending on the specific load. This puts a .44 Magnum rifle in a completely different league. The energy is roughly equivalent to that produced by the .30-30

The Ruger 77/44 utilizes a rotary magazine that holds four rounds, and feeding is flawless.

There are few rifles that are as easy to grasp and carry as a lever action.

Winchester, but with a much heavier bullet of .429-inch diameter. As a result, the .44 Magnum rifle is fully capable of taking large game at moderate ranges.

One limitation of a .44 Magnum rifle is that, with the velocity being comparatively low (for a rifle cartridge), the trajectory has a great deal of curvature. With a 240-grain bullet sighted to hit at the point of aim at 100 yards, the bullet rises 2 inches above the line of sight at midrange and will hit approximately 8 inches low at 150 yards.

One unique .44 Magnum load is the Hornady LEVERevolution that utilizes a 225-grain FTX bullet that features a flexible polymer tip. This load delivers over 1,800 fps from a rifle and, when sighted approximately 2 inches high at 75 yards, is on the point of aim at 125 yards and strikes only about 3 inches low at 150 yards. At that distance the remaining velocity is approximately 1,200 fps, giving an energy of over 750 ft/lbs. Coupled with a large diameter bullet weighing 225 grains, this load makes a .44 Magnum rifle a legitimate 150-yard rifle for hunting deer-size animals. That range opens many possibilities for hunting deer, hogs or black bear.

If smaller game or predators are the hunted species, the owner of a .44 Magnum rifle can simply use lower-powered .44 Special ammunition. For small pests at short ranges, shot cartridges are effective; CCI offers shot loads that utilize either #4 or #9 shot, and at short range they are pest poppers.

When using handloaded ammunition, the flexibility of a .44 Magnum rifle is enhanced to even greater levels. The entire range of power from mid-range .44 Special to full magnum persuasion is possible. There are components galore for the .44 Magnum shooter who handloads ammunition. Bullets are readily available in weights that range from 180 to 300 grains, and this range is extended on both ends by some specialty types. Several powders work for heavy loads in the big .44, among which are Alliant 2400, Hodgdon H110 and H4227, Winchester 296, Accurate No. 9 and IMR 4227. Recipes for loads are offered in profusion in all standard loading manuals, so it is not necessary to reproduce them. However, it is not possible to increase the power to any significant degree because of the case capacity and the already high-pressure limit of the cartridge. The versatility can certainly be enhanced significantly owing to the wide range of components.

A wide range of available projectiles make handloading the .44 Magnum a no-brainer. The highly regarded Swift A-Frame bullets are available in 240-, 280- and 300-grain versions. Nosler markets .44-caliber hollowpoints in 200-, 240- and 300-grain varieties, as well as a 240-grain soft point and full

metal jacketed in 220 and 250 grains. The highly regarded XTP bullet in 200, 240 and 300 grains, in addition to the 225-grain FTX polymer-tipped bullet, are available from Hornady. Speer offers an extensive line of .44-caliber bullets that includes 200- and 210-grain Gold Dot HP, 240-grain SP and HP, and 270-grain Gold Dot SP. Available .44-caliber bullets from Sierra include 180-, 210- and 240-grain hollowpoints, 220-grain full metal jacket and 300-grain soft point varieties. In addition to these jacketed bullets, many plated designs are available from Berry, Rainier and X-Treme bullets, and cast bullets are available from numerous sources. The point of this list is to illustrate that the owner of a .44 Magnum rifle can produce loads for anything from mice to bears.

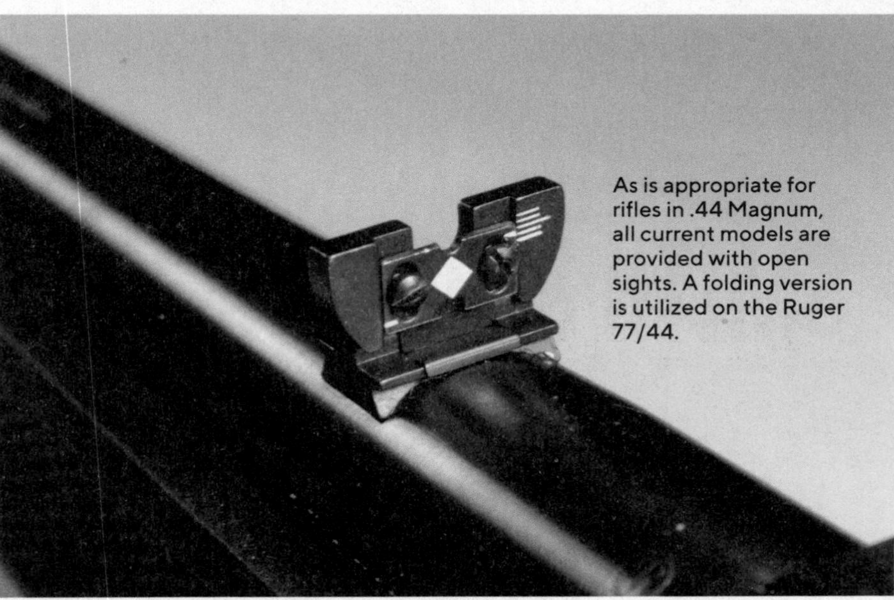

As is appropriate for rifles in .44 Magnum, all current models are provided with open sights. A folding version is utilized on the Ruger 77/44.

When it comes to .44 Magnum ammunition, the selection ranges from shot loads to heavy soft points.

One of the modern .44 Magnum loads is the LEVERevolution from Hornady. The polymer tip provides better velocity retention.

The Marlin 1894 has long been one of the most popular .44 Magnum rifles.

Henry Repeating Arms recently introduced a line of single-shot rifles and .44 Magnum is one of the calibers available.

THE INIMITABLE SMITH & WESSON COMBAT MAGNUM

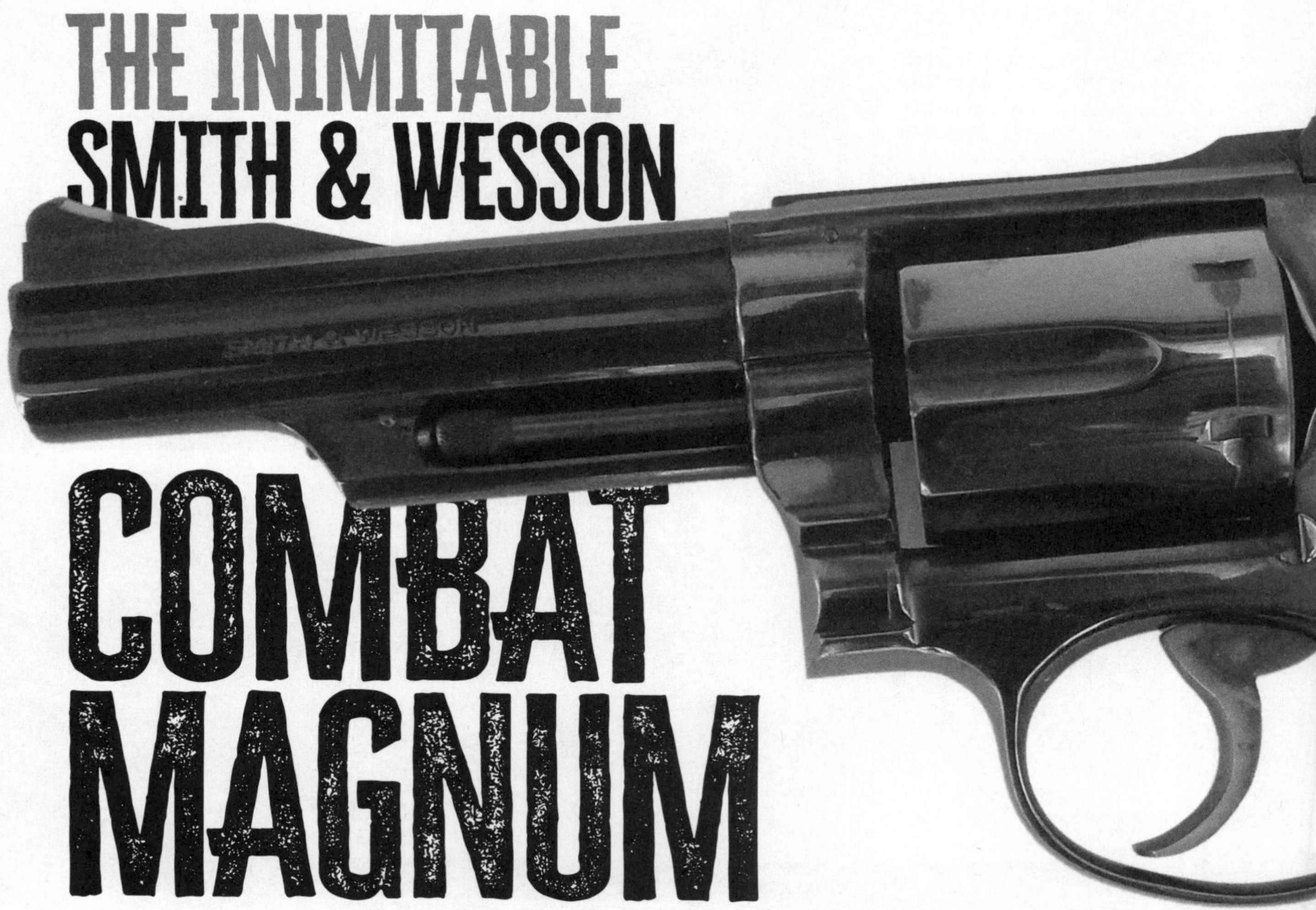

The K-Frame .357 Magnum is Still Going Strong

BY **ROBERT K. CAMPBELL**

It is surprising to some that handgun types well over 100 years old are not only in production, but flourishing. The Colt Single Action Army, introduced in 1873, is a popular recreational handgun that remains in service in Cowboy Action Shooting and as an outdoors handgun in improved versions. The 1911 pistol is still on the frontlines after more than a century of service. But there's another iconic revolver that doesn't get the attention it deserves. That's the Smith & Wesson Combat Magnum .357 Magnum revolver, a much-copied but never duplicated sixgun that has earned its place as a genuine working classic.

The S&W Combat Magnum, sometimes known as the Model 19 or Model 66, went into production in 1955 and was discontinued in 2005. The revolver has recently been reintroduced in a modern version. At the time of its introduction, it was the world's lightest .357 Magnum revolver. Intended for police service, the Combat Magnum became one of the most popular handguns of all time. It was the revolver everyone wanted, and arguably the finest service revolver ever fielded. In terms of power, accuracy, fit and finish, few modern service handguns equal it.

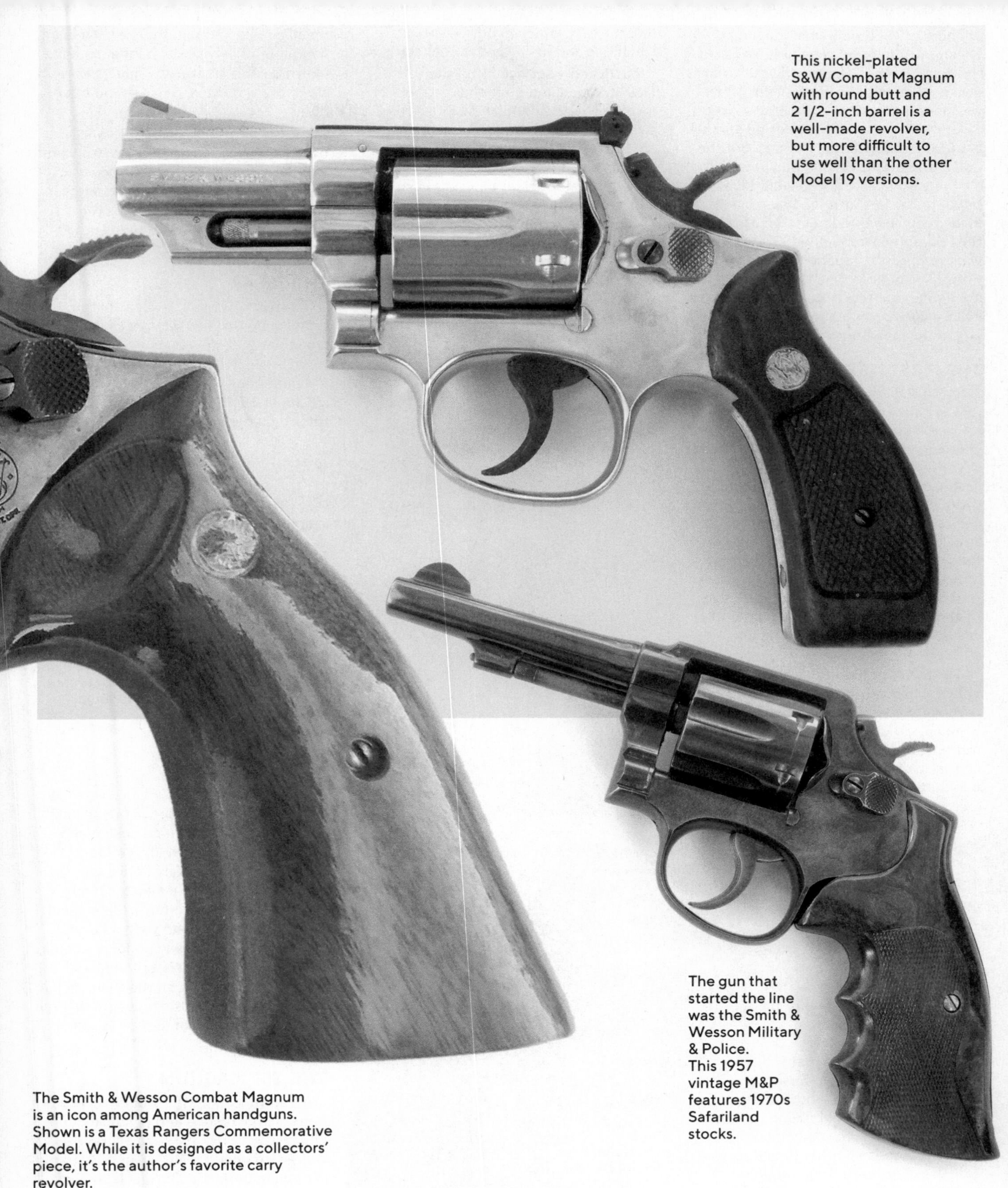

This nickel-plated S&W Combat Magnum with round butt and 2 1/2-inch barrel is a well-made revolver, but more difficult to use well than the other Model 19 versions.

The gun that started the line was the Smith & Wesson Military & Police. This 1957 vintage M&P features 1970s Safariland stocks.

The Smith & Wesson Combat Magnum is an icon among American handguns. Shown is a Texas Rangers Commemorative Model. While it is designed as a collectors' piece, it's the author's favorite carry revolver.

The story of the Combat Magnum began prior to 1899 when Colt pioneered the double-action (DA) swing-out cylinder revolver with its Model 1892, which was adopted by the United States Army. The Colt was not a robust design and did not fare well in military service. But the Colt's primary drawback was power. The .38 Long Colt cartridge jolted a 152-grain bullet to 750 fps. This loading proved inadequate in wound potential. During the Philippine War (1899–1902), Moro warriors proved capable of taking six or even 12 rounds of .38 Colt and continuing the fight. It matters little if the adversary eventually dies of his wounds if he kills you in the meantime!

THE FIRST M&P

Smith & Wesson developed the Military & Police (M&P) swing-out cylinder DA revolver to replace the Colt 1892 and compete with the newer, much-improved Colt revolvers. The first few S&W revolvers chambered the .38 Colt, but production quickly went to an improved cartridge, the .38 Smith & Wesson Special, or just .38 Special as it's known today. This cartridge used a 158-grain bullet at 850 fps. The .38 Special became the most successful revolver cartridge of all time. The .38 Special cylinder also accepts .38 Short and .38 Long Colt cartridges.

The medium-frame .38-caliber revolver became the most prolific service revolver in history. Government sales were curtailed as the military developed a .45-caliber self-loader, but police and civilian sales were brisk. With a 4-, 5- or 6-inch barrel, the M&P revolver became a common sidearm.

Smith & Wesson revolvers were immensely popular. But not everyone was happy about the cartridge. As one gun writer put it, the .38 was very popular with those who never had to shoot anyone. Another called the M&P the "gunfighter's gun of the 20th century" as many more fights involved it than all other police service calibers combined. With a solid hit, the .38 Special round-nose load proved capable of stopping an adversary about half the time. Many good cops were caught on the wrong end of that statistic.

A rare bird – a stainless M66 with round butt and 4-inch barrel.

Early in the service life of the M&P, target-sighted revolvers were introduced. Handgunners discovered two things about the .38 Special: The cartridge and the S&W revolvers that chambered it were very accurate, providing good accuracy for contests even at 100 yards. And second, the .38 Special cartridge had room for improvement by handloading. Elmer Keith designed a sharp-shouldered semi-wadcutter (SWC) bullet that kept most of the weight forward out of the cartridge case, allowing for greater powder capacity. Standard handloads could push a 160-grain SWC to 1,000 fps. Special grips, including the original Roper, were introduced that allowed comfortable shooting of such loads. Hollowpoint bullets were developed. Some loads reached 1,100 or even 1,200 fps. The M&P revolver was not built to take such loads. A number of .38 Special handguns were blown up and, in others, small parts took a beating and the revolvers went out of time.

For the first time, recoil tolerance became a concern. But outdoorsmen and working cops needed a more powerful load than the .38 Special. Penetration with .44 Special and .45 Colt factory loads wasn't much better than the .38 Special due to the soft lead bullets used.

THE .38-44

Smith & Wesson went back to the drawing board. The result was one of the finest hard-use revolvers ever manufactured — the Heavy Duty. It was simply a .44-caliber K-frame revolver with a .38 Special cylinder and barrel. With thick cylinders and a large frame, the Heavy Duty was capable of taking heavy handloads. A factory load designated .38-44 was introduced (.38 caliber/.44 frame). With a 158-grain bullet, this load could do 1,125 fps in a 4-inch barrel. Today, Buffalo Bore offers a .38-44 load that is a tad hotter and very accurate. The .38-44 armed many police agencies, and the Heavy Duty (later the Model 20) was manufactured until the 1960s. While a great revolver for the time, it was large, heavy and not as fast into action as lighter handguns.

Smith & Wesson's Heavy Duty is the direct ancestor of the Combat Magnum.

THE .357 MAGNUM

Meanwhile, S&W developed an even more powerful load and changed handgun history. The .38 Special cartridge was lengthened by 1/10 of an inch, to prevent chambering in .38 Special revolvers, and designated the .357 Magnum.

The new cartridge was a sensation.

The .357 Magnum fired a 158-grain SWC at 1,450 fps from an 8 3/8-inch barrel — 4-inch barrel velocity was around 1,250 fps. Chambered in a deluxe revolver on the .44 K frame, the new cartridge was used to take all manner of North American game. Introduced with a 3.5-inch barrel, the new revolver became a favorite of FBI agents and border patrolmen who could afford it. The magnum cost more than twice as much as the Heavy Duty.

The factory SWC bullet leaded badly after only a few shots, but anyone using this revolver had to be a handloader. Keith's .38-caliber 173-grain SWC HP was a popular bullet for the magnum. Eventually, the .357 became easier to come by, and Smith introduced the Highway Patrolman, an affordable version of the original.

Development of the S&W K frame continued with the introduction of the target-sighted Combat Masterpiece with 4-inch barrel and the K 38 with 6-inch barrel. With adjustable rear sights, ramp front sights, hand-filling stocks, and a target trigger and hammer, these are excellent handguns. The Combat Masterpiece was something of a prestige revolver well into the 1980s in agencies that limited officers to the .38-caliber revolver.

After World War II, S&W introduced the short action, which was pioneered by custom gunsmiths. These revolvers feature a shorter action that makes DA trigger work smoother and faster. With a shorter travel and more rapid reset, these .38s were winners on the target range and combat courses. The Combat Masterpiece was among the first of these new revolvers. The K frame was the company's bread and butter and best-selling handgun.

THE COMBAT MAGNUM

Carl Hellstrom, president of Smith & Wesson at the time, approached Bill Jordan concerning new service revolvers. Jordan was a very influential shooter, former Combat Marine, border patrolman and exhibition shooter. Hellstrom was interested in pushing S&W to the top, which he did, and the firearm he and Jordan brainstormed at the national shooting matches was one of the most important S&W handguns ever manufactured.

Jordan knew exactly what was needed. He recommended a lengthened cylinder of the Combat Masterpiece to accept the .357 Magnum cartridge. With target

Smith's Heavy Duty model is shown here above an early Military & Police .38.

The modern Model 66, true to the original but with improvements. This is a sturdy handgun.

Smith & Wesson's L-frame .44 Magnum leaves one pondering its application, but the company calls it a Combat Magnum.

In fast combat shooting, the Combat Magnum is well balanced. Recoil with magnum loads can be brisk, but the power dispensed is considerable.

In this high-ride holster from Nelson Holsters, the Combat Magnum is ready for a rapid presentation.

sights and a ramp front sight, this revolver would provide all the accuracy needed. It has a shrouded ejector rod. The new, short DA trigger is ideal for fast shooting. Jordan also recommended the revolver be supplied with target stocks to help control the recoil of the .357 Magnum cartridge. Officers could practice with .38 Special ammunition and load the .357 Magnum for duty.

Smith & Wesson engineers studied metallurgy and determined that the K-frame revolver could withstand the stress of the .357 Magnum cartridge. The result was the S&W Combat Magnum. This is the revolver that Jordan called a "peace officer's dream." It was particularly well received by highway patrol

The classic Tom Threepersons holster, produced by Rocking K Saddlery, is a classy option to tote the .357 Combat Magnum.

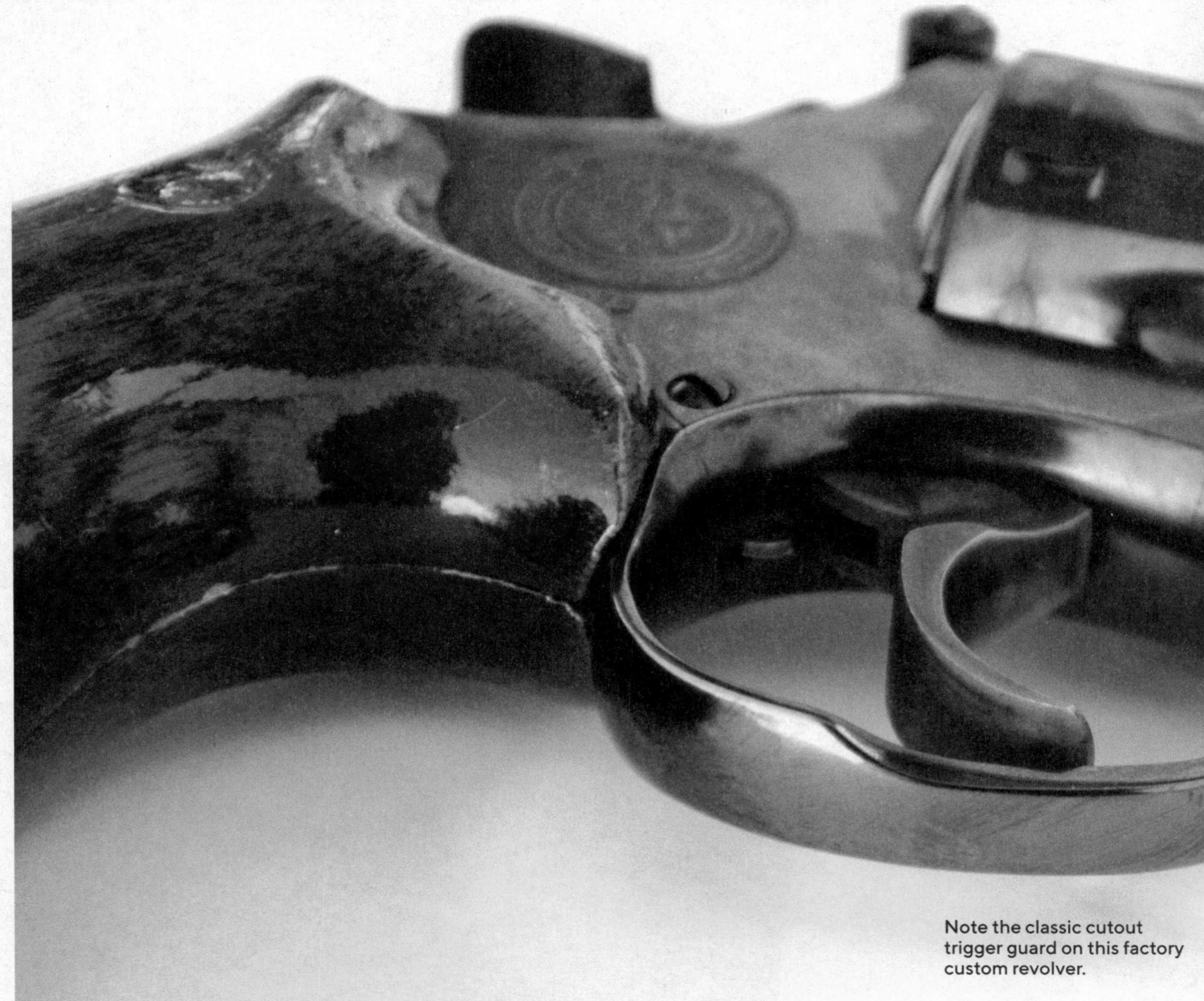

Note the classic cutout trigger guard on this factory custom revolver.

agencies that traditionally needed more vehicle penetration than urban officers. With its smooth DA trigger and red insert front sight, the Combat Magnum offers excellent first shot hit probability. A shroud protects the ejector rod from damage and hand-filling stocks allow excellent control.

According to a Police Marksman's Association study published in the 1990s, officers armed with the .357 Magnum revolver posted more hits for fewer shots fired than officers armed with the .38 revolver or 9mm and .45 ACP self-loaders. The .357 Magnum was an excellent man stopper — there were no complaints there. In 1957, S&W went to a numbering system to reference handguns while keeping the original named models as well. The Combat Magnum was given the Model 19 designation, and later stainless-steel revolvers were dubbed the Model 66. The Combat Magnum remained the premier service revolver for police agencies well into the 1980s.

NEW LOADS

Police agencies needed different loads for their revolvers. The 158-grain SWC used by outdoorsmen wasn't ideal for police work. The heavy 158-grain JHP (jacketed hollowpoint) used for taking deer wasn't a good service cartridge, either. Faster expansion and limited penetration were the goals. Interestingly, about half of the Combat Magnum revolvers in service were loaded with .38 Special ammunition. The .38 Special +P was developed to improve wound ballistics. The 110- and 125-grain jacketed hollowpoint loads were introduced. The most effective were those using a 158-grain lead SWC hollowpoint, not too different from handloads used during the 1930s.

A special +P+ load intended specifically for use in .357 Magnum revolvers was offered. The introduction of the 2 1/2-inch barrel Combat Magnum with its round butt and small grips gave officers a real problem in control with magnum loads. Few officers felt confident carrying this piece with full power loads. The service load was a .38 Special +P+

THE COMBAT MAGNUM CONTINUED TO ENJOY POPULAR USE, THOUGH, ESPECIALLY AMONG CIVILIAN SHOOTERS. DURING ITS LONG SERVICE LIFE, THE MOST POPULAR ISSUE REVOLVER WAS THE MODEL 66, A STAINLESS-STEEL COMBAT MAGNUM. THIS REVOLVER IS STILL IN USE WITH ELITE UNITS BASED ON ITS RELIABILITY, ACCURACY AND POWER.

firing a 110-grain JHP at 1,175 fps. This wasn't a full magnum, but hotter than any .38, and useful in the short-barreled revolvers.

Almost all of the Combat Magnum revolvers in police service used a 4-inch barrel. The 6-inch barrel revolver was also offered but seldom seen. Even rarer is the 4-inch Combat Magnum with round butt, but some were manufactured. With the popularity of the .357 Magnum, there were considerations that had to be addressed, especially with the use of the magnum in urban settings. The FBI adopted a policy that reflected the power of the magnum revolver. Agents were authorized to carry .357 Magnum wheelguns, but .38 Special ammunition was to be loaded.

In certain situations, .357 Magnum ammunition was authorized. The original 158-grain lead SWC was over-penetrative for urban work and leaded the barrel badly. With the development of jacketed hollowpoint bullets using a soft lead core surrounded by a thin copper jacket, the solution seemed at hand. The .38 Special loads with 110- to 125-grain bullets increased the wound potential of the .38 Special. These bullets crossed over well into .357 Magnum territory. Due to light weight and issues with bullet pull, the 110-grain projectile could not reach the velocity of the 125-grain JHP. A 110-grain JHP at 1,300 to 1,350 fps was an effective round, however, and was widely used at one time.

The powerful 125-grain JHP broke 1,380 to 1,450 fps. This is the single most effective service load ever issued. The 125-grain JHP proved effective and produced wounds resembling those from a high-powered rifle. The 125-grain JHP solved any problems associated with handgun wound potential. These loads were hard on the revolvers, however. When the Combat Magnum was introduced, Jordan and others recommended that practice regimen should consist of 20 rounds of .38 Special for each .357 Magnum cartridge. Court cases and liability concerns, as well as a realistic look at police training, led to qualification with the duty load. Some agencies practiced monthly, a high standard. They were well armed and well qualified and seldom missed with their magnum revolvers.

Revolver timing issues and wear and tear on the small parts became common. Smith & Wesson instituted several fixes, with a solid gas ring and other improvements. By the introduction of the Model 19-4 around 1975, the Combat Magnum was a much-improved revolver. But it was still a small-frame sixgun, basically a .357 Magnum on a .38 Special frame. The cutout for the ejector rod proved to be a weak point, and there were cracked frames in this area in high round-count handguns. This was the Achilles heel of the Combat Magnum and soon Smith introduced the L-frame revolver. It was a revolver with a frame midway in size between the K- and N-frame, but with a grip frame the same size as the K frame. The L-frame was a good revolver but came on the scene as police agencies were making a wholesale move to semi-auto pistols.

The Combat Magnum continued to enjoy popular use, though, especially among civilian shooters. During its long service life, the most popular issue revolver was the Model 66, a stainless-steel Combat Magnum. This revolver is still in use with elite units based on its reliability, accuracy and power. For example, the Navy SEALS keep the Model 66 Combat Magnum on hand for underwater duty. It is corrosion resistant and not dependent on perfect ammunition for function. It will come up shooting after a swim to the objective.

The Combat Magnum is a desirable handgun for home defense and for those wishing to own the finest medium-frame revolver ever built. The .357 Magnum cartridge is a powerful number, well suited to defense against man or beast.

In 2005, the Model 19 and Model 66 were discontinued after a 50-year production run. Demand had lessened, and expense was one reason. All revolvers are increasingly expensive to manufacture, at least the quality ones, and demand skill in hand fitting. The L-frame revolvers took the place in the lineup of the previous Combat Magnums. But today, the Model 66 has been reintroduced. This revolver features precision machining thanks to CNC technology. The new Model 66 features tight cylinders and cylinder throats and offers excellent accuracy potential. This revolver remains an excellent choice for all-around use.

A very different Combat Magnum was introduced in 2014. The Model 69

CHART 1 .38 SPECIAL VELOCITIES

.38 Special Factory Loads for the Combat Magnum

AMMUNITION	VELOCITY (fps)
Black Hills 100-grain Honey Badger	1,060
Buffalo Bore 158-grain SWC Outdoorsman	1,145
Double Tap 110-grain JHP	1,100
Federal Match 148-grain Wadcutter	770
Federal 129-grain Hydra Shock +P	1,070

CHART 2 .357 MAGNUM VELOCITIES

.357 Magnum Factory Loads for the Combat Magnum

AMMUNITION	VELOCITY (fps)
Black Hills 125-grain JHP	1,440
Buffalo Bore Low Flash Low Recoil 158-grain JHP	1,252
Buffalo Bore 180-grain Hard Cast FP	1,301
Federal 125-grain JHP	1,430
Federal 130-grain Hydra Shock	1,480
Federal Cast Core 180-grain	1,222
Fiocchi 158-grain XTP	1,121
Hornady 125-grain Critical Defense	1,383
Winchester 145-grain Silvertip	1,290

The famous red insert for the S&W front ramp sight.

is an L-frame revolver with a five-shot cylinder chambered for the .44 Magnum cartridge. This model is best served with .44 Special loads. It remains a formidable handgun for specialized use, but in my opinion is not nearly as versatile as the .357 models. As of 2018, the Combat Magnum is alive and well and remains very much appreciated.

A PERFECT REVOLVER

The Texas Rangers Commemorative, while designed as a collectors' piece, is my favorite carry revolver, and a good example of a Combat Magnum. It has certain modifications that I feel make it the best factory Combat Magnum ever offered. This Model 19-3 features the same S&W micro-click adjustable sights as any other Combat Magnum. It also has the high visibility red insert front sight that allowed so many officers to home in on the bad guys. The blued finish is flawless and bright after more than 40 years. The cylinder features the desirable recessed chambers. The action is very smooth. The trigger is a wide combat type with a smooth face, ideal for shooters schooled in staging the shot. There is an integral trigger stop. This action allows good accuracy well past 50 yards.

The trigger guard has the Bill Jordan-inspired thinned radius. Far superior to a cutaway trigger guard, this allows faster and sure trigger finger positioning. The grips are the much sought-after S&W smooth combat grips with a cutout on the left side for a speed loader. The gold inlay Texas State Seal is a nice touch. This revolver isn't a safe queen. When I need a powerful revolver, this is the one that rides with me. I have great confidence in its ability to get the job done. It has ridden with me to remote areas. It's usually loaded with a handload using the Hornady 125-grain XTP bullet over a stiff charge of H110 powder. It's good enough for who it is for.

I carry the revolver in a Tom Threepersons holster by Rocking K Saddlery when on the trail or just hiking for fun. This holster is a cut above the ordinary and offers real security and a high ride. When I carry the piece concealed, it rides in an Avenger-style holster from Nelson Holsters. With the belt loop keeping the handgun close to the body, and the high ride Avenger-style as properly executed by James Nelson, it's a first-class holster. If I had only one shot and had to stop the threat with that shot, it would be with a Combat Magnum.

PINNED AND RECESSED – DOES IT MATTER?

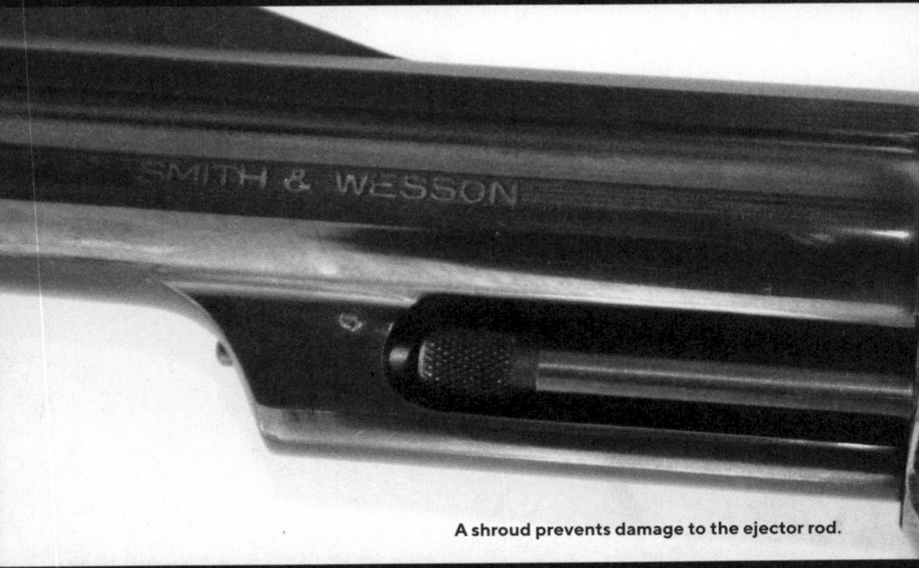

A shroud prevents damage to the ejector rod.

About Smith & Wesson revolvers, you will often hear the term "pinned and recessed." This simply means the revolver features a pinned barrel and recessed chambers in the cylinder. Collectors seem willing to pay extra for these features. For shooters, it should not matter, but some of the finest revolvers ever made have pinned barrels and recessed cylinders. Early S&W revolvers featured a barrel that screwed into the frame and a pin that kept the barrel rigid, preventing turning. This continued into modern production, although today's revolvers have a barrel shroud over the barrel. It was determined that the barrel did not need the pin for rigidity. The cylinder of magnum revolvers features countersunk cylinders to provide a degree of safety in the event of a burst cartridge case. The original S&W .357 – and other .357 Magnum revolvers manufactured prior to 1980 – used recessed cylinders. It was determined that with modern brass and loads the recessed chamber was not necessary. Eventually, S&W discontinued each of these features in modern products. While I like to have the recessed chamber, it isn't a deal breaker for an otherwise useful revolver.

28 GAUGE: THE MIGHTY MOUSE OF SHOTGUNS

Two handsome scaled-framed 28s, a Merkel 280 EL side-by-side, and a B. Rizzini Artemis over/under.

Singing the Praises of the 28-Gauge Underdog

BY **NICK HAHN**

Handgunners often refer to small pistols and revolvers chambered in what they consider ineffective calibers as "mouse guns." Many people refer to very heavy caliber rifles as "elephant guns," while the mild smaller-caliber rifles are often dubbed "rook rifles" or "garden guns." These latter guns are chambered in rounds that have a mild report and are meant for pest control. There are even shotguns designed for such use, chambered in bore sizes like 9mm smoothbore or the .36 caliber.

However, once you move up to the .410, it is no longer a garden gun but a legitimate target and game getter. But, the .410 is ignored by many game shooters and even the 28 gauge is shunted aside. It seems that many consider anything below 20 gauge as not quite up to the level of genuine game gun.

This Artemis over/under 28 gauge from B.Rizzini delivered a limit of Arizona doves.

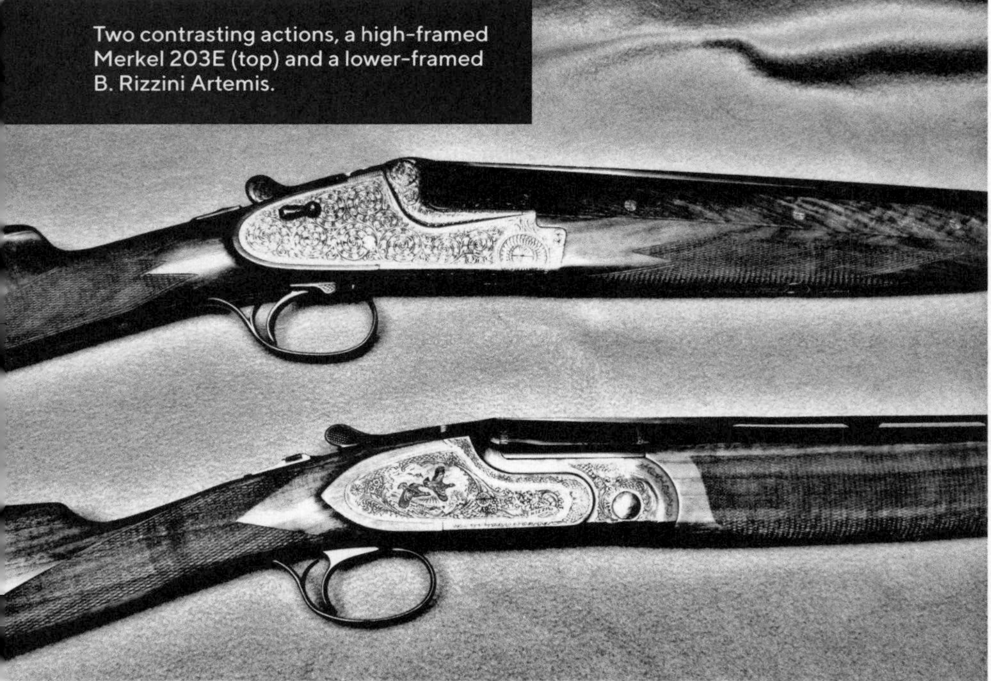
Two contrasting actions, a high-framed Merkel 203E (top) and a lower-framed B. Rizzini Artemis.

That is a mistake. The 28 gauge is a legitimate bore size, quite capable of taking practically anything with feathers.

From the 1940s to the 1960s, there was a popular cartoon character named Mighty Mouse. The tiny rodent cartoon character may have been small but had the strength and ability of mouse superhero — much bigger and stronger. Mighty Mouse became a part of our informal vocabulary and is now commonly used to indicate something small that is bigger and stronger than its size would imply. In the world of shotguns, the 28 gauge can rightly be called the Mighty Mouse, as it is often given almost mystical powers by gun writers. It hits harder than it should, many claim, or, "It is a perfectly balanced load," they say.

These are just some of the more popular attributes given to this diminutive bore size. I have been guilty of saying some of those things myself. There always seems to be a bit of hyperbole involved when the 28 gauge enters the discussion. It's a bore size that seems to capture the imagination of many because of its mild recoil yet sufficient power to handle most game. Also, the slender shape and light weight of guns no doubt contribute considerably to its attractiveness — especially to upland gunners who do a lot of walking.

The 28 gauge's popularity has had its highs and lows. Right now, it seems to be cresting, and there are more choices available than ever before. But, there is a catch — not all 28 gauges are created equal. Just as there are differences in larger-gauge shotguns, there are differences in the 28s as well. However, unlike the 12 gauge, which is generally built on its own frame, and the 20 gauge, which is also mostly built on its own frame, the 28 gauge has been largely relegated to the 20-gauge frame by some manufacturers.

But, there have always been gun makers that built 28s on their own frame, and these are the guns that are most attractive to upland gunners. The scaled-frame 28 gauges (variously called small frame, small action, dedicated frame, etc.) are some of the most visually appealing and wonderfully handling scatterguns.

Years ago, during the golden age of the American doubles, Parker Brothers made wonderful 28 gauges on 00-size frames. Other American gun makers also produced scaled 28-gauge doubles. Until recently, Ruger made a scaled-frame 28 over/under, and it was by far the most attractive of the Red Label models. Unfortunately, now the Red Label is no more. The Winchester Model 21 was never made in small frame when it was produced by Olin Corp. But today, Connecticut Shotgun Company makes its Model 21 in a scaled-frame 28.

To cut costs and simplify manufacturing post–WWII, most gun makers used 20-gauge frames, negating the primary advantages of a 28, those being smaller size and lighter weight. This practice didn't help the 28's popularity as a field gun. However, Remington came out with a downsized receiver on its popular Model 11-48 autoloader in 1952, which became an instant hit with skeet and game shooters. In 1969, Remington reduced the size of its popular Model 870 pump with a correctly sized 28 gauge. So, at

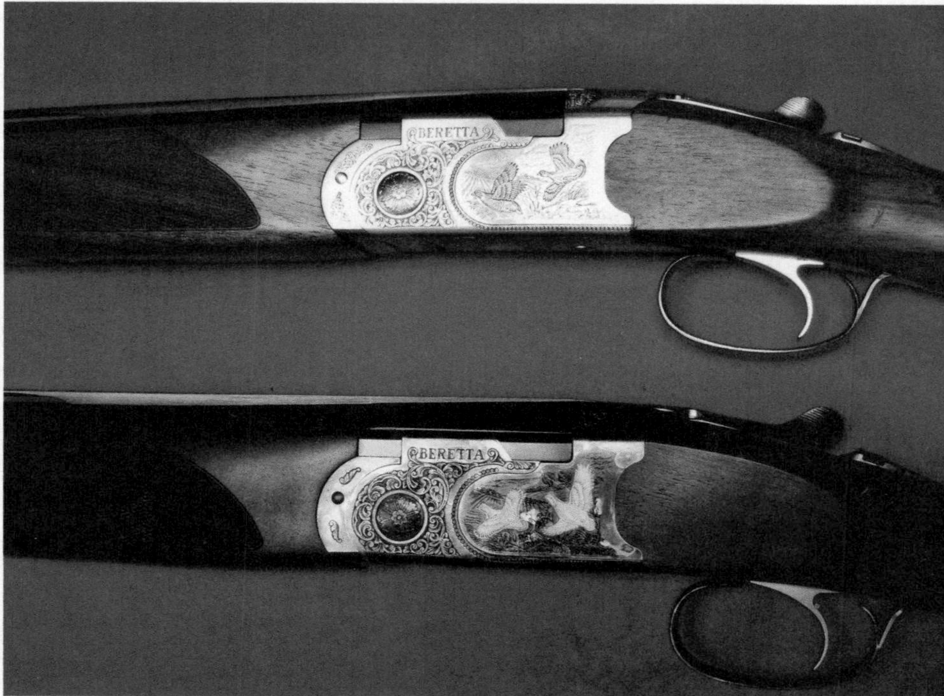

Two "baby frame" Beretta S687s. (Top) Silver Pigeon III; (bottom) Silver Pigeon V.

Current production Franchi 48AL 28 gauges. Although built on 20-gauge receivers, they are still slim and easy handling. (Top) Deluxe Model; (bottom) Standard Model.

least from the 1950s through the 1980s, Remington had proper-sized 28-gauge repeaters. By the late 1960s, Remington had discontinued the Model 11-48 and was making the legendary Model 1100 in small-frame 28. High Standard did make some smaller 28-gauge pump actions in the 1960s. But they were utility guns, and even the "deluxe" models could never compete with Remington.

In Europe, proper-sized 28s have been made since the gauge's beginning, but they were always pricey, handmade jobs. The Belgian Browning Superposed first appeared in 28 in 1960, but built on a 20-gauge frame. When the over/under shotgun boom took place with Japanese and Italian imports from the mid-1960s through the 1980s, 28 gauges were made by SKB, Nikko, Winchester, and Charles Daly, Miroku (later Browning Citori) from Japan and primarily Beretta and Franchi from Italy. But they were all on 20-gauge frames. Miroku made a limited number (500) of small-frame 28-gauge guns and supposedly 37 of these were imported into the U.S. by Charles Daly. But for whatever reason, Charles Daly decided not to include the gun in its line. A few that found their way into the hands of some lucky individuals bring a premium price on the used gun market today, at least twice as much as the Charles Daly 28 gauges on 20-gauge frames.

Just before they were discontinued in 1987, Winchester marketed some 101 O/Us (and Model 23 side-by-sides) on "baby frames" in 28 gauge and .410. Also, the same maker (Olin-Kodensha) made Parker Reproductions on 00 frames in 28. But that didn't last long. Today these guns, like the small-frame Miroku, cost more than the larger gauges or 28s built on 20-gauge frames. Of the European guns, Beretta also made 28 gauges, but on 20-gauge frames. However, the old Beretta S56 frames were small and slim enough that they made for a delightful 28. Also, there were always lesser-known (at the time) Italian makers, such as Poli, Rizzini and Zoli, that made very nice small-frame 28s, such as the ones sold by the old Abercrombie & Fitch, but they were never imported in large numbers. Of course, there were always the more expensive Italian and other European makers that sold scaled-frame 28s, but they were not very common or easily purchased by the average American.

This Parker Reproduction DHE Grade is built on the scaled 00-frame and in a very nice leather Emmebi case with a canvas over-case provided by the gun maker.

The 28 gauge has had a long history, perhaps not as long as the larger gauges, but they were made as early as the mid-1800s in England. W.W. Greener was a great proponent of the smallish gauge in the 19th century and published various testimonials by 28-gauge shooters. Some claimed that it shot "harder" and killed pigeons or game better than the 12 gauge! Naturally, they were all Greener guns. No one has ever accused William Wellington Greener of being modest about his products, and these 28-gauge testimonials were well documented in his book, THE GUN (and its development), first published in 1881. It has been republished 10 times since.

So, the 28 has been around, and shooters claimed all sorts of magical properties going back to the 19th century. The 28 gauge, by the way, was not invented by Parker Brothers as some Americans are prone to believe. Even the much-revered Jack O'Connor made that erroneous assumption, when he wrote in The Shotgun Book that Parker invented it in 1903. Parker Brothers made their first 28 gauge in 1903, but Greener was promoting it in the 1880s. It is not known exactly who first made the 28, but it was no doubt in England in the 1800s, and not Parker Brothers on this side of the pond.

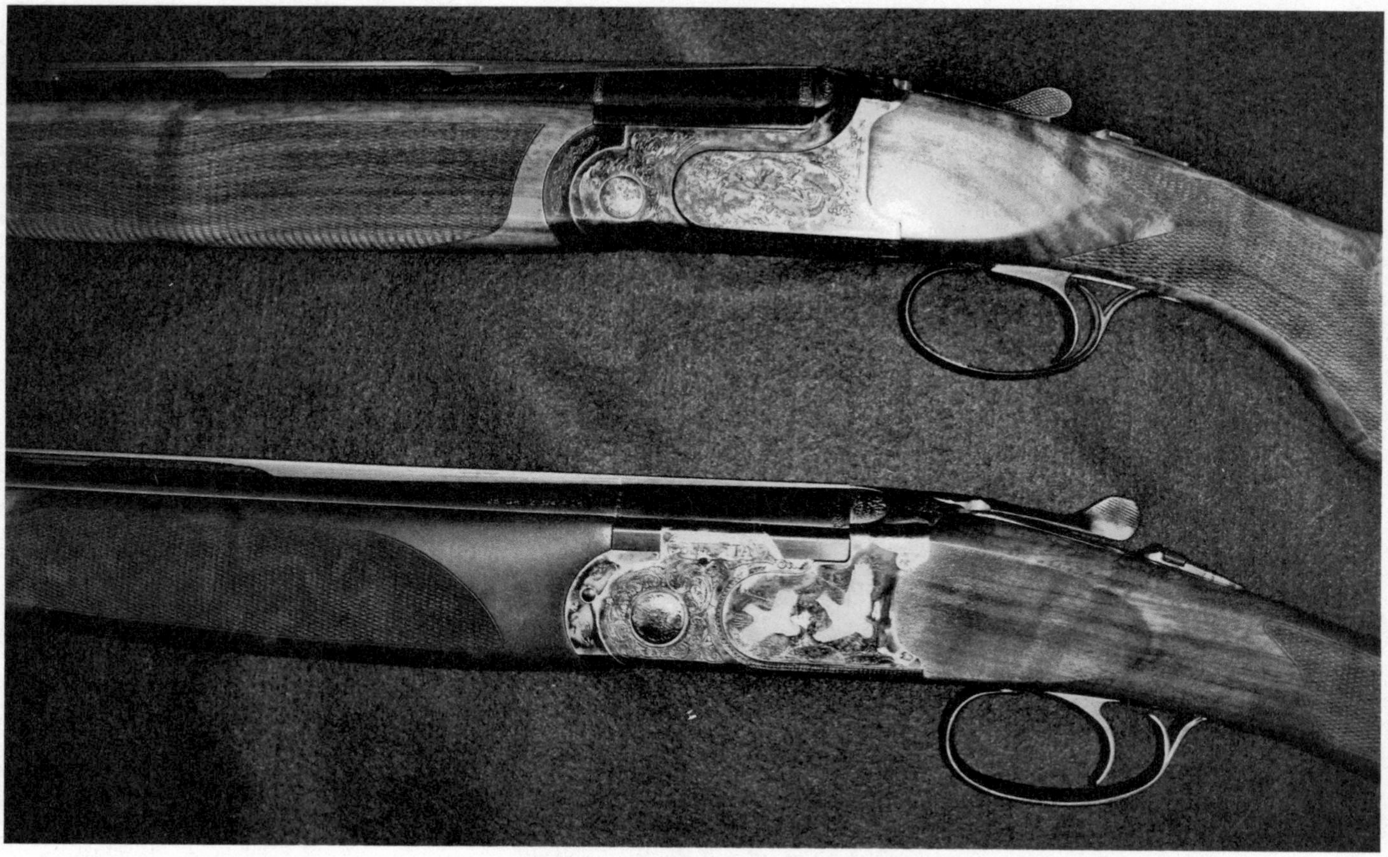

(above) Both the older (top) Beretta BL-4/S56E and the newer (bottom) Beretta S687 Silver Pigeon II are 28s built on 20-gauge frames.

Similarly, many American gun writers believe choke boring was invented in the 1870s by Fred Kemble, an Illinois duck hunter. However, records show that English gunmaker W.R. Pape filed a patent for choke boring in 1866. Pape, along with other English gunsmiths, experimented with choke boring as early as the 1850s. So, once again, it seems the British were the first, like in so many other areas of early shotgun development.

The appearance of plastic hulls and shot cups in the 1960s greatly improved shotgun performance. Although new load developments were concentrated on the two most popular gauges — the 12 and 20 — all bore sizes benefited from the use of plastic hulls and shot cups. But even before the development of the improved loads, the 28 gauge was still considered effective by many when it was loaded in paper hulls with felt wads. No less than arguably the greatest hunter of man-eating tigers, Jim Corbett, shot partridge and other game in his

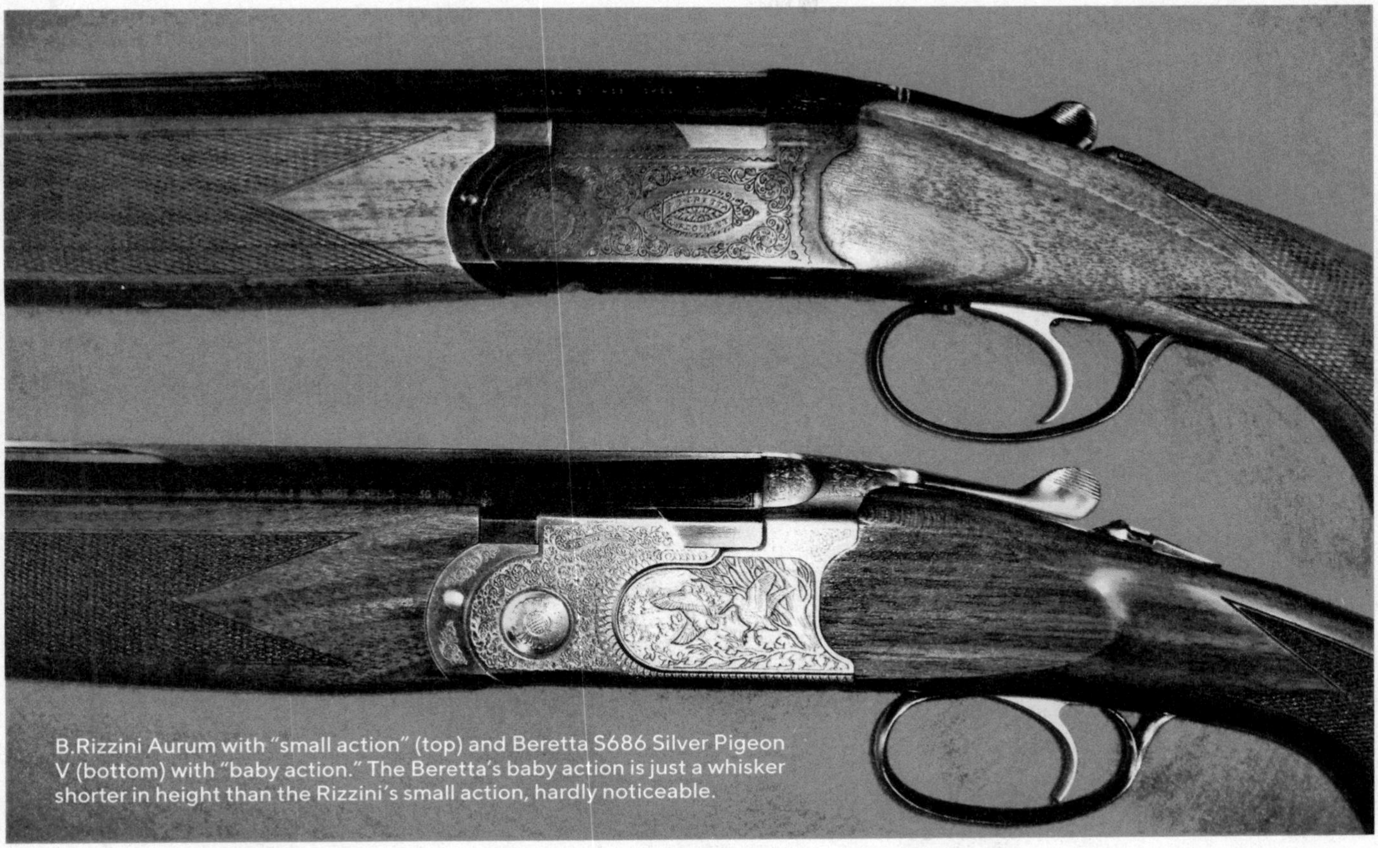

B.Rizzini Aurum with "small action" (top) and Beretta S686 Silver Pigeon V (bottom) with "baby action." The Beretta's baby action is just a whisker shorter in height than the Rizzini's small action, hardly noticeable.

A 28-gauge Franchi 48 AL with a pair of doves. This classic long-recoil autoloader dates to 1950 but has been made in 28 gauge since the late 1990s.

The Ithaca Model 37 was recently offered with a small 28-gauge frame.

beloved Kumaon foothills with a dainty little 28-gauge W.J. Jeffery box-lock double. Jack O'Connor, although known for being a rifleman, said that if he were left but with one gun to hunt the rest of his life, he would be perfectly happy with his little custom-made Arizaga 28-gauge double chasing pheasants in Idaho with his beloved Brittany, Mike.

The 28 is a wonderful gun for shooting within 40 yards, but only a very good shot would be able to shoot it consistently well over that distance. All one has to do is some patterning, and it won't take a genius to realize that the 28 gauge may have the same size pattern as a 12 or 20 gauge, but it is a much thinner pattern. After all, the number of pellets in 3/4 ounce of shot is less than in the 7/8 ounce of a 20 gauge, the 1 ounce of a 16, or the 1 1/8 ounce of a 12. As the distance increases, the pattern becomes thinner.

I had been interested in the 28 for many years but didn't really take up shooting it seriously until about 25 years ago. My first shooting experience with one was on a skeet range with a Remington Model 11-48 over half a century ago when I started my wife shooting. It was also during this period that I met two older gentlemen who shot them. One man shot a Beretta BL-4, which had just appeared on the U.S. market, imported by Garcia. This man mostly shot ducks and pheasants in the Sacramento Valley of California, and according to him, had no trouble knocking down those roosters or greenheads with the 28. The other man shot a Belgian-made side-by-side that he'd brought back from Europe as a war trophy. He claimed that his 28 gauge outshot his hunting partner's 12 gauge!

(above) The Remington Model 11-48 was the first autoloader built to scale for a 28 gauge. It is still as good as ever.

(below) The Ruger Red Label is a lovely, scaled 28 gauge, beautifully sculpted. Photo: Guns America

The lavish Benelli Legacy was built on a 28-gauge frame.

He had been shooting it since the end of the war, using the old paper hulls with felt wads. I didn't quite believe that his 28 outshot his friend's 12, but I knew he was an excellent shot and suspected he simply shot better than his partner, regardless of gauge.

Through the years, periodically I would enjoy shooting the 28 gauge. However, because I lived and worked abroad in various countries since the 1970s, ammunition was always a problem and I was restricted mostly to the 12 gauge. Even 20-gauge ammunition was hard to get, while the 28 was almost impossible to find in many of the countries. Despite the fact that I owned and shot 28s from time to time, it wasn't until the mid-1990s that I was able to start shooting it with any sort of regularity.

The landscape for the 28 gauge has changed considerably since the 1960s when I was first exposed to this bore size. Not only are there more choices in gun selection, but there have been new developments in 28-gauge loadings as well. Benelli came out with a new autoloader, the Ethos, and chambered it in the rare 3-inch 28 gauge. In collaboration with Benelli, Fiocchi started making 3-inch 28-gauge shells that carry a 1-1/16-ounce payload. That's a 12-gauge field load! To me, it seems to be a bit of overkill and defeating the purpose of a 28 gauge, but then, some apparently welcome this new "super magnum" 28. Actually, the 28-gauge Magnum with a 1-ounce loading has been around since the 1960s. Obviously, there are those who like the idea of a 28 gauge on steroids. Personally, if I want to shoot heavier loads, I will use a 20, 16 or 12.

Scaled-framed 28s are now widely available despite the fact that some makers are still using the larger 20-gauge frames. Beretta has been making the so-called "baby frames" for the 28 gauges and .410s for some time now. Other Italian makers, such as the various Rizzinis (B.Rizzini, I.Rizzini (FAIR) and E.Rizzini), currently all carry scaled frames. B.Rizzini even calls its models "small action."

Browning's Superposed was never made in small frame when it was in regular production. The 20-gauge frame was the smallest, and the Citori is still only made in the 20-sized frame. I'm somewhat surprised that Browning doesn't take advantage of the 28 gauge's current popularity and use the old Miroku "baby frame" blueprints to produce a small-frame 28-gauge Citori. FN did experiment with some (exactly two) very small-framed .410 Superposeds back in 1975–76, but never made them a regular production item. Today, the Browning Custom Shop does make scaled-frame 28 gauges, but of course those wonderful little jewels will cost you the price of a small car!

When it comes to repeaters, Remington and Ithaca are the only American gun makers that offer scaled-frame 28s today. Remington has been making the popular Model 870 as well as the Model 1100 in scaled-frame 28 gauge for more than 40 years. The newly resurrected Ithaca Gun Company now carries a lovely scaled-frame 28 in the Model 37 pump gun. That's about it for American gun makers. Mossberg has a small-framed .410 for their popular Model 500 pump series but does not offer any 28s. Browning does not make a scaled-frame 28-gauge repeater in any of its models. The Italians, most notably Beretta and

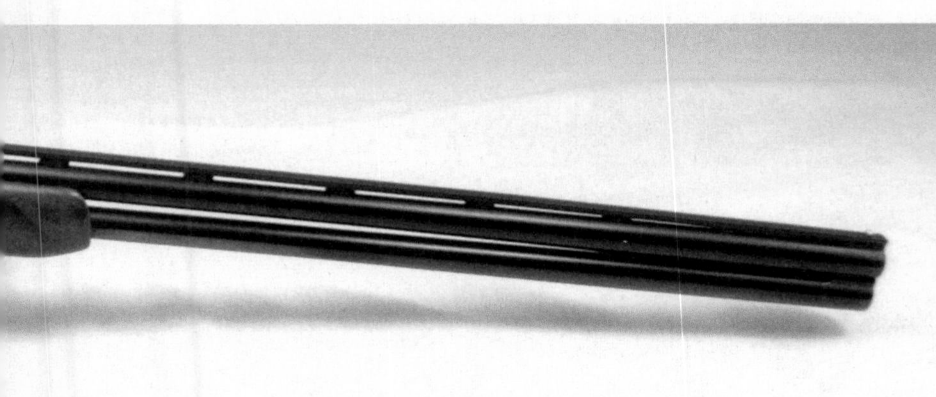

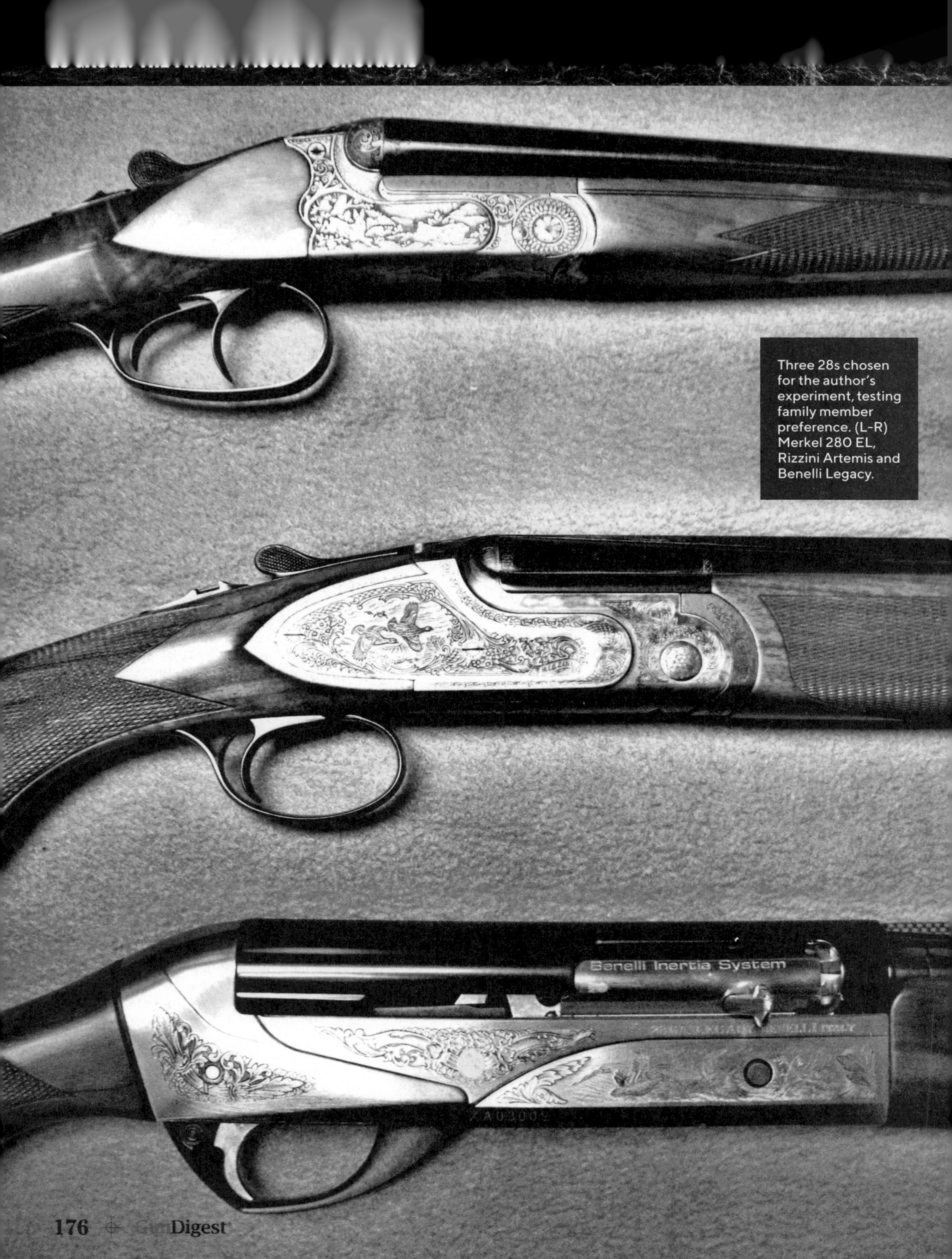

Three 28s chosen for the author's experiment, testing family member preference. (L-R) Merkel 280 EL, Rizzini Artemis and Benelli Legacy.

Benelli, produce scaled-frame 28-gauge autoloaders. The Beretta A400 Xplor 28 has a narrow receiver thickness of 1.420 inches, scaled for the 28 gauge. But it is lofty, unlike the Remington 1100 or 870 scaled frames, which are very low profiled. Because of the type of system (inertia) that Benelli employs, the receiver tends to be much larger than those of other systems. Still, the Benelli scaled-frame 28 has a receiver that is thin at around 1.330 inches, making it slimmer than the Beretta. Surprisingly, the Franchi 48AL 28, which is built on a 20-gauge receiver, has the smallest receiver. It measures 1.320 inches thick with a height of 2.25 inches and a length of 7.5 inches. So the Franchi 48 AL, although built on a 20-gauge frame, appears to be the thinnest and shortest of all Italian 28-gauge autoloaders.

Turkish-made shotguns have made a significant impact on the shotgun market recently. The Turkish guns began to make inroads in the lower price ranges during the last two decades. There are several U.S. gun manufacturers that import Turkish-made guns ranging from pure economy-grade doubles with extractors to more upscale versions with engraving and all the works, as well as gas- and inertia-operated autoloaders. These Turkish guns are also available in scaled frames for the 28 gauge. The Turks seem to be able to produce guns at the low end of the price range, yet still provide quality with decent wood and scaled frames.

There are those who don't seem to mind if the frame appears too large for the gauge. Some, in fact, prefer a 28 on a 20-gauge frame because the gun balances better for them. These shooters find the added bulk and weight of a 20-gauge receiver preferable to the smaller size and the feathery weight of the scaled-frame. This is especially true of those who travel to places like Argentina for "mega dove" shoots. They shoot hundreds if not thousands of rounds per outing, and take a pounding. There are 28s with 30-inch or longer barrels that are made for that type of shooting and weigh around 7 pounds. The heavier 28s are also popular with sporting clays shooters. In fact, there are special sporting clays models both in semi-auto and over/under configuration that have long barrels and weigh as much as a 12 gauge. Others prefer the 28 on a 12-gauge frame because they are skeet shooters who want the gun to feel the same when they are shooting all four categories.

But for most game shooters, the

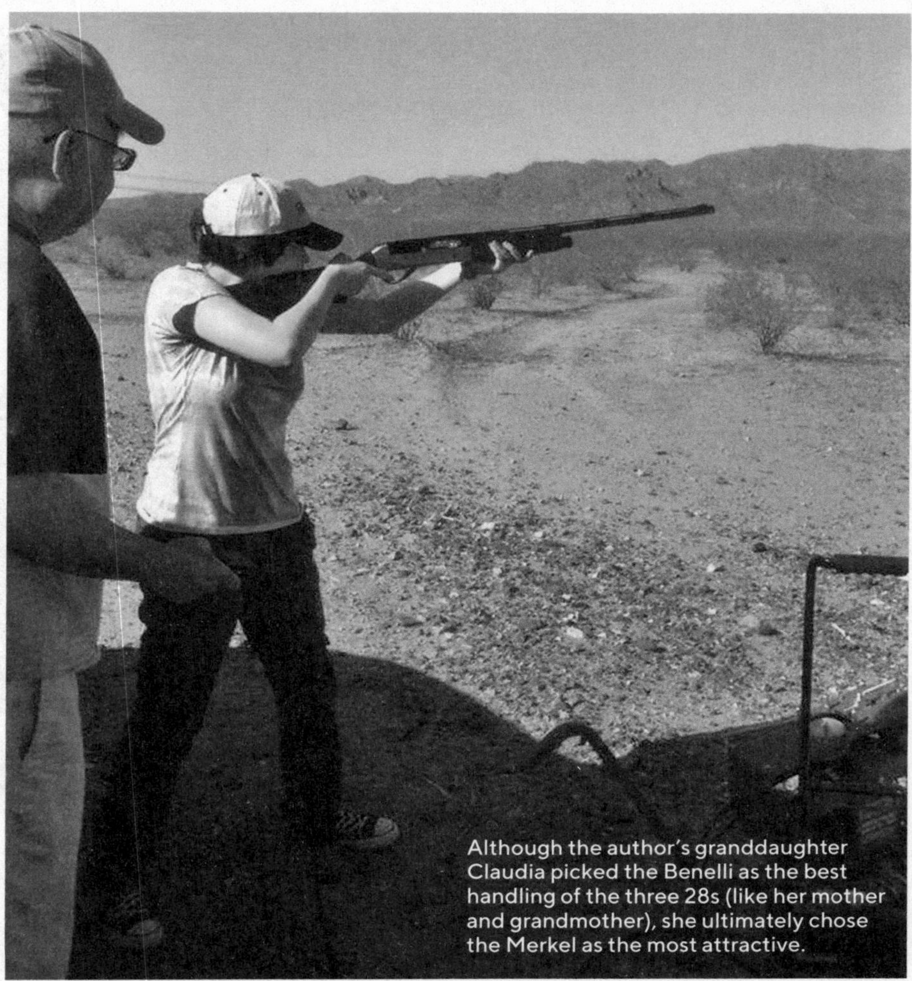

Although the author's granddaughter Claudia picked the Benelli as the best handling of the three 28s (like her mother and grandmother), she ultimately chose the Merkel as the most attractive.

scaled-frame 28 is their choice. It is lighter than the 20 and seems to kill birds just as well. It's slimmer and very comfortable to carry. In most upland hunting, one does far more walking than shooting. It's unlikely that an average hunter will burn more than a box of shells per outing, so why lug around a heavy gun? Besides, the scaled-frame 28 gauge just looks and feels right.

In my family, three generations of women started shooting shotguns with a 28 gauge. Many start young kids and women with a .410, though there is no shortage of women and boys who started with a 12. In fact, I myself started with a 12 gauge at the age of 13, because that's what everyone else shot, or at least that's what I thought. If I had to do it all over again, I would start with a smaller gauge, and not a heavy 12! For most young boys and girls, the 12 gauge is too much gun. On the other hand, the .410 is not a good choice. The .410 is an expert's gun and hard to shoot even for an experienced shotgunner, let alone a beginner. A 28 gauge, or a 20 gauge with light loads, is a much better choice for a beginner.

I started my wife with a 28-gauge Remington Model 11-48 autoloader, a skeet gun, back in 1967. About a quarter of a century later, I started my daughter when she was fourteen with a 28-gauge over/under, also a skeet gun. The latest was my granddaughter who started shooting a shotgun at sixteen with a 28-gauge Benelli Legacy. In the case of my granddaughter, it was especially appropriate to start her with a 28, since she is a small-framed, petite girl.

Recently, out of curiosity, I conducted an experiment of sorts, very unscientific, and not very inclusive, since it involved only three different shotguns. But I thought I would try it and see the results. I asked my wife, daughter and granddaughter each to pick their choice among the three 28-gauge shotguns that I placed before them. The guns were the Benelli Legacy autoloader, an over/under B.Rizzini Artemis, and a side-by-side Merkel 280 EL. They were each asked, without the opportunity to consult each other, to make their selection. The unscientific test consisted of basically two things. They were first asked to just look over and handle each gun and decide which one was most appealing to them visually, or aesthetically most pleasing. Next, they were asked to pick up and handle each gun and decide which one felt and handled the best. That was it. Not very scientific, but I thought I'd give it a try.

The author's daughter Natalie with a B.Rizzini Artemis 28 gauge.

My wife Jo, who has had experience with and been exposed to many different shotguns over the years, said almost immediately that she liked the Merkel best, that it looked the nicest, with the best engraving and wood. However, she said that the Benelli handled the best for her. My daughter Natalie, who also has had some experience and exposure to shotguns (although not as much as her mother), also liked the looks of the little Merkel, and like her mother, said that the Benelli felt the best for her as well. My granddaughter Claudia, who has the least exposure and experience with shotguns, looked over the three guns carefully, took the most time, then announced that she thought the Merkel was the nicest. She then went over the guns again, lifting and shouldering each and settled on the Benelli as the best handling for her. I wasn't surprised that she picked the Benelli because, in her case, that is the gun with which she learned to shoot.

It was interesting to note that all three, regardless of their experience and exposure to shotguns, thought the Merkel side-by-side was aesthetically most appealing. But at the same time, it seems that the Benelli autoloader felt the best for all three of them. Not much of an experiment, but there it is, the Merkel 280 EL wins the beauty contest while the Benelli is the winner for best handling characteristics, at least for these three ladies.

The 28 gauge is a wonderful bore size for all feathered game except for the very largest. It's not a turkey or a goose gun, although many of the bigger birds have been taken with a 28. But it can take ducks over decoys with proper loads (currently there are steel shot loadings as well as Bismuth available from several makers), and it will take pheasant over dogs without a problem. It has even become popular with some driven pheasant shooters in England, using 1-ounce loads. However, most of all, it is an ideal shotgun for upland hunting, especially when those long treks are required between occasional shots. To me, a scaled-framed 28 gauge is the perfect shotgun for upland game. It is truly the Mighty Mouse of shotguns!

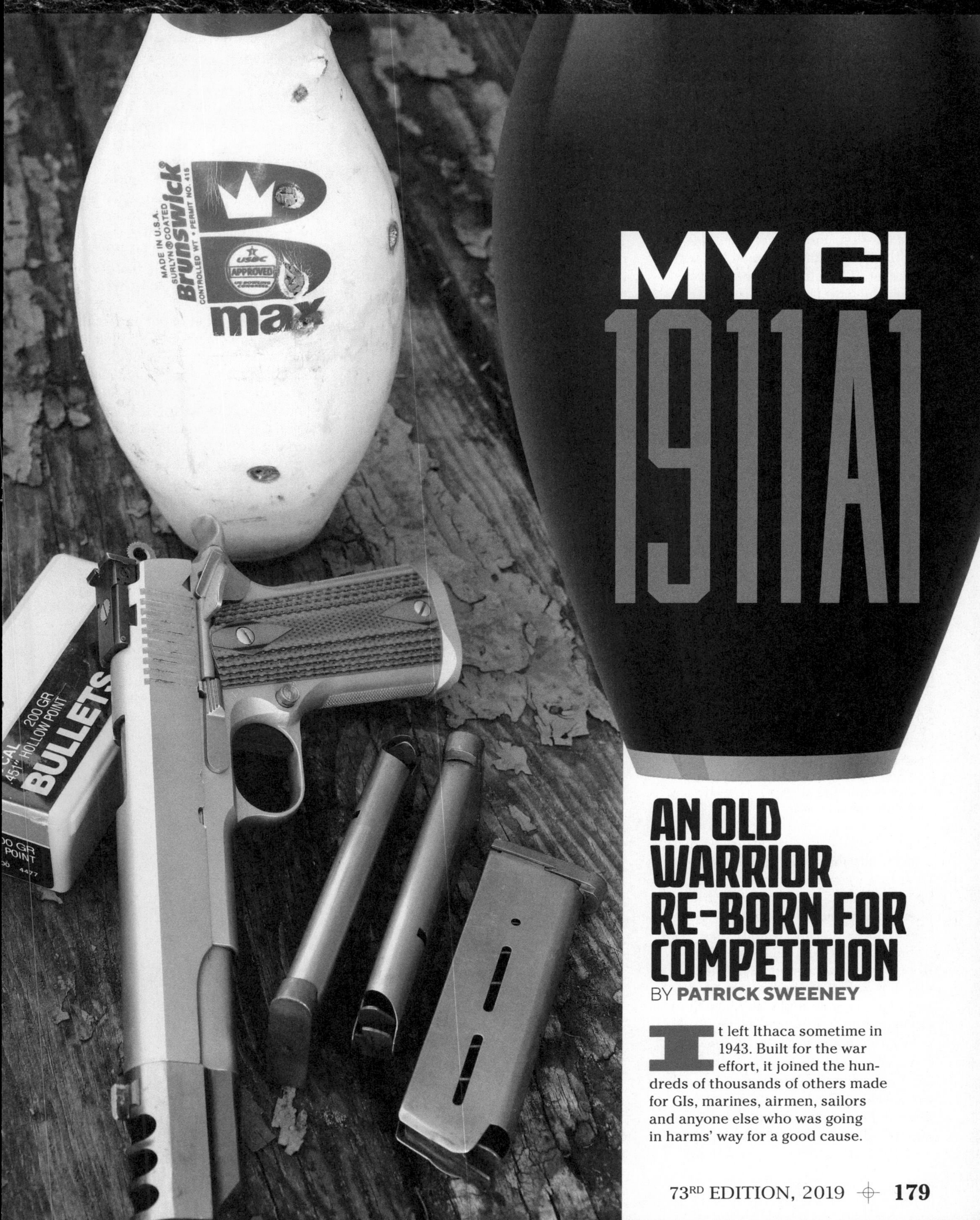

MY GI 1911A1

AN OLD WARRIOR RE-BORN FOR COMPETITION

BY **PATRICK SWEENEY**

It left Ithaca sometime in 1943. Built for the war effort, it joined the hundreds of thousands of others made for GIs, marines, airmen, sailors and anyone else who was going in harms' way for a good cause.

Between then and when I encountered it in 1977 at The Gun Room — a gun shop at which I was then employed — there's no way of knowing where it had been, what it had been through, or who had used it. But it was in pretty good shape, so it hadn't gone to awful places to be abused, at least. The shop only wanted $175 for it. Why did I buy it? I had discovered the new shooting sport called IPSC or International Practical Shooting Confederation, and as everyone "knew" back then, you didn't win matches with a revolver. (Little did I know that was wrong, and later I learned otherwise, to my great benefit.)

My boss at The Gun Room saw an opportunity for some PR. He had the local 1911 wizard, Frank Paris, build it up into a match-worthy pistol. Paris had been building bullseye guns for some time before then, and he and I had to go 'round a few times until he could get a front sight to stay on despite a steady diet of hardball-equivalent ammo. But he did great work, and I felt no need to change things for quite a few years.

The new five-pin setup for the Main Event. You need power to drive the pins off the table, and the author's trusty Ithaca certainly can do that.

I won the first IPSC match I ever entered with it. That was it, I was hooked. That was years before the formation of the USPSA (United States Practical Shooting Association), and when I started, all clubs were direct affiliates with the international organization. While I had a knack for it, I was a bit hobbled. You see, I was still loading on a single-stage press. This meant that I spent every weeknight loading the ammo I'd shoot on the weekends. One night was brass prep night, when I sorted and cleaned cases. The next, size all of them. The third, prime cases. The fourth, drop powder charges and seat bullets. The fifth, crimp cases, inspect and gauge. I was shooting maybe 200 rounds a week. That's ten thousand a year, but it meant I had no life outside of loading and shooting. Back then, that was fine. It did lead to problems, however.

One thing you need to know about WWII-era 1911A1s: the slides can be soft. Speedy wartime production called for acceptable shortcuts, one being a process called induction-hardening. Here, the slides were placed in an electric ring, and when the power was turned on, the ring (circling the slide) heated up, and in so-doing it heated the slide, but at the locking lugs. And only at the locking lugs. (Some makers used a dual-ring setup, and hardened slides at the locking lugs and the front, where the bushing notch was.) If you happen to see photos — or handle a WWII-era 1911A1 — you may notice that the finish is darker at the locking lugs area. They were hard enough for wartime, but not so for a steady diet of hot ammo, for IPSC competition and practice. It took me about four years to put enough ammo through it that the barrel and slide agreed on a mutual suicide pact. The slide peened the barrel lugs, and the barrel lugs chewed the slide. It stopped working.

The coup de gras on the slide and barrel combo came from Dillon. With the new RL-450 reloader (later I switched to a 550 and added a pair of Square Deals in "minor" calibers) I could greatly up my production rate. I went from scrambling to get close to 10,000 rounds a year, to averaging 35,000 a year and having a personal life as well. The switch and the new volume of ammo precipitated the need for a rebuild.

I replaced the upper half with a Bar-Sto barrel and slide from Caspian. I also added a compensator to the barrel because I needed it for IPSC, and this other new-to-me sport of bowling pin

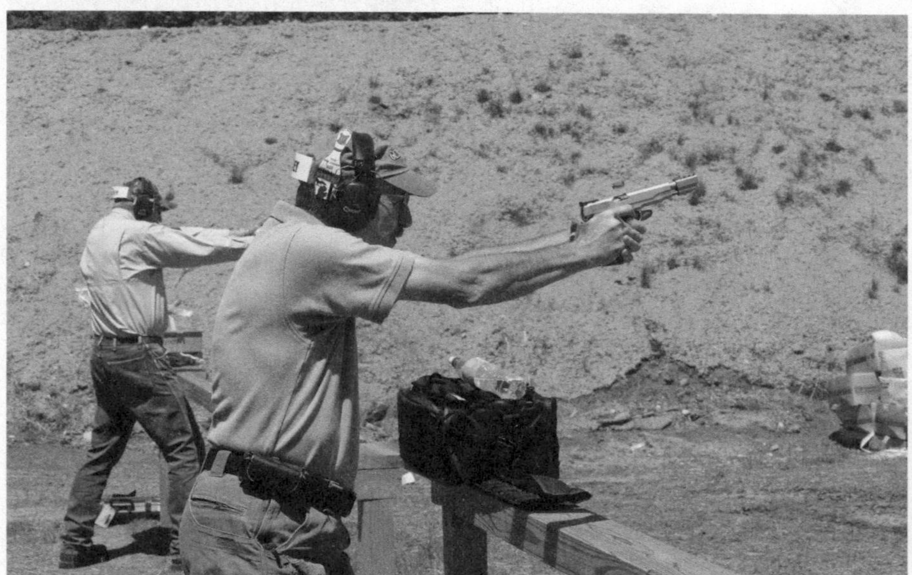
The author hard at work, slamming pins off the tables.

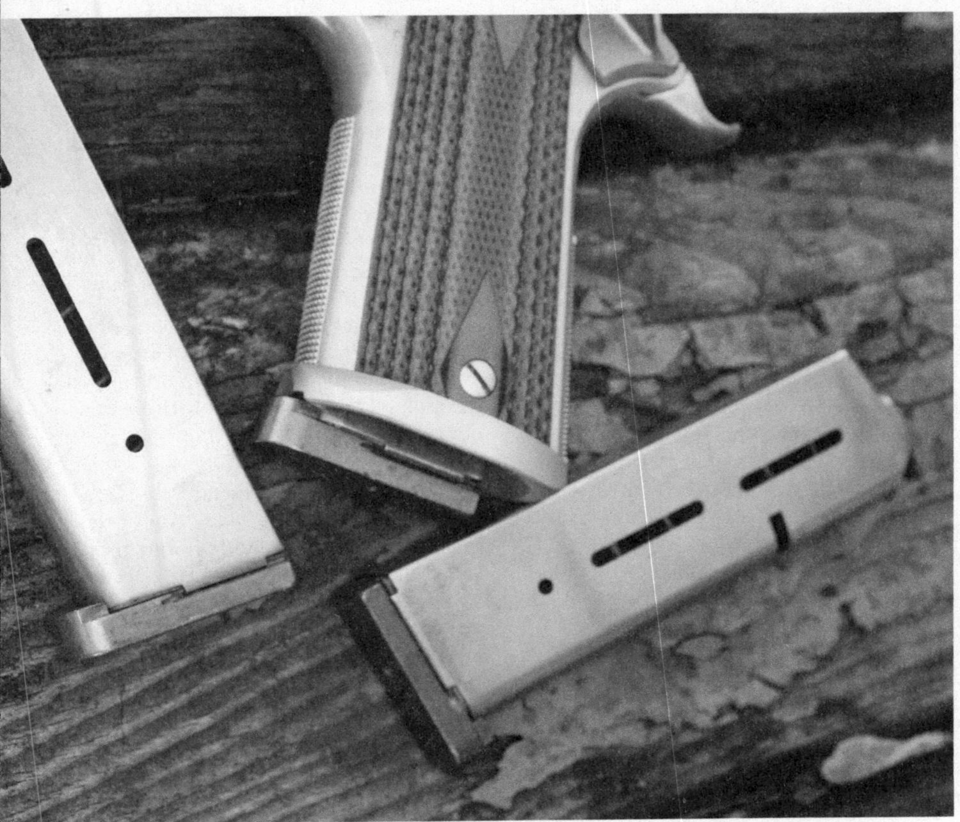

shooting. For IPSC, I needed a power factor (PF) of 185 (soon after lowered to 180, then 175 for a long time, now settled at 165), but for bowling pins I needed no less than a 195PF, and 200 was better yet. Power factor? Multiply weight in grains times velocity in feet per second and drop the last three zeros. For pins, I was hurling Speer 200-grain JHPs at 1,000 fps. For IPSC, I was shooting 200-grain H&G 68s at 900 fps. And I was putting three-quarters of a ton of lead a year into the backstops of the ranges I frequented.

In the late 1980s, I got tired of the various bolt-on mag-well funnels, and I installed my own. This involved silver-soldering gage steel to the sides of the mag-well opening. I then spent an inordinate amount of time grinding the outside to the contour of the grips, and the inside to a huge funnel, to speed reloads. I then had the frame hard-chromed, but left the slide blue, because that was the style then.

(left) Stan Chen put one of his new Gen2 mag-well funnels onto the author's Ithaca. If you shoot correctly, you don't need a reload. But when you do need one, you want one of these.

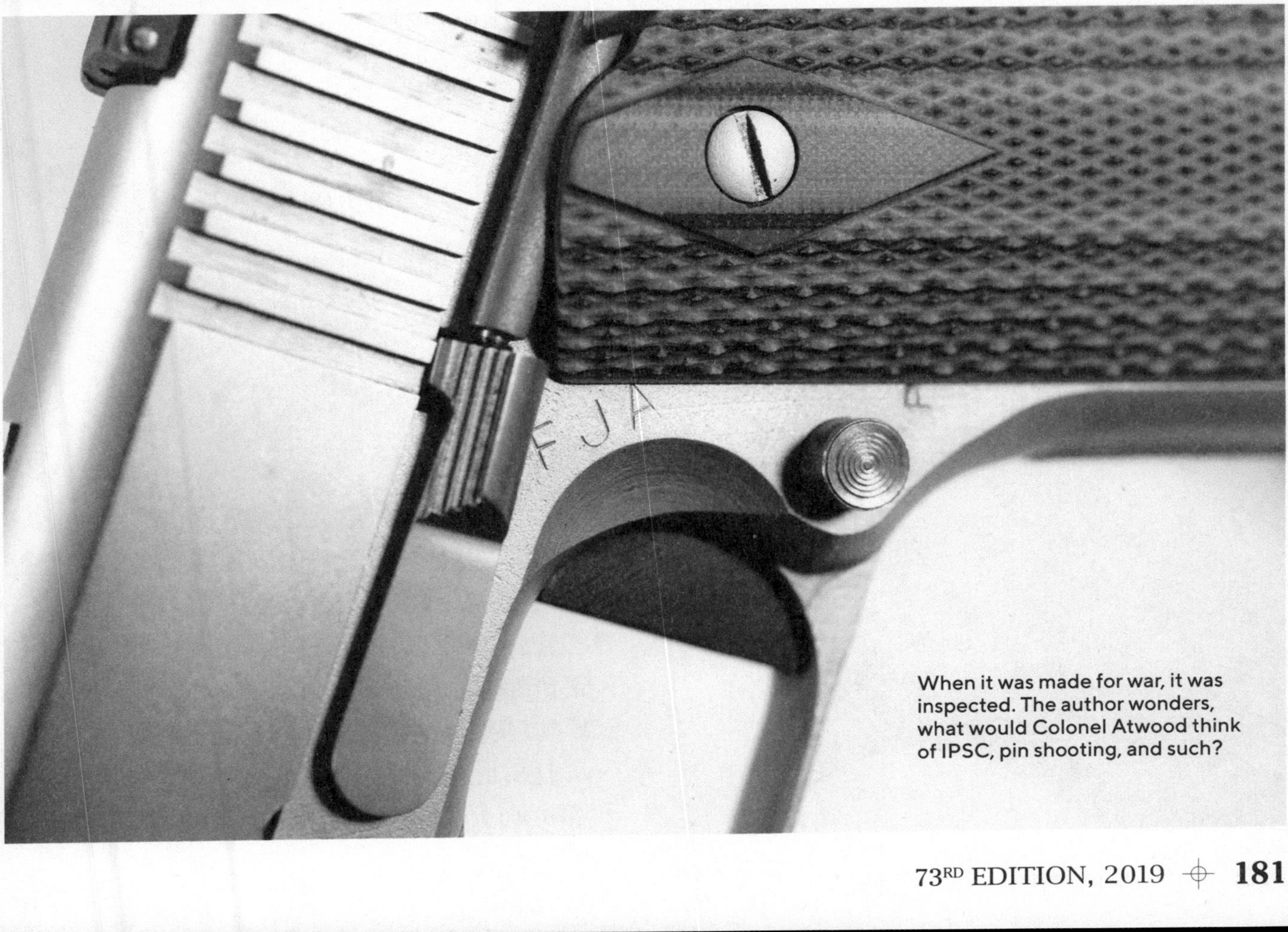

When it was made for war, it was inspected. The author wonders, what would Colonel Atwood think of IPSC, pin shooting, and such?

But, by the late 1980s, the writing was on the wall. IPSC competition, now in the U.S. under the aegis of the USPSA, pretty much required a .38 Super to win matches. A lot of us had been holding on as long as possible, loading up specialty .45 ACP ammo to feed gas to the muzzle brakes, but the Super always had an advantage there. And, it held two more rounds than a .45. That seems like no big deal now, but the difference between stepping to the line with a pistol that held 11 rounds, versus one that held nine, was huge by 1989. I built a single-stack Super, and soon after I had to build a hi-cap Super. The early 1990s was an equipment race, and IPSC/USPSA was still in the inflationary era. In the space of a few years I went from an eight-shot .45 to a 10-shot .38 Super, to an 18-shot, then a 23-shot .38 Super. And all the Supers had red-dot optics, not iron sights. I kept the original Ithaca and the original .38 Super single stack because I needed them for pin shooting. I also needed backup pistols, just in case.

I ended up needing the Ithaca as a backup when I went to the Gunsite Alumni Shoot in 1996. At the end of the match, my stock (as in no comp, brake, etc.) 1911 died a quick and mysterious death. I had to use my backup, my comp gun, in the shoot-off. Before you say "gamer, cheater!" ask yourself just how much work it is to draw a pistol that has essentially a seven-inch barrel from a Yaqui slide holster. No one complained, and anyone who had, I'd have gladly traded gear with them to see how a few practice draws went for them.

During the USPSA .38 Super era, I was still hurling vehicle-loads worth of bullets downrange through the Ithaca — so much so that I wore out the Bar-Sto barrel and had to replace it again. (Yes, I wore out a Bar-Sto barrel. Be afraid.) In went a Nowlin barrel, along with a bigger, more effective comp, fitted by my friend Ned Christiansen. Once the work was done and I was sure everything was running fine, I had the slide hard-chromed to match the frame. There were a few more years of pin shooting and then the Second Chance Pin Shoot closed operations after the 1998 season. The Ithaca languished in the safe, coming out now and then for special occasions, but not really seeing much work. A few years after the hibernation, I pulled it out to discover that one of the silver-soldered mag funnel straps had fallen off. How did that happen? When? Where? Oh well.

And then, oh frabjous day, the Pin Shoot came back. I dug out all the old gear, the old ammo, and managed to get in a modicum of practice. I did well enough to come home with a small measure of loot and glory.

When I learned that the Pin Shoot would be held again in 2018 and the two of us could get back into the swing of things, I had to decide: would I attempt to solder a replacement strap on, and go through all that work? Surely there has been improvement since then. And yes, Virginia, there has been.

A new friend, Stan Chen, had a magazine funnel that was already contoured, ready to be installed, and offered great looks without increased frame size. So, I shipped old Ithaca off to be brought up to date. While a new friend, Stan was not new in working on my guns. He had done an earlier version of his mag-well funnel on a stock 1911A1 of mine, from Springfield Armory.

I sent it off to Stan, and once it arrived the plan changed. It was going to take a bit more blending to make the new

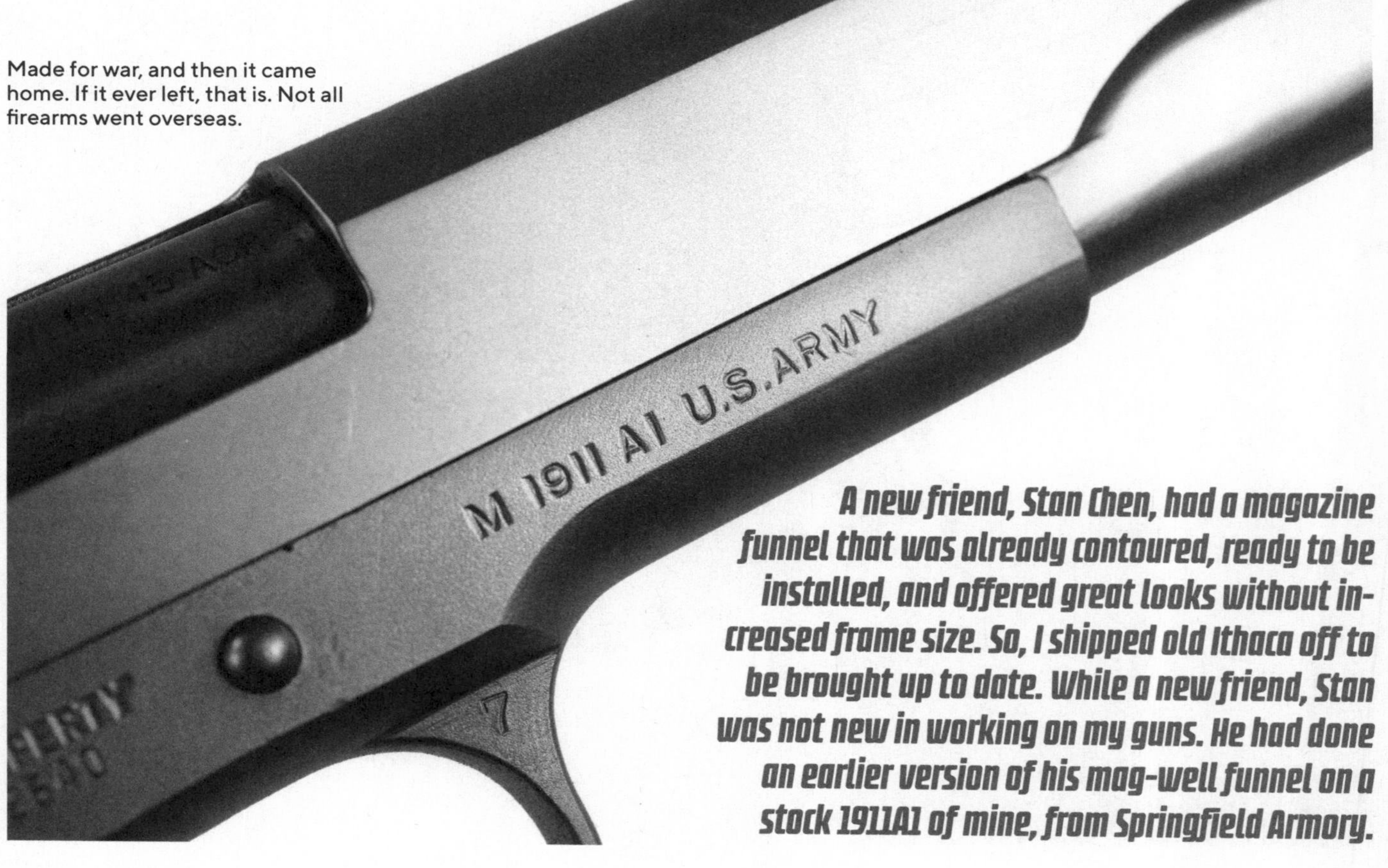

Made for war, and then it came home. If it ever left, that is. Not all firearms went overseas.

A new friend, Stan Chen, had a magazine funnel that was already contoured, ready to be installed, and offered great looks without increased frame size. So, I shipped old Ithaca off to be brought up to date. While a new friend, Stan was not new in working on my guns. He had done an earlier version of his mag-well funnel on a stock 1911A1 of mine, from Springfield Armory.

The Nowlin barrel in here is a relatively low-mileage one; it has not yet seen 100,000 rounds.

parts fit the old. The blending was going to end up grinding the hard-chrome off of the frame, in places that could not be hidden, and leave bare steel. So, did I want to have one of the new, hi-zoot finishes put on, or did I want them to hard-chrome it? Well, considering that the lower had survived all this time with a hard chrome job on it, that was easy. Back to classic HC.

If you have only ever seen the black oxide done over Tenifer, or the boron/silicon/Teflon/unobtainium finishes that are the current "this stuff rocks" choices, then hard chrome will come as a shock. Ever hear the term "fish-belly white"? That's hard chrome. There's no other color component, or depth to the finish, as you can see with the newer high-tech coatings. It was the best there was back then, and it still works, it just doesn't have the advantages that newer ones have. Still, it was what I wanted, so that was what Stan searched out and found. He has one hard-chrome shop left that he trusts, and if Stan trusts someone, then that's good enough for me.

What he put on the Ithaca was his new Gen2 mag funnel. The Gen2 is a mainspring housing with a mag funnel attached as an integral part. But unlike others, this is meant to go on a shortened frame. Stan trims the frame a bit shorter, machines a new mainspring housing retaining pin hole, and then blends it all to look good. The result is no longer than the original frame. On mine, he then hard chromed it and installed a pair of VZ G10 grips of the double-diamond style, in Hyena brown.

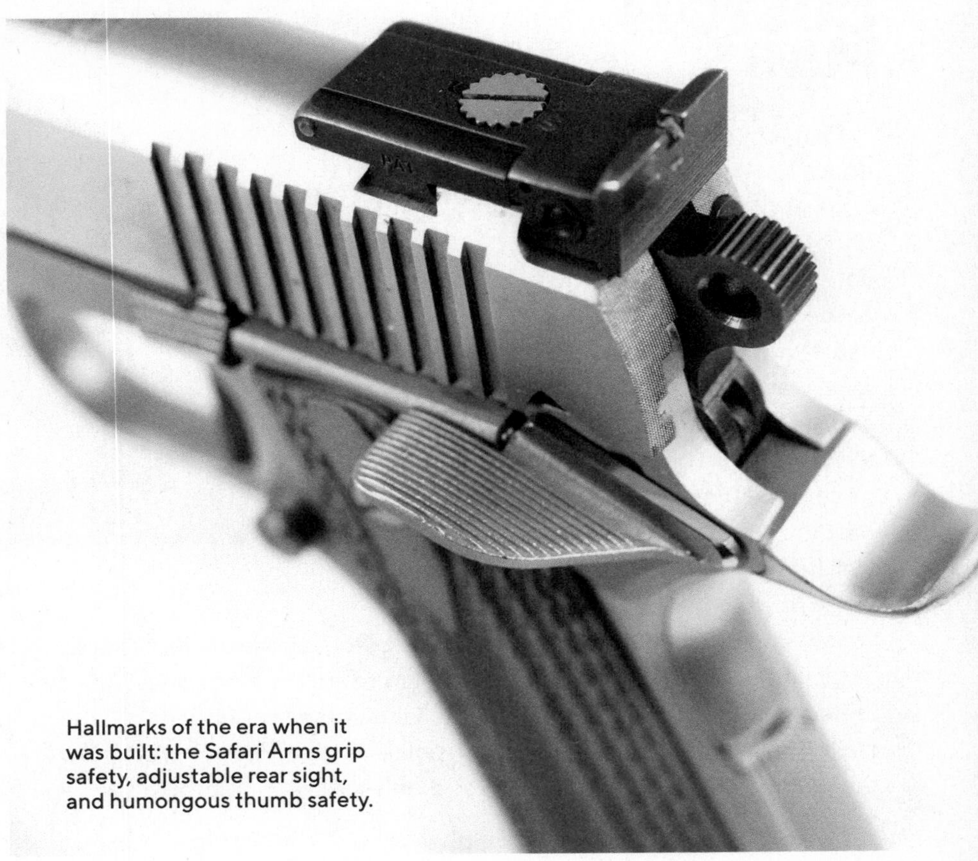

Hallmarks of the era when it was built: the Safari Arms grip safety, adjustable rear sight, and humongous thumb safety.

Cutting-edge 21st century, mated to retro 1980s IPSC. Beautiful.

The Ithaca is now complete. It has the best barrel, a Bar-Sto, complete with one of their comps on it. It has been worked on by two of the greatest 1911 'smiths to be found; Ned and Stan. It has served me admirably for 40 years, through eight USPSA Nationals, 15 Pin Shoots, a Buick-equivalent weight of bullets, and more recoil springs than I care to count, and has taught me many lessons.

The final disposition of this Ithaca is now in doubt. I mean, do I leave it to one of my heirs, or insist it accompany me into the ground in my casket? One thing is for sure, it will never be sold. One never knows what life has in store, or what the fates will require. I may end up living alone in a cardboard box, under a bridge. But if I am, despite everything else being gone, I'll still have the Ithaca.

After the author's 1998 pin shoot, he thought it was over for good. Now pin shoots are back, and life is good again.

DON'T LOSE SWEENEY'S CUSTOM MAGS!

Pistols need magazines. The Ithaca has its own set. These are original Wilson Combat 47s, with Shooting Star followers, up-to-date springs and replacement basepads. The basepads that came with the Wilson back then were plastic. To speed reloading and increase durability, I replaced the plastic with brass. The brass pads of the time were tall, to reach past the lips of bolt-on magazine-well funnels. I used a mill to trim these down, while keeping the weight and durability.

Once they were built and tested and worked 100 percent, I kept them with the Ithaca. If, sometime in the future, you see this pistol, ask the owner or seller, "Where are the magazines?" If you haven't read my obituary, call the police. If I don't have it, you know I didn't sell it, so something's wrong.

How the author's Ithaca rests in between pin shoots. In a soft case, with tested magazines at the ready.

P.O. ACKLEY: Trinidad, Colorado Gunsmith

The Outspoken P.O. Ackley Influenced More Than Just Wildcat Cartridges

BY **FRED ZEGLIN**

From 1945 to 1951 P.O. Ackley called Trinidad, Colorado his home after a very short stay in Cimarron, New Mexico where he and Ward Koozer had partnered with George Turner. The business in Cimarron went by the name of Ackley & Turner. That business manufactured the Turner Scope Mount, produced some rifle barrels and performed general gunsmithing services. Ackley found Cimarron to be isolated, which limited growth of the business. Turner stayed in Cimarron when the Ackley-Turner company dissolved.

Photo of the man himself, P.O. Ackley, from the collection of gunmaker Jerry Fisher. Fisher visited Ackley in the mid-1970s and remembers him talking about all facets of gunmaking. Making a living was a key subject in the discussion.

The limited edition Nosler Custom Rifle (NCR) is available in .280 Ackley Improved and two other standard chamberings — .300 WSM and .338 Win. Mag. — and is the top-tier rifle in the Ackley chambering from Nosler. The company's other M48 series rifles are also available in the popular 7mm Ackley Improved chamber.

Koozer and Ackley had met and worked together at the Ogden Arsenal during the war. Koozer, by his former wife's account, was in Cimarron with Ackley and continued their partnership in Trinidad. Ackley states that the selection of Trinidad was because it had several attributes that would benefit his business. He and his associates wanted a location that had rail service, mail facilities in all directions and was on the east side of the divide, which supposedly was better for mail order business. Upon moving to Trinidad, Ackley reformed his company as "Ackley, Koozer, and DeMiller Engineering Co."

160 Elm St., first location of Ackley business in Trinidad, Colorado.

The name on the shop windows is "P.O. Ackley and Company, Gun Makers." In 1947 the company was incorporated under the name, "P.O. Ackley, Inc." It was at this time in 1947 that Ward Koozer decided to leave the company. One of the primary investors in the corporation was A.T. "Doc" Kapelke, he was heavily involved in the negotiations when the corporation was later sold to Eastman.

Syracuse University records give an address for Ackley's business of 160 Elm St., Trinidad, Colorado in July of 1945. According to Ackley, when first opened in Trinidad, the business was located on Elm Street in a shop of about 4,000 square feet. He guessed that about six employees helped to build the business when it became established there. Anna Konuges-Floyd said that the back of the shop opened on an embankment, the employees used that bank to test fire finished projects.

Almost as soon as the doors were open in downtown Trinidad, the staff of Ackley's shop learned that there was a population of retired folks who lived within walking distance of the shop. Soon these duffers were hanging out and, of course, wasting time. This was at least a partial reason for building a new facility outside of town. Les Womack asked Ackley if the move helped with the unwanted visitors. "Nope," Ackley said ruefully, "they just brought their lunches!"

During his stay in Trinidad, Ackley ran what he called "one of the largest custom gun shops in the nation." He reportedly employed as many as 25 people during this time. The new company manufactured the Turner Mount under the name "Snap-in," made barrels, custom rifles and offered general gunsmithing.

Business came from all over the world, but mostly from the contiguous United States, Canada and Alaska. Amazingly, 20,000 to 25,000 letters were answered by P.O. Ackley, Inc., between 1947 and the sale of the business in 1951.

In the Trinidad City directory for 1948, P.O. Ackley had three addresses listed. The first is at 121 N. Commercial St. That specific address does not appear on any of the buildings on Commercial St. There is a bank, law offices and a couple of retail stores on the ground floor of the building. The notation next to Ackley's name for this address says, "Gun shop instructor Trinidad Jr. College." C.P. Donnelly mentioned that Cole Agee, the well-known engraver, worked for Ackley in Trinidad, and in Custom Built Rifles,

P.O. Ackley (left) with grandson Ron Pearson.

author Dick Simmons lists the Trinidad National Bank building as the address for Cole Agee in Trinidad. Likely Ackley rented this space for Agee to work in. Note: Cole Agee is in the group photo this chapter.

Ackley's home address, 316 Ash, was listed in the city directory as well; the listing reads, "P.O. Ackley (Winifred) pres & mgr P.O. Ackley Inc." Finally, P.O. Ackley Inc. is listed as being at 124 N. Chestnut. There is no building at that address as of this writing.

The old Ackley Home at 316 Ash Street, circa 2007.

This picture was taken in front of the Ackley shop at 160 Elm St. Back Row (left to right): unknown, unknown, Eugene Hopper, Perchoisky, unknown, Cole Agee, Ward Koozer. Second Row: Charles Rundel, Ann Konuges-Floyd, Glen Malin, Dick Adair, Kathy, P.O. Ackley, Earnest Parks. Front Row: Ruben Gutierrez, Bill Prator, O'Neal, Pano Ortiz, Paul Mayer.

Early in the fall of 1948, the P.O. Ackley, Inc. shop was moved outside of the city limits of Trinidad. The location was on Highway 12 west of town, Ackley had a new building built, out of which the company could operate. The new shop contained almost 12,000 square feet of space that included offices, store-rooms, vault, shipping rooms, tool rooms and more. That building burned down many years later (after Ackley, Inc. had been sold), and a new building was built on the foundation of the original.

It was in the new shop building that an accident took place that caused quite a stir. Anna Konuges-Floyd told about an explosion that injured two men. She said that the building was U-shaped, and she was leading a tour for some visitors at one end of the building. The two men were working with a grinder and there was a box on the floor with black powder in it. The sparks set off the powder and caused a small explosion, both guys were on fire and went outside and rolled on the ground while other employees used blankets to put out the fire. Anna ran to the office and called for the fire department only to find they were already on the way. Both men survived. This story was supported by another witness. The injuries were very minor.

While interviewing Anna Konuges-Floyd for this book I asked her what she learned from P.O. Ackley. "Actually, he was my first boss. Of course, I learned about how to deal with people and the public. P.O. would dictate letters to me in the evening, when he got tired of dictating he would often tell me about his experiences. For instance, he was head of the small arms department in Utah during the war. He would tell about the people he met and the places he had traveled. I was just a young girl of seventeen when I started working there, so I learned things I would have never learned. Because we lived in a very small town, and my father was an immigrant, although he worked hard and made a

(below) Location west of Trinidad that once was home to P.O. Ackley, Inc. The Ackley building burned to the ground, this new building was put up on part of the original foundation.

(bottom) Closeup of Bill Hause's rifle. Chambered in .224 Ackley Belted Express, it is a well- loved rifle still in amazing condition 60 years after it was built. Photo by Stan Trzoniec

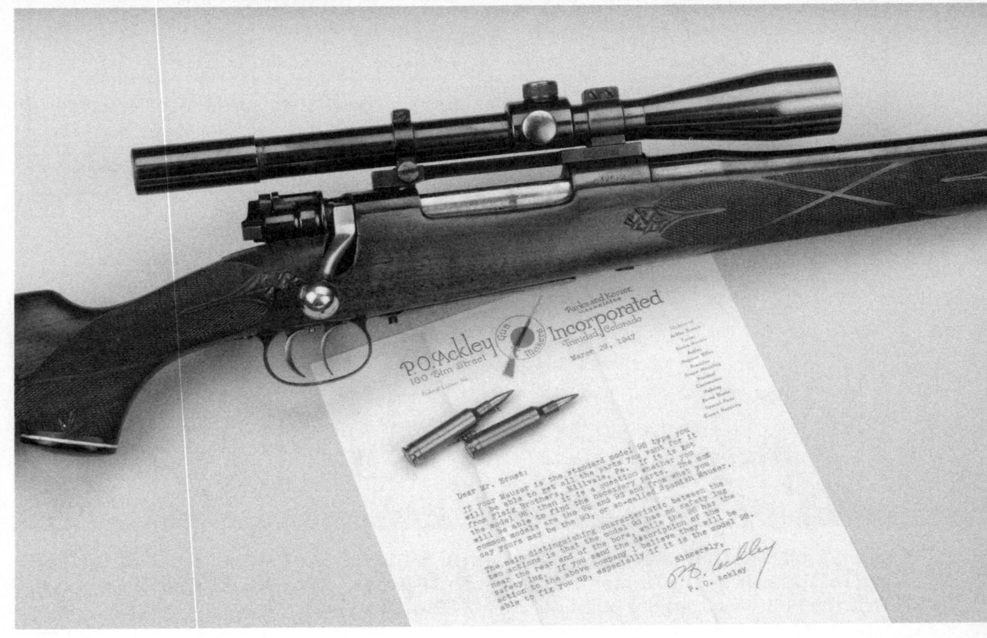

good life for us, we just were not exposed to a lot of culture. I learned from P.O. that whatever you wanted to do you did not have to wait to be dictated to by others, that you could make your own way. Also, he was very respectful of his mother, he saw after her all the time. He had no pretentions, everybody was equal."

Anna went on to say, "You know I had to learn to load my own ammunition. If we were going somewhere to go hunting or shooting, they made me take care of my own ammunition." Anna had a .228 Ackley Magnum, which she has now passed along to her son.

Ackley wrote to her years later when he was in Salt Lake City. "I hope you're in no hurry for your rifle," he said. Anna said, "That was our song in Trinidad. We told people, 'If you're in a hurry take your rifle back right away, we're not going to do the work on it.'" So, she understood that she would have to wait for the work. Customers being in a rush was nothing new, it seems.

"Today, P.O. is a busy man but not in the type of work that brings him greatest pleasure — for he would be happier doing his own work, with his own hands, in a small shop," said Roy Dunlap in 1950.

P.O. Ackley was known to buy out other gunsmiths from time to time, an example being the Turner Scope mount, or when he purchased the shop in Roseburg, Oregon at the start of his career from Ross King. In his Gunsmith column for *Guns & Ammo* magazine he wrote, "Arnold Terhaar made a few rifle actions, in fact, I have one of the prototypes myself which was never barreled. And some 25 or more years ago, I bought the tooling from Terhaar for his actions. Shortly thereafter we sold our corporation and all of this tooling went with the other equipment and I suppose it has been long since junked."

According to Charles Landis, P.O. Ackley, Inc. bought out Malcom Company, a scope maker. This would have dated prior to 1951 when Landis published his book on woodchuck hunting and rifles.

THE BIRTH OF THE FIRST GUNSMITHING SCHOOL IN THE UNITED STATES

Anna Konuges-Floyd said that she had been on a trip with the Ackleys and they had left a temporary secretary at the shop to take care of business. When they returned, the temp pointed at two desks in the office that were buried in mounds of mail and said, "They all want to know about the school." Anna laughed and said, "There wasn't any gunsmithing school at that time." Apparently, Jack O'Conner had answered a question from a reader in his column saying that he thought P.O. Ackley had started a school.

"We only had 'on the job' trainees, it was not a school," said Anna. It was in 1945 and '46, when these veterans returning from the war wrote P.O. Ackley wanting to be trained as gunsmiths. During that time he received 4,000 applications for on-the-job training, and the Trinidad Chamber of Commerce received another 1,000 letters according to one source. P.O. then approached the Trinidad State Junior College fathers about adding gunsmithing to its curriculum. The school agreed.

Dean C.O. Banta was head of the vocational school at Trinidad State Junior College and was enthusiastic about a gunsmithing curriculum. The new president, Dwight C. Baird, soon had Ackley on the staff to head up the department. A flurry of activity produced enough space and machine tools to start the course, and in January of 1947 the first group of students started class.

BARREL BLANKS

Unturned — Turned to specifications — Special target blanks

CHROME-MOLY **STAINLESS STEEL**

Barrels turned to specifications, threaded for standard actions and chambered for standard and many wild cat calibers.

SPECIAL

Barrels turned to specifications, chambered, unthreaded. Any length up to 29" by 1¼", any twist, longer blanks made to order. ALL TURNED BLANKS SEMI-POLISHED.

CUSTOM BUILT RIFLES

CONTROLLED EXPANSION BULLETS

Send for free circulars

P. O. ACKLEY INC. **Trinidad, Colorado**

Ad from a 1950 *American Rifleman* magazine.

Fisher's Peak was the view from Ackley's office at the P.O. Ackley, Inc. building, west of Trinidad. Today from the former site of the shop the peak is not visible, trees have grown across the highway from the building site, blocking the view.

P. O. ACKLEY IS NEWEST MEMBER OF FACULTY AT TRINIDAD JR. COLLEGE

Parker O. Ackley of Trinidad, nationally known gunsmith and operator of the Ackley Gun Factory in Trinidad, has been added to the faculty of Trinidad Junior College on a part-time basis.

Mr. Ackley is conducting a lecture and discussion course for members of the gunsmith class on the subject of "Modern Gunsmithing."

As a recognized authority on gunsmithing and the author of many articles on the manufacture and care of guns, Mr. Ackley will be able to give the college gunsmith students much valuable information.

Mr. Ackley moved to Trinidad two years ago and operates one of the most outstanding gunsmith shops in the United States. His famed Ackley gun barrels are noted for excellence and have obtained an international reputation for excellence and Mr. Ackley has become a recognized authority on the manufacture of guns and related problems.

Clipping from Trinidad State Junior College Archives. (*Tribune* April 30, 1947)

NEW GUNSMITHING SCHOOL MAKES THE ASSOCIATED PRESS WIRE SERVICE

Pottstown Mercury Newspaper
DATE 9 MAY 1947,
Pottstown, Montgomery, Pennsylvania

TRINIDAD, Colo., May 8, 1947 (AP) — A two-year course in gunsmith training, believed by the school authorities to be the first of its kind in the nation, is to be open late this month at Trinidad Junior college.

In announcing the new course, President Dwight C Baird said the college has received inquiries and applications from 22 states. Many of these came from former service men whose interest in firearms had been awakened during the war and who wanted to make a life's work as gunsmiths.

The idea for the new course came from P.O. Ackley, nationally known gunsmith and operator of a Trinidad gun shop. He received many inquiries from men wanting to learn his trade and, not wishing to undertake the training of apprentices himself, he referred the applicants to the college.

Similar articles ran in newspapers all over the country. A survey of newspapers turned up announcements about the new gunsmithing school in such diverse cities as Mansfield Ohio, Oakland California, Long Beach California, Joplin Missouri and even in the town where Ackley had gone to college, Syracuse, New York. A news release the week of April 10, 1949 prompted most of these as the articles read nearly identically. Headlines varied, however. "Gun Crazy Students Flocking to Trinidad Junior College," "Colorado Town Well Armed, Gunsmith Course Draws Hundreds of Students," "College Course for Trigger Happy," and "Gunsmith Class Grows."

In the March issue of the *American Rifleman* for 1950 there was an article that discussed the various gunsmithing schools available at the time and their programs. Trinidad was one of the schools visited and profiled in the article. There is a photo of Ackley lecturing and drawing an illustration on a blackboard along with a description of the courses, cost of attendance and the following: "P.O. Ackley, well-known as a commercial gunsmith and barrel-maker, conducts classes at Trinidad and works closely with the school in handling the entire course. Ackley received a Bachelor of Science degree from Syracuse University in 1927 [In agriculture, editor]; also attending Colorado A&M. Teaches theory of gunsmithing and metallurgy."

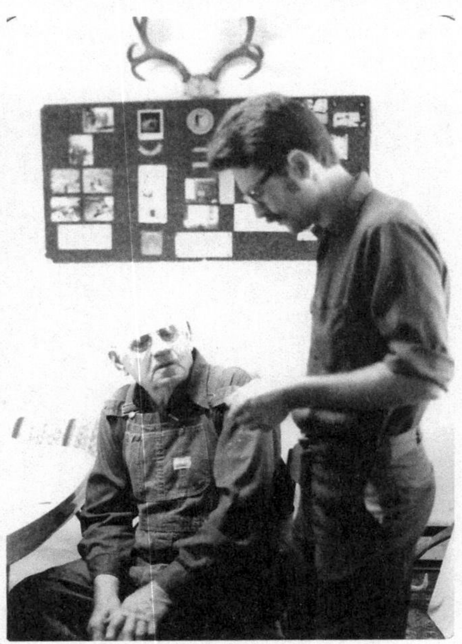

Dennis Bellm (right) consults P.O. Ackley.

Ackley worked at Trinidad State Junior College as an instructor, lecturing two hours a day in Theory of Gun Making and Metallurgy from 1947 to 1951. C.P. Donnelly was a student at Trinidad, graduating in 1947. Donnelly became well-known for the barrels he made under the business name of Siskiyou Rifle Works. He remembers how Ackley's business in Trinidad started out in an old Safeway store and later a building was built specifically to house the business.

According to Donnelly, when lecturing on firearm design, Ackley would disassemble a gun with his back to his students. He would also reassemble it in the same fashion, never showing them directly how it was done, but talking to them about the process. Then they'd have to figure it out on their own in lab. This was his way of forcing the students to become familiar with the gun they were studying.

Les Womack described Ackley's years of association with the students of Trinidad Junior College as a two-way street. The students supplied him with lots of enthusiastic help for his experiments. All he had to do was suggest an experiment, and everyone was ready to go. It was at this time that he ran a series of blow-up tests on military rifle actions to determine their strength and suitability for sporter conversion. Bill Hause stated that he did the record keeping for some of the blow-up tests. He said they started in September of 1950. This was an eye-opener and remains the only scientific approach made on the subject.

Ackley had been making up wildcat cartridges for many years, and now he encouraged students to experiment with most anything within the limits of safety. To keep a damper on the students' heady enthusiasm, he insisted on a chronograph report before accepting any ballistic data. "Figures don't lie, but liars do figure," Ackley said. The chronograph is an impartial judge.

Womack wrote further, "Adulation of one's professor is nothing new, but in Ackley's case the students at Trinidad felt it was more than justified. In spite of his 16-hour days, he was always available to anyone in need of help. He gave freely of any information he might have. He used to say that anybody in the gun business who thought he had a trade secret wasn't kidding anyone but himself."

Early in the course, Ackley pointed out

Cooper Rifles is yet another rifle maker turning out guns in Ackley chamberings, including this gorgeous Western Classic model.

Trinidad Trojan Tribune, January 15, 1947

GUNSMITHING COURSE WILL BE FIRST IN ENTIRE NATION

Details concerning the establishment of a two-year course in gunsmith training, believed to be the first course of its kind ever offered by a college in the United States, were announced today by officials of Trinidad Junior College who said applications for the course are now being received and the class will meet for the first time on either January 27 or February 3.

The announcement concerning the new course, which is expected to attract a capacity enrollment, dominated by veterans of World War II, was made by Dwight C. Baird, president of the college and C. O. Banta, dean of the vocational department.

Already inquiries and applications from students in 22 different states have been received, Dean Banta said, ranging from Massachusetts and New Hampshire to California, and from Montana to North Carolina. Veterans will be able to enroll under the GI Bill of Rights and Public Law 16.

Post-World War II left incredible numbers of men in need of a career after military service. That demand almost forced the creation of the gunsmith school at Trinidad.

Establishment of the gunsmith training course marks another "first" in vocational education pioneered by Trinidad Junior college.

There will be many strange faces at Trinidad Junior College Monday as 50 students arrive to attend the newest additions to our school, gunsmithing and handcraft classes.

At the present time 30 students have been accepted for gunsmithing and 20 are expected for hand-craft with many more applications pouring in.

The many arrivals come from many states which include Missouri, Kentucky, Idaho, Virginia, Massachusetts, Wisconsin, Pennsylvania, Illinois, Minnesota, Texas, Ohio, Colorado and Nebraska.

The first arrivals are Wilton L. Bose of Birch Tree, Mo., and Thomas C. Elliott of Corbin, Ky., who, luckily arrived early and have had no difficulties in securing rooms which now are creating quite a problem.

to the students that gunsmithing wasn't necessarily a road to riches. Since a gunsmith must be proficient at machining, wood working, heat treating and a myriad of other skills, the student must also be prepared to equip a shop. If not, did he have assurance of employment in an established shop upon graduation? Even if he had his own shop and equipment at the time, was he willing to put in long hours at low pay to make a living?

A simple love of firearms wasn't enough to pull one through, as the public wasn't disposed to pay a premium price for a man to work long hours on their weapons. As a hobby, you could take all the time you wanted, but gun work was done on a flat rate basis, and one must do the job as quickly as possible when one's bread and butter depended upon it. "If my wife hadn't had a good job, I would have starved to death long ago," Ackley used to say, only half in jest.

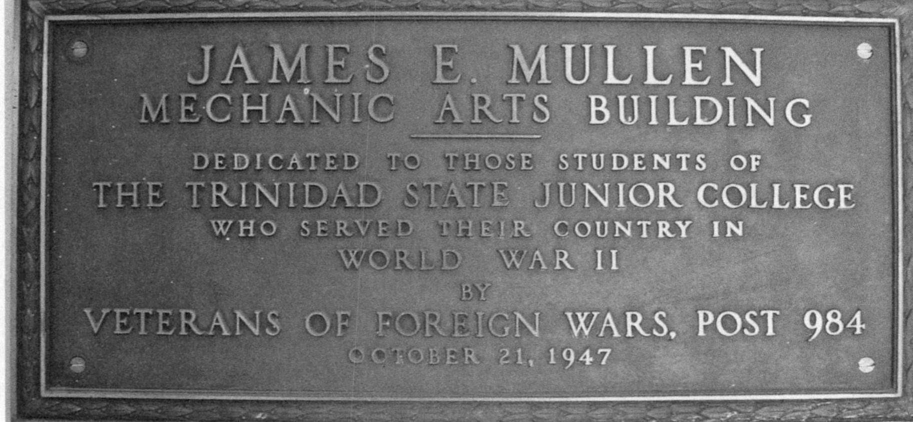

Dedication plaque for the Mullen Building, which still housed the Gunsmithing Department at TJSC in 2007.

60 YEARS LATER

While attending the 60th Reunion of the Gunsmithing Department at Trinidad State Junior College in June of 2007, I was able to interview Tom Elliot, the same man mentioned in the article above. He was a member of the first class to start in the Mullen Building on the Campus of TSJC. "The building was not finished when we moved in for classes," Elliot said. "The roof was not on the building yet, so when it rained or snowed the ceiling leaked."

The machine shop on the main floor of the Mullen Building has windows all along one wall and part of the rear wall. There is also a roll-up garage door at the rear that opens onto a grade. The shop is filled with lathes and other machinery and, according to Elliot, that room had workbenches all along the windows and a mix of machine tools that presumably were acquired by the school from war surplus, many of which Elliot did not know how to use. The instructors were DeMiller and Ackley.

"Ackley's Theory class stressed headspace, improved chamber designs and discussed both internal ballistics and external ballistics. Ackley tackled the subject of action strength, and in fact he had already performed some of his blow-up tests by that time. He talked about the Japanese action being the strongest he had tested. He discussed the .17 caliber and talked about the fact that bullets were not yet available to handle the velocity that it could generate, some would just blow up in the air in front of the gun. Some of the tests for the .17 included shooting at rail material from old railroad tracks. The .17 would blow straight through the track," recalled Elliot.

Mort Wilson graduated from the program in 1952, so his first year in school was Ackley's last year there. "Ackley taught strictly theory, he had a classroom in the Berg Building where he held court. That class had some theory, but it was more about supply sources and ballistics. He talked a lot about various calibers and tried to compare the ballistic performance from various calibers. For example, the .25-35 verses the .257 Roberts. It was somewhat of a ballistics class, of course we never had any chronographs, the best technical tool we had available was a ballistic pendulum.

"The one thing that stands out to me that Ackley never taught in theory class

[CONTINUED ON PAGE 193]

Tom Elliot stands in front of the historical display in the Mullen Building at TSJC. The rifle was built by P.O. Ackley, a custom 98 Mauser in .270 Winchester, and sports a Turner-Ackley scope mount.

Mort Wilson at the 60th reunion.

★ SPECIAL CARTRIDGES 

The illustration shows several special cartridges along with three well-known commercial loads for purposes of comparison; the three commercials being the .300 H. & H. Magnum, the .30-'06 and the .257 Roberts.

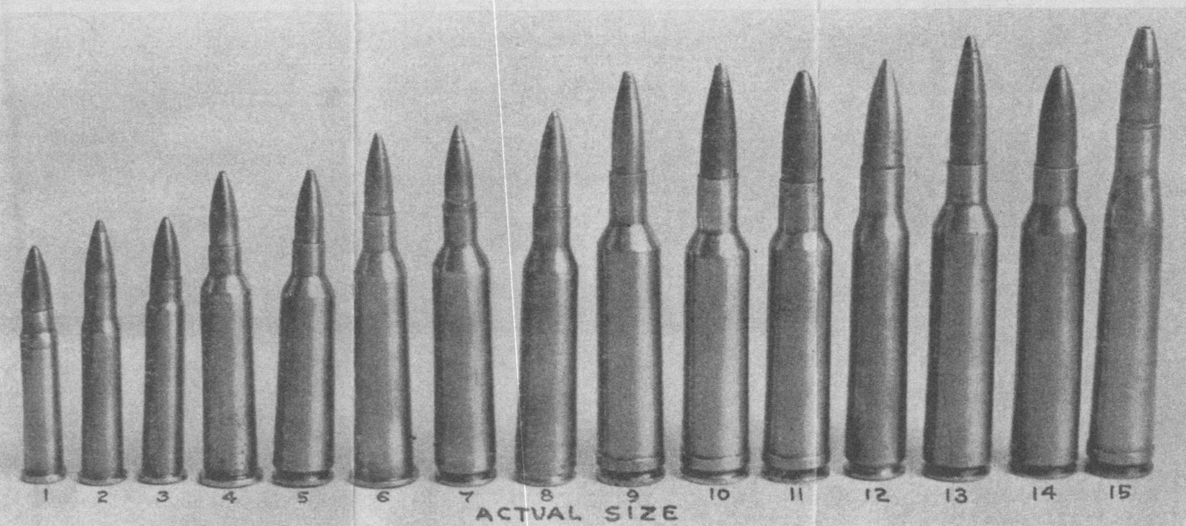

Nos.
1.—IMPROVED HORNET
2.—R-2 LOVELL
3.—IMPROVED LOVELL
4.—IMPROVED ZIPPER
5.—.22-250

Nos.
6.—.228 RIMMED MAGNUM
7.—.228 MAGNUM
8.—.257 ROBERTS
9.—.250 MAGNUM
10.—.270 MAGNUM

Nos.
11.—.30 MAGNUM
12.—.30-'06
13.—.270 NEWTON
14.—.30 NEWTON
15.—.300 H. & H. MAGNUM

THE "IMPROVED" HORNET

—is our own version of the Hornet and is a more efficient cartridge than the standard Hornet, being of a more modern design and having greater capacity. Factory loads can be fired in this chamber without trouble. Handloads can be loaded to considerably greater velocities than the standard type.

THE "IMPROVED" LOVELL

—is one of the latest versions of this popular cartridge. The capacity is about 2½ grains greater than the popular R-2 and the case is of a more modern design. Considerably higher velocities are possible with this one than with many of the earlier versions.

THE ".22-250"

—is probably the most efficient **light** bullet cartridge yet developed in the "Swift" class. Exceedingly high velocities can be attainted when loaded with light bullets. Velocities upwards of 4500 F.S. have been recorded. Fine with bullets weighing up to 55 grains. Almost any well-made standard action such as M/17 Springfield, M/98 Mauser, Etc., will handle this load without radical changes. This particular cartridge is known under several names and all are almost identical.

Ackley began marketing specialty work from the very beginning of his career.

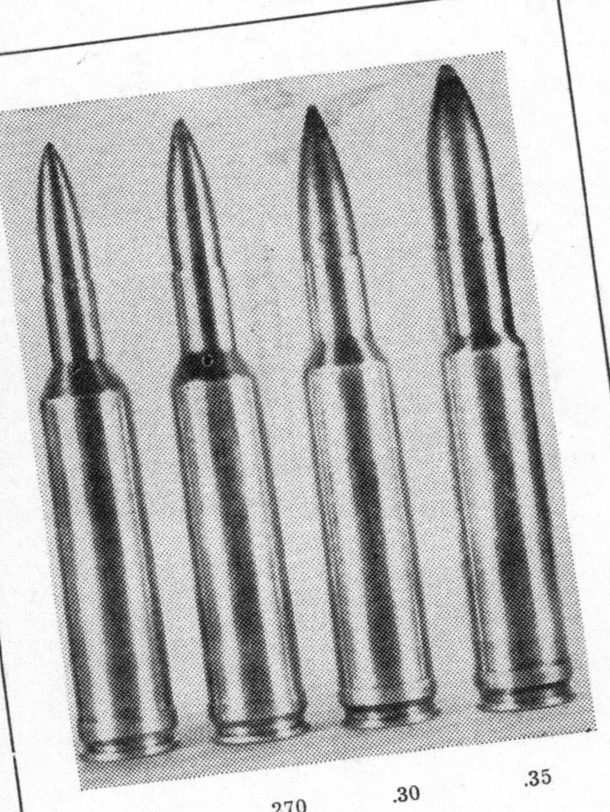

.250 .270 .30 .35

ACKLEY BELTED MAGNUMS

This series of magnums known as the Ackley Magnums are designed with the conventional 28 degree shoulder. This comparatively sharp shoulder has given exceedingly good results in both magnums and smaller calibers. These magnums are designed with an over all length short enough to work through standard actions without excessive alteration. The over all length is practically the same as the standard 30-06. They are designed with a comparatively long neck and straight body taper which results in reduced throat erosion and easy extraction.

The illustration shows these magnums in full size. It will be noted that the body dimensions are the same for all the Ackley Magnums, which means that the smaller ones can be rebored to the larger size without changing the chamber and headspace and have to be neck reamed only.

THE ACKLEY .250 MAGNUM. This popular load developes higher velocities than most of the wildcat calibers yet developed, including the .22 calibers. With the 115 grain Magnum bullet speeds of over 3400 fs. can be easily attained. With the 87 grain bullet, up to 4,000. With lighter bullet, speeds approaching 5,000 fs have been attained with experimental loads. The design of this super .250 caliber as well as its larger brothers is modern, yet conservative. The powder capacity is maximum for good efficiency, and the general design is conducive to easy extraction and minimum bolt thrust. Greater powder capacity is likely to reduce barrel life and lower efficiency. We feel that this design, although conservative, is the equal of any now available.

Average velocities will be found in the accompanying table.

THE ACKLEY .270 MAGNUM. The .270 Ackley Magnum is becoming increasingly popular. Bullets weighing from 100 grains to 180 grains can be used. Velocities range up to 3800 fs. Average velocities for various bullet weights will be found in the table at the bottom.

Bullet weights over 160 grains are not recommended. The 160 grain bullet is recommended only for the largest game. The 130 grain bullet is a good all round weight to use. The 100 grain bullet is recommended only for specialized shooting. It should not be used at the highest velocities except for big game where only a small number of shots will be used—otherwise the barrel life will be greatly reduced.

Barrel life is reasonably good with the heavier bullets; recoil is similar to the regular 30/06. The .270 Magnum is recommended as an ideal rifle for the largest game at long ranges, where flat trajectory and elimination of guess work is of prime importance.

This same case can be also furnished in 7 mm or .276.

.30 ACKLEY MAGNUM. This .30 Magnum developes ballistics the same as or better than the standard 300 H & H Magnum cartridge, as loaded by the various commercial ammunition manufacturers. It is recommended for use in shorter actions in preference to the full length magnum cartridges because no extensive alteration of the action is necessary, which results in a reduced margin of safety to a dangerous degree. This magnum will work through actions such as the 1903 Springfield or 1917 Enfield without any alteration with the exception of cutting out the bolt face to accommodate the larger head. It will work through any Model 98 actions with a minimum of alteration without any reduction of the margin of safety.

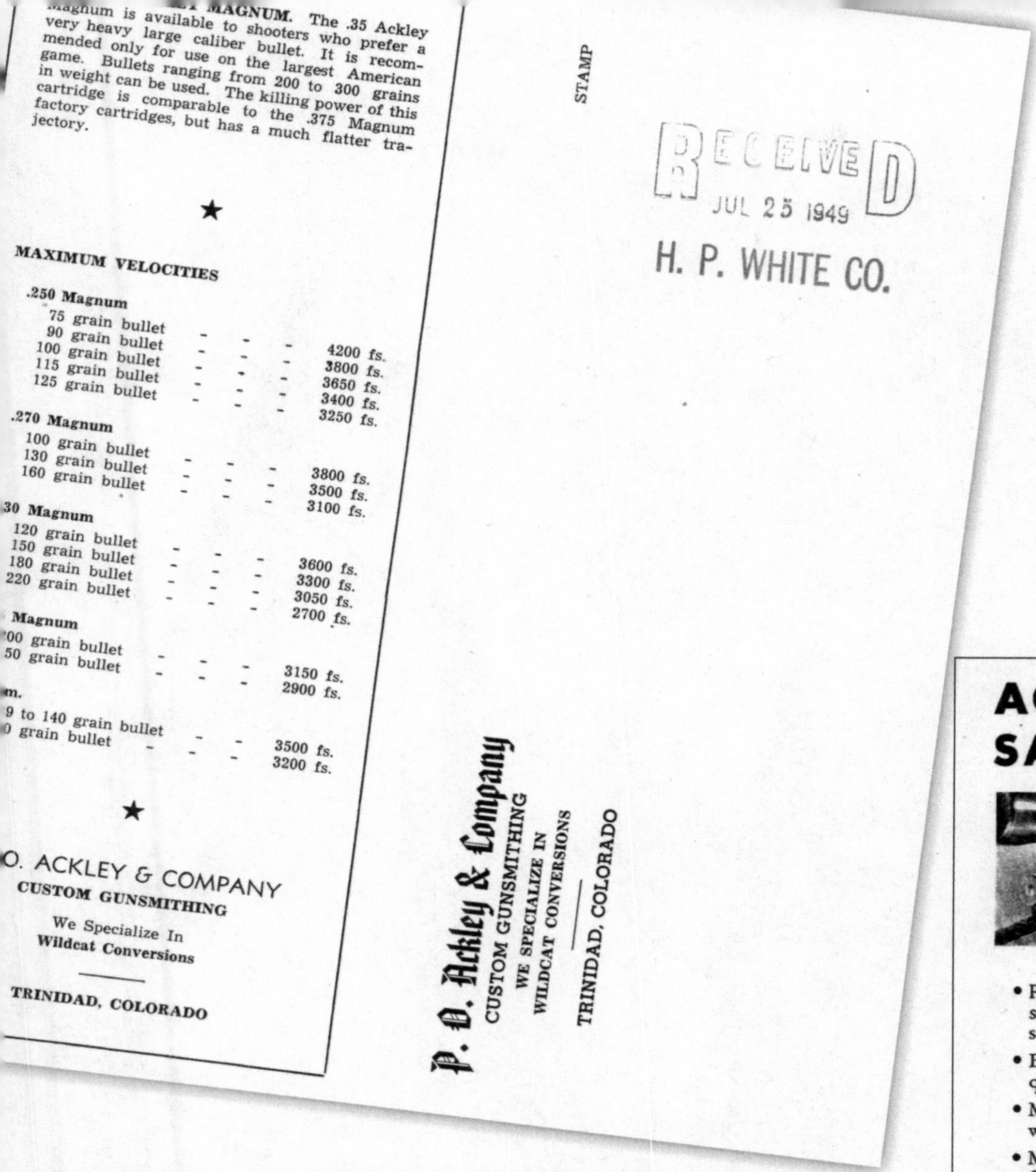

...Magnum is available to shooters who prefer a very heavy large caliber bullet. It is recommended only for use on the largest American game. Bullets ranging from 200 to 300 grains in weight can be used. The killing power of this cartridge is comparable to the .375 Magnum factory cartridges, but has a much flatter trajectory.

MAXIMUM VELOCITIES

.250 Magnum

75 grain bullet - - -	4200 fs.
90 grain bullet - - -	3800 fs.
100 grain bullet - - -	3650 fs.
115 grain bullet - - -	3400 fs.
125 grain bullet - - -	3250 fs.

.270 Magnum

100 grain bullet - - -	3800 fs.
130 grain bullet - - -	3500 fs.
160 grain bullet - - -	3100 fs.

30 Magnum

120 grain bullet - - -	3600 fs.
150 grain bullet - - -	3300 fs.
180 grain bullet - - -	3050 fs.
220 grain bullet - - -	2700 fs.

Magnum

00 grain bullet - - -	3150 fs.
50 grain bullet - - -	2900 fs.

m.

9 to 140 grain bullet - - -	3500 fs.
0 grain bullet - - -	3200 fs.

★

O. ACKLEY & COMPANY
CUSTOM GUNSMITHING
We Specialize In
Wildcat Conversions

TRINIDAD, COLORADO

STAMP

RECEIVED
JUL 25 1949
H. P. WHITE CO.

P. O. Ackley & Company
CUSTOM GUNSMITHING
WE SPECIALIZE IN
WILDCAT CONVERSIONS

TRINIDAD, COLORADO

(opposite) A sales pamphlet from P.O. Ackley, Inc., 1949. It's interesting to note that this date came from the files of H.P. White Co. The firm has a long history of performing scientific testing for the firearms industry. In some articles, primarily for *American Rifleman*, the H.P. White Co. performed tests on cartridges like Ackley's and provided data for the readers of the publication.

(above) Outside cover of the Ackley brochure.

was barrel making. I would have loved to learn about rifling design, and how to make the tools, how to figure the correct proportions to make an accurately rifled barrel. To my knowledge, he never discussed that material in class. He did talk some about cutters in general.

"Ackley's reputation drew a lot of people here to this program. He was very knowledgeable in the heat treatment of metals. I am a retired tool and die maker, so looking back on the time I spent sitting in P.O. Ackley's class and listening to him teach, I would say that if I weighed him in the balance, I would find him wanting as a teacher. He had built a good reputation prior to the war as a quality gunsmith. There were few well-known gunsmiths in the West at that time, being a barrel maker probably helped with Ackley's notoriety. His barrels were considered as good as any other maker available at that time. Articles in the pre-war years carried

ACKLEY LOW-LINE SAFETY . $6.00

"ON"

"OFF"

- Positively locks bolt, has positive stop, preventing interference with scope.
- Easy action; works through one-quarter turn.
- Made of hardened steel for longer wear.
- Made in left and right hand types for Model 98 Mauser; left hand only for Springfield and Model 54; special safeties for Model 93 Mauser.

The safety is held in position by means of a small pin, for which a small notch has to be cut in the bolt sleeve. This notch can be cut by means of a small hand grinder or needle file. If the notch is to be filed, it is usually necessary to anneal the sleeve at the point where the notch has to be cut. Care must be taken to cut the notch in the right position. Any gunsmith can quickly install this safety, or it can be installed by an individual who has the necessary grinder or tools.

Discount To Dealers and Jobbers

If your dealer is unable to supply you, write direct to

P. O. Ackley, Inc.
Trinidad, Colorado

Sales flyer for Ackley low scope safety.

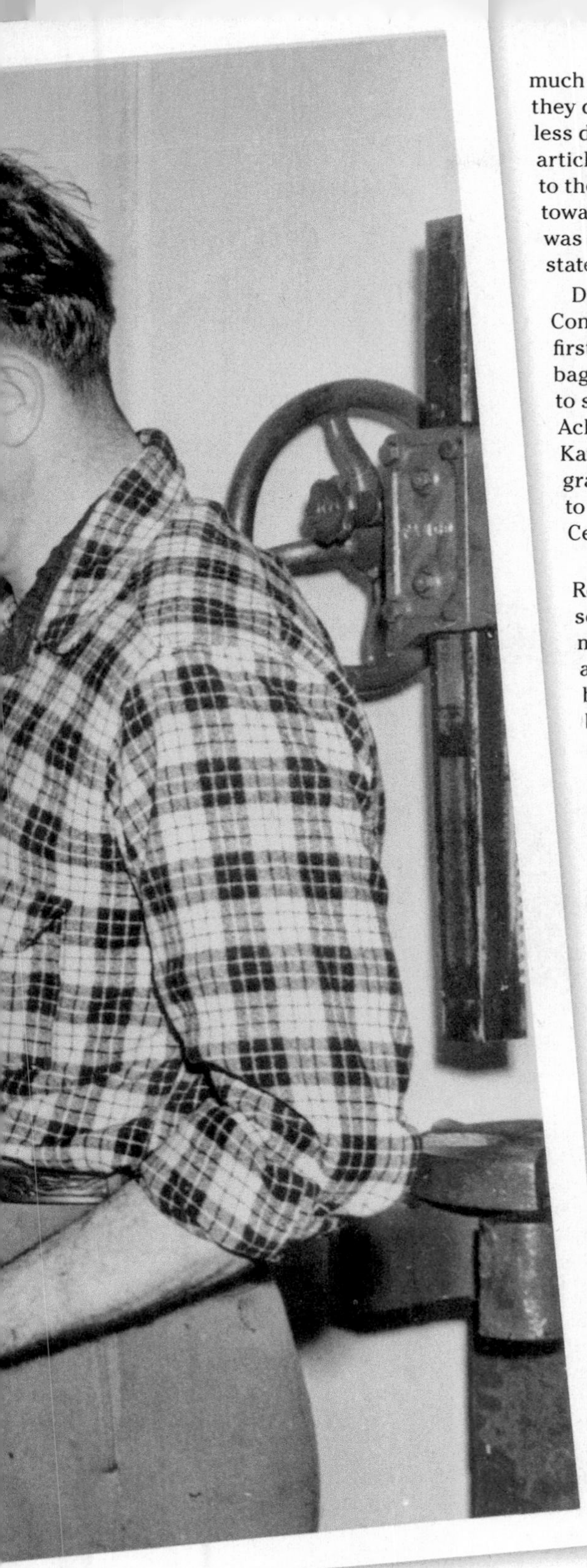

P.O. Ackley (left) and Russ Hightower inspecting rifles.

much more weight with readers than they do today, of course there were less distractions, no TV, etc. The articles written about Ackley prior to the war probably went a long way toward developing his reputation, he was friendly with several writers," stated Wilson.

Dennis Katona of Wallingford, Connecticut was a member of that first class in 1949. He packed his bags and headed out to Trinidad to study gunsmithing under P.O. Ackley. "The guy is an icon," said Katona, referring to Ackley. After graduating, Katona headed home to practice his new trade as a Certified Gunsmith.

In 1949, Ackley recommended Robert (Bob) G. West to the school in Trinidad. West first met Ackley in 1946, hung around a bit during the famous blow-up experiments and later became a close friend. West used Ackley barrels in his custom rifle business, located in Loveland, calling them "very good" quality. Trinidad State Junior College hired West as an instructor, he handled the second year shop students in the school. "I learned more from him than I would have been able to anywhere else," West said of Ackley. "He was never too busy to help with any problem that came up.

"He had a sharp, analytical mind and a memory like an elephant. He could quote loads by the hour. He had no secrets about the gun business. He was not egotistical or swell-headed about his fame or ability. He was just P.O."

West also told a story that, during his tenure at Trinidad, Roy Weatherby made a trip to the school. While there, he reportedly sat down with Ackley and West to discuss a problem he was having. According to West, he was working on his .257 Weatherby Magnum and having pressure problems. Ackley and West quipped to Weatherby, "Cut back on the powder charges." Weatherby responded, "You don't understand — this is a marketing problem. My cartridges are known for ultra-high velocities, I have to get that velocity."

Ackley and West explained that if Weatherby would freebore his chambers, pressures would be relieved to some extent and he would be able to reach his desired velocity with safe pressures. The rest, as they say, is history.

In support of this story, Anna Konuges-Floyd — who'd taken dictation and typed all of Ackley's letters — believed that "Roy Weatherby received a lot of assistance and advice from Ackley in developing the Weatherby line of cartridges, certainly more than he ever received credit for."

Roy F. Dunlap, author of the respected book, *Gunsmithing* wrote about Ackley in 1950, noting that, "P.O. Ackley has risen to be amongst those at the top in the gunsmithing field. A well-rounded education, plus a natural inquisitiveness do not allow him to accept unproved statements." Dunlap goes on to explain that, since moving to Trinidad after the war, Ackley's fame and business grew to the point that it paid for a new building and he had about 30 gunsmiths working in his shop. His modern cartridge designs ranged from the .17 Pee Wee through a whole hat full of improved calibers on up to his custom magnum calibers. The P.O. Ackley shop in Trinidad offered general gunsmithing, manufactured barrels, custom rifles, rebored barrels, manufactured scope mounts and safeties.

Ackley listed the tooling at P.O. Ackley Inc. "We have the usual run of machines for this type of shop. We have three automatic rifling machines, two deep-hole drilling machines (one is my original and the other is a Pratt & Whitney latest-type double-spindle machine). One of the rifling machines is a Pratt & Whitney exactly like the one used by Winchester, one is the latest-type Builder's machine and the other is the latest-type hydraulic machine of my own design. In addition, we have an old original hand-rifling machine. For barrel fitting, we have six small bench-type lathes, mostly Clausing and South Bend and a factory-type chambering machine. There are three small milling machines, a Quick-Way cylindrical grinder, a K.O. Lee universal cutter and tool grinder, several bench grinders, one large and one small drill press, a band saw, two automatic lapping machines (one of which is a gang machine, which will lap four barrels at a time), two punch presses, numerous bench vices and adequate tool room supplies. Of course, we have a little better than ordinary bluing set up for both stainless and alloy steels and a batch of good polishing equipment."

On pages 160 through 163 of Monty Kennedy's *Checkering and Carving of Gunstocks* (Stackpole Books, 1952) two of the checkering patterns used in the Ackley shop are depicted. That is not to say that Ackley himself cut these checkering patterns and carvings. By all accounts, including his own, Ackley did not do stock work personally, he always hired that work out.

During the years in Trinidad, Ackley's shop had many employees and work was divided by specialty. He employed Bill Prator, Glen Malin, Russell Hightower and Ward Koozer among others. All the men made and fitted barrels, while Hightower did the stock work. Apparently, Hightower was insulted that his name was not mentioned in Kennedy's book, even though he was a paid employee of P.O. Ackley, Inc. It's likely that Kennedy did not know the working arrangements in the Ackley shop and just requested examples of the work they did for his book.

P.O. Ackley and Bill Prator would get into arguments and Ackley would fire Prator. In a day or two he'd hire him back at a 10- to 12-cent per hour raise. According to Prator this happened at least twice. After years of working as Ackley's shop foreman, Bill Prator became head gunsmithing instructor at TSJC. During one of their arguments, Ackley told him that, "If he could make better barrel-making equipment, then he'd better do it!" Actually, Prator did just that, and those are the machines that the college used to train students to make barrels for many years.

According to Randy Selby, who was a student at Trinidad from 1969 to 1971, "Barrel making was listed as part of the curriculum at Trinidad. However, Bill hadn't taught the class for a time, so several of us, Horace Harvey of Montana, Pat Ratcliff, a 70 years young retired tool and die maker from Amarillo, Texas, and I struck a deal with Bill to teach the barrel-making class, if the three of us would help him. Pat obtained the steel from Texas and we cranked up the machines and made barrels. Mine shot 3/8-inch groups. Pat was a lot of help as he had 50 years of tool making under his belt. This was a highlight of my two years in Trinidad, along with the friendship of Pat, who lived to be 96 or 97 years old and we always kept in touch.

"Bill had made the deep-hole drill machine from the floor up, and even cast the castings for the head and other parts. The reaming machine was, as I remember it, made from an old lathe bed. The rifling machine was also built from the floor up by Bill. Things were a little crude, but every student was able to make a barrel. I managed to make two," said Selby. Bill Prator confirmed these details.

When in the shop at Trinidad State Junior College the author saw one of Bill Prator's rifling machines. The instructor, Keith Gipson and former instructor Dave Nolan, tell me they decided that this machine should be restored and that they hoped to offer barrel making as a class again at some point.

Thomas "Speedy" Gonzales was another instructor for the gunsmithing program at TSJC. He expressed the same concept that all the staff embraced — that the college has a rich history in gunsmithing and has contributed to the industry in very tangible ways.

The instructors at TSJC clearly understand the important history for which they have become the caretakers as they continue the mission of teaching the next generation gunsmiths and, equally important, craftsmanship.

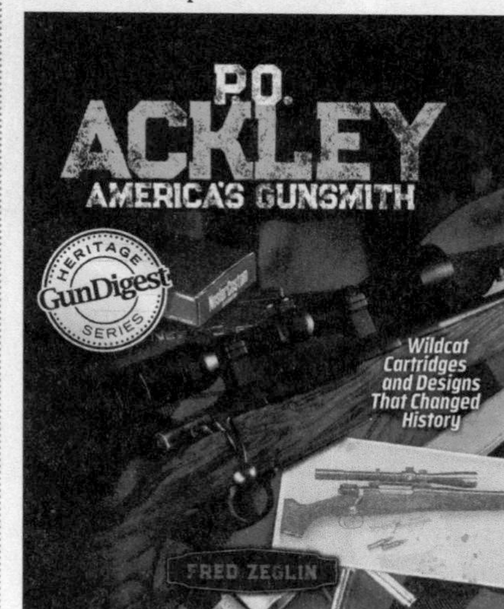

This article is an excerpt from P.O. Ackley: America's Gunsmith, available at GunDigestStore.com.

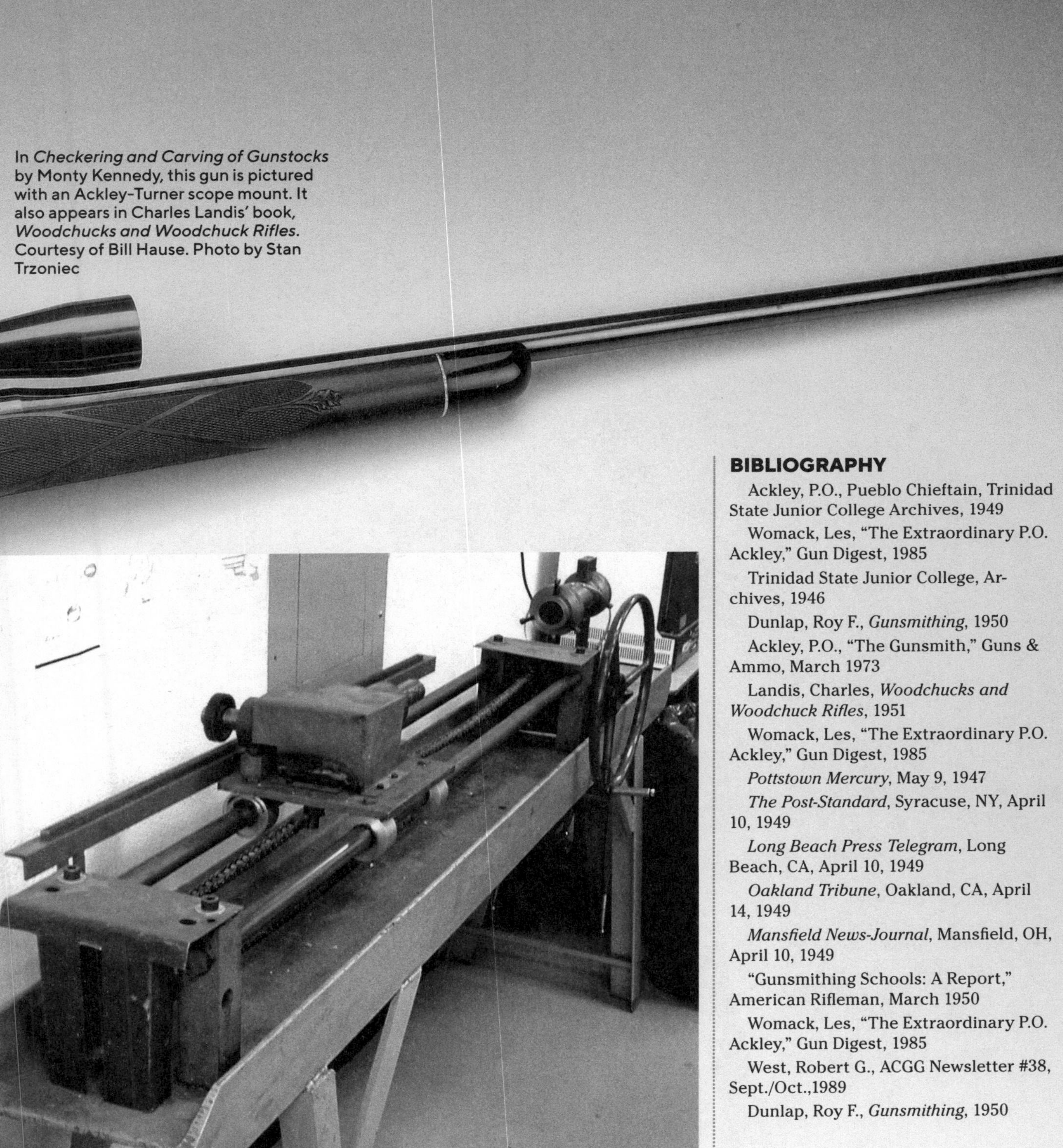

In *Checkering and Carving of Gunstocks* by Monty Kennedy, this gun is pictured with an Ackley-Turner scope mount. It also appears in Charles Landis' book, *Woodchucks and Woodchuck Rifles.* Courtesy of Bill Hause. Photo by Stan Trzoniec

Bill Prator built this rifling machine specifically to teach barrel making at TSJC.

BIBLIOGRAPHY

Ackley, P.O., Pueblo Chieftain, Trinidad State Junior College Archives, 1949

Womack, Les, "The Extraordinary P.O. Ackley," Gun Digest, 1985

Trinidad State Junior College, Archives, 1946

Dunlap, Roy F., *Gunsmithing*, 1950

Ackley, P.O., "The Gunsmith," Guns & Ammo, March 1973

Landis, Charles, *Woodchucks and Woodchuck Rifles*, 1951

Womack, Les, "The Extraordinary P.O. Ackley," Gun Digest, 1985

Pottstown Mercury, May 9, 1947

The Post-Standard, Syracuse, NY, April 10, 1949

Long Beach Press Telegram, Long Beach, CA, April 10, 1949

Oakland Tribune, Oakland, CA, April 14, 1949

Mansfield News-Journal, Mansfield, OH, April 10, 1949

"Gunsmithing Schools: A Report," American Rifleman, March 1950

Womack, Les, "The Extraordinary P.O. Ackley," Gun Digest, 1985

West, Robert G., ACGG Newsletter #38, Sept./Oct.,1989

Dunlap, Roy F., *Gunsmithing*, 1950

TAMING THE .45 COLT

Low-Recoil Loads are About the Fun of Shooting

BY NICK SISLEY

The author's Uberti Cattleman — very much a Colt 1873 Single Action Army lookalike — chambered in .45 Colt.

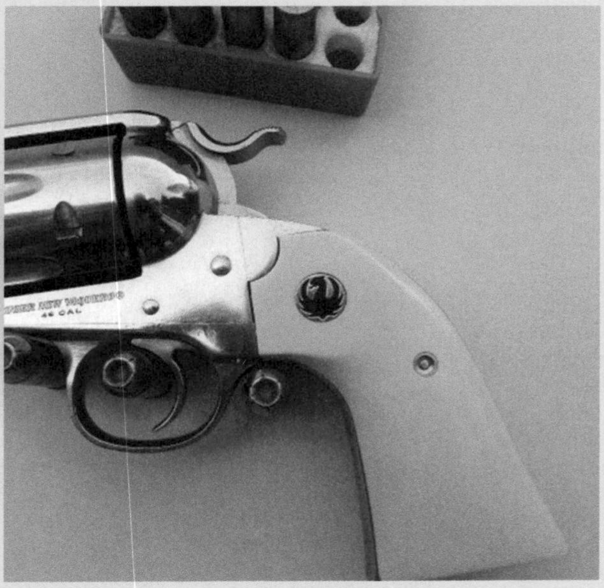

The Ruger Vaquero Bisley took a liking to Hornady XTP bullets (ideal for bigger loads if hunting) in .45 Colt. Note unique shape to the Bisley model grip.

A 255-grain bullet going out the muzzle at over 1,000 feet per second is not for the faint of heart. After shooting very many of these big loads, most handgunners will hang up their sixguns and call it a day. However, tone things down a touch, with that same 255-grain slug leaving the barrel around 800 fps, and you have pure shooting pleasure.

Recoil can eventually get to every shooter, no matter the brawn or mindset. The more you shoot, the more chance it will happen. Sure, if you're going to hunt critters with the cartridge you must shoot a load that's up to the job. But tame this load down and you'll regularly be able to shoot one of the most traditional and storied handgun loads ever developed.

Plenty has been written about .45 Colt history, but here's a brief synopsis. The cartridge was born about the time Samuel Colt's company came out with the 1873 Single Action Army (SAA) back in the black powder days. The .45 Colt was loaded only with black powder for decades, until smokeless came on the scene. But black powder factory loads and handloads continued for long thereafter. Even today, many reloaders love the thrill of that cloud of blue smoke that appears upon firing. Much has been written about the 1911 Colt .45 ACP and its long history as a favorite cartridge, but the .45 Colt is even longer-lived, born nearly four decades earlier.

The redoubtable Smith & Wesson Model 29 in .44 Magnum won't stand up to a long-term steady diet of those big magnum loads, but put 230-grain bullets down its barrel at say 800 fps, and it will last for decades and more. The same goes for a .45 Colt revolver. Ease off the velocity and pressure, and the gun will likely still be wonderful to shoot by your heirs.

Let's go back to the 1873 SAA, so often re-

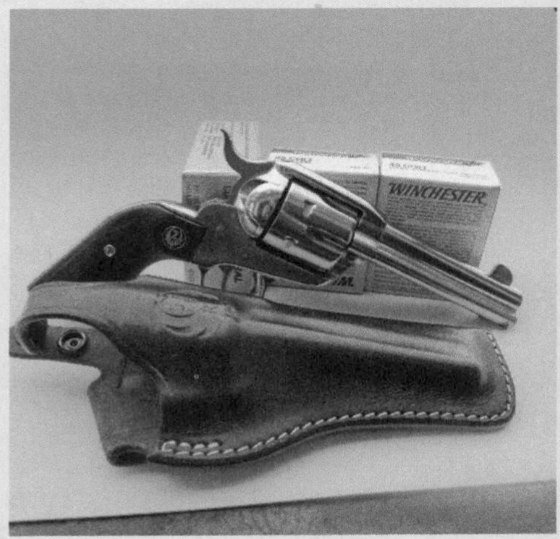

The Ruger Vaquero in highly polished stainless and a 4.62-inch barrel with .45 Colt factory loads.

ferred to as the Peacemaker. Colt still makes this gun in somewhat limited quantities, and SAA replicas have taken up the rest of the slack. Leading this replica pack would be the Ruger Vaquero models, but there are plenty of others these days — all available in .45 Colt.

The thing about the SAA-style is just that — style. Just looking at a Vaquero at your local gun shop is pleasing. When you pick up a SAA replica, even before you wrap your hands around the grip, a good feeling wells up in your heart. Here's a piece of firearms tradition that simply won't quit, despite being born over a century and a half ago. After double-checking the SAA (or Vaquero) is unloaded, your hand wraps around the grip and the sights are brought to bear on the gun shop's wild turkey hanging over the mantel, and there's a fresh new feeling. It's hard to put down such a gun without peeling out the dollars from your wallet or inflicting some damage to your plastic.

About the time the SAA was around 80 years young, television swelled the gun's popularity with the likes of Richard Boone as Paladin in "Have Gun, Will Travel", James Arness as Matt Dillon in "Gunsmoke", James Garner in "Maverick", and others. These cowboys of the silver screen all carried Single Action Army six-shooters. If you're as long in the tooth as I am you identify with these gents and their guns. I used to load wax bullets fired by only a primer in my Colt Single Action Army in those days for quick-draw practice, acting like a kid of 12 when I was already in my late 20s. Blame it on those TV episodes. Yes, that Colt SAA with which I practiced the quick draw was chambered in .45 Colt.

In the late 1980s, cowboy action shooting competition came on the scene formally under the Single Action Shooting Society (SASS), no doubt popularized in part because of renewed interest in the Single Action Army. (It also involves competition with shotguns and rifles of old.) Just a few of the cowboy action standards included no adjustable sights on SAA-style six-shooters, only five rounds could be chambered, shotguns and rifles had to be of a bygone era (or replicas), and cartridges had to be from that era. Original Colt Single Action Army guns escalated even more in value during this period (they were already at eye-popping prices), and Bill Ruger came on the scene with his Vaquero model. Additional SAA replica types were added that were made mainly in Italy, and still are.

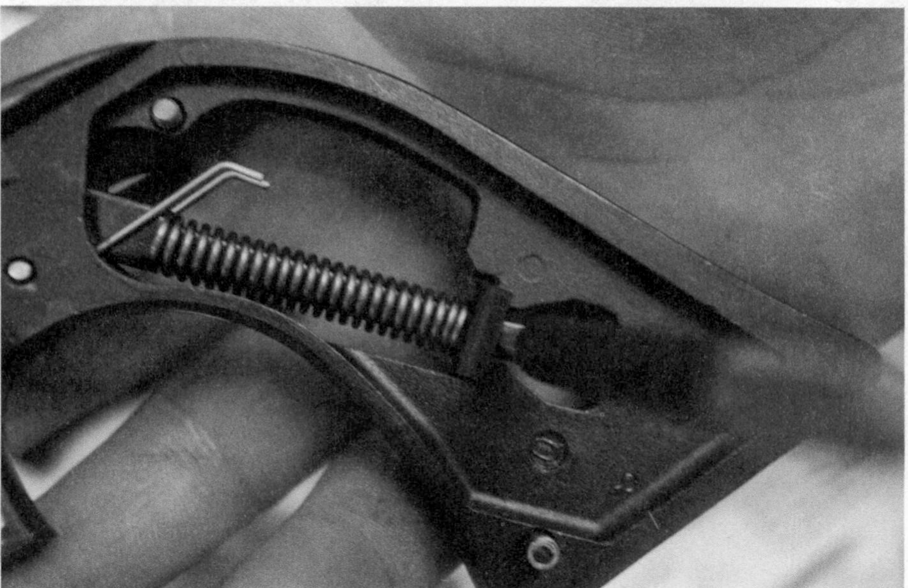

(top) Original Ruger Vaquero .45 Colt with 7.5-inch barrel, color case-hardened receiver, and blued barrel and cylinder.

(above) Changing the trigger spring on a Ruger Blackhawk can reduce the amount of pull and creep.

Before getting into the pleasure-to-shoot loads for the .45 Colt, let's look at some of these SAA replicas, starting with the Vaquero. Ruger offers this model in both blued and stainless versions, as well as the Bisley model with sharper grip angle, which is said to be better for competition shooting. From an eye-appeal standpoint, I love the original SAA style, but that's me. In .45 Colt, choose from a blued 5.5- or 4.62-inch barrel. Grips are of smart-looking walnut. Receiver, hammer and forged barrel material is alloy steel, and the gun weighs in at 40 ounces unloaded with 5.5-inch barrel.

If you're a SAA aficionado, you already know that with an original Colt SAA (and some of the replicas) the hammer must be pulled back to half cock before the cylinder can be rotated for loading and unloading with the loading gate open. Moving the trigger to half cock is not required with the Vaquero. This makes the Ruger unlike the Colt original, but, frankly, I like this Ruger feature. There are a few other minor differences.

My first Vaquero is no longer made. It's a blued version with 7.5-inch barrel and color case-hardened frame. The trigger was OK, but I had gunsmith Mike Crevar work on it. He did a beautiful job — no creep, very light pull. My second Vaquero, purchased recently, is in stainless with 4.62-inch barrel. For looks, I think this barrel length in a SAA is the best. Also, the stainless is brightly polished, which adds even more eye appeal. Many stainless-steel guns have a matte finish these days, which means considerably less labor time. Polishing to a high gloss is labor intensive. Crevar also worked on this gun's trigger. No one who tries them can believe just how excellent these Crevar-done Vaquero triggers feel.

Current Vaquero stainless offerings are the same, either 4.62- or 5.5-inch barrels. All other features are the same as in the blued model, plus the price is identical blued or stainless, $829 full retail. Not many pay suggested retail for anything these days, but I consider the Vaquero an outstanding value.

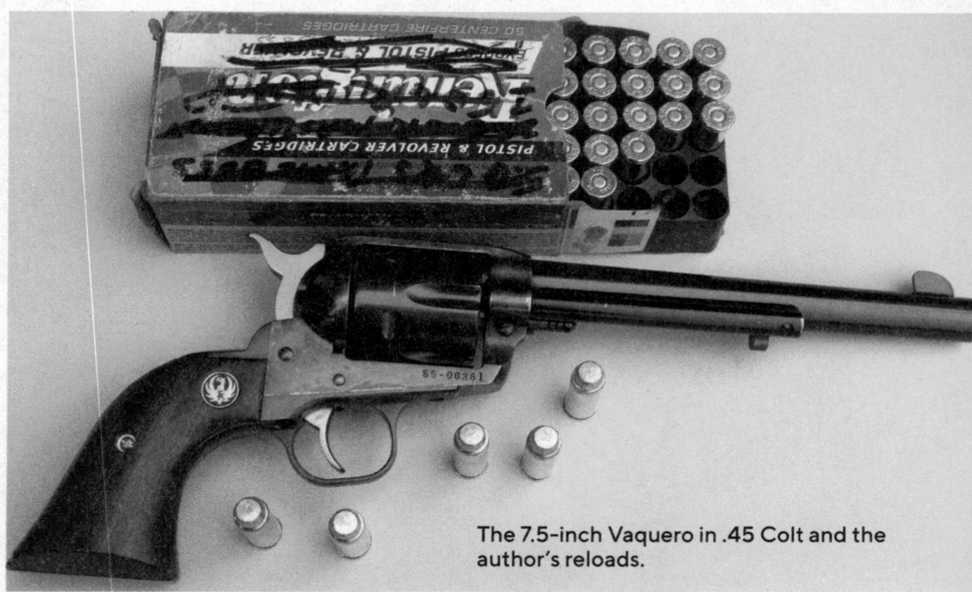

The 7.5-inch Vaquero in .45 Colt and the author's reloads.

The Uberti Cattleman in .45 Colt with one of the gun's best-shooting powders – Trail Boss.

Ruger also offers the New Model Blackhawk in .45 Colt. The blued renditions can be had with 4.62-, 5.5- and 7.5-inch barrels. This Blackhawk is similar in overall appearance to the Vaquero, but not the same. The Blackhawk has an adjustable rear and a different front sight, compared to the Vaquero's blade. Interestingly, the Blackhawk price is even lower at $669 suggested retail. Grips are black checkered hard rubber. This is another outstanding Ruger value.

Companies like Cimarron import a wide array of SAA types. A Cimarron in my possession is called the Teddy Roosevelt Commemorative in .45 Colt. This one has deeply etched engraving on the barrel, ejector housing, receiver, cylinder and grip. Further, it is finished in bright nickel plating. The engraving shows up so well on that bright steel. "TR" is engraved on the back of the receiver, just behind the cylinder. The finishing touch is mock ivory grips. The trigger, right from the factory, is crisp and under 3 pounds, but I love shooting it so well because it is extremely accurate.

AMERICAN EAGLE
CENTERFIRE CARTRIDGES

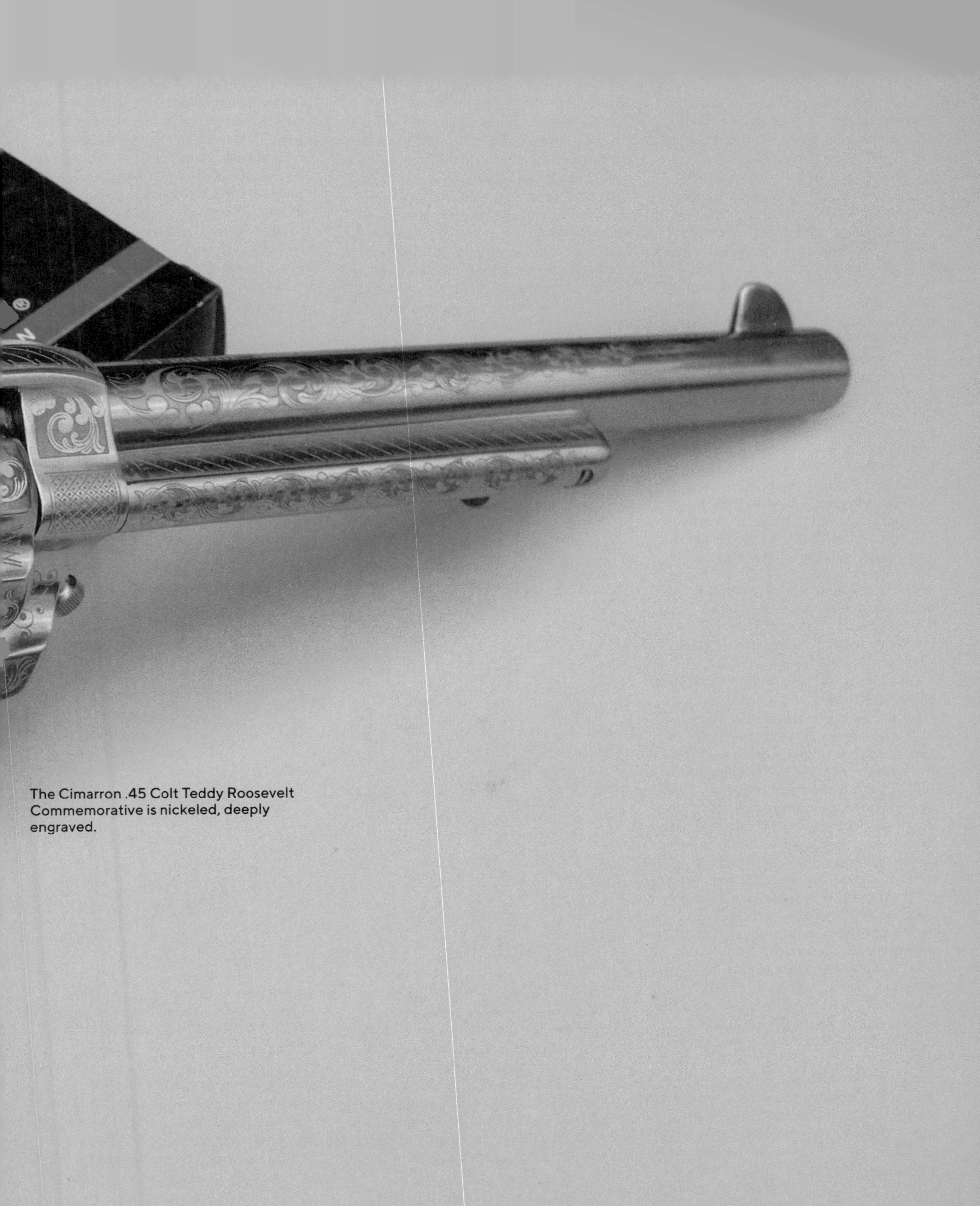

The Cimarron .45 Colt Teddy Roosevelt Commemorative is nickeled, deeply engraved.

Another Cimarron I have is the Earp Buntline in .45 Colt with 10-inch barrel. This one is from the "Hollywood" series. The Earp Buntline has a sterling silver grip inlay with "Wyatt Earp" engraved.

Uberti is in Italy, and markets guns in the USA on its own and through other U.S.-based gun companies. A .45 Colt Uberti SAA replica I bought several years ago is the Cattleman model. Typical of the early Colt SAA guns, the Cattleman has a blued barrel, cylinder and trigger guard, with a case-colored frame. Grips are of plain, uncheckered walnut. Barrel is 5.5 inches. Trigger is excellent with 3-pound pull.

Uberti has other SAA replicas, like the Stallion and several models of the El Patron SAA, plus non-SAA replicas of yesteryear. At Cimarron you'll find perhaps the longest list of SAA models anywhere. There are several models of the Eliminator SAA, as well as the Frontier models. Some can be engraved and/or outfitted with mock ivory grips. The Cimarron Hollywood series has deep interest among SAA replica buyers. Aptly named, some of the models in this series include the Rooster Shooter (John Wayne's SAA as Rooster Cogburn), and two models of The Man with No Name (Clint Eastwood Spaghetti Westerns) plus several more. All these Cimarron sixguns are offered in .45 Colt.

Reloading is germane to my existence. As a full-time gun writer I shoot a lot and, of course, reload most of the shells I shoot. For example, I've shot over 100,000 registered skeet targets and well over a million more clays preparing for skeet competition. I still shoot shotguns three to five days a week. Similarly, for the last 10 years, I've shot handguns three to five days a week. For the latter, my local range is only six miles away, making shooting convenient. While I shoot .22 rimfire rounds plenty, I also work with .38 Special, .44 Special and .45 Colt very often (firing 9mm, .357 Magnum, .44 Magnum and .45 ACP infrequently by comparison). At any rate, seldom does a day go by that I'm not reloading something and/or pulling the trigger.

Why do I love to reload? I enjoy sitting here at this keyboard using the old gray matter to string words together, but reloading gives me a break from using my brain power. This doesn't mean you leave your brain at idle when reloading. It's an endeavor that requires doing all phases of the operation perfectly. Still, reloading is relaxing and doesn't involve as much grueling concentration.

The bullet is paramount to fun reloading. Without a good bullet, you're stuck in the figurative mud. Many cast their own, which can be a bit cheaper, but I don't. I rely on Randy Moyer (www.moyerscastbullets.com) as he relies on his lead supplier to give him the same lead hardness time after time — Brinell Hardness 15. And, I stick with the same alloy for all the bullets I use for fun shooting in .45 Colt — Moyer's 255-grain semi-wadcutter. To reduce recoil even more, I could go to a lighter-weight .45-caliber bullet, but I guess being a traditionalist of the Old West I favor shooting the big bullets of yesteryear. Fresh from the box, these bullets are bright and shiny, and I almost never find one that has been deformed in transit. Bottom line: you need a good and reliable bullet maker unless you cast your own.

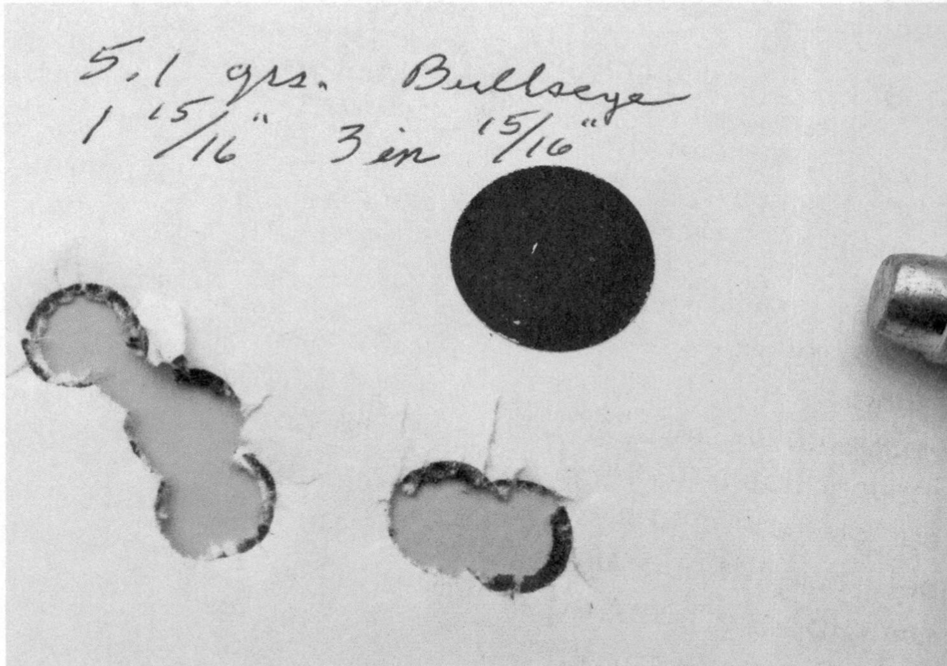

With 5.1 grains of Bullseye behind the Moyer .452 cast lead bullet, the author's sixgun produced this nice group at 25 yards.

The .45 Colt case is important as well. The usual suspects like Winchester, Remington, Federal, CCI, Hornady and others make fine cases. Often, you'll need to start with factory-loaded ammo, so just shoot them and take care of the cases. It's easy to do with a Single Action Army or any revolver chambered for the .45 Colt. A maker of excellent and very strong .45 Colt brass is Starline.

Powder is equally important, and it pays to start with several different options. Try buying in 1-pound cans. Old reliables include Unique and Bullseye, but there are newer pistol powders worth experimenting with, like Power Pistol, Trail Boss and others. Think faster-burning powders for the lower power loads, slower-burning propellants like 2400, 296 and others to pack into your higher velocity loads for hunting. There are plenty of large pistol primers from which to choose, as well as reloading die manufacturers.

Now let's get into reloading the .45 Colt with loads that won't rock your wrists, elbows or shoulders, or start you down the flinching road. I have two sets of reloading dies for the .45 Colt/.45 ACP. The inexpensive but excellent Lee dies are set for the .45 Colt, a set of Hornady dies are adjusted for the .45 ACP.

One load I've used often has been 5 grains of Trail Boss behind the Moyer cast 15 Brinell Hardness 255-grain semi-wadcutter (SWC). This is a soft load that shoots well at 25 yards with a velocity of a bit under 800 fps and relatively low pressure. I can shoot a box of 50 of these loads and never feel any fatigue or soreness in my wrists or hands, and I'm 80 years old and plagued with arthritis.

If you shoot your handgun a few times a year, sure, stick with the big loads. But what fun is shooting infrequently? The

CHART 1 .45 COLT VELOCITIES (BARREL CLEANED)

7 ½-Inch Ruger Vaquero 255-grain Moyer Lead SWC .452-Inch Diameter							
Powder	Vel. 1 (fps)	Vel. 2 (fps)	Vel. 3 (fps)	Vel. 4 (fps)	Vel. 5 (fps)	Max. Spread (fps)	Average (fps)
6 grains Power Pistol	842	864	822	811	810	54	829.8
8 grains Unique	942	927	943	955	964	37	946.2
6 grains Bullseye	897	908	907	911	909	12	906.4
5.8 grains WW 231	746	745	758	746	800	55	759.0
5 grains IMR Red	857	842	836	831	837	18	840.6
5 grains Trail Boss	769	795	796	786	776	27	784.4
Prochrony set 4 feet from muzzle off MTM rest. Barrel cleaned with Bore Snake after each 5-round group.							

idea I want to convey here is that .45 Colt shooting, and handgun shooting in general, should be a hoot. Granted, your pistol range might not be six miles away like mine, so when you go you probably want to shoot more than, say, 50 .22 rimfire loads and as many .45 Colts (or other centerfire cartridges). If that's true, I bet you don't want to pull off 100 .45 Colt loads at 950+fps. For me that's no fun, and I'm betting you're of the same mindset. It seems we are caught in the days of higher and higher velocity, greater and greater power. If you're hunting something, that's the path to follow. But with milder loads you can have so much more enjoyment shooting, and more often, too.

CHART 1b .45 COLT ACCURACY TESTS FOR CHART 1 LOADS

7 ½-Inch Ruger Vaquero 255-Grain Moyer Lead SWC .452-Inch Diameter	
Powder	5-Shot Group (inches)
6 grains Power Pistol	2.87
8 grains Unique	1.93
6 grains Bullseye	2.18
5.8 grains 231	1.93
5 grains IMR Red	2.75
5 grains Trail Boss	3.81

Five shots fired from a MTM rest at 25 yards. Barrel cleaned with a Bore Snake after each 5-shot group. Note: I decided to reduce the Power Pistol, Unique, Bullseye and IMR Red loads to see if accuracy would be affected, as well as get velocities in the 800-fps range. The WW 231 and Trail Boss loads at velocities of around 800 fps did present less felt recoil and more than adequate accuracy.

CHART 2 .45 COLT VELOCITIES (BARREL UNCLEANED)

7 ½-Inch Ruger Vaquero 255-grain Moyer Lead SWC .452-Inch Diameter							
Powder	Vel. 1 (fps)	Vel. 2 (fps)	Vel. 3 (fps)	Vel. 4 (fps)	Vel. 5 (fps)	Max. Spread (fps)	Average (fps)
5.5 grains Power Pistol	725	744	768	778	782	57	759
4.5 grains IMR Red	676	707	695	635	687	72	680
5.1 grains Bullseye	840	845	854	837	831	23	841.4
7 grains Unique	779	785	829	826	804	50	804.6
Prochrony set 4 feet from the muzzle, shot off a MTM rest. Barrel not cleaned between groups.							

Reducing the above velocities did not adversely affect accuracy. In most cases, accuracy was improved with the lighter loads. Further, despite so-called light loads, there were no squibs. From a subjective point of view (mine) there was significant increased felt recoil firing .45 Colt loads at 900 fps and faster, compared to loads in the 800-fps range. In addition, at 25 yards, accuracy was good with any of the six reloads around 800 fps.

CHART 2b .45 COLT ACCURACY TESTS FOR CHART 2 LOADS

7 ½-Inch Ruger Vaquero 255-Grain Moyer Lead SWC .452-Inch Diameter	
Powder	5-Shot Group (inches)
5.5 grains Power Pistol	4.18
4.5 grains IMR Red	1.75
5.1 grains Bullseye	1.93
7 grains Unique	2.75

Five shots fired from a MTM rest at 25 yards. Barrel left uncleaned between groups.

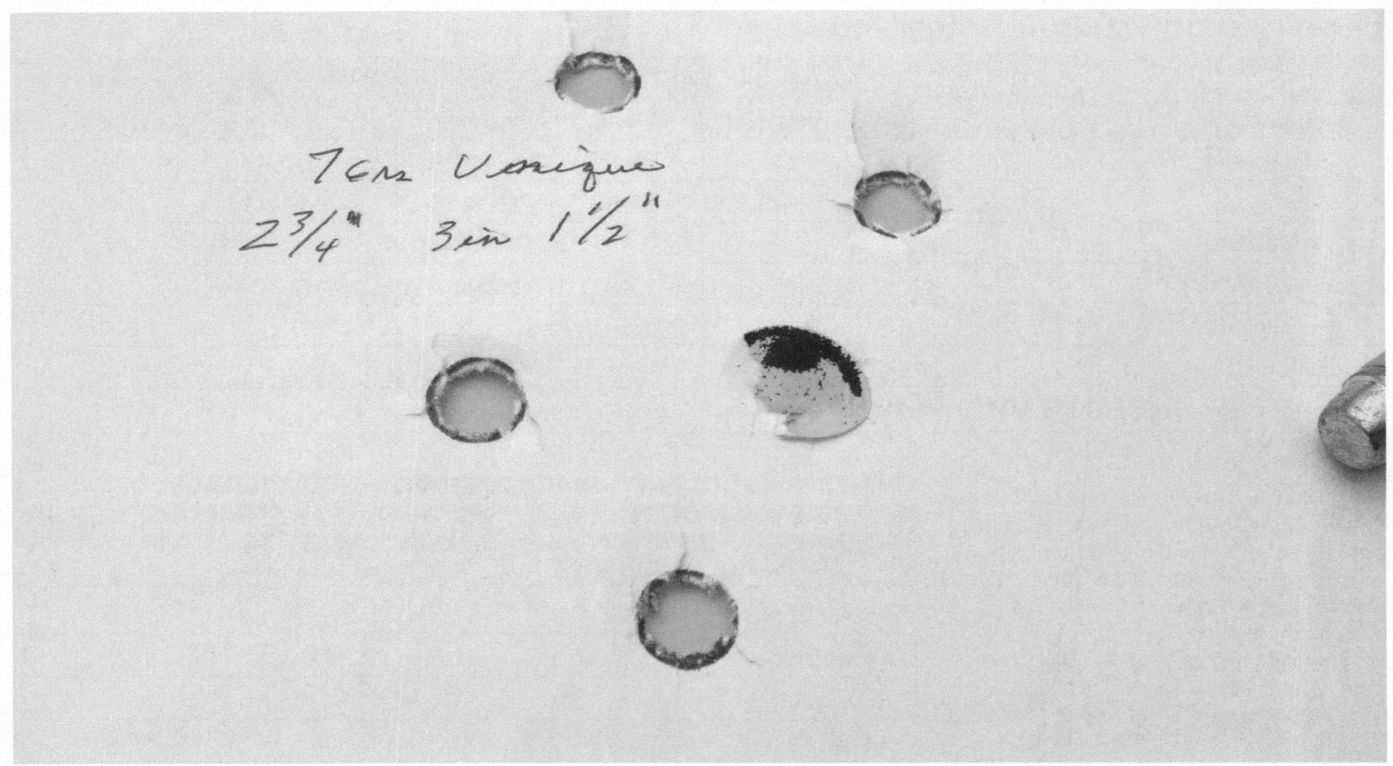

7 grains of Unique was behind this group at 25 yards for an average velocity of 804.6 fps.

YET ANOTHER ADVANTAGE WITH THESE LIGHTER LOADS IS THAT YOUR .45 COLT CASES WILL LAST A LOT LONGER FOR REPETITIVE RELOADING – THANKS TO VIRTUALLY NO CASE STRETCH OR RESULTANT TRIMMING. WITH BIG LOADS, CASES OBVIOUSLY STRETCH MORE, WHICH MEANS NOT ONLY CASE TRIMMING SOMEWHAT REGULARLY, BUT ALSO CASE LIFE IS DECREASED. TO REDUCE THE NUMBER OF CASE SPLITS AT THE NECK, I OPEN THE CASE MOUTHS MINIMALLY WHEN RELOADING.

For hunting big game, I wouldn't suggest any of these loads. Accuracy at 50, 75 and 100 yards has not been checked with any of these suggested lighter loads. When plinking at paper, I don't shoot at those longer ranges. In fact, most of my fun/practice shooting is done offhand at only 11 yards. Why 11 yards? That's where a big rock at my gun club range happens to be positioned. Just turns out to be 11 yards from the target holder. This is the type of close-range shooting this article covers. It's about making the big .45 more enjoyable, rather than being limited to shooting 50 or so high-velocity hunting-type loads every time you visit the range. I encourage you to shoot more. The only way I can do that with the big 255-grain loads in the .45 Colt, the cartridge we all love, is by shooting those heavy bullets out the muzzle at about 800 fps. I'm guessing you will feel the same way if you shoot often. I also hope to convince more shooters to try centerfire handguns as they are, quite literally, a blast.

With the Moyer 255-grain SWC .452-diameter bullets, I never get any barrel throat leading, let alone barrel leading, when kept in the territory of 800 fps. Big loads using lead bullets often do result in barrel leading, especially at the throat. The 15 Brinell Hardness I previously mentioned helps eliminate it at even higher velocities than 800 fps. These bullets are close in design to those old Elmer Keith helped develop for hunting. Consequently, feel free to use them in higher velocity loads for hunting.

Yet another advantage with these lighter loads is that your .45 Colt cases will last a lot longer for repetitive reloading — thanks to virtually no case stretch or resultant trimming. With big loads, cases obviously stretch more, which means not only case trimming somewhat regularly, but also case life is decreased. To reduce the number of case splits at the neck, I open the case mouths minimally when reloading. The Moyer 255-grain SWC bullets I suggest are beveled at the base, though slightly. This makes them easy to start the bullet somewhat into the case as you're ready to seat the bullet. Some bullets require significant case mouth opening, which will soon cause cracked necks.

There's nostalgic satisfaction in the tradition of shooting the .45 Colt, since the cartridge is older than dirt, nearing 150 years. There's a similar feeling about shooting, handling or even just looking at a revolver design that originated in 1873, even before that if we consider the Colt Walker, Colt 1860 Army and others. The latter were not SAA guns, but their design laid the foundation for the 1873 SAA. For a gun design to last that long and still be in production, Samuel Colt's company had to do something very right. If you don't shoot a .45 Colt in some version of the SAA, you should. And with the lighter loads suggested here, you'll grow to love shooting even more.

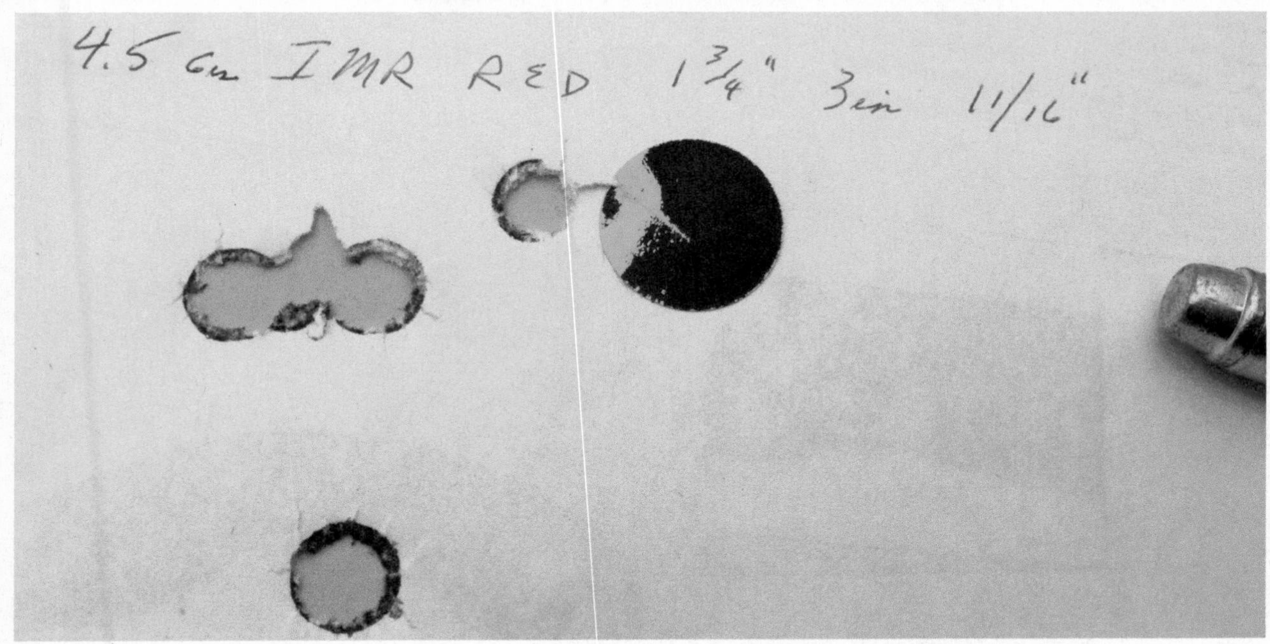

(above) 4.5 grains of IMR Red and the 255-grain lead bullet punched this group from the 7 ½-inch-barreled Ruger Vaquero.

(right) 5.5 grains of Power Pistol produced this outstanding 25-yard group.

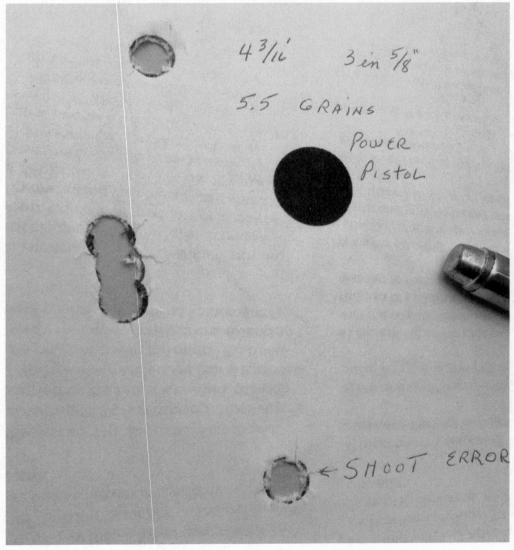

Grave of Demetrio Holguin, a traveler killed by the bandits during the raid on the Brite Ranch on Christmas Day, 1917.

GUNS OF THE BRITE RANCH RAID

Ranch Life on the Border During the Time of the Mexican Revolution Was Like a War Zone

BY **SHANE JAHN**

The revolution in Old Mexico began in 1910 and lasted for the better part of a decade. Stacks of books have been written on the subject, describing, dissecting and analyzing the complicated *Revolucion*. The big names of the violent struggle, men like Diaz, Madero, Villa, Huerta, Carranza and Zapata, are all remembered in history for one thing or another. It's unclear how many people died in the fighting, including soldiers, rebels and innocent civilians, but it was no small number, varying from one to two million.

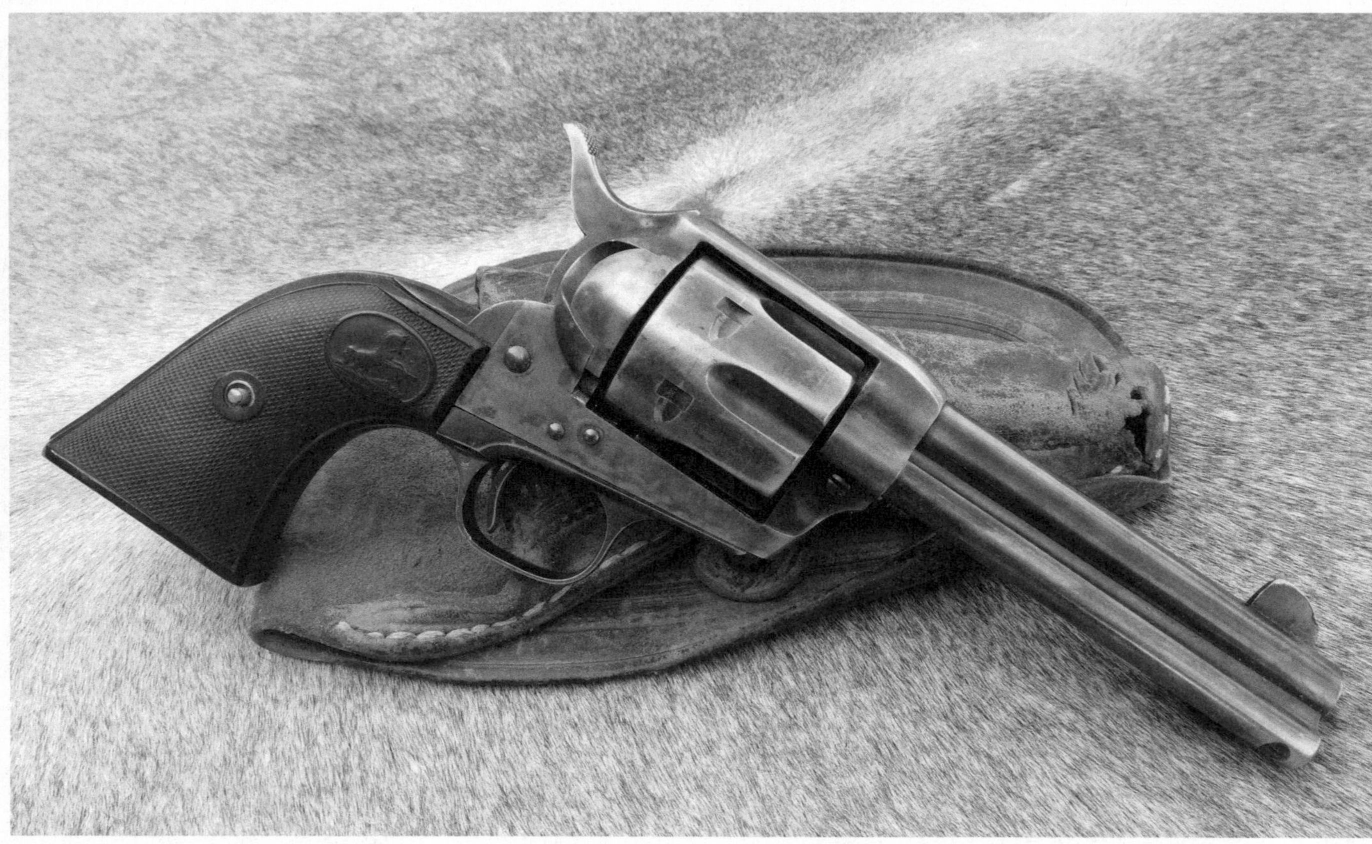

The Colt Single Action Army played a major role in the shootout at the Brite Ranch.

Pancho Villa's 1916 raid on Columbus, New Mexico, spurred the United States into action and unleashed strong characters like Pershing and Patton into Mexico, leading the U.S. Army in pursuit of combatants. During all of this turmoil south of the border, plenty of hell and havoc were wreaked on our side, from the Boca Chica on the Rio Grande to the deserts of New Mexico's boot heel. The wide-open country of the Big Bend Region of West Texas was no exception, with bandit raids occurring at Glenn Springs in 1916, the Brite Ranch in 1917, and the Neville Ranch in 1918, and numerous incidents in between that bear no name.

It appears that rogue murders and revenge killings went on back and forth by U.S. and Mexican shooters of various occupations and titles and many of the raids were, at least in part, made in retaliation. Other raids were made in efforts to acquire food and supplies like clothes, guns and ammunition — even livestock — and anything else that was needed to survive, profit from and contribute to the "cause" on the Mexican side of the Rio Grande.

Christmas morning 1917 likely started out like most winter days on the Brite Ranch, which was situated in the high desert country of Presidio County, Texas. That time of year the mornings are usually cold, with temperatures ranging from the teens to the thirties in the big, open valley known as Wild Horse Draw, which separates Mount Livermore and the Sierra Vieja Rim with miles of rolling, mostly open country. The ranch's main headquarters rests at the northeast base of Capote Peak, a Rock of Gibraltar-shaped sierra that looms over the region still known for its line-bred Hereford cattle.

Sam Neill, a Texan in his early 60s, having served as a customs agent and Texas Ranger, was at the Brite that morning to spend the holiday with his wife, daughter-in-law, and son, Van, who managed the ranch and lived on the sprawling cattle empire. Up early to start the wood-burning stoves and make morning coffee, Sam Neill gathered kindling to warm the house and returned to the kitchen where the cook had entered and had a hot cup awaiting him. Sitting to enjoy his early morning beverage and watch the morning come alive, he had no idea just how lively it was going to be.

Looking through the window toward the west, down the road to Candelaria, Neill saw six men riding abreast horseback, and coming fast. He watched for a moment, wondering who they could be and why the hurry. Then, as they neared the ranch headquarters, he knew. The men pulled their guns!

Neill dropped his coffee and ran for his rifle, a Winchester Model 1895, while yelling a warning to Van who was in another room of the house. Sam Neill went out to the corner of the yard as the riders pulled up their mounts, the leader yelling to his men, *Mata a los Americanos!* or "Kill the Americans!" He raised his Winchester and that was the last command the bandit gave that day, and forever.

At the shot, a small war erupted. Unknown to the Neills, more than forty banditos had hidden themselves around the adobe walls of the ranch compound and big earthen water dams nearby. It seems the bandits had done their homework and knew the usual ranch personnel numbers were low due to the holiday and ranch business. Owner Luke Brite was in Marfa and ranch cowboy and future Texas Ranger, Lee Trimble, was in El Paso with a load of cattle.

With hot lead in the air, Sam Neill got in three shots before a bullet zipped across his nose, knocking him down. He dove for the corner of the house but, after receiving too much enemy fire, retreated indoors. At some point during the fight he was also wounded in the right leg. From inside the adobe structure he and Van kept the bandits at bay, each shooting from inside opposite sides of the house, eventually running out of willing targets who would expose themselves for a shot. The bulk of the shooting went on for what Sam Neill later described as a "pretty squally" thirty minutes.

Capote Peak on Brite Ranch.

In the meantime, two young Mexican boys who worked on the ranch were taken captive by the bandits and one was released to send the Neill men an ultimatum to surrender or the house would be bombed. Neill's response was to "fly at it!" Seeing that a bomb threat was getting them nowhere, the bandits delivered another message: If the Neills quit shooting, they would too. They only wanted saddle horses and entry into the Brite Store, a post office and commissary of sorts that supplied ranch employees and folks in the area all things needed from food to clothes.

The Neills agreed and the shooting stopped, at least that which was directed toward them. Some of the surviving bandits had one of the captured boys take them to the horses that were located several miles away, east of the headquarters, in a canyon known as McKinley Wells, while others pilfered the store's supplies.

In the meantime, the mail stage came up from Candelaria, with a postman named Mickey Welch driving and two Mexican men on board. The bandits killed the two passengers and took Welch into the store where they hung him up by his feet and cut his throat. A neighbor, hearing the gunfire, came to investigate. Seeing the banditry in motion from a distance, he lit out to notify help.

Author's note: Decades later, around 1969 or 1970, the granddaughter of one of the murdered mail stage passengers contacted the Brite Ranch owners. Her family had never known what had happened to her grandfather, Demetrio Holguin, a mining engineer from the state of Durango. They simply knew he never arrived as planned in El Paso and suspected something terrible must have happened to him. While researching the bandit raids in college, she was finally able to put the pieces together. He was en route back to his wife and children when he was killed by the bandits raiding the Brite. One of the old ranch employees, who was a young man during the raid, remembered the general area where he was buried, and the family returned there each year to place flowers on his grave. His is the only grave marked after the raid.

Meanwhile, Reverend H.M. Bandy and his family arrived at the Brite Ranch, planning on having Christmas dinner with the Neills. Seeing that Bandy was a clergyman, and possibly due to the "cease fire" agreement made with Sam and Van, the bandits allowed them to enter the compound. Once getting his family inside the shelter of the sturdy adobe-walled home, the good reverend said a quick prayer and grabbed a rifle, prepared to defend his family and friends from the attackers, if need be.

The U.S. Cavalry was having Christmas dinner in the small town of Valentine, approximately 20 miles away, when they received word of the raid and jumped in a dozen vehicles — 1915 and 1916 model cars — owned by civilians, and headed to the Brite, taking about an hour to get there. Approximately 20 regular folks, all armed with rifles described in Robert Keil's book, *Bosque Bonito*, as "30-30 saddle guns," loaded up the soldiers and headed toward the fight. The Cavalrymen took their Springfield 1903 rifles with sixty rounds of ammunition, and each man carried a Colt 1911 .45 ACP and 21 rounds. Around 30 troops went, totaling 50 gunmen in all.

MUCH CONTROVERSY SURROUNDS THE VIOLENCE ON THE SOUTHWEST BORDER DURING THE TIMES AROUND THE MEXICAN REVOLUTION AND THE BANDIT RAIDS INTO THE UNITED STATES. VARIOUS SOURCES DIFFER SLIGHTLY IN SOME DETAILS, BUT IN THE END THE STORY IS THE SAME. MANY PEOPLE DIED, SOME DESERVINGLY, SOME NOT.

The Neills' 10-Guage Remington shotgun.

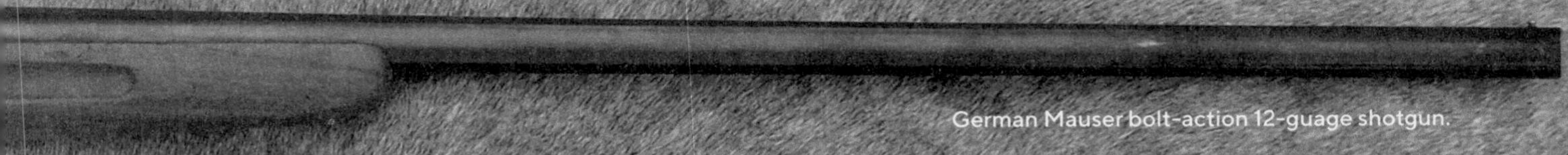

German Mauser bolt-action 12-guage shotgun.

dozen or so bandits were killed at the headquarters and before reaching the mountain pass and making good their escape down the Knight Trail, however temporary for some, to the semi-safety of their homeland. Some accounts put the number of slain bandits a bit higher.

(top) The Brite Ranch armory collection of rifles and shotguns.

(above) Van (left) and Sam Neill after the fight. Bullet strikes can be seen on the walls.

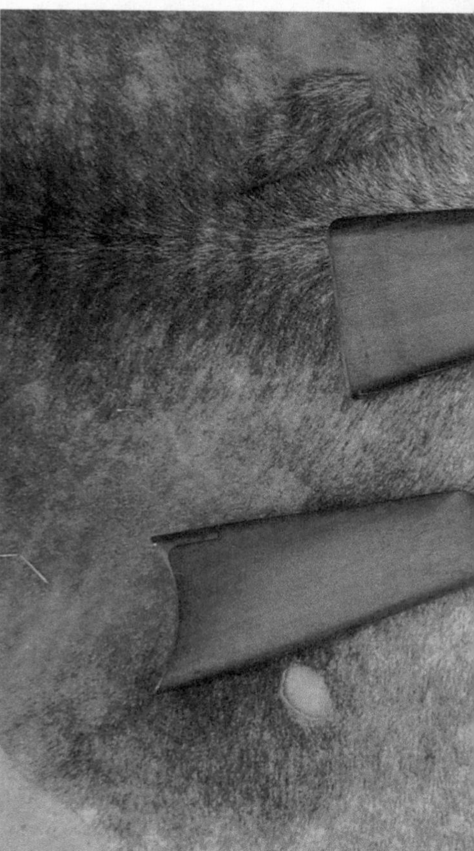

By the time the soldiers and locals approached the ranch, the bandits had gathered all they could haul from the store and around 25 head of Brite horses had been rounded up. Lookouts would have seen the dust from the automobiles coming for miles, alerting the raiders and allowing them ample time to start back on the trail for Old Mexico. Apparently, that's just what happened.

When the posse arrived at the headquarters, only dust could be seen from the fleeing invader's horses and the remuda they had stolen from rancher Luke Brite. The men got a quick brief from Van Neill and pursued the bandits via the automobiles toward the Sierra Vieja Rim, a colossal escarpment of lava rock uplift that rises several hundred feet from the Chihuahua desert floor. The dust from the running horses was so thick that it took a while before the posse could make out the bandits on horseback. The shooting started at extended ranges; men, horses and mules were hit on the Mexican's side. All in all, around a

THE GUNS

While the testimony given in the Congressional "Investigation of Mexican Affairs" about the bandit raids into the United States does not get into gun makes, models and calibers (the stuff we would like to know) we do have photos to determine what weapons were used during the Brite Ranch raid. Sam Neill is seen shortly after the ruckus with a bandage on his nose holding a Winchester Model 1895 lever action and wearing a Colt Single Action Army revolver in his gun belt, as is his son, Van.

Local history reveals that Sam Neill also used a double-barreled Remington 10 gauge with exposed hammers to good effect during the fight. As one can imagine, it makes sense that the Neills would have used any loaded gun handy during the shooting and reloaded at every opportunity. Another shotgun was reported to have seen action on that Christmas day as well, a bolt-action German Mauser in 12 gauge. An old photograph also shows a couple Winchester Model 1897 12 gauges that would have surely seen action if they were within arm's reach that day.

The U.S. soldiers who carried a handgun were issued the racehorse of the day (and still today) the Colt 1911 Government Model in .45 ACP. The Army's longarm was the venerable Springfield 1903 bolt-action rifle in .30-06 Springfield.

Most Texas Rangers during those times carried Colt Single Action Army revolvers. Calibers varied based on personal preference, but most favored the big bores in .45 Colt, .44 Special or .44-40 WCF/.44 WCF. Barrel lengths were another personal matter, with everything seen from 4 ¾- to 7 ½-inch sixguns. Favored rifles of the time were the Model 1895 and 1894 Winchester. Savage's Model 1899 was also popular among lawmen. Photos during the period of the bandit raids show a majority of Model 1895s. I suspect these rifles were chambered in .30-06 Springfield since that was the issued round for the Army. That would mean readily available ammunition for the lawmen if they had like-chambered rifles. The .30-40 Krag was popular as well.

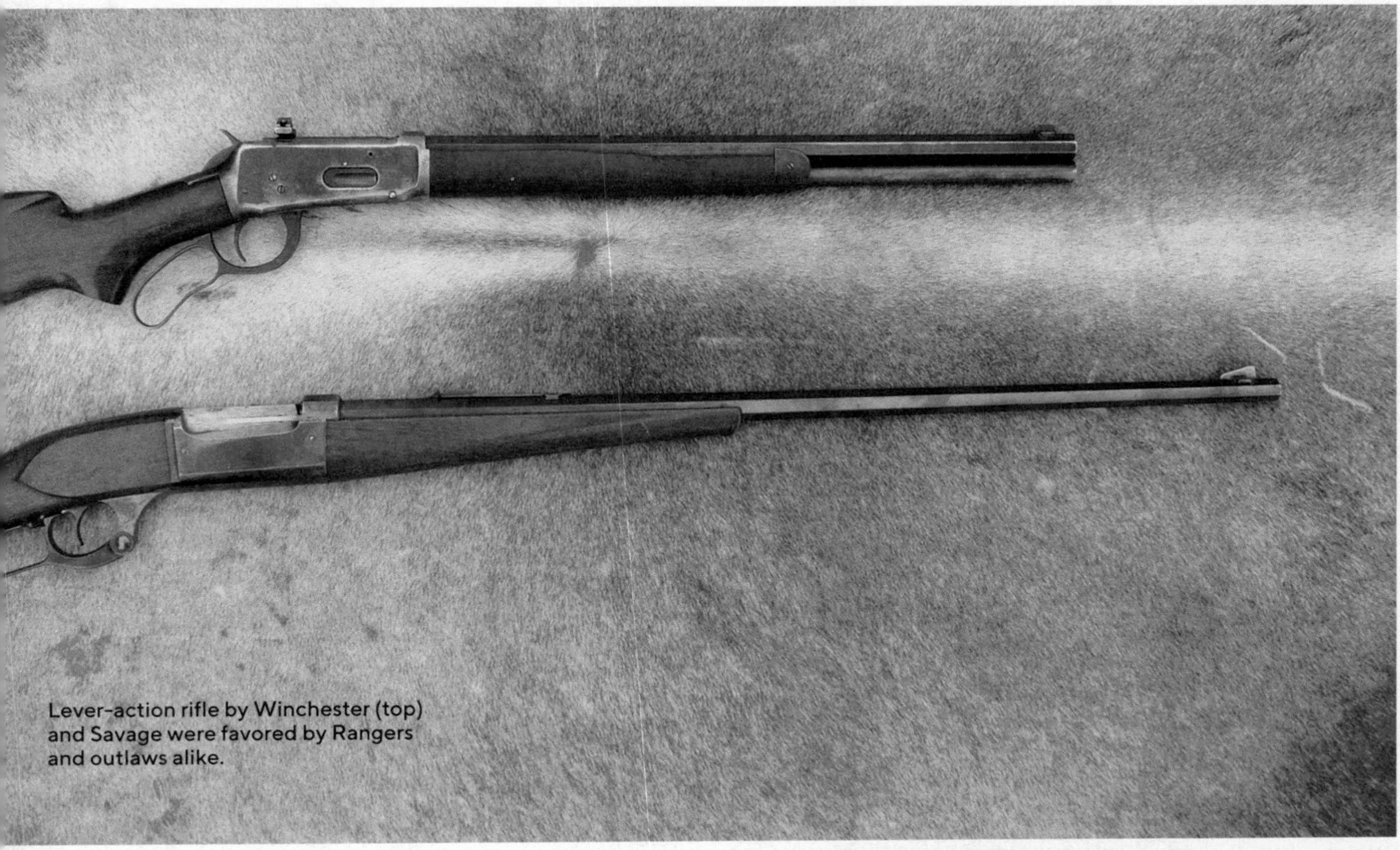

Lever-action rifle by Winchester (top) and Savage were favored by Rangers and outlaws alike.

The bandits — members of one side or another in the on-going Mexican Revolution — would have been carrying anything they could get their hands on. Photos show them with Remington rolling block single-shots, Mauser bolt guns and Winchester lever actions. Gunwriter, historian and retired lawman Sheriff Jim Wilson says the Mexicans favored the Winchester Model 1894 and Marlin 1893 in .30-30 WCF. The 1910 Mexican Mauser in 7x57 Mauser was very common, as well as Savage lever actions, Models 1895 and 1899, and Winchester models 1873, 1886, 1892 and 1895. Pretty much anything made during that era was used, it seems.

Texas Rangers, Brite Ranch cowboys, other ranchers and their rifles.

It is documented that Pancho Villa favored Colt's Bisley model as his carry gun, one being a 5 ½-incher in .44-40 wearing mother of pearl stocks. The Colt SAA was a main player for those who carried a handgun, but it's safe to say that any current handgun that could be obtained was used by the Mexicans.

I recall seeing a well-worn Model 1892 Winchester that a man once bought from an old Mexican vaquero down on this side of the Rio Grande. As the story went, the aged cowboy would have been a young man during the time of the revolution and moved to the U.S. later in life. When the buyer inquired about the numerous notches carved in the stock, the old man paused and replied, "javelina."

It was a terrible and vicious period in history. May we never see it repeated.

HANDGUNS FOR SENIOR SHOOTERS

You Don't Have to Beat Bad Guys Away with a Cane. Stay Armed and Ready No Matter What Life Throws Your Way

BY **AL DOYLE**

By choosing a handgun chambered in a mild-mannered round, and keeping up with practice, there's no reason age should stop you from being armed.

For folks who are aging or may have various physical limitations, the popular question, "What's the best gun for home defense?" is far too general. When age is a factor, making the right choice may go beyond what fits comfortably in your hand. Thus, the question for senior shooters is, what's the best handgun to keep Grandpa and Grandma safe from attackers who may view them as easy targets? Which models and what calibers can reasonably be shot, reloaded and controlled under stress by those with hand strength or vision problems?

Money can be a significant issue when shopping for a firearm, but age-related concerns might trump a stack of Ben Franklins. Even if you're able to afford that Les Baer custom 1911, arthritis and other health factors could make it necessary to limit exposure to recoil. The sunset years may not be the best time to obtain your first .454 Casull or .475 Linebaugh revolver. On the practical side, cashing in on old favorites that have become too hot to handle will provide funds to purchase guns that are more suitable to your current needs.

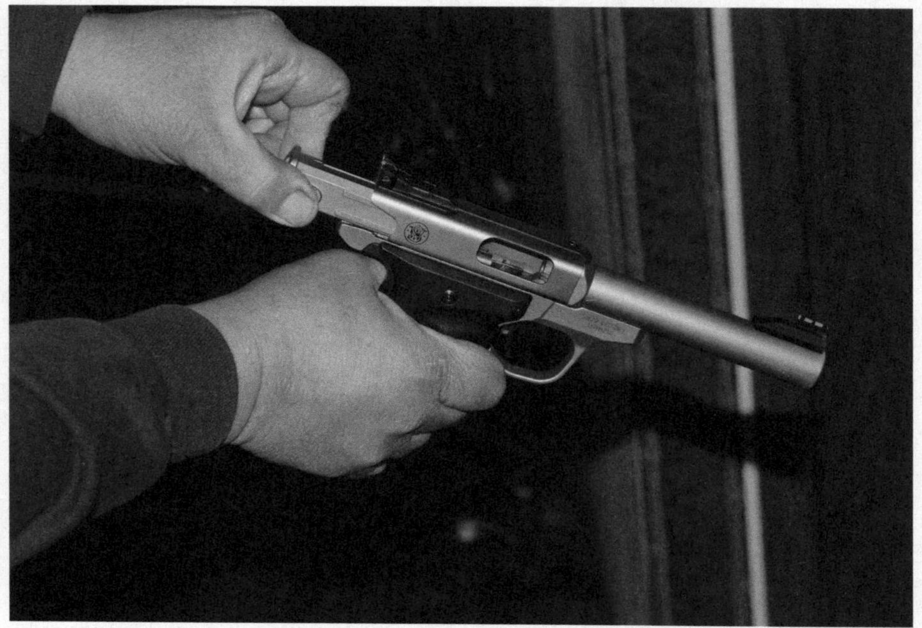

Chambering the Smith & Wesson Victory pistol is a two-fingered task.

"The problem is, I can't shoot nothing no more."

I overheard that grammar-challenged line from a 60-something visitor to a local gun show recently. The gentleman's remark is a common one among gray-haired gun enthusiasts. A better and more accurate way to describe the situation is, "I have to figure out what I can shoot."

A friend who is advising a widow is currently dealing with this dilemma. Her late husband left behind a collection that includes an AR-15, several Browning Hi Power 9mms and other desirable items. The lady is pro-gun and wants to keep a few pieces around for home defense.

The Smith & Wesson Victory has quickly become a popular .22 LR pistol. It may not be the ideal self-defense gun, but it's better than nothing.

Sadly, the limited hand strength of her youth has deteriorated due to arthritis and other persistent aches. Racking a Hi Power slide is out of the question. The moderate and normally manageable recoil of a 9mm would send spasms of pain through her shooting hand and wrist. What handgun option would be best for her?

A Ruger 10/22 is part of the estate, and it›s something the widow can and does handle with comfort. While a .22 LR surely isn›t the first choice for home defense, it may be the only option when larger calibers could cause genuine hurt and accuracy-destroying flinch. It's all too easy to pontificate about the "puny" rimfire, but age-related issues may substantially reduce the number of workable options.

The widow's advisor is also considering a Smith & Wesson .38 Special revolver as a keeper, but this classic firearm would need a Pachmayr or similar aftermarket grip to soak up recoil. Low-pressure wadcutters rather than amped-up +P rounds are going to be the ammunition of choice for the lady's sensitive hands.

You don't need to be a football player to load this Ruger Mark II.

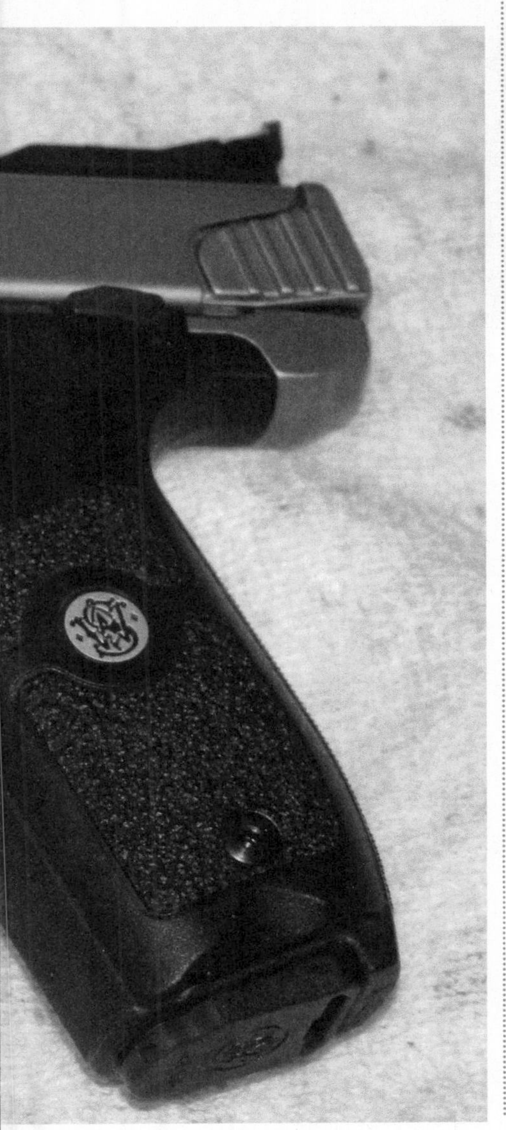

When asked to make a recommendation for the widow, I suggested a new or used Ruger Mark II, III or IV — the venerable rimfire pistol that launches the easy shooting .22 LR. Rounds can be chambered by using two fingers. Reliability is exceptional, and the Mark series is accurate. There are other options, though. The Smith & Wesson Victory comes with neon green three-dot sights that are ideal for older eyes, and it gobbles various brands of .22 ammo

There's nothing wrong with debating the merits of the .22LR cartridge for self-defense. But if the .22 is all you can handle shooting, it's better to have it on hand than to be defenseless. Photo: Federal Ammunition

Many gun owners would gladly reach for a stainless steel Smith & Wesson Model 15 in .38 Special.

without a problem. Like the Ruger, the Victory can be loaded easily by grasping it with a couple of fingers.

When it comes to home defense, relying on popular centerfire calibers — if health and physical ability allow — is a logical approach. With more than 25 years in the business, Tom Lauritzen of Lauritzen Enterprises in Wild Rose, Wisconsin, has sold thousands of pistols for protection, and he offered advice for the 60-plus crowd.

"I deal with the recoil and hand strength issue quite often," he said. "It isn›t just older people. My wife went with

Seniors aren't the only people who struggle with hand strength. Female shooters can face difficulty racking the slide on many popular semi-auto pistols. However, it can be overcome with lighter calibers and recoil springs, and some expert instruction.

If you can't handle the large calibers like you did in your younger years, don't be afraid to try small-caliber semi-auto handguns, such as the .380 Auto.

a 9mm Charter Arms Pitbull revolver because it has less recoil than a .38."

A loaded small-caliber handgun is better than a fake or even an unloaded one. Never bluff when armed, as merely brandishing a weapon with no willingness or ability to employ it may not be enough to deter a burglar or other invader. It could also land you in hot water with the authorities for brandishing a weapon, and even constitutes assault in some jurisdictions. Of course, no one wants to fire on another human, but it might be necessary for a life or death situation. Be well-informed on state and local laws regarding self-defense issues.

"If I come out of my bedroom with a gun, the intruder might run away," Lauritzen said. "If a woman has the exact same gun, she might get attacked because the bad guy feels he has the opportunity to take a gun from a woman since she won't shoot. That's a stereotype I don't believe, but many criminals do."

Income — or lack of it — can be a critical issue for senior citizens who need to obtain a pistol. Lauritzen stocks guns ranging from $150 to $3,000, and he recommended a trio of moderately priced options for those on fixed incomes.

"The Bersa Thunder in .380 ACP is a little over $300, and most women can operate the slide," he said. "Hornady Critical Duty .380 is a potent round. The Taurus 709 Slim is a lower-priced 9mm. The Walther CCP is one 9mm that many people can handle. It's a striker-fired pistol, and the slide is easy to rack."

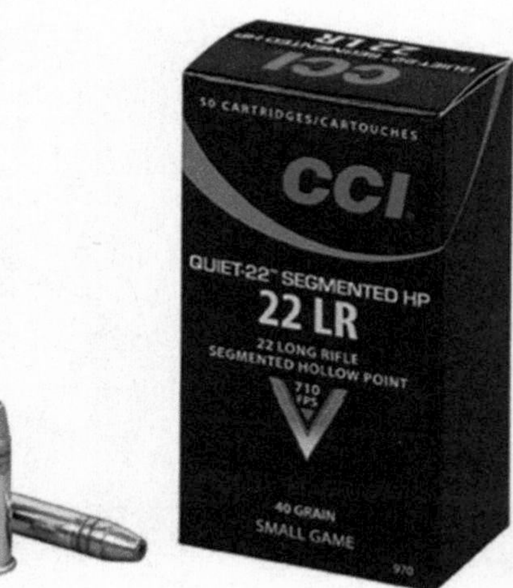

Rimfire ammo stuffed with segmented 40-grain hollowpoints, like these from CCI, is now widely available, is affordable to shoot for target practice, and offers low-recoil for fast follow-up shots. Don't discount it for personal protection. Photo: Federal Ammunition

The 9mm Luger, arguably America's most popular centerfire handgun caliber, is sufficient to make the proper impression when needed. "I have talked with police who have interviewed people who had 9mms pointed at them, and they swore it was a .45 or even a .50 caliber," Lauritzen said.

This veteran of the retail gun trade isn't reluctant to go smaller if physical limitations call for minimal recoil.

"I'll recommend a .22 for older people because they'll feel comfortable and confident with it," Lauritzen said. "A .22 is easy to shoot, and people will practice with it because the cost of ammo is so low."

It pays to think like a Marine when the situation gets tense and possibly dangerous. A Marine Corps recon sergeant who wishes to remain anonymous advises the over-60 crowd to have a plan when dealing with threats.

"In the Marine Corps School of Infantry, they teach two general modes of operation — attacking and raiding or defending a position," he said. "They involve different tasks. There are times when it's best to go straight at the enemy, but if you're not all that quick and agile, defend rather than attack. Hide in an ambush spot if possible."

Hunkering down in the bedroom or elsewhere with your chosen firearm and a phone is a lower-risk option than roaming through a dark house.

"If someone breaks in, get your weapon in hand and call 911," the Marine said. "You don't have to be a hero. If there is a lockable door between you and the assailant, lock it."

Think about possible scenarios and your reaction to them before the moment of truth arrives. This is especially critical if your physical mobility is limited.

"Just because you have a gun doesn't mean the bad guy's not going for you," he continued. "This is old data, but many [single-shot] Civil War muskets have been found loaded with three to five rounds in them because the soldiers were reluctant to shoot another person. It got them killed. You have to be willing to pull the trigger. Be mentally prepared. No hesitation, no freezing. Do what needs to be done all the way."

A 9mm and .45 ACP Glock loyalist since he began shooting, the sarge concurred with Lauritzen's willingness to recommend a .22 for those with less than average strength.

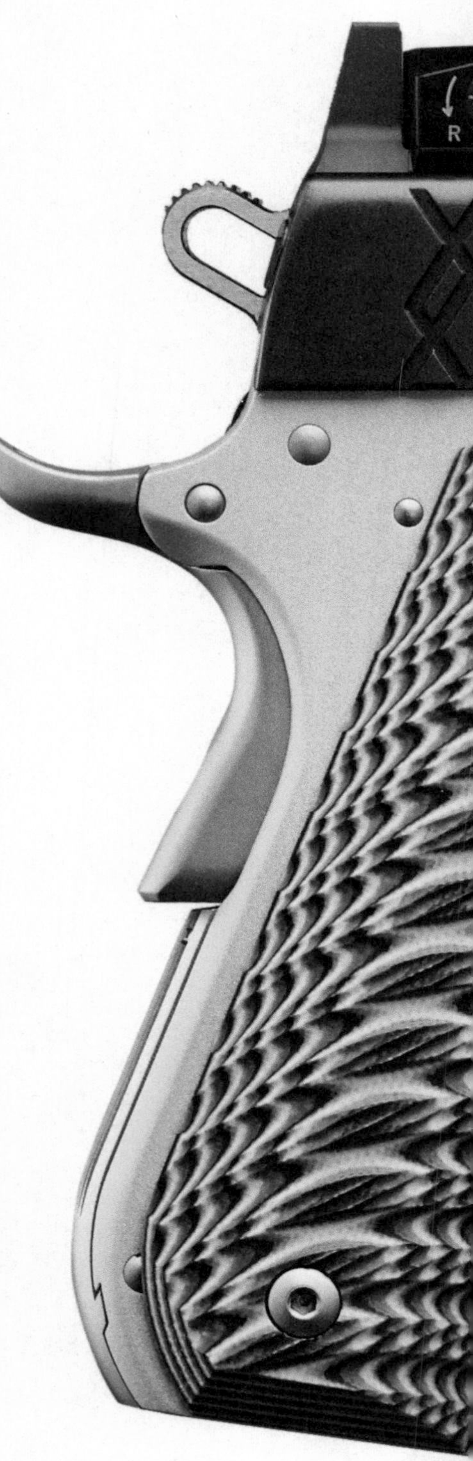

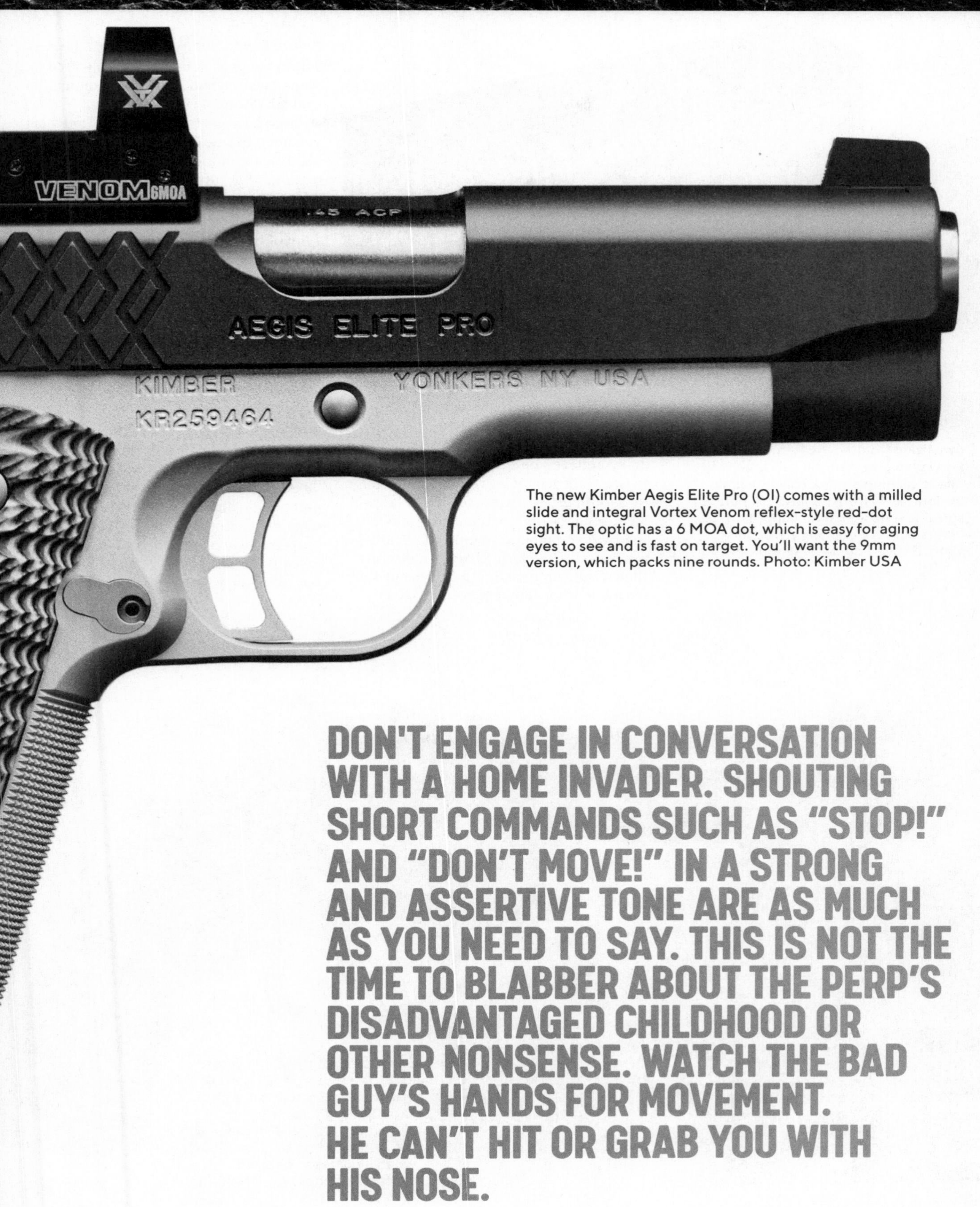

The new Kimber Aegis Elite Pro (OI) comes with a milled slide and integral Vortex Venom reflex-style red-dot sight. The optic has a 6 MOA dot, which is easy for aging eyes to see and is fast on target. You'll want the 9mm version, which packs nine rounds. Photo: Kimber USA

DON'T ENGAGE IN CONVERSATION WITH A HOME INVADER. SHOUTING SHORT COMMANDS SUCH AS "STOP!" AND "DON'T MOVE!" IN A STRONG AND ASSERTIVE TONE ARE AS MUCH AS YOU NEED TO SAY. THIS IS NOT THE TIME TO BLABBER ABOUT THE PERP'S DISADVANTAGED CHILDHOOD OR OTHER NONSENSE. WATCH THE BAD GUY'S HANDS FOR MOVEMENT. HE CAN'T HIT OR GRAB YOU WITH HIS NOSE.

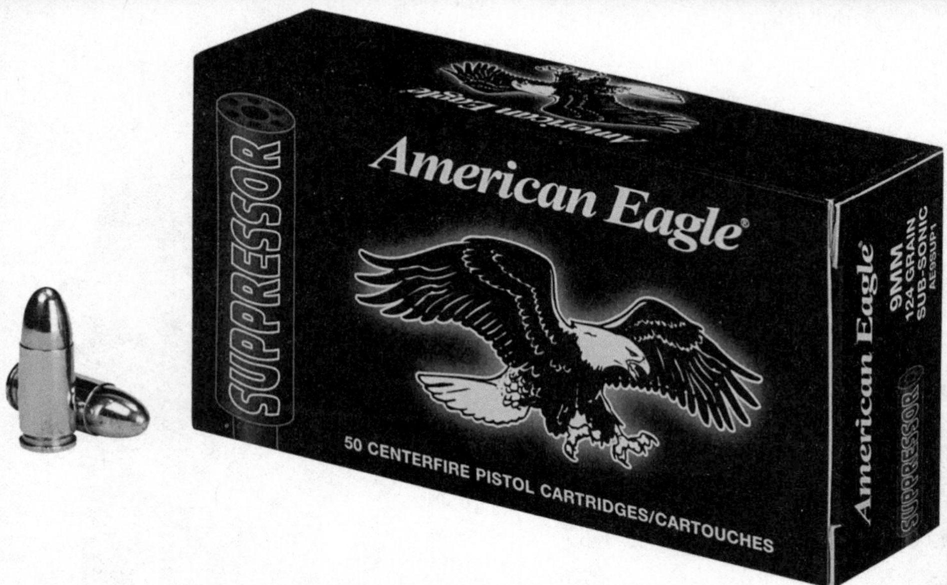

Downsizing from .45 ACP to 9mm is one easy way to give arthritic hands a break while remaining armed. This 124-grain sub-sonic FMJ from Federal's American Eagle line is designed for suppressor use, which makes it a good light-recoiling option. Photo: Federal Ammunition

"Its effect on people is not as small as many believe," he said. "That›s according to Greg Ellifritz's research and findings on shootings. The way I see it, the .22 will incapacitate or more. It has less recoil than larger calibers, so follow-up shots are faster." The Marine likes the discontinued but common Smith & Wesson 422 for those who want a concealed carry rimfire due to the pistol's slim profile.

Don›t engage in conversation with a home invader. Shouting short commands such as "Stop!" and "Don't move!" in a strong and assertive tone are as much as you need to say. This is not the time to blabber about the perp's disadvantaged childhood or other nonsense. Watch the bad guy's hands for movement. He can't hit or grab you with his nose.

If your skills are rusty or you have limited experience with guns, a wide range of classes from one-day sessions near home to nationally known schools such as Thunder Ranch, Gunsite, Front Sight and the Massad Ayoob Group provide training and ideas about dealing with potentially dangerous encounters. Consider such education as an investment in your well-being. Watching DVDs and online video by professionals in the field is a low-cost way to gain knowledge.

What other handguns will serve armed citizens of advanced years? Go shopping and handle different models to see what fits you best. Some self-appointed "experts" who specialize in bluster like to insist that their favorite gun is the only correct choice for everyone, but buying

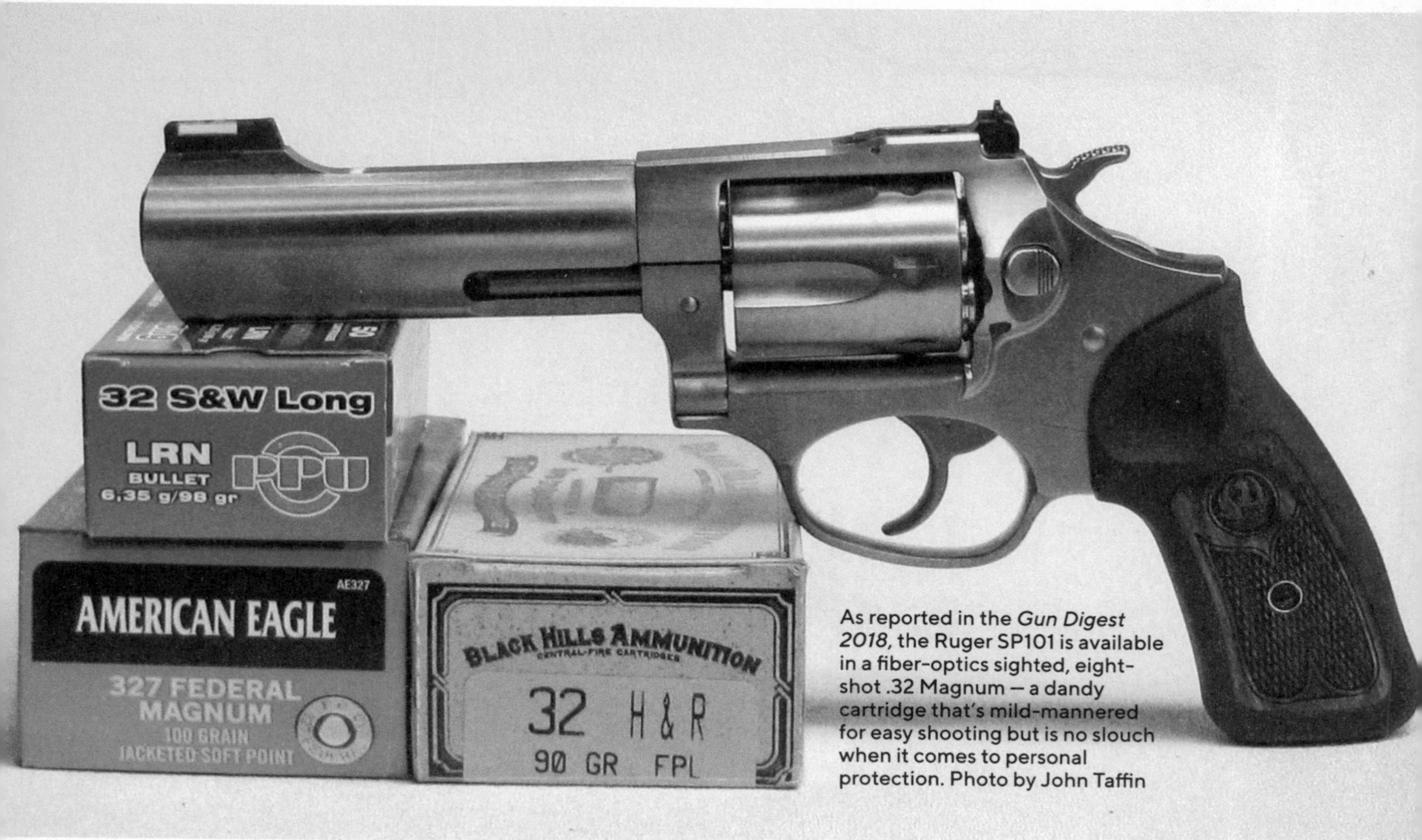

As reported in the *Gun Digest 2018*, the Ruger SP101 is available in a fiber-optics sighted, eight-shot .32 Magnum — a dandy cartridge that's mild-mannered for easy shooting but is no slouch when it comes to personal protection. Photo by John Taffin

the right pistol is much like choosing the perfect suit or dress. It should feel like it was made for you.

In addition to the previously mentioned brands, a wide range of well-made handguns by Beretta, Colt, Heckler & Koch, Kahr, Kel-Tec, SIG Sauer, Rock Island Arms/Armscor and Springfield Armory should be in stock at most gun merchants in America. Shopping around will provide a hands-on education that can't be duplicated online.

The plain iron sights that served well before you turned gray or bald may not be the answer today. Some pistols come with night sights or neon-colored fiber-optics, and these can provide a big boost to accuracy. Perhaps a gun you have owned for many years could be upgraded with aftermarket sights. Maybe it's time to really go modern and put a laser on your self-defense weapon. There are several new semi-auto handguns on the market that come equipped with reflex red-dot sights integral to the slide. These make target acquisition faster and reduce the number of planes your eye must assimilate when locking onto the target. Examples include the Glock 19 MOS, SIG Sauer P226 and P229 RX, Kimber Aegis Elite Pro (OI) and Beretta APX RDO.

If semi-autos can be a pain (literally) for older folks to handle, what about revolvers? Wheelguns are touted for their relative simplicity of operation. Like semi-autos, revolvers can be found at numerous price points and in all sorts of calibers, from the .22 LR on up to the .44 Magnum or larger.

Starting at the more affordable end of the scale, Taurus produces the Model 85 .38 "snubbie" in a variety of metal and polymer frames. Armscor .38s will do the job at a modest price, and Charter Arms offers a wide assortment of well-made little revolvers.

Ruger and Smith & Wesson products are as common as dirt, which is an indicator of their reliability. The .357 Magnum also accepts .38 Specials, and the less powerful round is a better choice for potential indoor usage. Just remember that muzzle flash from a .357 can be blinding indoors at 2 am.

Although short-barreled .38s have an obvious handiness, the 4-inch versions might be better for older eyes if the gun isn't going to be used for concealed carry away from home. If hand strength is an issue, find a .38 with a full hammer for easier single-action usage. Bobbed

The Beretta Model 86 Cheetah was a .380 ACP that employed a unique tip-up barrel arrangement for first-round loading, so racking the slide wasn't necessary. Sadly, the Cheetah is only available on the used market now, however Beretta does produce two current tip-up models, the Model 21 A Bobcat Inox in .22 LR, and the Model 3032 Tomcat Inox in .32 ACP. Photo courtesy Rock Island Auction Company

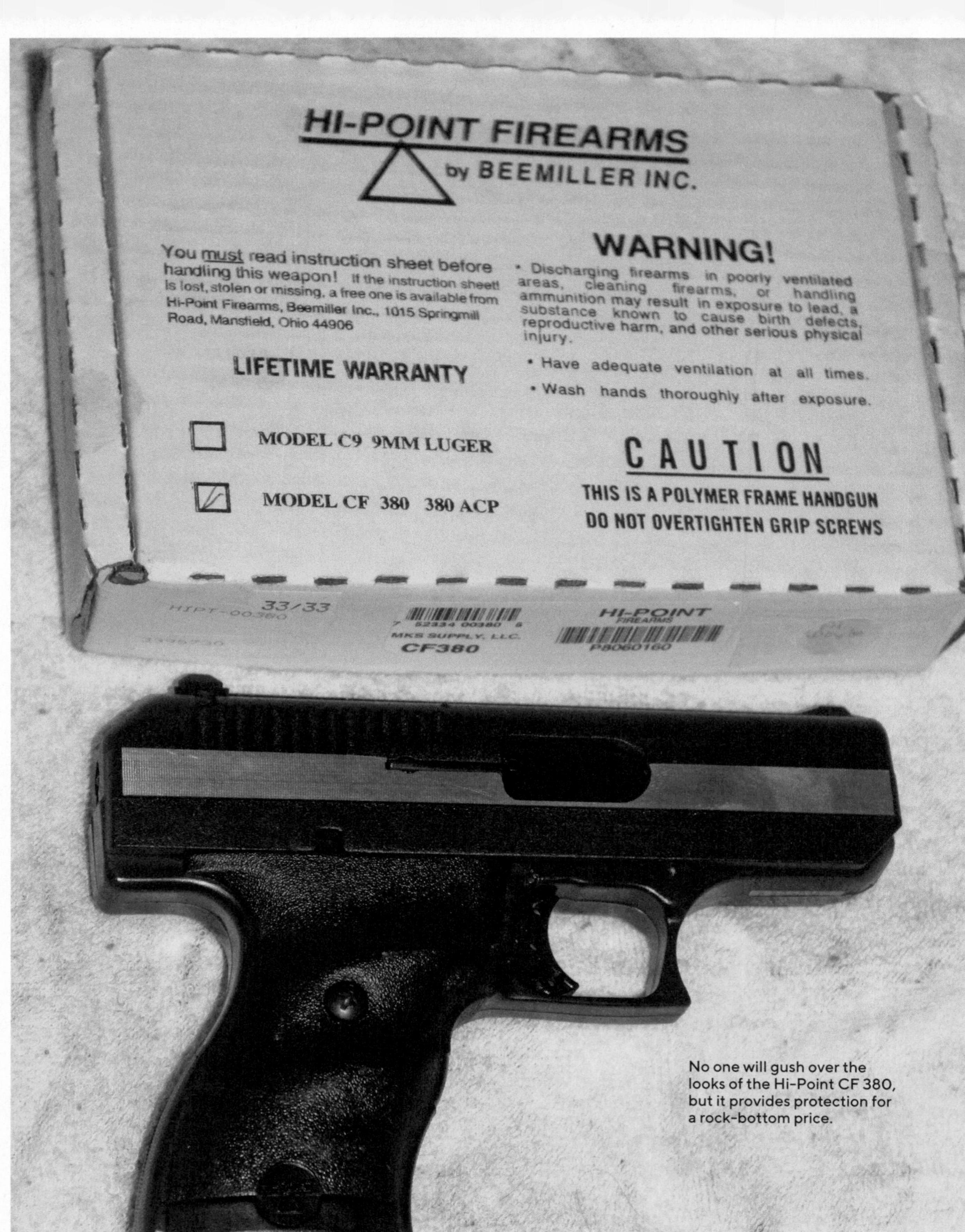

No one will gush over the looks of the Hi-Point CF 380, but it provides protection for a rock-bottom price.

hammers are great for CCW packing, but some older folks may have trouble with double-action shooting.

What about another caliber? It pays to listen to the experts. Big-bore revolver authority John Taffin and his finely crafted essay on .32-caliber wheelguns in the *2018 Gun Digest* is worth a read. Taffin and large handgun rounds have been synonymous for decades, but he isn't immune to the effects of aging. In his constant experimentation with revolvers, he developed "a small magnificent obsession" with several calibers that wouldn't have gotten his attention as a younger man. But, what can a .327 Federal Magnum, .32 H&R Magnum, .32 S&W Long or the .32 ACP do when a creep decides to attack?

The .32s combine modest recoil (think better accuracy) with enough punch to deal with unpleasant encounters. If a person can comfortably shoot something like a .40 Smith & Wesson, go for it. It's a different story for many people who long for the days when they were a snot-nosed punk of 50. As with everything else in life, it's a matter of doing the best you can in ever-changing circumstances.

Just about every gun owner has mentally played Sam Colt, John Browning or Bill Ruger at one time. In other words, they wanted to come up with a great gun design. What would be an ideal home defense piece for many older shooters? Such a gun was made in the past, but it didn't resonate with the public.

I refer to Beretta's Model 86 Cheetah, which is a full-sized .380 ACP semi-auto. This Italian-made firearm can be loaded by placing the first round in the tip-up barrel. Fill the single-stack magazine, slap it into place, and you have nine low-recoiling rounds on tap without having to rack a slide. The Model 86 is a rare sight today, available only on the used market, and prices reflect collectors' premiums.

Perhaps a reintroduced Beretta Cheetah would be a bigger seller in today's market with focused marketing and some modifications. They could replace the steel frame with polymer, top the barrel with high-visibility sights, and the Model 86 would become something well-suited for the 60-plus market, or anyone who has difficulty with standard semi-auto operation. Currently, the largest caliber pistol with a handy tip-up barrel is the Beretta 3032 Tomcat in .32 ACP.

PERHAPS A REINTRODUCED BERETTA CHEETAH WOULD BE A BIGGER SELLER IN TODAY'S MARKET WITH FOCUSED MARKETING AND SOME MODIFICATIONS. THEY COULD REPLACE THE STEEL FRAME WITH POLYMER, TOP THE BARREL WITH HIGH-VISIBILITY SIGHTS, AND THE MODEL 86 WOULD BECOME SOMETHING WELL-SUITED FOR THE 60-PLUS MARKET, OR ANYONE WHO HAS DIFFICULTY WITH STANDARD SEMI-AUTO OPERATION.

Although it doesn't have the unique loading method of the Tomcat, a brand-new pistol looks like it could be a good fit for those who answer to "Grandma" or "Grandpa." In his Guns America review, author Max Slowik refers to the Smith & Wesson M&P Shield 2.0 EZ as "an S&W Shield built for Grandpa." What makes this mid-sized piece so user-friendly?

Large, strategically placed serrations allow the gun to be loaded with relative ease. The single-stack magazine holds eight rounds, which is an improvement over pocket-sized .380s. Three-dot sights on a 3.6-inch barrel provide a boost in accuracy. The manufacturer's suggested retail price of $399 translates to $325 or less at the gun counter, a price that works well for those seniors who need to be careful spenders.

What about the retiree who literally must count every nickel? Is a baseball bat the only option?

It's a no-frills product for sure, but the Hi-Point CF 380 has very low recoil due to its chunky 29-ounce weight. Take a discount on the MSRP of $179, and Hi-Point brings centerfire pistol ownership to the masses. Although this .380 ACP is a reliable performer with a lifetime warranty, there is something else to consider.

The heavy slide can be difficult to pull back, so anyone with weaker hands may want to look elsewhere. This design feature means owners should give the CF 380 a longer break-in period than other pistols. Since extra rounds of practice will help with shooting skills, consider another box of ammo to be money well spent.

Don't give up on defending yourself if strength and vigor aren't what they were in the past. Adjust and adapt to current circumstances, and you won't have to nervously cower without the means of protection when trouble crosses your path.

GUNS o
THE GAN

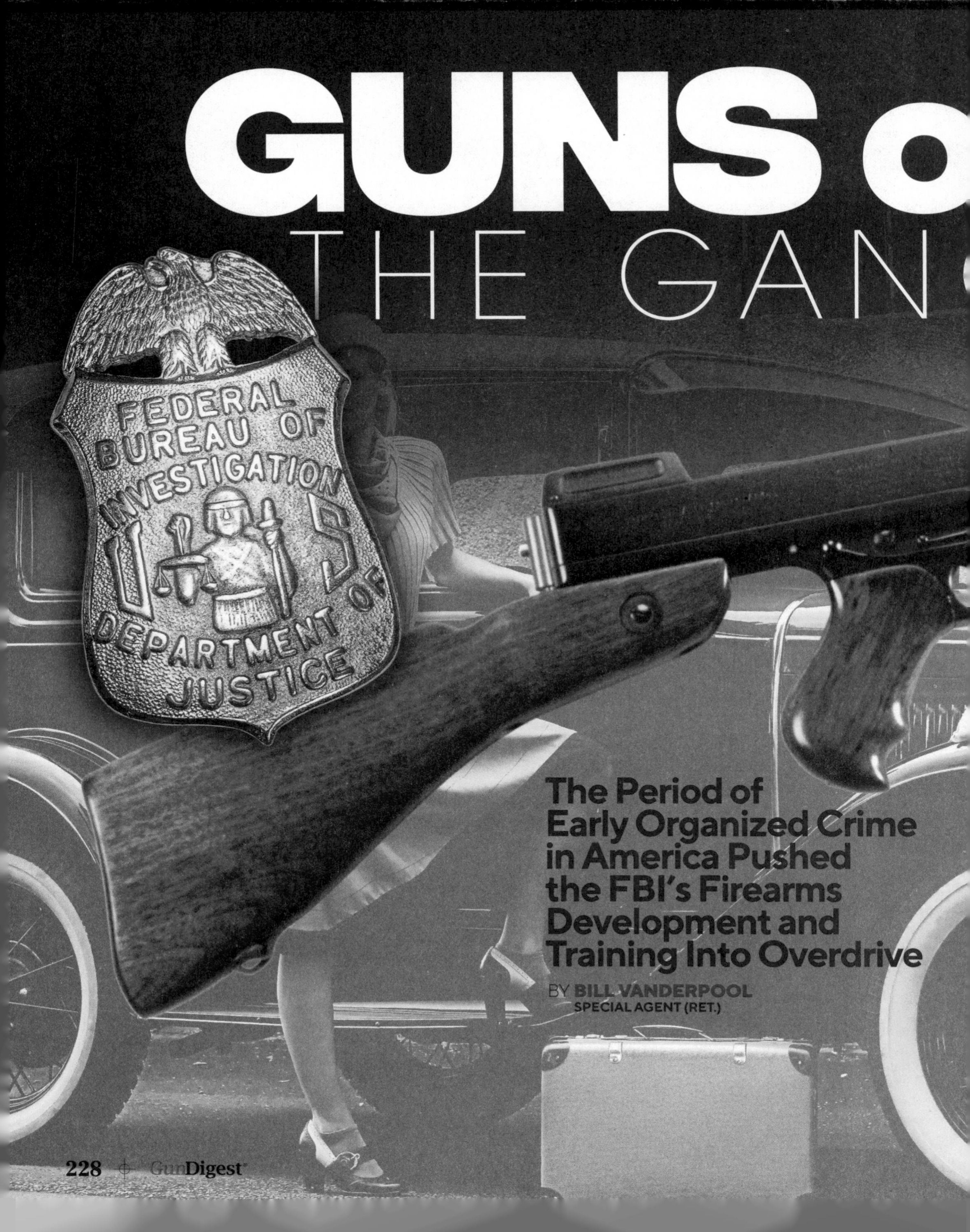

The Period of Early Organized Crime in America Pushed the FBI's Firearms Development and Training Into Overdrive

BY BILL VANDERPOOL
SPECIAL AGENT (RET.)

F THE FBI

STER ERA

Of all the weapons identified with the FBI, the Thompson submachine gun tops the list. Photo: FBI

(1931) K5440

National Prohibition, the birth of organized crime and the Great Depression all helped to fuel the lawless period of crime known as the gangster era well into the 1930s. Local law enforcement and the FBI were kept busy with bank robberies, kidnappings, mail thefts and escaped fugitives. Many of these crimes were not normally investigated by the Bureau but often a stolen car crossing a state line or other lesser federal violation opened the door to agents eager to get involved.

This S&W Model 19, heavily engraved, was presented to FBI Director Hoover in 1958 by William Sweet, a Smith & Wesson sales representative. Photo: Rock Island Auction Co.

John Dillinger's wanted poster

WANTED

JOHN HERBERT DILLINGER

On June 23, 1934, HOMER S. CUMMINGS, Attorney General of the United States, under the authority vested in him by an Act of Congress approved June 6, 1934, offered a reward of

$10,000.00

for the capture of John Herbert Dillinger or a reward of

$5,000.00

for information leading to the arrest of John Herbert Dillinger.

DESCRIPTION

Age, 32 years; Height, 5 feet 7-1/8 inches; Weight, 153 pounds; Build, medium; Hair, medium chestnut; Eyes, grey; Complexion, medium; Occupation, machinist; Marks and scars, 1/2 inch scar back left hand, scar middle upper lip, brown mole between eyebrows.

All claims to any of the aforesaid rewards and all questions and disputes that may
arise as among claimants to the foregoing rewards shall be passed upon by the Attorne
General and his decisions shall be final and conclusive. The right is reserved to di
vide and allocate portions of any of said rewards as between several claimants. No
part of the aforesaid rewards shall be paid to any official or employee of the Depar
ment of Justice.

If you are in possession of any information concerning the whereabouts of John
Herbert Dillinger, communicate immediately by telephone or telegraph collect to the
nearest office of the Division of Investigation, United States Department of Justic

Director Hoover used the print media to assist, gaining favorable publicity for his agents and the Bureau. Certain names appeared in headlines repeatedly: Lester Gillis, aka Baby Face Nelson, Charles "Pretty Boy" Floyd, and George F. Barnes, Jr., alias Machine Gun Kelly. Clyde Barrow teaming up with Bonnie Parker and Alvin Karpis, among many others, made the news. The Chicago Crime Commission named Al Capone as Public Enemy No. 1 according to authors William Helmer and Rick Mattix in their excellent study, *Public Enemies*.

By the early 1930s, special agents were armed with a variety of handguns, many personally owned. Many carried the Colt Official Police or the smaller Police Positive or Smith & Wesson M&P (Military and Police, later the Model 10) in .38 Special. Another popular weapon was the Colt Government Model of 1911 or 1911A1, in .45 Auto.

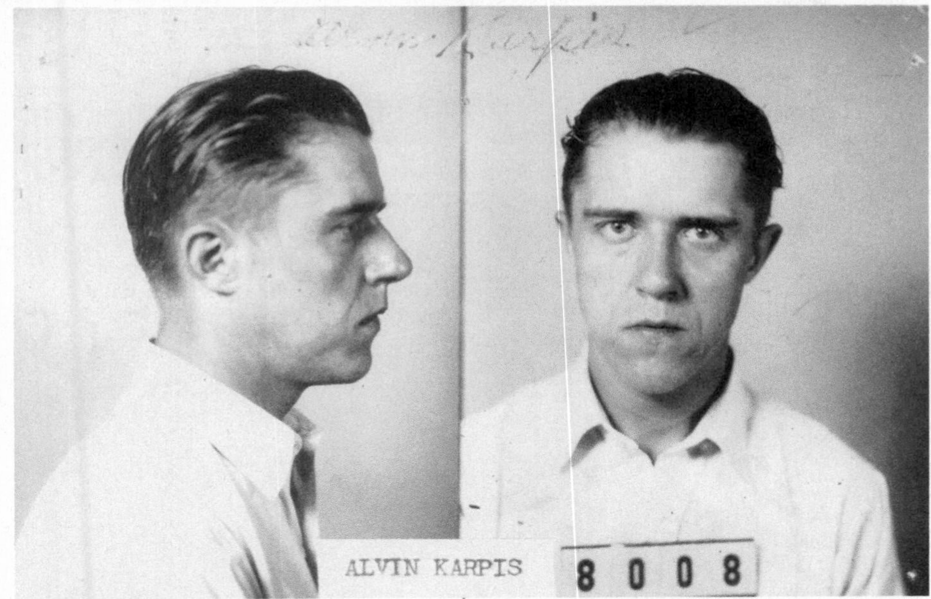

(left) Mug shot of Alvin Karpis.

(below left)) Baby Face Nelson's mug shot. He would kill two FBI Agents and countless civilians before he died. Photos: FBI

Back in the late 1920s, Colt had introduced a variation of their Government Model in .38 ACP caliber. That handgun shot the same ammunition as their earlier Model 1902, a rather light load. Eventually, ammunition manufacturers increased the power and velocity of the .38 ACP and called it the .38 Super, designed specifically for the stronger Government Model. Colt, in their rather overstated advertising, claimed their new model was "A Real He-Man Gun!" and continued, "That split second of danger, when every shot must reach its mark ... unfailing, unswerving ... calls for an arm that shoots fast, with deadly accuracy and telling results. Lives may hang in the balance..." Regardless of the hype, the FBI knew they faced opponents driving high-speed vehicles and often wearing so-called bulletproof vests. The issue .38 Special revolvers and .45 pistols could not penetrate these. The Bureau then purchased a number of the .38 Supers. One agency reference lists the .38 Super as being adopted in 1938. However, a letter signed by Director Hoover dated October 4, 1934 in answer to a police inquiry about what guns the Bureau used says otherwise. Hoover lists ".38-caliber Police Positive Special Revolver with a four inch barrel and the .38 super automatic pistol" as part of the Bureau arsenal. And a March 14, 1935 memo

Colt's .38 Super, based on the M1911 frame, proved to give better penetration through car bodies and the old-style body armor favored by gangsters. Photo: FBI

Colt's Official Police revolver in .38 Special was a primary Bureau-issue handgun in the mid-1930s.

The Police Positive was a smaller frame alternative popular with agents. It was issued in .38 Special.

Smith & Wesson's Military & Police was issued later and was liked for its excellent double action. It was also easier to gunsmith than the Colts. Photos: FBI

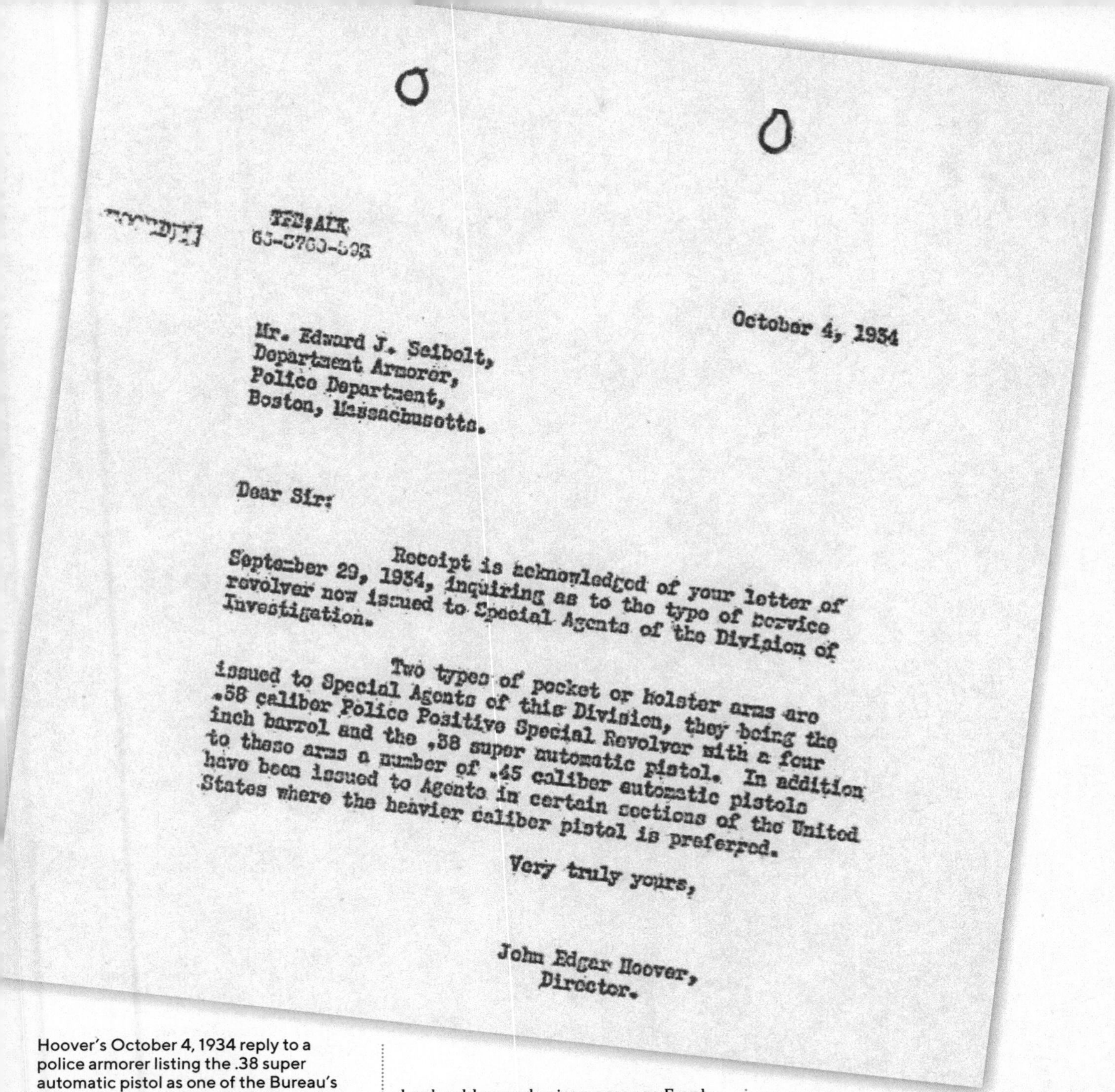

[illegible]

TFE:AIK
63-3760-393

October 4, 1934

Mr. Edward J. Seibolt,
Department Armorer,
Police Department,
Boston, Massachusetts.

Dear Sir:

Receipt is acknowledged of your letter of September 29, 1934, inquiring as to the type of service revolver now issued to Special Agents of the Division of Investigation.

Two types of pocket or holster arms are issued to Special Agents of this Division, they being the .38 caliber Police Positive Special Revolver with a four inch barrel and the .38 super automatic pistol. In addition to these arms a number of .45 caliber automatic pistols have been issued to Agents in certain sections of the United States where the heavier caliber pistol is preferred.

Very truly yours,

John Edgar Hoover,
Director.

Hoover's October 4, 1934 reply to a police armorer listing the .38 super automatic pistol as one of the Bureau's issue handguns. Photo: Larry Wack/FBI

from the Director orders the purchase of "four Clark #10 shoulder holsters for use with Colt Super-automatic pistols."

In 1933, two gunfights occurred that had a major effect on the Bureau's firearms policies. On June 17 at Kansas City's Union Station, Special Agent Raymond Caffrey and two local law enforcement officers were escorting convicted bank robber and prison escapee Frank Nash back to prison when gangsters appeared with Thompson submachine guns. There is still a question whether they were trying to free Nash or silence him. In the ensuing gunfight, Agent Caffrey, both local officers and Nash were killed. Two agents in another car were wounded. This became known as the Kansas City Massacre. Later studies of the shooting raised the question if Agent Caffrey, holding a 16-gauge Winchester Model 1897 shotgun with which he was unfamiliar, accidentally shot Nash and perhaps others. The aftermath of this shooting was immediately felt throughout the Bureau of Investigation.

Retired Special Agent Larry Wack, through the Freedom of Information Act (FOIA), has uncovered an impressive collection of memos from FBI files tracing the urgent acquisition of heavier firearms to equip agents following the event. On June 20, three days after the shooting, arrangements had already

The author's S&W Combat Magnum (Model 19). He carried it for seven of 11 years as a state investigator and 14 years with the FBI. It was later replaced with a SIG P228.

S.&W. .357 MAGNUM

been made for shipping two Thompson Model 1928s with 20-round magazines directly from Auto Ordnance to the Kansas City office. These guns were to be sent with "Cutts compensator with foregrip and sling strap." The Tommy guns were described in a later headquarters memo that date as "Model 28A_ U.S. Navy Model Thompson sub-machine guns, type XX 20 cartridge capacity, box magazine with Cutts compensator with foregrip and sling strap." Interestingly enough, the guns were shipped to Kansas City via air mail.

Another June 20 memo from Director Hoover instructs the Special Agent in Charge to contact the Kansas City PD for instruction on the new guns. The SAC was also advised to acquire "Forty-five colt special automatic pistol ball ammunition" locally. In a timely sales attempt, Colt contacted the Bureau with an offer to demonstrate their "Monitor" Automatic Machine Rifle in .30-06 caliber. The Monitor was a law enforcement version of the Browning Automatic Rifle used by the military. The Bureau wasn't interested at that time, the feeling being that the gun was too big and powerful for law enforcement use, but the agency would soon buy many to add to its arsenal.

Director Hoover soon received a letter from R. H. Colvin, Special Agent in Charge of the Little Rock office, referencing the shooting in Kansas City and the subsequent manhunt. In it he pleads to Hoover for additional firepower, stating, "It is imperative that we be equipped to meet them (the criminals) at least [as] well equipped in the way of arms. We have only the small light pistols furnished by the Bureau and which are entirely inadequate for the purpose." Colvin continues by suggesting the office get "one Thompson sub-machine gun, a couple of high-power rifles and about four 45 calibre [sic] Colts Automatic pistols and plenty of ammunition for each." He also says, "A sawed-off shotgun or two would also be useful. I hate to send agents out after these outlaws unless we can meet them on equal footing."

The Director must have built a fire under his advisors because on June 28, about a week later, a committee composed of T. F. Baughman, C. A. Appel and J. M. Keith reported back to him by memo, giving their firearms recommendations for the Bureau. The memo refers to their contacting experts from Army Ordnance, Metropolitan PD (Washington, DC) and others, with a list of suggested firearms. These were the Colt Police Positive revolver in .38 Special, the Army Springfield rifle in .30-06 (selected over the Monitor), a 12-Gauge "automatic" shotgun, either Winchester or Remington, cylinder bore with 20-inch barrel, and the Thompson submachine gun with magazines, including a 50-round type L per gun, with other accessories. The recommendation suggested issuing one each of the rifles and shotguns to each field office (except Honolulu) and one Thompson submachine gun to each office except two to certain larger offices.

Keith followed up on June 29 with more justification for the committee's choices and further described the rifle requested as a "N.R.A. type .30-06 caliber Springfield Sporter Rifle." He stated, "It shoots the high powered military boat-tailed bullet. It has the greatest penetration and the flattest projectory [sic] of any other modern rifle. The Sporter type has the rear peep-sight, which affords instant aiming and deadly accuracy at a distance of 500 or 600 yards. The tire could be shot from an automobile, the motor put out of commission or the gasoline tank punctured with this weapon."

Keith's justification for the shotgun was "… for urban work where snap shooting with deadly accuracy is

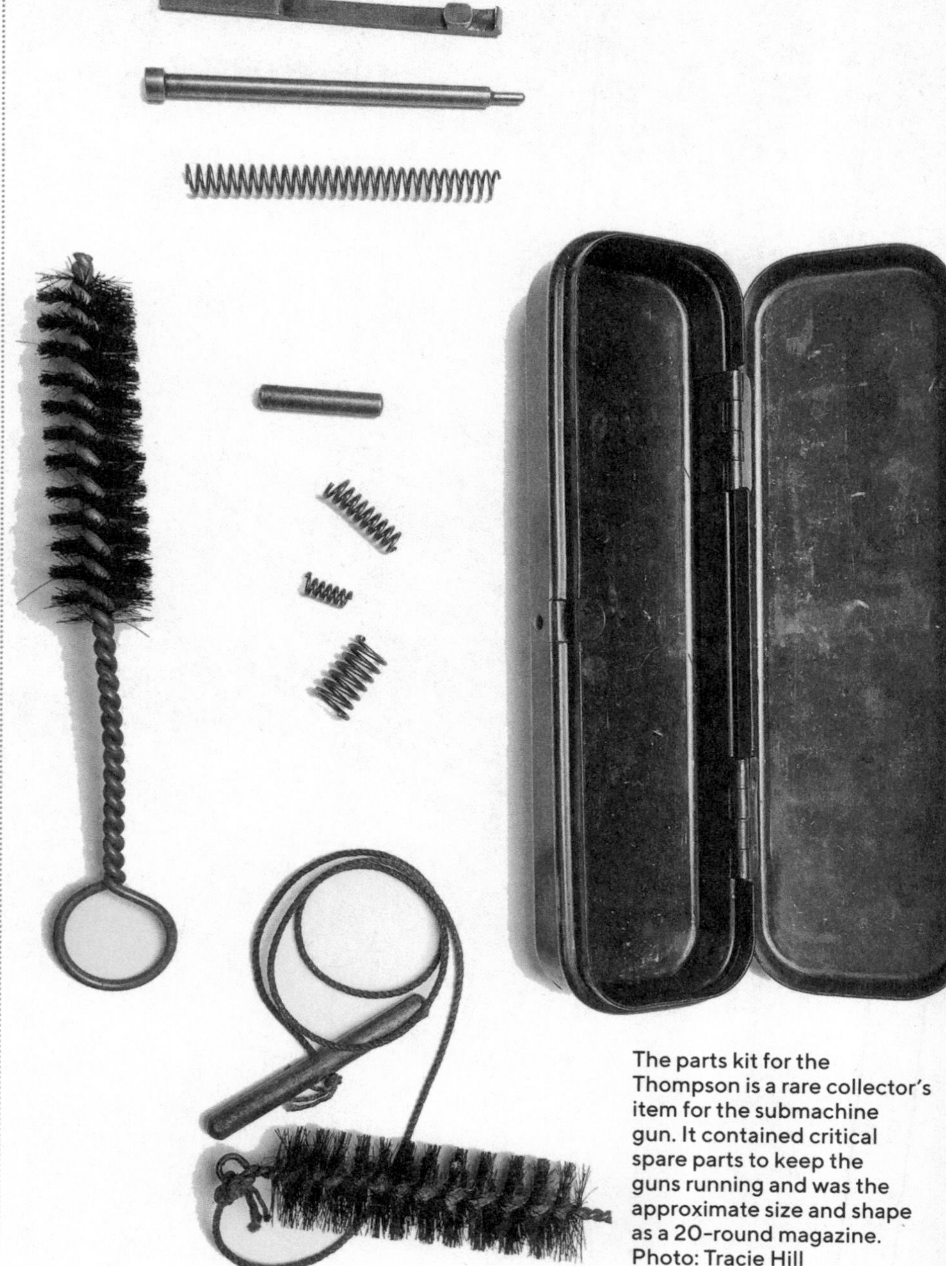

The parts kit for the Thompson is a rare collector's item for the submachine gun. It contained critical spare parts to keep the guns running and was the approximate size and shape as a 20-round magazine. Photo: Tracie Hill

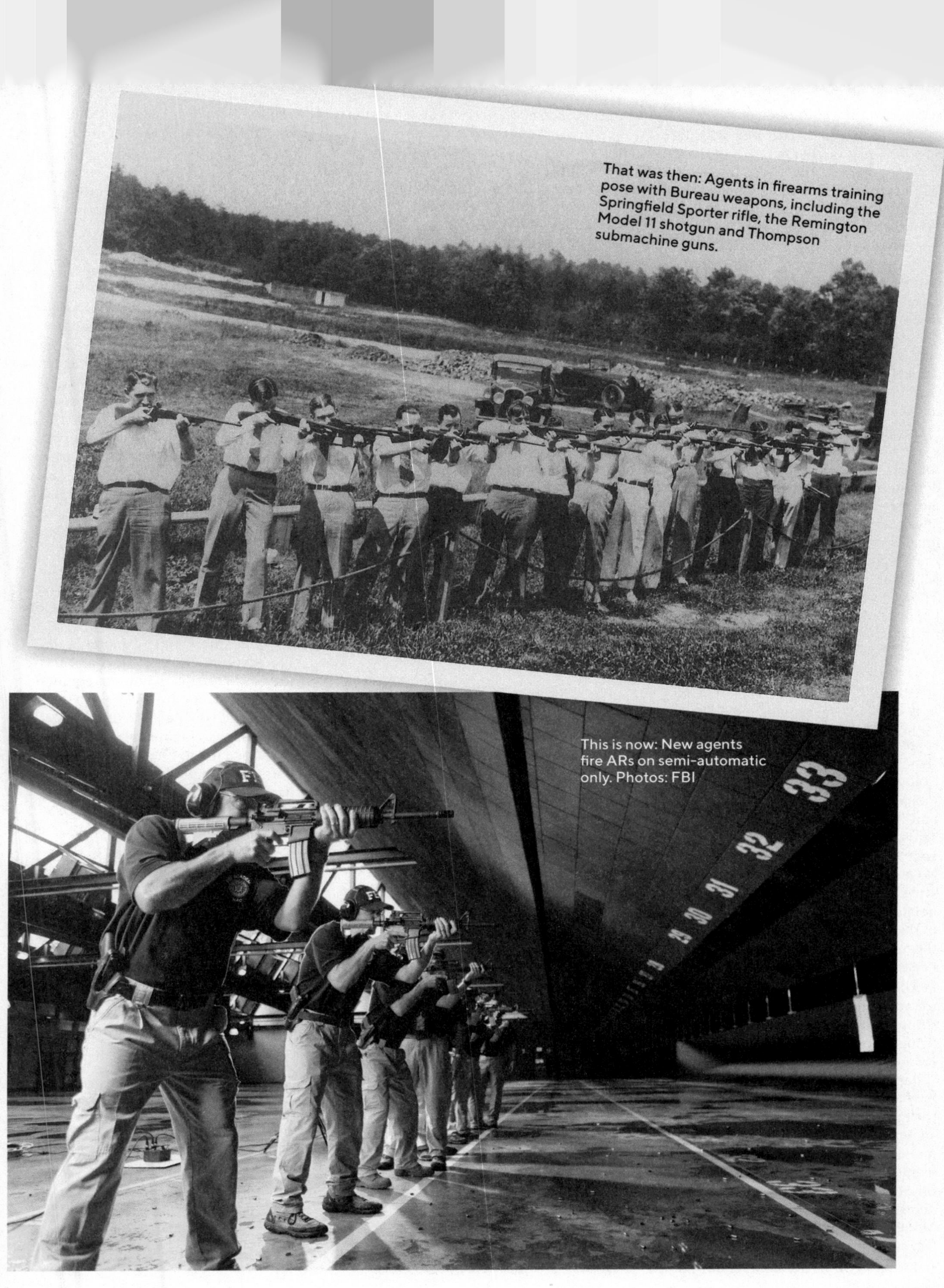

That was then: Agents in firearms training pose with Bureau weapons, including the Springfield Sporter rifle, the Remington Model 11 shotgun and Thompson submachine guns.

This is now: New agents fire ARs on semi-automatic only. Photos: FBI

required on the spur of the moment."

J. M. Keith, who at that time was the Special Agent in Charge (SAC) of the Washington Field Office (as opposed to HQ) continued his string of memos with one dated June 30 referring to a request from the Oklahoma City Field Office requesting .45 Colt automatics instead of .38 Special revolvers. Keith listed ballistics comparisons between the two calibers, "proving" the .38 was superior to the .45 with its 200-grain bullet weight. "However, it is to be noted that ordinary .38 Special ammunition, loaded with smokeless powder, gives better results than the best .45 Automatic Cartridge," he concluded.

On June 30, a purchase order was provided to Federal Laboratories, Washington, DC, for 20 Model 28AC Thompsons, equipped as previously. In addition, each gun was to include a canvas case for the 50-round drum magazine, another for four 20-round box magazines, one for the Thompson and a "Spare Parts Metal Kit Container, complete with Brush and Thong, Shorthandle Breach [sic] Cleaning Brush, Extracter, Firing Pin, Firing Pin Spring, Hammer Pin, Sear Spring, Sear Lever Spring and Trigger Spring."

The blizzard of memos continued into July. Field office heads were directed to assure all special agents, including accountants, were trained in the use of the revolver, and later the shotgun, rifle and "machine gun." An inventory was made of revolvers in the field and 162 Colt Police Positive revolvers in .38 Special and 184 holsters were purchased, to be sent directly to the offices. The revolvers cost $20.48 each and the holsters $1.00. No mention was made of the brand or style of holster except "soft leather belt holsters." Some discussion was made of the possibility of the agents keeping the revolvers stored in the office until needed, but this was, thankfully, vetoed.

A July 14 follow-up memo to the Director advised that the shotguns ordered be shipped to each field office directly from Bridgeport, Connecticut, indicating that Remington received the first purchase order. In addition, the Springfield Sporter Rifles would be shipped from the Springfield Armory, Springfield, Massachusetts on July 17. While the shotgun model wasn't mentioned, they were most likely Remington Model 11s. A mid-1930s photograph of agents in firearms training showed the distinctive hump of the Model 11.

By this time, steps were being taken to formalize firearms training for the Bureau. Forms were developed to report successful training by the agents with the various weapons. Another memo listed proposed safety rules for the indoor range in the basement of the Department of Justice. Written by Frank Baughman, the twelve range rules are very similar to those one might find posted today. The new range, which was located in the basement of the Department of Justice Building, even had a ventilation system.

In a memo dated June 26, 1934, F. X. Fay, Special Agent in Charge, New York, sent Director Hoover a memo describing a target carrier for indoor ranges that might be applicable to the Bureau. One was added to the range in the basement of the Department of Justice building.

On September 8, Frank Baughman reported to Director Hoover his visit to the National Rifle Association (located in the Barr Building, WDC) to obtain samples of their "Langrish" police silhouette target, which was described as the "outline of the body of a man from the head to the thighs." Also recommended by Baughman was the "special police target" described as 14 x 16 ¾ inches with a 5 ½-inch bullseye. The latter cost $10.00 per thousand.

E. F. Mitchell, in charge of the Police Training Section of NRA, also gave a supply of booklets to Baughman entitled *Manual of Police Revolver Instruction*, free of charge. Mitchell also offered to have qualified firearms instructors go to each Bureau field office and offer his services to the SAC. This would have been at no cost to the Bureau. It was not apparent if the offer was accepted.

About this time, an undated Monthly Report sample, probably written by Baughman, provides some indication of what courses the agents were using to qualify. Under Pistol, they were required to fire 10 shots slow fire at 15 yards, 10 shots slow fire at 25 yards and 10 rapid fire at 15 yards (two 5-round strings in 12 seconds each). There is no indication of what target was used, or the minimum score. The proposed form also listed courses of fire for other Bureau weapons:

12-Gauge Automatic Shotgun	(5 shots at 25 yards)
Thompson Submachine Gun:	(10 shots slow fire at 25 yards)
	(10 shots in bursts at 25 yards)
Gas Guns:	(No description)
.30-06 Bolt-Action Rifle:	(10 shots at 200 yards)
Monitor Automatic Rifle	(10 shots, single-shot action at 100 yards)
	(10 shots in short bursts at 100 yards)

Again, there was no description of the target used or the score required.

The proposed report also lists familiarization with the Vactuphone listening device, the dial number recording machine and latent fingerprinting.

By December 30 of that year, Bureau of Investigation agents and local detectives, including Jelly Bryce and Clarence Hurt, OKCPD, shot it out with bank robber Wilbur Underhill and his associates in Shawnee, Oklahoma. Underhill was mortally wounded and died a week later at McAlester prison. A photograph taken later the day of the shooting shows the law enforcement participants — Special Agent in Charge Ralph Colvin, Detective D. A. "Jelly" Bryce, Special Agent Paul Hansen, Detective Clarence Hurt and Special Agent Kelly Deaderick. Agent George Franklin, who was also in the shootout, was not in the photo, having escorted Underhill's girlfriend to the hospital. The photo shows Special Agent in Charge Colvin and a Thompson equipped with a 50-round drum magazine. Jelly Bryce carried one with a 20-round box mag. Agent Hansen had what appears to be a Remington auto shotgun. Clarence Hurt also carried a Thompson but one equipped with a horizontal foregrip, probably not Bureau issued. Special Agent Deaderick posed with a Thompson, which appears unloaded. It is not known which firearms were Bureau owned though all but Hurt's could have been. Interestingly, both Jelly Bryce and Clarence Hurt would join the Bureau of Investigation the following year (1934) along with fellow OKCPD detective Charles "Jerry" Campbell. Hurt had killed six men before joining the Bureau. He was one of three agents who shot John Dillinger. Jelly Bryce dropped three gangsters in his first year with Oklahoma City. Again, the reader is reminded that the detectives' appointments in 1934 were part of Hoover's program to enlist street cops and shooters into the agency, even without law or accounting degrees, or any degree at all.

Agent trainee firing the Glock 9mm in the prone position. Today's FBI handguns and training have come a long way since the days of the gangster era. Photo: FBI

THE FBI GETS EARLY NIGHT SIGHTS

About this time, an interesting accessory came to the attention of the FBI. The Special Agent in Charge of the Los Angeles office wrote the Director in a memo dated January 1, 1935 about a newly developed night sight for revolvers, Thompson submachine guns and shotguns. Co-invented by A. B. Scott and the movie actor Warren Baxter, it used a dry cell battery and a lens system to direct a clover leaf shaped light onto the target. Since the light was parallel to the barrel, the inventors claimed it could be used as a sighting device as well as lighting the target. The Automatic Nite Sight was described as "very compact," weighing less than 2 pounds and was "about five inches long by two and one-half inches high, and can very easily be slipped in the pocket when not in use."

Mr. Scott was quoted as only having made a few of these and that an associate of his was proceeding to Washington, DC, to demonstrate the device to the FBI. No record has been found that the FBI every purchased any of these lights.

I remember while attending National Academy in 1971 that Lester Limerick, then head gunsmith, showed me a Smith & Wesson Model 10 that had been modified to include night sights by drilling a very small hole in the front sight as well as in the frame on either side of the rear sight notch. A small battery in the stocks powered the lights.

After the Underhill shootout in December, 1933. Front row, L to R, FBI Special Agent in Charge Ralph Colvin and Detective D. A. "Jelly" Bryce, OKCPD. Back row, Special Agent Paul Hansen, Detective Clarence Hurt, OKCPD and Special Agent Kelly Deaderick. Not pictured was Special Agent George Franklin. Photo: FBI

This article is an excerpt from Guns of the FBI: A History of the FBI's Firearms and Training, available at GunDigest-Store.com.

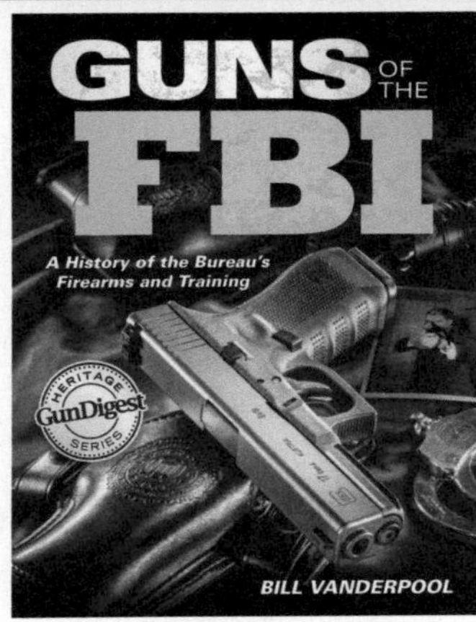

GUNS OF THE
FBI
A History of the Bureau's Firearms and Training
HERITAGE GunDigest SERIES
BILL VANDERPOOL

THE KIT GUN

A Classic Companion for the Trail

BY **ROBERT SADOWSKI**

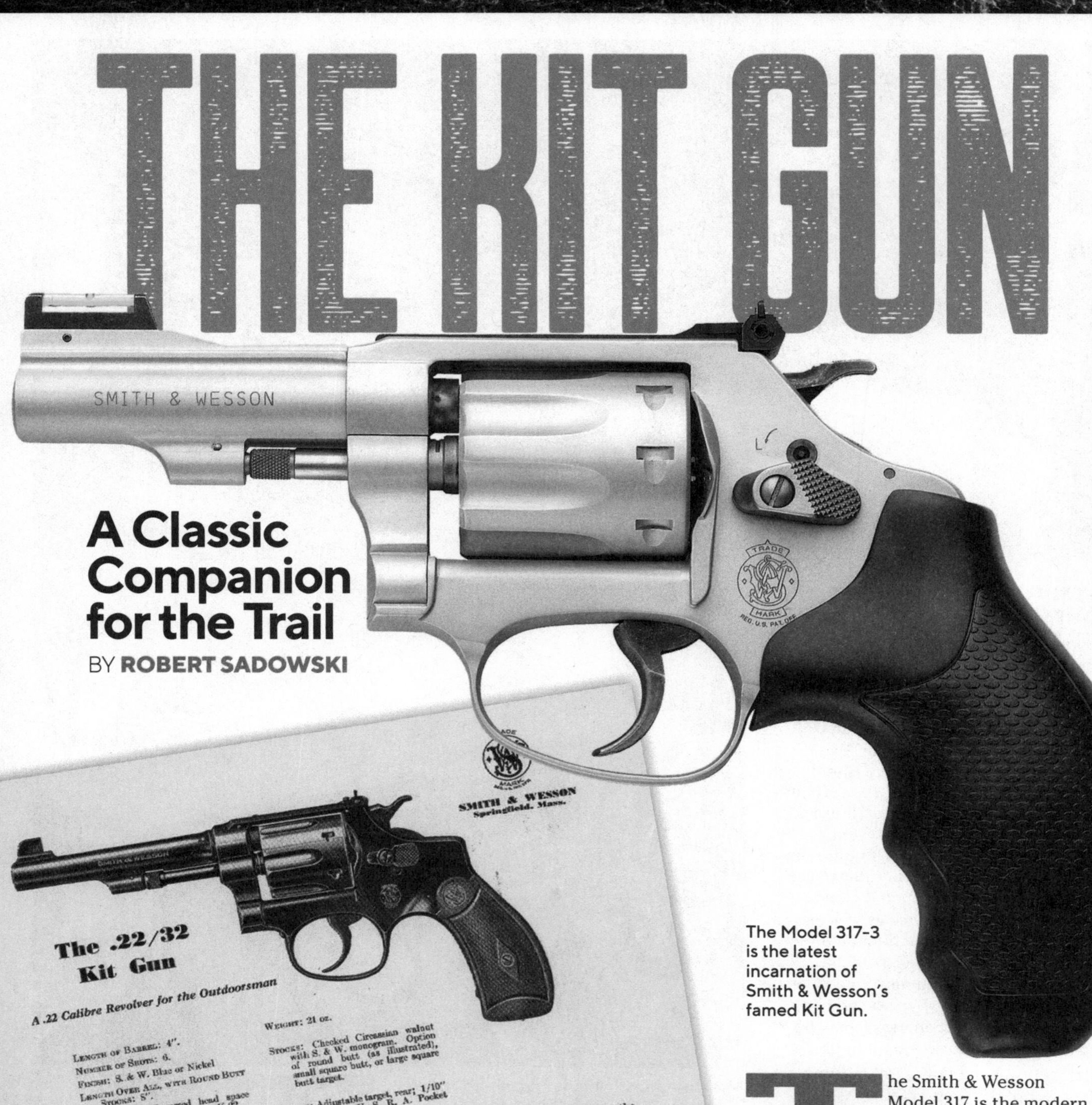

SMITH & WESSON
SMITH & WESSON Springfield, Mass.
The .22/32 Kit Gun
A .22 Calibre Revolver for the Outdoorsman
LENGTH OF BARREL: 4".
NUMBER OF SHOTS: 6.
FINISH: S. & W. Blue or Nickel
LENGTH OVER ALL, WITH ROUND BUTT STOCKS: 8".
CHAMBERING: Recessed head space as first used in our famous K-22.
AMMUNITION: All .22 rim fire cartridges from B. B. caps to .22 L. R. Regular and High Speed.
WEIGHT: 21 oz.
STOCKS: Checked Circassian walnut with S. & W. monogram. Option of round butt (as illustrated), small square butt, or large square butt target.
SIGHTS: Adjustable target, rear; 1/10" Patridge or U. S. R. A. Pocket Revolver, front.
The Kit Gun is designed for the man who loves the woods and streams. While compact for easy carrying in the pocket or kit bag, the barrel is long enough to give ample sight base for accurate shooting and to develop effective speed with the modern cartridges.
The adjustable target sights permit the use of different cartridges without the necessity of holding off the mark to compensate for varying points of impact.
In the illustration we show the round butt stock, as this is the most compact, and yet allows a comfortable hold with sufficient room between the front of the stock and rear of the trigger guard for the middle finger. At no extra cost this arm can be supplied with the large S. & W. target stock or the small square butt S. & W. Regulation Police stock.
Price $35.00

The Model 317-3 is the latest incarnation of Smith & Wesson's famed Kit Gun.

An advertisement from 1935 for the then-new .22-32 Kit Gun. Photo: Roy Jinks collection

The Smith & Wesson Model 317 is the modern benchmark in traditional kit gun design. When I was a kid, our camping kit consisted of an army surplus canvas tent, magnetic compass and a plastic garbage bag used as a ground cloth, among other surplus and homemade accoutrements. These days, my tent is lightweight water-resistant nylon, my compass a GPS, and I forego the homemade ground cloth for a blowup mattress. I also have a cordless coffee grinder. Expresso, anyone? As much as camping equipment has changed, the kit gun has remained consistent: a simple .22 rimfire revolver.

The green dot and V-notch are fine for informal plinking and small game hunting.

The kit gun we packed back then was a .22 LR and, as I recall, it was an H&R Sportsman break-top revolver. We shot all types of .22 rimfire ammo through it — shorts, longs, long rifles, shot loads, even blanks. Whatever .22 rimfire ammo I could scrounge, I would put through that H&R. One of the most important lessons from those formative days of camping, hiking and fishing was the lighter your stuff, the easier and faster it was to pack in and out. The modern-day Smith & Wesson Model 317 Kit Gun, while traditional, is a lot like modern outdoor equipment: lightweight, rugged, practical, safe and built for the long haul into the backcountry. The Model 317 keeps the traditional features that work and updates the rest.

Back in the day, a kit gun was included with the camping equipment, fishing tackle and hunting gear. Nearly every outdoor adventure into the big woods included one. The idea behind a kit gun was for sportsmen to have a small-caliber pistol while in the field. It could dispatch snakes and pesky critters that tried to raid your cooler. It also allowed you to plink at marauding soda cans and determine who had bragging rights around the campfire that night. Often the coup de grace to a wounded and tracked deer was accomplished by a hunter with a small-caliber pistol. I had friends who walked their traplines in the morning and carried a .22 LR revolver to dispatch a trapped fox, muskrat or mink.

Kit guns are generally small-frame .22 LR revolvers with barrel lengths of about 4 inches, adjustable sights and small grips. Even so, over the years the kit gun has evolved, and some would debate whether today's semi-automatic pistol could serve as a handy kit gun. I'd agree, but then I'd ask, can a semi-auto shoot birdshot, .22 Shorts or .22 Longs without manually racking the slide? I know the answer and you do, too.

(opposite and above) This petite J-frame has a nice grip that makes the Smith & Wesson 317-3 feel substantial without being bulky. It weighs just 11.7 ounces and has an 8-round capacity.

I spoke to Roy Jinks, Smith & Wesson's historian, who told me the year was about 1910 when a gun distributor named Phillip Bekeart ordered a special variation of the Smith & Wesson I-frame revolver. The I-frame was a small-frame revolver with a round butt, on which S&W built its .32 S&W-caliber Hand Ejector models. Bekeart wanted the company to chamber the I-frame revolver in .22 LR and add a more substantial grip and adjustable sights. Collectors refer to this revolver as the "Bekeart model" and, while it is suited for target shooting, it led S&W to develop the .22/.32 Kit Gun.

Basically, Smith & Wesson took the I-frame and chambered it as a 6-shot .22 LR. It was the first revolver to be named the Kit Gun and would become the benchmark for what would be known by the term. The .22/.32 Kit Gun evolved into the Model 34, which was made on the new J-frame. It was manufactured from 1953 through 1991. The Model 63 is the stainless version and is still produced to this day.

In 1997, the Model 317 Kit Gun appeared. Using a lightweight aluminum alloy frame — what S&W calls the AirLite — the Model 317 shed several ounces and gained two extra chambers over the Model 34. The Model 63 also gained the extra firepower, and became an 8-shot like the aluminum Model 317. The Model 317 was nearly a half a pound lighter than the Model 63. And lighter is better when in the field. It also incorporates a Hi-Viz green fiber optic front sight, which is hardly traditional but very practical. The front sight stands out for easy, fast sight alignment and does well for plinking. The sights are by no means precise.

The matte silver finish of the Model 317 wears well and does not require a lot of fuss like blued finish revolvers do. The grip is textured rubber with finger grooves and is large enough for an average-size adult to grip comfortably, yet allow a youngster a go at it, too.

The Model 317-3, which indicates the model has gone through three model revisions, is a true featherweight at 11.7 ounces. Smith machines a groove on the outside of the trigger guard to reduce weight. The weight is just one of the features that make the 317 a great kit

SPECIFICATIONS

Manufacturer: Smith & Wesson

Model: 317 Kit Gun

Produced: 1997–present

Caliber: .22 LR

Action: DA/SA

Barrel Length: 3.0 in.

Overall Length: 7.2 in.

Weight: 11.7 oz. (empty)

Sights: Hi-Viz fiber optic front/adj. rear

Finish: Matte silver

Grip: textured synthetic

Capacity: 8

MSRP: $759

(above) The 317 uses a hammer block, so if the revolver is dropped it will not fire. The chambers in the cylinder are recessed and the cylinder locks up tight.

(below) The Pathfinder Lite uses Charter Arm's trademark one-piece frame mated with a 2-inch barrel and checkered, finger-groove rubber grip.

gun. The grip is a perfect size to get your entire hand on the grip without curling a finger under the butt. The mechanism uses a hammer block, which prevents the revolver from firing if accidentally dropped on its snout or grip.

At the range, plinking and shooting the 317 for accuracy was a lot of fun. The cylinder locks up with precision and the single-action trigger is crisp. With 36-grain CPHP CCI Mini Mag ammo I averaged 0.67-inch groups using a rest at 10 yards. Whatever I feed this little revolver, it fires it and does it rather well.

Other manufacturers may not have "kit gun" in the model name designation but offer viable alternatives. The .22 LR Charter Arms Pathfinder is an economical example of a kit gun. It features no-nonsense fixed sights and a nice-size checkered rubber grip with a 6-shot capacity. It's a rugged revolver that won't break the bank and will fire nearly any .22 rimfire cartridge available.

One of my favorite kit guns is Ruger's Bearcat. This diminutive .22 LR single-action revolver has been in production since 1958, when the original version was introduced. In 1996, the New Model Bearcat was introduced, featuring a safety transfer bar. It comes in blued and

Ruger's New Model single-action Bearcat was introduced in 1996.

stainless models, and if you can't decide which one to buy, get them both. The Bearcat design is like the Remington Model 1853 cap-and-ball revolver except in a reduced scale. It offers plenty of grip to easily aim and is lightweight. This Bearcat got its name from the Stutz Bearcat automobile of the early 1900s that Bill Ruger admired. It features engraving of a bear and mountain lion on the unfluted cylinder.

The latest Ruger to more fully conform to the traditional definition of the kit gun is the LCRx. This .22 LR model, with the 3-inch barrel and adjustable rear sights, is a rival to the S&W Model 317. The LCRx weighs only 17.3 ounces and features an external hammer to fire in either single- or double-action mode. The 8-shot capacity cylinder is radically fluted to reduce weight, as is the aluminum frame.

The traditional kit gun is modern, lightweight, easy to pack and well suited for off-the-grid treks. Special thanks to Eastern Outfitters (easternoutfitter.com) of Hampstead, NC, for making this story possible.

The 6-shot cylinder of the Pathfinder has the chambers countersunk, so the rear of each cartridge is flush with the ejector.

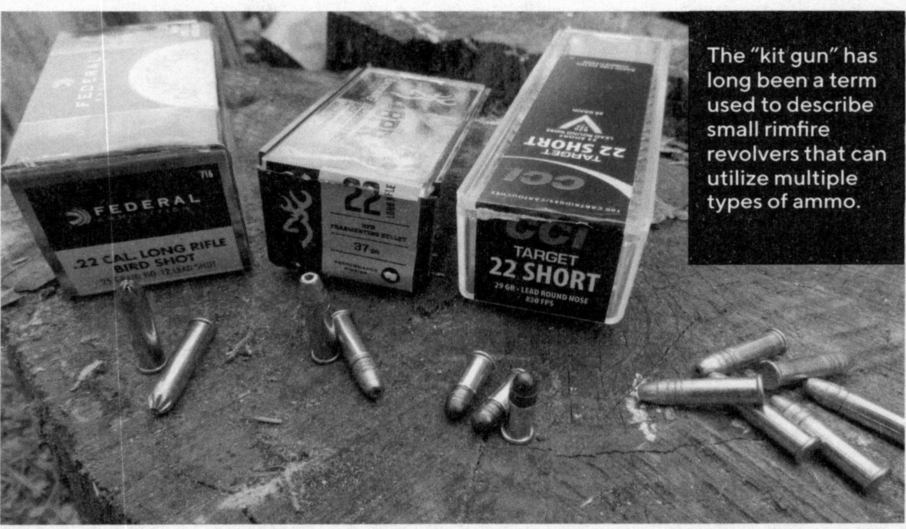

The "kit gun" has long been a term used to describe small rimfire revolvers that can utilize multiple types of ammo.

PERFORMANCE: SMITH & WESSON MODEL 317 KIT GUN

Load	Velocity (fps)	Energy (ft/lbs)	Best Accuracy (in.)	Average Accuracy (in.)
CCI Mini Mag 36-gr. CPHP	819	54	0.48	0.67
CCI Short Target 29-gr. LRN	707	32	0.87	1.0
Browning BPR 37-gr. Frag HP	1,008	83	0.86	0.88
Aguila Supermaximum 30-gr. CPHP	1,135	86	0.84	0.92
Winchester Power-Point 42-gr. CPHP	984	90	0.85	0.98

Bullet weight measured in grains, velocity in feet per second, energy in foot-pounds, taken 15 feet from the muzzle by a ProChrono digital chronograph. Accuracy in inches averaged from three 5-shot groups at 10 yards.

For rifle accuracy testing, a Hart Pedestal front rest was used, along with a Protektor 1 1/2-inch wide front sandbag and leather rear "bunny bag."

.22 LONG RIFLE ACCURACY REVISITED

Testing Accuracy Potential of Economy-Priced .22 Ammo

BY **MIKE THOMAS**

While I'm not a competitive rimfire shooter, I have always been intrigued with the accuracy potential of .22 Long Rifle ammunition. Except for an old, straight-out-of-the-box Model 41 Smith & Wesson .22 pistol, I have no rimfire target guns. And though my .22s are all of good quality, they are unmodified; none have accuracy enhancements.

In the 2003 edition of the *Gun Digest Annual* I wrote an article titled, "Practical Accuracy of .22 Long Rifle Ammunition." In that project, I used three handguns and three rifles and fired five, five-shot groups from each firearm with 24 samples of ammunition. Using a bench rest, rifle groups were shot from 50 yards and handgun groups from 25 yards.

In the years since that article was published, there have been many changes in .22 Long Rifle ammunition. Several of the products used in the original piece are no longer available, while some current offerings were not on the market then.

Most people who shoot .22s informally don't spend much time or attention on their selected ammunition. They have no need for expensive target rounds, even if they may be more accurate in a favorite rifle or handgun. These shooters are quite content with the bargain selections or a "bulk" product that costs anywhere from a nickel to a dime or slightly more per round. Quite often, the difference in group size between economical ammunition and the expensive stuff is small and only of importance to a competitor.

However, even the least serious of shooters have some interest in accuracy, even though they may never shoot paper targets from a bench rest. Such shooters still want to hit an intended target as consistently as possible. Without a minimal degree of accuracy, that's pretty much unachievable. Nonetheless, inexpensive rimfire ammo is often surprisingly accurate, capable of regular five-shot groups at 50 yards of under an inch using scoped rifles and around 2 1/2 to 3 inches at 25 yards with open-sighted handguns.

It is no coincidence that cheaper rimfire ammunition lacks the lot-to-lot consistency of more expensive products. One batch may shoot well, while the next one won't, a very common complaint with shooters. Manufacturers must make a profit

A Sugar Creek Gun Co. adjustable rest was used for handgun accuracy testing. The butt of the gun is not rested directly on the bag. The frame of gun, not the barrel, is rested on the front bag.

In the author's evaluation, 27 samples of .22 Long Rifle ammunition were used. These included subsonic, standard velocity, high velocity and hyper velocity products from a variety of manufacturers.

yet remain competitive in pricing — often very tough requirements. To produce top ammunition necessitates the best in equipment, operators, components and quality control, none of which are inexpensive.

If a "best" standard is relaxed in all these critical areas of manufacture, a reasonable level of "good" and affordable ammunition can be produced. It will not shoot as accurately as top-of-the-line .22 rimfire, but a decent batch will often do surprisingly well. That's satisfactory for the majority of rimfire shooters.

Some of the cheapest bulk ammunition is susceptible to various failures. Like others, I've experienced problem rounds, but less frequently than what some claim. These conditions are sometimes isolated to one lot but can be indicative of a faulty characteristic of a certain ammunition in general.

One failure I've noticed most often is a standard velocity or subsonic .22 ammo that won't reliably operate the action of a semi-automatic handgun or rifle. Another is a failure to fire. Several years ago, I bought a quantity of standard- and high-velocity ammunition of a certain brand to test for accuracy. At the time, the brand was very inexpensive and both types were accurate. No failures of any kind were encountered. Several years later, I purchased a few bricks of standard velocity from this maker. This batch didn't shoot as well as the first lot and I had numerous misfires, at least 5 percent, something I hadn't encountered before or since with any

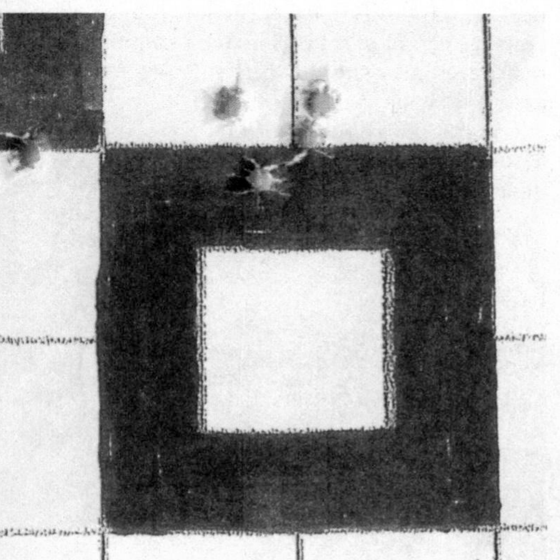

Many groups fired in the evaluation contained flyers. Depicted is such a group. Overall group size is more than doubled because of one flyer.

rimfire ammunition. Even a 1 percent failure to fire is too great. I mentioned this to a company representative for the brand at SHOT Show and he seemed quite surprised. I'm pretty sure my problem was restricted to one lot of ammo. I've since used the stuff without any problem, but accuracy from lot-to-lot is not always consistent.

This is not intended as a criticism of one manufacturer, because it can and does happen with any brand. For this article, I purchased some Federal Auto Match, an ammunition with which I had no experience. I had read about Auto Match on at least one Internet forum. From comments posted, the consensus was that it was supposedly among the worst, if not the worst .22 LR product available. Not only was it inaccurate, they claimed, but ignition was unreliable. However, five, five-shot groups fired at 50 yards from the Ruger 77/22 test rifle proved otherwise, averaging .56 inch. This was the best average group size of the 27 types of ammunition tested in the Ruger rifle! Ignition was fine.

Granted, a different lot of Auto Match may or may not shoot with this degree of accuracy. Regardless, it's never a waste of time to shoot some test groups with a new, unfamiliar ammunition. As for Internet information, lots of good stuff is available from experienced, knowledgeable shooters, but there may be just as much erroneous advice from others with little or no practical experience in the subject matter.

TEST GUNS

To test a wide spectrum of contemporary .22 LR, I used a Winchester Model 52 bolt-action reproduction that I purchased new in 1997. It is equipped with a Unertl Small Game scope of 6x. I bought two of these rifles with consecutive serial numbers at the same time. The other

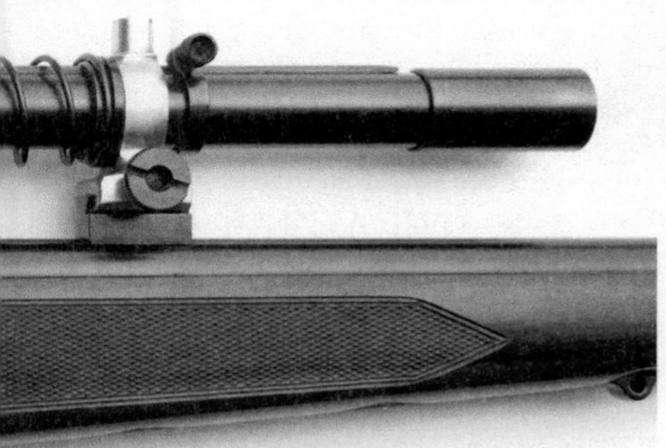

A Winchester Model 52 reproduction was one of two rifles used for group shooting. The scope is a Unertl 6X Small Game Scope. Long out of production, these remain excellent scopes. All adjustments are made using the rear mount with positive micrometer click adjustments.

A laminate wood, stainless-steel Ruger 77/22 was used in the rimfire evaluation. Scope is an old Weaver K-4 in 4X in Ruger factory rings.

RIFLES — AVERAGE GROUP SIZE IN INCHES

Ammunition	Winchester M52	Ruger 77/22	Average
Aguila HV 40 gr. (plated)	.84	.70	.77
Aguila SV 40 gr.	.78	.88	.83
Aguila Sub Sonic 40 gr.	.72	.78	.75
CCI Mini-Mag 36-gr. HV HP (plated)	.86	.70	.78
CCI Mini-Mag 40-gr. HV HP (plated)	.68	.88	.78
CCI Suppressor (subsonic) 45-gr. HP	.56	.60	.58
CCI Sub-Sonic 40-gr. HP	.71	1.04	.875
CCI Standard Velocity 40 gr.	.60	.74	.67
Federal Auto Match 40 gr.-HV	.80	.56	.68
Federal #510 40-gr. HV	.98	.76	.87
Federal #710 40-gr. HV (plated)	.92	1.02	.97
Federal #711B Target 40-gr. SV	.64	.58	.61
Federal #720 Hunter Match 40-gr. HV HP	.68	.98	.83
Federal #729 "275" bulk, 40-gr. HV	.76	.60	.68
Geco Match 40-gr. SV	.70	.70	.70
Geco Rifle 40-gr. SV	.86	.78	.82
Rem. Golden Bullet 40-gr. HV HP (plated)	.98	1.26	1.12
Rem. Subsonic 38-gr. HP	.98	.84	.91
Rem. Thunderbolt 40-gr. HV	.86	.94	.90
Rem. Viper 40-gr. Hyper Vel. (plated)	.92	1.10	1.01
Win. "235" bulk, 36-gr. HV HP (plated) 1.04	1.04	1.08	1.06
Win. Super X, 40-gr. PP HV HP (plated)	1.16	.74	.95
Win. Super X, Super Speed, 40-gr. HV (plated)	1.42	1.24	1.33
Win. Super X, 40-gr. Hyper Vel. HP (plated)	.62	.68	.65
Win. 42 Max PP, 42-gr. Hyper Vel. HP (plated)	1.10	1.38	1.24
Win. Wildcat 40-gr. HV	1.34	1.54	1.44
Average, Each Rifle	.83	.80	N/A

rifle was used in the 2003 Gun Digest article I previously mentioned. Both of these rifles show comparable accuracy.

The other rifle used for the ammunition evaluation was a Ruger 77/22, the stainless-steel/laminated wood stock version. It was purchased new in 1987 and is equipped with a steel K-4 Weaver (4x) scope. This is an old scope that's been in my possession for decades. It is likely from the 1960s or early '70s, but still offers a sharp image and ample magnification for a rimfire .22.

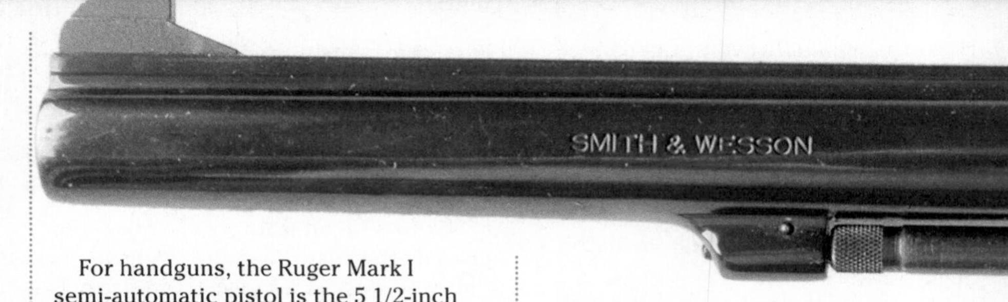

For handguns, the Ruger Mark I semi-automatic pistol is the 5 1/2-inch bull-barreled version. I purchased this one new from Gil Hebard Guns in 1976. The Model 17-4 Smith & Wesson revolver was bought new in 1982. This gun was used in the original 2003 article. All four firearms have been fired extensively. They show normal finish wear but appear to be mechanically sound.

HANDGUNS — AVERAGE GROUP SIZE IN INCHES

Ammunition	Smith & Wesson Model 17	Ruger MK1	Average
Aguila HV 40-gr. (plated)	3.12	1.96	2.54
Aguila SV 40-gr. (plated)	3.20	2.26	2.73
Aguila Sub Sonic 40 gr.	3.64	3.38	3.51
CCI Mini-Mag 36-gr. HV HP (plated)	2.70	2.74	2.72
CCI Mini-Mag 40-gr. HV HP (plated)	2.34	2.16	2.25
CCI SGB (Small Game Bullet) 40-gr. HV	2.44	2.46	2.45
CCI Suppressor (subsonic) 45-gr. HP	2.84	2.48	2.66
CCI Sub-Sonic 40-gr. HP	2.88	2.20	2.54
CCI Standard Velocity 40-gr.	2.50	2.10	2.30
Federal Auto Match 40 gr.	2.72	2.36	2.54
Federal #510 40-gr. HV	2.06	2.60	2.33
Federal #710 40-gr. HV (plated)	3.30	2.58	2.94
Federal #711B Target 40-gr. SV	1.76	1.80	1.78
Federal #720 Hunter Match 40-gr. HV HP	2.84	1.96	2.40
Federal #729 "275" bulk, 40-gr. HV	2.90	2.84	2.87
Geco Match 40-gr. SV	3.12	2.34	2.73
Geco Rifle 40-gr. SV	2.52	2.68	2.60
Rem. Golden Bullet 40-gr. HV HP (plated)	3.00	1.98	2.49
Rem. Subsonic 38-gr. HP	3.16	3.00	3.08
Rem. Thunderbolt 40-gr. HV	3.60	2.30	2.95
Rem. Viper 40-gr. Hyper Vel. (plated)	2.54	2.68	2.61
Win. "235" bulk, 36- gr. HV HP (plated)	2.46	2.14	2.30
Win. Super X 40-gr. PP HV HP (plated)	2.68	2.16	2.42
Win. Super X, Super Speed, 40-gr. HV (plated)	2.30	2.68	2.49
Win. Super X 40-gr. Hyper Vel. HP (plated)	4.24	2.64	3.44
Win. 42 Max PP, 42-gr. Hyper Vel. HP (plated)	2.74	2.52	2.63
Win. Wildcat 40-gr. HV	3.46	3.50	3.48
Average, Each Handgun	2.85	2.66	N/A

NOTE: All group size averages for test rifles are based on five, five-shot groups fired at 50 yards from a bench rest. Averages for handguns are based on five, five-shot groups fired at 25 yards from a bench rest. Group sizes were measured to the nearest tenth of an inch, then averaged on a calculator. Ambient temperatures ranged from approximately 32 degrees Fahrenheit to 55 degrees Fahrenheit. Any group that included a known, shooter-induced error was eliminated and re-fired before recording group size.

TEST CONCLUSIONS

While the recorded figures in the data tables tell the story, several aspects merit consideration. Most "large" group size averages resulted from one or more groups with a "flyer." The potential for flyers is greater with the cheaper ammunition, but not all of the really inexpensive stuff exhibited this characteristic. However, the next batch of the same ammo in some cases performed differently.

I normally buy CCI Standard Velocity by the case and shoot it in everything, including handguns and rifles. While not a "premium" high-priced product, CCI SV is more expensive than the bulk ammo. However, lot-to-lot consistency is often better than the cheaper stuff and well worth the price difference to some shooters. I have a few firearms where other ammunition provides better accuracy than the CCI, but the difference often isn't great. I find it easier to keep up with one ammunition and not have to adjust sights endlessly for different points of impact.

Regarding bullet trajectory and windage variance, this can vary greatly from one ammunition to the next. At very close range, one sight setting may be fine for a large variety of ammunition. However, at 25 yards with a handgun or 50 yards or more with rifles, the

This Smith & Wesson Model 17 with a 6-inch barrel was used for 25-yard group shooting.

A Ruger Mark I with 5 1/2-inch bull barrel was used in comparing the accuracy of the 27 loads used in the project.

difference in points of impact can be several inches. Windage variations are often not as great as elevation discrepancies. There are exceptions, but I've noticed that rifles sighted for CCI Standard Velocity will provide a point of impact an inch or higher at 50 yards when using hyper-velocity ammunition. With a subsonic round, point of impact may be two inches lower than CCI SV at the same distance. However, point of impact variance with handguns is usually less than with rifles at distances of, say, 25 yards.

I shoot a lot of rimfire ammunition and cannot buy into the alleged excessive "dirtiness" claimed about some rimfire ammo. Powder, bullet lubricant (grease, wax, etc.) and priming compound leave behind a residue. Other than slightly smudged fingertips, I have never seen evidence of any objectionable fouling, particularly the kind that would cause a malfunction like unreliable feeding or ejection. All guns used in this evaluation easily went several hundred rounds between cleanings. None appeared to be excessively dirty.

The Smith & Wesson Model 17 used in these trials has tight cylinder chambers, a characteristic of many S&W .22 rimfire revolvers. They become slightly tighter from normal fouling, but the gun remains functional. I've never seen this characteristic in a Colt rimfire revolver and they generally shoot at least as well as a Smith & Wesson.

My recommendation to anyone looking for good ammunition to shoot in rimfire handguns or rifles is to try at least ten ammo loadings. Get a good mix — standard velocity, high velocity, hollowpoint, plated and plain lead bullets. It's true that standard-velocity ammo is usually more accurate than high velocity, but not always. Some claim a particular gun will not shoot an unplated bullet well, but they may have only tried one or two. I've not been impressed with the accuracy of most subsonic rounds or hyper-velocity ammunition, but, as always, there are exceptions. They may be worth trying.

It's important to do all evaluations from a solid bench rest using good technique, 25 yards with handguns and 50 yards with rifles. Shoot at least five, five-shot groups before making any determination on accuracy. For most shooters, "flyers" that show up regularly during an evaluation will quickly eliminate an ammunition.

UBERTI BIRD'S HEAD SINGLE ACTIONS

BY **JIM DICKSON**

Classy Configuration for Constant Concealment

I have had a lot of experience with 3 1/2-inch barrel bird's head grip Colt single-action (SA) replicas, especially the old discontinued U.S. Firearms Double Eagle. Uberti now is making this configuration in two versions. I tested the Cattleman model imported by Taylor's & Co., Inc., and a Short Stroke CMS Kenda Lenseigne Pro imported by Stoeger. Either model in the bird's head grip configuration is made-to-order for concealed carry. The bird's head grip was a British design to prevent the handgun from imprinting in a pocket. It is very successful at that. The rounded back of the grip makes a small bulge through the clothing, whereas the 90- degree angle at the base of the grip on a conventional revolver raises a tell-tale sharp corner that fairly screams "Gun!"

The 3 1/2-inch barrel is long enough for balance and accuracy, but short enough for easy concealment. I have often carried this type of SA in my pocket and it looked just like I had a rag in there. Stuffing a rag in with it breaks up the outline even further for deep cover. When drawing the gun from the pocket, keep the thumb against the hammer spur to prevent it from snagging in the pocket lining. Of course, a pocket holster is even better and serves to keep lint and dirt out of the gun. El Paso Saddlery makes its famous horsehide

Holster. This extremely comfortable holster has a slight rearward cant that enables it to work well as a cross-draw holster when you are hunting with a long gun and don't want the pistol's hammer spur gouging out pieces of your gun stock wood. A cross-draw holster also works well when you must draw from a sitting position.

For inside-the-pants-carry, a Sticky Holster made for the Taurus Judge works best, as it can be positioned exactly as desired without fear of shifting. For a shoulder holster, I use one from El Paso Saddlery that is a reproduction of one that they made for the infamous gunfighter John Wesley Hardin. Extra ammo is carried in the El Paso pistol belt slides, holding six or 12 rounds, in classic cartridge loops that slide over the belt. Another option is Pacific Canvas and Leather's reproduction of the 1870s cavalry belt pouch for .45 Colt ammo.

No matter how you carry it, the bird's head grip configuration is infinitely easier to hide than the classic M1873 SAA, as well as more comfortable to carry when you must sit. I've always loved the look and feel of the classic original version and prefer it for open carry, but I would rather have the more compact bird's head grip 3 1/2-inch version for concealed carry. It's a pity that Colt and every single-action maker have

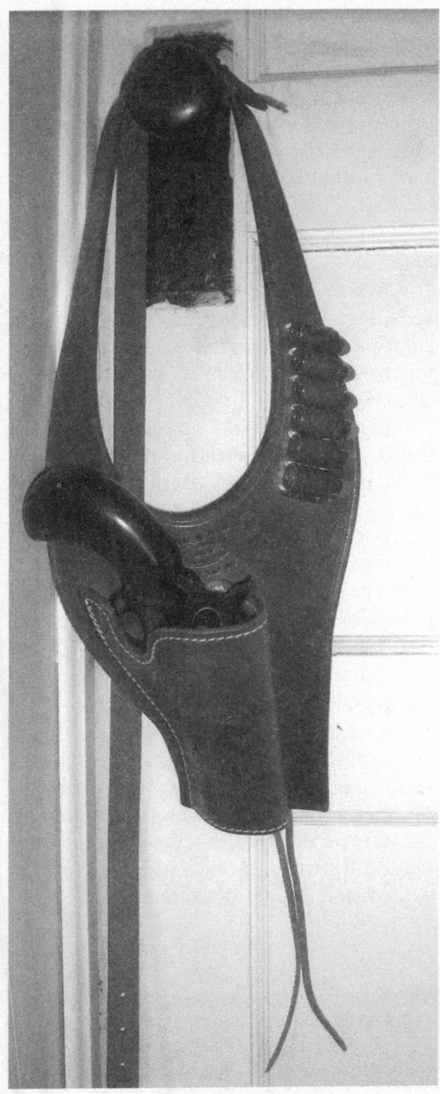

Uberti Cattleman in El Paso Saddlery shoulder holster like the one they made for John Wesley Hardin, the deadliest gunfighter of the Old West.

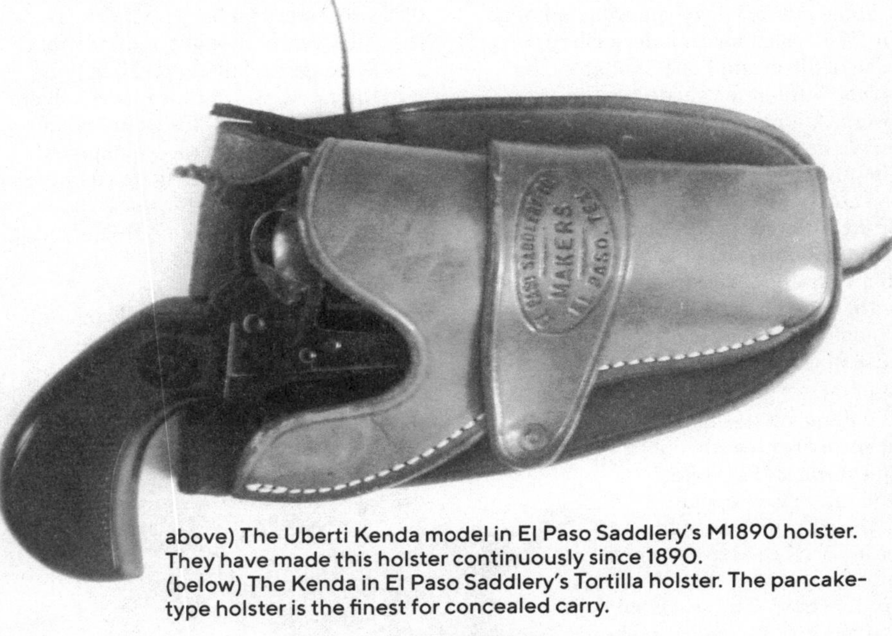

above) The Uberti Kenda model in El Paso Saddlery's M1890 holster. They have made this holster continuously since 1890.
(below) The Kenda in El Paso Saddlery's Tortilla holster. The pancake-type holster is the finest for concealed carry.

Pocket Max holster for these guns. There's a nub on the holster that ensures that the scabbard always stays in the pocket when the handgun is drawn. Wright Leather Works LLC also makes a very high-quality inside-the-pocket holster for this gun, with an extra layer of suede leather that wraps around the revolver.

I have a great many years of experience carrying single actions both openly and concealed. My preferred mode of carry is a pancake holster, like El Paso Saddlery's Tortilla model. The pancake is the most comfortable, fast, and concealable holster ever designed. For the traditionalist who wants classic SAA open carry, I like El Paso Saddlery's M1890

not always offered this configuration as a standard variation. Custom makers have offered it for years on a one-off custom basis, as it is not that bad a job to convert a standard gun, but why have the factories neglected it so? Colt's Custom Shop has made a lot of these over the years, but they have never been a standard factory item and the Custom Shop is not taking any orders at this time. Texas Longhorn Arms made the Texas Border Special with the bird's head grip, and they always made a top-quality gun for as long as they were in business. Today, Heritage Mfg. in the U.S. and Uberti in Italy make versions of the bird's head style as well as the standard M1873 SAA replicas.

Some may ask why you would choose an 1873 design for a modern carry gun. Ease of hitting and one-shot stopping power without felt recoil are the answers. A super lightweight gun of lesser power can kick so hard as to prevent effective second and third shots, yet lack the ability to stop a big enraged man or beast with one shot. The current generation of double-action only micro and mini .32s and .380s are impossible to hit with, out past double Derringer ranges. Combat effectiveness is sacrificed for ease of carry and concealment, but combat is why you carry.

Call me old-fashioned. I like a gun that I can easily hit with, out to 200 yards and beyond, and that has one-shot stopping power on man or beast. If you have to shoot more than once, "You in a heap o' trouble boy!" The so-called double-tap has cost police lives when faced with multiple assailants, as you run out of time and/or bullets before one of them gets you.

The Uberti-made Stoeger-imported Short Stroke Kenda CMS model.

You must be able to place one shot in the vitals and move on. A .45 Colt lets you do this.

You want power? The .45 Colt was designed to stop a charging cavalry horse with one shot. Over the years, it demonstrated that ability countless times on the Indian ponies the cavalry faced, and it was a staple for cowboys who needed to bring down a bucking bronco when their high-heeled boot got caught in the stirrup after they were thrown. The .45 Colt could be depended on to kill the bronc before he dragged you to death or smashed you against protruding rocks. It worked flawlessly on America's big bears and wolves as well. Trappers and backwoodsmen killed all North American big game with it. The U.S. Cavalry thought it great sport to ride alongside buffalo and bag them with their new M1873 Colt SAA revolvers. When the New Army .38s would not stop the Moros on Jihad in the Philippines, the .45 Colts brought them down in their tracks. You don't have to worry about being under-gunned for anything on this continent with the .45 Colt.

Ease of hitting has always been a strong point for the SAA revolvers, and the compact bird's head grip style is just as accurate and easy to hit with as the full-sized versions. While the double-action (DA) revolver is insignificantly faster for emptying the gun, it loses all speed advantage once you take time to point each shot at the target. The big difference is in how few people master precision DA shooting compared to how many can hit with SA shooting. This is what led Col. Colt to make all his early revolvers as SAs when the DA mechanism was already well established in pepperbox pistols.

When I picked up the test guns at Reeves Ace Hardware in Clayton, Georgia, it was like meeting old friends, for the single action and I go way back. Uberti guns have long been one of the principal Italian firms importing guns to the U.S. and its reputation is well known to American shooters. Both test guns are examples of the SAA bird's head grip in current production at a moderate price. Both were nicely polished and blued with color case-hardened frames. Trigger pulls were as perfect as you could ask for.

Screws in any gun can start backing out under prolonged fire, so I used a pair of screwdrivers specially made for Colt single actions by Peacemaker Specialties to keep them tight. These are an absolute necessity for shooting single actions, as the screws do work loose no matter who made the gun, and the handgun won't work when the screws come out. Lose a screw and you will be out of action until you can order a replacement from the maker. Screws also loosen up during dry firing, so keep checking them.

The base pin on a SA revolver is often difficult to pull out, and you can't take the cylinder out of the gun for cleaning until you do. I used the base pin puller from Peacemaker Specialties to take it out without risk of marring the finish, as often happens when a screwdriver is used to pry it out. On my own guns, I polish the base pin with 600 grit sandpaper where it goes into the cylinder until I can get it in and out without straining or using tools. Fortunately, the base pins on the Ubertis weren't that tight.

I fired close to 1,900 rounds of ammo, consisting of 18 different loads, to test the guns. These included the following:

AMMUNITION	Velocity (fps)
Black Hills 250-grain RNFP Cowboy	750
Hornady 185-grain FTX	950
Hornady 255-grain Cowboy	725
Barnes VOR-TX 200-grain XPB HP	1,050
CCI Big 4 .45 Colt Shotshells with 140 grains of #4 shot	-
Blazer 200-grain JHP Aluminum Case	-
Federal 225-grain Lead SWC HP	-
Load-X 205-grain RNFP Cowboy	-
Georgia Arms 200-grain Cowboy	750
Georgia Arms 250-grain Cowboy	725
Precision Cartridge 205-grain Lead	950
Precision Cartridge 250-grain FP Total Copper Jacket	725
Precision Cartridge 250-grain FP Total Copper Jacket	900
Fiocchi 250-grain LRNFP Cowboy	750
Sport Shooting 200-grain LRNFP	847
Armscor 255-grain Lead Cowboy Action	-
Aguila 200-grain Cowboy Action	600

A couple of comments: The Precision Cartridge 250-grain FP Total Copper Jacket load at 900 FPS is for use on bear and big game. At .45 caliber you already have a big enough hole. You need penetration on big game, not expansion, when using the .45 Colt. This load duplicates the original black powder load of 1873. Before you dismiss the cowboy loads for practice only, let me point out that the British .450 Boxer was a 225-grain bullet at 650-700 fps and the .455 Webley was a 265-grain bullet at 700 fps. Both loads were famous manstoppers. None of the ammo had a problem making 2-inch groups at 25 yards, but they didn't shoot to the same point of impact, due to the variation in loads.

In the course of firing all that ammo, I used an old toothbrush to clean the flecks of primer brass chips out of the firing pin orifice, as I don't like anything getting down in the lockwork. I don't ever remember having this occur when I was shooting the old copper primers in the black powder loads with their balloon head cases. Of course, these soft copper primers had their own problems. It was common for them to flow back into an oversized revolver firing pin hole when shooting .44-40 ammo where they could tie up the gun. Fortunately, that never happened with .45 Colt loads.

The Cattleman from Taylor's has the traditional high Colt hammer and the classic Colt grip rounded off into a bird's head shape. The polished wood grips are smooth as glass. In all my years I have never fired a single action that did not have checkered grips, so this was a new experience. I have never had a Colt single action move in my hand when I shot it, but those slick grips moved. I think they need to be checkered. I ended up gripping this gun a lot tighter than I normally do. Shooting the first cylinder, the hammer failed to strike the primer hard enough to leave a mark in it on the third shot. Apparently, the hammer and mainspring were not connecting properly on that shot. After that, it went back to firing normally from then on. Another new experience for the old SAA shooter.

At one point, the hammer would not cock, and the cylinder had to be jiggled before it would cock. A glance at the frame showed that the bolt screw had backed out again causing the problem. All part of shooting revolvers. Now you know why the only screws in a M1911A1 are the grip screws, and even they still have to be tightened. After this I began tightening all the screws on both guns after every box or two of shells and that solved the problem.

The second test gun is designed for shooters with smaller hands. This is Stoeger's Short Stroke CMS Kenda Lenseigne Pro. It has a lower hammer for smaller hands to reach, and a shorter hammer throw. Part of the backstrap is ground down and the brown plastic grips are kept as thin as possible. This model is named after Cowgirl Mounted Shooter Champion Kenda Lenseigne, who helped design it. Since people have different-size hands, this is a worthwhile variation. Personally, I would rather have the traditional thin grips and frame instead of changing the configuration of the top of the back of the grip. Still, this works with no drawbacks that I can find. As to which of these two guns is right for you, the answer is whichever fits your hand best.

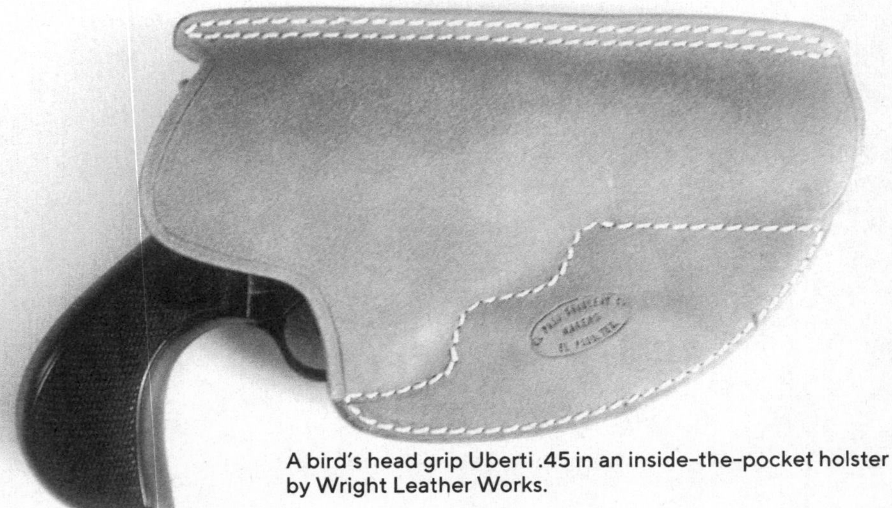

A bird's head grip Uberti .45 in an inside-the-pocket holster by Wright Leather Works.

At about one-third the price of a new Colt SAA, the Uberti single actions are going to continue to sell well. For those who carry concealed, one of these two bird's head models with 3 1/2-inch barrels is the best choice.

This early .44 Magnum was made in 1957, just before its designation was changed to the Model 29. The gun has all the original .44 Magnum features, including a serial number that begins with "S," a 6 1/2-inch pinned barrel, recessed cylinder and matte finish Goncalo Alves target grips. It's shown with a replica of "Dirty" Harry Callahan's badge, and an Original Dirty Harry Shoulder Holster that is still made by Lawman Leather Goods.

SMITH & WESSON MODEL 29

"The Most Powerful Handgun in the World." – Clint Eastwood in *Dirty Harry*

BY **RICK HACKER**

There are certain guns and cartridges that were literally made for each other. The Winchester Model 1873 and the .44-40, the Colt Government 1911 and the .45 ACP, and the M1 and the .30 Carbine are three that immediately come to mind. But more recently (a relative term, I admit) there was another, bigger, more powerful example, one that, like the Winchester '73, co-starred in its own movie and, as a result, became legendary. And that would be the Smith & Wesson Model 29 and the .44 Remington Magnum, a dynamic duo that everyone wanted to meet but few wanted to tangle with. I became one of the many who fell under their spell in the cinema, an infatuation that has lasted to this very day.

Although some may construe the Model 29 saga to be a chicken and egg scenario — that is, which came first, the gun or the cartridge — in this case it was

Capitalizing on the Model 29's fame, the S&W Model 57 (foreground) was made in the exact image of the Model 29 but was only offered in .41 Magnum. A midpoint cartridge between the .44 Magnum and the .357 Magnum, it never achieved the notoriety of its older brother. By comparison, the Model 629 (rear) — a stainless-steel version of the Model 29 — fared much better.

clearly the cartridge, chiefly born out of the exploits of a Salmon, Idaho, rancher named Elmer Keith, whose post–World War II handloading experiments based upon the .44 Special cartridge and his subsequent gun magazine articles about his shooting experiences helped start a series of events that would eventually create the .44 Magnum.

But Keith had a little help from his friends, namely a dedicated group (to which he belonged) of highly respected and experienced shooters — all enamored with the high-power potential of the .44 Special. This loosely knit cadre called themselves "The .44 Associates," and was composed of individuals such as Lawrence L. Newton, Phil Sharpe, Townsend Whelen, P.O. Ackley, Julian Hatcher and Skeeter Skelton. Their purpose was to share information about their individual activities aimed at stoking up the .44 Special to see if they could take it to a world of accelerated ballistics where no cartridge had gone before. Of course, there was no Internet in those days, so the U.S. Postal Service and the occasional phone call were the only means of communication with one another.

The .44 Special, in its factory loading, was then and still is an underpowered round that only reaches its potential on the handloading bench. Keith and his cronies were dedicated to pushing the cartridge to its limits and sometimes beyond, as was attested to by more than one blown cylinder. Developed in 1907 as a longer-cased, smokeless powder version of the .44 Russian, the .44 Special had been created by Smith & Wesson as the inaugural chambering for their New Century revolver, which was also known as the First Model Hand Ejector of 1908 or, more popularly, the Triple Lock. It was an ultra-sturdy, hefty double action built on what would eventually be called the N frame.

Introduced in 1907 — a year before the Triple Lock was brought out — the .44 Special was a smokeless powder loading that, it was discovered, was

By the very nature of the Model 29's size, holsters made for it, such as this Galco DAO rig, require a lot of leather. The gun shown is Smith & Wesson's Classic Model 29 reissue, which features a lockable internal action, something (thankfully) the original guns did not have.

The Model 29 requires a two-handed hold for optimum accuracy and control. Note the author's elbows are slightly bent and not locked, this to absorb the .44 Magnum's stout recoil.

far more accurate when velocities were kept at loadings that approximated the older black powder .44 Russian cartridge. Thus, accurate shooting triumphed over greater striking energy. That, of course, left plenty of room in the longer .44 Special case for more powder, making it the perfect candidate for Keith's ".44 Special Magnum" cartridge, as he called it.

When he finally achieved his hard-hitting goal, based upon a dramatically souped-up .44 Special, Keith managed to convince R.H. Coleman of the Remington Arms Company to produce the cartridge. But first the case was lengthened a tenth of an inch longer than the standard .44 Special, to prevent shooters from blowing up their guns (and possibly themselves) trying to fire the ultra-hot round in .44 Special revolvers. The result was the .44 Remington Magnum. In its initial loading, it held a semi-jacketed 240-grain flat-nosed bullet that thundered out of the barrel at 1,400 fps and struck with more than 750 ft-lbs of energy at 50 yards — almost double that of the .357 Magnum, which up until then really was the most powerful commercially available handgun cartridge in the world. Now that title was transferred to the .44 Magnum.

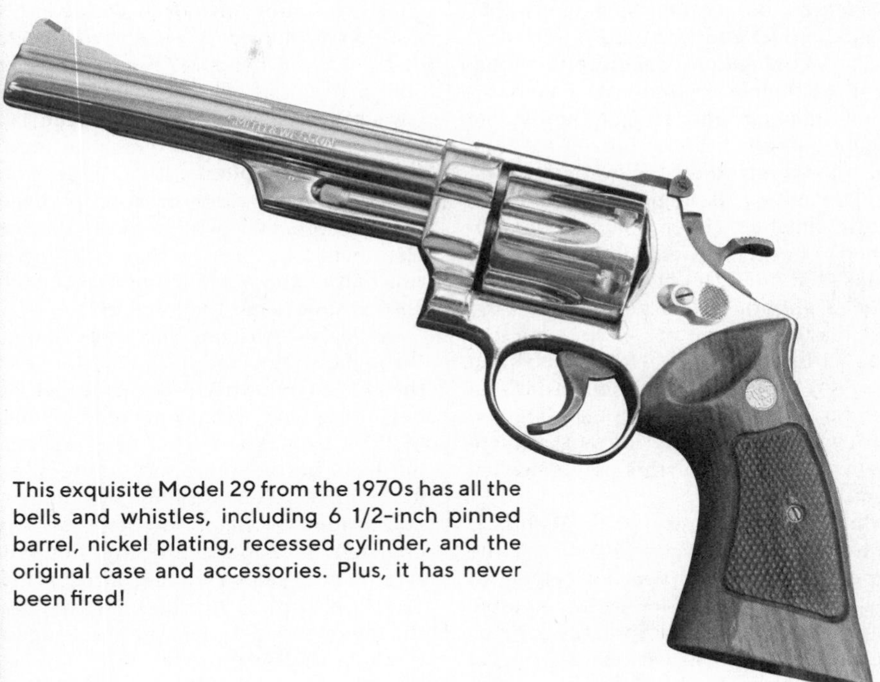

This exquisite Model 29 from the 1970s has all the bells and whistles, including 6 1/2-inch pinned barrel, nickel plating, recessed cylinder, and the original case and accessories. Plus, it has never been fired!

Originally, the Model 29 featured counterbored, recessed cylinder chambers to house the hefty .44 magnum cartridge. In 1981 this feature was eliminated, as it was unnecessary.

As for a handgun to launch this powerhouse projectile, going back to its .44 Special roots, Smith & Wesson had the perfect revolver, the Triple Lock, which had gone through Second and Third Model pre-war variations and now existed as the Hand Ejector Fourth Model, or 1950 Target (later known as the Model 24). But first some beefing up was needed to ready this wheelgun for the muscular .44 Magnum. A longer cylinder closed the gap between it and a thicker barrel, which bumped the weight of the gun to 48 ounces, a welcome improvement that helped tame the .44 Magnum's excessive recoil. In addition, the cylinder sported recessed chambers to enclose the cartridge heads (a feature which later proved unnecessary). All the internal parts, befitting the times, were hand honed. At last the .44 Magnum, as the gun was initially known (in acknowledgment of the only cartridge for which it would ever be chambered), was ready for prime time.

Five sequentially numbered prototypes, starting with serial number S121835, had been built in Smith & Wesson's Experimental Department, but the first actual production gun, serial number S130927 (with the "S" prefix denoting a hammer-block safety), was completed on December 15, 1955. One month later, on January 19, 1956, the .44 Magnum revolver was officially announced to the public. "Power — with Accuracy, in a proven caliber" the introductory ads trumpeted. "The first really

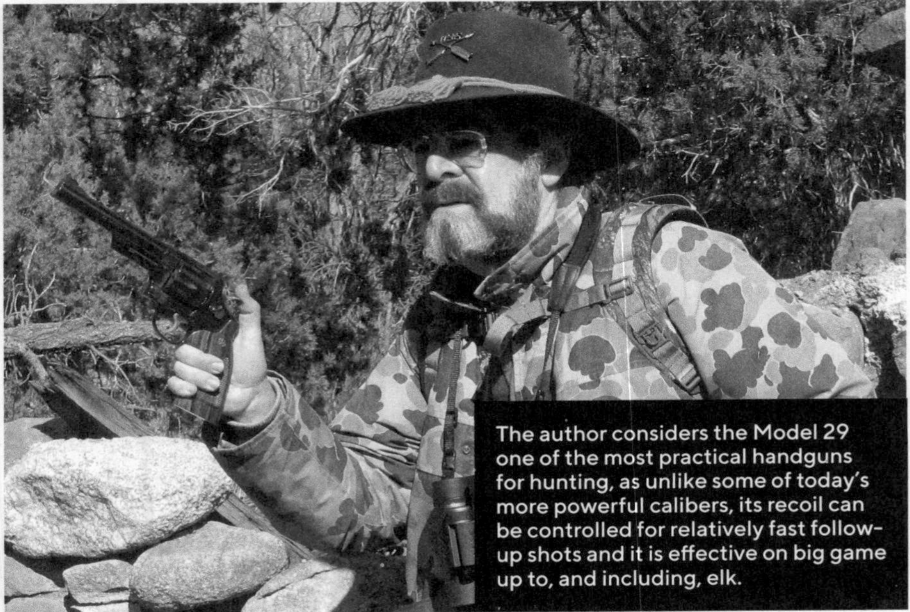

The author considers the Model 29 one of the most practical handguns for hunting, as unlike some of today's more powerful calibers, its recoil can be controlled for relatively fast follow-up shots and it is effective on big game up to, and including, elk.

NEW handgun development since Smith & Wesson pioneered the famous .357 Magnum over 20 years ago."

The .44 Magnum came in either blue or nickel finishes, along with casehardened hammer and trigger, adjustable sights and a 6 1/2-inch barrel; a 4-inch barrel was introduced a few months later. The massive handgun was fitted with matte finished (later changed to polished) checkered Goncalo Alves target grips that filled the hand for more controlled shooting. The gun was housed in a black wooden, satin-lined case that was embossed with ".44 Magnum" and the S&W logo on the lid. Included inside were a screwdriver and a cleaning rod with wire brush and cotton swab attachments. The price for this handsome assemblage was $140.

Julian Hatcher, who was Technical Editor of the *American Rifleman* at the time, and Elmer Keith each received .44 Magnums, as did a few other notable gun writers of the day. Soon the articles began appearing in various gun magazines, leading off with Hatcher's review in the March 1956 issue of the *American Rifleman*. Needless to say, the gun writers' reviews were laudatory, usually in awe of the .44 Magnum's workmanship and power, but often balking at the excessive recoil. Hunters snatched up the guns, no doubt enamored with Keith's writings, which included a verified tale of his having dropped a mule deer at 600 yards with a .44 Magnum. And some law enforcement officers liked the big cartridge's potential to crack an automobile's engine block with a single shot. However, many shooters soon realized that .44 Specials (which could also be chambered in the .44 Magnum) made this hefty handgun much more comfortable to shoot over the long term.

In 1957, due to a nomenclature change throughout the Smith & Wesson line, the .44 Magnum became the Model 29, beginning with serial number S179000. In 1958, to make the gun more appealing to target shooters and hunters, an 8 3/8-inch-barrel version was added, and in 1960 the black wooden case was changed to blond mahogany, but still retained the same cleaning accessories. The Gun Control Act of 1968 changed the Model 29's S-serial number designation to an N-frame prefix.

However, during the late 1960s the Model 29 saw its sales beginning to slip, and a lot of previously sold guns were finding themselves retired to safes or exchanged at the local sporting goods store for less punishing handguns. Although still cataloged, the Model 29 was effectively out of production and was now in danger of being discontinued altogether. But all that would dramatically change in 1971, when the blockbuster movie, *Dirty Harry*, starring Clint Eastwood as the rough and ready Inspector Harry Callahan, appeared on screen carrying a 6 1/2-inch Model 29 in a Bucheimer-Clark shoulder holster. Interestingly, when filming the movie and with S&W inventories low, the movie's producers had a difficult time seeking out Dirty Harry's 4-inch barreled Model 29 that screenwriter John Milius had called for in his original script. Consequently, a specially acquired 6 1/2-inch-barreled version from the factory made its movie debut.

"This is a .44 Magnum, the most powerful handgun in the world, and it can blow your head clean off," Eastwood hissed as the gun filled the screen in the film's opening monologue.

The rest is handgun history. Overnight, sales soared. That is, if you could find one for sale. Existing Model 29s on dealer's shelves began selling for as much as three times their then-current suggested retail price of $194. The big gun's feeding frenzy was heightened by subsequent Dirty Harry sequels, *Mag-*

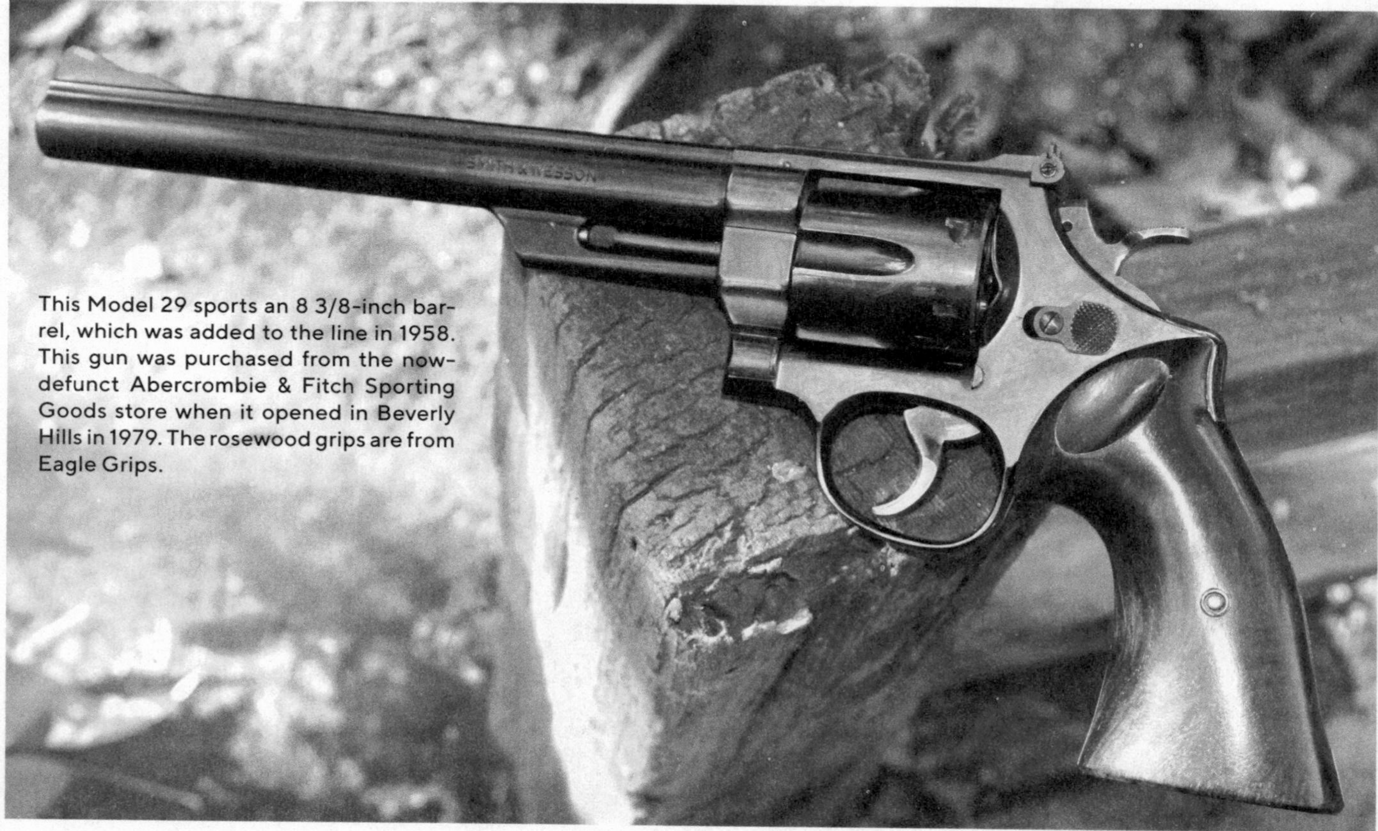

This Model 29 sports an 8 3/8-inch barrel, which was added to the line in 1958. This gun was purchased from the now-defunct Abercrombie & Fitch Sporting Goods store when it opened in Beverly Hills in 1979. The rosewood grips are from Eagle Grips.

The vast variety of .44 Magnum loads on today's market make the Model 29 a versatile gun for hunting and self-defense. Plus, you can shoot milder .44 Specials in it. The Model 29 shown is a newer Smith & Wesson Classics gun.

num Force (1973), *The Enforcer* (1976), *Sudden Impact* (1983), and finally, *The Dead Pool* (1988).

As a fledgling young gun writer back in the 1970s, I was not immune to the allure of the Model 29. After watching the first three Dirty Harry movies multiple times, and meeting Elmer Keith on numerous occasions, I simply *had* to have one. But even with my "insider's connections," they simply were not available — at least, not at the suggested retail price of the time at $354.50, let alone at any gun writer's hoped-for discount.

But then fate intervened. A new Abercrombie & Fitch (the original outdoor outfitter, not the urban outfitter it became) was about to open in Beverly Hills near where I lived. The year was 1979 and, in addition to pith helmets, tweed coats and golf clubs, the rumor was that the gun department was getting an allocation of three Model 29s for the grand opening, one in each barrel length — 4, 6 1/2, and 8 3/8 inches. And they would be selling them for their currently cataloged price!

Suffice to say, I was one of the first in line when the doors opened at 9 a.m., right behind two other guys who also were salivating over the prospect of acquiring a Model 29. We quickly compared notes and discovered we each had our sights set on a different barrel length, with me opting for the 8 3/8-inch version. So, rather than competing for the same gun, we formed a plan and when the doors opened, the three of us sprinted up the mezzanine steps, two at a time, rushed up to the gun counter like trail-weary cowboys bursting into a saloon, and slapped our money down. I promptly purchased the Model 29 with 8 3/8-inch barrel for $366 (the longer barrel always brought a premium). What made this acquisition even better was that I got the gun at a discounted price because the salesman couldn't find the mahogany case. Later, when I returned to pick up the revolver after California's mandatory waiting period, the case had been found, but A&F honored their discounted price.

I still have that gun, along with a few other Model 29s acquired over the years, including one of the original test guns sent to a gun writer in New York. After all, you can't have too many Model 29s. They are real attention-getters at the shooting range, especially when touching off full-house loads. They make, in my opinion, the ideal hunting handgun, sporting enough power to harvest a whitetail buck, but not so over-the-top in recoil that a fast follow-up shot can't be taken if needed. And in spite of some so-called pundits' opinions to the contrary, the Model 29 is a valid consideration for home defense, especially when loaded with less-penetrating cartridges such as Glaser Blue .44 Specials.

Over the years, the Model 29 underwent many variations before it was discontinued in 1999, only to be brought back today as a Smith & Wesson Classic that, reflecting our times, sports a lockable action and a corresponding telltale keyhole on the left side of the frame. But for me, nothing holds the aura, esteem and collectability of the original Model 29, which perpetuates a legacy started by the late Elmer Keith.

The current Model 29, part of Smith & Wesson's Classic line, available in 4- and 6 1/2-inch barrel models, can be easily identified by its keyhole lock on the left side of the frame, near the cylinder release latch. The scalloped grips are another instant giveaway. While these reissues are well made and are great shooters, they have little interest to collectors, nor do they carry the heftier price tags of the earlier guns.

THROUGH THE YEARS WITH A WINCHESTER MODEL 90

BY **JAMES E. HOUSE**

For about half a century, the Winchester Model 90 was a staple among rimfire rifles.

The Winchester Model 90 came into my family from a great uncle, a dentist, while visiting with my father and grandfather. The rifle was given to my grandfather, at least he thought so. Dad always said that the rifle was intended for him, which would have been logical since, to my knowledge, my grandfather used only a single-barrel shotgun. When my grandfather died in 1953, I am sure that he had never fired the old .22. While I was growing up, my grandparents lived a stone's throw from me, so the rifle stayed at my house. That rimfire, a Winchester Model 90 pump chambered for the .22 Short, was the only rifle in the family for many years.

It was a different time and place, for sure, and I had access to the rifle from an early age, as long as I bought my own ammunition. Odd jobs provided enough cash to keep a supply of .22 Shorts on hand. Living in a remote area, it was common practice to go home from school, pick up the .22 and head for the woods. In the summers, a lot of time was spent roaming the fields and woods with the Model 90. Living on a farm, meat processing was a regular event, and I sort of became the designated shooter.

For many years, the popular rimfire calibers were (left to right) .22 Short, .22 Long, .22 Long Rifle and .22 WRF. Versions of the Model 90 utilized all these calibers.

My older brother also used the rifle a lot, and at some point he let the magazine tube become unlatched and it fell out unnoticed. We used the rifle as a single-shot until I found the tube rusted and bent in a field about a year later, and with some work restored it to usable condition. Eventually, the leaf hammer spring broke and the rifle again became a single-shot, with a rubber band used to propel the hammer forward. Eventually the rifle was taken to a local gunsmith named Dutch Settlemoir for repair. Of course, living in that remote area seven miles from anywhere, we had no phone (and probably neither did Mr. Settlemoir). Communication was by mail because a phone was not available until my high school years, but eventually to my delight came a postcard with the message, "I have your Winchester up in good shape." I paid the $3 repair bill.

I looked on that old Winchester as *my* rifle and my father almost never used it. After the school years, I took the rifle with me and kept it for a few years, but eventually bought a bolt-action Winchester Model 69 and took the Model 90 back to my father. When he passed away several years ago, my brothers and I drew

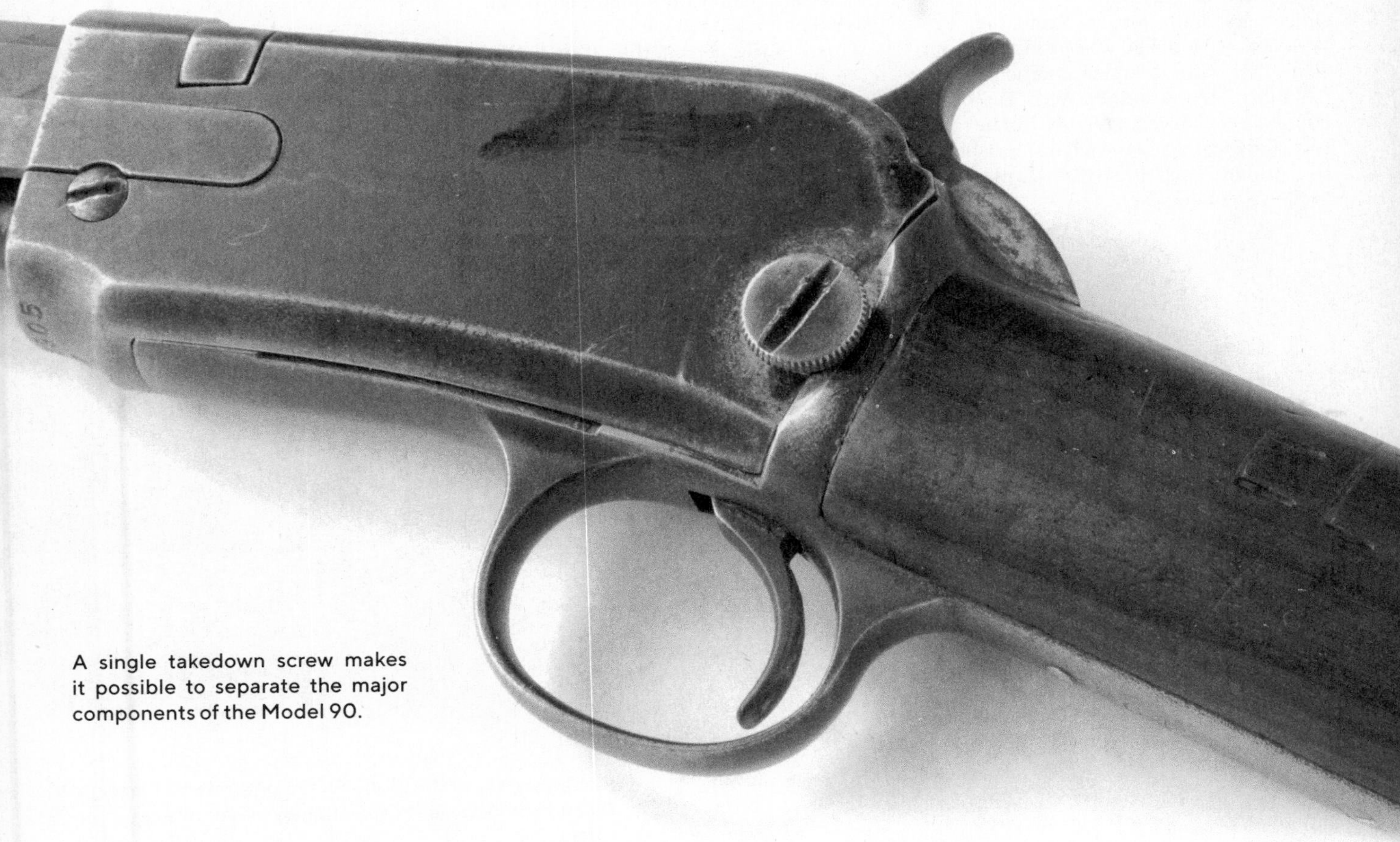

A single takedown screw makes it possible to separate the major components of the Model 90.

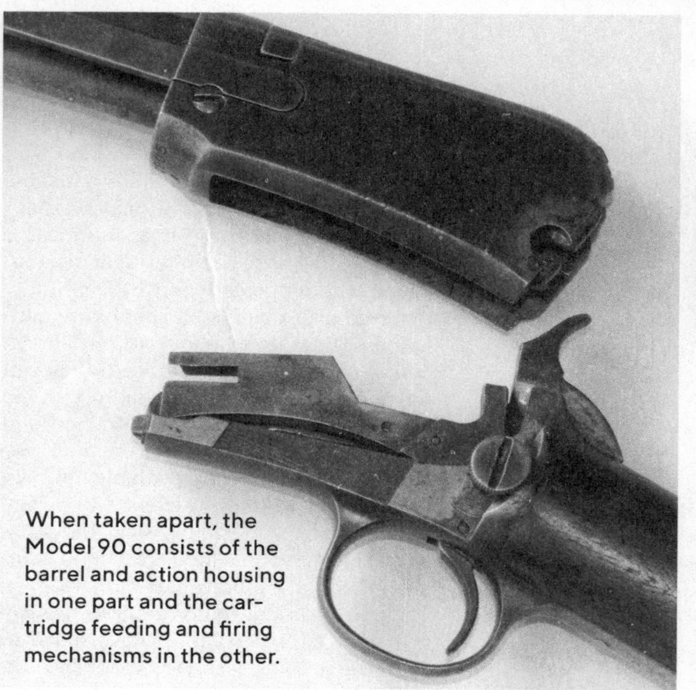
When taken apart, the Model 90 consists of the barrel and action housing in one part and the cartridge feeding and firing mechanisms in the other.

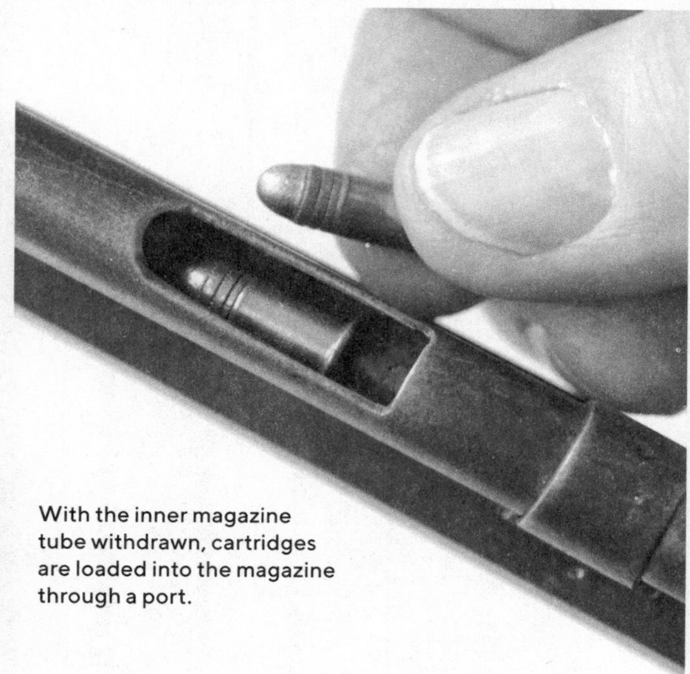
With the inner magazine tube withdrawn, cartridges are loaded into the magazine through a port.

numbers from a hat to see who got what. When my turn came, I picked the old Winchester Model 90, so at last it really did become my rifle.

Another of the superb firearms designed by John Moses Browning, the Winchester Model 90 was produced from 1890–1941, with versions chambered for .22 Short, .22 LR and .22 WRF. The octagon barrel, curved steel buttplate and tiny slide handle were characteristic of the design of rimfire rifles during that time period. Approximately 765,000 Model 90s were produced, but they are now considered to be collectible, so the price of a fairly nice specimen is rather high. The serial number on my Model 90 indicates that it was made in 1920.

Three variants of the Model 1890 were produced, the first being a solid-frame rifle made only from 1890–1892. In both the first and second versions, the breechblock moved between solid side panels, but the second version was a takedown model. The third variant was also a takedown model that had cutout notches in the sides of the receiver and locking lugs mated with these recesses. It utilized an adjustable rear sight. The rifle that is the subject of this article is a third variant. Both standard and deluxe versions of the second and third variants were available.

With the action being small, and the barrel rather long and heavy for a rimfire, the Model 90 has a "weight-forward"

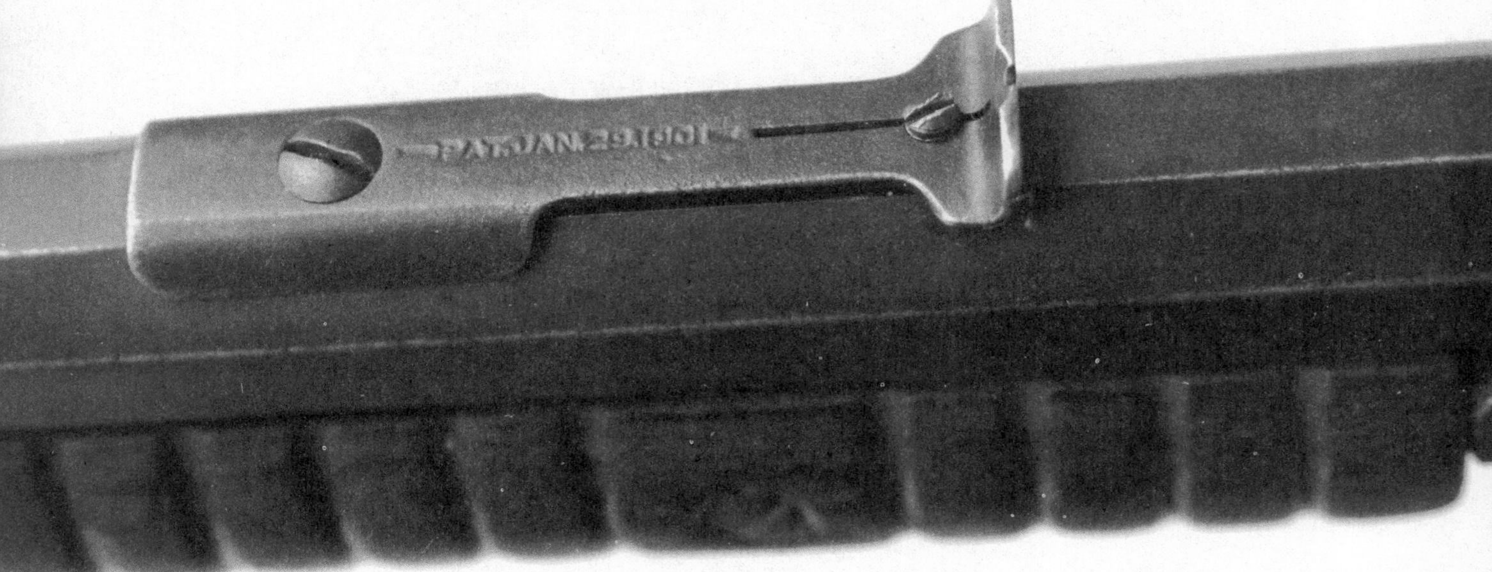

Some versions of the Model 90 incorporated a rear sight that was adjustable for elevation by means of a set screw.

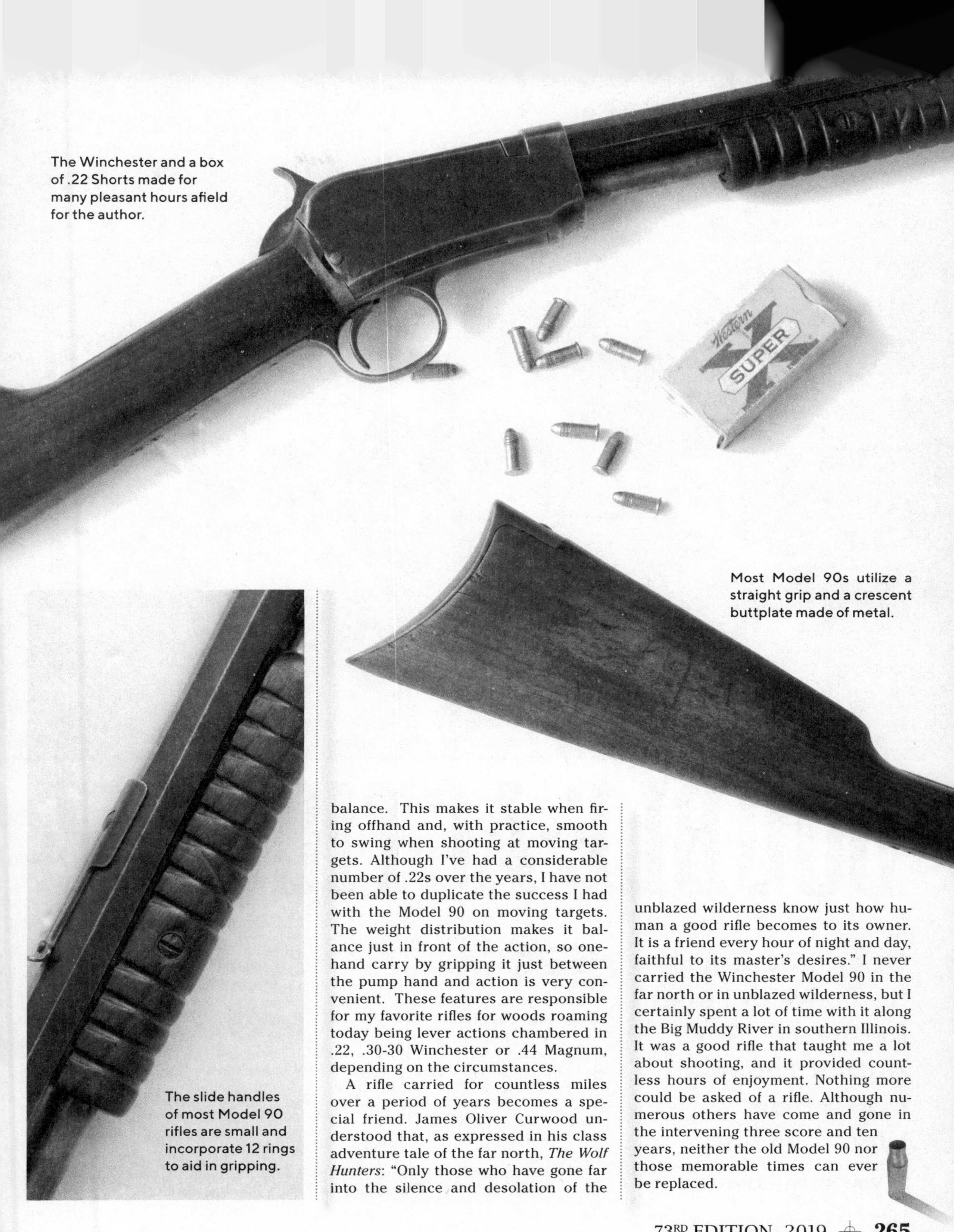

The Winchester and a box of .22 Shorts made for many pleasant hours afield for the author.

Most Model 90s utilize a straight grip and a crescent buttplate made of metal.

The slide handles of most Model 90 rifles are small and incorporate 12 rings to aid in gripping.

balance. This makes it stable when firing offhand and, with practice, smooth to swing when shooting at moving targets. Although I've had a considerable number of .22s over the years, I have not been able to duplicate the success I had with the Model 90 on moving targets. The weight distribution makes it balance just in front of the action, so one-hand carry by gripping it just between the pump hand and action is very convenient. These features are responsible for my favorite rifles for woods roaming today being lever actions chambered in .22, .30-30 Winchester or .44 Magnum, depending on the circumstances.

A rifle carried for countless miles over a period of years becomes a special friend. James Oliver Curwood understood that, as expressed in his class adventure tale of the far north, *The Wolf Hunters*: "Only those who have gone far into the silence and desolation of the unblazed wilderness know just how human a good rifle becomes to its owner. It is a friend every hour of night and day, faithful to its master's desires." I never carried the Winchester Model 90 in the far north or in unblazed wilderness, but I certainly spent a lot of time with it along the Big Muddy River in southern Illinois. It was a good rifle that taught me a lot about shooting, and it provided countless hours of enjoyment. Nothing more could be asked of a rifle. Although numerous others have come and gone in the intervening three score and ten years, neither the old Model 90 nor those memorable times can ever be replaced.

The author's .44 Magnum Redhawk has a 5 1/2-inch barrel. Ideal balance, one-hand control, lovely lines.

RUGER'S BEST DOUBLE-ACTION .44

One Good Gun: Redhawk or Super Redhawk? The Author Thought the Choice Would Be Easy

BY **WAYNE VAN ZWOLL**

Some people choose powerful firearms for the reason adolescent boys crave muscle-cars: image. My drift to 1911 pistols and large-frame revolvers was instead pragmatic. My pork-chop paws engulfed smaller handguns. Finger curled about the trigger like a shrimp, my leading knuckle crowded the muzzle. But to give pocket guns a fair shake, I ran the numbers. Ruger's LCP and LCR measure about 5.2 and 6.5 inches in length. My hand tapes 8.7.

Revolvers that fit me date to the 1840s, though I don't. Economic depression followed the panic of 1837. In 1841, Samuel Colt's Paterson plant closed. Colt found work with Samuel Morse, until in 1846, a visit from Samuel Walker of the Texas Rangers turned his attention again to guns. The resulting Walker Colt was a 4 1/2-pound .44, to be manufactured at Ely Whitney's plant. Few were shipped. Short months later, Captain Walker fell to a Mexican lance at the Battle of Juamantla.

War clouds fueled development of Colt's 1860 Army. The 1873 Peacemaker followed, an instant success. The .45 Long Colt, initially loaded with 28 grains black powder behind a 230-grain bul-

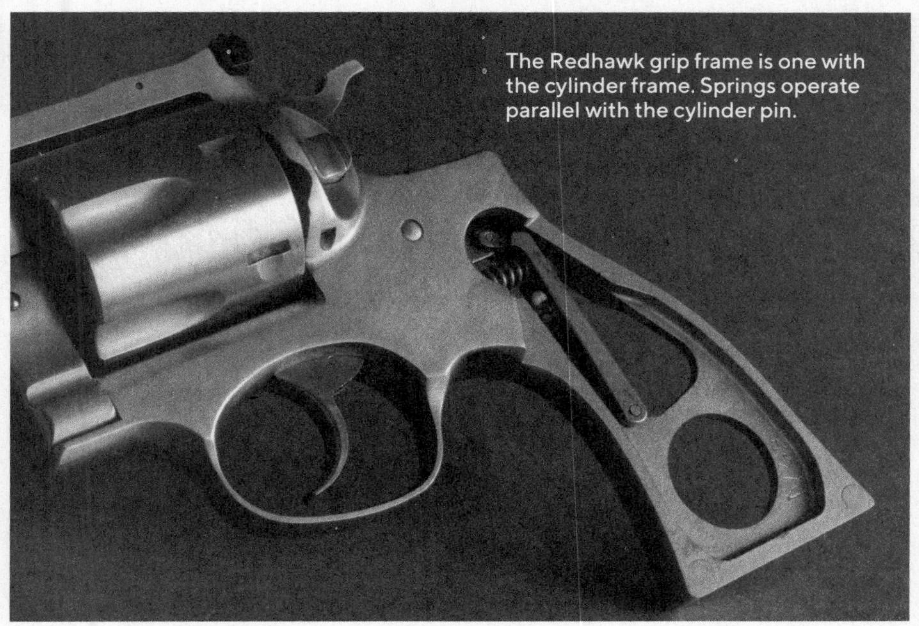

The Redhawk grip frame is one with the cylinder frame. Springs operate parallel with the cylinder pin.

let, earned its deadly reputation with a 40-grain charge, a 255-grain bullet. The U.S. Army adopted this single-action sidearm in 1875. Three years later, Colt bored its 1873 Model P Peacemaker Single Action Army for the .44-40, already available in Winchester's 1873 rifle. That dual chambering profited both firms, ensuring a ready supply of .44-40 ammunition across the West and absolving customers of packing two loads.

Meanwhile, Smith & Wesson saw promise in double-action revolvers. In 1905, a full decade after smokeless powder arrived, it built a .44 Special revolver for a black-powder load, 26 grains driving a 246-grain bullet through nine 7/8-inch pine boards! The .44 Hand Ejector appeared in 1907. The .44 Military Model of 1908 became the "Triple Lock," as it latched at the breech, forward of the extractor and between yoke and extractor shroud. Refinements followed. The Fourth Model, or 1950 Target, got the attention of an Idaho cowboy, who began crusading for a revolver cartridge to upstage the .357, announced in 1935 on S&W's .38/44 frame. Elmer Keith's .44 Special handloads presaged an even more potent round.

As the .357 got its zip from a case slightly longer than a .38 Special's, so the .44 Magnum gained its edge on the .44 Special. In 1954, Remington's first factory loads hurled 240-grain bullets at 1,350 fps, effectively doubling the blow of the .45 Colt. Smith added steel to its 1950 frame, hiking pistol heft from 40 to 47 ounces. The Model 29 .44 Magnum revolver went public in 1956.

Sturm, Ruger came late to the revolver game but quickly showed Bill Ruger's genius. The .357 Blackhawk appeared in 1955, the .44 a year later. These "Flattops" anchored a single-action series that's still strong at market. A medium-frame .357 double-action arrived in 1970, but the big news from Ruger that decade came at its end. During the NRA show in San Antonio in May 1979, the company unveiled its Redhawk, a six-shot DA .44 Magnum. That year was Sturm, Ruger's 30th — and most profitable. Sales reached $68.9 million, the net topping $7.9 million. Those figures surpassed 1978 returns by 15 and 13 percent. Clearly, Ruger was producing what shooters wanted.

Struggling into solvency after college, I wasn't then able to snare a .44 Redhawk. But it was soon in my sights, an alluring combination of strength and elegance, tradition and innovation.

Engineers Harry Sefried and Roy Melcher made the Redhawk what it is, but Harry credited Bill Ruger with the offset ejector rod. Breaking with tradition, it's not in the frame's center and doesn't rotate coaxially with the cylinder. So located, it permits a beefier frame next to the rod. The steel there is nearly twice as thick as it would have been with a frame-centered ejector. Another departure from the norm is the cylinder latch. Instead of a sliding tab, it's a button that releases when depressed. I prefer it, as firing with gloves on big hands can accidentally move a fore-and-aft latch.

The Redhawk's crane locks into the

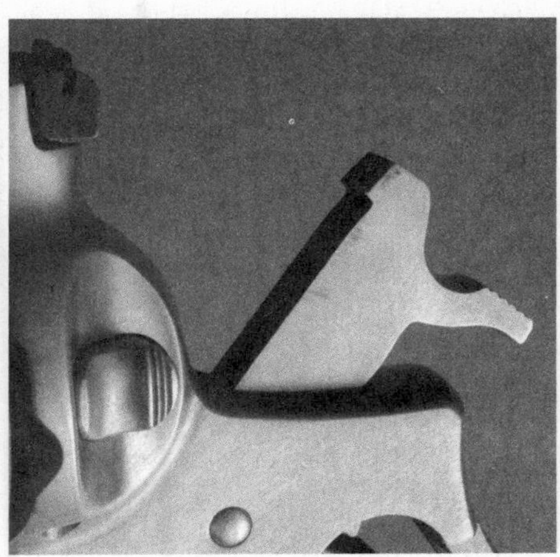

Redhawk and Super Redhawk share a flat-nose hammer and transfer bar, a push-button cylinder latch.

Sights are similar on Ruger's DA .44s. But the Redhawk's front is on a barrel rib, not an island ramp.

An adjustable, blued, square-notch sight (RH and SRH) contributes to a crisp picture, accurate aim.

For the Redhawk, author likes the Galco DAO (here) and Phoenix holsters. Note strap tab, tension screw.

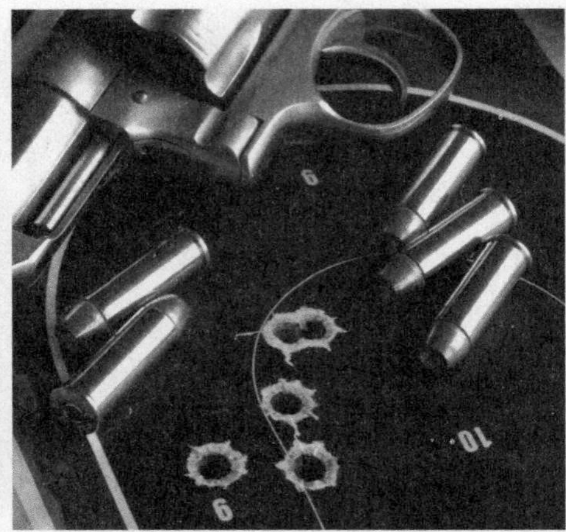

The Redhawk printed this 25-yard group with 210-grain Gold Dot ammo using iron sights.

Ruger's Redhawk now comes in .45 Colt, with full-moon clips for use with .45 ACP cartridges.

Short-barreled, round-butt versions of the Redhawk include this .44 Mag. Also offered in .357, .45.

frame, where it's held much more securely than if relegated to a forward under-barrel lug. Ruger described this as a "triple-locking" (not Triple Lock!) revolver, the cylinder secured "front, rear and bottom." In this respect, the Redhawk was more rugged than any other DA then on the market. Sefried observed the lockup "would last about indefinitely." The barrel has plenty of brawn, too, with 3/4x20-pitch threads.

A flat-nosed hammer falls on a transfer bar. A single coil spring powers two linkages: one to push the hammer, the other to return the trigger. Smith & Wesson DAs have two springs, a system Sefried said increases trigger pull without adding hammer thrust. Colt's two-legged flat spring yields a lighter pull but does not assist the hammer. Bill Ruger insisted on a trigger-weight setting "in the range of conventional double-action revolvers," so I shouldn't have been surprised when Redhawk pulls I weighed came in at 6 1/2 pounds SA and 11 DA. Both were smooth and *felt* lighter. According to Ruger engineers, the Redhawk reliably ignites primers with a DA pull as light as 7 pounds.

Introduced with barrel lengths of 5 1/2 and 7 1/2 inches, the .44 Magnum Redhawk arrived as the "logical evolution of the now-famous line of Ruger double-action revolvers." But it was also an "entirely new firearm, representing the most significant advance in the development of heavy frame double-action revolvers in many decades." The company also noted, "With the accuracy and power of the .44 Magnum cartridge [the Redhawk will] be widely used as a hunting revolver." It's since been chambered in .357 and .41 Magnum, and in .45 Colt. Ruger's latest catalog lists the .44 Magnum with hardwood grips and 5 1/2- and 7 1/2-inch barrels, including a Hunter model with scope ring dimples on the 7 1/2-inch rib. There's a .45 Colt/.45 ACP version with hardwood, a .45 Colt or .44 Magnum with Hogue Monogrips. Both have 4 1/4-inch barrels. A new round-butt, hardwood .357 holds eight shots behind a 2 3/4-inch barrel.

In past years, this pistol has been listed with blued chrome-moly steel, but now all versions are of brushed stainless. Sights are blued C-M. The replaceable front blade has a red plastic insert, the adjustable rear a white-outline square notch.

When life became unbearably hollow without a Redhawk, I yielded. The price had climbed well above the 1980 MSRP of $325. My consolation: it has kept rising. Good things seem never to go on sale, and I suspect the current figure ($1,079) will soon be eclipsed. I picked the 5 1/2-inch .44 because I like wood grips and think a 5 1/2-inch barrel gives a big revolver visual and physical balance. Recoil is more violent in shorter, lighter .44s, which also sacrifice sight radius. A 7 1/2-inch barrel brings heft from 49 to 54 ounces, quickly making the Redhawk a two-hand gun. Even if I almost always use two, it seems to me a handgun shouldn't require both.

Unlike later Ruger DAs built with separate grip frames, the Redhawk's grip is integral with the frame proper. There are no sideplates. You can disassemble the Redhawk without tools, but I used a screwdriver to release the grips. A pin fell — from where I could not tell. *Read the instructions, Dummy!* The manual confirmed what I'd suspected. The pin has no function in the assembled pistol; it secures the mainspring and strut during disassembly.

Firing the Redhawk won't put you to sleep, but the hardwood grips are thoughtfully shaped and mercifully smooth. They slip slightly in your hand as the gun rotates up in recoil, absorbing bite. While pliable rubber absorbs shock,

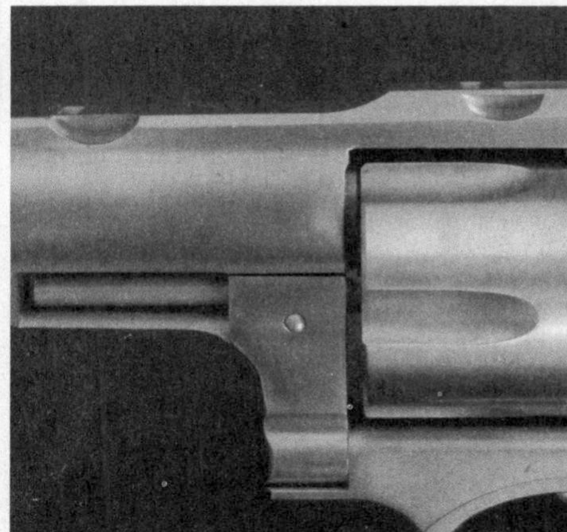

An extended, beefier, scope-friendly frame distinguishes the Super Redhawk. It differs inside too.

it also ensures that all the kick reaches you before it leaks energy moving the pistol. Redhawk sights give me the square, sharp image I like in irons.

In range trials, my Redhawk has printed pleasing groups with bullets of 180 to 300 grains. Nixing shots I pulled or wobbled out, I managed to threaten the 2-inch mark at 25 yards with the loads at hand.

Vertical spread *between* loads reflected the wide velocity range. Unlike rifles, handguns typically send heavier missiles higher into close targets. Trajectory disparities due to bullet speed and profile matter less than do exit points in the recoil cycle. Fast, light bullets exit early in the muzzle's climb. Slow, heavy bullets leave later.

For some time, I figured any DA enthusiast with a Ruger Redhawk had all the handgun he or she needed. But then a Super Redhawk followed me home.

Introduced in 1986, just seven years after its predecessor, the Super Redhawk distinguishes itself with an extended frame, essentially a barrel collar. Besides adding beef to the barrel-frame juncture, this frame has more steel in the top strap and around the ejector rod. It's long enough to support a scope. Ruger machined it for scope rings and has furnished them on every SRH except the Alaskan, with its 2 1/2-inch barrel. *That* fistful of recoil didn't debut with the first Super Redhawk, which featured hard synthetic grips with wood insets, and barrels of 7 1/2 and 9 1/2 inches, chambered only in .44 Magnum. Weights: 53 and 58 ounces.

The Super Redhawk embodies features of the Redhawk — same triple-locking cylinder and offset cylinder notches that dodge the thinnest points in the cylinder.

Scoped, a 52-ounce Super Redhawk becomes a two-hand gun. It's still a handgun, and easy to carry.

Same cylinder latch button and transfer bar ignition. The rear of the frame, the guard, trigger and hammer appear at a glance identical. Sights are the same too, albeit the SHR has an island ramp in the front, not a barrel-length rib. Both .44s have six-groove rifling with 1-in-20 right-hand twist.

Internally, however, the two revolvers are quite different. The Super Redhawk has the "peg" grip frame of Ruger's GP-100 instead of the Redhawk's traditional

Load	Group (in.)
Remington 180-gr. SJHP	2.1
Hornady 200-gr. XTP	2.2
Speer 210-gr. Gold Dot	1.9
Federal 240-gr. JHP	2.2
Winchester 250-gr. PTHP	2.4
Black Hills 300-gr. JHP	2.3

Bill Ruger is credited with designing a stout "triple-locking cylinder" that stays tight after much use.

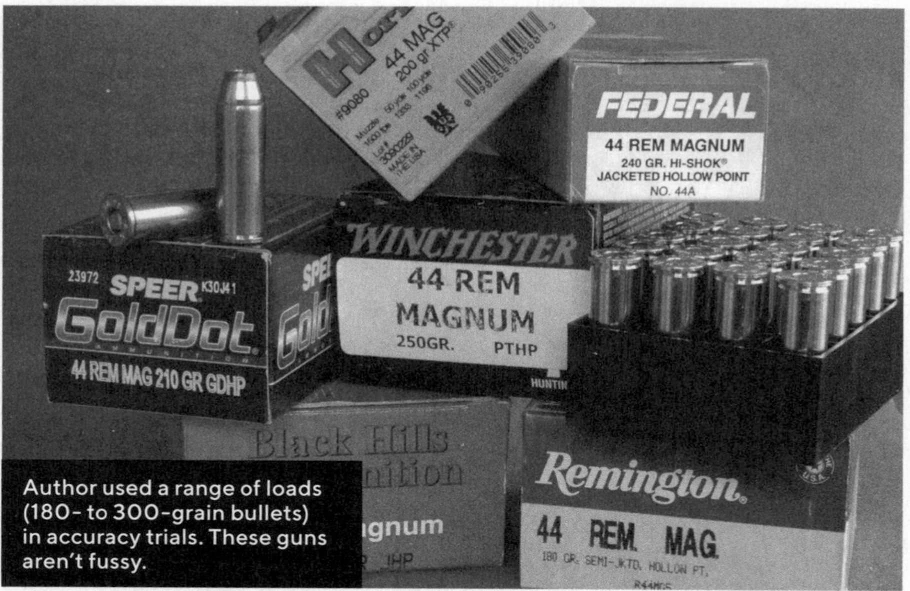

Author used a range of loads (180- to 300-grain bullets) in accuracy trials. These guns aren't fussy.

Steadying the Super Redhawk, author appreciates its smooth 4 3/4-pound trigger pull. Deer beware!

full-size grip frame. All three coil springs behind the standing breech of a Redhawk operate nearly parallel with the cylinder and barrel axes. The biggest spring in the Super Redhawk is pretty much centered in the grip and runs parallel to *it*.

The SRH has not been chambered in .357 Magnum or .45 Colt; but since its introduction, Ruger has added the .454 Casull, .480 Ruger, .41 Magnum and 10mm Auto to the original .44 Magnum chambering. Of course, you can fire .45 Colt ammo in revolvers bored for the Casull. While Super Redhawks in .44 Magnum, .41 Magnum and 10mm have the fluted cylinders of the original, .454s and .480s lack flutes. All SRHs now feature Hogue Tamer Monogrips, to help absorb recoil and ensure a secure hold with wet, cold or gloved hands.

Content with my 5 1/2-inch Redhawk, I had little need for its longer, heavier progeny. Then, short months ago as I write this, Ruger announced a "distributor exclusive" for AcuSport. This 52-ounce Super Redhawk, available through any dealer served by AcuSport, wore a 6 1/2-inch barrel. Long enough to tap the potential of the .44 Magnum, and wring hunting accuracy from iron sights or scope, it seemed to my eye a perfect match for the leggy SRH frame. *You don't have to need a revolver to buy one.* Though the price of Super Redhawks had risen from $510 at its debut to a starting MSRP of $1,159, I bit.

Revolvers have brought to bag only a few animals on my big game hunts, so by any measure I'm a rookie in this arena. But scoping the Super Redhawk

CARRYING ONE GOOD GUN

After slipping revolvers into fine leather from Don Hume, Bianchi and DeSantis, naming a "best" brand gets difficult. I won't — other than to say I lean ever more heavily toward Galco holsters. Besides an exhaustive selection of lined and unlined styles for autoloaders and SA and DA revolvers (alternatively in tan and Havana brown as well as black) the company lists belts, shoulder rigging, magazine and cartridge pouches — even handbags — of the high-quality, beautifully stitched leather that drew attention to it as The Famous Jackass Leather Company in the 1960s.

My Ruger Redhawk rides in a Galco DAO. An unlined belt holster of heavy steer hide, it's deep tan in color and has a retention strap with glove-friendly polymer release tab. A tension adjustment below the guard recess lets me tune its grip to the gun. Like other Galcos I've used, it provides glove-snug fit to the revolver. Slotted for belts to 1 3/4 inches, it has a double-stitched back and works with standard rake or cross-draw. Another holster option is the Galco Phoenix, with many of the same features, double retention screws and suede lining.

While Galco has belt holsters like the DAO to accommodate most popular frames and barrels, my pick for long hunting revolvers is the chest-borne, cross-draw Kodiak. It has adjustable torso rigging with Fastex buckle, retention strap with poly tab and 2-inch shoulder strap. A matching ammo carrier (loops or magazine pouch) attaches to the rig. In Havana brown, it's one of the most fetching holsters around. The Kodiak Hunter is slotted for scoped handguns and cradles my Super Redhawk. Like the Kodiak, it comes in right- and left-hand versions. *GalcoGunleather.com.*

Author prefers Galco's Kodiak and (here) Kodiak Hunter chest holsters for long, heavy revolvers.

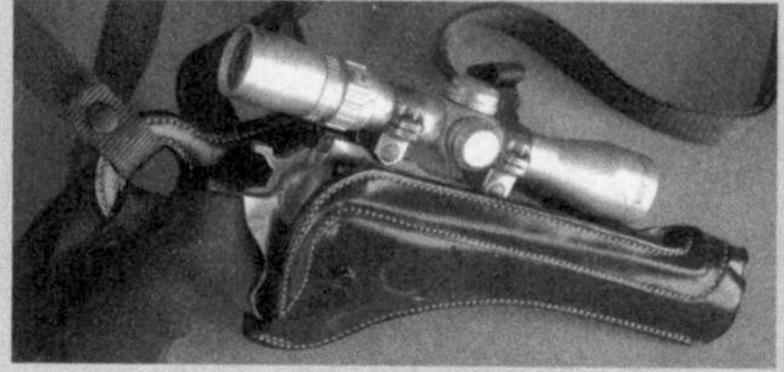
Galco's Kodiak Hunter has a reinforced slot for scoped guns, a padded shoulder strap, Fastex latch.

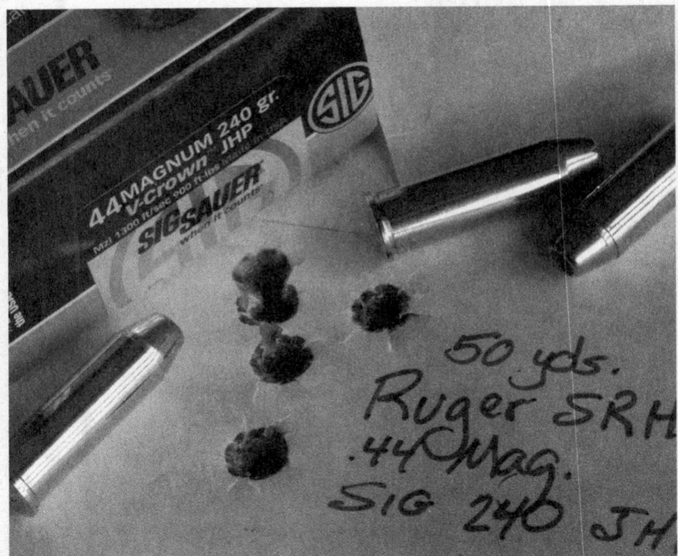

Rifle-like accuracy. The Super Redhawk shot this knot with SIG loads, nearly equaled it with others.

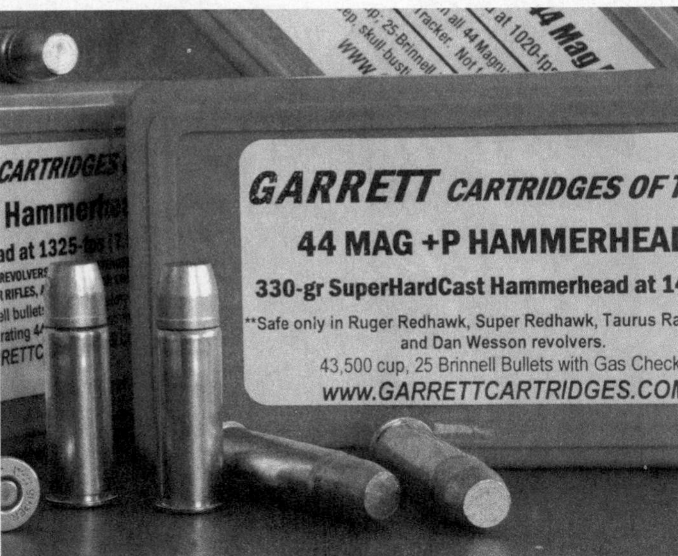

Potent .44 loads abound, but these Garrett options add extra muscle. Note label warnings, pressures.

with a Bushnell LER 2-6x variable gave it a lethal look indeed. So equipped, it was clearly a use-two-hands, find-a-rest handgun. Still, it balanced well and, unlike longer revolvers, this .44 felt more like a pistol than a carbine.

I usually zero big-bore handguns at 25 yards, for point-blank aim to 75. That's near the effective reach of traditional bullets at 1,100 to 1,400 fps. Federal, for example, loads a 280-grain Swift A-Frame to 1,170 fps. Zeroed at 25, it hits an inch high at 50 yards, 3.7 inches low at 75. Federal's 225-grain Barnes Expander at 1,280 fps reaches 50 yards just half an inch high and drops 2.8 inches at 75. These bullets fall 8.6 and 6.9 inches at 100.

After zeroing my Super Redhawk over a Caldwell bag, I tacked another target at a scope-friendly 50 yards and again took aim. Four bullets clustered inside 1.1 inches! Alas, fifth-shot gremlins would not be denied, and my final hollowpoint opened the group to 1.8. To my delight, a second series shot into 1.5 inches. I'm not skilled enough with a handgun to expect better. Nor is the SRH finicky. It herded all types and weights of bullets into snug knots. Black Hills 300-grain JHPs at 1,150 fps and 240-grain SIG JHPs at 1,300 delivered five-shot groups under 3 minutes of angle.

Now, 3-minute accuracy from a stock revolver with off-the-shelf ammunition would ordinarily put spring in my step. In this case, it posed a dilemma. I had just assured my editor at *Gun Digest* I could write compelling narrative about a revolver I prized above all others. One good gun. My Ruger Redhawk was now one of *two* good guns. Perhaps their common genesis, manufacture and features will ensure that both appear in the final copy. Both deserve the honor!

Even 300-grain bullets drilled tight groups. Predictably, heavy bullets struck higher than light ones.

BEAR STOPPER?

"We trailed the wounded brown bear tip-toe," the guide told me. "Slowly. A leaf ticked through the alders, and I jumped a foot. The bush got thicker. Just as I figured the risk was too great, he burst from the bushes. Like a tank but rocket-fast. My .44 was up and firing instantly, double action. The bear didn't flinch. It ran me over as I emptied the last chambers into its belly. It could've killed me, but probably just wanted out. We found it not far off, dead from the rifle wound." He paused. "I still pack that .44. It makes me feel good. It no longer makes me feel safe."

Powerful new loads for the .44 Magnum have made it more effective on heavy game. Besides the hollowpoint and softnose loads from major ammunition firms, you can get frisky options from the likes of Garrett, which catalogs hardcast 310-grain lead bullets at 1,100 fps (32,000 copper units of pressure) and 1,325 fps (38,000 CUP). A 330-grain Garrett Hammerhead at 1,400 fps is gas-checked and suitable only for the stoutest revolvers. At that level the .44 Magnum boasts the punch of the .454 Casull!

But even the Casull can fail to dissuade half-ton beasts hurtling toward you a few feet — and fewer seconds — away. At that distance, the difference between killing a bear and stopping it becomes startlingly apparent. And even a killing shot is much more difficult than self-styled gunslingers boast over their beer.

By all accounts, bear spray is a better stopper than revolver bullets.

Custom Shop | REMINGTON 700 7MM MAGNUM

The 7mm Magnum from Remington's Custom Shop, working with a pair of Swarovski's quality binoculars, resulted in a musk ox head on the wall and much meat for some residents of Nunavut.

Sometimes It Takes Years to Acquire a Coveted Firearm

BY **DICK WILLIAMS**

I look back on 1962 as a spectacular year. That was when I graduated from college, and the new 7mm Magnum cartridge was introduced in the Remington Model 700. Truth be told, I'm sure the world was more excited about the 7mm Mag. than it was about my graduation. But I celebrated the 7mm's arrival with the rest of the population by reading (and believing) everything that was written about it, how it was North America's new do-everything caliber. I swore I would one day own one and take exotic game with it. I had no idea it would take almost 50 years to fulfill that oath.

As I recall, there were several things working for the newest .284 caliber. First, it was a belted magnum, meaning it had the "magic belt" at the base of the cartridge case and enough powder capacity to launch even the caliber's heavier bullets at muzzle velocities of 3000 fps or more. Ballistic coefficients of the 7mm Magnum's most practical and useful bullets were higher than comparable projectiles in either the .270 Winchester or

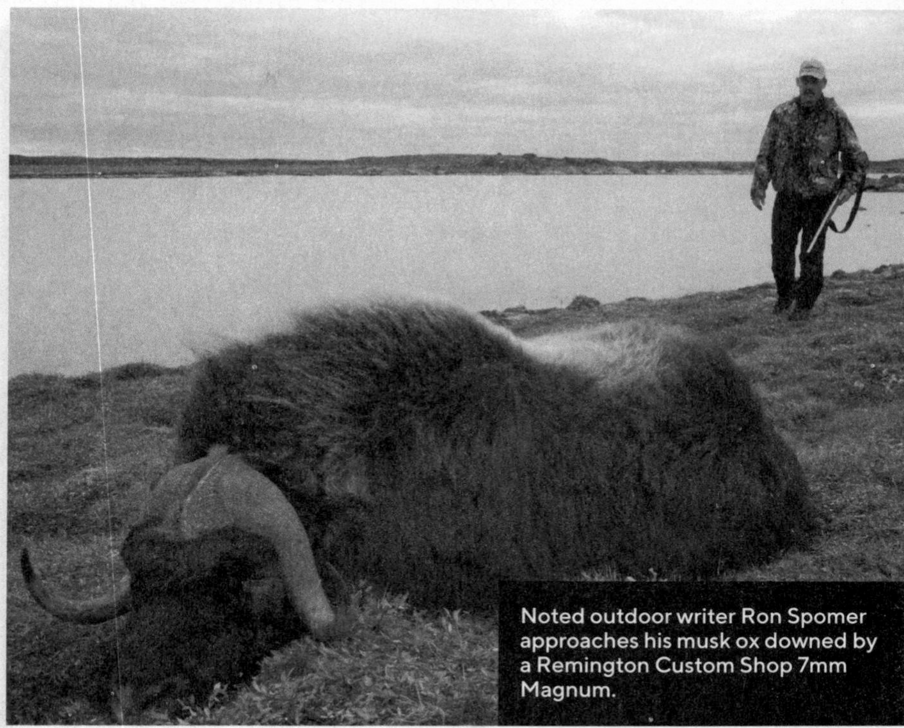

Noted outdoor writer Ron Spomer approaches his musk ox downed by a Remington Custom Shop 7mm Magnum.

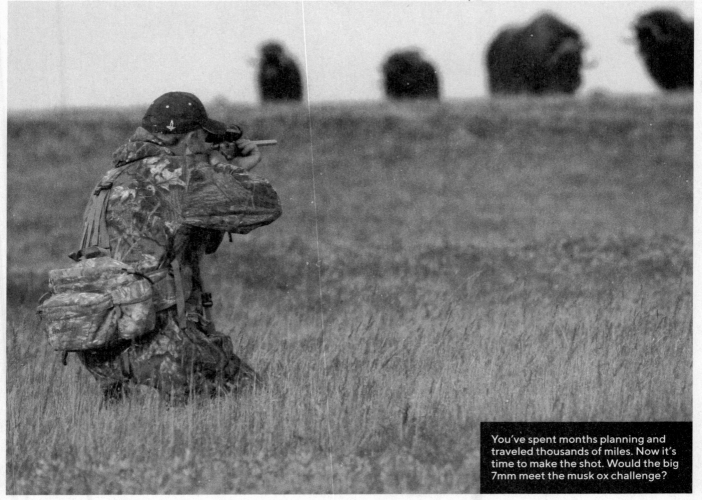

You've spent months planning and traveled thousands of miles. Now it's time to make the shot. Would the big 7mm meet the musk ox challenge?

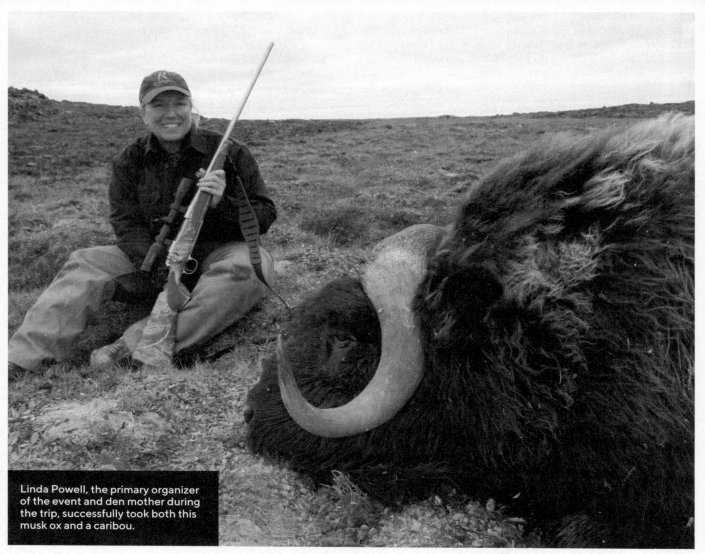

Linda Powell, the primary organizer of the event and den mother during the trip, successfully took both this musk ox and a caribou.

.30-06. The powder of choice for the new magnum was IMR4831, and I believe that surplus 4831 was still available when the 7mm was announced, meaning you could save more money when reloading for optimum performance.

Much of what was written on the 7mm Mag. was more about marketing than performance. The belted magnum was not a new concept, having been around since 1912 on the .375 H&H Magnum. Nor was the belt necessary for headspacing, since the 7mm had a sharp shoulder. Since then, belted cases have fallen out of favor, replaced by the craze for short, fat cases that work in shorter actions. But at the time of its introduction, the 7mm and other belted cartridges, like the .300 and .338 Winchester Magnums, did allow enhanced performance in a standard-length action. And the 7mm delivered the goods

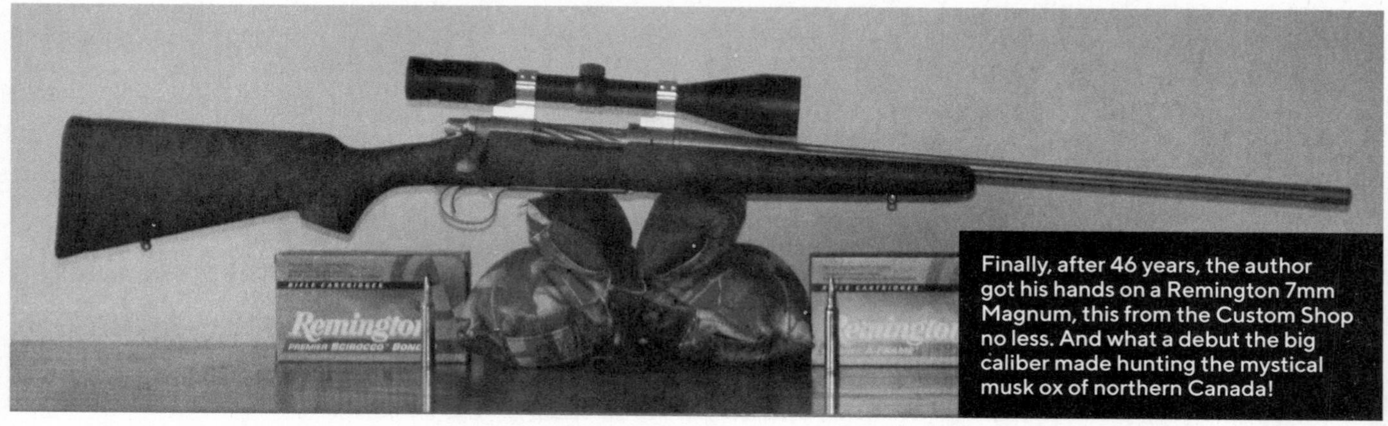
Finally, after 46 years, the author got his hands on a Remington 7mm Magnum, this from the Custom Shop no less. And what a debut the big caliber made hunting the mystical musk ox of northern Canada!

The big musk ox was the only animal the author has taken with a rifle that made it to his Wall of Memories. It hangs directly over his desk and is frequently looked upon for inspiration.

for hunters, as witnessed by it's becoming one of the most popular small- to medium-bore rifle calibers in America and other parts of the world.

Over the years, I became focused on handgun hunting but still managed to obtain and shoot various rifles. Had I been able to find a good, used 7mm Magnum on the market, I would have bought it. My lifelong hunting partner acquired a Sako in the caliber back in the late 1960s, which caused me to break the "Thou shalt not lust after your partner's rifle" hunting camp commandment. Into the 1970s and '80s I witnessed him take antelope and deer with that rifle and had to share the excitement vicariously. I tried talking him into a trade numerous times, my most fervent presentations taking place over adult beverages in hunting camps, but to no avail. Time passed.

In 1990, I made my first trip to Africa. For me it was a handgun-only hunt, but there was another client in camp who had brought a 7mm Magnum, and he used it to remarkable effect across a wide spectrum of animals. His first animal was a jackal spotted at about 50 yards. His aim was true, yet the small creature managed to run about 40 yards before folding up. I was having my first doubts about the 7mm Mag. until we examined the jackal and realized its entire chest cavity was empty of organs — the animal had run that distance dead on its feet! While I didn't witness additional action with the 7mm during that trip, my campmate used it to score several other trophies, including a couple of the larger antelope. I could feel my 30-year craving for the "magic magnum" returning.

In 2005, I went to work at Surefire where one of my jobs was organizing various events, including hunting trips with writers and other industry partners. A couple of years into the job, we were planning a musk ox hunt in northern Canada with Remington and Swarovski. Our marketing director was scheduled to go but had a last-minute conflict. When I was told I had to fill in for him, we had that classic, "Don't throw me in that briar patch!" dialogue. Guns furnished were Remington 700s topped with Swarovski scopes. After 45 years of fantasizing, I was being handed a 7mm Magnum to use on one of the most exotic hunts imaginable. Although he and I remain good friends to this day, on our occasional get-togethers he still sulks a bit over missing that trip.

There were six of us that made the journey north past the arctic circle to the small town of Nunavut, Canada, where we spent two days waiting for the weather to clear so we could fly another couple of hours to our hunting camp. As the saying goes, "We weren't at the end of the earth, but we could see it from our campsite." It was spectacular country. I wondered how primitive people could have survived there, particularly with only two months of decent weather the entire year.

Given Canada's issues with firearms, Remington had packaged all the rifles together for transport rather than sending individual guns to each hunter. It meant one world-renowned manufacturer would deal with Canadian government officials getting the rifles into the country, rather than six known "gun nuts" jumping through bureaucratic hoops real and imagined. It also meant that we couldn't sight in the rifles until after we reached camp. No problem. The Swarovski scopes had been securely mounted and suitable 7mm Remington Magnum ammo brought, including 150-grain Swift Scirocco and 160-grain Swift A-Frame PSP. I settled on the 150-grain Scirocco, figuring it would be excellent for anything I might encounter, save for grizzly. I didn't have a bear tag and was hoping none of the grizzlies had a Williams tag. Using the ATVs for bench rests, everyone was dialed in very quickly.

We were camped on a river, and while the hunters and ATVs had been flown in from Nunavut, some of the guides and camp personnel had made the trip via a power boat. Hunting would be spot and stalk from the ATVs or travel by boat to islands where herds of musk oxen had been seen. We also had caribou tags that proved much harder to fill than those for musk ox. Everyone in camp successfully took a musk ox, but only three of our group scored on caribou. We hunters kept those body parts that contributed to a trophy, and all the meat was harvested and taken back to Nunavut for distribution to town residents.

On the first day's hunt, my guide and I covered 30-plus miles on the Honda ATV. Riding that far over rough terrain sitting on a steel luggage rack with perhaps an inch of foam padding separating my butt from the rack took its toll on this old gun writer. When we became stuck in a small stream back near the camp, I had a lot of trouble trying to get off the machine. Fortunately, another guide came and helped pull us loose. During our travels we had seen a couple fearless members of the weasel family up close. Several hundred yards out a big, solitary grizzly wandered about. But no musk ox. And no caribou.

The next day I couldn't make myself get back on the luggage rack, so I rode the boat over to one of the islands and got lucky. After spotting a herd of musk oxen, we beached the boat half a mile away and began the stalk. I was able to get within 175 yards for the shot, but realized how difficult it was to pick a precise aiming point on the shaggy beasts. They're not huge — somewhere in the 350- to 400-pound range — but those winter coats tend to obscure the exact location of the vitals. I went for "center shoulder mass," and three shots later he was down. The musk ox, or *Umingmak* as it's known by the locals, is extremely tough for its size, but it does live in one of the world's harshest environments. Even so, this one was no match for the Model 700 — I'd finally scored with the 7mm.

The entertainment wasn't over. Back in camp, the hunters lived in a couple of wooden structures slightly above the river. The guides and camp staff (which included wives and kids) had a little tent city set up on the river bank. Everyone got involved in preparing the hides, heads and meat. For us the hunting was a sport, for them a matter of survival. When they have no clients, they are still out hunting throughout the good weather periods of their very brief summer.

It was a spectacular adventure, a true one-of-a-kind hunt. It didn't bother me that I didn't get a caribou. I've had other hunts in remote areas of Alaska, but nothing like this vast, empty land. I finally got my 7mm Magnum and used it on one of the more unique hunts in the world. As you might have guessed, the gun is not for sale.

A BROTHER'S 100-YEAR-OLD 1911

When rejoined with some of the original ammunition from the Korean War and WWII eras, this handgun excelled and exceeded the author's expectations.

BY **TOM TABOR**

There were many troubling things happening in our country during the 1960s and 1970s. It was a time of division for our country that produced many scars that linger today. But as bad as those times were, there was one favorable thing — the era of military surplus. The Vietnam War was starting to wind down and that resulted in the government having a surplus of items it needed to liquidate. In many cases, those products were better built and of higher quality than anything openly available on the civilian market — and the prices were great. Like many shooters, I took full advantage of those opportunities by buying a great deal of surplus rifle powder in bulk form, ammo cans, jackets, hats, various canvas bags and other gear, some of which still accompany me today into the field. But while this gear was an asset to many of us, the National Rifle Association fostered an even better opportunity for its membership. NRA brokered an agreement through the government for its members to buy from a large inventory of surplus military firearms at astronomically low prices.

The offer was that any NRA member could purchase one each of the following weapons: a 1903A3, an M1 Garand and M1 Carbine, and a Model 1911 .45 ACP. If memory serves, those prices ranged from about $14 up to around $24, dependent upon which firearm you selected. Those were darn low prices even back then and, as such, that opportunity captured the

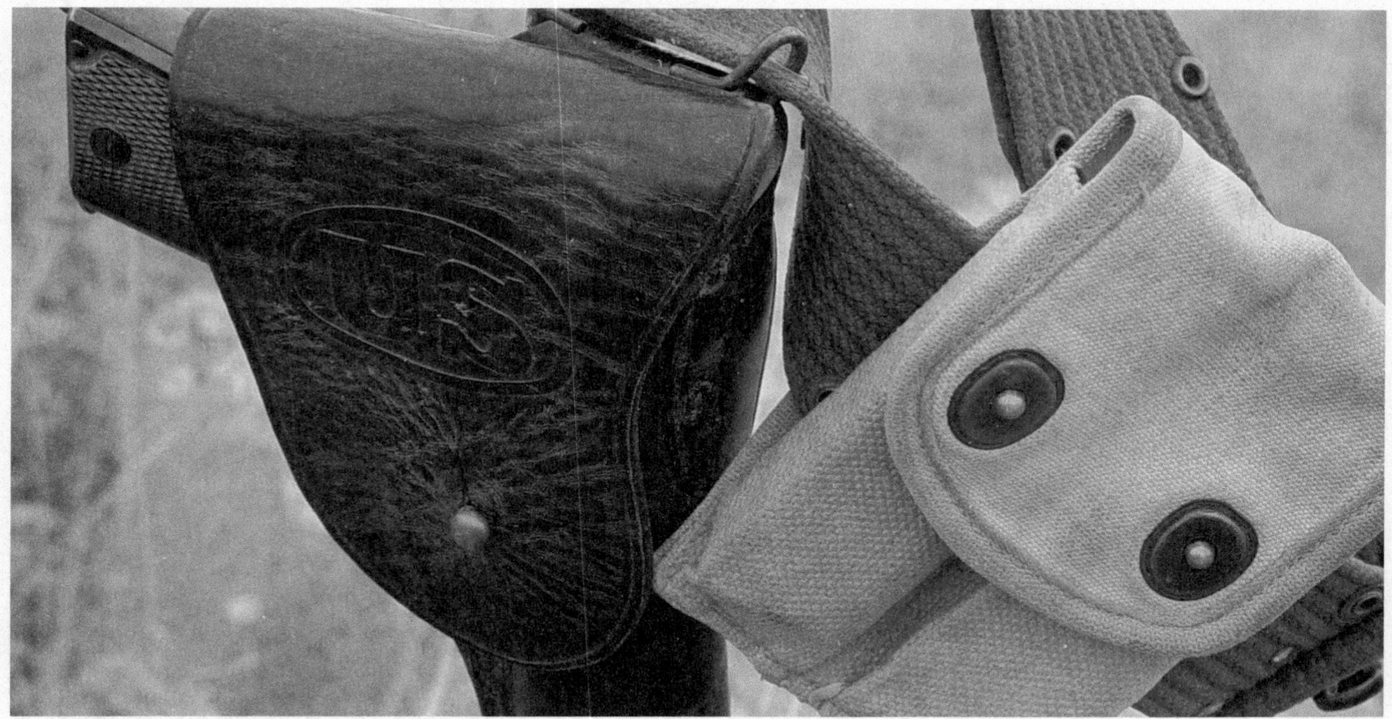

attention of a great many gun owners, including me. Unfortunately, even as low as those prices were, they wouldn't have been any further out of reach for me at that time if they had a price tag of $1000 or more. That's because I'd just been discharged from the U.S. Navy after my four-year enlistment and was on the verge of starting a new life as a family man. My wife and I were struggling just to keep ahead of the necessities of life and there simply wasn't any money left over for such a purchase. Consequently, I had to forgo that unprecedented opportunity, which I have regretted ever since.

On the other hand, my older brother Tony, who at the time was a little better off financially than me, rose to the occasion and purchased one of the Model 1911s for somewhere around $14.15. Shortly after, it arrived directly from the Anniston Army Deport via Railway Express.

I don't believe any handgun has a more prestigious reputation behind it

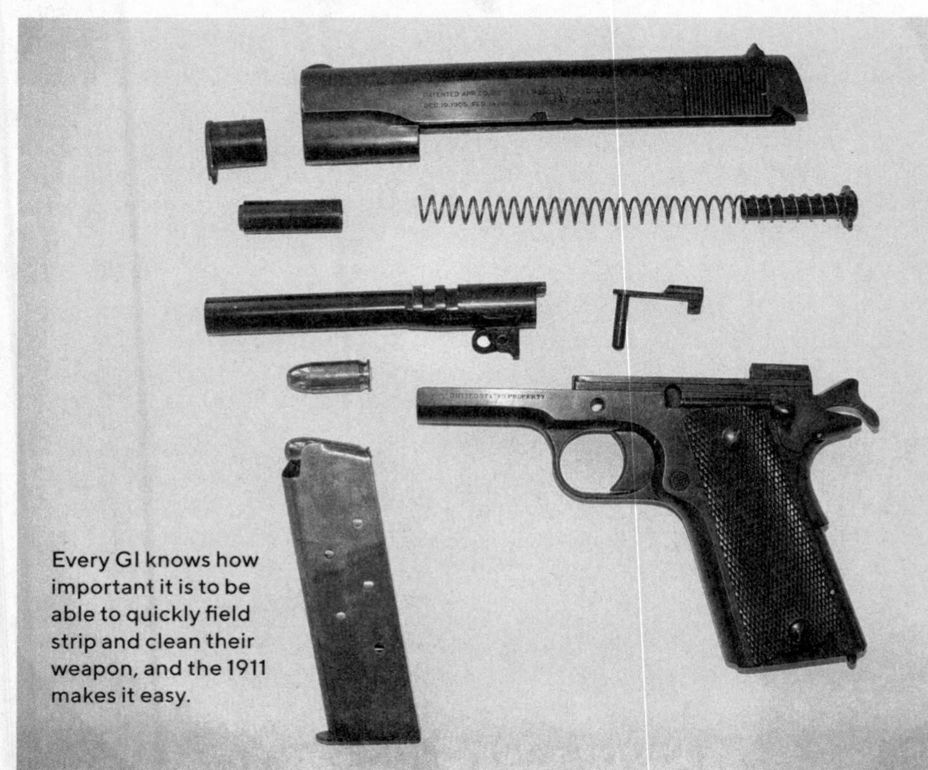

Every GI knows how important it is to be able to quickly field strip and clean their weapon, and the 1911 makes it easy.

The original grip of the military GI 1911 was made of checkered brown plastic. The long trigger and lack of a relief cut in the frame behind the trigger show this to be an early 1911, not a 1911A1.

than the John M. Browning-designed Model 1911. For over a century, it has played a pivotal role for our U.S. military troops. It was the handgun that many of our soldiers carried on their hip into battle during World Wars I and II, the Korean Conflict and Vietnam. And, more recently, it played a pivotal role for some of our specialized U.S. Army Special Forces and Marine Corps units involved in the Persian Gulf conflicts of Desert Storm, Operation Iraqi Freedom and Operation Enduring Freedom.

One of the distinct advantages of the military-issue 1911 is how easily repairable it is in the field. This is due to the lack of tolerances of the working mechanisms, which allow easy swapping of the parts even while on the battlefield. While this characteristic certainly doesn't lend itself to a high degree of shooting accuracy, that ability served our troops well in battle situations.

I once heard a high-ranking U.S. general being questioned as to why the 1911 had such a long tenure of use with the U.S. forces. I'm sorry to say, I can't recall which general that was, but his reply was a noteworthy one. He said that the military never considered the 1911 to be a tack-driving weapon and few enemies were ever actually shot or killed by one. However, he went on to say that they were considered worthwhile more for psychological reasons. Just the knowledge that a large-caliber handgun was strapped to the hip of a GI provided a significant degree of confidence when in battle, and that in itself was considered a desirable commodity in a battle-type situation.

As one would expect, the model name "1911" is indicative of the initial year of production. The Government Model continued to be produced for nearly six decades, ending in 1970. Over that time the model changed very little, but in 1923 a couple of improvements were made that included the replacement of the mainspring housing with a checkered arched housing and replacement grip safety spur with a longer one. These features are included on the M1911A1. Most of the government-issued handguns came with the typical parkerized finish, while the commercial versions were most often blued, with a letter "C" added to the serial numbers.

Over the years, to fulfill the needs of the military, Colt granted permission to various other manufacturers to produce the 1911, including Ithaca Gun Co., North American Arms Co. Ltd. (Canada), Remington Rand Co., Remington UMC, Singer

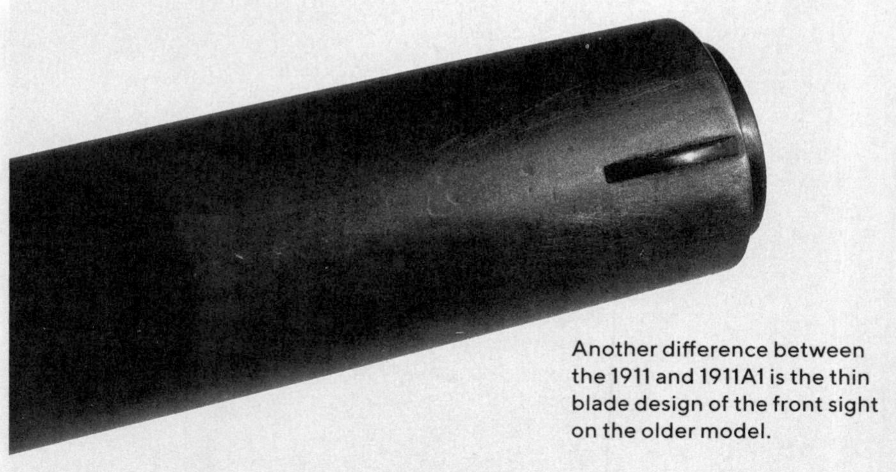

Another difference between the 1911 and 1911A1 is the thin blade design of the front sight on the older model.

This Model 1911 was built by Colt in 1917. Note the "United States Property" rollmark.

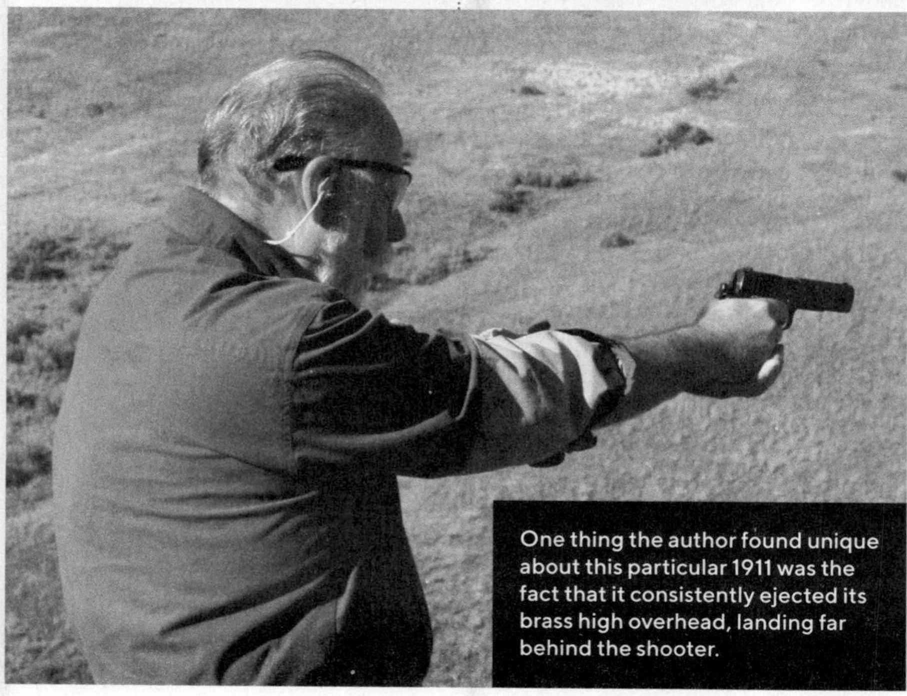

One thing the author found unique about this particular 1911 was the fact that it consistently ejected its brass high overhead, landing far behind the shooter.

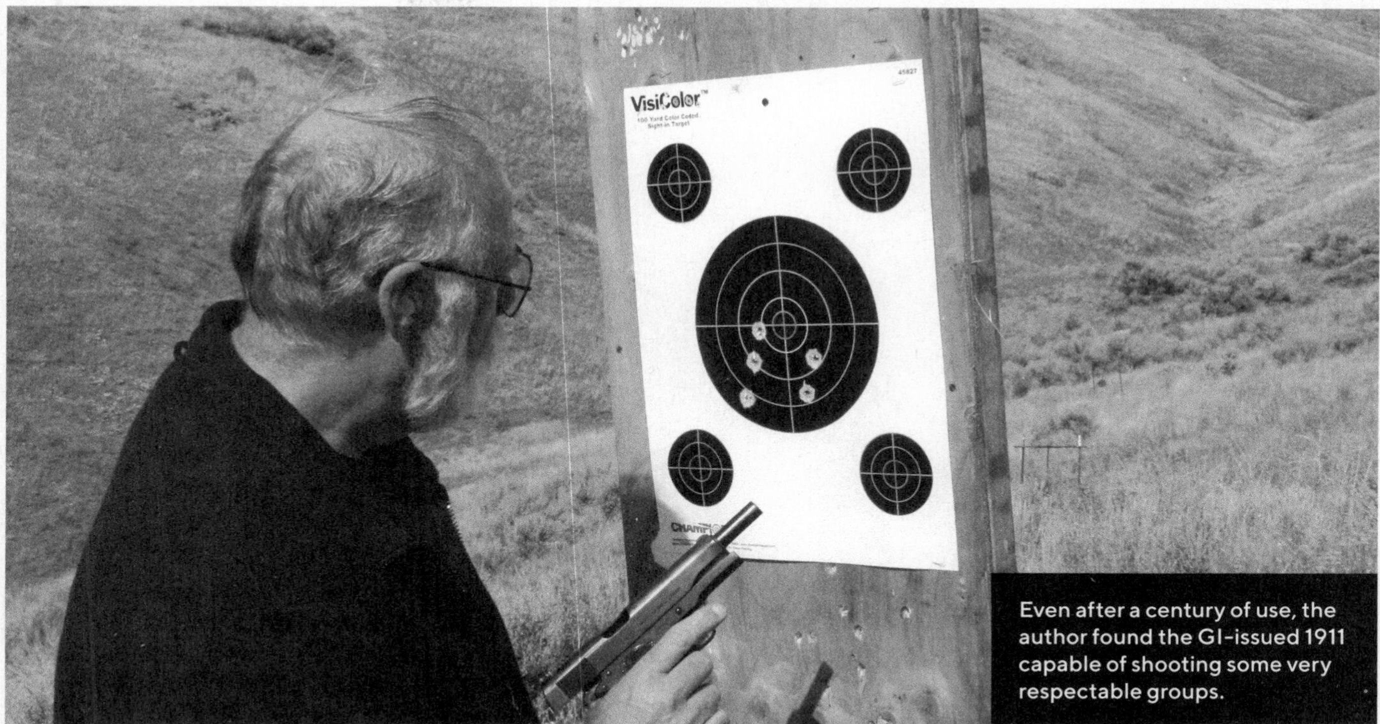

Even after a century of use, the author found the GI-issued 1911 capable of shooting some very respectable groups.

Sewing Machine Co., and Union Switch & Signal Company, and some were made at the Springfield Armory.

My Brother's GI 1911

Tony's blind purchase came with a certain amount of risk, even when acquired through the very respectable NRA. Nevertheless, when the 1911 finally arrived, he was pleasantly surprised by its nearly new condition. It was one of the earlier-produced 1911s — built more than 100 years ago in 1917 and, as such, it has become a cherished heirloom in his family. Sadly, however, he developed an urge to spiffy up its appearance and eventually shipped it off to a gunsmith to have the parkerizing removed and the gun blued. Even though that bluing added a certain amount of eye appeal, we both regret it wasn't kept in its original state.

I admit I foster a certain amount of jealousy over not being able to take advantage of those NRA sales years, but I have shot and used my brother's 1911 on many occasions and found it to be an absolutely remarkable firearm. Further adding to his gun's appeal is the fact that we were able to garner a few rounds of military surplus ammunition from the WWII and Korean timeframe. While it's always a bit bold to fire old ammunition when you have no knowledge of how those cartridges have been stored and handled, I couldn't resist seeing how the ol' warhorse 1911 would do when reunited with the shells of its era.

I began by first pulling a few of the bullets from those cartridges to inspect the contents. I was pleasantly surprised at what I found. The powder showed no obvious signs of clumping or attrition and I could not detect any unusual or acidic odors, which would have indicated a deterioration of the chemical composition of the powder. The powder essentially appeared as pristine as it must have been when loaded over seven decades earlier. While I certainly wouldn't recommend others do the same, I decided to reseat the bullets and head to the range for a reunion party of sorts between firearm and ammunition. What I found quite impressive was how the old cartridges shot every bit as well as the modern-day ammo I fired. The old stuff functioned perfectly in the gun, cycled reliably, and shot what I view as some remarkable groups.

One thing I found just a bit unusual was the fact that, while most semi-autos eject empty cases in a more lateral fashion out the ejection port and to the right, this 1911 launched them high overhead — depositing them quite some distance behind me. I wonder if this was a planned characteristic for a battle weapon or whether it was just an unforeseen characteristic of the design. I suppose it would make a certain amount of sense in a tight battle situation for the empties to be thrown far behind the shooter where there would be less chance of interfering with comrades.

The Way I See It

It seems like nearly every firearms manufacturer today is offering their own line of 1911s, many of which are beautiful and impressive weapons with a high degree of shooting accuracy. Likely, my brother Tony's model, as well as the other GI 1911s, would pale in comparison when it comes to overall accuracy. Nevertheless, none of those hold the historic significance that my brother's does. It's an asset that our country carried into battle and a firearm that I'm sure will stay in our family for many decades to come.

SPECIFICATIONS

MANUFACTURER: Colt's Manufacturing Company
MODEL: 1911
MANUFACTURED: 1917
CALIBER: .45 ACP
WEIGHT: 39 oz.
SIGHTS: Fixed rear and front
ACTION: Semi-auto, recoil operated, single action
BARREL LENGTH: 5 in.
OVERALL LENGTH: 8.5 in.
GRIPS: Checkered plastic
MAGAZINE: Z-stacked magazine holding 7 cartridges

A recent-production Deluxe Model 48 AL with Prince of Wales-style buttstock. Photo: GunsAmerica

FRANCHI 48 AL
THE WORLD'S LIGHTEST AUTOMATIC

BY **NICK HAHN**

Shotgun makers have always tried to come up with a lighter gun. A model may start out as an average 7 1/2-pound 12-gauge shotgun, but sooner or later there will be an attempt to lighten that gun if possible. Some models cannot be lightened without drastic changes and expense, so the lightening process never takes place. Others, from time to time, do undergo some weight-reducing mods.

The British mastered the art of lightening the double gun. Barrels were thinned, stocks hollowed, reducing a 12-gauge double to 6 pounds. The English gunmakers also reduced the weight of their doubles by producing shorter-chambered guns, like the 2-inchers that required less thickness in barrel walls and actions. They also made the "Twelve Twenties," a 12-gauge that started out normal size at the chamber/breech end but narrowed to a 20-gauge size at the muzzle. Since English doubles were essentially handmade, the lightening process was something that could take place under the judicious eye of the master gun maker as the shotgun was being built. With repeating shotguns, which are (with some rare exceptions) assembly line products, such care and attention could not be given, so a different approach had to take place.

Of all the leading autoloading shotguns on the market at the end of World War II, none weighed less than 7 1/2 pounds in 12 gauge, while most tipped the scales at well over 8. Very simply put, autoloaders were heavy. To get a light gun, one had to pay more and go for an imported double, since domestic doubles tended to be heavy as well. In 20 gauge, you could get a fairly light autoloader in the new Remington Model 11-48 at around 6 1/2 pounds, but there was nothing that could truly be called a featherweight autoloader.

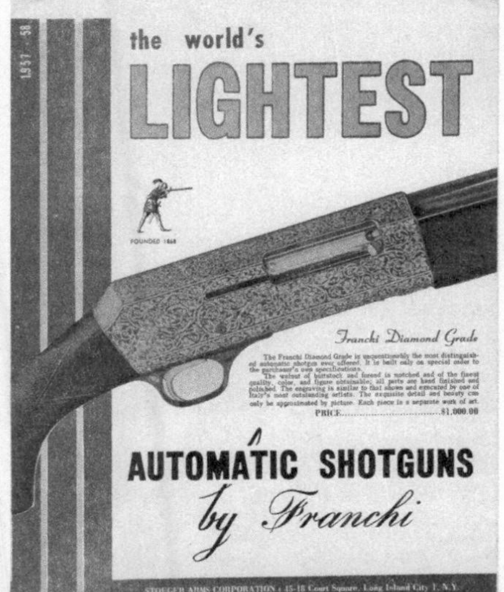

From the 1957 Franchi catalog, the custom-ordered Diamond Grade Model 48 AL featured hand engraving, hand fitting and finest-quality walnut.

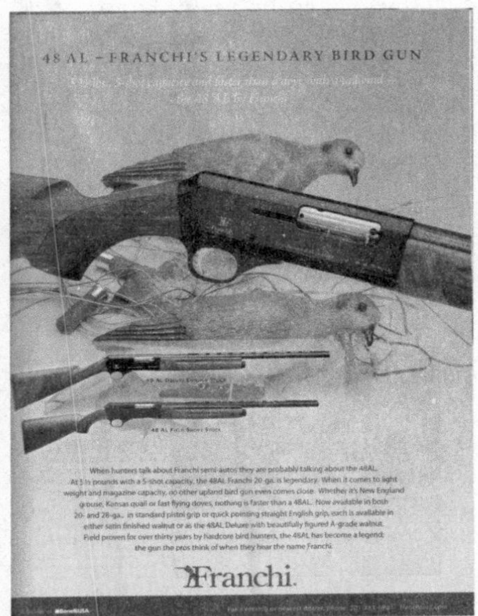

This advertisement features models of the Franchi 48 AL that were imported by Benelli from 1999 to 2016.

However, one autoloader that appeared shortly after the end of World War II was a true lightweight. It was the amazing Franchi 48 AL. The Franchi (pronounced "FRAHN-kee") 48 AL was advertised as the "World's LIGHTEST Automatic" shotgun, and at the time of its first appearance in America, and until more recent years, it was indeed the world's lightest. There may have been other autoloading shotguns that were lightweight — such as the Armalite AR-17 that weighed 5 1/2 pounds in 12 gauge — but none lasted very long. In contrast, the Franchi 48 AL lasted from 1948 until 2016 in the U.S. When the Luigi Franchi Company sold out, others continued to produce the gun. So, the 48 AL has been in continuous production since 1948, in one form or another.

The 48 AL is basically a modified and modernized version of Browning's long-recoil autoloader. The Franchi company knew they needed a repeating shotgun to be competitive in the post-war era, especially in the American market. So, they immediately launched into developing an autoloader as soon as the war ended. In 1948, Franchi introduced the new autoloader, the 48 AL; the numbers 48 stand for the year of the design, and the letters "A" for automatic and "L" for lightweight. At the same time, the company partnered with Stoeger to be the main importer of the shotgun into the United States.

The Franchi 48 AL appeared in the U.S. in late 1949, available in 12 gauge only, and was advertised to weigh 6 1/4 pounds. In reality, the gun weighed closer to 6 3/4 pounds, but you could get one that weighed close to 6 1/4 if you chose one with a short barrel without a rib. The 48 AL was not inexpensive. It started at $176.00 at a time when the Browning A-5 "Light Twelve" cost $153.50.

I first became aware of and interested in the Franchi 48 AL in the 1950s through the ads in the pages of the outdoor press of the day. However, it was way beyond the financial means of a kid whose aspiration to own a shotgun was mainly centered on single-barrel single-shots (possibly a bolt action!) sold by Sears and other inexpensive retailers. The Franchi was just too rich, although I drooled at the pictures and read all the articles about the gun and dreamed of owning one someday. But there was considerable interest in the new autoloader from those who could afford it. After a few years, Franchi wisely lowered its price to be more competitive, pricing it like the Browning, and managed to carve out a niche in the market among upland hunters.

On the left, the author's long-sought-after Eldorado 20 gauge, on the right a Benelli-import in 28.

To lower its price, Franchi began its 1953 line with a model that was not engraved. It was still a few bucks more than the Browning but was at least in the same ballpark. Also, in that same year, Franchi introduced a 20-gauge model that was slimmer and much lighter than the 12 gauge. Browning did not have a 20-gauge Auto 5 until five years later, and it weighed a little over a pound more than the Franchi. The Franchi 20 gauge weighed around 5 1/4 pounds and was an immediate hit with upland hunters. In a sense, it was the 20-gauge 48 AL that kept the Franchi competitive. Although the 12 gauge sold well, it was the 20 that was the biggest seller in the U.S. Franchi had the Standard model as its flagship, followed by the Hunter model, which had some game scenes line-engraved, and the Eldorado model, which was beautifully hand-engraved with Florentine scroll. It was the top-of-the-line of Franchi 48 ALs.

In 1958, Franchi introduced the Custom

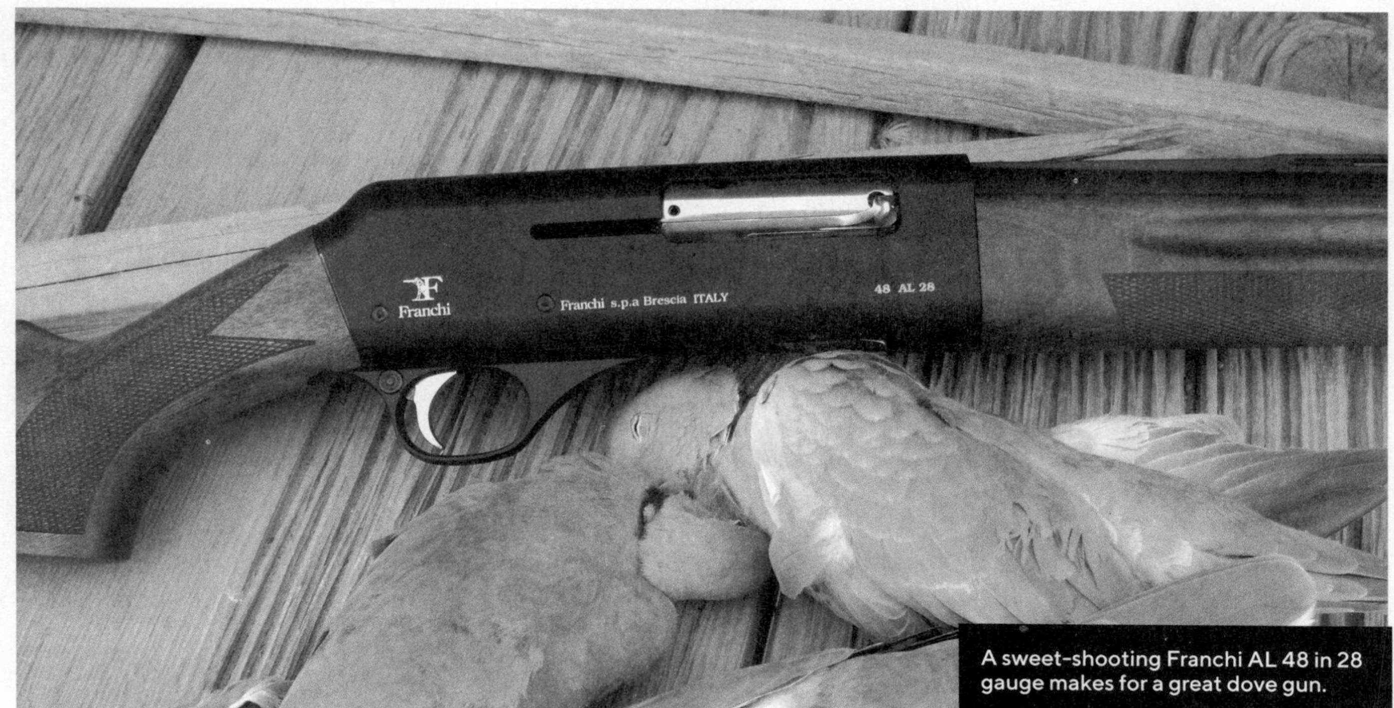

A sweet-shooting Franchi AL 48 in 28 gauge makes for a great dove gun.

Grade 48 ALs. These were entirely hand-built, gorgeously engraved and with exceptional wood. Concurrently with the introduction of the new Custom Grades, Franchi presented a Custom 48 AL autoloader to President Dwight Eisenhower. Naturally, the engraving was one of a kind. Eisenhower, who was an avid quail hunter, commented that it was the most beautiful shotgun that he had ever seen.

Despite American shooters' mistrust of alloy receivers, Franchi's receiver held up quite well, and in a way helped pave the way for acceptance of alloy receivers in America. But back in the day there were all kinds of unfounded rumors about alloy receivers blowing up or cracking. Franchi guaranteed its receivers for life and called them "Million Dollar Receivers!" So, despite the rumors of alloy failure, the Franchi quietly kept on selling.

I acquired my first Franchi 48 AL in 1969. It was a 20 gauge for which I paid $180. I was primarily an upland hunter at the time, so it suited me perfectly. I shot a lot of quail, snipe, dove and pheasant with that gun. I even managed to bag a few ducks that I jumped while upland gunning. By that time, there were other brands of lightweight autoloaders on the market. But to me, the Franchi was the best of the lot. Mine never failed, and I must have shot several thousand rounds of all kinds of ammo, including some questionable reloads.

In the early 1980s, Franchi sold the business and 48 ALs disappeared from the American market for a few years. Then, Beretta got into the business of expanding and acquiring other businesses. Beretta first bought the autoloader maker Benelli and, in turn, Benelli acquired Franchi in 1999.

Initially, the Benelli-imported Franchi 48 AL was available in 12, 20 and 28 gauges. But after a couple of years, the 12 was dropped for lack of sales and only the 20s and the 28s were imported. The new Benelli imports, with some minor changes, were made in two grades — Standard and Deluxe. There was also a fancier grade called the Fenice. Towards the end of the production period under Benelli, the manufacturing of 48 AL moved from Italy to Spain, at least for those guns that were imported by Benelli. Also, quite a few guns are found with "Made in Spain" marking on the receiver but with Italian barrels, sort of a mix-and-match arrangement.

Through the years, since my first Franchi 48 AL, I became interested in acquiring a higher-grade model. Franchi Custom Grades are literally impossible to get ahold of — at least I have never seen one offered for sale on the used gun market. The Hunter Grade was the most common upgrade that you could find both new and used. But I was interested in the Eldorado, which was rare, especially in 20. Apparently not that many were sold, and the model was discontinued in 1975, as were the Custom Grades.

Through the years I kept an eye out for an Eldorado 20 gauge. The 12-gauge models would turn up from time to time, but 20s were harder to find than the proverbial needle in a haystack. Finally, I located one about 20 years ago. It was reasonably priced, so I bought the gun sight unseen. The seller didn't know much about the gun. He didn't know it was an Eldorado model and just said that it was heavily engraved and described it as being in "pretty good shape." When I got it, I was pleasantly surprised that it was in excellent condition, showing hardly any use.

It was made in 1961, at a time when I could never dream of owning a Franchi 48 AL Eldorado. In 1961 it cost around $280.00, almost as much as a Browning Superposed over/under.

Today, after over half a century, the Franchi 48 AL is no longer imported into the U.S. However, many are available on the used market. It is a remarkable, old-school autoloader that was modernized to a point that it is still viable in this age of gas- and inertia-operated auto-loading shotguns. That says a lot for its design and durability. In Europe, lightweight shotguns have always been more popular than in America, and the Franchi 48 AL was always considered to be a premier autoloader. So, although it is no longer imported, this model will be around in the U.S. for a long time to come.

THE FANTASTIC LES BAER CONCEPT VI 1911

BY **ROBERT K. CAMPBELL**

How many handguns truly perform to your expectations? I'm talking about ones that operate with complete reliability. And are accurate — more accurate than you can hold? If you feel that the handgun is limiting your performance, you are among the top tier of shooters. If this describes you, then arguably you need a Les Baer handgun. Of the Les Baer line, you might want to take a gander at the Concept VI.

The 1911 is famous for its excellent hand fit, low bore axis and straight to the rear trigger compression. These attributes are not always reflected at their best in garden-variety handguns. After 40 years of firing 1911 pistols, my standards are high. I own several service-grade 1911s that give excellent service. My goal with the Les Baser Concept VI was to own a handgun that complemented my own skill and experience.

This is reflected in a price well over two thousand dollars. The pistol is worth its tariff, however, as it has lived up to its promise and then some. Over the past 12 months, I fired over 3,000 cartridges in this handgun without a single failure to feed, chamber, fire or eject. While I avoided burner-grade factory am-

The Les Baer Concept VI is a formidable handgun well worth its price.

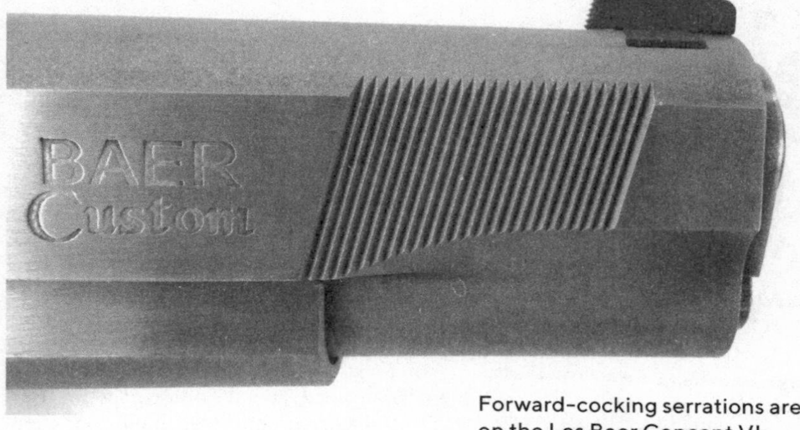

Forward-cocking serrations are well done on the Les Baer Concept VI.

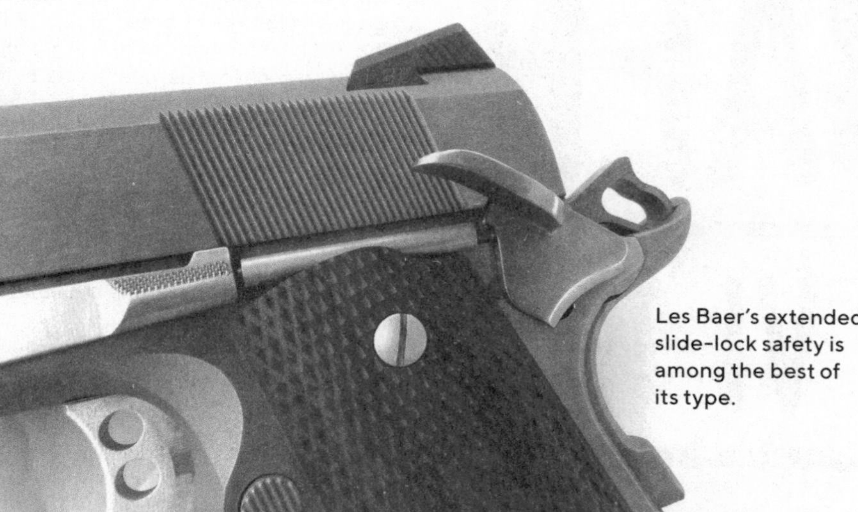
Les Baer's extended slide-lock safety is among the best of its type.

munition and handloads with low recoil impulse, this is impressive.

The pistol did not demand the specified break-in period. Using full-power handloads, the Concept VI came out of the box running and hasn't slowed down yet. I did not fire the piece as quickly as possible, in the "burnout" non-stop shooting torture test popularized on the Internet. This type of abuse doesn't prove anything. Handguns are meant to be cleaned and lubricated. Do so and they will last a lifetime.

Running a pistol dirty and dry will have an adverse effect on the machine and isn't an accurate representation of long-term reliability. I didn't waste ammunition in testing, but traveled to the range with a specific goal with each lot of ammo. Whether the goal was close quarters combat training or hitting a man-sized target at 100 yards, the pistol never failed to live up to my skill level. I have by no means discovered the full measure of the gun's accuracy. The Les Baer performed consistently and accurately.

The 30 LPI checkering gives the pistol excellent adhesion when firing.

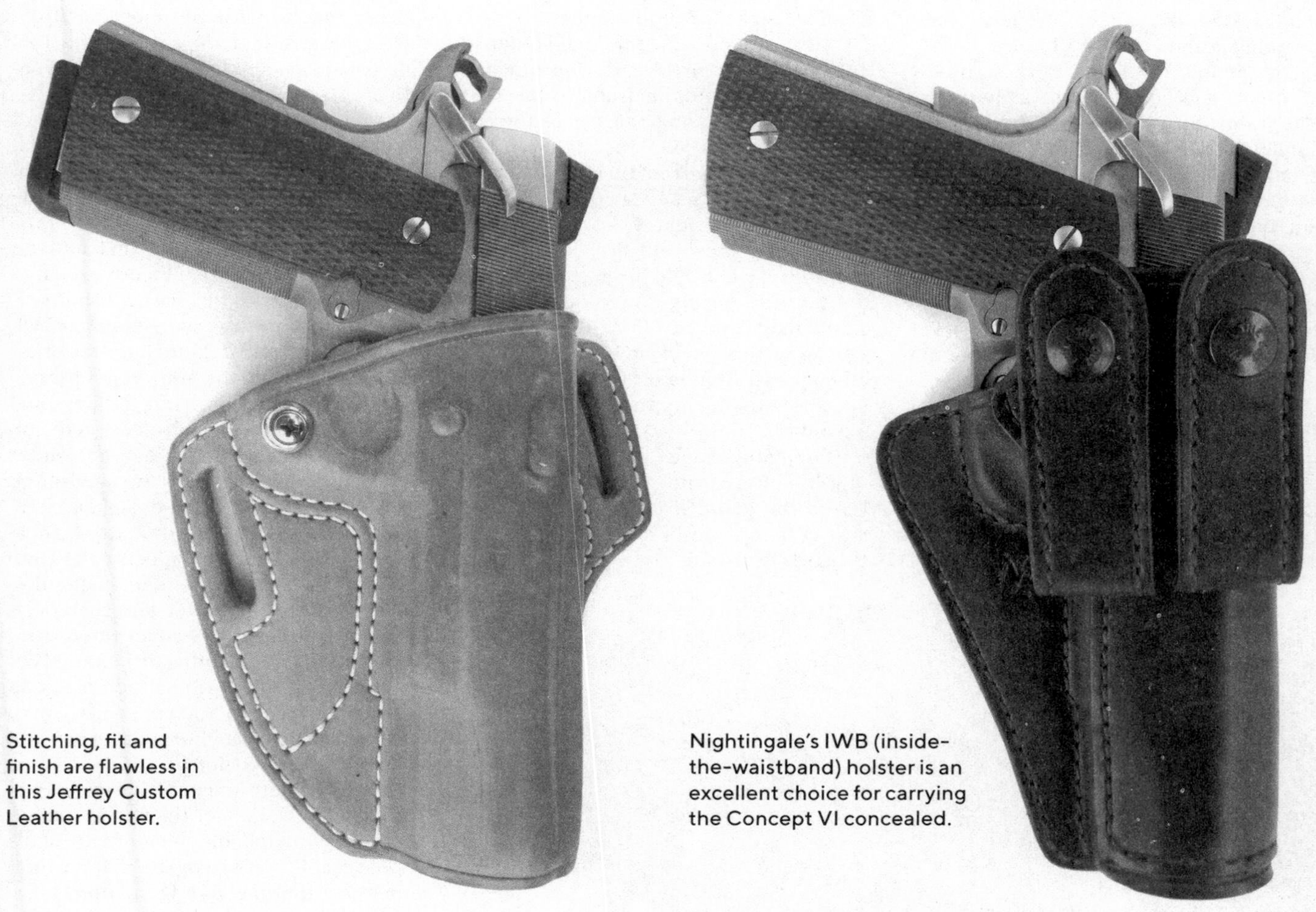

Stitching, fit and finish are flawless in this Jeffrey Custom Leather holster.

Nightingale's IWB (inside-the-waistband) holster is an excellent choice for carrying the Concept VI concealed.

Why the 1911 and why the Concept VI? I prefer the 1911-type handgun based on its good qualities. I don't use a 1911 because it is expected of me or because of a sense of history or emotional attachment, although these are important. I choose the 1911 based on performance. Speed to an accurate first shot, control during recoil, rapid shot recovery and practical combat accuracy are the long suits of the 1911.

Those choosing the 1911 are often dedicated handgunners and will exert the effort needed to master the handgun. The straight-to-the-rear trigger compression may be tuned to a very crisp let-off. I also like the peace of mind that comes with a positive slide lock and grip safety. The 1911 is flat and more easily concealed than other .45-caliber service pistols. The low bore axis sits low in the hand and limits muzzle flip.

Les Baer offers several variations on the 1911, including compact handguns and target sighted pistols. I chose the Concept VI after much thought. It's a stainless-steel gun with many good features. The slide-to-frame fit is excellent. The pistol is tight, very tight, out of the box, requiring some effort to rack the slide. The fit of the barrel, barrel lugs, barrel bushing and link is superb. I've done considerable work in fitting barrels, and the fit of the Les Baer is flawless.

The pistol features a crisp trigger action that breaks at 4 pounds. There is some take-up but no creep or backlash. It features excellent all-around combat sights. I prefer fixed sights for this application. I use the 230-grain bullet weight for most chores and it isn't difficult to properly sight the pistol with such a projectile. The Concept VI is properly regulated for 230-grain loads from the factory.

The slide is well finished, with cocking grooves both forward and in the conventional rear position. The hammer is skeletonized, and the trigger is a target type. The safety has a sharp indent with a positive snap as it locks into place. Modern 1911 handguns sometimes fit loose in this area, and that's the type of handgun you need to walk away from. The Les Baer is a fine example of proper fitting.

The grip safety is a modern beavertail type that leads the hand into the grip in speed drills and keeps the bore axis lower. The grip safety releases its hold on the trigger about halfway into compression. The frame features 30 line-per-inch (LPI) front strap checkering. In speed drills or when your hand is sweaty or cold, this is a great addition to the handgun. The pistol is supplied with a spare magazine. Les Baer magazines are well designed and present the bullet nose a little higher into the chamber than do GI-type 1911s.

I mentioned I did not experience any break-in malfunctions. If other shooters do, this is fairly standard for the Les Baer. Some years ago, I owned the Les Baer Monolith and experienced a handful of failures of the slide to go into battery when that pistol was new. These disappeared after perhaps 200 rounds. I lubricated the pistol liberally when breaking in the Concept VI.

For testing, my loads were standard hardball equivalent with a hardcast 230-grain round-nosed lead bullet over enough Titegroup for 830 fps. Alternately, an all-around load, the Magnus 225-grain flat point cast bullet hits hard and delivers impressive accuracy. I load it at 850 fps for pin shooting, target practice or long-range work. I've also experimented with the 200-grain semiwadcutter at 900 to 1,050 fps. While this, too, is an accurate bullet, it just seems the 230-grain weight works best for my needs.

When using these loads, I put my best foot forward and concentrated on marksmanship. Paper punching is a good thing and you must confirm sight regulation. But firing at small targets at known and unknown ranges is more a test of the marksman. The good sights, excellent balance and clean trigger break of the Les Baer make for good results.

I also practiced personal defense drills with the pistol. Drawing quickly, meeting the hands in front of the belt buckle, and shoving the pistol toward the target gave stellar results. Speed to a first hit is what the 1911 is all about. I usually practice smooth presentations from concealed carry ending in one shot. I also draw and fire double taps and address multiple targets. I don't see the point in hosing down a target with a full magazine of .45-caliber rounds. The first shot is most important, and all concentration is on making it count. I practice taking my time quickly to get a good hit.

The pistol comes with a guarantee of a 3-inch five-shot group at 50 yards. I fired the pistol from the Bullshooters rest, a handy aid in marksmanship. Fifty yards is a long poke for iron sights. I used my own handloads and backed up my results with the most accurate factory loads, including the Black Hills 230-grain jacketed hollowpoint and Federal's 230-grain Match.

At this point I've reached the limits of my shooting skills, and I cannot equal the factory guarantee, but I fired several five-shot groups with three shots inside 3 inches at 50 yards, with some fliers. Shooting from a solid rest isn't offhand shooting, but these results are excellent by any standard. At 25 yards, I shot several 1.5-inch groups with a single brilliantly clustered 1.25-inch group that made my day and the gun's reputation.

When I carry the pistol for personal defense it rides in a Professional holster from Jeffrey Custom Leather under a draping garment. This holster offers real speed and is a well-designed scabbard that presents an ideal draw angle and a good balance of speed and retention. When I must move to an inside-the-waistband (IWB) holster and the covering garment need only cover the pistol's handle, I use the Nightingale Leather IWB holster. With a dual loop attachment and hard boning, it's a fine concealed carry holster that is as comfortable as any and offers good concealment.

The Les Baer Concept VI is my idea of a perfect 1911. I'm not the perfect shooter, but the pistol complements the skills I possess. If you are in the market for a once-in-a-lifetime handgun, don't wait as long as I did. Give the Concept VI a whirl — I'd bet it gives your skills a run for their money, like it did mine.

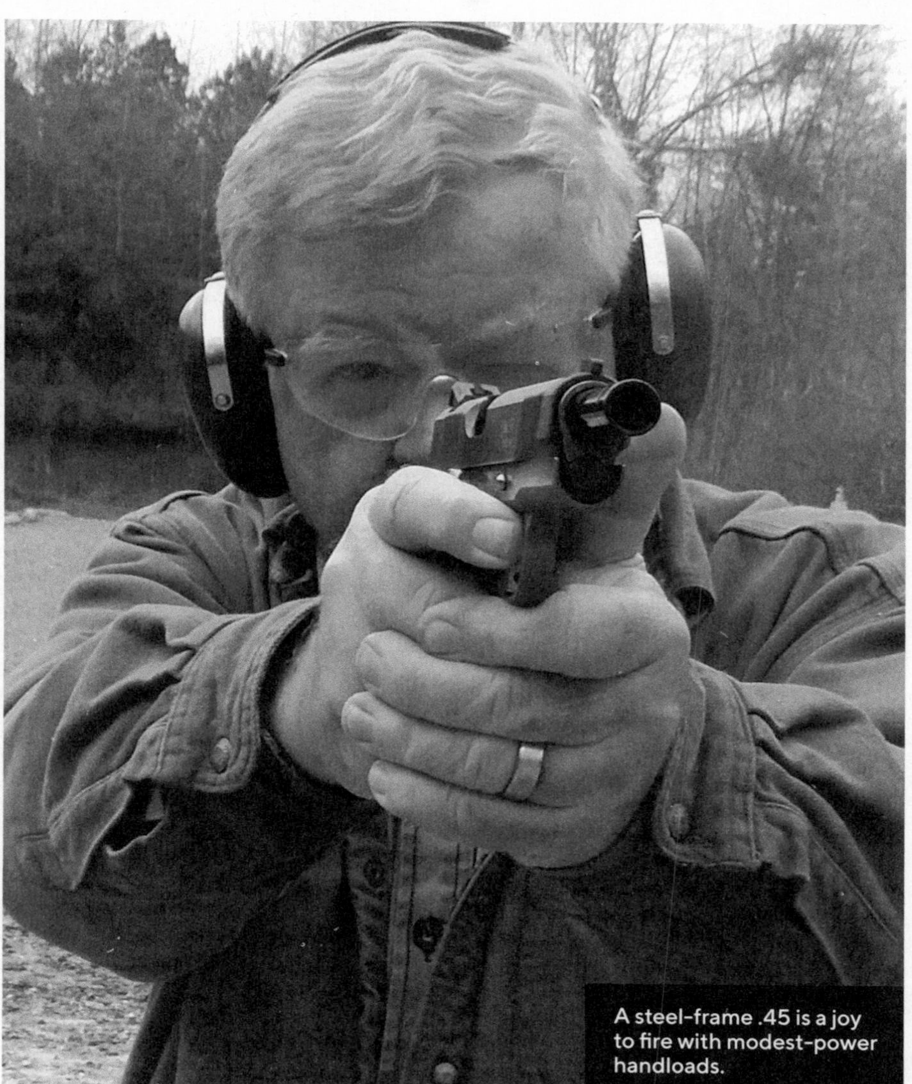
A steel-frame .45 is a joy to fire with modest-power handloads.

CONTACTS

Black Hills Ammunition
Black-Hills.com

Brownells.com (Bullshooters rest)
Brownells.com

Federal Cartridge Company
Federalpremium.com

Hodgdon Powder Company
Hodgdon.com

Jeffrey Custom Leather
JeffreyCustomLeather.com

Magnus Cast Bullets
Magnusbullets.com

Nightingale Leather
Nightingaleleather.com

Les Baer Inc.
LesBaer.com

Henry Single-Shot .243 Rifle

BY **AL DOYLE**

In a field where "tacticool" has become more than just a popular buzzword for marketers, why would a company produce a new line of firearms that could fit right in with the gun market of 1905? Check out the extensive selection of single-shot rifles and shotguns from Henry Repeating Arms that fits this description. These old-style singles come in five calibers — .223, .243, .308, .44 Magnum and .45-70 — and debuted in late 2017. Henry sent a .243 model for review, and several things were obvious even before I took the gun to the range.

The rifle's wood was dense, dark and nicely grained, which seems to be the rule with Henry products. At a time when black polymer stocks are quite popular, seeing wood on a rifle can be a flashback experience, and even more so when a prime cut has been turned into a stock. Likewise, the rich bluing was pleasing to the eye. Amazingly, all of this came on a gun with a manufacturer's suggested retail price of just $448.

It would be easy to assume that Henry obtains wood from the abundant tree crop near its Rice Lake, Wisconsin, assembly plant, but the company relies on other suppliers.

Henry's handy little single-shot rifles are available in blued or stainless steel, in a variety of common centerfire hunting calibers. Photos: Henry Repeating Arms

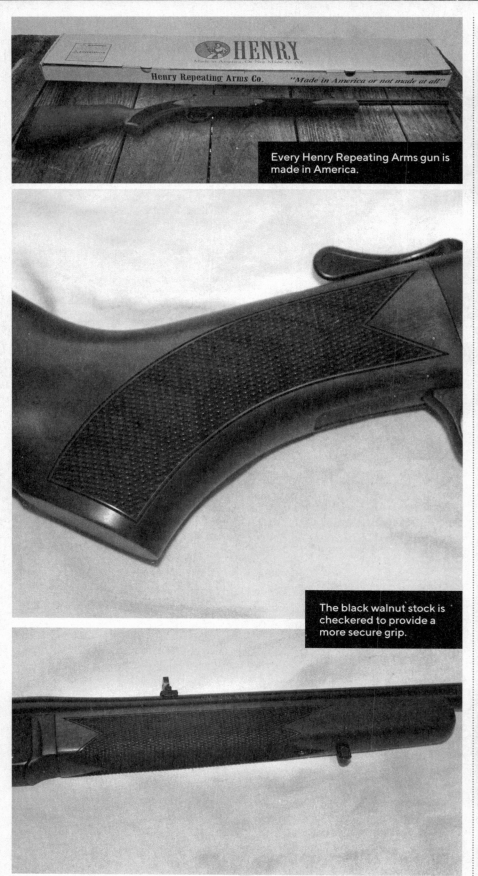

Every Henry Repeating Arms gun is made in America.

The black walnut stock is checkered to provide a more secure grip.

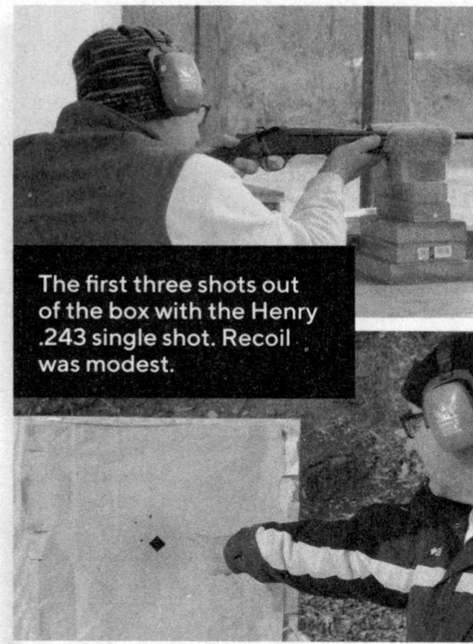

The first three shots out of the box with the Henry .243 single shot. Recoil was modest.

"We use American black walnut sourced from Missouri, Nebraska and Kansas," said Henry Arms owner Anthony Imperato. American is the operative word here, as Henry's motto is "Made in America, or not made at all."

Henry's new line of singles comes with an ambidextrous locking lever that opens the action when pushed to the left or right. Since there is no bolt in the face, this type of action is especially well suited for left-handers.

Upper Midwest winter weather made it difficult to take the rifle out for testing. A brief trip to the range on a blustery day provided some trigger time with the Henry. Giving up deer hunting many years ago meant I was rusty on shooting guns made for the field, so there was a certain eagerness to try this one out.

The mild recoil of the .243 Winchester cartridge combined with an ample rubber recoil pad made the Henry soft on the shoulder. Clearly, this single shot would be a good choice for a wide range of hunters. It's capable of bagging whitetail or mule deer, pronghorn antelope and small- to medium-sized hogs.

Testing was done with an adjustable folding rear leaf sight paired with a brass

Single-shot rifles work very well for left-handers.

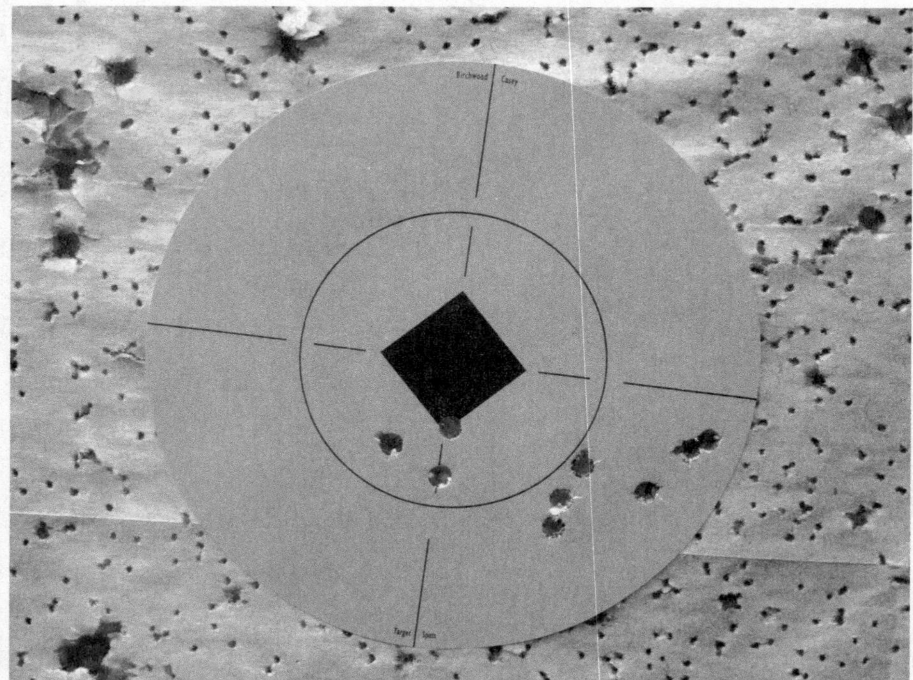

This target includes a trio of 3-shot groups from a benchrest at 50 yards. The two groups on the right were shot with Winchester 100-grain ammo, while the center triangle is from Remington 100-grain rounds.

Known for its lever-action rifles and carbines, Henry also makes a line of very classy and affordable single-shot shotguns, like this attractive brass receiver model. Photo: Henry Repeating Arms

bead at the tip of the barrel. This setup will work at short range, but the rifle comes drilled and tapped with three holes to accommodate optics mounts, so most hunters will opt for a scope mounted on a Weaver 82 rail. Some experimenters have gone to a red-dot sight on a Picatinny rail, which might seem odd on such an old-school rifle. It isn't difficult to visualize an adjustable peep sight on the Henry as a classier option.

My first few offhand shots were in the 2 1/2-inch range from 50 yards offhand, but cold and shooter error are to blame for groups opening up after that. Winchester and Remington 100-grain ammo was used. With more practice time in a warmer climate and the addition of a scope, there's no doubt the Henry has minute of angle potential.

The 22-inch barrel has a twist rate of 1:10 and, when combined with the short action of a single shot, makes for a dandy rifle that handles smoothly and carries nicely while hiking in the woods. I didn't put a gauge on the trigger, but it broke around 6 to 7 pounds — lighter than a double-action revolver. Generous checkering provides a firm grip, and everything was assembled to tight tolerances. My only complaint was Henry's choice of an extractor rather than an ejector for spent cases.

All calibers are available with steel frames, but collectors might prefer the brass-framed version available in .44 Magnum and .45-70. (The MSRP is $576 for brass models.) Henry also produces a brass-framed single-shot shotgun in 12, 20 and .410 gauges. Prices for steel and brass-framed shotguns are identical to the single-shot rifles.

One-round rifles are a niche market with dedicated fans. When Harrington & Richardson — the former leader in single-shot sales by volume — left that market a few years ago, it created a void that begged to be filled. Is that why Henry chose to add this new line of hunting arms?

"Consumers and some of our dealers asked us to make single shots," Imperato said. Since Henry is known for traditional lever-action rifles, extending the firm's line to single-shots makes sense.

Hunters who enjoy the challenge of going afield with just one round on tap have other reasons to opt for a single shot. These rifles are sleek and handle smoothly. A well-made single-shot is much more than a utilitarian game getter.

Looking for more of a hunting challenge? Take a Henry single-shot rifle or shotgun on your next trip. It combines simplicity and the art of the gunmaker.

Savage B22 F Rimfire Rifle

BY **TOM TABOR**

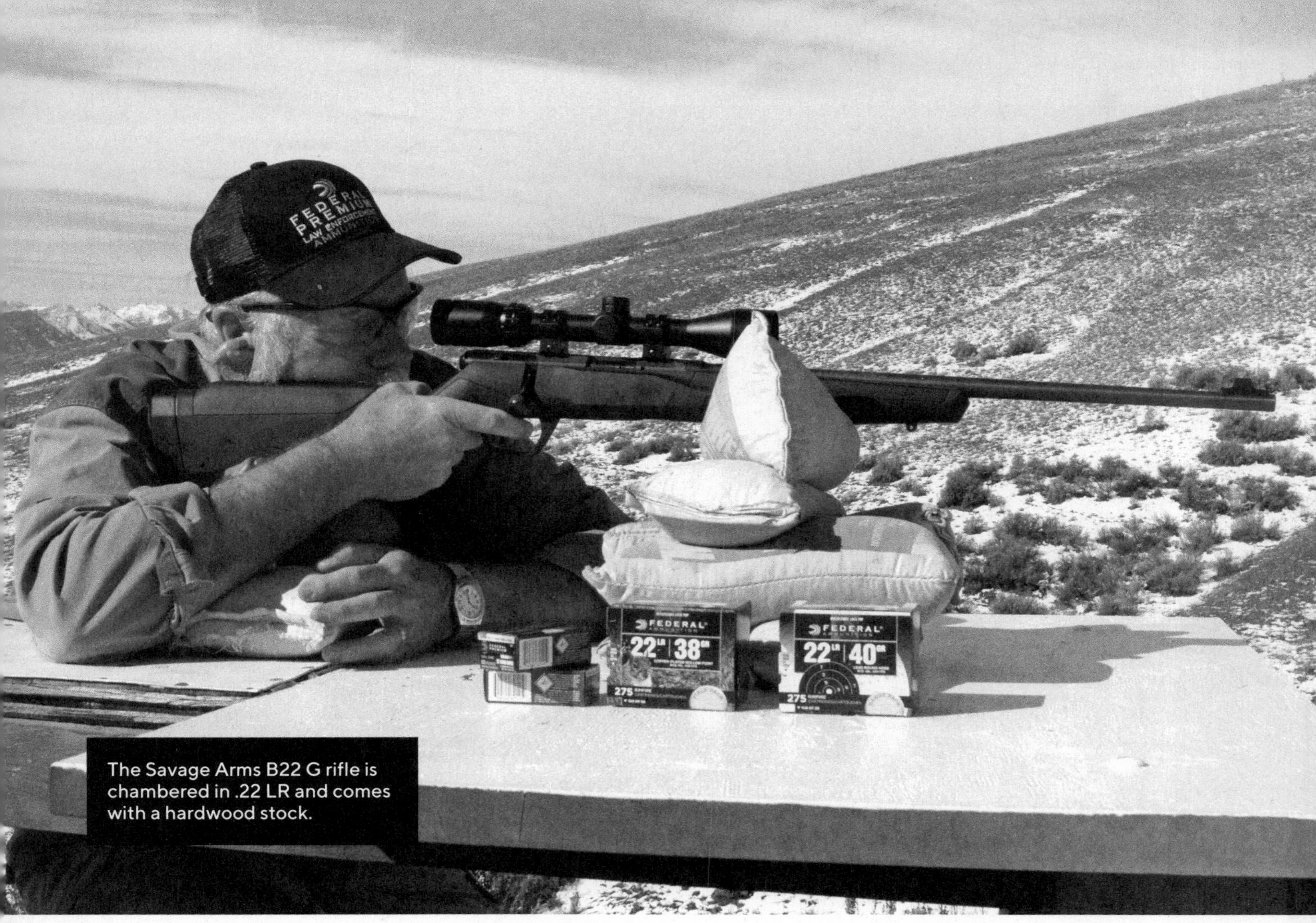

The Savage Arms B22 G rifle is chambered in .22 LR and comes with a hardwood stock.

In January 2013, Savage Arms introduced the first real competition to the phenomenally popular .17 HMR in the form of its new B-Mag bolt-action rifle. This was a brand-new rifle design that ushered in a more ballistically powerful rimfire cartridge — the .17 WSM (Winchester Super Magnum). To facilitate the project, an alliance was formed between Savage and Winchester, with the agreement that Savage would produce the new B-Mag rifles in that caliber and Winchester the ammunition. The result was a rifle that felt, handled and acted like a centerfire, yet was chambered for the new rimfire cartridge.

This powerful cartridge can launch the typical 20-grain .17-caliber bullet on its way nearly 28 percent faster than the .17 HMR. But if anyone thought that the .17 WSM was going to stifle the popularity of the .17 HMR, it's likely they were disappointed. While the .17 WSM B-Mag is still favored by some shooters today, I think it's safe to say it didn't rise to the expectations that some in the industry believed it would. What may be more important in the development of the B-Mag is the fact that it was essentially the first rifle in the company's new B-Series of firearms. And while there are many similarities between the ground-breaking B-Mag design and subsequent models, there are also some noteworthy differences. Possibly the most important of those is the fact that the B-Mag was designed to cock as the rifle bolt is being closed, while subsequent rifles in the series cock as the bolt is raised to eject the cartridge case.

Earlier, when I tested one of the B-Mag rifles, I found it took a certain amount of forward pressure against the bolt handle to close the action. While I didn't feel this

The .17 HMR-chambered B17 would be an excellent choice as a walkabout-style rifle for small game hunting and varmint shooting.

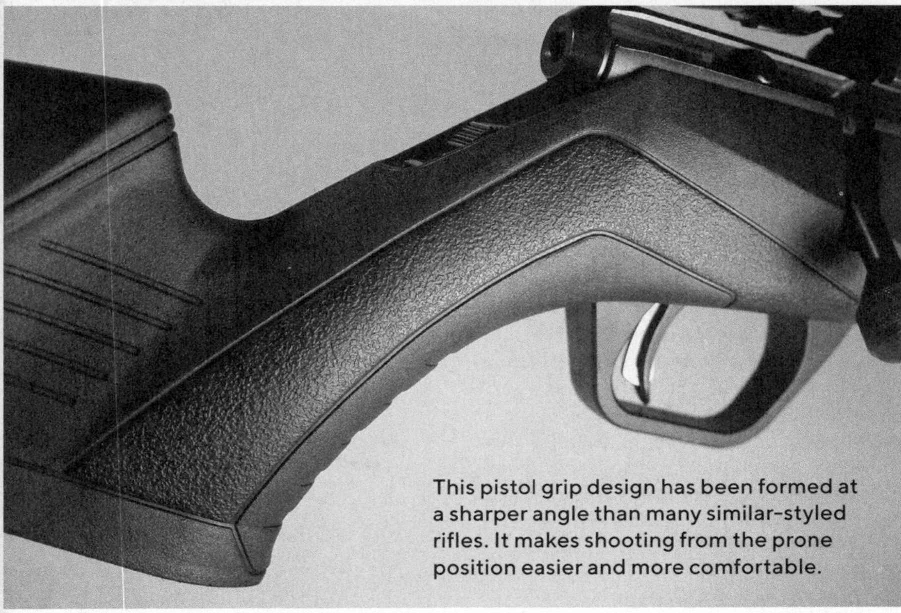

This pistol grip design has been formed at a sharper angle than many similar-styled rifles. It makes shooting from the prone position easier and more comfortable.

Savage Arms' rimfire B-Series rifles share many of the characteristics found in the company's centerfire line of rifles and are available with composite-style stocks.

The Savage Arms B22 G rifle is chambered in .22 LR and comes with a hardwood stock.

design was necessarily an unfavorable one, it did take me a while to get accustomed to that characteristic. However, some other shooters apparently found this trait a bit more annoying and voiced their concerns to Savage. I'm not sure whether those complaints were responsible for the design change in the latter B-Series models, but I view it generally as a favorable change.

Currently, there are three rimfire submodels within this latter B-Series lineup — the B22, B22 Magnum and B17. Those name designations reflect the cartridges the rifles are chambered to shoot, i.e. .22 LR, .22 WMR and .17 HMR. Within these sub-models there are a dozen configurations available, including those with composite stocks and three brand-new additions that have wood stocks. There is also a variety of barrel configurations from which to choose, including trim sporter-style barrels, heavy barrels, threaded heavy barrels (which have been made suppressor ready), stainless barrels and blued models. Like the company's popular A-Series rimfire rifles, all the B-Series guns feature a dependable 10-round rotary magazine. The safety on the B-Series has been conveniently located on the top of the receiver tang for easy accessibility while remaining in the shooting position. Also, in what I view to be a favorable characteristic, each rifle comes with the company's very popular Accu-Trigger.

To accommodate both the sporter and heavy barrel designs, Savage took the approach of making the barrel channel on the composite stock models large enough to accept either barrel diameter. Then, if the configuration called for a trim sporter barrel of smaller diameter, an insert made of the same stock material is screwed into the barrel channel. Obviously, this approach was taken as a cost-saving method to avoid having to inventory two separate style stocks, but I can see no downside to this approach, and when the insert is in place it would likely go unnoticed by most shooters.

Each B-Series rifle comes with a button-rifled 21-inch carbon-steel barrel with a twist rate appropriate to the cartridge. In this case, the B22 and B22 Magnum models come with a rate of twist of 1:16, while the B17s come equipped with 1:9-twist barrels. Like Savage's centerfire platform rifles, the B-Series features the same zero tolerance headspace design. In this case, each barrel is first threaded into its specific assigned action and the bolt is closed. Once that has been accomplished, a barrel locknut is tightened down in order to ensure the integrity of the perfect matching of those parts.

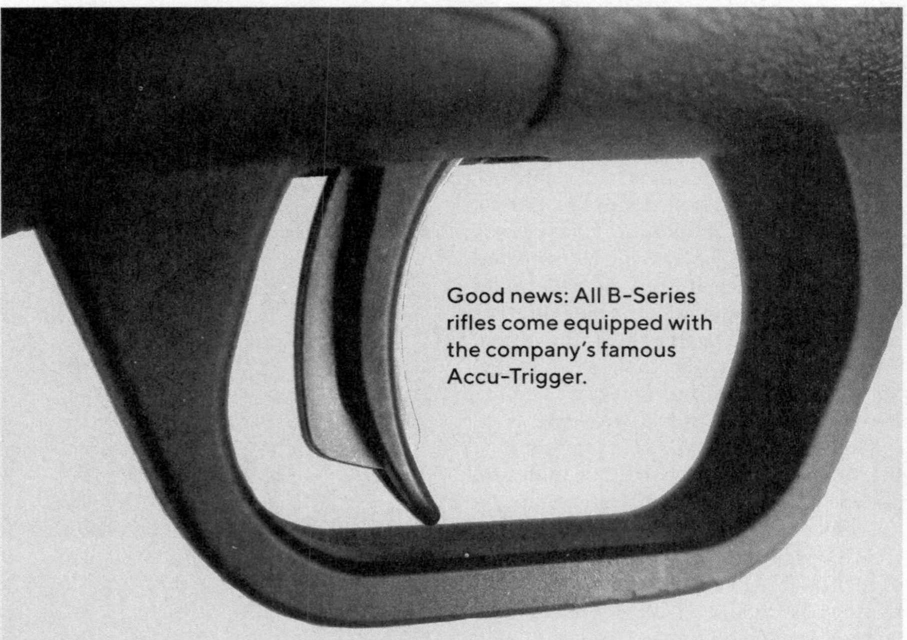

Good news: All B-Series rifles come equipped with the company's famous Accu-Trigger.

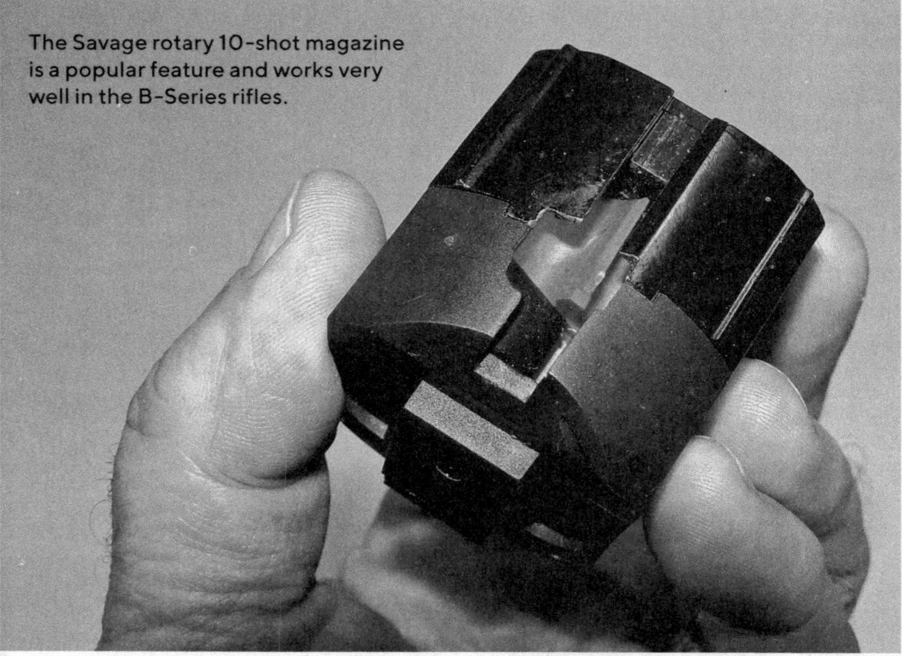

The Savage rotary 10-shot magazine is a popular feature and works very well in the B-Series rifles.

I obtained one of the Savage B-Series rifles in the sub-model B22 F, chambered in .22 LR. Like the other rifles in the B-Series it came equipped with an Accu-Trigger. I've always been a bit partial to this trigger, as it can be easily adjusted down to very light pull weights and still be safe and acceptable for field use. I found the factory had set the trigger to an average pull weight of only 2 pounds, 2-ounces, which I viewed as being nearly perfect for my needs, so I left it. Nevertheless, the ease at which this style of trigger can be adjusted is a real benefit that I frequently take full advantage of on my other Savage rifles. As is usually the case with Accu-Triggers, I found it to be crisp with little slop or pre-travel.

The fore-end of the stock was deeply grooved to accommodate the fingers of the shooter's off hand and both the fore-end and pistol grip are textured to discourage hand slippage. The angle of the pistol grip is slightly sharper than on many other similar-style stocks, making

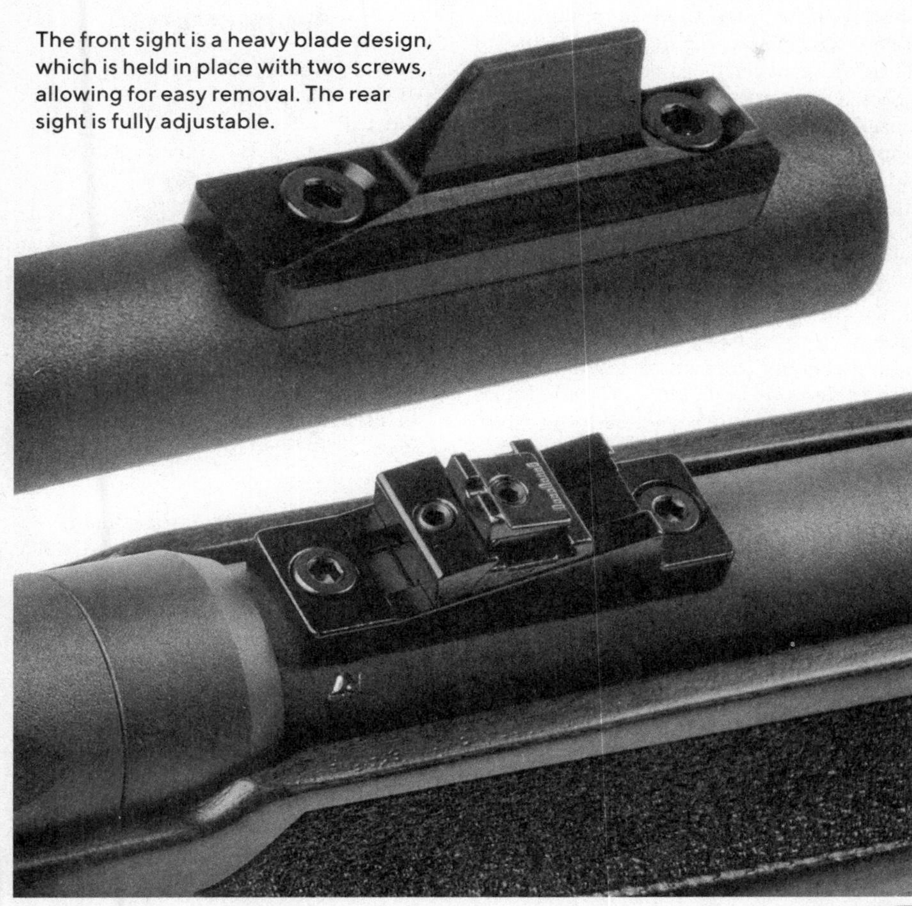

The front sight is a heavy blade design, which is held in place with two screws, allowing for easy removal. The rear sight is fully adjustable.

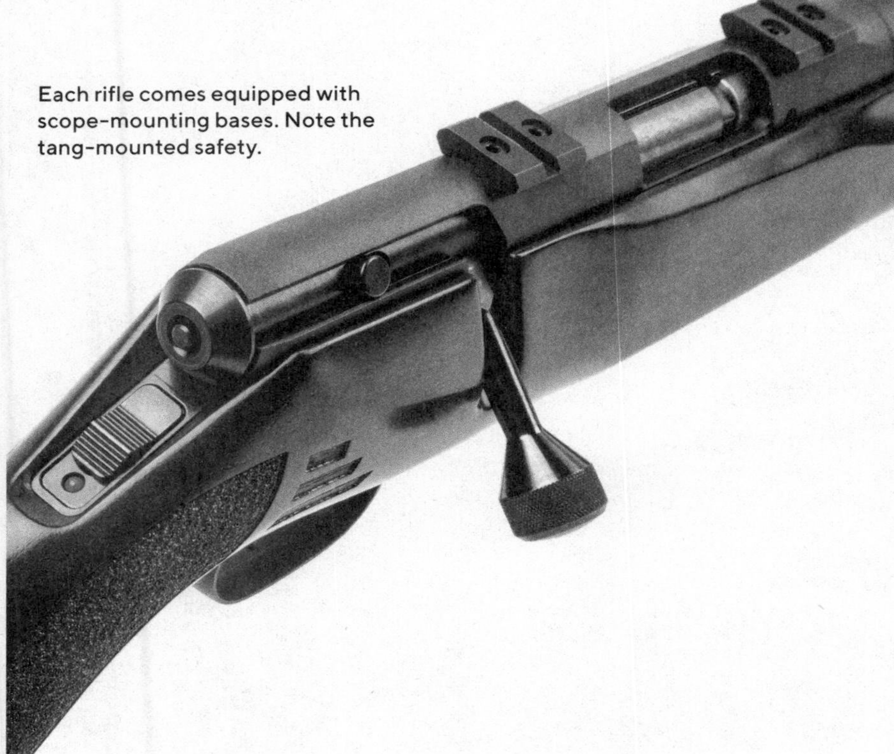

Each rifle comes equipped with scope-mounting bases. Note the tang-mounted safety.

shooting from the prone position easier and more comfortable. It also came with a slightly elevated comb, which helps to encourage better eye-to-scope alignment. And I found the rotary 10-shot magazine to be a favorable trait over the more typical banana-style magazines found on most other bolt-action rimfires. When in place, the magazine is flush with the bottom of the stock, blending in nicely and making it almost invisible to the eye. Like most new magazines, I found it to be a bit stiff to load, but after only a few loadings it loosened up considerably.

Even though my overall impression of the B-Series composite stocks is a favorable one, there was one feature that I found not so much to my liking: The trigger guard is formed as an integral part of the stock itself, molded in during the initial stock layup process. While this trend has become common in many of the low- to moderate-priced firearms today, it is one that I do not favor. I'm quite sure this design is cheaper to produce than the alternative of fabricating, inlet-

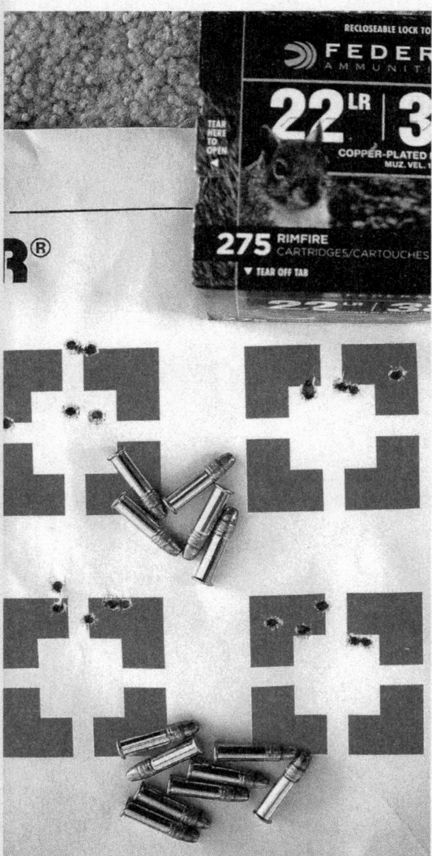

Even under less than hospitable shooting conditions, with wind gusting and extreme cold temperatures, the B22 F shot nice, tight groups.

ting and fitting a separate trigger guard piece and that is the reason for its growing popularity with manufacturers. Even though the trigger guard on the B22 F stock appeared durable and heavily constructed, if damage should occur to this area of the stock it could result in having to replace the entire stock rather than only the trigger guard.

The B22 F test rifle came with scope bases and, after mounting a Bushnell Banner 3-9X scope, I headed to a range to see how it would perform on paper. Sometimes even rimfire rifles prefer a particular type of ammunition or bullet design, so I chose to shoot three different Federal cartridges made up of different bullet weights and styles. That ammunition consisted of 38-grain copper-plated hollowpoints, 40-grain Hunter Match hollowpoints, and 40-grain lead round nose. The 38-grain cartridges were said to leave the muzzle at the relatively fast speed of 1,260 fps, while the other two generated the more standard .22 L.R. velocity of 1,200 fps.

Unfortunately, my range testing came at a time when less than hospitable conditions prevailed. Winds were gusty and temperatures frigid. Nevertheless, all the cartridges shot good groups. At 50 yards the ammunition with the 40-grain round-nose lead bullets seemed to group slightly better than the others, with the 5-shot groups averaging about 1 inch. The other cartridges came in with 5-shot group averages of about 1 1/2 inches. And possibly best of all, each of the cartridges impacted close to the same spot on the targets, making it possible to swap ammunition without necessarily worrying about repeatedly zeroing the rifle sights or scope reticles.

After sending several hundred rounds down the bore of the B22 F, I found the rifle performed flawlessly. The cartridges fed reliably from its rotary magazine and the empties ejected smoothly. I did find that the ejectors seemed to be a bit weak. Even though the empty cartridge cases always cleared the action as the bolt was opened, they usually landed only a short distance away. But because I recycle all my rimfire brass I found this characteristic made the retrieval of those empties easier.

Clearly, some compromises were made in the design and construction of the B-Series rimfire rifles. In most cases, those concessions were made to keep production costs and prices down. But in my opinion, those compromises have not severely affected the overall quality of these fine rifles. I found the favorable design of the zero tolerance headspacing to be a great feature, and the MSRP ranging from $281 to $413 for the composite-stocked models and $439 to $459 for the wood stock models certainly was appealing. In recent years, Savage Arms has come a long way when it comes to producing quality firearms and, in my opinion, the B-Series seems to be the perfect example of an equal balance between quality and the resulting savings to customers.

SPECIFICATIONS

MANUFACTURER: Savage Arms
MODEL: B-Series B22 F
CALIBER: .22 Long Rifle
BARREL: 21-inch button-rifled sporter barrel with a 1:16-inch twist
FINISH: Matte black
ACTION: Bolt
STOCK: Black ergonomic composite
TRIGGER: Savage Adjustable Accu-Trigger
SAFETY: Tang mounted
MAGAZINE: 10-shot removable rotary magazine
OVERALL LENGTH: 39 in.
LENGTH OF PULL: 13-1/2 in.
MSRP: $281.00 (B22 F)

The Savage Arms B22 F chambered in 22 LR is the perfect match when it comes to shooting ground squirrels.

THE TIPPMANN .44 MAGNUM ROLLING BLOCK RIFLE

BY **JIM DICKSON**

When I picked up the Tippmann rolling block rifle at Reeves Ace Hardware in Clayton, Georgia, my first impression was of an elegant 19th-century rifle but not a copy of the famed Remington rolling block. Tippmann Arms had definitely made its own version of this classic design. Instead of the 19th-century-style half octagon and half round barrel, this gun had a stepped round barrel that accomplished the same weight distribution and balance. The action was larger overall, deeper, and set at a steeper angle because it was originally designed for the Tippmann air rifle cartridges. The air rifle cartridges also needed a stronger hammer than the earlier Remington rolling blocks, and the hammer was made to a thicker, bolder design to fit the larger action. The result is not a copy of the classic Remington but an original Tippmann rolling block.

Tippmann's 8.5-pound .44 magnum rolling block hangs steady for offhand shooting and its 4-pound trigger pull gives it an accurate let-off. There is the traditional half-cock notch on the hammer to keep the hammer off the firing

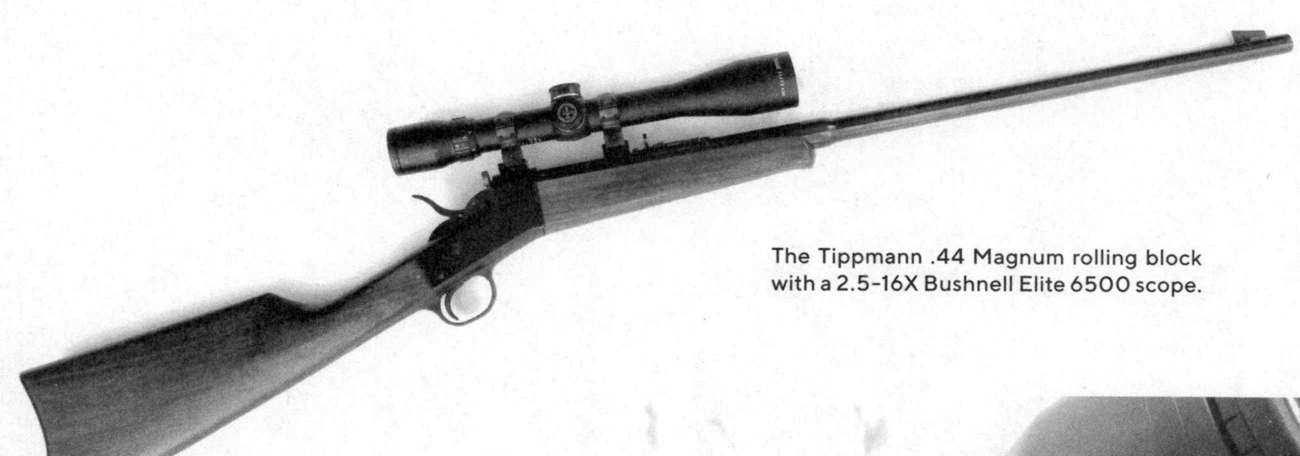

The Tippmann .44 Magnum rolling block with a 2.5-16X Bushnell Elite 6500 scope.

The rolling block action is shown open for loading.

pin when carrying the gun loaded. The 27-inch barrel has a 1 turn in 20-inch twist and the overall length is 43 inches. Length of pull is 13 1/2 inches and drop at heel is 3 7/8 inches. The gun is made of 4140 steel, except for the receiver, which is 1018. The wood is quality walnut and the slightly concave buttplate is steel with cross ribs instead of checkering. The satin finish is nicely blued. Everything is well made, a quality rifle. Instead of a leaf mainspring the Tippmann has a coil mainspring with the distinctive spongy feel of a modern coil.

The gun is also available in .357 magnum and .45-70 calibers, but I chose the .44 Magnum because it is a true all-around cartridge, capable of taking small game without ruining much meat, yet has also killed every species of big game in North America. The .357 Magnum makes a great small game gun but it is too small even for deer, in my opinion, much less larger animals. The .45-70 is great for deer and larger game but a lot of gun for squirrels and rabbits. The .44 Magnum is a true 19th-century meat gun, ready to shoot whatever size game presents itself for dinner.

In years past, this was a common hunting situation. You shot something, anything, or you went without supper. My late wife Betty and I faced the same sort of hunting in Alaska when we had trappers' licenses in the early 1980s and were living in a one-room log cabin. In the remote wilderness you really appreciate the simple reliability of a rolling block rifle as there is less to go wrong. This was one of the big reasons for the Remington rolling block's success and popularity on the American frontier.

TIPPMANN ROLLING BLOCK .44 MAGNUM TEST RESULTS

Qty. Fired	Load	Velocity (fps)	Penetration (Inches in ballistic gelatin)	Notes
100	Barnes Vor-Tx 225-gr. XPB HP	1,275	14-16	
60	Hornady 225-gr. FTX polymer-tip	1,410	16-18	
60	Hornady 240-gr. XTP JHP polymer-tip	1,350	18-20	
60	Hornady 300-gr. XTP polymer-tip	--	20+	
200	Black Hills 160-gr. Honeybadger	2,248*	27.75	*Out of a 20-inch barrel
40	Federal Fusion 240-gr. JHP	1,290	--	
40	Federal Premium 225-gr. Barnes Expander	1,280	--	
100	Federal American Eagle 240-gr. JHP	1,230	--	
50	Georgia Arms 240-gr. JHP "Deer Stopper"	1,325	--	
50	Georgia Arms 200-gr. "Deer Stopper"	1,650	--	
100	Load Up Ammunition.com 240-gr. Lead Flat Point	1,338	--	Coated bullet to prevent leading in the bore
100	Armscor 240-gr. Lead SWC Cowboy Action	1,080	--	In the .44 Magnum handgun allows a much faster second shot
50	Load-X 300-gr. FP	1,200	--	
40	Reed's Ammunition and Research 240-gr. soft point	1,500*	--	Factory velocity from 8.625-inch barrel
50	Reed's Ammunition and Research 300-gr. lead flat nose	1,340*	--	Factory velocity from 8.625-inch barrel
25	Precision Cartridge Co. 240-gr. lead SWC	--	--	
25	Precision Cartridge Co. 240-gr. JHP	--	--	
25	Precision Cartridge Co. 240-gr. flat point total copper jacket	--	--	
50	Sport Shooting 240-gr. plated hollowpoint	801	--	Best .44 Magnum load for rapid fire in a gunfight

The Tippmann points perfectly with the sights almost aligning themselves on the target. The gun is fun to shoot with little or no recoil, even with the heaviest 300-grain loads. The gun is so much fun to shoot that there needs to be a .22 version unless someone starts making .44 Magnums at the old price of .22s.

The action works smoothly, and extraction is positive just as you would expect. If you open the breech block sharply it will function as an ejector. The gun is quick and easy to hit targets while firing offhand and I like that. So many guns aren't.

With the 27-inch barrel, noise levels are far below those of the .44 Magnum when fired in a pistol and velocities are of course higher. This gun brings out the full hunting potential of the cartridge. I've always liked the .44 Magnum in a rifle, but it has too high a decibel level of noise and is too slow on follow-up shots for me to want it in a handgun. The inability to make a fast second shot is the reason that I have only known two veteran gunfighters who carried .44 Magnum handguns.

David Jones takes an offhand shot with the .44 Magnum rolling block.

My Betty always hunted with a Ruger .44 Mag. semi-auto carbine and never failed to make one-shot kills with it. I have seen the cartridge perform in a rifle over and over on game and it has always impressed. It's a meat hunter's gun in the tradition of the old Kentucky rifles but with more power. Daniel Boone and Davey Crockett could only dream of such a fine weapon for their purposes. Many old-time hunters went directly from Kentucky rifles to the Remington rolling blocks with complete satisfaction, except for the complaints about the newfangled cartridges making the gun more expensive to shoot. Nothing there has changed even today.

The important thing is that the tradition of the accurate single-shot long rifle is being upheld in the hunting field with this rifle. It is as steady on target as a fine Kentucky rifle and that's

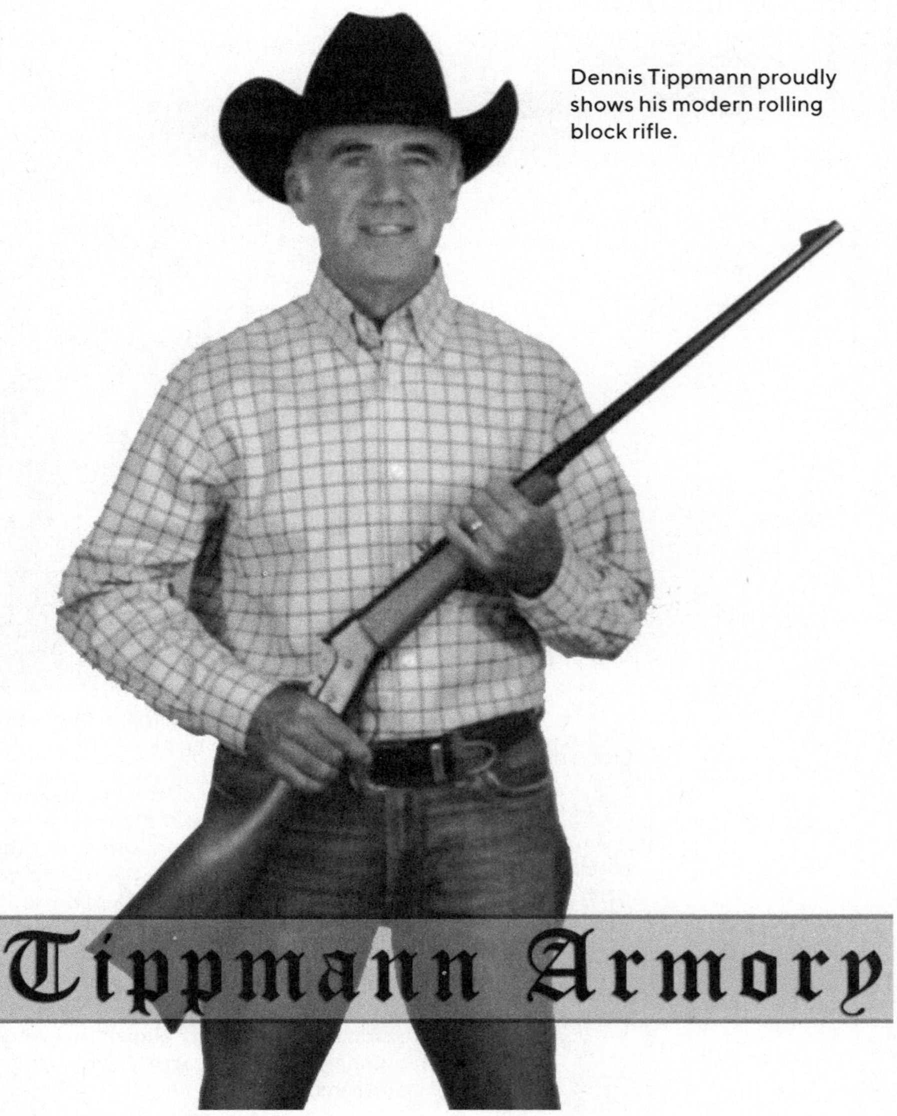

Dennis Tippmann proudly shows his modern rolling block rifle.

what a hunting gun needs to succeed in the field. Like the Kentucky rifles, the Tippmann rolling block has no sling swivels, as it's an offhand shooting gun and that's where it excels.

I fired 1,225 cartridges in my shooting test consisting of the following ammo. Velocities and penetration figures in ballistic gelatin are from the factories and would be higher from this 27-inch-barreled gun.

All the ammo tested proved superbly accurate in this sweet-shooting little rifle, but obviously with loads this different they did not all shoot to the same point of aim. That's why we have adjustable sights. The rifle comes with a buckhorn top and patridge bottom rear and a blade front sight. Using these iron sights, I put four shots into a 1-inch group at 50 yards using Reed's Ammunition and Research 240-grain ammunition. The rifle was fired from a Champion shooting rest.

Since the gun comes with hunting-style instead of target sights, I took advantage of the fact that it is drilled and tapped for scope mounts and comes with two mount bases. Using a Weaver gunsmith tool kit and the proper screwdriver bits for the gun, I mounted a Bushnell Elite 6500 2.5-16X scope and bore sighted it with a Bushnell magnetic bore sight. While a 16-power scope may seem excessive for a .44 Magnum, it sure makes seeing that 1-inch bullseye easier. For hunting, I would turn it down to 2.5X. The gun was placed in a Bullsbag Shooting Rest for accuracy tests. The rolling block proceeded to make 1-inch groups at 50 yards again. For this gun and cartridge that is excellent performance and far more accuracy than a gun built for offhand shooting requires.

Like almost all 1800s-era gun designs, the rolling block is put together with screws, which can back out under extensive shooting. I used an original M1870 combination tool to tighten them. After all that shooting, the rifle was cleaned with Shooter's Choice Bore Cleaner, Lead Remover and FP-10 Lubricant. These modern cleaners do a most efficient job.

When the Remington rolling block first came out, it took the world by storm. The action was so strong that no one ever succeeded in blowing out the breech. The Liege proof house in Belgium sure tried. They took a .50-70 rolling block and loaded it from breech to muzzle with 750 grains of black powder, 40 bullets and two wads. The gun took that monster demolition load without damage. The rolling block was seemingly indestructible.

At the 1867 Paris Imperial Exposition, the rolling block was unanimously selected by the High Commission on Firearms as "The finest rifle in the world." Denmark, Norway, Sweden, Spain, Egypt, Argentina, China, Austria, Italy and a host of South American countries adopted or bought large quantities of it. The U.S. made 33,000 at Springfield Armory for the Army and Navy. In terms of worldwide use, it was the AK-47 of the time. It was also a popular sporting rifle, as well as a mainstay of the professional buffalo hunters, working alongside the Sharps and trapdoor Springfields.

On the frontier it quickly made a name for itself when, in 1866, Nelson Story drove his cattle through Sioux territory when the Sioux were on the warpath. Nelson had bought 30 of the new Remington rolling blocks and their firepower enabled him to prevail against almost 20 to 1 odds in three separate mounted Indian attacks.

Alongside the Sharps, the Remington rolling block saw use on the American team that defeated the Irish for the World Championship in 1874. Henry Fulton, who shot the highest score on the American team, used a Remington rolling block.

The original Remington rolling block was one of the great rifles of history. And the fact that a new variation of it is being made by Tippmann Arms is a fitting tribute to a lasting design. The suggested retail price is $899. For anyone wanting to carry on the tradition of the Kentucky riflemen, but wanting the power and convenience of a cartridge gun, the Tippmann is an excellent choice.

FEDERAL TUNGSTEN SUPER SHOT

Some of the Hardest-Hitting Shotgun Ammunition Ever Made

BY **L.P. BREZNY**

It has been a dry spell for several years in the design and development of any new types of high-performance shotgun ammunition. When variations of basic tungsten shot had their run at the market, and other unique or at times quite standard load designs made their way to the sporting goods store shelves, the subject of a different load type seemed to have faded into smoothbore history. With the dawn of early 2017, something changed, and currently there are no less than three major variants in special high-performance shotshell loads being offered to hunters.

One of these is being marketed by Federal Cartridge, and this new direction is going to become the absolute optimum in ultra-high-performance standards down range. Tungsten Super Shot (TSS) as a pellet material is the heaviest shot type ever developed for hunting or defense. That alone says a great deal as to exactly where this subject is about to go. As a heavy pellet material, the kinetic en-

The author zeroing the Chiappa Triple-Barrel .410 turkey gun with a standard lead shot load prior to going afield.

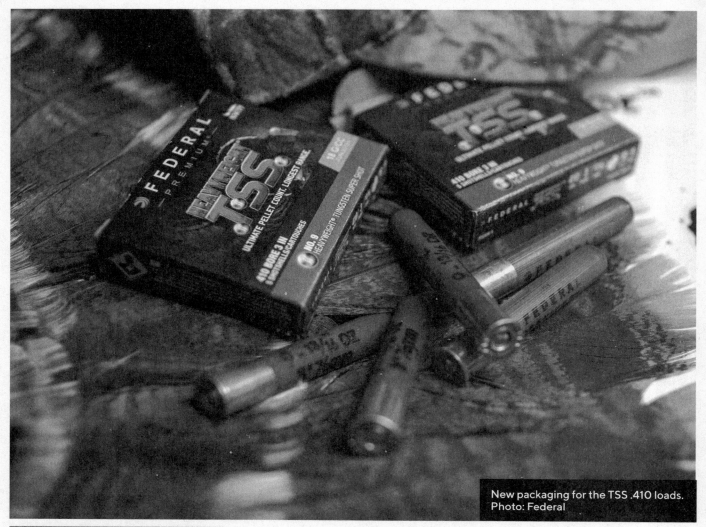

New packaging for the TSS .410 loads. Photo: Federal

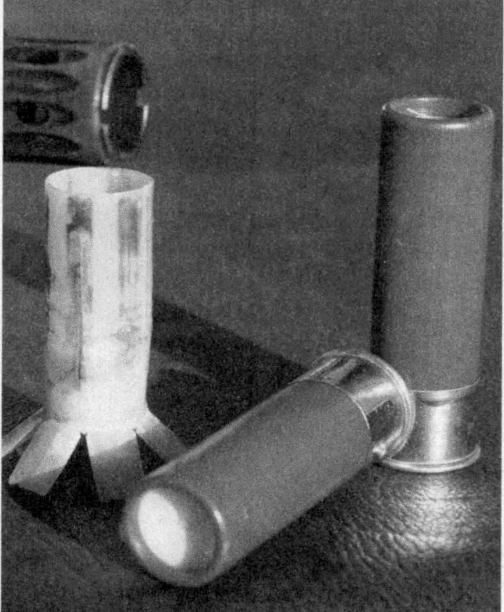

Prototype ammunition direct from Federal about three months ahead of release date. Note wad condition even when shooting ultra-hard pure tungsten shot.

ergy that this shot carries is very high, and it also retains wind-fighting ability as well as a stable line of flight to the target. There are no negatives with TSS ballistically, the only issue is that it is not cheap to produce or buy.

If there's one reason shotgunners haven't seen much of this shot type in use, it's the cost factor when matched against the massive number of other advanced and standard pellet types offered to shooters today. Federal, a company that can work through any and all development costs of new factory load offerings, decided it was time to bring out a factory version of the shot in an over-the-counter, commercially rolled package.

When Federal offered me the opportunity to take on the new load offerings in a couple of prototype shotshells several months ahead of the actual release date, I jumped at the chance. I already knew a good deal about TSS because we, meaning us old goose hunters, were loading it based on a unique double-walled steel shot 12-gauge wad, buffer and powder that had been retarded in terms of its active burn rate. That was back in the early days of non-toxic shot development. When handloaded in a #2 BB-, BBB- or T-size pellet, you ended up with a very hard-hitting long-range goose load. Effective range? 100+ yards, and that's no war story.

When you shoot TSS in big pellet sizes, you need to factor in required target lead, wind deflection, and pellet drop on low side shots. Even paying attention to your backstop down range is important here, as TSS has a massive shoot-through ability in larger pellet sizes. Several small outfits of the day tried to get on board by offering custom handloaded TSS ammunition, but again, the cost factor was always getting in the way of making a go of the endeavor.

Why TSS ammunition now? Without question there are many very good pellet types in equally good shotshell hulls

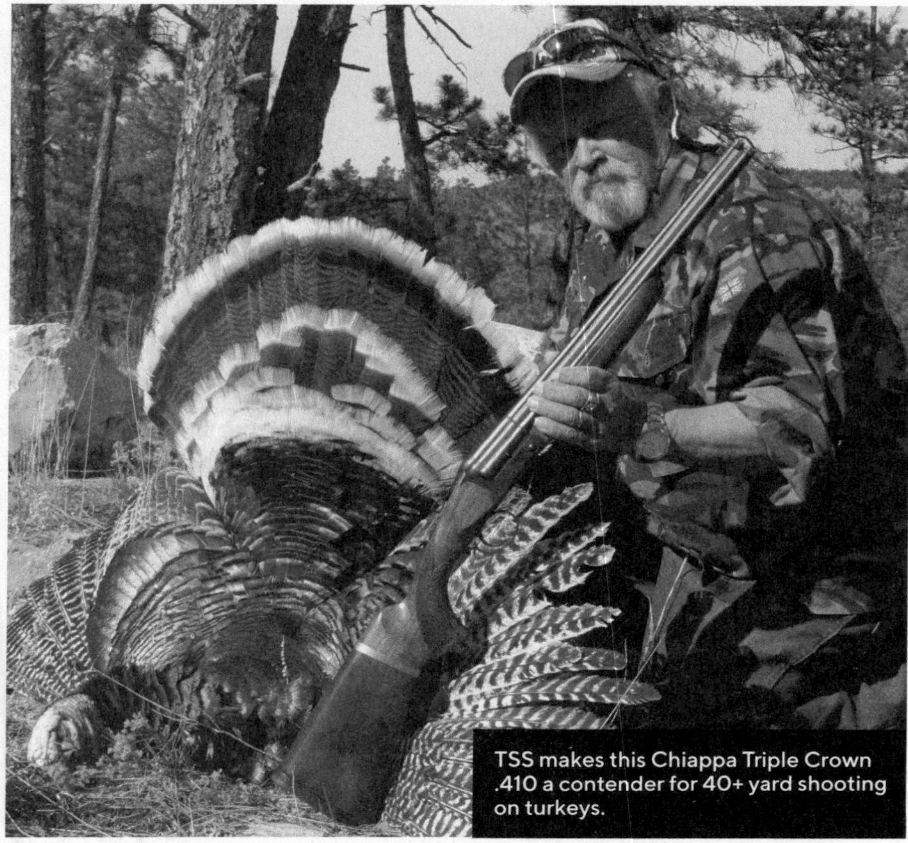

TSS makes this Chiappa Triple Crown .410 a contender for 40+ yard shooting on turkeys.

An author favorite during the TSS review, the Browning BPS 3-inch .410 with a full choke, has been a devastating harvesting system, but until now all bird shooting was inside 27 yards. TSS #9 shot at 18 density changes all that.

that can get the job done in the field. TSS is, for the most part, being marketed by Federal to the modern turkey hunter, as well as a secondary market of hunters of large, hard-to-bring-down warm target options. Examples include coyotes, pigs, badger and anything else that is large and gets in the way of the new load's payload charge. What we have here is a true specialty option as an over-the-counter cure for high-energy shotgunning.

Federal has taken a fresh look at turkey loads based on the use of TSS shot, which up to now was only offered to handloaders in bulk quantities. This high-density product (18 grams per cubic centimeter) is one of the heaviest materials in terms of individual pellet density that can be fired from a smoothbore firearm today. Live-fire testing of the new ammunition involved two prototype loads. The first was a 3-inch 12-gauge Heavyweight #9 TSS Flitecontrol wad turkey load, and the second a .410-gauge TSS #9 shot load. With a pellet density of 18 grams, this shot comes in at just two points double the density of pure black lead shot. In other words, a #9 pellet will do the work of a #5 lead shot pellet, but at a much greater pattern-filling pellet count. (A pellet density on target much like a handful of black pepper.)

Testing the first-generation prototype TSS #9 dust pellets by way of the new 3-inch 12-gauge turkey load indicated that penetration in ballistic gelatin at 40 yards was two and one-half times the penetration depth as standard lead shot of the same pellet size. The explanation above was borne out as it required a #5 plated lead shot pellet to get close to the penetration of the #9 TSS product. Federal TSS is without question some of the deadliest payload ever put in a factory loaded shotshell.

Being a real fan of the sub-gauge .410, I found it fascinating to see that at 30 yards the 3-inch .410 prototype load of #9 shot destroyed a turkey Birchwood Casey head/neck gobbler with a total clustered-up pellet contact count of 54 hits. The test gun was the Browning BPS, and the Invector Plus full choke. When pushed back to 40 yards, the same gun and load returned 27 pellet contact hits using a three-shot average. This compares with many standard lead shot turkey loads.

Moving to the 3-inch 12 gauge, the TSS #9 shot results at 40 yards were flat-out nuts to watch. When I fired on the 7-inch steel target, the stakes pulled loose from the ground and the target flipped over. The photo gobbler head and neck indi-

The Chiappa Charles Daly Triple Crown with a hard day's work completed.

cated that the pellet count was 56 hits, but I had missed to the left, and the main mass of shot — which was far too dense to ever count pellets — had turned the color-coded marker target pure white, and left the upper left corner totally shot away. The target heavy board backer had sustained a gaping 3-inch hole where the Federal Flitestopper wad had made an exit while still carrying some remaining shot in its base section.

Federal has scrapped all of their previous load offerings in turkey fodder, which even includes the very new 3rd Degree. Actually, the 3rd Degree shotshell will still be offered, but now makes use of a blended lead and TSS shot, and will be the only load even close to an advanced shot load being retained in all Federal turkey fodder for 2018 and beyond.

As luck would have it, I drew a 2017 fall tag for a prairie unit in western South Dakota. That was a big deal, because for the first time in my 20 years of hunting the Black Hills for Merriam turkeys, it was closed season in terms of fall birds. Because my remaining prototype ammu-

BACKRIDGE AMMUNITION ITX-13 SHOT STANDARD METRO

Pellet Weight (grs): 3.360
Effective SD: 0.0293
Pellet Diameter (in): Eq.~4
Standard SD: 0.0293

Range (yds)	Velocity (fps)	Energy (ft-lbs)	Time of Flight (sec)	Drop (in)	Wind Deflection (in/10mph)	45mph Lead (ft)
0	1,194	10.6	0.0000	0.0	0.0	0
5	1,101	9.0	0.0140	0.0	-0.1	0.9
10	1,021	7.8	0.0282	0.1	0.2	1.9
15	952	6.8	0.0435	0.3	0.7	2.9
20	891	5.9	0.0599	0.6	1.3	4.0
25	838	5.2	0.0773	1.0	2.1	5.1
30	791	4.7	0.0958	1.6	3.2	6.3
35	749	4.2	0.1154	2.2	4.4	7.6
40	713	3.8	0.1360	3.0	5.7	9.0
45	678	3.4	0.1576	4.0	7.3	10.4
50	646	3.1	0.1804	5.2	9.1	11.9
55	614	2.8	0.2043	6.6	11.3	13.5
60	585	2.6	0.2294	8.2	13.8	15.1
65	557	2.3	0.2557	10.0	16.6	16.9

#9 HIGH DENSITY "TUNGSTEN" SHOT FEDERAL TSS STANDARD METRO

Pellet Weight (grs): ~ 1.22
Pellet Diameter (in): Nom. 0.080

Range (yds)	Velocity (fps)	Energy (ft-lbs)	Time of Flight (sec)	Drop (in)	Wind Deflection (in/10mph)	45mph Lead (ft)
0	1,125	3.4	0.0000	0.0	0.0	0
5	1,036	2.9	0.0149	0.0	-0.1	1.0
10	960	2.5	0.0300	0.2	0.2	2.0
15	894	2.2	0.0463	0.4	0.7	3.1
20	837	1.9	0.0637	0.7	1.4	4.2
25	786	1.7	0.0823	1.2	2.3	5.4
30	742	1.5	0.1020	1.8	3.4	6.7
35	704	1.3	0.1229	2.5	4.6	8.1
40	667	1.2	0.1448	3.4	6.2	9.6
45	632	1.1	0.1680	4.6	8.0	11.1
50	600	1.0	0.1925	5.9	10.2	12.7
55	569	0.9	0.2182	7.5	12.6	14.4
60	540	0.8	0.2454	9.3	15.5	16.2

Note: Extremely small sample and some approximation involved, but results are indicative. Gun: .410 gauge with 3-inch shotshell, approx. 15/16-oz. shot. This data is generated by and is exclusive to Shot Data System and Ballistics Research & Development TM. Permission to use by any other data source must obtain from author or representative.

PAYLOAD TOTAL PELLET COUNT AND WEIGHTS FOR TSS SHOT

Gauge	Load/Pellets	Shot Weight (oz)	Notes
12-Gauge 3-Inch Magnum	#7 or #9 shot	1 ¾	--
12-Gauge 3.5-Inch Magnum	#7 or #9 shot	2-1/4	--
20-Gauge Magnum	#7 shot	1 ½	--
20-Gauge Low Recoil	#9 shot	1 ¾	--
410-Gauge 3 Inch	#9 shot	13/16	Load will stay with, or outshoot, standard 12-gauge 2 ¾- and 3-inch field loads in black lead shot or steel

#9 SST pellet carries the same energy as a pellet of #5 lead shot

13/16 oz. of #9 shot carries 295 pellets

1-1/8 oz. load carries 408 pellets
Comparison: 2 oz. load of #4 lead retains a total of 270 pellets

1-½ oz. TSS #7 carries 635 pellets.
(Increased pellet count and direct kinetic energy mass allows the .410 bore to stand with the larger shotshell gauge offerings)

Federal testing using 10-inch target

1-3/4 oz. #5 lead premium shotshell ammunition: 100 pellets in 10-inch circle at 40 yards

1-3/4 oz. load of #7 TSS will place 200 hits in a 10-inch circle at 40 yards

1 3/4 oz. of #9 (dust) will total 350 hits in a 10-inch circle at 40 yards.
#9 TSS is the same rated energy as #5 lead shot at any given range

*Data source Federal Cartridge.

nition was in short supply in all three of my test guns, the 3-inch 12 gauge in the SBE, the Chiappa Carbine Tri-Barrel, and the Browning 3-inch BPS .410 were the guns and loads of choice for the hunt.

When hunting open country prairie units in South Dakota, I often carry a scoped long-range coyote rifle, and also a short, lightweight scattergun. The triple-barrel Chiappa fit the bill perfectly as a backpack and calling shotgun, being that I could now count on the .410 well out to a crazy 72 yards (on large birds by ballistic gel measurement standards of 1.5-inch head/neck penetration in previous studies of the ultra-heavy-weight 18cc pellets). Secondly, the data coming in from Shot Data Systems indicated that, even in the very small #9 shot, this 18-density pellet was able to haul the mail well beyond any normal gunning range associated with taking the wild turkey. Not that I would ever shoot a bird at such ranges, but just knowing that the sub-gauge scattergun had all that horsepower gave me a warm, fuzzy feeling by the time I did pull up on an open prairie bird.

On a very cold December morning while hunting and calling song dogs along a wide section of brush-covered bottom badlands, I located several turkeys moving along a game trail just below me. The range was exactly 34 yards based on my Nikon LaserForce system, and after two weeks of searching out a target I decided to pull for the third bird in the group by way of the triple-barreled Chiappa short carbine shotgun. At the shot, consisting of one of the last two rounds of prototype TSS #9s I had with me, the bird took a neck hit, then rolled off the trail into a shallow depression never moving a feather. No nerve reaction, kicking or sign of life remained.

This was the first bird I had harvested with any .410 load past a measured 27 yards. Could I have stretched the shot farther? Yes, but after hunting two weeks without even a sighting of a bird, I didn't want to delay the hunt any longer with sub-zero weather closing in fast.

I believe it is safe to say that Federal has made a bold move taking on Tungsten Super Shot as a marketable shot type for high-performance loads. Without question, many dedicated turkey hunters are going to make the move to TSS. Any element of poor payload performance is a thing of the past when shooting this new product against a fine spring gobbler that hangs up just out of lead shot range.

COMPARISON OF STEEL, ITX, HEVI-SHOT, HEAVY WRIGHT 13, AND TSS. EFFECTIVE RANGE & PENETRATION BALLISTIC GEL. *SOURCE KPY BALLISTICS. MUZZLE VELOCITY 1,450 FPS ALL SAMPLES. ALL LOADS 1 OZ.

Shot Size	1.5-Inch Gel Penetration (yds)	2.25-Inch Gel Penetration (yds)
#4 Steel	31	N/A
#4 ITX 10	58.4	34.2
#4 Hevi Shot	87.8	58.7
#4 HW 13	103.5	72.3
#9 TSS	73.6	46.9
#7 TSS	117.1	83.7

NEW RIFLES

This Year's Rifle Crop Includes Plenty of Tempting Prospects for Hunters and Target Shooters

BY **WAYNE VAN ZWOLL**

Much of the shooting industry endured flat sales in 2017. Sporting rifles, in particular, languished on dealer racks. Even traffic in ARs slowed, as the confirmation of a Trump presidency all but erased the specter of new firearms restrictions — at least, briefly. Ammunition stocks built too, as panic buying and hoarding ground to a halt. Some gunmakers caught their breath in the R&D shop, or by tapping into buyer nostalgia with a return to classic designs. Not just 19th-century lever actions, but — courtesy Brownells — Vietnam-era M16-style battle rifles. After all, "retro" eventually applies to every firearm, as new shooters redefine the market. Many people who run businesses in our communities, teach our offspring and staff our government were born after the fall of Saigon. As for new products, long-range shooting continues to drive buyers to gun counters. Scopes that tap ballistic data on smartphones, with new, ballistically gifted loads like Federal's .22 Valkyrie and Hornady's 6.5 Precision Rifle Cartridge, woo millennial, tech-savvy shooters. For traditionalists, walnut stocks are appearing on rifles introduced with polymer. While at this writing 2018 has yet to confirm industry optimism evidenced at January's SHOT Show, the current rifle crop includes plenty of tempting prospects for hunters and target shooters of all ages.

Barrett

Dominant in .50-caliber circles, Barrett entered the competitive big game rifle arena last year with its Fieldcraft bolt action. Its clean lines and light weight (5 to 5 3/4 pounds) bring to mind rifles designed and built by Melvin Forbes of New Ultra Light Arms. (Melvin is still offering custom rifles from his ULA shop, but the line of Forbes rifles, produced briefly as a mass-produced alternative by a licensee, died on the vine.) Priced from $1,799 in 2018, the Barrett Fieldcraft comes in 10 chamberings, .243 to .30-06, including 6.5x55 and 6mm Creedmoor. barrett.net.

The Barrett Fieldcraft is ultralight and can be had in 10 popular chamberings. Photo: Barrett

Bergara

The name comes from the Spanish town of Bergara where, in 1999, a factory was producing rifle barrels for BPI Outdoors, which had just bought CVA (Connecticut Valley Arms). Four years later, BPI CEO Dudley McGarity grew that operation to furnish barrels for CVA. Other barrel contracts followed. Bergara then developed bolt-action rifles, most with actions on Remington 700 footprints. Proliferation of Bergaras has settled out into two series: the Premier and the B-14. Premiers include tactical and hunting styles, with chassis and carbon-fiber stocks in seven configurations, $1,715 to $2,800. New for 2018 are the Approach and HMR (Hunting Match Rifle) Pro, available now in 6mm Creedmoor and other short-action chamberings. Both feature No. 5 threaded barrels and detachable box magazines.

The Approach has a hand-laid synthetic stock, the HMR a molded stock with adjustable comb. The B-14 series, from $825, includes new Ridge and lightweight Hunter versions with SoftTouch finish on synthetic stocks. From .22-250 to .300 Win. Mag., they complement the walnut-stocked Timber and Woodsman rifles, and the stiff-barreled HMR and BMP (Bergara Match Precision), whose growing roster of chamberings now include 6mm Creedmoor. The 9 1/4-pound HMR lists for $1,150, the 11-pound BMP for $1,699, both with AICS detachable box magazines. Like B-14 sporters, they have a sliding plate extractor, plunger ejector, two-position safety and adjustable trigger. They accept Remington 700 scope bases. The BMP has an adjustable alloy stock and an exposed nut for quick barrel swaps.

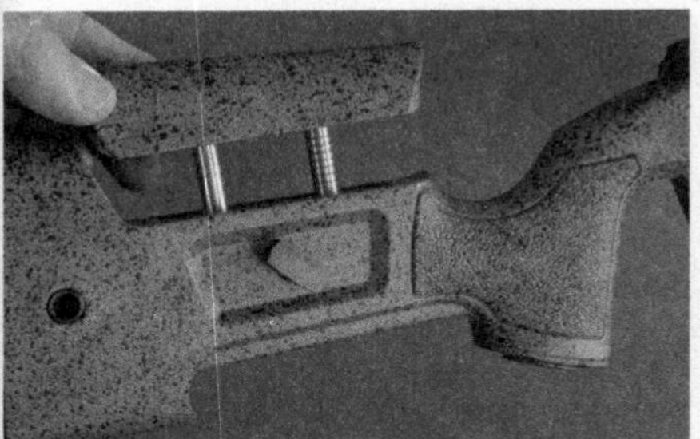

The stock of Bergara's B-14 HMR (Hunting/Match Rifle) is adjustable for length and comb height.

For 2018, Bergara offers new renditions of its accurate B-14 rifles with recessed, twin-lug bolts.

The author found Bergara's B-14 easy to shoot from hunting positions, and accurate. Note big bolt knob.

The first B-14 I fired was a 7-pound Woodsman, a .270 with 24-inch barrel and straight-combed, checkered walnut stock. A hinged floorplate secured an internal four-shot box. Handling, trigger pull and accuracy impressed me, so I followed up at the range with a new HMR in 6.5 Creedmoor. In a cosmetic departure from some "precision" rifles, the HMR's black-flecked, copper-hued prone stock doesn't look like tooling from a truck repair shop. Black spacers under a thick buttpad adjust length of pull. A thumb-screw on the side of the buttstock snugs the comb on twin pillars. The grip is long and steep, convex to fit the hollow of your palm. A toe hook helps you tug the butt into your shoulder. An alloy "mini-chassis" inside extends from below the comb nose several inches into the forestock.

The HMR is about as close as you'll get to a hunting and target rifle in one package. Despite its protrusions — toe hook, grip, magazine — it comes readily to hand. The long conical bolt knob accelerates cycling. The safety snicks firmly and quietly between two stops (it doesn't lock the bolt). The trigger on this 6.5 C arrived with an icicle-crisp 3-pound pull. The detachable box loads and feeds without fault. The follower serves as a single-loading platform, so you can feed the rifle by hand in long-range matches that require you to load singly. Predictably, this rifle easily held shots inside 1 MOA. Cleaning patches glided down the button-rifled bore. "Bergara holds bore diameter to within .0002 inch," says McGarity. "Each barrel is triple-honed and checked to ensure uniform hardness, end to end." bergarausa.com.

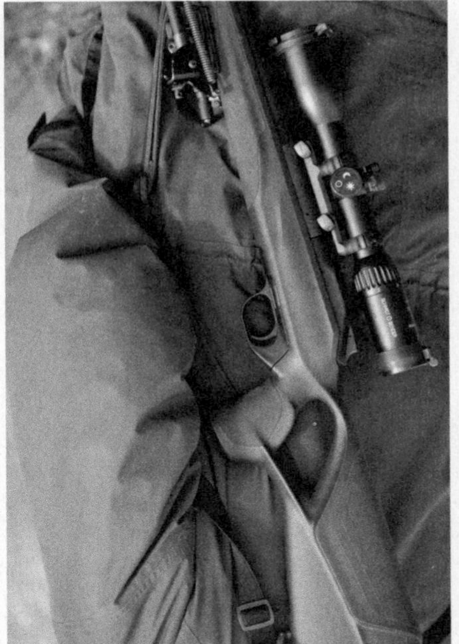

Blaser's R8 Professional Success is hugely popular in Europe. New versions grow the line for 2018.

Blaser

Top choice of many if not most European hunters, Blaser's straight-pull R8 rifle has become a series, expanded for 2018 with new thumbhole-stock "Success" models. Figured walnut with leather on grip and comb surfaces marks the Success Individual. The Carbon Success has leather too, on a carbon-fiber stock with clear finish. The new Success Ruthenium has a special hard coating on bolt, trigger and bolt knob. The R8 Long Range Professional Success in 6.5x47, 6.5/284, .300 Norma and .338 Lapua features a long, stiff barrel. A GRS model adds a fluted match barrel and laminated prone stock with open grip and adjustable comb. These and R8 Professional and Safari rifles — and a new R8 Silence with full-length suppressor — share the same action. The telescoping bolt has an expanding collet that locks to the barrel. It's strong enough to brook 120,000 psi of pressure. The aramid-reinforced magazine is cleverly designed into the trigger group, which is instantly detachable by hand. You can load the stack in the rifle or in your hand. A sliding tab inside the box locks it in the rifle. Trigger pull for R8s exported to the U.S. is set at 2.5 pounds. Stateside customers can special order the 1.6-pound "European" trigger, installed by Blaser. The R8's tang-mounted thumb-piece is a cocking switch, not a safety. Uncocked, the rifle is safe to carry with the chamber loaded.

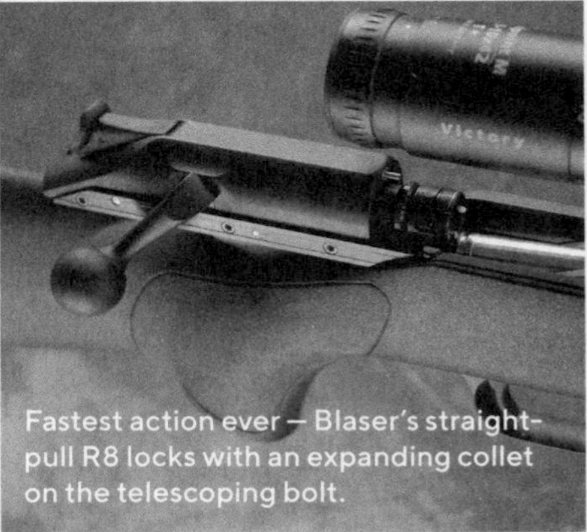

Fastest action ever — Blaser's straight-pull R8 locks with an expanding collet on the telescoping bolt.

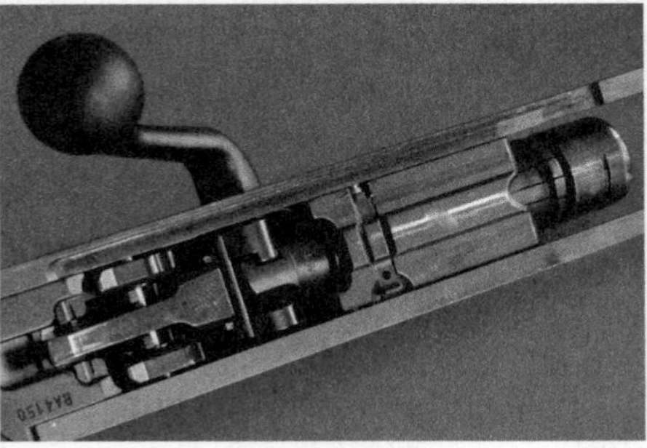

Blaser's R8 has a cocking switch, not a safety, so can be carried safely with a cartridge up the spout.

Blaser barrels are hammer-forged, with external plasma nitriding to ensure scope base dimples hold Blaser's QD mounts securely. Return-to-zero is positive. (I tested that by removing a scope, then snugging it back on and without adjustment hitting a 600-yard target!) R8 rifles I've used on the range and afield, in chamberings to .500 Jeffery, have performed without fault. No malfunctions, ever. The GRS long-range rifle delivers the reach of the .338 Lapua in a surprisingly nimble rifle that's a pleasure to fire from prone. The R8 Silence in .308 hops gently with a report mild enough to absolve you of earplugs on a hunt. But the slim suppressor is little thicker than a stiff barrel, and overall length doesn't exceed that of ordinary rifles with 22-inch barrels. No matter the variation, R8s consistently print groups well under a minute of angle — and are unsurpassed for fast repeat shots. This year, Blaser is making sure you get the most from your R8 by offering its own premier-quality Blaser-branded scopes, produced in Wetzlar by German Sports Optics. A recent visit to GSO, then to the Blaser plant at Isny, Germany, to fire R8 rifles fitted with the new scopes, convinced me they're not just cosmetically a perfect match for the R8, but like the rifle boast the best of German engineering and quality. blaser-usa.com.

This year, Blaser is cataloging its own top-quality scopes for the R8. They're built by GSO in Wetzlar.

Blaser rifles can be run easily from the shoulder without losing your position. Weather? No problem.

Browning

New X-Bolt Pro and X-Bolt Pro Long Range rifles from Browning have "burnt bronze" Cerakote-finished stainless barrels and actions. Gen 2 carbon fiber stocks feature grip texturing. A spiral-fluted bolt strips cartridges from detachable rotary magazines. Chamberings from 6mm Creedmoor to .300 Winchester come with 26-inch barrels and extended bolt knobs in the Long Range rifle, priced from $2,070. Shooters who revel in long names should fancy the new X-Bolt Hell's Canyon Speed Long Range McMillan, with McMillan Game Scout stock. Like the X-Bolt Pro and Pro Long Range, it has a threaded muzzle brake on a bronze-colored Cerakoted barrel of fluted stainless steel. It also shares four-screw X-Lock scope mounting and other features that define Browning's flagship bolt rifle. In 6mm and 6.5 Creedmoor, .300 WSM, .26 and .28 Nosler, and 7mm Rem. and .300 Win. Magnums, the new McMillan version is equipped with 26-inch barrels only, and A-TACS stock finish. Weight: 7 1/2 to 7 3/4 pounds. Price: $2,130 to $2,200. Laminated thumbhole stocks and stainless barrels on blued X-Bolt receivers define new Eclipse Hunter, Varmint and Target rifles ($1,200 to $1,400) with brake-equipped muzzles. Choose from 15 chamberings. Incidentally, the 6mm Creedmoor has been added to chambering lists for other X-Bolts. Barrels have a quick 1-in-7 1/2 twist for the long bullets that tap this 6mm's potential at distance. In rimfire rifles, Browning has a new version of its T-Bolt. The Laminated Target/Varmint Stainless, .22 LR, .22 WMR and .17 HMR, weighs 5 1/2 pounds with 22-inch threaded barrel. It lists for $940 (.22 LR) and $980. You can still get the classic Browning BL-22 in six variations, and the SA-22 autoloader in three grades. browning.com.

Christensen Arms

More than two decades ago, a doctorate in engineering helped Roland Christensen develop the first carbon fiber rifle barrel. A thin steel tube inside a lightweight carbon fiber shell provided the rigidity, strength and accuracy of heavier solid steel barrels. Christensen Arms now produces bolt-action and AR-style rifles barreled in carbon fiber and equipped with titanium muzzle brakes to further reduce weight. Chamberings from .223 to .375 H&H include the popular 6.5 Creedmoor and.338 Lapua in new ELR and Ultra ELR rifles. Pillar-bedded, prone-style stocks adjust for comb height and length of pull. Despite their stiff 27-inch barrels and magnum receivers, the most powerful of these long-range rifles weigh only 6 1/2 to 7 1/2 pounds. christensenarms.com.

The lightweight CZ 527 in .223 (and now 7.62x39 and 6.5 Grendel) is a fine "walking varminter.

The push-feed bolt of the new CZ 557, which replaces standard versions of the 550, has a stout extractor.

CZ

If you want a rimfire with a wood stock and the length and feel of a centerfire, CZ's 455 series of .22 bolt rifles is an obvious choice. A bonus: they shoot as accurately as match rifles! Not just mine, but the CZ owned by a good friend with a wall of shooting medals. The 455 design gives you interchangeable barrels, too. Last year, the company added its first stainless rimfire, in a black synthetic stock. For young shooters, there's the 455 Scout, with 12-inch hardwood stock and a short-threaded barrel. The centerfire stable has new entries from the petite 527 action to the 557 and 550. Besides .17 and .22 Hornet, .204, .222, .223 and 7.62x39, the 527 American is now bored to 6.5 Grendel. I carried one such 527 briefly last fall. The little Grendel, fashioned for AR-style actions, is a delight in this trim bolt rifle. All 527s ($665 to $787) boast single-set triggers. The larger 557 push-feed action that has supplanted the controlled-feed 550 in all but magnum versions now comes in a left-hand version at $865. The long action in .30-06 has a standard floorplate; the short action in .308 features a detachable box, like the 557 Varmint introduced last year. There's also a new 557 American in magnum chamberings: .26, .28 and .30 Nosler and .300 Win. Mag. Price: $849. Receivers on 557s and 550s are machined to accept CZ rings. The 550 is still the foundation for Safari Magnum and Safari Classics rifles — including the Safari Classics Express in "plains game" chamberings like the .270, .30-06 and .300 Win. Mag. cz-usa.com.

Dakota

One of the most elegant semi-custom rifles to come from a U.S. maker, the Dakota 76 Don Allen wrought from refinements to the early Winchester Model 70 action continues to climb in price. But all six versions — and the take-down 76 Traveler — still set standards for quality. A more affordable round-action Dakota 97 (four variations) now complements a mid-priced line of rifles on Nesika actions, also produced in the Dakota shop in a handful of variations. Single-shot enthusiasts can order a Miller or Dakota Model 10, or the "baby" Sharps the company builds to 80 percent scale on the famous 1874 Sharps design. After Remington acquired Dakota, it moved its Custom Shop and, later, a new Marlin Custom Shop, to Sturgis, giving the crew of talented men and women at Dakota's benches more than enough to do. The facility is still turning out top-quality firearms — and, I'm told, looking for skilled craftsmen. But these rifles aren't just rack queens. A Dakota 97 Outfitter took my most recent mountain goat, under tough conditions. Don Allen knew where to find lovely walnut, and how to fashion achingly beautiful rifles. But they were born to hunt. Still are. dakotaarms.com.

E.R Shaw

Want a choice of 90 chamberings, .17 to .458, in a made-to-order rifle for $1,400? Barrel maker E.R. Shaw has announced the Mark X bolt action, after a long incubation. The mechanism appears to be from Savage, which supplies an AccuTrigger (a Timney is your option). Barrel configurations and other specs are online for you to choose. Also from E.R. Shaw: a new AR-10 rifle of trim profile, with upper and lower of machined 7075-T6 alloy forgings. The barrel comes with the company's own muzzle brake; the bolt is nickel boron-coated. Price for this 9 1/2-pound rifle: $996. ershawbarrels.com.

Franchi

A long history of shotgun manufacture may have provided the momentum for Franchi's first bolt-action rifle, the Momentum. Actually, in Europe, where it was introduced last year at Germany's IWA trade show, the rifle is called the Horizon. There are minor differences — in barrel threading at the muzzle, for instance, and the addition of spiral fluting on the Horizon's full-diameter bolt body. But both feature the same push-feed mechanism, with recessed bolt face inside three locking lugs. A traditional internal box with hinged floorplate holds three cartridges. I'm told Franchi expects to sell most of the new rifles in .308 and .30-06. I've yet to fire one, though the 6 1/2-pound .30-06 I handled at the SHOT Show came to cheek easily. I noted it takes Remington 700 scope bases. I like the straight comb and thick recoil pad, the textured grip surfaces and palm-friendly bolt knob. I prefer standard sling studs to the rifle's integral tabs that don't allow swivels to swivel under sling pressure. At $609 (or $729 with a Burris Fullfield 3-9x40), the Momentum costs more than most entry-level bolt rifles from stateside companies — more, even than the Tikka T3. It's a bit less expensive than the new Sauer 100 and Mauser 18. franchiusa.com.

H-S Precision makes its rifles from scratch, from receiver (here in stages) to bolt, barrel and stock.

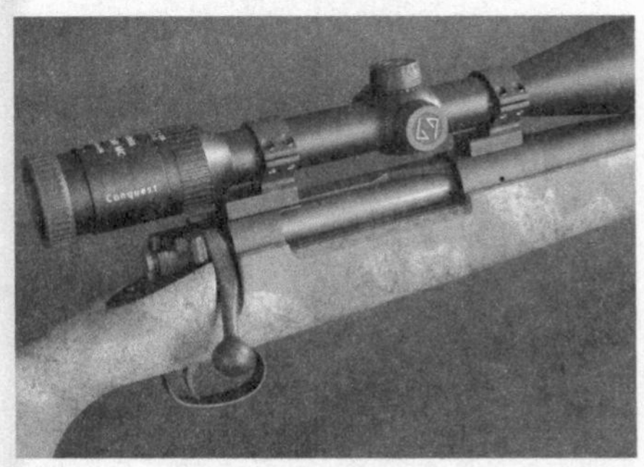

This sleek H-S Precision rifle has a cut-rifled barrel, a lightweight hand-laid stock with bedding rail.

H-S Precision

The South Dakota firm H-S Precision has expanded its line of late with heavy rifles for long, precise shots: The BCR in chamberings like 6mm BR has a single-shot action, 26-inch braked, fluted barrel and competition trigger. PLR long-range hunting rifles, 6.5x47 to .338 Lapua, feature prone stocks and 26-inch barrels but weigh only 8 pounds. Like most lighter H-S rifles, they have detachable box magazines. I prefer the more traditional SPR and SPL stock styles, which keep weights under 7 1/2 pounds with long barrels. Notably, H-S produces all major rifle components in-house — lock, stock and barrel. The twin-lug bolt actions are CNC-machined to very tight tolerances and wear finely adjustable triggers. Hand-laid carbon-fiber stocks incorporate alloy bedding blocks; 416R stainless barrels are cut-rifled and given 11-degree target crowns. H-S has enough variations in hunting, target and tactical series to justify your visit to hsprecision.com.

Henry Repeating Arms

B. Tyler Henry played a big role in developing the rifle of his name for Oliver Winchester and the nascent New Haven Repeating Arms Company. That was around 1860. Now Henry is a New Jersey-based company that manufactures modern rimfire and centerfire lever rifles with late-1800s profiles. Retailing at $470 and $570 in .22 LR and .22 WMR with traditional barrels, the recent Frontier model comes with threaded barrels for $502 and $596. Big Boy centerfire rifles chamber the .327 Federal and .41 Magnum, from $850. A hard-chromed All-Weather Big Boy in .357 and .44 Magnum and .45 Colt lists for $900. In my rack there's a large-frame Henry in .45-70 that shoots very accurately. Some months ago, the company announced the box-fed Long Ranger, bored for modern high-pressure cartridges: the .223, .243 and .308. The bolt has a six-lug rotating head and runs on a gear-and-pinion mechanism. Also new at gun counters: a hinged-breech, single-shot Henry with exposed hammer. Its 22-inch barrel in .223, .243 and .308 wears iron sights. Prices: $427 for a steel-breech version, $549 for brass. henryrifles.com.

Howa

The flagship rifle line of Legacy Sports International, Howa bolt rifles feature a push-feed action with a twin-lug bolt, two-stage trigger and three-position safety. The cylindrical receiver is very stout. Earlier Howas had traditional internal box magazines. The detachable boxes that replaced them on several models a few years ago are less appealing to me. The latch protrudes and is easy to trip accidentally. Howa stocks are of walnut and laminates, also synthetics mostly from Hogue. This

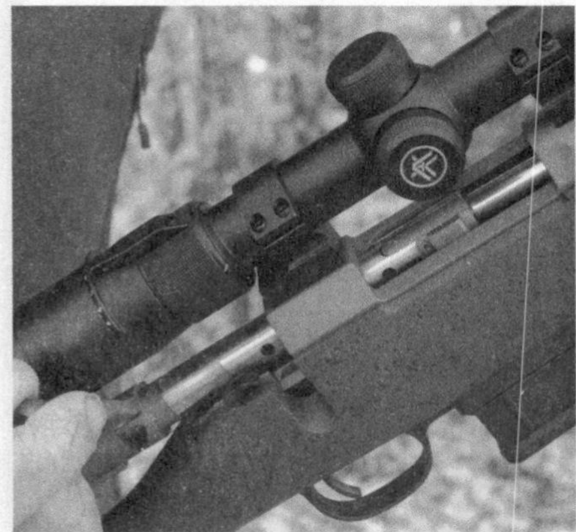

Howa's Alpine is one of several new rifles from Legacy Sports, including a Howa with H-S stock.

First mule deer! This hunter found her Howa rifle in 6.5 Creedmoor just right for a South Dakota buck.

year, you can get a Howa with one of the top-quality synthetic stocks from H-S Precision, with internal bedding block. Chamberings include 6mm Creedmoor.

Howa now offers barreled actions with 24- and heavy 26-inch barrels. They come with the sub-minute accuracy guarantee and lifetime warranty new last year for all Howa rifles bought in the U.S. Last spring, Legacy announced a Bell & Carlson-stocked Long Range rifle with heavy 26-inch barrel threaded at the muzzle. For 2018, there's a new KRG Bravo chassis rifle with aluminum backbone — plus an sAPC rifle with Australian-made chassis, and another chassis model scaled to Howa's Mini-Action. Specifically for long-range shooting, there's the Lithgow Arms LA105 "Woomera," an aboriginal word for "spear thrower." It's fitted with a heavy barrel and a Pic rail with 20 minutes of gain. Like Webley & Scott, Lithgow Arms is now part of the Legacy Sports family. Ditto the Escort brand that until recently represented shotguns only but now includes .22 rifles. Centerfire rifles in the Legacy Sports list come in chamberings from .223 to .300 Win. Mag., in various stock finishes and Cerakoting. Prices: from $529. Legacy offers packages too, with Howa rifles and Nikko Stirling scopes. legacysports.com.

Ithaca

Known for trap guns as well as double-barrel field shotguns, this venerable company roared back in my youth with the Model 37 pump. Now Ithaca has a precision rifle, its receiver machined from a billet of 4340, the bolt from 4140 chrome-moly. The race is EDM-cut for piston-slick bolt travel. Three action lengths accommodate cartridges as big as the .338 Lapua. The chassis stock adjusts for length and comb height. Customers can choose from a wide range of options and accessories. Ithaca also catalogs sporting rifles on the same action. ithacagun.com.

Jarrett

Several decades ago, a southern farmer began building rifles to compete on the benchrest circuit. Hunters soon found in Kenny Jarrett's rifles the accuracy and reach they craved for distant deer. Jarrett's "Beanfield Rifles" earned a national following. They still wear his hand-lapped barrels, but after using a variety of bolt actions, Jarrett has settled on an EDM-cut Tri-Lock action of his own design. Around it he has built a new single-shot Long Ranger rifle, its 27-inch barrel with a 1-in-9 twist for 190- and 220-grain match bullets from his flat-shooting .300 Jarrett cartridge. The Jewell trigger is set light, to help you drill the 4-inch knots Jarrett demands at 800 yards in his accuracy tests. jarrettrifles.com.

Kimber

Since the 84M's 1998 introduction, Kimber's bolt-rifle stable has grown to include L (long) and 8400 (magnum) actions. Lightweight Adirondack and Mountain Ascent sporters have joined laminate-stocked varminters and Talkeetna (synthetic) and Caprivi (walnut) dangerous game rifles. Classic Select and SuperAmerica 84s mollify those of us sweet on walnut. SoftTouch stocks distinguish new versions of synthetic lightweights like the Mountain Ascent and Subalpine (.308, .280 Ackley Improved, .30-06, .300 WSM, .300 Win. Mag.). New camo patterns like Gore's Optifade Subalpine and Optifade Open Country give rise to new sub-models of the 84 series. Kimber's Hunter, its first rifle with a detachable box, is priced well

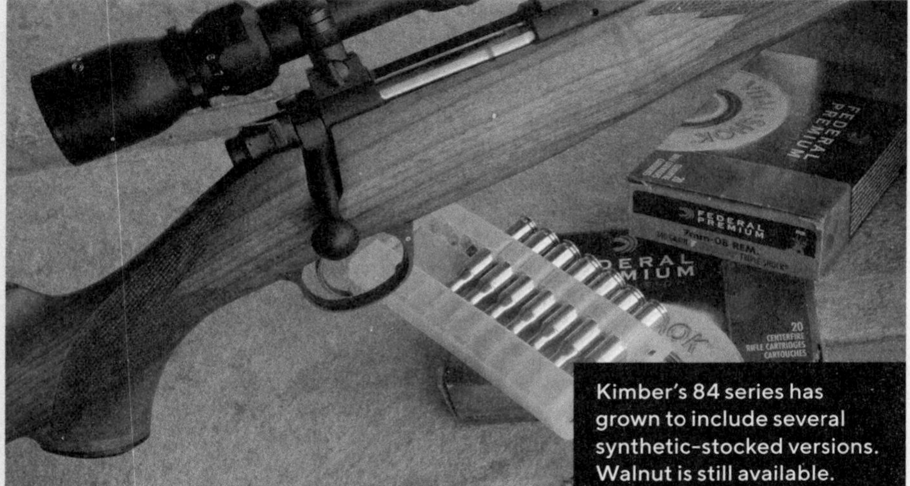

Kimber's 84 series has grown to include several synthetic-stocked versions. Walnut is still available.

Though most Kimber 84-series big game rifles weigh less than 6 pounds, they shoot tight groups.

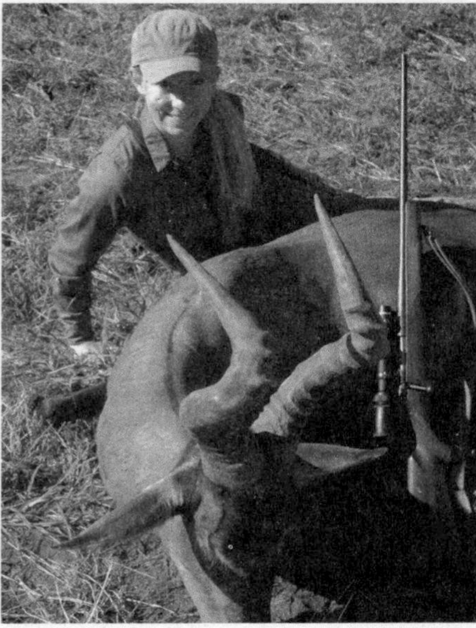

In Namibia, one shot from this hunter's Kimber in .308 ended her hunt for a fine red hartebeest.

below its kin — though it boasts the 84's lugs, extractor and three-position safety, 8-40 scope mount screws and an adjustable trigger. Cost savings come from its molded polymer stock, pillar-bedded to the satin-finished stainless-steel action. The 6 1/2-pound rifle debuted in .243, .257 Roberts, 6.5 Creedmoor, 7mm-08 and .308. It recently appeared in long-action form, too, for the .270, .280 Ackley Improved and .30-06. Big news for 2018 is on the other end of the cost spectrum: The Advanced Tactical SOC II in flat dark earth has a fully adjustable, chassis-style folding stock, five-shot detachable box, extended bolt knob, night vision mount and, of course, threaded barrel. Choose .308 or 6.5 Creedmoor. kimberamerica.com.

Marlin

Two pages of new lever rifles in the 2018 Marlin catalog include laminate-stocked stainless 1894 SBL (.44 Mag.) and CSBL (.357 Mag.) short rifles, rail-equipped and fitted with XS Ghost Ring sights spanning 16 1/2-inch barrels. The 1894 CST has a painted hardwood stock, is suppressor-ready. All three are priced at around $1,150. The 1894C ($788) and 1894CB ($1,092 with octagon barrel, Marble sights) are traditional straight-grip carbines. So is the resurrected Model 336 TDL Texan, with "B Grade" walnut for $999. It comes in .30-30 only. The Model 1895 Trapper in .45-70 with 16 1/2-inch barrel features black (painted hardwood) stock and Skinner sights for $1,123. This is an impressive roster of new firearms for Marlin, given last season's re-introduction of the 1894 Cowboy carbine and the announced return of the .444. Still to be seen: how many announcements become production runs, and how long new rifles last at market. The Remington shop is still finding its way in the production of lever rifles, but recent samples show better workmanship than the rifles boxed after Remington summarily moved production from North Haven to Ilion. Marlin custom rifles, built in Dakota's shop in Sturgis, South Dakota, show excellent materials and construction. On my most recent visit there, Marlins with exquisite wood and finish filled several racks. The actions were silky, triggers better than I've felt on any production-line Marlins in years. But they're expensive. Expect the Model 39, also built by the Dakota crew, to join Custom 336 and 1895 centerfires well above the $2,000 mark. Much more affordable are four new Marlin bolt-action rimfires, .22 LR and .22 WMR, pouring off production lines far from the northern prairie. marlinfirearms.com.

Mauser

The 1898 Mauser endures in rifles like the new Rigby Highland Stalker, built on Mauser actions produced at the Isny, Germany, plant responsible for Mauser-branded 98s that make rifle buffs salivate. In 2015, Mauser re-introduced its classic Magnum and Custom rifles. The double-square-bridge Magnum is pillar bedded with dual recoil lugs. Its billet-machined receiver has a deep magazine. A height-adjustable, banded front sight pairs with an express sight on an island. Point-pattern checkering adorns fine walnut with a black forend tip and a steel grip cap. The Custom version is similar, in standard chamberings, .22-250 to 9.3x64. Paul Mauser showed his genius before the 1898 action appeared. But the '98 captivated armies and sportsmen the world over. It was followed by Mausers of a different stripe. In 1966, the Model 66 used a telescoping bolt in a short receiver. Manufactured from 1974 to 1995, it followed the Model 3000, built by Heym for Mauser. The 77 had a detachable box, as did the three-lug 83 and its progeny, the Model 86, shipped stateside from 1989 to 1996. The SR 93, a 13-pound Mauser in .300 Win. Mag. had a *cast alloy* stock, an integrated bipod. Models 96 and 99, like the 225 and left-hand 226 (formerly KDF's K-15), had multiple-lug heads. The switch-barrel 2000, like Mauser's Lightning, was imported in 1998 only. Surviving late-model Mausers include the 03, introduced in 2003 as a take-down, switch-barrel rifle in 22 chamberings. Its six-lug bolt has interchangeable heads.

The M12, like the 03 named for its debut year, is more traditional and affordable, a gracefully proportioned rifle I had the pleasure of using on an Austrian hunt for chamois. That .270 was blessed with beautiful walnut. I appreciated the adjustable trigger, the flush detachable box easily loaded in the rifle through its generous port. The M12's full-diameter bolt is machined away for three pairs of lugs. The recessed bolt face has two plunger ejectors, an extractor in a forward lug. It has an M70-style three-position safety. All Mausers are now produced in Isny, along with Blaser and Sauer rifles. All three names are owned by the L&O Group. This January I happened to be in Isny as Mauser unveiled its newest rifle, the synthetic-stocked M18. Designed to compete with upscale entry-level rifles in the U.S., it was delivered to dealers in Germany in locked wooden crates not to be opened until the designated date. The suspense may have had its intended effect. Response has been positive, even for shooters hopelessly in love with the 98s that cost several times the M18's street price of around $650. This new rifle has an adjustable trigger, a three-position safety, a recessed, three-lug bolt head chiseled from the full-diameter body. The five-shot detachable box feeds 22- and 24-inch barrels. Mauser wisely configured the receiver to accept Remington 700 scope bases. Under a new Blaser-branded scope, I used factory ammunition to print 3/4-minute groups with the new Mauser 18. Great value from a great name. mauser.com.

Montana Rifle Company

Some years ago, Brian Sipe started making Winchester Model 70-style actions with investment-cast receivers, and manufacturing hand-lapped, button-rifled barrels for them. His son Jeff now runs the rifle enterprise and has trotted out a constant stream of new models, in chamberings to .338 Lapua and .505 Gibbs. Prices range into the mid-$3,000s. Timney triggers are standard. My 1999 Montana rifle in .280 is nimble and accurate. A stainless version in .375 has served me in Alaska and on dangerous game in Africa. Stocks of walnut and laminated wood give customers a choice, though the company's own synthetic stocks are top sellers. Cartridge lists include popular benchrest and Ackley rounds. Barrels from the Sipes' Montana Rifleman shop next door are still standard equipment. montanarifleco.com.

Mossberg

The MVP Precision is Mossberg's entry into the growing affordable long-range segment of the rifle market. Its Luth-AR MBA-3 adjustable buttstock complements the chassis atop a Magpul MOE grip up front. The 20- or 24-inch threaded barrel is of heavy contour and chambered in 6.5 Creedmoor and .308. Hunters enamored of traditional rifles should like the Revere, with its skip-checkered European walnut stock and rosewood caps. It's available in 6.5 Creedmoor, of course. So is the new Cerakoted Patriot, with its black synthetic stock. Choose from five other long- and short-action chamberings in both rifles. Mossberg has added the Patriot Super Bantam in .243 (it's also available in 7mm-08 and .308). The military look hasn't left the line. A new MVP Light Chassis rifle has short, stiff barrels in .223, 6.5 Creedmoor and .308. Per the new Precision, it comes with a Pic rail. So do MVP Tactical, Scout and Patrol rifles. Like all MVPs barreled for .308-size cartridges, they take the detachable boxes for M14s and AR-10s. Mossberg brings features of match-worthy precision rifles within reach of modest budgets. The flagship Patriot series of bolt rifles, in matte blue or Marinecote metal finish, with walnut, synthetic and laminated hunting-style stocks, are sturdy and accurate. Chamberings: .22-250 to .375 Ruger. My .375 Patriot handles like a wand, is reliable as sunrise, but costs less than any other dangerous game rifle I'd carry into the thickets! mossberg.com.

Nosler

All renditions of the Nosler 48 rifle employ the same push-feed bolt action. It has a three-position thumb safety, a recessed bolt face with Sako-style extractor, and plunger ejector flanked by twin locking lugs lapped for uniform contact. The adjustable trigger comes set for a 3- to 4-pound pull. Available in a wide range of popular chamberings — including the .22, .26, .28, .30 and .33 Nosler — the 48 feeds from an internal stack secured by a hinged floorplate. The Heritage version has a conservatively shaped walnut stock checkered 20 lpi in point patterns. The Patriot and Outfitter wear pillar- and glass-bedded synthetic stocks with alloy bedding rails. The Outfitter, designed for tough hunts for tough game, comes in seven chamberings, .308 to .458 Win. Mag. It has a blind magazine and open sights. Long-Range and Western rifles are Cerakoted. The Custom rifle offers a host of options, which you can specify online. nosler.com.

Proof Research

When it joined Jense Precision and Lone Wolf Rifle Stocks, Advanced Barrel Systems brought to the union a patent for carbon fiber-wrapped barrels six times stiffer and 10 times stronger than steel. Proof Research resulted, a firm for which 27,000-square-foot Montana facility is only part of its assets. Advanced Composites Division, in Dayton, Ohio, contributes composites developed in its work with the defense and aerospace industries. A partnership with Lawrence Barrels has added conventional stainless barrels to the Proof carbon fiber barrels that have tallied top scores in Palma, Sniper and Precision matches. Complete rifles include ARs and bolt-actions. Proof actions are wire EDM-cut, and pre-hardened before machining to hold tolerances. Bolts of 4340 chrome-moly have M16-type extractors, and threads for interchangeable knobs. The 7-pound Terminus bolt gun comes with a half-minute accuracy guarantee. My first three shots from a sample .308 cut one hole. An integral Pic rail with 20 minutes of gain keeps you from running out of dial. The 8 3/4-pound Tac II has a target-style, adjustable-comb stock and a detachable box. Proof spares nothing to satisfy the most demanding shooters. Its million-frame-per-second ballistics camera ensures the engineers don't miss anything in testing. proofresearch.com.

Quarter Minute Magnums

In their native Pennsylvania, they built accurate bolt rifles — a natural avocation where woodchuck shooting and benchrest matches followed development of the Kentucky rifle. The accuracy standard of half-inch groups at 200 yards may seem absurd. But after moving to western Idaho to indulge their lust for big game hunting, Scott and Vickie Harrold found that goal attainable, even with rifles weighing less than 8 pounds. Scott prefers BAT actions but uses Remington 700s too, fitted with cut-rifled, hand-lapped #5 Krieger barrels. He likes tight chambers and "just enough spin to stabilize long bullets." Neck-turned hulls perform best, he says, but he's built rifles for hunters who use factory ammo. McMillan HTG stocks and rails with 20 minutes gain are standard. The customer can specify the trigger. Scott installs brakes on request, noting, however, that they can affect accuracy. To ensure their concentricity, he buys BAT brakes undersize and bores them .020-inch over groove diameter. quarterminutemagnums.com.

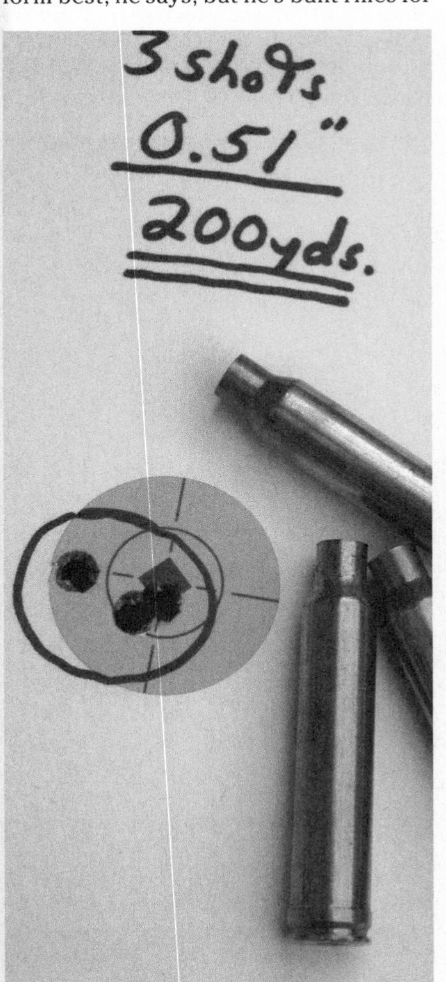

Quarter Minute Magnums, a Lewiston, Idaho shop, builds long-range rifles that shoot like this.

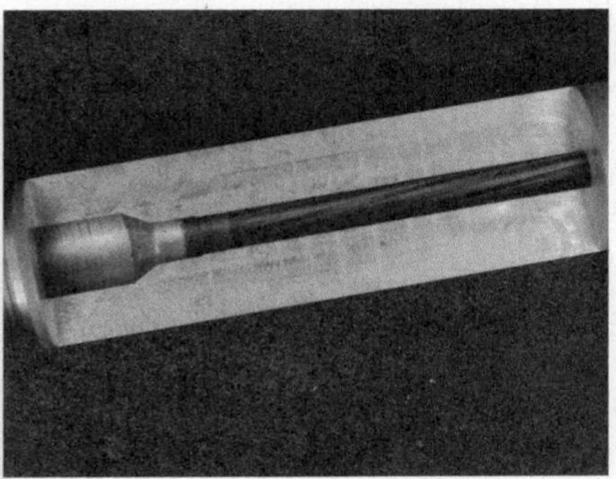
This cutaway of a Quarter Minute Magnum barrel shows its clean, minimum-diameter throat.

Remington

The theme for 2018 seems to be "suppressed," as three of the five rifles Remington notes as new in its catalog have short-threaded barrels. The Model Seven Threaded, 783 HBT (Heavy Barrel Threaded) and 597 Kryptek Threaded .22 join the Model 700 5R Threaded Gen 2 and 700 PCR (Precision Chassis Rifle). These latter two feature threaded barrels as well, but they're of "normal" length. The Model 700 5R boasts a stock by H-S Precision. The PCR in .260, 6.5 Creedmoor and .308 has a 24-inch barrel with 5R rifling and a Magpul PRS Gen 3 adjustable stock behind an alloy chassis. (The 700 *Tactical* Chassis, in .308, .300 Win. Mag., and .338 Lapua, has a TriNyte-coated stainless-barreled action, a Bell & Carlson stock. At $3,500, it lists for nearly triple the price of Model 700 Magpul rifles in .260 and .308.) The CDL Limited this year is a walnut-stocked stainless rifle in 6.5 Creedmoor. There's a new Long Range Stainless 700 in 7mm Rem. Mag., .300 Win. Mag. and .300 RUM. It features a 26-inch barrel, a Bell & Carlson M40 stock. This year, Remington has added the .338 Win. Mag. to the cartridge roster for its Model 700 American Wilderness Rifle, bringing the total chamberings to seven. The 6.5 Creedmoor has joined cartridge lists for the ADL and SPS. A replacement for the traditional M700 trigger, the X-Mark Pro delivers a 3 1/2-pound out-of-the-box pull. Cerberus Capital Management still controls the company. remington.com.

Rigby

In 1907, in the Kumaon District of India, Jim Corbett was presented with a Rigby bolt rifle for killing the Champawat tigress, a man-eater that by all reports had claimed more than 400 victims. That .275 has since returned to Rigby in London, where it has helped fuel a company revival.

The first John Rigby opened a gun shop in Dublin in 1775. His son William joined him to build dueling pistols, hunting rifles and shotguns. Eldest son William joined John in 1816. Two years later the elder Rigby died, and William invited his brother John Jason into the shop. John Jason died in 1845; but William Rigby lived until 1858, when *his* son John, then 29, assumed control of the company. In 1865, the enterprise moved to London as John Rigby & Co.,72 James Street, to sell "breech- and muzzle-loading guns, revolvers and ammunition." Rigby's first double rifle with "rising bite" lockup appeared in 1879. In 1887, the third-generation John Rigby worked on the .303 SMLE rifle. Then, with the gunpowder firm of Curtis & Harvey, he developed the powerful .450 NE 3 1/4" — a double-rifle round that after its 1898 debut would become a ballistic template for many dangerous-game cartridges.

About this time, Rigby also secured in Germany a 12-year exclusive license to sell Mauser actions and rifles across the U.K. and its colonies. Mauser's non-rotating extractor, engineered to prevent double-loading jams in battle, made this stout action popular with hunters, too. In 1899, Rigby requested a bigger action for its new .400/350 NE. Mauser responded with a magnum action. Three years later, the rimless .416 Rigby appeared. A century later it remains one of the most popular cartridges for African big game.

Rigby's fortunes have waxed and waned. Short years ago, the company hired a new Managing Director, Marc Newton, to revive Britain's oldest gunmaker. Newton lost no time getting support in this venture from Bernhard Knobel, who oversees Mauser production for the L&O Group in Isny, Germany. Mauser's 98 Magnum action soon begat the new Rigby Big Game rifle. Finished to pre-war standards of quality in London by gun-crafters with decades of experience, the new Rigby in .375, .416 and .450 was followed this past year by a lighter, slimmer rifle bored for the likes of the .275 Rigby (7mm Mauser). It's no coincidence that the new Highland Stalker bears close resemblance to the lithe rifle given to Jim Corbett in 1907. Available also in .308, .30-06, 8x57 and 9.3x62, it comes alive in hand and steadies quickly on target. Iron sights, a scope-friendly safety, and an adjustable trigger complement near-seamless fitting of lean, checkered Turkish walnut to the deep-black steel. johnrigbyandco.com.

Ruger

Over the last six years, Ruger's American centerfire bolt rifle has spawned a stream of variations, each proving again that the original price of $450 made this rifle the bargain of its decade for hunters who wanted a durable, reliable, but extremely accurate rifle. The first American I fired, under a Zeiss 3-9x40 Conquest, sent three 168-grain Hornadys into a 2 3/4-inch group *at 300 yards!* The knots got tighter. A 6.5 Creedmoor barrel on my American Predator is so accurate as to imperil horseflies on 100-yard paper. Last year, Ruger added the 6mm Creedmoor

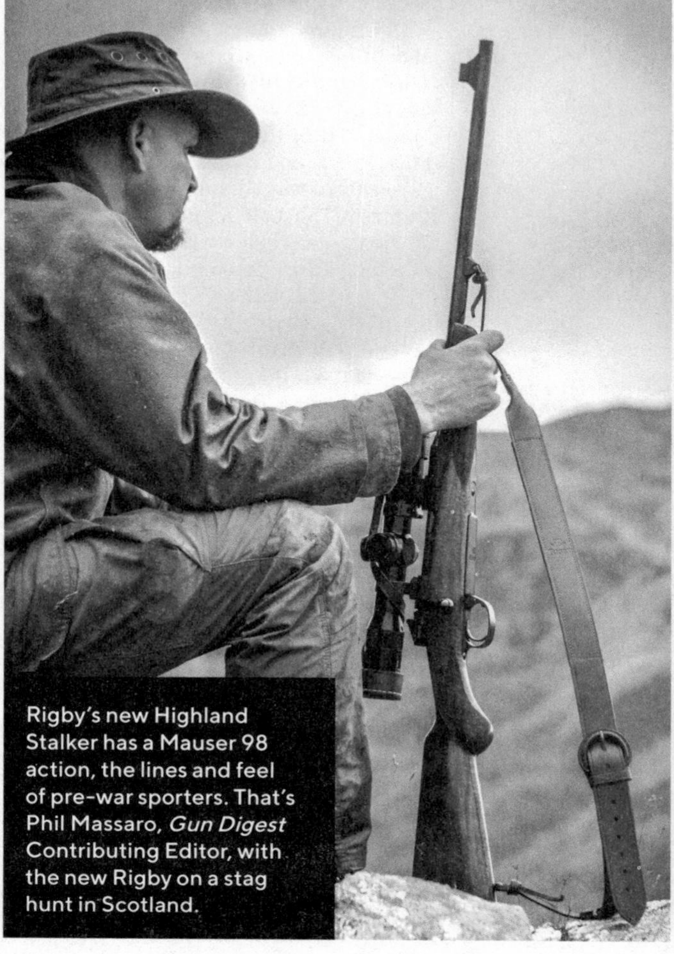

Rigby's new Highland Stalker has a Mauser 98 action, the lines and feel of pre-war sporters. That's Phil Massaro, *Gun Digest* Contributing Editor, with the new Rigby on a stag hunt in Scotland.

The .275 Rigby, a classic cartridge used by Jim Corbett, is the 7x57 Mauser by another name.

In London, Rigby fits fine walnut to Mauser actions. Hornady now offers .275 Rigby ammunition.

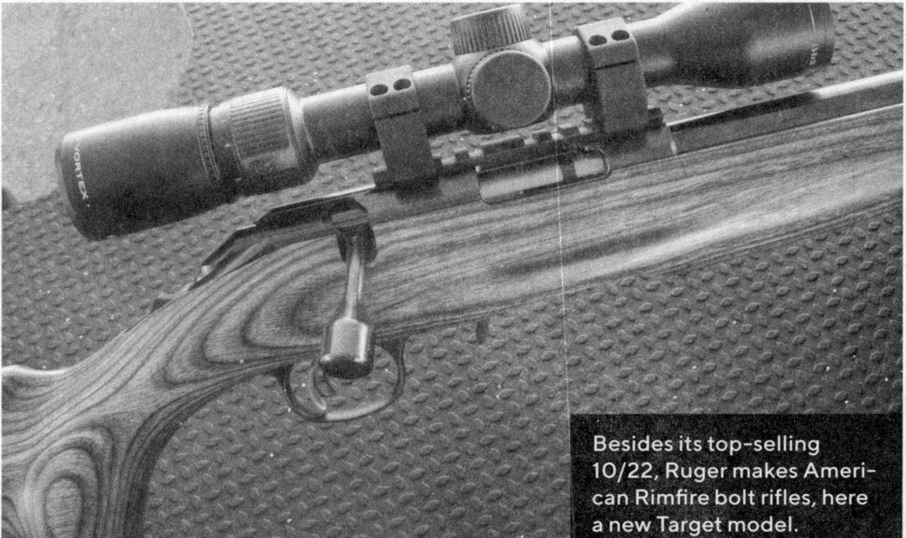
Besides its top-selling 10/22, Ruger makes American Rimfire bolt rifles, here a new Target model.

chambering, in an American Predator barrel rifled 1-in-7 3/4. For 2018, Predator magazine options include A1- and AR-style boxes, as well as the standard rotary box I still prefer. There's also a series of new Predators with stocks in Go Wild camo. New American Ranch rifles, and package rifles with Vortex Crossfire II scopes, have also appeared.

This year, Ruger has tweaked its RPR enough that the rifle qualifies as "new" in the catalog. It's available in .308, and in 6mm and 6.5 Creedmoor, at $1,599. In the AR-556 line, there's a fresh MPR in 5.56/.223with Magpul furniture and a 1-in-8 bore for $899. A lightweight version with a shorter, 16-inch barrel, retails at $849. Ruger's Hawkeye stable has a new entry, too: the Long-Range Target. It features a laminated stock painted bronze with black flecks. Adjustable for pull and comb height, it has a long, flat forend, a steep grip. The 24-inch heavy barrel, in .300 Win. Mag., wears a Ruger Hybrid Muzzle Brake. Fed by a detachable five-shot box mag, the receiver boasts a Pic rail with 20 minutes of angle to send your shots to the middle at distance without running you short of scope adjustment. The Long-Range Target lists for $1,279. Consistent with its limited availability the last few years, Ruger's elegant No. 1 single-shot comes this year in the "A" or Light Sporter configuration, in .450 Marlin. There's a less traditional alternative with stainless steel and a black laminate stock (no schnable) in .450 Bushmaster. MSRP for each: $1,899. Much more affordable is Ruger's ageless 10/22 autoloading .22 rimfire, which has sold into the millions and appears in myriad versions. Its new stablemate for 2018 is an American Rimfire in .22 LR, with 18-inch threaded barrel and laminated thumbhole stock, for $559. ruger.com.

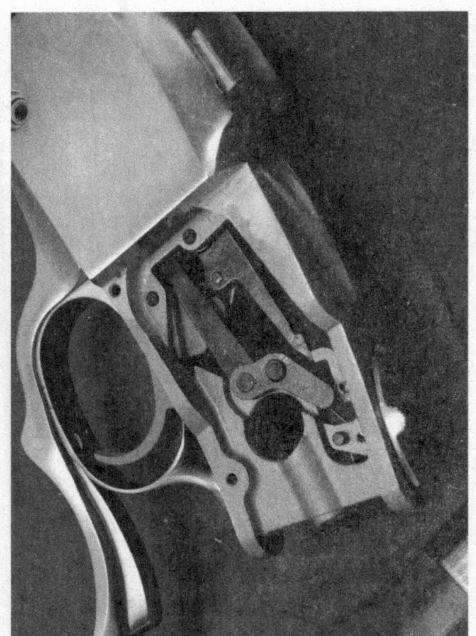
Ruger's No. 1, once a production-line rifle, is now made only in limited numbers and costs $1,899.

Sauer

Established in 1751, the German firm that now makes firearms for the L&O Group that also owns Mauser and Blaser has distinguished itself lately building rifles with the clean looks American shooters have come to consider, well, American! The upscale 404 and flagship Model 101 in various forms (like the "Forest" in my rack) has been joined by an expanding line of Model 100 bolt rifles priced from $899 for the CeraTech, in 14 chamberings, .222 to 9.3x62. The black synthetic stock is sleek and straight, with textured grip panels. The three-lug bolt with 60-degree lift complements a three-position safety, a trigger adjustable from 2.2 to 4.2 pounds. A detachable box magazine holds five rounds in a staggered stack. Long-range shooters will warm to the Fieldshoot and Pantera, perfectly stocked for prone shooting and the first rifles commercially bored for Hornady's hot new 6.5 PRC round, necked from the .300 RCM. I've fired these new Sauers and easily kept bullets well inside the 1-minute groups Sauer guarantees. sauer.de.

Author adores this iron-sighted Sauer 101 in 9.3x62, a smooth-cycling rifle that's very accurate.

Sauer's dual-purpose Pantera is the first rifle bored for Hornady's new 6.5 Precision Rifle Cartridge.

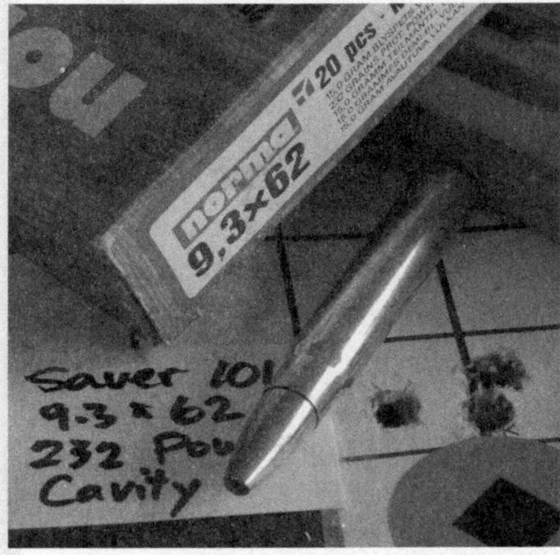

Power and accuracy — Sauer's nimble 101 in "nine-three" delivers both. The rifle has fine balance.

Savage

Sixty years after its debut, what started life as the Savage Model 110 (at $110!) still sells briskly. It was built with price in mind. A bolt-face extractor and plunger ejector, and a barrel nut for headspacing, reined in costs. Inexpensive synthetics have since replaced the original walnut stock. The tang safety was less a cost-control measure than a smart pitch to southpaws. It's as easy to use from the left shoulder as the right. Now it has three positions. Savage's jar-proof AccuTrigger, adjustable down to 1 1/2 pounds, appeared in 2003 and sparked an industry-wide search for safe but "easy" triggers. To distinguish among 110-based rifles, Savage adopted two-digit numbers for short actions, three-digit for long. Chrome-moly and stainless-steel hunting rifles are 11/111 and 16/116. Walnut-stocked Classics (14/114) include a .243 in my rack. It has taken several deer and printed groups as small as 0.35.

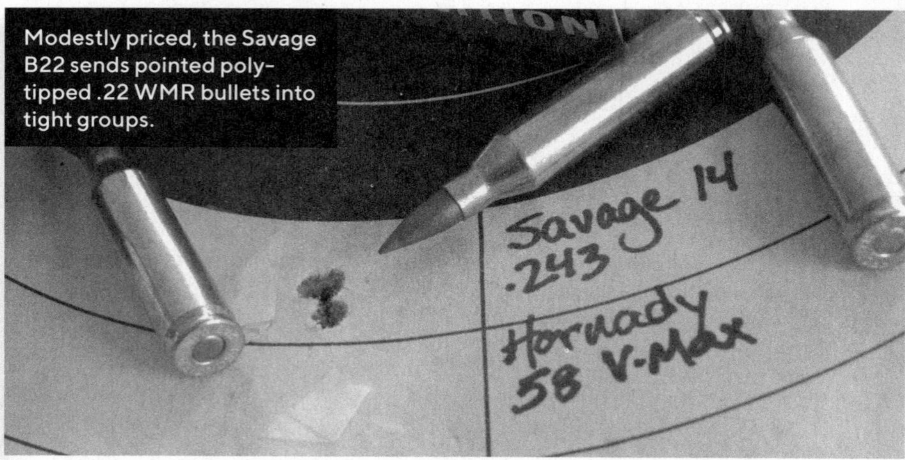

Modestly priced, the Savage B22 sends pointed poly-tipped .22 WMR bullets into tight groups.

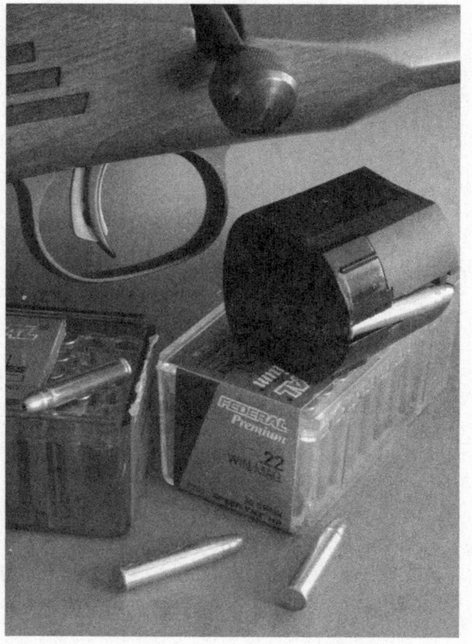

Savage's new B22 in .22 WMR has a rotary box magazine, a well-shaped stock and bolt knob, and AccuTrigger.

Recently, I used an engineering sample of a new Savage bolt rifle. Its stock has a longer, slimmer wrist, plus grooves for better purchase on checkered grip panels. Comb and recoil pad are detachable. Five combs of different heights interchange easily. Chevron-shaped butt spacers of three thicknesses fit snugly, each recessed to accept the rim of the next. They maintain the toe line of the stock, instead of changing it abruptly as do most spacers. Fitting the stock perfectly to my body and shooting style took a few short minutes. Next day, on the mountain, I spied a wink of tan through the black boles of a burn. By great good luck, I managed to intercept the moving elk and sent a Trophy Copper bullet. Recoil hid him as he crashed away. Suddenly, he tumbled down-slope, legs flailing loosely, to lodge against a calico, fire-stripped fir. Sleet from a fast-moving cloud pelted me as I quartered the animal.

The prototype handle on that rifle appears now as the AccuFit stock on eleven 110s — yes, they're again called 110s. The new-for-2018 roster features Hunter, Long-Range Hunter, Varmint Hunter, Bear Hunter, Wolverine, Predator, Hog Hunter, Tactical, Scout, Storm and Lightweight Storm variations, from $594. In budget-priced rifles, Savage has the new Model 110 Engage and Brush Hunter, and Axis II XP. Its line of precision rifles now includes the Model 10 APO. (Ashley Precision Ordnance supplies its Saber MRCS-AR folding chassis.) In 6.5 Creedmoor and .308, the 10 APO joins heavy-barrel rifles in Target and Law Enforcement groups. The new Stealth Evolution with bronze Cerakote finish on its alloy chassis comes in 12 chamberings from $1,799 (left-hand models, too). A similar Stealth in black comes with an alternative stock. The new Model 10 GRS in 6mm Creedmoor and other fast-steppers has a prone stock of traditional form. Rifles of MSR or AR-15 design increase by four this year. The MSR Valkyrie is bored for Federal's fresh .22 Valkyrie cartridge. It appears in the MSR 15 Recon Long Range Precision as well, with the 6.8 SPC and .22 Nosler. There's an MSR10 Long Range in 6mm Creedmoor, an MSR 10 Hunter in .338 Federal. Five rimfires, including a fine wood-stocked B22 in .22 WMR ($459), round out the new Savage offerings for 2018. savagearms.com.

Savage is backing off the proliferation of model numbers for 110-based rifles. Accuracy remains.

Steyr

Decades ago, the Steyr factory was turning out svelte Mannlicher-Schoenauer rifles. Current Steyr products lack that classic pre-war styling, but they're accurate rifles, with cold-hammer-forged barrels. The new Pro THB (Tactical Heavy Barrel) has a synthetic stock adjustable for length, and a five-round detachable box. It's chambered in .308, lists for $1,265. Also for 2018, Steyr has announced the Zephyr II rimfire rifle, in .22 LR, .17 HMR and .22

Steyr of Austria once fielded Mannlicher-Schoenauer rifles, that ancestry evident in modern Steyrs.

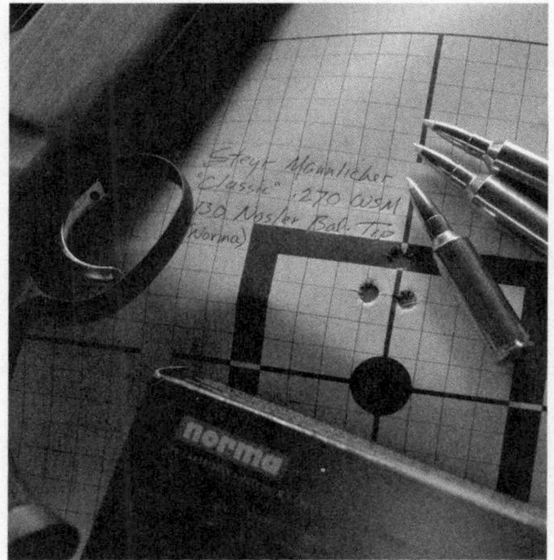

Author shot this 0.6-inch group with a Steyr Mannlicher Classic in .270 WSM — then took it hunting.

WMR. At just under six pounds with a 20-inch barrel, the rifle retails at $995. steyr-arms.com.

Tikka

Tikka has manufactured a wide range of items, from sewing machines to submachine guns. After WWII, it turned to hunting rifles and collaborated with another Finnish company, Sako, on a Model 555 bolt action. Later, Sako acquired Tikka (26 years its senior) and the shotgun firm Valmet. By 1989, production at Tikkakoski Works had moved to Sako's Riihimaki plant. Tikka sold its Whitetail rifle stateside during the 1990s, then, in 2003 introduced its new T3 to a welcoming market. The smooth-cycling, twin-lug bolt strips cartridges from a single-stack polymer box. A two-detent safety locks bolt and trigger, which adjusts from 2 to

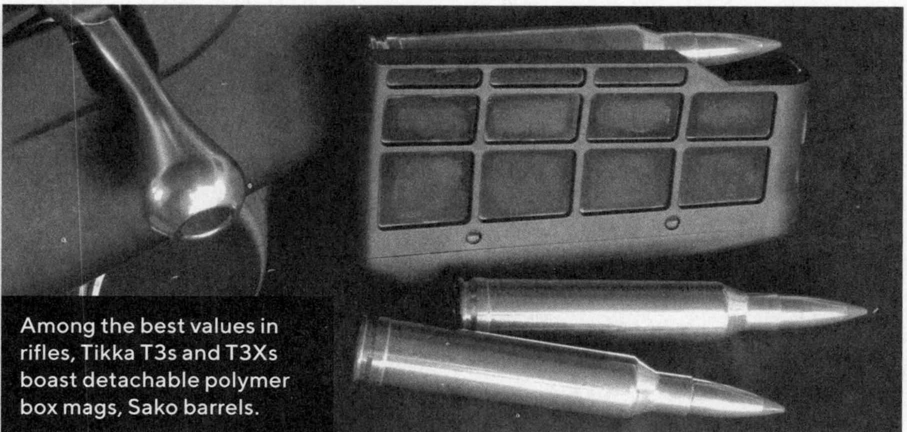

Among the best values in rifles, Tikka T3s and T3Xs boast detachable polymer box mags, Sako barrels.

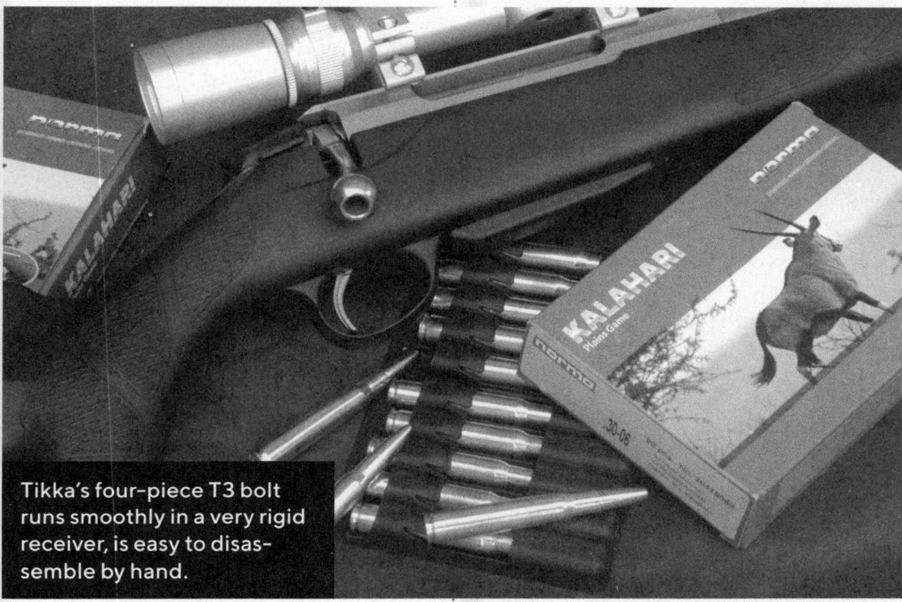

Tikka's four-piece T3 bolt runs smoothly in a very rigid receiver, is easy to disassemble by hand.

4 pounds. Range trials and hunts with T3s impressed me. Several rifles shot into 0.75 MOA. Behind a Norwegian elkhound in a Finnish forest, I spied a cow moose and fired offhand with my T3. Steam blew into the shadows. She spun and dropped. On another hunt, a bull paused in a narrow shot alley in the woods. Down he went to my shot. So did a whitetail later that week.

The T3 has many features of the costlier Sako 75 — including Sako barrels. Bolt stops suit the T3 action to different cartridge lengths. The T3 was succeeded in 2016 by the T3X, with a modular synthetic stock. Interchangeable slabs let you customize the grip. A robust recoil pad reduces the shock of violent loads; foam inserts in the butt muffle noise from the stock shell. The T3X's generous port permits easier single loading. Additional mounting holes anchor Picatinny rails. Tikka lists 19 configurations of the T3X, in chamberings from .204 Ruger. New for 2018 is the rimfire version, the T1X. It looks and handles much like a T3X, and its action has a similar bedding surface. The stock even accepts T3X grip shells. A 10-round detachable box comes with both .22 LR and .17 HMR rifles. It feeds a stainless bolt.

In Finland, game is managed by 300 state-sanctioned associations comprising around 2,370 clubs with 140,000 members. Hunters needn't join, but members get access to the best habitat in a country that puts 300,000 riflemen afield after moose. About 84 percent of the 22 million pounds of venison marketed annually in Finland is moose. Much of it is brought to earth with Tikka rifles. beretta.com.

Volquartsen

Now in its 44th year, this family-owned business uses CNC and wire-EDM machines to turn steel into slick-cycling autoloading rimfires that deliver one-hole accuracy. Volquartsen makes the only self-loading rifle I know for the hot

The author used this Volquartsen and a red-dot sight to down a fox squirrel. Racy stocks are standard.

.17 WSM rimfire. Its tungsten alloy bolt runs in a stainless receiver with integral rail. The rotary eight-shot magazine feeds a stiff 20-inch stainless barrel. Volquartsen's Fusion rifle lets you switch barrels from .22 LR to .22 WMR to .17 HMR without tools. Its counterweighted bolt reliably handles WMR and HMR ammo. Triggers break like icicles at just over 2 pounds. The Evolution gas-driven centerfire in .204 and .223 boasts a nitride-treated bolt in a stainless receiver. Volquartsen's colorful, sleekly contoured laminated stocks are not only eye-catching; they afford nimble handling and help you wring center hits from these super-accurate rifles in hunting positions. volquartsen.com.

Fastest 6.5? Your handloads probably won't beat factory fodder for Weatherby's latest magnum.

Weatherby

The Camilla, a short, lightweight rifle named for Roy Weatherby's wife and designed for women, got its field test three years ago when six "Safari Sisters" joined me for a Namibia hunt. This Vanguard model, priced at $849, now comes in five chamberings: .240 Wby., 6.5 Creedmoor, .270, .308 and .30-06. The Vanguard series has other new entries, too, like the Vanguard Adaptive Composite (VAC) in .223, 6.5 Creedmoor and .308. It has an adjustable target stock, a threaded barrel. For 2018, Weatherby is fielding a new Mark V Altitude, with carbon-fiber stock in 10 chamberings, 6.5 Creedmoor to .300 Wby. In both 6- and 9-lug actions ($3,000 and $3,200), the Altitude comes with 1-minute accuracy guarantee. So does the new Mark V KCR (Krieger Custom Rifle). Famous barrel-maker John Krieger is supplying his cut-rifled barrels for this rifle, with oversize bolt knob and black and Flat Dark Earth Cerakoting. Available in .257, 6.5-300, .300 and .30-378 Wby., the $3,600 KRC features a hand-laminated carbon-fiber stock with full-length bedding rail. weatherby.com.

Winchester

The Model 1866 "Yellow Boy" followed the Henry rifle resulting from the1855 purchase, by 40 New York investors, of a struggling firm that became the Volcanic Repeating Arms Company. Director Oliver F. Winchester moved the enterprise to New Haven, Connecticut. When in 1857 slow sales sent it into receivership, he bought all assets for $40,000 to establish the New Haven Arms Company and hired Benjamin Tyler Henry to improve the Volcanic rifle. The Henry rifle begat the 1866, with rear loading gate and wooden forend. Like other Winchester reproductions, the current Model 1866 is built by Miroku in Japan. This Short Rifle is of carefully fitted, its receiver, forend cap and crescent of polished brass. The 20-inch barrel in .44-40 or .38 Special has a folding-ladder sight. For 2018, the commemorative stable gets a new 1873 Carbine (it followed the '66) in .357, .44-40 and .45 Colt. Like the 1866, it lists for $1,300.

Now in several chamberings, the Camilla is named after Roy Weatherby's wife. It fits women well.

With new versions, Winchester's XPR (here in .325 WSM) is gaining on the costlier Model 70.

Cross-members stiffen the XPR forend. Note the inserted steel recoil lug; it engages a receiver slot.

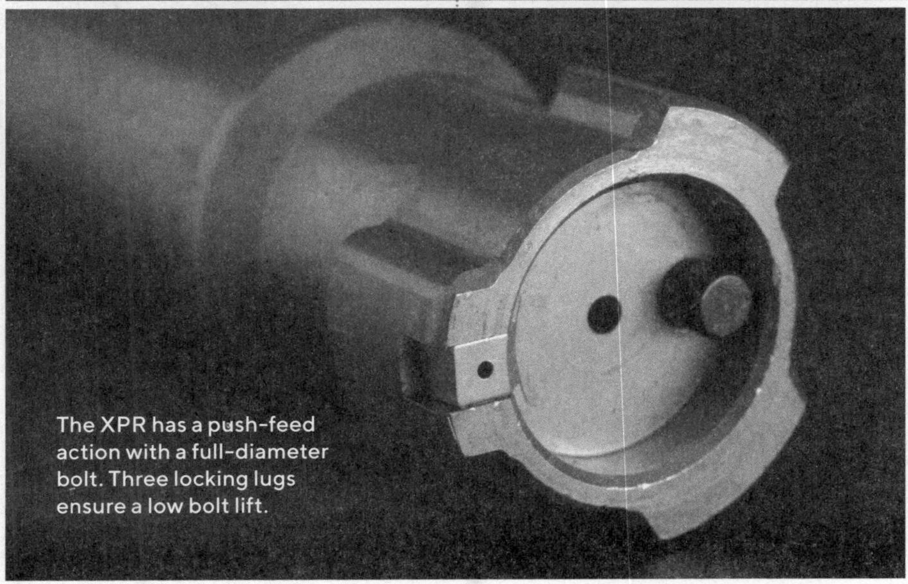
The XPR has a push-feed action with a full-diameter bolt. Three locking lugs ensure a low bolt lift.

In modern rifles, Winchester adds to the XPR bolt-action series that's taking market share from the firm's flagship Model 70. A new chassis-frame XPC precision rifle in .243, 6.5 Creedmoor and .308, with a Magpul PRS Gen 3 buttstock and 10-shot detachable box mag retails for $1,600. The 6.5 Creedmoor joins current cartridge rosters for XPR hunting rifles, and a walnut-stocked XPR Sporter makes its debut in 12 chamberings. Recent range trials with a synthetic-stocked XPR Hunter in .325 WSM impressed me. The button-rifled chrome-moly barrel is secured by a nut that economically ensures accurate headspacing. A full-diameter bolt recessed behind three locking lugs runs in a receiver machined from bar stock. Both are chrome-moly steel, the bolt body nickel Teflon-coated for smooth travel and easy 60-degree lift. The plunger ejector and lug-mounted extractor bracket a recessed bolt face. Cartridges push-feed from a single stack in a detachable polymer box. The ejection port is big enough for the occasional top feed by hand. A two-position sliding thumb safety locks the bolt. A tab in front lets you cycle the bolt without taking the rifle off safe. The M.O.A trigger on the XPR and current M70s is screw-adjustable for weight and over-travel. Perceived movement is minimal, consistent and smooth. Within an ounce of 3 pounds out of the box, the pull is the best I've felt for some time on a production-class bolt gun.

Scope-mount holes in the receiver accept stout 8-40 screws, a smarter choice than standard 6-48s (#6 diameter, 48 threads per inch) for the heavy scopes popular now. A slot in the receiver's belly engages the steel recoil bar in the polymer stock. Slim in profile, the fore-stock has internal cross-members to minimize flex. Textured panels on grip surfaces fore and aft keep cold hands from slipping. Internal ribs in a thick "Inflex Technology" buttpad mitigate recoil and direct the comb away from your face. I used a Leupold 2.5-8x36 scope in Talley rings for range tests with three Winchester loads: 175-grain Ballistic Silvertips, 200-grain AccuBonds, and 220-grain Power Max Bondeds. All landed, strangely enough, in the same place. Three-shot groups averaged 1.2 inches. Though half-minute knots seem common these days, I'm mighty satisfied with hunting rifles that consistently print into 1 1/4 MOA, as tight as I can hold in hunting conditions. While the XPR doesn't match the Model 70's long history or cosmetic appeal, it boasts the feel, fit and function of a hunting rifle to depend on. Its price makes it a bargain. winchesterguns.com.

The Dan Wesson 50th Anniversary 1911 has classy engraving and G10 grips that look like ivory.

NEW SEMI-AUTO HANDGUNS

BY **ROBERT SADOWSKI**

While the lion's share of pistols manufactured today are of the striker-fire variety, the innovations and improvements in the 1911 platform are widespread this year. Kimber, Springfield Armory, Dan Wesson, Remington, Taurus and others are providing options that range from officer-size to 6-inch-barreled full-size pistols. SIG, Canik, Ruger and others push the envelope on polymer striker-fire pistols with economical options for personal defense and concealed carry. The AR rifle platform lends itself well to a pistol and Springfield Armory, Bushmaster and other manufacturers have optimized these with abbreviated barrels and braces. The sad news coming out of Morgan, Utah, is that the Browning Hi Power is no longer in production. The Hi Power had been in production since 1935 and cataloged since 1954. Here is a look at new semi-automatic pistols introduced this year.

The SIG P220 in 10mm in new Legion variant.

The Kimber Micro 9 Desert Night.

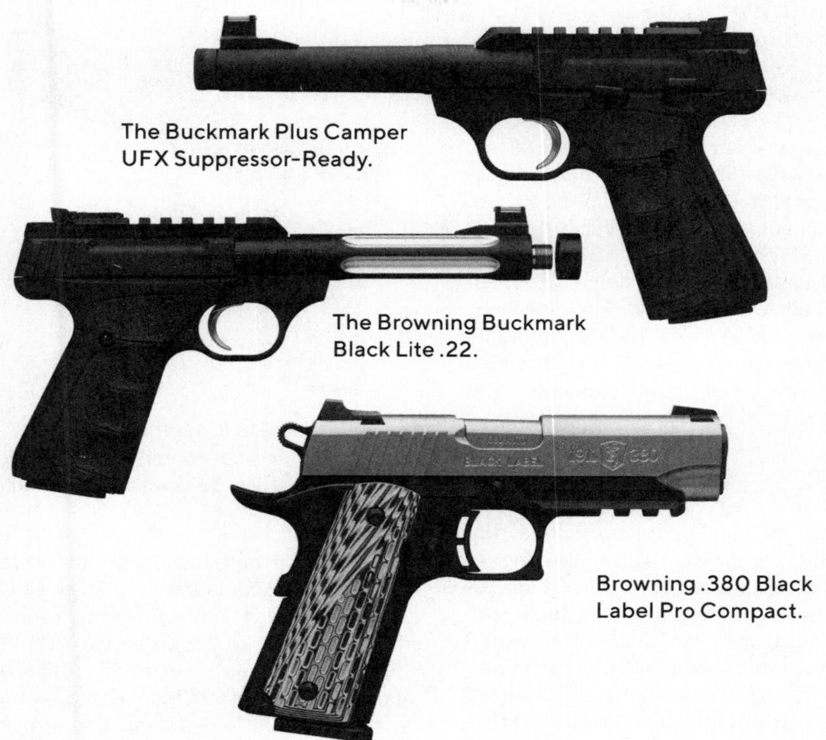

The Buckmark Plus Camper UFX Suppressor-Ready.

The Browning Buckmark Black Lite .22.

Browning .380 Black Label Pro Compact.

Browning

The 1911-380 Black Label series from Browning now includes four new Pro Stainless models: the Compact (MSRP: $799) with a 3.625-inch barrel and Full Size (MSRP: $799) with a 4.25-inch barrel. The Compact and Full Size also come in a Rail model (MSRP: $829) with accessory rail. These 85-percent-size 1911-platform pistols feature a stainless slide, polymer receiver, and grooved black/white G-10 composite grips. The Buck Mark Plus UFX (MSRP: $499) sports a threaded muzzle with a ½-28 thread spec and thread protector, matte blue finish, single-action trigger, UFX ambidextrous grips, Pro-Target white outline adjustable rear sight, TRUGLO/Marble Arms fiber-optic front sight and Picatinny top rail. The Buck Mark Plus Lite Flute UFX (MSRP: $620) has a heavily fluted 6-inch barrel with a threaded muzzle. It weighs just 5 ounces. browning.com

Bushmaster

Who needs an SBR and all that tax-stamp-document-hoop-jumping when there is the SquareDrop Pistol (MSRP: $1,399). Chambered in 5.56 NATO or .300 AAC BLK, this AR pistol sports a 7-, 9- or 10-inch barrel made of 4150 chrome-moly steel. It has a SquareDrop rail for free-floated accuracy and accessory mounting, plus an SB tactical arm brace. bushmaster.com

CZ-USA

The CZ-75/85 platform lends itself to modification and action pistol shooting, and the AccuShadow 2 (MSRP: $1,999) kicks it up a notch or two. It features a 1911-style AccuBushing that makes it capable of sub-3-inch groups at 50 yards. The Shadow 2 Black & Blue (MSRP: $1,299) is also built for competition on the SP-01 platform with a higher beavertail and undercut trigger guard, so the shooter's hand is as close to the bore axis as possible. Plus, with a contoured slide, most of the reciprocating mass is contained below the bore, equating to less muzzle flip. The trigger components have been tweaked for a smooth DA and crisp SA pull. The 9mm Scorpion EVO series now includes a compact EVO 3 S2 Micro pistol (MSRP: $1,149) with a 4-inch barrel and a collapsed length of just over 16 inches. This pint-sized pistol comes with a NoOsprey faux suppressor and telescoping SB Tactical arm brace. The SP-01 pistol is now available in a white nitride slide and FDE frame (MRSP: $539). The SP-01 can be had with an urban gray frame and suppressor-ready (MSRP: $549). The P-07 Compact (MSRP: $539) and Full Size (MSRP: $599) pistols are now available in an OD green frame. cz-usa.com

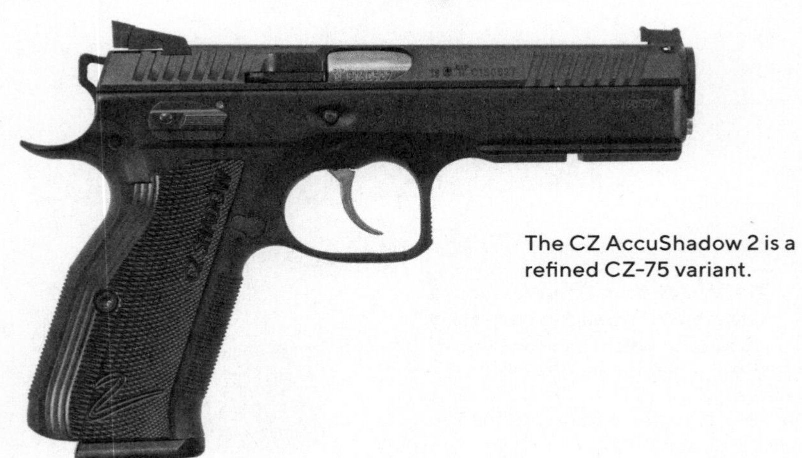

The CZ AccuShadow 2 is a refined CZ-75 variant.

Century Arms

The Canik TP9 SFT, imported by Century Arms.

Century Arms is the exclusive importer of Canik handguns, and the newest additions to the TP9 handgun series are the TP9SFL (MSRP: $520), a tactical version with a longer 5.2-inch barrel, the suppressor-ready variant TP9SFT (MSRP: $520), and the TP9SA Mod.2, which contains several upgrades like a refined slide profile, Warren Tactical sights and enhanced decocker. Plus, the new TP9SFX (MSRP: $550) is set up for competition shooting and is optics-ready for a red-dot reflex sight. As much as the AR platform lends itself to a pistol variant, so does the AK platform. The Draco NAK9 (MSRP: $725) is an AK-based 9mm handgun that is compatible with Glock 17 and 19 magazines. Century's 100-percent American-made AK-47 pistol line now includes the C39v2 Blade Pistol (MSRP: $950) with the Shockwave Blade stabilizing brace. centuryarms.com

Dan Wesson

Dan Wesson is commemorating a half-century of manufacturing firearms with a 50th Anniversary 1911 (MSRP: $2,999). This beauty has tasteful engraving on the slide and frame, a high-polish nitride finish, and G10 grips with the look of ivory. The newest 1911 series is the affordable Vigil series, built on a forged aluminum frame with a round-top stainless slide. The front and rear grip straps are checkered 25 lpi, and the butt is rounded for better and more comfortable carry. Four models include the full size (MSRP: $1,299), CCO (MSRP: $1,298) with 4.25-inch barrel, Commander (MSRP: $1,298), and Suppressor Ready (MSRP: $1,397) with a threaded 5.75-inch barrel. The Wraith (MSRP: $2,077) is a full-size 1911 with a threaded barrel and distressed finish. It is available in 9mm, 10mm or .45 ACP. The Discretion series gets a Commander model (MSRP: $2,142) and, like its big brother, has tall sights for use with a suppressor and a threaded barrel. The Specialist (MSRP: $2,012) full-size gets a distressed finish that has all the look of a hard-fought victory. The Officer-size ECO (MSRP: $1,662) features a 3.5-inch barrel and 7+1 capacity all with a new OD green finish. The A2 (MSRP: $1,363) is perhaps the closest Dan Wesson to look like a mil-spec 1911A1. The A2 wears a Parkerized finish and checkered double-diamond wood grips. cz-usa.com

Kimber

Kimber consistently pushes the 1911 envelope by manufacturing pistols that not only are aesthetically pleasing to the eye but also perform. The new KHX series of 1911s chambered in 9mm and .45 ACP feature hexagonal stair-stepped serrations on the slide at the muzzle and rear. The grips are Hogue's Enhanced MagGrip G10 that brings the grip texture to the mainspring housing and adds a laser sight. The KHX is available in an Ultra variant (MSRP: $1,259), Pro with rounded butt (MSRP: $1,259), Pro OR (MSRP: $1,087) that is optics-ready, a full-size Custom (MSRP: $1,259), and a Custom OR (MSRP: $1,087), which is also optics-ready. The new Aegis Elite line of 1911s features a two-tone finish with blued slide and matte stainless receivers. The slide serrations are an AEX pattern, and on OI (optics installed) models a Vortex Venom red-dot reflex sight is mounted. Aegis Elite variants include a subcompact Ultra (MSRP: $1,021), commander-size Pro (MSRP: $1,259) and Pro OI with red dot (MSRP: $1,395), full-size Custom (MSRP: $1,259) and Custom OI (MSRP: $1,395).

The new-for-2018 Kimber KHX Custom has racy-looking hexagonal stair-stepped serrations on the slide. Available in 9mm and .45 ACP.

The new special edition 1911 is the Hero Custom (MSRP: $987). It features a two-tone finish with a desert tan frame and black slide engraved with a U.S. flag. Other features include fiber-optic sights and Kryptek Highlander pattern grips. New to the popular .380 ACP Micro line is the Micro TLE (MSRP: $734) with black slide and frame, and green and black G10 grips. The Micro Eclipse (MSRP: $734) features a gray frame and stainless slide with brushed flats. The 9mm chambered Micro 9 now has a Covert variant (MSRP: $1,108) with gray slide and frame and Crimson Trace grips. The Micro 9 TLE (MSRP: $788) has a black slide and frame, and green and black G10 grips. To the Micro line Kimber added the new Micro Desert Night, featuring a matte black slide and desert tan receiver. Brown and black G-10 grips round out this little blaster. MSRP: $626. The Micro 9 Stainless Raptor takes the trademark raptor look and applies it to the Micro 9 platform. MSRP: $889. kimberamerica.com

The Dan Wesson Vigil Suppressor Ready 1911.

The Dan Wesson Discretion Commander.

The Wraith from Dan Wesson is a full-size 1911 threaded barrel and distressed finish. You can have it in 9mm, 10mm or .45 ACP.

The KHX Pro OR variant from Kimber is optics-ready.

Magnum Research

The iconic Desert Eagle Mark XIX Pistol (MSRP: $2,278) now features a casehardened finish, gold-plated trigger, walnut grip with engraved Desert Eagle logo, and Hogue rubber grips. Available in .357 Magnum or .44 Magnum. magnumresearch.com

Remington

This year, Big Green went all in on 1911s. The Model 1911 R1 Ultralight Executive (MSRP: $1,250) weighs under 31 ounces with a steel frame and has a fiber-optic front sight, laminated G10 grips and rounded butt. The Model 1911 R1 Ultralight Commander (MSRP: $849) has a traditional straight mainspring housing. The 10mm-chambered Model 1911 R1 Hunter FDE (MSRP: $1,340) has a 6-inch barrel and tough PVD DLC FDE frame and black slide. The Model 1911 R1 Recon (MSRP: $999) and Enhanced Double

The Remington R1 Ultralight Executive weighs less than 31 ounces, yet sports a steel frame.

The 9mm Subcompact Smoke R51 is now available in an interesting finish scheme.

Remington's RM380 subcompact can be had in bright blue finish. It has a DAO trigger, a winner for concealed carry.

Stack (MSRP: $999) are available in either 9mm or .45 ACP and are … double-stack platforms. The RP45 (MSRP: $418) is a polymer-frame, striker-fire chambered in .45 ACP with a 15+1 capacity. In the subcompact category is the RM380 Micro Carry Blue (MSRP: $348) with a DAO trigger and bright blue frame. The R51 9mm series now includes a Subcompact Smoke (MSRP: $408) with smoke-colored frame. remington.com

Ruger

The economical EC9s (MSRP: $299) from Ruger is easy on the wallet and hip for concealed carry. It's a polymer-frame striker fire chambered in 9mm with a 7+1 capacity. The Security-9 (MSRP: $379) is a compact-size polymer-frame, striker-fire pistol chambered in 9mm. It uses the same Secure Action that's also in the LCP II. The SR1911 series now includes a 9mm subcompact Lightweight Officer-style (MSRP: $979) with a 3.6-inch barrel and aluminum frame. It weighs 27.2 ounces unloaded. The 9mm SR1911 Target (MSRP: $1,020) is a full-size stainless variant with a 5-inch barrel and adjustable rear sight. At only 25 ounces, the new Mark IV 22/45

The Ruger EC9 carries a 7+1 payload of 9mm.

Ruger's new Security-9 is a compact-sized striker-fire that uses the firm's Secure Action.

(MSRP: $559) is built on a skeletonized aluminum receiver and covered with a diamond gray anodized finish — there is a threaded- and non-threaded-barrel variant. The Mark IV Target series now has a stainless version with a threaded barrel (MSRP: $699). ruger.com

SIG Sauer

The SIG P220 Legion is now available in 10mm (MSRP: $1,904) with the proprietary Legion gray coating and custom G10 grips and Legion medallion. Also joining the Legion series is the P226 RX (MSRP: $1,767) and P229 Legion RX Compact (MSRP: $1,685). Both feature the Legion treatment plus a SIG ROMEO1 red-dot sight. A new variation is the Select treatment, which is being applied to a variety of popular SIG pistols. The P229 Select Compact (MSRP: $1,195) offers the renowned P229 platform but with new G10 grips. The P238 series of .380ACP chambered 1911-inspired pistols now has a Select (MSRP: $738) model with a matte

The SIG P238 .380 ACP with "We the People" finish.

SIG's "We the People" finish applied to a very distressed-looking 1911.

If clearing out bullseyes is your game, the reintroduced SIG P210 Target will do the trick. It's a single-stack 9mm with adjustable rear sights and legendary accuracy.

gray finish and custom G10 grips. The P938 Select Micro-Compact (MSRP: $815) has the same Select treatment. The P938 Navy Micro-Compact (MSRP: $747) features a Navy frame and slide with rubber grips. The M17 (MSRP: $670), the military version of the P320, is set up like Uncle Sam ordered. The subcompact P365 (MSRP: $600) is a polymer frame, striker-fire pistol with a 10+1 round capacity in 9mm. In my opinion, SIG has reinvented the everyday carry pistol in the P365. The "We the People" finish treatment sports custom aluminum grips adorned with 50 stars (25 per side), a distressed finish on the stainless-steel slide and frame that includes patriotic engravings, such as 13 stars atop the slide, and "WE THE PEOPLE" and "1776" on the slide flats. This treatment has been applied to the 1911 (MSRP: $1,481), P938 (MSRP: $772) and P238 (MSRP: $728). Finally, SIG is reintroducing the legendary P210 as the P210 Target (MSRP: $1,699), a full-size single-stack 9mm with a crisp SAO trigger and adjustable rear sights. Consider this your new 9mm target pistol designed to shoot the black out of the target. sigsauer.com

Smith and Wesson

The M&P series now includes the economical M&P380 Shield EZ (MSRP: $399) chambered in .380 Auto and designed with an easy-to-rack slide, easy-to-load magazine and easy-to-clean design. It has a grip safety to make the pistol even safer. Also new to the M&P line is a Shield with an integrated Crimson Trace laser (MSRP: $549). The green laser is fitted into the dust cover of the frame and the handgun has the new M&P M2.0 trigger. A variant with a manual thumb safety is also available. smith-wesson.com

Smith & Wesson's M&P series now includes the M&P380 Shield EZ, which is chambered in .380 Auto and designed with an easy-to-rack slide.

Springfield Armory

Springfield's new Professional Series comes out of its custom shop with a long list of features like custom-fit slide, national match light rail frame, shortened dust cover, custom fit and fully supported ramp national match barrel and bushing, custom match hammer and sear, trigger tuned to 4 ½-pound pull, and a whole lot more. These are available in 9mm and .45 ACP and with a light rail (MSRP: $3,395) or without a rail (MSRP: $3,295). The next evolution of the acclaimed XD-S pistol is here. The latest addition to the XD-S Mod.2 series is called the 3.3-inch Single Stack .45 ACP (MSRP: $568). It features a higher hand position, enhanced grip texturing, thinner slide, an Ameriglo Pro-Glo front sight with tactical-rack rear sight. It's a subcompact pistol with a bark. Did you think all the interest in .380 ACP pistols had faded away? Not a chance. The 911 (MSRP: $599) is chambered in .380 ACP and has similar controls as a 1911 — shrunk down in size. It features a lightweight 7075 T6 aluminum frame and black Nitride or stainless 416 steel slide plus what Springfield calls Octo-Grip texturing of the front strap and mainspring housing to ensure a secure grip. G10 thinline grips adorn its sides. Expect a short trigger reset and crisp 5-pound trigger pull. The 911 comes with a Viridian grip laser (MSRP: $789).

The XD-E 3.3-inch Single Stack .45 ACP (MSRP: $568) is the XD-E on a more substantial diet of .45 ACP. The Saint AR-15 Pistol (MSRP: $989) is chambered in 5.56 NATO with a 7.5-inch barrel and overall length of 26.5 inches. It uses a direct impingement gas system, SB Tactical brace. Place this one on the short list for a new vehicle gun. It comes optics-ready. springfield-armory.com

Taurus

Taurus has taken its popular and economical 1911 platform and built an Officer Model (MSRP: $989) and Commander Model (MSRP: $609). Both are chambered in .45 ACP and feature a matte black finish and checkered polymer grips. The Commander has a 4.25-inch barrel and 8+1 capacity, while the Officer has a 3.5-inch barrel and 6+1 capacity. taurususa.com

Revolvers & Others

BY **MAX PRASAC**

They're seemingly outdated, singularly simplistic, boringly reliable, and they *just won't go away*. The revolver, in this modern day and age, is in a period of unmitigated vibrancy. If I sound like a broken record it's because every year brings us additional wheelguns, and despite the current plastic/polymer, high-capacity defensive craze, industry giants like Ruger keep indulging revolver loons like myself. And the hits just keep on coming.

The market for Colt Single Action Army replicas appears to be as lively as ever, while modern iterations of the single-action revolver by the likes of Magnum Research keep being refined and improved for a discerning public. Options are the name of the game and we all like our options! Meanwhile, new iterations of familiar double actions are being introduced frequently. Personal defense, particularly in this era of global uncertainty, is as

The Kimber K6S DCR weighs just 23 ounces, holds six shots of .357 Magnum.

popular a theme as ever and will probably never go out of style, as is evidenced by the new and improved defensive pistols available. Even so, the revolver is still very much a viable defensive firearm for carry or at home. Vibrant indeed.

So, it is with glee that I announce many new and improved revolvers and others.

Charter Arms

Founded in 1964, Charter Arms is headed by the third generation of Ecker family members, staying true to the spirit of this truly all-American firearms company. Known for producing double-action revolvers for more than half a decade in the heart of New England's "Gun Valley," Charter Arms entered the gun-building fray with the Undercover, a five-shot .38 Special that weighed in at only 16 ounces. Today, continuing with that theme, the firm produces a full line of DA revolvers for many purposes. Charter Arms revolvers feature one-piece frames (stronger than screw-on sideplate designs), a safe and completely blocked hammer system, and three place cylinder lock-up. Another plus is that they're 100 percent American-made.

Charter Arms offers 11 new models this year, starting with the Chameleon. An Undercover Lite model in .38 Special, it features a flashy iridescent finish that changes its exterior color depending on the angle and the light, appearing green, blue or purple.

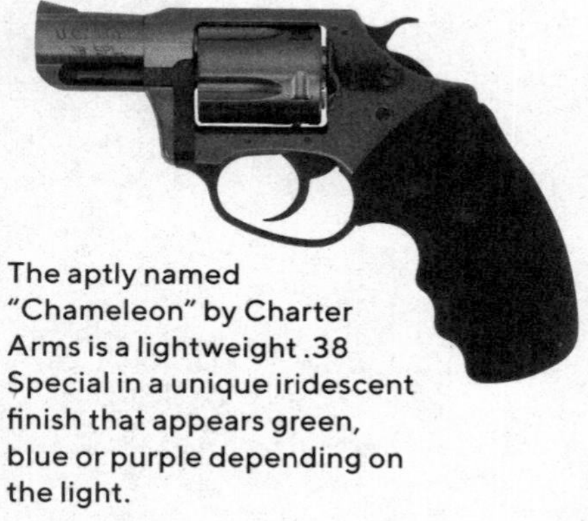

The aptly named "Chameleon" by Charter Arms is a lightweight .38 Special in a unique iridescent finish that appears green, blue or purple depending on the light.

The ubiquitous Bulldog line has two new members, one in .44 Special featuring a 6-inch barrel, the other with a 2 1/2-inch barrel chambered in .45 Colt. Both come in a stainless matte finish. The Pitbull line has a new member in 9mm featuring a 6-inch barrel and matte stainless finish. This revolver tips the scales at only 25 ounces empty. A new Undercover Lite in a high-polish magenta finish makes its debut this year, adding to the already impressive line of available finishes for the model. Like the others in its stable, this one is chambered in .38 Special.

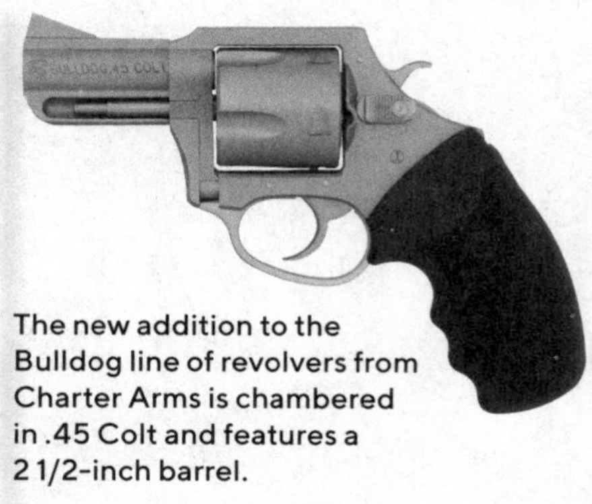

The new addition to the Bulldog line of revolvers from Charter Arms is chambered in .45 Colt and features a 2 1/2-inch barrel.

A new Undercover is making its debut with a 2-inch barrel, high polish finish and wooden grips. This .38 Special weighs only 16 ounces. The Pathfinder line is designed as an introductory revolver for new shooters. Three new .22 LR Pathfinder models are available — two with a 4.2-inch barrel finished in either pink or lavender, and one 2-inch model with a brushed aluminum finish. The 4.2-inch-barreled models feature an adjustable rear sight.

Lastly, there are two new Mag Pug revolvers available. The first with a 6-inch barrel, finished in a matte stainless steel and chambered in .357 Magnum, and the second featuring a 2 1/2-inch barrel but chambered in the potent .41 Magnum. This second model sports a matte stainless finish. charterarms.com

Cimarron

One thing I find remarkable about Cimarron is the constant evolution and expansion of its product line. Cimarron imports revolvers from both Uberti and Pietta. A complete line of replica Single Action Army revolvers is offered, along with black powder percussion models, open top and conversion revolvers, an impressive lineup that offers something for every enthusiast.

New this year is Sam Walker's Walker, an exact replica of the 1847 Texas Ranger Walker .44 black powder model. Commemorating the 200th anniversary of the Texas Rangers, it began selling in 2018 and will be available until the end of 2023. This big revolver is a six-shot single-action in .44 caliber with a 9-inch barrel, all steel frame, and replica markings. An added bonus: Cimarron will donate five percent of every sale to the Former Texas Ranger Foundation.

Also new is the "Percussion Peacemaker." The 1851 Navy replica features attractive laser engraving on a casehardened old silver frame, with a standard blued finish and one-piece walnut grip with diamond checkering. The percussion-style six-shot is available in .36 and .44 calibers with a 7 1/2-inch octagon barrel.

Another new model is the appropriately named "Bad Boy," a modern take on an old classic. The Bad Boy is a classic Model P design single-action revolver chambered in the powerful .44 Remington Magnum. It comes standard with an Army-style grip and a 6- or 8-inch octagon barrel. Available in a standard blue finish, smooth walnut one-piece grips, and a flat top with adjustable rear sight, the Bay Boy should prove popular. El Malo is a single-action revolver in either .357 Magnum or .45 Colt with a choice in barrel length of 4 3/4, 5 1/2, or 7 1/2 inches. The El Malo comes standard with a one-piece walnut grip, color casehardened frame, and blued cylinder and barrel. *cimarron-firearms.com*

This Cimarron is an exact replica of the 1847 Texas Ranger Walker commemorating the 200th anniversary of the Texas Rangers.

Cimarron's new Bad Boy SAA replica chambered in the hard-hitting .44 Remington Magnum cartridge.

Colt's new double-action Night Cobra .38 Special revolver features a matte black Diamond-Like Carbon (DLC) finish that is not only attractive but durable.

Colt

The company that really started it all still produces a version of the famous Single Action Army (SAA) of which virtually all modern single-action revolvers share DNA. One of the most iconic pieces of Americana, the Colt Single Action Army is probably the most recognizable guns in American film history.

While the Single Action Army is available today from Colt in several differing configurations — including the adjustable-sight version, the New Frontier — there is nothing new on the single-action front for 2019 from Colt.

The big news for 2017 was the return of a double-action revolver to the company's lineup, the new Colt Cobra double-action-only revolver. New for 2019 is the Night Cobra version. Like its stablemate, the Night Cobra retains the smooth DA trigger pull with a snag-free bobbed hammer. Custom Colt G10 grips provide comfort and a drag-free surface that won't hang up on clothing. The .38 Special is rated for +P ammunition and finished in an attractive matte black DLC (Diamond-Like Carbon) coating over stainless-steel construction. colt.com

Freedom Arms

Freedom Arms has the distinction of making some of the finest single-action revolvers in the industry. Demand and refinement is so high in Freedom, Wyoming, that the maker currently isn't releasing anything new on the revolver front.

These revolvers are the Rolls Royces of the single-action revolver world, and though a traditionally styled single-action revolver, the FA 83 is all modern on the inside and produced of 17-4PH stainless steel in a five-shot configuration. Freedom Arms prides itself on hand-assembling each unit to tight, exacting tolerances. It's a true "custom-built" production revolver.

Freedom likewise produces fine break-open, single-shot handguns designated the Model 2008. Available in a variety of calibers and three different barrel lengths — 10, 15 and 16 inches — the Model 2008 defines practical. All barrels are interchangeable, making caliber switches simple and they feature the excellent grip frame borrowed directly from the FA Model 83, which lends itself well to heavy recoil. Non-catalog barrel lengths are available for a fee. Four new cartridge/barrel configurations are available for 2018: .41 Magnum, .44 Magnum, .460 Smith & Wesson Magnum and 6.5 Creedmoor. While the barrels are interchangeable, they need fitting, a service that Freedom Arms provides. freedomarms.com

Freedom Arms' excellent Model 2008 single-shot pistol is available in four new calibers this year: .41 Mag, .44 Mag, .460 S&W Mag and 6.5 Creedmoor.

Heizer Defense

Heizer Defense packs a whole lot of punch in a small package with its PS1 Pocket Shotgun in .45 Colt/.410. The single-shot PS1 is a svelte package that weighs a mere 21 ounces, is less than 5 inches long and a lean 0.7-inch wide. There are four new popular defensive calibers in this platform, offering something for virtually everyone: 9mm, .40 S&W, .45 ACP and .38 Spl./.357 Magnum.

Heizer's popular PAK1, or "Pocket AK," chambered in 7.62x39. A whole lot of wallop in a diminutive package!

A couple of years ago, Heizer Defense announced the PAK1, and as the name suggests, the "pocket AK" is chambered in 7.62x39mm and comes with a ported barrel to keep muzzle flip to a bare minimum. A .300 Blackout version is in the works and should be available for 2019. Also available are interchangeable barrels, enabling the owner of any of the above pocket pistols to be chambered in any of the available calibers with a simple barrel swap, adding to the versatility of these pocket powerhouses. heizerdefense.com

Magnum Research

Born in 1999, Magnum Research entered the revolver building business with the introduction of the BFR — the "Biggest Finest Revolver" — chambered in the old warhorse .45-70 Government. Magnum Research has since redesigned its revolvers and today produces both long- and short-frame wheelguns in a range of calibers to suit just about everyone's needs. In this author's humble opinion, there is no wider assortment of hunting calibers offered under one roof than that of Magnum Research. There is literally something for everyone.

A subsidiary of Kahr Arms, Magnum Research of Minneapolis, Minnesota, offers a whole line of stainless-steel single-action revolvers in both standard caliber and a plethora of custom Precision Center offerings.

New to the party, and the first ever offering in a commercial revolver, is the .500 Linebaugh chambering. For the uninitiated, this cartridge started life as a cut-down .348 Winchester case (to 1.40 inches), necked up to .510-inch bullet diameter. As a big game cartridge, this one is near the top of the food chain when loaded accordingly. I had the pleasure of extensively testing the first prototype .500 Linebaugh and taking a game animal with it. Recoil is expectedly stout with most factory Buffalo Bore loads, but the accuracy exhibited was exceptional and the terminal effectiveness outstanding. Look for this chambering from the Magnum Research Precision Center custom shop, at least initially.

Also new about the time this book gets published is the six-shot, short-framed BFR in .44 Magnum. With a cylinder boasting the BFR's proportions, the engineers at Magnum Research decided to give the consumer an extra round in the cylinder — a welcome addition for sure. The .44 Magnum, which I consider a threshold cartridge, remains well represented.

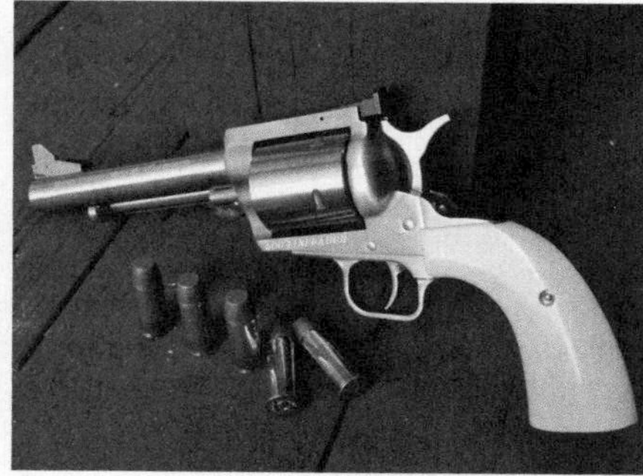

The all-new, first-ever production revolver in the legendary .500 Linebaugh chambering! Seen here with Magnum Research's outstanding Bisley grip frame. Photo: Author

Rumor has it, yet not confirmed, that Magnum Research is contemplating adding a .357 Magnum single-action revolver to the already impressive lineup. This will also (allegedly) be a six-shot configuration. It may be available soon — that's if it comes to fruition — allegedly!

These are big, no compromise, well-built revolvers that offer unparalleled accuracy and strength at a reasonable price point. magnumresearch.com

Smith & Wesson

Smith & Wesson has the distinction of building some of the finest DA revolvers in the world, bar none. Known for quality, fit and finish, as well as superb actions, S&W has a legacy of quality.

New this year is the Model 360. J-frames have been around since 1950, but this latest iteration is an all-modern revolver chambered in .357 Magnum and weighing just under 15 ounces empty. The five-shot wheelgun carries a 1.88-inch barrel with a red ramp front and a fixed rear sight. The barrel and cylinder are constructed of stainless steel, while the frame is scandium alloy.

A new revolver to come out of the Smith & Wesson Performance Center is the Model 686 six-shot .357 Magnum. It comes with a 4-inch barrel topped with a vented rib and an interchangeable front sight. The cylinder is unfluted, while trigger, trigger stop and hammer are chromed, and the action is tuned by the Performance Center. Another new model from the Performance Center is the 686 Plus, also in .357 Magnum, but this unfluted cylinder model has a seven-shot capacity. It's equipped with a 5-inch barrel with a vented rib and interchangeable front sight, tuned action and, like the new 686, comes with a chrome trigger, trigger stop and teardrop hammer. smith-wesson.com

Sturm, Ruger & Company

The big news for this year is the resurrection of the Bren Ten 10mm. Why is this of any concern to you, the revolver aficionado and what does this have to do with Ruger? It's because we are seeing the semi-auto-rooted 10mm finding its way into not one, but two Ruger DA revolvers. An odd marriage indeed, but it makes sense when you shoot these two new offerings.

First up is the Super Redhawk in 10mm. I was bitten by the Super Redhawk bug nearly two decades ago and immediately took notice of this latest version. It is a six-shot that comes with three full-moon clips to more easily load and unload. The barrel is 6 1/2 inches long, and it comes with attractive rubber grips with wooden inserts. I admit to having been a bit skeptical of this odd coupling, but that skepticism dissipated as soon as I shot it. The 10mm, loaded properly, is a potent cartridge, but when mated to a sturdy platform like the Super Redhawk, it becomes downright tame, making it perfect for the neophyte or recoil-sensitive veteran.

The other ten is a GP100 Match Champion with a 4.2-inch barrel. This is a very attractive package from a packability standpoint thanks to its proportional frame size. I got to spend some time with one and can report that I like it very much.

More GP100 goodness is on the horizon with the newly released seven-shot .357 Magnum. It's available in stainless steel with a 2 1/2-, 4.2- or 6-inch barrel, all with an adjustable rear sight. But there is more,

This new 10mm GP100 should prove popular. The balanced revolver has been frequently requested by the shooting public.

with the introduction of the GP100 in .327 Federal Magnum with either a 4.2- or 6-inch barrel. A whole slew of distributor exclusives is ready for prime time. One really jumped out at me and that is the blued steel GP100 in .44 Special with a 5-inch barrel. This is an exclusive offering from Lipsey's (lipseys.com).

Two new Redhawks are available for consideration this year — the 4.2- and 5.5-inch barreled eight-shot .357 Magnums. Yes, the Redhawk is a lot of gun for such a seemingly diminutive cartridge, but you get a full eight shots and the recoil from even the hottest magnum ammunition is nearly nonexistent. I got to shoot a few hundred rounds through one of these Redhawks and feel it is a nicely balanced package.

Ruger expanded the .357 Magnum Redhawk line with a 4.2-inch barreled revolver and one with a 5 1/2-inch barrel. The eight-shot revolver is seen here with a 4.2-inch barrel. Photo: Author

This Lipsey's dealer exclusive is just about the perfect, potent, packable package. The five-shot .480 Ruger Bisley features a 4 5/8-inch barrel and a Bisley grip frame. The author equipped his with Rowen Custom Grips in Turkish walnut. Photo: Author

Ruger's popular LCRx revolver is available in several new configurations this year. There is a .22 WMR offering with a 1.87-inch barrel with fixed sights, and another .22 WMR equipped with a 3-inch barrel and an adjustable rear sight. Two more new LCRxs are in the catalog, both with 1.87-inch barrels and fixed sights. One is available in .327 Federal Magnum, the other in 9mm. The latter comes with three full moon clips enabling rapid loading.

Not much newsworthy on the single-action front from Ruger, save for one distributor exclusive: the new Lipsey's .480 Ruger Super Blackhawk Bisley with 4 5/8-inch barrel. The five-shot Bisley is just about perfect in every way, chambered in a potent round and housed in a compact package. ruger.com

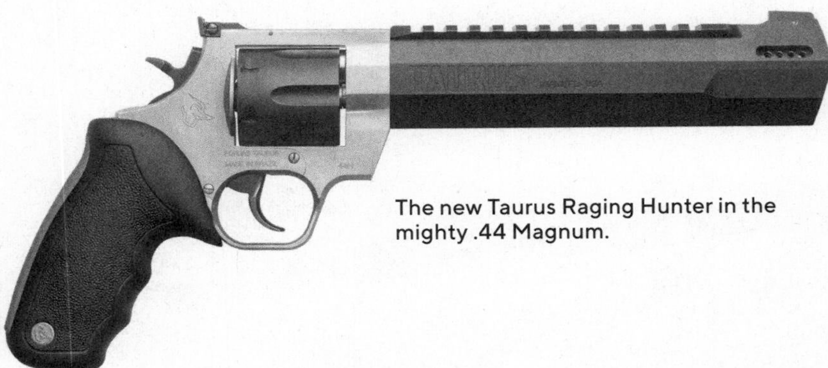
The new Taurus Raging Hunter in the mighty .44 Magnum.

Taurus

Taurus continues to offer a wide range of revolvers for personal defense, recreational shooting and hunting. There is something in its catalog for any handgun endeavor you choose. Made in Brazil, Taurus offers a full line of revolvers of different frame sizes and calibers. At Taurus, variety is the spice of life!

The extensive revolver line has been expanded with the addition of the new Model 856. What is the 856? It's a DA defensive revolver with a 2-inch barrel and available in both carbon and stainless steel with a matte blue or matte stainless finish. Weighing in at a mere 22 ounces, the 856 has a serrated ramp front sight and fixed rear. The six-shot .38 Special is easy to carry and conceal and is affordably priced with an MSRP of only $329.

Another addition is the multi-dimensional 692 seven-shot Multi-Caliber revolver. When equipped with the optional 3-inch barrel, it makes for a reliable everyday carry gun, and a great range tool with the optional 6 1/2-inch barrel. The new DA wheelgun features a seven-round capacity and can be changed from .38 Special/.357 Magnum to 9mm with a simple cylinder swap. It comes standard with an adjustable rear sight, spurred hammer, and Taurus' comfortable "Ribber Grip." The ported barrel aids with target acquisition for fast follow-up shots. Stellar clips come standard with each 692, and it can be had in matte blue or matte stainless finish.

The all-new 692 "Multi-Caliber" revolver from Taurus with cylinder swap capability. This revolver can go from .38 Special/.357 Magnum to 9mm with a simple cylinder swap.

The newest big-bore revolver from Brazil is the Raging Hunter in a unique stainless and blue two-tone finish, setting it apart from other Raging Bull revolvers. However, it can also be had in a matte blue low-glare finish. What truly sets it apart from its brethren is the Picatinny rail that is integral to the top of the barrel. I really like this system, as it allows you to equip it with an optic without disrupting the iron adjustable sights. If your optic dies for some reason in the field, you can simply remove it and your irons are ready to go. The barrel system is unique in that it has a steel sleeve inserted into an aluminum housing that cuts down on weight significantly, particularly considering the 8.375-inch barrel length. Despite the frame size and barrel length, the Raging Hunter comes in around 55 ounces empty and has a six-shot cylinder. The cushioned insert grips and porting cut down on felt recoil. Actually, the porting reduces muzzle rise, enabling faster target acquisition when multiple shots are required. For the handgun hunter this one appears to be a winner. taurususa.com

Taylor's & Company

The Taylor's & Company catalog is full of interesting and somewhat eclectic products for even the most discerning handgun aficionado. Of interest are the reproductions of the famous Howdah pistols that were used in the second half of the 1800s. These were designed to stop tigers from dragging poor unsuspecting individuals off of the backs of elephants. Also notable is the reproduction Le Mat Cavalry black powder pistol, featuring a nine-shot .44 caliber cylinder and a 20-gauge barrel in the cylinder center pin.

The black powder line of revolvers is rather extensive with several famous models, including the 1836 Paterson, 1848 Dragoon and 1847 Walker. The cartridge revolver segment of the Taylor's catalog is even more extensive, with many variations in 1873 Single Action Army replicas, as well as 1858 Remington Conversions and Schofield sixguns. An entire chapter could easily be dedicated to Taylor's & Company offerings.

The classic Taylor's Drifter SAA replica available in .357 Magnum or .45 Colt with three different octagon barrel lengths.

New for Taylor's is the Drifter model single action that is built on the new model cattleman frame. Differing from the standard cattleman is the octagon barrel available in several different lengths: 4 3/4, 5 1/2, and 7 1/2 inches. A true replica of the Single Action Army, it comes with a fixed blade front sight. Available in either .357 Magnum or .45 Colt chamberings, all three barrel lengths can be had with either. Taylor tuning is available for all Drifter configurations, a worthwhile option. taylorsfirearms.com

The Rock Island Armory Wanderer 12-gauge autoloader.

NEW SHOTGUNS

BY **JOHN HAVILAND**

Weather-resistant, bargain-priced and self-defense scatterguns that are short on both ends are the big trends in shotguns. However, a few new models will hearten hunters and target shooters who like the feel and look of an attractive gun when following the dogs or waiting their turn at the line.

Browning

Browning sells all manner of outdoor gear, but the company is synonymous with shotguns, and over/unders are its bread and butter. Several of Browning's stacked-barrel guns, autoloaders and pumps have had cosmetic improvements.

Browning's High Grade Program has entered its sixth year with a limited production of Citori 725 Field Grade VI 12- and 20-gauge over/unders. These guns feature gold-enhanced detailed engraving on a silver nitride steel receiver and

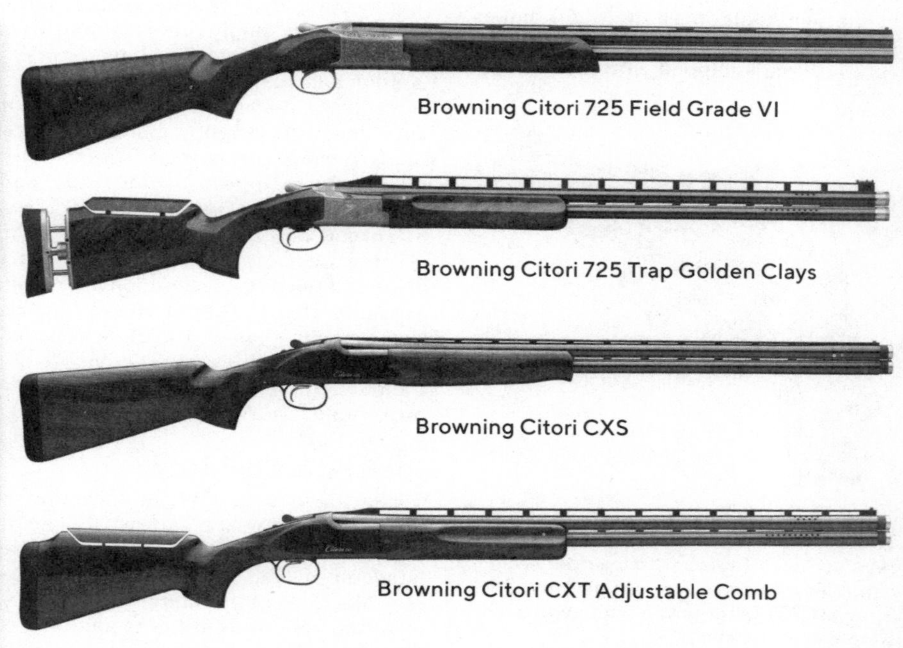

Browning Citori 725 Field Grade VI

Browning Citori 725 Trap Golden Clays

Browning Citori CXS

Browning Citori CXT Adjustable Comb

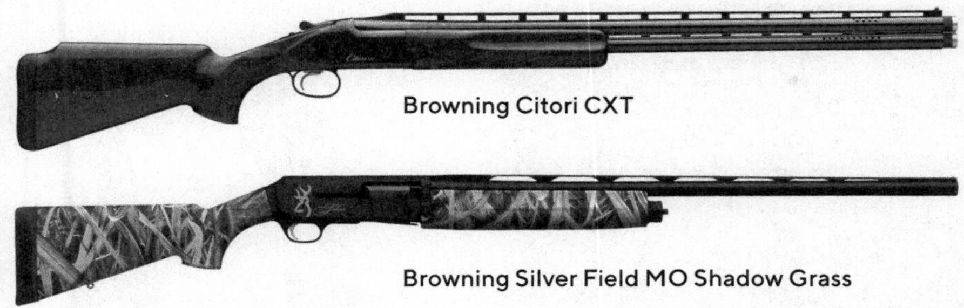

Browning Citori CXT

Browning Silver Field MO Shadow Grass

gloss oil-finished walnut stocks. Barrel lengths are 26 or 28 inches with a ventilated top rib and a front and middle white bead. The shotguns store in a canvas leather-trimmed case.

The Citori 725 Trap Golden Clays 12 gauge is similar in looks to the Field, but with the choice of 30- or 32-inch barrels with a HiViz Pro-Comp front sight and white middle bead. The Trap also has an adjustable Monte Carlo comb with a Gracoil Recoil Reduction System, and a Gracoil buttplate that adjusts for angle and position and is capped with a Pachmayr Decelerator XLT recoil pad.

There are two new CX Citori models. The Citori CXS 12 gauge has an adjustable comb and Schnabel-style forearm. Its blued-steel receiver is engraved with gold accents. Barrel lengths are 28, 30 or 32 inches. The Citori CXT is similar, with an adjustable comb or a raised cheekpiece and finger grooves in a semi-beavertail forearm. Barrels include a high-post floating rib, ventilated side rib, porting and a 70/30 point of impact.

The Cynergy CX over/under 12 gauge also wears an adjustable comb. The 60/40 point of impact of patterns make the CX good for hunting and target games. The matte blued finish 28-, 30- or 32-inch barrels have ventilated top and side ribs with white front and middle bead. The stock is Grade I walnut with a satin finish.

The Silver Field Composite autoloader's aluminum receiver is finished with a black/charcoal bi-tone finish. The composite stock and forearm have a non-glare matte black finish in Mossy Oak Shadow Grass camouflage. The Silver Field comes with either a 26- or 28-inch barrel with a 3- or 3.5-inch chamber.

The BPS Field Pump's steel receiver with ventilated rib barrel has a matte blued finish complementing a satin-finished walnut stock and forearm. The Field is chambered in 12, 16, 20, 28 and .410 bore. The 12, 20 and .410 have 3-inch chambers. All guns come with full (F), modified (M) and improved cylinder (IC) Invector choke tubes. browning.com

CZ-USA

CZ break-action guns include two over/under models for hunting and a side-by-side for those who like the sound of jingling spurs while shooting cowboy style. The Reaper Magnum is a turkey killer over/under and has 26-inch barrels cut with 12-gauge 3 1/2-inch chambers. Five extended choke tubes, including an extra F, come with the gun. That provides the option of a different choke in each barrel. Simply flip the barrel selector switch to make a close or long shot at a gobbler's head. The synthetic stock and forearm are veiled in Realtree Xtra Green camouflage and has detachable swivels at the front and back to add a sling. Optics clamp onto a top rail.

[The elegant CZ SCTP Sterling over/under's four-way adjustable comb fine tunes comb height and butt pitch. The shotgun is built on the Upland Sterling receiver and is chambered in 12 gauge with 28-inch barrels and F, IM, M, IC and C choke tubes. Panels of laser-cut stippling decorate the Turkish walnut forearm and stock and complement the chrome receiver.

The Sharp-Tail Coach side-by-side is a hammerless rendition of the Hammer Coach popular with cowboy action shooters. This new Coach has a single trigger and manual safety. The 20-inch barrels are choked cylinder bore in 12 or 20 gauge with 3-inch chambers. A Turkish walnut semi-beavertail forearm and stock finish the gun.

CZ builds several custom shotguns each year. The Supreme Field over/under incorporates many of the custom features of these with a lower price of $1,700. The shotgun's receiver is decorated with deep relief engraving cut by hand. The Grade III Turkish walnut stock and forearm have brilliant grain and panels of sharp checkering. The receiver finish is polished nickel chrome. Barrels are 28 inches in 12, 20 and 28 gauge with automatic ejectors and five extended choke tubes. cz-usa.com

Mossberg

Mossberg has added two 12-gauge models and one 20 gauge to its 590 Shockwave pump line. These sport a 14-inch barrel, five-round magazine and Raptor "bird's head" pistol grip. The 12-gauge models each weigh 5.3 pounds and include Cerakote Flat Dark Earth coating on the metal; there's also a new 590 Just In Case (JIC) with Cerakote Stainless metal finish. The JIC comes in a storage tube.

The 20-gauge model weighs a feather under five pounds with a matte blue metal finish. I shot target loads through the 20-gauge Shockwave and recoil was pleasant. Holding the gun waist high, a few shots were required to point it correctly to plaster targets at 20 yards. With my stance fixed, I let loose with the five rounds in the magazine.

Recently, I bought one of the original Mossberg JIC shotguns with the pistol-grip stock and 18.5-inch barrel. Mine is the Model 500 Mariner Cruiser pump 12 gauge. It fits in a 32.5-inch long and 6-inch wide thick-walled plastic tube with a capped thick rubber gasket on one end

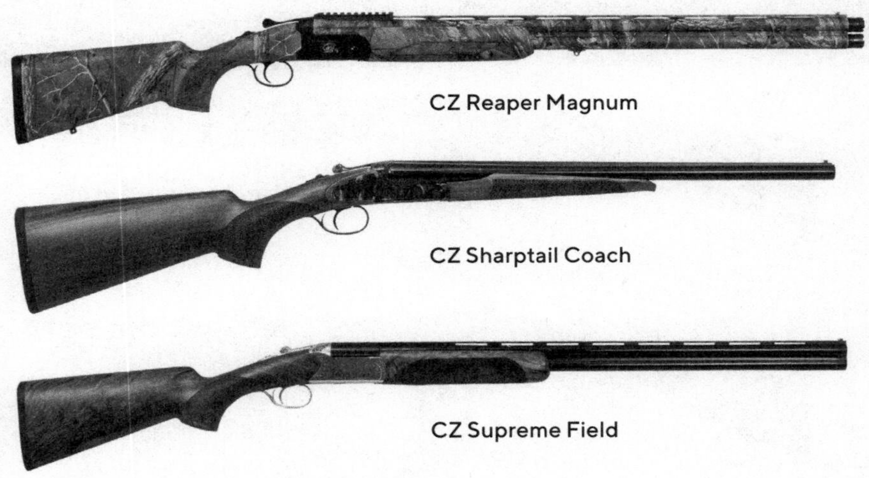

CZ Reaper Magnum

CZ Sharptail Coach

CZ Supreme Field

Mossberg 590M magazines hold from 5 to 20 12-gauge rounds.

A Mossberg 500 Mariner Cruiser pump-action Just In Case (JIC) shot a variety of 12-gauge shells from grouse loads to buckshot to slugs.

Mossberg 590 Mag Fed Pump

Mossberg 590 Mag Fed Tri-Rail

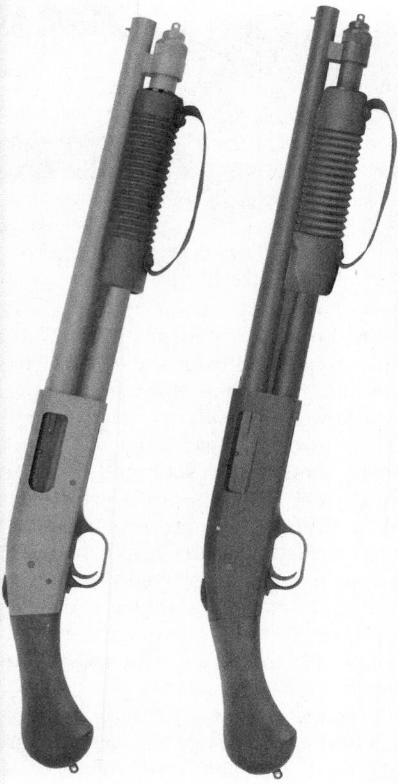

Mossberg Shockwave 12 Gauge

Mossberg Shockwave 20 Gauge

that tightens with a wingnut to seal the tube. The 28.75-inch long shotgun rests snugly in the tube with plenty of room remaining to store survival gear and plenty of extra shells.

I've shot the compact pump with a variety of shells. The 500's cylinder bore provides a full enough pattern shooting 1 1/8 ounces of 7 1/2 shot to pot grouse at 20 to 25 yards. D Dupleks Steelhead 1 1/8-oz. slugs hit right on aim at 15 yards. But aiming requires holding the gun at eye level with the arms extended. Recoil from the 5.5-pound gun is vicious, and unless you have strong arms the rear of the gun will leave a lasting impression on your face. Remington Buckshot 2 3/4-inch loads with nine 00 buckshot spread about a foot at 15 yards. That spread provides some aiming leeway and, with practice, I can hit a target with the gun held at waist level, pouring it on with the five shells in the magazine. The shotgun will always be close at hand either over my shoulder on a sling or stored in its case.

Detachable magazines are common on rifles, so why not shotguns? Even though the Mossberg 590M Mag-Fed pump retains a tube for the forearm to attach to, and usually doubles as a magazine, the gun comes with a detachable ten-shot double-stack magazine for 12-gauge 2 3/4-inch shells. Optional 5-, 15- and 20-round magazines cost $101 to $140. The reasons for a detachable magazine are a quick change of loads and fast reloads. The polymer magazine is made with steel feed lips and ribs that snap into notches in the gun's receiver, locking the magazine in place. A steel lever, at the front of the trigger guard, releases the mag.

The standard 590M has a cylinder bore 18.5-inch barrel, bead front sight and matte blue metal finish. The 590M Tri-Rail has a full-length rail on the bottom and each side of the forearm to attach sights and such, a cylinder bore Accu-Choke tube, heat shield around the barrel, and ghost ring rear sight.

I shot the standard 590M and the magazine easily snaps in and out of the bottom of the gun. The weight of the loaded magazine between my hands and the gun balances well. But it feels kind of strange to have that big magazine protruding out of the bottom of the gun.

The FLEX system of Tool-less Locking System (TLS) connectors and stocks, recoil pads and forearms enable adjusting the FLEX series of Mossberg shotguns for fit, style and use. The FLEX Conversion Kit does the same thing for standard Mossberg 500 and Maverick 88 pump-action shotguns in 12 and 20 gauge. Conversion Kits include all required hardware to customize the 500's and 88's stock and forearm. FLEX accessory components include 3/4-, 1 1/4- and 1 1/2-inch thick recoil pads, four synthetic forends, and standard full-length stocks with 12 1/2-, 13 1/2- and 14 1/4-inch length of pull, pistol grip, six-position adjustable tactical stock, and four-position adjustable, dual-comb hunting stock.

The bargain-priced Maverick 88 is available in three new 12-gauge models. The six- and eight-shot magazine models ($245) have a Flat Dark Earth-colored synthetic stock and forend, and the ATI top-folding stock version ($259) has a six-round magazine and black synthetic stock and forearm. Receivers and barrel surfaces on all three models feature a blued finish.

The Bantam SA-28 and SA-20 autoloaders have a 12.5-inch LOP and 24-inch barrel to better fit smaller shooters. The guns wear a walnut or synthetic stock and forearm. The walnut Bantam versions weigh a quarter-pound less, and the synthetic models a pound less than the standard SA guns. The Bantam models come with a Sport Set of F, M, IM, IM and C choke tubes. mossberg.com

Remington

Near as I can count, Remington currently makes 55 variations of its Model 870 and 870 Express pumps. At least a dozen of them are new this year, mostly tactical and magazine-fed guns.

Let's start with the detachable magazine models. Most of the 870 Detachable Magazine 12 gauges share a six-round detachable mag that fits in an aluminum well. Pushing a steel paddle at the front of the magazine releases the mag. Barrels are 18.5 inches with a fixed IC choke. A few highlights:

• The 870 DM has a black synthetic stock capped with a Super Cell recoil pad, and the forearm is a "corncob" that slides

Remington 870 Wingmaster Claro

Remington 870 DM Predator

Remington 870 DM Hardwood

Remington 870 DM Pistol Grip

Remington 870 TAC 14 Detachable Mag

Remington 870 TAC Magpul M Lock

Remington 870 TAC 14 Hardwood

back and forth on a tube that used to be the magazine.

• The 870 DM Hardwood is the same, but wears a stained hardwood stock and forearm.

• The 870 DM Magpul has a Magpul SGA stock with Super Cell recoil pad and Magpul MOE M-Lok forend. Sights are XS steel front and XS ghost ring rear clamped on a rail.

• The 870 DM Tactical Pistol Grip wears the same sights. Its extended tactical choke tube is ported. The stock has an AR-style grip.

• The Tactical/Predator sights are the same XS front and rear and it ships with a three- and six-round magazine. Its overmolded ShurShot thumbhole stock has a Super Cell recoil pad. Trulock extended choke tubes include a Boat Blaster and a Turkey/Predator. The gun is coated with Kryptek Highlander camouflage.

The 870 DM TAC-14 12 gauge is a whole different gun than the other DM models, or depending on how you look at it, nearly half the gun. Its cylinder bore 14-inch barrel and short Shockwave Raptor grip give it an overall length of 26.3 inches.

Other 870 TAC-14 guns use the regular magazine tube to hold 12- or 20-gauge shells. The TAC-14 Hardwood has a magazine extension that holds five 12-gauge shells with a Steel 870P handstop/sling mounted on the front of the magazine tube and a sling swivel mount on the end of the grip to hold a supplied sling. The 870 TAC-14 Marine Magnum has a nickel finish. The 870 TAC-14 Arm Brace carries five 12-gauge shells in an extended magazine. The Mesa Tactical stock has a Hogue OverMolded pistol grip and SB Tactical Arm Stabilizing Brace.

Maintaining tactical traits, the 870 Express Tactical 6 Position and Express Magpul have 18.5-inch cylinder bore barrels and tube magazines that hold up to six 12-gauge shells. The Tactical's front handle is corn cob-style and its adjustable Magpul CTR buttstock has a Hogue OverMolded vertical grip. The Magpul features an MOE M-Lok forearm and SGA stock.

The Versamax R12 autoloader comes with an IC fixed choke in an 18-inch barrel and low-profile rifle sights. The gun holds six 12-gauge shells in its tube magazine, which is extended with a shroud to mount lights and other accessories.

More traditional 870s include the Express .410 and Wingmaster Claro. The .410's 25-inch barrel has a fixed F choke and metal is finished in matte black. The Wingmaster polished blued 28-inch ribbed barrel and receiver go hand in hand with a high-gloss Claro walnut stock and forearm. A Supercell recoil pad, polished chrome bolt and gold trigger finish the gun. remington.com

Rock Island Armory

The lineup of new shotguns imported by Rock Island Armory includes a Traditional single-shot 12 gauge (top) and Over Under Plus 1 (below).

Rock Island is importing a variety of new 12-gauge shotguns, from traditional over/unders to a single-shot to an AR-lookalike. The Meriva pumps include the Standard 18.5-inch barrel with a slug choke. The black polymer stock wears a rubber buttpad. The Meriva 3 has an 18.5-inch barrel that comes with slug, F, M and IC choke tubes. Its polymer buttstock sports a vertical grip. Metal is finished in marine chrome.

The Rock Island Armory VR-60 12 gauge looks similar to a large AR-type rifle.

The autoloading Lion has five models. The Lion Conceal is covered with Muddy Girl camouflage and its 28-inch barrel comes with F, M and IC chokes. The Lion Sport is similar, but its metal is an anodized red. The Wanderer and Elegance are also the same gun, but with a walnut stock and forearm, and the Elegance is engraved. The Lion Tactical SA has a muzzle brake and F, M and IC chokes. The rear sight is a ghost ring aperture and the polymer buttstock has a vertical grip.

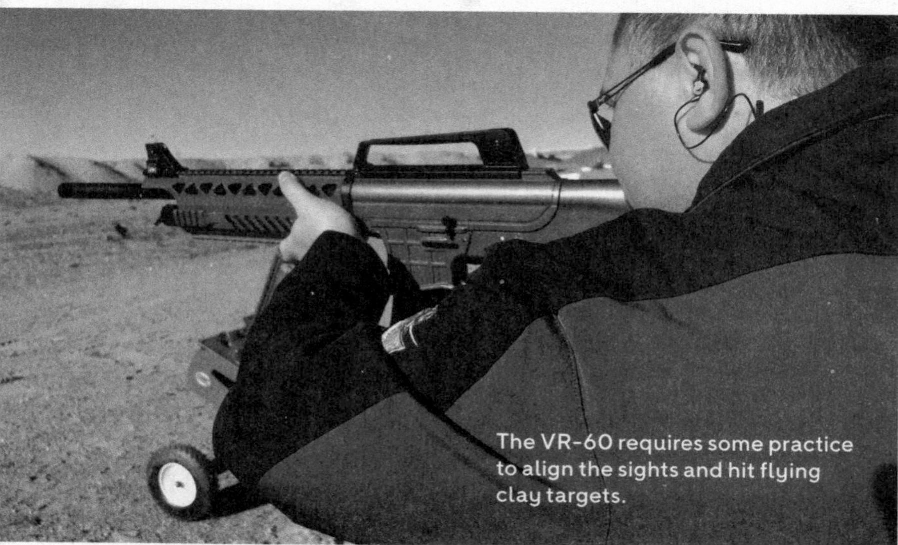

The VR-60 requires some practice to align the sights and hit flying clay targets.

The Rock Island Armory Lion Conceal autoloader is covered with Muddy Girl camouflage.

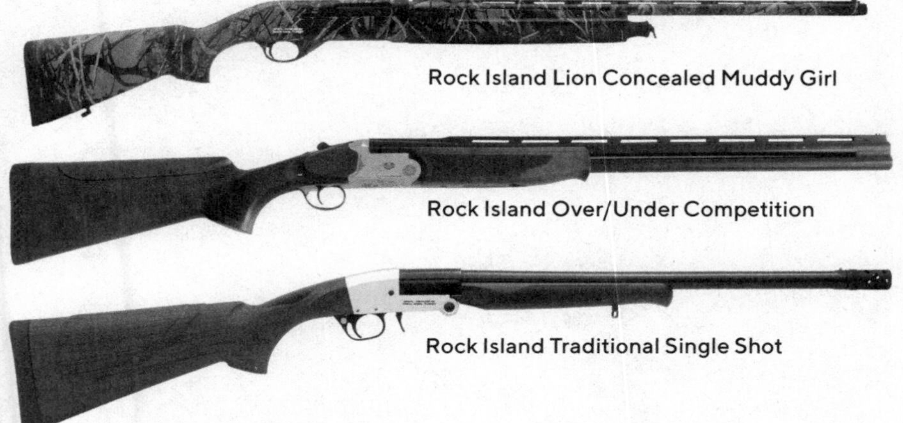

Rock Island Lion Concealed Muddy Girl

Rock Island Over/Under Competition

Rock Island Traditional Single Shot

The Over/Under Plus sports a silver-anodized receiver with hand engraving. A walnut stock and forearm complete the gun. It comes with F, M and IC chokes for its 28-inch barrels.

The Over/Under Competition wears a nickel-chrome finish on its receiver. I shot the Competition at clay targets and did quite well.

However, about all I hit was the ground while attempting to shoot the VR-60, which looks like an AR-type rifle. The gun's high sights just did not point well for me and I had a difficult time finding flying clays. The three models of the VR-60 have five-shot detachable magazines and a 20-inch barrel with a F, M and IC choke tubes. The guns can be had in black, red or brown finish. The Bull Rocket is similar, but in a bullpup design with a cylinder choke.

The Traditional single-shot 12 gauge has a muzzle brake on its 20-inch barrel. Its synthetic stock and forearm are colored with a walnut paint. armscor.com

Winchester

Winchester continues to expand its Super X4 autoloader and Super X pump lines with new slug guns, turkey getters and all things camouflage. The Super X4 Cantilever Buck has a 22-inch barrel that handles 2 3/4- and 3-inch slugs. A Truglo fiber-optic front sight and adjustable rear provide a bright sight picture. A Weaver-style cantilever rail provides an option for mounting optics. Spacers, fitted between the Inflex Technology recoil pad, allow you to adjust length of pull of the synthetic black stock with a round grip. The Super X4 Universal Hunter's receiver is drilled and tapped for mounting optics and offers a choice of a 24-, 26- or 28-inch barrel with a chrome-plated chamber and bore, and Invector-Plus choke tubes. Mossy Oak Break-Up Country camouflage covers the gun.

The Super X Turkey Hunter and Long Beard 12- and 20-gauge pumps have a 24-inch barrel and are masked in Mossy Oak Obsession camo. The Turkey Hunter has an Invector-Plus Extra-Full turkey choke tube, while an Extra-Full extended choke screws into the muzzle of the Long Beard. winchesterguns.com

The Winchester 101 Classic field-style over/under shotgun wears Grade III European walnut and intricate receiver engraving. The gun is a 2018 SHOT Show special.

Winchester SX4 Cantilever Buck

Winchester Universal Hunter

Winchester SXP Long Beard

Winchester SXP Turkey Hunter

NEW OPTICS

BY **TOM TABOR**

In the recent past, shooting optics essentially fell into one of two basic categories — scopes or binoculars. But that has all changed. Today, the category includes much more diversity within those two groups of products, as well as additional types of optics that were never available.

Just a couple of decades ago, no one would have envisioned a rangefinder could be purchased for a couple of hundred dollars that would allow you to accurately range your game at a quarter of a mile away, or even farther in some cases. Nevertheless, we now have that capability, and in packages that can easily fit in the palm of your hand. In the shooting world, that itself is an impressive accomplishment, but now that same technology has been incorporated into riflescopes and binoculars.

We now have extremely efficient night vision equipment available to us, heat-seeking optics that can both see game during times of poor or non-existent light conditions and locate blood trails. All these capabilities and many more are now at our disposal and priced to fit in a family budget.

Scopes, binoculars and other optics frequently come today with greater magnification capabilities, possess overall better clarity, in many cases are smaller and lighter in weight and are more durable than those of the past. Some have warranties assuring a lifetime of reliable and trouble-free service. This is an exciting time in the optics world. Here are a few of those fine products that are now on store shelves and awaiting your attention.

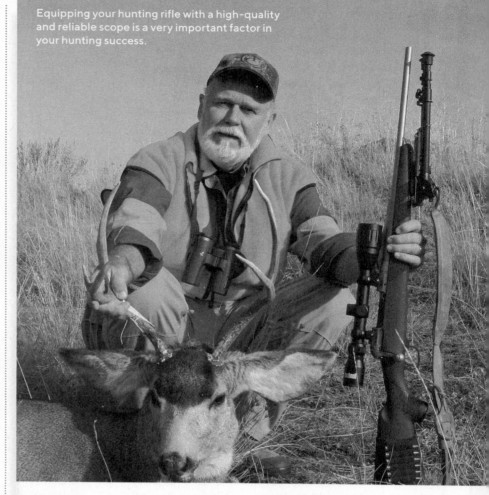

Equipping your hunting rifle with a high-quality and reliable scope is a very important factor in your hunting success.

Aimpoint

Aimpoint is frequently recognized as the worldwide leader when it comes to red-dot sighting technology. Further adding to that reputation is the company's newest addition, the Aimpoint Micro S-1. This sight is designed for use on shotguns with ventilated ribs. The Micro S-1 comes in a compact, low-profile design that can benefit hunters seeking such game as turkeys, deer or other similar game. It can also be used to improve your performance when hunting waterfowl or upland birds, or even when shooting clay targets. Its innovative carbon fiber reinforced mounting system allows you to attach the sight at any point along the rib where it sits in the lowest possible optical axis. Included are eight interchangeable adapter plates to fit most standard shotgun ribs. MSRP: $804.00. aimpoint.com

Aimpoint's new Micro S-1 sight is specifically designed for use on shotguns and can be easily attached to most ventilated ribs.

Burris

The Greeley, Colorado, firm of Burris has recently introduced the RT-6 1-6x24 riflescope, which is shorter than most 1-4x scopes. This would a great scope for 3-Gun events due its quick-to-point capabilities. Its features include an illuminated reticle with 11 intensity settings and a Ballistic AR mil reticle with trajectory compensation out to 600 yards. Its 30mm main tube has been nitrogen filled and comes in a matte finish. MSRP runs $230.79 for the scope alone, while the RT-6 1-6x24 Combo, including a FastFire 3 PEPR Mount, is available for $373.66. burrisoptics.com

Bushnell

At SHOT Show, Bushnell invited a few outdoor writers to preview the company's extensive new optics lines. Fortunately, I was one of those individuals, but like all of the others in the group, I was sworn to secrecy until the company released those products for sale later in the year. We were all ushered into a room where the products lined the walls and shelves. If nothing else, we were impressed by the sheer volume of new products. The quality of those products, consisting of binoculars, firearm scopes, spotting scopes and rangefinders, impressed us all. Even though at this writing some new optics are not yet available to the public, they will be by the time this *Gun Digest* goes to print. While there are far too many products to cover here, one great example lies in the category the company refers to as its Forge series, which consists of binoculars, riflescopes and spotting scopes.

The new ambidextrous Transition 3x Magnifier is designed specifically for Bushnell's TRS-25, but it can be used effectively with most other red-dot sights.

Bushnell's new 10x42 Forge binos come attractively colored in a combination of brown and black and are of a quality that assures a lifetime of use.

The Bushnell Forge 4.5-27x50 riflescope is a versatile choice for a wide range of shooters.

Bushnell's Forge binoculars will be available in four sizes: 10x30, 8x42, 10x42 and 15x56. Every element in the optical path of these binoculars comes with the very best coatings. The EXO Barrier bonds to the exterior lens to repel water, oil, dust and debris even in the worst weather conditions. The Ultra Wide Band Coating is an anti-reflection product for the lenses and prism to ensure the brightest images. And the PC3 Phase Coating, which is applied to the prisms, enhances resolution and contract. Forge binocular MSRPs range from $349.99 to $799.99.

Forge riflescopes come with side parallax adjustment, precision exposed locking zero-stop turrets, scope covers, a 2 1/2-inch sun shade, fully multi-coated optics including the Bushnell EXO Barrier and Ultra Wide Band Coatings and a 30mm main tube, and they are waterproof and fog proof. They are available in a wide variety of different reticle and optical choices within three basic magnification range groups: 2.5-15x50, 3-18x50 and 4.5-27x50. MSRPs for Forge riflescopes range from $749.99 up to $949.99.

The Forge 20-60x80 spotting scope with the 45-degree angled eyepiece would make a good choice when it comes to extended viewing periods.

Spotting scopes in the Forge line are available in three models: 10-50x60 Terrain, 20-60x80 Roof Prism with a straight eyepiece and 20-60x80 Roof Prism with a 45-degree angled eyepiece. All feature Extra-Low ED Prime Glass lenses that are protected by EXO Barrier to repel any crud you can imagine, and all of the optics are fully-multi-coated. MSRPs for Forge spotting scopes range from $1,149.99 up to $1,199.99.

Other late-breaking products from Bushnell include two models to the company's already extensive AR Optics line. These are a caliber-specific Accelerate 3x prism sight and an ambidextrous Transition 3x Magnifier. The Transition 3x Magnifier is designed to benefit the Bushnell TRS-25 but it can be used in conjunction with most any red-dot sight. It is waterproof, fog proof and shock proof. The Accelerate 3x prism sight carries a MSRP of $349.99 while the Transition 3x Magnifier runs $258.95.

With the 6.5 Creedmoor continuing to increase in popularity, particularly among long-distance shooters, Bushnell's new AR Optics 4.5-18x40 scope with the Drop Zone 6.5 Creedmoor reticle could be a good match. In this case, the reticle is designed to maximize the Creedmoor's performance by providing holdover points for shots out to 600 yards. Tactical-style target turrets allow for fast adjustments and the side parallax focus dial permits you to quickly adjust image clarity at any range. Multi-coated optics provide bright, crisp sight images, and a 1-inch main tube housing crafted from aircraft-grade aluminum ensures durability coupled with light weight. MSRP for the 4.5-18x40 Drop Zone 6.5 Creedmoor is $323.45.

Bushnell has also added an optic for those MSR shooters favoring the .300 Blackout. The new AR Optics 1-4x24

The Bushnell Engage line includes both riflescopes and binoculars.

scope includes a specially designed DropZone .300 Blackout illuminated reticle, which features holdover points calibrated to both subsonic and supersonic .300 Blackout ballistics. This scope's first focal plane design performs like a high-performance red-dot when set on low power, but when turned up to 4x magnification provides holdover points out to 300 yards. MSRP: $386.95

Bushnell has recently announced a new optics series called the Engage Optics Scopes and Binocular Line. Engage riflescopes feature a new look, upgraded features and a brand-new Deploy MOA reticle with 1-MOA windage and elevation hashmarks. Nine magnification configurations are available ranging from 2-7x36 up to 6-24x50. All feature Butler Creek Flip Caps, the Deploy MOA Reticle and Bushnell's Ironclad Warranty. Five models come with a 1-inch tube in a low-profile design, capped elevation and windage turrets, while the additional four models have rugged 30mm tubes and the new Tool-less Xero Reset Locking Turrets. bushnell.com

FLIR

In many ways, FLIR has set the standard when it comes to thermal imaging, a classic example of which is the ThermoSight Pro Thermal Imaging Weapon System. This device is a compact sight that has been equipped with the company's shot-activated video recording and patent pending High Visibility Technology (HVT). It's powered by the new FLIR Boson Core, featuring a 12 µm pixel pitch sensor, on-chip video processing and an uncompressed video signal fed directly to a high definition 1280x960 display. The Thermal Sight Pro gives clean thermal imagery under any light condition from low contrast daylight to total darkness, and in smoke, haze, light fog or rain.

There are three models available, each offering thermal resolution of 320x240, and all come packed in an aircraft-aluminum alloy body. These units allow you to register memorable moments with onboard video recording and image capture capabilities, while managing them with Bluetooth 4.0 and USB-C connectivity. Internal storage capacity permits the storing of up to four hours of video or 1,000 still images. The three 4x digital zoom models consist of the FLIR ThemoSight Pro PTS233, which comes equipped with 19mm lens and a 12-degree field-of-view; the PTS533 with 50mm lens and a 4.5-degree field-of-view; and the PTS733 with 75mm lens and a 3-degree field-of-view. The PTS233 models are available for $2,199 MSRP. flir.com

Leica

Some shooters prefer the no-nonsense approach inherent in a non-illuminated riflescope and that is where Leica's three new Magnus scopes come into play. They're available in 1.5-10x42, 1.8-12x50 and 2.4-16x56, and are priced at a lower entry point than the company's illuminated versions. They all come with the proven optical quality that Leica is best known for, including the company's no tool turret scale zeroing, approximately 91 percent light transmission, and high-contrast sighting even under unfavorable light conditions. They also have an optimal eye relief of 3.5 inches, diopter compensation of -4/+3 dpt, applied AquaDura lens coatings, and are waterproof and fog proof down to depths of 13.1 feet. MSRPs vary from $1,799 up to $2,199.

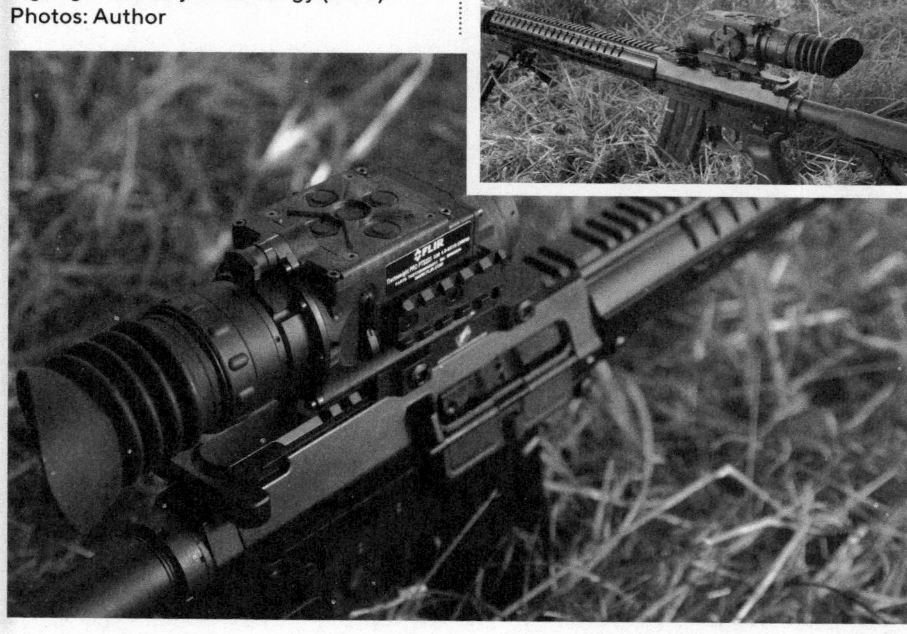

The FLIR ThermoSight Pro Thermal Imaging Weapon System has been equipped with the company's shot-activated video recording, and patent pending High Visibility Technology (HVT). Photos: Author

Leica has expanded its Premium Entry-Level Series Binoculars to include a couple of new choices: the Trinovid 8x32 HD and the 10x32 HD. Both come with a guarantee of exceptionally bright and clear view, pin-sharp resolution, plus superb color fidelity and contrast. As is the case with the top Leica models, the lenses of the Trinovid binoculars feature an effective water-resistant and dirt-repellent coating. Diopter corrections can be conveniently and easily made using the right eyepiece. Personal settings for the eye-relief distance can be accomplished using the built-in four click-stop settings. MSRP for the Trinovid 8x32 HD is $849, and $899 for the Trinovid 10x32 HD model. leica-camera.com

Leupold & Stevens

Leupold continues to grow its popular Mark 8 series of riflescopes with a new model — the Mark 8 3.5-25x56. This scope couples the sharp optical quality that precision and long-range shooters depend upon with the abilities inherent in some new performance-driven additions. Now weighing in at just 32.5 ounces, this latest Mark 8 still delivers the same ruggedness and reliability of the other scopes in the series, but with less weight. Also new to the Mark 8 line are the simplified ZeroLock dials for both windage and elevation, allowing "no-look" adjustments to be made to lock them in place. The Mark 8 3.5-25x56 is available in a variety of reticles, such as the Tactical Milling Reticle (TMR), Combat Competition Hunter (CCH) and TReMoR3. All these scopes offer front focal plane reticles, a 35mm main tube, 90 MOA adjustment for elevation and a generous amount of eye relief. MSRP runs $3,899.99 for the non-illuminated reticle Mark 8 3.5-25x56, $5,374.99 for the illuminated model.

Also new at the Beaverton, Oregon-based Leupold is the new line of VX-5HD optics. These riflescopes feature a 5x erector assembly and are now available in 1-5x, 2-10x and 3-15x models. These come equipped with the company's Twilight Max Light Management System intended to deliver crisp, clear images even in low-light situations without compromising the scope's ability to reduce glare when exposed to harsh midday sun. They also come with Leupold's new CDS-ZL2 adjustments, which offer a secure locking dial calibrated to your exact rifle and load using the Custom Dial System, a 30mm main-tube and a variety of different reticle choices. MSRPs range from $909.99 to $1,429.99. leupold.com

Leupold's newest addition to the Mark 8 series riflescopes is the 3.5-25x56.

Meopta

The new Meopta MeoAce (Meo Aiming Compact Equipment) 3x20 Tactical Sight is designed for use with rifles chambered in 5.56 NATO and 7.62x39, or 7.62x51 NATO/.308 Winchester when using the 5.56 side of the reticle and firing 180-grain bullets. This scope provides precision aiming out to 400 meters and is night vision compatible with illuminated reticles adjustable to twelve brightness intensity settings. Meopta's proprietary MeoBright multi-coating lenses eliminate glare and reflections while the hydrophobic MeoDrop coatings ensure a high level of visual clarity during adverse weather conditions. The MeoAce 3x20 carries an MSRP of $1,299.99 and optical accessories are available.

Also new from Meopta is the MeoRed T 1x30 Reflex Sight. It comes with unlimited eye relief to enable fast, accurate target acquisition. The MeoRed T was developed primarily for today's AR/MSR platforms and has a 1.5 MOA illuminated red-dot reticle with twelve intensity settings. For rugged, light weight, it comes housed in an aircraft-grade aluminum body. MSRP is $999.99 and optional accessories are available for purchase separately.

Meopta's MeoMag 3x Magnifier is designed for use with red-dot sights and would be an ideal match to the MeoRed T, MeoRed T-mini, MeoSight III, M-RAD or other similar units, but it can also double as a stand-alone monocular. Meopta's propriety MeoBright lens multi-coating cuts glare and reflections and its hydrophobic MeoDrop lens coatings ensure a high level of visual clarity even in the most adverse of weather conditions. MSRP runs $999.99. meoptausa.com

The Meopta MeoAce 3x20 illuminated reticle Tactical Sight is designed for use on rifles chambered in 5.56 NATO and 7.62x39 (or 7.62x51 NATO/.308 Winchester in 180-grain loads when using the 5.56 side of the reticle), which is accurate up to 400 meters.

Meopta's new MeoRed T 1x30 Reflex Sight was designed as a primary optic on today's AR/MSR platform rifles.

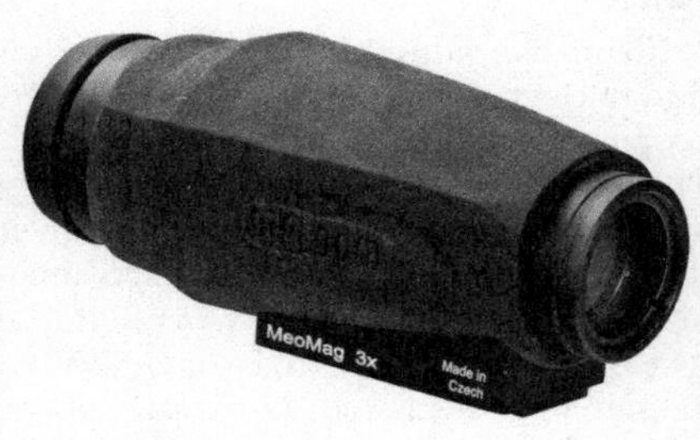

The Meopta 3x Magnifier would be ideal for use with any of the company's red-dot sights or other similarly styled optics.

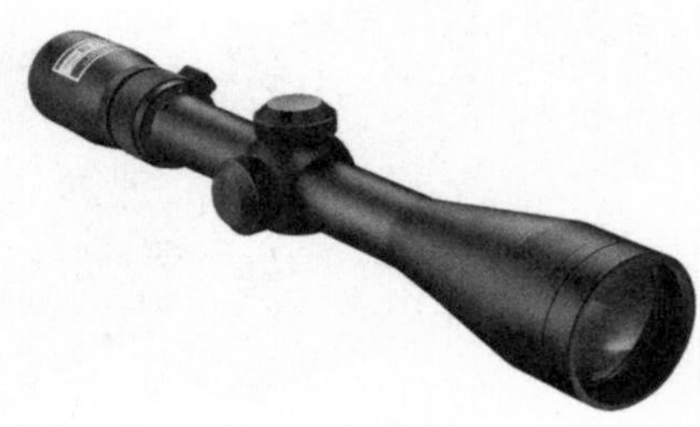

The Nikon Buckmaster II riflescope lineup now includes a 3-9x50 Matte BDC model, which would be a good choice for any hunter.

The new Nikon Black X1000 4-16x50 and 6-24x50 riflescopes are available with either X-MRAD or X-MOA tactical-style reticles, making them a solid option for precision shooters.

Nikon

Nikon has added yet one more addition to the company's Buckmaster II riflescope lineup — the 3-9x50 Matte BDC. This scope couples the long-range aiming simplicity inherent in a BDC reticle, yet it is conservatively priced and accompanied by a lifetime warranty. Through the use of Nikon's Spot On Ballistic Match Technology (available as a free app or online program) you can optimize the Buckmaster II 3-9x50 BDC scope to precisely match an individual cartridge and load. It comes with the company's Spring-Loaded Instant Zero-Reset turrets, which can be easily returned to the zero-mark after sight-in for enhanced confidence. Its generous eye relief, a waterproof, fog proof and shock proof construction, and a fixed 100-yard parallax setting combine to make the Buckmaster II a good choice for general hunting. And like all Nikon riflescopes, it is backed by Nikon's Limited Lifetime Warranty and No Fault Repair/Replacement Policy. MSRP for the Buckmaster II 3-9x50 BDC riflescope runs $179.95.

Specifically designed around the needs of American shooters, Nikon's new Black riflescope series provides a diverse choice. For precision rifle shooters, the company's new X1000 is available in a choice of 4-16x50 and 6-24x50 models. Both are available in either X-MRAD or X-MOA tactical-style reticles. These provide you with a visually clean, yet highly functional way of estimating range and hold-over. However, AR and MSR shooters looking for rapid-action targeting capabilities might find the Black Force1000 1-4x24 riflescope to their liking. It comes with capped turrets and SpeedForce illuminated double horseshoe reticles. The center portion of these reticles serves as a quick reference for reaction-speed target acquisition and engagement and a quick way of establishing moving target leads. The SpeedForce MOA reticle integrates BDC circles and hashmarks for precise intermediate-range target holdovers. Black series scopes come with a 30mm main tube made of aircraft-grade aluminum alloy that has been Type 3 hard anodized for ruggedness and resistance to damage. MSRPs for the Black series scopes range from $399.95 to $649.95.

Nikon's LaserForce Rangefinding Binocular is equipped with built-in laser ranging capabilities capable of measuring distances as close as 10 yards all the way out to 1,900 yards. These binoculars come with instantaneous readouts on a crisp OLED display with four levels of brightness, making it easily readable under virtually any light condition. They feature ED (extra-low dispersion) Glass, which has been fully multilayer-coated and include Nikon's ID (Incline/Decline) Technology compensation for angle and slope bullet trajectory compensation. Currently, these binoculars are available in 10x42 at $1,199.95 MSRP. nikonsportoptics.com

Nikon's Black Force1000 1-4x24 riflescope is primarily designed with AR shooters in mind.

Nikon's LaserForce Rangefinding Binocular is capable of ranging targets out to 1,900 yards.

Swarovski

Swarovski Optik produces sporting sights and optics that many shooters and hunters consider some of the highest quality in the world. Specifically targeting the needs of American shooters, Swarovski Optik North America, a subsidiary of the Austrian-based company, has recently brought to market its newest product — the BTX Binocular Spotting Scope. This scope essentially merges the benefits associated with binocular-style optics with those of a spotting scope. This unique concept uses the visual power of both eyes, enabling the observer to take full advantage of their entire vision capabilities. The result is an optic that eliminates eye strain, particularly when longer duration viewing is called for. Its built-in adjustable forehead rest and an aiming aid integrated above the right eyepiece permits you to more quickly locate your viewing target. The BTX is compatible with all objective modules in the Swarovski Optik ATX/STX family. An example of this flexibility would be to use the ME 1.7x magnification extender to quickly increase the BTX's magnification to 50x or 60x. MSRP for the BTX eyepiece module is $3,077.00 with the modular objective lens ranging from $1,143.00 for the 65mm up to $2,288.00 for the 95mm. swarovskioptik.com

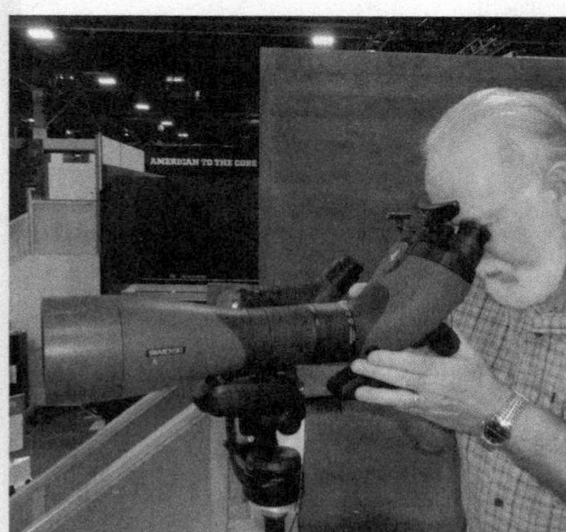

In the author's opinion, when it comes to long stints of viewing, Swarovski's new BTX Binocular Spotting Scope would be perfect.

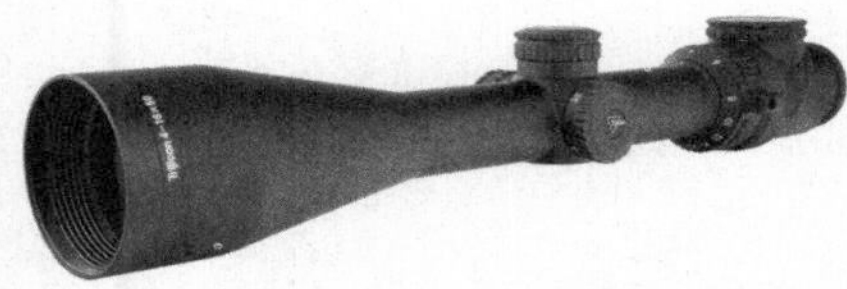

Trijicon's battery-free 4-16X50 AccuPoint riflescope is the latest edition to the company's AccuPoint series. With it, your shooting is extended under any light conditions.

The new RMR Type 2 Miniature Reflex Sight from Trijicon was designed for handguns and all extreme usage platforms.

Trijicon

Trijicon has created another Brilliant Aiming Solution with introduction of the new 4-16x50 AccuPoint riflescope. This latest model in the AccuPoint series gives tactical marksmen, long-range hunters and precision rifle shooters the ability to accurately extend their range under any light condition all in a battery-free environment. It's built around a fiber-optic, tritium-illuminated reticle, which helps when it comes to quick target acquisition. It's a dual-illumination system that automatically adjusts the illumination brightness based on the available ambient light, but its built-in override capabilities permit you to adjust the brightness manually if desired, too. Windage and elevation adjustments are made in 0.25 MOA or 0.1-mil increments with a full 80 MOA downrange adjustment potential. The side parallax control allows easy adjustment of focus while keeping your eyes locked on the target. The new 4-16x AccuPoint is available in six of the most popular AccuPoint reticles, including the classic duplex crosshair (green), MOA-dot crosshair (green), MIL-dot crosshair (green) and triangle post (red, green or amber). All are in the 2nd focal plane, offering pinpoint accuracy at any magnification setting. The MSRP for the 4-16x50 AccuPoint is $1,399.

Also new from Trijicon is the RMR Type 2 Miniature Reflex Sight. This sight was designed for handguns and all extreme usage platforms. It deploys new electronics that help to bolster a high degree of durability under the harshest of environments and heaviest recoil. It includes a Button Lock Out Mode that prevents accidental adjustments from occurring to the brightness setting. It's constructed of 7075-T6 aluminum developed to MIL-spec standards and weighs only 1.2-ounces. Trijicon considers the Trijicon RMR Type 2 to be the most rugged and durable reflex sight on the market today. MSRP runs $699. trijicon.com

Zeiss

Zeiss has recently introduced its new line of riflescopes — the Conquest V6 Series. The Conquest V6 scopes feature a 6x variable magnification range and new ballistic lockable turrets, and come with a choice of reticles including the ZBR and ZMOA. The scopes utilize FL lens and T lens coatings to achieve a light transmission of 92 percent, while the LotuTec water-repellant lens coating keeps the exterior lenses clean and clear.

Built in Germany, these scopes are currently available in three 30mm main tube models: 1-6x24, 3-18x50 and 5-30x50. They come with a machined magnification ring with finer adjustment than previous versions of the Conquest line and include an updated ergonomic turret design for speed and versatility in the field. With the large, forgiving eyebox and fine reticle in the second image plane, the V6 encourages rapid target acquisition with minimum target subtension coverage. Zeiss has also integrated its own intelligent motion sensors into the 1-6x24 model. The sensors automatically deactivate the illuminated dot as soon as you put the rifle down, then reactivate it as the rifle is brought back up to take aim. MSRPs for the Conquest V6 riflescopes range from $1,549.99 to $1,899.99.

Zeiss' new Victory Pocket binoculars are currently available in two sizes: 8x25 and 10x25. Weighing in at only 10 ounces makes these binos a perfect choice for long days in the field. They are the first pocket binoculars to utilize FL-Lenses and produce enhanced resolution and edge-to-edge sharpness with the lowest color fringing in their class. They also are said to provide the widest field of view currently available in their class at 8x magnification. A field of view of 390 feet at 1,000 yards and a near focus range of only 6 feet make the Victory Pocket 8x25 a versatile choice at $749.99 MSRP. And for the person looking for a bit more magnification, the Victory Pocket 10x25 is available for $799.99 MSRP. zeiss.com/us/sports-optics

Zeiss's 3-18x50 is one of three new scopes within the new Conquest V6 Series (shown here) and accompanied by 1-6x24 and 5-30x50 models. These scopes are built in Germany and come with a machined magnification ring with finer adjustment than previous versions of the Conquest line.

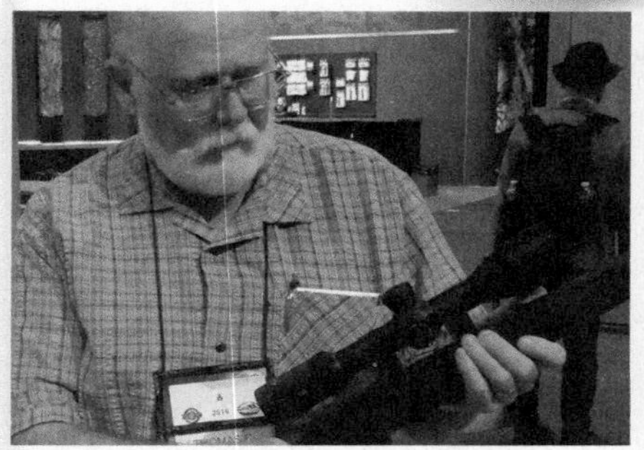

Conquest V6 Series riflescopes offer advantages not inherent in the previous Conquest scopes.

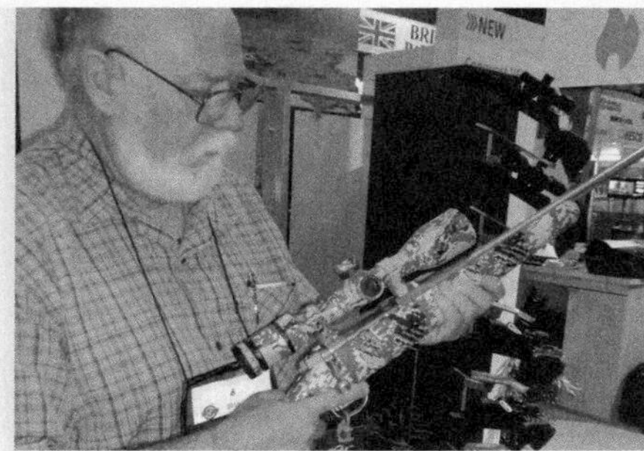

Camo finishes are available for this year's Conquest V6 Series scopes through Zeiss's custom shop.

Cimarron has introduced replica copies of the Walker Revolver using the original company numbers, like "C 47," in a 1,000-pistol run between now and 2023. Capt. Samuel Hamilton Walker was largely responsible for Colt's reworking the fragile design of the Colt Patterson into what became the later Walker and Colt Dragoon revolvers.

MUZZLELOADERS & BLACKPOWDER CARTRIDGE GUNS

Building on Old Foundations

BY **WM. HOVEY SMITH**

Civil War replicas dominated the new muzzleloading gun category at the 40th Anniversary SHOT Show. These guns continue the trend of authentic replicas for today's shooters. Traditions introduced four rifles and one smoothbore, while Davide Pedersoli presented an Austrian Lorenz rifle. Hunters were almost forgotten. Dixie Gun Works, working with Pedersoli, arranged for flint and percussion versions of a single-barreled 12-gauge shotgun to fill a gap in the market for traditional guns of this type. By far the flashiest piece at the show was a flintlock side-by-side shotgun exhibited by Petersoli.

Cimarron Firearms

Often a go-to place for Cowboy Action Shooters, Cimarron introduced a Teddy Roosevelt 1876 Rifle with engravings, a half-round barrel, half magazine and deluxe wood. This lever action is chambered in the original .45-75 caliber. Cimarron's intention was to judge demand to see if the rifle should be added to its line. This bottlenecked cartridge uses a 350-grain bullet compared to the .45-60's 300-grain projectile.

I once owned a Winchester 1876 in .45-60 and developed a fondness for the rifle and its easy-to-reload cartridge, which can be made by trimming common .45-70 brass. I asked if a plain half-magazine, half-round version might be made in .45-60, and was given an am-

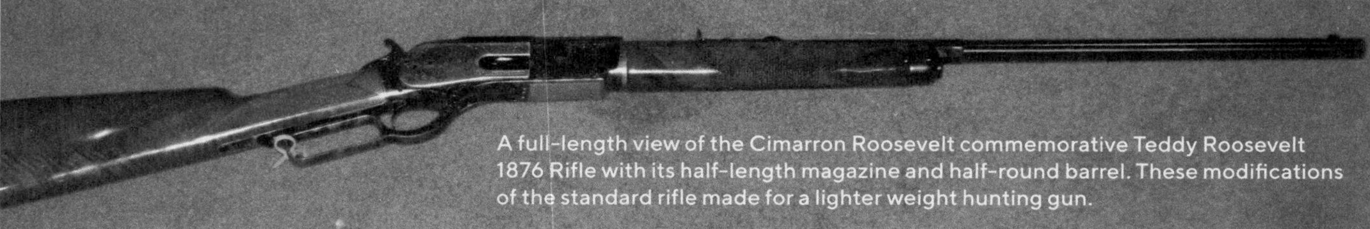
A full-length view of the Cimarron Roosevelt commemorative Teddy Roosevelt 1876 Rifle with its half-length magazine and half-round barrel. These modifications of the standard rifle made for a lighter weight hunting gun.

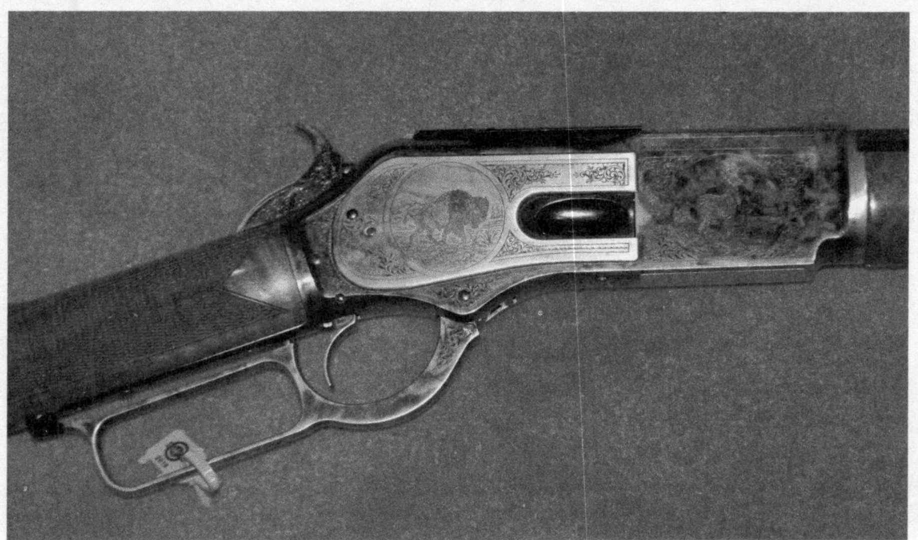
The 1876 Centennial lever-action rifle used an enlarged version of the 1873 Winchester action to chamber more powerful cartridges. The Cimarron Teddy Roosevelt rifle is made with fancy wood, heavily engraved and chambered for the .45-75 bottlenecked cartridge. Roosevelt wrote about this rifle in his book, *Ranch Life and The Hunting Trail.*

biguous reply. Because of its 300-grain bullet, the .45-60 was considered a deer and black bear round, compared to the 400- to 500-grain bullets for heavier game used in the .45-70 cartridge in the Winchester 1886 lever action. Cimarron offers standard-weight versions of the 1876 in both .45-caliber cartridges as well as the .50-95, which was the least popular of the three chamberings.

An exacting replica of Col. Sam Walker's Colt Walker pistols just missed making the show. These will be produced in a run of 1,000 guns and marked identically with the originals using company markings. The big .44s will be sold starting this year and continue through 2023. Cimarron will donate 5 percent of the sale price to the Former Texas Rangers Foundation. The retail price of $678.75 will allow Colt collectors to put a near-exact replica in their collection, at much less cost than an original. cimarron-firearms.com

CVA

New this year from CVA are two variations of the Apex rifle, the Long Range and the Prairie. These guns feature longer barrels and a money back guarantee that their Bergara barrels will shoot better than any other drop-barrel muzzleloader. The Long Range has a 30-inch barrel compared to the Prairie's 28 inches, and the Mountain Rifle's 25-inch tube. The entire Apex line has been progressively improved over the years. Augmentations now include a hand-detachable breech plug, thumb-hole stock, rubber overmolds, a palm-saver grip and recoil pad.

While some are still available, the Optima Muzzleloading Pistol is to be discontinued. With the demise of Tradition's Vortex last year, and of the muzzleloading version of the Thompson/Center Encore before that, there are no factory makers of in-line muzzleloading pistols for hunting big game. In the Encore and Optima handguns, I often use a load of 100 grains of powder and a 370-grain T/C Maxi-Ball bullet, which will penetrate 27 inches of American or African game. While some traditionally styled pistols may also be used for hunting, they cannot tolerate such a powerful load and lack easy mounting of optical sights. bpioutdoors.com

Davide Pedersoli

The Italian gunmaker in Gardone produces the widest variety of muzzleloading and replica cartridge guns made, and does so almost entirely in their factory in northern Italy. The wood, mostly American walnut, comes in as blanks, the barrels as steel rods. These are used to make exacting replicas, using originals as patterns. Modern CNC machines are employed so the same equipment can make a muzzleloader one day and a cartridge gun the next.

Stefano Pedersoli holding Davide Pedersoli's double-barreled Beautiful Hunter flintlock.

Davide Pedersoli's Double Barrel Flintlock with a side view of the engraved lock.

The Davide Pedersoli 13.9mm Lorenz Austrian musket. The original was used in large numbers by both the U.S. and Confederate forces during the American Civil War. This gun has an excellent reputation in Europe as a service target rifle when used with the correct paper-patched bullets. As in the U.S., regular matches are held in Europe for blackpowder firearms of all sorts, which are climaxed by an international competition.

Undoubtedly, the engraved Beautiful Hunter flintlock double-barreled shotgun attracted the most attention. The gun is 20 gauge with plumb-browned barrels and heavily engraved locks. The 27.5-inch barrels are chrome-lined and choked improved cylinder and modified. The touchholes on the display gun were plugged, indicating that it had never been fired.

Many who saw the new double said that they liked it, but would they like it sufficiently to buy it at a price of $1,965? I have no interest in the engraved model that was shown, but I would like a shooters-grade gun, and said as much. Initial production will be of the engraved model, which will mostly wind up as a decorative item rather than as a hunting gun. Pity.

Among international shooters, the 1854 Austrian Lorenz has the reputation of being among the best-shooting service rifles of the mid-1800s. Unlike the minié ball used in the American Springfield rifle, the Lorenz uses a paper-patched solid-based lead bullet with two large grease grooves. As cast, the bullet is 13.7mm and, with two wraps of paper, reaches the bore size of 13.9mm. The paper is also lubed to help load the rifle. The approximately .54-caliber bore gave Confederate supply officers fits, because they had units armed with the gun, which added yet another specialized bullet to supply among the 50-odd other sizes used by the South's forces. The Lorenz will have a suggested retail price of $1,950. Pedersoli is also developing a mold to cast bullets for the rifle.

These rifles in Union combat units were replaced as quickly as possible with Springfields, and were often reissued to rear-guard units. Individual Confederate soldiers (with their hodge-podge of guns and ammo) generally did not like the Lorenz, primarily because they seldom had proper ammunition. The best they could hope for was that the projectile would exit the bore and go somewhere towards the enemy. Otherwise, the 9-pound gun and bayonet made a serviceable pike. davide-pedersoli.com

Dixie Gun Works

In collaboration with Pedersoli, Dixie's Charles Kirkland has arranged production of a single-barreled, cylinder bore 12-gauge shotgun for training use by organizations like the 4-H, Boy Scouts of America and others who have shooting programs. "They could get muzzleloading rifles and handguns for their programs, but there were no replica muzzleloading shotguns on the market that they could afford," Kirkland said.

The Dixie/Pedersoli Scout shotgun is available from Dixie in both left- and right-handed percussion and as a right-handed flintlock. It has a walnut stock, octagon-to-round barrel with two sight pins. However, it is not equipped with a ramrod or provisions to mount one. Asked why this apparent oversight was made, Kirkland said the guns were designed to be used at shooting ranges where a robust range rod would be used to load them. Despite this, we hunters need a ramrod on our shotguns, and I can think of no period 12-gauge single-barreled shotgun that did not have them, unless it was in a cased set. The suggested retail price of the gun ranges from $665.00 for the percussion to $699.99 for the flintlock version. Kirkland said a reduced program price would be given to shooter-training organizations. I had a chance to briefly hunt with the flintlock, which is described at the end of this report. dixiegunworks.com

Knight Rifles

Knight Rifles, maker of super-accurate bolt-action and striker-fired muzzleloaders, has continued the same line that they offered last year. Among the muzzleloaders that have attracted the most attention are the 6.5-pound Ultra-Lite with its modern-age composite stock, the Mountaineer in a choice of .45, .50 or .52 calibers and the Disc Extreme offered in the same calibers. Knight has a variety of stock options.

The company still offers its striker-fired guns, which are direct descendants of Tony Knight's original MK-85. These include the Bighorn, Littlehorn and Wolverine. The Littlehorn has a 12.5-inch stock for youngsters and small adults. Knight's TK-2000 remains the most powerful muzzleloading shotgun in recent production, with the capability of taking loads of two ounces of shot. knightrifles.com

Taylor's & Company

With a booth awash with almost every muzzleloading and black powder firearm associated with the opening of the American West, Taylor's now offers Pietta's 1862 Sheriff's model, which is a 5-inch .44 percussion revolver with engraving that includes a star on the barrel shank. Options include simulated ivory or wooden grips.

Besides being a seller of guns to the Cowboy Action Shooting market from nearly every European maker, Taylor's also has guns with larger than standard grips, custom revolver turning, custom 1911s, leather, target rifles for long-range black-powder shooting and the accessories to make everything work. Its offerings also include guns that the cowboys

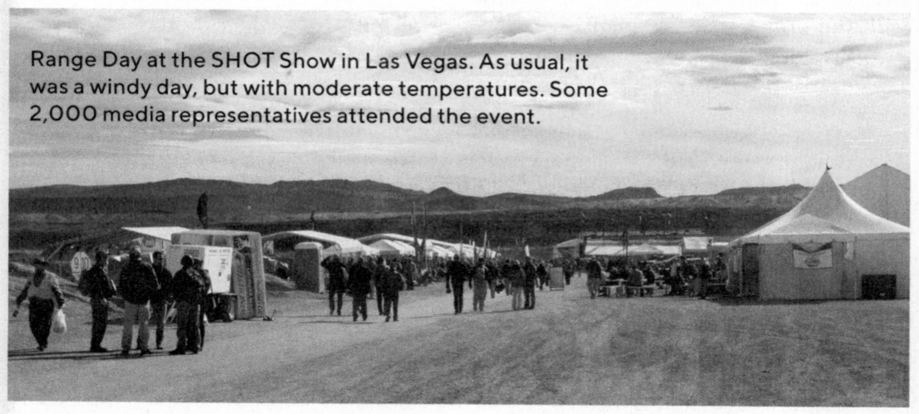

Range Day at the SHOT Show in Las Vegas. As usual, it was a windy day, but with moderate temperatures. Some 2,000 media representatives attended the event.

The engraved Pietta Sheriff's model from Taylor's & Company is a .44-caliber shortened barrel revolver engraved with a star on the barrel shank. It is offered in either imitation ivory or wooden grips.

wish that they could have had, such as lever actions chambered for the .45 Long Colt, triple-barreled shotguns and a pistol-grip 12-gauge Model 1887 lever-action shotgun. taylorsfirearms.com

Thompson/Center Arms

Since Thompson/Center Arms was purchased by Smith & Wesson, there have been more reductions in the firm's muzzleloading products. The only new version of a gun that was shown at SHOT Show was a camo and weather-coated version of Michael Waddell's Triumph Bone Collector series. Waddell started as a champion turkey caller and cameraman at the Realtree camouflage company in Columbus, Georgia, and over the years has become an outdoor personality in his own right. Not only does he still hunt turkey, but he has also participated in well over 100 big game hunts from both behind and in front of the camera.

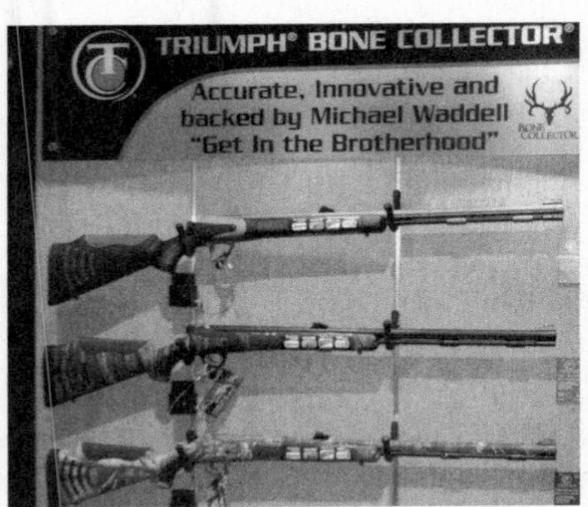

Thompson/Center Arms' new Triumph Bone Collector is inspired by Michael Waddell's hunting exploits. The muzzleloaders feature three different camo patterns. The series is based on the Triumph's falling barrel action, which is activated by an under-lever beneath the trigger guard.

Waddell's Triumph Bone Collector is among the simplest of the modern drop-barrel muzzleloaders. The barrel swings down by operating a lever under the trigger guard, it has a quick-detachable breech, uses 209 primers and can employ charges of up to 150 grains of pelletized or other black powders or equivelent substitutes. It also has a relieved muzzle that makes it easy to load. New features? It's now available in Realtree Edge and Realtree's Original Pattern camouflage. The Triumph employs a Flex-Tech recoil-reducing stock and fiber optic sights. It's priced between $638 and $679 and is among T/Cs best-selling muzzleloaders. smith-wesson.com

Traditions

Traditions' new line of American Civil War guns are made by Chiappa and were first shown at the SHOT Show last year. They include smoothbore and rifled versions of the .69-caliber 1842 Springfield with an armory-bright polish, the .58-caliber 1853 Enfield with blued barrel, the .58-caliber 1861 Springfield with its bright-polished finish and the 1863 Zouave with its blued finish and brass patchbox. The Zouave — with its shorter 33-inch barrel and blued finish — is more commonly seen in the hunting woods than the others. It was one of the first of the replica muzzleloading rifled-muskets made and has been produced by many firms over the decades.

These Chiappas are some of the most authentic replica muzzleloaders yet made and have period stamps and markings. They are not inexpensive and are priced between $1,000 and $1,200. They are also available as fully inletted kits for between $800 and $950. I have assembled some of Traditions' other kits and found that the parts drop in with minimal fitting. The steel barrels needed only a little extra polishing to remove clamp marks and scratches. traditionsfirearms.com

Powder and Bullets

Hodgdon has introduced a new pelletized powder, Triple7even FireStar, which has several new aspects. The pellets are ribbed to increase the surface burn area, it takes three pellets to equal a 100-grain charge and they leave only a little water-soluble residue. A warning on the package states that three pellets is a maximum load. Even though manufacturers may recommend three or more Pyrodex or other pellets in their guns, Hodgdon's recommendations are for a maximum of a 100-grain equivalent charge for pelletized powders. The single exception is for the 60-grain Triple7even Maximum Pellets where two may be used.

In limited testing, the new pellets shot well, and the gun cleaned up with water and a little scrubbing. These pellets are sold in packages of 10 sealed plastic tubes containing 60 pellets. This product has the potential of being more water re-

Hodgdon's TripleSeven FireStar pellets have hexagonal ribs to provide greater surface area for more rapid and cleaner combustion. Three of the new pellets are required to equal a 100-grain charge. These pellets yield a slightly higher velocity than other 100-grain pellet charges, have little residue and only need water to clean.

sistant than Hodgdon's boxed cylindrical Triple7even pellets.

Traditions has introduced three new .50-caliber muzzleloading bullets: The saboted Smackdown 170-grain bullet designed for rapid expansion on deer-sized game, the Carnivore with a protected point for improved ballistics and the XR in 200-, 230- and 250-grain weights for enhanced long-range performance.

Harvester showed, but did not have ready for sales, a close copy of the PowerBelt design. Production of these bullets was said to start before the end of 2018.

Other Makers

Gunmakers who had no changes in their line included Chiappa and Uberti, who have extensive lines of Civil War-era and early cartridge guns for reenactors and Cowboy Action Shooters. Remington, maker of the Model 700 Ultimate Muzzleloader, also had no new products. This muzzleloader is a single-shot version of the Model 700 rifle and is offered in wood and synthetic-stocked versions.

Report from the Field

Former Warrant Officer Carson Miller shot one of my "almost muzzleloaders" and two others as we tried to find a black powder rifle that he could shoot well enough to hunt deer. He felt relieved when I sent him back to get a Remington Model 700, since he usually used this bolt-action gun. He thought that I was sending him after a cartridge rifle and was somewhat shocked that this 700 was also a front-stuffer — the Remington Model 700 Ultimate Muzzleloader.

Miller is working on a book examining how older hunters can extend their hunting life by decades. One adaptation is to use muzzleloading guns that can be loaded to provide soft-shooting hunting tools. Now in his late 60s, he's beginning to experience some of the ills of age, including a tremor, impaired vision and a flinch. The gun that he shot most often was the Vietnam War-era M60 machine gun, which he qualified with as a helicopter pilot in the 1970s. This was the first time he had ever fired a muzzleloader, and he was having trouble.

On his first hunt, he tried my .577 Snider swinging-block rifle and a Markesberry .50-caliber with iron sights. Of the two, he shot the Markesberry much better, but missed two deer with it. On his second trip, I sighted in a Remington Genesis .50-caliber muzzleloader with a thumb-hole stock. He never shot that gun, but stuck with the scope-sighted Ultimate Muzzleloader shooting a charge of 90 grains of Pyrodex RS and PowerBelt's 295-grain hollowpoint. This is a comfortable, adequate load to shoot in this rifle, which is rated for a charge of 200 grains of powder and a saboted 150-grain copper bullet.

Miller's experiences illustrated some of the diversity available in modern muzzleloaders and big-bore single-shot rifles that may be legally used during muzzleloading seasons in Mississippi and Louisiana. Between used guns and new products offered at the 2018 SHOT Show, muzzleloaders and products are available for shooters of all ages.

A New Kind of Scout

In trying out new muzzleloaders, I opt for the least expensive gun in the line or the most difficult model to shoot. My theory is that if these guns work, then it is likely that the more expensive ones will perform as well. The Dixie-Pedersoli Scout 12-gauge flintlock cylinder bore shotgun arrived two weeks after the SHOT Show. Although big game season had closed, there was time to get in a couple of quick small game hunts.

I already had all the components that I needed to work up a load for the 5 1/2-pound gun. This is a very light weight for a 12 bore, and I opted for a 1-ounce load of shot. A volume-equivalent of powder was 78 grains of Olde Eynsford FFg black powder, on top of which I used a 1/4-inch card wad and a 1/2-inch fiber cushion wad, the shot and a 13-gauge over-shot wad. European-bored 12-gauge barrels are often a little tighter than their American equivalents, hence the smaller over-shot wad. This load shot well and performed even better at 30 yards when I put the shot in a shot cup with the excess space filled by a bit of torn plastic bag. (See the testing on a YouTube video at https://youtu.be/7zBlLbn0hcA.)

A spell of rainy weather was not helpful. The result was that I bagged three squirrels with four shots. On the first, I aimed off the head and killed it with shot from the pattern's fringe, so as not to riddle the squirrel. On the other two, I placed from 7 to 10 pellets in the animals killing them cleanly. (This hunt also produced a video at https://youtu.be/eRHN6EScffo.)

This minimalist gun uses a small flintlock, does not come with a ramrod or provisions for mounting one and has inexpensive furniture but shoots well. I also tested the factory recommended load of 72 grains of powder and 1 1/8 ounces of shot, which I also found to be effective on squirrels. I intend to use an equivalent load of HeviShot on turkey next spring.

Rural Free Delivery Hog

My RFD wild hog came while my bladesmith, Paul Hjort, and I were working in my shop getting some knives ready for a coming show. Hearing loud and persistent barking by my dogs, I found that they had bayed a wild hog in my backyard. I had taken a repaired Woodman .50-caliber break-barrel muzzleloader on several hunts in Georgia and Florida as described in the *2017 Gun Digest* but had not managed to put any game in front of it. Now there was a 125-pound hog standing in my yard.

We may take wild hogs on private lands in Georgia year-around. Because hogs are an ever-present possibility, I still had the Woodman loaded with 90 grains of Blackhorn 209 and a saboted 250-grain copper Markesbery Beast Buster bullet, which has a very deep hollowpoint like some Barnes copper bullets. While the dogs kept the sow engaged, I went into the house and grabbed the rifle.

The hog outweighed both of my dogs put together and appeared to regard them with contempt. The sow continued feeding while they were barking their heads off. When I returned, the three of them had moved about 30 yards across the yard. I went to a corner of a shed, turned on the red-dot sight and braced against the building. I had to wait until the dogs moved to offer a clear shot. When I fired, the hog collapsed. Good thing too, as I had no reloads; although I had stuffed my 1858 Remington Sheriff's Model .44 revolver into my belt as I walked out the door.

My shot entered low in the neck, passed through the spine and raked through the body. The recovered bullet, traveling at 1,750 fps., expanded to 0.75 inch and tore a ragged hole through bone and flesh. Paul helped me put the hog on my skinning tripod, and I processed it with a thin-bladed boning knife that I had just re-handled in the shop. By the next day, parts of the hog that had not been cooked on the grill were in my freezer. You can see a video about the hog hunt on YouTube "Adventures in Rural Knife Making with Hera, Hog and Half-Dog Fred" at: https://youtu.be/ckKxXtMhCJo.

With its weight of slightly under 6 pounds, the Woodman rifle makes a handy muzzleloader for stalking and treestand hunting. It's rated for 150-grain loads of black powder, but its light weight makes it far more comfortable to shoot with loads of 100 grains of powder and 300-grain bullets, which are adequate for whitetails and hogs out to 150 yards.

The author with his RFD (Rural Free Delivery) wild hog taken with the Woodman .50-caliber rifle using a load of 8 grains of Blackhorn 209 powder and a hollowpoint Markesbery 250-grain Beast Buster bullet at a speed of 1,750 fps. This copper-bronze bullet is quite similar to those sold by Barnes and other makers. The projectile worked well and expanded to about .75 caliber. The author is all set to get some pork chops.

The Old Man Speaks with Authority

The Old Man, a Mark III .577 Snider rifle from the Royal Arsenal of Nepal, had been on periodic hunts since I purchased it from Atlanta Cutlery in 2012. I had cleaned the gun and first shot it with an antique ammo brand briefly offered by Cabela's, and then using much more accurate reloads done by a Canadian reloader. Prepared as I might be, I had not managed to see any game when I was hunting. When Miller arrived, I brought out my "modern gun" again for him to try, but he did not shoot well with the Snider rifle.

Just to confirm that the Old Man could still do its stuff, I shot a 1.5-inch group at 50 yards centered about 12 inches high above the bull. This is certainly not MOA shooting, but sufficiently accurate to take close-range deer. I took the gun to one of my favorite hunting locations on Georgia's Ossabaw Island, but did not see any game.

During a hunt when I was back at home, the Snider took a tumble out of a stand. As the gun fell, the hammer caught on one of the rungs of the aluminum ladder and came to full cock. The gun hit hard enough to jam a two-inch plug of sand into the barrel. The arm of the tumbler that connects it to the mainspring snapped in two. Fortunately, IMA, International Military Arms, in New Jersey, had a replacement lock for the 1854 Enfield, which would more-or-less interchange with the Snider lock, and I ordered one. After I cleaned the lock and extracted the tumbler, I found that it would fit but the lower portion of the cone on the hammer had to be cut away to allow it to fully strike the rifle's firing pin.

In the waning light of a cold January evening, two does walked into one of my food plots where I had a tower stand. As the deer approached, I raised the gun, cocked the hammer and attempted to sight in on one of the deer. The thin-bladed front sight was almost invisible. I held low on the deer for the 60-yard shot. The trigger pull on the new tumbler felt a little different, but the break was smooth. The deer collapsed at the shot. In a few seconds it had expired. The big slug had hit high, as expected, and penetrated the spine. You can see a video about this hunt at: https://youtu.be/Ju6l5Cg1CPA.

The Old Man does not speak often, but when it does it speaks with authority. The problem is that no company now loads factory ammunition for it. Ammo can be produced by trimming about 0.75 inch from 24-gauge brass cases, according to the late Frank Barnes in his *Cartridges of the World*. He suggested loads with bullets weighing 480 grains and charges of 70-73 grains of Fg to replicate the military load. Barnes reported this load as having a muzzle velocity of 1,250 fps and a muzzle energy of 1,666 ft-lbs. The load I was using generated 1,600 ft-lbs — a little less than full power.

Original military cartridges used a bullet that was hollow-based and at first had an exposed wooden plug in a hollow-pointed bullet, and later a closed hollow void underneath the bullet nose. This complex bullet construction was used in an attempt to improve accuracy. The Cabela's loads that I first tried in the rifle shot terribly, with bullets hitting the target sideways. The Canadian reloads shot much better and gave me the confidence that I could use it to take close-range game, a sentiment that Barnes had expressed.

Some British still shoot Snider rifles in competition and a few take them hunting. The lack of factory ammunition hinders their more widespread use, unlike the many contemporary loadings of the .45-70 Government in the U.S. for the Allin-action Springfield rifles. Bullets and cases for the .577 and .577-450 rounds, and many other obsolete rimfire (reloadable) and centerfire cartridges, may be ordered by telephone from Texas manufacturer Bob Hayley at (940) 888-3352.

Carson "Jay" Miller shooting the Mark III .577 Snider rifle. The author took a small deer with this gun, but Carson was having trouble shooting it well. The rifle, with its 480-grain bullet and load of 70 grains of blackpowder, has moderate recoil and the shot pushed Miller backward. The load produces about 1,600 ft-lbs of muzzle energy and can take North American deer and hogs at close range, although these guns typically shoot about a foot high at 50 yards.

This Mark III Snider rifle was used to take a small Georgia deer, which is shown here wrapped for the freezer. The deer, shot at about 40 yards, went down instantly. The 480-grain bullet generated 1,600 ft-lbs. It passed through the spine of the animal, resulting in a very quick kill.

AIRGUNS: NEW OPTIONS ABOUND FOR HUNTING AND TARGET

BY **RICK EUTSLER**

The Gamo Swarm Maxxim is a break-barrel, multi-shot PCP air rifle that has changed industry standards and upped the ante.

Airguns have come a long way in the last few decades. Today's manufacturers are delivering power and performance along with value that has never before been seen. In this year's annual roundup, we identify a few airgun brands that stand out in the crowd.

Air Arms

Air Arms was founded in 1983 with a focus to create the best airguns in the world. Air Arms embarked on creating some truly exceptional, precision PCP (Pre-Charged Pneumatic) and spring-powered air rifles for the U.K. and world markets. There is no part of an Air Arms product that is not carefully considered and meticulously crafted to the highest standards, and yet its products are still offered at a price point that shooters can afford.

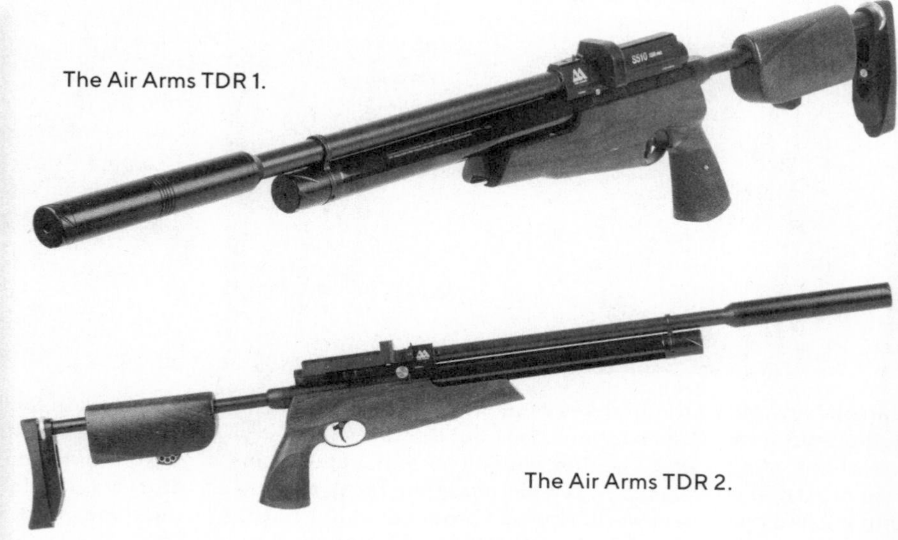

The Air Arms TDR 1.

The Air Arms TDR 2.

The Air Arms product lines stretch from heirloom-quality spring-type airguns designed to last for generations, to Olympic-class PCP pistols and rifles. Its line of spring-type airguns are arguably the most accurately built in the world. The TX200 has won more springer field target competitions than nearly all other contenders combined. It's unbelievably beautiful — from the custom walnut stock to bluing so deep you'd swear it was black glass. There's no equal in the market, other than maybe the Air Arms Pro Sport.

This level of craftsmanship extends to Air Arms' full line of PCP air rifles as well. The core design is the S510 series. Offered in various models and stock types, this system has proven to be wonderfully reliable, smooth and incredibly accurate. Whether you're a benchrest or competitive field target shooter, or small game hunter, there is a perfect fit for your needs in the S510 line.

In the world of field target competition, Air Arms continuously occupies the top of the leaderboard. For those not familiar with field target, it's one of the most popular competitive disciplines in the airgunning world. It requires exceptional skill and knowledge of ballistics, trajectory, and reading the dynamics of your environment. With all that already going on, your equipment must never let you down. Air Arms has created several purpose-built products for those competing at any field target level. If you want to be competitive, then you want to be shooting an Air Arms air rifle.

New for 2018, the concern introduced the S510 TDR FAC rifle. This version converts the S510 into an amazingly portable take-down field airgun. Coming in at only 6.2 pounds, it's designed from the ground up for small game hunting. The S510 TDR has features that include a fully adjustable two-stage trigger, Lothar Walther match barrel, integrated barrel shroud with fixed moderator, 10-shot rotary magazine, indexing power adjuster, and smooth side lever cocking system. Simply put, the S510 TDR is a dream to shoot. Air Arms has brought to market some amazing air rifles and is set to continue that tradition into 2018 and beyond. www.air-arms.co.uk

Ataman Airguns

Ataman is based out of Russia and long known for building high-quality precision airguns. Ataman entered the U.S. airgun market about three years ago in earnest. Imported and supported by Air Venturi based out of Ohio, Ataman airguns come in a variety of shapes, styles and configurations. One thing they all have in common, however, is exceptional build quality, performance and accuracy.

All Ataman airguns are built around precision accuracy, which starts with match barrels, exceptional regulators and fully adjustable match triggers that adjust down to ounces of pull weight. It's very difficult to properly regulate big-bore airguns, but Ataman has hit the nail on the head with its line of .35-caliber models generating extreme spreads of only 4 or 5 feet per second across 10 full power shots. Ataman takes things to the next level by setting up each caliber to operate at optimal efficiency based on the most accurate pellet. Operating at 300 bar (approximately 4,400 psi), Ataman can dial in the regulator for each caliber. This kind of precision performance gives shooters the ultimate advantage for bench shooting or hunting.

While Ataman makes airguns in many different styles, it's this writer's opinion that there are two that really stand out: the M2R Tactical Carbine Compact and the AP16 multi-shot pistol. The M2R Tactical Carbine Compact is available in .22, .25, .30 and .35 calibers. It features an AR-style adjustable folding buttstock, pistol grip walnut stock, buttery-smooth side lever action and multi-shot rotary magazine. A fully shrouded and moderated barrel keeps things quiet for backyard shooting or stealthy hunting excursions. Regardless of the outing, the M2R Tactical Carbine Compact is a favorite.

Perhaps the most impressive Ataman airgun is the AP16 pistol. It's very difficult to create a small form factor pistol with the power and accuracy to be a viable hunting airgun. But Ataman has managed to do just that. Utilizing a high-pressure cylinder and setting the regulator for optimal power and shot count, the AP16 in .22 caliber delivers nearly 21 identical shots in the 14 ft-lbs range. This makes the AP16 stand out above all others in this category. With so much to offer U.S. airgunners, it's no wonder Ataman is a premier brand. atamanguns.com

Daystate Airguns

Daystate is a high-end maker of airguns that are distributed worldwide. The firm's philosophy has always been quality over raw quantity, and that's reflected in its products. Starting back in the early 1970s, Daystate began building airguns designed to exceed shooter expectations.

With roots in the U.K., the company's

The Ataman AP16 Regulated Compact Air Pistol has a familiar 1911 grip.

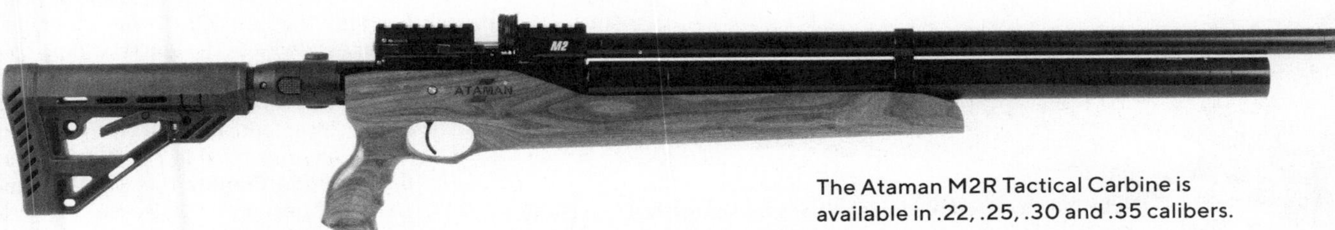

The Ataman M2R Tactical Carbine is available in .22, .25, .30 and .35 calibers.

The Daystate Hunstman has a fully adjustable trigger, smooth rear cocking system and 10-shot rotary magazine.

Daisy Red Ryder — still going strong, Ralphie!

developers had to learn how to do more with less due to the various restrictions placed on airguns. The standard air rifle there can only generate up to 12 ft-lbs without the need of an FAC License. This means that precision engineering and accuracy must rule the day if the company's airguns are going to be effective on the bench or in the field. While we in the U.S. are accustomed to simply turning up the power *ad nauseam*, often at the expense of accuracy and durability, our fellow airgunners across the pond have learned how to use that limited 12 ft-lbs exceptionally well. But Daystate is not content with just building 12 ft-lb airguns.

Currently, Daystate's focus has been branching out into higher power airguns and larger calibers, like the new .30-cal. variants. This focus is a direct result of the demand from markets like the U.S. where consumers want more power and more variety, all without compromising build quality and accuracy. Daystate has really attacked this challenge full force, introducing "smart guns" that leverage user-adjustable modern electronic valving systems that use only a fraction of the air consumed — air normally wasted by mechanical valve systems. These systems are already available on flagship models like the Pulsar and Renegade. But the most critical component to this challenge is to never forsake the core philosophy of building exceptionally crafted airguns, something Daystate continues as it holds true to its roots.

On the other end of the scale, Daystate has also proven that you don't have to go "totally tech" to see amazing results. Good design and consistent execution is key. The Huntsman Regal XL is designed around solid, practical, consistent engineering. Even though it's the entry-level product, the Italian walnut stock (available in right- or left-hand configurations), fully adjustable trigger, smooth rear cocking system and 10-shot rotary magazine deliver consistent shots through the usable shot curve with amazing accuracy. It's no wonder Daystate is considered by some to be one of the finest airgun makers in the world. daystate.com

Gamo USA/Daisy Airguns

Nearly every airgunner in the U.S. — maybe even in the world — has handled, shot or at least is aware of the venerable Daisy Red Ryder. This iconic airgun is forever cemented into our national heritage. Where the Colt Single Action may have won the West, the Daisy Red Ryder won the hearts and minds of many generations of shooters worldwide.

The partnership of Gamo USA and Daisy Airguns has created an amazing combination. Daisy is firmly ingrained and committed to youth shooters, with a focus on gun safety education through the company's scholastic programs, inflatable ranges, and the Daisy Nationals, the most prestigious BB gun competition in the world. Gamo USA holds a firm advantage in the market when it comes to affordable, powerful and accurate adult precision airguns. This one-two punch makes Gamo USA/ Daisy Outdoor Products a major force in the domestic airgun market.

While most people see its airguns as entry-level learning tools for young shooters, Daisy is the official licensee of Winchester Air Rifles. At SHOT Show 2018, Daisy launched the new Winchester line of big-bore air rifles. The Winchester Model 70-35 and 70-45 create an entirely new space for the company in the U.S. airgun market. The Winchester Model 70-35 is a perfect blend of power and shot count, designed to deliver 12 shots in .35 caliber with sufficient power (up to 134 ft-lbs at the muzzle) and accuracy to take down medium-sized game and predators out to 100 yards. The Winchester Model 70-45 is a .45-caliber precision air rifle that pushes over 200 ft-lbs of energy at the muzzle, enough for deer and hogs out to 50 yards. But, it's not just about performance. As with the undeniable look of Daisy BB guns, it was critical that these new Winchesters were instantly recognizable as Winchester rifles. These new big-bore hunting air rifles from Winchester are a testament to the long-standing commitment to heritage and tradition.

Last year, Gamo took break-barrels to a new level, introducing the first truly functional and reliable multi-shot break-barrel airgun. Frankly, this was the game-changing product of 2017, and it left all other break-barrel manufacturers scrambling to catch up. The Swarm Maxxim

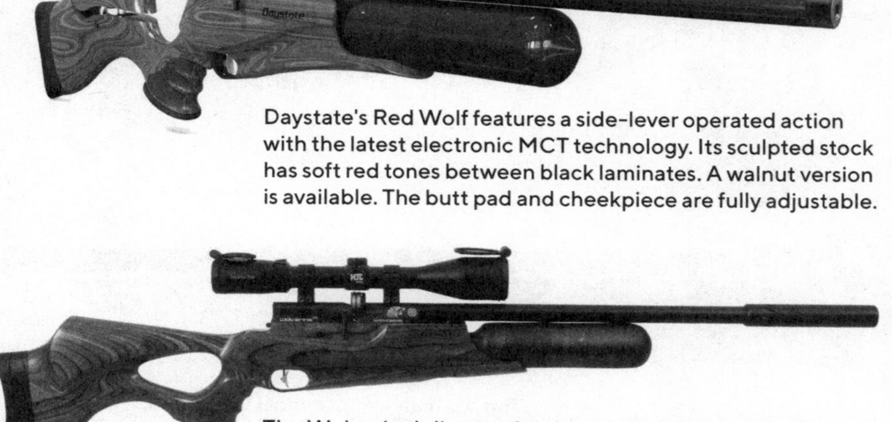
Daystate's Red Wolf features a side-lever operated action with the latest electronic MCT technology. Its sculpted stock has soft red tones between black laminates. A walnut version is available. The butt pad and cheekpiece are fully adjustable.

The Wolverine's lineage has been extended to include an air regulated action and side-lever cocking. A gray laminate or walnut thumbhole stock is offered.

The Gamo Swarm Magnum is a .22-caliber air rifle capable of 1,000+ fps velocity and 100-yard effective range.

takes the multi-shot capability and accuracy of a PCP air rifle and puts it into an extremely lightweight and affordable package. In 2018, Gamo USA expanded the Swarm line with the new .22-caliber Swarm Magnum. This true 1,000+ fps, 100-yard capable, multi-shot break-barrel airgun is set to dominate this segment of the market in 2018. Looking at all they've accomplished so far, it's undeniable that this new marriage of Gamo USA and Daisy Outdoor Products is set to create some amazing new airguns for a whole new generation of shooters. www.gamousa.com

Umarex

Umarex, whose U.S. division is based in Fort Smith, Arkansas, is the go-to brand for all things action pistol related. Creating officially licensed products under names like Colt, Ruger, Smith & Wesson, Beretta, Walther and now Glock, there's no bigger player in this exclusive airgun space. Attention to detail is what sets the outfit apart. Creating quality products that rival the look, weight, feel and function of originals is what it's all about — and there's nobody that does it better than Umarex. But that's not all they're known for.

Umarex is set to launch the new Hammer .50-caliber big-bore PCP in mid- to late-2018. What makes this product launch so special is the fact that it opens a whole new world of airgun capabilities that were previously only achievable through specialized, custom-manufactured, one-of-a-kind airguns. The Hammer is said to deliver more than 700 ft-lbs at the muzzle and is capable of taking not just traditional game like whitetail deer, but also exceptionally large game like elk, bear and even wildebeest. And that's not just theory, Umarex has already done it on the TV show *American Airgunner*. Moreover, the Hammer will be assembled with mostly U.S.-made parts, and quality tested at a facility in Fort Smith, Arkansas. Once launched, the Hammer should be the most powerful production airgun on store shelves, and at a price point that is truly affordable. This revolutionary big-bore airgun is changing the longstanding perception of airguns and opening many new doors across the country with state game and fish agencies. More and more states are seeing airguns as truly viable hunting options, changing their state laws, and creating space for airgunners to get into the big game hunting world.

In that spirit of delivering exceptional performance at an unbelievable value, back in 2017 Umarex USA introduced the Gauntlet PCP. It's obvious that Umarex was on a mission to create something that was extremely affordable, yet also amazingly capable. The Gauntlet has features such as a removable air reservoir with integrated precision regulator, 10-shot rotary magazine (8 shots in .25), shrouded and suppressed barrel, and a fully adjustable trigger. These features rival airguns costing three and four times as much, yet the Gauntlet stands its ground. New for 2018, Umarex will introduce the much-anticipated .25-caliber version of the Gauntlet.

So, whether you are a cowboy action shooter, big game hunter, backyard plinker or small game hunter, Umarex USA has an airgun that is sure to fit your exact need. www.umarexusa.com

You Can't Shoot Without Air and Pellets

As PCP airguns become more and more popular, the need to source high-pressure air (HPA) is greater. Moreover, today's PCP airguns need higher pressure than traditional SCUBA tanks, which makes sourcing HPA even more challenging. In 2017, Air Venturi launched its pioneering, personal HPA compressor. This water-cooled compressor finally put the concept of personal HPA on the map in a meaningful, affordable and sustainable way. Other companies are trying to catch up and there are many options on the market these days, but none have really matched the Air Venturi Compressor. In response to market demand, Air Venturi has continued pushing forward with the development of new, even more affordable personal HPA compressors. New for 2018, the concern will launch its Nomad compressor. The model brings personal HPA to an entirely new level. Set to retail at only $500, this little device will run off 110V OR 12V power (Yes, it will run off a car battery!), making it the perfect field companion. It's designed to direct-fill PCP airguns at a reasonable and reliable rate, topping off a typical airgun in just a couple of minutes. Essentially, this new technology changes everything in the airgun world, making PCP airguns an everyday option for shooters everywhere.

The very handy Air Venturi Nomad compressor.

But HPA is not all you need. You've got to have quality ammo for your airgun. Companies like H&N and JSB continue to produce precision ammo for the masses. Available in an amazing variety of shapes, sizes, calibers and weights, the possibilities are almost limitless. From match-grade precision wadcutters, to deep hollowpoint pellets, to metal-tipped pellets for maximum penetration and expansion, there's no doubt that the right pellet for every airgunner and every airgun is out there.

The new age of airgunning is here. We are seeing advances in technology, performance, power, accuracy and affordability across the board. Companies are building some amazing products for an entirely new generation of shooters. It really is a great time to be an airgunner!

AMMUNITION, BALLISTICS AND COMPONENTS

BY **PHIL MASSARO**

There were a lot of interesting ammunition and reloading-related items released for this year and plenty to be excited about. We've got new cartridges, powders for reloading, expanded ammunition lines and component bullets — all making an interesting crop of goodies. There's no doubt our ammunition is getting better each year, and this year is no exception.

Federal .224 Valkyrie

Probably one of the hottest releases this year is Federal's smokin' new .22 centerfire, the .224 Valkyrie. Based on a shortened 6.8 SPC Remington cartridge, the Valkyrie is designed to give the best long-range performance available from a .22 centerfire and do it from an AR-15 platform. Built around the 90-grain Sierra MatchKing — with an incredible G1 BC of 0.563 and velocity of 2,700 fps — the Valkyrie makes a perfectly viable 1,000-yard cartridge with minimal recoil. Testing the cartridge in Las Vegas, I was easily making hits at over 800 yards, and was able to watch my own vapor trail. Federal offers the Valkyrie in the 90-grain MatchKing load, as well as a 90-grain Fusion for hunters, a 60-grain Nosler Ballistic Tip for dusting varmints and in its American Eagle line as a 75-grain TMJ, which sells at a very attractive price point. I think you'll be hearing a lot of positive feedback about this cartridge. federalpremium.com

Hornady DGX Bonded Ammunition and Bullets

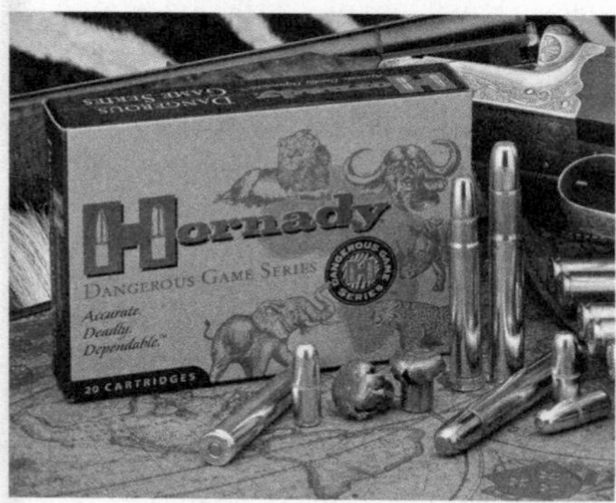

African safari is one of my passions, and Hornady has been instrumental in keeping those big safari rifles fueled. Hornady gave us the DGX (Dangerous Game eXpanding) and DGS (Dangerous Game Solid) bullets in its safari line, a pair of bullets that printed very well and offered a similar point of impact. There were some field reports, however, that the softpoint DGX was a bit too soft, and was lacking in the penetration department. Hornady has now countered those field reports with the DGX Bonded bullet — featuring a thick copper jacket chemically bonded to the core to slow expansion and guarantee deep penetration. The new bullet uses a jacket of 0.098 inch, and a good round-nose meplat. Combined with the DGS solid, hunters are now better equipped for elephant, Cape buffalo, hippo and brown bear alike. The DGX Bonded is available in 9.3x74R, .375 H&H, .375 Ruger, .450/400 NE 3", .404 Jeffery, .416 Remington Magnum, .416 Ruger, .416 Rigby, .500/416 NE, .450 Rigby, .450 NE, .458 Winchester Magnum, .458 Lott, .470 NE and .500 NE. Also available in component form in .375, .410, .416, .423 (for the .404 Jeffery), .458, .474 and .510-inch bullets for those who prefer to handload their dangerous game ammunition. hornady.com/ammunition

Redding Premium Die Sets for Handgun Cartridges

Those who handload pistol ammunition have a reason to smile this year. Redding has put together its Premium Die Set for handgun cartridges and it's a great value. Using the Titanium Carbide sizing die — no lubrication needed — resizing brass is a quick and simple procedure. The Special Expander Die is an eye-opener, as it uses a unique expander to prepare the brass cases to receive the projectile. What's more, the expander has a proprietary coating that will not get gunked up with brass flakes, or any other dirty concoction of lube and metal filings. Finally, there is Redding's famous micrometer seating die, which allows for predictable, fine adjustments to the seating depth of bullets, and quick changes to those depths. These die sets are wonderfully accurate and make perfect sense whether you load single-stage or on a progressive. Available in 9mm Luger, .38 Spl./.357 Mag, .40 S&W/10mm Auto, .44 Spec./.44 Mag, .45 ACP and .45 Colt. redding-reloading.com

Winchester Deer Season XP Copper Impact

All-copper bullets have earned a definite place in the market and have come quite a long way from the earliest designs. The jacket cannot separate from the core because there is neither; it's one homogenous design. Winchester has hopped on board,

offering its Deer Season XP line with an all-copper bullet. If you recall, Winchester's Deer Season XP line features a large polymer tip (black for the lead core bullets) and a deep hollowpoint for the rapid expansion that will switch a deer's nervous system off. The Deer Season XP Copper Impact will give a bit better structural integrity and still maintain the deep penetration associated with the monometal construction. To differentiate from the original Deer Season XP line, Winchester employs a bright red polymer tip. Being all copper, light-for-caliber bullets can be employed without fear of bullet breakup, along with a healthy muzzle velocity. Deer Season XP Copper Impact is available in .243 Winchester (85 grain), .270 Winchester (130 grain), .308 Winchester, .30-06 Springfield and .300 Winchester Magnum (both 150 grain). winchester.com

Hornady 6.5 PRC

Warning, we've got another 6.5mm cartridge to choose from, and it's looking like it has the potential to stick around. The 6.5 PRC (named for the Precision Rifle Competition) is sort of the "big brother" to the 6.5 Creedmoor, driving the 143-grain ELD-X at a muzzle velocity of 2,960 fps, a full 250 fps faster than the Creedmoor. Based on the .300 Ruger Compact Magnum case necked down to hold 6.5mm bullets, the 6.5 PRC has a trajectory similar to the .300 Winchester Magnum (with 180-grain bullets), but with better wind deflection values. At

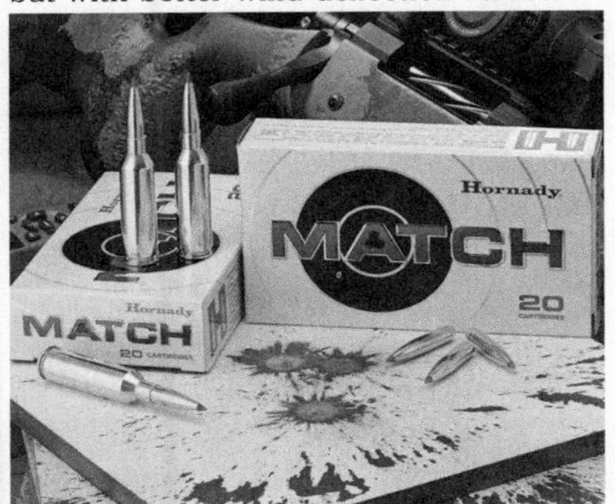

this writing, there are only a handful of rifles in production, but I'd be willing to bet by the time you read these words there will be many more available. While it has a performance level very similar to the 6.5-284 Norma, only time will tell how many of the 6.5mms will stay relevant, but I think the PRC has a damned good shot. Available with 143-grain ELD-X expanding bullet and 147-grain ELD-Match target bullet. hornady.com/ammunition

CCI Mini-Mag Segmented

If you're a devotee of the rimfire cartridges, I'd be willing to bet you're familiar with the Mini-Mag line of ammunition, long renowned for its accuracy. The Mini-Mag is now available with the CCI 40-grain segmented bullet, designed to break into three separate segments upon impact. I've used this bullet in the Quiet-22 line, shooting into ballistic gel, as well as eradicating varmints. I can attest to the effectiveness of the design, and in the Mini-Mag line it should become a squirrel's worst nightmare! cci-ammunition.com

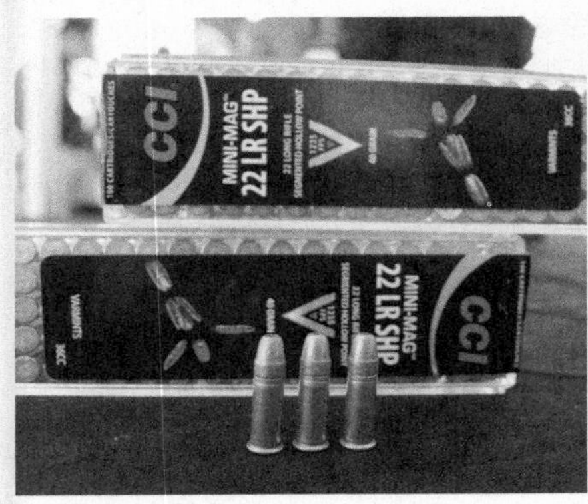

IMR Enduron Powder — IMR8133

Hodgdon, which acquired the revered IMR brand of smokeless powder, has done extensive research and development into temperature insensitive powders. The Enduron line proved itself with the original trio of IMR4166, IMR4451 and IMR7977, giving very uniform results irrespective of temperature, making the traveling sportsman's life much easier. The fourth, IMR4955, mimicked the performance of the tried and true IMR4831. This year brings us IMR8133, a slow-burning powder for the big magnum cases. With a burn rate similar (but not interchangeable with) Hodgdon's RETUMBO, IMR8133 is perfect for the .300 Remington Ultra Magnum, .30 Nosler and 7mm STW. I can only imagine that many of the huge Weatherby cases would be well-served by it. The same ben-

eficial features of the Enduron line are all there: copper-fouling elimination, temperature insensitivity and excellent load density for those big cases. If it performs anything like its other four siblings, it'll quickly become a staple. Available in 1- and 8-lb. containers. hodgdon.com

Sierra MatchKing 6.5mm 150-Grain Bullet

Sierra has been in the match-grade bullet business for over 70 years, so I think they know what they're doing. Its MatchKing has been the long-range shooter's friend for decades and is the benchmark against which all other bullets are measured. The various 6.5mm cartridges — with the potential to use those high BC heavy-for-caliber bullets — have always mated well with the Sierra bullet lineup. This year, Sierra releases product No. 1755, the 150-grain 6.5mm bullet with a G1 BC of 0.713 (until velocities drop below 1,760 fps) for serious long-range performance. One caveat: this bullet will require a 1:7.5-inch twist rate or faster to be properly stabilized. sierrabullets.com

Federal Heavyweight TSS Turkey Loads

Federal has been at the forefront of turkey ammunition for quite some time, and with good reason: some of the guys over

there are absolutely nuts for turkey hunting. This year Federal introduces its Heavyweight TSS shotshells, using the Tungsten Super Shot pellets, and a different mindset. When I started hunting turkeys in the mid-1980s, heavy payloads of large shot were completely *en vogue*, but that seems to be changing. TSS pellets are an alloy comprised mostly of tungsten, and according to Federal are 56 percent denser than lead. This translates to more retained energy downrange, which correlates to more kills. Furthermore — to deviate from the older mindset — smaller shot sizes can be utilized to get the job done. Again, as a youth, 7 1/2, 8 and 9 shot were reserved for clay birds and maybe ruffed grouse; when made of the TSS alloy, small shot sizes become a perfectly viable tool for gobblers. Smaller shot equates to more pellets downrange, increasing the chances of a solid hit, and I'll take all the little advantages I can get. The Federal Heavyweight TSS uses the Flitestopper wad, proven to be effective in both the Black Cloud and 3rd Degree line, and is designed around loads of either No. 7 or No. 9 shot. It's available in 12-ga. 3 inch (1 3/4 oz.), 12-ga. 3 1/2 inch (2 1/4 oz.), 20-ga. 3 inch (1 1/2 oz. No. 7) and even in .410 bore (13/16 oz. of No. 9). Heavyweight TSS comes in five-packs, with a portion of the proceeds going to the National Wild Turkey Federation. federalpremium.com

Hornady Precision Hunter

Making a gigantic splash with the ELD-X bullet, Hornady followed suit with the Precision Hunter line, offering the sleek hunting bullet in its loaded ammunition line. Based on the success of the initial developments, Hornady has expanded the line. With a very high ballistic coefficient, and bullets that run on the heavier side of average for a given caliber, the

ELD-X bullet will get the job done in a multitude of different hunting situations, from near to far. This year's new offerings include nine new calibers. Included are 6mm Creedmoor (103 grain); .25-06 Remington (110 grain); .257 Weatherby Magnum (110 grain); 6.5 PRC (143 grain); .270 WSM (145 grain); .280 Ackley Improved (162 grain), 7mm WSM (162 grain), .338 Winchester Magnum (230 grain) and .338 Lapua (270 grain). As is usual with Hornady developers, they are thinking about not just those newer, long-range cartridges, but of the hunter with a rifle that he or she has loved for some time and wants to extend its capabilities by feeding it modern bullets. I especially like that they've decided to give the .270 and 7mm WSM cartridges a breath of life. I know many owners of rifles in those calibers who've complained (and rightfully so) about ammunition availability. hornady.com/ammunition

Winchester Xtended Range Bismuth

Waterfowl hunters have long had to deal with the shortcomings of steel shot: it doesn't carry as well as lead, doesn't pattern as well as lead and doesn't hit as hard as lead. However, the toxicity of lead submerged in bodies of water is a reality and is therefore no longer an option. However, there are alternatives that give good performance without endangering the ecosystem. Winchester has announced the release of its Xtended Range Bismuth shotshells in 3-inch 12 gauge, loaded with 1 5/8 oz. of No. 5 Bismuth at a muzzle velocity of 1,200 fps. Winchester has once again employed its Shot-Lok technology — which essentially uses an epoxy resin to hold the shot column in place, breaking apart during flight — to keep the pattern as tight as possible. It also prevents the bismuth shot from fracturing during the violent passage from chamber to barrel. However, the Winchester Xtended Range Bismuth is not just a waterfowl load. It works perfectly on turkey, and even on upland birds in areas where the use of lead shot is prohibited. It seems that the need for lead-alternative ammunition is only going to rise, and it's good to see companies like Winchester answering the call. winchester.com

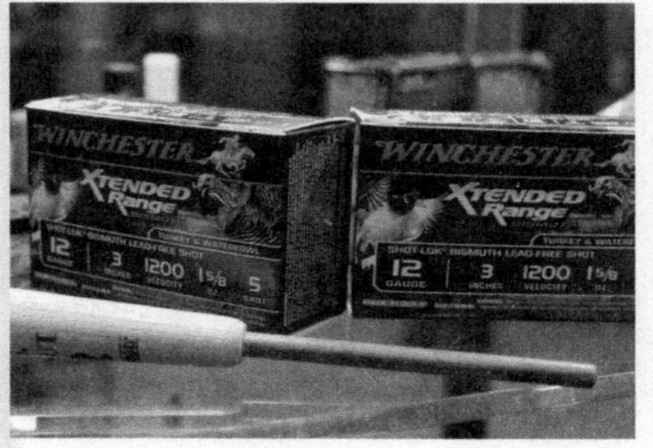

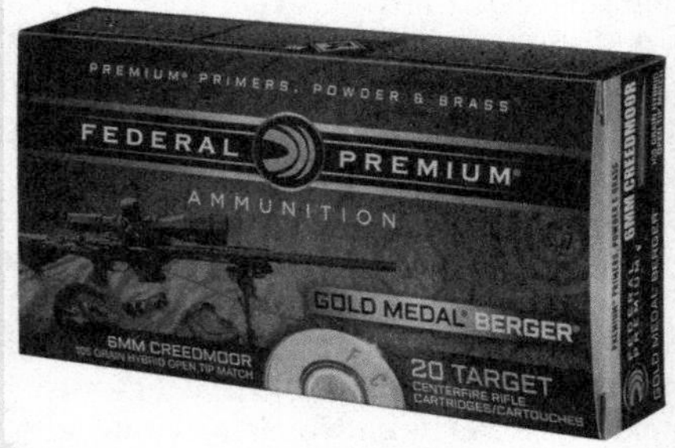

Federal Gold Medal Match 6mm Creedmoor

The 6.5 Creedmoor has had the shooting industry in a tizzy for a decade now, and while some are tired of hearing it, the design has its merits. The 6.5's little brother, the 6mm Creedmoor is gaining an equally stellar reputation, especially in the PRC circles as it offers a perfectly viable long-range trajectory with virtually no recoil. To maximize trajectories and minimize wind deflection, you'll need a bullet that has a high BC value, in other words a sleek design that will slice through the air. I'm certain you're familiar with those bullets that feature the long, tapering o-gives. They are great at traveling through the atmosphere, but not so great at the initial engagement of rifling. Berger has solved the issue, with a hybrid bullet design that blends both tangent and secant o-give styles for a best-of-both-worlds solution. Federal Premium is now loading that Berger bullet in its Gold Medal ammunition line for the 6mm Creedmoor for 2018. Using a 105-grain Berger Hybrid bullet — with the famous J4 jacket, known for its concentricity — the new Federal 6mm Creedmoor Gold Medal load will have the steel singing in the next zip code with no issues at all. Whether it's an AR-platform rifle or your favorite bolt gun, Federal Gold Medal ammo will get the job done. federalpremium.com

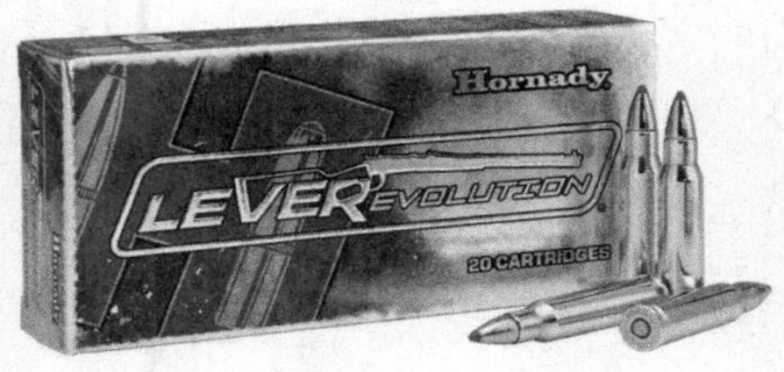

Hornady LEVERevolution .307 Winchester Ammunition

The allure of lever-action rifles will never leave us, no matter how many technological advances are made in the field of firearms. Winchester's release of the .307 Winchester in 1982 in the Big Bore 94 rifle gave shooters the performance of a .308 Winchester (a rimless cartridge) in a rimmed, lever-friendly cartridge. Hornady has further revolutionized lever-action ammunition with its FTX (Flex Tip Expanding) bullet —a spitzer that is safe to use in a tubular magazine. Hornady .307 Winchester ammunition uses a 160-grain FTX bullet at 2,650 fps, giving the lever-action shooter an unprecedented trajectory from a cartridge designed for a tubular magazine. When zeroed at 200 yards, the Hornady bullet will be only 10 inches low at 300 yards; that's a game-changer for sure. hornady.com/ammunition

Federal Premium 9mm Hydra-Shok Deep

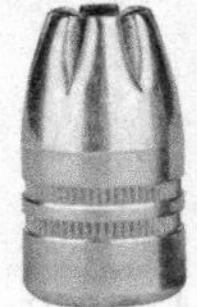

Making its debut in 1989, the Hydra-Shok bullet was a revolutionary design, one that many shooters have come to rely upon. However, bullet technology is continually evolving and improving. Now Federal has given the Hydra-Shok a facelift, introducing the Hydra-Shok Deep. With a redesigned core that gives penetration qualities that more closely match FBI requirements, the new bullet plows 15 inches of penetration into bare ballistic gelatin along with good expansion to end a threat quickly. This equates to a 50 percent increase in penetration compared to the original design (a 70 percent increase was noted in the FBI Protocol tests). The notched jacket and unique center post are retained, but the terminal ballistics of this bullet will make an already good design even better. The initial offering is a 135-grain 9mm Luger load, with other calibers following shortly. federalpremium.com

Federal Power-Shok Copper

Federal's simple lead-free hollowpoint design is an oft-overlooked solution to many hunting problems. It expands consistently, yields great penetration and has been seriously accurate in many of my rifles. The lead-free movement is on — there's no denying that — and the Power-Shok Copper is perfectly applicable in those areas that prohibit the use of lead ammunition. This year, Federal has expanded the line to include a 180-grain load for both the .300 Winchester Magnum and .300 Winchester Short Magnum. Federal has employed the lead-free Catalyst primer in the deal; it certainly doesn't get much more 'green' than this. federalpremium.com

Browning BXS Rifle Ammunition

Browning's ammunition line has been excellent, the stuff is consistent and accurate. This year, the line has been expanded to include the BXS rifle cartridges, made with an all-copper polymer-tip bullet for reliable expansion. Using nickel-plated cases — to avoid corrosion and assist in smooth feeding — the BXS line is a great choice for deer, bear and all larger big game animals. Available in 6.5 Creedmoor, .270 Winchester, 7mm Remington Magnum, .308 Winchester, .30-06 Springfield, .300 WSM and .300 Winchester Magnum. browningammo.com

Speer No. 15 Handloading Manual

I love a new reloading manual, and with the sheer quantities of new powders available on the market, we definitely need new data. The *Speer No. 15 Manual* does exactly that. In the 948 pages between the hard-

covers, there's a lot of good and relevant stuff. All the popular calibers are covered (and yes, there's good data on the 6.5 and 6mm Creedmoor) along with the new IMR Enduron and Alliant Reloder powders. The front of the manual handles the basic how-to of reloading, and each cartridge listing has some unique features, such as the height the bullet would reach if fired straight up and the maximum distance the bullet would travel at an optimum elevation. While the manual covers only Speer bullets, which are some fine offerings in and of themselves, the data inside can be (carefully) used for load development with other bullet brands. The *Speer No. 15 Manual* is a welcome addition to my reloading shelf. speer-ammo.com

CCI .17 HMR VNT Ammunition

The .17 HMR still makes a great small game rifle, though its popularity seems to have waned as of late. It has virtually no recoil, yet packs enough punch to take rabbits, squirrels, prairie dogs and woodchucks. CCI has mated the 17-grain Speer VNT bullet with the HMR case, resulting in a load that will deliver near-explosive performance. The polymer-tipped bullet leaves the muzzle at 2,650 fps — a bit faster than most loads on the market — to take full advantage of the thinly jacketed Speer VNT. The yellow polymer tip increases the BC, allowing the shooter to make those distant shots just a bit easier. Available in 50-packs, the CCI VNT load is a sure winner. cci-ammunition.com

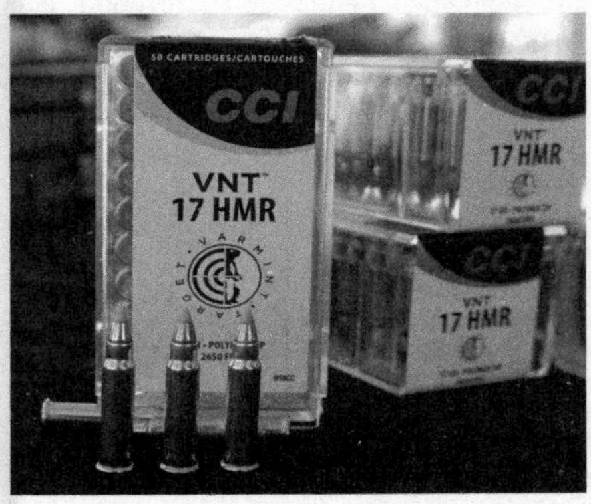

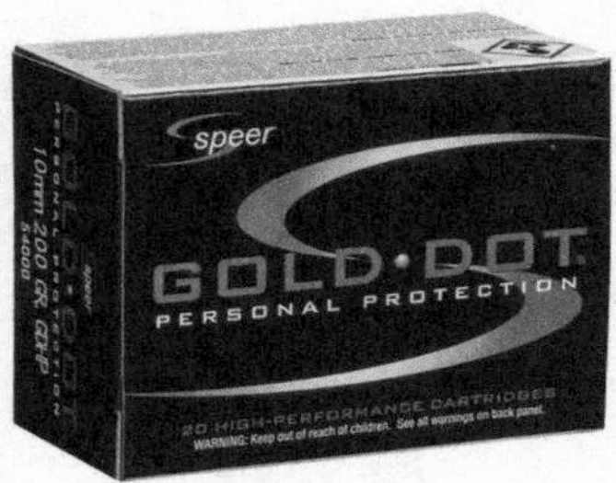

Speer Gold Dot Personal Protection 10mm Ammo

The Speer Gold Dot bullet has an impeccable reputation in the defensive handgun world, and with good reason: It's a sound design, delivering not only excellent accuracy, but terminal ballistics you can bet your life on. I've handloaded a ton of it throughout the years, but now Speer has added the 10mm Auto to its list of factory ammunition. Built around the 200-grain Gold Dot hollowpoint and driven at a muzzle velocity of 1,100 fps, Speer Handgun Personal Protection ammo will allow the Big Ten to roar. Undoubtedly, the 10mm Auto is a fierce handgun cartridge, and for those who handle it well it makes a fantastic choice. Speer Gold Dot ammo will stand up to the velocity of the 10mm Auto and be a perfect companion to the Ten. speer-ammo.com

Federal Edge TLR Ammunition

Last year's announcement of Federal's Edge TLR was an important development for those who chase long-range accuracy and terminal performance. Designed as a hunting bullet that can be relied upon for consistent expansion to distances that are farther than we should actually be shooting at game, it was released in the common .30-caliber cartridges: .308 Winchester, .30-06 Springfield, .300 Winchester Magnum and .300 Winchester Short Magnum.

I've tested that ammunition and it was more than accurate, and I'm happy to announce that it is no longer just available in .30 caliber. There are three new offerings for this year, opening up the product line to many more hunters. The .270 Winchester and .270 Winchester Short Magnum crowd can enjoy the 140-grain Edge TLR, while

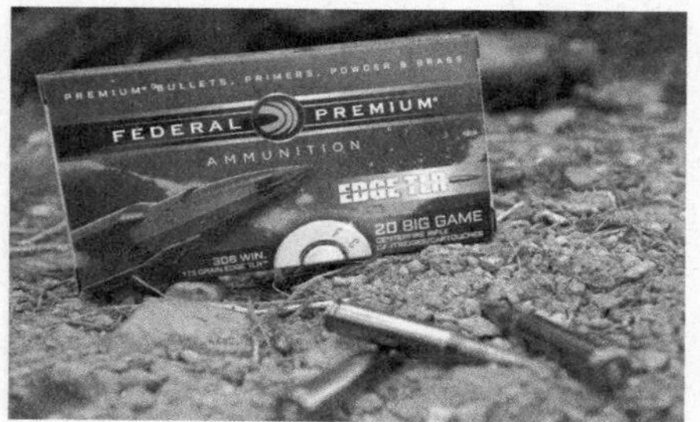

the multitude of 7mm Remington Magnum shooters can now use the famous translucent blue tip on a 155-grain 7mm bullet. The same small lead core at the front of the bullet is maintained, as is the bonded core design and AccuChannel groove, to reduce friction. The high ballistic coefficient of these bullets will fare very well on the windy plains of Wyoming, or from one side of the canyon to the other in Colorado. federalpremium.com

Western Powders Handloading Manual

Western Powders — including the Accurate, Ramshot, Blackhorn and Extreme brands — has been vastly overlooked, in my opinion. The Western Powders Handloading Manual is more than just a collection of recipes; it offers the basic how-to and then delves into more advanced techniques for the reloader. While these topics are dealt with briefly, they will — at the very least — spark the reader to dig deeper into these techniques, and further their knowledge of handloading ammunition. The recipes themselves give a useful cross-section of bullet brands, types and weights for each cartridge covered, and are organized by the powder applicable for the cartridge. All the necessary info is there, including the gear used to develop the test data, starting and maximum loads, pressures generated and cartridge overall length. I've had Western Powders come to my rescue on more than one rifle that just wouldn't shoot anything well, and I'm glad this resource is available from the horse's mouth. westernpowders.com

RCBS Brass Boss

Case preparation can be a total chore — or a labor of love, depending how you view it — requiring many different steps in the process. RCBS has taken all the necessary tools and rolled them up into one compact, easy-to-use device that runs on a variable speed electric motor. Sparing your elbow grease for other processes, the Brass Boss has six rotating heads, and comes with the tool heads for inside chamfer (it even comes with the VLD chamfer tool), outside deburring tool, primer pocket cleaner (small/large), military crimp remover (small/large), primer pocket uniformer

(small/large) and case neck brushes. At the rear of the unit are two fixed-speed heads for case neck brushes, for a total of eight functions. This unit is similar in design to the rear section of the Universal Case Prep Station (which had a case length trimmer on the front), and after using it for years I can attest to how easy it makes the prep work. Power cord included. rcbs.com

Federal Trophy Bonded Bear Claw and Sledgehammer Solids

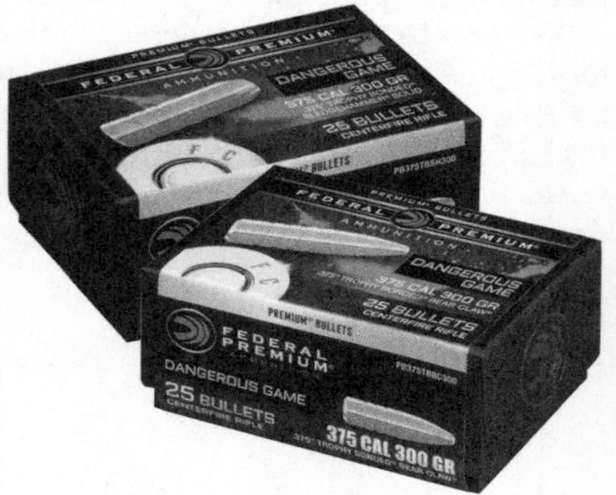

Jack Carter designed what many dangerous game hunters consider to be one of the finest bullets ever: the Trophy Bonded Bear Claw. Paired with the Sledgehammer Solid (non-expanding bullet), the hunter is well served for anything that walks on this planet. Federal has loaded it in its excellent factory ammunition, but this year we handloaders can smile, as they have released the bullet in component form, allowing those of us who tailor our own ammo to take full advantage of the wonderful terminal ballistics this pair will provide. Available in .375 caliber (250 and 300 grains), .416 caliber (400 grains), .458 caliber (500 grains) and .474 caliber for the .470 NE (500 grains). federalpremium.com

The Lyman Long Range Precision Rifle Reloading Handbook

The Precision Rifle Competition and Extended Long Range matches have served to bolster the already huge interest in long-

range shooting. With long-distance shooting comes the need for uber-accurate rifles, and they are often fueled by handloaded ammunition. Lyman introduces its *Long Range Precision Rifle Reloading Handbook*, focused on those cartridges used for this type of shooting and on the bullets designed to give the best ballistic coefficients. Sierra, Berger, Hornady and Lapua bullets are included, along with articles by today's top long-range shooters. If you're new to this facet of shooting, or a seasoned veteran, Lyman's new *Reloading Handbook* will only help your game, offering insights to developing the most accurate loads possible. Printed in full color, it's a must-have for your reloading library. lymanproducts.com

Alliant Green Dot and Red Dot

Wait, what? Haven't we had these powders for as long as anyone can remember? Well, Alliant has updated these industry staples to provide cleaner-burning characteristics, yet give the same time-honored performance that so many shotgunners have come to expect. Red Dot is perfect for full-house 12-gauge target loads, and Green Dot still provides those great light trap loads, as well as so many other shotgun applications. Available in 1-, 4-, and 8-pound canisters. alliantpowder.com/

Browning BXD Shotshells

Browning has expanded its BXD line of waterfowl shotshells this year, offering No. 3 shot in both 12 and 20 gauge. The 3-inch 12-gauge load uses 1 1/4 oz. of plated steel shot at a velocity of 1,450 fps, and the 3-inch 20-gauge load delivers a payload of 1 oz. of No. 3 steel shot at 1,300 fps, for dense patterns and neck-breaking power. A long-

range wad and plated shot keep your shot-string where you need it, resulting in cleaner kills and bigger smiles when the decoys are being pulled up. browningammo.com

Nosler RDF

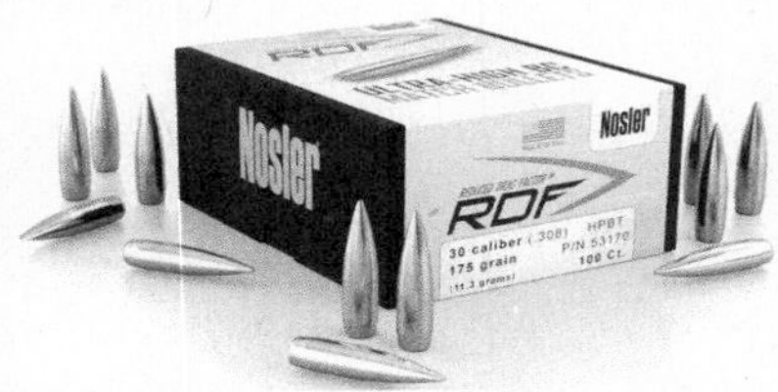

Nosler has expanded its RDF (Reduced Drag Factor) bullet line for long-range shooting fans. New bullet offerings include an 85-grain .224, 130-grain 6.5mm, 185-grain 7mm (the first in this caliber) and a 210-grain .308. The RDF line has proven to be extremely accurate, with a very small hollowpoint and a sleek, long boat tail design. Delivering premium bullet performance since 1948, Nosler has continued to stay on the forefront of projectile design and engineering. RDF bullets are available in 100- and 500-count boxes. nosler.com

Federal Component Brass

It's been some time since I've seen Federal brass available; I regularly purchased its component cases for my reloading projects. I'm very happy to announce that Federal brass is once again available to the reloader! Pistol cases available are .327 Federal, 9mm Luger, .40 S&W and .45 ACP. Rifle calibers include .223 Rem., .22-250 Rem., .224 Valkyrie, .243 Win., .270 Win., .270 WSM, 7mm Rem. Mag., .30-30 Win., .308 Win., .30-06, .300 Win. Mag., .300 WSM and .338 Federal. The case shoulders and necks are annealed for long life. federalpremium.com

Hornady Match Ammo

The ELD Match bullet is one serious piece of gear, and when loaded in Hornady Match ammunition gives hair-splitting accuracy. Hornady has seen the wisdom in further expanding the line this year, offering the aforementioned 6.5 PRC, and two hot .30s. The .300 Winchester Magnum is loaded with the 195-grain ELD Match at 2,930 fps, and the blazing .300 Norma Magnum has the 225-grain ELD Match at 2,850 fps. We're all familiar with the capabilities of the .300 Winchester, but I can attest to the accuracy capabilities of the new .300 Norma Magnum; simply put it's a winner. It has been adopted by some of our military shooters, and that alone should be reason enough to get behind it. Top it with the ELD Match, and it will become even more effective as a serious long-range cartridge. hornady.com/ammunition

Federal Trophy Bonded Tipped Bullets

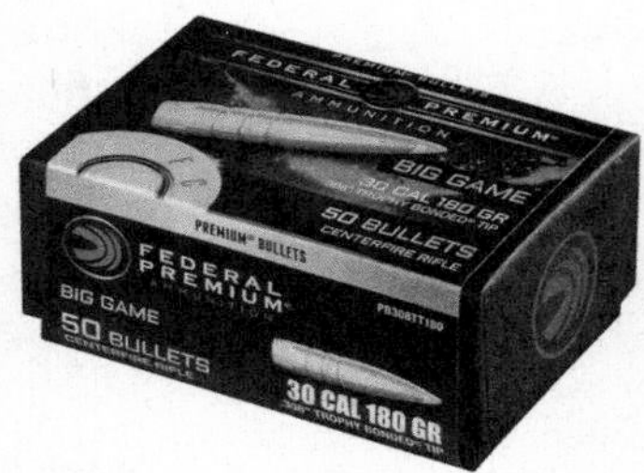

Federal, long famous for loading the finest bullets of other brands in its factory ammunition, has made a lot of headway with its own bullets. The Trophy Bonded Tip has the small lead core up front, chemically bonded to the thick copper jacket, and that rear copper shank that gives such good penetration. But this version has a sleek o-give, polymer tip and a boat tail, in addition to a grooved shank to minimize barrel fouling. I like how this bullet shoots and love its terminal ballistics. And now it's available as a component bullet, so reloaders can enjoy the performance as well. Available in .277-inch (.270) diameter (130 and 140 grains), .284 (7mm) diameter (140 and 160 grains) and .308 (165 and 180 grains), in 50-count boxes. federalpremium.com

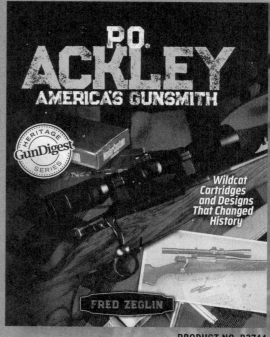

Many manufacturers do not supply suggested retail prices. Others did not get their pricing to us before press time. All pricing can vary dependent on the exact brand and style of ammo selected and/or the retail outlet from which you make your purchase. Pricing has been rounded to the nearest dollar and represents our best estimate of average pricing. An * after the cartridge means these loads are available with Nosler Partition or Swift A-Frame bullets. Listed pricing may or may not reflect this bullet type. ** = these are packed 50 to box, all others are 20 to box. Wea. Mag.= Weatherby Magnum. Spfd. = Springfield. A-Sq. = A-Square. N.E.=Nitro Express.

Cartridge	Bullet Wgt. Grs.	VELOCITY (fps)					ENERGY (ft. lbs.)					TRAJ. (in.)				Est. Price/box
		Muzzle	100 yds.	200 yds.	300 yds.	400 yds.	Muzzle	100 yds.	200 yds.	300 yds.	400 yds.	100 yds.	200 yds.	300 yds.	400 yds.	
17, 22																
17 Hornet	15.5	3860	2924	2159	1531	1108	513	294	160	81	42	1.4	0.0	-9.1	-33.7	NA
17 Hornet	20	3650	3078	2574	2122	1721	592	421	294	200	131	1.10	0.0	-6.4	-20.6	NA
17 Hornet	25	3375	2842	2367	1940	1567	632	448	311	209	136	1.4	0	24.8	56.3	NA
17 Remington Fireball	20	4000	3380	2840	2360	1930	710	507	358	247	165	1.6	1.5	-2.8	-13.5	NA
17 Remington Fireball	25	3850	3280	2780	2330	1925	823	597	429	301	206	0.9	0.0	-5.4	NA	NA
17 Remington	20	4200	3544	2978	2477	2029	783	558	394	272	183	0	-1.3	-6.6	-17.6	NA
17 Remington	25	4040	3284	2644	2086	1606	906	599	388	242	143	+2.0	+1.7	-4.0	-17.0	$17
4.6x30 H&K	30	2025	1662	1358	1135	1002	273	184	122	85	66	0	-12.7	-44.5	—	NA
4.6x30 H&K	40	1900	1569	1297	1104	988	320	218	149	108	86	0	-14.3	-39.3	—	NA
204 Ruger (Hor)	24	4400	3667	3046	2504	2023	1032	717	494	334	218	0.6	0	-4.3	-14.3	NA
204 Ruger (Fed)	32 Green	4030	3320	2710	2170	1710	1155	780	520	335	205	0.9	0.0	-5.7	-19.1	NA
204 Ruger	32	4125	3559	3061	2616	2212	1209	900	666	486	348	0	-1.3	-6.3	—	NA
204 Ruger	32	4225	3632	3114	2652	2234	1268	937	689	500	355	.6	0.0	-4.2	-13.4	NA
204 Ruger	40	3900	3451	3046	2677	2336	1351	1058	824	636	485	.7	0.0	-4.5	-13.9	NA
204 Ruger	45	3625	3188	2792	2428	2093	1313	1015	778	589	438	1.0	0.0	-5.5	-16.9	NA
5.45x39mm	60	2810	2495	2201	1927	1677	1052	829	645	445	374	1.0	0.0	-9.2	-27.7	NA
221 Fireball	40	3100	2510	1991	1547	1209	853	559	352	212	129	0	-4.1	-17.3	-45.1	NA
221 Fireball	50	2800	2137	1580	1180	988	870	507	277	155	109	+0.0	-7.0	-28.0	0.0	$14
22 Hornet (Fed)	30 Green	3150	2150	1390	990	830	660	310	130	65	45	0.0	-6.6	-32.7	NA	NA
22 Hornet	34	3050	2132	1415	1017	852	700	343	151	78	55	+0.0	-6.6	-15.5	-29.9	NA
22 Hornet	35	3100	2278	1601	1135	929	747	403	199	100	67	+2.75	0.0	-16.9	-60.4	NA
22 Hornet	40	2800	2397	2029	1698	1413	696	510	366	256	177	0	-4.6	-17.8	-43.1	NA
22 Hornet	45	2690	2042	1502	1128	948	723	417	225	127	90	+0.0	-7.7	-31.0	0.0	$27**
218 Bee	46	2760	2102	1550	1155	961	788	451	245	136	94	+0.0	-7.2	-29.0	0.0	$46**
222 Rem.	35	3760	3125	2574	2085	1656	1099	759	515	338	213	1.0	0.0	-6.3	-20.8	NA
222 Rem.	50	3345	2930	2553	2205	1886	1242	953	723	540	395	1.3	0	-6.7	-20.6	NA
222 Remington	40	3600	3117	2673	2269	1911	1151	863	634	457	324	+1.07	0.0	-6.13	-18.9	NA
222 Remington	50	3140	2602	2123	1700	1350	1094	752	500	321	202	+2.0	-0.4	-11.0	-33.0	$11
222 Remington	55	3020	2562	2147	1773	1451	1114	801	563	384	257	+2.0	-0.4	-11.0	-33.0	$12
222 Rem. Mag.	40	3600	3140	2726	2347	2000	1150	876	660	489	355	1.0	0	-5.7	-17.8	NA
222 Rem. Mag.	50	3340	2917	2533	2179	1855	1238	945	712	527	382	1.3	0	-6.8	-20.9	NA
222 Rem. Mag.	55	3240	2748	2305	1906	1556	1282	922	649	444	296	+2.0	-0.2	-9.0	-27.0	$14
22 PPC	52	3400	2930	2510	2130	NA	1335	990	730	525	NA	+2.0	1.4	-5.0	0.0	NA
223 Rem.	35	3750	3206	2725	2291	1899	1092	799	577	408	280	1.0	0	-5.7	-18.1	NA
223 Rem.	35	4000	3353	2796	2302	1861	1243	874	607	412	269	0.8	0	-5.3	-17.3	NA
223 Rem.	64	2750	2368	2018	1701	1427	1074	796	578	411	289	2.4	0	-11	-34.1	NA
223 Rem.	75	2790	2562	2345	2139	1943	1296	1093	916	762	629	1.5	0	-8.2	-24.1	NA
223 Remington	40	3650	3010	2450	1950	1530	1185	805	535	340	265	+2.0	+1.0	-6.0	-22.0	$14
223 Remington	40	3800	3305	2845	2424	2044	1282	970	719	522	371	0.84	0.0	-5.34	-16.6	NA
223 Remington (Rem)	45 Green	3550	2911	2355	1865	1451	1259	847	554	347	210	2.5	2.3	-4.3	-21.1	NA
223 Remington	50	3300	2874	2484	2130	1809	1209	917	685	504	363	1.37	0.0	-7.05	-21.8	NA
223 Remington	52/53	3330	2882	2477	2106	1770	1305	978	722	522	369	+2.0	+0.6	-6.5	-21.5	$14
223 Remington (Win)	55 Green	3240	2747	2304	1905	1554	1282	921	648	443	295	1.9	0.0	-8.5	-26.7	NA
223 Remington	55	3240	2748	2305	1906	1556	1282	922	649	444	296	+2.0	-0.2	-9.0	-27.0	$12
223 Remington	60	3100	2712	2355	2026	1726	1280	979	739	547	397	+2.0	+0.2	-8.0	-24.7	$16
223 Remington	62	3000	2700	2410	2150	1900	1240	1000	800	635	495	1.60	0.0	-7.7	-22.8	NA
223 Remington	64	3020	2621	2256	1920	1619	1296	977	723	524	373	+2.0	-0.2	-9.3	-23.0	$14
223 Remington	69	3000	2720	2460	2210	1980	1380	1135	925	750	600	+2.0	+0.8	-5.8	-17.5	$15
223 Remington	75	2790	2554	2330	2119	1926	1296	1086	904	747	617	2.37	0.0	-8.75	-25.1	NA
223 Rem. Super Match	75	2930	2694	2470	2257	2055	1429	1209	1016	848	703	1.20	0.0	-6.9	-20.7	NA
223 Remington	77	2750	2584	2354	2169	1992	1293	1110	948	804	679	1.93	0.0	-8.2	-23.8	NA
223 WSSM	55	3850	3438	3064	2721	2402	1810	1444	1147	904	704	0.7	0.0	-4.4	-13.6	NA
223 WSSM	64	3600	3144	2732	2356	2011	1841	1404	1061	789	574	1.0	0.0	-5.7	-17.7	NA
5.56 NATO	55	3130	2740	2382	2051	1750	1196	917	693	514	372	1.1	0	-7.3	-23.0	NA
5.56 NATO	75	2910	2676	2543	2242	2041	1410	1192	1002	837	693	1.2	0	-7.0	-21.0	NA
224 Wea. Mag.	55	3650	3192	2780	2403	2057	1627	1244	943	705	516	+2.0	+1.2	-4.0	-17.0	$32

Cartridge	Bullet Wgt. Grs.	VELOCITY (fps)					ENERGY (ft. lbs.)					TRAJ. (in.)				Est. Price/box
		Muzzle	100 yds.	200 yds.	300 yds.	400 yds.	Muzzle	100 yds.	200 yds.	300 yds.	400 yds.	100 yds.	200 yds.	300 yds.	400 yds.	
22 Nosler	55	3350	2965	2615	2286	1984	1370	1074	833	638	480	0	-2.5	-10.1	-24.4	
22 Nosler	77	2950	2672	2410	2163	1931	1488	1220	993	800	637	0	-3.4	-12.8	-29.7	
224 Valkyrie	90	2700	2542	2388	2241	2098	1457	1291	1140	1003	880	1.9	0	-8.1	-23.2	NA
224 Valkyrie	75	3000	2731	2477	2237	2010	1499	1242	1022	833	673	1.6	0	-7.3	-21.5	NA
224 Valkyrie	60	3300	2930	2589	2273	1797	1451	1144	893	688	522	1.3	0	-6.5	-19.8	NA
225 Winchester	55	3570	3066	2616	2208	1838	1556	1148	836	595	412	+2.0	+1.0	-5.0	-20.0	$19
22-250 Rem.	35	4450	3736	3128	2598	2125	1539	1085	761	524	351	6.5	0	-4.1	-13.4	NA
22-250 Rem.	40	4000	3320	2720	2200	1740	1420	980	660	430	265	+2.0	+1.8	-3.0	-16.0	$14
22-250 Rem.	40	4150	3553	3033	2570	2151	1530	1121	817	587	411	0.6	0	-4.4	-14.2	NA
22-250 Rem.	45 Green	4000	3293	2690	2159	1696	1598	1084	723	466	287	1.7	1.7	-3.2	-15.7	NA
22-250 Rem.	50	3725	3264	2641	2455	2103	1540	1183	896	669	491	0.89	0.0	-5.23	-16.3	NA
22-250 Rem.	52/55	3680	3137	2656	2222	1832	1654	1201	861	603	410	+2.0	+1.3	-4.0	-17.0	$13
22-250 Rem.	60	3600	3195	2826	2485	2169	1727	1360	1064	823	627	+2.0	+2.0	-2.4	-12.3	$19
22-250 Rem.	64	3425	2988	2591	2228	1897	1667	1269	954	705	511	1.2	0	-6.4	-20.0	NA
220 Swift	40	4200	3678	3190	2739	2329	1566	1201	904	666	482	+0.51	0.0	-4.0	-12.9	NA
220 Swift	50	3780	3158	2617	2135	1710	1586	1107	760	506	325	+2.0	+1.4	-4.4	-17.9	$20
220 Swift	50	3850	3396	2970	2576	2215	1645	1280	979	736	545	0.74	0.0	-4.84	-15.1	NA
220 Swift	50	3900	3420	2990	2599	2240	1688	1298	992	750	557	0.7	0	-4.7	-14.5	NA
220 Swift	55	3800	3370	2990	2630	2310	1765	1390	1090	850	650	0.8	0.0	-4.7	-14.4	NA
220 Swift	55	3650	3194	2772	2384	2035	1627	1246	939	694	506	+2.0	+2.0	-2.6	-13.4	$19
220 Swift	60	3600	3199	2824	2475	2156	1727	1364	1063	816	619	+2.0	+1.6	-4.1	-13.1	$19
22 Savage H.P.	70	2868	2510	2179	1874	1600	1279	980	738	546	398	0	-4.1	-15.6	-37.1	NA
22 Savage H.P.	71	2790	2340	1930	1570	1280	1225	860	585	390	190	+2.0	-1.0	-10.4	-35.7	NA
6mm (24)																
6mm BR Rem.	100	2550	2310	2083	1870	1671	1444	1185	963	776	620	+2.5	-0.6	-11.8	0.0	$22
6mm Norma BR	107	2822	2667	2517	2372	2229	1893	1690	1506	1337	1181	+1.73	0.0	-7.24	-20.6	NA
6mm Creedmoor	108	2786	2618	2456	2299	2149	1861	1643	1446	1267	1106	1.5	0	-6.6	-18.9	$26
6mm PPC	70	3140	2750	2400	2070	NA	1535	1175	895	665	NA	+2.0	+1.4	-5.0	0.0	NA
243 Winchester	55	4025	3597	3209	2853	2525	1978	1579	1257	994	779	+0.6	0.0	-4.0	-12.2	NA
243 Win.	58	3925	3465	3052	2676	2330	1984	1546	1200	922	699	0.7	0	-4.4	-13.8	NA
243 Winchester	60	3600	3110	2660	2260	1890	1725	1285	945	680	475	+2.0	+1.8	-3.3	-15.5	$17
243 Win.	70	3400	3020	2672	2350	2050	1797	1418	1110	858	653	0	-2.5	-9.7	—	NA
243 Winchester	70	3400	3040	2700	2390	2100	1795	1435	1135	890	685	1.1	0.0	-5.9	-18.0	NA
243 Winchester	75/80	3350	2955	2593	2259	1951	1993	1551	1194	906	676	+2.0	+0.9	-5.0	-19.0	$16
243 Win.	80	3425	3081	2763	2468	2190	2984	1686	1357	1082	852	1.1	0	-5.7	-17.1	NA
243 Win.	87	2800	2574	2359	2155	1961	1514	1280	1075	897	743	1.9	0	-8.1	-23.8	NA
243 Win.	95	3185	2908	2649	2404	2172	2140	1784	1480	1219	995	1.3	0	-6.3	-18.6	NA
243 W. Superformance	80	3425	3080	2760	2463	2184	2083	1684	1353	1077	847	1.1	0.0	-5.7	-17.1	NA
243 Winchester	85	3320	3070	2830	2600	2380	2080	1770	1510	1280	1070	+2.0	+1.2	-4.0	-14.0	$18
243 Winchester	90	3120	2871	2635	2411	2199	1946	1647	1388	1162	966	1.4	0.0	-6.4	-18.8	NA
243 Winchester*	100	2960	2697	2449	2215	1993	1945	1615	1332	1089	882	+2.5	+1.2	-6.0	-20.0	$16
243 Winchester	105	2920	2689	2470	2261	2062	1988	1686	1422	1192	992	+2.5	+1.6	-5.0	-18.4	$21
243 Light Mag.	100	3100	2839	2592	2358	2138	2133	1790	1491	1235	1014	+1.5	0.0	-6.8	-19.8	NA
243 WSSM	55	4060	3628	3237	2880	2550	2013	1607	1280	1013	794	0.6	0.0	-3.9	-12.0	NA
243 WSSM	95	3250	3000	2763	2538	2325	2258	1898	1610	1359	1140	1.2	0.0	-5.7	-16.9	NA
243 WSSM	100	3110	2838	2583	2341	2112	2147	1789	1481	1217	991	1.4	0.0	-6.6	-19.7	NA
6mm Remington	80	3470	3064	2694	2352	2036	2139	1667	1289	982	736	+2.0	+1.1	-5.0	-17.0	$16
6mm R. Superformance	95	3235	2955	2692	2443	3309	2207	1841	1528	1259	1028	1.2	0.0	-6.1	-18.0	NA
6mm Remington	100	3100	2829	2573	2332	2104	2133	1777	1470	1207	983	+2.5	+1.6	-5.0	-17.0	$16
6mm Remington	105	3060	2822	2596	2381	2177	2105	1788	1512	1270	1059	+2.5	+1.1	-3.3	-15.0	$21
240 Wea. Mag.	87	3500	3202	2924	2663	2416	2366	1980	1651	1370	1127	+2.0	+2.0	-2.0	-12.0	$32
240 Wea. Mag.	100	3150	2894	2653	2425	2207	2202	1860	1563	1395	1082	1.3	0	-6.3	-18.5	NA
240 Wea. Mag.	100	3395	3106	2835	2581	2339	2559	2142	1785	1478	1215	+2.5	+2.8	-2.0	-11.0	$43
25-20 Win.	86	1460	1194	1030	931	858	407	272	203	165	141	0.0	-23.5	0.0	0.0	$32**
25-45 Sharps	87	3000	2677	2385	2112	1859	1739	1384	1099	862	668	1.1	0	-7.4	-22.6	$25
25-35 Win.	117	2230	1866	1545	1282	1097	1292	904	620	427	313	+2.5	-4.2	-26.0	0.0	$24
250 Savage	100	2820	2504	2210	1936	1684	1765	1392	1084	832	630	+2.5	+0.4	-9.0	-28.0	$17
257 Roberts	100	2980	2661	2363	2085	1827	1972	1572	1240	965	741	+2.5	-0.8	-5.2	-21.6	$20
257 Roberts	122	2600	2331	2078	1842	1625	1831	1472	1169	919	715	+2.5	0.0	-10.6	-31.4	$21
257 Roberts+P	100	3000	2758	2529	2312	2105	1998	1689	1421	1187	984	1.5	0	-7.0	-20.5	NA
257 Roberts+P	117	2780	2411	2071	1761	1488	2009	1511	1115	806	576	+2.5	-0.2	-10.2	-32.6	$18
257 Roberts+P	120	2780	2560	2360	2160	1970	2060	17 50	1480	1240	1030	+2.5	+1.2	-6.4	-23.6	$22

Cartridge	Bullet Wgt. Grs.	VELOCITY (fps)					ENERGY (ft. lbs.)					TRAJ. (in.)				Est. Price/box
		Muzzle	100 yds.	200 yds.	300 yds.	400 yds.	Muzzle	100 yds.	200 yds.	300 yds.	400 yds.	100 yds.	200 yds.	300 yds.	400 yds.	
257 R. Superformance	117	2946	2705	2478	2265	2057	2253	1901	1595	1329	1099	1.1	0.0	-5.7	-17.1	**NA**
25-06 Rem.	87	3440	2995	2591	2222	1884	2286	1733	1297	954	686	+2.0	+1.1	-2.5	-14.4	**$17**
25-06 Rem.	90	3350	3001	2679	2378	2098	2243	1790	1434	1130	879	1.2	0	-6.0	-18.3	**NA**
25-06 Rem.	90	3440	3043	2680	2344	2034	2364	1850	1435	1098	827	+2.0	+1.8	-3.3	-15.6	**$17**
25-06 Rem.	100	3230	2893	2580	2287	2014	2316	1858	1478	1161	901	+2.0	+0.8	-5.7	-18.9	**$17**
25-06 Rem.	117	2990	2770	2570	2370	2190	2320	2000	1715	1465	1246	+2.5	+1.0	-7.9	-26.6	**$19**
25-06 Rem.*	120	2990	2730	2484	2252	2032	2382	1985	1644	1351	1100	+2.5	+1.2	-5.3	-19.6	**$17**
25-06 Rem.	122	2930	2706	2492	2289	2095	2325	1983	1683	1419	1189	+2.5	+1.8	-4.5	-17.5	**$23**
25-06 R. Superformance	117	3110	2861	2626	2403	2191	2512	2127	1792	1500	1246	1.4	0.0	-6.4	-18.9	**NA**
25 WSSM	85	3470	3156	2863	2589	2331	2273	1880	1548	1266	1026	1.0	0.0	-5.2	-15.7	**NA**
25 WSSM	115	3060	2844	2639	2442	2254	2392	2066	1778	1523	1398	1.4	0.0	-6.4	-18.6	**NA**
25 WSSM	120	2990	2717	2459	2216	1987	2383	1967	1612	1309	1053	1.6	0.0	-7.4	-21.8	**NA**
257 Wea. Mag.	87	3825	3456	3118	2805	2513	2826	2308	1870	1520	1220	+2.0	+2.7	-0.3	-7.6	**$32**
257 Wea. Mag.	90	3550	3184	2848	2537	2246	2518	2026	1621	1286	1008	1.0	0	-5.3	-16.0	**NA**
257 Wea. Mag.	100	3555	3237	2941	2665	2404	2806	2326	1920	1576	1283	+2.5	+3.2	0.0	-8.0	**$32**
257 Wea. Mag.	110	3330	3069	2823	2591	2370	2708	2300	1947	1639	1372	1.1	0	-5.5	-16.1	**NA**
257 Scramjet	100	3745	3450	3173	2912	2666	3114	2643	2235	1883	1578	+2.1	+2.77	0.0	-6.93	**NA**
6.5																
6.5 Grendel	123	2590	2420	2256	2099	1948	1832	1599	1390	1203	1037	1.8	0	-8.6	-25.1	**NA**
6.5x47 Lapua	123	2887	NA	2554	NA	2244	2285	NA	1788	NA	1380	NA	4.53	0.0	-10.7	**NA**
6.5x50mm Jap.	139	2360	2160	1970	1790	1620	1720	1440	1195	985	810	+2.5	-1.0	-13.5	0.0	**NA**
6.5x50mm Jap.	156	2070	1830	1610	1430	1260	1475	1155	900	695	550	+2.5	-4.0	-23.8	0.0	**NA**
6.5x52mm Car.	139	2580	2360	2160	1970	1790	2045	1725	1440	1195	985	+2.5	0.0	-9.9	-29.0	**NA**
6.5x52mm Car.	156	2430	2170	1930	1700	1500	2045	1630	1285	1005	780	+2.5	-1.0	-13.9	0.0	**NA**
6.5x52mm Carcano	160	2250	1963	1700	1467	1271	1798	1369	1027	764	574	+3.8	0.0	-15.9	-48.1	**NA**
6.5x55mm Swe.	93	2625	2350	2090	1850	1630	1425	1140	905	705	550	2.4	0.0	-10.3	-31.1	**NA**
6.5x55mm Swe.	123	2750	2570	2400	2240	2080	2065	1810	1580	1370	1185	1.9	0.0	-7.9	-22.9	**NA**
6.5x55mm Swe.*	139/140	2850	2640	2440	2250	2070	2525	2170	1855	1575	1330	+2.5	+1.6	-5.4	-18.9	**$18**
6.5x55mm Swe.	140	2550	NA	NA	NA	NA	2020	NA	NA	NA	NA	0.0	0.0	0.0	0.0	**$18**
6.5x55mm Swe.	140	2735	2563	2397	2237	2084	2325	2041	1786	1556	1350	1.9	0	-8.0	-22.9	**NA**
6.5x55mm Swe.	156	2650	2370	2110	1870	1650	2425	1950	1550	1215	945	+2.5	0.0	-10.3	-30.6	**NA**
260 Rem.	100	3200	2917	2652	2402	2165	2273	1889	1561	1281	1041	1.3	0	-6.3	-18.6	**NA**
260 Rem.	130	2800	2613	2433	2261	2096	2262	1970	1709	1476	1268	1.8	0	-7.7	-22.2	**NA**
260 Remington	125	2875	2669	2473	2285	2105	2294	1977	1697	1449	1230	1.71	0.0	-7.4	-21.4	**NA**
260 Remington	140	2750	2544	2347	2158	1979	2351	2011	1712	1448	1217	+2.2	0.0	-8.6	-24.6	**NA**
6.5 Creedmoor	120	3020	2815	2619	2430	2251	2430	2111	1827	1574	1350	1.4	0.0	-6.5	-18.9	**NA**
6.5 Creedmoor	120	3050	2850	2659	2476	2300	2479	2164	1884	1634	1310	1.4	0	-6.3	-18.3	**NA**
6.5 Creedmoor	140	2550	2380	2217	2060	1910	2021	1761	1527	1319	1134	2.3	0	-9.4	-27.0	**NA**
6.5 Creedmoor	140	2710	2557	2410	2267	2129	2283	2033	1805	1598	1410	1.9	0	-7.9	-22.6	**NA**
6.5 Creedmoor	140	2820	2654	2494	2339	2190	2472	2179	1915	1679	1467	1.7	0.0	-7.2	-20.6	**NA**
6.5 C. Superformance	129	2950	2756	2570	2392	2221	2492	2175	1892	1639	1417	1.5	0.0	-6.8	-19.7	**NA**
6.5x52R	117	2208	1856	1544	1287	1104	1267	895	620	431	317	0	-8.7	-32.2	—	**NA**
6.5x57	131	2543	2295	2060	1841	1638	1882	1532	1235	986	780	0	-5.1	-18.5	-42.1	**NA**
6.5 PRC	143	2960	2808	2661	2519	2381	2782	2503	2248	2014	1800	1.5	0	-6.4	-18.2	**NA**
6.5 PRC	147	2910	2775	2645	2518	2395	2764	2514	2281	2069	1871	1.5	0	-6.5	-18.4	**NA**
6.5-284 Norma	142	3025	2890	2758	2631	2507	2886	2634	2400	2183	1982	1.13	0.0	-5.7	-16.4	**NA**
6.5-284 Norma	156	2790	2531	2287	2056	-	2697	2220	1812	1465	-	1.9	0	-8.6	-	**NA**
6.71 (264) Phantom	120	3150	2929	2718	2517	2325	2645	2286	1969	1698	1440	+1.3	0.0	-6.0	-17.5	**NA**
6.5 Rem. Mag.	120	3210	2905	2621	2353	2102	2745	2248	1830	1475	1177	+2.5	+1.7	-4.1	-16.3	**Disc.**
264 Win. Mag.	100	3400	3104	2828	2568	2322	2566	2139	1775	1464	1197	1.1	0	-5.4	-16.1	**NA**
264 Win. Mag.	125	3200	2978	2767	2566	2373	2841	2461	2125	1827	1563	1.2	0	-5.8	-16.8	**NA**
264 Win. Mag.	130	3100	2900	2709	2526	2350	2773	2427	2118	1841	1594	1.3	0	-6.1	-17.6	**NA**
264 Win. Mag.	140	3030	2782	2548	2326	2114	2854	2406	2018	1682	1389	+2.5	+1.4	-5.1	-18.0	**$24**
6.5 Nosler	129	3400	3213	3035	2863	2698	3310	2957	2638	2348	2085	0.9	0	-4.7	-13.6	**NA**
6.5 Nosler	140	3300	3118	2943	2775	2613	3119	2784	2481	2205	1955	1.0	0	-5.0	-14.6	**NA**
6.71 (264) Blackbird	140	3480	3261	3053	2855	2665	3766	3307	2899	2534	2208	+2.4	+3.1	0.0	-7.4	**NA**
6.5-300 Weatherby Magnum	127	3531	3309	3099	2898	2706	-	3088	2707	2368	2065	0	-1.68	-6.98	-16.43	**NA**
6.5-300 Weatherby Magnum	130	3476	3267	3084	2901	2726	-	3097	2746	2430	2145	0	-1.74	-7.14	-16.68	**NA**
6.5-300 Weatherby Magnum	140	3395	3122	2866	2624	2394	-	3030	2552	2139	1781	0	-2.04	-8.24	-19.36	**NA**
6.8 REM SPC	90	2840	2444	2083	1756	1469	1611	1194	867	616	431	2.2	0	-3.9	-32.0	**NA**
6.8 REM SPC	110	2570	2338	2118	1910	1716	1613	1335	1095	891	719	2.4	0.0	-6.3	-20.8	**NA**
6.8 REM SPC	120	2460	2250	2051	1863	1687	1612	1349	1121	925	758	2.3	0	-10.5	-31.1	**NA**

Cartridge	Bullet Wgt. Grs.	VELOCITY (fps)					ENERGY (ft. lbs.)					TRAJ. (in.)				Est. Price/box
		Muzzle	100 yds.	200 yds.	300 yds.	400 yds.	Muzzle	100 yds.	200 yds.	300 yds.	400 yds.	100 yds.	200 yds.	300 yds.	400 yds.	
6.8mm Rem.	115	2775	2472	2190	1926	1683	1966	1561	1224	947	723	+2.1	0.0	-3.7	-9.4	NA
27																
270 Win. (Rem.)	115	2710	2482	2265	2059	NA	1875	1485	1161	896	NA	0.0	4.8	-17.3	0.0	NA
270 Win.	120	2675	2288	1935	1619	1351	1907	1395	998	699	486	2.6	0	-12.0	-37.4	NA
270 Win.	140	2940	2747	2563	2386	2216	2687	2346	2042	1770	1526	1.8	0	-6.8	-19.8	NA
270 Win. Supreme	130	3150	2881	2628	2388	2161	2865	2396	1993	1646	1348	1.3	0.0	-6.4	-18.9	NA
270 Win. Supreme	150	2930	2693	2468	2254	2051	2860	2416	2030	1693	1402	1.7	0.0	-7.4	-21.6	NA
270 W. Superformance	130	3200	2984	2788	2582	2393	2955	2570	2228	1924	1653	1.2	0.0	-5.7	-16.7	NA
270 Winchester	100	3430	3021	2649	2305	1988	2612	2027	1557	1179	877	+2.0	+1.0	-4.9	-17.5	$17
270 Winchester	130	3060	2776	2510	2259	2022	2702	2225	1818	1472	1180	+2.5	+1.4	-5.3	-18.2	$17
270 Winchester	135	3000	2780	2570	2369	2178	2697	2315	1979	1682	1421	+2.5	+1.4	-6.0	-17.6	$23
270 Winchester*	140	2940	2700	2480	2260	2060	2685	2270	1905	1590	1315	+2.5	+1.8	-4.6	-17.9	$20
270 Winchester*	150	2850	2585	2336	2100	1879	2705	2226	1817	1468	1175	+2.5	+1.2	-6.5	-22.0	$17
270 WSM	130	3275	3041	2820	2609	2408	3096	2669	2295	1564	1673	1.1	0.0	-5.5	-16.1	NA
270 WSM	140	3125	2865	2619	2386	2165	3035	2559	2132	1769	1457	1.4	0.0	-6.5	-19.0	NA
270 WSM	150	3000	2795	2599	2412	2232	2997	2601	2250	1937	1659	1.5	0	-6.6	-19.2	NA
270 WSM	150	3120	2923	2734	2554	2380	3242	2845	2490	2172	1886	1.3	0.0	-5.9	-17.2	NA
270 Wea. Mag.	100	3760	3380	3033	2712	2412	3139	2537	2042	1633	1292	+2.0	+2.4	-1.2	-10.1	$32
270 Wea. Mag.	130	3375	3119	2878	2649	2432	3287	2808	2390	2026	1707	+2.5	-2.9	-0.9	-9.9	$32
270 Wea. Mag.	130	3450	3194	2958	2732	2517	3435	2949	2525	2143	1828	1.0	0	-4.9	-14.5	NA
270 Wea. Mag.*	150	3245	3036	2837	2647	2465	3507	3070	2681	2334	2023	+2.5	+2.6	-1.8	-11.4	$47
7mm																
7mm BR	140	2216	2012	1821	1643	1481	1525	1259	1031	839	681	+2.0	-3.7	-20.0	0.0	$23
275 Rigby	140	2680	2455	2242	2040	1848	2233	1874	1563	1292	1062	2.2	0	-9.1	-26.5	NA
7mm Mauser*	139/140	2660	2435	2221	2018	1827	2199	1843	1533	1266	1037	+2.5	0.0	-9.6	-27.7	$17
7mm Mauser	139	2740	2556	2379	2209	2046	2317	2016	1747	1506	1292	1.9	0	-8.1	-23.3	NA
7mm Mauser	154	2690	2490	2300	2120	1940	2475	2120	1810	1530	1285	+2.5	+0.8	-7.5	-23.5	$17
7mm Mauser	175	2440	2137	1857	1603	1382	2313	1774	1340	998	742	+2.5	-1.7	-16.1	0.0	$17
7x30 Waters	120	2700	2300	1930	1600	1330	1940	1405	990	685	470	+2.5	-0.2	-12.3	0.0	$18
7mm-08 Rem.	120	2675	2435	2207	1992	1790	1907	1579	1298	1057	854	2.2	0	-9.4	-27.5	NA
7mm-08 Rem.	120	3000	2725	2467	2223	1992	2398	1979	1621	1316	1058	+2.0	0.0	-7.6	-22.3	$18
7mm-08 Rem.	139	2840	2608	2387	2177	1978	2489	2098	1758	1463	1207	1.8	0	-7.9	-23.2	NA
7mm-08 Rem.*	140	2860	2625	2402	2189	1988	2542	2142	1793	1490	1228	+2.5	+0.8	-6.9	-21.9	$18
7mm-08 Rem.	154	2715	2510	2315	2128	1950	2520	2155	1832	1548	1300	+2.5	+1.0	-7.0	-22.7	$23
7-08 R. Superformance	139	2950	2857	2571	2393	2222	2686	2345	2040	1768	1524	1.5	0.0	-6.8	-19.7	NA
7x64mm	173	2526	2260	2010	1777	1565	2452	1962	1552	1214	941	0	-5.3	-19.3	-44.4	NA
7x64mm Bren.	140	2950	2710	2483	2266	2061	2705	2283	1910	1597	1320	1.5	0.0	-2.9	-7.3	$24.50
7x64mm Bren.	154	2820	2610	2420	2230	2050	2720	2335	1995	1695	1430	+2.5	+1.4	-5.7	-19.9	NA
7x64mm Bren.*	160	2850	2669	2495	2327	2166	2885	2530	2211	1924	1667	+2.5	+1.6	-4.8	-17.8	$24
7x64mm Bren.	175	2650	2445	2248	2061	1883	2728	2322	1964	1650	1378	2.2	0	-9.1	-26.4	$24.50
7x65mmR	173	2608	2337	2082	1844	1626	2613	2098	1666	1307	1015	0	-4.9	-17.9	-41.9	NA
275 Rigby	139	2680	2456	2242	2040	1848	2217	1861	1552	1284	1054	2.2	0	-9.1	-26.5	NA
284 Winchester	150	2860	2595	2344	2108	1886	2724	2243	1830	1480	1185	+2.5	+0.8	-7.3	-23.2	$24
280 R. Superformance	139	3090	2890	2699	2516	2341	2946	2578	2249	1954	1691	1.3	0.0	-6.1	-17.7	NA
280 Rem.	139	3090	2891	2700	2518	2343	2947	2579	2250	1957	1694	1.3	0	-6.1	-17.7	NA
280 Remington	140	3000	2758	2528	2309	2102	2797	2363	1986	1657	1373	+2.5	+1.4	-5.2	-18.3	$17
280 Remington*	150	2890	2624	2373	2135	1912	2781	2293	1875	1518	1217	+2.5	+0.8	-7.1	-22.6	$17
280 Remington	160	2840	2637	2442	2556	2078	2866	2471	2120	1809	1535	+2.5	+0.8	-6.7	-21.0	$20
280 Remington	165	2820	2510	2220	1950	1701	2913	2308	1805	1393	1060	+2.5	+0.4	-8.8	-26.5	$17
280 Ack. Imp.	140	3150	2946	2752	2566	2387	3084	2698	2354	2047	1772	1.3	0	-5.8	-17.0	NA
280 Ack. Imp.	150	2900	2712	2533	2360	2194	2800	2450	2136	1855	1603	1.6	0	-7.0	-20.3	NA
280 Ack. Imp.	160	2950	2751	2561	2379	2205	3091	2686	2331	2011	1727	1.5	0	-6.9	-19.9	NA
7x61mm S&H Sup.	154	3060	2720	2400	2100	1820	3200	2520	1965	1505	1135	+2.5	+1.8	-5.0	-19.8	NA
7mm Dakota	160	3200	3001	2811	2630	2455	3637	3200	2808	2456	2140	+2.1	+1.9	-2.8	-12.5	NA
7mm Rem. Mag.	139	3190	2986	2791	2605	2427	3141	2752	2405	2095	1817	1.2	0	-5.7	-16.5	NA
7mm Rem. Mag. (Rem.)	140	2710	2482	2265	2059	NA	2283	1915	1595	1318	NA	0.0	-4.5	-1.57	0.0	NA
7mm Rem. Mag.*	139/140	3150	2930	2710	2510	2320	3085	2660	2290	1960	1670	+2.5	+2.4	-2.4	-12.7	$21
7mm Rem. Mag.	150/154	3110	2830	2568	2320	2085	3221	2667	2196	1792	1448	+2.5	+1.6	-4.6	-16.5	$21
7mm Rem. Mag.*	160/162	2950	2730	2520	2320	2120	3090	2650	2250	1910	1600	+2.5	+1.8	-4.4	-17.8	$34
7mm Rem. Mag.	165	2900	2699	2507	2324	2147	3081	2669	2303	1978	1689	+2.5	+1.2	-5.9	-19.0	$28
7mm Rem Mag.	175	2860	2645	2440	2244	2057	3178	2718	2313	1956	1644	+2.5	+1.0	-6.5	-20.7	$21
7 R.M. Superformance	139	3240	3033	2836	2648	2467	3239	2839	2482	2163	1877	1.1	0.0	-5.5	-15.9	NA

Cartridge	Bullet Wgt. Grs.	VELOCITY (fps)					ENERGY (ft. lbs.)					TRAJ. (in.)				Est. Price/box
		Muzzle	100 yds.	200 yds.	300 yds.	400 yds.	Muzzle	100 yds.	200 yds.	300 yds.	400 yds.	100 yds.	200 yds.	300 yds.	400 yds.	
7 R.M. Superformance	154	3100	2914	2736	2565	2401	3286	2904	2560	2250	1970	1.3	0.0	-5.9	-17.2	**NA**
7mm Rem. SA ULTRA MAG	140	3175	2934	2707	2490	2283	3033	2676	2277	1927	1620	1.3	0.0	-6	-17.7	**NA**
7mm Rem. SA ULTRA MAG	150	3110	2828	2563	2313	2077	3221	2663	2188	1782	1437	2.5	2.1	-3.6	-15.8	**NA**
7mm Rem. SA ULTRA MAG	160	2850	2676	2508	2347	2192	2885	2543	2235	1957	1706	1.7	0	-7.2	-20.7	**NA**
7mm Rem. SA ULTRA MAG	160	2960	2762	2572	2390	2215	3112	2709	2350	2029	1743	2.6	2.2	-3.6	-15.4	**NA**
7mm WSM	140	3225	3008	2801	2603	2414	3233	2812	2438	2106	1812	1.2	0.0	-5.6	-16.4	**NA**
7mm WSM	160	2990	2744	2512	2081	1883	3176	2675	2241	1864	1538	1.6	0.0	-7.1	-20.8	**NA**
7mm Wea. Mag.	139	3300	3091	2891	2701	2519	3361	2948	2580	2252	1958	1.1	0	-5.2	-15.2	**NA**
7mm Wea. Mag.	140	3225	2970	2729	2501	2283	3233	2741	2315	1943	1621	+2.5	+2.0	-3.2	-14.0	**$35**
7mm Wea. Mag.	140	3340	3127	2925	2732	2546	3467	3040	2659	2320	2016	0	-2.1	-8.2	-19	**NA**
7mm Wea. Mag.	150	3175	2957	2751	2553	2364	3357	2913	2520	2171	1861	0	-2.5	-9.6	-22	**NA**
7mm Wea. Mag.	154	3260	3023	2799	2586	2382	3539	3044	2609	2227	1890	+2.5	+2.8	-1.5	-10.8	**$32**
7mm Wea. Mag.*	160	3200	3004	2816	2637	2464	3637	3205	2817	2469	2156	+2.5	+2.7	-1.5	-10.6	**$47**
7mm Wea. Mag.	165	2950	2747	2553	2367	2189	3188	2765	2388	2053	1756	+2.5	+1.8	-4.2	-16.4	**$43**
7mm Wea. Mag.	175	2910	2693	2486	2288	2098	3293	2818	2401	2033	1711	+2.5	+1.2	-5.9	-19.4	**$35**
7.21(.284) Tomahawk	140	3300	3118	2943	2774	2612	3386	3022	2693	2393	2122	2.3	3.2	0.0	-7.7	**NA**
7mm STW	140	3300	3086	2889	2697	2513	3384	2966	2594	2261	1963	0	-2.1	-8.5	-19.6	**NA**
7mm STW	140	3325	3064	2818	2585	2364	3436	2918	2468	2077	1737	+2.3	+1.8	-3.0	-13.1	**NA**
7mm STW	150	3175	2957	2751	2553	2364	3357	2913	2520	2171	1861	0	-2.5	-9.6	-22	**NA**
7mm STW	175	2900	2760	2625	2493	2366	3267	2960	2677	2416	2175	0	-3.1	-11.2	-24.9	**NA**
7mm STW Supreme	160	3150	2894	2652	2422	2204	3526	2976	2499	2085	1727	1.3	0.0	-6.3	-18.5	**NA**
7mm Rem. Ultra Mag.	140	3425	3184	2956	2740	2534	3646	3151	2715	2333	1995	1.7	1.6	-2.6	-11.4	**NA**
7mm Rem. Ultra Mag.	160	3225	3035	2854	2680	2512	3694	3273	2894	2551	2242	0	-2.3	-8.8	-20.2	**NA**
7mm Rem. Ultra Mag.	174	3040	2896	2756	2621	2490	3590	3258	2952	2669	2409	0	-2.6	-9.9	-22.2	**NA**
7mm Firehawk	140	3625	3373	3135	2909	2695	4084	3536	3054	2631	2258	+2.2	+2.9	0.0	-7.03	**NA**
7.21 (.284) Firebird	140	3750	3522	3306	3101	2905	4372	3857	3399	2990	2625	1.6	2.4	0.0	-6.0	**NA**
.28 Nosler	160	3300	3114	2930	2753	2583	3883	3444	3049	2693	2371	1.1	0	-5.1	-14.9	**$78**
30																
300 ACC Blackout	110	2150	1886	1646	1432	1254	1128	869	661	501	384	0	-8.3	-29.6	-67.8	**NA**
300 AAC Blackout	125	2250	2031	1826	1636	1464	1404	1145	926	743	595	0	-7	-24.4	-54.8	**NA**
300 AAC Blackout	220	1000	968	-	-	-	488	457	-	-	-	0	-	-	-	**-**
30 Carbine	110	1990	1567	1236	1035	923	977	600	373	262	208	0.0	-13.5	0.0	0.0	**$28****
30 Carbine	110	2000	1601	1279	1067	—	977	626	399	278	—	0	-12.9	-47.2	—	**NA**
300 Whisper	110	2375	2094	1834	1597	NA	1378	1071	822	623	NA	3.2	0.0	-13.6	NA	**NA**
300 Whisper	208	1020	988	959	NA	NA	480	451	422	NA	NA	0.0	-34.10	NA	NA	**NA**
303 Savage	190	1890	1612	1327	1183	1055	1507	1096	794	591	469	+2.5	-7.6	0.0	0.0	**$24**
30 Remington	170	2120	1822	1555	1328	1153	1696	1253	913	666	502	+2.5	-4.7	-26.3	0.0	**$20**
7.62x39mm Rus.	123	2360	2049	1764	1511	1296	1521	1147	850	623	459	3.4	0	-14.7	-44.7	**NA**
7.62x39mm Rus.	123/125	2300	2030	1780	1550	1350	1445	1125	860	655	500	+2.5	-2.0	-17.5	0.0	**$13**
30-30 Win.	55	3400	2693	2085	1570	1187	1412	886	521	301	172	+2.0	0.0	-10.2	-35.0	**$18**
30-30 Win.	125	2570	2090	1660	1320	1080	1830	1210	770	480	320	-2.0	-2.6	-19.9	0.0	**$13**
30-30 Win.	140	2500	2198	1918	1662	—	1943	1501	1143	858	—	2.9	0	-12.4	—	**NA**
30-30 Win.	150	2390	2040	1723	1447	1225	1902	1386	989	697	499	0.0	-7.5	-27.0	-63.0	**NA**
30-30 Win. Supreme	150	2480	2095	1747	1446	1209	2049	1462	1017	697	487	0.0	-6.5	-24.5	0.0	**NA**
30-30 Win.	160	2300	1997	1719	1473	1268	1879	1416	1050	771	571	+2.5	-2.9	-20.2	0.0	**$18**
30-30 Win. Lever Evolution	160	2400	2150	1916	1699	NA	2046	1643	1304	1025	NA	3.0	0.2	-12.1	NA	**NA**
30-30 PMC Cowboy	170	1300	1198	1121	—	—	638	474	—	—	—	0.0	-27.0	0.0	0.0	**NA**
30-30 Win.*	170	2200	1895	1619	1381	1191	1827	1355	989	720	535	+2.5	-5.8	-23.6	0.0	**$13**
300 Savage	150	2630	2354	2094	1853	1631	2303	1845	1462	1143	886	+2.5	-0.4	-10.1	-30.7	**$17**
300 Savage	150	2740	2499	2272	2056	1852	2500	2081	1718	1407	1143	2.1	0	-8.8	-25.8	**NA**
300 Savage	180	2350	2137	1935	1754	1570	2207	1825	1496	1217	985	+2.5	-1.6	-15.2	0.0	**$17**
30-40 Krag	180	2430	2213	2007	1813	1632	2360	1957	1610	1314	1064	+2.5	-1.4	-13.8	0.0	**$18**
7.65x53mm Arg.	180	2590	2390	2200	2010	1830	2685	2280	1925	1615	1345	+2.5	0.0	-27.6	0.0	**NA**
7.5x53mm Argentine	150	2785	2519	2269	2032	1814	2583	2113	1714	1376	1096	+2.0	0.0	-8.8	-25.5	**NA**
308 Marlin Express	140	2800	2532	2279	2040	1818	2437	1992	1614	1294	1207	2.0	0	-8.7	-25.8	**NA**
308 Marlin Express	160	2660	2430	2226	2026	1836	2513	2111	1761	1457	1197	3.0	1.7	-6.7	-23.5	**NA**
307 Winchester	150	2760	2321	1924	1575	1289	2530	1795	1233	826	554	+2.5	-1.5	-13.6	0.0	**Disc.**
7.5x55 Swiss	180	2650	2450	2250	2060	1880	2805	2390	2020	1700	1415	+2.5	+0.6	-8.1	-24.9	**NA**
7.5x55mm Swiss	165	2720	2515	2319	2132	1954	2710	2317	1970	1665	1398	+2.0	0.0	-8.5	-24.6	**NA**
30 Remington AR	123/125	2800	2465	2154	1867	1606	2176	1686	1288	967	716	2.1	0.0	-9.7	-29.4	**NA**
308 Winchester	55	3770	3215	2726	2286	1888	1735	1262	907	638	435	-2.0	+1.4	-3.8	-15.8	**$22**
308 Win.	110	3165	2830	2520	2230	1960	2447	1956	1551	1215	938	1.4	0	-6.9	-20.9	**NA**

Cartridge	Bullet Wgt. Grs.	VELOCITY (fps)					ENERGY (ft. lbs.)					TRAJ. (in.)				Est. Price/box
		Muzzle	100 yds.	200 yds.	300 yds.	400 yds.	Muzzle	100 yds.	200 yds.	300 yds.	400 yds.	100 yds.	200 yds.	300 yds.	400 yds.	
308 Win. PDX1	120	2850	2497	2171	NA	NA	2164	1662	1256	NA	NA	0.0	-2.8	NA	NA	NA
308 Winchester	150	2820	2533	2263	2009	1774	2648	2137	1705	1344	1048	+2.5	+0.4	-8.5	-26.1	$17
308 W. Superformance	150	3000	2772	2555	2348	1962	2997	2558	2173	1836	1540	1.5	0.0	-6.9	-20.0	NA
308 Win.	155	2775	2553	2342	2141	1950	2650	2243	1887	1577	1308	1.9	0	-8.3	-24.2	NA
308 Win.	155	2850	2640	2438	2247	2064	2795	2398	2047	1737	1466	1.8	0	-7.5	-22.1	NA
308 Winchester	165	2700	2440	2194	1963	1748	2670	2180	1763	1411	1199	+2.5	0.0	-9.7	-28.5	$20
308 Winchester	168	2680	2493	2314	2143	1979	2678	2318	1998	1713	1460	+2.5	0.0	-8.9	-25.3	$18
308 Win. Super Match	168	2870	2647	2462	2284	2114	3008	2613	2261	1946	1667	1.7	0.0	-7.5	-21.6	NA
308 Win. (Fed.)	170	2000	1740	1510	NA	NA	1510	1145	860	NA	NA	0.0	0.0	0.0	0.0	NA
308 Winchester	178	2620	2415	2220	2034	1857	2713	2306	1948	1635	1363	+2.5	0.0	-9.6	-27.6	$23
308 Win. Super Match	178	2780	2609	2444	2285	2132	3054	2690	2361	2064	1797	1.8	0.0	-7.6	-21.9	NA
308 Winchester*	180	2620	2393	2178	1974	1782	2743	2288	1896	1557	1269	+2.5	-0.2	-10.2	-28.5	$17
30-06 Spfd.	55	4080	3485	2965	2502	2083	2033	1483	1074	764	530	+2.0	+1.9	-2.1	-11.7	$22
30-06 Spfd. (Rem.)	125	2660	2335	2034	1757	NA	1964	1513	1148	856	NA	0.0	-5.2	-18.9	0.0	NA
30-06 Spfd.	125	2700	2412	2143	1891	1660	2023	1615	1274	993	765	2.3	0	-9.9	-29.5	NA
30-06 Spfd.	125	3140	2780	2447	2138	1853	2736	2145	1662	1279	953	+2.0	+1.0	-6.2	-21.0	$17
30-06 Spfd.	150	2910	2617	2342	2083	1853	2820	2281	1827	1445	1135	+2.5	+0.8	-7.2	-23.4	$17
30-06 Superformance	150	3080	2848	2617	2417	2216	3159	2700	2298	1945	1636	1.4	0.0	-6.4	-18.9	NA
30-06 Spfd.	152	2910	2654	2413	2184	1968	2858	2378	1965	1610	1307	+2.5	+1.0	-6.6	-21.3	$23
30-06 Spfd.*	165	2800	2534	2283	2047	1825	2872	2352	1909	1534	1220	+2.5	+0.4	-8.4	-25.5	$17
30-06 Spfd.	168	2710	2522	2346	2169	2003	2739	2372	2045	1754	1497	+2.5	+0.4	-8.0	-23.5	$18
30-06 M1 Garand	168	2710	2523	2343	2171	2006	2739	2374	2048	1758	1501	2.3	0	-8.6	-24.6	NA
30-06 Spfd. (Fed.)	170	2000	1740	1510	NA	NA	1510	1145	860	NA	NA	0.0	0.0	0.0	0.0	NA
30-06 Spfd.	178	2720	2511	2311	2121	1939	2924	2491	2111	1777	1486	+2.5	+0.4	-8.2	-24.6	$23
30-06 Spfd.*	180	2700	2469	2250	2042	1846	2913	2436	2023	1666	1362	-2.5	0.0	-9.3	-27.0	$17
30-06 Superformance	180	2820	2630	2447	2272	2104	3178	2764	2393	2063	1769	1.8	0.0	-7.6	-21.9	NA
30-06 Spfd.	220	2410	2130	1870	1632	1422	2837	2216	1708	1301	988	+2.5	-1.7	-18.0	0.0	$17
30-06 High Energy	180	2880	2690	2500	2320	2150	3315	2880	2495	2150	1845	+1.7	0.0	-7.2	-21.0	NA
30 T/C	150	2920	2696	2483	2280	2087	2849	2421	2054	1732	1450	1.7	0	-7.3	-21.3	NA
30 T/C Superformance	150	3000	2772	2555	2348	2151	2997	2558	2173	1836	1540	1.5	0.0	-6.9	-20.0	NA
30 T/C Superformance	165	2850	2644	2447	2258	2078	2975	2560	2193	1868	1582	1.7	0.0	-7.6	-22.0	NA
300 Rem SA Ultra Mag	150	3200	2901	2622	2359	2112	3410	2803	2290	1854	1485	1.3	0.0	-6.4	-19.1	NA
300 Rem SA Ultra Mag	165	3075	2792	2527	2276	2040	3464	2856	2339	1898	1525	1.5	0.0	-7	-20.7	NA
300 Rem SA Ultra Mag	180	2960	2761	2571	2389	2214	3501	3047	2642	2280	1959	2.6	2.2	-3.6	-15.4	NA
300 Rem. SA Ultra Mag	200	2800	2644	2494	2348	2208	3841	3104	2761	2449	2164	0	-3.5	-12.5	-27.9	NA
7.82 (308) Patriot	150	3250	2999	2762	2537	2323	3519	2997	2542	2145	1798	+1.2	0.0	-5.8	-16.9	NA
300 RCM	150	3265	3023	2794	2577	2369	3550	3043	2600	2211	1870	1.2	0	-5.6	-16.5	NA
300 RCM Superformance	150	3310	3065	2833	2613	2404	3648	3128	2673	2274	1924	1.1	0.0	-5.4	-16.0	NA
300 RCM Superformance	165	3185	2964	2753	2552	2360	3716	3217	2776	2386	2040	1.2	0.0	-5.8	-17.0	NA
300 RCM Superformance	180	3040	2840	2649	2466	2290	3693	3223	2804	2430	2096	1.4	0.0	-6.4	-18.5	NA
300 WSM	150	3300	3061	2834	2619	2414	3628	3121	2676	2285	1941	1.1	0.0	-5.4	-15.9	NA
300 WSM	180	2970	2741	2524	2317	2120	3526	3005	2547	2147	1797	1.6	0.0	-7.0	-20.5	NA
300 WSM	180	3010	2923	2734	2554	2380	3242	2845	2490	2172	1886	1.3	0	-5.9	-17.2	NA
300 WSM	190	2875	2729	2588	2451	2319	3486	3142	2826	2535	2269	0	3.2	-11.5	-25.7	NA
308 Norma Mag.	180	2975	2787	2608	2435	2269	3536	3105	2718	2371	2058	0	-3	-11.1	-25.0	NA
308 Norma Mag.	180	3020	2820	2630	2440	2270	3645	3175	2755	2385	2050	+2.5	+2.0	-3.5	-14.8	NA
300 Dakota	200	3000	2824	2656	2493	2336	3996	3542	3131	2760	2423	+2.2	+1.5	-4.0	-15.2	NA
300 H&H Mag.	180	2870	2678	2494	2318	2148	3292	2866	2486	2147	1844	1.7	0	-7.3	-21.6	NA
300 H&H Magnum*	180	2880	2640	2412	2196	1990	3315	2785	2325	1927	1583	+2.5	+0.8	-6.8	-21.7	$24
300 H&H Mag.	200	2750	2596	2447	2303	2164	3357	2992	2659	2355	2079	1.8	0	-7.6	-21.8	NA
300 H&H Magnum	220	2550	2267	2002	1757	NA	3167	2510	1958	1508	NA	-2.5	-0.4	-12.0	0.0	NA
300 Win. Mag.	150	3290	2951	2636	2342	2068	3605	2900	2314	1827	1424	+2.5	+1.9	-3.8	-15.8	$22
300 WM Superformance	150	3400	3150	2914	2690	2477	3850	3304	2817	2409	2043	1.0	0.0	-5.1	-15.0	NA
300 Win. Mag.	165	3100	2877	2665	2462	2269	3522	3033	2603	2221	1897	+2.5	+2.4	-3.0	-16.9	$24
300 Win. Mag.	178	2900	2760	2568	2375	2191	3509	3030	2606	2230	1897	+2.5	+1.4	-5.0	-17.6	$29
300 Win. Mag.	178	2960	2770	2588	2413	2245	3463	3032	2647	2301	1992	1.5	0	-6.7	-19.4	NA
300 WM Super Match	178	2960	2770	2587	2412	2243	3462	3031	2645	2298	1988	1.5	0.0	-6.7	-19.4	NA
300 Win. Mag.*	180	2960	2745	2540	2344	2157	3501	3011	2578	2196	1859	+2.5	+1.2	-5.5	-18.5	$22
300 WM Superformance	180	3130	2927	2732	2546	2366	3917	3424	2983	2589	2238	1.3	0.0	-5.9	-17.3	NA
300 Win. Mag.	190	2885	1691	2506	2327	2156	3511	3055	2648	2285	1961	+2.5	+1.2	-5.7	-19.0	$26
300 Win. Mag.	195	2930	2760	2596	2438	2286	3717	3297	2918	2574	2262	1.5	0	-6.7	-19.4	NA
300 Win. Mag.*	200	2825	2595	2376	2167	1970	3545	2991	2508	2086	1742	-2.5	+1.6	-4.7	-17.2	$36

Cartridge	Bullet Wgt. Grs.	VELOCITY (fps)					ENERGY (ft. lbs.)					TRAJ. (in.)				Est. Price/box
		Muzzle	100 yds.	200 yds.	300 yds.	400 yds.	Muzzle	100 yds.	200 yds.	300 yds.	400 yds.	100 yds.	200 yds.	300 yds.	400 yds.	
300 Win. Mag.	220	2680	2448	2228	2020	1823	3508	2927	2424	1993	1623	+2.5	0.0	-9.5	-27.5	**$23**
30 Nosler	180	3200	3004	2815	2635	2462	4092	3606	3168	2774	2422	0	-2.4	-9.1	-20.9	**NA**
30 Nosler	210	3000	2868	2741	2617	2497	4196	3836	3502	3193	2906	0	-2.7	-10.1	-22.5	**NA**
300 Rem. Ultra Mag.	150	3450	3208	2980	2762	2556	3964	3427	2956	2541	2175	1.7	1.5	-2.6	-11.2	**NA**
300 Rem. Ultra Mag.	150	2910	2686	2473	2279	2077	2820	2403	2037	1716	1436	1.7	0.0	-7.4	-21.5	**NA**
300 Rem. Ultra Mag.	165	3350	3099	2862	2938	2424	4110	3518	3001	2549	2152	1.1	0	-5.3	-15.6	**NA**
300 Rem. Ultra Mag.	180	3250	3037	2834	2640	2454	4221	3686	3201	2786	2407	2.4	0.0	-3.0	-12.7	**NA**
300 Rem. Ultra Mag.	180	2960	2774	2505	2294	2093	3501	2971	2508	2103	1751	2.7	2.2	-3.8	-16.4	**NA**
300 Rem. Ultra Mag.	200	3032	2791	2562	2345	2138	4083	3459	2916	2442	2030	1.5	0.0	-6.8	-19.9	**NA**
300 Rem. Ultra Mag.	210	2920	2790	2665	2543	2424	3975	3631	3311	3015	2740	1.5	0	-6.4	-18.1	**NA**
30 Nosler	180	3200	3004	2815	2635	2462	4092	3606	3168	2774	2422	0	-2.4	-9.1	-20.9	**NA**
30 Nosler	210	3000	2868	2741	2617	2497	4196	3836	3502	3193	2906	0	-2.7	-10.1	-22.5	**NA**
300 Wea. Mag.	100	3900	3441	3038	2652	2305	3714	2891	2239	1717	1297	+2.0	+2.6	-0.6	-8.7	**$32**
300 Wea. Mag.	150	3375	3126	2892	2670	2459	3794	3255	2786	2374	2013	1.0	0	-5.2	-15.3	**NA**
300 Wea. Mag.	150	3600	3307	3033	2776	2533	4316	3642	3064	2566	2137	+2.5	+3.2	0.0	-8.1	**$32**
300 Wea. Mag.	165	3140	2921	2713	2515	2325	3612	3126	2697	2317	1980	1.3	0	-6.0	-17.5	**NA**
300 Wea. Mag.	165	3450	3210	3000	2792	2593	4360	3796	3297	2855	2464	+2.5	+3.2	0.0	-7.8	**NA**
300 Wea. Mag.	178	3120	2902	2695	2497	2308	3847	3329	2870	2464	2104	+2.5	-1.7	-3.6	-14.7	**$43**
300 Wea. Mag.	180	3330	3110	2910	2710	2520	4430	3875	3375	2935	2540	+1.0	0.0	-5.2	-15.1	**NA**
300 Wea. Mag.	190	3030	2830	2638	2455	2279	3873	3378	2936	2542	2190	+2.5	+1.6	-4.3	-16.0	**$38**
300 Wea. Mag.	220	2850	2541	2283	1964	1736	3967	3155	2480	1922	1471	+2.5	+0.4	-8.5	-26.4	**$35**
300 Pegasus	180	3500	3319	3145	2978	2817	4896	4401	3953	3544	3172	+2.28	+2.89	0.0	-6.79	**NA**
300 Norma Magnum	215	3017	2881	2748	2618	2491	4346	3963	3605	3272	2963	NA	NA	NA	NA	**$85**
300 Norma Magnum	230	2934	2805	2678	2555	2435	4397	4018	3664	3334	3028	NA	NA	NA	NA	**$85**
300 Norma Magnum	225	2850	2731	2615	2502	2392	4058	3726	3417	3128	2859	1.6	0	-6.7	-18.9	**NA**
31																
32-20 Win.	100	1210	1021	913	834	769	325	231	185	154	131	0.0	-32.3	0.0	0.0	**$23****
303 British	150	2685	2441	2211	1993	1789	2401	1985	1628	1323	1066	2.2	0	-9.3	-27.4	**NA**
303 British	180	2460	2124	1817	1542	1311	2418	1803	1319	950	687	+2.5	-1.8	-16.8	0.0	**$18**
303 Light Mag.	150	2830	2570	2325	2094	1884	2667	2199	1800	1461	1185	+2.0	0.0	-8.4	-24.6	**NA**
7.62x54mm Rus.	146	2950	2730	2520	2320	NA	2820	2415	2055	1740	NA	+2.5	+2.0	-4.4	-17.7	**NA**
7.62x54mm Rus.	174	2800	2607	2422	2245	2075	3029	2626	2267	1947	1664	1.8	0	-7.8	-22.4	**NA**
7.62x54mm Rus.	180	2580	2370	2180	2000	1820	2650	2250	1900	1590	1100	+2.5	0.0	-9.8	-28.5	**NA**
7.7x58mm Jap.	150	2640	2399	2170	1954	1752	2321	1916	1568	1271	1022	+2.3	0.0	-9.7	-28.5	**NA**
7.7x58mm Jap.	180	2500	2300	2100	1920	1750	2490	2105	1770	1475	1225	+2.5	0.0	-10.4	-30.2	**NA**
8mm																
8x56 R	205	2400	2188	1987	1797	1621	2621	2178	1796	1470	1196	+2.9	0.0	-11.7	-34.3	**NA**
8x57mm JS Mau.	165	2850	2520	2210	1930	1670	2965	2330	1795	1360	1015	+2.5	+1.0	-7.7	0.0	**NA**
32 Win. Special	165	2410	2145	1897	1669	NA	2128	1685	1318	1020	NA	2.0	0.0	-13.0	-19.9	**NA**
32 Win. Special	170	2250	1921	1626	1372	1175	1911	1393	998	710	521	+2.5	-3.5	-22.9	0.0	**$14**
8mm Mauser	170	2360	1969	1622	1333	1123	2102	1464	993	671	476	+2.5	-3.1	-22.2	0.0	**$18**
8mm Mauser	196	2500	2338	2182	2032	1888	2720	2379	2072	1797	1552	2.4	0	-9.8	-27.9	**NA**
325 WSM	180	3060	2841	2632	2432	2242	3743	3226	2769	2365	2009	+1.4	0.0	-6.4	-18.7	**NA**
325 WSM	200	2950	2753	2565	2384	2210	3866	3367	2922	2524	2170	+1.5	0.0	-6.8	-19.8	**NA**
325 WSM	220	2840	2605	2382	2169	1968	3941	3316	2772	2300	1893	+1.8	0.0	-8.0	-23.3	**NA**
8mm Rem. Mag.	185	3080	2761	2464	2186	1927	3896	3131	2494	1963	1525	+2.5	+1.4	-5.5	-19.7	**$30**
8mm Rem. Mag.	220	2830	2581	2346	2123	1913	3912	3254	2688	2201	1787	+2.5	+0.6	-7.6	-23.5	**Disc.**
33																
338 Federal	180	2830	2590	2350	2130	1930	3200	2670	2215	1820	1480	1.8	0.0	-8.2	-23.9	**NA**
338 Marlin Express	200	2565	2365	2174	1992	1820	2922	2484	2099	1762	1471	3.0	1.2	-7.9	-25.9	**NA**
338 Federal	185	2750	2550	2350	2160	1980	3105	2660	2265	1920	1615	1.9	0.0	-8.3	-24.1	**NA**
338 Federal	210	2630	2410	2200	2010	1820	3225	2710	2265	1880	1545	2.3	0.0	-9.4	-27.3	**NA**
338 Federal MSR	185	2680	2459	2230	2020	1820	2950	2460	2035	1670	1360	2.2	0.0	-9.2	-26.8	**NA**
338-06	200	2750	2553	2364	2184	2011	3358	2894	2482	2118	1796	+1.9	0.0	-8.22	-23.6	**NA**
330 Dakota	250	2900	2719	2545	2378	2217	4668	4103	3595	3138	2727	+2.3	+1.3	-5.0	-17.5	**NA**
338 Lapua	250	2900	2685	2481	2285	2098	4668	4002	2416	2899	2444	1.7	0	-7.3	-21.3	**NA**
338 Lapua	250	2963	2795	2640	2493	NA	4842	4341	3881	3458	NA	+1.9	0.0	-7.9	0.0	**NA**
338 Lapua	285	2745	2616	2491	2369	2251	4768	4331	3926	3552	3206	1.8	0	-7.4	-21	**NA**
338 Lapua	300	2660	2544	2432	2322	-	4715	4313	3940	3592	-	1.9	0	-7.8	-	**NA**
338 RCM Superformance	185	2980	2755	2542	2338	2143	3647	3118	2653	2242	1887	1.5	0.0	-6.9	-20.3	**NA**
338 RCM Superformance	200	2950	2744	2547	2358	2177	3846	3342	2879	2468	2104	1.6	0.0	-6.9	-20.1	**NA**
338 RCM Superformance	225	2750	2575	2407	2245	2089	3778	3313	2894	2518	2180	1.9	0.0	-7.9	-22.7	**NA**

Cartridge	Bullet Wgt. Grs.	VELOCITY (fps)					ENERGY (ft. lbs.)					TRAJ. (in.)				Est. Price/box
		Muzzle	100 yds.	200 yds.	300 yds.	400 yds.	Muzzle	100 yds.	200 yds.	300 yds.	400 yds.	100 yds.	200 yds.	300 yds.	400 yds.	
338 WM Superformance	185	3080	2850	2632	2424	2226	3896	3337	2845	2413	2034	1.4	0.0	-6.4	-18.8	NA
338 Win. Mag.	200	3030	2820	2620	2429	2246	4077	3532	3049	2621	2240	1.4	0	-6.5	-18.9	NA
338 Win. Mag.*	210	2830	2590	2370	2150	1940	3735	3130	2610	2155	1760	+2.5	+1.4	-6.0	-20.9	$33
338 Win. Mag.*	225	2785	2517	2266	2029	1808	3871	3165	2565	2057	1633	+2.5	+0.4	-8.5	-25.9	$27
338 WM Superformance	225	2840	2758	2582	2414	2252	4318	3798	3331	2911	2533	1.5	0.0	-6.8	-19.5	NA
338 Win. Mag.	230	2780	2573	2375	2186	2005	3948	3382	2881	2441	2054	+2.5	+1.2	-6.3	-21.0	$40
338 Win. Mag.*	250	2660	2456	2261	2075	1898	3927	3348	2837	2389	1999	+2.5	+0.2	-9.0	-26.2	$27
338 Ultra Mag.	250	2860	2645	2440	2244	2057	4540	3882	3303	2794	2347	1.7	0.0	-7.6	-22.1	NA
338 Lapua Match	250	2900	2760	2625	2494	2366	4668	4229	3825	3452	3108	1.5	0.0	-6.6	-18.8	NA
338 Lapua Match	285	2745	2623	2504	2388	2275	4768	4352	3966	3608	3275	1.8	0.0	-7.3	-20.8	NA
33 Nosler	225	3025	2856	2687	2525	2369	4589	4074	3608	3185	2803	0	-2.8	-10.4	-23.4	NA
33 Nosler	265	2775	2661	2547	2435	2326	4543	4167	3816	3488	3183	0	-3.4	-12.2	-26.8	NA
33 Nosler	300	2550	2445	2339	2235	2134	4343	3981	3643	3327	3033	0	-4.3	-15	-32.6	NA
8.59(.338) Galaxy	200	3100	2899	2707	2524	2347	4269	3734	3256	2829	2446	3	3.8	0.0	-9.3	NA
340 Wea. Mag.*	210	3250	2991	2746	2515	2295	4924	4170	3516	2948	2455	+2.5	+1.9	-1.8	-11.8	$56
340 Wea. Mag.*	250	3000	2806	2621	2443	2272	4995	4371	3812	3311	2864	+2.5	+2.0	-3.5	-14.8	$56
338 A-Square	250	3120	2799	2500	2220	1958	5403	4348	3469	2736	2128	+2.5	+2.7	-1.5	-10.5	NA
338-378 Wea. Mag.	225	3180	2974	2778	2591	2410	5052	4420	3856	3353	2902	3.1	3.8	0.0	-8.9	NA
338 Titan	225	3230	3010	2800	2600	2409	5211	4524	3916	3377	2898	+3.07	+3.8	0.0	-8.95	NA
338 Excalibur	200	3600	3361	3134	2920	2715	5755	5015	4363	3785	3274	+2.23	+2.87	0.0	-6.99	NA
338 Excalibur	250	3250	2922	2618	2333	2066	5863	4740	3804	3021	2370	+1.3	0.0	-6.35	-19.2	NA
34, 35																
348 Winchester	200	2520	2215	1931	1672	1443	2820	2178	1656	1241	925	+2.5	-1.4	-14.7	0.0	$42
357 Magnum	158	1830	1427	1138	980	883	1175	715	454	337	274	0.0	-16.2	-33.1	0.0	$25**
35 Remington	150	2300	1874	1506	1218	1039	1762	1169	755	494	359	+2.5	-4.1	-26.3	0.0	$16
35 Remington	200	2080	1698	1376	1140	1001	1921	1280	841	577	445	+2.5	-6.3	-17.1	-33.6	$16
35 Remington	200	2225	1963	1722	1505	—	2198	1711	1317	1006	—	3.8	0	-15.6	—	NA
35 Rem. Lever Evolution	200	2225	1963	1721	1503	NA	2198	1711	1315	1003	NA	3.0	-1.3	-17.5	NA	NA
356 Winchester	200	2460	2114	1797	1517	1284	2688	1985	1434	1022	732	+2.5	-1.8	-15.1	0.0	$31
356 Winchester	250	2160	1911	1682	1476	1299	2591	2028	1571	1210	937	+2.5	-3.7	-22.2	0.0	$31
358 Winchester	200	2475	2180	1906	1655	1434	2720	2110	1612	1217	913	2.9	0	-12.6	-37.9	NA
358 Winchester	200	2490	2171	1876	1619	1379	2753	2093	1563	1151	844	+2.5	-1.6	-15.6	0.0	$31
358 STA	275	2850	2562	2292	2039	NA	4958	4009	3208	2539	NA	+1.9	0.0	-8.6	0.0	NA
350 Rem. Mag.	200	2710	2410	2130	1870	1631	3261	2579	2014	1553	1181	+2.5	-0.2	-10.0	-30.1	$33
35 Whelen	200	2675	2378	2100	1842	1606	3177	2510	1958	1506	1145	+2.5	-0.2	-10.3	-31.1	$20
35 Whelen	200	2910	2585	2283	2001	1742	3760	2968	2314	1778	1347	1.9	0	-8.6	-25.9	NA
35 Whelen	225	2500	2300	2110	1930	1770	3120	2650	2235	1870	1560	+2.6	0.0	-10.2	-29.9	NA
35 Whelen	250	2400	2197	2005	1823	1652	3197	2680	2230	1844	1515	+2.5	-1.2	-13.7	0.0	$20
358 Norma Mag.	250	2800	2510	2230	1970	1730	4350	3480	2750	2145	1655	+2.5	+1.0	-7.6	-25.2	NA
358 STA	275	2850	2562	229*2	2039	1764	4959	4009	3208	2539	1899	+1.9	0.0	-8.58	-26.1	NA
9.3mm																
9.3x57mm Mau.	232	2362	2058	1778	1528	NA	2875	2182	1630	1203	NA	0	-6.8	-24.6	NA	NA
9.3x57mm Mau.	286	2070	1810	1590	1390	1110	2710	2090	1600	1220	955	+2.5	-2.6	-22.5	0.0	NA
370 Sako Mag.	286	3550	2370	2200	2040	2880	4130	3570	3075	2630	2240	2.4	0.0	-9.5	-27.2	NA
9.3x62mm	232	2625	2302	2002	1728	-	2551	2731	2066	1539	-	2.6	0	-11.3	-	NA
9.3x62mm	250	2550	2376	2208	2048	—	3609	3133	2707	2328	—	0	-5.4	-17.9	—	NA
9.3x62mm	286	2360	2155	1961	1778	1608	3537	2949	2442	2008	1642	0	-6.0	-21.1	-47.2	NA
9.3x62mm	286	2400	2163	1941	1733	—	3657	2972	2392	1908	—	0	-6.7	-22.6	—	NA
9.3x64mm	286	2700	2505	2318	2139	1968	4629	3984	3411	2906	2460	+2.5	+2.7	-4.5	-19.2	NA
9.3x72mmR	193	1952	1610	1326	1120	996	1633	1112	754	538	425	0	-12.1	-44.1	—	NA
9.3x74mmR	250	2550	2376	2208	2048	—	3609	3133	2707	2328	—	0	-5.4	-17.9	—	NA
9.3x74Rmm	286	2360	2136	1924	1727	1545	3536	2896	2351	1893	1516	0.0	-6.1	-21.7	-49.0	NA
375																
375 Winchester	200	2200	1841	1526	1268	1089	2150	1506	1034	714	527	+2.5	-4.0	-26.2	0.0	$27
375 Winchester	250	1900	1647	1424	1239	1103	2005	1506	1126	852	676	+2.5	-6.9	-33.3	0.0	$27
376 Steyr	225	2600	2331	2078	1842	1625	3377	2714	2157	1694	1319	2.5	0.0	-10.6	-31.4	NA
376 Steyr	270	2600	2372	2156	1951	1759	4052	3373	2787	2283	1855	2.3	0.0	-9.9	-28.9	NA
375 Dakota	300	2600	2316	2051	1804	1579	4502	3573	2800	2167	1661	+2.4	0.0	-11.0	-32.7	NA
375 N.E. 2-1/2"	270	2000	1740	1507	1310	NA	2398	1815	1362	1026	NA	+2.5	-6.0	-30.0	0.0	NA
375 Flanged	300	2450	2150	1886	1640	NA	3998	3102	2369	1790	NA	+2.5	-2.4	-17.0	0.0	NA
375 Ruger	250	2890	2675	2471	2275	2088	4636	3973	3388	2873	2421	1.7	0	-7.4	-21.5	NA
375 Ruger	260	2900	2703	2514	2333	—	4854	4217	3649	3143	—	0	-4.0	-13.4	—	NA

Cartridge	Bullet Wgt. Grs.	VELOCITY (fps)					ENERGY (ft. lbs.)					TRAJ. (in.)				Est. Price/box
		Muzzle	100 yds.	200 yds.	300 yds.	400 yds.	Muzzle	100 yds.	200 yds.	300 yds.	400 yds.	100 yds.	200 yds.	300 yds.	400 yds.	
375 Ruger	270	2840	2600	2372	2156	1951	4835	4052	3373	2786	2283	1.8	0.0	-8.0	-23.6	**NA**
375 Ruger	300	2660	2344	2050	1780	1536	4713	3660	2800	2110	1572	2.4	0.0	-10.8	-32.6	**NA**
375 Flanged NE	300	2400	2103	1829	NA	NA	3838	2947	2228	NA	NA	0	-6.4	-	-	**NA**
375 H&H Magnum	250	2890	2675	2471	2275	2088	4636	3973	3388	2873	2421	1.7	0	-7.4	-21.5	**NA**
375 H&H Magnum	250	2670	2450	2240	2040	1850	3955	3335	2790	2315	1905	+2.5	-0.4	-10.2	-28.4	**NA**
375 H&H Magnum	270	2690	2420	2166	1928	1707	4337	3510	2812	2228	1747	+2.5	0.0	-10.0	-29.4	**$28**
375 H&H Mag.	270	2800	2562	2337	2123	1921	4700	3936	3275	2703	2213	1.9	0	-8.3	-24.3	**NA**
375 H&H Magnum*	300	2530	2245	1979	1733	1512	4263	3357	2608	2001	1523	+2.5	-1.0	-10.5	-33.6	**$28**
375 H&H Mag.	300	2660	2345	2052	1782	1539	4713	3662	2804	2114	1577	2.4	0	-10.8	-32.6	**NA**
375 H&H Hvy. Mag.	270	2870	2628	2399	2182	1976	4937	4141	3451	2150	1845	+1.7	0.0	-7.2	-21.0	**NA**
375 H&H Hvy. Mag.	300	2705	2386	2090	1816	1568	4873	3793	2908	2195	1637	+2.3	0.0	-10.4	-31.4	**NA**
375 H&H Mag.	350	2300	2052	1821	-	-	4112	3273	2578	-	-	0	-6.7	-	-	**NA**
375 Rem. Ultra Mag.	270	2900	2558	2241	1947	1678	5041	3922	3010	2272	1689	1.9	2.7	-8.9	-27.0	**NA**
375 Rem. Ultra Mag.	260	2950	2750	2560	2377	—	5023	4367	3783	3262	—	0	-3.8	-12.9	—	**NA**
375 Rem. Ultra Mag.	300	2760	2505	2263	2035	1822	5073	4178	3412	2759	2210	2.0	0.0	-8.8	-26.1	**NA**
375 Wea. Mag.	260	3000	2798	2606	2421	—	5195	4520	3920	3384	—	0	-3.6	-12.4	—	**NA**
375 Wea. Mag.	300	2700	2420	2157	1911	1685	4856	3901	3100	2432	1891	+2.5	-.04	-10.7	0.0	**NA**
378 Wea. Mag.	260	3100	2894	2697	2509	—	5547	4834	4199	3633	—	0	-4.2	-14.6	—	**NA**
378 Wea. Mag.	270	3180	2976	2781	2594	2415	6062	5308	4635	4034	3495	+2.5	+2.6	-1.8	-11.3	**$71**
378 Wea. Mag.	300	2929	2576	2252	1952	1680	5698	4419	3379	2538	1881	+2.5	+1.2	-7.0	-24.5	**$77**
375 A-Square	300	2920	2626	2351	2093	1850	5679	4594	3681	2917	2281	+2.5	+1.4	-6.0	-21.0	**NA**
38-40 Win.	180	1160	999	901	827	764	538	399	324	273	233	0.0	-33.9	0.0	0.0	**$42****
40, 41																
400 A-Square DPM	400	2400	2146	1909	1689	NA	5116	2092	3236	2533	NA	2.98	0.0	-10.0	NA	**NA**
400 A-Square DPM	170	2980	2463	2001	1598	NA	3352	2289	1512	964	NA	2.16	0.0	-11.1	NA	**NA**
408 CheyTac	419	2850	2752	2657	2562	2470	7551	7048	6565	6108	5675	-1.02	0.0	1.9	4.2	**NA**
405 Win.	300	2200	1851	1545	1296		3224	2282	1589	1119		4.6	0.0	-19.5	0.0	**NA**
450/400-3"	400	2050	1815	1595	1402	NA	3732	2924	2259	1746	NA	0.0	NA	-33.4	NA	**NA**
416 Ruger	400	2400	2151	1917	1700	NA	5116	4109	3264	2568	NA	0.0	-6.0	-21.6	0.0	**NA**
416 Dakota	400	2450	2294	2143	1998	1859	5330	4671	4077	3544	3068	+2.5	-0.2	-10.5	-29.4	**NA**
416 Taylor	375	2350	2021	1722	na	na	4600	3403	2470	NA	NA	0	-7	NA	NA	**NA**
416 Taylor	400	2350	2117	1896	1693	NA	4905	3980	3194	2547	NA	+2.5	-1.2	15.0	0.0	**NA**
416 Hoffman	400	2380	2145	1923	1718	1529	5031	4087	3285	2620	2077	+2.5	-1.0	-14.1	0.0	**NA**
416 Rigby	350	2600	2449	2303	2162	2026	5253	4661	4122	3632	3189	+2.5	-1.8	-10.2	-26.0	**NA**
416 Rigby	400	2370	2210	2050	1900	NA	4990	4315	3720	3185	NA	+2.5	-0.7	-12.1	0.0	**NA**
416 Rigby	400	2400	2115	1851	1611	—	5115	3973	3043	2305	—	0	-6.5	-21.8	—	**NA**
416 Rigby	400	2415	2156	1915	1691	—	5180	4130	3256	2540	—	0	-6.0	-21.6	—	**NA**
416 Rigby	410	2370	2110	1870	1640	NA	5115	4050	3165	2455	NA	+2.5	-2.4	-17.3	0.0	**$110**
416 Rem. Mag.*	350	2520	2270	2034	1814	1611	4935	4004	3216	2557	2017	+2.5	-0.8	-12.6	-35.0	**$82**
416 Rem. Mag.	400	2400	2142	1901	1679	—	5116	4076	3211	2504	—	3.1	0	-12.7	—	**NA**
416 Rem. Mag.	450	2150	1925	1716	-	-	4620	3702	2942	-	-	0	-7.8	-	-	**NA**
416 Wea. Mag.*	400	2700	2397	2115	1852	1613	6474	5104	3971	3047	2310	+2.5	0.0	-10.1	-30.4	**$96**
10.57 (416) Meteor	400	2730	2532	2342	2161	1987	6621	5695	4874	4147	3508	+1.9	0.0	-8.3	-24.0	**NA**
500/416 N.E.	400	2300	2092	1895	1712	—	4697	3887	3191	2602	—	0	-7.2	-24.0	—	**NA**
500/416 N.E.	410	2325	2062	1817	-	-	4620	3735	2996	NA	NA	0	-6.7	-	-	**NA**
404 Jeffrey	400	2150	1924	1716	1525	NA	4105	3289	2614	2064	NA	+2.5	-4.0	-22.1	0.0	**NA**
404 Jeffrey	400	2300	2053	1823	1611	—	4698	3743	2950	2306	—	0	-6.8	-24.1	—	**NA**
404 Jeffery	400	2350	2020	1720	1458	—	4904	3625	2629	1887	—	0	-6.5	-21.8	—	**NA**
404 Jeffery	450	2150	1946	1755	-	-	4620	3784	3078	-	-	0	-7.6	-	-	**NA**
425, 44																
425 Express	400	2400	2160	1934	1725	NA	5115	4145	3322	2641	NA	+2.5	-1.0	-14.0	0.0	**NA**
44-40 Win.	200	1190	1006	900	822	756	629	449	360	300	254	0.0	-33.3	0.0	0.0	**$36****
44 Rem. Mag.	210	1920	1477	1155	982	880	1719	1017	622	450	361	0.0	-17.6	0.0	0.0	**$14**
44 Rem. Mag.	240	1760	1380	1114	970	878	1650	1015	661	501	411	0.0	-17.6	0.0	0.0	**$13**
444 Marlin	240	2350	1815	1377	1087	941	2942	1753	1001	630	472	+2.5	-15.1	-31.0	0.0	**$22**
444 Marlin	265	2120	1733	1405	1160	1012	2644	1768	1162	791	603	+2.5	-6.0	-32.2	0.0	**Disc.**
444 Mar. Lever Evolution	265	2325	1971	1652	1380	NA	3180	2285	1606	1120	NA	3.0	-1.4	-18.6	NA	**NA**
444 Mar. Superformance	265	2400	1976	1603	1298	NA	3389	2298	1512	991	NA	4.1	0.0	-17.8	NA	**NA**
45																
45-70 Govt.	250	2025	1616	1285	1068	—	2276	1449	917	634	—	6.1	0	-27.2	—	**NA**
45-70 Govt.	300	1810	1497	1244	1073	969	2182	1492	1031	767	625	0.0	-14.8	0.0	0.0	**$21**
45-70 Govt. Supreme	300	1880	1558	1292	1103	988	2355	1616	1112	811	651	0.0	-12.9	-46.0	-105.0	**NA**

Cartridge	Bullet Wgt. Grs.	VELOCITY (fps)					ENERGY (ft. lbs.)					TRAJ. (in.)				Est. Price/box
		Muzzle	100 yds.	200 yds.	300 yds.	400 yds.	Muzzle	100 yds.	200 yds.	300 yds.	400 yds.	100 yds.	200 yds.	300 yds.	400 yds.	
45-70 Govt.	325	2000	1685	1413	1197	—	2886	2049	1441	1035	—	5.5	0	-23.0	—	**NA**
45-70 Lever Evolution	325	2050	1729	1450	1225	NA	3032	2158	1516	1083	NA	3.0	-4.1	-27.8	NA	**NA**
45-70 Govt. CorBon	350	1800	1526	1296			2519	1810	1307			0.0	-14.6	0.0	0.0	**NA**
45-70 Govt.	405	1330	1168	1055	977	918	1590	1227	1001	858	758	0.0	-24.6	0.0	0.0	**$21**
45-70 Govt. PMC Cowboy	405	1550	1193	—	—	—	1639	1280	—	—	—	0.0	-23.9	0.0	0.0	**NA**
45-70 Govt. Garrett	415	1850	—	—	—	—	3150	—	—	—	—	3.0	-7.0	0.0	0.0	**NA**
45-70 Govt. Garrett	530	1550	1343	1178	1062	982	2828	2123	1633	1327	1135	0.0	-17.8	0.0	0.0	**NA**
450 Bushmaster	250	2200	1831	1508	1480	1073	2686	1860	1262	864	639	0.0	-9.0	-33.5	0.0	**NA**
450 Marlin	325	2225	1887	1587	1332	—	3572	2570	1816	1280	—	4.2	0	-18.1	—	**NA**
450 Marlin	350	2100	1774	1488	1254	1089	3427	2446	1720	1222	922	0.0	-9.7	-35.2	0.0	**NA**
450 Mar. Lever Evolution	325	2225	1887	1585	1331	NA	3572	2569	1813	1278	NA	3.0	-2.2	-21.3	NA	**NA**
457 Wild West Magnum	350	2150	1718	1348	NA	NA	3645	2293	1413	NA	NA	0.0	-10.5	NA	NA	**NA**
450/500 N.E.	400	2050	1820	1609	1420	—	3732	2940	2298	1791	—	0	-9.7	-32.8	—	**NA**
450 N.E. 3-1/4"	465	2190	1970	1765	1577	NA	4952	4009	3216	2567	NA	+2.5	-3.0	-20.0	0.0	**NA**
450 N.E.	480	2150	1881	1635	1418	—	4927	3769	2850	2144	—	0	-8.4	-29.8	—	**NA**
450 N.E. 3-1/4"	500	2150	1920	1708	1514	NA	5132	4093	3238	2544	NA	+2.5	-4.0	-22.9	0.0	**NA**
450 No. 2	465	2190	1970	1765	1577	NA	4952	4009	3216	2567	NA	+2.5	-3.0	-20.0	0.0	**NA**
450 No. 2	500	2150	1920	1708	1514	NA	5132	4093	3238	2544	NA	+2.5	-4.0	-22.9	0.0	**NA**
450 Ackley Mag.	465	2400	2169	1950	1747	NA	5947	4857	3927	3150	NA	+2.5	-1.0	-13.7	0.0	**NA**
450 Ackley Mag.	500	2320	2081	1855	1649	NA	5975	4085	3820	3018	NA	+2.5	-1.2	-15.0	0.0	**NA**
450 Rigby	500	2350	2139	1939	1752	—	6130	5079	4176	3408	—	0	-6.8	-22.9	—	**NA**
450 Rigby	550	2100	1887	1690	-	-	5387	4311	3425	-	-	0	-8.3	-	-	**NA**
458 Win. Magnum	400	2380	2170	1960	1770	NA	5030	4165	3415	2785	NA	+2.5	-0.4	-13.4	0.0	**$73**
458 Win. Magnum	465	2220	1999	1791	1601	NA	5088	4127	3312	2646	NA	+2.5	-2.0	-17.7	0.0	**NA**
458 Win. Magnum	500	2040	1823	1623	1442	1237	4620	3689	2924	2308	1839	+2.5	-3.5	-22.0	0.0	**$61**
458 Win. Mag.	500	2140	1880	1643	1432	—	5084	3294	2996	2276	—	0	-8.4	-29.8	—	**NA**
458 Win. Magnum	510	2040	1770	1527	1319	1157	4712	3547	2640	1970	1516	+2.5	-4.1	-25.0	0.0	**$41**
458 Lott	465	2380	2150	1932	1730	NA	5848	4773	3855	3091	NA	+2.5	-1.0	-14.0	0.0	**NA**
458 Lott	500	2300	2029	1778	1551	—	5873	4569	3509	2671	—	0	-7.0	-25.1	—	**NA**
458 Lott	500	2300	2062	1838	1633	NA	5873	4719	3748	2960	NA	+2.5	-1.6	-16.4	0.0	**NA**
460 Short A-Sq.	500	2420	2175	1943	1729	NA	6501	5250	4193	3319	NA	+2.5	-0.8	-12.8	0.0	**NA**
460 Wea. Mag.	500	2700	2404	2128	1869	1635	8092	6416	5026	3878	2969	+2.5	+0.6	-8.9	-28.0	**$72**
475																
500/465 N.E.	480	2150	1917	1703	1507	NA	4926	3917	3089	2419	NA	+2.5	-4.0	-22.2	0.0	**NA**
470 Rigby	500	2150	1940	1740	1560	NA	5130	4170	3360	2695	NA	+2.5	-2.8	-19.4	0.0	**NA**
470 Nitro Ex.	480	2190	1954	1735	1536	NA	5111	4070	3210	2515	NA	+2.5	-3.5	-20.8	0.0	**NA**
470 N.E.	500	2150	1885	1643	1429	—	5132	3945	2998	2267	—	0	-8.9	-30.8	—	**NA**
470 Nitro Ex.	500	2150	1890	1650	1440	1270	5130	3965	3040	2310	1790	+2.5	-4.3	-24.0	0.0	**$177**
475 No. 2	500	2200	1955	1728	1522	NA	5375	4243	3316	2573	NA	+2.5	-3.2	-20.9	0.0	**NA**
50, 58																
50 Alaskan	450	2000	1729	1492	NA	NA	3997	2987	2224	NA	NA	0.0	-11.25	NA	NA	**NA**
500 Jeffery	570	2300	1979	1688	1434	—	6694	4958	3608	2604	—	0	-8.2	-28.6	—	**NA**
505 Gibbs	525	2300	2063	1840	1637	NA	6166	4922	3948	3122	NA	+2.5	-3.0	-18.0	0.0	**NA**
505 Gibbs	570	2100	1893	1701	-	-	5583	4538	3664	-	-	0	-8.1	-	-	**NA**
505 Gibbs	600	2100	1899	1711	-	-	5877	4805	3904	-	-	0	-8.1	-	-	**NA**
500 N.E.	570	2150	1889	1651	1439	—	5850	4518	3450	2621	—	0	-8.9	-30.6	—	**NA**
500 N.E.-3"	570	2150	1928	1722	1533	NA	5850	4703	3752	2975	NA	+2.5	-3.7	-22.0	0.0	**NA**
500 N.E.-3"	600	2150	1927	1721	1531	NA	6158	4947	3944	3124	NA	+2.5	-4.0	-22.0	0.0	**NA**
495 A-Square	570	2350	2117	1896	1693	NA	5850	4703	3752	2975	NA	+2.5	-1.0	-14.5	0.0	**NA**
495 A-Square	600	2280	2050	1833	1635	NA	6925	5598	4478	3562	NA	+2.5	-2.0	-17.0	0.0	**NA**
500 A-Square	600	2380	2144	1922	1766	NA	7546	6126	4920	3922	NA	+2.5	-3.0	-17.0	0.0	**NA**
500 A-Square	707	2250	2040	1841	1567	NA	7947	6530	5318	4311	NA	+2.5	-2.0	-17.0	0.0	**NA**
500 BMG PMC	660	3080	2854	2639	2444	2248	13688		500 yd. zero			+3.1	+3.9	+4.7	+2.8	**NA**
577 Nitro Ex.	750	2050	1793	1562	1360	NA	6990	5356	4065	3079	NA	+2.5	-5.0	-26.0	0.0	**NA**
577 Tyrannosaur	750	2400	2141	1898	1675	NA	9591	7633	5996	4671	NA	+3.0	0.0	-12.9	0.0	**NA**
600, 700																
600 N.E.	900	1950	1680	1452	NA	NA	7596	5634	4212	NA	NA	+5.6	0.0	0.0	0.0	**NA**
700 N.E.	1200	1900	1676	1472	NA	NA	9618	7480	5774	NA	NA	+5.7	0.0	0.0	0.0	**NA**
50 BMG																
50 BMG	624	2952	2820	2691	2566	2444	12077	11028	10036	9125	8281	0	-2.9	-10.6	-23.5	**NA**
50 BMG Match	750	2820	2728	2637	2549	2462	13241	12388	11580	10815	10090	1.5	0.0	-6.5	-18.3	**NA**

Notes: Blanks are available in 32 S&W, 38 S&W and 38 Special. "V" after barrel length indicates test barrel was vented to produce ballistics similar to a revolver with a normal barrel-to-cylinder gap. Ammo prices are per 50 rounds except when marked with an ** which signifies a 20 round box; *** signifies a 25-round box. Not all loads are available from all ammo manufacturers. Listed loads are those made by Remington, Winchester, Federal, and others. DISC. is a discontinued load. Prices are rounded to the nearest whole dollar and will vary with brand and retail outlet.

Cartridge	Bullet Wgt. Grs.	VELOCITY (fps)			ENERGY (ft. lbs.)			Mid-Range Traj. (in.)		Bbl. Lgth. (in).	Est. Price/ box
		Muzzle	50 yds.	100 yds.	Muzzle	50 yds.	100 yds.	50 yds.	100 yds.		
22, 25											
221 Rem. Fireball	50	2650	2380	2130	780	630	505	0.2	0.8	10.5"	**$15**
25 Automatic	35	900	813	742	63	51	43	NA	NA	2"	**$18**
25 Automatic	45	815	730	655	65	55	40	1.8	7.7	2"	**$21**
25 Automatic	50	760	705	660	65	55	50	2.0	8.7	2"	**$17**
30											
7.5mm Swiss	107	1010	NA	NA	240	NA	NA	NA	NA	NA	**NEW**
7.62x25 Tokarev	85	1647	1458	1295	512	401	317	0	-3.2	4.75	
7.62mmTokarev	87	1390	NA	NA	365	NA	NA	0.6	NA	4.5"	**NA**
7.62 Nagant	97	790	NA	NA	134	NA	NA	NA	NA	NA	**NEW**
7.63 Mauser	88	1440	NA	NA	405	NA	NA	NA	NA	NA	**NEW**
30 Luger	93	1220	1110	1040	305	255	225	0.9	3.5	4.5"	**$34**
30 Carbine	110	1790	1600	1430	785	625	500	0.4	1.7	10"	**$28**
30-357 AeT	123	1992	NA	NA	1084	NA	NA	NA	NA	10"	**NA**
32											
32 NAA	80	1000	933	880	178	155	137	NA	NA	4"	**NA**
32 S&W	88	680	645	610	90	80	75	2.5	10.5	3"	**$17**
32 S&W Long	98	705	670	635	115	100	90	2.3	10.5	4"	**$17**
32 Short Colt	80	745	665	590	100	80	60	2.2	9.9	4"	**$19**
32 H&R	80	1150	1039	963	235	192	165	NA	NA	4"	**NA**
32 H&R Magnum	85	1100	1020	930	230	195	165	1.0	4.3	4.5"	**$21**
32 H&R Magnum	95	1030	940	900	225	190	170	1.1	4.7	4.5"	**$19**
327 Federal Magnum	85	1400	1220	1090	370	280	225	NA	NA	4-V	**NA**
327 Federal Magnum	100	1500	1320	1180	500	390	310	-0.2	-4.50	4-V	**NA**
32 Automatic	60	970	895	835	125	105	95	1.3	5.4	4"	**$22**
32 Automatic	60	1000	917	849	133	112	96			4"	**NA**
32 Automatic	65	950	890	830	130	115	100	1.3	5.6	NA	**NA**
32 Automatic	71	905	855	810	130	115	95	1.4	5.8	4"	**$19**
8mm Lebel Pistol	111	850	NA	NA	180	NA	NA	NA	NA	NA	**NEW**
8mm Steyr	112	1080	NA	NA	290	NA	NA	NA	NA	NA	**NEW**
8mm Gasser	126	850	NA	NA	200	NA	NA	NA	NA	NA	**NEW**
9mm, 38											
380 Automatic	60	1130	960	NA	170	120	NA	1.0	NA	NA	**NA**
380 Automatic	75	950	NA	NA	183	NA	NA	NA	NA	3"	**$33**
380 Automatic	85/88	990	920	870	190	165	145	1.2	5.1	4"	**$20**
380 Automatic	90	1000	890	800	200	160	130	1.2	5.5	3.75"	**$10**
380 Automatic	95/100	955	865	785	190	160	130	1.4	5.9	4"	**$20**
38 Super Auto +P	115	1300	1145	1040	430	335	275	0.7	3.3	5"	**$26**
38 Super Auto +P	125/130	1215	1100	1015	425	350	300	0.8	3.6	5"	**$26**
38 Super Auto +P	147	1100	1050	1000	395	355	325	0.9	4.0	5"	**NA**
38 Super Auto +P	115	1130	1016	938	326	264	225	1	-9.5	-	**NA**
9x18mm Makarov	95	1000	930	874	211	182	161	NA	NA	4"	**NEW**
9x18mm Ultra	100	1050	NA	NA	240	NA	NA	NA	NA	NA	**NEW**
9x21	124	1150	1050	980	365	305	265	NA	NA	4"	**NA**
9x21 IMI	123	1220	1095	1010	409	330	281	-3.15	—	5.0	**NA**
9x23mm Largo	124	1190	1055	966	390	306	257	0.7	3.7	4"	**NA**
9x23mm Win.	125	1450	1249	1103	583	433	338	0.6	2.8	NA	**NA**
9mm Steyr	115	1180	NA	NA	350	NA	NA	NA	NA	NA	**NEW**
9mm Luger	80	1445	–	–	–	385	–	–	–	–	**NA**
9mm Luger	88	1500	1190	1010	440	275	200	0.6	3.1	4"	**$24**
9mm Luger	90	1360	1112	978	370	247	191	NA	NA	4"	**$26**
9mm Luger	92	1325	1117	991	359	255	201	-3.2	—	4.0	**NA**
9mm Luger	95	1300	1140	1010	350	275	215	0.8	3.4	4"	**NA**
9mm Luger	100	1180	1080	NA	305	255	NA	0.9	NA	4"	**NA**
9mm Luger Guard Dog	105	1230	1070	970	355	265	220	NA	NA	4"	**NA**
9mm Luger	115	1155	1045	970	340	280	240	0.9	3.9	4"	**$21**

Cartridge	Bullet Wgt. Grs.	VELOCITY (fps)			ENERGY (ft. lbs.)			Mid-Range Traj. (in.)		Bbl. Lgth. (in).	Est. Price/ box
		Muzzle	50 yds.	100 yds.	Muzzle	50 yds.	100 yds.	50 yds.	100 yds.		
9mm Luger	123/125	1110	1030	970	340	290	260	1.0	4.0	4"	$23
9mm Luger	124	1150	1040	965	364	298	256	-4.5	—	4.0	NA
9mm Luger	135	1010	960	918	306	276	253	—	—	4.0	NA
9mm Luger	140	935	890	850	270	245	225	1.3	5.5	4"	$23
9mm Luger	147	990	940	900	320	290	265	1.1	4.9	4"	$26
9mm Luger +P	90	1475	NA	NA	437	NA	NA	NA	NA	NA	NA
9mm Luger +P	115	1250	1113	1019	399	316	265	0.8	3.5	4"	$27
9mm Federal	115	1280	1130	1040	420	330	280	0.7	3.3	4"V	$24
9mm Luger Vector	115	1155	1047	971	341	280	241	NA	NA	4"	NA
9mm Luger +P	124	1180	1089	1021	384	327	287	0.8	3.8	4"	NA
38											
38 S&W	146	685	650	620	150	135	125	2.4	10.0	4"	$19
38 S&W Short	145	720	689	660	167	153	140	-8.5	—	5.0	NA
38 Short Colt	125	730	685	645	150	130	115	2.2	9.4	6"	$19
39 Special	100	950	900	NA	200	180	NA	1.3	NA	4"V	NA
38 Special	110	945	895	850	220	195	175	1.3	5.4	4"V	$23
38 Special	110	945	895	850	220	195	175	1.3	5.4	4"V	$23
38 Special	130	775	745	710	175	160	120	1.9	7.9	4"V	$22
38 Special Cowboy	140	800	767	735	199	183	168			7.5" V	NA
38 (Multi-Ball)	140	830	730	505	215	130	80	2.0	10.6	4"V	$10**
38 Special	148	710	635	565	165	130	105	2.4	10.6	4"V	$17
38 Special	158	755	725	690	200	185	170	2.0	8.3	4"V	$18
38 Special +P	95	1175	1045	960	290	230	195	0.9	3.9	4"V	$23
38 Special +P	110	995	925	870	240	210	185	1.2	5.1	4"V	$23
38 Special +P	125	975	929	885	264	238	218	1	5.2	4"	NA
38 Special +P	125	945	900	860	250	225	205	1.3	5.4	4"V	#23
38 Special +P	129	945	910	870	255	235	215	1.3	5.3	4"V	$11
38 Special +P	130	925	887	852	247	227	210	1.3	5.50	4"V	NA
38 Special +P	147/150	884	NA	NA	264	NA	NA	NA	NA	4"V	$27
38 Special +P	158	890	855	825	280	255	240	1.4	6.0	4"V	$20
357											
357 SIG	115	1520	NA	NA	593	NA	NA	NA	NA	NA	NA
357 SIG	124	1450	NA	NA	578	NA	NA	NA	NA	NA	NA
357 SIG	125	1350	1190	1080	510	395	325	0.7	3.1	4"	NA
357 SIG	135	1225	1112	1031	450	371	319	—	—	4.0	NA
357 SIG	147	1225	1132	1060	490	418	367	—	—	4.0	NA
357 SIG	150	1130	1030	970	420	355	310	0.9	4.0	NA	NA
356 TSW	115	1520	NA	NA	593	NA	NA	NA	NA	NA	NA
356 TSW	124	1450	NA	NA	578	NA	NA	NA	NA	NA	NA
356 TSW	135	1280	1120	1010	490	375	310	0.8	3.5	NA	NA
356 TSW	147	1220	1120	1040	485	410	355	0.8	3.5	5"	NA
357 Mag., Super Clean	105	1650									NA
357 Magnum	110	1295	1095	975	410	290	230	0.8	3.5	4"V	$25
357 (Med.Vel.)	125	1220	1075	985	415	315	270	0.8	3.7	4"V	$25
357 Magnum	125	1450	1240	1090	585	425	330	0.6	2.8	4"V	$25
357 Magnum	125	1500	1312	1163	624	478	376	—	—	8.0	NA
357 (Multi-Ball)	140	1155	830	665	420	215	135	1.2	6.4	4"V	$11**
357 Magnum	140	1360	1195	1075	575	445	360	0.7	3.0	4"V	$25
357 Magnum FlexTip	140	1440	1274	1143	644	504	406	NA	NA	NA	NA
357 Magnum	145	1290	1155	1060	535	430	360	0.8	3.5	4"V	$26
357 Magnum	150/158	1235	1105	1015	535	430	360	0.8	3.5	4"V	$25
357 Mag. Cowboy	158	800	761	725	225	203	185				NA
357 Magnum	165	1290	1189	1108	610	518	450	0.7	3.1	8-3/8"	NA
357 Magnum	180	1145	1055	985	525	445	390	0.9	3.9	4"V	$25
357 Magnum	180	1180	1088	1020	557	473	416	0.8	3.6	8"V	NA
357 Mag. CorBon F.A.	180	1650	1512	1386	1088	913	767	1.66	0.0		NA
357 Mag. CorBon	200	1200	1123	1061	640	560	500	3.19	0.0		NA
357 Rem. Maximum	158	1825	1590	1380	1170	885	670	0.4	1.7	10.5"	$14**
40, 10mm											
40 S&W	120	1150	–	–	352	–	–	–	—	–	$38
40 S&W	125	1265	1102	998	444	337	276	-3.0	–	4.0	NA

Cartridge	Bullet Wgt. Grs.	VELOCITY (fps)			ENERGY (ft. lbs.)			Mid-Range Traj. (in.)		Bbl. Lgth. (in).	Est. Price/ box
		Muzzle	50 yds.	100 yds.	Muzzle	50 yds.	100 yds.	50 yds.	100 yds.		
40 S&W	135	1140	1070	NA	390	345	NA	0.9	NA	4"	**NA**
40 S&W Guard Dog	135	1200	1040	940	430	325	265	NA	NA	4"	**NA**
40 S&W	155	1140	1026	958	447	362	309	0.9	4.1	4"	**$14*** **
40 S&W	165	1150	NA	NA	485	NA	NA	NA	NA	4"	**$18*** **
40 S&W	175	1010	948	899	396	350	314	—	—	4.0	**NA**
40 S&W	180	985	936	893	388	350	319	1.4	5.0	4"	**$14*** **
40 S&W	180	1000	943	896	400	355	321	4.52	—	4.0	**NA**
40 S&W	180	1015	960	914	412	368	334	1.3	4.5	4"	**NA**
400 Cor-Bon	135	1450	NA	NA	630	NA	NA	NA	NA	5"	**NA**
10mm Automatic	155	1125	1046	986	436	377	335	0.9	3.9	5"	**$26**
10mm Automatic	155	1265	1118	1018	551	430	357	—	—	5.0	**NA**
10mm Automatic	170	1340	1165	1145	680	510	415	0.7	3.2	5"	**$31**
10mm Automatic	175	1290	1140	1035	650	505	420	0.7	3.3	5.5"	**$11** **
10mm Auto. (FBI)	180	950	905	865	361	327	299	1.5	5.4	4"	**$16** **
10mm Automatic	180	1030	970	920	425	375	340	1.1	4.7	5"	**$16** **
10mm Auto H.V.	180	1240	1124	1037	618	504	430	0.8	3.4	5"	**$27**
10mm Automatic	200	1160	1070	1010	495	510	430	0.9	3.8	5"	**$14** **
10.4mm Italian	177	950	NA	NA	360	NA	NA	NA	NA	NA	**NEW**
41 Action Exp.	180	1000	947	903	400	359	326	0.5	4.2	5"	**$13** **
41 Rem. Magnum	170	1420	1165	1015	760	515	390	0.7	3.2	4"V	**$33**
41 Rem. Magnum	175	1250	1120	1030	605	490	410	0.8	3.4	4"V	**$14** **
41 (Med. Vel.)	210	965	900	840	435	375	330	1.3	5.4	4"V	**$30**
41 Rem. Magnum	210	1300	1160	1060	790	630	535	0.7	3.2	4"V	**$33**
41 Rem. Magnum	240	1250	1151	1075	833	706	616	0.8	3.3	6.5V	**NA**
44											
44 S&W Russian	247	780	NA	NA	335	NA	NA	NA	NA	NA	**NA**
44 Special	210	900	861	825	360	329	302	5.57	—	6.0	**NA**
44 Special FTX	165	900	848	802	297	263	235	NA	NA	2.5"	**NA**
44 S&W Special	180	980	NA	NA	383	NA	NA	NA	NA	6.5"	**NA**
44 S&W Special	180	1000	935	882	400	350	311	NA	NA	7.5"V	**NA**
44 S&W Special	200	875	825	780	340	302	270	1.2	6.0	6"	**$13** **
44 S&W Special	200	1035	940	865	475	390	335	1.1	4.9	6.5"	**$13** **
44 S&W Special	240/246	755	725	695	310	285	265	2.0	8.3	6.5"	**$26**
44-40 Win.	200	722	698	676	232	217	203	-3.4	-23.7	4.0	**NA**
44-40 Win.	205	725	689	655	239	216	195	—	—	7.5	**NA**
44-40 Win.	210	725	698	672	245	227	210	-11.6	—	5.5	**NA**
44-40 Win.	225	725	697	670	263	243	225	-3.4	-23.8	4.0	**NA**
44-40 Win. Cowboy	225	750	723	695	281	261	242				**NA**
44 Rem. Magnum	180	1610	1365	1175	1035	745	550	0.5	2.3	4"V	**$18** **
44 Rem. Magnum	200	1296	1193	1110	747	632	548	-.5	-6.2	6.0	**NA**
44 Rem. Magnum	200	1400	1192	1053	870	630	492	0.6	NA	6.5"	**$20**
44 Rem. Magnum	200	1500	1332	1194	999	788	633	—	—	7.5	**NA**
44 Rem. Magnum	210	1495	1310	1165	1040	805	635	0.6	2.5	6.5"	**$18** **
44 Rem. Mag. FlexTip	225	1410	1240	1111	993	768	617	NA	NA	NA	**NA**
44 (Med. Vel.)	240	1000	945	900	535	475	435	1.1	4.8	6.5"	**$17**
44 R.M. (Jacketed)	240	1180	1080	1010	740	625	545	0.9	3.7	4"V	**$18** **
44 R.M. (Lead)	240	1350	1185	1070	970	750	610	0.7	3.1	4"V	**$29**
44 Rem. Magnum	250	1180	1100	1040	775	670	600	0.8	3.6	6.5"V	**$21**
44 Rem. Magnum	250	1250	1148	1070	867	732	635	0.8	3.3	6.5"V	**NA**
44 Rem. Magnum	275	1235	1142	1070	931	797	699	0.8	3.3	6.5"	**NA**
44 Rem. Magnum	300	1150	1083	1030	881	781	706	—	—	7.5	**NA**
44 Rem. Magnum	300	1200	1100	1026	959	806	702	NA	NA	7.5"	**$17**
44 Rem. Magnum	330	1385	1297	1220	1406	1234	1090	1.83	0.00	NA	**NA**
44 Webley	262	850	—	—	—	—	—	—	—	—	**NA**
440 CorBon	260	1700	1544	1403	1669	1377	1136	1.58	NA	10"	**NA**
45, 50											
450 Short Colt/450 Revolver	226	830	NA	NA	350	NA	NA	NA	NA	NA	**NEW**
45 S&W Schofield	180	730	NA	NA	213	NA	NA	NA	NA	NA	**NA**
45 S&W Schofield	230	730	NA	NA	272	NA	NA	NA	NA	NA	**NA**
45 G.A.P.	165	1007	936	879	372	321	283	-1.4	-11.8	5.0	**NA**
45 G.A.P.	185	1090	970	890	490	385	320	1.0	4.7	5"	**NA**

Cartridge	Bullet Wgt. Grs.	VELOCITY (fps)			ENERGY (ft. lbs.)			Mid-Range Traj. (in.)		Bbl. Lgth. (in).	Est. Price/ box
		Muzzle	50 yds.	100 yds.	Muzzle	50 yds.	100 yds.	50 yds.	100 yds.		
45 G.A.P.	230	880	842	NA	396	363	NA	NA	NA	NA	**NA**
45 Automatic	150	1050	NA	NA	403	NA	NA	NA	NA	NA	**$40**
45 Automatic	165	1030	930	NA	385	315	NA	1.2	NA	5"	**NA**
45 Automatic Guard Dog	165	1140	1030	950	475	390	335	NA	NA	5"	**NA**
45 Automatic	185	1000	940	890	410	360	325	1.1	4.9	5"	**$28**
45 Auto. (Match)	185	770	705	650	245	204	175	2.0	8.7	5"	**$28**
45 Auto. (Match)	200	940	890	840	392	352	312	2.0	8.6	5"	**$20**
45 Automatic	200	975	917	860	421	372	328	1.4	5.0	5"	**$18**
45 Automatic	230	830	800	675	355	325	300	1.6	6.8	5"	**$27**
45 Automatic	230	880	846	816	396	366	340	1.5	6.1	5"	**NA**
45 Automatic +P	165	1250	NA	NA	573	NA	NA	NA	NA	NA	**NA**
45 Automatic +P	185	1140	1040	970	535	445	385	0.9	4.0	5"	**$31**
45 Automatic +P	200	1055	982	925	494	428	380	NA	NA	5"	**NA**
45 Super	185	1300	1190	1108	694	582	504	NA	NA	5"	**NA**
45 Win. Magnum	230	1400	1230	1105	1000	775	635	0.6	2.8	5"	**$14****
45 Win. Magnum	260	1250	1137	1053	902	746	640	0.8	3.3	5"	**$16****
45 Win. Mag. CorBon	320	1150	1080	1025	940	830	747	3.47			**NA**
455 Webley MKII	262	850	NA	NA	420	NA	NA	NA	NA	NA	**NA**
45 Colt FTX	185	920	870	826	348	311	280	NA	NA	3"V	**NA**
45 Colt	200	1000	938	889	444	391	351	1.3	4.8	5.5"	**$21**
45 Colt	225	960	890	830	460	395	345	1.3	5.5	5.5"	**$22**
45 Colt + P CorBon	265	1350	1225	1126	1073	884	746	2.65	0.0		**NA**
45 Colt + P CorBon	300	1300	1197	1114	1126	956	827	2.78	0.0		**NA**
45 Colt	250/255	860	820	780	410	375	340	1.6	6.6	5.5"	**$27**
454 Casull	250	1300	1151	1047	938	735	608	0.7	3.2	7.5"V	**NA**
454 Casull	260	1800	1577	1381	1871	1436	1101	0.4	1.8	7.5"V	**NA**
454 Casull	300	1625	1451	1308	1759	1413	1141	0.5	2.0	7.5"V	**NA**
454 Casull CorBon	360	1500	1387	1286	1800	1640	1323	2.01	0.0		**NA**
460 S&W	200	2300	2042	1801	2350	1851	1441	0	-1.60	NA	**NA**
460 S&W	260	2000	1788	1592	2309	1845	1464	NA	NA	7.5"V	**NA**
460 S&W	250	1450	1267	1127	1167	891	705	NA	NA	8.375-V	**NA**
460 S&W	250	1900	1640	1412	2004	1494	1106	0	-2.75	NA	**NA**
460 S&W	300	1750	1510	1300	2040	1510	1125	NA	NA	8.4-V	**NA**
460 S&W	395	1550	1389	1249	2108	1691	1369	0	-4.00	NA	**NA**
475 Linebaugh	400	1350	1217	1119	1618	1315	1112	NA	NA	NA	**NA**
480 Ruger	325	1350	1191	1076	1315	1023	835	2.6	0.0	7.5"	**NA**
50 Action Exp.	300	1475	1251	1092	1449	1043	795	-	-	6"	**NA**
50 Action Exp.	325	1400	1209	1075	1414	1055	835	0.2	2.3	6"	**$24****
500 S&W	275	1665	1392	1183	1693	1184	854	1.5	NA	8.375	**NA**
500 S&W	300	1950	1653	1396	2533	1819	1298	—	—	8.5	**NA**
500 S&W	325	1800	1560	1350	2340	1755	1315	NA	NA	8.4-V	**NA**
500 S&W	350	1400	1231	1106	1523	1178	951	NA	NA	10"	**NA**
500 S&W	400	1675	1472	1299	2493	1926	1499	1.3	NA	8.375	**NA**
500 S&W	440	1625	1367	1169	2581	1825	1337	1.6	NA	8.375	**NA**
500 S&W	500	1300	1178	1085	1876	1541	1308	—	—	8.5	**NA**
500 S&W	500	1425	1281	1164	2254	1823	1505	NA	NA	10"	**NA**

Note: The actual ballistics obtained with your firearm can vary considerably from the advertised ballistics. Also, ballistics can vary from lot to lot with the same brand and type load.

Cartridge	Bullet Wt. Grs.	Velocity (fps) 22-1/2" Bbl.		Energy (ft. lbs.) 22-1/2" Bbl.		Mid-Range Traj. (in.)	Muzzle Velocity
		Muzzle	100 yds.	Muzzle	100 yds.	100 yds.	6" Bbl.
17 Aguila	20	1850	1267	NA	NA	NA	NA
17 Hornady Mach 2	15.5	2050	1450	149	75	NA	NA
17 Hornady Mach 2	17	2100	1530	166	88	0.7	NA
17 HMR Lead Free	15.5	2550	1901	NA	NA	.90	NA
17 HMR TNT Green	16	2500	1642	222	96	NA	NA
17 HMR	17	2550	1902	245	136	NA	NA
17 HMR	17	2650	NA	NA	NA	NA	NA
17 HMR	20	2375	1776	250	140	NA	NA
17 Win. Super Mag.	20 Tipped	3000	2504	400	278	0.0	NA
17 Win. Super Mag.	20 JHP	3000	2309	400	237	0.0	NA
17 Win. Super Mag.	25 Tipped	2600	2230	375	276	0.0	NA
5mm Rem. Rimfire Mag.	30	2300	1669	352	188	NA	24
22 Short Blank	—	—	—	—	—	—	—
22 Short CB	29	727	610	33	24	NA	706
22 Short Target	29	830	695	44	31	6.8	786
22 Short HP	27	1164	920	81	50	4.3	1077
22 Colibri	20	375	183	6	1	NA	NA
22 Super Colibri	20	500	441	11	9	NA	NA
22 Long CB	29	727	610	33	24	NA	706
22 Long HV	29	1180	946	90	57	4.1	1031
22 LR Pistol Match	40	1070	890	100	70	4.6	940
22 LR Shrt. Range Green	21	1650	912	127	NA	NA	NA
CCI Quiet 22 LR	40	710	640	45	36	NA	NA
22 LR Sub Sonic HP	38	1050	901	93	69	4.7	NA
22 LR Segmented HP	40	1050	897	98	72	NA	NA
22 LR Standard Velocity	40	1070	890	100	70	4.6	940
22 LR AutoMatch	40	1200	990	130	85	NA	NA
22 LR HV	40	1255	1016	140	92	3.6	1060
22 LR Silhoutte	42	1220	1003	139	94	3.6	1025
22 SSS	60	950	802	120	86	NA	NA
22 LR HV HP	40	1280	1001	146	89	3.5	1085
22 Velocitor GDHP	40	1435	–	–	–	NA	NA
22LR CCI Copper	21	1850	–	–	–	–	–
22 LR Segmented HP	37	1435	1080	169	96	2.9	NA
22 LR Hyper HP	32/33/34	1500	1075	165	85	2.8	NA
22 LR Expediter	32	1640	NA	191	NA	NA	NA
22 LR Stinger HP	32	1640	1132	191	91	2.6	1395
22 LR Lead Free	30	1650	NA	181	NA	NA	NA
22 LR Hyper Vel	30	1750	1191	204	93	NA	NA
22 LR Shot #12	31	950	NA	NA	NA	NA	NA
22 WRF LFN	45	1300	1015	169	103	3	NA
22 Win. Mag. Lead Free	28	2200	NA	301	NA	NA	NA
22 Win. Mag.	30	2200	1373	322	127	1.4	1610
22 Win. Mag. V-Max BT	33	2000	1495	293	164	0.60	NA
22 Win. Mag. JHP	34	2120	1435	338	155	1.4	NA
22 Win. Mag. JHP	40	1910	1326	324	156	1.7	1480
22 Win. Mag. FMJ	40	1910	1326	324	156	1.7	1480
22 Win. Mag. Dyna Point	45	1550	1147	240	131	2.60	NA
22 Win. Mag. JHP	50	1650	1280	300	180	1.3	NA
22 Win. Mag. Shot #11	52	1000	—	NA	—	—	NA

NOTES: * = 10 rounds per box. ** = 5 rounds per box. Pricing variations and number of rounds per box can occur with type and brand of ammunition. Listed pricing is the average nominal cost for load style and box quantity shown. Not every brand is available in all shot size variations. Some manufacturers do not provide suggested list prices. All prices rounded to nearest whole dollar. The price you pay will vary dependent upon outlet of purchase. # = new load spec this year; "C" indicates a change in data.

Dram Equiv.	Shot Ozs.	Load Style	Shot Sizes	Brands	Avg. Price/ box	Velocity (fps)
10 Gauge 3-1/2" Magnum						
Max	2-3/8	magnum blend	5, 6, 7	Hevi-shot	NA	1200
4-1/2	2-1/4	premium	BB, 2, 4, 5, 6	Win., Fed., Rem.	$33	1205
Max	2	premium	4, 5, 6	Fed., Win.	NA	1300
4-1/4	2	high velocity	BB, 2, 4	Rem.	$22	1210
Max	18 pellets	premium	00 buck	Fed., Win.	$7**	1100
Max	1-7/8	Bismuth	BB, 2, 4	Bis.	NA	1225
Max	1-3/4	high density	BB, 2	Rem.	NA	1300
4-1/4	1-3/4	steel	TT, T, BBB, BB, 1, 2, 3	Win., Rem.	$27	1260
Mag	1-5/8	steel	T, BBB, BB, 2	Win.	$27	1285
Max	1-5/8	Bismuth	BB, 2, 4	Bismuth	NA	1375
Max	1-1/2	hypersonic	BBB, BB, 2	Rem.	NA	1700
Max	1-1/2	heavy metal	BB, 2, 3, 4	Hevi-Shot	NA	1500
Max	1-1/2	steel	T, BBB, BB, 1, 2, 3	Fed.	NA	1450
Max	1-3/8	steel	T, BBB, BB, 1, 2, 3	Fed., Rem.	NA	1500
Max	1-3/8	steel	T, BBB, BB, 2	Fed., Win.	NA	1450
Max	1-3/4	slug, rifled	slug	Fed.	NA	1280
Max	24 pellets	Buckshot	1 Buck	Fed.	NA	1100
Max	54 pellets	Super-X	4 Buck	Win.	NA	1150
12 Gauge 3-1/2" Magnum						
Max	2-1/4	premium	4, 5, 6	Fed., Rem., Win.	$13*	1150
Max	2	Lead	4, 5, 6	Fed.	NA	1300
Max	2	Copper plated turkey	4, 5	Rem.	NA	1300
Max	18 pellets	premium	00 buck	Fed., Win., Rem.	$7**	1100
Max	1-7/8	Wingmaster HD	4, 6	Rem.	NA	1225
Max	1-7/8	heavyweight	5, 6	Fed.	NA	1300
Max	1-3/4	high density	BB, 2, 4, 6	Rem.		1300
Max	1-7/8	Bismuth	BB, 2, 4	Bis.	NA	1225
Max	1-5/8	blind side	Hex, 1, 3	Win.	NA	1400
Max	1-5/8	Hevi-shot	T	Hevi-shot	NA	1350
Max	1-5/8	Wingmaster HD	T	Rem.	NA	1350
Max	1-5/8	high density	BB, 2	Fed.	NA	1450
Max	1-5/8	Blind side	Hex, BB, 2	Win.	NA	1400
Max	1-5/8	high density	BB, 2	Fed.	NA	1450
Max	1-5/8	Blind side	Hex, BB, 2	Win.	NA	1400
Max	1-3/8	Heavyweight	2, 4, 6	Fed.	NA	1450
Max	1-3/8	steel	T, BBB, BB, 2, 4	Fed., Win., Rem.	NA	1450
Max	1-1/2	FS steel	BBB, BB, 2	Fed.	NA	1500
Max	1-1/2	Supreme H-V	BBB, BB, 2, 3	Win.	NA	1475

Dram Equiv.	Shot Ozs.	Load Style	Shot Sizes	Brands	Avg. Price/ box	Velocity (fps)
12 Gauge 3-1/2" Magnum *(cont.)*						
Max	1-3/8	H-speed steel	BB, 2	Rem.	NA	1550
Max	1-1/4	Steel	BB, 2	Win.	NA	1625
Max	24 pellets	Premium	1 Buck	Fed.	NA	1100
Max	54 pellets	Super-X	4 Buck	Win.	NA	1050
12 Gauge 3" Magnum						
4	2	premium	BB, 2, 4, 5, 6	Win., Fed., Rem.	$9*	1175
4	1-7/8	premium	BB, 2, 4, 6	Win., Fed., Rem.	$19	1210
4	1-7/8	duplex	4x6	Rem.	$9*	1210
Max	1-3/4	turkey	4, 5, 6	Fed., Fio., Win., Rem.	NA	1300
Max	1-3/4	high density	BB, 2, 4	Rem.	NA	1450
Max	1-5/8	high density	BB, 2	Fed.	NA	1450
Max	1-5/8	Wingmaster HD	4, 6	Rem.	NA	1227
Max	1-5/8	high velocity	4, 5, 6	Fed.	NA	1350
4	1-5/8	premium	2, 4, 5, 6	Win., Fed., Rem.	$18	1290
Max	1-1/2	Wingmaster HD	T	Rem.	NA	1300
Max	1-1/2	Hevi-shot	T	Hevi-shot	NA	1300
Max	1-1/2	high density	BB, 2, 4	Rem.	NA	1300
Max	1-1/2	slug	slug	Bren.	NA	1604
Max	1-5/8	Bismuth	BB, 2, 4, 5, 6	Bis.	NA	1250
4	24 pellets	buffered	1 buck	Win., Fed., Rem.	$5**	1040
4	15 pellets	buffered	00 buck	Win., Fed., Rem.	$6**	1210
4	10 pellets	buffered	000 buck	Win., Fed., Rem.	$6**	1225
4	41 pellets	buffered	4 buck	Win., Fed., Rem.	$6**	1210
Max	1-3/8	heavyweight	5, 6	Fed.	NA	1300
Max	1-3/8	high density	B, 2, 4, 6	Rem. Win.	NA	1450
Max	1-3/8	slug	slug	Bren.	NA	1476
Max	1-3/8	blind side	Hex, 1, 3, 5	Win.	NA	1400
Max	1-1/4	slug, rifled	slug	Fed.	NA	1600
Max	1-3/16	saboted	slug	Bren.	NA	1476
Max	7/8	slug, rifled	slug	Rem.	NA	1875
Max	1-1/8	low recoil	BB	Fed.	NA	850
Max	1-1/8	steel	BB, 2, 3, 4	Fed., Win., Rem.	NA	1550
Max	1-1/16	high density	2, 4	Win.	NA	1400
Max	1	steel	4, 6	Fed.	NA	1330
Max	1-3/8	buckhammer	slug	Rem.	NA	1500

Dram Equiv.	Shot Ozs.	Load Style	Shot Sizes	Brands	Avg. Price/ box	Velocity (fps)
12 Gauge 3" Magnum *(cont.)*						
Max	1	TruBall slug	slug	Fed.	NA	1700
Max	1	slug, rifled	slug, magnum	Win., Rem.	$5**	1760
Max	1-3/8	buckhammer	slug	Rem.	NA	1500
Max	1	saboted slug	slug	Rem., Win., Fed.	$10**	1550
Max	385 grs.	partition gold	slug	Win.	NA	2000
Max	1-1/8	Rackmaster	slug	Win.	NA	1700
Max	300 grs.	XP3	slug	Win.	NA	2100
3-5/8	1-3/8	steel	BBB, BB, 1, 2, 3, 4	Win., Fed., Rem.	$19	1275
Max	1-1/8	snow goose FS	BB, 2, 3, 4	Fed.	NA	1635
Max	1-1/8	steel	BB, 2, 4	Rem.	NA	1500
Max	1-1/8	steel	T, BBB, BB, 2, 4, 5, 6	Fed., Win.	NA	1450
Max	1-1/8	steel	BB, 2	Fed.	NA	1400
Max	1-1/8	FS lead	3, 4	Fed.	NA	1600
Max	1-3/8	Blind side	Hex, BB, 2	Win.	NA	1400
4	1-1/4	steel	T, BBB, BB, 1, 2, 3, 4, 6	Win., Fed., Rem.	$18	1400
Max	1-1/4	FS steel	BBB, BB, 2	Fed.	NA	1450
12 Gauge 2-3/4"						
Max	1-5/8	magnum	4, 5, 6	Win., Fed.	$8*	1250
Max	1-3/8	lead	4, 5, 6	Fiocchi	NA	1485
Max	1-3/8	turkey	4, 5, 6	Fio.	NA	1250
Max	1-3/8	steel	4, 5, 6	Fed.	NA	1400
Max	1-3/8	Bismuth	BB, 2, 4, 5, 6	Bis.	NA	1300
3-3/4	1-1/2	magnum	BB, 2, 4, 5, 6	Win., Fed., Rem.	$16	1260
Max	1-1/4	blind side	Hex, 2, 5	Win.	NA	1400
Max	1-1/4	Supreme H-V	4, 5, 6, 7-1/2	Win. Rem.	NA	1400
3-3/4	1-1/4	high velocity	BB, 2, 4, 5, 6, 7-1/2, 8, 9	Win., Fed., Rem., Fio.	$13	1330
Max	1-1/4	high density	B, 2, 4	Win.	NA	1450
Max	1-1/4	high density	4, 6	Rem.	NA	1325
3-1/4	1-1/4	standard velocity	6, 7-1/2, 8, 9	Win., Fed., Rem., Fio.	$11	1220
Max	1-1/8	Hevi-shot	5	Hevi-shot	NA	1350
3-1/4	1-1/8	standard velocity	4, 6, 7-1/2, 8, 9	Win., Fed., Rem., Fio.	$9	1255
Max	1-1/8	steel	2, 4	Rem.	NA	1390
Max	1	steel	BB, 2	Fed.	NA	1450
3-1/4	1	standard velocity	6, 7-1/2, 8	Rem., Fed., Fio., Win.	$6	1290
3-1/4	1-1/4	target	7-1/2, 8, 9	Win., Fed., Rem.	$10	1220
3	1-1/8	spreader	7-1/2, 8, 8-1/2, 9	Fio.	NA	1200

Dram Equiv.	Shot Ozs.	Load Style	Shot Sizes	Brands	Avg. Price/ box	Velocity (fps)
12 Gauge 2-3/4" *(cont.)*						
3	1-1/8	target	7-1/2, 8, 9, 7-1/2x8	Win., Fed., Rem., Fio.	$7	1200
2-3/4	1-1/8	target	7-1/2, 8, 8-1/2, 9, 7-1/2x8	Win., Fed., Rem., Fio.	$7	1145
2-3/4	1-1/8	low recoil	7-1/2, 8	Rem.	NA	1145
2-1/2	26 grams	low recoil	8	Win.	NA	980
2-1/4	1-1/8	target	7-1/2, 8, 8-1/2, 9	Rem., Fed.	$7	1080
Max	1	spreader	7-1/2, 8, 8-1/2, 9	Fio.	NA	1300
3-1/4	28 grams (1 oz)	target	7-1/2, 8, 9	Win., Fed., Rem., Fio.	$8	1290
3	1	target	7-1/2, 8, 8-1/2, 9	Win., Fio.	NA	1235
2-3/4	1	target	7-1/2, 8, 8-1/2, 9	Fed., Rem., Fio.	NA	1180
3-1/4	24 grams	target	7-1/2, 8, 9	Fed., Win., Fio.	NA	1325
3	7/8	light	8	Fio.	NA	1200
3-3/4	8 pellets	buffered	000 buck	Win., Fed., Rem.	$4**	1325
4	12 pellets	premium	00 buck	Win., Fed., Rem.	$5**	1290
3-3/4	9 pellets	buffered	00 buck	Win., Fed., Rem., Fio.	$19	1325
3-3/4	12 pellets	buffered	0 buck	Win., Fed., Rem.	$4**	1275
4	20 pellets	buffered	1 buck	Win., Fed., Rem.	$4**	1075
3-3/4	16 pellets	buffered	1 buck	Win., Fed., Rem.	$4**	1250
4	34 pellets	premium	4 buck	Fed., Rem.	$5**	1250
3-3/4	27 pellets	buffered	4 buck	Win., Fed., Rem., Fio.	$4**	1325
		PDX1	1 oz. slug, 3-00 buck	Win.	NA	1150
Max	1 oz	segmenting, slug	slug	Win.	NA	1600
Max	1	saboted slug	slug	Win., Fed., Rem.	$10**	1450
Max	1-1/4	slug, rifled	slug	Fed.	NA	1520
Max	1-1/4	slug	slug	Lightfield		1440
Max	1-1/4	saboted slug	attached sabot	Rem.	NA	1550
Max	1	slug, rifled	slug, magnum	Rem., Fio.	$5**	1680
Max	1	slug, rifled	slug	Win., Fed., Rem.	$4**	1610
Max	1	sabot slug	slug	Sauvestre		1640
Max	7/8	slug, rifled	slug	Rem.	NA	1800
Max	400	plat. tip	sabot slug	Win.	NA	1700
Max	385 grains	Partition Gold Slug	slug	Win.	NA	1900
Max	385 grains	Core-Lokt bonded	sabot slug	Rem.	NA	1900
Max	325 grains	Barnes Sabot	slug	Fed.	NA	1900

Dram Equiv.	Shot Ozs.	Load Style	Shot Sizes	Brands	Avg. Price/ box	Velocity (fps)
12 Gauge 2-3/4" *(cont.)*						
Max	300 grains	SST Slug	sabot slug	Hornady	NA	2050
Max	3/4	Tracer	#8 + tracer	Fio.	NA	1150
Max	130 grains	Less Lethal	.73 rubber slug	Lightfield	NA	600
Max	3/4	non-toxic	zinc slug	Win.	NA	NA
3	1-1/8	steel target	6-1/2, 7	Rem.	NA	1200
2-3/4	1-1/8	steel target	7	Rem.	NA	1145
3	1#	steel	7	Win.	$11	1235
3-1/2	1-1/4	steel	T, BBB, BB, 1, 2, 3, 4, 5, 6	Win., Fed., Rem.	$18	1275
3-3/4	1-1/8	steel	BB, 1, 2, 3, 4, 5, 6	Win., Fed., Rem., Fio.	$16	1365
3-3/4	1	steel	2, 3, 4, 5, 6, 7	Win., Fed., Rem., Fio.	$13	1390
Max	7/8	steel	7	Fio.	NA	1440
16 Gauge 2-3/4"						
3-1/4	1-1/4	magnum	2, 4, 6	Fed., Rem.	$16	1260
3-1/4	1-1/8	high velocity	4, 6, 7-1/2	Win., Fed., Rem., Fio.	$12	1295
2-3/4	1-1/8	standard velocity	6, 7-1/2, 8	Fed., Rem., Fio.	$9	1185
2-1/2	1	dove	6, 7-1/2, 8, 9	Fio., Win.	NA	1165
Max	1	Bismuth	4, 6	Rio	NA	1200
Max	15/16	steel	2, 4	Fed., Rem.	NA	1300
Max	7/8	steel	2, 4	Win.	$16	1300
3	12 pellets	buffered	1 buck	Win., Fed., Rem.	$4**	1225
Max	4/5	slug, rifled	slug	Win., Fed., Rem.	$4**	1570
Max	.92	sabot slug	slug	Sauvestre	NA	1560
20 Gauge 3" Magnum						
3	1-1/4	premium	2, 4, 5, 6, 7-1/2	Win., Fed., Rem.	$15	1185
Max	1-1/4	Wingmaster HD	4, 6	Rem.	NA	1185
3	1-1/4	turkey	4, 6	Fio.	NA	1200
Max	1-1/4	Hevi-shot	2, 4, 6	Hevi-shot	NA	1250
Max	1-1/8	high density	4, 6	Rem.	NA	1300
Max	18 pellets	buck shot	2 buck	Fed.	NA	1200
Max	24 pellets	buffered	3 buck	Win.	$5**	1150

Dram Equiv.	Shot Ozs.	Load Style	Shot Sizes	Brands	Avg. Price/ box	Velocity (fps)
20 Gauge 3" Magnum *(cont.)*						
2-3/4	20 pellets	buck	3 buck	Rem.	$4**	1200
Max	1	hypersonic	2, 3, 4	Rem.	NA	Rem.
3-1/4	1	steel	1, 2, 3, 4, 5, 6	Win., Fed., Rem.	$15	1330
Max	1	blind side	Hex, 2, 5	Win.	NA	1300
Max	7/8	steel	2, 4	Win.	NA	1300
Max	7/8	FS lead	3, 4	Fed.	NA	1500
Max	1-1/16	high density	2, 4	Win.	NA	1400
Max	1-1/16	Bismuth	2, 4, 5, 6	Bismuth	NA	1250
Mag	5/8	saboted slug	275 gr.	Fed.	NA	1900
Max	3/4	TruBall slug	slug	Fed.	NA	1700
Max	3/4	TruBall slug	slug	Fed.	NA	1700
20 Gauge 2-3/4"						
2-3/4	1-1/8	magnum	4, 6, 7-1/2	Win., Fed., Rem.	$14	1175
2-3/4	1	high velocity	4, 5, 6, 7-1/2, 8, 9	Win., Fed., Rem., Fio.	$12	1220
Max	1	Bismuth	4, 6	Bis.	NA	1200
Max	1	Hevi-shot	5	Hevi-shot	NA	1250
Max	1	Supreme H-V	4, 6, 7-1/2	Win. Rem.	NA	1300
Max	1	FS lead	4, 5, 6	Fed.	NA	1350
Max	7/8	Steel	2, 3, 4	Fio.	NA	1500
2-1/2	1	standard velocity	6, 7-1/2, 8	Win., Rem., Fed., Fio.	$6	1165
2-1/2	7/8	clays	8	Rem.	NA	1200
2-1/2	7/8	promotional	6, 7-1/2, 8	Win., Rem., Fio.	$6	1210
2-1/2	1	target	8, 9	Win., Rem.	$8	1165
Max	7/8	clays	7-1/2, 8	Win.	NA	1275
2-1/2	7/8	target	8, 9	Win., Fed., Rem.	$8	1200
Max	3/4	steel	2, 4	Rem.	NA	1425
2-1/2	7/8	steel - target	7	Rem.	NA	1200
1-1/2	7/8	low recoil	8	Win.	NA	980
Max	1	buckhammer	slug	Rem.	NA	1500
Max	5/8	Saboted Slug	Copper Slug	Rem.	NA	1500
Max	20 pellets	buffered	3 buck	Win., Fed.	$4	1200

Dram Equiv.	Shot Ozs.	Load Style	Shot Sizes	Brands	Avg. Price/ box	Velocity (fps)
20 Gauge 2-3/4" *(cont.)*						
Max	5/8	slug, saboted	slug	Win.,	$9**	1400
2-3/4	5/8	slug, rifled	slug	Rem.	$4**	1580
Max	3/4	saboted slug	copper slug	Fed., Rem.	NA	1450
Max	3/4	slug, rifled	slug	Win., Fed., Rem., Fio.	$4**	1570
Max	.9	sabot slug	slug	Sauvestre		1480
Max	260 grains	Partition Gold Slug	slug	Win.	NA	1900
Max	260 grains	Core-Lokt Ultra	slug	Rem.	NA	1900
Max	260 grains	saboted slug	platinum tip	Win.	NA	1700
Max	3/4	steel	2, 3, 4, 6	Win., Fed., Rem.	$14	1425
Max	250 grains	SST slug	slug	Hornady	NA	1800
Max	1/2	rifled, slug	slug	Rem.	NA	1800
Max	67 grains	Less lethal	2/.60 rubber balls	Lightfield	NA	900
28 Gauge 3"						
Max	7/8	tundra tungsten	4, 5, 6	Fiocchi	NA	TBD

Dram Equiv.	Shot Ozs.	Load Style	Shot Sizes	Brands	Avg. Price/ box	Velocity (fps)
28 Gauge 2-3/4"						
2	1	high velocity	6, 7-1/2, 8	Win.	$12	1125
2-1/4	3/4	high velocity	6, 7-1/2, 8, 9	Win., Fed., Rem., Fio.	$11	1295
2	3/4	target	8, 9	Win., Fed., Rem.	$9	1200
Max	3/4	sporting clays	7-1/2, 8-1/2	Win.	NA	1300
Max	3/4	Bismuth	5, 7	Rio	NA	1250
Max	5/8	steel	6, 7	NA	NA	1300
Max	5/8	slug		Bren.	NA	1450
410 Bore 3"						
Max	11/16	high velocity	4, 5, 6, 7-1/2, 8, 9	Win., Fed., Rem., Fio.	$10	1135
Max	9/16	Bismuth	5, 7	Rio	NA	1175
Max	3/8	steel	6	NA	NA	1400
		judge	5 pellets 000 Buck	Fed.	NA	960
		judge	9 pellets #4 Buck	Fed.	NA	1100
Max	Mixed	Per. Defense	3DD/12BB	Win.	NA	750
410 Bore 2-1/2"						
Max	1/2	high velocity	4, 6, 7-1/2	Win., Fed., Rem.	$9	1245
Max	1/5	slug, rifled	slug	Win., Fed., Rem.	$4**	1815
1-1/2	1/2	target	8, 8-1/2, 9	Win., Fed., Rem., Fio.	$8	1200
Max	1/2	sporting clays	7-1/2, 8, 8-1/2	Win.	NA	1300
Max		Buckshot	5-000 Buck	Win.	NA	1135
		judge	12-bb's, 3 disks	Win.	NA	TBD
Max	Mixed	Per. Defense	4DD/16BB	Win.	NA	750
Max	42 grains	Less lethal	4/.41 rubber balls	Lightfield	NA	1150

ACCU-TEK AT-380 II ACP
Caliber: 380 ACP. **Capacity:** 6-round magazine. **Barrel:** 2.8 in. **Weight:** 23.5 oz. **Length:** 6.125 in. overall. **Grips:** Textured black composition. **Sights:** Blade front,rear adjustable for windage. **Features:** Made from 17-4 stainless steel, has an exposed hammer, manual firing-pin safety block and trigger disconnect. Magazine release located on the bottom of the grip. American made, lifetime warranty. Comes with two 6-round stainless steel magazines and a California-approved cable lock. Introduced 2006. Made in USA by Excel Industries.
Price: Satin stainless **$289.00**

ACCU-TEK HC-380
Similar to AT-380 II except has a 13-round magazine.
Price: **$330.00**

ACCU-TEK LT-380
Similar to AT-380 II except has a lightweight aluminum frame. **Weight:** 15 ounces.
Price: **$324.00**

AMERICAN CLASSIC 1911-A1
Caliber: .45 ACP. **Capacity:** 7+1 magazine **Barrel:** 5 in. **Grips:** Checkered walnut. **Sights:** Fixed. **Finish:** Blue or hard chromed. A .22 LR version is also available. Other variations include Trophy model with adjustable sights, two-tone finish.
Price: .... **$609.00–$819.00**

AMERICAN CLASSIC COMMANDER
Caliber: .45 ACP. Same features as 1911-A1 model except is Commander size with 4.25-in. barrel.
Price: .... **$624.00–$795.00**

AMERICAN TACTICAL IMPORTS MILITARY 1911
Caliber: .45 ACP. **Capacity:** 7+1 magazine. **Barrel:** 5 in. **Grips:** Textured mahogany. **Sights:** Fixed military style. **Finish:** Blue. Also offered in Commander and Officer's sizes and Enhanced model with additional features.
Price: .... **$500.00–$899.00**

AMERICAN TACTICAL IMPORTS GSG 1911
Caliber: .22 LR. **Capacity:** 10+1 magazine. **Weight:** 34 oz. Other features and dimensions similar to centerfire 1911.
Price: **$299.95**

AUTO-ORDNANCE 1911A1
Caliber: 45 ACP. **Capacity:** 7-round magazine. **Barrel:** 5 in. **Weight:** 39 oz. **Length:** 8.5 in. overall. **Grips:** Brown checkered plastic with medallion. **Sights:** Blade front, rear drift-adjustable for windage. **Features:** Same specs as 1911A1 military guns-parts interchangeable. Frame and slide blued; each radius has non-glare finish. Introduced 2002. Made in USA by Kahr Arms.
Price: 1911PKZSE Parkerized, plastic grips **$688.00**
Price: 1911PKZSEW Parkerized, wood grips **$705.00**
Price: 1911BKOW Black matte finish, wood grips **$750.00**

BAER H.C. 40
Caliber: 40 S&W. **Capacity:** 18- round magazine. **Barrel:** 5 in. **Weight:** 37 oz. **Length:** 8.5 in. overall. **Grips:** Wood. **Sights:** Low-mount adjustable rear sight with hidden rear leaf, dovetail front sight. **Features:** Double-stack Caspian frame, beavertail grip safety, ambidextrous thumb safety, 40 S&W match barrel with supported chamber, match stainless steel barrel bushing, lowered and flared ejection port, extended ejector, match trigger fitted, integral mag well, bead blast blued finish on lower, polished sides on slide. Introduced 2008. Made in USA by Les Baer Custom, Inc.
Price: **$2,960.00**

BAER 1911 BOSS .45
Caliber: .45 ACP. **Capacity:** 8+1 capacity. **Barrel:** 5 in. **Weight:** 37 oz. **Length:** 8.5 in. overall. **Grips:** Premium Checkered Cocobolo Grips. **Sights:** Low-Mount LBC Adj. Sight, Red Fiber Optic Front. **Features:** Speed Trgr, Beveled Mag Well, Rounded for Tactical. Rear cocking serrations on the slide, Baer fiber optic front sight (red), flat mainspring housing, checkered at 20 LPI, extended combat safety, Special tactical package, chromed complete lower, blued slide, (2) 8-round premium magazines.
Price: **$2,560.00**

BAER 1911 CUSTOM CARRY
Caliber: .45 ACP. **Capacity:** 7- or 10-round magazine. **Barrel:** 5 in. **Weight:** 37 oz. **Length:** 8.5 in. overall. **Grips:** Checkered walnut. **Sights:** Baer improved ramp-style dovetailed front, Novak low-mount rear. **Features:** Baer forged NM frame, slide and barrel with stainless bushing. Baer speed trigger with 4-lb. pull. Partial listing shown. Made in USA by Les Baer Custom, Inc.
Price: Custom Carry 5, blued **$2,190.00**
Price: Custom Carry 5, stainless **$2,290.00**
Price: Custom Carry 4 Commanche-length, blued **$2,190.00**
Price: Custom Carry 4 Commanche-length, .38 Super **$2,550.00**

BAER 1911 ULTIMATE RECON
Caliber: .45 ACP. **Capacity:** 7- or 10-round magazine. **Barrel:** 5 in. **Weight:** 37 oz. **Length:** 8.5 in. overall. **Grips:** Checkered cocobolo. **Sights:** Baer improved ramp-style dovetailed front, Novak low-mount rear. **Features:** NM Caspian frame, slide and barrel with stainless bushing. Baer speed trigger with 4-lb. pull. Includes integral Picatinny rail and Sure-Fire X-200 light. Made in USA by Les Baer Custom, Inc. Introduced 2006.
Price: Bead blast blued **$2,650.00**
Price: Bead blast chrome **$2,910.00**

BAER 1911 PREMIER II
Calibers: .38 Super, 400 Cor-Bon, .45 ACP. **Capacity:** 7- or 10-round magazine. **Barrel:** 5 in. **Weight:** 37 oz. **Length:** 8.5 in. overall. **Grips:** Checkered rosewood, double diamond pattern. **Sights:** Baer dovetailed front, low-mount Bo-Mar rear with hidden leaf. **Features:** Baer NM forged steel frame and barrel with stainless bushing, deluxe Commander hammer and sear, beavertail grip safety with pad, extended ambidextrous safety; flat mainspring housing; 30 LPI checkered front strap. Made in USA by Les Baer Custom, Inc.
Price: 5 in. .45 ACP **$2,180.00**
Price: 5 in. 400 Cor-Bon **$2,380.00**
Price: 5 in. .38 Super **$2,620.00**
Price: 6 in. .45 ACP, 400 Cor-Bon, .38 Super, From **$2,390.00**
Price: Super-Tac, .45 ACP, 400 Cor-Bon, .38 Super, From **$2,650.00**

BAER 1911 S.R.P.
Caliber: .45 ACP. **Barrel:** 5 in. **Weight:** 37 oz. **Length:** 8.5 in. overall. **Grips:** Checkered walnut. **Sights:** Trijicon night sights. **Features:** Similar to the F.B.I. contract gun except uses Baer forged steel frame. Has Baer match barrel with supported chamber, complete tactical action. Has Baer Ultra Coat finish. Introduced 1996. Made in USA by Les Baer Custom, Inc.
Price: Government or Commanche Length **$2,840.00**

BAER 1911 STINGER
Calibers: .45 ACP or .38 Super. **Capacity:** 7-round magazine. **Barrel:** 5 in. **Weight:** 34 oz. **Length:** 8.5 in. overall. **Grips:** Checkered cocobolo. **Sights:** Baer dovetailed front, low-mount Bo-Mar rear with hidden leaf. **Features:** Baer NM frame. Baer Commanche slide, Officer's style grip frame, beveled mag well. Made in USA by Les Baer Custom, Inc.
Price: .45 ACP .... **$2,240.00–$2,310.00**
Price: .38 Super **$2,840.00**

BAER 1911 PROWLER III
Caliber: .45 ACP. **Capacity:** 8-round magazine. **Barrel:** 5 in. **Weight:** 34 oz. **Length:** 8.5 in. overall. **Grips:** Checkered cocobolo. **Sights:** Baer dovetailed front, low-mount Bo-Mar rear with hidden leaf. **Features:** Similar to Premier II with tapered cone stub weight, rounded corners. Made in USA by Les Baer Custom, Inc.
Price: Blued **$2,910.00**

BAER HEMI 572
Caliber: .45 ACP. Based on Les Baer's 1911 Premier I pistol and inspired by Chrysler 1970 Hemi Cuda muscle car. **Features:** Double serrated slide, Baer fiber optic front sight with green insert, VZ black recon grips with hex-head screws, hard chrome finish on all major components, Dupont S coating on barrel, trigger, hammer, ambi safety and other controls.
Price: **$2,690.00**

BAER ULTIMATE MASTER COMBAT
Calibers: .45 ACP or .38 Super. A full house competition 1911 offered in 8 variations including 5 or 6-inch barrel, PPC Distinguished or Open class, Bullseye Wadcutter class and others. Features include double serrated slide, fitted slide to frame, checkered front strap and trigger guard, serrated rear of slide, extended ejector, tuned extractor, premium checkered grips, blued finish and two 8-round magazines.
Price: Compensated .45 .... **$3,240.00**
Price: Compensated. 38 Super **$3,390.00**

BERETTA M92/96 A1 SERIES
Calibers: 9mm, .40 S&W. **Capacities:** 15-round magazine; .40 S&W, 12 rounds (M96 A1). **Barrel:** 4.9 in. **Weight:** 33-34 oz. **Length:** 8.5 in. **Sights:** Fiber optic front, adjustable rear. **Features:** Same as other models in 92/96 family except for addition of accessory rail.
Price: **$775.00**

BERETTA MODEL 92FS
Caliber: 9mm. **Capacity:** 10-round magazine. **Barrels:** 4.9 in., 4.25 in. (Compact). **Weight:** 34 oz. **Length:** 8.5 in. overall. **Grips:** Checkered black plastic. **Sights:** Blade front, rear adjustable for windage. Tritium night sights available. **Features:** Double action. Extractor acts as chamber loaded indicator, squared trigger guard, grooved front and backstraps, inertia firing pin. Matte or blued finish. Introduced 1977. Made in USA
Price: **$699.00**
Price: Inox **$850.00**

BERETTA M9 .22 LR
Caliber: .22 LR. **Capacity:** 10 or 15-round magazine. **Features:** Black Brunitron finish, interchangeable grip panels. Similar to centerfire 92/M9 with same operating controls, lighter weight (26 oz.).
Price: **$430.00**

BERETTA MODEL U22 NEOS

Caliber: .22 LR. **Capacity:** 10-round magazine. **Barrels:** 4.5 in. and 6 in. **Weights:** 32 oz.; 36 oz. **Length:** 8.8 in./10.3 in. **Sights:** Target. **Features:** Integral rail for standard scope mounts, light, perfectly weighted, 100 percent American made by Beretta.

Price: Blue **$325.00**
Price: Inox **$350.00**

BERETTA MODEL PX4 STORM

Calibers: 9mm, 40 S&W. **Capacities:** 17 (9mm Para.); 14 (40 S&W). **Barrel:** 4 in. **Weight:** 27.5 oz. **Grips:** Black checkered w/3 interchangeable backstraps. **Sights:** 3-dot system coated in Superluminova; removable front and rear sights. **Features:** DA/SA, manual safety/hammer decocking lever (ambi) and automatic firing pin block safety. Picatinny rail. Comes with two magazines (17/10 in 9mm Para. and 14/10 in 40 S&W). Removable hammer unit. American made by Beretta. Introduced 2005.

Price: 9mm or .40.......... **$650.00**
Price: .45 ACP **$700.00**
Price: .45 ACP SD (Special Duty).......... **$1,150.00**

BERETTA MODEL PX4 STORM SUB-COMPACT

Calibers: 9mm, 40 S&W. **Capacities:** 13 (9mm); 10 (40 S&W). **Barrel:** 3 in. **Weight:** 26.1 oz. **Length:** 6.2 in. overall. **Grips:** NA. **Sights:** NA. **Features:** Ambidextrous manual safety lever, interchangeable backstraps included, lock breech and tilt barrel system, stainless steel barrel, Picatinny rail.

Price: **$650.00**

BERETTA MODEL M9

Caliber: 9mm. **Capacity:** 15. **Barrel:** 4.9 in. **Weights:** 32.2-35.3 oz. **Grips:** Plastic. **Sights:** Dot and post, low profile, windage adjustable rear. **Features:** DA/SA, forged aluminum alloy frame, delayed locking-bolt system, manual safety doubles as decocking lever, combat-style trigger guard, loaded chamber indicator. Comes with two magazines (15/10). American made by Beretta. Introduced 2005.

Price: **$675.00**

BERETTA MODEL M9A1

Caliber: 9mm. **Capacity:** 15. **Barrel:** 4.9 in. **Weights:** 32.2-35.3 oz. **Grips:** Plastic. **Sights:** Dot and post, low profile, windage adjustable rear. **Features:** Same as M9, but also includes integral Mil-Std-1913 Picatinny rail, has checkered front and backstrap. Comes with two magazines (15/10). American made by Beretta. Introduced 2005.

Price: **$775.00**

BERETTA M9A3

Caliber: 9mm. **Capacity:** 10 or 15. **Features:** Same general specifications as M9A1 with safety lever able to be converted to decocker configuration. Flat Dark Earth finish. Comes with three magazines, Vertec-style thin grip.

Price: **$1,100.00**

BERETTA NANO

Caliber: 9mm. **Capacity:** 6-round magazine. **Barrel:** 3.07 in. **Weight:** 17.7 oz. **Length:** 5.7 in. overall. **Grips:** Polymer. **Sights:** 3-dot low profile. **Features:** Double-action only, striker fired. Replaceable grip frames.

Price: **$475.00**

BERETTA PICO
Caliber: .380 ACP. **Capacity:** 6-round magazine. **Barrel:** 2.7 in. **Weight:** 11.5 oz. **Length:** 5.1 in. overall. **Grips:** Integral with polymer frame. Interchangeable backstrap. **Sights:** White outline rear. **Features:** Adjustable, quick-change. Striker-fired, double-action only operation. Ambidextrous magazine release and slide release. Ships with two magazines, one flush, one with grip extension. Made in the USA.
Price: **$399.00**

BERSA THUNDER 45 ULTRA COMPACT
Caliber: .45 ACP. **Barrel:** 3.6 in. **Weight:** 27 oz. **Length:** 6.7 in. overall. **Grips:** Anatomically designed polymer. **Sights:** White outline rear. **Features:** Double action; firing pin safeties, integral locking system. Available in matte, satin nickel, gold, or duo-tone. Introduced 2003. Imported from Argentina by Eagle Imports, Inc.
Price: Thunder 45, matte blue **$500.00**
Price: Thunder 45, duo-tone **$550.00**

BERSA THUNDER 380 SERIES
Caliber: .380 ACP. **Capacity:** 7 rounds. **Barrel:** 3.5 in. **Weight:** 23 oz. **Length:** 6.6 in. overall. **Features:** Otherwise similar to Thunder 45 Ultra Compact. 380 DLX has 9-round capacity. 380 Concealed Carry has 8-round capacity. Imported from Argentina by Eagle Imports, Inc.
Price: Thunder Matte **$335.00**
Price: Thunder Satin Nickel **$355.00**
Price: Thunder Duo-Tone **$355.00**
Price: Thunder Duo-Tone with Crimson Trace Laser Grips **$555.00**

BERSA THUNDER 9 ULTRA COMPACT/40 SERIES
Calibers: 9mm, 40 S&W. **Barrel:** 3.5 in. **Weight:** 24.5 oz. **Length:** 6.6 in. overall. **Features:** Otherwise similar to Thunder 45 Ultra Compact. 9mm Para. High Capacity model has 17-round capacity. 40 High Capacity model has 13-round capacity. Imported from Argentina by Eagle Imports, Inc.
Price: **$500.00**

BERSA THUNDER 22
Caliber: .22 LR. **Capacity:** 10-round magazine. **Weight:** 19 oz. **Features:** Similar to Thunder .380 Series except for caliber. Alloy frame and slide. Finish: Matte black, satin nickel or duo-tone.
Price: **$320.00**

BERSA THUNDER PRO XT
Caliber: 9mm. **Capacity:** 17-round magazine. **Barrel:** 5 in. **Weight:** 34 oz. **Grips:** Checkered black polymer. **Sights:** Adjustable rear, dovetail fiber optic front. **Features:** Available with matte or duo-tone finish. Traditional double/single action design developed for competition. Comes with five magazines.
Price: **$923.00**

BROWNING 1911-22 COMPACT
Caliber: .22 LR **Capacity:** 10-round magazine. **Barrel:** 3.625 in. **Weight:** 15 oz. **Length:** 6.5 in. overall. **Grips:** Brown composite. **Sights:** Fixed. **Features:** Slide is machined aluminum with alloy frame and matte blue finish. Blowback action and single action trigger with manual thumb and grip safeties. Works, feels and functions just like a full-size 1911. It is simply scaled down and chambered in the best of all practice rounds: .22 LR for focus on the fundamentals.
Price: **$600.00**

BROWNING 1911-22 A1
Caliber: .22 LR, **Capacity:** 10-round magazine. **Barrel:** 4.25 in. **Weight:** 16 oz. **Length:** 7.0625 in. overall. **Grips:** Brown composite. **Sights:** Fixed. **Features:** Slide is machined aluminum with alloy frame and matte blue finish. Blowback action and single action trigger with manual thumb and grip safeties. Works, feels and functions just like a full-size 1911. It is simply scaled down and chambered in the best of all practice rounds: .22 LR for focus on the fundamentals.
Price: **$600.00**

BROWNING 1911-22 BLACK LABEL
Caliber: .22 LR. **Capacity:** 10-round magazine. **Barrels:** 4.25 in. or 3.625 in. (Compact model). **Weight:** 14 oz. overall. **Features:** Other features are similar to standard 1911-22 except for this model's composite/polymer frame, extended grip safety, stippled black laminated grip, skeleton trigger and hammer. Available with accessory rail (shown). Suppressor Ready model has threaded muzzle protector, 4.875-inch barrel.
Price: **$640.00**
Price: With Rail.. **$670.00**
Price: Suppressor Ready model.. **$740.00**

BROWNING 1911-22 POLYMER DESERT TAN
Caliber: .22 LR. **Capacity:** 10-round magazine. **Barrels:** 4.25 in. or 3.625 in. **Weight:** 13–14 oz. overall. **Features:** Other features are similar to standard 1911-22 except for this model's composite/polymer frame. Also available with pink composite grips.
Price: **$580.00**

BROWNING 1911-380
Caliber: .380 ACP. **Capacity:** 8-round magazine. **Barrels:** 4.25 in. or 3.625 in. (Compact). **Weight:** 16 to 17.5 oz. **Features:** Aluminum or stainless slide, polymer frame with or without rail. Features are virtually identical to those on the 1911-22. 1911-380 Pro has three-dot combat or night sights, G10 grips, accessory rail. Medallion Pro has checkered walnut grips.
Price: **$670.00**
Price: Pro, Medallion Pro.. **$800.00–$910.00**

BROWNING HI POWER
No longer in production, although some Hi Powers may still be available at a limited number of dealers. **Caliber:** 9mm. **Capacity:** 13-round magazine. **Barrel:** 4.625 in. **Weight:** 32 oz. **Length:** 7.75 in. **Grips:** Checkered walnut (standard model), textured and grooved polymer (Mark III). **Sights:** Fixed

low-profile 3-dot (Mark III), fixed or adjustable low profile (standard model). **Features:** Single-action operation with ambidextrous thumb safety, forged steel frame and slide. Made in Belgium.
Price: Mark III **$1,110.00**
Price: Fixed Sights **$1,120.00**
Price: Standard, Adjustable sights **$1,200.00**

BROWNING BUCK MARK CAMPER UFX
Caliber: .22 LR. **Capacity:** 10-round magazine. **Barrel:** 5.5-in. tapered bull. **Weight:** 34 oz. **Length:** 9.5 in. overall. **Grips:** Overmolded Ultragrip Ambidextrous. **Sights:** Pro-Target adjustable rear, ramp front. **Features:** Matte blue receiver, matte blue or stainless barrel.
Price: Camper UFX **$390.00**
Price: Camper UFX stainless **$430.00**

BROWNING BUCK MARK HUNTER
Caliber: .22 LR. **Capacity:** 10-round magazine. **Barrel:** 7.25-in. heavy tapered bull. **Weight:** 38 oz. **Length:** 11.3 in. overall. **Grips:** Cocobolo target. **Sights:** Pro-Target adjustable rear, Tru-Glo/Marble's fiber-optic front. Integral scope base on top rail. Scope in photo not included. **Features:** Matte blue.
Price: **$500.00**

BROWNING BUCK PRACTICAL URX
Caliber: .22 LR. **Capacity:** 10-round magazine. **Barrels:** 5.5-in. tapered bull or 4-in. slab-sided (Micro). **Weight:** 34 oz. **Length:** 9.5 in. overall. **Grips:** Ultragrip RX Ambidextrous. **Sights:** Pro-Target adjustable rear, Tru-Glo/Marble's fiber-optic front. **Features:** Matte gray receiver, matte blue barrel.
Price: **$479.00**
Price: Stainless **$470.00**
Price: Micro **$470.00**

BROWNING BUCK MARK PLUS UDX
Caliber: .22 LR. **Capacity:** 10-round magazine. **Barrel:** 5.5-in. slab-sided. **Weight:** 34 oz. **Length:** 9.5 in. overall. **Grips:** Walnut Ultragrip DX Ambidextrous or rosewood. **Sights:** Pro-Target adjustable rear, Tru-Glo/Marble's fiber-optic front. **Features:** Matte blue or stainless.
Price: **$550.00**
Price: Stainless **$600.00**

BROWNING BUCK MARK FIELD TARGET SUPPRESSOR READY
Caliber: .22 LR. **Capacity:** 10-round magazine. **Barrel:** 5.5-in. heavy bull, suppressor ready. **Grips:** Cocobolo target. **Sights:** Pro-Target adjustable rear, Tru-Glo/Marble's fiber-optic front. Integral scope base on top rail. Scope in photo not included. **Features:** Matte blue.
Price: **$600.00**

CHIAPPA 1911-22
Caliber: .22 LR. **Capacity:** 10-round magazine. **Barrel:** 5 in. **Weight:** 33.5 oz. **Length:** 8.5 in. **Grips:** Two-piece wood. **Sights:** Fixed. **Features:** A faithful replica of the famous John Browning 1911A1 pistol. Fixed barrel design. Available in black, OD green or tan finish. Target and Tactical models have adjustable sights.
Price: From .... **$269.00–$408.00**

CHIAPPA M9-22 STANDARD
Caliber: .22 LR. **Barrel:** 5 in. **Weight:** 2.3 lbs. **Length:** 8.5 in. **Grips:** Black molded plastic or walnut. **Sights:** Fixed front sight and windage adjustable rear sight. **Features:** The M9 9mm has been a U.S. standard-issue service pistol since 1990. Chiappa's M9-22 is a replica of this pistol in 22 LR. The M9-22 has the same weight and feel as its 9mm counterpart but has an affordable 10-shot magazine for the .22 Long Rifle cartridge, which makes it a true rimfire reproduction. Comes standard with steel trigger, hammer assembly and a 1/2x28 threaded barrel.
Price: **$339.00**

CHIAPPA M9-22 TACTICAL
Caliber: .22 LR. **Barrel:** 5 in. **Weight:** 2.3 lbs. **Length:** 8.5 in. **Grips:** Black molded plastic. **Sights:** Fixed front sight and Novak-style rear sights. **Features:** The M9-22 Tactical model comes with a faux suppressor (this ups the "cool factor" on the range and extends the barrel to make it even more accurate). It also has a 1/2x28 thread adaptor that can be used with a legal suppressor.
Price: **$419.00**

CHRISTENSEN ARMS 1911 SERIES
Calibers: .45 ACP, .40 S&W, 9mm. **Barrels:** 3.7 in., 4.3 in., 5.5 in. **Features:** All models are built on a titanium frame with hand-fitted slide, match-grade barrel, tritium night sights and G10 Operator grip panels.
Price: .... **$1,995.00–$3,799.00**

CITADEL M-1911
Calibers: .45 ACP, 9mm. **Capacity:** 7 (.45), 8 (9mm). **Barrels:** 5 or 3.5 in (.45 & 9mm only). **Weight:** 2.3 lbs. **Length:** 8.5 in. **Grips:** Checkered wood or Hogue wrap-around polymer. **Sights:** Low-profile combat fixed rear, blade front. **Finish:** Matte black, brushed or polished nickel. **Features:** Extended grip safety, ambidextrous safety and slide release. Built by Armscor (Rock Island Armory) in the Philippines and imported by Legacy Sports.
Price: Matte black **$592.00**
Price: Matte black, Hogue grips **$630.00**
Price: Brushed nickel **$681.00**
Price: Polished nickel **$700.00**

CIMARRON MODEL 1911
Caliber: .45 ACP. **Barrel:** 5 in. **Weight:** 37.5 oz. **Length:** 8.5 in. overall. **Grips:** Checkered walnut. **Features:** A faithful reproduction of the original pattern of the Model 1911 with Parkerized finish and lanyard ring. Polished or nickel finish available.
Price: **$541.00**

CIMARRON MODEL 1911 WILD BUNCH
Caliber: .45 ACP. **Barrel:** 5 in. **Weight:** 37.5 oz. **Length:** 8.5 in. overall. **Grips:** Checkered walnut. **Features:** Original WWI 1911 frame with flat mainspring housing, correct markings, polished blue finish, comes with tanker shoulder holster.
Price: **$842.00**

COBRA ENTERPRISES FS32, FS380
Calibers: .32 ACP or .380 ACP. **Capacity:** 7 rounds. **Barrel:** 3.5 in. **Weight:** 2.1 lbs. **Length:** 6.375 in. overall. **Grips:** Black molded synthetic integral with frame. **Sights:** Fixed. Made in USA by Cobra Enterprises of Utah, Inc.
Price: .... **$138.00–$250.00**

COBRA ENTERPRISES PATRIOT SERIES
Calibers: .380, 9mm or .45 ACP. **Capacities:** 6-, 7- or 10-round magazine. **Barrel:** 3.3 in. **Weight:** 20 oz. **Length:** 6 in. overall. **Grips:** Black polymer. **Sights:** Fixed. **Features:** Bright chrome, satin nickel or black finish. Made in USA by Cobra Enterprises of Utah, Inc.
Price: .... **$349.00–$395.00**

COBRA DENALI
Caliber: .380 ACP. **Capacity:** 5 rounds. **Barrel:** 2.8 in. **Weight:** 22 oz. **Length:** 5.4 in. **Grips:** Black molded synthetic integral with frame. **Sights:** Fixed. **Features:** Made in USA by Cobra Enterprises of Utah, Inc.
Price: **$179.00**

COLT MODEL 1991 MODEL O
Caliber: .45 ACP. **Capacity:** 7-round magazine. **Barrel:** 5 in. **Weight:** 38 oz. **Length:** 8.5 in. overall. **Grips:** Checkered black composition. **Sights:** Ramped blade front, fixed square notch rear, high profile. **Features:** Matte finish. Continuation of serial number range used on original G.I. 1911A1 guns. Comes with one magazine and molded carrying case. Introduced 1991. Series 80 firing system.
Price: Blue **$799.00**
Price: Stainless **$879.00**

COLT XSE SERIES MODEL O COMBAT ELITE
Caliber: .45 ACP. **Capacity:** 8-round magazine. **Barrel:** 5 in. **Grips:** Checkered, double-diamond rosewood. **Sights:** Three white-dot Novak. **Features:** Brushed stainless receiver with blued slide; adjustable, two-cut aluminum trigger; extended ambidextrous thumb safety; upswept beavertail with palm swell; elongated slot hammer.
Price: **$1,100.00**

COLT LIGHTWEIGHT COMMANDER
Calibers: .45 ACP, 8-shot, 9mm (9 shot). **Barrel:** 4.25 in. **Weight:** 26 oz. alloy frame, 33 oz. (steel frame). **Length:** 7.75 in. overall. **Grips:** G10 Checkered Black Cherry. **Sights:** Novak White Dot front, Low Mount Carry rear. **Features:** Blued slide, black anodized frame. Aluminum alloy frame.
Price: **$999.00**
Price: Combat Commander w/steel frame **$949.00**

COLT DEFENDER

Caliber: .45 ACP (7-round magazine), 9mm (8-round). **Barrel:** 3 in. **Weight:** 22.5 oz. **Length:** 6.75 in. overall. **Grips:** Pebble-finish rubber wraparound with finger grooves. **Sights:** White dot front, snag-free Colt competition rear. **Features:** Stainless or blued finish; aluminum frame; combat-style hammer; Hi-Ride grip safety, extended manual safety, disconnect safety. Introduced 1998. Made in USA by Colt's Mfg. Co., Inc.

Price: Stainless **$899.00**

Price: Blue **$949.00**

COLT SERIES 70

Caliber: .45 ACP. **Barrel:** 5 in. **Weight:** 37.5 oz. **Length:** 8.5 in. **Grips:** Rosewood with double diamond checkering pattern. **Sights:** Fixed. **Features:** Custom replica of the Original Series 70 pistol with a Series 70 firing system, original roll marks. Introduced 2002. Made in USA by Colt's Mfg. Co., Inc.

Price: Blued **$899.00**

Price: Stainless **$979.00**

COLT 38 SUPER

Caliber: .38 Super. **Barrel:** 5 in. **Weight:** 36.5 oz. **Length:** 8.5 in. **Grips:** Wood with double diamond checkering pattern. **Finish:** Bright stainless. **Sights:** 3-dot. **Features:** Beveled magazine well, standard thumb safety and service-style grip safety. Introduced 2003. Made in USA. by Colt's Mfg. Co., Inc.

Price: **$1,499.00**

COLT MUSTANG POCKETLITE

Caliber: .380 ACP. **Capacity:** 6-round magazine. **Barrel:** 2.75 in. **Weight:** 12.5 oz. **Length:** 5.5 in. **Grips:** Black composite. **Finish:** Brushed stainless. **Features:** Thumb safety, firing-pin safety block. Introduced 2012.

Price: **$599.00**

COLT MUSTANG LITE

Caliber: .380 ACP. Similar to Mustang Pocketlite except has black polymer frame.

Price: **$499.00**

COLT MUSTANG XSP

Caliber: .380 ACP. **Features:** Similar to Mustang Pocketlite except has polymer frame, black diamond or bright stainless slide, squared trigger guard, accessory rail, electroless nickel finished controls.

Price: Bright Stainless..................................... **$528.00**

Price: Black Diamond-Like Carbon finish..................................... **$672.00**

COLT RAIL GUN

Caliber: .45 ACP. **Capacity:** (8+1). **Barrel:** 5 in. **Weight:** 40 oz. **Length:** 8.5 in. **Grips:** Rosewood double diamond. **Sights:** White dot front and Novak rear. **Features:** 1911-style semi-auto. Stainless steel frame and slide, front and rear slide serrations, skeletonized trigger, integral accessory rail, Smith & Alexander upswept beavertail grip palm swell safety, tactical thumb safety, National Match barrel.

Price: **$1,199.00**

COLT SPECIAL COMBAT GOVERNMENT CARRY MODEL

Calibers: .45 ACP (8+1), .38 Super (9+1). **Barrel:** 5 in. **Weight:** NA. **Length:** 8.5 in. **Grips:** Black/silver synthetic. **Sights:** Novak front and rear night sights. **Features:** 1911-style semi-auto. Skeletonized three-hole trigger, slotted hammer, Smith & Alexander upswept beavertail grip palm swell safety and extended magazine well, Wilson tactical ambidextrous safety. Available in blued, hard chrome, or blued/satin-nickel finish, depending on chambering. Marine pistol has desert tan Cerakote stainless steel finish, lanyard loop.

Price: **$2,095.00**

COLT GOVERNMENT MODEL 1911A1 .22

Caliber: .22 LR. **Capacity:** 12-round magazine. **Barrel:** 5 in. **Weight:** 36 oz. **Features:** Made in Germany by Walther under exclusive arrangement with Colt Manufacturing Company. Blowback operation. All other features identical to original, including manual and grip safeties, drift-adjustable sights.

Price: **$399.00**

COLT COMPETITION PISTOL
Calibers: .45 ACP, .38 Super or 9mm Para. Full-size Government Model with 5-inch national match barrel, dual-spring recoil operating system, adjustable rear and fiber optic front sights, custom G10 Colt logo grips.
Price: **$999.00**
Price: 38 Super **$1,099.00**

COLT SERIES 70 NATIONAL MATCH GOLD CUP
Caliber: .45 ACP. **Barrel:** 5 in. national match. **Weight:** 37 oz. **Length:** 8.5 in. **Grips:** Checkered walnut with gold medallions. **Sights:** Adjustable Bomar rear, target post front. Finish: blued. **Features:** Flat top slide, flat mainspring housing. Wide three-hole aluminum trigger.
Price: .... **$1,299.00.**

COLT GOLD CUP TROPHY Calibers: .45 ACP or 9mm. Updated version of the classic Colt target and service pistol first introduced in the late 1950s to give shooters a serious competition pistol out of the box. Features include an undercut trigger guard, upswept beavertail grip safety and dual-spring recoil system. Checkering on the front and rear of the grip strap is 25 LPI with blue G10 grips. The new Gold Cup Trophy is built on the Series 70 firing system. Re-introduced to the Colt catalog in 2017.
Price: .... **$1,699.00.**

CZ 75 B
Calibers: 9mm, .40 S&W. **Capacity:** 10-round magazine. **Barrel:** 4.7 in. **Weight:** 34.3 oz. **Length:** 8.1 in. overall. **Grips:** High impact checkered plastic. **Sights:** Square post front, rear adjustable for windage; 3-dot system. **Features:** Single action/double action; firing pin block safety; choice of black polymer, matte or high-polish blue finishes. All-steel frame. B-SA is a single action with a drop-free magazine. Imported from the Czech Republic by CZ-USA.
Price: 75 B **$625.00**
Price: 75 B, stainless **$783.00**
Price: 75 B-SA **$661.00**

CZ 75 BD DECOCKER
Similar to the CZ 75B except has a decocking lever in place of the safety lever. All other specifications are the same. Introduced 1999. Imported from the Czech Republic by CZ-USA.
Price: 9mm, black polymer **$612.00**

CZ 75 B COMPACT
Similar to the CZ 75 B except has 14-round magazine in 9mm, 3.9-in. barrel and weighs 32 oz. Has removable front sight, non-glare ribbed slide top. Trigger guard is squared and serrated; combat hammer. Introduced 1993. Imported from the Czech Republic by CZ-USA.
Price: 9mm, black polymer **$631.00**
Price: 9mm, dual tone or satin nickel **$651.00**
Price: 9mm. D PCR Compact, alloy frame **$651.00**

CZ P-07 DUTY
Calibers: .40 S&W, 9mm. **Capacity:** 16+1. **Barrel:** 3.8 in. **Weight:** 27.2 oz. **Length:** 7.3 in. overall. **Grips:** Polymer black Polycoat. **Sights:** Blade front, fixed groove rear. **Features:** The ergonomics and accuracy of the CZ 75 with a totally new trigger system. The new Omega trigger system simplifies the CZ 75 trigger system, uses fewer parts and improves the trigger pull. In addition, it allows users to choose between using the handgun with a decocking lever (installed) or a manual safety (included) by a simple parts change. The polymer frame design of the Duty and a new sleek slide profile (fully machined from bar stock) reduce weight, making the P-07 Duty a great choice for concealed carry.
Price: **$524.00**

CZ P-09 DUTY
Calibers: 9mm, .40 S&W. **Capacity:** 19 (9mm), 15 (.40). **Features:** High-capacity version of P-07. Accessory rail, interchangeable grip backstraps, ambidextrous decocker can be converted to manual safety.
Price: **$544.00**

CZ 75 TACTICAL SPORT
Similar to the CZ 75 B except the CZ 75 TS is a competition ready pistol designed for IPSC standard division (USPSA limited division). Fixed target sights, tuned single-action operation, lightweight polymer match trigger with adjustments for take-up and overtravel, competition hammer, extended magazine catch, ambidextrous manual safety, checkered walnut grips, polymer magazine well, two-tone finish. Introduced 2005. Imported from the Czech Republic by CZ-USA.
Price: 9mm, 20-shot mag. **$1,310.00**
Price: .40 S&W, 16-shot mag. **$1,310.00**

CZ 75 SP-01
Similar to NATO-approved CZ 75 Compact P-01 model. Features an integral 1913 accessory rail on the dust cover, rubber grip panels, black Polycoat finish, extended beavertail, new grip geometry with checkering on front and back straps, and double or single action operation. Introduced 2005. The Shadow variant designed as an IPSC "production" division competition firearm. Includes competition hammer, competition rear sight and fiber-optic front sight, modified slide release, lighter recoil and mainspring for use with "minor power factor" competition ammunition. Includes Polycoat finish and slim walnut grips. Finished by CZ Custom Shop. Imported from the Czech Republic by CZ-USA.
Price: SP-01 Standard **$680.00**
Price: SP-01 Shadow Target II **$1,638.00**

CZ 97 B
Caliber: .45 ACP. **Capacity:** 10-round magazine. **Barrel:** 4.85 in. **Weight:** 40 oz. **Length:** 8.34 in. overall. **Grips:** Checkered walnut. **Sights:** Fixed. **Features:** Single action/double action; full-length slide rails; screw-in barrel bushing; linkless barrel; all-steel construction; chamber loaded indicator; dual transfer bars. Introduced 1999. Imported from the Czech Republic by CZ-USA.
Price: Black polymer **$707.00**
Price: Glossy blue **$727.00**

CZ 97 BD DECOCKER
Similar to the CZ 97 B except has a decocking lever in place of the safety lever. Tritium night sights. Rubber grips. All other specifications are the same. Introduced 1999. Imported from the Czech Republic by CZ-USA.
Price: 9mm, black polymer **$816.00**

CZ 2075 RAMI/RAMI P
Calibers: 9mm, .40 S&W. **Barrel:** 3 in. **Weight:** 25 oz. **Length:** 6.5 in. overall. **Grips:** Rubber. **Sights:** Blade front with dot, white outline rear drift adjustable for windage. **Features:** Single action/double action; alloy or polymer frame, steel slide; has laser sight mount. Imported from the Czech Republic by CZ-USA.
Price: 9mm, alloy frame, 10- and 14-shot magazines **$671.00**
Price: .40 S&W, alloy frame, 8-shot magazine **$671.00**
Price: RAMI P, polymer frame, 9mm, .40 S&W **$612.00**

CZ P-01
Caliber: 9mm. **Capacity:** 14-round magazine. **Barrel:** 3.85 in. **Weight:** 27 oz. **Length:** 7.2 in. overall. **Grips:** Checkered rubber. **Sights:** Blade front with dot, white outline rear drift adjustable for windage. **Features:** Based on the CZ 75, except with forged aircraft-grade aluminum alloy frame. Hammer forged barrel, decocker, firing-pin block, M3 rail, dual slide serrations, squared trigger guard, re-contoured trigger, lanyard loop on butt. Serrated front and backstrap. Introduced 2006. Imported from the Czech Republic by CZ-USA.
Price: CZ P-01 .... **$680.00**

CZ 805 BREN S1
Calibers: 5.56 NATO or .300 AAC Blackout. **Capacity:** 30-round capacity. **Barrel:** 11 in. **Weight:** 6.7 lbs. **Features:** Semi-automatic version of 9mm. 20-round magazine. Semi-automatic version of Czech military large-frame pistol. Uses AR-type magazines. Aluminum frame, adjustable sights, accessory rails.
Price: **$1,799.00**

CZ SCORPION EVO

Caliber: 9mm. **Capacity:** 20-round magazine. **Features:** Semi-automatic version of CZ Scorpion Evo submachine gun. Ambidextrous controls, adjustable sights, accessory rails.

Price: $849.00

DAN WESSON DW RZ-10

Caliber: 10mm. **Capacity:** 9-round magazine. **Barrel:** 5 in. **Grips:** Diamond checkered cocobolo. **Sights:** Bo-Mar-style adjustable target sight. **Weight:** 38.3 oz. **Length:** 8.8 in. overall. **Features:** Stainless steel frame and serrated slide. Series 70-style 1911, stainless steel frame, forged stainless steel slide. Commander-style match hammer. Reintroduced 2005. Made in USA by Dan Wesson Firearms, distributed by CZ-USA.

Price: 10mm, 8+1 .... $1,558.00

DAN WESSON DW RZ-45 HERITAGE

Caliber: .45 ACP. **Capacity:** 7-round magazine. **Weight:** 36 oz. **Length:** 8.8 in. overall. Similar to the RZ-10 Auto except in .45 ACP.

Price: 10mm, 8+1 .... $1,428.00

DAN WESSON VALOR 1911

Calibers: 9mm, .40 S&W, .45 ACP. **Barrel:** 5 in. **Grips:** Slim Line G10. **Sights:** Heinie Ledge Straight Eight adjustable night sights. **Weight:** 2.4 lbs. **Length:** 8.8 in. overall. **Features:** The defensive-style Valor is a base stainless 1911 with matte black finish. Other features include forged stainless frame and match barrel with 25 LPI checkering and undercut trigger guard, adjustable defensive night sights, and Slim Line VZ grips. Silverback model has polished stainless slide and matte black frame Made in USA by Dan Wesson Firearms, distributed by CZ-USA.

Price: $2,012.00
Price: 10mm $2,271.00
Price: Silverback .... $1,883.00–$2,064.00

DAN WESSON SPECIALIST

Caliber: .45 ACP. **Capacity:** 8-round magazine. **Barrel:** 5 in. **Grips:** G10 VZ Operator II. **Sights:** Single amber tritium dot rear, green lamp with white target ring front sight. **Features:** Integral Picatinny rail, 25 LPI frontstrap checkering, undercut trigger guard, ambidextrous thumb safety, extended mag release and detachable two-piece mag well.

Price: $1,701.00

DAN WESSON V-BOB

Caliber: .45 ACP. **Capacity:** 8-round magazine. **Barrel:** 4.25 in. **Weight:** 34 oz. **Length:** 8 in. **Grips:** Slim Line G10. **Sights:** Heinie Ledge Straight-Eight Night Sights. **Features:** Black matte or stainless finish. Bobtail forged grip frame with 25 LPI checkering front and rear.

Price: $2,077.00

DAN WESSON VALKYRIE

Caliber: .45 ACP. **Barrel:** 4.25 in. **Length:** 7.75 in. **Grips:** Slim Line G10. **Sights:** Tritium Night Sights. **Features:** Similar to V-Bob except has Commander-size slide on Officer-size frame.

Price: $2,012.00

DAN WESSON POINTMAN

Calibers: 9mm, .38 Super, .45 ACP. **Capacity:** 8 or 9-round magazine. **Barrel:** 5 in. **Length:** 8.5 in. **Grips:** Double-diamond cocobolo. **Sights:** Adjustable rear and fiber optic front. **Features:** Undercut trigger guard, checkered front strap, serrated rib on top of slide.

Price: .45, .38 Super $1,597.00
Price: 9mm $1,558.00

DAN WESSON A2

Caliber: .45 ACP. **Capacity:** 8-round magazine capacity. Limited production model based on traditional 1911A1 design. **Features:** Modern fixed combat sights, lowered/flared ejection port, double-diamond walnut grips. Introduced 2017.

Price: $1,363.00

Prices given are believed to be accurate at time of publication however, many factors affect retail pricing so exact prices are not possible.

DESERT EAGLE 1911 G
Caliber: .45 ACP. **Capacity:** 8-round magazine. **Barrels:** 5 in. or 4.33 in. (DE1911C Commander size), or 3.0 in. (DE1911U Undercover). **Grips:** Double diamond checkered wood. **Features:** Extended beavertail grip safety, checkered flat mainspring housing, skeletonized hammer and trigger, extended mag release and thumb safety, stainless full-length guide road, enlarged ejection port, beveled mag well and high-profile sights. Comes with two 8-round magazines.
Price: $904.00
Price: Undercover.. $1,019.00

DESERT EAGLE MARK XIX
Calibers: .357 Mag., 9 rounds; .44 Mag., 8 rounds; .50 AE, 7 rounds. **Barrels:** 6 in., 10 in., interchangeable. **Weight:** 62 oz. (.357 Mag.); 69 oz. (.44 Mag.); 72 oz. (.50 AE) **Length:** 10.25-in. overall (6-in. bbl.). **Grips:** Polymer; rubber available. **Sights:** Blade-on-ramp front, combat-style rear. Adjustable available. **Features:** Interchangeable barrels; rotating three-lug bolt; ambidextrous safety; adjustable trigger. Military epoxy finish. Satin, bright nickel, chrome, brushed, matte or black-oxide finishes available. 10-in. barrel extra. Imported from Israel by Magnum Research, Inc.
Price: .... $1,572.00–$2,060.00

BABY DESERT EAGLE III
Calibers: 9mm, .40 S&W, .45 ACP. **Capacities:** 10-, 12- or 15-round magazines. **Barrels:** 3.85 in. or 4.43 in. **Weights:** 28–37.9 oz. **Length:** 7.25–8.25 overall. **Grips:** Ergonomic polymer. **Sights:** White 3-dot system. **Features:** Choice of steel or polymer frame with integral rail; slide-mounted decocking safety. Upgraded design of Baby Eagle II series.
Price: .... $646.00–$691.00

DESERT EAGLE L5
Caliber: .357 Magnum. **Capacity:** 9+1. **Barrel:** 5 in. **Weight:** 50 oz. **Length:** 9.7 in. **Features:** Steel barrel, frame and slide with full Weaver-style accessory rail and integral muzzle brake. Gas-operated rotating bolt, single-action trigger, fixed sights.
Price: From $1,790.00

DESERT EAGLE MR9, MR40
Caliber: 9mm, (15-round magazine) or .40 S&W (11 rounds). **Barrel:** 4.5 in. **Weight:** 25 oz. **Length:** 7.6 in. overall. **Sights:** Three-dot rear sight adjustable for windage, interchangeable front sight blades of different heights. **Features:** Polymer frame, locked breech, striker-fired design with decocker/safety button on top of slide, three replaceable grip palm swells, Picatinny rail. Made in Germany by Walther and imported by Magnum Research. Introduced 2014.
Price: $559.00

DIAMONDBACK DB380
Caliber: .380 ACP. **Capacity:** 6+1. **Barrel:** 2.8 in. **Weight:** 8.8 oz. **Features:** ZERO-Energy striker firing system with a mechanical firing pin block, steel magazine catch, windage-adjustable sights. Frames available with several color finish options.
Price: .... $290.00–$350.00

DIAMONDBACK DB9
Caliber: 9mm. **Capacity:** 6+1. **Barrel:** 3 in. **Weight:** 11 oz. **Length:** 5.60 in. **Features:** Other features similar to DB380 model.
Price: .... $290.00–$350.00

DIAMONDBACK DB FS NINE
Caliber: 9mm. **Capacity:** 15+1. **Barrel:** 4.75 in. **Weight:** 21.5 oz. **Length:** 7.8 in. **Features:** Double-action, striker-fired model with polymer frame and stainless steel slide. Flared mag well, extended magazine base pad, ergonomically contoured grip, fixed 3-dot sights, front and rear slide serrations, integral MIL-STD 1913 Picatinny rail.
Price: $483.00

DOUBLESTAR 1911 SERIES
Caliber: .45 ACP. **Capacity:** 8-round magazine. **Barrels:** 3.5 in., 4.25 in., 5 in. **Weights:** 33–40 oz. **Grips:** Cocobolo wood. **Sights:** Novak LoMount 2 white-dot rear, Novak white-dot front. **Features:** Single action, M1911-style with forged frame and slide of 4140 steel, stainless steel barrel machined from bar stock by Storm Lake, funneled mag well, accessory rail, black Nitride finish.
Price: .... **$1,364.00–$2,242.00**

EAA WITNESS FULL SIZE
Calibers: 9mm, .38 Super. **Capacity:** 18-round magazine; .40 S&W, 10mm, 15-round magazine; .45 ACP, 10-round magazine. **Barrel:** 4.5 in. **Weight:** 35.33 oz. **Length:** 8.1 in. overall. **Grips:** Checkered rubber. **Sights:** Undercut blade front, open rear adjustable for windage. **Features:** Double-action/single-action trigger system; round trigger guard; frame-mounted safety. Available with steel or polymer frame. Also available with interchangeable .45 ACP and .22 LR slides. Steel frame introduced 1991. Polymer frame introduced 2005. Imported from Italy by European American Armory.
Price: Steel frame **$607.00**
Price: Polymer frame **$571.00**
Price: 45/22 .22 LR, full-size steel frame, blued **$752.00**

EAA WITNESS COMPACT
Caliber: 9mm. **Capacity:** 14-round magazine; .40 S&W, 10mm, 12-round magazine; .45 ACP, 8-round magazine. **Barrel:** 3.6 in. **Weight:** 30 oz. **Length:** 7.3 in. overall. **Features:** Available with steel or polymer frame (shown). All polymer frame Witness pistols are capable of being converted to other calibers. Otherwise similar to full-size Witness. Imported from Italy by European American Armory.
Price: Polymer frame **$571.00**
Price: Steel frame **$607.00**

EAA WITNESS-P CARRY
Caliber: 9mm. **Capacity:** 17-round magazine; 10mm, 15-round magazine; .45 ACP, 10-round magazine. **Barrel:** 3.6 in. **Weight:** 27 oz. **Length:** 7.5 in. overall. **Features:** Otherwise similar to full-size Witness. Polymer frame introduced 2005. Imported from Italy by European American Armory.
Price: **$711.00**

EAA WITNESS PAVONA COMPACT POLYMER
Calibers: .380 ACP (13-round magazine), 9mm (13) or .40 S&W (9). **Barrel:** 3.6 in. **Weight:** 30 oz. **Length:** 7 in. overall. **Features:** Designed primarily for women with fine-tuned recoil and hammer springs for easier operation, a polymer frame with integral checkering, contoured lines and in black, charcoal, blue, purple or magenta with silver or gold sparkle.
Price: .... **$476.00–$528.00**

EAA WITNESS ELITE 1911
Caliber: .45 ACP. **Capacity:** 8-round magazine. **Barrel:** 5 in. **Weight:** 32 oz. **Length:** 8.58 in. overall. **Features:** Full-size 1911-style pistol with either steel or polymer frame. Also available in Commander or Officer's models with 4.25- or 3.5-in. barrel, polymer frame.
Price: **$580.00**
Price: Commander or Officer's Model............ **$627.00**

EAA SAR B6P
Caliber: 9mm. Based on polymer frame variation of CZ 75 design. Manufactured by Sarsilmaz in Turkey. Features similar to Witness series.
Price: .... **$407.00–$453.00**

EAA SAR K2-45
Caliber: .45 ACP. **Barrel:** 4.7 in. **Weight:** 2.5 lbs. **Features:** Similar to B6P with upgraded features. Built by Sarsilmaz for the Turkish military. Features include a cocked and locked carry system, ergonomically designed grip, steel frame and slide construction, adjustable rear sight, extended beaver tail, serrated trigger guard and frame, removable dove-tail front sight, auto firing pin block and low barrel axis for reduced felt recoil.
Price: **$849.00**

ED BROWN CLASSIC CUSTOM
Caliber: .45 ACP. **Capacity:** 7-round magazine. **Barrel:** 5 in. **Weight:** 40 oz. **Grips:** Cocobolo wood. **Sights:** Bo-Mar adjustable rear, dovetail front. **Features:** Single action, M1911 style, custom made to order, stainless frame and slide available. Special mirror-finished slide.
Price: From **$3,695.00**

ED BROWN KOBRA AND KOBRA CARRY
Caliber: .45 ACP. **Capacity:** 7-round magazine. **Barrels:** 5 in. (Kobra); 4.25 in. (Kobra Carry). **Weight:** 39 oz. (Kobra); 34 oz. (Kobra Carry). **Grips:** Hogue exotic wood. **Sights:** Ramp, front; fixed Novak low-mount night sights, rear. **Features:** Snakeskin pattern serrations on forestrap and mainspring housing, dehorned edges, beavertail grip safety.
Price: Kobra K-SS, From **$2,695.00**
Price: Kobra Carry, From **$2,945.00**

ED BROWN KOBRA CARRY LIGHTWEIGHT
Caliber: .45 ACP. **Capacity:** 7-round magazine. **Barrel:** 4.25 in. (Commander model slide). **Weight:** 27 oz. **Grips:** Hogue exotic wood. **Sights:** 10-8 Performance U-notch plain black rear sight with .156-in. notch for fast acquisition of close targets. Fixed dovetail front night sight with high-visibility white outlines. **Features:** Aluminum frame and bobtail housing. Matte finished Gen III coated slide for low glare, with snakeskin on rear of slide only. Snakeskin pattern serrations on forestrap and mainspring housing, dehorned edges, beavertail grip safety. LW insignia on slide, which stands for Lightweight.
Price: Kobra Carry Lightweight **$3,495.00**

ED BROWN EXECUTIVE SERIES
Similar to other Ed Brown products, but with 25-LPI checkered frame and mainspring housing. Various finish, sight and grip options.
Price: .... **$2,695.00–$3,395.00**

ED BROWN SPECIAL FORCES
Similar to other Ed Brown products, but with ChainLink treatment on forestrap and mainspring housing. Entire gun coated with Gen III finish. Square cut serrations on rear of slide only. Dehorned. Introduced 2006. Available with various finish, sight and grip options.
Price: From .... **$2,156.00–$4,675.00**

ED BROWN SPECIAL FORCES CARRY
Similar to the Special Forces basic models. Features a 4.5-in. Commander Bobtail frame. Weighs approx. 35 oz. Fixed dovetail 3-dot night sights with high-visibility white outlines.
Price: From **$2,695.00**

EXCEL ARMS MP-22
Caliber: .22 WMR. **Capacity:** 9-round magazine. **Barrel:** 8.5-in. bull barrel. **Weight:** 54 oz. **Length:** 12.875 in. overall. **Grips:** Textured black composition. **Sights:** Fully adjustable target sights. **Features:** Made from 17-4 stainless steel, comes with aluminum rib, integral Weaver base, internal hammer, firing pin block. American made, lifetime warranty. Comes with two 9-round stainless steel magazines and a California-approved cable lock. .22 WMR Introduced 2006. Made in USA by Excel Arms.
Price: **$477.00**

EXCEL ARMS MP-5.7
Caliber: 5.7x28mm. **Capacity:** 9-round magazine. **Features:** Blowback action. Other features similar to MP-22. Red-dot optic sights, scope and rings are optional.
Price: **$615.00**
Price: With optic sights........ **$685.00**
Price: With scope and rings........ **$711.00**

FIRESTORM 380
Caliber: .380 ACP. **Capacity:** 7+1. **Barrel:** 3.5 in. **Weight:** 20 oz. **Length:** 6.6 in. **Sights:** Fixed, white outline system. **Grips**: Rubber. **Finish:** Black matte. **Features:** Traditional DA/SA operation.
Price: **$270.00**

FMK 9C1 G2
Caliber: 9mm. **Capacity:** 10+1 or 14+1. **Barrel:** 4 in. **Overall length:** 6.85 in. **Weight:** 23.45 oz. **Finish:** Black, Flat Dark Earth or pink. **Sights:** Interchangeable Glock compatible. **Features:** Available in either single action or double action only. Polymer frame, high-carbon steel slide, stainless steel barrel. Very low bore axis and shock absorbing backstrap are said to result in low felt recoil. DAO model has Fast Action Trigger (FAT) with shorter pull and reset. Made in the USA.
Price: **$409.95**

FN FNS SERIES
Caliber: 9mm. **Capacity:** 17-round magazine, .40 S&W (14-round magazine). **Barrels:** 4 in. or 3.6 in. (Compact). **Weights:** 25 oz. (9mm), 27.5 oz. (.40). **Length:** 7.25 in. **Grips:** Integral polymer with two interchangeable backstrap inserts. **Features:** Striker fired, double action with manual safety, accessory rail, ambidextrous controls, 3-dot night sights.
Price: **$599.00**

FN FNX SERIES
Calibers: 9mm, .40 S&W. **Capacities:** 17-round magazine, .40 S&W (14 rounds), .45 ACP (10 or 14 rounds). **Barrels:** 4 in. (9mm and .40), 4.5 in. .45. **Weights:** 22–32 oz. (.45). **Lengths:** 7.4, 7.9 in. (.45). **Features:** DA/SA operation with decocking/manual safety lever. Has external extractor with loaded-chamber indicator, front and rear cocking serrations, fixed 3-dot combat sights.
Price: 9mm, .40 .... **$699.00**
Price: .45 ACP **$824.00**

FN FNX .45 TACTICAL
Similar to standard FNX .45 except with 5.3-in. barrel with threaded muzzle, polished chamber and feed ramp, enhanced high-profile night sights, slide cut and threaded for red-dot sight (not included), MIL-STD 1913 accessory rail, ring-style hammer.
Price: **$1,400.00**

FN FIVE-SEVEN
Caliber: 5.7x28mm. **Capacity:** 10- or 20-round magazine. **Barrel:** 4.8 in. **Weight:** 23 oz. **Length:** 8.2 in. **Features:** Adjustable three-dot system. Single-action polymer frame, chambered for low-recoil 5.7x28mm cartridge.
Price: **$1,349.00**

GLOCK 17/17C
Caliber: 9mm. **Capacities:** 17/19/33-round magazines. **Barrel:** 4.49 in. **Weight:** 22.04 oz. (without magazine). **Length:** 7.32 in. overall. **Grips:**

Black polymer. **Sights:** Dot on front blade, white outline rear adjustable for windage. **Features:** Polymer frame, steel slide; double-action trigger with Safe Action system; mechanical firing pin safety, drop safety; simple takedown without tools; locked breech, recoil operated action. ILS designation refers to Internal Locking System. Adopted by Austrian armed forces 1983. NATO approved 1984. Model 17L has 6-inch barrel, ported or non-ported, slotted and relieved slide, checkered grip with finger grooves, no accessory rail. Imported from Austria by Glock, Inc. USA.
Price: From **$599.00**
Price: 17L **$750.00**
Price: 17 Gen 4 .... **$649.00**
Price: 17 Gen 5 .... **$599.99**

GLOCK GEN4 SERIES
In 2010, a new series of Generation 4 pistols was introduced with several improved features. These included a multiple backstrap system offering three different size options, short, medium or large frame; reversible and enlarged magazine release; dual recoil springs; and RTF (Rough Textured Finish) surface. Some recent models are only available in Gen 4 configuration.

GEN 5 SERIES
A new frame design was introduced in 2017 named Generation 5. The finger grooves were removed for more versatility and the user can customize the grip by using different backstraps, as with the Gen 4 models. A flared mag well and a cutout at the front of the frame give the user more speed during reloading. There is a reversible and enlarged magazine catch, changeable by users, as well as the ambidextrous slide stop lever to accommodate left- and right-handed operators. The rifling and crown of the barrel are slightly modified for increased precision. As of 2018, Gen 5 variants are available in Glock Models 17, 19, 26 and 34.

GLOCK 19/19C
Caliber: 9mm. **Capacities:** 15/17/19/33-round magazines. **Barrel:** 4.02 in. **Weight:** 20.99 oz. (without magazine). **Length:** 6.85 in. overall. Compact version of Glock 17. Imported from Austria by Glock, Inc.
Price: **$599.00**
Price: 19 Gen 4 .... **$649.00**
Price: 19 Gen 5 .... **$749.00**

GLOCK 20/20C 10MM
Caliber: 10mm. **Capacity:** 15-round magazine. **Barrel:** 4.6 in. **Weight:** 27.68 oz. (without magazine). **Length:** 7.59 in. overall. **Features:** Otherwise similar to Model 17. Imported from Austria by Glock, Inc. Introduced 1990.
Price: From **$637.00**
Price: 20 Gen 4 .... **$687.00**

GLOCK MODEL 20 SF SHORT FRAME
Caliber: 10mm. **Barrel:** 4.61 in. with hexagonal rifling. **Weight:** 27.51 oz. **Length:** 8.07 in. overall. **Sights:** Fixed. **Features:** Otherwise similar to the Model 20 but with short-frame design, extended sight radius.
Price: **$637.00**

GLOCK 21/21C
Caliber: .45 ACP. **Capacity:** 13-round magazine. **Barrel:** 4.6 in. **Weight:** 26.28 oz. (without magazine). **Length:** 7.59 in. overall. **Features:** Otherwise similar to the Model 17. Imported from Austria by Glock, Inc. Introduced 1991. SF version has tactical rail, smaller diameter grip, 10-round magazine capacity. Introduced 2007.
Price: From **$637.00**
Price: 21 Gen 4 .... **$687.00**

GLOCK 22/22C
Caliber: .40 S&W. **Capacities:** 15/17-round magazine. **Barrel:** 4.49 in. **Weight:** 22.92 oz. (without magazine). **Length:** 7.32 in. overall. **Features:** Otherwise similar to Model 17, including pricing. Imported from Austria by Glock, Inc. Introduced 1990.
Price: From **$599.00**
Price: 22C **$649.00**
Price: 22 Gen 4 .... **$649.00**

GLOCK 23/23C
Caliber: .40 S&W. **Capacities:** 13/15/17-round magazine. **Barrel:** 4.02 in. **Weight:** 21.16 oz. (without magazine). **Length:** 6.85 in. overall. **Features:** Otherwise similar to the Model 22, including pricing. Compact version of Glock 22. Imported from Austria by Glock, Inc. Introduced 1990.
Price: **$599.00**
Price: 23C Compensated **$621.00**
Price: 23 Gen 4 .... **$649.00**

GLOCK 24/24C
Caliber: .40 S&W. **Capacities:** 10/15/17 or 22-round magazine. **Features:** Similar to Model 22 except with 6.02-inch barrel, ported or non-ported, trigger pull recalibrated to 4.5 lbs.
Price: From **$750.00**

GLOCK 26
Caliber: 9mm. **Capacities:** 10/12/15/17/19/33-round magazine. **Barrel:** 3.46 in. **Weight:** 19.75 oz. **Length:** 6.29 in. overall. Subcompact version of Glock 17. Imported from Austria by Glock, Inc.
Price: **$599.00**
Price: 26 Gen 4 .... **$649.00**
Price: 26 Gen 5 .... **$749.00**

GLOCK 27
Caliber: .40 S&W. **Capacities:** 9/11/13/15/17-round magazine. **Barrel:** 3.46 in. **Weight:** 19.75 oz. (without magazine). **Length:** 6.29 overall. **Features:** Otherwise similar to the Model 22, including pricing. Subcompact version of Glock 22. Imported from Austria by Glock, Inc. Introduced 1996.
Price: From **$599.00**
Price: 27 Gen 4 .... **$649.00**

GLOCK 29 GEN 4
Caliber: 10mm. **Capacities:** 10/15-round magazine. **Barrel:** 3.78 in. **Weight:** 24.69 oz. (without magazine). **Length:** 6.77 in. overall. **Features:** Otherwise similar to the Model 20, including pricing. Subcompact version of the Glock 20. Imported from Austria by Glock, Inc. Introduced 1997.
Price: Fixed sight **$637.00**

GLOCK MODEL 29 SF SHORT FRAME
Caliber: 10mm. **Barrel:** 3.78 in. with hexagonal rifling. **Weight:** 24.52 oz. **Length:** 6.97 in. overall. **Sights:** Fixed. **Features:** Otherwise similar to the Model 29 but with short-frame design, extended sight radius.
Price: **$637.00**

GLOCK 30 GEN 4
Caliber: .45 ACP. **Capacities:** 9/10/13-round magazines. **Barrel:** 3.78 in. **Weight:** 23.99 oz. (without magazine). **Length:** 6.77 in. overall. **Features:** Otherwise similar to the Model 21, including pricing. Subcompact version of the Glock 21. Imported from Austria by Glock, Inc. Introduced 1997. SF version has tactical rail, octagonal rifled barrel with a 1:15.75 rate of twist, smaller diameter grip, 10-round magazine capacity. Introduced 2008.
Price: **$637.00**
Price: 30 SF (short frame) **$637.00**

GLOCK 30S
Caliber: .45 ACP. **Capacity:** 10-round magazine. **Barrel:** 3.78 in. **Weight:** 20 oz. **Length:** 7 in. **Features:** Variation of Glock 30 with a Model 36 slide on a Model 30SF frame (short frame).
Price: **$637.00**

GLOCK 31/31C
Caliber: .357 Auto. **Capacities:** 15/17-round magazine. **Barrel:** 4.49 in. **Weight:** 23.28 oz. (without magazine). **Length:** 7.32 in. overall. **Features:** Otherwise similar to the Model 17. Imported from Austria by Glock, Inc.
Price: From **$599.00**
Price: 31 Gen 4 .... **$649.00**

GLOCK 32/32C
Caliber: .357 Auto. **Capacities:** 13/15/17-round magazine. **Barrel:** 4.02 in. **Weight:** 21.52 oz. (without magazine). **Length:** 6.85 in. overall. **Features:** Otherwise similar to the Model 31. Compact. Imported from Austria by Glock, Inc.
Price: **$599.00**
Price: 32 Gen 4 .... **$649.00**

GLOCK 33
Caliber: .357 Auto. **Capacities:** 9/11/13/15/17-round magazine. **Barrel:** 3.46 in. **Weight:** 19.75 oz. (without magazine). **Length:** 6.29 in. overall. **Features:** Otherwise similar to the Model 31. Subcompact. Imported from Austria by Glock, Inc.
Price: From **$599.00**
Price: 33 Gen 4 .... **$614.00**

GLOCK 34
Caliber: 9mm. **Capacities:** 17/19/33-round magazine. **Barrel:** 5.32 in. **Weight:** 22.9 oz. **Length:** 8.15 in. overall. **Features:** Competition version of Glock 17 with extended barrel, slide, and sight radius dimensions. Available with MOS (Modular Optic System).
Price: From **$679.00**
Price: MOS **$840.00**
Price: 34 Gen 4 .... **$729.00**
Price: 34 Gen 5 .... **$899.00**

GLOCK 35
Caliber: .40 S&W. **Capacities:** 15/17-round magazine. **Barrel:** 5.32 in. **Weight:** 24.52 oz. (without magazine). **Length:** 8.15 in. overall. **Sights:** Adjustable. **Features:** Otherwise similar to the Model 22. Competition version of the Glock 22 with extended barrel, slide and sight radius dimensions. Available with MOS (Modular Optic System). Introduced 1996.
Price: From **$679.00**
Price: MOS **$840.00**
Price: 35 Gen 4 .... **$729.00**

GLOCK 36
Caliber: .45 ACP. **Capacity:** 6-round magazine. **Barrel:** 3.78 in. **Weight:** 20.11 oz. (without magazine). **Length:** 6.77 overall. **Sights:** Fixed. **Features:** Single-stack magazine, slimmer grip than Glock 21/30. Subcompact. Imported from Austria by Glock, Inc. Introduced 1997.
Price: **$637.00**

GLOCK 37
Caliber: .45 GAP. **Capacity:** 10-round magazine. **Barrel:** 4.49 in. **Weight:** 25.95 oz. (without magazine). **Length:** 7.32 overall. **Features:** Otherwise similar to the Model 17. Imported from Austria by Glock, Inc. Introduced 2005.
Price: **$614.00**
Price: 37 Gen 4 .... **$664.00**

GLOCK 38
Caliber: .45 GAP. **Capacities:** 8/10-round magazine. **Barrel:** 4.02 in. **Weight:** 24.16 oz. (without magazine). **Length:** 6.85 overall. **Features:** Otherwise similar to the Model 37. Compact. Imported from Austria by Glock, Inc.
Price: **$614.00**

GLOCK 39
Caliber: .45 GAP. **Capacities:** 6/8/10-round magazine. **Barrel:** 3.46 in. **Weight:** 19.33 oz. (without magazine). **Length:** 6.3 overall. **Features:** Otherwise similar to the Model 37. Subcompact. Imported from Austria by Glock, Inc.
Price: **$614.00**

GLOCK 40 GEN 4
Caliber: 10mm. **Features:** Similar features as the Model 41 except for 6.01-in. barrel. Includes MOS optics.
Price: **$840.00**

GLOCK 41 GEN 4
Caliber: .45 ACP. **Capacity:** 13-round magazine. **Barrel:** 5.31 in. **Weight:** 27 oz. **Length:** 8.9 in. overall. **Features:** This is a long-slide .45 ACP Gen4 model introduced in 2014. Operating features are the same as other Glock models. Available with MOS (Modular Optic System).
Price: **$749.00**
Price: MOS **$840.00**

Prices given are believed to be accurate at time of publication however, many factors affect retail pricing so exact prices are not possible.

GLOCK 42 GEN 4

Caliber: .380 ACP. **Capacity:** 6-round magazine. **Barrel:** 3.25 in. **Weight:** 13.8 oz. **Length:** 5.9 in. overall. **Features:** This single-stack, slimline sub-compact is the smallest pistol Glock has ever made. This is also the first Glock pistol made in the USA.

Price: **$499.00**

GLOCK 43 GEN 4

Caliber: 9mm. **Capacity:** 6+1. **Barrel:** 3.39 in. **Weight:** 17.95 oz. **Length:** 6.26 in. **Height:** 4.25 in. **Width:** 1.02 in. **Features:** Newest member of Glock's Slimline series with single-stack magazine.

Price: **$599.00**

GRAND POWER P-1 MK7

Caliber: 9mm. **Capacity:** 15+1 magazine. **Barrel:** 3.7 in. **Weight:** 26 oz. **Features:** Compact DA/SA pistol featuring frame-mounted safety, steel slide and frame and polymer grips. Offered in several variations and sizes. Made in Slovakia and imported by Eagle Imports.

Price: **$449.99**

GUNCRAFTER INDUSTRIES NO. 1

Calibers: .45 ACP or .50 GI. **Capacity:** 7-round magazine. **Features:** 1911-style series of pistols best known for the proprietary .50 GI chambering. Offered in several common 1911 variations. No. 1 has 5-inch heavy match-grade barrel, 7-round magazine, Parkerized or hard chrome finish, checkered grips and frontstrap, Heinie slant tritium sights. Other models include Commander-style, Officer's Model, Long Slide w/6-inch barrel and several 9mm and .38 Super versions.

Price: .... **$2,695.00–$4,125.00**

HECKLER & KOCH USP

Calibers: 9mm, .40 S&W, .45 ACP. **Capacities:** 15-round magazine; .40 S&W, 13-shot magazine; 45 ACP, 12-shot magazine. **Barrels:** 4.25–4.41 in. **Weight:** 1.65 lbs. **Length:** 7.64–7.87 in. overall. **Grips:** Non-slip stippled black polymer. **Sights:** Blade front, rear adjustable for windage. **Features:** New HK design with polymer frame, modified Browning action with recoil reduction system, single control lever. Special "hostile environment" finish on all metal parts. Available in SA/DA, DAO, left- and right-hand versions. Introduced 1993. .45 ACP Introduced 1995. Imported from Germany by Heckler & Koch, Inc.

Price: USP .45 .... **$1,033.00**

Price: USP .40 and USP 9mm **$952.00**

HECKLER & KOCH USP COMPACT

Calibers: 9mm, .357 SIG, .40 S&W, .45 ACP. **Capacities:** 13-round magazine; .40 S&W and .357 SIG, 12-shot magazine; .45 ACP, 8-shot magazine. **Features:** Similar to the USP except the 9mm, .357 SIG and .40 S&W have 3.58-in. barrels, measure 6.81 in. overall and weigh 1.47 lbs. (9mm). Introduced 1996. .45 ACP measures 7.09 in. overall. Introduced 1998. Imported from Germany by Heckler & Koch, Inc.

Price: USP Compact .45 .... **$1,040.00**

Price: USP Compact 9mm, .40 S&W **$992.00**

HECKLER & KOCH USP45 TACTICAL

Calibers: .40 S&W, .45 ACP. **Capacities:** 13-round magazine; .45 ACP, 12-round magazine. **Barrels:** 4.90-5.09 in. **Weight:** 1.9 lbs. **Length:** 8.64 in. overall. **Grips:** Non-slip stippled polymer. **Sights:** Blade front, fully adjustable target rear. **Features:** Has extended threaded barrel with rubber O-ring; adjustable trigger; extended magazine floorplate; adjustable trigger stop; polymer frame. Introduced 1998. Imported from Germany by Heckler & Koch, Inc.

Price: USP Tactical .45 .... **$1,352.00**

Price: USP Tactical .40 .... **$1,333.00**

HECKLER & KOCH USP COMPACT TACTICAL
Caliber: .45 ACP. **Capacity:** 8-round magazine. **Features:** Similar to the USP Tactical except measures 7.72 in. overall, weighs 1.72 lbs. Introduced 2006. Imported from Germany by Heckler & Koch, Inc.
Price: USP Compact Tactical **$1,352.00**

HECKLER & KOCH HK45
Caliber: .45 ACP. **Capacity:** 10-round magazine. **Barrel:** 4.53 in. **Weight:** 1.73 lbs. **Length:** 7.52 in. overall. **Grips:** Ergonomic with adjustable grip panels. **Sights:** Low profile, drift adjustable. **Features:** Polygonal rifling, ambidextrous controls, operates on improved Browning linkless recoil system. Available in Tactical and Compact variations.
Price: USP Tactical .45 .... **$1,193.00–$1,392.00**

HECKLER & KOCH MARK 23 SPECIAL OPERATIONS
Caliber: .45 ACP. **Capacity:** 12-round magazine. **Barrel:** 5.87 in. **Weight:** 2.42 lbs. **Length:** 9.65 in. overall. **Grips:** Integral with frame; black polymer. **Sights:** Blade front, rear drift adjustable for windage; 3-dot. **Features:** Civilian version of the SOCOM pistol. Polymer frame; double action; exposed hammer; short recoil, modified Browning action. Introduced 1996. Imported from Germany by Heckler & Koch, Inc.
Price: **$2,299.00**

HECKLER & KOCH P30 AND P30L
Calibers: 9mm, .40 S&W. **Capacities:** 13- or 15-round magazines. **Barrels:** 3.86 in. or 4.45 in. (P30L) **Weight:** 26–27.5 oz. **Length:** 6.95, 7.56 in. overall. **Grips:** Interchangeable panels. **Sights:** Open rectangular notch rear sight with contrast points. **Features:** Ergonomic features include a special grip frame with interchangeable backstrap inserts and lateral plates, allowing the pistol to be individually adapted to any user. Browning-type action with modified short recoil operation. Ambidextrous controls include dual slide releases, magazine release levers and a serrated decocking button located on the rear of the frame (for applicable variants). A Picatinny rail molded into the front of the frame. The extractor serves as a loaded-chamber indicator.
Price: P30 .... **$1,099.00**
Price: P30L Variant 2 Law Enforcement Modification (LEM) enhanced DAO **$1,149.00**
Price: P30L Variant 3 Double Action/Single Action (DA/SA) with Decocker **$1,108.00**

HECKLER & KOCH P2000
Calibers: 9mm, .40 S&W. **Capacities:** 13-round magazine; .40 S&W, 12-shot magazine. **Barrel:** 3.62 in. **Weight:** 1.5 lbs. **Length:** 7 in. overall. **Grips:** Interchangeable panels. **Sights:** Fixed Patridge style, drift adjustable for windage, standard 3-dot. **Features:** Incorporates features of HK USP Compact pistol, including Law Enforcement Modification (LEM) trigger, double-action hammer system, ambidextrous magazine release, dual slide-release levers, accessory mounting rails, recurved, hook trigger guard, fiber-reinforced polymer frame, modular grip with exchangeable backstraps, nitro-carburized finish, lock-out safety device. Introduced 2003. Imported from Germany by Heckler & Koch, Inc.
Price: **$799.00**

HECKLER & KOCH P2000 SK
Calibers: 9mm, .357 SIG, .40 S&W. **Capacities:** 10-round magazine; .40 S&W and .357 SIG, 9-round magazine. **Barrel:** 3.27 in. **Weight:** 1.3 lbs. **Length:** 6.42 in. overall. **Sights:** Fixed Patridge style, drift adjustable. **Features:** Standard accessory rails, ambidextrous slide release, polymer frame, polygonal bore profile. Smaller version of P2000. Introduced 2005. Imported from Germany by Heckler & Koch, Inc.
Price: **$799.00**

HECKLER & KOCH VP9/VP 40
Calibers: 9mm, .40 S&W. **Capacities:** 10- or 15-round magazine. .40 S&W (10 or 13). **Barrel:** 4.09 in. **Weight:** 25.6 oz. **Length:** 7.34 in. overall. **Sights:** Fixed 3-dot, drift adjustable. **Features:** Striker-fired system with HK enhanced light pull trigger. Ergonomic grip design with interchangeable backstraps and side panels.
Price: **$719.00**

HI-POINT FIREARMS MODEL 9MM COMPACT
Caliber: 9mm. **Capacity:** 8-round magazine. **Barrel:** 3.5 in. **Weight:** 25 oz. **Length:** 6.75 in. overall. **Grips:** Textured plastic. **Sights:** Combat-style

adjustable 3-dot system; low profile. **Features:** Single-action design; frame-mounted magazine release; polymer frame. Scratch-resistant matte finish. Introduced 1993. Comps are similar except they have a 4-in. barrel with muzzle brake/compensator. Compensator is slotted for laser or flashlight mounting. Introduced 1998. Made in USA by MKS Supply, Inc.
Price: C-9 9mm **$199.00**

HI-POINT FIREARMS MODEL 380 POLYMER
Caliber: .380 ACP. **Capacities:** 10- and 8-round magazine. **Weight:** 25 oz. **Features:** Similar to the 9mm Compact model except chambered for adjustable 3-dot sights. Polymer frame. Action locks open after last shot. Trigger lock.
Price: CF-380 .... **$179.00**

HI-POINT FIREARMS 40 AND 45 SW/POLYMER
Calibers: .40 S&W, .45 ACP. **Capacities:** .40 S&W, 8-round magazine; .45 ACP, 9 rounds. **Barrel:** 4.5 in. **Weight:** 32 oz. **Length:** 7.72 in. overall. **Sights:** Adjustable 3-dot. **Features:** Polymer frames, last round lock-open, grip-mounted magazine release, magazine disconnect safety, integrated accessory rail, trigger lock. Introduced 2002. Made in USA by MKS Supply, Inc.
Price: **$219.00**

HIGH STANDARD HS-22
Caliber: .22 Long Rifle **Capacity:** 10-round magazine. **Barrels:** 5.5-in. bull or slab-sided. **Weight:** 44 oz. **Length:** 9.5 in. **Grips:** Wood. **Sights:** Adjustable. **Finish:** Flat black or Parkerized gray. **Features:** Removable aluminum rib, adjustable trigger, various custom options available.
Price: From **$900.00**

ITHACA 1911
Caliber: .45 ACP. **Capacity:** 7-round capacity. **Barrels:** 4.25 or 5 in. **Weight:** 35 or 40 oz. **Sights:** Fixed combat or fully adjustable target. **Grips:** Checkered cocobolo with Ithaca logo. Classic 1911A1 style with enhanced features including match-grade barrel, lowered and flared ejection port, extended beavertail grip safety, hand-fitted barrel bushing, two-piece guide rod, checkered front strap.
Price: **$1,575.00**

IVER JOHNSON EAGLE
Calibers: 9mm, .45 ACP. **Features:** Series of 1911-style pistols made in typical variations including full-size (Eagle), Commander (Hawk), Officer's (Thrasher) sizes in .45 ACP and 9mm. Many finishes available, including Cerakote, polished stainless, pink and several snakeskin variations.
Price: .... **$608.00–$959.00**

KAHR CM SERIES
Calibers: 9mm, .40 S&W, .45 ACP. **Capacities:** 9mm (6+1), .40 S&W (6+1). .45 ACP (5+1). CM45 Model is shown. **Barrels:** 3 in., 3.25 in. (45) **Weights:** 15.9–17.3 oz. **Length:** 5.42 in. overall. **Grips:** Textured polymer with integral steel rails molded into frame. **Sights:** CM9093, Pinned in polymer sight; PM9093, drift-adjustable, white bar-dot combat. **Features:** A conventional rifled barrel instead of the match-grade polygonal barrel on Kahr's PM series; the CM slide stop lever is MIM (metal-injection-molded) instead of machined; the CM series slide has fewer machining operations and uses simple engraved markings instead of roll marking. The CM series are shipped with one magazine instead of two. The slide is machined from solid 416 stainless with a matte finish, each gun is shipped with one 6-round stainless steel magazine with a flush baseplate. Magazines are U.S.-made, plasma welded, tumbled to remove burrs and feature Wolff springs. The magazine catch in the polymer frame is all metal and will not wear out on the stainless steel magazine after extended use.
Price: **$460.00**

KAHR MK SERIES MICRO

Similar to the K9/K40 except is 5.35 in. overall, 4 in. high, with a 3.08 in. barrel. Weighs 23.1 oz. Has snag-free bar-dot sights, polished feed ramp, dual recoil spring system, DAO trigger. Comes with 5-round flush baseplate and 6-shot grip extension magazine. Introduced 1998. Made in USA by Kahr Arms.

Price: M9093 MK9, matte stainless steel **$911.00**
Price: M9093N MK9, matte stainless steel, tritium night sights **$1,017.00**
Price: M9098 MK9 Elite 2003, stainless steel **$991.00**
Price: M4043 MK40, matte stainless steel **$911.00**
Price: M4043N MK40, matte stainless steel, tritium night sights **$1,115.00**
Price: M4048 MK40 Elite 2003, stainless steel **$991.00**

KAHR P SERIES

Calibers: .380 ACP, 9mm, .40 S&W, 45 ACP. **Capacity:** 7-shot magazine. **Features:** Similar to K9/K40 steel frame pistol except has polymer frame, matte stainless steel slide. Barrel length 3.5 in.; overall length 5.8 in.; weighs 17 oz. Includes two 7-shot magazines, hard polymer case, trigger lock. Introduced 2000. Made in USA by Kahr Arms.

Price: KP9093 9mm **$762.00**
Price: KP4043 .40 S&W **$762.00**
Price: KP4543 .45 ACP **$829.00**
Price: KP3833 .380 ACP (2008) **$667.00**

KAHR KP GEN 2 PREMIUM SERIES

Calibers: 9mm, .45 ACP. **Capacities:** KP9 9mm (7-shot magazine), KP45 .45 ACP (6 shots). **Barrel**: 3.5 in. **Features:** Black polymer frame, matte stainless slide, Tru-Glo Tritium fiber optic sights, short trigger, accessory rail.

Price: **$976.00**

KAHR TP GEN 2 PREMIUM SERIES

Calibers: 9mm, .45 ACP. **Capacities:** TP9 9mm (8-shot magazine), TP45 .45 ACP (7 or 8 shots). **Barrels:** 4, 5, or 6 in. **Features:** Model with 4-inch barrel has features similar to KP GEN 2. The 5-inch model has front and rear slide serrations, white 3-dot sights, mount for reflex sights. The 6-inch model has the same features plus comes with Leupold Delta Point Reflex sight.

Price: **$976.00**
Price: 5-inch bbl **$1,015.00**
Price: 6-inch bbl **$1,566.00**

KAHR CT 9/40/45 SERIES

Calibers: 9mm, .40 S&W, .45 ACP. **Capacities:** 9mm (8+1), .40 S&W (6+1) .45 ACP (7+1). **Barrel:** 4 in. **Weights:** 20–25 oz. **Length:** 5.42 in. overall. **Grips:** Textured polymer with integral steel rails molded into frame. **Sights:** Drift adjustable, white bar-dot combat. **Features:** Same as Kahr CM Series.

Price: **$460.00**

KAHR CT 380

Caliber: .380 ACP. **Capacity:** (7+1). **Barrel:** 3 in. **Weight**: 14 oz. Other features similar to CT 9/40/45 models.

Price: **$419.00**

KAHR K SERIES

Calibers: K9: 9mm, 7-shot; K40: .40 S&W, 6-shot magazine. **Barrel:** 3.5 in. **Weight:** 25 oz. **Length:** 6 in. overall. **Grips:** Wraparound textured soft polymer. **Sights:** Blade front, rear drift adjustable for windage; bar-dot combat style. **Features:** Trigger-cocking double-action mechanism with passive firing pin block. Made of 4140 ordnance steel with matte black finish. Contact maker for complete price list. Introduced 1994. Made in USA by Kahr Arms.

Price: K9093C K9, matte stainless steel **$855.00**
Price: K9093NC K9, matte stainless steel w/tritium night sights **$985.00**
Price: K9094C K9 matte blackened stainless steel **$891.00**
Price: K9098 K9 Elite 2003, stainless steel **$932.00**
Price: K4043 K40, matte stainless steel **$855.00**
Price: K4043N K40, matte stainless steel w/tritium night sights **$985.00**
Price: K4044 K40, matte blackened stainless steel **$891.00**
Price: K4048 K40 Elite 2003, stainless steel **$932.00**

KAHR PM SERIES

Calibers: 9mm, .40 S&W, .45 ACP. **Capacity:** 7-round magazine. **Features:** Similar to P-Series pistols except has smaller polymer frame (Polymer Micro). Barrel length 3.08 in.; overall length 5.35 in.; weighs 17 oz. Includes two 7-shot magazines, hard polymer case, trigger lock. Introduced 2000. Made in USA by Kahr Arms.

Price: PM9093 PM9 .... **$810.00**
Price: PM4043 PM40 .... **$810.00**
Price: PM4543 PM45 .... **$880.00**

Prices given are believed to be accurate at time of publication however, many factors affect retail pricing so exact prices are not possible.

KAHR T SERIES

Calibers: 9mm, .40 S&W. **Capacities:** T9: 9mm, 8-round magazine; T40: .40 S&W, 7-round magazine. **Barrel:** 4 in. **Weight:** 28.1–29.1 oz. **Length:** 6.5 in. overall. **Grips:** Checkered Hogue Pau Ferro wood grips. **Sights:** Rear: Novak low-profile 2-dot tritium night sight, front tritium night sight. **Features:** Similar to other Kahr makes, but with longer slide and barrel upper, longer butt. Trigger cocking DAO; locking breech; Browning-type recoil lug; passive striker block; no magazine disconnect. Comes with two magazines. Introduced 2004. Made in USA by Kahr Arms.

Price: KT9093 T9 matte stainless steel **$857.00**
Price: KT9093-NOVAK T9, "Tactical 9," Novak night sight **$980.00**
Price: KT4043 40 S&W............ **$857.00**

KAHR CW SERIES

Caliber: 9mm, .40 S&W, .45 ACP. **Capacities:** 9mm, 7-round magazine; .40 S&W and .45 ACP, 6-round magazine. **Barrels:** 3.5 and 3.64 in. **Weight:** 17.7–18.7 oz. **Length:** 5.9–6.36 in. overall. **Grips:** Textured polymer. Similar to P-Series, but CW Series have conventional rifling, metal-injection-molded slide stop lever, no front dovetail cut, one magazine. CW40 introduced 2006. Made in USA by Kahr Arms.

Price: CW9093 CW9 .... **$449.00**
Price: CW4043 CW40 .... **$449.00**
Price: CW4543 CW45 .... **$449.00**

KAHR P380

Caliber: .380 ACP. **Capacity:** 6+1. **Features:** Very small DAO semi-auto pistol. Features include 2.5-in. Lothar Walther barrel; black polymer frame with stainless steel slide; drift adjustable white bar/dot combat/sights; optional tritium sights; two 6+1 magazines. Overall length 4.9 in., weight 10 oz. without magazine.

Price: Standard sights **$667.00**
Price: Night sights............ **$792.00**

KAHR CW380

Caliber: .380 ACP. **Capacity:** 6-round magazine. **Barrel:** 2.58 in. **Weight:** 11.5 oz. **Length:** 4.96 in. **Grips:** Textured integral polymer. **Sights:** Fixed white-bar combat style. **Features:** DAO. Black or purple polymer frame, stainless slide.

Price: **$419.00**

KAHR TIG SPECIAL EDITION

Caliber: 9mm. **Capacity:** 8 rounds. **Weight:** 18.5 oz. **Barrel:** 4 in. (Sub-compact model). **Features:** Limited Special Edition to support Beyond the Battlefield Foundation founded by John "Tig" Tiegen and his wife to provide support for wounded veterans. Tiegen is one of the heroes of the Benghazi attack in 2012. Kryptek Typhon finish on frame, black Teracote finish on slide engraved with Tiegen signature, Tig logo and BTB logo. Production will be limited to 1,000 pistols. Part of the proceeds from the sale of each firearm will be donated to the Beyond the Battlefield Foundation by Kahr Firearms Group.

Price: **$541.00**

KEL-TEC P-11

Caliber: 9mm. **Capacity:** 10-round magazine. **Barrel:** 3.1 in. **Weight:** 14 oz. **Length:** 5.6 in. overall. **Grips:** Checkered black polymer. **Sights:** Blade front, rear adjustable for windage. **Features:** Ordnance steel slide, aluminum frame. DAO trigger mechanism. Introduced 1995. Made in USA by Kel-Tec CNC Industries, Inc.

Price: From **$340.00**

KEL-TEC PF-9
Caliber: 9mm. **Capacity:** 7 rounds. **Weight:** 12.7 oz. **Sights:** Rear sight adjustable for windage and elevation. **Barrel:** 3.1 in. **Length:** 5.85 in. **Features:** Barrel, locking system, slide stop, assembly pin, front sight, recoil springs and guide rod adapted from P-11. Trigger system with integral hammer block and the extraction system adapted from P-3AT. Mil-Std-1913 Picatinny rail. Made in USA by Kel-Tec CNC Industries, Inc.
Price: From **$356.00**

KEL-TEC P-32
Caliber: .32 ACP. **Capacity:** 7-round magazine. **Barrel:** 2.68. **Weight:** 6.6 oz. **Length:** 5.07 overall. **Grips:** Checkered composite. **Sights:** Fixed. **Features:** Double-action-only mechanism with 6-lb. pull; internal slide stop. Textured composite grip/frame.
Price: From **$326.00**

KEL-TEC P-3AT
Caliber: .380 ACP. **Capacity:** 7-round magazine **Weight:** 7.2 oz. **Length:** 5.2. **Features:** Lightest .380 ACP made; aluminum frame, steel barrel.
Price: From **$331.00**

KEL-TEC PLR-16
Caliber: 5.56mm NATO. **Capacity:** 10-round magazine. **Weight:** 51 oz. **Sights:** Rear sight adjustable for windage, front sight is M-16 blade. **Barrel:** 9.2 in. **Length:** 18.5 in. **Features:** Muzzle is threaded 1/2x28 to accept standard attachments such as a muzzle brake. Except for the barrel, bolt, sights and mechanism, the PLR-16 pistol is made of high-impact glass fiber reinforced polymer. Gas-operated semi-auto. Conventional gas-piston operation with M-16 breech locking system. MIL-STD-1913 Picatinny rail. Made in USA by Kel-Tec CNC Industries, Inc.
Price: Blued **$682.00**

KEL-TEC PLR-22
Caliber: .22 LR. **Capacity:** 26-round magazine. **Length:** 18.5 in. overall. 40 oz. **Features:** Semi-auto pistol based on centerfire PLR-16 by same maker. Blowback action. Open sights and Picatinny rail for mounting accessories; threaded muzzle.
Price: **$400.00**

KEL-TEC PMR-30
Caliber: .22 Magnum (.22WMR). **Capacity:** 30 rounds. **Barrel:** 4.3 in. **Weight:** 13.6 oz. **Length:** 7.9 in. overall. **Grips:** Glass reinforced Nylon (Zytel). **Sights:** Dovetailed aluminum with front & rear fiber optics. **Features:** Operates on a unique hybrid blowback/locked-breech system. It uses a double-stack magazine of a new design that holds 30 rounds and fits completely in the grip of the pistol. Dual opposing extractors for reliability, heel magazine release to aid in magazine retention, Picatinny accessory rail under the barrel, Urethane recoil buffer, captive coaxial recoil springs. The barrel is fluted for light weight and effective heat dissipation. PMR30 disassembles for cleaning by removal of a single pin.
Price: **$455.00**

KIMBER MICRO CDP
Caliber: .380 ACP. **Capacity:** 6-round magazine. **Barrel:** 2.75 in. **Weight:** 17 oz. **Grips:** Double diamond rosewood. Mini 1911-style single action with no grip safety.
Price: **$951.00**

KIMBER MICRO CRIMSON CARRY
Caliber: .380 ACP. **Capacity:** 6-round magazine. **Barrel:** 2.75 in. **Weight:** 13.4 oz. **Length:** 5.6 in **Grips:** Black synthetic, double diamond. **Sights:** Fixed low profile. **Finish:** Matte black. **Features:** Aluminum frame with satin silver finish, steel slide, carry-melt treatment, full-length guide rod, rosewood Crimson Trace Lasergrips.
Price: **$747.00**

KIMBER MICRO TLE
Caliber: .380 ACP. **Features:** Similar to Micro Crimson Carry. **Features:** Black slide and frame. Green and black G10 grips.
Price: **$734.00**

KIMBER MICRO RAPTOR
Caliber: .380 ACP **Capacity:** 6-round magazine. **Sights:** Tritium night sights. **Finish:** Stainless. **Features:** Variation of Micro Carry with Raptor-style scalloped "feathered" slide serrations and grip panels.
Price: **$842.00**

KIMBER COVERT SERIES
Caliber: .45 ACP **Capacity:** 7-round magazine. **Barrels:** 3, 4 or 5 in. **Weight:** 25–31 oz. **Grips:** Crimson Trace laser with camo finish. **Sights:** Tactical wedge 3-dot night sights. **Features:** Made in the Kimber Custom Shop.

Finish: Kimber Gray frame, matte black slide, black small parts. Carry Melt treatment. Available in three frame sizes: Custom, Pro and Ultra.
Price: **$1,457.00**

KIMBER CUSTOM II
Caliber: 9mm, .45 ACP. **Barrel:** 5 in. **Weight:** 38 oz. **Length:** 8.7 in. overall. **Grips:** Checkered black rubber, walnut, rosewood. **Sights:** Dovetailed front and rear, Kimber low profile adjustable or fixed sights. **Features:** Slide, frame and barrel machined from steel or stainless steel. Match-grade barrel, chamber and trigger group. Extended thumb safety, beveled magazine well, beveled front and rear slide serrations, high ride beavertail grip safety, checkered flat mainspring housing, kidney cut under trigger guard, high cut grip, match-grade stainless steel barrel bushing, polished breechface, Commander-style hammer, lowered and flared ejection port, Wolff springs, bead blasted black oxide or matte stainless finish. Introduced in 1996. Made in USA by Kimber Mfg., Inc.
Price: Custom II **$871.00**

KIMBER CUSTOM TLE II
Caliber: .45 ACP or 10mm. **Features:** TLE (Tactical Law Enforcement) version of Custom II model plus night sights, frontstrap checkering, threaded barrel, Picatinny rail.
Price: .45 ACP **$1,007.00**
Price: 10mm **$1,028.00**

KIMBER STAINLESS II
Same features as Custom II except has stainless steel frame.
Price: Stainless II .45 ACP **$998.00**
Price: Stainless II 9mm **$1,016.00**
Price: Stainless II .45 ACP w/night sights................ **$1,141.00**
Price: Stainless II Target .45 ACP (stainless, adj. sight) **$1,108.00**

KIMBER PRO CARRY II
Calibers: 9mm, .45 ACP. **Features:** Similar to Custom II, has aluminum frame, 4-in. bull barrel fitted directly to the slide without bushing. Introduced 1998. Made in USA by Kimber Mfg., Inc.
Price: Pro Carry II, .45 ACP **$837.00**
Price: Pro Carry II, 9mm **$857.00**
Price: Pro Carry II w/night sights **$977.00**

KIMBER SAPPHIRE PRO II
Caliber: 9mm. **Capacity:** 9-round magazine. **Features:** Similar to Pro Carry II, 4-inch match-grade barrel. Striking two-tone appearance with satin silver aluminum frame and high polish bright blued slide. Grips are blue/black G-10 with grooved texture. Fixed Tactical Edge night sights. From the Kimber Custom Shop.
Price: **$1,652.00**

KIMBER RAPTOR II
Caliber: .45 ACP. **Capacities:** .45 ACP (8-round magazine, 7-round (Ultra and Pro models). **Barrels:** 3, 4 or 5 in. **Weight:** 25–31 oz. **Grips:** Thin milled rosewood. **Sights:** Tactical wedge 3-dot night sights. **Features:** Made in the Kimber Custom Shop. Matte black or satin silver finish. Available in three frame sizes: Custom (shown), Pro and Ultra.
Price: .... **$1,434.00–$1,568.00**

KIMBER ULTRA CARRY II
Calibers: 9mm, .45 ACP. **Features:** Lightweight aluminum frame, 3-in. match-grade bull barrel fitted to slide without bushing. Grips 0.4-in. shorter. Light recoil spring. Weighs 25 oz. Introduced in 1999. Made in USA by Kimber Mfg., Inc.
Price: Stainless Ultra Carry II .45 ACP **$919.00**
Price: Stainless Ultra Carry II 9mm **$1,016.00**
Price: Stainless Ultra Carry II .45 ACP with night sights **$1,039.00**

KIMBER GOLD MATCH II
Caliber: .45 ACP. **Features:** Similar to Custom II models. Includes stainless steel barrel with match-grade chamber and barrel bushing, ambidextrous thumb safety, adjustable sight, premium aluminum trigger, hand-checkered double diamond rosewood grips. Barrel hand-fitted for target accuracy. Made in USA by Kimber Mfg., Inc.
Price: Gold Match II .45 ACP................ **$1,393.00**
Price: Gold Match Stainless II .45 ACP **$1,574.00**

KIMBER CDP II SERIES

Calibers: 9mm, .45 ACP. **Features:** Similar to Custom II but designed for concealed carry. Aluminum frame. Standard features include stainless steel slide, fixed Meprolight tritium 3-dot (green) dovetail-mounted night sights, match-grade barrel and chamber, 30 LPI frontstrap checkering, two-tone finish, ambidextrous thumb safety, hand-checkered double diamond rosewood grips. Introduced in 2000. Made in USA by Kimber Mfg., Inc.

Price: Ultra CDP II 9mm (2008) **$1,359.00**
Price: Ultra CDP II .45 ACP **$1,318.00**
Price: Compact CDP II .45 ACP **$1,318.00**
Price: Pro CDP II .45 ACP **$1,318.00**
Price: Custom CDP II (5-in. barrel, full length grip) **$1,318.00**

KIMBER CDP

Calibers: 9mm, .45 ACP. **Barrel:** 3, 4 or 5 in. **Weight:** 25–31 oz. **Features:** Aluminum frame, stainless slide, 30 LPI checkering on backstrap and trigger guard, low profile tritium night sights, Carry Melt treatment. **Sights:** Hand checkered rosewood or Crimson Trace Lasergrips. Introduced in 2017.

Price: **$1,173.00**
Price: With Crimson Trace Lasergrips **$1,473.00**

KIMBER ECLIPSE II SERIES

Calibers: .38 Super, 10 mm, .45 ACP. **Features:** Similar to Custom II and other stainless Kimber pistols. Stainless slide and frame, black oxide, two-tone finish. Gray/black laminated grips. 30 LPI frontstrap checkering. All models have night sights; Target versions have Meprolight adjustable Bar/Dot version. Made in USA by Kimber Mfg., Inc.

Price: Eclipse Ultra II (3-in. barrel, short grip) **$1,350.00**
Price: Eclipse Pro II (4-in. barrel, full-length grip) **$1,350.00**
Price: Eclipse Custom II 10mm **$1,350.00**
Price: Eclipse Target II (5-in. barrel, full-length grip, adjustable sight) **$1,393.00**

KIMBER TACTICAL ENTRY II

Caliber: 45 ACP. **Capacity:** 7-round magazine. **Barrel:** 5 in. **Weight:** 40 oz. **Length:** 8.7 in. overall. **Features:** 1911-style semi-auto with checkered frontstrap, extended magazine well, night sights, heavy steel frame, tactical rail.

Price: **$1,490.00**

KIMBER TACTICAL CUSTOM HD II

Caliber: .45 ACP. **Capacity:** 7-round magazine. **Barrel:** 5 in. match-grade. **Weight:** 39 oz. **Length:** 8.7 in. overall. **Features:** 1911-style semiauto with night sights, heavy steel frame.

Price: **$1,387.00**

KIMBER SUPER CARRY PRO

Caliber: .45 ACP. **Capacity:** 8-round magazine. **Features:** 1911-style semi-auto pistol. Ambidextrous thumb safety; Carry Melt profiling; full-length guide rod; aluminum frame with stainless slide; satin silver finish; super carry serrations; 4-inch barrel; micarta laminated grips and tritium night sights.

Price: **$1,596.00**

KIMBER SUPER CARRY HD SERIES

Caliber: .45 ACP. **Features:** Designated as HD (Heavy Duty), each is chambered in .45 ACP and features a stainless steel slide and frame, premium KimPro II finish and night sights with cocking shoulder for one-hand operation. Like the original Super Carry pistols, HD models have directional serrations on slide, frontstrap and mainspring housing for unequaled control under recoil. A round heel frame and Carry Melt treatment make them comfortable to carry and easy to conceal.

KIMBER SUPER CARRY ULTRA HD

Caliber: .45 ACP. **Capacity:** 7-round magazine. **Barrel:** 3 in. **Weight:** 32 oz. **Length:** 6.8 in. overall. **Grips:** G-10, Checkered with border. **Sights:** Night sights with cocking shoulder radius 4.8 in. **Features:** Rugged stainless slide and frame with KimPro II finish. Aluminum match-grade trigger with a factory setting of approximately 4-5 pounds.

Price: **$1,699.00**

Prices given are believed to be accurate at time of publication however, many factors affect retail pricing so exact prices are not possible.

KIMBER SUPER CARRY PRO HD
Caliber: .45 ACP. **Capacity:** 8-round magazine. **Barrel:** 4 in. **Weight:** 35 oz. **Length:** 7.7 in. overall. **Features:** Same as Super Carry Ultra HD model.
Price: **$1,699.00**

KIMBER SUPER CARRY CUSTOM HD
Caliber: .45 ACP. **Capacity:** 8-round magazine. **Barrel:** 5. **Weight:** 38 oz. **Length:** 8.7 overall. **Grips:** G-10, Checkered with border. **Sights:** Night sights with cocking shoulder radius 4.8 in. **Features:** Rugged stainless steel slide and frame with KimPro II finish. Aluminum match grade trigger with a factory setting of approximately 4-5 pounds.
Price: **$1,625.00**

KIMBER ULTRA CDP II
Calibers: 9mm, .45 ACP. **Capacities:** 7-round magazine (9 in 9mm). **Features:** Compact 1911-style pistol; ambidextrous thumb safety; carry melt profiling; full-length guide rod; aluminum frame with stainless slide; satin silver finish; checkered frontstrap; 3-inch barrel; rosewood double diamond Crimson Trace laser grips; tritium 3-dot night sights.
Price: **$1,603.00**

KIMBER STAINLESS ULTRA TLE II
Caliber: .45 ACP. **Capacity:** 7-round magazine. **Features:** 1911-style semi-auto pistol. Features include full-length guide rod; aluminum frame with stainless slide; satin silver finish; checkered frontstrap; 3-in. barrel; tactical gray double diamond grips; tritium 3-dot night sights.
Price: **$1,136.00**

KIMBER ROYAL II
Caliber: .45 ACP. **Capacity:** 7-round magazine. **Barrel:** 5 in. **Weight:** 38 oz. **Length:** 8.7 in. overall. **Grips:** Solid bone-smooth. **Sights:** Fixed low profile. **Features:** A classic full-size pistol wearing a charcoal blue finish complimented with solid bone grip panels. Front and rear serrations. Aluminum match-grade trigger with a factory setting of approximately 4–5 pounds.
Price: **$1,785.00**

KIMBER MASTER CARRY SERIES
Caliber: .45 ACP. **Capacity:** 8-round magazine, 9mm (Pro only). **Barrels:** 5 in. (Custom), 4 in. (Pro), 3 in. (Ultra) **Weight:** 25–30 oz. **Grips:** Crimson Trace Laser. **Sights:** Fixed low profile. **Features:** Matte black KimPro slide, aluminum round heel frame, full-length guide rod.
Price: **$1,497.00**

KIMBER WARRIOR SOC

Caliber: .45 ACP. **Capacity:** 7-round magazine. **Barrel:** 5 in threaded for suppression. **Sights:** Fixed Tactical Wedge tritium. **Finish:** Dark Green frame, Flat Dark Earth slide. **Features:** Full-size 1911 based on special series of pistols made for USMC. Service melt, ambidextrous safety.

Price: **$1,392.00**

KIMBER SUPER JAGARE

Caliber: 10mm. **Capacity:** 8+1. **Barrel:** 6 in, ported. **Weight:** 42 oz. **Finish:** Stainless steel KimPro, Charcoal gray frame, diamond-like carbon coated slide. Slide is ported. **Sights:** Delta Point Pro Optic. **Grips:** Micarta. Frame has rounded heel, high cut trigger guard. Designed for hunting.

Price: **$2,688.00**

KIMBER KHX SERIES

Calibers: .45 ACP, 9mm. **Capacity:** 8+1. **Features:** This series is offered in Custom, Pro and Ultra sizes. **Barrels:** 5-, 4- or 3-inch match-grade stainless steel. **Weights:** 25–38 oz. **Finishes:** Stainless steel frame and slide with matte black KimPro II finish. Stepped hexagonal slide and top-strap serrations. **Sights:** Green and red fiber optic and Hogue Laser Enhanced MagGrip G10 grips and matching mainspring housings. Pro and Ultra models have rounded heel frames. Optics Ready (OR) models available in Custom and Pro sizes with milled slide that accepts optics plates for Vortex, Trijicon and Leupold red-dot sights.

Price: Custom OR .45 ACP **$1,087.00**
Price: Custom OR 9mm **$1,108.00**
Price: Custom, Pro or Ultra .45 .... **$1,259.00**
Price: Custom, Pro or Ultra 9mm **$1,279.00**

KIMBER AEGIS ELITE SERIES

Calibers: 9mm, .45 ACP. **Features:** Offered in Custom, Pro and Ultra sizes with 5-, 4.25- or 3-in. barrels. Sights: Green or red fiber optic or Vortex Venom red dot on OI (Optics Installed) models (shown). Grips: G10. Features: Satin finish stainless steel frame, matte black or gray slide, front and rear AEX slide serrations.

Price: .45 ACP **$1,021.00**
Price: 9mm **$1,041.00**
Price: .45 OI **$1,375.00**
Price: 9mm OI **$1,395.00**

LIONHEART LH9 MKII

Caliber: 9mm. **Capacities:** 15-round magazine. LH9C Compact, 10 rounds. **Barrel:** 4.1 in. **Weight:** 26.5 oz. **Length:** 7.5 in **Grips:** One-piece black polymer with textured design. **Sights:** Fixed low profile. Novak LoMount sights available. **Finish:** Cerakote Graphite Black or Patriot Brown. **Features:** Hammer-forged heat-treated steel slide, hammer-forged aluminum frame. Double-action PLUS action.

Price: **$695.00**
Price: Novak sights **$749.00**

LLAMA MAX-1

Calibers: .38 Super, .45 ACP. **Barrel:** 5 in. **Weight:** 37 oz. **Sights:** Mil-spec. fixed. **Features:** Standard size and features of the 1911A1 full-size model. Lowered ejection port, matte blue or hard chrome finish. Imported from the Philippines by Eagle Imports. Introduced in 2016.

Price: **$565.00**

Prices given are believed to be accurate at time of publication however, many factors affect retail pricing so exact prices are not possible.

LLAMA MICRO MAX
Caliber: .380 ACP. **Capacity:** 7-round magazine. **Weight:** 23 oz. **Sights:** Novak style rear, fiber optic front. **Grips:** Wood or black synthetic. **Features:** A compact 1911-style pistol with 3.75-in. barrel. Skeletonized hammer and trigger, double slide serrations, comes with two 7-shot magazines. Imported from the Philippines by Eagle Imports.
Price: **$468.00**

MAC 3011 SSD TACTICAL
Caliber: .45 ACP. **Capacity:** 14+1 magazine. **Barrel:** 5-in. match-grade bull. **Sights**: Bomar-type fully adjustable rear, dovetail front. **Weight:** 46 oz. **Finish:** Blue. **Grips:** Aluminum. **Features:** Checkered frontstrap serrations, skeletonized trigger and hammer, flared and lowered ejection port, ambidextrous safety. Imported from the Philippines by Eagle Imports.
Price: **$1,136.00**

MAC 1911 BOB CUT
Caliber: .45 ACP. **Capacity:** 8+1 magazine. **Barrel:** 4.25 in. Commander-size 1911 design. **Sights**: Novak-type fully adjustable rear, dovetail front. **Weight:** 34.5 oz. **Finish:** Blue or hard chrome. **Grips:** Custom hardwood. **Features:** Stippled frontstrap, skeletonized trigger and hammer, flared and lowered ejection port, bobtail grip frame. Imported from the Philippines by Eagle Imports.
Price: **$902.00**

MAC 1911 BULLSEYE
Caliber: .45 ACP **Capacity:** 8+1 magazine. **Barrel**: 6-in. match-grade bull. **Sights**: Bomar-type fully adjustable rear, dovetail front. **Weight:** 46 oz. **Finish:** Blue or hard chrome. **Grips:** Hardwood. **Features:** Checkered frontstrap, skeletonized trigger and hammer, flared and lowered ejection port, wide front and rear slide serrations. Imported from the Philippines by Eagle Imports.
Price: **$1,219.00**

NIGHTHAWK CUSTOM T4
Calibers: 9mm, .45 ACP **Capacities:** .45 ACP, 7- or 8-round magazine; 9mm, 9 or 10 rounds; 10mm, 9 or 10 rounds. **Barrels:** 3.8, 4.25 or 5 in. **Weights:** 28–41 ounces, depending on model. **Features:** Manufacturer of a wide range of 1911-style pistols in Government Model (full-size), Commander and Officer's frame sizes. Shown is T4 model, introduced in 2013 and available only in 9mm.
Price: From .... **$3,495.00–$3,695.00**

NIGHTHAWK CUSTOM GRP
Calibers: 9mm, 10mm, .45 ACP. **Capacity:** 8-round magazine. **Features:** Global Response Pistol (GRP). Black, Sniper Gray, green, Coyote Tan or Titanium Blue finish. Match-grade barrel and trigger, choice of Heinie or Novak adjustable night sights.
Price: **$3,095.00**

NIGHTHAWK CUSTOM SHADOW HAWK
Caliber: 9mm. **Barrels:** 5 in. or 4.25 in. **Features:** Stainless steel frame with black Nitride finish, flat-faced trigger, high beavertail grip safety, checkered frontstrap, Heinie Straight Eight front and rear titanium night sights.
Price: **$3,795.00**

NIGHTHAWK CUSTOM WAR HAWK
Caliber: .45 ACP. **Barrels:** 5 in. or 4.25 in. **Features:** One-piece mainspring housing and mag well, Everlast Recoil System, Hyena Brown G10 grips.
Price: **$3,895.00**

NIGHTHAWK CUSTOM BOB MARVEL 1911
Calibers: 9mm or .45 ACP. **Barrel:** 4.25-in. bull barrel. **Features:** Everlast Recoil System, adjustable sights, match trigger, black Melonite finish.
Price: **$4,395.00**

NIGHTHAWK CUSTOM DOMINATOR
Caliber: .45 ACP. **Capacity:** 8-round magazine. **Features:** Stainless frame, black Perma Kote slide, cocobolo double-diamond grips,, front and rear slide serrations, adjustable sights.
Price: **$3,595.00**

NIGHTHAWK CUSTOM SILENT HAWK
Caliber: .45 ACP. **Capacity:** 8-round magazine. **Barrel:** 4.25 in. **Features:** Commander recon frame, G10 black and gray grips. Designed to match Silencerco silencer, not included with pistol.
Price: **$4,295.00**

NIGHTHAWK CUSTOM HEINIE LONG SLIDE
Calibers: 10mm, .45 ACP. **Barrel:** Long slide 6-in. **Features:** Cocobolo wood grips, black Perma Kote finish, adjustable or fixed sights, frontstrap checkering.
Price: **$3,895.00**

NIGHTHAWK CUSTOM BROWNING HI POWER
Caliber: 9mm. **Capacity:** 13-round magazine. **Features:** Nighthawk hasn't reinvented the classic high-capacity pistol but has improved it. Features include hand textured frame, trigger guard, slide top and rear, extended beavertail, contoured mag well, Heinie slant pro rear sight with a Nighthawk 14K gold bead front, crowned barrel, crisp 4-lb. trigger job, Cerakote Satin finish, select cocobolo checkered grips. Comes with two 13-round magazines.
Price: **$3,195.00**

NIGHTHAWK CUSTOM BORDER SPECIAL
Caliber: .45 ACP **Capacity:** 8+1 magazine. **Barrel:** 4.25-in. match grade. **Weight:** 34 oz. **Sights:** Heinie Black Slant rear, gold bead front. **Grips:** Cocobolo double diamond**. Finish:** Cerakote Elite Midnight black. **Features:** Commander-size steel frame with bobtail concealed carry grip. Scalloped frontstrap and mainspring housing. Serrated slide top. Rear slide serrations only. Crowned barrel flush with bushing.
Price: **$3,650.00**

NORTH AMERICAN ARMS GUARDIAN DAO
Calibers: .25 NAA, .32 ACP, .380 ACP, .32 NAA. **Capacity:** 6-round magazine. **Barrel:** 2.49 in. **Weight:** 20.8 oz. **Length:** 4.75 in. overall. **Grips:** Black polymer. **Sights:** Low-profile fixed. **Features:** DAO mechanism. All stainless steel construction. Introduced 1998. Made in USA by North American Arms. The .25 NAA is based on a bottle-necked .32 ACP case, and the .32 NAA is on a bottle-necked .380 ACP case.
Price: .25 NAA, 32 ACP **$409.00**
Price: .32 NAA, .380 ACP **$486.00**

PHOENIX ARMS HP22, HP25
Calibers: .22 LR, .25 ACP. **Capacities:** .22 LR, 10-shot (HP22), .25 ACP, 10-shot (HP25). **Barrel:** 3 in. **Weight:** 20 oz. **Length:** 5.5 in. overall. **Grips:** Checkered composition. **Sights:** Blade front, adjustable rear. **Features:** Single action, exposed hammer; manual hold-open; button magazine release. Available in satin nickel,matte blue finish. Introduced 1993. Made in USA by Phoenix Arms.
Price: With gun lock **$162.00**
Price: HP Range kit with 5-in. bbl., locking case and accessories (1 Mag) **$207.00**
Price: HP Deluxe Range kit with 3- and 5-in. bbls., 2 mags, case **$248.00**

REMINGTON R1
Caliber: .45 ACP. **Capacity:** 7-round magazine. **Barrels:** 5 in. (Full-size); 4.25 in. (Commander). **Weight:** 38.5 oz., 31 oz. (Ultralite). **Grips:** Double diamond walnut. **Sights:** Fixed, dovetail front and rear, 3-dot. **Features:** Flared and lowered ejection port. Comes with two magazines.
Price: Full-size or Commander **$774.00**
Price: Stainless **$837.00**
Price: Ultralite Commander........ **$849.00**

REMINGTON R1 LIMITED
Calibers: 9mm, .40 S&W, .45 ACP (Double-stack only). **Capacity:** 19+1 magazine. **Barrel:** 5 in. **Grips:** G10 VZ Operator**. Weight:** 38 oz. **Features:** Stainless steel frame and slide. Double Stack Model has 19-shot capacity.
Price: **$1,250.00**
Price: Limited Double Stack........ **$1,399.00**

REMINGTON R1 RECON
Calibers: 9mm, .45 ACP. **Barrel:** 4.25-in. match grade. **Features:** Double-stack stainless steel frame and slide. G10 VZ Operator grips, skeletonized trigger, ambidextrous safety, PVD coating, Tritium night sights, wide front and rear serrations, checkered mainspring housing and frontstrap.
Price: **$1,275.00**

REMINGTON R1 TACTICAL
Caliber: .45 ACP. **Barrel:** 5-in. **Sights:** Trijicon night sights. **Features:** Single- or double-stack frame. Threaded barrel available on double-stack model. Adjustable trigger. Other features same as Recon.
Price: **$1,250.00**
Price: Threaded barrel........ **$1,275.00**

Prices given are believed to be accurate at time of publication however, many factors affect retail pricing so exact prices are not possible.

REMINGTON R1 HUNTER
Caliber: 10mm. **Capacity:** 8-round magazine. **Barrel:** 6-in. match grade. **Sights:** Fully adjustable. **Finish:** Stainless steel. Comes with two 8-shot magazines, Operator II VZ G10 grips.
Price: $1,310.00

REMINGTON R1 ENHANCED
Calibers: .45 ACP, 9mm. **Capacities:** Same features as standard R1 except 8-shot magazine (.45), 9-shot (9mm). Stainless satin black oxide finish, wood laminate grips and adjustable rear sight. Other features include forward slide serrations, fiber optic front sight. Available with threaded barrel.
Price: $903.00
Price: Stainless $990.00
Price: Threaded barrel.. $959.00
Price: With Crimson Trace Laser Sight.. $1,129.00
Price: Enhanced Double Stack $999.00

REMINGTON R1 CARRY
Caliber: .45 ACP. **Capacity:** 8-round magazine. **Barrel:** 5 in. or 4.25 in. (Carry Commander). **Weight:** 35–39 oz. **Grips:** Cocobolo. **Sights:** Novak-type drift-adjustable rear, tritium-dot front sight. **Features:** Skeletonized trigger. Comes with one 8- and one 7-round magazine.
Price: $1,067.00

REMINGTON RM380
Caliber: .380 ACP. **Capacity:** 6-round magazine. **Barrel:** 2.9 in. **Length:** 5.27 in. **Height:** 3.86 in. **Weight:** 12.2 oz. **Sights:** Fixed and contoured. **Grips:** Glass-filled nylon with replaceable panels. **Features:** Double-action-only operation, all-metal construction with aluminum frame, stainless steel barrel, light dual recoil spring system, extended beavertail. Introduced in 2015.
Price: Light blue/black two-tone $348.00
Price: Black finish $436.00
Price: With Crimson Trace Laser Sight.. $638.00

REMINGTON RP9/RP45
Calibers: 9mm, .45 ACP. **Capacities:** 10- or 18-round magazine. **Barrel:** 4.5 in. **Weight:** 26.4 oz. **Sights:** Drift adjustable front and rear. **Features:** Striker-fired polymer frame model with Picatinny rail. Interchangeable backstraps. Smooth, light trigger pull with short reset, trigger safety. Easy loading double-stack magazine.
Price: $418.00

REMINGTON R51
Caliber: 9mm. **Capacity:** 7-round magazine. **Barrel:** 3.4 in. **Sights:** Fixed low profile. **Weight:** 22 oz. **Features:** Skeletonized trigger with crisp, light pull. Aluminum frame with black stainless slide. Redesigned and improved variation of 2014 model, which was recalled. Reintroduced in 2017.
Price: $448.00

REPUBLIC FORGE 1911
Calibers: .45 ACP, 9mm, .38 Super, .40 S&W, 10mm. **Features:** A manufacturer of custom 1911-style pistols offered in a variety of configurations, finishes and frame sizes, including single- and double-stack models with many options. Made in Texas.
Price: From $2,795.00

ROBERTS DEFENSE 1911 SERIES
Caliber: .45 ACP. **Capacity:** 8-round magazine. **Barrels:** 5, 4.25 or 3.5 in. **Weights:** 26–38 oz. **Sights:** Novak-type drift-adjustable rear, tritium-dot or fiber optic front sight. **Features:** Skeletonized trigger. Offered in four model variants with many custom features and options. Made in Wisconsin by Roberts Defense.
Price: Recon **$2,370.00**
Price: Super Grade **$2,270.00**
Price: Operator **$2,350.00**

ROCK ISLAND ARMORY 1911A1-45 FSP
Calibers: 9mm, .38 Super, .45 ACP. **Capacities:**.45 ACP (8 rounds), 9mm Parabellum, .38 Super (9 rounds**). Features:** 1911-style semi-auto pistol. Hard rubber grips, 5-inch barrel, blued, Duracoat or two-tone finish, drift-adjustable sights. Nickel finish or night sights available.
Price: From **$538.00**

ROCK ISLAND ARMORY 1911A1-FS MATCH
Caliber: .45 ACP. **Barrels:** 5 in. or 6 in. **Features:** 1911 match-style pistol. Features fiber optic front and adjustable rear sights, skeletonized trigger and hammer, extended beavertail, double diamond checkered walnut grips.
Price: **$877.00**

ROCK ISLAND ARMORY 1911A1-.22 TCM
Caliber: .22 TCM. **Capacity:** 17-round magazine. **Barrel:** 5 in. **Weight:** 36 oz. **Length:** 8.5 in. **Grips:** Polymer. **Sights:** Adjustable rear. **Features:** Chambered for high velocity .22 TCM rimfire cartridge. Comes with interchangeable 9mm barrel.
Price: **$960.00**

ROCK ISLAND ARMORY PRO MATCH ULTRA "BIG ROCK"
Caliber: 10mm. **Capacity:** 8- or 16-round magazine. **Barrel:** 6 in. **Weight:** 40 oz. **Length:** 8.5 in. **Grips:** VZ G10. **Sights:** Fiber optic front, adjustable rear. **Features:** Two magazines, upper and lower accessory rails, extended beavertail safety.
Price: **$1,187.00**
Price: High capacity model **$1,340.00**

ROCK ISLAND ARMORY MAP & MAPP
Caliber: 9mm. **Capacity:** 16-round magazine. **Barrel:** 3.5 (MAPP) or 4 in (MAP). Browning short recoil action-style pistols with: integrated front sight; snag-free rear sight; single- & double-action trigger; standard or ambidextrous rear safety; polymer frame with accessory rail.
Price: **$500.00**

ROCK ISLAND ARMORY XT22
Calibers: .22 LR, .22 Magnum. **Capacities:** 10- or 15-round magazine. **Barrel:** 5 in. **Weight:** 38 oz. **Features:** The XT-22 is the only .22 1911 with a forged 4140 steel slide and a one piece 4140 chrome moly barrel. Available as a .22/.45 ACP combo.
Price: **$600.00**
Price: .22 LR/.45 combo **$900.00**

ROCK ISLAND ARMORY BABY ROCK 380
Caliber: .380 ACP. **Capacity:** 7-round magazine. **Features:** Blowback operation. An 85 percent-size version of 1911-A1 design with features identical to full-size model.
Price: **$460.00**

ROCK RIVER ARMS LAR-15/LAR-9
Calibers: .223/5.56mm NATO, 9mm. **Barrels:** 7 in., 10.5 in. Wilson chrome moly, 1:9 twist, A2 flash hider, 1/2x28 thread. **Weights:** 5.1 lbs. (7-in. barrel), 5.5 lbs. (10.5-in. barrel). **Length:** 23 in. overall. **Stock:** Hogue rubber grip. **Sights:** A2 front. **Features:** Forged A2 or A4 upper, single stage trigger, aluminum free-float tube, one magazine. Similar 9mm Para. LAR-9 also available. From Rock River Arms, Inc.
Price: LAR-15 7 in. A2 AR2115 .... **$1,175.00**
Price: LAR-15 10.5 in. A4 AR2120 .... **$1,055.00**
Price: LAR-9 7 in. A2 9mm2115 .... **$1,320.00**

ROCK RIVER ARMS TACTICAL PISTOL
Caliber: .45 ACP. **Features:** Standard-size 1911 pistol with rosewood grips, Heinie or Novak sights, Black Cerakote finish.
Price: **$2,200.00**

ROCK RIVER ARMS LIMITED MATCH
Calibers: .45 ACP, 40 S&W, .38 Super, 9mm**. Barrel:** 5 in. **Sights:** Adjustable rear, blade front. **Finish:** Hard chrome. **Features:** National Match frame with beveled magazine well, front and rear slide serrations, Commander Hammer, G10 grips.
Price: **$3,600.00**

ROCK RIVER ARMS CARRY PISTOL
Caliber: .45 ACP. **Barrel:** 5 in. **Sights:** Heinie. **Finish:** Parkerized. **Grips:** Rosewood. **Weight:** 39 oz.
Price: **$1,600.00**

ROCK RIVER ARMS 1911 POLY
Caliber: .45 ACP. **Capacity:** 7-round magazine. **Barrel:** 5 in. **Weight:** 33 oz. **Sights:** Fixed. **Features:** Full-size 1911-style model with polymer frame and steel slide.
Price: **$925.00**

RUGER AMERICAN PISTOL
Calibers: 9mm, .45 ACP. **Capacities:** 10 or 17 (9mm), 10 (.45 ACP). **Barrels:** 4.2 in. (9), 4.5 in. (.45). **Lengths:** 7.5 or 8 in. **Weights:** 30–31.5 oz. **Sights:** Novak LoMount Carry 3-Dot. **Finish:** Stainless steel slide with black Nitride finish. **Grip:** One-piece ergonomic wrap-around module with adjustable palm swell and trigger reach. **Features:** Short take-up trigger with positive re-set, ambidextrous mag release and slide stop, integrated trigger safety, automatic sear block system, easy takedown. Introduced in 2016.
Price: **$579.00**

RUGER AMERICAN COMPACT PISTOL
Caliber: 9mm. **Barrel:** 3.5 in. **Features:** Compact version of American Pistol with same general specifications.
Price: **$579.00**

Prices given are believed to be accurate at time of publication however, many factors affect retail pricing so exact prices are not possible.

RUGER SR9 /SR40
Calibers: 9mm, .40 S&W. **Capacities:** 9mm (17-round magazine), .40 S&W (15). **Barrel:** 4.14 in. **Weights:** 26.25, 26.5 oz. **Grips:** Glass-filled nylon in two color options — black or OD Green, w/flat or arched reversible backstrap. **Sights:** Adjustable 3-dot, built-in Picatinny-style rail. **Features:** Semi-auto in six configurations, striker-fired, through-hardened stainless steel slide brushed or blackened stainless slide with black grip frame or blackened stainless slide with OD Green grip frame, ambidextrous manual 1911-style safety, ambi. mag release, mag disconnect, loaded chamber indicator, Ruger cam block design to absorb recoil, comes with two magazines. 10-shot mags available. Introduced 2008. Made in USA by Sturm, Ruger & Co.
Price: SR9 (17-Round), SR9-10 (SS) **$569.00**

RUGER SR9C/SR40C COMPACT
Calibers: 9mm, .40 S&W. **Capacities:** 10- and 17-round magazine. **Barrels:** 3.4 in. (SR9C), 3.5 in. (SR40C). **Weight:** 23.4 oz. **Features:** Features include 1911-style ambidextrous manual safety; internal trigger bar interlock and striker blocker; trigger safety; magazine disconnector; loaded chamber indicator; two magazines, one 10-round and the other 17-round; 3.5-in. barrel; 3-dot sights; accessory rail; brushed stainless or blackened allow finish.
Price: **$569.00**

RUGER SECURITY-9
Caliber: 9mm. **Capacity:** 10- or 15-round magazine. **Barrel:** 4 in. **Weight:** 21 oz. **Sights:** Drift-adjustable 3-dot. Striker-fired polymer-frame compact model. Uses the same Secure Action as LCP II. Bladed trigger safety plus external manual safety.
Price: **$379.00**

RUGER SR45
Caliber: .45 ACP. **Capacity:** 10-round magazine. **Barrel:** 4.5 in. **Weight:** 30 oz. **Length:** 8 in. **Grips:** Glass-filled nylon with reversible flat/arched backstrap. **Sights:** Adjustable 3-dot. **Features:** Same features as SR9.
Price: **$569.00**

RUGER LC9S
Caliber: 9mm. **Capacity:** 7+1. **Barrel:** 3.12 in. **Grips:** Glass-filled nylon. **Sights:** Adjustable 3-dot. **Features:** Brushed stainless slide, black glass-filled grip frame, blue alloy barrel finish. Striker-fired operation with smooth trigger pull. Integral safety plus manual safety. Aggressive frame checkering with smooth "melted" edges. Slightly larger than LCS380. LC9S Pro has no manual safety.
Price: **$479.00**

RUGER LC380
Caliber: .380 ACP. Other specifications and features identical to LC9.
Price: **$479.00**
Price: LaserMax laser grips **$529.00**
Price: Crimson Trace Laserguard **$629.00**

RUGER LCP
Caliber: .380. **Capacity:** 6-round magazine. **Barrel:** 2.75 in. **Weight:** 9.4 oz. **Length:** 5.16 in. **Grips:** Glass-filled nylon. **Sights:** Fixed, drift adjustable or integral Crimson Trace Laserguard.
Price: Blued **$259.00**
Price: Stainless steel slide **$289.00**
Price: Viridian-E Red Laser sight **$349.00**
Price: Custom w/drift adjustable rear sight **$269.00**

RUGER LCP II
Caliber: .380. **Capacity:** 6-round magazine. **Barrel:** 2.75 in. **Weight:** 10.6 oz. **Length:** 5.16 in. **Grips:** Glass-filled nylon. **Sights:** Fixed. **Features:** Last round fired holds action open. Larger grip frame surface provides better recoil distribution. Finger grip extension included. Improved sights for superior visibility. Sights are integral to the slide, hammer is recessed within slide.
Price: **$349.00**

RUGER EC9S
Caliber: 9mm. **Capacity:** 7-shot magazine. **Barrel:** 3.125 in. Striker-fired polymer frame. **Weight:** 17.2 oz.
Price: **$299.00**

RUGER CHARGER
Caliber: .22 LR. **Capacity:** 15-round BX-15 magazine. **Features:** Based on famous 10/22 rifle design with pistol grip stock and fore-end, scope rail, bipod. Black laminate stock. Silent-SR Suppressor available. Add $449. NFA regulations apply. Reintroduced with improvements and enhancements in 2015.
Price: Standard **$309.00**
Price: Takedown **$419.00**

RUGER MK IV COMPETITION

RUGER MARK IV TARGET

RUGER MARK IV SERIES
Caliber: .22 LR. **Capacity:** 10-round magazine. **Barrels:** 5.5 in, 6.875 in. Target model has 5.5-in. bull barrel, Hunter model 6.88-in. fluted bull, Competition model 6.88-in. slab-sided bull. **Weight:** 33–46 oz. **Grips:** Checkered or target laminate. **Sights:** Adjustable rear, blade or fiber-optic front (Hunter). **Features:** Updated design of Mark III series with one-button takedown. Introduced 2016. Modern successor of the first Ruger pistol of 1949.
Price: Standard **$449.00**
Price: Target (blue) **$529.00**
Price: Target (stainless) **$689.00**
Price: Hunter .... **$769.00–$799.00**
Price: Competition **$749.00**

RUGER 22/45 MARK IV

RUGER 22/45 MARK IV PISTOL
Caliber: .22 LR. **Features:** Similar to other .22 Mark IV autos except has Zytel grip frame that matches angle and magazine latch of Model 1911 .45 ACP pistol. Available in 4.4-, 5.5-in. bull barrels. Comes with extra

Prices given are believed to be accurate at time of publication however, many factors affect retail pricing so exact prices are not possible.

magazine, plastic case, lock. Molded polymer or replaceable laminate grips. **Weight:** 25–33 oz. **Sights:** Adjustable. Updated design of Mark III with one-button takedown. Introduced 2016.
Price: $409.00
Price: 4.4-in. bull threaded barrel w/rails $529.00
Price: Lite w/aluminum frame, rails $549.00

RUGER SR22
Caliber: .22 LR. **Capacity:** 10-round magazine. **Barrel:** 3.5 in. **Weight:** 17.5 oz. **Length:** 6.4 in. **Sights:** Adjustable 3-dot. **Features:** Ambidextrous manual safety/decocking lever and mag release. Comes with two interchangeable rubberized grips and two magazines. Black or silver anodize finish. Available with threaded barrel.
Price: Black $439.00
Price: Silver $459.00
Price: Threaded barrel $479.00

RUGER SR1911
Caliber: .45. **Capacity:** 8-round magazine. **Barrel:** 5 in. (3.5 in. Officer Model) **Weight:** 39 oz. **Length:** 8.6 in., 7.1 in. **Grips:** Slim checkered hardwood. **Sights:** Novak LoMount Carry rear, standard front. **Features:** Based on Series 70 design. Flared and lowered ejection port. Extended mag release, thumb safety and slide-stop lever, oversized grip safety, checkered backstrap on the flat mainspring housing. Comes with one 7-round and one 8-round magazine.
Price: $939.00

RUGER SR1911 CMD
Caliber: .45 ACP. **Barrel:** 4.25 in. **Weight:** 29.3 (aluminum), 36.4 oz. (stainless). **Features:** Commander-size version of SR1911. Other specifications and features are identical to SR1911.
Price: Low glare stainless $939.00
Price: Anodized aluminum two-tone.......... $979.00

RUGER SR1911 TARGET
Calibers: 9mm, .45 ACP. **Capacities:** .45 and 10mm (8-round magazine), 9mm (9 shot). **Barrel:** 5 in. **Weight:** 39 oz. **Sights:** Bomar adjustable. **Grips:** G10 Deluxe checkered. **Features:** Skeletonized hammer and trigger, satin stainless finish. Introduced in 2016.
Price: $1,019.00

RUGER SR1911 OFFICER
Caliber: 9mm. **Capacity:** 8-round magazine. **Barrel:** 3.6 in. **Weight:** 27 oz. **Features:** Compact variation of SR1911 Series. Black anodized aluminum frame, stainless slide, skeletonized trigger, Novak 3-dot Night Sights, G10 deluxe checkered G10 grips.
Price: $979.00

SCCY CPX
Caliber: 9mm. **Capacity:** 10-round magazine. **Barrel:** 3.1 in. **Weight:** 15 oz. **Length:** 5.7 in. overall. **Grips:** Integral with polymer frame. **Sights:** 3-dot system, rear adjustable for windage. **Features:** Zytel polymer frame, steel slide, aluminum alloy receiver machined from bar stock. DAO with consistent 9-pound trigger pull. Concealed hammer. Available with (CPX-1) or without (CPX-2) manual thumb safety. Introduced 2014. Made in USA by SCCY Industries.
Price: Black carbon.......... $334.00
Price: Stainless/blue two-tone $339.00

SEECAMP LWS 32/380 STAINLESS DA
Calibers: .32 ACP, .380 ACP. **Capacity:** 6-round magazine. **Barrel:** 2 in., integral with frame. **Weight:** 10.5 oz. **Length:** 4.125 in. overall. **Grips:** Glass-filled nylon. **Sights:** Smooth, no-snag, contoured slide and barrel top. **Features:** Aircraft quality 17-4 PH stainless steel. Inertia-operated firing pin. Hammer fired DAO. Hammer automatically follows slide down to safety rest position after each shot, no manual safety needed. Magazine safety disconnector. Polished stainless. Introduced 1985. From L.W. Seecamp.
Price: .32 .... $446.25
Price: .380 .... $795.00

SIG SAUER 1911

Calibers: .45 ACP, .40 S&W. **Capacities:** .45 ACP, .40 S&W. 8- and 10-round magazine. **Barrel:** 5 in. **Weight:** 40.3 oz. **Length:** 8.65 in. overall. **Grips:** Checkered wood grips. **Sights:** Novak night sights. Blade front, drift adjustable rear for windage. **Features:** Single-action 1911. Hand-fitted dehorned stainless steel frame and slide; match-grade barrel, hammer/sear set and trigger; 25-LPI front strap checkering, 20-LPI mainspring housing checkering. Beavertail grip safety with speed bump, extended thumb safety, firing pin safety and hammer intercept notch. Introduced 2005. XO series has contrast sights, Ergo Grip XT textured polymer grips. STX line available from Sig Sauer Custom Shop; two-tone 1911, non-railed, Nitron slide, stainless frame, burled maple grips. Polished cocking serrations, flat-top slide, mag well. Carry line has Siglite night sights, lanyard attachment point, gray diamondwood or rosewood grips, 8+1 capacity. Compact series has 6+1 capacity, 7.7 OAL, 4.25-in. barrel, slim-profile wood grips, weighs 30.3 oz. Ultra Compact in 9mm or .45 ACP has 3.3-in. barrel, low-profile night sights, slim-profile gray diamondwood or rosewood grips. 6+1 capacity. 1911 C3 is a 6+1 compact .45 ACP, rosewood custom wood grips, two-tone and Nitron finishes. Weighs 30 oz. unloaded, lightweight alloy frame. Length is 7.7 in. Now offered in more than 30 different models with numerous options for frame size, grips, finishes, sight arrangements and other features. From SIG Sauer, Inc.

Price: Nitron **$1,174.00**
Price: Tacops.................. **$1,221.00**
Price: XO Black **$1,010.00**
Price: STX **$1,244.00**
Price: Nightmare **$1,244.00**
Price: Carry Nightmare **$1,195.00**
Price: Compact C3 .... **$1,010.00**
Price: Ultra Compact **$1,119.00**
Price: Max **$1,663.00**
Price: Spartan **$1,397.00**
Price: Super Target **$1,609.00**
Price: Traditional Stainless Match Elite **$1,164.00**

SIG SAUER P220

Caliber: .45 ACP, 10mm. **Capacity:** 7- or 8-round magazine. **Barrel:** 4.4 in. **Weight:** 27.8 oz. **Length:** 7.8 in. overall. **Grips:** Checkered black plastic. **Sights:** Blade front, drift adjustable rear for windage. Optional Siglite night sights. **Features:** Double action. Stainless steel slide, Nitron finish, alloy frame, M1913 Picatinny rail; safety system of decocking lever, automatic firing pin safety block, safety intercept notch, and trigger bar disconnector. Squared combat-type trigger guard. Slide stays open after last shot. Introduced 1976. P220 SAS Anti-Snag has dehorned stainless steel slide, front Siglite night sight, rounded trigger guard, dust cover, Custom Shop wood grips. Equinox line is Custom Shop product with Nitron stainless slide with a black hard-anodized alloy frame, brush-polished flats and nickel accents. Truglo tritium fiber-optic front sight, rear Siglite night sight, gray laminated wood grips with checkering and stippling. From SIG Sauer, Inc.

Price: **$1,087.00**
Price: P220 Elite 10mm **$1,422.00**
Price: P220 Elite Stainless **$1,359.00**
Price: P220 Super Match.................. **$1,467.00**
Price: P220 Combat Threaded Barrel.................. **$1,282.00**
Price: Legion 10mm.................. **$1,904.00**

SIG SAUER P225 A-1

Caliber: 9mm. **Capacity:** 8-round magazine. **Barrels:** 3.6 or 5 in. **Weight:** 30.5 oz. **Features:** Shorter and slim-profile version of P226 with enhanced short reset trigger, single-stack magazine.

Price: **$1,122.00**
Price: Night sights.................. **$1,236.00**

Prices given are believed to be accurate at time of publication however, many factors affect retail pricing so exact prices are not possible.

SIG SAUER P226
Calibers: 9mm, .40 S&W. **Barrel:** 4.4 in. **Length:** 7.7 in. overall. **Features:** Similar to the P220 pistol except has 4.4-in. barrel, measures 7.7 in. overall, weighs 34 oz. DA/SA or DAO. Many variations available. Snap-on modular grips. Legion series has improved short reset trigger, contoured and shortened beavertail, relieved trigger guard, higher grip, other improvements. From SIG Sauer, Inc.
Price: From $1,087.00
Price: Elite $1,481.00
Price: Combat $1,289.00
Price: Tactical Operations (TACOPS) $1,329.00
Price: Engraved $1,631.00
Price: Legion $1,428.00
Price: RX w/Romeo 1 Reflex sight $1,685.00
Price: MK25 Navy Version $1,187.00

SIG SAUER P227
Caliber: .45 ACP. **Capacity:** 10-round magazine. **Features:** Same general specifications and features as P226 except chambered for .45 ACP and has double-stack magazine.
Price: .... $1,087.00–$1,350.00

SIG SAUER P229 DA
Caliber: Similar to the P220 except chambered for 9mm (10- or 15-round magazines), .40 S&W, (10- or 12-round magazines). **Barrels:** 3.86-in. barrel, 7.1 in. overall length and 3.35 in. height. **Weight:** 32.4 oz. **Features:** Introduced 1991. Snap-on modular grips. Frame made in Germany, stainless steel slide assembly made in U.S.; pistol assembled in U.S. Many variations available. Legion series has improved short reset trigger, contoured and shortened beavertail, relieved trigger guard, higher grip, other improvements. From SIG Sauer, Inc.
Price: P229, From $1,085.00
Price: P229 Legion $1,413.00
Price: P229 Select $1,195.00

SIG SAUER SP2022
Calibers: 9mm, .357 SIG, .40 S&W. **Capacities:** 10-, 12-, or 15-round magazines. **Barrel:** 3.9 in. **Weight:** 30.2 oz. **Length:** 7.4 in. overall. **Grips:** Composite and rubberized one-piece. **Sights:** Blade front, rear adjustable for windage. Optional Siglite night sights. **Features:** Polymer frame, stainless steel slide; integral frame accessory rail; replaceable steel frame rails; left- or right-handed magazine release, two interchangeable grips. From SIG Sauer, Inc.
Price: $642.00

SIG SAUER P238
Caliber: .380 ACP. **Capacity:** 6-round magazine. **Barrel:** 2.7 in. **Weight:** 15.4 oz. **Length:** 5.5 in. overall. **Grips:** Hogue G-10 and Rosewood grips. **Sights:** Contrast/Siglite night sights. **Features:** All-metal beavertail-style frame.
Price: $723.00
Price: Desert Tan $738.00
Price: Polished $798.00
Price: Rose Gold $932.00
Price: Emperor Scorpion $801.00

SIG SAUER P320
Calibers: 9mm, .357 SIG, .40 S&W, .45 ACP. **Capacities:** 15 or 16 rounds (9mm), 13 or 14 rounds (.357 or .40). **Barrels:** 3.6 in. (Subcompact), 3.9 in. (Carry model) or 4.7 in. (Full size). **Weights:** 26–30 oz. **Lengths:** 7.2 or 8.0 in overall. **Grips:** Interchangeable black composite. **Sights:** Blade front, rear adjustable for windage. Optional Siglite night sights. **Features:** Striker-fired DAO, Nitron finish slide, black polymer frame. Frame size and calibers are interchangeable. Introduced 2014. Made in USA by SIG Sauer, Inc.
Price: Full size $679.00
Price: Carry (shown) $679.00

SIG SAUER P320 SUBCOMPACT
Calibers: 9mm, .40 S&W. **Barrel:** 3.6 in. **Features:** Accessory rail. Other features similar to Full-Size and Carry models.
Price: $679.00

SIG SAUER MODEL 320 RX
Caliber: 9mm. **Capacity:** 17-round magazine. **Barrels:** 4.7 in. or 3.9 in. **Features:** Full and Compact size models with ROMEO1 Reflex sight, accessory rail, stainless steel frame and slide. XFive has improved control ergonomics, bull barrel, 21-round magazines.
Price: $952.00
Price: XFive $1,005.00

SIG SAUER P365

Caliber: 9mm. **Barrel:** 3.1 in. **Weight:** 17.8 oz. **Features:** Micro-compact striker-fired model with 10-round magazine, stainless steel frame and slide, XRAY-3 day and night sights fully textured polymer grip.

Price: **$599.00**

SIG SAUER MPX

Calibers: 9mm, .357 SIG, .40 S&W. **Capacities:** 10, 20 or 30 rounds. **Barrel:** 8 in. **Weight:** 5 lbs **Features:** Semi-auto AR-style gun with closed, fully locked short-stroke pushrod gas system.

Price: From **$2,016.00**

SIG SAUER P938

Calibers: 9mm, .22 LR. **Capacities:** 9mm (6-shot mag.), .22 LR (10-shot mag.). **Barrel:** 3.0 in. **Weight:** 16 oz. **Length:** 5.9 in. **Grips:** Rosewood, Blackwood, Hogue Extreme, Hogue Diamondwood. **Sights:** Siglite night sights or Siglite rear with Tru-Glo front. **Features:** Slightly larger version of P238.

Price: .... **$760.00–$1,195.00**
Price: .22 LR **$656.00**

SMITH & WESSON M&P SERIES

Calibers: .22 LR, 9mm, .357 Sig, .40 S&W. **Capacities, full-size models:** 12 rounds (.22), 17 rounds (9mm), 15 rounds (.40). **Compact models:** 12 (9mm), 10 (.40). **Barrels:** 4.25, 3.5 in. **Weights:** 24, 22 oz. **Lengths:** 7.6, 6.7 in. **Grips:** Polymer with three interchangeable palm swell grip sizes. **Sights:** 3 white-dot system with low-profile rear. **Features:** Zytel polymer frame with stainless steel slide, barrel and structural components. VTAC (Viking Tactics) model has Flat Dark Earth finish, VTAC Warrior sights. Compact models available with Crimson Trace Lasergrips. Numerous options for finishes, sights, operating controls.

Price: **$569.00**
Price: (VTAC) **$799.00**
Price: (Crimson Trace) .... **$699.00–$829.00**
Price: M&P 22 .... **$389.00–$419.00**

SMITH & WESSON M&P PRO SERIES C.O.R.E.

Calibers: 9mm, .40 S&W. **Capacities:** 17 rounds (9mm), 15 rounds (.40). **Barrels:** 4.25 in. (M&P9, M&P40), or 5 in. (M&P9L, M&P40L). **Features:** Based on the Pro series line of competition-ready firearms, the C.O.R.E. models (Competition Optics Ready Equipment) feature a slide engineered to accept six popular competition optics (Trijicon RMR, Leupold Delta Point, Jpoint, Doctor, C-More STS, Insight MRDS). Optics not included. Other features identical to standard M&P9 and M&P40 models.

Price: **$769.00**

SMITH & WESSON M&P 45

Caliber: .45 ACP. **Capacity:** 8 or 10 rounds. **Barrel length:** 4 or 4.5 in. **Weight:** 26, 28 or 30 oz. **Features:** Available with or without thumb safety. **Finish:** Black or Dark Earth Brown. **Features:** M&P model offered in three frame sizes.

Price: .... **$599.00–$619.00**
Price: Threaded barrel kit **$719.00**

SMITH & WESSON M&P M2.0 SERIES

Calibers: 9mm, .40 S&W, .45 ACP. **Capacities:** 17 rounds (9mm), 15 rounds (.40), 10 rounds (.45). **Barrels:** 4.25, 4.5 or 4.6 in. (.45 only). **Weights:** 25 –27 oz. **Finishes**: Armornite Black or Flat Dark Earth. **Grip:** Textured polymer with 4 interchangeable modular inserts. Second Generation of M&P Pistol series. Introduced in 2017.

Price: **$599.00**

SMITH & WESSON M&P 9/40 SHIELD

Calibers: 9mm, .40 S&W. **Capacities:** 7- and 8-round magazine (9mm); 6-round and 7-round magazine (.40). **Barrel:** 3.1 in. **Length:** 6.1 in. **Weight:** 19 oz. **Sights:** 3-white-dot system with low-profile rear. Features: Ultra-compact, single-stack variation of M&P series. Available with or without thumb safety. Crimson Trace Green Laserguard available.

Price: **$449.00**
Price: CT Green Laserguard **$589.00**

SMITH & WESSON M&P 45 SHIELD

Caliber: .45 ACP. **Barrel:** 3.3 in. Ported model available. **Weight:** 20–23 oz. **Sights:** White dot or tritium night sights. Comes with one 6-round and one 7-round magazine.

Price: **$479.00**
Price: Tritium night sights **$579.00**
Price: Ported barrel **$609.00**

SMITH & WESSON MODEL SD9 VE/SD40 VE

Calibers: .40 S&W, 9mm. **Capacities:** 10+1, 14+1 and 16+1 **Barrel:** 4 in. **Weight:** 39 oz. **Length:** 8.7 in. **Grips:** Wood or rubber. **Sights:** Front: Tritium Night Sight, Rear: Steel Fixed 2-Dot. **Features:** SDT (Self Defense Trigger) for optimal, consistent pull first round to last, standard Picatinny-style rail, slim ergonomic textured grip, textured finger locator and aggressive front and backstrap texturing with front and rear slide serrations.

Price: **$389.00**

Prices given are believed to be accurate at time of publication however, many factors affect retail pricing so exact prices are not possible.

SMITH & WESSON MODEL SW1911

Calibers: .45 ACP, 9mm. **Capacities:** 8 rounds (.45), 7 rounds (subcompact .45), 10 rounds (9mm). **Barrels:** 3, 4.25, 5 in. **Weights:** 26.5–41.7 oz. **Lengths:** 6.9–8.7 in. **Grips:** Wood, wood laminate or synthetic. Crimson Trace Lasergrips available. **Sights:** Low-profile white dot, tritium night sights or adjustable. **Finish:** Black matte, stainless or two-tone. **Features:** Offered in three different frame sizes. Skeletonized trigger. Accessory rail on some models. Compact models have round-butt frame. Pro Series have 30 LPI checkered frontstrap, oversized external extractor, extended mag well, full-length guide rod, ambidextrous safety.

Price: Standard Model E Series, From **$979.00**
Price: Crimson Trace grips **$1,149.00**
Price: Pro Series .... **$1,459.00–$1,609.00**
Price: Scandium Frame E Series **$1,449.00**

SMITH & WESSON BODYGUARD 380

Caliber: .380 Auto. **Capacity:** 6+1. **Barrel:** 2.75 in. **Weight:** 11.85 oz. **Length:** 5.25 in. **Grips:** Polymer. **Sights:** Integrated laser plus drift-adjustable front and rear. **Features:** The frame of the Bodyguard is made of reinforced polymer, as is the magazine base plate and follower, magazine catch and trigger. The slide, sights and guide rod are made of stainless steel, with the slide and sights having a Melonite hardcoating.

Price: **$449.00**

SPHINX SDP

Caliber: 9mm. **Capacity:** 15-shot magazine. **Barrel:** 3.7 in. **Weight:** 27.5 oz. **Length:** 7.4 in. **Sights:** Defiance Day & Night Green fiber/tritium front, tritium 2-dot red rear. **Features:** DA/SA with ambidextrous decocker, integrated slide position safety, aluminum MIL-STD 1913 Picatinny rail, Blued alloy/steel or stainless. Aluminum and polymer frame, machined steel slide. Offered in several variations. Made in Switzerland and imported by Kriss USA.

Price: From **$999.00**

SPRINGFIELD ARMORY EMP ENHANCED MICRO

Calibers: 9mm, 40 S&W. **Capacity:** 9-round magazine. **Barrel:** 3-inch stainless steel match grade, fully supported ramp, bull. **Weight:** 26 oz. **Length:** 6.5 in. overall. **Grips:** Thinline cocobolo hardwood. **Sights:** Fixed low-profile combat rear, dovetail front, 3-dot tritium. **Features:** Two 9-round stainless steel magazines with slam pads, long aluminum match-grade trigger adjusted to 5 to 6 lbs., forged aluminum alloy frame, black hardcoat anodized finish; dual spring full-length guide rod, forged satin-finish stainless steel slide. Introduced 2007. Champion has 4-inch barrel, fiber optic front sight, three 10-round magazines, Bi-Tone finish.

Price: .... **$1,104.00–$1,249.00**
Price: Champion **$1,179.00**

SPRINGFIELD ARMORY XD SERIES

Calibers: 9mm, .40 S&W, .45 ACP. **Barrels:** 3, 4, 5 in. **Weights:** 20.5-31 oz. **Lengths:** 6.26-8 overall. **Grips:** Textured polymer. **Sights:** Varies by model; Fixed sights are dovetail front and rear steel 3-dot units. **Features:** Three sizes in X-Treme Duty (XD) line: Sub-Compact (3-in. barrel), Service (4-in. barrel), Tactical (5-in. barrel). Three ported models available. Ergonomic polymer frame, hammer-forged barrel, no-tool disassembly, ambidextrous magazine release, visual/tactile loaded chamber indicator, visual/tactile striker status indicator, grip safety, XD gear system included. Introduced 2004. XD 45 introduced 2006. Compact line introduced 2007. Compact is shipped with one extended magazine (13) and one compact magazine (10). XD Mod.2 Sub-Compact has newly contoured slide and redesigned serrations, stippled grip panels, fiber-optic front sight. From Springfield Armory.

Price: Sub-Compact OD Green 9mm/40 S&W, fixed sights **$508.00**
Price: Compact .45 ACP, 4 barrel, Bi-Tone finish **$607.00**
Price: Service Black 9mm/.40 S&W, fixed sights **$541.00**
Price: Service Black .45 ACP, external thumb safety **$638.00**
Price: V-10 Ported Black 9mm/.40 S&W **$608.00**
Price: XD Mod.2 .... **$565.00**
Price: XD OSP w/Vortex Venom Red Dot Sight **$724.00**

SPRINGFIELD ARMORY XD(M) SERIES

Calibers: 9mm, .40 S&W, .45 ACP. **Barrels:** 3.8 or 4.5 in. **Sights:** Fiber optic front with interchangeable red and green filaments, adjustable target rear. **Grips:** Integral polymer with three optional backstrap designs. **Features:** Variation of XD design with improved ergonomics, deeper and longer slide serrations, slightly modified grip contours and texturing. Black polymer frame, forged steel slide. Black and two-tone finish options.

Price: .... **$623.00–$779.00**

SPRINGFIELD ARMORY MIL-SPEC 1911A1

Caliber: .45 ACP. **Capacity:** 7-round magazine. **Barrel:** 5 in. **Weights:** 35.6–39 oz. **Lengths:** 8.5–8.625 in. overall. **Finish:** Stainless steel. **Features:** Similar to Government Model military .45.

Price: Mil-Spec Parkerized, 7+1, 35.6 oz. **$785.00**
Price: Mil-Spec Stainless Steel, 7+1, 36 oz. **$889.00**

SPRINGFIELD ARMORY TACTICAL RESPONSE

Caliber: .45 ACP. **Features:** Similar to 1911A1 except .45 ACP only, checkered frontstrap and main-spring housing, Novak Night Sight combat rear sight and matching dove-tailed front sight, tuned, polished extractor, oversize barrel link; lightweight speed trigger and combat action job, match barrel and bushing, extended ambidextrous thumb safety and fitted beavertail grip safety. Checkered Cocobolo wood grips, comes with two

Wilson 7-shot magazines. Frame is engraved "Tactical" both sides of frame with "TRP" Introduced 1998. TRP-Pro Model meets FBI specifications for SWAT Hostage Rescue Team.
Price: **$1,646.00**
Price: Operator with adjustable Trijicon night sights........ **$1,730.00**

SPRINGFIELD ARMORY RANGE OFFICER
Calibers: 9mm, .45 ACP. **Barrels:** 5-in. stainless match grade. Compact model has 4 in. barrel. **Sights:** Adjustable target rear, post front. **Grips:** Double diamond checkered walnut. **Weights:** 40 oz., 28 oz. (compact). **Features:** Operator model has fiber optic sights.
Price: **$936.00**
Price: Compact........ **$899.00**
Price: Stainless finish........ **$1,045.00**
Price: Operator........ **$1,029.00**

SPRINGFIELD ARMORY CHAMPION OPERATOR LIGHTWEIGHT
Caliber: .45 ACP. **Barrel:** 4-in. stainless match-grade bull barrel. **Sights:** 3-dot Tritium combat profile. **Grips:** Double diamond checkered cocobolo with Cross Cannon logo. **Features:** Alloy frame with integral rail, extended ambi thumb safety and trigger, lightweight Delta hammer.
Price: **$1,050.00**

SPRINGFIELD ARMORY 911
Caliber: .380 ACP. **Barrel:** 2.7-in. stainless steel. **Sights:** 3-dot Tritium combat profile. **Weight:** 12.6 oz. **Grips:** Grooved Hogue G10. **Features:** Alloy frame, stainless steel slide. Springfield Armory's smallest pistol to date.
Price: **$599.00**

STEYR M-A1 SERIES
Calibers: 9mm, .40 S&W. **Capacities:** 9mm (15 or 17-round capacity) or .40 S&W (10-12). **Barrels:** 3.5 in. (MA-1), 4.5 in. (L-A1), 3 in. (C-A1). **Weight:** 27 oz. **Sights:** Fixed with white outline triangle. **Grips:** Black synthetic. Ergonomic low-profile for reduced muzzle lift. **Features:** DAO striker-fired operation.
Price: M-A1........ **$575.00**
Price: C-A1 compact model........ **$575.00**
Price: L-A1 full-size model........ **$575.00**
Price: S-A1 subcompact model........ **$575.00**

STOEGER COMPACT COUGAR
Caliber: 9mm. **Capacity:** 13+1. **Barrel:** 3.6 in. **Weight:** 32 oz. **Length:** 7 in. **Grips:** Wood or rubber. **Sights:** Quick read 3-dot. **Features:** DA/SA with a matte black finish. The ambidextrous safety and decocking lever is easily accessible to the thumb of a right- or left-handed shooter.
Price: **$469.00**

STI INTERNATIONAL
This company manufactures a wide selection of 1911-style semi-auto pistols chambered in .45 ACP, 9mm, .357 SIG, 10mm and .38 Super. Barrel lengths are offered from 3.0 to 6.0 in. Listed here are several of the company's more than 20 current models. Numerous finish, grip and sight options are available.
Price: 5.0 Trojan........ **$1,499.00**
Price: 5.0 Apeiro........ **$2,999.00**
Price: Costa Carry Comp........ **$3,699.00**
Price: H.O.S.T. Single stack........ **$2,699.00**
Price: H.O.S.T. Double stack........ **$3,199.00**
Price: DVC 3-Gun........ **$2,999.00**
Price: DVC Limited........ **$3,199.00**
Price: DVC Open........ **$3,999.00**
Price: HEXTAC Series........ **$2,199.00**

TAURUS CURVE

Caliber: .380 ACP. **Capacity:** 6+1. **Barrel:** 2.5 in. **Weight:** 10.2 oz. **Length:** 5.2 in. **Features:** Unique curved design to fit contours of the body for comfortable concealed carry with no visible "printing" of the firearm. Double-action only. Light and laser are integral with frame.

Price: **$404.00**

TAURUS MODEL 1911

Calibers: 9mm, .45 ACP. **Capacities:** .45 ACP 8+1, 9mm 9+1. **Barrel:** 5 in. **Weight:** 33 oz. **Length:** 8.5 in. **Grips:** Checkered black. **Sights:** Heinie straight 8. **Features:** SA. Blued, stainless steel, duotone blue and blue/gray finish. Standard/Picatinny rail, standard frame, alloy frame and alloy/Picatinny rail. Introduced in 2007. Imported from Brazil by Taurus International.

Price: 1911B, Blue **$719.00**
Price: 1911B, Walnut grips **$866.00**
Price: 1911SS, Stainless Steel **$907.00**
Price: 1911SS-1, Stainless Steel w/rail..................... **$945.00**
Price: 1911 DT, Duotone Blue **$887.00**

TAURUS MODEL 92

Caliber: 9mm. **Capacity:** 10- or 17-round magazine. **Barrel:** 5 in. **Weight:** 34 oz. **Length:** 8.5 in. overall. **Grips:** Checkered rubber, rosewood, mother of pearl. **Sights:** Fixed notch rear. 3-dot sight system. Also offered with micrometer-click adjustable night sights. **Features:** DA, ambidextrous 3-way hammer drop safety, allows cocked and locked carry. Blued, stainless steel, blued with gold highlights, stainless steel with gold highlights, forged aluminum frame, integral key-lock. .22 LR conversion kit available. Imported from Brazil by Taurus International.

Price: 92B **$513.00**
Price: 92SS **$529.00**

TAURUS SLIM PT-709

Caliber: 9mm. **Capacity:** 7+1. **Weight:** 19 oz. **Length:** 6.24 in. width less than an inch. **Features:** Compact DA/SA semi-auto pistol in polymer frame; blued or stainless slide; SA/DA trigger pull; low-profile fixed sights.

Price: **$319.00**
Price: Stainless..................... **$339.00**

TAURUS SLIM 740

Caliber: .40 S&W. **Capacity:** 6+1. **Barrel:** 3.2 in. **Weight:** 19 oz. **Length:** 6.24 in. overall. **Grips:** Polymer Grips. **Features:** DA with stainless steel finish.

Price: **$319.00**
Price: Stainless..................... **$339.00**

TAURUS SPECTRUM

Caliber: .380. **Barrel:** 2.8 in. **Weight:** 10 oz. **Length:** 5.4 in. **Sights:** Low-profile integrated with slide. **Features:** Polymer frame with stainless steel slide. Many finish combinations with various bright colors. Made in the USA. Introduced in 2017.

Price: .... **$289.00–$305.00**

Prices given are believed to be accurate at time of publication however, many factors affect retail pricing so exact prices are not possible.

TRISTAR 100 /120 SERIES
Calibers: 9mm, .40 S&W (C-100 only). **Capacities:** 15 (9mm), 11 (.40). **Barrels:** 3.7–4.7 in. **Weights:** 26–30 oz. **Grips:** Checkered polymer. **Sights:** Fixed. **Finishes:** Blue or chrome. **Features:** Alloy or steel frame. SA/DA. A series of pistols based on the CZ 75 design. Imported from Turkey.
Price: From .... **$460.00–$490.00**

TURNBULL MODEL 1911
Caliber: .45 ACP. **Features:** An accurate reproduction of 1918-era Model 1911 pistol. Forged slide with appropriate shape and style. Late-style sight with semi-circle notch. Early-style safety lock with knurled undercut thumb piece. Short, wide checkered spur hammer. Hand-checkered double-diamond American Black Walnut grips. Hand polished with period correct Carbonia charcoal bluing. Custom made to order with many options. Made in the USA by Doug Turnbull Manufacturing Co.
Price: From **$2,625.00**

WALTHER P99 AS
Calibers: 9mm, .40 S&W. **Capacities:** 15 or 10 rounds (9mm), 10 or 8 rounds (.40). **Barrels:** 3.5 or 4 in. **Weights:** 21–26 oz. **Lengths:** 6.6–7.1 in. **Grips:** Polymer with interchangeable backstrap inserts. **Sights:** Adjustable rear, blade front with three interchangeable inserts of different heights. **Features:** Offered in two frame sizes, standard and compact. DA with trigger safety, decocker, internal striker safety, loaded chamber indicator. Made in Germany.
Price: **$629.00**

WALTHER PK380
Caliber: .380 ACP. **Capacity:** 8-round magazine. **Barrel:** 3.66 in. **Weight:** 19.4 oz. **Length:** 6.5 in. **Sights:** Three-dot system, drift adjustable rear. **Features:** DA with external hammer, ambidextrous mag release and manual safety. Picatinny rail. Black frame with black or nickel slide.
Price: **$399.00**
Price: Nickel slide **$449.00**

WALTHER PPK/S
Caliber: .22 LR. **Capacities:** 10+1 (.22), 7+1 (.380). **Barrel:** 3.3 in **Weight:** 22 oz. **Length:** 6.1 in **Grips:** Checkered plastic. **Sights:** Fixed. Made in Germany.
Price: (.22 blue) **$400.00**
Price: (.22 nickel) **$430.00**

WALTHER PPQ M2
Calibers: 9mm, .40 S&W, .45 ACP, .22 LR. **Capacities:** 9mm, (15-round magazine), .40 S&W (11). .45 ACP, 22 LR (PPQ M2 .22). **Barrels:** 4 or 5 in. **Weight:** 24 oz. **Lengths:** 7.1, 8.1 in. **Sights:** Drift-adjustable. **Features:** Quick Defense trigger, firing pin block, ambidextrous slidelock and mag release, Picatinny rail. Comes with two extra magazines, two interchangeable frame backstraps and hard case. Navy SD model has threaded 4.6-in. barrel. M2 .22 has aluminum slide, blowback operation, weighs 19 ounces.
Price: 9mm, .40 .... **$649.00–$749.00**
Price: M2 .22 .... **$429.00**
Price: .45 .... **$699.00–$799.00**

WALTHER CCP
Caliber: 9mm. **Capacity:** 8-round magazine. **Barrel:** 3.5 in. **Weight:** 22 oz. **Length:** 6.4 in. **Features:** Thumb-operated safety, reversible mag release, loaded chamber indicator. Delayed blowback gas-operated action provides less recoil and muzzle jump, and easier slide operation. Available in all black or black/stainless two-tone finish.
Price: From .... **$469.00–$499.00**

Prices given are believed to be accurate at time of publication however, many factors affect retail pricing so exact prices are not possible.

WALTHER PPS
Calibers: 9mm, 40 S&W. **Capacities:** 6-, 7-, 8-round magazines for 9mm; 5-, 6-, 7-round magazines for 40 S&W. **Barrel:** 3.2 in. **Weight:** 19.4 oz. **Length:** 6.3 in. overall. **Stocks:** Stippled black polymer. **Sights:** Picatinny-style accessory rail, 3-dot low-profile contoured sight. **Features:** PPS — "Polizeipistole Schmal" or Police Pistol Slim. Measures 1.04-in. wide. Ships with 6- and 7-round magazines. Striker-fired action, flat slide stop lever, alternate backstrap sizes. QuickSafe feature decocks striker assembly when backstrap is removed. Loaded chamber indicator. Introduced 2008.
Price: **$629.00**

WALTHER P22
Caliber: .22 LR. **Barrels:** 3.4, 5 in. **Weights:** 19.6 oz. (3.4), 20.3 oz. (5). **Lengths:** 6.26, 7.83 in. **Sights:** Interchangeable white dot, front, 2-dot adjustable, rear. **Features:** A rimfire version of the Walther P99 pistol, available in nickel slide with black frame, Desert Camo or Digital Pink Camo frame with black slide.
Price: From **$379.00**
Price: Nickel slide/black frame, or black slide/camo frame **$449.00**

WALTHER CREED
Caliber: 9mm. **Capacity:** 16+1. **Barrel:** 4 in. **Weight:** 27 oz. **Sights:** 3-dot system. Features: Polymer frame with ergonomic grip, Picatinny rail, pre-cocked DA trigger, front and rear slide serrations with non-slip surface. Comes with two magazines. Similar to the discontinued PPX. Made in Germany.
Price: **$349.00**

WILSON COMBAT ELITE SERIES
Calibers: 9mm, .38 Super, .40 S&W; .45 ACP. **Barrel:** Compensated 4.1-in. hand-fit, heavy flanged cone match grade. **Weight:** 36.2 oz. **Length:** 7.7 in. overall. **Grips:** Cocobolo. **Sights:** Combat Tactical yellow rear tritium inserts, brighter green tritium front insert. **Features:** High-cut frontstrap, 30 LPI checkering on frontstrap and flat mainspring housing, High-Ride Beavertail grip safety. Dehorned, ambidextrous thumb safety, extended ejector, skeletonized ultra light hammer, ultralight trigger, Armor-Tuff finish on frame and slide. Introduced 1997. Made in USA by Wilson Combat. This manufacturer offers more than 100 different 1911 models ranging in price from about $2,800 to $5,000. XTAC and Classic 6-in. models shown. Prices show a small sampling of available models.
Price: Classic, From **$3,300.00**
Price: CQB, From **$2,865.00**
Price: Hackathorn Special **$3,750.00**
Price: Tactical Carry **$3,750.00**
Price: Tactical Supergrade **$5,045.00**
Price: Bill Wilson Carry Pistol **$3,850.00**
Price: Ms. Sentinel **$3,875.00**
Price: Hunter 10mm, .460 Rowland **$4,100.00**
Price: Beretta Brigadier Series, From **$1,095.00**
Price: X-Tac Series, From **$2,760.00**
Price: Texas BBQ Special, From **$4,960.00**

BAER 1911 ULTIMATE MASTER COMBAT

Calibers: .38 Super, 400 Cor-Bon, .45 ACP (others available). **Capacity:** 10-shot magazine. **Barrels:** 5, 6 in. Baer National Match. **Weight:** 37 oz. **Length:** 8.5 in. overall. **Grips:** Checkered cocobolo. **Sights:** Baer dovetail front, low-mount Bo-Mar rear with hidden leaf. **Features:** Full-house competition gun. Baer forged NM blued steel frame and double serrated slide; Baer triple port, tapered cone compensator; fitted slide to frame; lowered, flared ejection port; Baer reverse recoil plug; full-length guide rod; recoil buff; beveled magazine well; Baer Commander hammer, sear; Baer extended ambidextrous safety, extended ejector, checkered slide stop, beavertail grip safety with pad, extended magazine release button; Baer speed trigger. Made in USA by Les Baer Custom, Inc.

Price: .45 ACP Compensated **$3,240.00**
Price: .38 Super Compensated **$3,390.00**
Price: 5-in. Standard barrel **$3,040.00**
Price: 5-in. barrel .38 Super or 9mm **$3,140.00**
Price: 6-in. barrel........ **$3,140.00**
Price: 6-in. barrel .38 Super or 9mm **$3,220.00**

BAER 1911 NATIONAL MATCH HARDBALL

Caliber: .45 ACP. **Capacity:** 7-round magazine. **Barrel:** 5 in. **Weight:** 37 oz. **Length:** 8.5 in. overall. **Grips:** Checkered walnut. **Sights:** Baer dovetail front with under-cut post, low-mount Bo-Mar rear with hidden leaf. **Features:** Baer NM forged steel frame, double serrated slide and barrel with stainless bushing; slide fitted to frame; Baer match trigger with 4-lb. pull; polished feed ramp, throated barrel; checkered frontstrap, arched mainspring housing; Baer beveled magazine well; lowered, flared ejection port; tuned extractor; Baer extended ejector, checkered slide stop; recoil buff. Made in USA by Les Baer Custom, Inc.

Price: **$2,310.00**

BAER 1911 PPC OPEN CLASS

Caliber: .45 ACP, 9mm. **Barrel:** 6 in, fitted to frame. **Sights:** Adjustable PPC rear, dovetail front. **Grips:** Checkered Cocobola. **Features:** Designed for NRA Police Pistol Combat matches. Lowered and flared ejection port, extended ejector, polished feed ramp, throated barrel, frontstrap checkered at 30 LPI, flat serrated mainspring housing, Commander hammer, front and rear slide serrations. 9mm has supported chamber.

Price: **$2,695.00**
Price: 9mm w/supported chamber **$3,095.00**

BAER 1911 BULLSEYE WADCUTTER

Similar to National Match Hardball except designed for wadcutter loads only. Polished feed ramp and barrel throat; Bo-Mar rib on slide; full-length recoil rod; Baer speed trigger with 3.5-lb. pull; Baer deluxe hammer and sear; Baer beavertail grip safety with pad; flat mainspring housing checkered 20 LPI. Blue finish; checkered walnut grips. Made in USA by Les Baer Custom, Inc.

Price: From **$2,390.00**

COLT GOLD CUP NM SERIES

Caliber: .45 ACP. **Capacity:** 8-round magazine. **Barrel:** 5-inch National Match. **Weight:** 37 oz. **Length:** 8.5. **Grips:** Checkered wraparound rubber composite with silver-plated medallions or checkered walnut grips with gold medallions. **Sights:** Target post dovetail front, Bomar fully adjustable rear. **Features:** Adjustable aluminum wide target trigger, beavertail grip safety, full-length recoil spring and target recoil spring, available in blued finish or stainless steel.

Price: (blued) **$1,299.00**
Price: (stainless) **$1,350.00**

COLT COMPETITION PISTOL

Calibers: .45 ACP, 9mm or .38 Super. **Capacities:** 8 or 9-shot magazine. **Barrel:** 5 in. National Match. **Weight:** 39 oz. Length: 8.5 in. **Grips:** Custom Blue Colt G10. **Sights:** Novak adjustable rear, fiber optic front. A competition-ready pistol out of the box at a moderate price. Blue or satin nickel finish. Series 80 firing system. O Series has stainless steel frame and slide with Cerakote gray frame and black slide, competition trigger, gray/black G-10 grips, front and rear slide serrations.

Price: .... **$949.00–$1,099.00**
Price: Competition O series........ **$2,499.00**

CZ 75 TS CZECHMATE

Caliber: 9mm. **Capacity:** 20-round magazine. **Barrel:** 130mm. **Weight:** 1360 g **Length:** 266mm overall. **Features:** The handgun is custom built, therefore the quality of workmanship is fully comparable with race pistols built directly to IPSC shooters' wishes. Individual parts and components are excellently match fitted, broke-in and tested. Every handgun is outfitted with a four-port compensator, nut for shooting without a compensator, the slide stop with an extended finger piece, the slide stop without a finger piece, ergonomic grip panels from aluminum with a new type pitting and side mounting provision with the C-More red-dot sight. For shooting without a red-dot sight there is included a standard target rear sight of Tactical Sports type, package contains also the front sight.

Price: **$3,317.00**

CZ 75 TACTICAL SPORTS

Calibers: 9mm,.40 S&W. **Capacities:** 17-20-round magazines. **Barrel:** 114mm. **Weight:** 1270 g **Length:** 225mm overall. **Features:** Semi-automatic handgun with a locked breech. This model is designed for competition shooting in accordance with world IPSC (International Practical Shooting Confederation) rules and regulations. The CZ 75 TS pistol model design stems from the standard CZ 75 model. However, this model features a number of special modifications, which are usually required for competitive handguns: SA trigger mechanism, match trigger made of plastic featuring option for trigger travel adjustments before discharge (using upper screw), and for overtravel (using bottom screw). The adjusting screws are set by the manufacturer — sporting hammer specially adapted for a reduced trigger pull weight, an extended magazine catch, grip panels made of walnut, guiding funnel made of plastic for quick inserting of the magazine into pistol's frame. Glossy blued slide, silver Polycoat frame. Packaging includes 3 magazines.

Price: **$1,310.00**

DAN WESSON CHAOS
Caliber: 9mm. **Capacity:** 21-round magazine. **Barrel:** 5 in. **Weight:** 3.20 lbs. **Length:** 8.75 in. overall. **Features:** A double-stack 9mm designed for 3-Gun competition.
Price: **$3,829.00**

DAN WESSON HAVOC
Calibers: 9mm, .38 Super. **Capacity:** 21-round magazine. **Barrel:** 4.25 in. **Weight:** 2.20 lbs. **Length:** 8 in. overall. **Features:** The Havoc is based on an "All Steel" Hi-capacity version of the 1911 frame. It comes ready to compete in Open IPSC/USPSA division. The C-more mounting system offers the lowest possible mounting configuration possible, enabling extremely fast target acquisition. The barrel and compensator arrangement pair the highest level of accuracy with the most effective compensator available.
Price: **$4,299.00**

EAA WITNESS ELITE GOLD TEAM
Calibers: 9mm, 9x21, .38 Super, .40 S&W, .45 ACP. **Barrel:** 5.1 in. **Weight:** 44 oz. **Length:** 10.5 in. overall. **Grips:** Checkered walnut, competition-style. **Sights:** Square post front, fully adjustable rear. **Features:** Triple-chamber cone compensator; competition SA trigger; extended safety and magazine release; competition hammer; beveled magazine well; beavertail grip. Hand-fitted major components. Hard chrome finish. Match-grade barrel. From EAA Custom Shop. Introduced 1992. Limited designed for IPSC Limited Class competition. Features include full-length dust-cover frame, funneled magazine well, interchangeable front sights. Stock (2005) designed for IPSC Production Class competition. Match introduced 2006. Made in Italy, imported by European American Armory.
Price: Gold Team **$2,406.00**
Price: Stock, 4.5 in. barrel, hard-chrome finish **$1,263.00**
Price: Limited Custom Xtreme **$2,502.00**
Price: Witness Match Xtreme **$2,335.00**
Price: Witness Stock III Xtreme **$2.252.00**

DAN WESSON MAYHEM
Caliber: .40 S&W. **Capacity:** 18-round magazine. **Barrel:** 6 in. **Weight:** 2.42 lbs. **Length:** 8.75 in. overall. **Features:** The Mayhem is based on an "All-Steel" Hi-capacity version of the 1911 frame. It comes ready to compete in Limited IPSC/USPSA division or fulfill the needs of anyone looking for a superbly accurate target-grade 1911. The 6-in. bull barrel and tactical rail add to the static weight, or "good weight." A 6-in. long slide for added sight radius and enhanced pointability, but that would add to the "bad weight" so the 6-in. slide has been lightened to equal the weight of a 5 in. The result is a 6 in. long slide that balances and feels like a 5 in. but shoots like a 6 in. The combination of the all-steel frame with industry leading parts delivers the most well-balanced, softest shooting 6-in. limited gun on the market.
Price: **$3,899.00**

DAN WESSON TITAN
Caliber: 10mm. **Capacity:** 21-round magazine. **Barrel:** 4.25 in. **Weight:** 1.62 lbs. **Length:** 8 in. overall. **Features:** The Titan is based on an "All Steel" Hi-capacity version of the 1911 frame. The rugged HD night sights are moved forward and recessed deep into the slide yielding target accuracy and extreme durability. The Snake Scale serrations' aggressive 25 LPI checkering, and the custom competition G-10 grips ensure controllability even in the harshest of conditions. The combination of the all-steel frame, bull barrel and tactical rail enhance the balance and durability of this formidable target-grade Combat handgun.
Price: **$3,829.00**

FREEDOM ARMS MODEL 83 .22 FIELD GRADE SILHOUETTE CLASS
Caliber: .22 LR. **Capacity:** 5-round cylinder. **Barrel:** 10 in. **Weight:** 63 oz. **Length:** 15.5 in. overall. **Grips:** Black Micarta. **Sights:** Removable Patridge front blade; Iron Sight Gun Works silhouette rear click-adjustable for windage and elevation (optional adj. front sight and hood). **Features:** Stainless steel, matte finish, manual sliding-bar safety system; dual firing pins, lightened hammer for fast lock time, pre-set trigger stop. Introduced 1991. Made in USA by Freedom Arms.
Price: Silhouette Class **$2,762.00**

FREEDOM ARMS MODEL 83 CENTERFIRE SILHOUETTE MODELS
Calibers: 357 Mag., .41 Mag., .44 Mag. **Capacity:** 5-round cylinder. **Barrel:** 10 in., 9 in. (.357 Mag. only). **Weight:** 63 oz. (41 Mag.). **Length:** 15.5 in., 14.5 in. (.357 only). **Grips:** Pachmayr Presentation. **Sights:** Iron Sight Gun Works silhouette rear sight, replaceable adjustable front sight blade with hood. **Features:** Stainless steel, matte finish, manual sliding-bar safety system. Made in USA by Freedom Arms.
Price: Silhouette Models, From **$2,460.00**

HIGH STANDARD SUPERMATIC TROPHY TARGET

Caliber: .22 LR. **Capacity:** 9-round mag. **Barrels:** 5.5-in. bull or 7.25-in. fluted. **Weights:** 44–46 oz. **Lengths:** 9.5–11.25 in. overall. **Stock:** Checkered hardwood with thumb rest. **Sights:** Undercut ramp front, frame-mounted micro-click rear adjustable for windage and elevation; drilled and tapped for scope mounting. **Features:** Gold-plated trigger, slide lock, safety-lever and magazine release; stippled front grip and backstrap; adjustable trigger and sear. Barrel weights optional. From High Standard Manufacturing Co., Inc.
Price: 5.5-in. barrel **$1,070.00**
Price: 7.25-in. barrel **$1,205.00**

HIGH STANDARD VICTOR TARGET

Caliber: .22 LR. **Capacity:** 10-round magazine. **Barrels:** 4.5 in. or 5.5 in. polished blue; push-button takedown. **Weight:** 46 oz. **Length:** 9.5 in. overall. **Stock:** Checkered walnut with thumb rest. **Sights:** Undercut ramp front, micro-click rear adjustable for windage and elevation. Also available with scope mount, rings, no sights. **Features:** Stainless steel frame. Full-length vent rib. Gold-plated trigger, slide lock, safety-lever and magazine release; stippled front grip and backstrap; polished blue slide; adjustable trigger and sear. Comes with barrel weight. From High Standard Manufacturing Co., Inc.
Price: 4.5- or 5.5-in. barrel, vented sight rib, scope base **$1,050.00**

KIMBER SUPER MATCH II

Caliber: .45 ACP. **Capacity:** 8-round magazine. **Barrel:** 5 in. **Weight:** 38 oz. **Length:** 8.7 in. overall. **Grips:** Rosewood double diamond. **Sights:** Blade front, Kimber fully adjustable rear. **Features:** Guaranteed to shoot 1-in. groups at 25 yards. Stainless steel frame, black KimPro slide; two-piece magazine well; premium aluminum match-grade trigger; 30 LPI frontstrap checkering; stainless match-grade barrel; ambidextrous safety; special Custom Shop markings. Introduced 1999. Made in USA by Kimber Mfg., Inc.
Price: **$2,313.00**

RUGER MARK IV TARGET

Caliber: .22 LR. **Capacity:** 10-round magazine. **Barrel:** 5.5-in. heavy bull. **Weight:** 35.6 oz. **Grips:** Checkered synthetic or laminate. **Sights:** .125 blade front, micro-click rear, adjustable for windage and elevation, loaded chamber indicator; integral lock, magazine disconnect. Plastic case with lock included.
Price: (blued) **$529.00**
Price: (stainless) **$689.00**

SMITH & WESSON MODEL 41 TARGET

Caliber: .22 LR. **Capacity:** 10-round magazine. **Barrels:** 5.5 in., 7 in. **Weight:** 41 oz. (5.5-in. barrel). **Length:** 10.5 in. overall (5.5-in. barrel). **Grips:** Checkered walnut with modified thumb rest, usable with either hand. **Sights:** .125 in. Patridge on ramp base; micro-click rear-adjustable for windage and elevation. **Features:** .375 in. wide, grooved trigger; adjustable trigger stop drilled and tapped.
Price: .... **$1,369.00–$1,619.00**

STI APEIRO

Calibers: 9mm, .40 S&W, .45 ACP. **Features:** 1911-style semi-auto pistol with Schuemann "Island" barrel; patented modular steel frame with polymer grip; high capacity double-stack magazine; stainless steel ambidextrous thumb safeties and knuckle relief high-rise beavertail grip safety; unique sabertooth rear cocking serrations; 5-inch fully ramped, fully supported "Island" bull barrel, with the sight milled in to allow faster recovery to point of aim; custom engraving on the polished sides of the (blued) stainless steel slide; stainless steel mag well; STI adjustable rear sight and Dawson fiber optic front sight; blued frame.
Price: **$2,999.00**

STI EAGLE 5.0, 6.0
Calibers: 9mm, 9x21, .38 & .40 Super, .40 S&W, 10mm, .45 ACP. **Capacity:** 10-round magazine. **Barrels:** 5-, 6-in. bull. **Weight:** 34.5 oz. **Length:** 8.62 in. overall. **Grips:** Checkered polymer. **Sights:** STI front, Novak or Heinie rear. **Features:** Standard frames plus 7 others; adjustable match trigger; skeletonized hammer; extended grip safety with locator pad. Introduced 1994. Made in USA by STI International.
Price: (5.0 Eagle).. **$2,099.00**

STI STEELMASTER
Caliber: 9mm minor, comes with one 126mm magazine. **Barrel:** 4.15 in. **Weight:** 38.9 oz. **Length:** 9.5 in. overall. **Features:** Based on the renowned STI race pistol design, the SteelMaster is a shorter and lighter pistol that allows for faster target acquisition with reduced muzzle flip and dip. Designed to shoot factory 9mm (minor) ammo, this gun delivers all the advantages of a full-size race pistol in a smaller, lighter, faster-reacting and less violent package. The Steelmaster is built on the patented modular steel frame with polymer grip. It has a 4.15-in. classic slide which has been flat topped. Slide lightening cuts on the front and rear further reduce weight while "Sabertooth" serrations further enhance the aesthetics of this superior pistol. It also uses the innovative Trubor compensated barrel, which has been designed to eliminate misalignment of the barrel and compensator bore or movement of the compensator on the barrel. The shorter Trubor barrel system in the SteelMaster gives an even greater reduction in muzzle flip, and the shorter slide decreases overall slide cycle time allowing the shooter to achieve faster follow-up shots. The SteelMaster is mounted with a C-More, 6-minute, red-dot scope with blast shield and thumb rest. Additional enhancements include aluminum mag well, stainless steel ambidextrous safeties, stainless steel high rise grip safety, STI "Spur" hammer, STI RecoilMaster guide rod system and checkered frontstrap and mainspring housing.
Price: **$2,799.00**

STI TROJAN
Calibers: 9mm, .38 Super, .40 S&W, .45 ACP. **Barrel:** 5 in., 6 in. **Weight:** 36 oz. **Length:** 8.5 in. **Grips:** Rosewood. **Sights:** STI front with STI adjustable rear. **Features:** Stippled frontstrap, flat-top slide, one-piece steel guide rod.
Price: (Trojan 5) **$1,499.00**
Price: (Trojan 6, not available in .38 Super) **$1,555.00**

STI TRUBOR
Calibers: 9mm 'Major', 9x23, .38 Super (USPSA, IPSC). **Barrel:** 5 in. with integrated compensator. **Weight:** 41.3 oz. (including scope and mount) **Length:** 10.5 in. overall. **Features:** Built on the patented modular steel frame with polymer grip, the STI Trubor utilizes the Trubor compensated barrel, which is machined from one piece of 416 rifle-grade stainless steel. The Trubor is designed to eliminate misalignment of the barrel and compensator bore or movement of the compensator along the barrel threads, giving the shooter a more consistent performance and reduced muzzle flip. True to 1911 tradition, the Trubor has a classic scalloped slide with front and rear cocking serrations on a forged steel slide (blued) with polished sides, aluminum mag well, stainless steel ambidextrous safeties, stainless steel high rise grip safety, full-length guide rod, checkered frontstrap and checkered mainspring housing. With mounted C-More Railway sight included with the pistol.
Price: **$2,999.00**

Prices given are believed to be accurate at time of publication however, many factors affect retail pricing so exact prices are not possible.

CHARTER ARMS BULLDOG
Caliber: .44 Special. **Capacity:** 5-round cylinder. **Barrel:** 2.5 in. **Weight:** 21 oz. **Sights:** Blade front, notch rear. **Features:** Soft-rubber pancake-style grips, shrouded ejector rod, wide trigger and hammer spur. American made by Charter Arms.
Price: Blued **$409.00**
Price: Stainless **$422.00**
Price: Target Bulldog, 4 barrel, 23 oz. **$479.00**

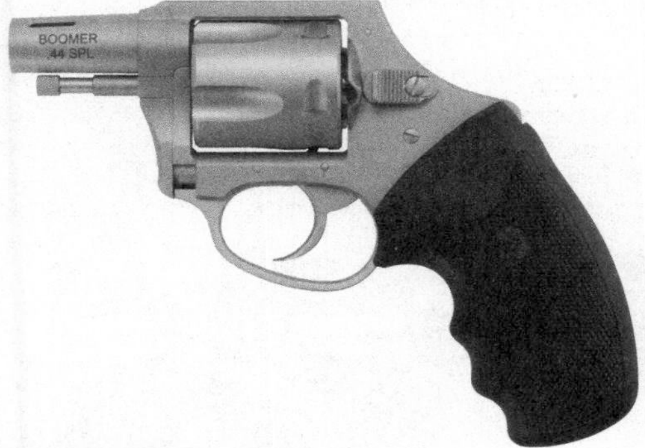

CHARTER ARMS BOOMER
Caliber: .44 Special. **Capacity:** 5-round cylinder. **Barrel:** 2 in., ported. **Weight:** 20 oz. **Grips:** Full rubber combat. **Sights:** Fixed.
Price: Blued **$443.00**

CHARTER ARMS POLICE BULLDOG
Caliber: .38 Special. **Capacity:** 6-round cylinder. **Barrel:** 4.2 in. **Weight:** 26 oz. **Sights:** Blade front, notch rear. Large frame version of Bulldog design.
Price: Blued **$408.00**

CHARTER ARMS CHIC LADY & CHIC LADY DAO
Caliber: .38 Special. **Capacity:** 5-round cylinder. **Barrel:** 2 in. **Weight:** 12 oz. **Grip:** Combat. **Sights:** Fixed. **Features:** 2-tone pink or lavender & stainless with aluminum frame. American made by Charter Arms.
Price: Chic Lady **$473.00**
Price: Chic Lady DAO **$483.00**

CHARTER UNDERCOVER LITE
Caliber: .38 Special +P. **Capacity:** 5-round cylinder. **Barrel:** 2 in. **Weight:** 12 oz. **Grip:** Full. **Sights:** Fixed. **Features:** 2-tone pink & stainless with aluminum frame. Constructed of tough aircraft-grade aluminum and steel, the Undercover Lite offers rugged reliability and comfort. This ultra-lightweight 5-shot .38 Special features a 2-in. barrel, fixed sights and traditional spurred hammer. American made by Charter Arms.
Price: **$397.00**

CHARTER ARMS CRIMSON UNDERCOVER
Caliber: .38 Special +P. **Capacity:** 5-round cylinder. **Barrel:** 2 in. **Weight:** 16 oz. **Grip:** Crimson Trace. **Sights:** Fixed. **Features:** Stainless finish and frame. American made by Charter Arms.
Price: **$577.00**

CHARTER ARMS OFF DUTY
Caliber: .38 Special. **Barrel:** 2 in. **Weight:** 12.5 oz. **Sights:** Blade front, notch rear. **Features:** 5-round cylinder, aluminum casting, DAO with concealed hammer. Also available with semi-concealed hammer. American made by Charter Arms.
Price: Aluminum **$404.00**
Price: Crimson Trace Laser grip **$657.00**

CHARTER ARMS MAG PUG
Caliber: .357 Mag. **Capacity:** 5-round cylinder. **Barrel:** 2.2 in. **Weight:** 23 oz. **Sights:** Blade front, notch rear. **Features:** American made by Charter Arms.
Price: Blued or stainless **$400.00**
Price: 4.4-in. full-lug barrel........ **$470.00**
Price: Crimson Trace Laser Grip........ **$609.00**

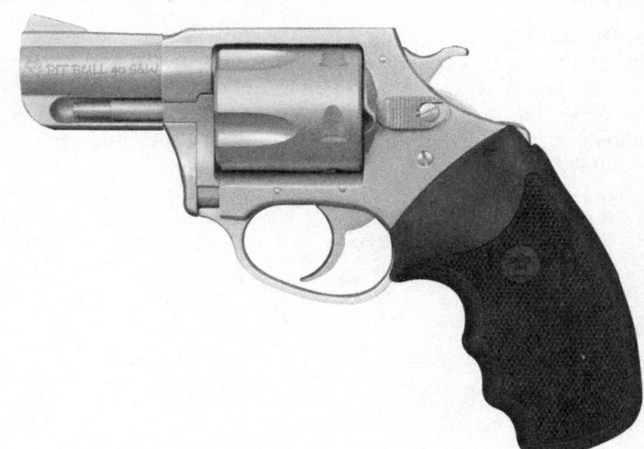

CHARTER ARMS PITBULL
Calibers: 9mm, 40 S&W, .45 ACP. **Capacity:** 5-round cylinder. **Barrel:** 2.2 in. **Weights:** 20–22 oz. **Sights:** Fixed rear, ramp front. **Grips:** Rubber. **Features:** Matte stainless steel frame or Nitride frame. Moon clips not required for 9mm, .45 ACP.
Price: 9mm **$502.00**
Price: .40 S&W **$489.00**
Price: .45 ACP **$489.00**

CHARTER ARMS SOUTHPAW
Caliber: .38 Special +P. **Capacity:** 5-round cylinder. **Barrel:** 2 in. **Weight:** 12 oz. **Grips:** Rubber Pachmayr style. **Features:** Snubnose, matte black aluminum alloy frame with stainless steel cylinder. Cylinder latch and crane assembly are on right side of frame for convenience of left-hand shooters.
Price: **$419.00**

CHARTER ARMS PATHFINDER
Calibers: .22 LR or .22 Mag. **Capacity:** 6-round cylinder. **Barrel:** 2 in., 4 in. **Weights:** 20 oz. (12 oz. Lite model). **Grips:** Full. **Sights:** Fixed or adjustable (Target). **Features:** Stainless finish and frame.
Price .22 LR **$365.00**
Price .22 Mag **$367.00**
Price: Lite **$379.00**
Price: Target **$409.00**

CHARTER ARMS UNDERCOVER
Caliber: .38 Special +P. **Capacity:** 6-round cylinder. **Barrel:** 2 in. **Weight:** 12 oz. **Sights:** Blade front, notch rear. **Features:** American made by Charter Arms.
Price: Blued **$346.00**

CHARTER ARMS UNDERCOVER SOUTHPAW
Caliber: .38 Spec. +P. **Capacity:** 5-round cylinder. **Barrel:** 2 in. **Weight:** 12 oz. **Sights:** NA. **Features:** Cylinder release is on the right side and the cylinder opens to the right side. Exposed hammer for both SA and DA. American made by Charter Arms.
Price: **$419.00**

CHIAPPA RHINO
Calibers: .357 Magnum, 9mm, .40 S&W. **Features:** 2-, 4-, 5- or 6-inch barrel; fixed or adjustable sights; visible hammer or hammerless design. **Weights:** 24–33 oz. Walnut or synthetic grips with black frame; hexagonal-shaped cylinder. Unique design fires from bottom chamber of cylinder.
Price: From **$1,139.00**

COBRA SHADOW
Caliber: .38 Special +P. **Capacity:** 5 rounds. **Barrel:** 1.875 in. **Weight:** 15 oz. Aluminum frame with stainless steel barrel and cylinder. **Length:** 6.375 in. **Grips:** Rosewood, black rubber or Crimson Trace Laser. **Features:** Black anodized, titanium anodized or custom colors including gold, red, pink and blue.
Price: **$369.00**
Price: Rosewood grips **$434.00**
Price: Crimson Trace Laser grips **$625.00**

COLT COBRA
Caliber: .38 Special. **Capacity:** 6 rounds. **Sights:** Fixed rear, fiber optic red front. **Grips:** Hogue rubbed stippled with finger grooves. **Weight**: 25 oz. **Finish:** Matte stainless. Same name as classic Colt model made from 1950–1986 but totally new design. Introduced in 2017.
Price: **$699.00**

COLT NIGHT COBRA
Caliber; .38 Special. **Capacity:** 6 rounds. **Grips:** Black synthetic VC G10. **Sight:** Tritium front night sight. DAO operation with bobbed hammer. Features a linear leaf spring design for smooth DA trigger pull.
Price: **$899.00**

COMANCHE II-A
Caliber: .38 Special. **Capacity:** 6-round cylinder. **Barrels:** 3 or 4 in. **Weights:** 33, 35 oz. **Lengths:** 8, 8.5 in. overall. **Grips:** Rubber. **Sights:** Fixed. **Features:** Blued finish, alloy frame. Distributed by SGS Importers.
Price: **$220.00**

DAN WESSON 715
Caliber: .357 Magnum. **Capacity:** 6-round cylinder. **Barrel:** 6-inch heavy barrel with full lug. **Weight:** 38 oz. **Lengths:** 8, 8.5 in. overall. **Grips:** Hogue rubber with finger grooves. **Sights:** Adjustable rear, interchangeable front blade. **Features:** Stainless steel. Interchangeable barrel assembly. Reintroduced in 2014. 715 Pistol Pack comes with 4-, 6- and 8-in. interchangeable barrels.
Price: From **$1,558.00**
Price: Pistol Pack **$1,999.00**

EAA WINDICATOR
Calibers: .38 Special, .357 Mag **Capacity:** 6-round cylinder. **Barrels:** 2 in., 4 in. **Weight:** 30 oz. (4 in.). **Length:** 8.5 in. overall (4 in. bbl.). **Grips:** Rubber with finger grooves. **Sights:** Blade front, fixed rear. **Features:** Swing-out cylinder; hammer block safety; blue or nickel finish. Introduced 1991. Imported from Germany by European American Armory.
Price: .38 Spec. from **$354.00**
Price: .357 Mag, steel frame from **$444.00**

KIMBER K6S
Caliber: .357 Magnum. **Capacity:** 6-round cylinder. **Barrel:** 2-inch full lug. **Grips:** Gray rubber. **Finish:** Satin stainless. Kimber's first revolver, claimed to be world's lightest production 6-shot .357 Magnum. DAO design with non-stacking match-grade trigger. Introduced 2016. CDP model has laminated checkered rosewood grips, Tritium night sights, two-tone black DLC/brushed stainless finish, match grade trigger.
Price: **$878.00**
Price: 3-in. Barrel **$899.00**
Price: Deluxe Carry w/Medallion grips **$1,088.00**
Price: Custom Defense Package **$1,155.00**
Price: Crimson Trace Laser Grips **$1,177.00**

KORTH USA
Calibers: .22 LR, .22 WMR, .32 S&W Long, .38 Special, .357 Mag., 9mm. **Capacity:** 6-shot. **Barrels:** 3, 4, 5.25, 6 in. **Weights:** 36–52 oz. **Grips:** Combat, Sport: Walnut, Palisander, Amboina, Ivory. **Finish:** German Walnut, matte with oil finish, adjustable ergonomic competition style. **Sights:** Adjustable Patridge (Sport) or Baughman (Combat), interchangeable and adjustable rear w/Patridge front (Target) in blue and matte. **Features:** DA/SA, 3 models, over 50 configurations, externally adjustable trigger stop and weight, interchangeable cylinder, removable wide-milled trigger shoe on Target model. Deluxe models are highly engraved editions. Available finishes include high polish blued finish, plasma coated in high polish or matte silver, gold, blue or charcoal. Many deluxe options available. From Korth USA.
Price: From **$8,000.00**
Price: Deluxe Editions, from **$12,000.00**

KORTH SKYHAWK
Caliber: 9mm. **Barrels:** 2 or 3 in. **Sights:** Adjustable rear with gold bead front. **Grips:** Hogue with finger grooves. **Features:** Polished trigger, skeletonized hammer. Imported by Nighthawk Custom.
Price: **$1,699.00**

ROSSI R461/R462
Caliber: .357 Mag. **Capacity:** 6-round cylinder. **Barrel:** 2 in. **Weight:** 26–35 oz. **Grips:** Rubber. **Sights:** Fixed. **Features:** DA/SA, +P-rated frame, blue carbon or high polish stainless steel, patented Taurus Security System.
Price: Blue carbon finish **$349.00**
Price: Stainless finish **$359.00**

ROSSI MODEL R971/R972
Caliber: 357 Mag. +P. **Capacity:** 6-round cylinder. **Barrel:** 4 in., 6 in. **Weight:** 32 oz. **Length:** 8.5 or 10.5 in. overall. **Grips:** Rubber. **Sights:** Blade front, adjustable rear. **Features:** SA/DA action. Patented key-lock Taurus Security System; forged steel frame. Introduced 2001. Made in Brazil by Amadeo Rossi. Imported by BrazTech/Taurus.
Price: Model R971 (blued finish, 4-in. bbl.) **$399.00**
Price: Model R972 (stainless steel finish, 6-in. bbl.) **$429.00**

ROSSI MODEL 351/851
Similar to Model R971/R972, chambered for .38 Special +P. Blued finish, 4-inch barrel. Introduced 2001. Made in Brazil by Amadeo Rossi. From BrazTech/Taurus.
Price: **$349.00**

RUGER GP-100
Calibers: .357 Mag., .327 Federal Mag, .44 Special **Capacities:** 6- or 7-round cylinder, .327 Federal Mag (7-shot), .44 Special (5-shot), .22 LR, (10-shot). **Barrels:** 3-in. full shroud, 4-in. full shroud, 6-in. full shroud. (.44 Special offered only with 3-in. barrel.) **Weights:** 36–45 oz. **Sights:** Fixed; adjustable on 4- and 6-in. full shroud barrels. **Grips:** Ruger Santoprene Cushioned Grip with Goncalo Alves inserts. **Features:** Uses action, frame features of both the Security-Six and Redhawk revolvers. Full-length, short ejector shroud. Satin blue and stainless steel.
Price: Blued **$769.00**
Price: Satin stainless **$799.00**
Price: .22 LR **$829.00**

Price: .44 Spl.. **$829.00**
Price: 7-round cylinder, 327 Fed or .357 Mag **$899.00**

RUGER GP-100 MATCH CHAMPION
Calibers: 10mm Magnum, .357 Mag. **Capacity:** 6-round cylinder. **Barrel:** 4.2-in. half shroud, slab-sided. **Weight:** 38 oz. **Sights:** Fixed rear, fiber optic front. **Grips:** Hogue Stippled Hardwood. **Features:** Satin stainless steel finish.
Price: Blued **$969.00**

RUGER LCR
Calibers: .22 LR (8-round cylinder), .22 WMR, .38 Special and .357 Mag., 5-round cylinder. **Barrel:** 1.875 in. **Weights:** 13.5–17.10 oz. **Length:** 6.5 in. overall. **Grips:** Hogue Tamer or Crimson Trace Lasergrips. **Sights:** Pinned ramp front, U-notch integral rear. **Features:** The Ruger Lightweight Compact Revolver (LCR), a 13.5 ounce, small frame revolver with a smooth, easy-to-control trigger and highly manageable recoil.
Price: .22 LR, .22 WMR, .38 Spl., iron sights **$579.00**
Price: 9mm, .327, .357, iron sights.. **$669.00**
Price: .22 LR, .22WMR, .38 Spl. Crimson Trace Lasergrip **$859.00**
Price: 9mm, .327, .357, Crimson Trace Lasergrip **$949.00**

Prices given are believed to be accurate at time of publication however, many factors affect retail pricing so exact prices are not possible.

RUGER LCRX

Calibers: .38 Special +P, 9mm, .327 Fed. Mag., .22 WMR. **Barrels:** 1.875 in. or 3 in. **Features:** Similar to LCR except this model has visible hammer, adjustable rear sight. The 3-inch barrel model has longer grip. 9mm comes with three moon clips.

Price: **$579.00**
Price: .327 Mag., .357 Mag., 9mm **$699.00**

RUGER SP-101

Calibers: .22 LR (6 shot); .327 Federal Mag. (6-shot), .38 Spl, .357 Mag. (5-shot). **Barrels:** 2.25, 3 1/16, 4.2 in (.327 Mag.). **Weights:** 25–30 oz. **Sights:** Adjustable or fixed, rear; fiber-optic or black ramp front. **Grips:** Ruger Cushioned Grip with inserts. **Features:** Compact, small frame, double-action revolver. Full-length ejector shroud. Stainless steel only.

Price: Fixed sights **$719.00**
Price: Adjustable rear, fiber optic front sights **$769.00**

RUGER REDHAWK

Calibers: .44 Rem. Mag., .45 Colt and .45 ACP/.45 Colt combo. **Capacity:** 6-round cylinder. **Barrels:** 2.75, 4.2, 5.5, 7.5 in. (.45 Colt in 4.2 in. only.) **Weight:** 54 oz. (7.5 bbl.). **Length:** 13 in. overall (7.5-in. barrel). **Grips:** Square butt cushioned grip panels. TALO Distributor exclusive 2.75-in. barrel stainless model has round butt, wood grips. **Sights:** Interchangeable Patridge-type front, rear adjustable for windage and elevation. **Features:** Stainless steel, brushed satin finish, blued ordnance steel. 9.5 sight radius. Introduced 1979.

Price: **$1,079.00**
Price: Hunter Model 7.5-in. bbl. **$1,159.00**
Price: TALO 2.75 in. model **$1,069.00**

Prices given are believed to be accurate at time of publication however, many factors affect retail pricing so exact prices are not possible.

RUGER SUPER REDHAWK

Calibers: 10mm, .44 Rem. Mag., .454 Casull, .480 Ruger. **Capacities:** 5- or 6-round cylinder. **Barrels:** 2.5 in. (Alaskan), 5.5 in., 6.5 in. (10mm), 7.5 in. or 9.5 in. **Weight:** 44–58 oz. **Length:** 13 in. overall (7.5-in. barrel). **Grips:** Hogue Tamer Monogrip. **Features:** Similar to standard Redhawk except has heavy extended frame with Ruger Integral Scope Mounting System on wide topstrap. Wide hammer spur lowered for better scope clearance. Incorporates mechanical design features and improvements of GP-100. Ramp front sight base has Redhawk-style interchangeable insert sight blades, adjustable rear sight. Alaskan model has 2.5-inch barrel. Satin stainless steel and low-glare stainless finishes. Introduced 1987.

Price: .44 Magnum, 10mm **$1,159.00**
Price: .454 Casull, .480 Ruger **$1,199.00**

SMITH & WESSON GOVERNOR

Calibers: .410 Shotshell (2.5 in.), .45 ACP, .45 Colt. **Capacity:** 6 rounds. **Barrel:** 2.75 in. **Length:** 7.5 in., (2.5 in. barrel). **Grip:** Synthetic. **Sights:** Front: Dovetailed tritium night sight or black ramp, rear: fixed. **Grips:** Synthetic. **Finish:** Matte black or matte silver (Silver Edition). **Weight:** 29.6 oz. **Features:** Capable of chambering a mixture of .45 Colt, .45 ACP and .410 gauge 2.5-inch shotshells, the Governor is suited for both close and distant encounters, allowing users to customize the load to their preference. Scandium alloy frame, stainless steel cylinder. Packaged with two full moon clips and three 2-shot clips.

Price: **$869.00**
Price: w/Crimson Trace Laser Grip **$1,179.00**

SMITH & WESSON J-FRAME

The J-frames are the smallest Smith & Wesson wheelguns and come in a variety of chamberings, barrel lengths and materials as noted in the individual model listings.

SMITH & WESSON 60LS/642LS LADYSMITH

Calibers: .38 Special +P, .357 Mag. **Capacity:** 5-round cylinder. **Barrels:** 1.875 in. (642LS); 2.125 in. (60LS) **Weights:** 14.5 oz. (642LS); 21.5 oz. (60LS); **Length:** 6.6 in. overall (60LS). **Grips:** Wood. **Sights:** Black blade, serrated ramp front, fixed notch rear. 642 CT has Crimson Trace Laser Grips. **Features:** 60LS model has a Chiefs Special-style frame. 642LS has Centennial-style frame, frosted matte finish, smooth combat wood grips. Introduced 1996. Comes in a fitted carry/storage case. Introduced 1989. Made in USA by Smith & Wesson.

Price: (642LS) **$499.00**
Price: (60LS) **$759.00**
Price: (642 CT) **$699.00**

SMITH & WESSON MODEL 63

Caliber: .22 LR **Capacity:** 8-round cylinder. **Barrel:** 3 in. **Weight:** 26 oz. **Length:** 7.25 in. overall. **Grips:** Black synthetic. **Sights:** Hi-Viz fiber optic front sight, adjustable black blade rear sight. **Features:** Stainless steel construction throughout. Made in USA by Smith & Wesson.

Price: **$769.00**

SMITH & WESSON MODEL 442/637/638/642 AIRWEIGHT

Caliber: .38 Special +P. **Capacity:** 5-round cylinder. **Barrels:** 1.875 in., 2.5 in. **Weight:** 15 oz. **Length:** 6.375 in. overall. **Grips:** Soft rubber. **Sights:** Fixed, serrated ramp front, square notch rear. **Features:** A family of J-frame .38 Special revolvers with aluminum-alloy frames. Model 637; Chiefs Special-style frame with exposed hammer. Introduced 1996. Models 442, 642; Centennial-style frame, enclosed hammer. Model 638, Bodyguard style, shrouded hammer. Comes in a fitted carry/storage case. Introduced 1989. Made in USA by Smith & Wesson.

Price: From **$469.00**
Price: Laser Max Frame Mounted Red Laser sight **$539.00**

SMITH & WESSON MODELS 637 CT/638 CT

Similar to Models 637, 638 and 642 but with Crimson Trace Laser Grips.

Price: **$699.00**

Prices given are believed to be accurate at time of publication however, many factors affect retail pricing so exact prices are not possible.

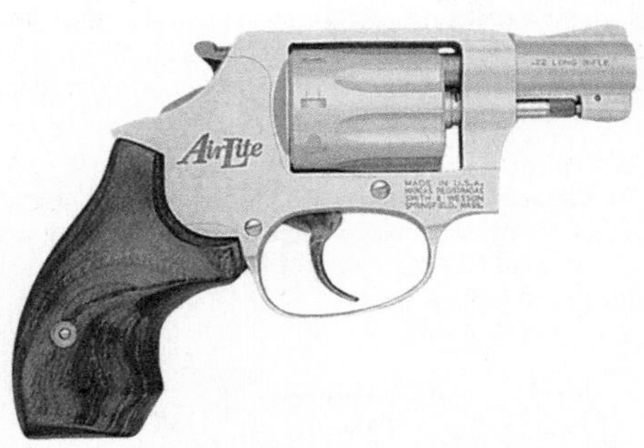

SMITH & WESSON MODEL 317 AIRLITE
Caliber: .22 LR. **Capacity:** 8-round cylinder. **Barrel:** 1.875 in. **Weight:** 10.5 oz. **Length:** 6.25 in. overall (1.875-in. barrel). **Grips:** Rubber. **Sights:** Serrated ramp front, fixed notch rear. **Features:** Aluminum alloy, carbon and stainless steels, Chiefs Special-style frame with exposed hammer. Smooth combat trigger. Clear Cote finish. Model 317 Kit Gun has adjustable rear sight, fiber optic front. Introduced 1997.
Price: **$759.00**

SMITH & WESSON MODEL 340/340PD AIRLITE SC CENTENNIAL
Calibers: .357 Mag., 38 Special +P. **Capacity:** 5-round cylinder. **Barrel:** 1.875 in. **Weight:** 12 oz. **Length:** 6.375 in. overall (1.875-in. barrel). **Grips:** Rounded butt rubber. **Sights:** Black blade front, rear notch **Features:** Centennial-style frame, enclosed hammer. Internal lock. Matte silver finish. Scandium alloy frame, titanium cylinder, stainless steel barrel liner. Made in USA by Smith & Wesson.
Price: **$1,019.00**

SMITH & WESSON MODEL 351PD
Caliber: .22 Mag. **Capacity:** 5-round cylinder. **Barrel:** 1.875 in. **Weight:** 10.6 oz. **Length:** 6.25 in. overall (1.875-in. barrel). **Sights:** HiViz front sight, rear notch. **Grips:** Wood. **Features:** 7-shot, aluminum-alloy frame. Chiefs Special-style frame with exposed hammer. Nonreflective matte-black finish. Internal lock. Made in USA by Smith & Wesson.
Price: **$759.00**

SMITH & WESSON MODEL 360/360PD AIRLITE CHIEF'S SPECIAL
Calibers: .357 Mag., .38 Special +P. **Capacity:** 5-round cylinder. **Barrel:** 1.875 in. **Weight:** 12 oz. **Length:** 6.375 in. overall (1.875-in. barrel). **Grips:** Rounded butt rubber. **Sights:** Black blade front, fixed rear notch. **Features:** Chief's Special-style frame with exposed hammer. Internal lock. Scandium alloy frame, titanium cylinder, stainless steel barrel. Made in USA by Smith & Wesson.
Price: **$1,019.00**

SMITH & WESSON BODYGUARD 38
Caliber: .38 Special +P. **Capacity:** 5-round cylinder. **Barrel:** 1.9 in. **Weight:** 14.3 oz. **Length:** 6.6 in. **Grip:** Synthetic. **Sights:** Front: Black ramp, Rear: fixed, integral with backstrap. Plus: Integrated laser sight. **Finish:** Matte black. **Features:** The first personal protection series that comes with an integrated laser sight.
Price: **$539.00**

SMITH & WESSON MODEL 640 CENTENNIAL DA ONLY
Calibers: .357 Mag., .38 Special +P. **Capacity:** 5-round cylinder. **Barrel:** 2.125 in. **Weight:** 23 oz. **Length:** 6.75 in. overall. **Grips:** Uncle Mike's Boot grip. **Sights:** Tritium Night Sights. **Features:** Stainless steel. Fully concealed hammer, snag-proof smooth edges. Internal lock.
Price: **$839.00**

SMITH & WESSON MODEL 649 BODYGUARD
Caliber: .357 Mag., .38 Special +P. **Capacity:** 5-round cylinder. **Barrel:** 2.125 in. **Weight:** 23 oz. **Length:** 6.625 in. overall. **Grips:** Uncle Mike's Combat. **Sights:** Black pinned ramp front, fixed notch rear. **Features:** Stainless steel construction, satin finish. Internal lock. Bodyguard style, shrouded hammer. Made in USA by Smith & Wesson.
Price: **$729.00**

SMITH & WESSON K-FRAME/L-FRAME
The K-frame series are mid-size revolvers and the L-frames are slightly larger.

SMITH & WESSON MODEL 10 CLASSIC
Caliber: .38 Special. **Capacity:** 6-round cylinder. **Features:** Bright blued steel frame and cylinder, checkered wood grips, 4-inch barrel and fixed sights. The oldest model in the Smith & Wesson line, its basic design goes back to the original Military & Police Model of 1905.
Price: **$739.00**

SMITH & WESSON MODEL 17 MASTERPIECE CLASSIC
Caliber: .22 LR. **Capacity:** 6-round cylinder. **Barrel:** 6 in. **Weight:** 40 oz. **Grips:** Checkered wood. **Sights:** Pinned Patridge front, micro-adjustable rear. Updated variation of K-22 Masterpiece of the 1930s.
Price: **$989.00**

SMITH & WESSON MODEL 48 CLASSIC
Same specifications as Model 17 except chambered in .22 Magnum (.22 WMR) and is available with a 4- or 6-inch barrel.
Price: .... **$949.00–$989.00**

SMITH & WESSON MODEL 64/67
Caliber: .38 Special +P. **Capacity:** 6-round cylinder **Barrel:** 3 in. **Weight:** 33 oz. **Length:** 8.875 in. overall. **Grips:** Soft rubber. **Sights:** Fixed, .125-in. serrated ramp front, square notch rear. Model 67 is similar to Model 64 except for adjustable sights. **Features:** Satin finished stainless steel, square butt.
Price: From .... **$689.00–$749.00**

SMITH & WESSON MODEL 66
Caliber: .357 Magnum. **Capacity:** 6-round cylinder. **Barrel:** 4.25 in. **Weight:** 36.6 oz. **Grips:** Synthetic. **Sights:** White outline adjustable rear, red ramp front. **Features:** Return in 2014 of the famous K-frame "Combat Magnum" with stainless finish.
Price: **$849.00**

SMITH & WESSON MODEL 69
Caliber: .44 Magnum. **Capacity:** 5-round cylinder. **Barrel:** 4.25 in. **Weight:** 37 oz. **Grips:** Checkered wood. **Sights:** White outline adjustable rear, red ramp front. **Features:** L-frame with stainless finish, 5-shot cylinder, introduced in 2014.
Price: **$989.00**

SMITH & WESSON MODEL 617
Caliber: .22 LR. **Capacity:** 10-round cylinder. **Barrel:** 6 in. **Weight:** 44 oz. **Length:** 11.125 in. **Grips:** Soft rubber. **Sights:** Patridge front, adjustable rear. Drilled and tapped for scope mount. **Features:** Stainless steel with satin finish. Introduced 1990.
Price: From **$829.00**

SMITH & WESSON MODEL 686/686 PLUS
Caliber: .357 Mag/.38 Special. **Capacity:** 6 (686) or 7 (Plus). **Barrels:** 6 in. (686), 3 or 6 in. (686 Plus), 4 in. (SSR). **Weight:** 35 oz. (3 in. barrel). **Grips:** Rubber. Sights: White outline adjustable rear, red ramp front. Features: Satin stainless frame and cylinder. Stock Service Revolver (SSR) has tapered underlug, interchangeable front sight, high-hold ergonomic wood grips, chamfered charge holes, custom barrel w/recessed crown, bossed mainspring.
Price: 686 .... **$829.00**
Price: Plus **$849.00**
Price: SSR **$999.00**

SMITH & WESSON MODEL 986 PRO
Caliber: 9mm. **Capacity:** 7-round cylinder **Barrel:** 5-in. tapered underlug. **Features:** SA/DA L-frame revolver chambered in 9mm. Features similar to 686 PLUS Pro Series with 5-inch tapered underlug barrel, satin stainless finish, synthetic grips, adjustable rear and Patridge blade front sight.
Price: **$1,149.00**

SMITH & WESSON M&P R8
Caliber: .357 Mag. **Capacity:** 8-round cylinder. **Barrel:** 5-in. half lug with accessory rail. **Weight:** 36.3 oz. **Length:** 10.5 in. **Grips:** Black synthetic. **Sights:** Adjustable v-notch rear, interchangeable front. **Features:** Scandium alloy frame, stainless steel cylinder.
Price: **$1,329.00**

Prices given are believed to be accurate at time of publication however, many factors affect retail pricing so exact prices are not possible.

SMITH & WESSON N-FRAME
These large-frame models introduced the .357, .41 and .44 Magnums to the world.

SMITH & WESSON MODEL 25 CLASSIC
Calibers: .45 Colt or .45 ACP. **Capacity:** 6-round cylinder. **Barrel:** 6.5 in. **Weight:** 45 oz. **Grips:** Checkered wood. **Sights:** Pinned Patridge front, micro-adjustable rear.
Price: **$1,019.00**

SMITH & WESSON MODEL 27 CLASSIC
Caliber: .357 Magnum. **Capacity:** 6-round cylinder. **Barrels:** 4 or 6.5 in. **Weight:** 41.2 oz. **Grips:** Checkered wood. **Sights:** Pinned Patridge front, micro-adjustable rear. Updated variation of the first magnum revolver, the .357 Magnum of 1935.
Price: (4 in.) **$1,019.00**
Price: (6.5 in.) **$1,059.00**

SMITH & WESSON MODEL 29 CLASSIC
Caliber: .44 Magnum **Capacity:** 6-round cylinder. **Barrel:** 4 or 6.5 in. **Weight:** 48.5 oz. **Length:** 12 in. **Grips:** Altamont service walnut. **Sights:** Adjustable white-outline rear, red ramp front. **Features:** Carbon steel frame, polished-blued or nickel finish. Has integral key lock safety feature to prevent accidental discharges. Original Model 29 made famous by "Dirty Harry" character played in 1971 by Clint Eastwood.
Price: .... **$999.00–$1,169.00**

SMITH & WESSON MODEL 57 CLASSIC
Caliber: .41 Magnum. **Capacity:** 6-round cylinder. **Barrel:** 6 in. **Weight:** 48 oz. **Grips:** Checkered wood. **Sights:** Pinned red ramp, micro-adjustable rear.
Price: **$1,009.00**

SMITH & WESSON MODEL 329PD ALASKA BACKPACKER
Caliber: .44 Magnum. **Capacity:** 6-round cylinder. **Barrel:** 2.5 in. **Weight:** 26 oz. **Length:** 9.5 in. **Grips:** Synthetic. **Sights:** Adj. rear, HiViz orange-dot front. **Features:** Scandium alloy frame, blue/black finish, stainless steel cylinder.
Price: From **$1,159.00**

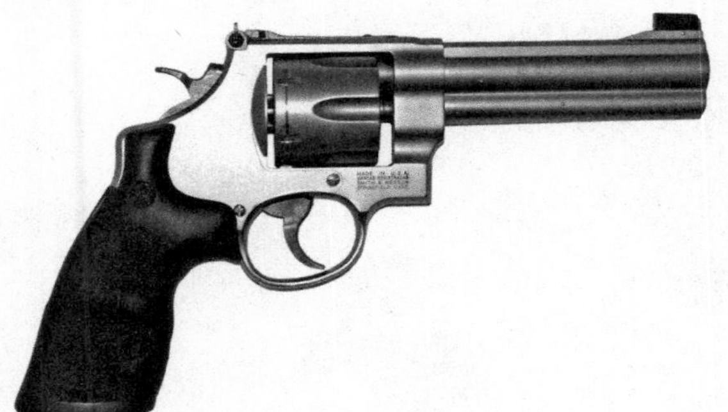

SMITH & WESSON MODEL 625/625JM
Caliber: .45 ACP. **Capacity:** 6-round cylinder. **Barrels:** 4 in., 5 in. **Weight:** 43 oz. (4-in. barrel). **Length:** 9.375 in. overall (4-in. barrel). **Grips:** Soft rubber; wood optional. **Sights:** Patridge front on ramp, S&W micrometer click rear adjustable for windage and elevation. **Features:** Stainless steel construction with .400-in. wide semi-target hammer, .312-in. smooth combat trigger; full lug barrel. Glass beaded finish. Introduced 1989. Jerry Miculek Professional (JM) Series has .265-in. wide grooved trigger, special wooden Miculek Grip, five full moon clips, gold bead Patridge front sight on interchangeable front sight base, bead blast finish. Unique serial number run. Mountain Gun has 4-in. tapered barrel, drilled and tapped, Hogue Rubber Monogrip, pinned black ramp front sight, micrometer click-adjustable rear sight, satin stainless frame and barrel weighs 39.5 oz.
Price: 625 or 625JM **$1,074.00**

SMITH & WESSON MODEL 629
Calibers: .44 Magnum, .44 S&W Special. **Capacity:** 6-round cylinder. **Barrels:** 4 in., 5 in., 6.5 in. **Weight:** 41.5 oz. (4-in. bbl.). **Length:** 9.625 in. overall (4-in. bbl.). **Grips:** Soft rubber; wood optional. **Sights:** .125-in. red ramp front, white outline rear, internal lock, adjustable for windage and elevation. Classic similar to standard Model 629, except Classic has full-lug 5-in. barrel, chamfered front of cylinder, interchangeable red ramp front sight with adjustable white outline rear, Hogue grips with S&W monogram, drilled and tapped for scope mounting. Factory accurizing and endurance packages. Introduced 1990. Classic Power Port has Patridge front sight and adjustable rear sight. Model 629CT has 5-in. barrel, Crimson Trace Hoghunter Lasergrips, 10.5 in. OAL, 45.5 oz. weight. Introduced 2006.
Price: From **$949.00**

SMITH & WESSON X-FRAME
These extra-large X-frame S&W revolvers push the limits of big-bore handgunning.

SMITH & WESSON MODEL 500
Caliber: 500 S&W Magnum. **Capacity:** 5-round cylinder. **Barrels:** 4 in., 6.5 in., 8.375 in. **Weight:** 72.5 oz. **Length:** 15 in. (8.375-in. barrel). **Grips:** Hogue Sorbothane Rubber. **Sights:** Interchangeable blade, front, adjustable rear. **Features:** Recoil compensator, ball detent cylinder latch, internal lock. 6.5-in.-barrel model has orange-ramp dovetail Millett front sight, adjustable black rear sight, Hogue Dual Density Monogrip, .312-in. chrome trigger with overtravel stop, chrome tear-drop hammer, glass bead finish. 10.5-in.-barrel model has red ramp front sight, adjustable rear sight, .312-in. chrome trigger with overtravel stop, chrome teardrop hammer with pinned sear, hunting sling. Compensated Hunter has .400-in. orange ramp dovetail front sight, adjustable black blade rear sight, Hogue Dual Density Monogrip, glass bead finish w/black clear coat. Made in USA by Smith & Wesson.
Price: From **$1,299.00**

SMITH & WESSON MODEL 460V
Caliber: 460 S&W Magnum (Also chambers .454 Casull, .45 Colt). **Capacity:** 5-round cylinder. **Barrels:** 7.5 in., 8.375-in. gain-twist rifling. **Weight:** 62.5 oz. **Length:** 11.25 in. **Grips:** Rubber. **Sights:** Adj. rear, red ramp front. **Features:** Satin stainless steel frame and cylinder, interchangeable compensator. 460XVR

Prices given are believed to be accurate at time of publication however, many factors affect retail pricing so exact prices are not possible.

(X-treme Velocity Revolver) has black blade front sight with interchangeable green Hi-Viz tubes, adjustable rear sight. 7.5-in.-barrel version has Lothar-Walther barrel, 360-degree recoil compensator, tuned Performance Center action, pinned sear, integral Weaver base, non-glare surfaces, scope mount accessory kit for mounting full-size scopes, flashed-chromed hammer and trigger, Performance Center gun rug and shoulder sling. Interchangeable Hi-Viz green dot front sight, adjustable black rear sight, Hogue Dual Density Monogrip, matte-black frame and shroud finish with glass-bead cylinder finish, 72 oz. Compensated Hunter has teardrop chrome hammer, .312-in. chrome trigger, Hogue Dual Density Monogrip, satin/matte stainless finish, HiViz interchangeable front sight, adjustable black rear sight. XVR introduced 2006.
Price: 460V **$1,369.00**
Price: 460XVR, from **$1,369.00**

SUPER SIX CLASSIC BISON BULL
Caliber: .45-70 Government. **Capacity:** 6-round cylinder. **Barrel:** 10in. octagonal with 1:14 twist. **Weight:** 6 lbs. **Length:** 17.5 in. overall. **Grips:** NA. **Sights:** Ramp front sight with dovetailed blade, click-adjustable rear. **Features:** Manganese bronze frame. Integral scope mount, manual cross-bolt safety.
Price: **$1,500.00**

TAURUS MODEL 17 TRACKER
Caliber: .17 HMR. **Capacity:** 7-round cylinder. **Barrel:** 6.5 in. **Weight:** 45.8 oz. **Grips:** Rubber. **Sights:** Adjustable. **Features:** Double action, matte stainless, integral key-lock.
Price: From **$539.00**

TAURUS MODEL 992 TRACKER
Calibers: .22 LR with interchangeable .22 WMR cylinder. **Capacity:** 9-round cylinder. **Barrel:** 4 or 6.5 in with ventilated rib. **Features:** Adjustable rear sight, blued or stainless finish.
Price: Blue **$591.00**
Price: Stainless **$627.00**

TAURUS MODEL 44SS
Caliber: .44 Magnum. **Capacity:** 5-round cylinder. **Barrel:** 4-in. ported. **Weight:** 34 oz. **Grips:** Rubber. **Sights:** Adjustable. **Features:** Double action. Integral key-lock. Introduced 1994. Finish: Matte stainless. Imported from Brazil by Taurus International Manufacturing, Inc.
Price: From **$769.00**

TAURUS MODEL 65
Caliber: .357 Magnum. **Capacity:** 6-round cylinder. **Barrel:** 4-in. full underlug. **Weight:** 38 oz. **Length:** 10.5 in. overall. **Grips:** Soft rubber. **Sights:** Fixed. **Features:** Double action, integral key-lock. Matte blued or stainless. Imported by Taurus International.
Price: Blued **$519.00**
Price: Stainless **$569.00**

TAURUS MODEL 66
Similar to Model 65, 4 in. or 6 in. barrel, 7-round cylinder, adjustable rear sight. Integral key-lock action. Imported by Taurus International.
Price: Blue **$579.00**
Price: Stainless **$629.00**

TAURUS MODEL 82 HEAVY BARREL
Caliber: .38 Special. **Capacity:** 6-round cylinder. **Barrel:** 4 in., heavy. **Weight:** 36.5 oz. **Length:** 9.25 in. overall. **Grips:** Soft black rubber. **Sights:** Serrated ramp front, square notch rear. **Features:** Double action, solid rib, integral key-lock. Imported by Taurus International.
Price: From **$499.00**

TAURUS MODEL 85FS
Caliber: .38 Special. **Capacity:** 5-round cylinder. **Barrel:** 2 in. **Weights:** 17–24.5 oz., titanium 13.5–15.4 oz. **Grips:** Rubber, rosewood or mother of pearl. **Sights:** Ramp front, square notch rear. **Features:** Spurred hammer. Blued, matte stainless, blue with gold accents, stainless with gold accents; rated for +P ammo. Integral keylock. Some models have titanium frame. Introduced 1980. Imported by Taurus International.
Price: From **$379.00**

TAURUS 380 MINI
Caliber: .380 ACP. **Capacity:** 5-round cylinder w/moon clip. **Barrel:** 1.75 in. **Weight:** 15.5 oz. **Length:** 5.95 in. **Grips:** Rubber. **Sights:** Adjustable rear, fixed front. **Features:** DAO. Available in blued or stainless finish. Five Star (moon) clips included.
Price: Blued **$459.00**
Price: Stainless **$489.00**

TAURUS MODEL 45-410 JUDGE
Calibers: 2.5-in. .410/.45 LC, 3-in. .410/.45 LC. **Barrels:** 3 in., 6.5 in. (blued finish). **Weights:** 35.2 oz., 22.4 oz. **Length:** 7.5 in. **Grips:** Ribber rubber. **Sights:** Fiber Optic. **Features:** DA/SA. Matte stainless and ultra-lite stainless finish. Introduced in 2007. Imported from Brazil by Taurus International.
Price: From **$589.00**

TAURUS JUDGE PUBLIC DEFENDER POLYMER
Caliber: .45 Colt/.410 (2.5 in.). **Capacity:** 5-round cylinder. **Barrel:** 2.5-in. **Weight:** 27 oz. **Features:** SA/DA revolver with 5-round cylinder; polymer frame; Ribber rubber-feel grips; fiber-optic front sight; adjustable rear sight; blued or stainless cylinder; shrouded hammer with cocking spur; blued finish.
Price: From **$509.00**

TAURUS RAGING JUDGE MAGNUM
Calibers: .454 Casull, .45 Colt, 2.5-in. and 3-in. .410. **Barrels:** 3 or 6 in. **Features:** SA/DA revolver with fixed sights with fiber-optic front; blued or stainless steel finish; vent rib for scope mounting (6-in. only); cushioned Raging Bull grips.
Price: **$1,089.00**

Prices given are believed to be accurate at time of publication however, many factors affect retail pricing so exact prices are not possible.

TAURUS MODEL 627 TRACKER
Caliber: .357 Magnum. **Capacity:** 7-round cylinder. **Barrels:** 4 or 6.5 in. **Weights:** 28.8, 41 oz. **Grips:** Rubber. **Sights:** Fixed front, adjustable rear. **Features:** Double-action. Stainless steel, Shadow Gray or Total Titanium; vent rib (steel models only); integral key-lock action. Imported by Taurus International.
Price: From **$709.00**

TAURUS MODEL 444 ULTRA-LIGHT
Caliber: .44 Magnum. **Capacity:** 5-round cylinder. **Barrels:** 2.5 or 4 in. **Weight:** 28.3 oz. **Grips:** Cushioned inset rubber. **Sights:** Fixed red-fiber optic front, adjustable rear. **Features:** UltraLite titanium blue finish, titanium/alloy frame built on Raging Bull design. Smooth trigger shoe, 1.760-in. wide, 6.280-in. tall. Barrel rate of twist 1:16, 6 grooves. Introduced 2005. Imported by Taurus International.
Price: **$792.00**

TAURUS MODEL 444/454 RAGING BULL SERIES
Calibers: .44 Magnum, .454 Casull. **Barrels:** 2.25 in., 5 in., 6.5 in., 8.375 in. **Weight:** 53–63 oz. **Length:** 12 in. overall (6.5 in. barrel). **Grips:** Soft black rubber. **Sights:** Patridge front, adjustable rear. **Features:** DA, ventilated rib, integral key-lock. Most models have ported barrels. Introduced 1997. Imported by Taurus International.
Price: 444 .... **$753.00**
Price: 454 .... **$1,109.**

TAURUS RAGING HUNTER
Caliber: .44 Magnum. **Capacity:** 6-round cylinder. **Barrel:** 8.375 in. **Sights:** Adjustable rear, fixed front. **Grips:** Soft rubber with cushioned inset. **Weight:** 55 oz. **Features:** DA, ventilated rib. Imported by Taurus International.
Price: **$919.00**

TAURUS MODEL 605 PLY
Caliber: .357 Magnum. **Capacity:** 5-round cylinder. **Barrel:** 2 in. **Weight:** 20 oz. **Grips:** Rubber. **Sights:** Fixed. **Features:** Polymer frame steel cylinder. Blued or stainless. Introduced 1995. Imported by Taurus International.
Price: Blued **$460.00**
Price: Stainless **$507.00**

TAURUS MODEL 650 CIA
Calibers: .357 Magnum/.38 Special +P only. **Capacity:** 5-round cylinder. **Barrel:** 2 in. **Weight:** 24.5 oz. **Grips:** Rubber. **Sights:** Ramp front, square notch rear. **Features:** DAO, blued finish, integral key-lock, internal hammer. Introduced 2001. From Taurus International.
Price: From **$539.00**

TAURUS MODEL 905
Caliber: 9mm. **Capacity:** 5-round cylinder. **Barrel:** 2 in. **Features:** Small-frame revolver with rubber boot grips, fixed sights, choice of exposed or concealed hammer. Blued or stainless finish.
Price: Blued **$509.00**
Price: Stainless **$559.00**

TAURUS MODEL 692
Calibers: .38 Special/.357 Magnum or 9mm. **Capacity:** 7-round cylinder. **Barrels:** 3 or 6.5 in, ported. **Sights:** Adjustable rear, fixed front. **Grip:** "Ribber" textured. **Finish:** Matte blued or stainless. **Features:** Caliber can be changed with a swap of the cylinders which are non-fluted.
Price: **$659.00**

CIMARRON 1872 OPEN TOP
Calibers: .38, .44 Special, .44 Colt, .44 Russian, .45 LC, .45 S&W Schofield. **Barrels:** 5.5 in. and 7.5 in. **Grips:** Walnut. **Sights:** Blade front, fixed rear. **Features:** Replica of first cartridge-firing revolver. Blued finish; Navy-style brass or steel Army-style frame. Introduced 2001 by Cimarron F.A. Co.
Price: Navy model **$529.00**
Price: Army **$550.00**

CIMARRON 1875 OUTLAW
Calibers: .357 Magnum, .38 Special, .44 W.C.F., .45 Colt, .45 ACP. **Barrels:** 5.5 in. and 7.5 in. **Weight:** 2.5–2.6 lbs. **Grip:** 1-piece walnut. **Features:** Standard blued finish with color casehardened frame. Replica of 1875 Remington model. Available with dual .45 Colt/.45 ACP cylinder.
Price: **$578.00**
Price: Dual Cyl. **$686.00**

CIMARRON MODEL 1890
Caliber: .357 Magnum, .38 Special, .44 W.C.F., .45 Colt, .45 ACP. **Barrel:** 5.5 in. **Weight:** 2.4-2.5 lbs. **Grip:** 1-piece walnut. **Features:** Standard blued finish with standard blue frame. Replica of 1890 Remington model. Available with dual .45 Colt/.45 ACP cylinder.
Price: **$606.00**
Price: Dual Cylinder **$702.00**

CIMARRON BISLEY MODEL SINGLE-ACTION
Calibers: .357 Magnum, .44 WCF, .44 Special, .45. **Features:** Similar to Colt Bisley, special grip frame and trigger guard, knurled wide-spur hammer, curved trigger. Introduced 1999. Imported by Cimarron F.A. Co.
Price: From **$636.00**

CIMARRON LIGHTNING SA
Calibers: .22 LR, .32-20/32 H&R dual cyl. combo, .38 Special, .41 Colt. **Barrels:** 3.5 in., 4.75 in., 5.5 in. **Grips:** Smooth or checkered walnut. **Sights:** Blade front. **Features:** Replica of the Colt 1877 Lightning DA. Similar to Cimarron Thunderer, except smaller grip frame to fit smaller hands. Standard blued, charcoal blued or nickel finish with forged, old model, or color casehardened frame. Dual cylinder model available with .32-30/.32 H&R chambering. Introduced 2001. From Cimarron F.A. Co.
Price: From .... **$503.00–$565.00**
Price: .32-20/.32 H&R dual cylinder **$649.00**

CIMARRON MODEL P SAA
Calibers: .32 WCF, .38 WCF, .357 Magnum, .44 WCF, .44 Special, .45 Colt and .45 ACP. **Barrels:** 4.75, 5.5, 7.5 in. **Weight:** 39 oz. **Length:** 10 in. overall (4.75-in. barrel). **Grips:** Walnut. **Sights:** Blade front. **Features:** Old model black-powder frame with Bullseye ejector, or New Model frame. Imported by Cimarron F.A. Co.
Price: From **$550.00**

CIMARRON MODEL "P" JR.
Calibers: .22 LR, .32-20, .32 H&R, 38 Special **Barrels:** 3.5, 4.75, 5.5 in. **Grips:** Checkered walnut. **Sights:** Blade front. **Features:** Styled after 1873 Colt Peacemaker, except 20 percent smaller. Blue finish with color case-hardened frame; Cowboy action. Introduced 2001. From Cimarron F.A. Co.
Price: From **$480.00**

CIMARRON ROOSTER SHOOTER
Calibers: .357, .45 Colt and .44 W.C.F. **Barrel:** 4.75 in. **Weight:** 2.5 lbs. **Grip:** 1-piece orange finger grooved. **Features:** A replica of John Wayne's Colt Single Action Army model used in many of his great Westerns including his Oscar-winning performance in "True Grit," where he brings the colorful character Rooster Cogburn to life.
Price: **$909.00**

CIMARRON THUNDERER
Calibers: .357 Magnum, .44 WCF, .45 Colt. **Capacity:** 6-round cylinder. **Features:** Doc Holiday combo comes with leather shoulder holster, ivory handled dagger. Gun and knife have matching serial numbers. Made by Uberti.
Price: From .... **$575.00–$948.00**
Price: Combo **$1,559.00**

CIMARRON THUNDERSTORM
Caliber: .45 Colt. **Barrels:** 3.5 or 4.75 in. **Grips:** Model P or Thunderer, checkered wood. **Finish:** Blue or stainless. Action job including U.S.-made competition springs. Designed for Cowboy Action Shooting. Available with Short Stroke action.
Price: Blued **$753.00**
Price: Stainless **$948.00**
Price: Short Stroke Action **$779.00**

CIMARRON FRONTIER
Calibers: .357 Magnum, .44 WCF, .45 Colt. **Barrels:** 3.5, 4.75, 5.5 or 7.5 in. **Features:** Basic SAA design. Choice of Old Model or Pre-War frame. Blued or stainless finish. Available with Short Stroke action.
Price: Blued **$530.00**
Price: Stainless **$723.00**
Price: Short Stroke Action **$598.00**

CIMARRON U.S.V. ARTILLERY MODEL SINGLE-ACTION

Caliber: .45 Colt. **Barrel:** 5.5 in. **Weight:** 39 oz. **Length:** 11.5 in. overall. **Grips:** Walnut. **Sights:** Fixed. **Features:** U.S. markings and cartouche, casehardened frame and hammer. Imported by Cimarron F.A. Co.

Price: Blued finish.............................. **$594.00**
Price: Original finish **$701.00**

CIMARRON BAD BOY

Caliber: .44 Magnum. **Features:** Single Action Army-style revolver with 6- or 8-in. octagon barrel, standard blued finish, smooth walnut one-piece grip, flat-top frame with adjustable rear sight. Introduced 2018.

Price: **$688.00**

COLT NEW FRONTIER

Calibers: .357 Magnum, .44 Special and .45 Colt. **Barrels:** 4.75 in., 5.5 in., and 7.5 in. **Grip:** Walnut. **Features:** From 1890 to 1898, Colt manufactured a variation of the venerable Single Action Army with a uniquely different profile. The "Flattop Target Model" was fitted with an adjustable leaf rear sight and blade front sights. Colt has taken this concept several steps further to bring shooters a reintroduction of a Colt classic. The New Frontier has that sleek flattop design with an adjustable rear sight for windage and elevation and a target ready ramp-style front sight. The guns are meticulously finished in Colt Royal Blue on both the barrel and cylinder, with a case-colored frame. Additional calibers available through Colt Custom Shop.

Price: **$1,899.00**

COLT SINGLE ACTION ARMY

Calibers: .357 Magnum, .45 Colt. **Capacity:** 6-round cylinder. **Barrels:** 4.75, 5.5, 7.5 in. **Weight:** 40 oz. (4.75-in. barrel). **Length:** 10.25 in. overall (4.75-in. barrel). **Grips:** Black Eagle composite. **Sights:** Blade front, notch rear. **Features:** Available in full nickel finish with nickel grip medallions, or Royal Blue with color casehardened frame. Reintroduced 1992. Additional calibers available through Colt Custom Shop.

Price: Blued **$1,599.00**
Price: Nickel.............................. **$1,799.00**

EAA BOUNTY HUNTER SA

Calibers: .22 LR/.22 WMR, .357 Mag., .44 Mag., .45 Colt. **Capacities:** 6. 10-round cylinder available for .22LR/.22WMR. **Barrels:** 4.5 in., 7.5 in. **Weight:** 2.5 lbs. **Length:** 11 in. overall (4.625 in. barrel). **Grips:** Smooth walnut. **Sights:** Blade front, grooved topstrap rear. **Features:** Transfer bar safety; 3-position hammer; hammer-forged barrel. Introduced 1992. Imported by European American Armory

Price: Centerfire, blued or case-hardened **$478.00**
Price: Centerfire, nickel **$515.00**
Price: .22 LR/.22 WMR, blued **$343.00**
Price: .22LR/.22WMR, nickel **$380.00**
Price: .22 LR/.22WMR, 10-round cylinder **$465.00**

EMF 1875 OUTLAW

Calibers: .357 Magnum, .44-40, .45 Colt. **Barrels:** 7.5 in., 9.5 in. **Weight:** 46 oz. **Length:** 13.5 in. overall. **Grips:** Smooth walnut. **Sights:** Blade front, fixed groove rear. **Features:** Authentic copy of 1875 Remington with firing pin in hammer; color casehardened frame, blued cylinder, barrel, steel backstrap and trigger guard. Also available in nickel, factory engraved. Imported by E.M.F. Co.

Price: All calibers **$520.00**
Price: Laser Engraved **$800.00**

EMF 1873 GREAT WESTERN II

Calibers: .357 Magnum, .45 Colt, .44/40. **Barrels:** 3.5 in., 4.75 in., 5.5 in., 7.5 in. **Weight:** 36 oz. **Length:** 11 in. (5.5-in. barrel). **Grips:** Walnut. **Sights:** Blade front, notch rear. **Features:** Authentic reproduction of the original 2nd Generation Colt single-action revolver. Standard and bone casehardening. Coil hammer spring. Hammer-forged barrel.

Price: 1873 Californian .... **$545.00–$560.00**
Price: 1873 Custom series, bone or nickel, ivory-like grips **$689.90**
Price: 1873 Stainless steel, ivory-like grips **$589.90**
Price: 1873 Paladin **$560.00**
Price: Deluxe Californian with checkered walnut grips **$660.00**
Price: Buntline with stag grips.............................. **$810.00**

EMF 1873 DAKOTA II

Caliber: .357 Magnum, 45 Colt. **Barrel:** 4.75 in. **Grips:** Walnut. **Finish:** black.
Price: **$460.00**

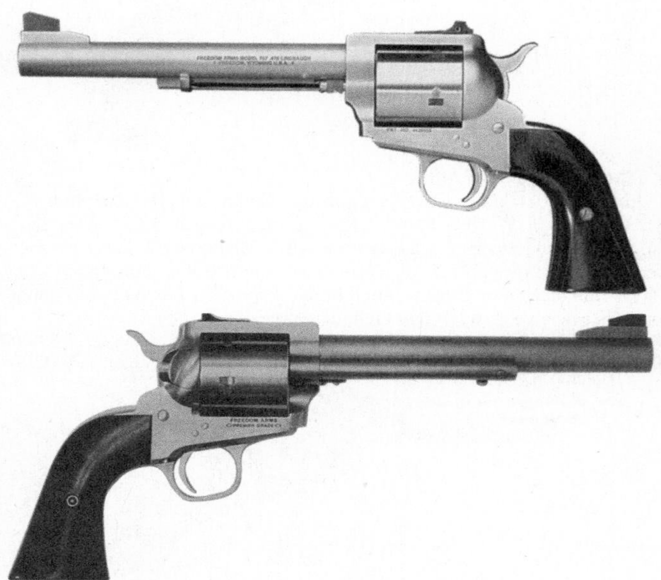

FREEDOM ARMS MODEL 83 PREMIER GRADE

Calibers: .357 Magnum, 41 Magnum, .44 Magnum, .454 Casull, .475 Linebaugh, .500 Wyo. Exp. **Capacity:** 5-round cylinder. **Barrels:** 4.75 in., 6 in., 7.5 in., 9 in. (.357 Mag. only), 10 in. (except .357 Mag. and 500 Wyo. Exp.) **Weight:** 53 oz. (7.5-in. bbl. in .454 Casull). **Length:** 13 in. (7.5 in. bbl.). **Grips:** Impregnatedhardwood. **Sights:** Adjustable rear with replaceable front sight. Fixed rear notch and front blade. **Features:** Stainless steel construction with brushed finish; manual sliding safety bar. Micarta grips optional. 500 Wyo. Exp. Introduced 2006. Lifetime warranty. Made in USA by Freedom Arms, Inc.
Price: From **$2,738.00**

FREEDOM ARMS MODEL 83 FIELD GRADE

Calibers: .22 LR, .357 Magnum, .41 Magnum, .44 Magnum, .454 Casull, .475 Linebaugh, .500 Wyo. Exp. **Capacity:** 5-round cylinder. **Barrels:** 4.75 in., 6 in., 7.5 in., 9 in. (.357 Mag. only), 10 in. (except .357 Mag. and .500 Wyo. Exp.) **Weight:** 56 oz. (7.5-in. bbl. in .454 Casull). **Length:** 13.1 in. (7.5 in. bbl.). **Grips:** Pachmayr standard, impregnated hardwood or Micarta optional. **Sights:** Adjustable rear with replaceable front sight. Model 83 frame. All stainless steel. Introduced 1988. Made in USA by Freedom Arms Inc.
Price: From **$2,332.00**

FREEDOM ARMS MODEL 97 PREMIER GRADE

Calibers: .17 HMR, .22 LR, .32 H&R, .327 Federal, .357 Magnum, 6 rounds; .41 Magnum, .44 Special, .45 Colt. **Capacity:** 5-round cylinder. **Barrels:** 4.25 in., 5.5 in., 7.5 in., 10 in. (.17 HMR, .22 LR, .32 H&R). **Weight:** 40 oz. (5.5 in. .357 Mag.). **Length:** 10.75 in. (5.5 in. bbl.). **Grips:** Impregnated hardwood; Micarta optional. **Sights:** Adjustable rear, replaceable blade front. Fixed rear notch and front blade. **Features:** Stainless steel construction, brushed finish, automatic transfer bar safety system. Introduced in 1997. Lifetime warranty. Made in USA by Freedom Arms.
Price: From **$2,148.00**

HERITAGE ROUGH RIDER

Calibers: .22 LR, 22 LR/22 WMR combo, .357 Magnum .44-40, .45 Colt. **Capacity:** 6-round cylinder. **Barrels:** 3.5 in., 4.75 in., 5.5 in., 7.5 in. **Weights:** 31–38 oz. **Grips:** Exotic cocobolo laminated wood or mother of pearl; bird's head models offered. **Sights:** Blade front, fixed rear. Adjustable sight on 4.75 in. and 5.5 in. models. **Features:** Hammer block safety. Transfer bar with Big Bores. High polish blue, black satin, silver satin, casehardened and stainless finish. Introduced 1993. Made in USA by Heritage Mfg., Inc.
Price: Rimfire calibers, From **$200.00**
Price: Centerfire calibers, From **$450.00**

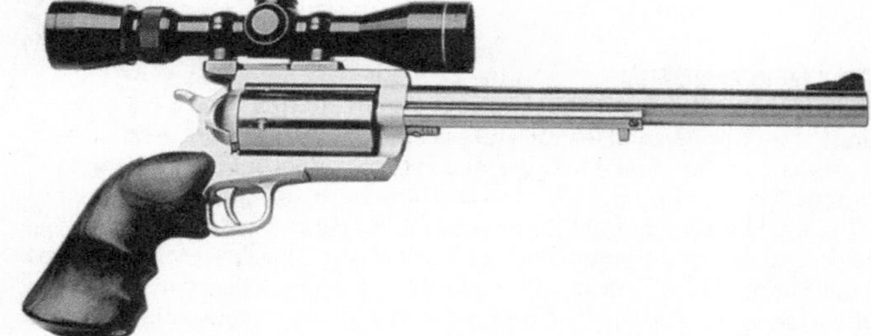

MAGNUM RESEARCH BFR SINGLE ACTION

Calibers: .44 Magnum, .444 Marlin, .45-70, .45 Colt/.410, .450 Marlin, .454 Casull, .460 S&W Magnum, .480 Ruger/.475 Linebaugh, .500 Linebaugh, .500 JRH, .500 S&W, .30-30. **Barrels:** 6.5 in., 7.5 in. and 10 in. **Weights:** 3.6–5.3 lbs. **Grips:** Black rubber. **Sights:** Rear sights are the same configuration as the Ruger revolvers. Many aftermarket rear sights will fit the BFR. Front sights are machined by Magnum in four heights and anodized flat black. The four heights accommodate all shooting styles, barrel lengths and calibers. All sights are interchangeable with each BFR's. **Features:** Crafted in the USA, the BFR single-action 5-shot stainless steel revolver frames are CNC machined inside and out from a pre-heat treated investment casting.

This is done to prevent warping and dimensional changes or shifting that occurs during the heat treat process. Magnum Research designed the frame with large calibers and substantial recoil in mind, built to close tolerances to handle the pressure of true big-bore calibers. The BFR is equipped with a transfer bar safety feature that allows the gun to be carried safely with all five chambers loaded.
Price: **$1,184.00**

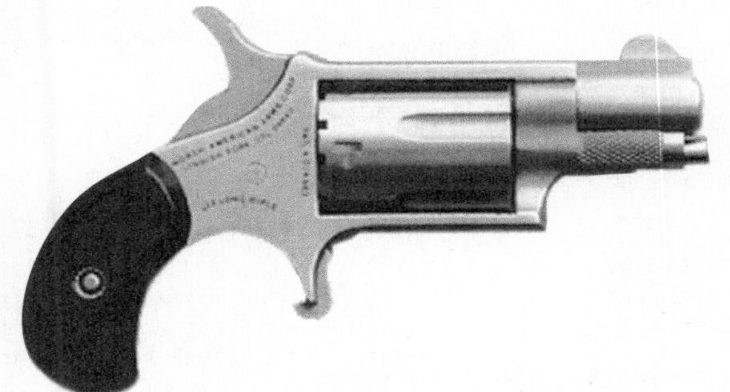

NORTH AMERICAN ARMS MINI
Calibers: .22 Short, 22 LR, 22 WMR. **Capacity:** 5-round cylinder. **Barrels:** 1.125 in., 1.625 in. **Weight:** 4–6.6 oz. **Length:** 3.625 in., 6.125 in. overall. **Grips:** Laminated wood. **Sights:** Blade front, notch fixed rear. **Features:** All stainless steel construction. Polished satin and matte finish. Engraved models available. From North American Arms.
Price: .22 Short, .22 LR **$226.00**
Price: .22 WMR **$236.00**

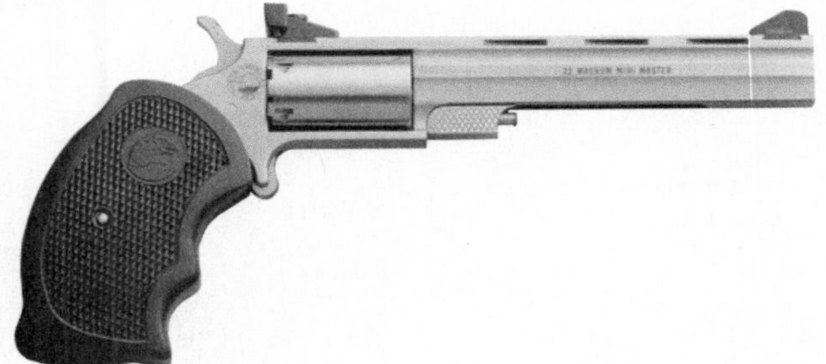

NORTH AMERICAN ARMS MINI-MASTER
Calibers: .22 LR, .22 WMR. **Capacity:** 5-round cylinder. **Barrel:** 4 in. **Weight:** 10.7 oz. **Length:** 7.75 in. overall. **Grips:** Checkered hard black rubber. **Sights:** Blade front, white outline rear adjustable for elevation, or fixed. **Features:** Heavy vented barrel; full-size grips. Non-fluted cylinder. Introduced 1989.
Price: .... **$284.00–$349.00**

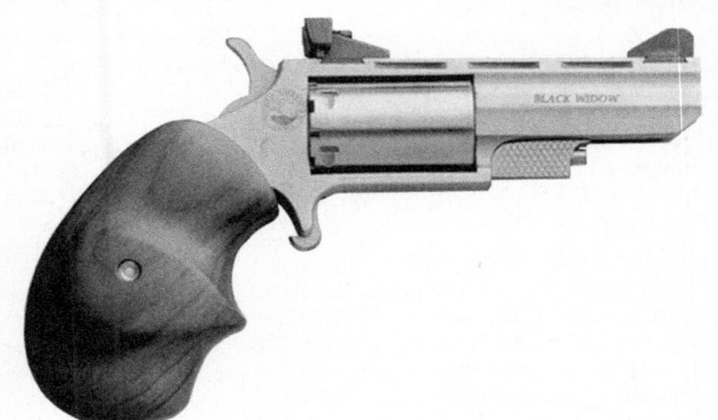

NORTH AMERICAN ARMS BLACK WIDOW
Similar to Mini-Master, 2-in. heavy vent barrel. Built on .22 WMR frame. Non-fluted cylinder, black rubber grips. Available with Millett low-profile fixed sights or Millett sight adjustable for elevation only. Overall length 5.875 in., weighs 8.8 oz. From North American Arms.
Price: Adjustable sight, .22 LR or .22 WMR **$352.00**
Price: Fixed sight, .22 LR or .22 WMR **$288.00**

NORTH AMERICAN ARMS "THE EARL" SINGLE-ACTION
Calibers: .22 Magnum with .22 LR accessory cylinder. **Capacity:** 5-round cylinder. **Barrel:** 4 in. octagonal. **Weight:** 6.8 oz. **Length:** 7.75 in. overall. **Grips:** Wood. **Sights:** Barleycorn front and fixed notch rear. **Features:** Single-action mini-revolver patterned after 1858-style Remington percussion revolver. Includes a spur trigger and a faux loading lever that serves as cylinder pin release.
Price: .... **$298.00, $332.00 (convertible)**

RUGER NEW MODEL SINGLE-SIX SERIES
Calibers: .22 LR, .17 HMR. Convertible and Hunter models come with extra cylinder for .22 WMR. **Capacity:** 6. **Barrels:** 4.62 in., 5.5 in., 6.5 in. or 9.5 in. **Weight:** 35–42 oz. **Finish:** Blued or stainless. **Grips:** Black checkered hard rubber, black laminate or hardwood (stainless model only). Single-Six .17 Model available only with 6.5-in. barrel, blue finish, rubber grips. Hunter Model available only with 7.5-in. barrel, black laminate grips and stainless finish.
Price: (blued).. **$629.00**
Price: (stainless) **$699.00**

RUGER SINGLE-TEN AND RUGER SINGLE-NINE SERIES
Calibers: .22 LR, .22 WMR. **Capacities:** 10 (.22 LR Single-Ten), 9 (.22 Mag Single-Nine). **Barrels:** 5.5 in. (Single-Ten), 6.5 in. (Single-Nine). **Weight:** 38–39 oz. **Grips:** Hardwood Gunfighter. **Sights:** Williams Adjustable Fiber Optic.
Price: **$699.00**

RUGER NEW MODEL BLACKHAWK/ BLACKHAWK CONVERTIBLE
Calibers: .30 Carbine, .357 Magnum/.38 Special, .41 Magnum, .44 Special, .45 Colt. **Capacity:** 6-round cylinder. **Barrels:** 4.625 in., 5.5 in., 6.5 in., 7.5 in. (.30 carbine and .45 Colt). **Weights:** 36–45 oz. **Lengths:** 10.375 in. to 13.5 in. **Grips:** Rosewood or black checkered. **Sights:** .125-in. ramp front, micro-click rear adjustable for windage and elevation. **Features:** Rosewood grips, Ruger transfer bar safety system, independent firing pin, hardened chrome-moly steel frame, music wire springs through-out. Case and lock included. Convertibles come with extra cylinder.
Price: (blued).. **$669.00**
Price: (Convertible, .357/9mm)... **$749.00**
Price: (Convertible, .45 Colt/.45 ACP) **$749.00**
Price: (stainless, .357 only)... **$799.00**

RUGER BISLEY SINGLE ACTION
Calibers: .44 Magnum. and .45 Colt. **Barrel:** 7.5-in. barrel. **Length:** 13.5 in. **Weight:** 48–51 oz. Similar to standard Blackhawk, hammer is lower with smoothly curved, deeply checkered wide spur. The trigger is strongly curved with wide smooth surface. Longer grip frame. Adjustable rear sight, ramp-style front. Unfluted cylinder and roll engraving, adjustable sights. Plastic lockable case. Orig. fluted cylinder introduced 1985; discontinued 1991. Unfluted cylinder introduced 1986.
Price: **$899.00**

RUGER NEW MODEL SUPER BLACKHAWK

Caliber: .44 Magnum/.44 Special. **Capacity:** 6-round cylinder. **Barrel:** 4.625 in., 5.5 in., 7.5 in., 10.5 in. bull. **Weight:** 45–55 oz. **Length:** 10.5 in. to 16.5 in. overall. **Grips:** Rosewood. **Sights:** .125-in. ramp front, micro-click rear adjustable for windage and elevation. **Features:** Ruger transfer bar safety system, fluted or unfluted cylinder, steel grip and cylinder frame, round or square back trigger guard, wide serrated trigger, wide spur hammer. With case and lock.

Price: **$829.00**

RUGER NEW MODEL SUPER BLACKHAWK HUNTER

Caliber: .44 Magnum. **Capacity:** 6-round cylinder. **Barrel:** 7.5 in., full-length solid rib, unfluted cylinder. **Weight:** 52 oz. **Length:** 13.625 in. **Grips:** Black laminated wood. **Sights:** Adjustable rear, replaceable front blade. **Features:** Reintroduced Ultimate SA revolver. Includes instruction manual, high-impact case, set of medium scope rings, gun lock, ejector rod as standard. Bisley-style frame available.

Price: (Hunter, Bisley Hunter) **$959.00**

RUGER NEW VAQUERO SINGLE-ACTION

Calibers: .357 Magnum, .45 Colt. **Capacity:** 6-round cylinder. **Barrel:** 4.625 in., 5.5 in., 7.5 in. **Weight:** 39–45 oz. **Length:** 10.5 in. overall (4.625 in. barrel). **Grips:** Rubber with Ruger medallion. **Sights:** Fixed blade front, fixed notch rear. **Features:** Transfer bar safety system and loading gate interlock. Blued model color casehardened finish on frame, rest polished and blued. Engraved model available. Gloss stainless. Introduced 2005.

Price: **$829.00**

RUGER NEW MODEL BISLEY VAQUERO

Calibers: .357 Magnum, .45 Colt. **Capacity:** 6-round cylinder. **Barrel:** 5.5-in. **Length:** 11.12 in. **Weight:** 45 oz. **Features:** Similar to New Vaquero but with Bisley-style hammer and grip frame. Simulated ivory grips, fixed sights.

Price: **$899.00**

RUGER NEW BEARCAT SINGLE-ACTION

Caliber: .22 LR. **Capacity:** 6-round cylinder. **Barrel:** 4 in. **Weight:** 24 oz. **Length:** 9 in. overall. **Grips:** Smooth rosewood with Ruger medallion. **Sights:** Blade front, fixed notch rear. Distributor special edition available with adjustable sights. **Features:** Reintroduction of the Ruger Bearcat with slightly lengthened frame, Ruger transfer bar safety system. Available in blued finish only. Rosewood grips. Introduced 1996 (blued), 2003 (stainless). With case and lock.

Price: SBC-4, blued **$639.00**
Price: KSBC-4, satin stainless **$689.00**

TAYLOR'S CATTLEMAN SERIES

Calibers: .357 Magnum or 45 Colt. **Barrels:** 4.75 in., 5.5 in., or 7.5 in. **Features:** Series of Single Action Army-style revolvers made in many variations.

Price: Gunfighter w/blued & color case finish........ **$526.00**
Price: Stainless **$665.00**
Price: Nickel........ **$616.00**
Price: Charcoal blued **$591.00**
Price: Bird's Head 3.5- or 4.5-in. bbl., walnut grips **$516.00**
Price: Engraved (shown)........ **$852.00**

UBERTI 1851–1860 CONVERSION

Calibers: .38 Special, .45 Colt. **Capacity:** 6-round engraved cylinder. **Barrels:** 4.75 in., 5.5 in., 7.5 in., 8 in. **Weight:** 2.6 lbs. (5.5-in. bbl.). **Length:** 13 in. overall (5.5-in. bbl.). **Grips:** Walnut. **Features:** Brass backstrap, trigger guard; color casehardened frame, blued barrel, cylinder. Introduced 2007. Imported from Italy by Stoeger Industries.

Price: 1851 Navy **$569.00**
Price: 1860 Army **$589.00**

Prices given are believed to be accurate at time of publication however, many factors affect retail pricing so exact prices are not possible.

UBERTI 1871–1872 OPEN TOP
Calibers: .38 Special, .45 Colt. **Capacity:** 6-round engraved cylinder. **Barrels:** 4.75 in., 5.5 in., 7.5 in. **Weight:** 2.6 lbs. (5.5-in. bbl.). **Length:** 13 in. overall (5.5-in. bbl.). **Grips:** Walnut. **Features:** Blued backstrap, trigger guard; color casehardened frame, blued barrel, cylinder. Introduced 2007. Imported from Italy by Stoeger Industries.
Price: .... **$539.00–$569.00**

UBERTI 1873 CATTLEMAN SINGLE-ACTION
Caliber: .45 Colt. **Capacity:** 6-round cylinder. **Barrels:** 4.75 in., 5.5 in., 7.5 in. **Weight:** 2.3 lbs. (5.5-in. bbl.). **Length:** 11 in. overall (5.5-in. bbl.). **Grips:** Styles: Frisco (pearl styled); Desperado (buffalo horn styled); Chisholm (checkered walnut); Gunfighter (black checkered), Cody (ivory styled), one-piece walnut. **Sights:** Blade front, groove rear. **Features:** Steel or brass backstrap, trigger guard; color casehardened frame, blued barrel, cylinder. NM designates New Model plunger-style frame; OM designates Old Model screw cylinder pin retainer. Imported from Italy by Stoeger Industries.
Price: 1873 Cattleman Frisco **$849.00**
Price: 1873 Cattleman Desperado (2006) **$849.00**
Price: 1873 Cattleman Chisholm (2006) **$579.00**
Price: 1873 Cattleman NM, blued 4.75 in. barrel **$649.00**
Price: 1873 Cattleman NM, Nickel finish, 7.5 in. barrel **$849.00**
Price: 1873 Cattleman Cody **$859.00**

UBERTI 1873 CATTLEMAN BIRD'S HEAD SINGLE ACTION
Calibers: .357 Magnum, .45 Colt. **Capacity:** 6-round cylinder. **Barrels:** 3.5 in., 4 in., 4.75 in., 5.5 in. **Weight:** 2.3 lbs. (5.5-in. bbl.). **Length:** 10.9 in. overall (5.5-in. bbl.). **Grips:** One-piece walnut. **Sights:** Blade front, groove rear. **Features:** Steel or brass backstrap, trigger guard; color casehardened frame, blued barrel, fluted cylinder. Imported from Italy by Stoeger Industries.
Price: **$569.00**

UBERTI CATTLEMAN .22
Caliber: .22 LR. **Capacity:** 6- or 12-round cylinder. **Barrel:** 5.5 in. **Grips:** One-piece walnut. **Sights:** Fixed. **Features:** Blued and casehardened finish, steel or brass backstrap/trigger guard.
Price: (brass backstrap, trigger guard) **$509.00**
Price: (steel backstrap, trigger guard) **$529.00**
Price: (12-round model, steel backstrap, trigger guard) **$559.00**

UBERTI 1873 BISLEY SINGLE-ACTION
Calibers: .357 Magnum, .45 Colt (Bisley); .22 LR and .38 Special. (Stallion), both with 6-round fluted cylinder. **Barrels:** 4.75 in., 5.5 in., 7.5 in. **Weight:** 2–2.5 lbs. **Length:** 12.7 in. overall (7.5-in. barrel). **Grips:** Two-piece walnut. **Sights:** Blade front, notch rear. **Features:** Replica of Colt's Bisley Model. Polished blued finish, color casehardened frame. Introduced 1997. Imported by Stoeger Industries.
Price: 1873 Bisley, 7.5-in. barrel **$599.00**

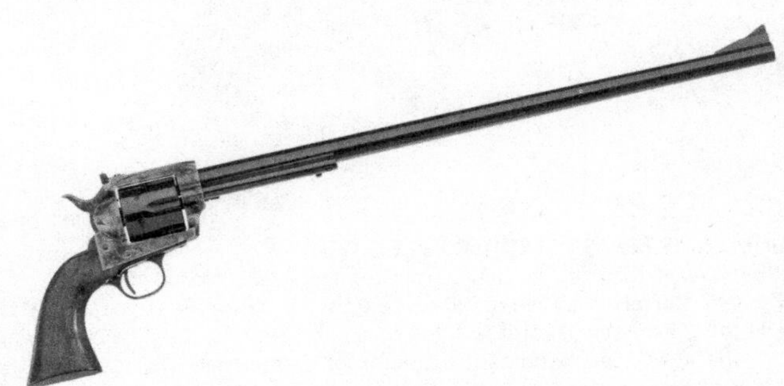

UBERTI 1873 BUNTLINE AND REVOLVER CARBINE SINGLE-ACTION
Caliber: .357 Magnum, .44-40, .45 Colt. **Capacity:** 6. **Barrel:** 18 in. **Length:** 22.9–34 in. **Grips:** Walnut pistol grip or rifle stock. **Sights:** Fixed or adjustable. **Features:** Imported from Italy by Stoeger Industries.
Price: 1873 Revolver Carbine, 18-in. bbl., 34 in. OAL **$729.00**
Price: 1873 Cattleman Buntline Target, 18-in. bbl. 22.9 in. OAL **$639.00**

UBERTI OUTLAW, FRONTIER, AND POLICE
Caliber: .45 Colt. **Capacity:** 6-round cylinder. **Barrels:** 5.5 in., 7.5 in. **Weight:** 2.5–2.8 lbs. **Length:** 10.8 in. to 13.6 in. overall. **Grips:** Two-piece smooth walnut. **Sights:** Blade front, notch rear. **Features:** Cartridge version of 1858 Remington percussion revolver. Nickel and blued finishes. Fluted cylinder. Imported by Stoeger Industries.
Price: 1875 Outlaw, nickel finish **$659.00**
Price: 1875 Frontier, blued finish **$559.00**
Price: 1890 Police, blued finish **$599.00**

UBERTI 1870 SCHOFIELD-STYLE TOP BREAK
Calibers: .38 Special, .44 Russian, .44-40, .45 Colt. **Capacity:** 6-round cylinder. **Barrels:** 3.5 in., 5 in., 7 in. **Weight:** 2.4 lbs. (5-in. barrel) **Length:** 10.8 in. overall (5-in. barrel). **Grips:** Two-piece smooth walnut or pearl. **Sights:** Blade front, notch rear. **Features:** Replica of Smith & Wesson Model 3 Schofield. Single-action, top break with automatic ejection. Polished blued finish (first model). Introduced 1994. Imported by Stoeger Industries.
Price: **$1,429.00**

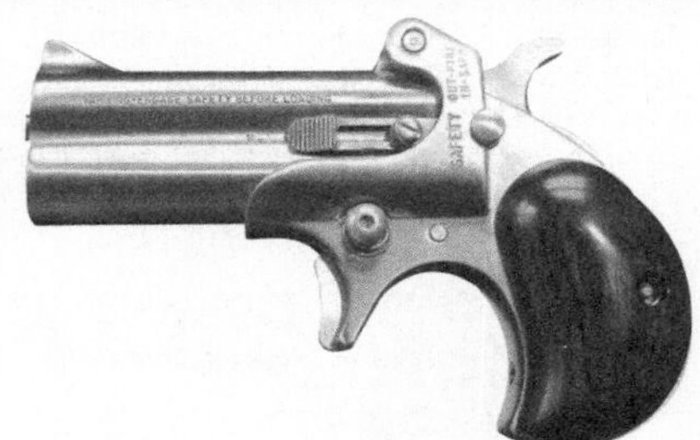

AMERICAN DERRINGER MODEL 1

Calibers: All popular handgun calibers plus .45 Colt/.410 Shotshell. **Capacity:** 2, (.45-70 model is single shot). **Barrel:** 3 in. **Overall length:** 4.82 in. **Weight:** 15 oz. **Features:** Manually operated hammer-block safety automatically disengages when hammer is cocked. Texas Commemorative has brass frame and is available in .38 Special, .44-40. or .45 Colt.
Price: .... **$635.00–$735.00**
Price: Texas Commemorative **$835.00**

AMERICAN DERRINGER MODEL 8

Calibers: .45 Colt/.410 shotshell. **Capacity:** 2. **Barrel:** 8 in. **Weight:** 24 oz.
Price: **$915.00**
Price: High polish finish **$1,070.00**

AMERICAN DERRINGER DA38

Calibers: .38 Special, .357 Magnum, 9mm Luger. **Barrel:** 3.3 in. **Weight:** 14.5 oz. **Features:** DA operation with hammer-block thumb safety. Barrel, receiver and all internal parts are made from stainless steel.
Price: .... **$690.00–$740.00**

BOND ARMS TEXAS DEFENDER DERRINGER

Calibers: Available in more than 10 calibers, from .22 LR to .45 LC/.410 shotshells. **Barrel:** 3 in. **Weight:** 20 oz. **Length:** 5 in. **Grips:** Rosewood. **Sights:** Blade front, fixed rear. **Features:** Interchangeable barrels, stainless steel firing pins, cross-bolt safety, automatic extractor for rimmed calibers. Stainless steel construction, brushed finish. Right or left hand.
Price: **$493.00**
Price: Interchangeable barrels, .22 LR thru .45 LC, 3 in. **$139.00**
Price: Interchangeable barrels, .45 LC, 3.5 in. .... **$159.00–$189.00**

BOND ARMS RANGER II

Caliber: .45 LC/.410 shotshells or .357 Magnum/.38 Special. **Barrel:** 4.25 in. **Weight:** 23.5 oz. **Length:** 6.25 in. **Features:** This model has a trigger guard. Intr. 2011. From Bond Arms.
Price: **$673.00**

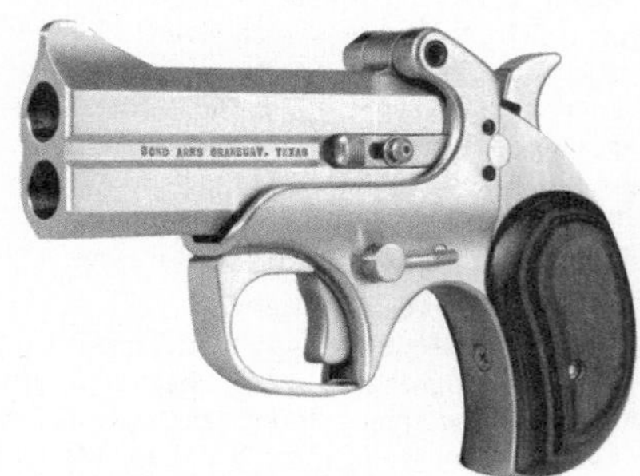

BOND ARMS CENTURY 2000 DEFENDER

Calibers: .45 LC/.410 shotshells. or .357 Magnum/.38 Special. **Barrel:** 3.5 in. **Weight:** 21 oz. **Length:** 5.5 in. **Features:** Similar to Defender series.
Price: **$517.00**

BOND ARMS COWBOY DEFENDER

Calibers: From .22 LR to .45 LC/.410 shotshells. **Barrel:** 3 in. **Weight:** 19 oz. **Length:** 5.5 in. **Features:** Similar to Defender series. No trigger guard.
Price: **$493.00**

BOND ARMS SNAKE SLAYER

Calibers: .45 LC/.410 shotshell (2.5 in. or 3 in.). **Barrel:** 3.5 in. **Weight:** 21 oz. **Length:** 5.5 in. **Grips:** Extended rosewood. **Sights:** Blade front, fixed rear. **Features:** Single-action; interchangeable barrels; stainless steel firing pin. Introduced 2005.
Price: **$568.00**

BOND ARMS SNAKE SLAYER IV

Calibers: .45 LC/.410 shotshell (2.5 in. or 3 in.). **Barrel:** 4.25 in. **Weight:** 22 oz. **Length:** 6.25 in. **Grips:** Extended rosewood. **Sights:** Blade front, fixed rear. **Features:** Single-action; interchangeable barrels; stainless steel firing pin. Introduced 2006.
Price: **$613.00**

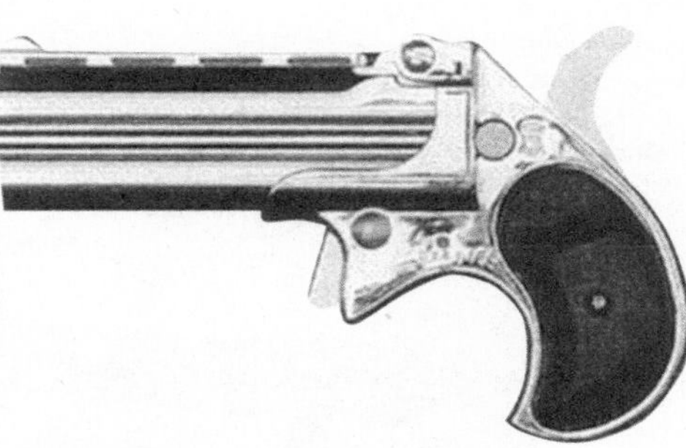

COBRA BIG-BORE DERRINGERS

Calibers: .22 WMR, .32 H&R Mag., .38 Special, 9mm Para., .380 ACP. **Barrel:** 2.75 in. **Weight:** 14 oz. **Length:** 4.65 in. overall. **Grips:** Textured black or white synthetic or laminated rosewood. **Sights:** Blade front, fixed notch rear. **Features:** Alloy frame, steel-lined barrels, steel breechblock. Plunger-type safety with integral hammer block. Black, chrome or satin finish. Introduced 2002. Made in USA by Cobra Enterprises of Utah, Inc.
Price: **$187.00**

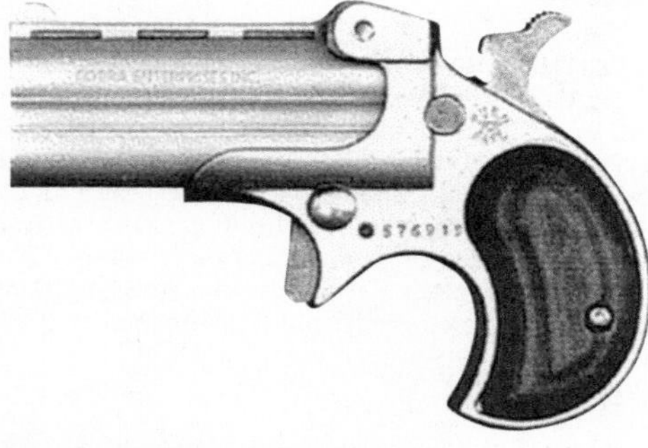

COBRA STANDARD SERIES DERRINGERS

Calibers: .22 LR, .22 WMR, .25 ACP, .32 ACP. **Barrel:** 2.4 in. **Weight:** 9.5 oz. **Length:** 4 in. overall. **Grips:** Laminated wood or pearl. **Sights:** Blade front, fixed notch rear. **Features:** Choice of black powder coat, satin nickel or chrome finish. Introduced 2002. Made in USA by Cobra Enterprises of Utah, Inc.
Price: **$169.00**

COBRA LONG-BORE DERRINGERS

Calibers: .22 WMR, .38 Special, 9mm. **Barrel:** 3.5 in. **Weight:** 16 oz. **Length:** 5.4 in. overall. **Grips:** Black or white synthetic or rosewood. **Sights:** Fixed. **Features:** Chrome, satin nickel, or black Teflon finish. Introduced 2002. Made in USA by Cobra Enterprises of Utah, Inc.
Price: **$187.00**

Prices given are believed to be accurate at time of publication however, many factors affect retail pricing so exact prices are not possible.

COBRA TITAN .45 LC/.410 DERRINGER
Calibers: .45 LC, .410 or 9mm, 2-round capacity. **Barrel:** 3.5 in. **Weight:** 16.4 oz. **Grip:** Rosewood. **Features:** Standard finishes include: satin stainless, black stainless and brushed stainless. Made in USA by Cobra Enterprises of Utah, Inc.
Price: **$399.00**

COMANCHE SUPER SINGLE-SHOT
Calibers: .45 LC/.410 **Barrel:** 10 in. **Sights:** Adjustable. **Features:** Blue finish, not available for sale in CA, MA. Distributed by SGS Importers International, Inc.
Price: **$240.00**

DOUBLETAP DERRINGER
Calibers: .45 Colt or 9mm **Barrel:** 3 in. **Weight:** 12 oz. **Length:** 5.5 in. **Sights:** Adjustable. **Features:** Over/under, two-barrel design. Rounds are fired individually with two separate trigger pulls. Tip-up design, aluminum frame.
Price: **$499.00**

HEIZER PS1 POCKET SHOTGUN
Calibers: .45 Colt or .410 shotshell. Single-shot. **Barrel:** Tip-up, 3.25 in. **Weight:** 22 oz. **Length:** 5.6 in. **Width:** .742 in **Height:** 3.81 in. **Features:** Available in several finishes. Standard model is matte stainless or black. Also offered in Hedy Jane series for the women in pink or in two-tone combinations of stainless and pink, blue, green, purple. Includes interchangeable AR .223 barrel. Made in the USA by Heizer Industries.
Price: **$499.00**

HEIZER POCKET AR
Caliber: .223 Rem./5.56 NATO. Single shot. **Barrel:** 3.75 in., ported or non-ported. **Length:** 6.375 in. **Weight:** 23 oz. **Features:** Similar to PS1 pocket shotgun but chambered for .223/5.56 rifle cartridge.
Price: **$339.00**

HEIZER PAK1
Caliber: 7.2x39. Similar to Pocket AR but chambered for 7.62x39mm. Single shot. **Barrel:** 3.75 in., ported or unported. **Length:** 6.375 in. **Weight:** 23 oz.
Price: **$339.00**

Prices given are believed to be accurate at time of publication however, many factors affect retail pricing so exact prices are not possible.

HENRY MARE'S LEG

Calibers: .22 LR, .22 WMR, .357 Magnum, .44 Magnum, .45 Colt. **Capacities:** 10 rounds (.22 LR), 8 rounds (.22 WMR), 5 rounds (others). **Barrel:** 12.9 in. **Length:** 25 in. **Weight:** 4.5 lbs. (rimfire) to 5.8 lbs. (centerfire calibers). **Features:** Lever-action operation based on Henry rifle series and patterned after gun made famous in Steve McQueen's 1950s TV show, "Wanted: Dead or Alive." Made in the USA.

Price: .22 LR..**$462.00**
Price: .22 WMR **$473.00**
Price: Centerfire calibers **$1,024.00**

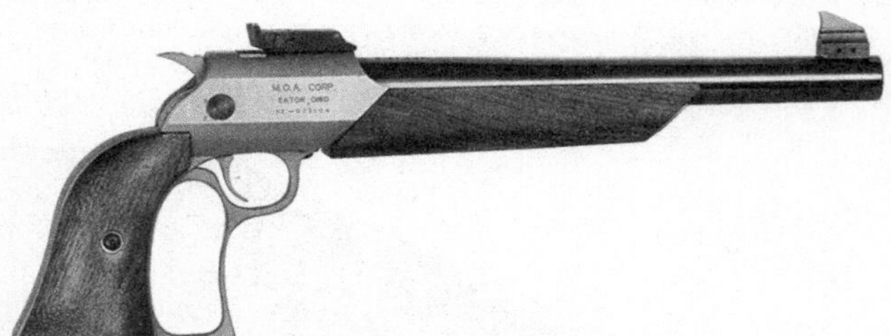

MAXIMUM SINGLE-SHOT

Calibers: .22 LR, .22 Hornet, .22 BR, .22 PPC, 223 Rem., .22-250, 6mm BR, 6mm PPC, .243, .250 Savage, 6.5mm-35M, .270 MAX, .270 Win., 7mm TCU, 7mm BR, 7mm-35, 7mm INT-R, 7mm-08, 7mm Rocket, 7mm Super-Mag., .30 Herrett, .30 Carbine, .30-30, .308 Win., 30x39, .32-20, .350 Rem. Mag., .357 Mag., .357 Maximum, .358 Win., .375 H&H, .44 Mag., .454 Casull. **Barrel:** 8.75 in., 10.5 in., 14 in. **Weight:** 61 oz. (10.5-in. bbl.); 78 oz. (14-in. bbl.). **Length:** 15 in., 18.5 in. overall (with 10.5- and 14-in. bbl., respectively). **Grips:** Smooth walnut stocks and fore-end. Also available with 17-finger-groove grip. **Sights:** Ramp front, fully adjustable open rear. **Features:** Falling block action; drilled and tapped for M.O.A. scope mounts; integral grip frame/receiver; adjustable trigger; Douglas barrel (interchangeable). Introduced 1983. Made in USA by M.O.A. Corp.

Price: **$1,062.00**

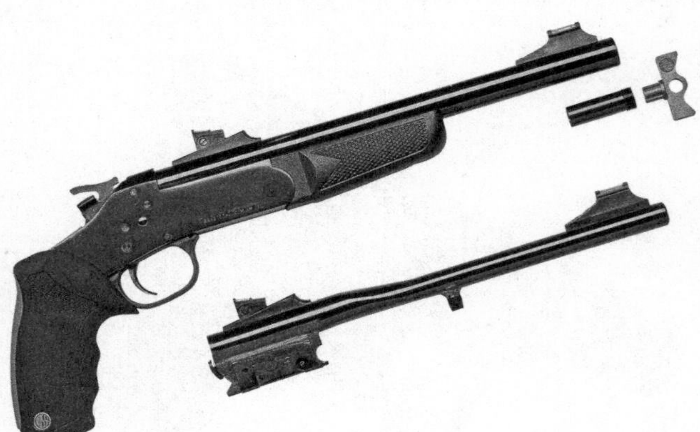

ROSSI MATCHED PAIR, "DUAL THREAT PERFORMER"

Calibers: .22LR, .44 Magnum, .223, .243. .410, 20 gauge, single shot. Interchangeable rifle and shotgun barrels in various combinations. **Sights:** Fiber optic front sights, adjustable rear. **Features:** Two-in-one pistol system with single-shot simplicity. Removable choke and cushioned grip with a Taurus Security System.

Price: .22/.410 from **$345.00**

THOMPSON/CENTER ENCORE PRO HUNTER

Calibers: .223, .308. Single shot, break-open design. **Barrel:** 15 in. **Weight:** 4.25–4.5 lbs. **Grip:** Walnut on blued models, rubber on stainless. Matching fore-end. **Sights:** Adjustable rear, ramp front. **Features:** Interchangeable barrels, adjustable trigger. Pro Hunter has "Swing Hammer" to allow reaching the hammer when the gun is scoped. Other Pro Hunter features include fluted barrel.

Price: From **$779.00**

THOMPSON/CENTER G2 CONTENDER

Calibers: .22 LR or .357 Magnum. A second generation Contender pistol maintaining the same barrel interchangeability with older Contender barrels and their corresponding forends (except Herrett fore-end). The G2 frame will not accept old-style grips due to the change in grip angle. Incorporates an automatic hammer block safety with built-in interlock. Features include trigger adjustable for overtravel, adjustable rear sight; ramp front sight blade, blued steel finish.

Price: From **$729.00**

Prices given are believed to be accurate at time of publication however, many factors affect retail pricing so exact prices are not possible.

ALEXANDER ARMS AR SERIES

Calibers: .17 HMR, 5.56 NATO, 6.5 Grendel, .300 AAC, .338 Lapua Mag., .50 Beowulf. This manufacturer produces a wide range of AR-15 type rifles and carbines. **Barrels:** 16, 18, 20 or 24 in. Models are available for consumer, law enforcement and military markets. Depending on the specific model, features include forged flattop receiver with Picatinny rail, button-rifled stainless steel barrels, composite free-floating handguard, A2 flash hider, M4 collapsible stock, gas piston operating system.

Price: .17 HMR **$1,210.00**
Price: 5.56 NATO **$1,349.00**
Price: 6.5 Grendel .... **$1,540.00–$1,750.00**
Price: .300 AAC **$1,349.00**
Price: .50 Beowulf .... **$1,375.00–$1,750.00**

ALEXANDER ARMS ULFBERHT

Caliber: .338 Lapua Mag. Custom-designed adjustable gas-piston operating system. **Barrel:** 27.5-in. chrome moly with three-prong flash hider. **Stock:** Magpul PRS. **Length:** 41.25 in. (folded), 50 in. (extended stock). **Weight:** 19.8 lbs.

Price: **$5,800.00**

M-15 LIGHT TACTICAL CARBINE

Calibers: .223 Rem., 6.8 SPC, 7.62x39mm. **Capacity:** 30-round magazine. **Barrel:** 16 in. heavy chrome lined; 1:7 in. twist, flash suppressor. **Weight:** 6 lbs. **Length:** 36 in. overall. **Stock:** Green or black composition. **Sights:** Standard A2. **Features:** Forged flattop receiver with Picatinny rail, 10-in. aluminum KeyMod handguard, anodize aluminum supper/lower receiver, flip-up sights. Introduced in 2016.

Price: **$999.00**

ARMALITE AR-10 PRC 260

Caliber: .260 Rem. **Barrel:** 20-in. ceramic coated stainless steel threaded with Surgeon/AWC PSR muzzle brake flash suppressor. **Weight:** 11.5 lbs. **Features:** Magpul PSR stock with adjustable comb and length of pull, 15-in. aluminum free-floating quadrail, forward assist, Timney trigger, ambidextrous safety and charging handle. Introduced in 2017.

Price: From **$3,560.00**

ARMALITE AR-10 3-GUN COMPETITION RIFLE

Calibers: 7.62x1mm/.308 Win. **Capacity:** 25-round magazine. **Barrel:** 18-in. stainless steel. **Weight:** 8.9 lbs. **Features:** MBA-1 buttstock with adjustable comb and length of pull, 15-in. free-floating 3-Gun handguard, Raptor charging handle, Timney trigger, ambidextrous safety.

Price: **$2,199.00**

EAGLE-15 VERSATILE SPORTING RIFLE (VSR)

Caliber: .223 Rem/5.56x45 NATO (.223 Wylde chamber). **Capacity:** 30-shot Magpul PMAG. **Barrel:** 16-in. chrome moly with flash suppressor. **Stock**: 6-position collapsible with free-float rail system, rubberized grip. **Weight:** 6.6 lbs. **Features:** Carbine length gas system, 15-in. handguard with Key Mod attachments, forged lower and flat-top upper, Picatinny rail.

Price: **$800.00**

ARSENAL, INC. SLR-107F

Caliber: 7.62x39mm. **Barrel:** 16.25 in. **Weight:** 7.3 lbs. **Stock:** Left-side folding polymer stock. **Sights:** Adjustable rear. **Features:** Stamped receiver, 24mm flash hider, bayonet lug, accessory lug, stainless steel heat shield, two-stage trigger. Introduced 2008. Made in USA by Arsenal, Inc.

Price: SLR-107FR, includes scope rail **$1,099.00**

ARSENAL, INC. SLR-107CR

Caliber: 7.62x39mm. **Barrel:** 16.25 in. **Weight:** 6.9 lbs. **Stock:** Left-side folding polymer stock. **Sights:** Adjustable rear. **Features:** Stamped receiver, front sight block/gas block combination, 500-meter rear sight, cleaning rod, stainless steel heat shield, scope rail, and removable muzzle attachment. Introduced 2007. Made in USA by Arsenal, Inc.

Price: SLR-107CR **$1,119.00**

ARSENAL, INC. SLR-106CR

Caliber: 5.56 NATO. **Barrel:** 16.25 in. Steyr chrome-lined barrel, 1:7 twist rate. **Weight:** 6.9 lbs. **Stock:** Black polymer folding stock with cutout for scope rail. Stainless steel heat shield handguard. **Sights:** 500-meter rear sight and rear sight block calibrated for 5.56 NATO. Warsaw Pact scope rail. **Features:** Uses Arsenal, Bulgaria, Mil-Spec receiver, two-stage trigger, hammer and disconnector. Polymer magazines in 5- and 10-round capacity in black and green, with Arsenal logo. Others are 30-round black waffles, 20- and 30-round versions in clear/smoke waffle, featuring the "10" in a double-circle logo of Arsenal, Bulgaria. Ships with 5-round magazine, sling, cleaning kit in a tube, 16 in. cleaning rod, oil bottle. Introduced 2007. Made in USA by Arsenal, Inc.

Price: SLR-106CR **$1,200.00**

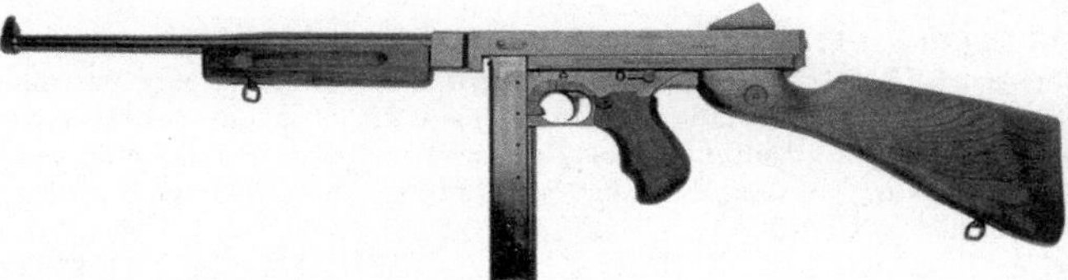

AUTO-ORDNANCE 1927A-1 THOMPSON

Caliber: .45 ACP. **Barrel:** 16.5 in. **Weight:** 13 lbs. **Length:** About 41 in. overall (Deluxe). **Stock:** Walnut stock and vertical fore-end. **Sights:** Blade front, open rear adjustable for windage. **Features:** Recreation of Thompson Model 1927. Semi-auto only. Deluxe model has finned barrel, adjustable rear sight and compensator; Standard model has plain barrel and military sight. Available with 100-round drum or 30-round stick magazine. Made in USA by Auto-Ordnance Corp., a division of Kahr Arms.

Price: Deluxe w/stick magazine **$1,544.00**
Price: Deluxe w/drum magazine **$2,061.00**
Price: Lightweight model w/stick mag **$1,325.00**

AUTO-ORDNANCE 1927 A-1 COMMANDO

Similar to the 1927 A-1 except has Parkerized finish, black-finish wood butt, pistol grip, horizontal fore-end. Comes with black nylon sling. Introduced 1998. Made in USA by Auto-Ordnance Corp., a division of Kahr Arms.

Price: T1-C **$1,393.00**

AUTO ORDNANCE M1 CARBINE

Caliber: .30 Carbine (15-shot magazine). **Barrel:** 18 in. **Weight:** 5.4 to 5.8 lbs. **Length:** 36.5 in. **Stock:** Wood or polymer. **Sights:** Blade front, flip-style rear. **Features:** A faithful recreation of the military carbine.

Price: **$899.00**
Price: Folding stock **$989.00**

BARRETT MODEL 82A-1 SEMI-AUTOMATIC
Calibers: .416 Barret, 50 BMG. **Capacity:** 10-shot detachable box magazine. **Barrel:** 29 in. **Weight:** 28.5 lbs. **Length:** 57 in. overall. **Stock:** Composition with energy-absorbing recoil pad. **Sights:** Scope optional. **Features:** Semiautomatic, recoil operated with recoiling barrel. Three-lug locking bolt; muzzle brake. Adjustable bipod. Introduced 1985. Made in USA by Barrett Firearms.
Price: From **$9,119.00**

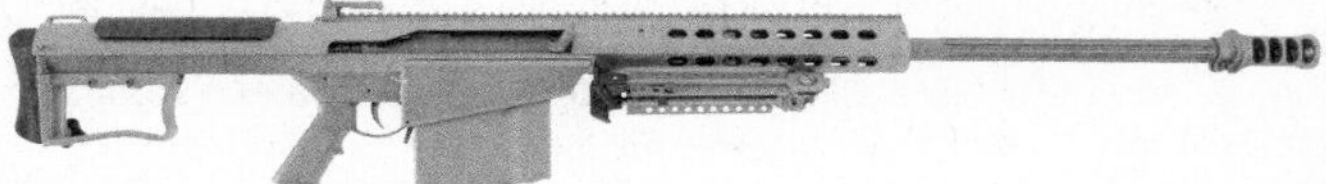

BARRETT M107A1
Caliber: 50 BMG. **Capacity:** 10-round detachable magazine. **Barrels:** 20 or 29 in. **Sights:** 27-in. optics rail with flip-up iron sights. **Weight:** 30.9 lbs. **Finish:** Flat Dark Earth. **Features:** Four-port cylindrical muzzle brake. Quick-detachable Barrett QDL Suppressor. Adjustable bipod and monopod.
Price: **$12,281.00**

BARRETT MODEL REC7 GEN II
Calibers: 5.56 (.223), 6.8 Rem. SPC. **Capacity:** 30-round magazine. **Barrel:** 16 in. **Sights:** ARMS rear, folding front. Weight: 28.7 lbs. **Features:** AR-style configuration with standard 17-4 stainless piston system, two-position forward venting gas plug, chrome-lined gas block, A2 flash hider, 6-position MOE stock.
Price: **$2,759.00**

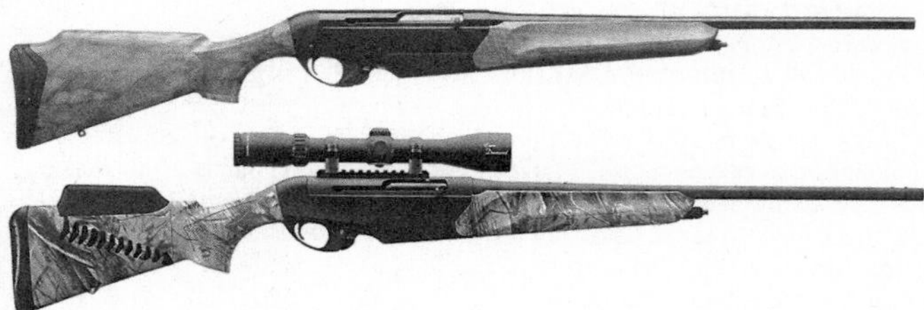

BENELLI R1
Calibers: .30-06 (4+1), .300 Win Mag (3+1), .338 Win Mag (3+1). **Weight:** 7.1 lbs. **Length:** 43.75 in. to 45.75 in. **Stock:** Select satin walnut or synthetic. **Sights:** None. **Features:** Auto-regulating gas-operated system, three-lug rotary bolt, interchangeable barrels, optional recoil pads. Introduced 2003. Imported from Italy by Benelli USA.
Price: **$1,019.00**

BERETTA ARX 100
Caliber: 5.56 NATO. **Capacity:** 30-round. Accepts AR magazines. **Barrel:** 16 in. with flash suppressor and quick changeability. **Features:** Ambidextrous controls, Picatinny quad rail system.
Price: **$1,600.00**

BERETTA CX4 STORM CARBINE Calibers: 9mm, 40 S&W, .45 ACP. **Barrel:** 16.6 in. **Stock**: Black synthetic with thumbhole. **Sights:** Ghost ring. **Features**: Blowback single action, ambidextrous controls, Picatinny quad rail system. Reintroduced in 2017.
Price: **$800.00**

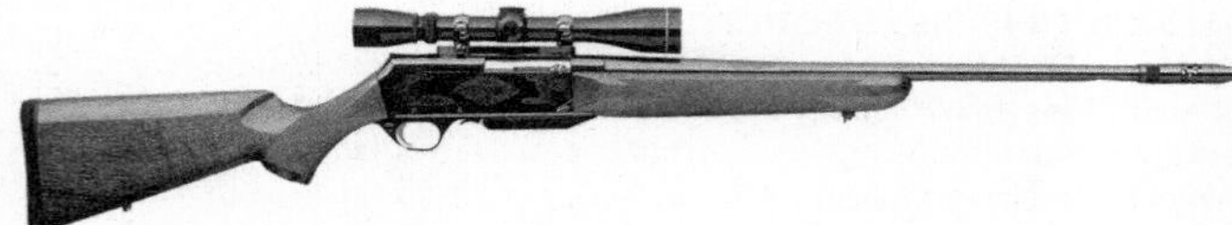

BROWNING BAR SAFARI AND SAFARI W/BOSS SEMI-AUTO
Calibers: Safari: .25-06 Rem., .270 Win., 7mm Rem. Mag., .30-06, .308 Win., .300 Win. Mag., .338 Win. Mag. Safari w/BOSS: .270 Win., 7mm Rem. Mag., .30-06 Spfl., .300 Win. Mag., .338 Win. Mag. **Barrels:** 22–24 in. round tapered. **Weights:** 7.4–8.2 lbs. **Lengths:** 43–45 in. overall. **Stock:** French walnut pistol grip stock and fore-end, hand checkered. **Sights:** No sights. **Features:** Has new bolt release lever; removable trigger assembly with larger trigger guard; redesigned gas and buffer systems. Detachable 4-round box magazine. Scroll-engraved receiver is tapped for scope mounting. BOSS barrel vibration modulator and muzzle brake system available. Mark II Safari introduced 1993. Made in Belgium.
Price: BAR MK II Safari, From **$1,230.00**
Price: BAR Safari w/BOSS, From **$1,400.00**

BROWNING BAR MK III SERIES
Calibers: .243 Win., 7mm-08, .270 Win., .270 WSM, 7mm Rem., .308 Win, .30-06, .300 Win. Mag., .300 WSM. **Capacities:** Detachable 4 or 5-shot magazine. **Barrel:** 22, 23 or 24 in.es. **Stock:** Grade II checkered walnut, shim adjustable. Camo stock with composite gripping surfaces available. Stalker model has composite stock. **Weight:** 7.5 lbs. **Features:** Satin nickel alloy with high relief engraving, stylized fore-end.
Price: **$1,240.00**
Price: Camo **$1,380.00**
Price: Stalker **$1,270.00**

BROWNING BAR MK 3 DBM
Caliber: .308 Win. **Capacity:** 10-round detachable magazine. **Barrel:** 18 in. **Stock**: Black composite. Other features similar to standard BAR MK III.
Price: **$1,470.00**

BUSHMASTER ACR
Calibers: 5.56mm, 6.5mm, 6.8mm. **Capacity:** 30-round polymer magazine. **Barrels:** All three calibers are available with 10.5 in., 14.5 in., 16.5 in. and 18 in. barrels. **Weights:** 14.5 in. bbl. 7 lbs. **Lengths:** 14.5 in. bbl. with stock folded: 25.75 in. with stock deployed (mid) 32.625 in., 10.5 in. bbl. with stock folded: 21.312 in., with stock deployed (mid): 27.875 in., with stock deployed and extended: 31.75 in., Folding Stock Length of Pull — 3 in. **Stock:** Fixed high-impact composite A-frame stock with rubber butt pad and sling mounts. **Features:** Cold hammer-forged barrels with Melonite coating for extreme long life. A2 birdcage-type hider to control muzzle flash and adjustable, two-position, gas piston-driven system for firing suppressed or unsuppressed, supported by hardened internal bearing rails. The Adaptive Combat Rifle (ACR) features a tool-less, quick-change barrel system available in 10.5 in., 14.5 in. and 16.5 in. and in multiple calibers. Multi-caliber bolt carrier assembly quickly and easily changes from .223/5.56mm NATO to 6.8mm Rem SPC (spec II chamber). Free-floating MIL-STD 1913 monolithic top rail for optic mounting. Fully ambidextrous controls including magazine release, bolt catch and release, fire selector and nonreciprocating charging handle. High-impact composite handguard with heat shield; accepts rail inserts. High-impact composite lower receiver with textured magazine well and modular grip storage. Fire Control: Semi and full auto two-stage standard AR capable of accepting drop-in upgrade. Magazine: Optimized for MagPul PMAG Accepts standard NATO/M-16 magazines.
Price: Basic Folder Configuration **$2,149.00**
Price: ACR Enhanced **$2,249.00**

BUSHMASTER HEAVY-BARRELED CARBINE
Caliber: 5.56/.223. **Barrel:** 16 in. **Weights:** 6.93–7.28 lbs. **Length:** 32.5 in. overall. **Features:** AR-style carbine with chrome-lined heavy profile vanadium steel barrel, fixed or removable carry handle, six-position telestock.
Price: **$895.00**
Price: A3 with removable handle **$1,420.00**

BUSHMASTER 450 RIFLE AND CARBINE
Caliber: .450 Bushmaster. **Capacity:** 5-round magazine. **Barrels:** 20 in. (rifle), 16 in. (carbine). **Weights:** 8.3 lbs. (rifle), 8.1 lbs. (carbine). **Length:** 39.5 in. overall (rifle), 35.25 in. overall (carbine). **Features:** AR-style with chrome-lined chrome-moly barrel, synthetic stock, Izzy muzzle brake.
Price: Carbine **$1,285.00**
Price: Rifle **$1,300.00**

BUSHMASTER TARGET
Caliber: 5.56/.223. **Capacity:** 30-round magazine. **Barrels:** 20 or 24 in. heavy or standard. **Weights:** 8.43–9.29 lbs. **Lengths:** 39.5or 43.5 **Features:** Semiauto AR-style with chrome-lined or stainless steel 1:9 in. twist barrel, fixed or removable carry handle, manganese phosphate finish.
Price: .... **$969.00–$1,000.00**

BUSHMASTER M4A3 TYPE CARBINE
Caliber: 5.56/.223. **Capacity:** 30-round magazine. **Barrel:** 16 in. **Weights:** 6.22–6.7 lbs. **Lengths:** 31–32.5 in. overall. **Features:** AR-style carbine with chrome-moly vanadium steel barrel, Izzy-type flash hider, six-position telestock, various sight options, standard or multi-rail handguard, fixed or removable carry handle.
Price: **$1,100.00**

BUSHMASTER QUICK RESPONSE CARBINE
Caliber: 5.56/223. **Capacity:** 10-round magazine. **Barrel:** 16 in. chrome moly superlight contour with Melonite finish. **Features:** Mini red-dot detachable sight, 6-position collapsible stock, A2-type flash hider. Introduced in 2016.
Price: **$769.00**

CENTURY INTERNATIONAL AES-10 HI-CAP
Caliber: 7.62x39mm. **Capacity:** 30-shot magazine. **Barrel:** 23.2 in. **Weight:** NA. **Length:** 41.5 in. overall. **Stock:** Wood grip, fore-end. **Sights:** Fixed notch rear, windage-adjustable post front. **Features:** RPK-style, accepts standard double-stack AK-type mags. Side-mounted scope mount, integral carry handle, bipod. Imported by Century Arms Int'l.
Price: AES-10, From **$450.00**

CENTURY INTERNATIONAL GP WASR-10 HI-CAP
Caliber: 7.62x39mm. **Capacity:** 30-round magazine. **Barrel:** 16.25 in. 1:10 right-hand twist. **Weight:** 7.2 lbs. **Length:** 34.25 in. overall. **Stock:** Wood laminate or composite, grip, fore-end. **Sights:** Fixed notch rear, windage-adjustable post front. **Features:** Two 30-rd. detachable box magazines, cleaning kit, bayonet. Version of AKM rifle; U.S. parts added for BATFE compliance. Threaded muzzle, folding stock, bayonet lug, compensator, Dragunov stock available. Made in Romania by Cugir Arsenal. Imported by Century Arms Int'l.
Price: GP WASR-10, From **$450.00**

CENTURY INTERNATIONAL M70AB2 SPORTER
Caliber: 7.62x39mm. **Capacity:** 30-shot magazine. **Barrel:** 16.25 in. **Weight:** 7.5 lbs. **Length:** 34.25 in. overall. **Stocks:** Metal grip, wood fore-end. **Sights:** Fixed notch rear, windage-adjustable post front. **Features:** Two 30-rd. double-stack magazine, cleaning kit, compensator, bayonet lug and bayonet. Paratrooper-style Kalashnikov with under-folding stock. Imported by Century Arms Int'l.
Price: M70AB2, From **$480.00**

CMMG MK SERIES
Calibers: 5.56 NATO, .308 Win., 7.62x39, .300 BLK. This company manufactures a wide range of AR and AK style rifles and carbines. Many AR/AK options offered. Listed are several variations of CMMG's many models. Made in the USA.
Price: MK4 LEM .223 .... **$995.00**
Price: MK3 .308 .... **$1,595.00**
Price: MK47 AKS8 7.62x39 (shown) **$1,650.00**
Price: MK4 RCE .300 BLK **$1,500.00**

CMMG MKW ANVIL
Caliber: .458 SOCOM. **Barrel:** 16.1 in. CMMG SV Muzzle Brake**. Weight:** 7.5 lbs. **Stock:** M4 with A2 pistol grip, 6 position mil-spec receiver extension. Introduced in 2017.
Price: From **$1,850.00**

CMMG Mk4 DTR2
Caliber: .224 Valkyrie. **Capacity:** 10-round magazine (6.8 magazine). **Barrel:** 24 in. threaded. CMMG SV Muzzle Brake**. Weight:** 9.2 lbs. **Stock:** Magpul PRS with MOE Pistol grip4 with A2 pistol grip. **Features:** Model is engineered to deliver on this new cartridge's promise of long-range accuracy and high-energy performance.
Price: From **$1,699.95**

COLT LE6920
Caliber: 5.56 NATO. **Barrel:** 16.1-in. chrome lined. **Sights:** Adjustable. Based on military M4. **Features:** Magpul MOE handguard, carbine stock, pistol grip, vertical grip. Direct gas/locking bolt operating system.
Price: From .... **$849.00–$1,099.00**

COLT LE6940
Caliber: 5.56 NATO. Similar to LE1920 with Magpul MBUS backup sight, folding front, four accessory rails. One-piece monolithic upper receiver has continuous Mil-Spec rail from rear of upper to the front sight. Direct gas (LE6940) or articulating link piston (LE6940P) system.
Price: LE6940 .... **$1,399.00**

COLT L36960-CCU
Caliber: 5.56 NATO. **Capacity:** 30-round magazine. **Barrel:** 16-in. **Stock:** Magpul MOE SL with pistol grip. **Weight:** 6.7 lbs. **Features:** Combat Unit Carbine with 30-shot magazine. Aluminum receiver with black finish, mid-length gas system, optics ready.
Price: **$1,299.00**

COLT EXPANSE M4
Caliber: 5.56 NATO. **Capacity:** 30 rounds. **Barrel:** 16.1 in. **Sights:** Adjustable front post. Comes optics ready. **Weight:** 6.4 lbs. Flattop Picatinny rail. **Stock:** Adjustable M4 with A2-style grip. Economy priced AR. Introduced in 2016.
Price: **$799.00**

COLT MARC 901 MONOLITHIC
Caliber: .308. **Capacity:** 20 rounds. **Barrels:** 16.1 or 18 in. heavy fully floated with bayonet lug, flash hider. **Stock:** Adjustable VLTOR. **Sights:** Mil-spec flip up. **Weight:** 9.4 pounds. **Features:** One-piece flattop upper receiver with Picatinny rail, ambidextrous controls, matte black finish. Carbine model has muzzle brake, retractable Bravo stock, full-length Picatinny rail. Tubular handguard with 3 rails.
Price: **$1,999.00**
Price: Carbine **$1,399.00**

DANIEL DEFENSE AR SERIES
Caliber: 5.56 NATO/.223. **Capacity:** 20-round Magpul PMAG magazine. **Barrels:** 16 or 18 in.es. Flash suppressor. **Weight:** 7.4 lbs. **Lengths:** 34.75–37.85 in. overall. **Stock:** Glass-filled polymer with Soft Touch overmolding. Pistol grip. **Sights:** None. **Features:** Lower receiver is Mil-Spec with enhanced and flared magazine well, QD swivel attachment point. Upper receiver has M4 feed ramps. Lower and upper CNC machined of 7075-T6 aluminum, hard coat anodized. Shown is MK12, one of many AR variants offered by Daniel Defense. Made in the USA
Price: From....................**$1,599.00**
Price: DD5VI 7.62/.308....................**$3.044.00**

DPMS VARMINT SERIES
Calibers: .204 Ruger, .223. **Barrels:** 16 in., 20 in. or 24 in. bull or fluted profile. **Weights:** 7.75–11.75 lbs. **Lengths:** 34.5–42.25 in. overall. **Stock:** Black Zytel composite. **Sights:** None. **Features:** Flattop receiver with Picatinny top rail; hardcoat anodized receiver; aluminum free-float tube handguard; many options. From DPMS Panther Arms.
Price: ....**$939.00–$1,229.00**

DPMS PRAIRIE PANTHER
Calibers: 5.56 NATO or 6.8 SPC. **Barrels:** 20-in. 416 stainless fluted heavy 1:8 in. barrel. **Features:** Phosphate steel bolt; free-floated carbon fiber handguard; flattop upper with Picatinny rail; aluminum lower; two 30-round magazines; skeletonized Zytel stock; Choice of matte black or one of several camo finishes.
Price: ....**$1,269.00–$1,289.00**

DPMS MK12
Caliber: .308 Win./7.62 NATO. **Barrel:** 18 in. **Weight:** 8.5 lbs. **Sights:** Midwest Industry flip-up. **Features:** 4-rail free floating handguard, flash hider, extruded 7029 T6 A3 Flattop receiver.
Price: **$1,759.00**

DPMS 3G2
Calibers: .223/5.56, 6.5 Creedmoor. **Barrel:** 16 in. **Weight:** 7.1 lbs. **Stock:** Magpul STR with Hogue rubber pistol grip. **Sights:** Magpul Gen 2 BUS. **Features:** Miculek Compensator, two-stage fire control. M111 Modular handguard allows placement of sights on top rail or 45-degree angle.
Price: From....................**$1,129.00–$1,239.00**

DPMS LITE HUNTER
Calibers: .243, .260 Rem., .308, .338 Federal. **Barrel:** 20 in. stainless. **Weight:** 8 pounds. **Stock:** Standard A2. **Features:** Two-stage match trigger. Hogue pistol grip. Optics ready top rail.
Price: **$1,499.00**

DPMS .300 AAC BLACKOUT
Caliber: .300 AAC Blackout. **Barrel:** 16-in. heavy 4150 chrome-lined. **Weight:** 7 pounds. **Stock:** Adjustable 6-position.
Price: **$1,199.00**

DPMS ORACLE
Calibers: .223/5.56 or .308/7.62. **Barrel:** 16 in. **Weights:** 6.2 (.223), 8.3 (308). Standard AR-15 fire control with A3 flattop receiver. **Finish:** Matte black or A-TACS camo.
Price: .223 ATACS....................**$739, $849**
Price: .308 ATACS....................**$1,099, $1,189**

DPMS GII SERIES
Caliber: .308 Win./7.62 NATO. **Barrels:** 16, 18 in. **Weight:** From 7.25 lbs. Features: promoted as the lightest .308 AR available. Features include new extractor and ejector systems, and improved steel feed ramp. New bolt geometry provides better lock-up and strength. Offered in several configurations.
Price: AP4 (shown)....................**$1,499.00**
Price: Recon....................**$1,759.00**
Price: SASS....................**$2,379.00**
Price: Hunter....................**$1,699.00**
Price: Bull....................**$1,759.00**
Price: MOE....................**$1,599.00**

Prices given are believed to be accurate at time of publication however, many factors affect retail pricing so exact prices are not possible.

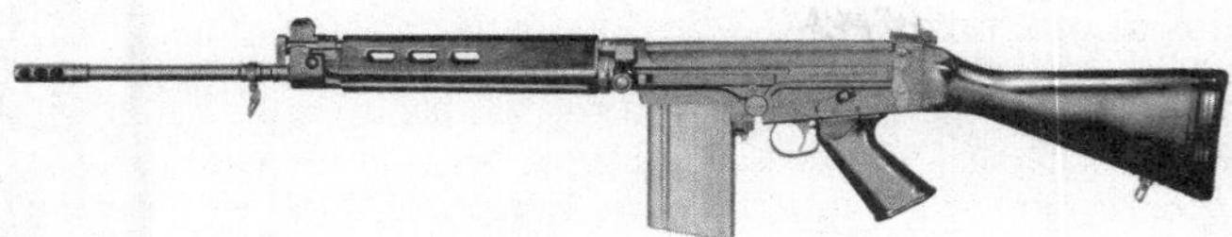

DSA SA58 STANDARD

Caliber: .308 Win. **Barrel:** 21 in. bipod cut w/threaded flash hider. **Weight:** 8.75 lbs. **Length:** 43 in. **Stock:** Synthetic, X-Series or optional folding para stock. **Sights:** Elevation-adjustable post front, windage-adjustable rear peep. **Features:** Fully adjustable short gas system, high-grade steel or 416 stainless upper receiver. Made in USA by DSA, Inc.

Price: From **$1,700.00**

DSA SA58 CARBINE

Caliber: .308 Win. **Barrel:** 16.25 in. bipod cut w/threaded flash hider. **Features:** Carbine variation of FAL-style rifle. Other features identical to SA58 Standard model. Made in USA by DSA, Inc.

Price: **$1,700.00**

DSA SA58 TACTICAL CARBINE

Caliber: .308 Win. **Barrel:** 16.25 in. fluted with A2 flash hider. **Weight:** 8.25 lbs. **Length:** 36.5 in. **Stock:** Synthetic, X-Series or optional folding para stock. **Sights:** Elevation-adjustable post front, windage-adjustable match rear peep. **Features:** Shortened fully adjustable short gas system, high-grade steel or 416 stainless upper receiver. Made in USA by DSA, Inc.

Price: **$1,975.00**

DSA SA58 MEDIUM CONTOUR

Caliber: .308 Win. **Barrel:** 21 in. w/threaded flash hider. **Weight:** 9.75 lbs. **Length:** 43 in. **Stock:** Synthetic military grade. **Sights:** Elevation-adjustable post front, windage-adjustable match rear peep. **Features:** Gas-operated semiauto with fully adjustable gas system, high-grade steel receiver. Made in USA by DSA, Inc.

Price: **$1,700.00**

DSA ZM4 AR SERIES

Caliber: .223/5.56 NATO. **Weight:** 9 pounds. **Features:** Standard Flattop rifle features include 20-in., chrome moly heavy barrel with A2 flash hider. Mil-Spec forged lower receiver, forged flattop or A2 upper. Fixed A2 stock. Carbine variations are also available with 16-in. barrels and many options.

Price: Standard Flat-Top **$820.00**
Price: MRC Multi-Role Carbine **$1,275.00**
Price: Mid Length Carbine **$834.00**
Price: Flat-Top with rail **$850.00**

EXCEL ARMS MR-22

Caliber: .22 WMR. **Capacity:** 9-shot magazine. **Barrel:** 18 in. fluted stainless steel bull barrel. **Weight:** 8 lbs. **Length:** 32.5 in. overall. **Grips:** Textured black polymer. **Sights:** Fully adjustable target sights. **Features:** Made from 17-4 stainless steel, aluminum shroud w/Weaver rail, manual safety, firing-pin block, last-round bolt-hold-open feature. Four packages with various equipment available. American made, lifetime warranty. Comes with one 9-round stainless steel magazine and a California-approved cable lock. Introduced 2006. Made in USA by Excel Arms.

Price: MR-22 .22 WMR **$538.00**

EXCEL ARMS X-SERIES

Caliber: .22 LR, 5.7x28mm (10 or 25-round); .30 Carbine (10 or 20-round magazine). 9mm (10 or 17 rounds). **Barrel:** 18 in. **Weight:** 6.25 lbs. **Length:** 34 to 38 in. **Features:** Available with or without adjustable iron sights. Blow-back action (5.57x28) or delayed blow-back (.30 Carbine).

Price: .22 LR **$504.00**
Price: 5.7x28 or 9mm .... **$795.00–$916.00**

FN15 SERIES

Caliber: 5.56x45. **Capacity:** 20 or 30 rounds. **Barrels:** 16 in., 18 in., 20 in. **Features:** AR-style rifle/carbine series with most standard features and options.

Price: Tactical II (also in .300 BLK) **$1,599.00**
Price: Standard rifle **$1,149.00**
Price: Sporting **$1,749.00**
Price: DMR II **$1,999.00**
Price: Carbine **$1,149.00**
Price: Competition **$2,240.00**
Price: Military Collector **$1,749.00**

FN 15 TACTICAL CARBINE FDA P-LOK

Caliber: 5.56x45mm. **Capacity:** 30-shot PMAG. **Barrel**: 16-in. free-floating and chrome-lined with FN 3-prong flash hider. **Stock:** B5 Systems buttstock and grip. **Weight**: 7.2 lbs. **Finish:** Flat Dark Earth. **Features:** P-LOK handguard, M-LOK accessory mounting system, hard anodized aluminum flat-top receiver with Picatinny rail, forward assist.

Price: **$1,499.00**

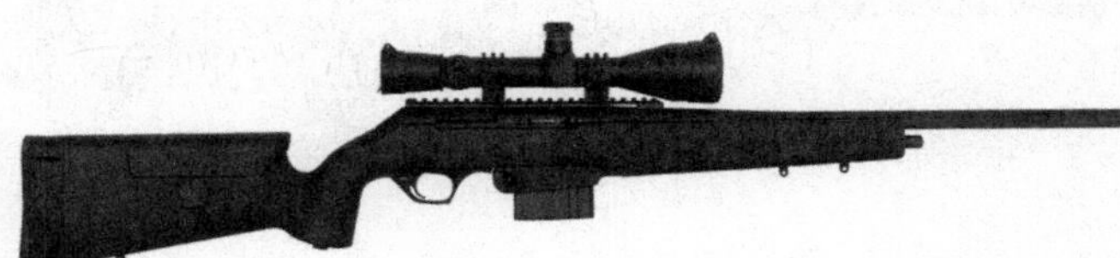

FNH FNAR COMPETITION

Caliber: .308 Win. **Capacity:** 10-shot magazine. **Barrel:** 20 in. fluted. **Weight:** 8.9 lbs. **Length:** 41.25 in. overall. **Sights:** None furnished. Optical rail atop receiver, three accessory rails on fore-end. **Stock:** Adjustable for comb height, length of pull, cast-on and cast-off. Blue/gray laminate. Based on BAR design.

Price: **$1,767.00**

FNH SCAR 16S Caliber: 5.56mm/.223. **Capacities:** 10 or 30 rounds. **Barrel:** 16.25 in. **Weight:** 7.25 lbs. **Lengths:** 27.5–37.5 in. (extended stock). **Stock:** Telescoping, side-folding polymer. Adjustable cheekpiece, A2 style pistol grip. **Sights:** Adjustable folding front and rear. **Features:** Hard anodized aluminum receiver with four accessory rails. Ambidextrous safety and mag release. Charging handle can be mounted on right or left side. Semi-auto version of newest service rifle of U.S. Special Forces.
Price: **$3,299.00**

FNH SCAR 17S Caliber: 7.62x51 NATO/.308. **Capacities:** 10 or 30 rounds. **Barrel:** 16.25 in. **Weight:** 8 lbs. **Lengths:** 28.5–38.5 in. (extended stock). **Features:** Other features the same as SCAR 16S.
Price: **$3,499.00**

FRANKLIN ARMORY 3 GR-L Caliber: 5.56mm/.223. **Capacities:** 10 or 30 rounds. **Barrel:** 18 in. fluted with threaded muzzle crown. **Weight:** 7.25 lbs. **Stock:** Magpul PRS. Adjustable comb and length of pull. **Features:** Hard anodized Desert Smoke upper receiver with full-length Picatinny rail. One of many AR type rifles and carbines offered by this manufacturer. Made in the USA.
Price: **$2,310.00**

HECKLER & KOCH MODEL MR556A1
Caliber: .223 Remington/5.56 NATO. **Capacity:** 10+1. **Barrel:** 16.5 in. **Weight:** 8.9 lbs. **Lengths:** 33.9–37.68 in. **Stock:** Black synthetic adjustable. **Features:** Uses the gas piston system found on the HK 416 and G26, which does not introduce propellant gases and carbon fouling into the rifle's interior.
Price: **$3,295.00**

HECKLER & KOCH MODEL MR762A1
Caliber: Similar to Model MR556A1 except chambered for 7.62x51mm/.308 Win. cartridge. **Weight:** 10 lbs. w/empty magazine. **Lengths:** 36–39.5 in. **Features:** Variety of optional sights are available. Stock has five adjustable positions.
Price: **$3,995.00**

HIGH STANDARD HSA-15
Calibers: .223 Remington/5.56 NATO or .300 AAC Blackout. **Capacity:** 30-round magazine. **Barrels:** A2 style with 16 or 20 in. **Features:** Fixed or collapsible stock, adjustable sights. Series of AR-style models offered in most variations with popular options. Made by High Standard Manufacturing Co.
Price: .... **$785.00–$1,250.00**

HI-POINT CARBINE SERIES
Calibers: .380 ACP, 9mm Para. .40 S&W, 10mm, (10-round magazine); .45 ACP (9-round). **Barrels:** 16.5 in. (17.5 in. for .40 S&W and .45). **Weight:** 4.5–7 lbs. **Length:** 31.5 in. overall. **Stock:** Black polymer, camouflage. **Sights:** Protected post front, aperture rear. Integral scope mount. **Features:** Grip-mounted magazine release. Black or chrome finish. Sling swivels. Available with laser or red-dot sights, RGB 4X scope, forward grip. Introduced 1996. Made in USA by MKS Supply, Inc.
Price: .380 ACP, From **$315.00**
Price: 9mm (995TS), From **$315.00**
Price: .40 S&W (4095TS), From **$315.00**
Price: .45 ACP (4595TS), From **$319.00**
Price: 10mm (1095TS), From **$389.00**

INLAND M1 1945 CARBINE
Caliber: .30 Carbine. **Capacity:** 15 rounds. **Barrel:** 18 in. **Weight:** 5 lbs. 3 oz. **Features:** A faithful reproduction of the last model that Inland manufactured in 1945, featuring a type 3 bayonet lug/barrel band, adjustable rear sight, push button safety, and walnut stock. Scout Model has 16.5-in. barrel, flash hider, synthetic stock with accessory rail. Made in the USA.
Price: **$1,299.00**
Price: Scout Model **$1,449.00**

JP ENTERPRISES LRP-07
Calibers: .308 Win, .260 Rem., 6.5 Creedmoor, .338 Federal. **Barrels:** 16–22 in., polished stainless with compensator. **Buttstock:** A2, ACE ARFX, Tactical Tactical Intent Carbine, Magpul MOE. **Grip:** Hogue Pistol Grip. **Features:** Machined upper and lower receivers with left-side charging system. MKIII Hand Guard. Adjustable gas system.
Price: From............ **$3,299.00**

JP ENTERPRISES JP-15
Calibers: .223, .204 Ruger, 6.5 Grendel, .300 Blackout, .22 LR. **Barrels:** 18 or 24-in. **Buttstock:** Synthetic modified thumbhole or laminate thumbhole. **Grip:** Hogue Pistol grip. Basic AR-type general-purpose rifle with numerous options.
Price: From............ **$1,999.00**

KALASHNIKOV USA
Caliber: 7.62x39mm. **Capacity:** 30-round magazine. AK-47 series made in the USA in several variants and styles. **Barrel:** 16.25 in. **Weight:** 7.52 lbs.
Price: US132S Synthetic stock **$799.00**
Price: US132W Wood carbine **$836.00**

KEL-TEC RFB
Caliber: 7.62 NATO/.308. 20-round FAL-type magazine. **Barrel:** 18 in. with threaded muzzle, A2-style flash hider. **Weight:** 8 lbs. **Features:** A bullpup short-stroke gas piston operated carbine with ambidextrous controls, reversible operating handle, Mil-Spec Picatinny rail.
Price: **$1,927.00**

KEL-TEC SU-16 SERIES
Caliber: 5.56 NATO/.223. **Capacity:** 10-round magazine. **Barrels:** 16 or 18.5 in. **Weights:** 4.5–5 lbs. **Features:** Offering in several rifle and carbine variations.
Price: From............ **$682.00–$900.00**

Prices given are believed to be accurate at time of publication however, many factors affect retail pricing so exact prices are not possible.

LARUE TACTICAL OBR
Calibers: 5.56 NATO/.223, 7.62 NATO/.308 Win. **Barrels:** 16.1 in., 18 in. or 20 in. **Weights:** 7.5–9.25 lbs. **Features:** Manufacturer of several models of AR-style rifles and carbines. Optimized Battle Rifle (OBR) series is made in both NATO calibers. Many AR-type options available. Made in the USA
Price: OBR 5.56 .... **$2,245.00**
Price: OBR 7.62 .... **$3,370.00**

LEWIS MACHINE & TOOL (LMT)
Calibers: 5.56 NATO/.223, 7.62 NATO/.308 Win. **Barrels:** 16.1 in., 18 in. or 20 in. **Weights:** 7.5–9.25 lbs. **Features:** Manufacturer of a wide range of AR-style carbines with many options. SOPMOD stock, gas piston operating system, monolithic rail platform, tactical sights. Made in the USA by Lewis Machine & Tool.
Price: Standard 16 .... **$1,649.00**
Price: Comp 16, flattop receiver **$1,685.00**
Price: CQB Series from **$2,399.00**
Price: Sharpshooter Weapons System **$6,499.00**

LES BAER CUSTOM ULTIMATE AR 223
Caliber: .223. **Barrels:** 18 in., 20 in., 22 in., 24 in. **Weights:** 7.75–9.75 lbs. **Length:** NA. **Stock:** Black synthetic. **Sights:** None furnished; Picatinny-style flattop rail for scope mounting. **Features:** Forged receiver; Ultra single-stage trigger (Jewell two-stage trigger optional); titanium firing pin; Versa-Pod bipod; chromed National Match carrier; stainless steel, hand-lapped and cryo-treated barrel; guaranteed to shoot .5 or .75 MOA, depending on model. Made in USA by Les Baer Custom Inc.
Price: Super Varmint Model .... **$2,640.00–$2870.00**
Price: Super Match Model .... **$2,740.00–$2960.00**
Price: M4 Flattop model **$2,790.00**
Price: IPSC Action Model **$2,890.00**
Price: LBC-AR (.264 LBC-AR) **$2,640.00**

LES BAER ULTIMATE MATCH/SNIPER
Caliber: .308 Win. **Barrels:** 18 or 20 in. **Features:** Magpul stock, Enforcer muzzle brake.
Price: **$3,940.00**
Price: Ultimate Monolith SWAT Model **$4,390.00**

LR 300S
Caliber: 5.56 NATO. **Capacity:** 30-shot magazine. **Barrel:** 16.5 in.; 1:9 in. twist. **Weights:** 7.4–7.8 lbs. **Length:** NA. **Stock:** Folding. **Sights:** YHM flip front and rear. **Features:** Flattop receive, full-length top Picatinny rail. Phantom flash hider, multi sling mount points, field strips with no tools. Made in USA from Z-M Weapons.
Price: AXL, AXLT **$2,139.00**
Price: NXL **$2,208.00**

LWRC INTERNATIONAL M6 SERIES
Calibers: 5.56 NATO, .224 Valkyrie, .6.5 Creedmoor, 6.8 SPC, 7.62x51mm, .300 BLK. **Capacity:** 30-shot magazine. Features: This company makes a complete line of AR-15 type rifles operated by a short-stroke, gas piston system. A wide variety of stock, sight and finishes are available. Colors include black, Flat Dark Earth, Olive Drab Green, Patriot Brown.
Price: M6A2 .... **$2,217.00**
Price: M6-SPR (Special Purpose Rifle) **$2,479.00**
Price: REPR (Shown) **$5,139.00**
Price: SIX8 A5 6.8 SPC .... **$2,600.00–$2,750.00**
Price: IC-DI 224 Valkyrie **$1,995.00**

MOSSBERG MMR SERIES Caliber: 5.56 NATO. **Capacity:** 10 or 30 rounds. GIO system. **Barrel:** 16 or 18 in. with A2-style muzzle brake. **Features:** Picatinny rail, black synthetic stock, free-floating stainless barrel. Offered in several variants. Pro and Optics Ready have JM Pro match trigger. Optics Ready has 6-position stock with FLEX pad, Magpul MOE grip and trigger guard. Introduced in 2016.
Price: MMR Carbine **$938.00**
Price: MMR Tactical Optics Ready **$1,253.00**
Price: MMR Pro **$1,393.00**

REMINGTON LE R4 OPERATOR NEW MEXICO
Caliber: .223. **Capacity:** 30-round magazine. **Barrel:** 16 in. with twist rate of 1:7 for heavier, longer bullets. **Weight:** 6.5 lbs. **Length:** 33.25–36.25 in. **Stock:** Magpul SL. **Sights:** Troy Industries front and rear folding battle sights. **Features:** AR-style with direct impingement gas operation. Carbine length system with mil-spec forged receiver, single-stage mil-spec trigger. Designed for a LE agency in New Mexico. Introduced in 2016 by Remington Law Enforcement Division.
Price: **$1,299.00**

ROCK RIVER ARMS LAR SERIES
Calibers: .223/5.56, .308/7.62, 6.8 SPC, .458 SOCOM, 9mm and .40 S&W. **Features:** These AR-15 type rifles and carbines are available with a very wide range of options. Virtually any AR configuration is offered including tactical, hunting and competition models. Some models are available in left-hand versions.
Price: .... **$1,035.00–$1,845.00**

RUGER AR-556
Caliber: 5.56 NATO. **Capacity:** 30-round magazine. **Features:** Basic AR M4-style Modern Sporting Rifle with direct impingement operation, forged aluminum upper and lower receivers, and cold hammer-forged chrome-moly steel barrel with M4 feed ramp cuts. Other features include Ruger Rapid Deploy folding rear sight, milled F-height gas block with post front sight, telescoping 6-position stock and one 30-round Magpul magazine. Introduced in 2015. MPR (Multi Purpose Rifle) model has 18-in. barrel with muzzle brake, flat-top upper, 15-in. free-floating handguard with Magpul M-LOK accessory slots, Magpul MOE SL collapsible buttstock and MOE grip.
Price: **$799.00**
Price: MPR **$899.00**

RUGER PC CARBINE
Caliber: 9mm. **Capacity:** 17 rounds. Interchangeable magazine wells for Ruger and Glock magazines. **Barrel:** 16.12-in. threaded and fluted. **Stock:** Glass-filled nylon synthetic. **Sights:** Adjustable ghost-ring rear, protected-blade front. **Weight:** 6.8 lbs. **Features:** Reversible magazine release and charging handle. Dead-blow action reduces felt recoil. Receiver has integrated Picatinny rail.
Price: **$649.00**

RUGER SR-556/SR-762
Calibers: 5.56 NATO or 7.62 NATO/.308. (SR-762 model). **Features:** AR-style semi-auto rifle with two-stage piston; quad rail handguard; Troy Industries sights; black synthetic fixed or telescoping buttstock; 16.12-in. 1:9 in. twist steel barrel with birdcage; 10- or 30-round detachable box magazine; black matte finish overall. SR-556 has takedown feature.
Price: SR-556........ **$2,199.00**
Price: SR-762 .... **$2,349.00**

RUGER MINI-14 RANCH RIFLE
Calibers: .223 Rem., .300 Blackout (Tactical Rifle). **Capacity:** 5-shot or 20-shot detachable box magazine. **Barrel:** 18.5 in. Rifling twist 1:9 in. **Weights:** 6.75–7 lbs. **Length:** 37.25 in. overall. **Stocks:** American hardwood, steel reinforced, or synthetic. **Sights:** Protected blade front, fully adjustable Ghost Ring rear. **Features:** Fixed piston gas-operated, positive primary extraction. New buffer system, redesigned ejector system. Ruger S100RM scope rings included on Ranch Rifle. Heavier barrels added in 2008, 20-round magazine added in 2009.
Price: Mini-14/5, Ranch Rifle, blued, wood stock **$999.00**
Price: K-Mini-14/5, Ranch Rifle, stainless, scope rings **$1,069.00**
Price: Mini-14 Target Rifle: laminated thumbhole stock, heavy crowned 22 in. stainless steel barrel, other refinements **$1,259.00**
Price: Mini-14 ATI Stock: Tactical version of Mini-14 but with six-position collapsible stock or folding stock, grooved pistol grip. Multiple Picatinny optics/accessory rails **$1,089.00**
Price: Mini-14 Tactical Rifle: Similar to Mini-14 but with 16.12 in. barrel with flash hider, black synthetic stock, adjustable sights **$1,019.00**

RUGER MINI THIRTY
Caliber: Similar to the Mini-14 rifle except modified to chamber the 7.62x39 Russian service round. **Weight:** 6.75 lbs. **Barrel:** Has 6-groove barrel with 1:10 in. twist. **Features:** Ruger Integral Scope Mount bases and protected blade front, fully adjustable Ghost Ring rear. Detachable 5-shot staggered box magazine. 20-round magazines available. Stainless or matte black alloy w/synthetic stock. Introduced 1987.
Price: Matte black finish **$1,069.00**
Price: Stainless **$1,089.00**
Price: Stainless w/20-round mag **$1,139.00**

SAVAGE MSR 15/MSR 10
Calibers: AR-style series chambered in 5.56 NATO (Patrol and Recon), 6.5 Creedmoor or .308 Win. (MSR 10 Hunter and Long Range). **Barrels:** 16.1 in. (Patrol and Recon), 16 or 18 in. (Hunter), 20 or 22 in. (Long Range). Wylde chamber on Patrol and Recon models. Hunter and Long Range models have muzzle brake.
Price: Patrol **$869.00**
Price: Recon (shown) **$994.00**
Price: MSR 10 Long Range **$2,284.00**
Price: MSR 10 Hunter........ **$1,481.00**

SIG-SAUER MCX
Calibers: 5.56 NATO, 7.62x39mm or .300 Blackout. **Features:** AR-style rifle. Modular system allows switching between calibers with conversion kit. Features include a 16 in. barrel, aluminum KeyMod handguards, ambi controls and charging handle, choice of side-folding or telescoping stock, auto-regulating gas system to all transition between subsonic and supersonic loads.
Price: **$2,131.00**
Price: With conversion kit **$2,188.00**

SIG 516 PATROL
Caliber: 5.56 NATO. **Features:** AR-style rifle with included 30-round magazine, 16-in. chrome-lined barrel with muzzle brake; free-floating, aluminum quad Picatinny rail, Magpul MOE adjustable stock, black anodized or Flat Dark Earth finish, various configurations available.
Price: From........ **$1,888.00**

SIG-SAUER SIG716 TACTICAL PATROL
Caliber: 7.62 NATO/.308 Win. **Features:** AR-10 type rifle. Gas-piston operation with 3-round-position (4-position optional) gas valve; 16-, 18- or 20-in. chrome-lined barrel with threaded muzzle and nitride finish; free-floating aluminum quad rail fore-end with four M1913 Picatinny rails; telescoping buttstock; lower receiver is machined from a 7075-T6 Aircraft grade aluminum forging; upper receiver, machined from 7075-T6 aircraft grade aluminum with integral M1913 Picatinny rail. DMR has free-floating barrel, two-stage match-grade trigger, short-stroke pushrod operating system.
Price: **$2,385.00**
Price: Designated Marksman (DMR) **$3,108.00**

Prices given are believed to be accurate at time of publication however, many factors affect retail pricing so exact prices are not possible.

SMITH & WESSON M&P15
Caliber: 5.56mm NATO/.223. **Capacity:** 30-shot steel magazine. **Barrel:** 16 in., 1:9 in. twist. **Weight:** 6.74 lbs., w/o magazine. **Lengths:** 32–35 in. overall. **Stock:** Black synthetic. **Sights:** Adjustable post front sight, adjustable dual aperture rear sight. **Features:** 6-position telescopic stock, thermo-set M4 handguard. 14.75 in. sight radius. 7-lbs. (approx.) trigger pull. 7075 T6 aluminum upper, 4140 steel barrel. Chromed barrel bore, gas key, bolt carrier. Hard-coat black-anodized receiver and barrel finish. OR (Optics Ready) model has no sights. TS model has Magpul stock and folding sights. Made in USA by Smith & Wesson.
Price: Sport Model **$739.00**
Price: OR Model **$1,069.00**
Price: TS model **$1,569.00**

SMITH & WESSON M&P15-300
Calibers: .300 Whisper/.300 AAC Blackout. **Features:** Other specifications the same of 5.56 models.
Price: **$1,119.00**

SMITH & WESSON MODEL M&P15 VTAC Caliber: .223 Remington/5.56 NATO. **Capacity:** 30-round magazine. **Barrel:** 16 in. **Weight:** 6.5 lbs. **Length:** 35 in. extended, 32 in. collapsed, overall. **Features:** Six-position CAR stock. Surefire flash-hider and G2 light with VTAC light mount; VTAC/JP handguard; JP single-stage match trigger and speed hammer; three adjustable Picatinny rails; VTAC padded two-point adjustable sling.
Price: **$1,949.00**

SMITH & WESSON M&P15PC CAMO
Caliber: 223 Rem/5.56 NATO, A2 configuration. **Capacity:** 10-round magazine. **Barrel:** 20 in. stainless with 1:8 in. twist. **Weight:** 8.2 lbs. **Length:** 38.5 in. overall. **Features:** AR-style, no sights but integral front and rear optics rails. Two-stage trigger, aluminum lower. Finished in Realtree Advantage Max-1 camo.
Price: **$1,589.00**

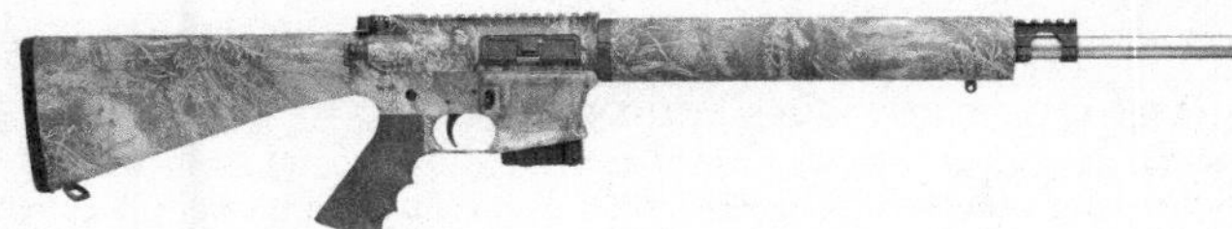

SMITH & WESSON M&P10
Caliber: .308 Win. **Capacity:** 10 rounds. **Barrel:** 18 in. **Weight:** 7.7 pounds. **Features:** 6-position CAR stock, black hard anodized finish. Camo finish hunting model available w/5-round magazine.
Price: **$1,619.00**
Price: (Camo) **$1,729.00**

SPRINGFIELD ARMORY M1A
Caliber: 7.62mm NATO (.308). **Capacities:** 5- or 10-shot box magazine. **Barrel:** 25.062 in. with flash suppressor, 22 in. without suppressor. **Weight:** 9.75 lbs. **Length:** 44.25 in. overall. **Stock:** American walnut with walnut-colored heat-resistant fiberglass handguard. Matching walnut handguard available. Also available with fiberglass stock. **Sights:** Military, square blade front, full click-adjustable aperture rear. **Features:** Commercial equivalent of the U.S. M-14 service rifle with no provision for automatic firing. From Springfield Armory.
Price: SOCOM 16 .... **$1,987.00**
Price: Scout Squad, From **$1,850.00**
Price: Standard M1A, From **$1,685.00**
Price: Loaded Standard, From **$1,847.00**
Price: National Match, From **$2,434.00**
Price: Super Match (heavy premium barrel) about **$2,965.00**
Price: Tactical, From .... **$3,619.00–$4,046.00**

SPRINGFIELD ARMORY SAINT Caliber: 5.56 NATO. **Capacity:** 30-round magazine. **Barrel:** 16 in., 1:8 twist. **Weight:** 6 lbs., 11 oz. **Sights:** AR2-style fixed post front, flip-up aperture rear. **Features:** Mid-length gas system, BCM 6-position stock, Mod 3 grip PMT KeyMod handguard 7075 T6 aluminum receivers. Springfield Armory's first entry into AR category. Introduced 2016.
Price: **$899.00**

STAG ARMS AR-STYLE SERIES
Calibers: 5.56 NATO/.223, 6.8 SPC, 9mm Parabellum. Ten. **Capacities:** 20- or 30-shot magazine. **Features:** This manufacturer offers more than 25 AR-style rifles or carbines with many optional features including barrel length and configurations, stocks, sights, rail systems and both direct impingement and gas piston operating systems. Left-hand models are available on some products. Listed is a sampling of Stag Arms models.
Price: Model 1 .... **$949.00**
Price: Model 2T Carbine (Tactical) **$1,130.00**
Price: Model 3 Carbine **$895.00**
Price: Model 3G Rifle **$1,459.00**
Price: Model 5 Carbine (6.8) **$1,045.00**
Price: Stag 7 Hunter (6.8) **$1,055.00**
Price: Model 9 (9mm) **$990.00**

STONER SR-15 MOD2
Caliber: .223. **Capacity:** 30-round magazine. **Barrel:** 18 in. **Weight:** 7.6 lbs. **Length:** 38 in. overall. **Stock:** Mag-Pul MOE. **Sights:** Post front, fully adjustable rear (300-meter sight). **Features:** URX-4 upper receiver; two-stage trigger, 30-round magazine. Black finish. Made in USA by Knight's Mfg.
Price: **$2,700.00**

STONER SR-25 ACC
Caliber: 7.62 NATO. **Capacities:** 10- or 20-shot steel magazine. **Barrel:** 16 in. with flash hider. **Weight:** 8.5 lbs. **Features:** Shortened, non-slip handguard; drop-in two-stage match trigger, removable carrying handle, ambidextrous controls, matte black finish. Made in USA by Knight's Mfg. Co.
Price: **$5,300.00**

WILSON COMBAT TACTICAL
Caliber: 5.56mm NATO. **Capacity:** Accepts all M-16/AR-15 Style Magazines, includes one 20-round magazine. **Barrel:** 16.25 in., 1:9 in. twist, match-grade fluted. **Weight:** 6.9 lbs. **Length:** 36.25 in. overall. **Stock:** Fixed or collapsible. **Features:** Free-float ventilated aluminum quad-rail handguard, Mil-Spec Parkerized barrel and steel components, anodized receiver, precision CNC-machined upper and lower receivers, 7075 T6 aluminum forgings. Single-stage JP Trigger/ Hammer Group, Wilson Combat Tactical muzzle brake, nylon tactical rifle case. M-4T version has flat-top receiver for mounting optics, OD green furniture, 16.25 in. match-grade M-4 style barrel. SS-15 Super Sniper Tactical Rifle has 1-in-8 twist, heavy 20 in. match-grade fluted stainless steel barrel. Made in USA by Wilson Combat.
Price: .... **$2,225.00–$2,450.00**

BIG HORN ARMORY MODEL 89 RIFLE AND CARBINE
Caliber: .500 S&W Mag. **Capacities:** 5- or 7-round magazine. **Features:** Lever-action rifle or carbine chambered for .500 S&W Magnum. 22- or 18-in. barrel; walnut or maple stocks with pistol grip; aperture rear and blade front sights; recoil pad; sling swivels; enlarged lever loop; magazine capacity 5 (rifle) or 7 (carbine) rounds.
Price: **$2,424.00**

BIG HORN ARMORY MODEL 90 SERIES

Calibers: .460 S&W, .454 Casull. Features similar to Model 89. Several wood and finish upgrades available.
Price: Rifle .460 w/22-in. bbl., From **$3,024.00**
Price: Carbine .460 w/18-in. bbl., From **$2,849.00**
Price: 90A rifle, .454, 22-in. bbl., From **$2,949.00**
Price: 90A carbine, .454, 18-in. bbl., From.................................. **$2,774.00**

BROWNING BLR

Features: Lever action with rotating bolt head, multiple-lug breech bolt with recessed bolt face, side ejection. Rack-and-pinion lever. Flush-mounted detachable magazines, with 4+1 capacity for magnum cartridges, 5+1 for standard rounds. **Barrel:** Button-rifled chrome-moly steel with crowned muzzle. **Stock:** Buttstocks and fore-ends are American walnut with grip and forend checkering. Recoil pad installed. **Trigger:** Wide-groove design, trigger travels with lever. Half-cock hammer safety; fold-down hammer. **Sights:** Gold bead on ramp front; low-profile square-notch adjustable rear. **Features:** Blued barrel and receiver, high-gloss wood finish. Receivers are drilled and tapped for scope mounts, swivel studs included. Action lock provided. Introduced 1996. Imported from Japan by Browning.

BROWNING BLR LIGHTWEIGHT W/PISTOL GRIP, SHORT AND LONG ACTION; LIGHTWEIGHT '81, SHORT AND LONG ACTION

Calibers: Short Action, 20 in. Barrel: .22-250 Rem., .243 Win., 7mm-08 Rem., .308 Win., .358, .450 Marlin. **Calibers: Short Action, 22 in. Barrel:** .270 WSM, 7mm WSM, .300 WSM, .325 WSM. **Calibers: Long Action 22 in. Barrel:** .270 Win., .30-06. **Calibers: Long Action 24 in. Barrel:** 7mm Rem. Mag., .300 Win. Mag. **Weights:** 6.5–7.75 lbs. **Lengths:** 40–45 in. overall. **Stock:** New checkered pistol grip and Schnabel forearm. Lightweight '81 differs from Pistol Grip models with a Western-style straight grip stock and banded forearm. Lightweight w/Pistol Grip Short Action and Long Action introduced 2005. Model '81 Lightning Long Action introduced 1996.
Price: Lightweight w/Pistol Grip Short Action, From...................... **$1,020.00**
Price: Lightweight w/Pistol Grip Long Action **$1,100.00**
Price: Lightweight '81 Short Action **$960.00**
Price: Lightweight '81 Long Action **$1,040.00**
Price: Lightweight '81 Takedown Short Action, From **$1,040.00**
Price: Lightweight '81 Takedown Long Action, From **$1,120.00**
Price: Lightweight stainless .... **$1,100.00–$1,180.00**
Price: Stainless Takedown .... **$1,230.00–$1,300.00**
Price: Gold Medallion w/nickel finish, engraving .... **$1,470.00–$1,550.00**

CHIAPPA MODEL 1892 RIFLE

Calibers: .38 Special/357 Magnum, .38-40, .44-40, .44 Mag., .45 Colt. **Barrels:** 16 in. (Trapper), 20 in. round and 24 in. octagonal (Takedown). **Weight:** 7.7 lbs. **Stock:** Walnut. **Sights:** Blade front, buckhorn. Trapper model has interchangeable front sight blades. **Features:** Finishes are blue/case colored. Magazine capacity is 12 rounds with 24 in. bbl.; 10 rounds with 20 in. barrel; 9 rounds in 16 in. barrel. Mare's Leg models have 4-shot magazine, 9- or 12-in. barrel.
Price: From.. **$1,409.00**
Price: Takedown.. **$1,539.00**
Price: Trapper **$1,359.00**
Price: Mare's Leg, from... **$1,489.00**

CHIAPPA MODEL 1886

Caliber: .45-70. **Barrels:** 16, 18.5, 22, 26 in. Replica of famous Winchester model offered in several variants.
Price: Rifle **$1,759.00**
Price: Carbine **$1,669.00**
Price: Kodiak **$1,969.00**

CIMARRON 1860 HENRY CIVIL WAR MODEL

Calibers: .44 WCF, .45 LC. **Capacity:** 12-round magazine. **Barrel:** 24 in. (rifle). **Weight:** 9.5 lbs. **Length:** 43 in. overall (rifle). **Stock:** European walnut. **Sights:** Bead front, open adjustable rear. **Features:** Brass receiver and buttplate. Uses original Henry loading system. Copy of the original rifle. Charcoal blued finish optional. Introduced 1991. Imported by Cimarron F.A. Co.
Price: From... **$1,600.00**

CIMARRON 1866 WINCHESTER REPLICAS

Calibers: .38 Special, .357 Magnum, .45 LC, .32 WCF, .38 WCF, .44 WCF. **Barrels:** 24 in. (rifle), 20 in. (short rifle), 19 in. (carbine), 16 in. (trapper). **Weight:** 9 lbs. **Length:** 43 in. overall (rifle). **Stock:** European walnut. **Sights:** Bead front, open adjustable rear. **Features:** Solid brass receiver, buttplate, fore-end cap. Octagonal barrel. Copy of the original Winchester '66 rifle. Introduced 1991. Imported by Cimarron F.A. Co.
Price: 1866 Sporting Rifle, 24 in. barrel, From **$1,226.00**
Price: 1866 Short Rifle, 20 in. barrel, From **$1,226.00**
Price: 1866 Carbine, 19 in. barrel, From **$1,364.00**
Price: 1866 Trapper, 16 in. barrel, From **$1,203.00**

CIMARRON 1873 SHORT RIFLE

Calibers: .357 Magnum, .38 Special, .32 WCF, .38 WCF, .44 Special, .44 WCF, .45 Colt. **Barrel:** 20 in. tapered octagon. **Weight:** 7.5 lbs. **Length:** 39 in. overall. **Stock:** Walnut. **Sights:** Bead front, adjustable semi-buckhorn rear. **Features:** Has half "button" magazine. Original-type markings, including caliber, on barrel and elevator and "Kings" patent. Trapper Carbine (.357 Mag., .44 WCF, .45 Colt). From Cimarron F.A. Co.
Price: **$1,272.00**
Price: Trapper Carbine 16-in. bbl. **$1,242.00**

CIMARRON 1873 DELUXE SPORTING

Similar to the 1873 Short Rifle except has 24-in. barrel with half-magazine.
Price: **$1,378.00**

CIMARRON 1873 LONG RANGE SPORTING

Calibers: .44 WCF, .45 Colt. **Barrel:** 30 in., octagonal. **Weight:** 8.5 lbs. **Length:** 48 in. overall. **Stock:** Walnut. **Sights:** Blade front, semi-buckhorn ramp rear. Tang sight optional. **Features:** Color casehardened frame; choice of modern blued-black or charcoal blued for other parts. Barrel marked "Kings Improvement." From Cimarron F.A. Co.
Price: **$1,325.10**

EMF 1866 YELLOWBOY LEVER ACTIONS

Calibers: .38 Special, .44-40, .45 LC. **Barrels:** 19 in. (carbine), 24 in. (rifle). **Weight:** 9 lbs. **Length:** 43 in. overall (rifle). **Stock:** European walnut. **Sights:** Bead front, open adjustable rear. **Features:** Solid brass frame, blued barrel, lever, hammer, buttplate. Imported from Italy by EMF.
Price: Rifle... **$1,175.00**

EMF MODEL 1873 LEVER-ACTION

Calibers: .32/20, .357 Magnum, .38/40, .44-40, .45 Colt. **Barrels:** 18 in., 20 in., 24 in., 30 in. **Weight:** 8 lbs. **Length:** 43.25 in. overall. **Stock:** European walnut. **Sights:** Bead front, rear adjustable for windage and elevation. **Features:** Color casehardened frame (blued on carbine). Imported by EMF.
Price: **$1,250.00**

HENRY ORIGINAL RIFLE

Caliber: .44-40. **Capacity:** 13-round magazine. **Barrel:** 24 in. **Weight:** 9 lbs. **Stock:** Straight-grip fancy American walnut with hardened brass buttplate. **Sights:** Folding ladder rear with blade front. **Finish:** Hardened brass receiver with blued steel barrel. **Features:** Virtually identical to the original 1860 version except for the caliber. Each serial number has prefix " BTH" in honor of Benjamin Tyler Henry, the inventor of the lever-action repeating rifle that went on to become the most legendary firearm in American history. Introduced in 2014 by Henry Repeating Arms. Made in the USA.
Price: **$2,415.00**

Prices given are believed to be accurate at time of publication however, many factors affect retail pricing so exact prices are not possible.

HENRY .45-70
Caliber: .45-70. **Capacity:** 4-round magazine. **Barrel:** 18.5 in. **Weight:** 7 lbs. **Stock:** Pistol grip walnut. **Sights:** XS Ghost Rings with blade front.
Price: **$850.00**

HENRY BIG BOY LEVER-ACTION CARBINE
Calibers: .327 Fed. Magnum, .357 Magnum/.38 Special, .41 Magnum, .44 Magnum/.44 Special, .45 Colt. **Capacity:** 10-shot tubular magazine. **Barrel:** 20 in. octagonal, 1:38 in. right-hand twist. **Weight:** 8.68 lbs. **Length:** 38.5 in. overall. **Stock:** Straight-grip American walnut, brass buttplate. **Sights:** Marbles fully adjustable semi-buckhorn rear, brass bead front. **Features:** Brasslite receiver not tapped for scope mount. Available in several Deluxe, engraved and other special editions. All Weather has round barrel, hardwood stock, chrome satin finish. Made in USA by Henry Repeating Arms.
Price: **$945.00**
Price: All Weather **$1,050.00**
Price: Engraved Special Editions from **$1,470.00**

HENRY .30/30 LEVER-ACTION CARBINE
Same as the Big Boy except has straight grip American walnut, .30-30 only, 6-shot. Receivers are drilled and tapped for scope mount. Made in USA by Henry Repeating Arms.
Price: H009 Blued receiver, round barrel **$850.00**
Price: H009B Brass receiver, octagonal barrel **$949.95**

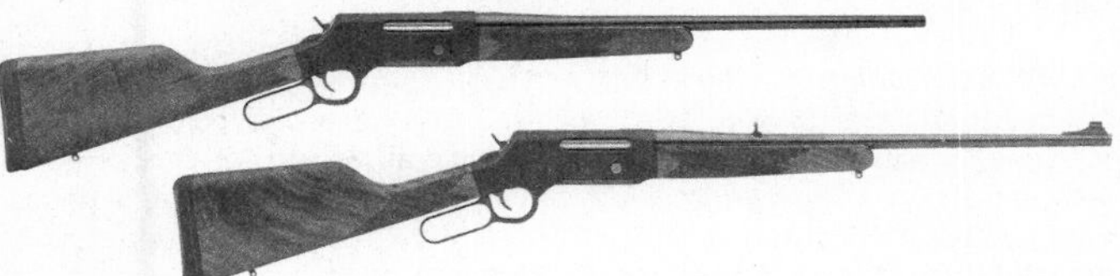

HENRY LONG RANGER
Calibers: .223 Rem., .243 Win., 308 Win. **Capacities:** 5 (.223), 4 (.243, .308). **Barrel:** 20 in. **Stock:** Straight grip, checkered walnut with buttpad, oil finish, swivel studs. **Features:** Geared action, side ejection, chromed steel bolt with 6 lugs, flush fit detachable magazine.
Price: **$1,066.00**

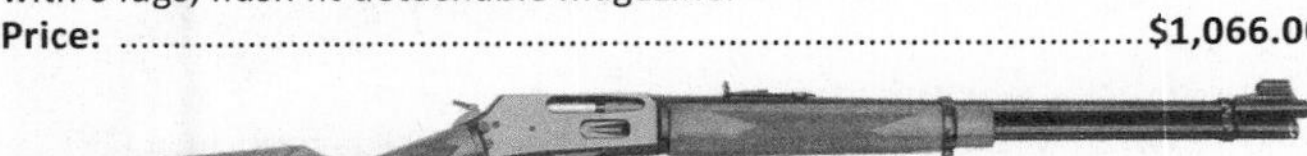

MARLIN MODEL 336C LEVER-ACTION CARBINE
Calibers: .30-30 or .35 Rem. **Capacity:** 6-shot tubular magazine. **Barrel:** 20 in. Micro-Groove. **Weight:** 7 lbs. **Length:** 38.5 in. overall. **Stock:** Checkered American black walnut, capped pistol grip. Mar-Shield finish; rubber buttpad; swivel studs. **Sights:** Ramp front with wide-scan hood, semi-buckhorn folding rear adjustable for windage and elevation. **Features:** Hammer-block safety. Receiver tapped for scope mount, offset hammer spur; top of receiver sandblasted to prevent glare. Includes safety lock. The latest variation of Marlin's classic lever gun that originated in 1937.
Price: **$635.00**

MARLIN MODEL 336SS LEVER-ACTION CARBINE
Caliber: .30-30 only. **Capacity:** 6-shot. **Features:** Same as the 336C except receiver, barrel and other major parts are machined from stainless steel. receiver tapped for scope. Includes safety lock.
Price: **$779.00**

MARLIN MODEL 336W LEVER-ACTION
Similar to the Model 336C except has walnut-finished, cut-checkered Maine birch stock; blued steel barrel band has integral sling swivel; no front sight hood; comes with padded nylon sling; hard rubber butplate. Introduced 1998. Includes safety lock. Made in USA by Marlin.
Price: **$548.00**

MARLIN 336BL
Caliber: .30-30. **Capacity:** 6-shot full-length tubular magazine. Barrel: 18-in. blued with Micro-Groove rifling (12 grooves). Features: Lever-action rifle. Finger lever; side ejection; blued steel receiver; hammer block safety; brown laminated hardwood pistol-grip stock with fluted comb; cut checkering; deluxe recoil pad; blued swivel studs.
Price: **$667.00**

MARLIN MODEL 336XLR
Caliber: .30-30. **Features:** Similar to Model 336C except has a 24-in. stainless barrel with Ballard-type cut rifling, stainless steel receiver and other parts, laminated hardwood stock with pistol grip, nickel-plated swivel studs. Chambered for .30-30 Win. with Hornady spire-pointed Flex-Tip cartridges. Includes safety lock. Introduced 2006.
Price: Model 336XLR **$969.00**

MARLIN MODEL 1894C
Caliber: .44 Special/.44 Magnum, 10-round tubular magazine. **Barrel:** 20 in. Ballard-type rifling. **Weight:** 6 lbs. **Length:** 37.5 in. overall. **Stock:** Checkered American black walnut, straight grip and fore-end. Mar-Shield finish. Rubber rifle buttpad; swivel studs. **Sights:** Wide-Scan hooded ramp front, semi-buckhorn folding rear adjustable for windage and elevation. **Features:** Hammer-block safety. Receiver tapped for scope mount, offset hammer spur, solid top receiver sandblasted to prevent glare. Includes safety lock.
Price: **$789.00**

MARLIN MODEL 1894 COWBOY
Calibers: .357 Magnum, .44 Magnum, .45 Colt. **Capacity:** 10-round magazine. **Barrel:** 20 in. tapered octagon, deep cut rifling. **Weight:** 7.5 lbs. **Length:** 41.5 in. overall. **Stock:** Straight grip American black walnut, hard rubber buttplate, Mar-Shield finish. **Sights:** Marble carbine front, adjustable Marble semi-buckhorn rear. **Features:** Squared finger lever; straight grip stock; blued steel fore-end tip. Designed for Cowboy Shooting events. Introduced 1996. Includes safety lock. Made in USA by Marlin.
Price: **$1,093.00**

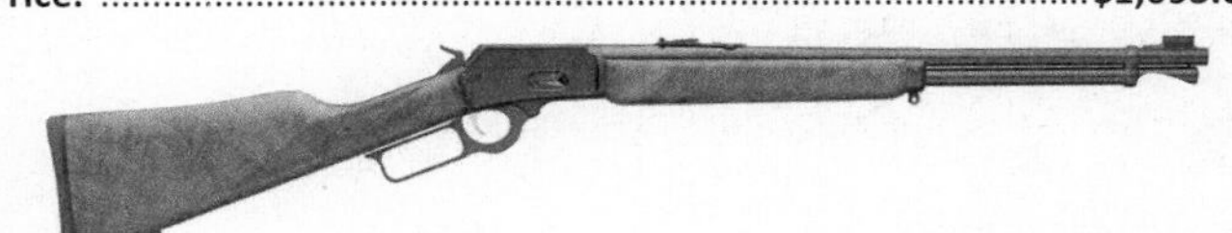

MARLIN 1894 DELUXE
Caliber: .44 Magnum/.44 Special. **Capacity:** 10-shot tubular magazine. **Features:** Squared finger lever; side ejection; richly polished deep blued metal surfaces; solid top receiver; hammer block safety; #1 grade fancy American black walnut straight-grip stock and fore-end; cut checkering; rubber rifle buttpad; Mar-Shield finish; blued steel fore-end cap: swivel studs; deep-cut Ballard-type rifling (6 grooves).
Price: **$950.00**

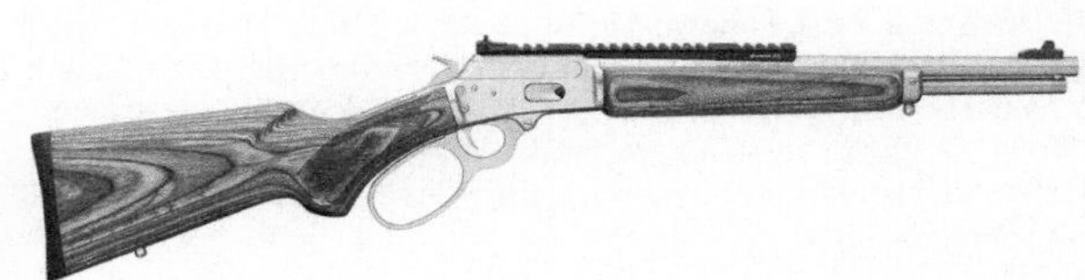

MARLIN 1894 SBL
Caliber: .44 Magnum. **Capacity:** 6-round tubular magazine. **Features:** 16.5-in. barrel, laminated stock, stainless finish, large lever, accessory rail, XS Ghost Ring sights.
Price: **$1,146.00**

MARLIN MODEL 1895 LEVER-ACTION
Caliber: .45-70 Govt. **Capacity:** 4-shot tubular magazine. **Barrel:** 22 in. round. **Weight:** 7.5 lbs. **Length:** 40.5 in. overall. **Stock:** Checkered American black walnut, full pistol grip. Mar-Shield finish; rubber buttpad; quick detachable swivel studs. **Sights:** Bead front with Wide-Scan hood, semi-buckhorn folding rear adjustable for windage and elevation. **Features:** Hammer-block safety. Solid receiver tapped for scope mounts or receiver sights; offset hammer spur. Includes safety lock.
Price: **$745.00**

MARLIN MODEL 1895G GUIDE GUN LEVER-ACTION
Similar to Model 1895 with deep-cut Ballard-type rifling; straight-grip walnut stock. Overall length is 37 in., weighs 7 lbs. Introduced 1998. Includes safety lock. Made in USA by Marlin.
Price: **$750.00**

MARLIN MODEL 1895GS GUIDE GUN
Caliber: .45-70 Govt. **Capacity:** 4 rounds. **Features:** Similar to Model 1895G except receiver, barrel and most metal parts are machined from stainless steel. Chambered for .45-70 Govt., 4-shot, 18.5 in. barrel. Overall length is 37 in., weighs 7 lbs. Introduced 2001. Includes safety lock. Made in USA by Marlin.
Price: **$896.00**

MARLIN MODEL 1895 SBLR
Caliber: .45-70 Govt. **Features:** Similar to Model 1895GS Guide Gun but with stainless steel barrel (18.5 in.), receiver, large loop lever and magazine tube. Black/gray laminated buttstock and fore-end, XS ghost ring rear sight, hooded ramp front sight, receiver/barrel-mounted top rail for mounting accessory optics. Chambered in .45-70 Government. Overall length is 42.5 in., weighs 7.5 lbs.
Price: **$1,232.00**

MARLIN MODEL 1895 COWBOY LEVER-ACTION
Similar to Model 1895 except has 26-in. tapered octagon barrel with Ballard-type rifling, Marble carbine front sight and Marble adjustable semi-buckhorn rear sight. Receiver tapped for scope or receiver sight. Overall length is 44.5 in., weighs about 8 lbs. Introduced 2001. Includes safety lock. Made in USA by Marlin.
Price: **$899.00**

MARLIN 1895GBL
Caliber: .45-70 Govt. **Features:** Lever-action rifle with 6-shot, full-length tubular magazine; 18.5-in. barrel with deep-cut Ballard-type rifling (6 grooves); big-loop finger lever; side ejection; solid-top receiver; deeply blued metal surfaces; hammer block safety; pistol-grip two-tone brown laminate stock with cut checkering; ventilated recoil pad; Mar-Shield finish, swivel studs.
Price: **$786.00**

MOSSBERG 464 LEVER ACTION
Caliber: .30-30 Win. **Capacity:** 6-round tubular magazine. **Barrel:** 20 in. round. **Weight:** 6.7 lbs. **Length:** 38.5 in. overall. **Stock:** Hardwood with straight or pistol grip, quick detachable swivel studs. **Sights:** Folding rear sight, adjustable for windage and elevation. **Features:** Blued receiver and barrel, receiver drilled and tapped, two-position top-tang safety. Available with straight grip or semi-pistol grip. Introduced 2008. From O.F. Mossberg & Sons, Inc.
Price: **$572.00**
Price: SPX Model w/tactical stock and features **$540.00**

NAVY ARMS 1873 RIFLE
Calibers: .357 Magnum, .45 Colt. **Capacity:** 12-round magazine. **Barrels:** 20 in., 24.25 in., full octagonal. **Stock:** Deluxe checkered American walnut. **Sights:** Gold bead front, semi-buckhorn rear. **Features:** Turnbull color casehardened frame, rest blued. Full-octagon barrel. Available exclusively from Navy Arms. Made by Winchester.
Price: **$2,500.00**

NAVY ARMS 1892 SHORT RIFLE
Calibers: .45 Colt, .44 Magnum. **Capacity:** 10-round magazine. **Barrel:** 20 in. full octagon. **Stock:** Checkered Grade 1 American walnut. **Sights:** Marble's Semi-Buckhorn rear and gold bead front. **Finish:** Color casehardened.
Price: **$2,500.00**

NAVY ARMS LIGHTNING RIFLE
Calibers: .45 Colt, .357 Magnum. Replica of the Colt Lightning slide-action rifle of the late 19th and early 20th centuries. **Barrel:** Octagon 20 or 24 in. **Stock:** Checkered Grade 1 American walnut. **Finish:** Color casehardened.
Price: **$2,500.00**

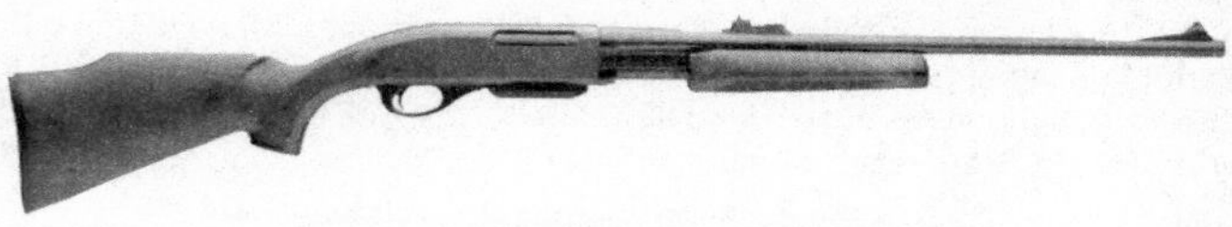

REMINGTON MODEL 7600 PUMP ACTION
Calibers: .270 Win., .30-06, .308. **Barrels:** 22 in. round tapered or 18.5 in. (Carbine). **Weight:** 7.5 lbs. **Length:** 42.6 in. overall. **Stock:** Cut-checkered walnut pistol grip and fore-end, Monte Carlo with full cheekpiece. Satin or high-gloss finish. **Sights:** Gold bead front sight on matte ramp, open step adjustable sporting rear. **Features:** Redesigned and improved version of the Model 760. Detachable 4-round magazine. Crossbolt safety. Receiver tapped for scope mount. Introduced 1981.
Price: 7600 .... **$918.00**

ROSSI R92 LEVER-ACTION CARBINE
Calibers: .38 Special/.357 Magnum, .44 Magnum., .44-40 Win., .45 Colt. Barrels: 16or 20 in. with round barrel, 20 or 24 in. with octagon barrel. Weight: 4.8–7 lbs. Length: 34–41.5 in. Features: Blued or stainless finish. Various options available in selected chamberings (large lever loop, fiber-optic sights, cheekpiece).
Price: Blued **$624.00**
Price: Stainless **$690.00**

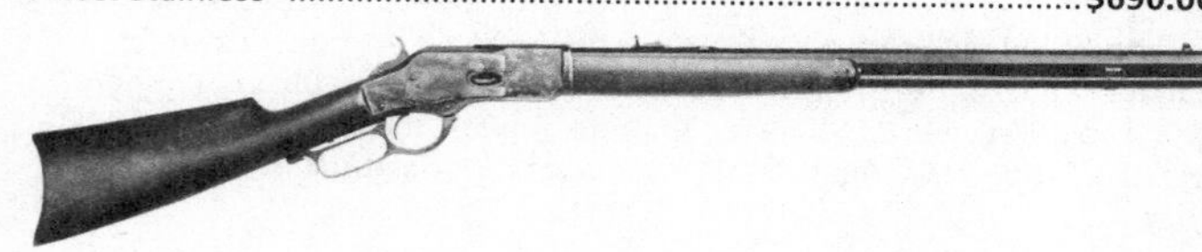

UBERTI 1873 SPORTING RIFLE
Calibers: .357 Magnum, .44-40, .45 Colt. **Barrels:** 16.1 in. round, 19 in. round or 20 in., 24.25 in. octagonal. **Weight:** Up to 8.2 lbs. **Length:** Up to 43.3 in. overall. **Stock:** Walnut, straight grip and pistol grip. **Sights:** Blade front adjustable for windage, open rear adjustable for elevation. **Features:** Color casehardened frame, blued barrel, hammer, lever, buttplate, brass elevator. Imported by Stoeger Industries.
Price: Carbine 19-in. bbl. **$1,219.00**
Price: Trapper 16.1-in. bbl. **$1,259.00**
Price: Carbine 18-in. half oct. bbl. **$1,309.00**
Price: Short Rifle 20-in. bbl. **$1,259.00**
Price: Sporting Rifle, 24.25-in. bbl. **$1,259.00**
Price: Special Sporting Rifle, A-grade walnut **$1,399.00**

Prices given are believed to be accurate at time of publication however, many factors affect retail pricing so exact prices are not possible.

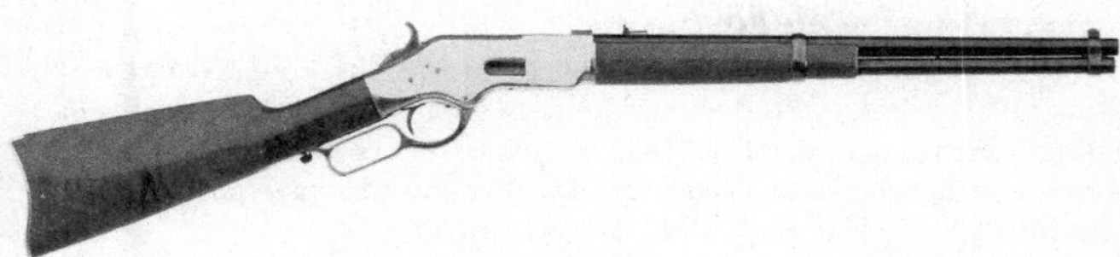

UBERTI 1866 YELLOWBOY CARBINE, SHORT, RIFLE
Calibers: .38 Special, .44-40, .45 Colt. **Barrel:** 24.25 in. octagonal. **Weight:** 8.2 lbs. **Length:** 43.25 in. overall. **Stock:** Walnut. **Sights:** Blade front adjustable for windage, rear adjustable for elevation. **Features:** Frame, buttplate, fore-end cap of polished brass, balance charcoal blued. Imported by Stoeger Industries.
Price: 1866 Yellowboy Carbine, 19-in. round barrel........................**$1,119.00**
Price: 1866 Yellowboy Short Rifle, 20-in. octagonal barrel **$1,169.00**
Price: 1866 Yellowboy Rifle, 24.25-in. octagonal barrel **$1,169.00**

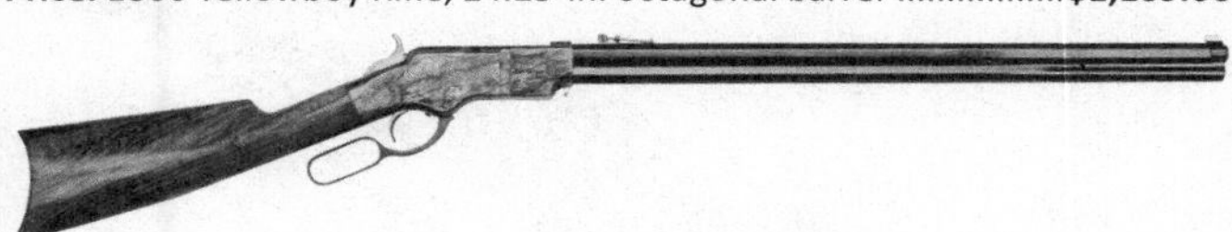

UBERTI 1860 HENRY
Calibers: .44-40, .45 Colt. **Barrel:** 24.25 in. half-octagon. **Weight:** 9.2 lbs. **Length:** 43.75 in. overall. **Stock:** American walnut. **Sights:** Blade front, rear adjustable for elevation. Imported by Stoeger Industries.
Price: 1860 Henry Trapper, 18.5-in. barrel, brass frame.................**$1,429.00**
Price: 1860 Henry Rifle Iron Frame, 24.25-in. barrel **$1,459.00**

WINCHESTER MODEL 94 SHORT RIFLE
Calibers: .30-30, .38-55. **Barrel:** 20 in. **Weight:** 6.75 lbs. **Sights:** Semi-buckhorn rear, gold bead front. **Stock:** Walnut with straight grip. Fore-end has black grip cap. Also available in Trail's End takedown design in .450 Marlin or .30-30.
Price: **$1,230.00**
Price: (Takedown) **$1,460.00**

WINCHESTER MODEL 94 CARBINE
Same general specifications as M94 Short Rifle except for curved buttplate and fore-end barrel band.
Price: **$1,200.00**

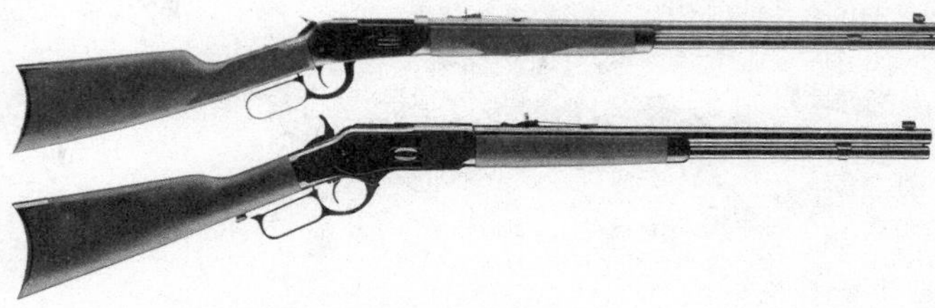

WINCHESTER MODEL 94 SPORTER
Calibers: .30-30, .38-55. **Barrel:** 24 in. **Weight:** 7.5 lbs. **Features:** Same features of Model 94 Short Rifle except for crescent butt and steel buttplate, 24 in. half-round, half-octagon barrel, checkered stock.
Price: **$1,400.00**

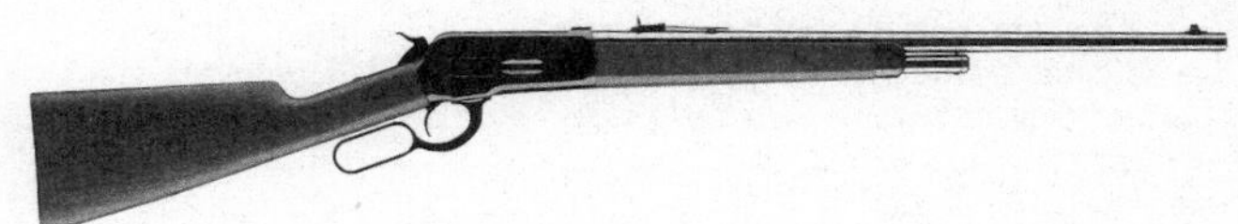

WINCHESTER 1873 SHORT RIFLE
Calibers: .357 Magnum, .44-40, .45 Colt. **Capacities:** Tubular magazine holds 10 rounds (.44-40, .45 Colt), 11 rounds (.38 Special). **Barrel:** 20 in. **Weight:** 7.25 lbs. **Sights:** Marble semi-buckhorn rear, gold bead front. Tang is drilled and tapped for optional peep sight. **Stock:** Satin finished, straight-grip walnut with steel crescent buttplate and steel fore-end cap. Tang safety. A modern version of the "Gun That Won the West."
Price: **$1,300.00**

WINCHESTER MODEL 1886 SHORT RIFLE
Caliber: .45-70. **Barrel:** 24 in. **Weight:** 8.4 lbs. **Sights:** Adjustable buckhorn rear, blade front. **Stock:** Grade 1 walnut with crescent butt.
Price **$1,340.00**

WINCHESTER MODEL 1892 CARBINE
Calibers: .357 Magnum, .44 Magnum, .44-40, .45 Colt. **Barrel:** 20 in. **Weight:** 6 lbs. **Stock:** Satin finished walnut with straight grip, steel fore-end strap. **Sights:** Marble semi-buckhorn rear, gold bead front. Other features include saddle ring and tang safety.
Price: **$1,260.00**
Price: 1892 Short Rifle...**$1,070.00**

ARMALITE AR-30A1
Calibers: .300 Win. Mag., .338 Lapua. **Capacity:** 5 rounds. **Barrels:** 24 in. (.300 Win.), 26 in. (.338 Lapua), competition grade. **Weight:** 12.8 lbs. **Length:** 46 in. **Stock:** Standard fixed. **Sights:** None. Accessory top rail included. **Features:** Bolt-action rifle. Muzzle brake, ambidextrous magazine release, large ejection port makes single loading easy, V-block patented bedding system, bolt-mounted safety locks firing pin. Target versions have adjustable stock. AR-31 is in .308 Win., accepts AR-10 double-stack magazines, has adjustable pistol grip stock.
Price: **$3,460.00**
Price: AR-31.. **$3,460.00**

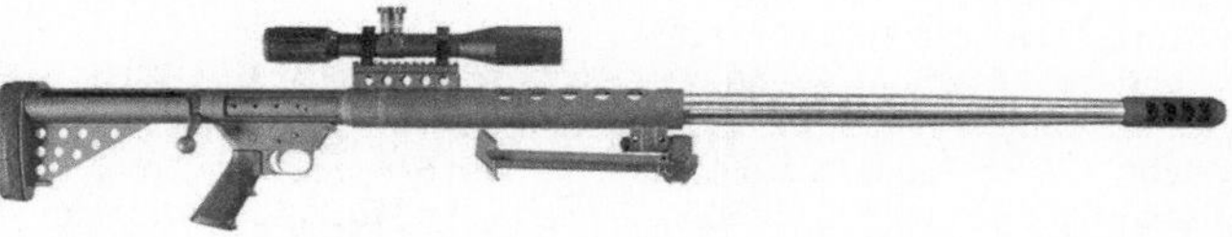

ARMALITE AR-50A1
Caliber: .50 BMG, .416 Barrett. **Capacity:** Bolt-action single-shot. **Barrel:** 30 in. with muzzle brake. National Match model (shown) has 33-in. fluted barrel. **Weight:** 34.1 lbs. **Stock:** Three-section. Extruded fore-end, machined vertical grip, forged and machined buttstock that is vertically adjustable. National Match model (.50 BMG only) has V-block patented bedding system, Armalite Skid System to ensure straight-back recoil.
Price: **$3,359.00**
Price: National Match................................ **$4,230.00**

BARRETT MODEL 95
Caliber: 50 BMG. **Capacity:** 5-round magazine. **Barrel:** 29 in. **Weight:** 23.5 lbs. **Length:** 45 in. overall. **Stock:** Energy-absorbing recoil pad. **Sights:** Scope optional. **Features:** Bolt-action, bullpup design. Disassembles without tools; extendable bipod legs; match-grade barrel; muzzle brake. Introduced 1995. Made in USA by Barrett Firearms Mfg., Inc.
Price: From.. **$6,670.00**

BARRETT MODEL 98B Caliber: .338 Lapua Magnum. **Capacity:** 10-round magazine. **Barrel:** 26 in. fluted or 20 in. **Weight:** 13.5 lbs. **Length:** 49.8 in. **Features:** Comes with two magazines, bipod, monopod, side accessory rail, hard case. Fieldcraft model chambered in .260 Rem., 6.5 Creedmoor, 7mm Rem., .308Win., .300 Win Mag. Tactical Model in .308, .300 Win Mag., .338 Lapua. Fieldcraft Lightweight Hunting Rifle in .22-250, .243, 6.5 Creedmoor, .25-06, 6.5x55 Swede, .270 Win., 7mm-08, .308, .30-06.
Price: From.. **$4,850.00**
Price: Fieldcraft Model, From.................... **$3,750.00**
Price: Fieldcraft Lightweight Hunting Rifle **$1,799.00**
Price: Tactical Model, From........................ **$4,419.00**

BARRETT MODEL 99 SINGLE SHOT
Calibers: .50 BMG., .416 Barrett. **Barrel:** 33 in. **Weight:** 25 lbs. **Length:** 50.4 in. overall. **Stock:** Anodized aluminum with energy-absorbing recoil pad. **Sights:** None furnished; integral M1913 scope rail. **Features:** Bolt action; detachable bipod; match-grade barrel with high-efficiency muzzle brake. Introduced 1999. Made in USA by Barrett Firearms.
Price: From.. **$3,999.00–$4,199.00**

BARRETT MRAD
Calibers: .260 Rem., 6.5 Creedmoor, .308 Win., .300 Win. Mag., .338 Lapua Magnum. **Capacity:** 10-round magazine. **Barrels:** 20 in., 24 in. or 26 in. fluted or heavy. **Features:** User-interchangeable barrel system, folding stock, adjustable cheekpiece, 5-position length of pull adjustment button, match-grade trigger, 22-in. optics rail.
Price: .... **$5,850.00–$6,000.00**

BERGARA B-14 SERIES
Calibers: 6.5 Creedmoor, .270 Win., 7mm Rem. Mag., .308 Win., .30-06, .300 Win. Mag. **Barrels:** 22 or 24 in. **Weight:** 7 lbs. **Features:** Synthetic with Soft touch finish, recoil pad, swivel studs, adjustable trigger, choice of detachable mag or hinged floorplate. Made in Spain.
Price: **$825.00**
Price: Walnut Stock..................................... **$945.00**
Price: Premier Series, From......................... **$2,190.00**
Price: Hunting and Match Rifle (HMR), From.......... **$1,150.00**

BERGARA BCR SERIES Calibers: Most popular calibers from .222 Rem. to .300 Win. Mag **Barrels:** 18, 22, 24 or 26 in. Various options available.
Price: BCR23 Sport Hunter from **$3,950.00**
Price: BCR24 Varmint Hunter from **$4,100.00**
Price: BCR25 Long Range Hunter from **$4,350.00**
Price: BCR27 Competition from **$4,950.00**

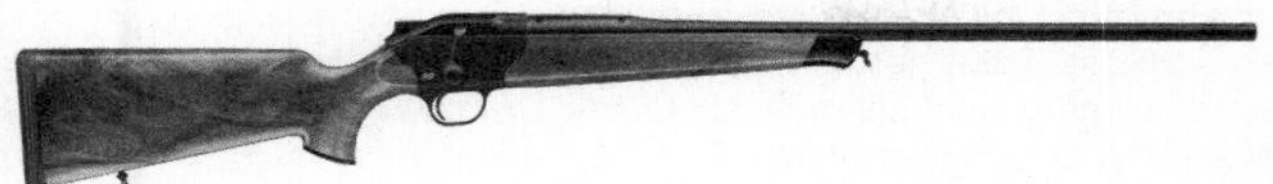

BLASER R-8 SERIES

Calibers: Available in virtually all standard and metric calibers from .222 Rem. to 10.3x60R. Straight-pull bolt action. **Barrels:** 20.5, 23, or 25.75 in. **Weights:** 6.375–8.375 lbs. **Lengths:** 40 in. overall (22 in. barrel). **Stocks:** Synthetic or Turkish walnut. **Sights:** None furnished; drilled and tapped for scope mounting. **Features:** Thumb-activated safety slide/cocking mechanism; interchangeable barrels and bolt heads. Many optional features. Imported from Germany by Blaser USA.

Price: From **$3,787.00**

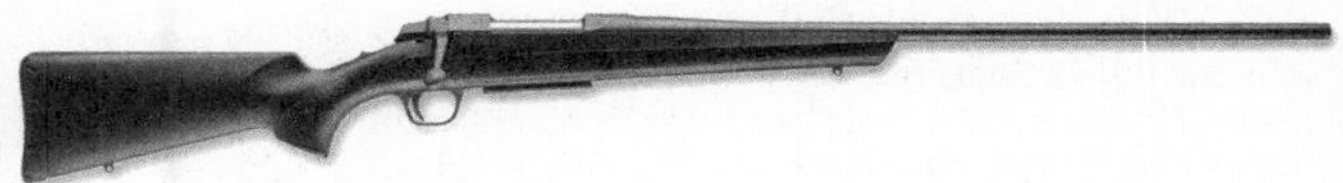

BROWNING AB3 COMPOSITE STALKER

Calibers: .243, 6.5 Creedmoor, .270 Win., .270 WSM, 7mm-08, 7mm Rem. Mag., .30-06, .300 Win. Mag., .300 WSM or .308 Win. **Barrels:** 22 in, 26 in. for magnums. **Weights:** 6.8–7.4 lbs. **Stock:** Matte black synthetic. **Sights:** None. Picatinny rail scope mount included.

Price: **$600.00**

Price: Micro Stalker **$600.00**

Price: Hunter.......... **$670.00**

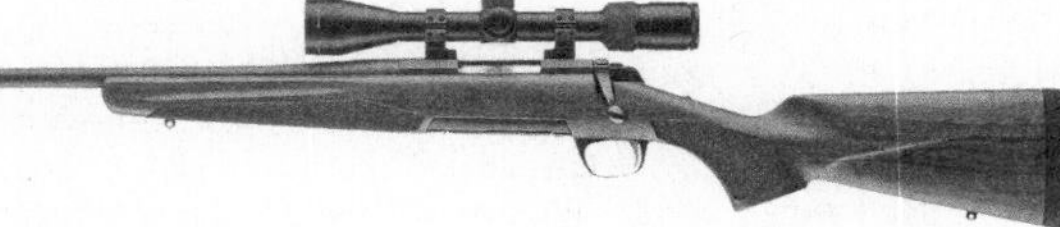

BROWNING X-BOLT HUNTER

Calibers: .223, .22-250, .243 Win., 6mm Creedmoor, 6.5 Creedmoor, .25-06 Rem., .270 Win., .270 WSM, .280 Rem., 7mm Rem. Mag., 7mm WSM, 7mm-08 Rem., .308 Win., .30-06, .300 Win. Mag., .300 WSM, .325 WSM, .338 Win. Mag., .375 H&H Mag. **Barrels:** 22 in., 23 in., 24 in., 26 in., varies by model. Matte blued or stainless free-floated barrel, recessed muzzle crown. **Weights:** 6.3–7 lbs. **Stocks:** Hunter and Medallion models have black walnut stocks; Composite Stalker and Stainless Stalker models have composite stocks. Inflex Technology recoil pad. **Sights:** None, drilled and tapped receiver, X-Lock scope mounts. **Features:** Adjustable three-lever Feather Trigger system, polished hard-chromed steel components, factory pre-set at 3.5 lbs., alloy trigger housing. Bolt unlock button, detachable rotary magazine, 60-degree bolt lift, three locking lugs, top-tang safety, sling swivel studs. Introduced 2008.

Price: Standard calibers **$900.00**

Price: Magnum calibers **$950.00**

Price: Left-hand models.......... **$940.00–$980.00**

BROWNING X-BOLT MICRO MIDAS

Calibers: .243 Win., 6mm Creedmoor, 6.5 Creedmoor, 7mm-08 Rem., .308 Win., .22-250 Rem. .270 WSM, .300 WSM. **Barrel:** 20 in. **Weight:** 6 lbs.,1 oz. **Length:** 37.625–38.125 in. overall. **Stock:** Satin finish checkered walnut or composite. **Sights:** Hooded front and adjustable rear. **Features:** Steel receiver with low-luster blued finish. Glass bedded, drilled and tapped for scope mounts. Barrel is free-floating and hand chambered with target crown. Bolt-action with adjustable Feather Trigger and detachable rotary magazine. Compact 12.5 in. length of pull for smaller shooters, designed to fit smaller-framed shooters like youth and women. This model has all the same features as the full-size model with sling swivel studs installed and Inflex Technology recoil pad. (Scope and mounts not included).

Price: **$860.00**

Price: Composite stock **$940.00**

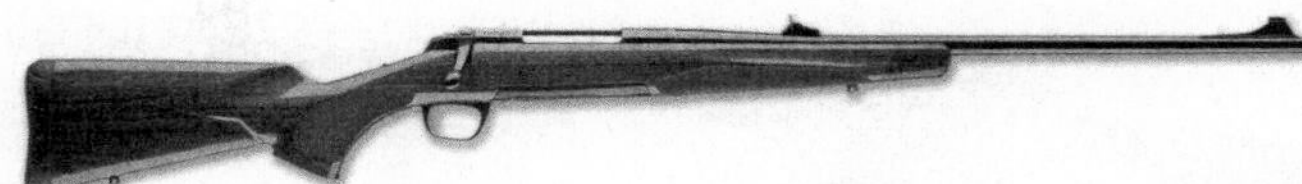

BROWNING X-BOLT MEDALLION

Calibers: Most popular calibers from .223 Rem. to .375 H&H. **Barrels:** 22, 24 or 26 in. free-floated. **Features:** Engraved receiver with polished blue finish, gloss finished and checkered walnut stock with rosewood grip and fore-end caps, detachable rotary magazine. Medallion Maple model has AAA-grade maple stock.

Price: **$1,040.00**

Price: Medallion Maple **$1,070.00**

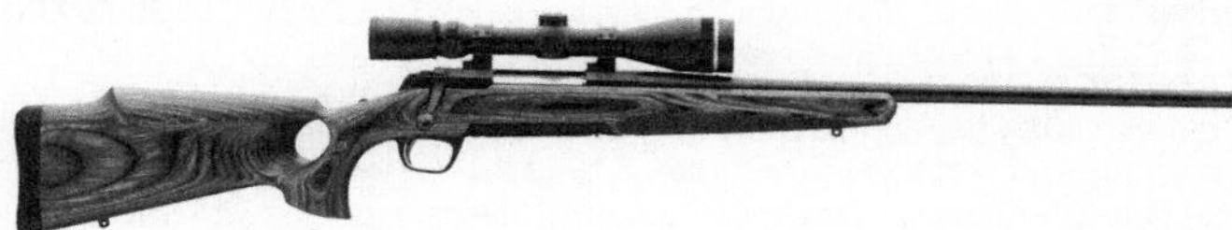

BROWNING X-BOLT ECLIPSE HUNTER

Calibers: Most popular calibers from .223 Rem. to .300 WSM. Same general features of X-Bolt series except for its laminated thumbhole stock.

Price: **$1,200.00**

Price: Varmint and Target models.......... **$1,400.00**

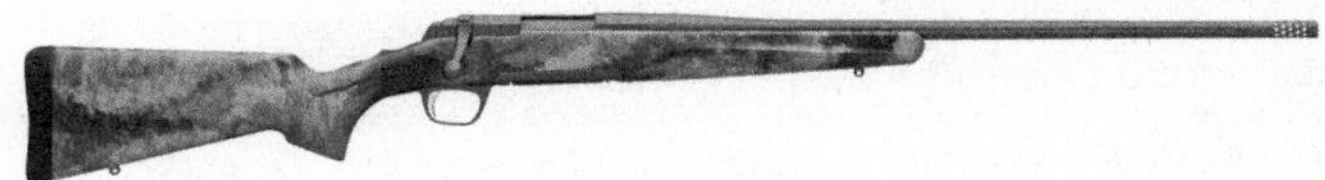

BROWNING X-BOLT HELL'S CANYON

Calibers: .243 Win., 26 Nosler, 6.5 Creedmoor, .270 Win., .270 WSM, 7mm-08 Rem., 7mm Rem. Mag., .308 Win., .30-06, .300 Win. Mag., .300 WSM. **Barrels:** 22–26-in. fluted and free-floating with muzzle brake or thread protector. **Stock:** A-TACS AU Camo composite with checkered grip panels. **Features:** Detachable rotary magazine, adjustable trigger, Cerakote Burnt Bronze finish on receiver and barrel.

Price: .... **$1,200.00–$1,270.00**

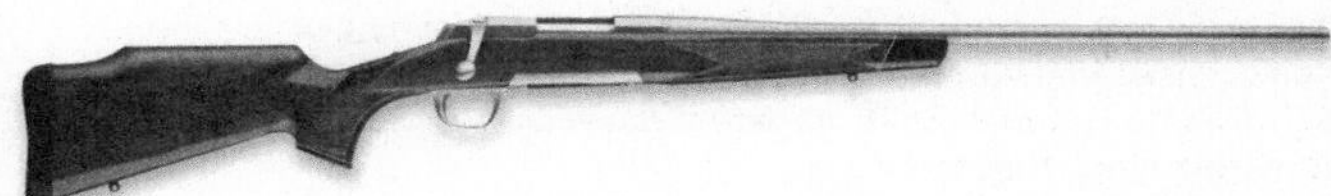

BROWNING X-BOLT WHITE GOLD

Calibers: Eighteen popular calibers from .223 Rem. to .338 Win. Mag. Same general features of X-Bolt series plus polished stainless steel barrel, receiver, bolt and trigger. Gloss-finished finely checkered walnut Monte Carlo-style stock with rosewood grip and fore-end caps.

Price: .... **$1,420.00–$1,540.00**

BROWNING X-BOLT PRO SERIES

Calibers: 6mm Creedmoor, 6.5 Creedmoor, 26 Nosler, 28 Nosler, .270 Win., 7mm Rem. Mag., .308 Win., .30-06., .300 Win. Mag. Detachable rotary magazine. **Barrels:** 22–26 in. Stainless steel, fluted with threaded/removable muzzle brake. **Weights:** 6–7.5 lbs. **Finish:** Cerakote Burnt Bronze. **Stock:** Second generation carbon fiber with palm swell, textured gripping surfaces. Adjustable trigger, top tang safety, sling swivel studs. Long Range has heavy sporter-contour barrel, proprietary lapping process.

Price: X-Bolt Pro.......... **$2,070.00–$2,130.00**

Price: X-Bolt Pro Long Range .... **$2,100.00–$2,180.00**

BUSHMASTER BA50 BOLT-ACTION

Caliber: .50 Browning BMG. **Capacity:** 10-round magazine. **Barrels:** 30 in. (rifle), 22 in. (carbine). **Weight:** 30 lbs. (rifle), 27 lbs. (carbine). **Length:** 58 in. overall (rifle), 50 in. overall (carbine). **Features:** Free-floated Lothar Walther barrel with muzzle brake, Magpul PRS adjustable stock.

Price: **$5,657.00**

CHEYTAC M-200

Caliber: .408 CheyTac. **Capacity:** 7-round magazine. **Barrel:** 30 in. **Length:** 55 in. stock extended. **Weight:** 27 lbs. (steel barrel); 24 lbs. (carbon-fiber barrel). **Stock:** Retractable. **Sights:** None, scope rail provided. **Features:** CNC-machined receiver, attachable Picatinny rail M-1913, detachable barrel, integral bipod, 3.5-lb. trigger pull, muzzle brake. Made in USA by CheyTac, LLC.

Price: From..... **$11,700.00**

COOPER FIREARMS OF MONTANA

This company manufacturers bolt-action rifles in a variety of styles and in almost any factory or wildcat caliber. Features of the major model sub-category/styles are listed below. Several other styles and options are available. Classic: Available in all models. AA Claro walnut stock with 4-panel hand checkering, hand-rubbed oil-finished wood, Pachmayr pad, steel grip cap and standard sling swivel studs. Barrel is chrome-moly premium match grade Wilson Arms. All metal work has matte finish. Custom Classic: Available in all models. AAA Claro walnut stock with shadow-line beaded cheek-piece, African ebony tip, Western fleur wrap-around hand checkering, hand-rubbed oil-finished wood, Pachmayr pad, steel grip cap and standard sling swivel studs. Barrel is chrome-moly premium match grade Wilson Arms. All metal work has high gloss finish. Western Classic: Available in all models. AAA+ Claro walnut stock. Selected metal work is highlighted with case coloring. Other features same as Custom Classic. Mannlicher: Available in all models. Same features as Western Classic with full-length stock having multi-point wrap-around hand checkering. Varminter: Available in Models 21, 22, 38, 52, 54 and 57-M. Same features as Classic except heavy barrel and stock with wide fore-end, hand-checkered grip.

COOPER MODEL 21

Calibers: Virtually any factory or wildcat chambering in the .223 Rem. family is available including: .17 Rem., .19-223, Tactical 20, .204 Ruger, .222 Rem, .222 Rem. Mag., .223 Rem, .223 Rem AI, 6x45, 6x47. Single shot. **Barrels:** 22–24 in. for Classic configurations, 24–26 in. for Varminter configurations. **Weights:** 6.5–8.0 lbs., depending on type. **Stock:** AA-AAA select claro walnut, 20 LPI checkering. **Sights:** None furnished. **Features:** Three front locking-lug, bolt-action, single-shot. Action: 7.75 in. long, Sako extractor. Button ejector. Fully adjustable single-stage trigger. Options include wood upgrades, case-color metalwork, barrel fluting, custom LOP, and many others.

Price: Classic **$2,225.00**
Price: Custom Classic..... **$2,595.00**
Price: Western Classic. **$3,455.00**
Price: Varminter..... **$2,295.00**
Price: Mannlicher **$4,395.00**

COOPER MODEL 22

Calibers: Virtually any factory or wildcat chambering in the mid-size cartridge length including: .22-250 Rem., .22-250 Rem. AI, .25-06 Rem., .25-06 Rem. AI, .243 Win., .243 Win. AI, .220 Swift, .250/3000 AI, .257 Roberts, .257 Roberts AI, 7mm-08 Rem., 6mm Rem., .260 Rem., 6x284, 6.5x284, .22 BR, 6mm BR, .308 Win. Single shot. **Barrels:** 24 in. or 26 in. stainless match in Classic configurations. 24 in. or 26 in. in Varminter configurations. **Weight:** 7.5–8.0 lbs. depending on type. **Stock:** AA-AAA select claro walnut, 20 LPI checkering. **Sights:** None furnished. **Features:** Three front locking-lug bolt-action single shot. Action: 8.25 in. long, Sako-style extractor. Button ejector. Fully adjustable single-stage trigger. Options include wood upgrades, case-color metalwork, barrel fluting, custom LOP, and many others.

Price: Classic **$2,225.00**
Price: Custom Classic..... **$2,595.00**
Price: Western Classic. **$3,455.00**
Price: Varminter..... **$2,225.00**
Price: Mannlicher **$4,495.00**

COOPER MODEL 38

Calibers: .22 Hornet family of cartridges including the .17 Squirrel, .17 He Bee, .17 Ackley Hornet, .17 Mach IV, .19 Calhoon, .20 VarTarg, .221 Fireball, .22 Hornet, .22 K-Hornet, .22 Squirrel, .218 Bee, .218 Mashburn Bee. Single shot. **Barrels:** 22 in. or 24 in. in Classic configurations, 24 in. or 26 in. in Varminter configurations. **Weights:** 6.5–8.0 lbs. depending on type. **Stock:** AA-AAA select claro walnut, 20 LPI checkering. **Sights:** None furnished. **Features:** Three front locking-lug bolt-action single shot. Action: 7 in. long, Sako-style extractor. Button ejector. Fully adjustable single-stage trigger. Options include wood upgrades, case-color metalwork, barrel fluting, custom LOP, and many others.

Price: Classic **$2,195.00**
Price: Custom Classic..... **$2,595.00**
Price: Western Classic. **$3,455.00**
Price: Varminter..... **$2,225.00**
Price: Mannlicher **$4,395.00**

COOPER MODEL 52

Calibers: .30-06, .270 Win., .280 Rem, .25-06, .284 Win., .257 Weatherby Mag., .264 Win. Mag., .270 Weatherby Mag., 7mm Remington Mag., 7mm Weatherby Mag., 7mm Shooting Times Westerner, .300 Holland & Holland, .300 Win. Mag., .300 Weatherby Mag., .308 Norma Mag., 8mm Rem. Mag., .338 Win. Mag., .340 Weatherby V. Three-shot magazine. **Barrels:** 22 in. or 24 in. in Classic configurations, 24 in. or 26 in. in Varminter configurations. **Weight:** 7.75–8 lbs. depending on type. **Stock:** AA-AAA select claro walnut, 20 LPI checkering. **Sights:** None furnished. **Features:** Three front locking-lug bolt-action single shot. Action: 7 in. long, Sako style extractor. Button ejector. Fully adjustable single-stage trigger. Options include wood upgrades, case-color metalwork, barrel fluting, custom LOP, and many others.

Price: Classic. **$2,275.00**
Price: Custom Classic..... **$3,195.00**
Price: Western Classic. **$3,895.00**
Price: Jackson Game..... **$2,355.00**
Price: Jackson Hunter **$2,225.00**
Price: Excalibur. **$2,275.00**
Price: Mannlicher **$4,995.00**

COOPER MODEL 54

Calibers: .22-250, .243 Win., .250 Savage, .260 Rem., 7mm-08, .308 Win. and similar length cartridges. Features are similar to those of the Model 52.

Price: Classic. **$2,275.00**
Price: Custom Classic..... **$3,195.00**
Price: Western Classic. **$3,895.00**
Price: Jackson Game..... **$2,355.00**
Price: Jackson Hunter **$2,225.00**
Price: Excalibur. **$2,275.00**
Price: Mannlicher **$4,995.00**

COOPER MODEL 58 DANGEROUS GAME

Calibers: .404 Jeffery, .416 Rigby, .458 Lott, 505 Gibbs. Built for the world's most dangerous game. Controlled round feed, Timney trigger, AA or AAA Claro checkered walnut stock, rollover cheekpiece, ebony fore-end tip, color casehardened finish and other high-grade features available on various models.

Price: Classic. **$3,095.00**
Price: Custom Classic..... **$4,255.00**
Price: Western Classic. **$4,595.00**
Price: Jackson Game..... **$3,195.00**
Price: Mannlicher **$5,695.00**

Prices given are believed to be accurate at time of publication however, many factors affect retail pricing so exact prices are not possible.

CZ 527 LUX BOLT-ACTION
Calibers: .17 Hornet, .204 Ruger, .22 Hornet, .222 Rem., .223 Rem. **Capacity:** 5-round magazine. **Barrels:** 23.5 in. standard or heavy. **Weight:** 6 lbs., 1 oz. **Length:** 42.5 in. overall. **Stock:** European walnut with Monte Carlo. **Sights:** Hooded front, open adjustable rear. **Features:** Improved mini-Mauser action with non-rotating claw extractor; single set trigger; grooved receiver. Imported from the Czech Republic by CZ-USA.
Price: Brown laminate stock.. **$733.00**
Price: Model FS, full-length stock, cheekpiece **$827.00**

CZ 527 AMERICAN BOLT-ACTION
Similar to the CZ 527 Lux except has classic-style stock with 18 LPI checkering; free-floating barrel; recessed target crown on barrel. No sights furnished. Introduced 1999. Imported from the Czech Republic by CZUSA.
Price: From.. **$733.00**

CZ 550 FS MANNLICHER
Calibers: .22-250 Rem., .243 Win., 6.5x55, 7x57, 7x64, .308 Win., 9.3x62, .270 Win., 30-06. **Barrel:** Free-floating; recessed target crown. **Weight:** 7.48 lbs. **Length:** 44.68 in. overall. **Stock:** American classic-style stock with 18 LPI checkering or FS (Mannlicher). **Sights:** No sights furnished. **Features:** Improved Mauser-style action with claw extractor, fixed ejector, square bridge dovetailed receiver; single set trigger. Introduced 1999. Imported from the Czech Republic by CZ-USA.
Price: FS (full stock) **$894.00**
Price: American, from... **$827.00**

CZ 550 SAFARI MAGNUM/AMERICAN SAFARI MAGNUM Similar to CZ 550 American Classic. **Calibers:** .375 H&H Mag., .416 Rigby, .458 Win. Mag., .458 Lott. Overall length is 46.5 in. **Barrel:** 25 in. **Weight:** 9.4 lbs., 9.9 lbs (American). **Features:** Hooded front sight, express rear with one standing, two folding leaves. Imported from the Czech Republic by CZ-USA.
Price: Safari Magnum **$1,215.00**
Price: American Safari Field ....**$1,215.00–$1,348.00**
Price: American Kevlar **$1,714.00**

CZ 550 VARMINT
Similar to CZ 550 American Classic. **Calibers:** .308 Win. and .22-250. **Stock:** Kevlar, laminated. **Length:** 46.7 in. **Barrel:** 25.6 in. **Weight:** 9.1 lbs. Imported from the Czech Republic by CZ-USA.
Price: **$865.00**
Price: Kevlar **$1,037.00**
Price: Laminated **$966.00**

CZ 550 MAGNUM H.E.T. High Energy Tactical model similar to CZ 550 American Classic. **Caliber:** .338 Lapua. Length: 52 in. **Barrel:** 28 in. **Weight:** 14 lbs. **Features:** Adjustable sights, satin blued barrel. Imported from the Czech Republic by CZ-USA.
Price: **$3,929.00**

CZ 550 ULTIMATE HUNTING
Similar to CZ 550 American Classic. **Caliber:** .300 Win Mag. **Length:** 44.7 in. **Barrel:** 23.6 in. **Weight:** 7.7 lbs. **Stock:** Kevlar. **Features:** Nightforce 5.5-20x50 scope included. Imported from the Czech Republic by CZ-USA.
Price: **$3,458.00**

CZ 557
Calibers: .243 Win., 6.5x55, .270 Win., .308 Win., .30-06. **Capacity:** 5+1. **Barrel:** 20.5 in. **Stock:** Satin finished walnut or Manners carbon fiber with textured grip and fore-end. **Sights:** None on Sporter model. **Features:** Forged steel receiver has integral scope mounts. Magazine has hinged floorplate. Trigger is adjustable. Push-feed action features short extractor and plunger style ejector. Varmint model (.243, .308) has 25.6-in. barrel, detachable box magazine.
Price: Sporter, walnut stock **$832.00**
Price: Synthetic stock **$779.00**
Price: Varmint model..**$865.00**

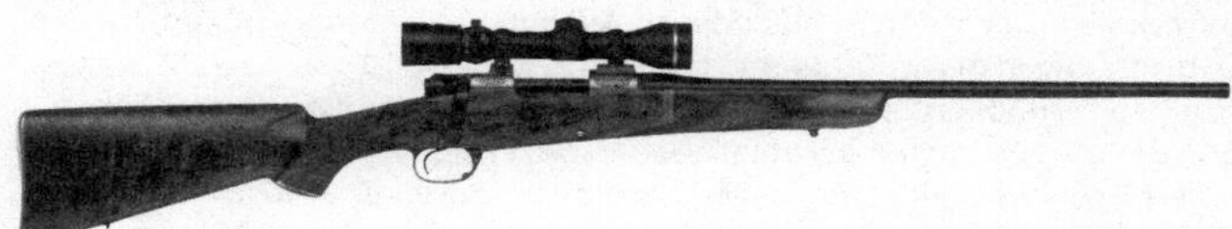

DAKOTA 76 TRAVELER TAKEDOWN
Calibers: .257 Roberts, .25-06 Rem., 7x57, .270 Win., .280 Rem., .30-06, .338-06, .35 Whelen (standard length); 7mm Rem. Mag., .300 Win. Mag., .338 Win. Mag., .416 Taylor, .458 Win. Mag. (short magnums); 7mm, .300, .330, .375 Dakota Magnums. **Barrel:** 23 in. **Weight:** 7.5 lbs. **Length:** 43.5 in. overall. **Stock:** Medium fancy-grade walnut in classic style. Checkered grip and fore-end; solid buttpad. **Sights:** None furnished; drilled and tapped for scope mounts. **Features:** Threadless disassembly. Uses modified Model 76 design with many features of the Model 70 Winchester. Left-hand model also available. Introduced 1989. African chambered for .338 Lapua Mag., .404 Jeffery, .416 Rigby, .416 Dakota, .450 Dakota, 4-round magazine, select wood, two stock cross-bolts. 24-in. barrel. Weighs 9-10 lbs. Ramp front sight, standing leaf rear. Introduced 1989. Made in USA by Dakota Arms, Inc.
Price: Traveler...**$7,240.00**
Price: Safari Traveler..**$9,330.00**
Price: African Traveler **$10,540.00**

DAKOTA 76 CLASSIC
Caliber: .257 Roberts, .270 Win., .280 Rem., .30-06, 7mm Rem. Mag., .338 Win. Mag., .300 Win. Mag., .375 H&H, .458 Win. Mag. **Barrel:** 23 in. **Weight:** 7.5 lbs. **Length:** 43.5 in. overall. **Stock:** Medium fancy-grade walnut in classic style. Checkered pistol grip and fore-end; solid buttpad. **Sights:** None furnished; drilled and tapped for scope mounts. **Features:** Has many features of the original Winchester Model 70. One-piece rail trigger guard assembly; steel grip cap. Model 70-style trigger. Many options available. Left-hand rifle available at same price. Introduced 1988. From Dakota Arms, Inc.
Price: From...**$6,030.00**
Price: Professional Hunter...**$7,995.00**
Price: Safari Grade...**$8,010.00**

DAKOTA MODEL 97
Calibers: .22-250, .375 Dakota Mag. **Barrels:** 22 in., 24 in. **Weight:** 6.1–6.5 lbs. **Length:** 43 in. overall. **Stock:** Fiberglass. **Sights:** Optional. **Features:** Matte blue finish, black stock. Right-hand action only. Introduced 1998. Made in USA by Dakota Arms, Inc.
Price: From...**$3,720.00**
Price: All Weather (stainless)..**$4,050.00**
Price: Outfitter Takedown **$5,150.00**
Price: Varminter...**$4,820.00**

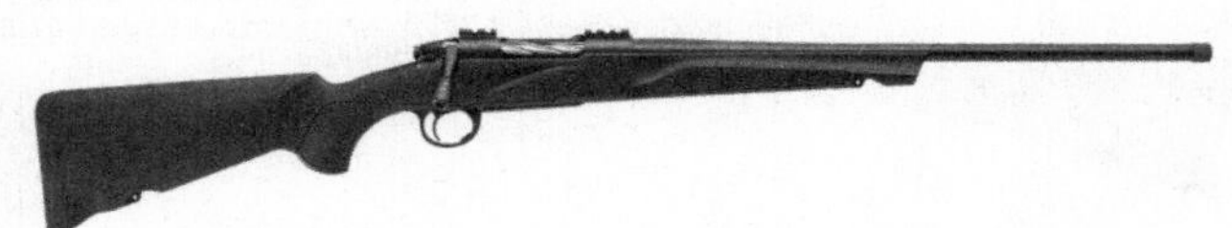

FRANCHI MOMENTUM
Calibers: .243 Win., 6.5 Creedmoor, .270 Win., .308 Win., .30-06, .300 Win. Mag. **Barrels:** 22 or 24 in. **Weights:** 6.5–7.5 lbs. **Stock:** Black synthetic with checkered gripping surface, recessed sling swivel studs, TSA recoil pad. **Sights:** None. **Features:** Available with Burris Fullfield II 3-9X40mm scope.
Price: Varminter....................$609.00
Price: With Burris 3-9X scope....................$729.00

HOWA M-1500 RANCHLAND COMPACT
Calibers: .223 Rem., .22-250 Rem., .243 Win., .308 Win. and 7mm-08. **Barrel:** 20 in. #1 contour, blued finish. **Weight:** 7 lbs. **Stock:** Hogue Overmolded in black, OD green, Coyote Sand colors. 13.87-in. LOP. **Sights:** None furnished; drilled and tapped for scope mounting. **Features:** Three-position safety, hinged floorplate, adjustable trigger, forged one-piece bolt, M-16-style extractor, forged flat-bottom receiver. Also available with Nikko-Stirling Nighteater 3-9x42 riflescope. Introduced in 2008. Imported from Japan by Legacy Sports International.
Price: Rifle Only....................$652.00
Price: Rifle with 3-9x42 Nighteater scope....................$762.00

HOWA/HOGUE KRYPTEK RIFLE
Calibers: Most popular calibers from .204 Ruger to .375 Ruger. **Barrel:** 20, 22 or 24 in., blue or stainless. **Stock:** Hogue overmolded in Kryptek Camo. **Features:** Three-position safety, two-stage match trigger, one-piece bolt with two locking lugs.
Price: $672.00
Price: Magnum calibers $700.00
Price: Stainless from $736.00

HOWA ALPINE MOUNTAIN RIFLE
Calibers: .243 Win., 6.5 Creedmoor, 7mm-08, .308 Win. **Barrel:** 20 in. **Weight:** 5.7 lbs. **Stock:** OD Green synthetic. **Features:** Two-stage HACT trigger, Cerakote finish on barrel and action, Pachmyr Decelerator pad.
Price: Stainless, From $1,188.00

H-S PRECISION PRO-SERIES 2000
Calibers: 30 different chamberings including virtually all popular calibers. Made in hunting, tactical and competition styles with many options. **Barrels:** 20 in., 22 in., 24 in. or 26 in. depending on model and caliber. Hunting models include the Pro-Hunter Rifle (PHR) designed for magnum calibers with built-in recoil reducer and heavier barrel; Pro-Hunter Lightweight (PHL) with slim, fluted barrel; Pro-Hunter Sporter (SPR) and Pro-Hunter Varmint (VAR). Takedown, Competition and Tactical variations are available. **Stock:** H-S Precision synthetic stock in many styles and colors with full-length bedding block chassis system. Made in USA
Price: PHR....................$3,795.00
Price: PHL....................$3,895.00
Price: SPR....................$3,495.00
Price: SPL Sporter....................$3,595.00
Price: VAR....................$3,595.00
Price: PTD Hunter Takedown....................$3,595.00
Price: STR Short Tactical....................$3,895.00
Price: HTR Heavy Tactical....................$3,895.00
Price: Competition....................$3,895.00

KENNY JARRETT RIFLES
Calibers: Custom built in virtually any chambering including .223 Rem., .243 Improved, .243 Catbird, 7mm-08 Improved, .280 Remington, .280 Ackley Improved, 7mm Rem. Mag., .284 Jarrett, .30-06 Springfield, .300 Win. Mag., .300 Jarrett, .323 Jarrett, .338 Jarrett, .375 H&H, .416 Rem., .450 Rigby, other modern cartridges. Numerous options regarding barrel type and weight, stock styles and material. **Features:** Tri-Lock receiver. Talley rings and bases. Accuracy guarantees and custom loaded ammunition. Newest series is the Shikar featuring 28-year aged American Black walnut hand-checkered stock with Jarrett-designed stabilizing aluminum chassis. Accuracy guaranteed to be .5 MOA with standard calibers, .75 MOA with magnums.
Price: Shikar Series $10,320.00
Price: Signature Series....................$8,320.00
Price: Long Ranger Series....................$8,320.00
Price: Ridge Walker Series....................$8,320.00
Price: Wind Walker $8,320.00
Price: Original Beanfield (customer's receiver) $6,050.00
Price: Professional Hunter $11,070.00
Price: SA/Custom $7,000.00

KIMBER MODEL 8400
Calibers: .25-06 Rem., .270 Win., 7mm, .30-06, .300 Win. Mag., .338 Win. Mag., or .325 WSM. **Capacity:** 4. **Barrel:** 24 in. **Weights:** 6 lbs., 3 oz.–6 lbs., 10 oz. **Length:** 43.25 in. **Stocks:** Claro walnut or Kevlar-reinforced fiberglass. **Sights:** None; drilled and tapped for bases. **Features:** Mauser claw extractor, two-position wing safety, action bedded on aluminum pillars and fiberglass, free-floated barrel, match-grade adjustable trigger set at 4 lbs., matte or polished blue or matte stainless finish. Introduced 2003. Sonora model (2008) has brown laminated stock, hand-rubbed oil finish, chambered in .25-06 Rem., .30-06, and .300 Win. Mag. Weighs 8.5 lbs., measures 44.50 in. overall length. Front swivel stud only for bipod. Stainless steel bull barrel, 24 in. satin stainless steel finish. Made in USA by Kimber Mfg. Inc.
Price: Classic $1,223.00
Price: Classic Select Grade, French walnut stock (2008) $1,427.00
Price: SuperAmerica, AAA walnut stock $2,240.00
Price: Patrol Tactical....................$2,447.00
Price: Montana $1,427.00

KIMBER MODEL 8400 CAPRIVI
Similar to Model 8400. **Calibers:** .375 H&H, .416 Remington and .458 Lott. **Capacity:** 4-round magazine. **Stock:** Claro walnut or Kevlar-reinforced fiberglass. Features twin steel crossbolts in stock, AA French walnut, pancake cheekpiece, 24 LPI wrap-around checkering, ebony fore-end tip, hand-rubbed oil finish, barrel-mounted sling swivel stud. **Features:** Bolt-action rifle. 3-leaf express sights. Howell-type rear sling swivel stud and a Pachmayr Decelerator recoil pad in traditional orange color. Introduced 2008. Made in USA by Kimber Mfg. Inc.
Price: From $3,263.00
Price: Special Edition, From $5,031.00

KIMBER MODEL 8400 TALKEETNA
Similar to Model 8400. **Caliber:** .375 H&H. **Capacity:** 4-round magazine. **Weight:** 8 lbs. **Length:** 44.5 in. **Stock:** Synthetic. **Features:** Free-floating match-grade barrel with tapered match-grade chamber and target crown, three-position wing safety acts directly on the cocking piece for greatest security, and Pachmayr Decelerator. Made in USA by Kimber Mfg. Inc
Price: $2,175.00

KIMBER MODEL 84M
Calibers: .22-250 Rem., .204 Ruger, .223 Rem., .243 Win., .257 Roberts., .260 Rem., 7mm-08 Rem., .308 Win. **Capacity:** 5. **Barrels:** 22 in., 24 in., 26 in. **Weight:** 5 lbs., 10 oz.–10 lbs. **Lengths:** 41–45 in. **Stock:** Claro walnut, checkered with steel grip cap; synthetic or gray laminate. **Sights:** None; drilled and tapped for bases. **Features:** Mauser claw extractor, three-position wing safety, action bedded on aluminum pillars, free-floated barrel, match-grade trigger set at 4 lbs., matte blue finish. Includes cable lock. Introduced 2001. Montana (2008) has synthetic stock, Pachmayr Decelerator recoil pad, stainless steel 22-in. sporter barrel. Adirondack has Kevlar white/black Optifade Forest camo stock, 18-in. barrel with threaded muzzle, weighs less than 5 lbs. Made in USA by Kimber Mfg. Inc.
Price: Classic $1,223.00
Price: Varmint $1,291.00
Price: Montana $1,427.00
Price: Adirondak $1,768.00

KIMBER MODEL 84M HUNTER
Calibers: .243 Win., .257 Roberts., 6.5 Creedmoor, 7mm-08, .308 Win. **Capacity:** 3 + 1, removable box type. **Barrel:** 22 in. **Weight:** 6.5 lbs. **Stock:** FDE Polymer with recoil pad, pillar bedding. **Finish:** Stainless. Other features include Mauser-type claw extractor, M70-type 3-position safety, adjustable trigger.
Price: **$885.00**

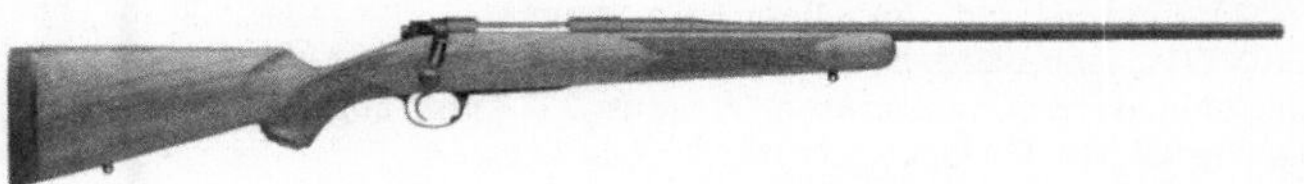

KIMBER MODEL 84L CLASSIC
Calibers: .270 Win., .30-06. **Capacity:** 5-round magazine. **Features:** Bolt-action rifle. 24-in. sightless matte blue sporter barrel; hand-rubbed A-grade walnut stock with 20 LPI panel checkering; pillar and glass bedding; Mauser claw extractor; 3-position M70-style safety; adjustable trigger.
Price: **$1,427.00**

KIMBER ADVANCED TACTICAL SOC/SRC II
Calibers: 6.5 Creedmoor, .308 Win. SRC chambered only in .308. **Capacity:** 5-round magazine. **Barrel:** 22-in. (SOC) stainless steel, (18 in. (SRC) with threaded muzzle. **Stock:** Side-folding aluminum with adjustable comb. **Features:** Stainless steel action, matte black or Flat Dark Earth finish. 3-position Model 70-type safety.
Price: **$2,449.00**

MAUSER M-03 SERIES
Calibers: .243, 6.5x55SE, .270 Win., 7x64mm, 7mm Rem. Mag., .308 Win., .30-06, .300 Win Mag., 8x57mm IS, .338 Win. Mag. 9.3x62mm. **Capacity:** 5-round magazine. **Barrels:** 22 in., 18.5 in. (Trail Model). **Stock:** Grade 2 walnut with ebony tip, or synthetic. **Features**: Classic Mauser design with Mag Safe magazine lock, adjustable rear and ramp front sights.
Price: Extreme (synthetic) **$3,745.00**
Price: Pure (walnut) **$4,941.00**
Price: Trail (polymer w/orange pads) **$4,410.00**

MAUSER M-12 PURE
Calibers: .22-250, .243, 6.5x55SE, .270 Win., 7x64mm, 7mm Rem. Mag., .308 Win., .30-06, .300 Win Mag., 8x57mm IS, .338 Win. Mag. 9.3x62mm. **Capacity:** 5-round magazine. **Barrel:** 22 in. **Sights:** Adjustable rear, blade front. **Stock:** Walnut with ebony fore-end tip.
Price: **$1,971.00**

MAUSER M-18
Calibers: .243, .270 Win., 7mm Rem. Mag., .308 Win., .30-06, .300 Win Mag. **Capacity:** 5-round magazine. **Barrel:** 21.75 or 24.5 in. **Weight**: 6.5 lbs. **Stock:** Polymer 2 with grip inlays. **Features:** Adjustable trigger, 3-position safety, recessed 3-lug bolt head chiseled from full diameter body.
Price: **$699.00**

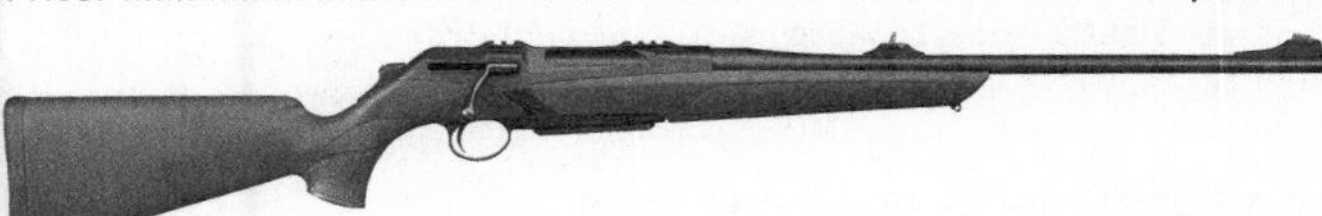

MERKEL RX HELIX Calibers: .223 Rem., .243 Rem., 6.5x55, 7mm-08, .308 Win., .270 Win., .30-06, 9.3x62, 7mm Rem. Mag., .300 Win. Mag., .270 WSM, .300 WSM, .338 Win. Mag. **Features:** Straight-pull bolt action. Synthetic stock on Explorer model. Walnut stock available in several grades. Factory engraved models available. Takedown system allows switching calibers in minutes.
Price: Explorer, synthetic stock, From **$3,360.00**
Price: Walnut stock, From **$3,870.00**

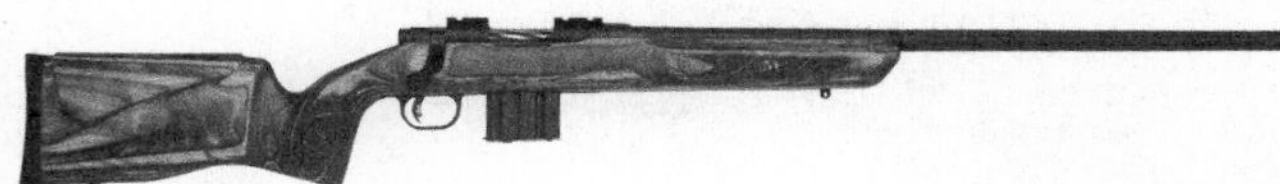

MOSSBERG MVP SERIES
Caliber: .223/5.56 NATO. **Capacity:** 10-round AR-style magazines. **Barrels:** 16.25-in. medium bull, 20-in. fluted sporter. **Weight:** 6.5–7 lbs. **Stock:** Classic black textured polymer. **Sights:** Adjustable folding rear, adjustable blade front. **Features:** Available with factory mounted 3-9x32 scope, (4-16x50 on Varmint model). FLEX model has 20-in. fluted sporter barrel, FLEX AR-style 6-position adjustable stock. Varmint model has laminated stock, 24-in. barrel. Thunder Ranch model has 18-in. bull barrel, OD Green synthetic stock.
Price: Patrol Model **$732.00**
Price: Patrol Model w/scope **$863.00**
Price: FLEX Model **$764.00**
Price: FLEX Model w/scope **$897.00**
Price: Thunder Ranch Model **$755.00**
Price: Predator Model **$732.00**
Price: Predator Model w/scope **$872.00**
Price: Varmint Model **$753.00**
Price: Varmint Model w/scope **$912.00**
Price: Long Range Rifle (LR) **$974.00**

MOSSBERG PATRIOT
Calibers: .22-250, .243 Win., .25-06, .270 Win., 7mm-08, .7mm Rem., .308 Win., .30-06, .300 Win. Mag., .38 Win. Mag., .375 Ruger. **Capacities:** 4- or 5-round magazine. **Barrels:** 22-in. sporter or fluted. **Stock:** Walnut, laminate, camo or synthetic black. **Weights:** 7.5–8 lbs. **Finish:** Matte blued. **Sights:** Adjustable or none. Some models available with 3-9x40 scope. Other features include patented Lightning Bolt Action Trigger adjustable from 2 to 7 pounds, spiral-fluted bolt. Not all variants available in all calibers. Introduced in 2015.
Price: Walnut stock **$438.00**
Price: Walnut with premium Vortex Crossfire scope **$649.00**
Price: Synthetic stock **$396.00**
Price: Synthetic stock with standard scope **$436.00**
Price: Laminate stock w/iron sights **$584.00**
Price: Deer THUG w/Mossy Oak Infinity Camo stock **$500.00**
Price: Bantam, From **$396.00**

MOSSBERG PATRIOT NIGHT TRAIN
Calibers: .308 Win. or .300 Win. Mag. Features: Tactical model with Silencerco Saker Muzzle brake, 6-24x50 scope with tactical turrets, green synthetic stock with Neoprene comb-raising kit. **Weight:** 9 lbs.
Price: Night Train with 6-24x50 scope **$811.00**

NESIKA SPORTER RIFLE
Calibers: .260 Rem., 6.5x284, 7mm-08, .280 Rem., 7mm Rem. Mag., 308 Win., .30-06, .300 Win. Mag. **Barrels:** 24 or 26 in. Douglas air-gauged stainless. **Stock:** Composite with aluminum bedding block. **Sights:** None, Leupold QRW bases. **Weight:** 8 lbs. **Features:** Timney trigger set at 3 pounds, receiver made from 15-5 stainless steel, one-piece bolt from 4340 CM steel. Guaranteed accuracy at 100 yards.
Price: $3,499.00
Price: Long Range w/heavy bbl., varmint stock $3,999.00
Price: Tactical w/28î bbl., muzzle brake, adj. stock $4,499.00

NEW ULTRA LIGHT ARMS
Calibers: Custom made in virtually every current chambering. **Barrel:** Douglas, length to order. **Weights:** 4.75–7.5 lbs. **Length:** Varies. **Stock:** Kevlar graphite composite, variety of finishes. **Sights:** None furnished; drilled and tapped for scope mounts. **Features:** Timney trigger, hand-lapped action, button-rifled barrel, hand-bedded action, recoil pad, sling-swivel studs, optional Jewell trigger. Made in USA by New Ultra Light Arms.
Price: Model 20 Ultimate Mountain Rifle $3,500.00
Price: Model 20 Ultimate Varmint Rifle $3,500.00
Price: Model 24 Ultimate Plains Rifle $3,600.00
Price: Model 28 Ultimate Alaskan Rifle $3,900.00
Price: Model 40 Ultimate African Rifle $3,900.00

NOSLER MODEL 48 SERIES
Calibers: Offered in most popular calibers including .280 Ackley Improved and 6.5-284 wildcats. **Barrel:** 24 in. Long Range 26 in. **Weight:** 7.25–8 lbs. **Stock:** Walnut or composite. Custom Model is made to order with several optional features.
Price: Heritage $1,895.00
Price: Custom Model from $2,495.00
Price: Long Range $2,495.00

REMINGTON MODEL 700 CDL CLASSIC DELUXE
Calibers: .243 Win., .270 Win., 7mm-08 Rem., 7mm Rem. Mag., .30-06, .300 Win. Mag. **Barrels:** 24 in. or 26-in. round tapered. **Weights:** 7.4–7.6 lbs. **Lengths:** 43.6–46.5 in. overall. **Stocks:** Straight-comb American walnut stock, satin finish, checkering, right-handed cheekpiece, black fore-end tip and grip cap, sling swivel studs. **Sights:** None. **Features:** Satin blued finish, jeweled bolt body, drilled and tapped for scope mounts. Hinged-floorplate magazine capacity: 4, standard calibers; 3, magnum calibers. SuperCell recoil pad, cylindrical receiver, integral extractor. Introduced 2004. CDL SF (stainless fluted) chambered for .260 Rem., .257 Wby. Mag., .270 Win., .270 WSM, 7mm-08 Rem., 7mm Rem. Mag., .30-06, .300 WSM. Left-hand versions introduced 2008 in six calibers. Made in U.S. by Remington Arms Co., Inc.
Price: Standard Calibers, From ....$1,029.00–$1,089.00
Price: CDL SF, From $1,226.00

REMINGTON MODEL 700 BDL
Calibers: .243 Win., .270 Win., 7mm Rem. Mag., .30-06, **Barrels:** 22 in., 24 in., 26-in. round tapered. **Weights:** 7.25–7.4 lbs. **Lengths:** 41.6–46.5 in. overall. **Stock:** Walnut. Gloss-finish pistol grip stock with skip-line checkering, black forend tip and grip cap with white line spacers. Quick-release floorplate. **Sights:** Gold bead ramp front; hooded ramp, removable step-adjustable rear with windage screw. **Features:** Side safety, receiver tapped for scope mounts, matte receiver top, quick detachable swivels.
Price: Standard Calibers $994.00

REMINGTON MODEL 700 SPS
Calibers: .22-250 Rem., 6.8 Rem SPC, .223 Rem., .243 Win., .270 Win., .270 WSM, 7mm-08 Rem., 7mm Rem. Mag., 7mm Rem. Ultra Mag., .30-06, .308 Win., .300 WSM, .300 Win. Mag., .300 Rem. Ultra Mag. Barrels: 20 in., 24 in. or 26 in. carbon steel. Weights: 7–7.6 lbs. Lengths: 39.6–46.5 in. overall. **Stock:** Black synthetic, sling swivel studs, SuperCell recoil pad. Woodtech model has walnut decorated synthetic stock with overmolded grip patterns. Camo stock available. **Sights:** None. **Barrel:** Bead-blasted 416 stainless steel. **Features:** Introduced 2005. SPS Stainless replaces Model 700 BDL Stainless Synthetic. Plated internal fire control component. SPS DM features detachable box magazine. SPS Varmint includes X-Mark Pro trigger, 26-in. heavy contour barrel, vented beavertail fore-end, dual front sling swivel studs. Made in U.S. by Remington Arms Co., Inc.
Price: From ....$724.00–$838.00

REMINGTON 700 SPS TACTICAL
Calibers: .223 .300 AAC Blackout and .308 Win. **Features:** 20-in. heavy-contour tactical-style barrel; dual-point pillar bedding; black synthetic stock with Hogue overmoldings; semi-beavertail fore-end; X-Mark Pro adjustable trigger system; satin black oxide metal finish; hinged floorplate magazine; SuperCell recoil pad.
Price: From ....$788.00–$842.00

REMINGTON 700 VTR A-TACS CAMO
Calibers: .223 and .308 Win. **Features:** ATACS camo finish overall; triangular contour 22-in. barrel has an integral muzzle brake; black overmold grips; 1:9 in. twist (.223 caliber), or 1:12 in. (.308) twist.
Price: $930.00

REMINGTON MODEL 700 VLS
Calibers: .204 Ruger, .223 Rem., .22-250 Rem., .243 Win., .308 Win. **Barrel:** 26-in. heavy contour barrel (0.820-in. muzzle O.D.), concave target-style barrel crown. **Weight:** 9.4 lbs. **Length:** 45.75 in. overall. **Stock:** Brown laminated stock, satin finish, with beavertail fore-end, grip cap, rubber buttpad. **Sights:** None. **Features:** Introduced 1995. Made in U.S. by Remington Arms Co., Inc.
Price: $1,056.00

REMINGTON MODEL 700 SENDERO SF II
Calibers: .25-06 Rem., .264 Win. Mag., 7mm Rem. Mag., 7mm Rem. Ultra Mag, .300 Win. Mag., .300 Rem. Ultra Mag. **Barrel:** Satin stainless 26-in. heavy contour fluted. **Weight:** 8.5 lbs. **Length:** 45.75 in. overall. **Stock:** Black composite reinforced with aramid fibers, beavertail fore-end, palm swell. **Sights:** None. **Features:** Aluminum bedding block. Drilled and tapped for scope mounts, hinged floorplate magazines. Introduced 1996. Made in U.S. by Remington Arms Co., Inc.
Price: $1,500.00

REMINGTON MODEL 700 VTR SERIES
Calibers: .204 Ruger, .22-250, .223 Rem., .243 Win., .308 Win. **Barrel:** 22-in. triangular counterbored with integrated muzzle brake. **Weight:** 7.5 lbs. **Length:** 41.625 in. overall. **Features:** Olive drab overmolded or Digital Tiger TSP Desert Camo stock with vented semi-beavertail fore-end, tactical-style dual swivel mounts for bipod, matte blue on exposed metal surfaces.
Price: From .... **$825.00–$980.00**

REMINGTON MODEL 700 VARMINT SF
Calibers: .22-250, .223, .220 Swift, .308 Win. **Barrel:** 26-in. stainless steel fluted. **Weight:** 8.5 lbs. **Length:** 45.75 in. **Features:** Synthetic stock with ventilated forend, stainless steel/trigger guard/floorplate, dual tactical swivels for bipod attachment.
Price: **$991.00**

REMINGTON MODEL 700 MOUNTAIN SS
Calibers: .25-06, .270 Win., .280 Rem., 7mm-08, .308 Win., .30-06. **Barrel:** 22 in. **Length:** 40.6 in. **Weight:** 6.5 lbs. **Features:** Satin stainless finish, Bell & Carlson Aramid Fiber stock.
Price: **$1,135.00**

REMINGTON MODEL 700 XCR TACTICAL
Calibers: .308 Win., .300 Win. Mag., 338 Lapua Mag. Detachable box magazine. **Barrel:** 26-in. varmint contour, fluted and free floating. **Features:** Tactical, long-range precision rifle with Bell & Carlson Tactical stock in OD Green, full-length aluminum bedding, adjustable X-Mark Pro trigger. Muzzle brake on .338 Lapua model.
Price: **$1,540.00**

REMINGTON MODEL 700 AWR
Calibers: .270 Win., .30-06, .300 Win. Mag., .300 Rem. Ultra Mag., .338 RUM, .338 Win. Mag. **Barrel:** 24- or 26-in. free floating. **Features:** Adjustable trigger, fiberglass stock. American Wilderness Rifle.
Price: **$1,150.00**

REMINGTON MODEL 783
Calibers: .223 Rem., .22-250, .243 Win., .270 Win., 7mm Rem. Mag., .308 Win., .30-06, .300 Win. Mag. **Barrel:** 22 in. **Stock:** Synthetic. **Weight:** 7–7.25 lbs. **Finish:** Matte black. **Features:** Adjustable trigger with two-position trigger-block safety, magnum contour button-rifle barrel, cylindrical receiver with minimum-size ejection port, pillar-bedded stock, detachable box magazine, 90-degree bolt throw.
Price: **$399.00**
Price: Compact with 18.25- or 20-in. bbl. **$399.00**
Price: Mossy Oak Breakup camo stock **$451.00**

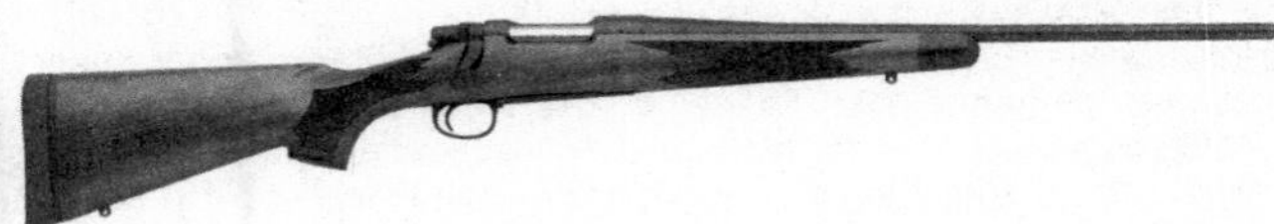

REMINGTON MODEL SEVEN CDL
Calibers: .243, .260 Rem., 7mm-08, .308 Win. **Barrel:** 20 in. **Weight:** 6.5 lbs. **Length:** 39.25 in. **Stock:** Walnut with black fore-end tip, satin finish. **Features:** Lightweight barrel has 16.5-in. barrel with threaded muzzle, synthetic camo stock, is available in .300 AAC Blackout chambering.
Price: CDL **$1,039.00**
Price: Synthetic stock **$731.00**
Price: Synthetic stock/stainless **$838.00**
Price: Lightweight/threaded **$795.00**

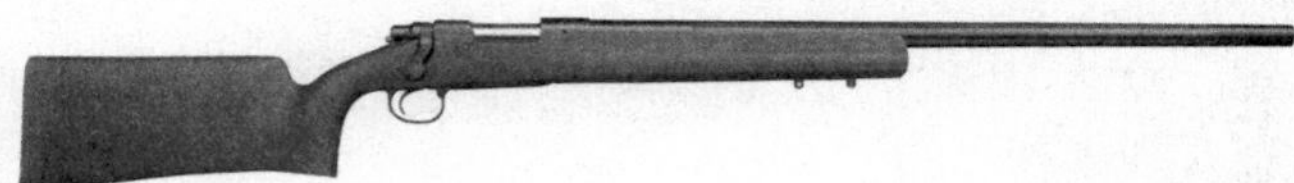

REMINGTON 40-XB TACTICAL
Caliber: .308 Win. **Features:** Stainless steel bolt with Teflon coating; hinged floorplate; adjustable trigger; 27.25-in. tri-fluted 1:14 in. twist barrel; H-S Precision Pro Series tactical stock, black color with dark green spiderweb; two front swivel studs; one rear swivel stud; vertical pistol grip. From the Remington Custom Shop.
Price: **$2,995.00**

REMINGTON 40-XB RANGEMASTER
Calibers: Almost any caliber from .22 BR Rem. to .300 Rem. Ultra Mag. Single-shot or repeater. **Features:** Stainless steel bolt with Teflon coating; hinged floorplate; adjustable trigger; 27.25-in. tri-fluted 1:14 in. twist barrel; walnut stock. From the Remington Custom Shop.
Price: **$2,595.00**

REMINGTON 40-XS TACTICAL SERIES
Caliber: .338 Lapua Magnum. **Features:** 416 stainless steel Model 40-X 24-in. 1:12 in. twist barreled action; black polymer coating; McMillan A3 series stock with adjustable length of pull and adjustable comb; adjustable trigger and Sunny Hill heavy-duty, all-steel trigger guard; Tactical Weapons System has Harris bi-pod with quick adjust swivel lock, Leupold Mark IV 3.5-10x40 long range M1 scope with Mil-Dot reticle, Badger Ordnance all-steel Picatinny scope rail and rings, military hard case, Turner AWS tactical sling. From the Remington Custom Shop.
Price: .308 Win. **$4,400.00**
Price: .338 Lapua **$4,950.00**
Price: Tactical Weapons System, From **$7,731.00**

ROCK ISLAND ARMORY TCM
Caliber: .22 TCM. **Capacity:** 5-round magazine, interchangeable with .22 TCM 17-round pistol magazine. **Barrel:** 22.75 in. **Weight:** 6 lbs. **Features:** Introduced in 2013. Manufactured in the Philippines and imported by Armscor Precision International.
Price: **$450.00**

RUGER PRECISION RIFLE
Calibers: 6mm Creedmoor, 6.5 Creedmoor, .308 Win. **Capacity:** 10-round magazine. **Barrel:** Medium contour, 20 in. (.308), 24 in. (6.5). **Stock:** Folding with adjustable length of pull and comb height. Soft rubber buttplate, sling attachment points, Picatinny bottom rail. **Weight:** 9.7–11 lbs. **Features:** Three lug one-piece CNC-machined bolt with oversized handle, dual cocking cams; multi-magazine interface works with Magpul, DPMS, SR-25, M110, AICS and some M14 magazines; CNC-machined 4140 chrome-moly steel upper; Ruger Marksman adjustable trigger with wrench stored in bolt shroud; comes with two 10-round Magpul magazines. Introduced in 2016.
Price: **$1,599.00**
Price: With muzzle brake **$1,799.00**

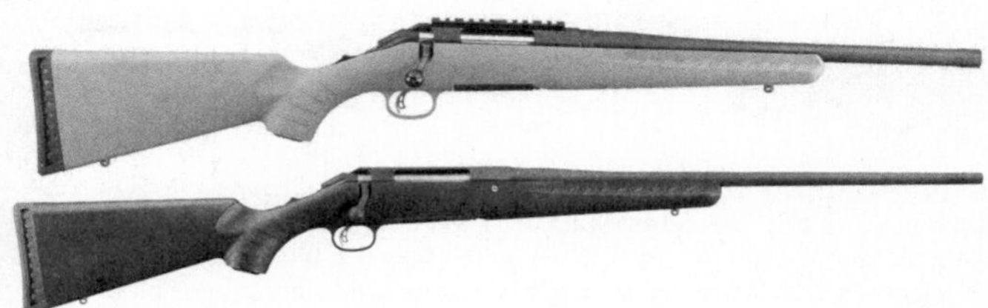

RUGER AMERICAN RIFLE

Calibers: .22-250, .243, 7mm-08, .308, .270 Win., .30-06, .300 Win. Mag. Capacity: 4-round rotary magazine. **Barrels:** 22 in. or 18 in. (Compact). **Length:** 42.5 in. **Weight:** 6.25 lbs. **Stock:** Black composite. **Finish:** Matte black or matte stainless (All Weather model). **Features:** Tang safety, hammer-forged free-floating barrel. Available with factory mounted Redfield Revolution 4x scope. Ranch model has Flat Dark Earth composite stock, Predator has Moss Green composite stock, both chambered in several additional calibers to standard model.

Price: Standard or compact **$489.00**
Price: With scope **$639.00**
Price: Ranch or Predator model **$529.00**
Price: .300 Win. Mag. **$699.00**

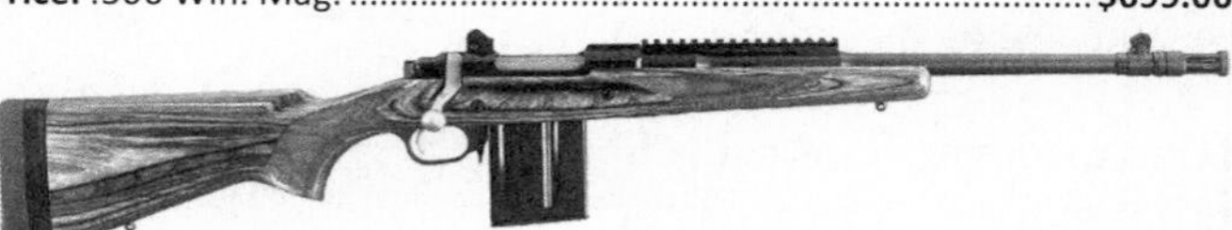

RUGER GUNSITE SCOUT RIFLE

Caliber: .308 Win. **Capacity:** 10-round magazine. **Barrel:** 16.5 in. **Weight:** 7 lbs. **Length:** 38–39.5 in. **Stock:** Black laminate. **Sights:** Front post sight and rear adjustable. **Features:** Gunsite Scout Rifle is a credible rendition of Col. Jeff Cooper's "fighting carbine" scout rifle. The Ruger Gunsite Scout Rifle is a platform in the Ruger M77 family. While the Scout Rifle has M77 features such as controlled round feed and integral scope mounts (scope rings included), the 10-round detachable box magazine is the first clue this isn't your grandfather's Ruger rifle. The Ruger Gunsite Scout Rifle has a 16.5-in. medium contour, cold hammer-forged, alloy steel barrel with a Mini-14 protected nonglare post front sight and receiver mounted, adjustable ghost ring rear sight for out-of-the-box usability. A forward-mounted Picatinny rail offers options in mounting an assortment of optics, including scout scopes available from Burris and Leupold, for "both eyes open" sighting and super-fast target acquisition.

Price: **$1,139.00**
Price: (stainless) **$1,199.00**

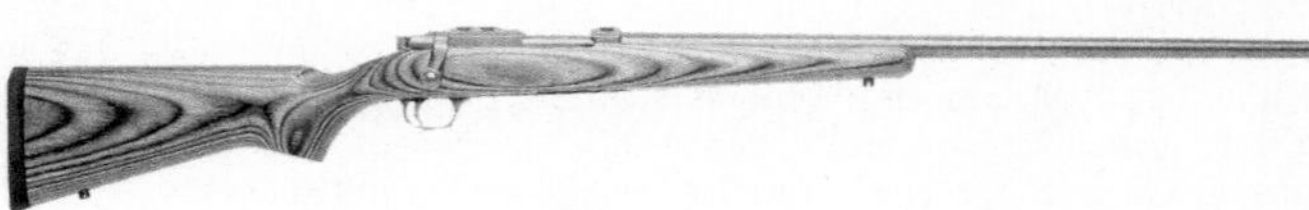

RUGER MODEL 77 SERIES

Calibers: .17 Hornet, .22 Hornet, .357 Magnum, .44 Magnum. Capacities: 4–6 rounds. **Barrel:** 18.5 in. (.357 and .44 Mag,), 20 or 24 in. (.17 Hornet and .22 Hornet). **Weight:** 5.5–7.5 lbs. **Stock:** American walnut, black synthetic, Next G1 Vista Camo or Green Mountain laminate.

Price: 77/17, Green Mtn. laminate stock **$969.00**
Price: 77/22, Green Mtn. laminate stock **$969.00**
Price: 77/22, walnut stock **$939.00**
Price: 77/357, 77/44, black synthetic stock **$999.00**
Price: 77/44, Next G1 Vista camo **$1,060.00**

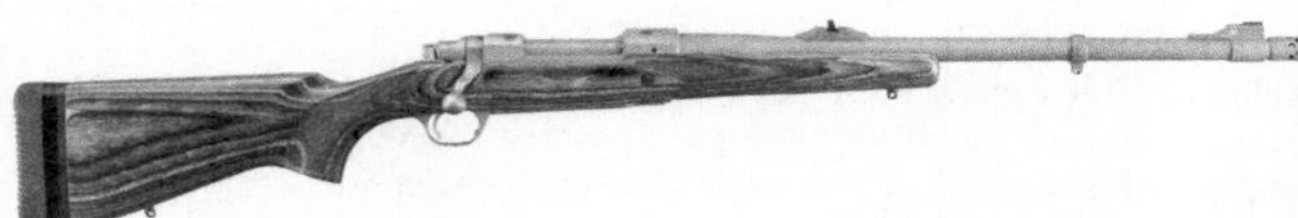

RUGER GUIDE GUN

Calibers: .30-06, .300 Win. Mag., .338 Win. Mag., .375 Ruger, .416 Ruger. **Capacities:** 3 or 4 rounds. **Barrel:** 20 in. with barrel band sling swivel and removable muzzle brake. **Weights:** 8–8.12 pounds. **Stock:** Green Mountain laminate. **Finish:** Hawkeye matte stainless. **Sights:** Adjustable rear, bead front. Introduced 2013.

Price: **$1,269.00**

RUGER HAWKEYE

Calibers: .204 Ruger, .223 Rem., .243 Win., .270 Win., 6.5 Creedmoor, 7mm/08, 7mm Rem. Mag., .308 Win., .30-06, .300 Win. Mag., .338 Win. Mag., .375 Ruger, .416 Ruger. **Capacities:** 4-round magazine, except 3-round magazine for magnums; 5-round magazine for .204 Ruger and .223 Rem. **Barrels:** 22 in., 24 in. **Weight:** 6.75–8.25 lbs. **Length:** 42–44.4 in. overall. **Stock:** American walnut, laminate or synthetic. FTW has camo stock, muzzle brake. Long Range Target has adjustable target stock, heavy barrel. **Sights:** None furnished. Receiver has Ruger integral scope mount base, Ruger 1 in. rings. **Features:** Includes Ruger LC6 trigger, new red rubber recoil pad, Mauser-type controlled feeding, claw extractor, 3-position safety, hammer-forged steel barrels, Ruger scope rings. Walnut stocks have wrap-around cut checkering on the forearm, and more rounded contours on stock and top of pistol grips. Matte stainless all-weather version features synthetic stock. Hawkeye African chambered in .375 Ruger, .416 Ruger and has 23-in. blued barrel, checkered walnut stock, windage-adjustable shallow V-notch rear sight, white bead front sight. Introduced 2007.

Price: Standard, right- and left-hand **$939.00**
Price: Compact **$939.00**
Price: Laminate Compact **$999.00**
Price: Compact Magnum **$969.00**
Price: VT Varmint Target **$1,139.00**
Price: Predator **$1,139.00**
Price: African with muzzle brake **$1,279.00**
Price: FTW Hunter **$1,279.00**
Price: Long Range Target **$1,279.00**

SAKO TRG-22 TACTICAL RIFLE

Calibers: 6.5 Creedmoor, .308 Winchester (TRG-22). For TRG-22A1 add .260 Rem. TRG-42 only available in .300 Win. Mag., or .338 Lapua. **Features:** Target-grade Cr-Mo or stainless barrels with muzzle brake; three locking lugs; 60-degree bolt throw; adjustable two-stage target trigger; adjustable or folding synthetic stock; receiver-mounted integral 17mm axial optics rails with recoil stop-slots; tactical scope mount for modern three-turret tactical scopes (30 and 34 mm tube diameter); optional bipod. 22A1 has folding stock with two-hinge design, M-LOK fore-end, full aluminum middle chassis.

Price: TRG-22 .... **$3,495.00**
Price: TRG-22A1 .... **$6,725.00**
Price: TRG-42 .... **$4,550.00**

SAKO MODEL 85

Calibers: .22-250 Rem., .243 Win., .25-06 Rem., .260 Rem., 6.5x55mm, .270 Win., .270 WSM, 7mm-08 Rem., 7x64, .308 Win., .30-06; 7mm WSM, .300 WSM, .338 Federal, 8x57IS, 9.3x62. **Barrels:** 22.4 in., 22.9 in., 24.4 in. **Weight:** 7.75 lbs. **Length:** NA. **Stock:** Polymer, laminated or high-grade walnut, straight comb, shadow-line cheekpiece. **Sights:** None furnished. **Features:** Controlled-round feeding, adjustable trigger, matte stainless or nonreflective satin blue. Offered in a wide range of variations and models. Introduced 2006. Imported from Finland by Beretta USA.

Price: Grey Wolf **$1,725.00**
Price: Black Bear **$1,850.00**
Price: Kodiak **$1,950.00**
Price: Varmint Laminated **$2,025.00**
Price: Classic **$2,275.00**
Price: Bavarian .... **$2,200.00–$2,300.00**
Price: Bavarian carbine, Full-length stock **$2,400.00**
Price: Brown Bear **$2,175.00**

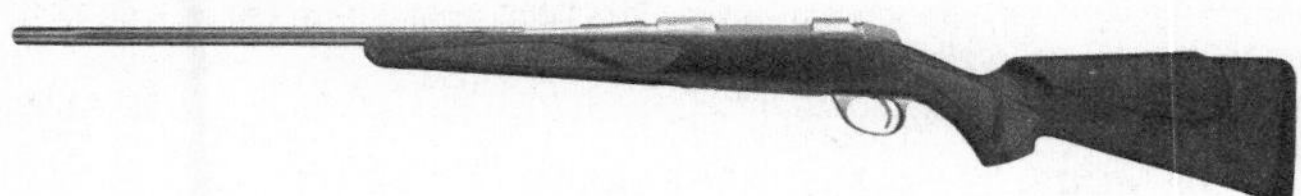

SAKO 85 FINNLIGHT

Similar to the Model 85 but chambered in .243 Win., .25-06, .260 Rem., 6.5 Creedmoor, .270 Win., .270 WSM, .300 WSM, .30-06, .300 WM, .308 Win., 6.5x55mm, 7mm Rem Mag., 7mm-08. **Weights:** 6 lbs., 3 oz.–6 lbs. 13 oz. **Features:** Stainless steel barrel and receiver, black synthetic stock. Finnlight II has composite stock with carbon fiber bedding, adjustable comb.

Price: **$1,800.00**
Price: Finnlight II **$2,475.00**

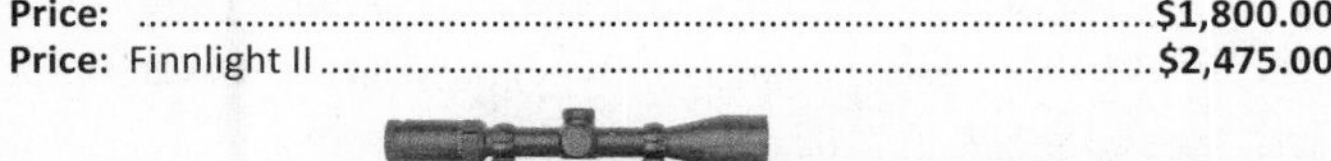

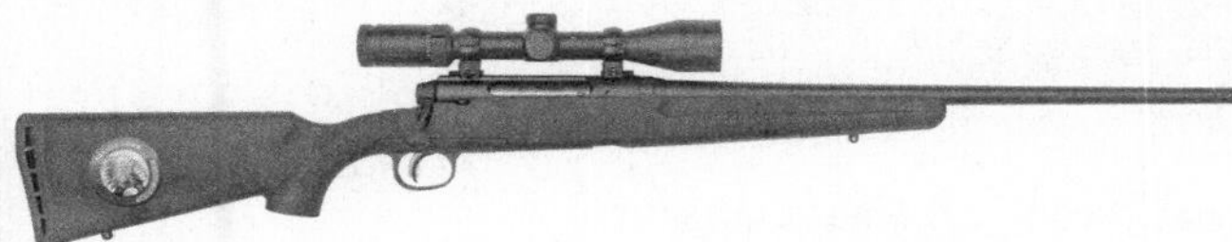

SAVAGE AXIS SERIES

Calibers: .243 Win., 6.5 Creedmoor, 7mm-08 Rem., .308 Win., .25-06 Rem., .270 Win, .30-06, .223 Rem., .22-250 Rem. **Barrel:** 22 in. **Weight:** 6.5 lbs. **Length:** 43.875 in. **Stock:** Black synthetic or camo, including pink/black Muddy Girl. **Sights:** Drilled and tapped for scope mounts. Several models come with factory mounted Weaver Kaspa 3-9x40 scope. **Features:** Available with black matte or stainless finish

Price: From .... **$363.00–$525.00**

SAVAGE MODEL 25 VARMINTER

Calibers: .17 Hornet, .22 Hornet, .222 Rem., .204 Ruger, .223 Rem. Capacity: 4-round magazine. **Barrel:** 24-in. medium-contour fluted barrel with recessed target crown, free-floating sleeved barrel, dual pillar bedding. **Weight:** 8.25 lbs. **Length:** 43.75 in. overall. **Stock:** Brown laminate with beavertail-style fore-end. Thumbhole stock available. **Sights:** Weaver-style bases installed. **Features:** Diameter-specific action built around the .223 Rem. bolt head dimension. Three locking lugs, 60-degree bolt lift, AccuTrigger adjustable from 2.5–3.25 lbs. Walking Varminter has black synthetic or camo stock, 22-in. barrel. **Weight:** 7.15 lbs. **Length:** 41.75 in. Introduced 2008. Made in USA by Savage Arms, Inc.

Price: From .... **$774.00–$824.00**
Price: Walking Varminter .... **$619.00–$671.00**

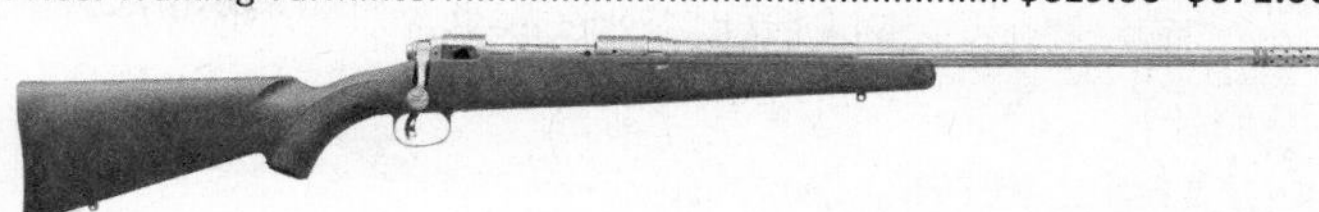

SAVAGE CLASSIC SERIES MODEL 14/114

Calibers: .243 Win., 7mm-08 Rem., .308 Win., .270 Win., 7mm Rem. Mag., .30-06, .300 Win. Mag. **Capacities:** 3- or 4-round magazine. **Barrels:** 22 in. or 24 in. **Weight:** 7–7.5 lbs. **Length:** 41.75–43.75 in. overall (Model 14 short action); 43.25–45.25 in. overall (Model 114 long action). **Stock:** Satin lacquer American walnut with ebony fore-end, wraparound checkering, Monte Carlo comb and cheekpiece. **Sights:** None furnished. Receiver drilled and tapped for scope mounting. **Features:** AccuTrigger, matte blued barrel and action, hinged floorplate.

Price: From **$979.00**

SAVAGE MODEL 12 VARMINT/TARGET SERIES

Calibers: .204 Ruger, .223 Rem., .22-250 Rem. Capacity: 4-shot magazine. **Barrel:** 26 in. stainless barreled action, heavy fluted, free-floating and button-rifled barrel. **Weight:** 10 lbs. **Length:** 46.25 in. overall. **Stock:** Dual pillar bedded, low profile, black synthetic or laminated stock with extra-wide beavertail fore-end. **Sights:** None furnished; drilled and tapped for scope mounting. **Features:** Recessed target-style muzzle. AccuTrigger, oversized bolt handle, detachable box magazine, swivel studs. Model 112BVSS has heavy target-style prone laminated stock with high comb, Wundhammer palm swell, internal box magazine. Model 12VLP DBM has black synthetic stock, detachable magazine, and additional chamberings in .243, .308 Win., .300 Win. Mag. Model 12FV has blued receiver. Model 12BTCSS has brown laminate vented thumbhole stock. Made in USA by Savage Arms, Inc.

Price: 12 FCV **$780.00**
Price: 12 BVSS **$1,146.00**
Price: 12 Varminter Low Profile (VLP) **$1,181.00**
Price: 12 Long Range Precision **$1,288.00**
Price: 12 BTCSS Thumbhole stock **$1,293.00**
Price: 12 Long Range Precision Varminter **$1,554.00**
Price: 12 F Class **$1,648.00**
Price: 12 Palma **$2,147.00**

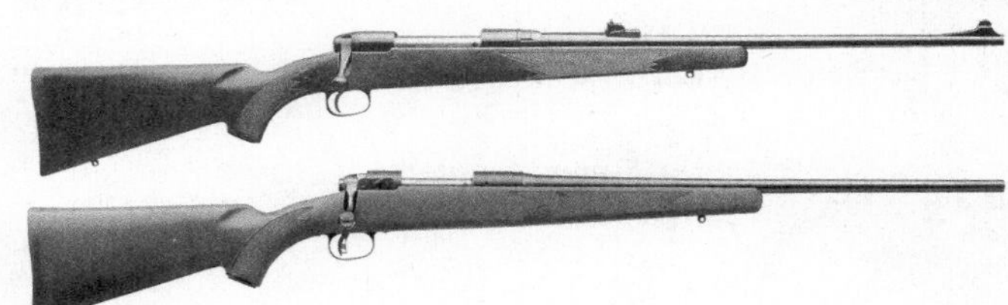

SAVAGE MODEL 11/111 HUNTER SERIES

Calibers: .223 Rem., .22-250 Rem., .243 Win., 6.5 Creedmoor, .260 Rem., 6.5x284 Norma, .338 Lapua, 7mm-08 Rem., .308 Win. **Capacities:** 2- or 4-round magazine; .25-06 Rem., .270 Win., 7mm Rem. Mag., .30-06, .300 Win. Mag., (long action Model 111), 3- or 4-round magazine. **Barrels:** 20 in., 22 in. or 24 in.; blued free-floated barrel. **Weights:** 6.5–6.75 lbs. **Lengths:** 41.75–43.75 in. overall (Model 11); 42.5–44.5 in. overall (Model 111). **Stock:** Graphite/fiberglass filled composite or hardwood. **Sights:** Ramp front, open fully adjustable rear; drilled and tapped for scope mounting. **Features:** Three-position top tang safety, double front locking lugs. Introduced 1994. Made in USA by Savage Arms, Inc.

Price: From .... **$684.00–$1,421.00**

SAVAGE MODEL 10 GRS

Calibers: 6.5 Creedmoor, .308 Win. **Stock:** Synthetic with adjustable comb, vertical pistol grip. **Sights:** None. Picatinny rail atop receiver. **Features:** Designed primarily for Law Enforcement. Detachable box magazine.

Price: **$1,450.00**

SAVAGE MODEL 10FP/110FP LAW ENFORCEMENT SERIES

Calibers: .223 Rem., .308 Win. (Model 10), 4-round magazine; .25-06 Rem., .300 Win. Mag., (Model 110), 3- or 4-round magazine. **Barrel:** 24 in.; matte blued free-floated heavy barrel and action. **Weight:** 6.5–6.75 lbs. **Length:** 41.75–43.75 in. overall (Model 10); 42.5–44.5 in. overall (Model 110). **Stock:** Black graphite/fiberglass composition, pillar-bedded, positive checkering. **Sights:** None furnished. Receiver drilled and tapped for scope mounting. **Features:** Black matte finish on all metal parts. Double swivel studs on the fore-end for sling and/or bipod mount. Right- or left-hand. Model 110FP introduced 1990. Model 10FP introduced 1998. Model 10FCP HS has HS Precision black synthetic tactical stock with molded alloy bedding system, Leupold 3.5-10x40 black matte scope with Mil Dot reticle, Farrell Picatinny Rail Base, flip-open lens covers, 1.25-in. sling with QD swivels, Harris bipod, Storm heavy-duty case. Made in USA by Savage Arms, Inc.

Price: Model 10FCP McMillan, McMillan fiberglass tactical stock.. **$1,591.00**
Price: Model 10FCP-HS HS Precision, HS Precision tactical stock ... **$1,315.00**
Price: Model 10FCP ... **$925.00**
Price: Model 10FLCP, left-hand model, standard stock or Accu-Stock ... **$975.00**
Price: Model 10FCP SR ... **$785.00**
Price: Model 10 Precision Carbine ... **$952.00**

SAVAGE 110 BA STEALTH

Calibers: .300 win, Mag., or .338 Lapua Mag. **Capacities:** Detachable 5- or 6-round box magazine. **Barrel:** 24 in. with threaded muzzle. **Stock:** Fab Defense GLR Shock buttstock, M-LOK fore-end. **Weight:** 11.125 lbs. **Features:** Adjustable AccuTrigger, Picatinny rail. Stealth Evolution has fluted heavy barrel, 10-round magazine, adjustable length of pull stock, Flat Dark Earth finish.

Price: Stealth ... **$1,484.00**
Price: Stealth, .338 Lapua ... **$1,624.00**
Price: Evolution ... **$1,999.00**
Price: Evolution, .338 Lapua ... **$2,149.00**

SAVAGE MODEL 10 PREDATOR HUNTER

Calibers: .204 Ruger. .223, .22-250, .243, .260 Rem., 6.5 Creedmoor, **6.5x284 Norma. Barrel:** 22 in. medium-contour. **Weight:** 7.25 lbs. **Length:** 43 in. overall. **Stock:** Synthetic with Mossy Oak Max-1 Camo coverage. **Features:** AccuTrigger, oversized bolt handle, right or left-hand action.

Price: ... **$999.00**

SAVAGE MODEL 110 PREDATOR

Calibers: .204 Ruger. .223, .22-250, .243, .260 Rem., 6.5 Creedmoor. Capacity: 4-round magazine. **Barrels:** 22 or 24 in. threaded heavy contour. **Weight:** 8.5 lbs. **Stock:** AccuStock with Mossy Oak Max-1 camo finish, soft grip surfaces, adjustable length of pull.

Price: ... **$899.00**

SAVAGE MODEL 110 HUNTER SERIES

Calibers: .204 Ruger. .223, .22-250, .243, ,25-06, .260 Rem., 6.5 Creedmoor, .270 Win., 7mm-08 Rem., .280 Ackley Imp., .308 Win., .30-06, .300 Win. Mag. **Capacities:** 3- or 4-round magazine. **Barrels:** 22 or 24. in. **Weight:** 8.5 lbs. **Stock:** AccuStock with gray finish, soft grip surfaces, adjustable length of pull.

Price: Hunter ... **$749.00**
Price: Bear Hunter (.300 WSM, .338 Fed., .375 Ruger ... **$999.00**
Price: Hog Hunter (20 in. bbl. open sights) ... **$594.00**
Price: Brush Hunter (20-in. bbl., .338 Win., .375 Rug.) ... **$784.00**
Price: Long Range Hunter (26 in. bbl., muzzle brake) ... **$1,099.00**

SAVAGE MODEL 110 TACTICAL

Caliber: .308 Win. **Capacity:** 10-round magazine. **Barrels:** 20 or 24 in. threaded and fluted heavy contour. **Weight:** 8.65 lbs. **Stock:** AccuStock with soft grip surfaces, AccuFit system. Features: Top Picatinny rail, right- or left-hand operation.

Price: ... **$784.00**
Price: Tactical Desert (6mm, 6.5 Creedmoor, FDE finish ... **$769.00**

SAVAGE MODEL 12 PRECISION TARGET SERIES BENCHREST

Calibers: .308 Win., 6.5x284 Norma, 6mm Norma BR. **Barrel:** 29-in. ultra-heavy. **Weight:** 12.75 lbs. **Length:** 50 in. overall. **Stock:** Gray laminate. **Features:** New Left-Load, Right-Eject target action, Target AccuTrigger adjustable from approx. 6 oz. to 2.5 lbs. oversized bolt handle, stainless extra-heavy free-floating and button-rifled barrel.

Price: ... **$1,629.00**

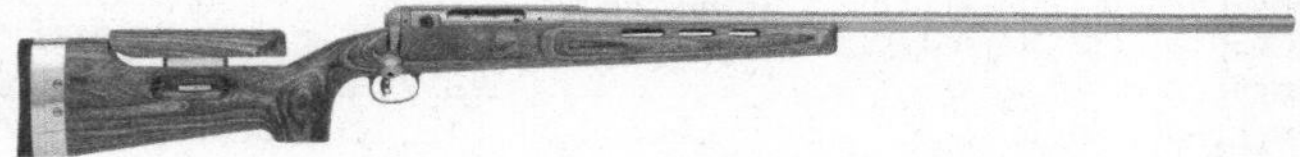

SAVAGE MODEL 12 PRECISION TARGET PALMA

Similar to Model 12 Benchrest but in .308 Win. only, 30-in. barrel, multi-adjustable stock, weighs 13.3 lbs.

Price: ... **$2,147.00**

SAVAGE MODEL 12 F CLASS TARGET RIFLE

Similar to Model 12 Benchrest but chambered in 6 Norma BR, 30-in. barrel, weighs 13.3 lbs.

Price: ... **$1,648.00**

SAVAGE MODEL 12 F/TR TARGET RIFLE

Similar to Model 12 Benchrest but in .308 Win. only, 30-in. barrel, weighs 12.65 lbs.

Price: ... **$1,538.00**

SAVAGE MODEL 112 MAGNUM TARGET

Caliber: .338 Lapua Magnum. Single shot. **Barrel:** 26-in. heavy with muzzle brake. **Stock:** Wood laminate. **Features:** AccuTrigger, matte black finish, oversized bolt handle, pillar bedding.

Price: ... **$1,177.00**

STEYR PRO HUNTER

Similar to the Classic Rifle except has ABS synthetic stock with adjustable butt spacers, straight comb without cheekpiece, palm swell, Pachmayr 1 in. swivels. Special 10-round magazine conversion kit available. Introduced 1997. Imported from Austria by Steyr Arms, Inc.

Price: From ... **$1,150.00–$1,377.00**

Prices given are believed to be accurate at time of publication however, many factors affect retail pricing so exact prices are not possible.

STEYR SCOUT
Calibers: .223, .243, 7mm-08, .308 Win. **Capacity:** 5- or 10-shot magazine. **Barrel:** 19 in. fluted. **Weight:** 6.5 lbs. **Length:** NA. **Stock:** Gray Zytel. **Sights:** Pop-up front and rear. **Features:** Luggage case, scout sling, two stock spacers, two magazines. Introduced 1998. Imported from Austria by Steyr Arms, Inc.
Price: **$1,725.00**

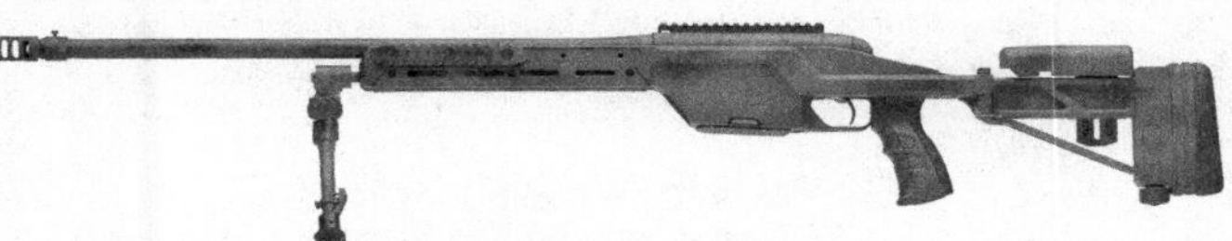

STEYR SSG08
Calibers: .243 Win., 7.62x51 NATO (.308Win), 7.62x63B (.300 Win Mag)., .338 Lapua Mag. Capacity: 10-round magazine. **Barrels:** 20, 23.6 or 25.6 in. **Stock:** Dural aluminum folding stock black with .280 mm long UIT-rail and various Picatinny rails. **Sights:** Front post sight and rear adjustable. **Features:** High-grade aluminum folding stock, adjustable cheekpiece and buttplate with height marking, and an ergonomical exchangeable pistol grip. Versa-Pod, muzzle brake, Picatinny rail, UIT rail on stock and various Picatinny rails on fore-end, and a 10-round HC-magazine. SBS rotary bolt action with four frontal locking lugs, arranged in pairs. Cold-hammer-forged barrels are available in standard or compact lengths.
Price: **$5,899.00**

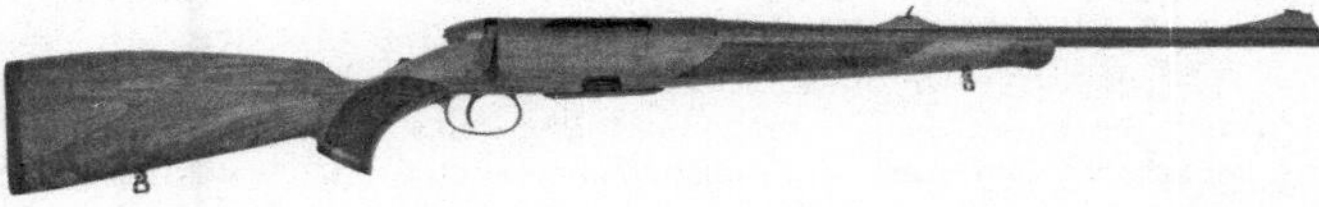

STEYR SM 12
Calibers: .243, 6.5x55SE, .270 Win., 7mm-08 Rem., .308 Win., .30-06, .300 Win. Mag, .300 WSM, 9.3x62mm. **Barrels:** 20-in. blue or 25-in. stainless. **Stock:** Walnut with checkered grip and fore-end. Available in half or full-length configurations. **Sights:** Adjustable rear, ramp front with bead. Stainless barrel has no sights. **Features:** Sling swivels, Bavarian cheekpiece, hand-cocking system operated by thumb manually cocks firing mechanism.
Price: Standard-length stock.................................. **$2,545.00**
Price: Full length (Mannlicher).................................. **$2,750.00**

THOMPSON/CENTER DIMENSION
Calibers: .204 Ruger, .223 Rem., .22-250 Rem., .243 Win., .270 Win., 7mm Rem. Mag., .308 Win., .30-06, .300 Win. Mag. **Capacity:** 3-round magazine. **Barrels:** 22 or 24 in. **Weight:** NA. **Length:** NA. **Stock:** Textured grip composite with adjustment spacers. **Features:** Calibers are interchangeable between certain series or "families" — .204/.223; .22-250/.243/7mm-08/.308; .270/.30-06; 7mm Rem. Mag./.300 Win. Mag. Introduced in 2012.
Price: **$689.00**

THOMPSON/CENTER VENTURE
Calibers: .270 Win., 7mm Rem. Mag., .30-06, .300 Win. Mag. **Capacity:** 3-round magazine. **Barrel:** 24 in., 20 in. (Compact). **Weight:** 7.5 lbs. **Stock:** Composite. **Sights:** None, Weaver-style base. **Features:** Standard-length action with Nitride fat bolt design, externally adjustable trigger, two-position safety, textured grip. Introduced 2009.
Price: **$537.00**

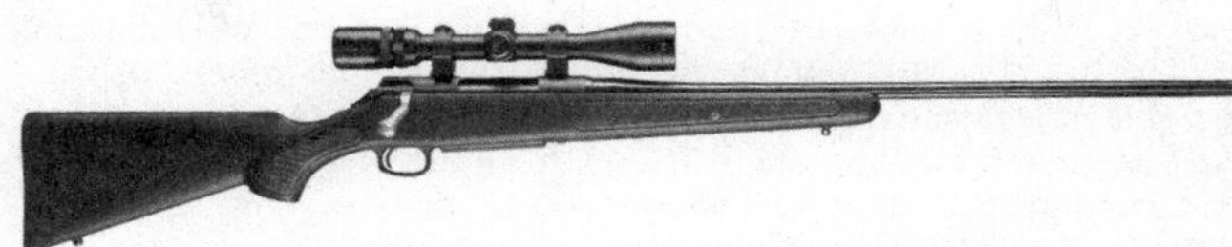

THOMPSON/CENTER VENTURE MEDIUM ACTION
Calibers: .204, .22-250, .223, .243, 7mm-08, .308 and 30TC. **Capacity:** 3+1 detachable nylon box magazine. **Features:** Bolt-action rifle with a 24-in. crowned medium weight barrel, classic-styled composite stock with inlaid traction grip panels, adjustable 3.5- to 5-pound trigger along with a drilled and tapped receiver (bases included). **Weight:** 7 lbs. **Length:** 43.5 in.
Price: **$537.00**

THOMPSON/CENTER VENTURE PREDATOR PDX
Calibers: .204, .22-250, .223, .243, .308. **Weight:** 8 lbs. **Length:** 41.5 in. **Features:** Bolt-action rifle similar to Venture medium action but with heavy, deep-fluted 22-in. barrel and Max-1 camo finish overall.
Price: From.. **$638.00**

TIKKA T3X SERIES Calibers: Virtually any popular chambering including .204 Ruger .222 Rem., .223 Rem., .243 Win., .25-06, 6.5x55 SE, .260 Rem, .270 Win., .260 WSM, 7mm-08, 7mm Rem. Mag., .308 Win., .30-06, .300 Win. Mag., .300 WSM. **Barrels:** 20, 22.4, 24.3 in. **Stock:** Checkered walnut, laminate or modular synthetic with interchangeable pistol grips. Newly designed recoil pad. **Features:** Offered in a variety of different models with many options. Left-hand models available. One minute-of-angle accuracy guaranteed. Introduced in 2016. Made in Finland by Sako. Imported by Beretta USA.
Price: Hunter from.................................. **$875.00**
Price: Lite from (shown).................................. **$725.00**
Price: Varmint from.................................. **$950.00**
Price: Laminate stainless.................................. **$1,050.00**
Price: Forest.................................. **$1,000.00**
Price: Tac A1 (shown).................................. **$1,899.00**
Price: Compact Tactical Rifle, From.................................. **$1,150.00**

WEATHERBY MARK V
Calibers: Deluxe version comes in all Weatherby calibers plus .243 Win., .270 Win., 7mm-08 Rem., .30-06, .308 Win. **Barrels:** 24 in., 26 in., 28 in. **Weights:** 6.75–10 lbs. **Lengths:** 44–48.75 in. overall. **Stock:** Walnut, Monte Carlo with cheekpiece; high luster finish; checkered pistol grip and fore-end; recoil pad. **Sights:** None furnished. **Features:** 4 models with Mark V action and wood stocks; other common elements include cocking indicator; adjustable trigger; hinged floorplate, thumb safety; quick detachable sling swivels. Lazermark same as Mark V Deluxe except stock has extensive oak leaf pattern laser carving on pistol grip and fore-end; chambered in Wby. Magnums .257, .270 Win., 7mm., .300, .340, with 26 in. barrel. Sporter is same as the Mark V Deluxe without the embellishments. Metal has low-luster blue, stock is Claro walnut with matte finish, Monte Carlo comb, recoil pad. Chambered for these Wby. Mags: .257, .270 Win., 7mm, .300, .340. Other chamberings: 7mm Rem. Mag., .300 Win. Introduced 1993. Six Mark V models come with synthetic stocks. Ultra Lightweight rifles weigh 5.75 to 6.75 lbs.; 24 in., 26 in. fluted stainless barrels with recessed target crown; Bell & Carlson stock with CNC-machined aluminum bedding plate and tan "spider web" finish, skeletonized handle and sleeve. Available in .243 Win., .25-06 Rem., .270 Win., 7mm-08 Rem., 7mm Rem. Mag., .280 Rem, .308 Win., .30-06, .300 Win. Mag. Wby. Mag chamberings: .240, .257, .270 Win., 7mm,

.300. Accumark uses Mark V action with heavy-contour 26 in. and 28 in. stainless barrels with black oxidized flutes, muzzle diameter of .705 in. No sights, drilled and tapped for scope mounting. Stock is composite with matte gel-coat finish, full-length aluminum bedding Hasblock. Weighs 8.5 lbs. Chambered for these Wby. Mags: .240, .257, .270, 7mm, .300, .340, .338-378, .30-378. Other chamberings: .22-250, .243 Win., .25-06 Rem., .270 Win., .308 Win., 7mm Rem. Mag., .300 Win. Mag. Altitude] has 22-, 24-, 26-, 28-in. fluted stainless steel barrel, Monte Carlo carbon fiber composite stock with raised comb, Kryptek Altitude camo. Tacmark has 28-in. free-floated fluted barrel with Accubrake, fully adjustable stock, black finish. Safari Grade has fancy grade checkered French walnut stock with ebony fore-end and grip cap, adjustable express rear and hooded front sights, from the Weatherby Custom Shop. Made in USA.

Price: Mark V Deluxe **$2,700.00**
Price: Mark V Lazermark **$2,800.00**
Price: Mark V Sporter **$1,800.00**
Price: Mark V Ultra Lightweight **$2,300.00**
Price: Mark V Accumark .... **$2,300.00–$2,700.00**
Price: Mark V Altitude .... **$3,000.00–$3,700.00**
Price: Mark V Safari Grade Custom .... **$6,900.00–$7,600.00**
Price: Mark V Tacmark **$4,100.00**

WEATHERBY VANGUARD II SERIES

Calibers: .240, .257, and .300 Wby Mag. **Barrel:** 24 in. matte black. **Weights:** 7.5–8.75 lbs. **Lengths:** 44–46.75 in. overall. **Stock:** Raised comb, Monte Carlo, injection-molded composite stock. **Sights:** None furnished. **Features:** One-piece forged, fluted bolt body with three gas ports, forged and machined receiver, adjustable trigger, factory accuracy guarantee. Vanguard Stainless has 410-Series stainless steel barrel and action, bead blasted matte metal finish. Vanguard Deluxe has raised comb, semi-fancy-grade Monte Carlo walnut stock with maplewood spacers, rosewood fore-end and grip cap, polished action with high-gloss blued metalwork. Vanguard Synthetic Package includes Vanguard Synthetic rifle with Bushnell Banner 3-9x40 scope mounted and boresighted, Leupold Rifleman rings and bases, Uncle Mikes nylon sling, and Plano PRO-MAX injection-molded case. Sporter has Monte Carlo walnut stock with satin urethane finish, fineline diamond point checkering, contrasting rosewood fore-end tip, matte-blued metalwork. Sporter SS metalwork is 410 Series bead-blasted stainless steel. Vanguard Youth/Compact has 20 in. No. 1 contour barrel, short action, scaled-down nonreflective matte black hardwood stock with 12.5-in. length of pull, and full-size, injection-molded composite stock. Chambered for .223 Rem., .22-250 Rem., .243 Win., 7mm-08 Rem., .308 Win. Weighs 6.75 lbs.; OAL 38.9 in. Sub-MOA Matte and Sub-MOA Stainless models have pillar-bedded Fiberguard composite stock (Aramid, graphite unidirectional fibers and fiberglass) with 24-in. barreled action; matte black metalwork, Pachmayr Decelerator recoil pad. Sub-MOA Stainless metalwork is 410 Series bead-blasted stainless steel. Sub-MOA Varmint guaranteed to shoot 3-shot group of .99 in. or less when used with specified Weatherby factory or premium (non-Weatherby calibers) ammunition. Hand-laminated, tan Monte Carlo composite stock with black spiderwebbing; CNC-machined aluminum bedding block, 22 in. No. 3 contour barrel, recessed target crown. Varmint Special has tan injection-molded Monte Carlo composite stock, pebble grain finish, black spiderwebbing. 22 in. No. 3 contour barrel (.740-in. muzzle dia.), bead blasted matte black finish, recessed target crown. Back Country has two-stage trigger, pillar-bedded Bell & Carlson stock, 24-in. fluted barrel, three-position safety. WBY-X Series comes with choice of several contemporary camo finishes (Bonz, Black Reaper, Kryptek, Hog Reaper, Whitetail Bonz, Blaze, GH2 "Girls Hunt Too") and is primarily targeted to younger shooters. Made in USA.

Price: Vanguard Synthetic **$649.00**
Price: Vanguard Synthetic DBM .... **$749.00–$899.00**
Price: Vanguard Stainless **$799.00**
Price: Vanguard Deluxe, 7mm Rem. Mag., .300 Win. Mag. **$1,149.00**
Price: Vanguard Synthetic Package, .25-06 Rem. **$999.00**
Price: Vanguard Sporter **$849.00**
Price: Vanguard Youth/Compact **$599.00**
Price: Vanguard S2 Back Country **$1,399.00**
Price: Vanguard Black Reaper **$749.00**
Price: Vanguard RC (Range Certified) **$1,199.00**
Price: Vanguard Varmint Special **$849.00**
Price: Camilla (designed for women shooters) **$849.00**
Price: Lazerguard (Laser carved AA-grade walnut stock) **$1,199.00**
Price: H-Bar (tactical series) from .... **$1,149.00–$1,449.00**
Price: Weatherguard **$749.00**

Price: Modular Chassis **$1,519.00**
Price: Dangerous Game Rifle (DGR) .375 H&H **$1,299.00**
Price: Safari (.375 or .30-06) **$1,199.00**

WINCHESTER MODEL 70 SUPER GRADE

Calibers: .270 Win., .270 WSM, 7mm Rem. Mag., .30-06, .300 Win Mag., .300 WSM, .338 Win. Mag. **Capacities:** 5 rounds (short action) or 3 rounds (long action). **Barrels:** 24 in. or 26 in. blued. **Weights:** 8–8.5 lbs. **Features:** Full fancy Grade IV/V walnut stock with shadow-line cheekpiece, controlled round feed with claw extractor, Pachmayr Decelerator pad. No sights but drilled and tapped for scope mounts.

Price: .... **$1,440.00–$1,480.00**

WINCHESTER MODEL 70 ALASKAN

Calibers: .30-06, .300 Win. Mag., .338 Win. Mag., .375 H&H Magnum. **Barrel:** 25 in **Weight:** 8.8 lbs. **Sights:** Folding adjustable rear, hooded brass bead front. **Stock:** Satin finished Monte Carlo with cut checkering. **Features:** Integral recoil lug, Pachmayr Decelerator recoil pad.

Price: **$1,400.00**

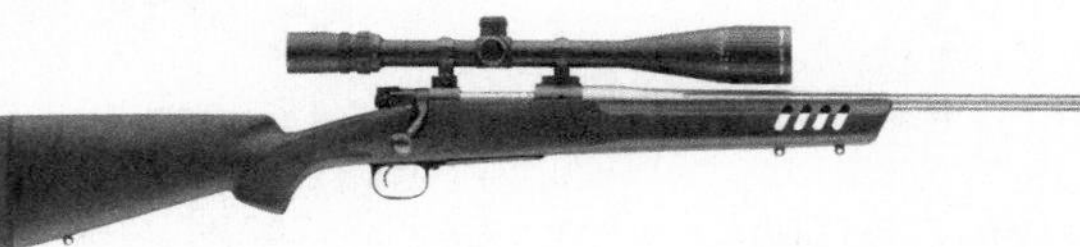

WINCHESTER MODEL 70 COYOTE LIGHT

Calibers: .22-250, .243 Win., .308 Win., .270 WSM, .300 WSM and .325 WSM. **Capacities:** 5-round magazine (3-round mag. in .270 WSM, .300 WSM and .325 WSM). **Barrel:** 22-in. fluted stainless barrel (24 in. in .270 WSM, .300 WSM and .325 WSM). **Weight:** 7.5 lbs. **Length:** NA. **Features:** Composite Bell and Carlson stock, Pachmayr Decelerator pad. Controlled round feeding. No sights but drilled and tapped for mounts.

Price: .... **$1,270.00–$1,310.00**

WINCHESTER MODEL 70 FEATHERWEIGHT

Calibers: .22-250, .243, 7mm-08, .308, .270 WSM, 7mm WSM, .300 WSM, .325 WSM, .25-06, .270, .30-06, 7mm Rem. Mag., .300 Win. Mag., .338 Win. Mag. **Capacities:** 5 rounds (short action) or 3 rounds (long action). **Barrels:** 22-in. blued (24 in. in magnum chamberings). **Weights:** 6.5–7.25 lbs. **Length:** NA. **Features:** Satin-finished checkered Grade I walnut stock, controlled round feeding. Pachmayr Decelerator pad. No sights but drilled and tapped for scope mounts.

Price: **$1,010.00**

WINCHESTER MODEL 70 SPORTER

Calibers: .270 WSM, 7mm WSM, .300 WSM, .325 WSM, .25-06, .270, .30-06, 7mm Rem. Mag., .300 Win. Mag., .338 Win. Mag. **Capacities:** 5 rounds (short action) or 3 rounds (long action). **Barrels:** 22 in., 24 in. or 26 in. blued. **Weights:** 6.5–7.25 lbs. **Length:** NA. **Features:** Satin-finished checkered Grade I walnut stock with sculpted cheekpiece, controlled round feeding. Pachmayr Decelerator pad. No sights but drilled and tapped for scope mounts.

Price: **$1,010.00**

WINCHESTER MODEL 70 SAFARI EXPRESS

Calibers: .375 H&H Magnum, .416 Remington, .458 Win. Mag. **Barrel:** 24 in. **Weight:** 9 lbs. **Sights:** Fully adjustable rear, hooded brass bead front. **Stock:** Satin finished Monte Carlo with cut checkering, deluxe cheekpiece. **Features:** Forged steel receiver with double integral recoil lugs bedded front and rear, dual steel crossbolts, Pachmayr Decelerator recoil pad.

Price: **$1,560.00**

WINCHESTER XPR

Calibers: .270 Win., .30-06, .300 Win. Mag., .338 Win. Mag. **Capacities:** Detachable box magazine holds 3 to 5 rounds. **Barrels:** 24 or 26 in. **Stock:** Black polymer with Inflex Technology recoil pad. **Weight:** Approx. 7 lbs. **Finish:** Matte blue. **Features:** Bolt unlock button, nickel coated Teflon bolt.

Price: **$549.99**
Price: Mossy Oak Break-Up Country camo stock **$600.00**
Price: With Vortex II 3-9x40 scope **$710.00**
Price: XPR Hunter Camo (shown) **$600.00**

Prices given are believed to be accurate at time of publication however, many factors affect retail pricing so exact prices are not possible.

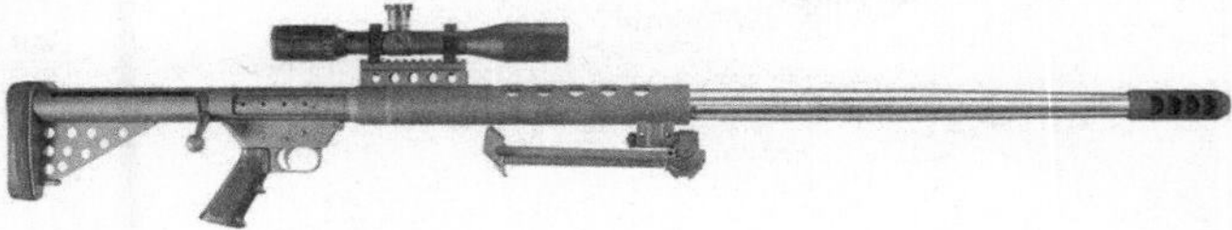

ARMALITE AR-50
Caliber: .50 BMG **Barrel:** 31 in. **Weight:** 33.2 lbs. **Length:** 59.5 in. **Stock:** Synthetic. **Sights:** None furnished. **Features:** A single-shot bolt-action rifle designed for long-range shooting. Available in left-hand model. Made in USA by Armalite.
Price: **$3,359.00**

BALLARD 1875 1 1/2 HUNTER
Caliber: Various calibers. **Barrel:** 26–30 in. **Weight:** NA **Length:** NA. **Stock:** Hand-selected classic American walnut. **Sights:** Blade front, Rocky Mountain rear. **Features:** Color casehardened receiver, breechblock and lever. Many options available. Made in USA by Ballard Rifle & Cartridge Co.
Price: **$3,250.00**

BALLARD 1875 #3 GALLERY SINGLE SHOT
Caliber: Various calibers. **Barrel:** 24–28 in. octagonal with tulip. **Weight:** NA. **Length:** NA. **Stock:** Hand-selected classic American walnut. **Sights:** Blade front, Rocky Mountain rear. **Features:** Color casehardened receiver, breechblock and lever. Many options available. Made in USA by Ballard Rifle & Cartridge Co.
Price: **$3,300.00**

BALLARD 1875 #4 PERFECTION
Caliber: Various calibers. **Barrels:** 30 in. or 32 in. octagon, standard or heavyweight. **Weights:** 10.5 lbs. (standard) or 11.75 lbs. (heavyweight bbl.) **Length:** NA. **Stock:** Smooth walnut. **Sights:** Blade front, Rocky Mountain rear. **Features:** Rifle or shotgun-style buttstock, straight grip action, single- or double-set trigger, "S" or right lever, hand polished and lapped Badger barrel. Made in USA by Ballard Rifle & Cartridge Co.
Price: **$3,950.00**

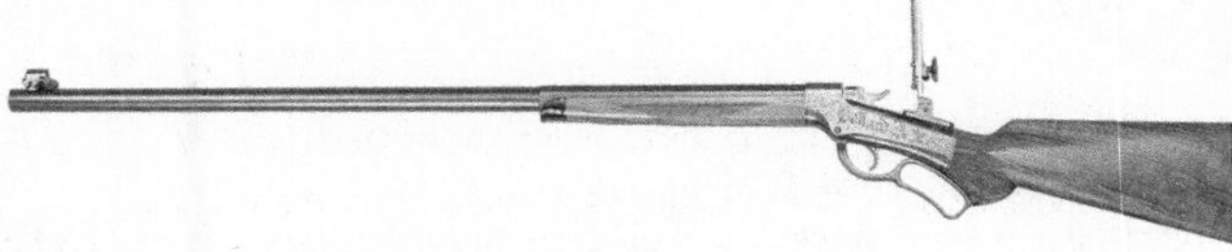

BALLARD 1875 #7 LONG RANGE
Calibers: .32-40, .38-55, .40-65, .40-70 SS, .45-70 Govt., .45-90, .45-110. **Barrels:** 32 in., 34 in. half-octagon. **Weight:** 11.75 lbs. **Length:** NA. **Stock:** Walnut; checkered pistol grip shotgun butt, ebony fore-end cap. **Sights:** Globe front. **Features:** Designed for shooting up to 1,000 yards. Standard or heavy barrel; single or double-set trigger; hard rubber or steel buttplate. Introduced 1999. Made in USA by Ballard Rifle & Cartridge Co.
Price: From........ **$3,600.00**

BALLARD 1875 #8 UNION HILL
Calibers: Various calibers. **Barrel:** 30-in. half-octagon. **Weight:** About 10.5 lbs. **Length:** NA. **Stock:** Walnut; pistol grip butt with cheekpiece. **Sights:** Globe front. **Features:** Designed for 200-yard offhand shooting. Standard or heavy barrel; double-set triggers; full loop lever; hook Schuetzen buttplate. Introduced 1999. Made in USA by Ballard Rifle & Cartridge Co.
Price: From........ **$4,175.00**

BALLARD MODEL 1885 LOW WALL SINGLE SHOT RIFLE
Calibers: Various calibers. **Barrels:** 24–28 in. **Weight:** NA. **Length:** NA. **Stock:** Hand-selected classic American walnut. **Sights:** Blade front, sporting rear. **Features:** Color casehardened receiver, breechblock and lever. Many options available. Made in USA by Ballard Rifle & Cartridge Co.
Price: **$3,300.00**

BALLARD MODEL 1885 HIGH WALL STANDARD SPORTING SINGLE SHOT
Calibers: Various calibers. **Barrels:** Lengths to 34 in. **Weight:** NA. **Length:** NA. **Stock:** Straight-grain American walnut. **Sights:** Buckhorn or flattop rear, blade front. **Features:** Faithful copy of original Model 1885 High Wall; parts interchange with original rifles; variety of options available. Introduced 2000. Made in USA by Ballard Rifle & Cartridge Co.
Price: **$3,300.00**

BALLARD MODEL 1885 HIGH WALL SPECIAL SPORTING SINGLE SHOT
Calibers: Various calibers. **Barrels:** 28–30 in. octagonal. **Weight:** NA. **Length:** NA. **Stock:** Hand-selected classic American walnut. **Sights:** Blade front, sporting rear. **Features:** Color casehardened receiver, breechblock and lever. Many options available. Made in USA by Ballard Rifle & Cartridge Co.
Price: **$3,600.00**

BROWN MODEL 97D SINGLE SHOT
Calibers: Available in most factory and wildcat calibers from .17 Ackley Hornet to .375 Winchester. **Barrels:** Up to 26 in., air-gauged match grade. **Weight:** About 5 lbs., 11 oz. **Stock:** Sporter style with pistol grip, cheekpiece and Schnabel fore-end. **Sights:** None furnished; drilled and tapped for scope mounting. **Features:** Falling-block action gives rigid barrel-receiver matting; polished blue/black finish. Hand-fitted action. Standard and custom made-to-order rifles with many options. Made in USA by E. Arthur Brown Co., Inc.
Price: Standard model........ **$1,695.00**

C. SHARPS ARMS MODEL 1875 TARGET & SPORTING RIFLE
Calibers: .38-55, .40-65, .40-70 Straight or Bottlenecks, .45-70, .45-90. **Barrel:** 30-in. heavy tapered round. **Weight:** 11 lbs. **Length:** NA. **Stock:** American walnut. **Sights:** Globe with post front sight. **Features:** Long Range Vernier tang sight with windage adjustments. Pistol grip stock with cheek rest; checkered steel buttplate. Introduced 1991. From C. Sharps Arms Co.
Price: Without sights........ **$1,425.00**
Price: With blade front & buckhorn rear barrel sights **$1,525.00**
Price: With standard tang & globe w/post & ball front sights **$1,725.00**
Price: With deluxe vernier tang & globe w/spirit level & aperture sights **$1,825.00**
Price: With single set trigger, add **$125.00**

C. SHARPS ARMS 1875 CLASSIC SHARPS
Similar to New Model 1875 Sporting Rifle except 26 in., 28 in. or 30 in. full octagon barrel, crescent buttplate with toe plate, Hartford-style fore-end with cast German silver nose cap. Blade front sight, Rocky Mountain buckhorn rear. Weighs 10 lbs. Introduced 1987. From C. Sharps Arms Co.
Price: **$1,775.00**

C. SHARPS ARMS 1874 BRIDGEPORT SPORTING
Calibers: .38-55 to .50-3.25. **Barrel:** 26 in., 28 in., 30-in. tapered octagon. **Weight:** 10.5 lbs. **Length:** 47 in. **Stock:** American black walnut; shotgun butt with checkered steel buttplate; straight grip, heavy fore-end with Schnabel tip. **Sights:** Blade front, buckhorn rear. Drilled and tapped for tang sight. **Features:** Double-set triggers. Made in USA by C. Sharps Arms.
Price: **$1,995.00**

C. SHARPS ARMS NEW MODEL 1885 HIGHWALL
Calibers: .22 LR, .22 Hornet, .219 Zipper, .25-35 WCF, .32-40 WCF, .38-55 WCF, .40-65, .30-40 Krag, .40-50 ST or BN, .40-70 ST or BN, .40-90 ST or BN, .45-70 Govt. 2-1/10 in. ST, .45-90 2-4/10 in. ST, .45-100 2-6/10 in. ST, .45-110 2-7/8 in. ST, .45-120 3-1/4 in. ST. **Barrels:** 26 in., 28 in., 30 in., tapered full octagon. **Weight:** About 9 lbs., 4 oz. **Length:** 47 in. overall. **Stock:** Oil-finished American walnut; Schnabel-style fore-end. **Sights:** Blade front, buckhorn rear. Drilled and tapped for optional tang sight. **Features:** Single trigger; octagonal receiver top; checkered steel buttplate; color casehardened receiver and buttplate, blued barrel. Many options available. Made in USA by C. Sharps Arms Co.
Price: From........ **$1,975.00**

C. SHARPS ARMS 1885 HIGHWALL SCHUETZEN RIFLE
Calibers: .30-30, .32-40, .38-55, .40-50. **Barrels:** 24, 26, 28 or 30 in. Full tapered octagon. **Stock:** Straight grain American walnut with oil finish, pistol grip, cheek rest. **Sights:** Globe front with aperture set, long-range fully adjustable tang sight with Hadley eyecup. **Finish:** Color casehardened receiver group, buttplate and bottom tang, matte blue barrel. Single set trigger.
Price: From **$2,875.00**

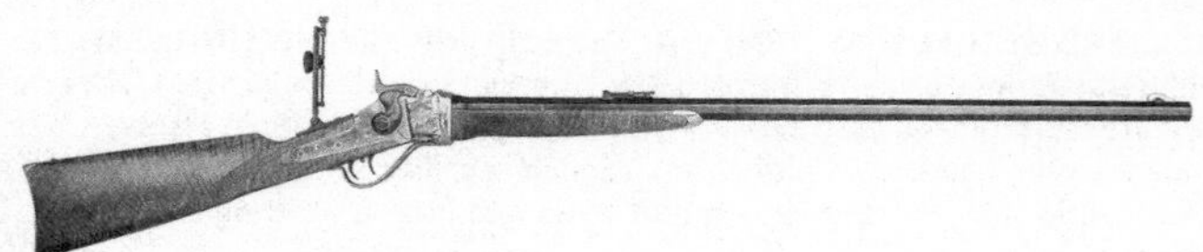

CIMARRON BILLY DIXON 1874 SHARPS SPORTING
Calibers: .45-70, .45-90, .50-70. **Barrel:** 32-in. tapered octagonal. **Weight:** NA. **Length:** NA. **Stock:** European walnut. **Sights:** Blade front, Creedmoor rear. **Features:** Color casehardened frame, blued barrel. Hand-checkered grip and fore-end; hand-rubbed oil finish. Made by Pedersoli. Imported by Cimarron F.A. Co.
Price: From **$2,141.70**

CIMARRON MODEL 1885 HIGH WALL
Calibers: .38-55, .40-65, .45-70 Govt., .45-90, .45-120, .30-40 Krag, .348 Winchester, .405 Winchester. **Barrel:** 30-in. octagonal. **Weight:** NA. **Length:** NA. **Stock:** European walnut. **Sights:** Bead front, semi-buckhorn rear. **Features:** Replica of the Win.ester 1885 High Wall rifle. Color casehardened receiver and lever, blued barrel. Curved buttplate. Optional double-set triggers. Introduced 1999. Imported by Cimarron F.A. Co.
Price: From **$1,097.00**
Price: With pistol grip, adj. sights, From **$1,277.00**
Price: Deluxe model, double-set triggers **$1,450.00**

CIMARRON MODEL 1885 LOW WALL
Calibers: .22 Hornet, .32-20, .38-40, .44-40, .45 Colt. **Barrel:** 30-in. octagonal. **Weight:** NA. **Length:** NA. **Stock:** European walnut. **Sights:** Bead front, semi-buckhorn rear. **Features:** Replica of the Winchester 1885 Low Wall rifle. Color casehardened receiver, blued barrel. Curved buttplate. Optional double-set triggers. Introduced 1999. Imported by Cimarron F.A. Co.
Price: From **$1,023.00**

CIMARRON ADOBE WALLS ROLLING BLOCK
Caliber: .45-70 Govt. **Barrel:** 30-in. octagonal. **Weight:** 10.33 lbs. **Length:** NA. **Stock:** Hand-checkered European walnut. **Sights:** Bead front, semi-buckhorn rear. **Features:** Color casehardened receiver, blued barrel. Curved buttplate. Double-set triggers. Made by Pedersoli. Imported by Cimarron F.A. Co.
Price: From **$1,740.00**

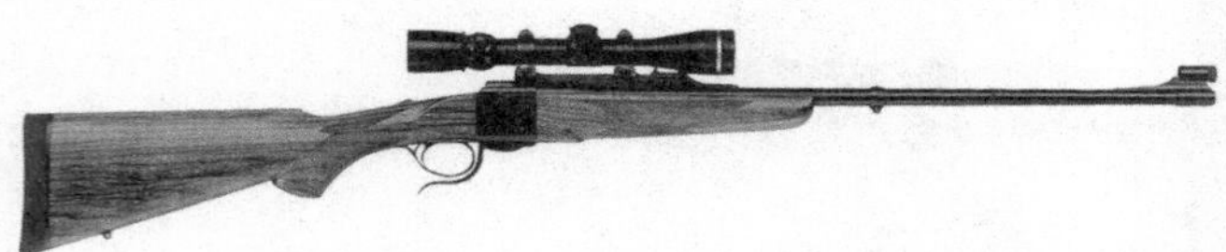

DAKOTA ARMS MODEL 10
Calibers: Most rimmed and rimless commercial calibers. **Barrel:** 23 in. **Weight:** 6 lbs. **Length:** 39.5 in. overall. **Stock:** Medium fancy grade walnut in classic style. Standard or full-length Mannlicher-style. Checkered grip and fore-end. **Sights:** None furnished. Drilled and tapped for scope mounting. **Features:** Falling block action with underlever. Top tang safety. Removable trigger plate for conversion to single set trigger. Introduced 1990. Made in USA by Dakota Arms.
Price: From **$5,260.00**
Price: Deluxe from **$6,690.00**

DAKOTA ARMS SHARPS
Calibers: Virtually any caliber from .17 Ackley Hornet to .30-40 Krag. **Features:** 26-in. octagon barrel, XX-grade walnut stock with straight grip and tang sight. Many options and upgrades are available.
Price: From **$4,490.00**

EMF PREMIER 1874 SHARPS
Calibers: .45-70, .45-110, .45-120. **Barrel:** 32 in., 34 in.. **Weight:** 11–13 lbs. **Length:** 49 in., 51 in. overall. **Stock:** Pistol grip, European walnut. **Sights:** Blade front, adjustable rear. **Features:** Superb quality reproductions of the 1874 Sharps Sporting Rifles; casehardened locks; double-set triggers; blue barrels. Imported from Pedersoli by EMF.
Price: Business Rifle **$1,585.00**
Price: Down Under Sporting Rifle, Patchbox, heavy barrel **$2,405.00**
Price: Silhouette, pistol-grip **$1,899.90**
Price: Super Deluxe Hand Engraved **$3,600.00**
Price: Competition Rifle **$2,200.00**

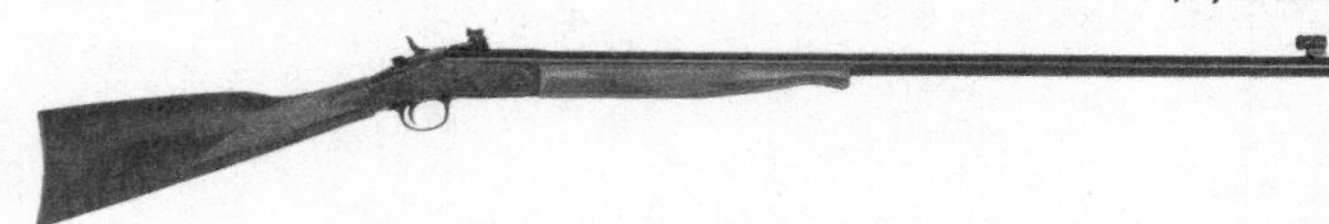

H&R BUFFALO CLASSIC
Calibers: .45 Colt or .45-70 Govt. **Barrel:** 32 in. heavy. **Weight:** 8 lbs. **Length:** 46 in. overall. **Stock:** Cut-checkered American black walnut. **Sights:** Williams receiver sight; Lyman target front sight with 8 aperture inserts. **Features:** Color casehardened Handi-Rifle action with exposed hammer; color casehardened crescent buttplate; 19th-century checkering pattern. Introduced 1995. Made in USA by H&R 1871, Inc.
Price: Buffalo Classic Rifle **$479.00**

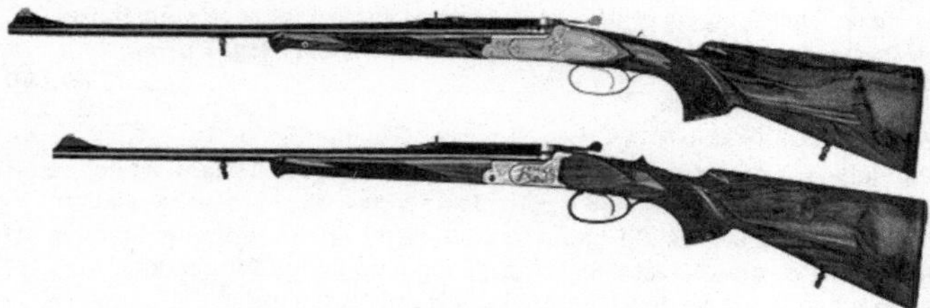

KRIEGHOFF HUBERTUS SINGLE-SHOT
Calibers: .222, .22-250, .243 Win., .270 Win., .308 Win., .30-06, 5.6x50R Mag., 5.6x52R, 6x62R Freres, 6.5x57R, 6.5x65R, 7x57R, 7x65R, 8x57JRS, 8x75RS, 9.3x74R, 7mm Rem. Mag., .300 Win. Mag. **Barrels:** 23.5 in. Shorter lengths available. **Weight:** 6.5 lbs. **Length:** 40.5 in. **Stock:** High-grade walnut. **Sights:** Blade front, open rear. **Features:** Break-open loading with manual cocking lever on top tang; takedown; extractor; Schnabel forearm; many options. Imported from Germany by Krieghoff International Inc.
Price: Hubertus single shot, From **$7,295.00**
Price: Hubertus, magnum calibers **$8,295.00**

MERKEL K1 MODEL LIGHTWEIGHT STALKING
Calibers: .243 Win., .270 Win., 7x57R, .308 Win., .30-06, 7mm Rem. Mag., .300 Win. Mag., 9.3x74R. **Barrel:** 23.6 in. **Weight:** 5.6 lbs. unscoped. **Stock:** Satin-finished walnut, fluted and checkered; sling-swivel studs. **Sights:** None (scope base furnished). **Features:** Franz Jager single-shot break-open action, cocking/uncocking slide-type safety, matte silver receiver, selectable trigger pull weights, integrated, quick detach 1 in. or 30mm optic mounts (optic not included). Extra barrels are an option. Imported from Germany by Merkel USA.
Price: Jagd Stalking Rifle **$3,795.00**
Price: Jagd Stutzen Carbine **$4,195.00**
Price: Extra barrels **$1,195.00**

MILLER ARMS
Calibers: Virtually any caliber from .17 Ackley Hornet to .416 Remington. Falling block design with 24-in. premium match-grade barrel, express sights, XXX-grade walnut stock and fore-end with 24 LPI checkering. Made in several styles including Classic, Target and Varmint. Many options and upgrades are available. From Dakota Arms.
Price: From **$5,590.00**

ROSSI SINGLE-SHOT SERIES
Calibers: .223 Rem., .243 Win., .44 Magnum. **Barrel:** 22 in. **Weight:** 6.25 lbs. **Stocks:** Black Synthetic Synthetic with recoil pad and removable cheek piece. **Sights:** Adjustable rear, fiber optic front, scope rail. Some models have scope rail only. **Features:** Single-shot break open, positive ejection, internal transfer bar mechanism, manual external safety, trigger block system, Taurus Security System, Matte blue finish.
Price: **$307.00**

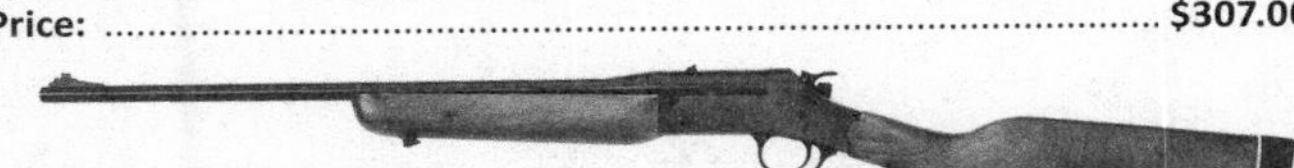

ROSSI MATCHED PAIRS
Gauges/Calibers: .410-bore or 20-gauge shotgun barrel with interchangeable rifle barrel in either .223 Rem., .243 Win. or .44 Mag. **Barrel:** 23 in. shotgun, 28 in. rifle. **Weights:** 5–6.3 lbs. **Stock:** Black synthetic. **Sights:** Bead front on shotgun barrel, fully adjustable front and rear on rifle barrel, top rail mounted for scope, fully adjustable fiber optic sights. **Features:** Single-shot break open, internal transfer bar mechanism, manual external safety, blue finish, trigger block system, Taurus Security System. Rimfire models are also available.
Price: **$352.00**

RUGER NO. 1 SERIES
This model is currently available only in select limited editions each year. For 2018 there are two chamberings offered — .450 Bushmaster and .450 Marlin. Features for the .450 Bushmaster model include a 20-in. stainless steel barrel with muzzle brake, no sights, and a black laminate stock. The .450 Marlin model has a 20-in. satin blue finish, blade sights, and an American walnut stock. Features common to most variants of the No. 1 include a falling block mechanism and under lever, sliding tang safety, integral scope mounts machined on the steel quarter rib, sporting-style recoil pad, grip cap and sling swivel studs.
Price: **$1,899.00**

SHILOH CO. SHARPS 1874 LONG RANGE EXPRESS
Calibers: .38-55, .40-50 BN, .40-70 BN, .40-90 BN, .40-70 ST, .40-90 ST, .45-70 Govt. ST, .45-90 ST, .45-110 ST, .50-70 ST, .50-90 ST. **Barrel:** 34-in. tapered octagon. **Weight:** 10.5 lbs. **Length:** 51 in. overall. **Stock:** Oil-finished walnut (upgrades available) with pistol grip, shotgun-style butt, traditional cheek rest, Schnabel fore-end. **Sights:** Customer's choice. **Features:** Re-creation of the Model 1874 Sharps rifle. Double-set triggers. Made in USA by Shiloh Rifle Mfg. Co.
Price: **$2,059.00**
Price: Sporter Rifle No. 1 (similar to above except with 30-in. barrel, blade front, buckhorn rear sight) **$2,059.00**
Price: Sporter Rifle No. 3 (similar to No. 1 except straight-grip stock, standard wood) **$1,949.00**

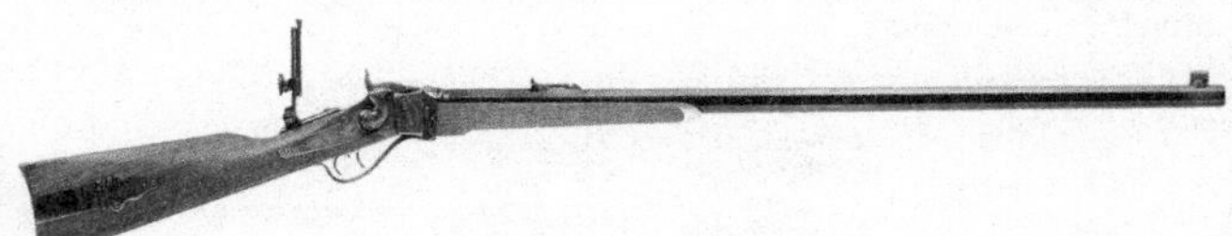

SHILOH CO. SHARPS 1874 QUIGLEY
Calibers: .45-70 Govt., .45-110. **Barrel:** 34-in. heavy octagon. **Stock:** Military-style with patch box, standard-grade American walnut. **Sights:** Semi-buckhorn, interchangeable front and midrange vernier tang sight with windage. **Features:** Gold inlay initials, pewter tip, Hartford collar, case color or antique finish. Double-set triggers.
Price: **$3,533.00**

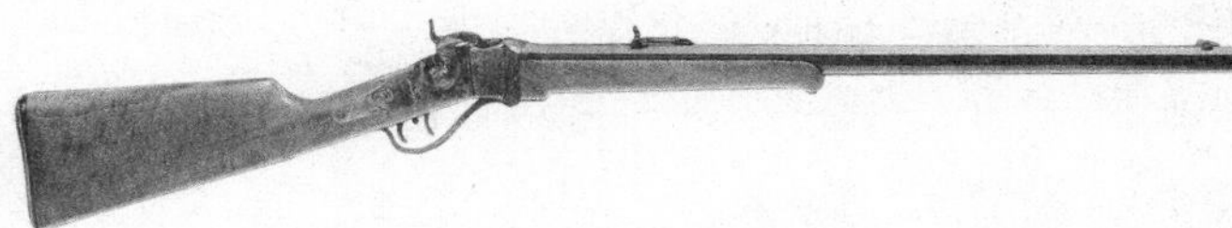

SHILOH CO. SHARPS 1874 SADDLE
Calibers: .38-55, .40-50 BN, .40-65 Win., .40-70 BN, .40-70 ST, .40-90 BN, .40-90 ST, .44-77 BN, .44-90 BN, .45-70 Govt. ST, .45-90 ST, .45-100 ST, .45-110 ST, .45-120 ST, .50-70 ST, .50-90 ST. **Barrels:** 26 in. full or half octagon. **Stock:** Semi-fancy American walnut. Shotgun style with cheek rest. **Sights:** Buckhorn and blade. **Features:** Double-set trigger, numerous custom features can be added.
Price: **$2,044.00**

SHILOH CO. SHARPS 1874 MONTANA ROUGHRIDER
Calibers: .38-55, .40-50 BN, .40-65 Win., .40-70 BN, .40-70 ST, .40-90 BN, .40-90 ST, .44-77 BN, .44-90 BN, .45-70 Govt. ST, .45-90 ST, .45-100 ST, .45-110 ST, .45-120 ST, .50-70 ST, .50-90 ST. **Barrels:** 30 in. full or half octagon. **Stock:** American walnut in shotgun or military style. **Sights:** Buckhorn and blade. **Features:** Double-set triggers, numerous custom features can be added.
Price: **$2,059.00**

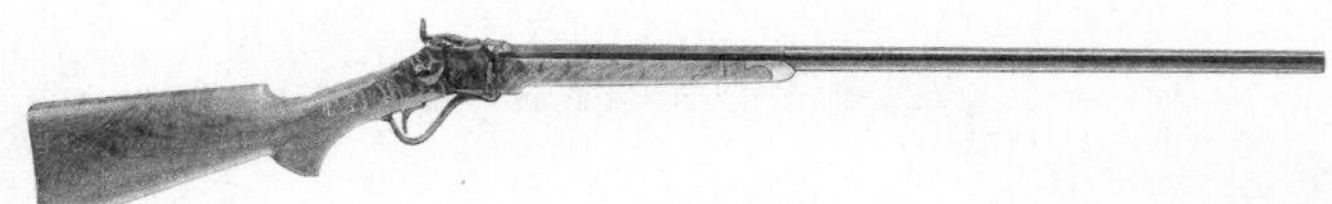

SHILOH CO. SHARPS CREEDMOOR TARGET
Calibers: .38-55, .40-50 BN, .40-65 Win., .40-70 BN, .40-70 ST, .40-90 BN, .40-90 ST, .44-77 BN, .44-90 BN, .45-70 Govt. ST, .45-90 ST, .45-100 ST, .45-110 ST, .45-120 ST, .50-70 ST, .50-90 ST. **Barrel:** 32 in. half round-half octagon. **Stock:** Extra fancy American walnut. Shotgun style with pistol grip. **Sights:** Customer's choice. **Features:** Single trigger, AA finish on stock, polished barrel and screws, pewter tip.
Price: **$3,105.00**

THOMPSON/CENTER ENCORE PRO HUNTER PREDATOR RIFLE
Calibers: .204 Ruger, .223 Remington, .22-250 and .308 Winchester. **Barrel:** 28-in. deep-fluted interchangeable. **Length:** 42.5 in. **Weight:** 7.75 lbs. **Stock:** Composite buttstock and fore-end with non-slip inserts in cheekpiece, pistol grip and fore-end. Realtree Advantage Max-1 camo finish overall. Scope is not included.
Price: **$882.00**

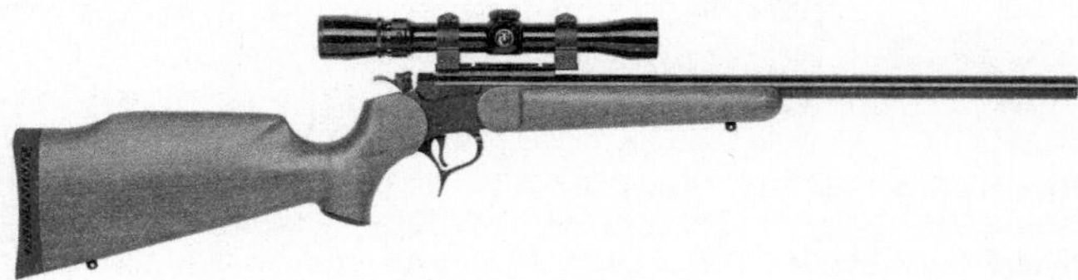

THOMPSON/CENTER G2 CONTENDER
Calibers: .204 Ruger, .223 Rem., 6.8 Rem. 7-30 Waters, .30-30 Win. **Barrel:** 23-in. interchangeable with blued finish. **Length:** 36.75 in. **Stock:** Walnut. **Sights:** None. Weight: 5.5 pounds. Reintroduced in 2015. Interchangeable barrels available in several centerfire and rimfire calibers.
Price: **$769.00**

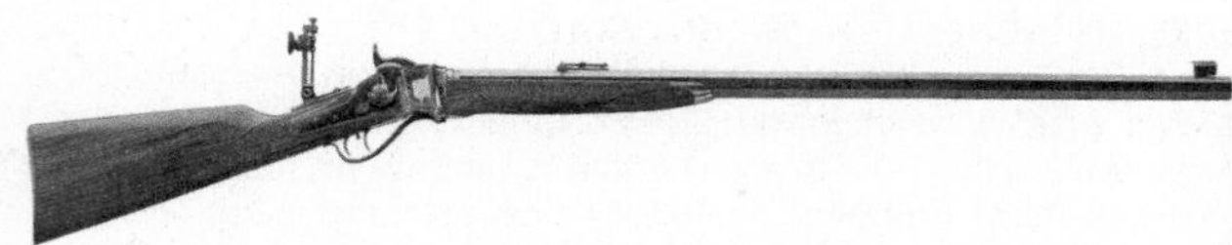

UBERTI 1874 SHARPS SPORTING
Caliber: .45-70 Govt. **Barrels:** 30 in., 32 in., 34 in. octagonal. **Weight:** 10.57 lbs. with 32 in. barrel. **Lengths:** 48.9 in. with 32 in. barrel. **Stock:** Walnut. **Sights:** Dovetail front, Vernier tang rear. **Features:** Cut checkering, case-colored finish on frame, buttplate, and lever. Imported by Stoeger Industries.
Price: Standard Sharps **$1,919.00**
Price: Special Sharps **$2,019.00**
Price: Deluxe Sharps **$3,269.00**
Price: Down Under Sharps **$2,719.00**
Price: Long Range Sharps **$2,719.00**
Price: Buffalo Hunter Sharps **$2,620.00**
Price: Sharps Cavalry Carbine **$2,020.00**
Price: Sharps Extra Deluxe **$5,400.00**
Price: Sharps Hunter **$1,699.00**

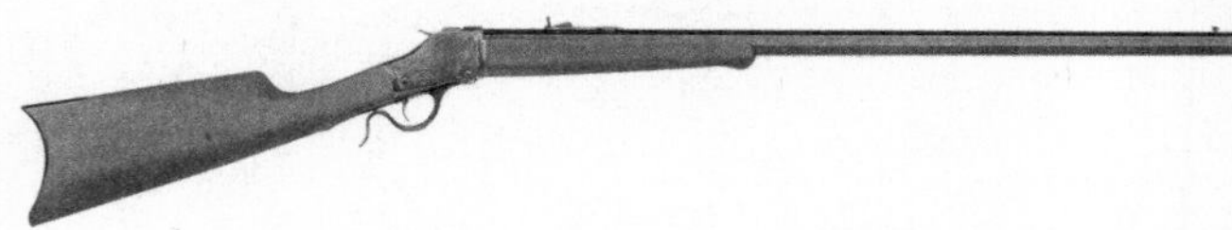

UBERTI 1885 HIGH-WALL SINGLE-SHOT
Calibers: .45-70 Govt., .45-90, .45-120. **Barrels:** 28–32 in. **Weights:** 9.3–9.9 lbs. **Lengths:** 44.5–47 in. overall. **Stock:** Walnut stock and fore-end. **Sights:** Blade front, fully adjustable open rear. **Features:** Based on Winchester High-Wall design by John Browning. Color casehardened frame and lever, blued barrel and buttplate. Imported by Stoeger Industries.
Price: From .... **$1,079.00–$1,279.00**

UBERTI SPRINGFIELD TRAPDOOR RIFLE/CARBINE
Caliber: .45-70 Govt., single shot **Barrel:** 22 or 32.5 in. **Features:** Blued steel receiver and barrel, casehardened breechblock and buttplate. **Sights:** Creedmoor style.
Price: Springfield Trapdoor Carbine, 22 in. barrel **$1,749.00**
Price: Springfield Trapdoor Army, 32.5 in. barrel **$2,019.00**

BAIKAL MP94 COMBO GUN
Calibers/Gauges: Over/under style with 12-gauge shotgun barrel over either a .223 or .308 rifle barrel. **Barrels:** 19.7 in. **Stock:** Checkered walnut. **Sights:** Adjustable rear, ramp front with bead. Picatinny or 11mm scope rail. **Features:** Four choke tubes for shotgun barrel. Double triggers. Made in Russia by Baikal and imported by U.S. Sporting Goods, Inc.
Price: **$790.00**

BAIKAL MP221 DOUBLE RIFLE
Calibers: .30-06 or .45-70 side-by-side double rifle. **Barrels:** 23.5 in. **Stock:** Checkered walnut. **Sights:** Adjustable rear, ramp front with bead. Picatinny or 11mm scope rail. **Features:** Double triggers, extractors, adjustable barrel regulation. Made in Russia by Baikal and imported by U.S. Sporting Goods Inc.
Price: **$1,155.00**

BERETTA S686/S689 O/U RIFLE SERIES
Calibers: .30-06, 9.3x74R. **Barrels:** 23 in. O/U boxlock action. Single or double triggers. EELL Grade has better wood, moderate engraving.
Price: .... **$4,200.00–$9,000.00**
Price: EELL Diamond Sable grade, From **$12,750.00**

BRNO MODEL 802 COMBO GUN
Calibers/Gauges: .243 Win., .308 or .30-06/12 ga. Over/Under. **Barrels:** 23.6 in. **Weight:** 7.6 lbs. **Length:** 41 in. **Stock:** European walnut. **Features:** Double trigger, shotgun barrel is improved-modified chokes. Imported by CZ USA.
Price: **$2,087.00**

BRNO EFFECT
Caliber: .30-06 Single Shot.......... **$1,585.00**

BRNO STOPPER
Caliber: .458 Win. Over/Under **$5,554.00**

FAUSTI CLASS EXPRESS
Calibers: .30-06, .30R Blaser, 8x57 JRS, 9.3x74R, .444 Marlin, .45-70 Govt. Over/Under. **Barrels:** 24 in. **Weight:** 7.5 lbs. **Length:** 41 in. **Stock:** Oil-finished Grade A walnut. Pistol grip, Bavarian or Classic. **Sights:** Folding leaf rear, fiber optic front adjustable for elevation. **Features:** Inertia single or double trigger, automatic ejectors. Made in Italy and imported by Fausti USA.
Price: **$4,990.00**
Price: SL Express w/hand engraving, AA wood.......... **$7,600.00**

HOENIG ROTARY ROUND ACTION DOUBLE
Calibers: Most popular calibers. Over/Under design. **Barrels:** 22–26 in. **Stock:** English Walnut; to customer specs. **Sights:** Swivel hood front with button release (extra bead stored in trap door grip cap), express-style rear on quarter-rib adjustable for windage and elevation; scope mount. **Features:** Round action opens by rotating barrels, pulling forward. Inertia extractor system, rotary safety blocks strikers. Single lever quick-detachable scope mount. Simple takedown without removing fore-end. Introduced 1997. Custom rifle made in USA by George Hoenig.
Price: From.......... **$22,500.00**

HOENIG ROTARY ROUND ACTION COMBINATION
Calibers: Most popular calibers and shotgun gauges. Over/Under design with rifle barrel atop shotgun barrel. **Barrel:** 26 in. **Weight:** 7 lbs. **Stock:** English Walnut to customer specs. **Sights:** Front ramp with button release blades. Foldable aperture tang sight windage and elevation adjustable. Quarter-rib with scope mount. **Features:** Round action opens by rotating barrels, pulling forward. Inertia extractor; rotary safety blocks strikers. Simple takedown without removing forend. Custom rifle made in USA by George Hoenig.
Price: From.......... **$27,500.00**

HOENIG VIERLING FOUR-BARREL COMBINATION
Calibers/gauges: Two 20-gauge shotgun barrels with one rifle barrel chambered for .22 Long Rifle and another for .223 Remington. Custom rifle made in USA by George Hoenig.
Price: **50,000.00**

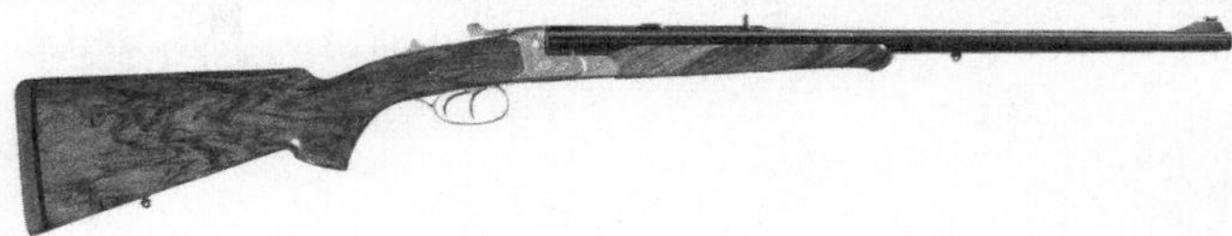

KRIEGHOFF CLASSIC DOUBLE
Calibers: 7x57R, 7x65R, .308 Win., .30-06, 8x57 JRS, 8x75RS, 9.3x74R, .375NE, .500/.416NE, .470NE, .500NE. **Barrel:** 23.5 in. **Weight:** 7.3–11 lbs. **Stock:** High grade European walnut. Standard model has conventional rounded cheekpiece, Bavaria model has Bavarian-style cheekpiece. **Sights:** Bead front with removable, adjustable wedge (.375 H&H and below), standing leaf rear on quarter-rib. **Features:** Boxlock action; double triggers; short opening angle for fast loading; quiet extractors; sliding, self-adjusting wedge for secure bolting; Purdey-style barrel extension; horizontal firing pin placement. Many options available. Introduced 1997. Imported from Germany by Krieghoff International.
Price: **$10,995.00**
Price: Engraved sideplates, add **$4,000.00**
Price: Extra set of rifle barrels, add.......... **$6,300.00**
Price: Extra set of 20-ga., 28 in. shotgun barrels, add.......... **$4,400.00**

KRIEGHOFF CLASSIC BIG FIVE DOUBLE RIFLE
Similar to the standard Classic except available in .375 H&H, .375 Flanged Mag. N.E., .416 Rigby, .458 Win., 500/416 NE, 470 NE, 500 NE. Has hinged front trigger, nonremovable muzzle wedge, Universal Trigger System, Combi Cocking Device, steel trigger guard, specially weighted stock bolt for weight and balance. Many options available. Introduced 1997. Imported from Germany by Krieghoff International.
Price: **$13,995.00**
Price: Engraved sideplates, add **$4,000.00**
Price: Extra set of 20-ga. shotgun barrels, add.......... **$5,000.00**
Price: Extra set of rifle barrels, add.......... **$6,300.00**

LEBEAU-COURALLY EXPRESS SXS
Calibers: 7x65R, 8x57JRS, 9.3x74R, .375 H&H, .470 N.E. **Barrel:** 24–26 in. **Weights:** 7.75–10.5 lbs. **Stock:** Fancy French walnut with cheekpiece. **Sights:** Bead on ramp front, standing left express rear on quarter-rib. **Features:** Holland & Holland-type sidelock with automatic ejectors; double triggers. Built to order only. Imported from Belgium by Wm. Larkin Moore and Griffin & Howe.
Price: **$45,000.00**

MERKEL BOXLOCK DOUBLE
Calibers: 5.6x52R, .243 Winchester, 6.5x55, 6.5x57R, 7x57R, 7x65R, .308 Win., .30-06, 8x57 IRS, 9.3x74R. **Barrel:** 23.6 in. **Weight:** 7.7 oz. **Length:** NA. **Stock:** Walnut, oil finished, pistol grip. **Sights:** Fixed 100 meter. **Features:** Anson & Deeley boxlock action with cocking indicators, double triggers, engraved color casehardened receiver. Introduced 1995. Imported from Germany by Merkel USA.
Price: Model 140-2, From Approx.......... **$13,000.00**
Price: Model 141 Small Frame SXS Rifle; built on smaller frame, chambered for 7mm Mauser, .30-06, or 9.3x74R From Approx.. .... **$11,000.00**
Price: Model 141 Engraved; fine hand-engraved hunting scenes on silvered receiver From Approx. **$13,500.00**

SAVAGE MODEL 42
Calibers/Gauges: Break-open over/under design with .22 LR or .22 WMR barrel over a .410 shotgun barrel. Under-lever operation. **Barrel:** 20 in. **Stock:** Synthetic black matte. **Weight:** 6.1 lbs. **Sights:** Adjustable rear, bead front. Updated variation of classic Stevens design from the 1940s.
Price **$485.00**

BROWNING BUCK MARK SEMI-AUTO

Caliber: .22 LR. **Capacity:** 10+1. **Action:** A rifle version of the Buck Mark Pistol; straight blowback action; machined aluminum receiver with integral rail scope mount; manual thumb safety. **Barrel:** Recessed crowns. **Stock:** Stock and forearm with full pistol grip. **Features:** Action lock provided. Introduced 2001. Four model name variations for 2006, as noted below. **Sights:** FLD Target, FLD Carbon, and Target models have integrated scope rails. Sporter has Truglo/Marble fiber-optic sights. Imported from Japan by Browning.

Price: FLD Target, 5.5 lbs., bull barrel, laminated stock **$720.00**
Price: Target, 5.4 lbs., blued bull barrel, wood stock **$700.00**
Price: Sporter, 4.4 lbs., blued sporter barrel w/sights **$700.00**

BROWNING SA-22 SEMI-AUTO 22

Caliber: .22 LR. **Capacity:** Tubular magazine in buttstock holds 11 rounds. **Barrel:** 19.375 in. **Weight:** 5 lbs. 3 oz. **Length:** 37 in. overall. **Stock:** Checkered select walnut with pistol grip and semi-beavertail fore-end. **Sights:** Gold bead front, folding leaf rear. **Features:** Engraved receiver with polished blue finish; crossbolt safety; easy takedown for carrying or storage. The Grade VI is available with either grayed or blued receiver with extensive engraving with gold-plated animals: right side pictures a fox and squirrel in a woodland scene; left side shows a beagle chasing a rabbit. On top is a portrait of the beagle. Stock and fore-end are of high-grade walnut with a double-bordered cut checkering design. Introduced 1956. Made in Belgium until 1974. Currently made in Japan by Miroku.

Price: Grade I, scroll-engraved blued receiver **$700.00**
Price: Grade VI BL, gold-plated engraved blued receiver **$1,580.00**

CITADEL M-1 CARBINE

Caliber: .22LR. **Capacity:** 10-round magazine. **Barrel:** 18 in. **Weight:** 4.8 lbs. **Length:** 35 in. **Stock:** Wood or synthetic in black or several camo patterns. **Features:** Built to the exacting specifications of the G.I. model used by U.S. infantrymen in both WWII theaters of battle and in Korea. Used by officers as well as tankers, drivers, artillery crews, mortar crews, and other personnel. Weight, barrel length and OAL are the same as the "United States Carbine, Caliber .30, M1," its official military designation. Made in Italy by Chiappa. Imported by Legacy Sports.

Price: Synthetic stock, black. **$316.00**
Price: Synthetic stock, camo. **$368.00**
Price: Wood stock. **$400.00**

CZ MODEL 512

Calibers: .22 LR/.22 WMR. **Capacity:** 5-round magazines. **Barrel:** 20.5 in. **Weight:** 5.9 lbs. **Length:** 39.3 in. **Stock:** Beech. **Sights:** Adjustable. **Features:** The modular design is easily maintained, requiring only a coin as a tool for field stripping. The action of the 512 is composed of an aluminum alloy upper receiver that secures the barrel and bolt assembly and a fiberglass reinforced polymer lower half that houses the trigger mechanism and detachable magazine. The 512 shares the same magazines and scope rings with the CZ 455 bolt-action rifle.

Price: .22 LR **$480.00**
Price: .22 WMR **$510.00**

H&K 416-22

Caliber: .22 LR. **Capacity:** 10- or 20-round magazine. **Features:** Blowback semi-auto rifle styled to resemble H&K 416 with metal upper and lower receivers; rail interface system; retractable stock; pistol grip with storage compartment; on-rail sights; rear sight adjustable for wind and elevation; 16.1-in. barrel. Also available in pistol version with 9-in. barrel. Made in Germany by Walther under license from Heckler & Koch and imported by Umarex.

Price: **$599.00**

H&K MP5 A5

Caliber: .22 LR. **Capacity:** 10- or 25-round magazine **Features:** Blowback semi-auto rifle styled to resemble H&K MP5 with metal receiver; compensator; bolt catch; NAVY pistol grip; on-rail sights; rear sight adjustable for wind and elevation; 16.1-in. barrel. Also available in pistol version with 9-in. barrel. Also available with SD-type fore-end. Made in Germany by Walther under license from Heckler & Koch. Imported by Umarex.

Price: **$499.00**
Price: MP5 SD.. **$599.00**

HENRY U.S. SURVIVAL AR-7 22

Caliber: .22 LR. **Capacity:** 8-shot magazine. **Barrel:** 16 in. steel lined. **Weight:** 2.25 lbs. **Stock:** ABS plastic. **Sights:** Blade front on ramp, aperture rear. **Features:** Takedown design stores barrel and action in hollow stock. Light enough to float on water. Dark gray or camo finish. Comes with two magazines. Introduced 1998. From Henry Repeating Arms Co.

Price: H002B Black finish **$290.00**
Price: H002C Camo finish **$350.00**

KEL-TEC SU-22CA

Caliber: .22 LR. **Capacity:** 26-round magazine. **Barrel:** 16.1 in. **Weight:** 4 lbs. **Length:** 34 in. **Features:** Blowback action, crossbolt safety, adjustable front and rear sights with integral picatinny rail. Threaded muzzle.

Price: **$547.00**

Prices given are believed to be accurate at time of publication however, many factors affect retail pricing so exact prices are not possible.

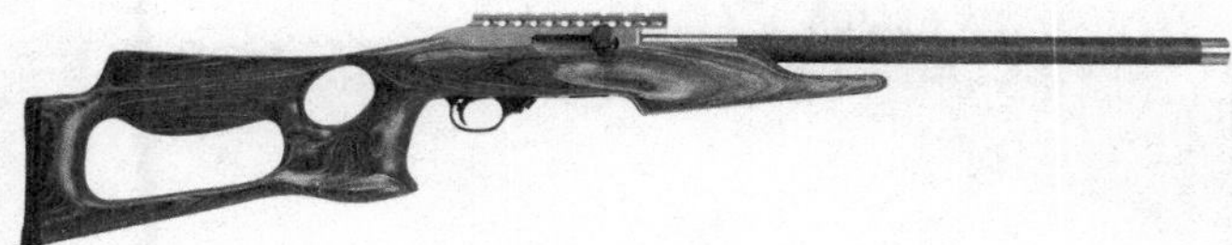

MAGNUM RESEARCH MLR22 SERIES

Calibers: .22 WMR or .22 LR. **Capacity:** 10-shot magazine. **Barrel:** 17 in. graphite. **Weight:** 4.45 lbs. **Length:** 35.5 in. overall. **Stock:** Hogue OverMolded synthetic or Laminated Thumbhole (Barracuda model). **Sights:** Integral scope base. **Features:** French grey anodizing, match bolt, target trigger. .22 LR rifles use factory Ruger 10/22 magazines. 4-5 lbs. average trigger pull. Barracuda model has Laminated Thumbhole stock, 19-in. barrel. Introduced: 2007. From Magnum Research, Inc.

Price: .22 LR Hogue OverMolded stock **$669.00**
Price: .22 LR Barracuda w/Thumbhole stock **$819.00**
Price: .22 WMR Hogue OverMolded stock **$791.00**
Price: .22 WMR Barracuda w/Thumbhole stock **$935.00**

MARLIN MODEL 60

Caliber: .22 LR. **Capacity:** 14-round tubular magazine. **Barrel:** 19 in. round tapered. **Weight:** About 5.5 lbs. **Length:** 37.5 in. overall. **Stock:** Press-checkered, laminated Maine birch with Monte Carlo, full pistol grip; black synthetic or Realtree Camo. **Sights:** Ramp front, open adjustable rear. Matted receiver is grooved for scope mount. **Features:** Last-shot bolt hold-open. Available with factory mounted 4x scope.

Price: Laminate **$209.00**
Price: Model 60C camo **$246.00**
Price: Synthetic **$201.00**

MARLIN MODEL 60SS SELF-LOADING RIFLE

Same as the Model 60 except breech bolt, barrel and outer magazine tube are made of stainless steel; most other parts are either nickel-plated or coated to match the stainless finish. Monte Carlo stock is of black/gray Maine birch laminate, and has nickel-plated swivel studs, rubber buttpad. Introduced 1993.

Price: **$315.00**

MARLIN 70PSS PAPOOSE STAINLESS

Caliber: .22 LR. **Capacity:** 7-shot magazine. **Barrel:** 16.25 in. stainless steel, Micro-Groove rifling. **Weight:** 3.25 lbs. **Length:** 35.25 in. overall. **Stock:** Black fiberglass-filled synthetic with abbreviated fore-end, nickel-plated swivel studs, molded-in checkering. **Sights:** Ramp front with orange post, cut-away Wide Scan hood; adjustable open rear. Receiver grooved for scope mounting. **Features:** Takedown barrel; crossbolt safety; manual bolt hold-open; last shot bolt hold-open; comes with padded carrying case. Introduced 1986. Made in USA by Marlin.

Price: **$345.00**

MARLIN MODEL 795

Caliber: .22. **Capacity:** 10-round magazine. **Barrel:** 18 in. with 16-groove Micro-Groove rifling. **Sights:** Ramp front sight, adjustable rear. Receiver grooved for scope mount. **Stock:** Black synthetic, hardwood, synthetic thumbhole, solid pink, pink camo, or Mossy Oak New Break-up camo finish. **Features:** Last shot hold-open feature. Introduced 1997. SS is similar to Model 795 except stainless steel barrel. Most other parts nickel-plated. Adjustable folding semi-buckhorn rear sights, ramp front high-visibility post and removable cutaway wide scan hood. Made in USA by Marlin Firearms Co.

Price: **$183.00**
Price: Stainless **$262.00**

MOSSBERG BLAZE SERIES

Caliber: .22 LR. **Capacities:** 10 or 25 rounds. **Barrel:** 16.5 in. **Sights:** Adjustable. **Weights:** 3.5–4.75 lbs. **Features:** A series of lightweight polymer rifles with several finish options and styles. Green Dot Combo model has Dead Ringer greet dot sight. Blaze 47 has AK-profile with adjustable fiber optic rear and raised front sight, ambidextrous safety, and a choice of wood or synthetic stock.

Price: **$196.00**
Price: Muddy Girl camo **$262.00**
Price: Wildfire camo **$262.00**
Price: Kryptek Highlander camo **$283.00**
Price: Blaze 47 synthetic stock **$346.00**
Price: Blaze 47 wood stock **$397.00**

MOSSBERG MODEL 702 PLINKSTER

Caliber: .22 LR. **Capacity:** 10-round magazine. **Barrel:** 18 in. free-floating. **Weights:** 4.1–4.6 lbs. **Sights:** Adjustable rifle. Receiver grooved for scope mount. **Stock:** Wood or black synthetic. **Features:** Ergonomically placed magazine release and safety buttons, crossbolt safety, free gun lock. Made in USA by O.F. Mossberg & Sons, Inc.

Price: From **$190.00**

MOSSBERG MODEL 715T SERIES

Caliber: .22 LR. **Capacity:** 10- or 25-round magazine. **Barrel:** 16.25 or 18 in. with A2-style muzzle brake. **Weight:** 5.5 lbs. **Features:** AR style offered in several models. Flattop or A2 style carry handle.

Price: Black finish **$375.00**
Price: Muddy Girl camo **$430.00**

REMINGTON MODEL 552 BDL DELUXE SPEEDMASTER

Calibers: .22 Short (20 rounds), Long (17) or LR (15) tubular magazine. **Barrel:** 21-in. round tapered. **Weight:** 5.75 lbs. **Length:** 40 in. overall. **Stock:** Walnut. Checkered grip and fore-end. **Sights:** Adjustable rear, ramp front. **Features:** Positive crossbolt safety in trigger guard, receiver grooved for tip-off mount. Operates with .22 Short, Long or Long Rifle cartridges. Classic design introduced in 1957.

Price: **$707.00**

REMINGTON 597

Calibers: .22 LR, 10 rounds; or .22 WMR, 8 rounds. **Barrel:** 20 in. **Weight:** 5.5 lbs. **Length:** 40 in. overall. **Stock:** Black synthetic or camo coverage in several patterns. TVP has laminated, contoured thumbhole stock. **Sights:** Big game. **Features:** Matte black metal finish or stainless, nickel-plated bolt. Receiver is grooved and drilled and tapped for scope mounts. Introduced 1997. Made in USA by Remington.

Price: Standard model, synthetic stock **$213.00**
Price: Synthetic w/Scope **$257.00**
Price: Camo from **$306.00**

RUGER 10/22 AUTOLOADING CARBINE

Caliber: .22 LR. **Capacity:** 10-round rotary magazine. **Barrel:** 18.5 in. round tapered (16.12 in. compact model). **Weight:** 5 lbs. (4.5, compact). **Length:** 37.25 in., 34 in. (compact) overall. **Stock:** American hardwood with pistol grip and barrel band, or synthetic. **Sights:** Brass bead front, folding leaf rear adjustable for elevation. **Features:** Available with satin black or stainless finish on receiver and barrel. Detachable rotary magazine fits flush into stock, crossbolt safety, receiver tapped and grooved for scope blocks or tip-off mount. Scope base adaptor furnished with each rifle. Made in USA by Sturm, Ruger & Co.

Price: Wood stock **$309.00**
Price: Synthetic stock **$309.00**
Price: Stainless, synthetic stock **$339.00**
Price: Compact model, fiber-optic front sight **$359.00**

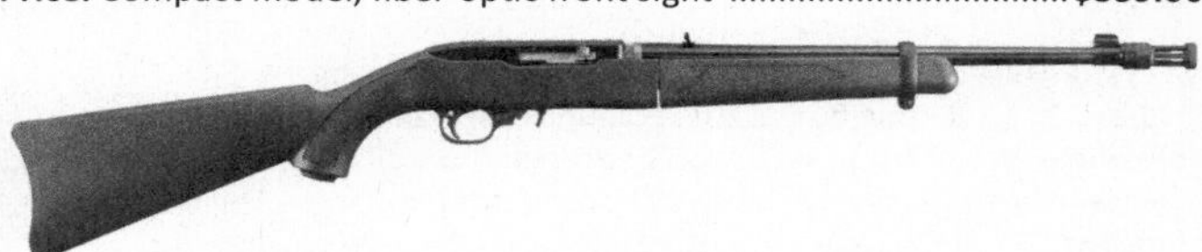

RUGER 10/22 TAKEDOWN RIFLE

Caliber: .22 LR. **Capacity:** 10-round rotary magazine. **Barrels:** 18.5 in. stainless, or 16.6 in. satin black threaded with suppressor. Easy takedown feature enables quick separation of the barrel from the action by way of a recessed locking lever, for ease of transportation and storage. **Stock:** Black synthetic. **Sights:** Adjustable rear, gold bead front. **Weight:** 4.66 pounds. Comes with backpack carrying bag.

Price: Stainless **$439.00**
Price: Satin black w/flash suppressor **$459.00**
Price: Threaded barrel **$629.00**
Price: With Silent-SR suppressor **$1,078.00**

RUGER 10/22 SPORTER

Same specifications as 10/22 Carbine except has American walnut stock with hand-checkered pistol grip and fore-end, straight buttplate, sling swivels, 18.9-in. barrel, and no barrel band.

Price: **$419.00**

RUGER 10/22-T TARGET RIFLE

Similar to the 10/22 except has 20-in. heavy, hammer-forged barrel with tight chamber dimensions, improved trigger pull. **Weight:** 7.5 lbs. **Stock:** Black or brown laminated hardwood, dimensioned for optical sights. No iron sights supplied. Introduced 1996.

Price: From **$550.00**
Price: Stainless from **$589.00**

RUGER SR-22 RIFLE

AR-style semiauto rifle chambered in .22 LR, based on 10/22 action. Features include all-aluminum chassis replicating the AR-platform dimensions between the sighting plane, buttstock height and grip; Picatinny rail optic mount includes a six-position, telescoping M4-style buttstock (on a Mil-Spec diameter tube); Hogue Monogrip pistol grip; buttstocks and grips interchangeable with any AR-style compatible option; round, mid-length handguard mounted on a standard-thread AR-style barrel nut; precision-rifled, cold hammer forged 16.125-in. alloy steel barrel capped with an SR-556/Mini-14 flash suppressor.

Price: **$709.00**

SAVAGE A17 SERIES

Calibers: .17 HMR, .22 WMR. **Capacity:** 10-round rotary magazine. **Barrel:** 22 in. **Weight:** 5.4–5.6 lbs. **Features:** Delayed blowback action, Savage AccuTrigger, synthetic or laminated stock. Target model has heavy barrel, sporter or thumbhole stock. Also available in .22 WMR (A22 Model.) Introduced in 2016.

Price: Standard model **$473.00**
Price: Sporter (Gray laminate stock) **$574.00**
Price: Target Sporter **$571.00**
Price: Target Thumbhole **$631.00**
Price: A22 .22 WMR **$465.00**

SAVAGE MODEL 64G

Caliber: .22 LR. **Capacity:** 10-round magazine. **Barrels:** 20 in., 21 in. **Weight:** 5.5 lbs. **Lengths:** 40 in., 41 in. **Stock:** Walnut-finished hardwood with Monte Carlo-type comb, checkered grip and fore-end. **Sights:** Bead front, open adjustable rear. Receiver grooved for scope mounting. **Features:** Thumb-operated rotating safety. Blue finish. 64 SS has stainless finish. Side ejection, bolt hold-open device. Introduced 1990. Made in Canada, from Savage Arms.

Price: 64 G **$221.00**
Price: 64 F **$175.00**
Price: 64 FSS **$264.00**
Price: 64 TR-SR **$360.00**

SMITH & WESSON M&P15-22 SERIES

Caliber: .22 LR. **Capacities:** 10- or 25-round magazine. **Barrel:** 15.5 in., 16 in. or 16.5 in. **Stock:** 6-position telescoping or fixed. **Features:** A rimfire version of AR-derived M&P tactical autoloader. Operates with blowback action. Quad-mount Picatinny rails, plain barrel or compensator, alloy upper and lower, matte black metal finish. Kryptek Highlander or Muddy Girl camo finishes available.

Price: Standard **$449.00**
Price: Kryptek Highlander or Muddy Girl camo **$499.00**
Price: MOE Model with Magpul sights, stock and grip **$609.00**
Price: Performance Center upgrades, threaded barrel **$789.00**

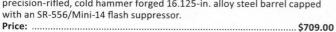

BROWNING BL-22

Caliber: .22 LR. **Capacity:** Tubular magazines, 15+1. **Action:** Short-throw lever action, side ejection. Rack-and-pinion lever. **Barrel:** Recessed muzzle. **Stock:** Walnut, two-piece straight-grip Western style. **Trigger:** Half-cock hammer safety; fold-down hammer. **Sights:** Bead post front, folding-leaf rear. Steel receiver grooved for scope mount. **Weight:** 5–5.4 lbs. **Length:** 36.75–40.75 in. overall. **Features:** Action lock provided. Introduced 1996. FLD Grade II Octagon has octagonal 24-in. barrel, silver nitride receiver with scroll engraving, gold-colored trigger. FLD Grade I has satin-nickel receiver, blued trigger, no stock checkering. FLD Grade II has satin-nickel receivers with scroll engraving; gold-colored trigger, cut checkering. Both introduced 2005. Grade I has blued receiver and trigger, no stock checkering. Grade II has gold-colored trigger, cut checkering, blued receiver with scroll engraving. Imported from Japan by Browning.

Price: BL-22 Grade I/II, From .... **$620.00–$700.00**
Price: BL-22 FLD Grade I/II, From .... **$660.00–$750.00**
Price: BL-22 FLD, Grade II Octagon **$980.00**

HENRY LEVER-ACTION RIFLES

Caliber: .22 Long Rifle (15 shot), .22 Magnum (11 shots), .17 HMR (11 shots). **Barrel:** 18.25 in. round. **Weight:** 5.5–5.75 lbs. **Length:** 34 in. overall (.22 LR). **Stock:** Walnut. **Sights:** Hooded blade front, open adjustable rear. **Features:** Polished blue finish; full-length tubular magazine; side ejection; receiver grooved for scope mounting. Introduced 1997. Made in USA by Henry Repeating Arms Co.

Price: H001 Carbine .22 LR **$360.00**
Price: H001L Carbine .22 LR, Large Loop Lever **$375.00**
Price: H001Y Youth model (33 in. overall, 11-round .22 LR) **$360.00**
Price: H001M .22 Magnum, 19.25 in. octagonal barrel, deluxe walnut stock **$500.00**
Price: H001V .17 HMR, 20 in. octagonal barrel, Williams Fire Sights **$500.00**

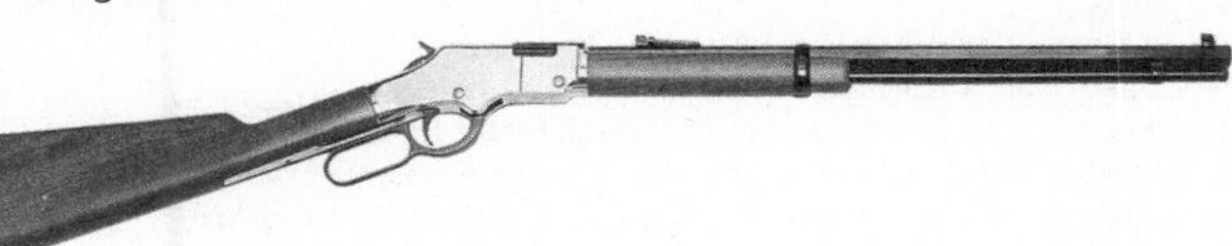

HENRY LEVER-ACTION OCTAGON FRONTIER MODEL

Same as lever rifles except chambered in .17 HMR, .22 Short/Long/LR, .22 Magnum. **Barrel:** 20 in. octagonal. **Sights:** Marble's fully adjustable semi-buckhorn rear, brass bead front. **Weight:** 6.25 lbs. Made in USA by Henry Repeating Arms Co.

Price: H001T Lever Octagon **$450.00**
Price: H001TM Lever Octagon .22 Magnum **$550.00**

HENRY GOLDEN BOY SERIES

Calibers: .17 HMR, .22 LR (16-shot), .22 Magnum. **Barrel:** 20 in. octagonal. **Weight:** 6.25 lbs. **Length:** 38 in. overall. **Stock:** American walnut. **Sights:** Blade front, open rear. **Features:** Brasslite receiver, brass buttplate, blued barrel and lever. Introduced 1998. Made in USA from Henry Repeating Arms Co.

Price: H004 .22 LR **$550.00**
Price: H004M .22 Magnum **$595.00**
Price: H004V .17 HMR **$615.00**
Price: H004DD .22 LR Deluxe, engraved receiver **$1,585.00**

HENRY SILVER BOY

Calibers: 17 HMR, .22 S/L/LR, .22 WMR. **Capacities:** Tubular magazine. 12 rounds (.17 HMR and .22 WMR), 16 rounds (.22 LR), 21 rounds (.22 Short). **Barrel:** 20 in. **Stock:** American walnut with curved buttplate. **Finish:** Nickel receiver, barrel band and buttplate. **Sights:** Adjustable buckhorn rear, bead front. Silver Eagle model has engraved scroll pattern from early original Henry rifle. Offered in same calibers as Silver Boy. Made in USA from Henry Repeating Arms Company.

Price: .22 S/L/LR **$600.00**
Price: .22 WMR **$650.00**
Price: .17 HMR **$675.00**
Price: Silver Eagle .... **$850.00–$900.00**

HENRY PUMP ACTION

Caliber: .22 LR. **Capacity:** 15 rounds. **Barrel:** 18.25 in. **Weight:** 5.5 lbs. **Length:** NA. **Stock:** American walnut. **Sights:** Bead on ramp front, open adjustable rear. **Features:** Polished blue finish; receiver grooved for scope mount; grooved slide handle; two barrel bands. Introduced 1998. Made in USA from Henry Repeating Arms Co.

Price: H003T .22 LR **$550.00**
Price: H003TM .22 Magnum **$595.00**

MOSSBERG MODEL 464 RIMFIRE

Caliber: .22 LR. **Capacity:** 14-round tubular magazine. **Barrel:** 20-in. round blued. **Weight:** 5.6 lbs. **Length:** 35.75 in. overall. **Features:** Adjustable sights, straight grip stock, plain hardwood straight stock and fore-end. Lever-action model.

Price: **$485.00**

REMINGTON 572 BDL DELUXE FIELDMASTER PUMP

Calibers: .22 Short (20), .22 Long (17) or .22 LR (15), tubular magazine. **Barrel:** 21 in. round tapered. **Weight:** 5.5 lbs. **Length:** 40 in. overall. **Stock:** Walnut with checkered pistol grip and slide handle. **Sights:** Big game. **Features:** Crossbolt safety; removing inner magazine tube converts rifle to single shot; receiver grooved for tip-off scope mount. Another classic rimfire, this model has been in production since 1955.

Price: **$723.00**

ANSCHUTZ MODEL 64 MP

Caliber: .22 LR. **Capacity:** 5-round magazine. **Barrel:** 25.6-in. heavy match. **Weight:** 9 lbs. **Stock:** Multipurpose hardwood with beavertail fore-end. **Sights:** None. Drilled and tapped for scope or receiver sights. **Features:** Model 64S BR (benchrest) has 20-in. heavy barrel, adjustable two-stage match-grade trigger, flat beavertail stock. Imported from Germany by Steyr Arms.

Price: **$1,399.00**
Price: Model 64 S BR.......... **$1,539.00**

ANSCHUTZ 1416D/1516D CLASSIC

Calibers: .22 LR (1416D888), .22 WMR (1516D). **Capacity:** 5-round magazine. **Barrel:** 22.5 in. **Weight:** 6 lbs. **Length:** 41 in. overall. **Stock:** European hardwood with walnut finish; classic style with straight comb, checkered pistol grip and fore-end. **Sights:** Hooded ramp front, folding leaf rear. **Features:** Uses Match 64 action. Adjustable single-stage trigger. Receiver grooved for scope mounting. Imported from Germany by Steyr Arms.

Price: 1416D KL, .22 LR **$1,099.00**
Price: 1416D KL Classic left-hand **$1,199.00**
Price: 1516D KL, .22 WMR.......... **$1,169.00**
Price: 1416D, thumbhole stock **$1,599.00**

ANSCHUTZ 1710D CUSTOM

Caliber:.22 LR. **Capacity:** 5-round magazine. **Barrels:** 23.75- or 24.25-in. heavy contour. **Weights:** 6.5–7.375 lbs. **Length:** 42.5 in. overall. **Stock:** Select European walnut. **Sights:** Hooded ramp front, folding leaf rear; drilled and tapped for scope mounting. **Features:** Match 54 action with adjustable single-stage trigger; roll-over Monte Carlo cheekpiece, slim fore-end with Schnabel tip, Wundhammer palm swell on pistol grip, rosewood grip cap with white diamond insert; skip-line checkering on grip and fore-end. Introduced 1988. Imported from Germany by Steyr Arms.

Price: From.......... **$2,195.00**
Price: Meistergrade w/high grade walnut stock.......... **$2,595.00**

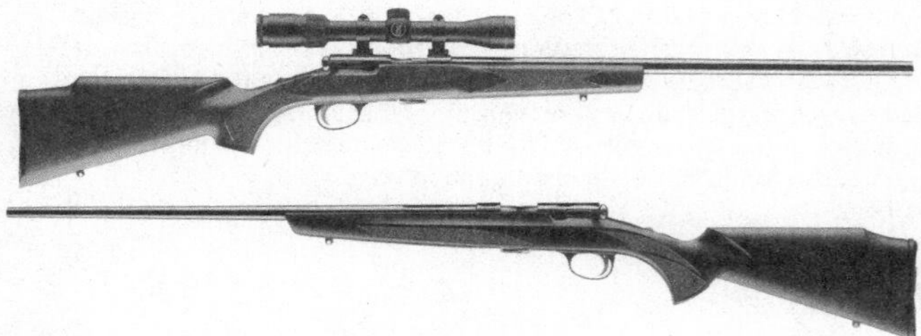

BROWNING T-BOLT RIMFIRE

Calibers: .22 LR, .17 HMR, .22 WMR. **Capacity:** 10-round rotary box double helix magazine. **Barrel:** 22-in. free-floating, semi-match chamber, target muzzle crown. **Weight:** 4.8 lbs. **Length:** 40.1 in. overall. **Stock:** Walnut, maple or composite. **Sights:** None. **Features:** Straight-pull bolt action, three-lever trigger adjustable for pull weight, dual action screws, sling swivel studs. Crossbolt lockup, enlarged bolt handle, one-piece dual extractor with integral spring and red cocking indicator band, gold-tone trigger. Top-tang, thumb-operated two-position safety, drilled and tapped for scope mounts. Varmint model has raised Monte Carlo comb, heavy barrel, wide forearm. Introduced 2006. Imported from Japan by Browning. Left-hand models added in 2009.

Price: .22 LR, From.......... **$750.00–$780.00**
Price: Composite Target .... **$780.00–$800.00**
Price: .17 HMR/.22 WMR, From .... **$790.00–$830.00**

COOPER MODEL 57-M REPEATER

Calibers: .22 LR, .22 WMR, .17 HMR, .17 Mach. **Barrel:** 22 in. or 24 in. **Weight:** 6.5–7.5 lbs. **Stock:** Claro walnut, 22 LPI hand checkering. **Sights:** None furnished. **Features:** Three rear locking lug, repeating bolt-action with 5-round magazine for .22 LR; 4-round magazine for .22 WMR and 17 HMR. Fully adjustable trigger. Left-hand models add $150 to base rifle price. 0.250-in. group rimfire accuracy guarantee at 50 yards; 0.5-in. group centerfire accuracy guarantee at 100 yards. Options include wood upgrades, case-color metalwork, barrel fluting, custom LOP, and many others.

Price: Classic **$2,295.00**
Price: Custom Classic.......... **$2,695.00**
Price: Western Classic **$3,455.00**
Price: Schnabel **$2,455.00**
Price: Jackson Squirrel.......... **$2,395.00**
Price: Jackson Hunter **$2,255.00**
Price: Mannlicher **$4,395.00**

CZ 452 AMERICAN

Similar to the CZ 452 M 2E Lux except has classic-style stock of Circassian walnut; 22.5-in. free-floating barrel with recessed target crown; receiver dovetail for scope mounting. No open sights furnished. Introduced 1999. Imported from the Czech Republic by CZ-USA.

Price: .22 LR, .22 WMR **$463.00**
Price: Scout/Youth model w/16 in. barrel.......... **$312.00**

CZ 455 AMERICAN

Calibers: .17 HMR, .22 LR, .22 WMR. **Capacity:** 5-round magazine. **Barrel:** 20.5 in. **Weight:** 6.1 lbs. **Length:** 38.2 in. **Stock:** Walnut. **Sights:** None. Integral 11mm dovetail scope base. **Features:** Adjustable trigger. Six versions available including blue laminate with thumbhole stock, Varmint model with 0.866-in. heavy barrel, full-length Mannlicher walnut stock, and others. American Combo Package includes interchangeable barrel to switch calibers.

Price: From .... **$421.00–$565.00**

DAVEY CRICKETT SINGLE SHOT

Calibers: .22 LR, .22 WMR, single-shot. **Barrel:** 16.125 in. **Weight:** About 2.5 lbs. **Length:** 30 in. overall. **Stock:** American walnut. **Sights:** Post on ramp front, peep rear adjustable for windage and elevation. **Features:** Drilled and tapped for scope mounting using special Chipmunk base. Engraved model also available. Made in USA Introduced 1982. Formerly Chipmunk model. From Keystone Sporting Arms.

Price: From.......... **$171.00**

HENRY MINI BOLT YOUTH RIFLE

Caliber: .22 LR, single-shot youth gun. **Barrel:** 16 in. stainless, 8-groove rifling. **Weight:** 3.25 lbs. **Length:** 30 in., LOP 11.5 in. **Stock:** Synthetic, pistol grip, wraparound checkering and beavertail forearm. Available in black finish or bright colors. **Sights:** William Fire sights. **Features:** One-piece bolt configuration manually operated safety.

Price: **$275.00**

Prices given are believed to be accurate at time of publication however, many factors affect retail pricing so exact prices are not possible.

MARLIN MODEL XT-17 SERIES

Caliber: .17 HRM. **Capacity:** 4- and 7-round, two magazines included. **Barrel:** 22 in. **Weight:** 6 lbs. **Stock:** Black synthetic with palm swell, stippled grip areas, or walnut-finished hardwood with Monte Carlo comb. Laminated stock available. **Sights:** Adjustable rear, ramp front. Drilled and tapped for scope mounts. **Features:** Adjustable trigger. Blue or stainless finish.

Price: .... **$269.00–$429.00**

MARLIN MODEL XT-22 SERIES

Calibers: .22 Short, .22 Long, .22 LR. **Capacities:** Available with 7-shot detachable box magazine or tubular magazine (17 to 22 rounds). **Barrels:** 22 in. Varmint model has heavy barrel. **Weight:** 6 lbs. **Stock:** Black synthetic, walnut-finished hardwood, walnut or camo. Tubular model available with two-tone brown laminated stock. **Finish:** Blued or stainless. **Sights:** Adjustable rear, ramp front. Some models have folding rear sight with a hooded or high-visibility orange front sight. **Features:** Pro-Fire Adjustable Trigger, Micro-Groove rifling, thumb safety with red cocking indicator. The XT-22M series is chambered for .22 WMR. Made in USA by Marlin Firearms Co.

Price: From .... **$221.00–$340.00**

Price: XT-22M .... **$240.00–$270.00**

MEACHAM LOW-WALL

Calibers: Any rimfire cartridge. **Barrels:** 26–34 in. **Weight:** 7-15 lbs. **Sights:** none. Tang drilled for Win. base, .375 in. dovetail slot front. **Stock:** Fancy eastern walnut with cheekpiece; ebony insert in forearm tip. **Features:** Exact copy of 1885 Winchester. With most Winchester factory options available including double-set triggers. Introduced 1994. Made in USA by Meacham T&H Inc.

Price: From.. **$4,999.00**

MOSSBERG MODEL 817

Caliber: .17 HMR. **Capacity:** 5-round magazine. **Barrel:** 21-in. free-floating bull barrel, recessed muzzle crown. **Weight:** 4.9 lbs. (black synthetic), 5.2 lbs. (wood). **Stock:** Black synthetic or wood; length of pull, 14.25 in. **Sights:** Factory-installed Weaver-style scope bases. **Features:** Blued or brushed chrome metal finishes, crossbolt safety, gun lock. Introduced 2008. Made in USA by O.F. Mossberg & Sons, Inc.

Price: .... **$212.00–$253.00**

MOSSBERG MODEL 801/802

Caliber: .22 LR **Capacity:** 10-round magazine. **Barrel:** 18 in. free-floating. Varmint model has 21-in. heavy barrel. **Weight:** 4.1–4.6 lbs. **Sights:** Adjustable rifle. Receiver grooved for scope mount. **Stock:** Black synthetic. **Features:** Ergonomically placed magazine release and safety buttons, crossbolt safety, free gun lock. 801 Half Pint has 12.25-in. LOP, 16-in. barrel and weighs 4 lbs. Hardwood stock; removable magazine plug.

Price: Plinkster.. **$223.00**

Price: Half Pint.. **$223.00**

Price: Varmint.. **$223.00**

NEW ULTRA LIGHT ARMS 20RF

Caliber: .22 LR, single-shot or repeater. **Barrel:** Douglas, length to order. **Weight:** 5.25 lbs. **Length:** Varies. **Stock:** Kevlar/graphite composite, variety of finishes. **Sights:** None furnished; drilled and tapped for scope mount. **Features:** Timney trigger, hand-lapped action, button-rifled barrel, hand-bedded action, recoil pad, sling-swivel studs, optional Jewell trigger. Made in USA by New Ultra Light Arms.

Price: 20 RF single shot.. **$1,800.00**

Price: 20 RF repeater **$1,850.00**

ROSSI MATCHED PAIR SINGLE-SHOT/SHOTGUN

Calibers/Gauges: .17 HMR rifle with interchangeable 12- or 20-gauge shotgun barrel. **Barrels:** 23 in. (rifle), 28 in. (shotgun). **Weights:** 5.25–6.25 lbs. **Stock:** Hardwood (brown or black finish). **Sights:** Fully adjustable front and rear. **Features:** Break-open breech, transfer-bar manual safety. Youth Model has .17 HMR or .22 LR rifle barrel with interchangeable .410 shotgun. Introduced 2001. Imported by BrazTech International.

Price: From.. **$298.00**

Price: Youth Model, From **$245.00**

RUGER AMERICAN RIMFIRE RIFLE

Calibers: .17 HMR, .22 LR,.22 WMR. **Capacity:** 10-round rotary magazine. **Barrels:** 22-in., or 18-in. threaded. **Sights:** Williams fiber optic, adjustable. **Stock:** Composite with interchangeable comb adjustments, sling swivels. Adjustable trigger.

Price: **$359.00**

Price: With Silent R Suppressor.. **$449.00**

RUGER 77/22 RIMFIRE

Calibers: .22 LR, .22 WMR. **Capacities:** .22 LR, 10-shot magazine; .22 WMR, 9-shot magazine. **Barrels:** 20 in. or 24 in. (stainless model only). **Weights:** 6.0–6.5 lbs. (20 in. bbl.); 7.5 lbs. (24 in. bbl.). **Length:** 39.25 in. overall (20 in. bbl.). **Stock:** Checkered American walnut or synthetic, stainless sling swivels. **Sights:** Plain barrel with integral scope mounting system complete with 1-in. Ruger rings. **Features:** Mauser-type action uses Ruger's famous rotary magazine. Three-position safety, simplified bolt stop, patented bolt-locking system. Uses the dual-screw barrel attachment system of the 10/22 rifle.

Price: Blue finish w/walnut or synthetic stock.. **$979.00**

Price: Stainless steel w/walnut stock **$1,069.00**

RUGER 77/17 RIMFIRE

Caliber: .17 HMR. **Capacity:** 9-round rotary magazine. **Barrels:** 22–24 in. **Weights:** 6.5–7.5 lbs. **Length:** 41.25–43.25 in. overall. **Stock:** Checkered American walnut, laminated hardwood; stainless sling swivels. **Sights:** None. Integral scope mounting system with 1-in. Ruger rings. **Features:** Mauser-type action uses Ruger's rotary magazine. Three-position safety, simplified bolt stop, patented bolt-locking system. Uses the dual-screw barrel attachment system of the 10/22 rifle. Introduced 2002.

Price: Blue finish w/walnut stock.. **$979.00**

Price: Stainless steel w/laminate stock **$1,069.00**

SAKO FINNFIRE II

Calibers: .22 LR or .17 HMR. **Capacity:** 6-round magazine. **Barrel:** 22 in. **Weight:** 6.3 lbs. **Stock:** Checkered American walnut, oil-finished with cheekpiece, rubber buttpad, sling swivels. **Sights:** Adjustable or fixed rear, bead front. Made in Finland and imported by Beretta USA.

Price: **$1,100.00**

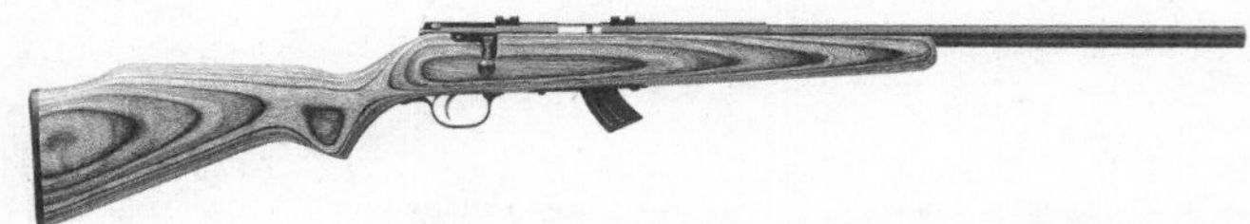

SAVAGE MARK II BOLT-ACTION

Calibers: .22 LR, .17 HMR. **Capacity:** 10-round magazine. **Barrel:** 20.5 in. **Weight:** 5.5 lbs. **Length:** 39.5 in. overall. **Stock:** Walnut-finished hardwood with Monte Carlo-type comb, checkered grip and fore-end. Camo or OD Green stock available. **Sights:** Bead front, open adjustable rear. Receiver grooved for scope mounting. **Features:** Thumb-operated rotating safety. Blue finish. Introduced 1990. Made in Canada, from Savage Arms, Inc.

Price: .... **$228.00–$280.00**
Price: Varmint w/heavy barrel **$242.00**
Price: Camo stock **$280.00**
Price: OD Green stock........ **$291.00**

SAVAGE MARK II-FSS STAINLESS RIFLE

Similar to the Mark II except has stainless steel barreled action and black synthetic stock with positive checkering, swivel studs, and 20.75-in. free-floating and button-rifled barrel with magazine. Weighs 5.5 lbs. Introduced 1997. Imported from Canada by Savage Arms, Inc.

Price: **$336.00**

SAVAGE MODEL 93G MAGNUM BOLT ACTION

Caliber: .22 WMR. **Capacity:** 5-round magazine. **Barrel:** 20.75 in. **Weight:** 5.75 lbs. **Length:** 39.5 in. overall. **Stock:** Walnut-finished hardwood with Monte Carlo-type comb, checkered grip and fore-end. **Sights:** Bead front, adjustable open rear. Receiver grooved for scope mount. **Features:** Thumb-operated rotary safety. Blue finish. Introduced 1994. Made in Canada, from Savage Arms.

Price: Model 93G **$285.00**
Price: Model 93F (as above with black graphite/fiberglass stock) **$364.00**
Price: Model 93 BSEV, thumbhole stock........ **$646.00**

SAVAGE MODEL 93FSS MAGNUM RIFLE

Similar to Model 93G except stainless steel barreled action and black synthetic stock with positive checkering. Weighs 5.5 lbs. Introduced 1997. Imported from Canada by Savage Arms, Inc.

Price: **$353.00**

SAVAGE MODEL 93FVSS MAGNUM

Similar to Model 93FSS Magnum except 21-in. heavy barrel with recessed target-style crown, satin-finished stainless barreled action, black graphite/fiberglass stock. Drilled and tapped for scope mounting; comes with Weaver-style bases. Introduced 1998. Imported from Canada by Savage Arms, Inc.

Price: **$364.00**

SAVAGE B-MAG

Caliber: .17 Win. Super Magnum. **Capacity:** 8-round rotary magazine. **Stock:** Synthetic. **Weight:** 4.5 pounds. Chambered for new Winchester .17 Super Magnum rimfire cartridge that propels a 20-grain bullet at approximately 3,000 fps. **Features:** Adjustable AccuTrigger, rear locking lugs, new and different bolt-action rimfire design that cocks on close of bolt. New in 2013.

Price: **$402.00**
Price: Stainless steel receiver and barrel........ **$433.00**
Price: Heavy Bbl. Laminate stock **$547.00**

SAVAGE BRJ SERIES

Similar to Mark II, Model 93 and Model 93R17 rifles but features spiral fluting pattern on a heavy barrel, blued finish and Royal Jacaranda wood laminate stock.

Price: Mark II BRJ, .22 LR **$519.00**
Price: Model 93 BRJ, .22 Mag........ **$542.00**
Price: Model 93 R17 BRJ, .17 HMR **$542.00**

SAVAGE TACTICAL RIMFIRE SERIES

Similar to Savage Model BRJ series semi-auto rifles but with matte finish and a tactical-style wood stock.

Price: Mark II TR, .22 LR **$533.00**
Price: Mark II TRR, .22 LR, three-way accessory rail **$627.00**
Price: Model 93R17 TR, .17 HMR **$558.00**
Price: Model 93R17 TRR, .17 HMR, three-way accessory rail **$654.00**

SAVAGE B SERIES

Calibers: .17 HMR, .22 LR, 22 WMR. **Capacity:** 10-round rotary magazine. **Barrel:** 21 in. (16.25 in. threaded heavy barrel on Magnum FV-SR Model). **Stock:** Black synthetic with target-style vertical pistol grip. **Weight:** 6 lbs. Features include top tang safety, Accutrigger. Introduced in 2017.

Price: From........ **$281.00–$394.00**

ANSCHUTZ 1903 MATCH
Caliber: .22 LR. **Capacity:** Single-shot. **Barrel:** 21.25 in. **Weight:** 8 lbs. **Length:** 43.75 in. overall. **Stock:** Walnut-finished hardwood with adjustable cheekpiece; stippled grip and fore-end. **Sights:** None furnished. **Features:** Uses Anschutz Match 64 action. A medium weight rifle for intermediate and advanced Junior Match competition. Available from Champion's Choice.
Price: Right-hand **$1,195.00**

ANSCHUTZ 64-MP R SILHOUETTE
Caliber: .22 LR. **Capacity:** 5-round magazine. **Barrel:** 21.5-in. medium heavy; 0.875-in. diameter. **Weight:** 8 lbs. **Length:** 39.5 in. overall. **Stock:** Walnut-finished hardwood, silhouette-type. **Sights:** None furnished. **Features:** Uses Match 64 action. Designed for metallic silhouette competition. Stock has stippled checkering, contoured thumb groove with Wundhammer swell. Two-stage #5098 trigger. Slide safety locks sear and bolt. Introduced 1980. Available from Champion's Choice.
Price: 64-MP R **$1,100.00**
Price: 64-S BR Benchrest **$1,327.00**

ANSCHUTZ 2007 MATCH RIFLE
Uses same action as the Model 2013 but has a lighter barrel. European walnut stock in right-hand, true left-hand or extra-short models. Sights optional. Available with 19.6-in. barrel with extension tube, or 26 in., both in stainless or blued. Introduced 1998. Available from Champion's Choice.
Price: Right-hand, blued, no sights.. **$2,795.00**

ANSCHUTZ 1827BT FORTNER BIATHLON
Caliber: .22 LR. **Capacity:** 5-round magazine. **Barrel:** 21.7 in. **Weight:** 8.8 lbs. with sights. **Length:** 40.9 in. overall. **Stock:** European walnut with cheekpiece, stippled pistol grip and fore-end. **Sights:** Optional globe front specially designed for Biathlon shooting, micrometer rear with hinged snow cap. **Features:** Uses Super Match 54 action and nine-way adjustable trigger; adjustable wooden buttplate, biathlon butthook, adjustable hand-stop rail. Uses Anschutz/Fortner system straight-pull bolt action, blued or stainless steel barrel. Introduced 1982. Available from Champion's Choice.
Price: From.. **$3,450.00**

ANSCHUTZ SUPER MATCH SPECIAL MODEL 2013
Caliber: .22 LR. **Capacity:** single-shot. **Barrel:** 25.9 in. **Weight:** 13 lbs. **Length:** 41.7–42.9 in. **Stock:** Adjustable aluminum. **Sights:** None furnished. **Features:** 2313 aluminum-silver/blue stock, 500mm barrel, fast lock time, adjustable cheekpiece, heavy action and muzzle tube, with handstop and standing riser block. Introduced in 1997. Available from Champion's Choice.
Price: From **$4,200.00**

ANSCHUTZ 1912 SPORT
Caliber: .22 LR. **Barrel:** 26 in. match. **Weight:** 11.4 lbs. **Length:** 41.7 in. overall. **Stock:** Non-stained thumbhole stock adjustable in length with adjustable buttplate and cheekpiece adjustment. Flat fore-end raiser block 4856 adjustable in height. Hook buttplate. **Sights:** None furnished. **Features:** in. Free rifle in. for women. Smallbore model 1907 with 1912 stock: Match 54 action. Delivered with: Hand stop 6226, fore-end raiser block 4856, screwdriver, instruction leaflet with test target. Available from Champion's Choice.
Price: **$2,995.00**

ANSCHUTZ 1913 SUPER MATCH RIFLE
Same as the Model 1911 except European walnut International-type stock with adjustable cheekpiece, or color laminate, both available with straight or lowered fore-end, adjustable aluminum hook buttplate, adjustable hand stop, weighs 13 lbs., 46 in. overall. Stainless or blued barrel. Available from Champion's Choice.
Price: Right-hand, blued, no sights, walnut stock.. **$3,750.00**

ANSCHUTZ 1907 STANDARD MATCH RIFLE
Same action as Model 1913 but with 0.875-in. diameter 26-in. barrel (stainless or blues). **Length:** 44.5 in. overall. **Weight:** 10.5 lbs. **Stock:** Choice of stock configurations. Vented fore-end. Designed for prone and position shooting ISU requirements; suitable for NRA matches. Also available with walnut flat-forend stock for benchrest shooting. Available from Champion's Choice.
Price: Right-hand, blued, no sights.. **$2,385.00**

ARMALITE AR-10(T)
Caliber: .308 Win. **Capacity:** 10-round magazine. **Barrel:** 24 in. target-weight Rock 5R custom. **Weight:** 10.4 lbs. **Length:** 43.5 in. overall. **Stock:** Green or black composition; N.M. fiberglass handguard tube. **Sights:** Detachable handle, front sight, or scope mount available. Comes with international-style flattop receiver with Picatinny rail. **Features:** National Match two-stage trigger. Forged upper receiver. Receivers hard-coat anodized. Introduced 1995. Made in USA by Armalite, Inc.
Price: Black **$1,700.00**
Price: AR-10, .338 Federal **$1,800.00**

ARMALITE M15 A4 CARBINE 6.8 & 7.62X39
Calibers: 6.8 Rem., 7.62x39. **Barrel:** 16 in. chrome-lined with flash suppressor. **Weight:** 7 lbs. **Length:** 26.6 in. **Features:** Front and rear picatinny rails for mounting optics, two-stage tactical trigger, anodized aluminum/phosphate finish.
Price: **$1,107.00**

BLASER R93 LONG RANGE SPORTER 2
Caliber: .308 Win. Capacity: 10-round magazine. **Barrel:** 24 in. **Weight:** 10.4 lbs. **Length:** 44 in. overall. **Stock:** Aluminum with synthetic lining. **Sights:** None furnished; accepts detachable scope mount. **Features:** Straight-pull bolt action with adjustable trigger; fully adjustable stock; quick takedown; corrosion resistant finish. Introduced 1998. Imported from Germany by Blaser USA.
Price: **$4,400.00**

BUSHMASTER A2/A3 TARGET
Calibers: 5.56 NATO, .223 Rem. **Capacity:** 30-round magazine. **Barrels:** 20 in., 24 in. **Weight:** 8.43 lbs. (A2); 8.78 lbs. (A3). **Length:** 39.5 in. overall (20 in. barrel). **Stock:** Black composition; A2 type. **Sights:** Adjustable post front, adjustable aperture rear. **Features:** Patterned after Colt M-16A2. Chrome-lined barrel with manganese phosphate exterior. Available in stainless barrel. Made in USA by Bushmaster Firearms Co.
Price: A2 .... **$969.00**
Price: A3 with carrying handle **$999.00**

REMINGTON 40-XB RANGEMASTER TARGET

Calibers: 15 calibers from .22 BR Remington to .300 Win. Mag. **Barrel:** 27.25 in. **Weight:** 11.25 lbs. **Length:** 47 in. overall. **Stock:** American walnut, laminated thumbhole or Kevlar with high comb and beavertail fore-end stop. Rubber nonslip buttplate. **Sights:** None. Scope blocks installed. **Features:** Adjustable trigger. Stainless barrel and action. Receiver drilled and tapped for sights. Model 40-XB Tactical (2008) chambered in .308 Win., comes with guarantee of 0.75-in. maximum 5-shot groups at 100 yards. **Weight:** 10.25 lbs. Includes Teflon-coated stainless button-rifled barrel, 1:14 in. twist, 27.25-in. long, three longitudinal flutes. Bolt-action repeater, adjustable 40-X trigger and precision machined aluminum bedding block. Stock is H-S Precision Pro Series synthetic tactical stock, black with green web finish, vertical pistol grip. From Remington Custom Shop.

Price: 40-XB KS, aramid fiber stock, single shot **$2,863.00**
Price: 40-XB KS, aramid fiber stock, repeater **$3,014.00**
Price: 40-XB Tactical .308 Win. **$2,992.00**

REMINGTON 40-XBBR KS

Calibers: Five calibers from .22 BR to .308 Win. **Barrel:** 20 in. (light varmint class), 24 in. (heavy varmint class). **Weight:** 7.25 lbs. (light varmint class); 12 lbs. (heavy varmint class). **Length:** 38 in. (20-in. bbl.), 42 in. (24-in. bbl.). **Stock:** Aramid fiber. **Sights:** None. Supplied with scope blocks. **Features:** Unblued benchrest with stainless steel barrel, trigger adjustable from 1.5 lbs. to 3.5 lbs. Special 2-oz. trigger extra cost. Scope and mounts extra. From Remington Custom Shop.

Price: Single shot **$3,950.00**

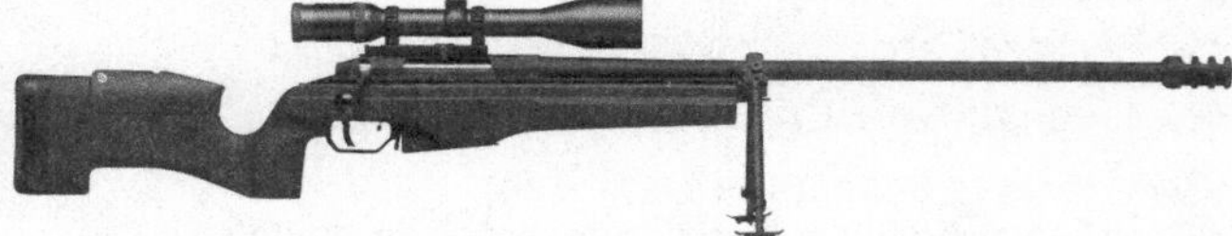

REMINGTON 40-XC KS TARGET

Caliber: 7.62 NATO. **Capacity:** 5-shot. **Barrel:** 24 in., stainless steel. **Weight:** 11 lbs. without sights. **Length:** 43.5 in. overall. **Stock:** Aramid fiber. **Sights:** None furnished. **Features:** Designed to meet the needs of competitive shooters. Stainless steel barrel and action. From Remington Custom Shop.

Price: **$3,067.00**

SAKO TRG-22 BOLT-ACTION

Calibers: .308 Win., 10-shot magazine, .338 Lapua. **Capacity:** 5-round magazine. **Barrel:** 26 in. **Weight:** 10.25 lbs. **Length:** 45.25 in. overall. **Stock:** Reinforced polyurethane with fully adjustable cheekpiece and buttplate. **Sights:** None furnished. Optional quick-detachable, one-piece scope mount base, 1 in. or 30mm rings. **Features:** Resistance-free bolt, free-floating heavy stainless barrel, 60-degree bolt lift. Two-stage trigger is adjustable for length, pull, horizontal or vertical pitch. TRG-42 has similar features but has long action and is chambered for .338 Lapua. Imported from Finland by Beretta USA.

Price: TRG-22 ....**$3,495.00**
Price: TRG-22 with folding stock **$6,075.00**
Price: TRG-42 ....**$4,445.00**
Price: TRG-42 with folding stock **$7,095.00**

SPRINGFIELD ARMORY M1A SUPER MATCH

Caliber: .308 Win. **Barrel:** 22 in., heavy Douglas Premium. **Weight:** About 11 lbs. **Length:** 44.31 in. overall. **Stock:** Heavy walnut competition stock with longer pistol grip, contoured area behind the rear sight, thicker butt and fore-end, glass bedded. **Sights:** National Match front and rear. **Features:** Has figure-eight-style operating rod guide. Introduced 1987. From Springfield Armory.

Price: Approx **$2,956.00**

SPRINGFIELD ARMORY M1A/M-21 TACTICAL MODEL

Similar to M1A Super Match except special sniper stock with adjustable cheekpiece and rubber recoil pad. Weighs 11.6 lbs. From Springfield Armory.

Price: **$3,619.00**

STI SPORTING COMPETITION

Caliber: 5.56 NATO. Features: AR-style semi-auto rifle with 16-in. 410 stainless 1:8 in. twist barrel; mid-length gas system; Nordic Tactical Compensator and JP Trigger group; custom STI Valkyrie handguard and gas block; flattop design with picatinny rail; anodized finish with black Teflon coating. Also available in Tactical configuration.

Price: **$1,455.00**

TIME PRECISION .22 RF BENCH REST

Caliber: .22 LR. **Capacity:** Single-shot. **Barrel:** Shilen match-grade stainless. **Weight:** 10 lbs. with scope. **Length:** NA. **Stock:** Fiberglass. Pillar bedded. **Sights:** None furnished. **Features:** Shilen match trigger removable trigger bracket, full-length steel sleeve, aluminum receiver. Introduced 2008. Made in USA by Time Precision.

Price: From **$2,200.00**

Prices given are believed to be accurate at time of publication however, many factors affect retail pricing so exact prices are not possible.

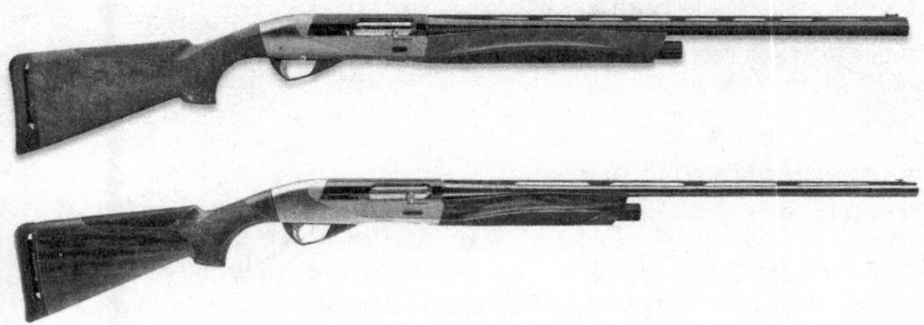

BENELLI ETHOS

Gauges: 12 ga., 20 ga., 28 ga. 3 in. **Capacity:** 4+1. **Barrel:** 28 in. (Full, Mod., Imp. Cyl., Imp. Mod., Cylinder choke tubes). **Weights:** 6.5 lbs. (12 ga.), 5.3–5.7 (20 & 28 ga.). **Length:** 49.5 in. overall (28 in. barrel). **Stock:** Select AA European walnut with satin finish. **Sights:** Red bar fiber optic front, with three interchangeable inserts, metal middle bead. **Features:** Utilizes Benelli's Inertia Driven system. Recoil is reduced by Progressive Comfort recoil reduction system within the buttstock. Twelve and 20-gauge models cycle all 3-inch loads from light 7/8 oz. up to 3-inch magnums. Also available with nickel-plated engraved receiver. Imported from Italy by Benelli USA, Corp.

Price: **$1,999.00**
Price: Engraved nickel-plated (shown) **$2,199.00**
Price: 20 or 28 ga. (engraved, nickel plated only) **$2,199.00**

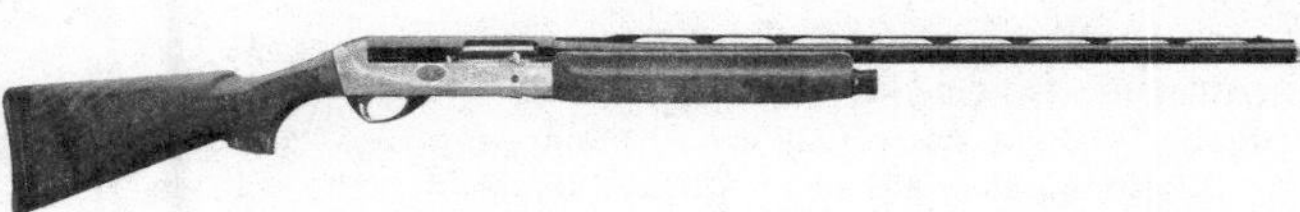

BENELLI LEGACY SPORT

Gauges: 12 ga., 20 ga. (2 3/4- and 3-inch) gauge. **Weight:** 6.3 (20 ga.)–7.5 lbs. **Features:** Inertia Driven system; sculptured nickel finished lower receiver with classic game scene etchings; highly polished blued upper receiver; AA-Grade walnut stock; (A-grade on Sport II); gel recoil pad; ported 24- or 26-in. barrel, Crio chokes.

Price: **$2,439.00**
Price: Legacy Sport II **$1,899.00**

BENELLI ULTRA LIGHT

Gauges: 12 ga., 20 ga., 28 ga. 3 in. chamber (12, 20), 2 3/4 in. (28). **Barrels:** 24 in., 26 in. Mid-bead sight. **Weights:** 5.2–6 lbs. **Features:** Similar to Legacy line. Drop adjustment kit allows the stock to be custom fit without modifying the stock. WeatherCoat walnut stock. Lightened receiver, shortened magazine tube, carbon-fiber rib and grip cap. Introduced 2008. Imported from Italy by Benelli USA, Corp.

Price: 12 and 20 ga. **$1,699.00**
Price: 28 ga. **$1,799.00**

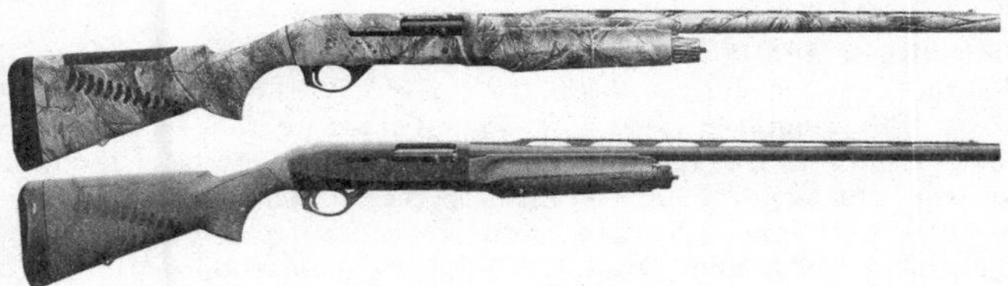

BENELLI M2 FIELD

Gauges: 20 ga., 12 ga., 3 in. chamber. **Barrels:** 21 in., 24 in., 26 in., 28 in. **Weights:** 5.4–7.2 lbs. Length: 42.5–49.5 in. overall. **Stock:** Synthetic, Advantage Max-4 HD, Advantage Timber HD, APG HD. **Sights:** Red bar. **Features:** Uses the Inertia Driven bolt mechanism. Vent rib. Comes with set of five choke tubes. Imported from Italy by Benelli USA.

Price: Synthetic stock 12 ga. **$1,499.00**
Price: Camo stock 12 ga. **$1,549.00**
Price: Synthetic stock 20 ga. **$1,499.00**
Price: Camo stock 20 ga. **$1,599.00**
Price: Rifled slug .... **$1,469.00–$1,589.00**
Price: Left-hand 12 ga. **$1409.00**
Price: Left-hand model 20 ga. **$1519.00**

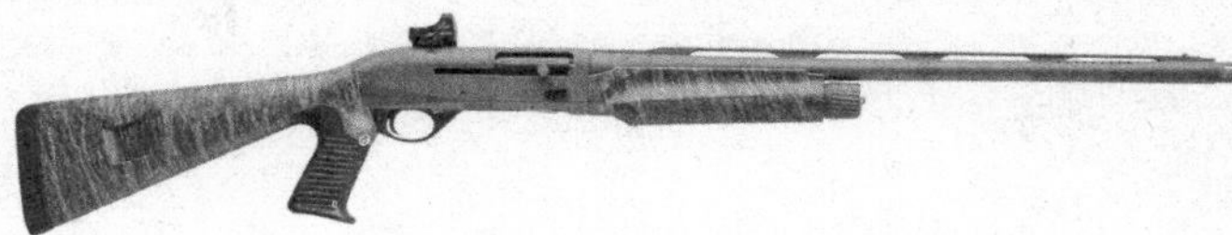

BENELLI M2 TURKEY EDITION

Gauges: 12 ga. and 20 ga., Full, Imp. Mod, Mod., Imp. Cyl., Cyl. choke tubes. **Barrel:** 24 in. **Weight:** 7 lbs. **Stock:** 12 ga. model has ComfortTech with pistol grip, Bottomland/Cerakote finish. 20 ga. has standard stock with Realtree APG finish. **Features:** From the Benelli Performance Shop.

Price: 20 ga. standard stock **$2,599.00**
Price: 12 ga. pistol grip stock **$3,399.00**

BENELLI MONTEFELTRO

Gauges: 12 ga. and 20 ga. Full, Imp. Mod, Mod., Imp. Cyl., Cyl. choke tubes. **Barrels:** 24 in., 26 in., 28 in. **Weights:** 5.3–7.1 lbs. **Stock:** Checkered walnut with satin finish. **Lengths:** 43.6–49.5 in. overall. **Features:** Burris FastFire II sight. Uses the Inertia Driven rotating bolt system with a simple inertia recoil design. Finish is blued. Introduced 1987.

Price: Standard Model **$1,139.00**
Price: Left Hand Model **$1,229.00**
Price: Silver **$1,779.00**

BENELLI SUPER BLACK EAGLE III

Gauge: 12 ga., 3 1/2 inch. Latest evolution of Super Black Eagle. Comfort Tech stock with adjustable comb, 22 synthetic chevrons, gel recoil pad. Offered with several camo finishes, black synthetic or satin walnut. Left-hand model available. Introduced in 2017.

Price: **$1,899.00**
Price: Camo finish **$1,999.00**
Price: Rifle Slug **$1,499.00**

BENELLI CORDOBA

Gauges: 20 ga., 12 ga., 3-in. chamber. **Capacity:** 4+1. **Barrels:** 28 in., 30 in., ported, 10mm sporting rib. **Weights:** 7.2–7.3 lbs. **Lengths:** 49.6–51.6 in. **Features:** Designed for high-volume sporting clays and Argentina dove shooting. Inertia-driven action, Extended Sport CrioChokes. Ported. Imported from Italy by Benelli USA.

Price: Field Models .... **$2,069.00–$2,099.00**
Price: Performance Shop Model .... **$2,719.00–$2,829.00**

BENELLI SUPERSPORT & SPORT II

Gauges: 20 ga., 12 ga., 3-in. chamber. **Capacity:** 4+1. **Barrels:** 28 in., 30 in., ported, 10mm sporting rib. **Weight:** 7.2–7.3 lbs. **Lengths:** 49.6–51.6 in. **Stock:** Carbon fiber, ComforTech (Supersport) or walnut (Sport II). **Sights:** Red bar front, metal midbead. Sport II is similar to the Legacy model except has nonengraved dual tone blued/silver receiver, ported wide-rib barrel, adjustable buttstock, and functions with all loads. Walnut stock with satin finish. Introduced 1997. **Features:** Designed for high-volume sporting clays. Inertia-driven action, Extended CrioChokes. Ported. Imported from Italy by Benelli USA.

Price: SuperSport **$2,199.00**
Price: Sport II **$1,899.00**

BENELLI VINCI

Gauge: 12 ga., 3-in. **Barrels:** 24–28-inch ribbed. Tactical model available with 18.5-in. barrel. **Finishes:** Black, MAX-4HD or APG HD; synthetic contoured stocks; optional Steady-Grip model. **Weight:** 6.7–6.9 lbs. **Features:** Gas-operated action. Modular disassembly; interchangeable choke tubes. Picatinny rail, pistol grip, ghost ring sight.

Price: .... **$1,449.00–$2,199.00**

BENELLI SUPER VINCI
Gauge: 12 ga.. 2 3/4 in., 3 in. and 3 1/2 in. **Capacity:** 3+1. **Barrels:** 26 in., 28 in. **Weights:** 6.9–7 lbs. **Lengths:** 48.5–50.5 in. **Stock:** Black synthetic, Realtree Max4 and Realtree APG. **Features:** Crio Chokes: C,IC,M,IM,F. Length of Pull: 14.375 in. Drop at Heel: 2 in. Drop at Comb: 1.375 in. **Sights:** Red bar front sight and metal bead mid-sight. Minimum recommended load: 3-dram, 1 1/8 oz. loads (12 ga.). Receiver drilled and tapped for scope mounting. Imported from Italy by Benelli USA., Corp.
Price: Black Synthetic Comfortech **$1,799.00**
Price: Camo **$1,899.00**

BERETTA A300 OUTLANDER
Gauge: 12 ga., 3-in. **Capacity:** 3+1. Operates with 2 3/4-in. shells. **Barrel:** 28 in. with Mobilechoke system. **Stock:** Synthetic, camo or wood. **Weight:** 7.1 pounds. **Features:** Based on A400 design but at a lower price.
Price: .... **$775.00–$850.00**

BERETTA A400 XPLOR UNICO
Gauge: 12 ga.. 2 3/4 to 3 1/2-inch shells. **Barrels:** 26- or 28-inch "Steelium" with interchangeable choke tubes. **Features:** Self-regulation gas-operated shotgun. Optional Kick-Off hydraulic damper. Anodized aluminum receiver; sculpted, checkered walnut buttstock and fore-end.
Price: **$1,755.00**
Price: With Kick-Off recoil reduction system **$1,855.00**

BERETTA A400 XCEL SPORTING
Gauge: 12 ga. 3-in. chamber. **Barrels:** 28 in., 30 in. 32 in. **Weight:** 7.5 lbs. **Stock:** Walnut and polymer. **Features:** Gas operated. In addition to A400 specifications and features, the Sporting model has aqua blue receiver. Optional Gun Pod electronic system gives digital readout of air temperature, ammunition pressure, number of rounds fired.
Price: **$1,745.00**
Price: With Kick-Off system **$1,845.00**

BERETTA A400 ACTION
Gauges: 12 ga., 20 (3 in.) or 28 ga. (2 3/4-in. chamber). **Barrels:** 28 in., 30 in. **Weight:** 5.3 (28 ga.) to 6.7 lbs. **Stock:** Walnut and polymer combination. **Features:** Gas-operating Blink operating system can reportedly fire 4 rounds in less than one second. Kick-Off hydraulic recoil reduction system reduces felt recoil up to 70 percent.
Price: **$1,600.00**
Price: With Kick-Off system **$1,655.00**

BROWNING A5
Gauges: 12 ga., 3 or 3 1/2; 16 ga., 2 3/4 in. (Sweet Sixteen). **Barrels:** 26 in., 28 in. or 30 in. **Weights:** 6.6–7 lbs. **Lengths:** 47.25–51.5 in. **Stock:** Gloss finish walnut with 22 LPI checkering, black synthetic or camo. Adjustable for cast and drop. **Features:** Operates on Kinematic short-recoil system, totally different than the classic Auto-5 long-recoil action manufactured from 1903–1999. Lengthened forcing cone, three choke tubes (IC, M, F), flat ventilated rib, brass bead front sight, ivory middle bead. Available in Mossy Oak Duck Blind or Break-up Infinity camo. Ultimate Model has satin finished aluminum alloy receiver with light engraving of pheasants on left side, mallards on the right. Gloss blued finish, Grade III oil-finished walnut stock. Wicked Wing has Cerakote Burnt Bronze finish on receiver and barrel, Mossy Oak Shadow Grass Blades camo on stock.
Price: A5 Hunter **$1,630.00**
Price: A5 Hunter 3 1/2 in. **$1,760.00**
Price: A5 Stalker (synthetic) **$1,500.00**
Price: A5 Stalker 3 1/2 in. **$1,580.00**
Price: A5 Ultimate **$1,990.00**
Price: A5 Sweet Sixteen **$1,700.00**
Price: A5 Wicked Wing **$1,830.00**

BROWNING MAXUS HUNTER
Gauges: 12 ga., 3 in. and 3 1/2 in. **Barrels:** 26 in., 28 in. and 30 in. Flat ventilated rib with fixed cylinder choke; stainless steel; matte finish. **Weight:** 7 lbs. 2 oz. **Length:** 40.75 in. **Stock:** Gloss finish walnut stock with close radius pistol grip, sharp 22 LPI checkering, Speed Lock Forearm, shim adjustable for length of pull, cast and drop. **Features:** Vector Pro-lengthened forcing cone, three Invector-Plus choke tubes, Inflex Technology recoil pad, ivory front bead sight, One 1/4 in. stock spacer. Strong, lightweight aluminum alloy receiver with durable satin nickel finish & laser engraving (pheasant on the right, mallard on the left). All-Purpose Hunter has Mossy Oak Break-Up Country Camo, Duratouch coated composite stock. Wicked Wing has Cerakote Burnt Bronze finish on receiver and barrel, Mossy Oak Shadow Grass Blades camo on stock.
Price: 3 in. **$1,550.00**
Price: 3 1/2 in. **$1,700.00**
Price: All-Purpose Hunter **$1,740.00**
Price: Maxus Wicked Wing **$1,740.00**

BROWNING MAXUS SPORTING
Gauge: 12 ga., 3 in. **Barrels:** 28 in., 30 in. flat ventilated rib. **Weight:** 7 lbs. 2 oz. **Length:** 49.25 in.–51.25 in. **Stock:** Gloss finish high grade walnut stock with close radius pistol grip, Speed Lock forearm, shim adjustable for length of pull, cast and drop. **Features:** Laser engraving of game birds transforming into clay birds on the lightweight alloy receiver. Quail are on the right side, and a mallard duck on the left. The Power Drive Gas System reduces recoil and cycles a wide array of loads. It's available in a 28 in. or 30 in. barrel length. The high-grade walnut stock and forearm are generously checkered, finished with a deep, high gloss. The stock is adjustable and one .250-in. stock spacer is included. For picking up either clay or live birds quickly, the HiViz Tri-Comp fiber-optic front sight with mid-bead ivory sight does a great job, gathering light on the most overcast days. Vector Pro-lengthened forcing cone, five Invector-Plus choke tubes, Inflex Technology recoil pad, HiViz Tri-Comp fiber-optic front sight, ivory mid-bead sight, one .250-in. stock spacer.
Price: **$1,760.00**
Price: Golden Clays **$2,070.00**

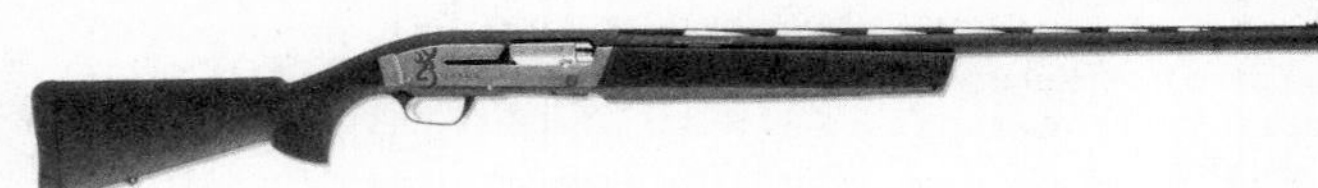

BROWNING MAXUS SPORTING CARBON FIBER
Gauge: 12 ga., 3 in. **Barrels:** 28 in., 30 in. flat ventilated rib. **Weights:** 6 lbs. 15 oz.–7 lbs. **Length:** 49.25–51.25 in. **Stock:** Composite stock with close radius pistol grip, Speed Lock forearm, textured gripping surfaces, shim adjustable for length of pull, cast and drop, carbon fiber finish, Dura-Touch Armor Coating. **Features:** Strong, lightweight aluminum alloy, carbon fiber finish on top and bottom. The stock is finished with Dura-Touch Armor Coating for a secure, non-slip grip when the gun is wet. It has the Browning exclusive Magazine Cut-Off, a patented Turn-Key Magazine Plug and Speed Load Plus. Deeply finished look of carbon fiber and Dura-Touch Armor Coating. Vector Pro-lengthened forcing cone, five Invector-Plus choke tubes, Inflex Technology recoil pad, HiViz Tri-Comp fiber-optic front sight, ivory mid-bead sight, one .250-in. stock spacer.
Price: **$1,550.00**

Prices given are believed to be accurate at time of publication however, many factors affect retail pricing so exact prices are not possible.

BROWNING MAXUS RIFLED DEER STALKER
Gauge: 12 ga. 3 in. **Barrel:** 22 in. thick-walled, fully rifled for slug ammunition only. **Weight:** 7 lbs. 3 oz. **Length:** 43.25 in. **Stock:** Composite stock with close radius pistol grip, Speed Lock forearm, textured gripping surfaces, shim adjustable for length of pull, cast and drop, matte black finish Dura-Touch Armor Coating. **Features:** Stock is adjustable for length of pull, cast and drop. Cantilever scope mount, one .250-in. stock spacer. Available with Mossy Oak Break-up Country camo full coverage.
Price: **$1,520.00**
Price: Mossy Oak Break-Up Country camo **$1,640.00**

BROWNING GOLD LIGHT 10 GAUGE
Gauge: 10 ga. 3 1/2 in. **Capacity:** 4 rounds. **Barrels:** 24 (NWTF), 26 or 28 in. **Stock:** Composite with Dura-Cote Armor coating. Mossy Oak camo (Break-Up Country or Shadow Grass Blades). **Weight:** Approx. 9.5 pounds. Gas operated action, aluminum receiver, three standard Invector choke tubes. Receiver is drilled and tapped for scope mount. National Wild Turkey Foundation model has Hi-Viz 4-in-1 fiber optic sight, NWTF logo on buttstock.
Price: Mossy Oak Camo finishes **$1,740.00**
Price: NWTF Model **$1,870.00**

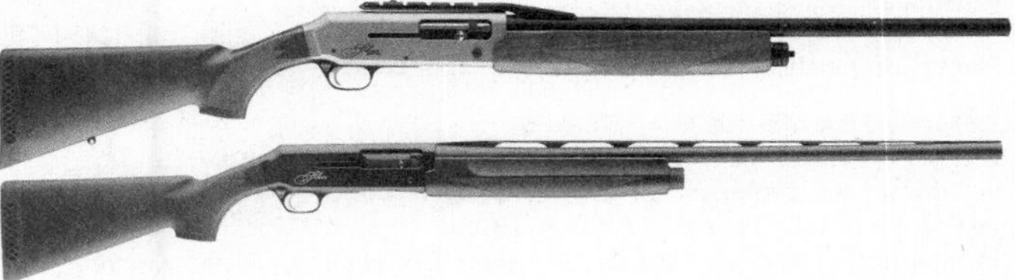

BROWNING SILVER
Gauges: 12 ga., 3 in. or 3 1/2 in.; 20 ga., 3 in. chamber. **Barrels:** 26 in., 28 in., 30 in. Invector Plus choke tubes. **Weights:** 7 lbs., 9 oz. (12 ga.), 6 lbs., 7 oz. (20 ga.). **Stock:** Satin finish walnut. **Features:** Active Valve gas system, semi-humpback receiver. Invector Plus choke system, three choke tubes. Imported by Browning.
Price: Silver Hunter, 12 ga., 3 1/2 in. **$1,360.00**
Price: Silver Hunter, 20 ga., 3 in., intr. 2008 ...... **$1,200.00**
Price: Silver Sporting, 12 ga., 2 3/4 in., intr. 2009 ...... **$1,320.00**
Price: Silver Sporting Micro, 12 ga., 2 3/4 in., intr. 2008 ...... **$1,320.00**
Price: Silver Rifled Deer, Mossy Oak New Break-Up, 12 ga., 3 in., intr. 2008 ...... **$1,460.00**
Price: Silver Rifled Deer Stalker, 12 ga., 3 in., intr. 2008 ...... **$1,310.00**

CHARLES DALY MODEL 600
Gauges: 12 ga. or 20 ga. (3 in.) or 28 ga. (2 3/4 in.). **Capacity:** 5+1. **Barrels:** 26 in., 28 in. (20 and 28 ga.), 26 in., 28 in. or 30 in. (12 ga.). Three choke tubes provided (Rem-Choke pattern). **Stock:** Synthetic, wood or camo. Features: Comes in several variants including Field, Sporting Clays, Tactical and Trap. Left-hand models available. Uses gas-assisted recoil operation. Imported from Turkey.
Price: Field **$480.00**
Price: Superior w/walnut stock (shown) **$597.00**
Price: Sporting **$858.00**
Price: Tactical **$685.00**

CHARLES DALY MODEL 635 MASTER MAG
Gauge: 12 ga., 3 1/2 in. **Barrels:** 24 in., 26 in., 28 in. Ported. **Stock:** Synthetic with full camo coverage. **Features:** Similar to Model 600 series.
Price: From **$665.00**

CZ MODEL 712/720
Gauges: 12 ga., 20 ga. **Capacity:** 4+1. **Barrel:** 26 in. **Weight:** 6.3 lbs. **Stock:** Turkish walnut with 14.5 in. length of pull. **Features:** Chrome-lined barrel with 3-inch chamber, ventilated rib, five choke tubes. Matte black finish.
Price: 712 12 ga. ...... **$499.00–$699.00**
Price: 720 20 ga. ...... **$516.00–$599.00**

ESCORT WATERFOWL EXTREME SEMI-AUTO
Gauges: 12 ga. or 20 ga., 2 3/4 in. through 3 1/2 in. **Capacity:** 5+1. **Barrel:** 28 in. **Weight:** 7.4 lbs. **Length:** 48 in. **Stock:** Composite stock with close radius pistol grip; Speed Lock forearm; textured gripping surfaces; shim adjustable for length of pull, cast and drop; Realtree Max4 or AP camo finish; Dura-Touch Armor Coating. **Sights:** HiVis MagniSight fiber-optic, magnetic sight to enhance sight acquisition in lowlight conditions. **Features:** The addition of non-slip grip pads on the fore-end and pistol grip provide a superior hold in all weather conditions. Smart-Valve gas pistons regulate gas blowback to cycle every round — from 2 3/4-inch range loads through 3 1/2-inch heavy magnums. Escorts also have Fast-loading systems that allow one-handed round changes without changing aiming position. Left-hand models available at no increase in price.
Price: Black/Synthetic **$551.00**
Price: Realtree Camo **$736.00**
Price: 3 1/2-in. Black/Synthetic **$649.00**
Price: 3 1/2-in. Realtree Camo **$815.00**

FABARM XLR5 VELOCITY AR
Gauge: 12 ga. **Barrels:** 30 or 32 in. **Weight:** 8.25 lbs. **Features:** Gas-operated model designed for competition shooting. Unique adjustable rib that allows a more upright shooting position. There is also an adjustable trigger shoe, magazine cap adjustable weight system. Five interchangeable choke tubes. Imported from Italy by Fabarm USA.
Price: From ...... **$2,755.00–$3,300.00**
Price: FR Sporting ...... **$1,990.00–$2,165.00**
Price: LR (Long Rib) ...... **$2,260.00–$2,800.00**

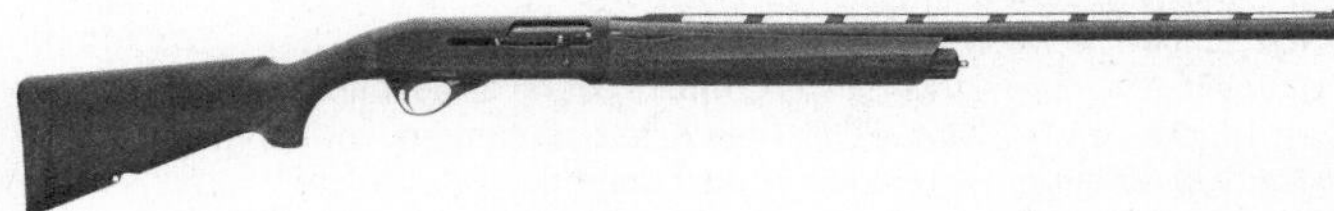

FRANCHI AFFINITY
Gauges: 12 ga., 20 ga. Three-inch chamber also handles 2 3/4-inch shells. **Barrels:** 26 in., 28 in., 30 in. (12 ga.), 26 in. (20 ga.). 30-in. barrel available only on 12-ga. Sporting model. **Weights:** 5.6–6.8 pounds. **Stocks:** Black synthetic or Realtree Camo. Left-hand versions available.
Price: Synthetic **$849.00**
Price: Synthetic left-hand action **$899.00**
Price: Camo **$949.00**
Price: Sporting **$1,149.00**

FRANCHI INTENSITY
Gauge: 12 ga. 3 1/2-in. chamber. **Barrels:** 26 in., 28 in., 30 in. (IC, Mod., Full choke tubes). **Weight:** 6.8 lbs. **Stock:** Black synthetic or camo.
Price: Synthetic **$1,099.00**
Price: Camo **$1,199.00**

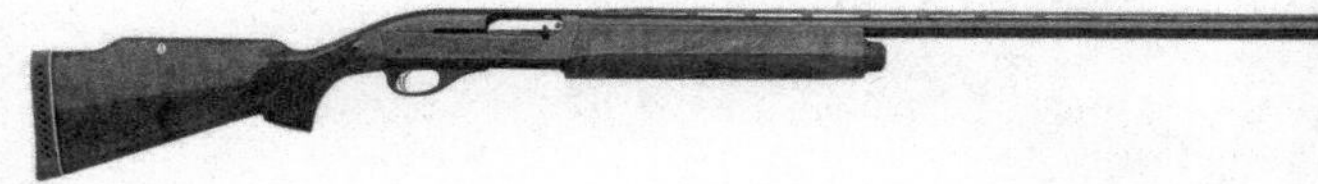

MOSSBERG 930

Gauge: 12 ga., 3 in. **Capacity:** 4-shell magazine. **Barrels:** 24 in., 26 in., 28 in., over-bored to 10-gauge bore dimensions; factory ported, Accu-Choke tubes. **Weight:** 7.5 lbs. **Length:** 44.5 in. overall (28-in. barrel). **Stock:** Walnut or synthetic. Adjustable stock drop and cast spacer system. **Sights:** Turkey Taker fiber-optic, adjustable windage and elevation. Front bead fiber-optic front on waterfowl models. **Features:** Self-regulating gas system, dual gas-vent system and piston, EZ-Empty magazine button, cocking indicator. Interchangeable Accu-Choke tube set (IC, Mod, Full) for waterfowl and field models. XX-Full turkey Accu-Choke tube included with turkey models. Ambidextrous thumb-operated safety, Uni-line stock and receiver. Receiver drilled and tapped for scope base attachment, free gun lock. Introduced 2008. From O.F. Mossberg & Sons, Inc.

Price: Turkey, From $630.00
Price: Waterfowl, From $782.00
Price: Combo, From $744.00
Price: Field, From $685.00
Price: Slugster, From $678.00
Price: Turkey Pistolgrip; Mossy Oak Infinity Camo $735.00
Price: Tactical; 18.5-in. tactical barrel, black synthetic stock and matte black finish $739.00
Price: SPX; no muzzle brake, M16-style front sight, ghost ring rear sight, pistol grip stock, 8-shell extended magazine $1,012.00
Price: Home Security/Field Combo; 18.5 in. Cylinder bore barrel and 28 in. ported Field barrel; black synthetic stock and matte black finish $693.00
Price: High Performance (13-round magazine)........ $974.00

MOSSBERG MODEL 935 MAGNUM

Gauge: 12 ga. 3 in. and 3 1/2-in., interchangeable. **Barrels:** 22 in., 24 in., 26 in., 28in. **Weights:** 7.25–7.75 lbs. **Lengths:** 45–49 in. overall. **Stock:** Synthetic. **Features:** Gas-operated semi-auto models in blued or camo finish. Fiber-optics sights, drilled and tapped receiver, interchangeable Accu-Mag choke tubes.

Price: 935 Magnum Turkey Pistol grip; full pistol grip stock $1,032.00
Price: 935 Magnum Grand Slam: 22 in. barrel $928.00
Price: 935 Magnum Waterfowl: 26 in. or 28 in. barrel $760.00
Price: 935 Magnum Turkey/Deer Combo: interchangeable 24 in. Turkey barrel, Mossy Oak New Break-up camo overall $1,000.00
Price: 935 Magnum Waterfowl/Turkey Combo: 24 in. Turkey and 28 in. Waterfowl barrels, Mossy Oak New Break-up finish overall $1,000.00

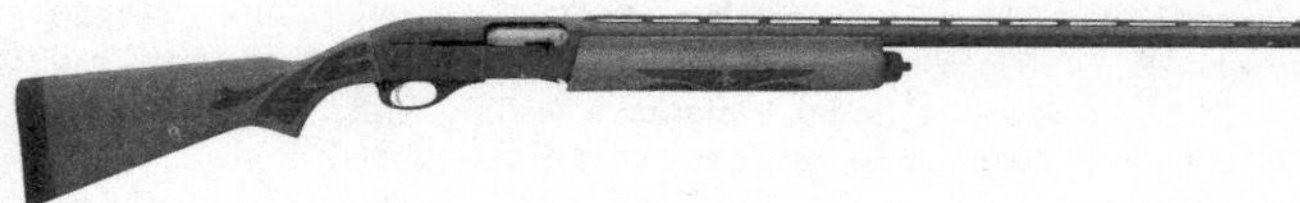

MOSSBERG SA-20

Gauge: 20 ga. **Barrels:** 20 in. (Tactical), 26 in. or 28 in. **Weight:** 5.5–6 lbs. **Stock:** Black synthetic. Gas operated action, matte blue finish. Tactical model has ghost-ring sight, accessory rail.

Price: From........ $580.00–$633.00

REMINGTON MODEL 11-87 SPORTSMAN

Gauges: 12 ga., 20 ga., 3 in. **Barrels:** 26 in., 28 in., RemChoke tubes. Standard contour, vent rib. **Weights:** 7.75–8.25 lbs. Lengths: 46–48 in. overall. **Stock:** American walnut with satin finish. **Sights:** Single bead front. **Features:** Matte-black metal finish, magazine cap swivel studs.

Price: $748.00

REMINGTON MODEL 1100 CLASSIC

Gauges: 12 ga., 20 ga. or 28 ga. **Barrels:** 28 in. (12 ga.), 26 in. (20), 25 in. (28). Features: Part of the Remington American Classics Collection honoring Remington's most enduring firearms. American walnut B-grade stock with classic white line spacer and grip caps, ventilated recoil pad the white line spacer and white diamond grip cap. Machine-cut engraved receiver has tasteful scroll pattern with gold inlay retriever and "American Classic" label. Limited availability.

Price: $1,686.00

REMINGTON MODEL 1100 200TH YEAR ANNIVERSARY

Gauge: 12 ga. **Barrel:** 28 in. **Features:** C-grade American walnut stock with *fleur-de-lis* checkering. Receiver has classic engraving pattern, gold inlay. Limited edition of 2,016 guns to honor the Remington company's 200th anniversary — the oldest firearms manufacturer in the USA. Limited availability.

Price: $1,999.00

REMINGTON MODEL 1100 COMPETITION MODELS

Gauges: .410 bore, 28 ga., 20 ga., 12 ga. **Barrels:** 26 in., 27 in., 28 in., 30 in. light target contoured vent rib barrel with twin bead target sights. **Stock:** Semi-fancy American walnut stock and fore-end, cut checkering, high gloss finish. **Features:** Classic Trap has 30-inch barrel and weighs approximately 8.25 pounds. Sporting Series is available in all four gauges with 28-inch barrel in 12 and 20 gauge, 27 in. in 28 and .410. **Weights:** 6.25–8 pounds. Competition Synthetic model has synthetic stock with adjustable comb, case and length. Five Briley Target choke tubes. High-gloss blued barrel, Nickel-Teflon finish on receiver and internal parts. **Weight:** 8.1 pounds.

Price: Classic Trap $1,334.00
Price: Sporting Series, From $1,252.00
Price: Competition Synthetic: $1,305.00

REMINGTON VERSA MAX SERIES

Gauge: 12 ga., 2 3/4 in., 3 in., 3 1/2 in. **Barrels:** 26 in. and 28 in. flat ventilated rib. **Weights:** 7.5–7.7 lbs. **Length:** 40.25 in. **Stock:** Synthetic. **Features:** Reliably cycles 12-gauge rounds from 2 3/4 in. to 3 1/2 in. magnum. Versaport gas system regulates cycling pressure based on shell length. Reduces recoil to that of a 20-gauge. Self-cleaning. Continuously cycled thousands of rounds in torture test. Synthetic stock and fore-end with grey overmolded grips. Drilled and tapped receiver. Enlarged trigger guard opening and larger safety for easier use with gloves. TriNyte Barrel and Nickel Teflon plated internal components offer extreme corrosion resistance. Includes 5 Flush Mount Pro Bore Chokes (Full, Mod, Imp Mod Light Mod, IC)

Price: Sportsman, From $1,066.00
Price: Synthetic, From $1,427.00
Price: Tactical, From $1,456.00
Price: Waterfowl, From $1,765.00
Price: Camo, From $1,664.00

REMINGTON MODEL V3

Gauge: 12 ga., 3 in. **Capacity:** 3+1 magazine. **Barrels:** 26 or 28 in. **Features:** The newest addition to the Remington shotgun family operates on an improved VersaPort gas system, claimed to offer the least recoil of any 12-ga. autoloader. Operating system is located in front of the receiver instead of the fore-end, resulting in better weight distribution than other autoloaders, and improved handling qualities. **Stock:** Walnut, black synthetic, or camo. Designed to function with any 2 3/4- or 3-in. ammo. Made in the USA by Remington.

Price: Synthetic black........ $895.00
Price: Walnut or camo........ $995.00

Prices given are believed to be accurate at time of publication however, many factors affect retail pricing so exact prices are not possible.

SKB MODEL IS300
Gauge: 12 ga., 2-3/4- and 3-in. loads. **Capacity:** 4+1 magazine. **Barrels:** 26 in., 28 in. or 30 in. with 3 choke tubes IC, M, F. **Stock:** Black synthetic, oil-finished walnut or camo. **Weight:** 6.7–7.3 pounds. **Features:** Inertia-driven operating system. Target models have adjustable stock dimensions including cast and drop. Made in Turkey and imported by GU, Inc.
Price: Synthetic **$625.00**
Price: Walnut or Camo Field **$715.00**
Price: Walnut Target **$870.00**
Price: RS300 Target with adjustable stock **$1,000.00**

SKB MODEL HS 300
Gauges: 12 ga. or 20 ga. **Barrel:** 26 or 28 in. **Stock:** Checkered walnut or camo finish. **Weight:** 7 lbs. Features: Gas-operated design. Introduced in 2017.
Price: Walnut stock **$750.00**
Price: Camo stock **$780.00**

STEVENS S1200
Gauge: 12 ga., 3 in. **Capacity:** 5. **Barrel:** 26 in. with ventilated rib, 5 choke tubes. **Weight:** 6.8 lbs. **Stock:** Black synthetic, camo or walnut. **Features:** Inertia operating system, bottom loading. Introduced in 2016.
Price: Synthetic stock **$571.00**
Price: Walnut **$685.00**
Price: Camo stock **$629.00**

STOEGER MODEL 3000
Gauge: 12 ga., 2 3/4- and 3-in. loads. Minimum recommended load 3-dram, 1 1/8 ounces. **Capacity:** 4+1 magazine. Inertia-driven operating system. **Barrels:** 26 or 28 in. with 3 choke tubes IC, M, XF. **Weights:** 7.4–7.5 lbs. **Finish:** Black synthetic or camo (Realtree APG or Max-4). M3K model is designed for 3-Gun competition and has synthetic stock, 24-in. barrel, modified loading port.
Price: Synthetic **$599.00**
Price: Walnut or Camo **$649.00**
Price: M3K **$699.00**
Price: 3000R rifled slug model **$649.00**

STOEGER MODEL 3020
Gauge: 20 ga., 2 3/4- or 3-in. loads. **Features:** This model has the same general specifications as the Model 3000 except for its chambering and weight of 5.5 to 5.8 pounds.
Price: Synthetic **$599.00**
Price: Camo **$649.00**

STOEGER MODEL 3500
Gauge: 12 ga. 2 3/4-, 3- and 3 1/2-in. loads. Minimum recommended load 3-dram, 1-1/8 ounces. **Barrels:** 24 in., 26 in. or 28 in. Choke tubes for IC, M, XF. **Weights:** 7.4–7.5 pounds. **Finish:** Black synthetic or camo (Realtree APG or Max-4). **Features:** Other features similar to Model 3000.
Price: Synthetic **$679.00**
Price: Camo **$799.00**

TRISTAR VIPER G2
Gauges: 12 ga., 20 ga. 2 3/4 in. or 3 in. interchangeably. Capacity: 5-round magazine. **Barrels:** 26 in., 28 in. (carbon fiber only offered in 12-ga. 28 in. and 20-ga. 26 in.). **Stock:** Wood, black synthetic, Mossy Oak Duck Blind camouflage, faux carbon fiber finish (2008) with the new Comfort Touch technology. **Features:** Magazine cutoff, vent rib with matted sight plane, brass front bead (camo models have fiber-optic front sight), shot plug included, and 3 Beretta-style choke tubes (IC, M, F). Viper synthetic, Viper camo have swivel studs. Five-year warranty. Viper Youth models have shortened length of pull and 24 in. barrel. Sporting model has ported barrel, checkered walnut stock with adjustable comb. Imported by Tristar Sporting Arms Ltd.
Price: From **$519.00**
Price: Camo models, From **$609.00**
Price: Silver Model .... **$639.00–$689.00**
Price: Youth Model **$550.00**
Price: Sporting Model **$800.00**

TRISTAR VIPER MAX
Gauge: 12. 3 1/2 in. **Barrel:** 24–30 in., threaded to accept Benelli choke tubes. Gas-operated action. Offered in several model variants. Introduced in 2017.
Price: **$730.00**

WEATHERBY SA-SERIES
Gauges: 12 ga., 20 ga., 3 in. **Barrels:** 26 in., 28 in. flat ventilated rib. **Weight:** 6.5 lbs. **Stock:** Wood and synthetic. **Features:** The SA-08 is a reliable workhorse that lets you move from early season dove loads to late fall's heaviest waterfowl loads in no time. Available with wood and synthetic stock options in 12- and 20-gauge models, including a scaled-down youth model to fit 28 ga. Comes with 3 application-specific choke tubes (SK/IC/M). Made in Turkey.
Price: SA-08 Upland **$799.00**
Price: SA-08 Synthetic **$649.00**
Price: SA-08 Waterfowler 3.0 .... **$799.00**
Price: SA-08 Synthetic Youth **$649.00**
Price: SA-08 Deluxe **$849.00**
Price: Element Deluxe w/inertia operated action, AA walnut **$1,099.00**

WEATHERBY SA-459
Gauges: 12 ga., 20 ga., 3 in. **Capacities:** 5 or 8 round. **Barrels:** 18.5 in. (Tactical) or 21.25 in. (Turkey). **Features:** Tactical model has Picatinny rail, pistol grip synthetic stock, ghost ring rear and M16-type front sight. Turkey model has fiber optic front sight, Realtree Xtra Green camo finish full coverage.
Price: Tactical model **$699.00**
Price: Turkey model **$799.00**

WINCHESTER SUPER X3
Gauge: 12 ga., 3 in. and 3 1/2 in. **Barrels:** 26 in., 28 in., .742-in. back-bored; Invector Plus choke tubes. **Weights:** 7–7.25 lbs. **Stock:** Composite, 14.25 in. x 1.75 in. x 2 in. Mossy Oak New Break-Up camo with Dura-Touch Armor Coating. Pachmayr Decelerator buttpad with hard heel insert, customizable length of pull. **Features:** Alloy magazine tube, gunmetal grey Perma-Cote UT finish, self-adjusting Active Valve gas action, lightweight recoil spring system. Electroless nickel-plated bolt, three choke tubes, two length-of-pull stock spacers, drop and cast adjustment spacers, sling swivel studs. Introduced 2006. Made in Belgium, assembled in Portugal.
Price: Field **$1,070.00**
Price: Black Shadow 3 1/2 .... **$1,000.00–$1,070.00**
Price: Universal Hunter 3 1/2 .... **$1,160.00–$1,230.00**
Price: Waterfowl Hunter **$1,200.00**
Price: Sporting, adj. comb **$1,700.00**
Price: Cantilever Buck **$1,150.00**
Price: Coyote, pistol grip composite stock **$1,200.00**
Price: Long Beard, pistol grip camo stock **$1,270.00**
Price: Ultimate Sporting Adjustable **$1,870.00**
Price: Composite Sporting **$1,680.00**

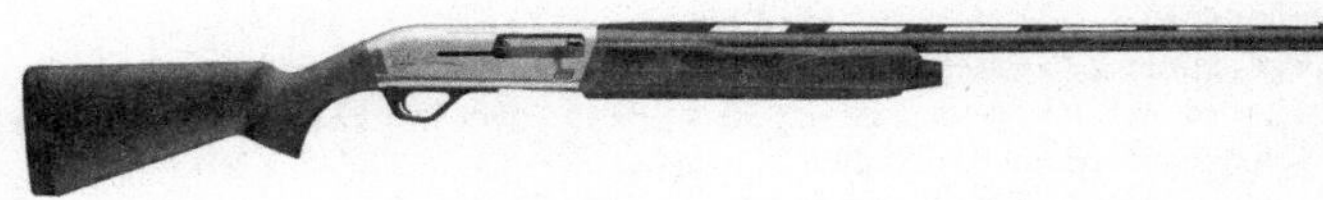

WINCHESTER SUPER X4
Gauge: 12 ga., 3 in. and 3 1/2 in. **Capacity:** 4-round magazine. **Barrels:** 22 in., 24 in., 26 in. or 28 in. Invector Plus Flush choke tubes. **Weight:** 6 lbs. 10 oz. **Stock:** Synthetic with rounded pistol grip and textured gripping surfaces, or satin finished checkered grade II/III Turkish walnut. Length-of-pull spacers. Several camo finishes available. **Features:** TruGlo fiber optic front sight, Inflex Technology recoil pad, active valve system, matte blue barrel, matte black receiver. Offered in Standard, Field, Compact, Waterfowl, Cantilever Buck, Cantilever Turkey models.
Price: From .... **$800.00–$1,070.00.**

Prices given are believed to be accurate at time of publication however, many factors affect retail pricing so exact prices are not possible.

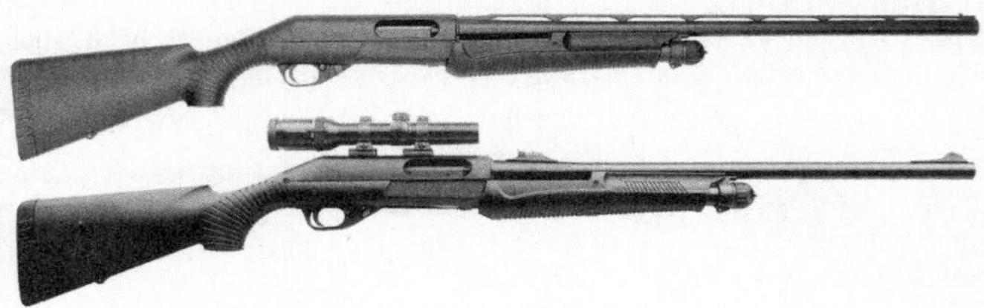

BENELLI SUPERNOVA

Gauge: 12 ga. 3 1/2 in. Capacity: 4-round magazine. **Barrels:** 24 in., 26 in., 28 in. **Lengths:** 45.5–49.5 in. **Stock:** Synthetic; Max-4, Timber, APG HD (2007). **Sights:** Red bar front, metal midbead. **Features:** 2 3/4 in., 3 in. chamber (3 1/2 in. 12 ga. only). Montefeltro rotating bolt design with dual action bars, magazine cutoff, synthetic trigger assembly, adjustable combs, shim kit, choice of buttstocks. Introduced 2006. Imported from Italy by Benelli USA.

Price: **$549.00**
Price: Camo stock **$669.00**
Price: Rifle slug model .... **$829.00–$929.00**

BENELLI NOVA

Gauges: 12 ga., 20 ga. **Capacity:** 4-round magazine. **Barrels:** 24 in., 26 in., 28 in. **Stock:** Black synthetic, Max-4, Timber and APG HD. **Sights:** Red bar. **Features:** 2 3/4 in., 3 in. (3 1/2 in. 12 ga. only). Montefeltro rotating bolt design with dual action bars, magazine cut-off, synthetic trigger assembly. Introduced 1999. Field & Slug Combo has 24 in. barrel and rifled bore; open rifle sights; synthetic stock; weighs 8.1 lbs. Imported from Italy by Benelli USA.

Price: Max-5 camo stock **$559.00**
Price: H20 model, black synthetic, matte nickel finish **$669.00**
Price: Tactical, 18.5-in. barrel, Ghost Ring sight **$459.00**
Price: Black synthetic youth stock, 20 ga. **$469.00**

BROWNING BPS

Gauges: 10 ga., 12 ga., 3 1/2 in.; 12 ga., 16 ga., or 20 ga., 3 in. (2 3/4 in. in target guns), 28 ga., 2 3/4 in., 5-shot magazine, .410, 3 in. chamber. **Barrels:** 10 ga. 24 in. Buck Special, 28 in., 30 in., 32 in. Invector; 12 ga., 20 ga. 22 in., 24 in., 26 in., 28 in., 30 in., 32 in. (Imp. Cyl., Mod. or Full), .410 26 in. (Imp. Cyl., Mod. and Full choke tubes.) Also available with Invector choke tubes, 12 or 20 ga. Upland Special has 22-in. barrel with Invector tubes. BPS 3 in. and 3 1/2 in. have back-bored barrel. **Weight:** 7 lbs., 8 oz. (28 in. barrel). Length: 48.75 in. overall (28 in. barrel). **Stock:** 14.25 in. x 1.5 in. x 2.5 in. Select walnut, semi-beavertail fore-end, full pistol grip stock. **Features:** All 12 ga. 3 in. guns except Buck Special and game guns have back-bored barrels with Invector Plus choke tubes. Bottom feeding and ejection, receiver top safety, high post vent rib. Double action bars eliminate binding. Vent rib barrels only. All 12 and 20 ga. guns with 3 in. chamber available with fully engraved receiver flats at no extra cost. Each gauge has its own unique game scene. Introduced 1977. Stalker is same gun as the standard BPS except all exposed metal parts have a matte blued finish and the stock has a black finish with a black recoil pad. Available in 10 ga. (3 1/2 in.) and 12 ga. with 3 in. or 3 1/2 in. chamber, 22 in., 28 in., 30 in. barrel with Invector choke system. Introduced 1987. Rifled Deer Hunter is similar to the standard BPS except has newly designed receiver/magazine tube/barrel mounting system to eliminate play, heavy 20.5-in. barrel with rifle-type sights with adjustable rear, solid receiver scope mount, "rifle" stock dimensions for scope or open sights, sling swivel studs. Gloss or matte finished wood with checkering, polished blue metal. Medallion model has additional engraving on receiver, polished blue finish, AA/AAA grade walnut stock with checkering. All-Purpose model has Realtree AP camo on stock and fore-end, HiVis fiber optic sights. Introduced 2013. Imported from Japan by Browning.

Price: Field, Stalker models, From .... **$600.00–$700.00**
Price: Camo coverage **$820.00**
Price: Deer Hunter **$830.00**
Price: Deer Hunter Camo **$870.00**
Price: Magnum Hunter (3 1/2 in.) .... **$800.00–$1,030.00**
Price: Medallion **$830.00**
Price: Trap **$840.00**

BROWNING BPS 10 GAUGE SERIES

Similar to the standard BPS except completely covered with Mossy Oak Shadow Grass camouflage. Available with 26- and 28-in. barrel. Introduced 1999. Imported by Browning

Price: Mossy Oak camo **$950.00**
Price: Synthetic stock, Stalker **$800.00**

BROWNING BPS NWTF TURKEY SERIES

Similar to the standard BPS except has full coverage Mossy Oak Break-Up Infinity camo finish on synthetic stock, fore-end and exposed metal parts. Offered in 12 ga., 3 in. or 3 1/2 in., or 10 ga. 24-in. bbl. has extra-full choke tube and HiViz fiber-optic sights. Introduced 2001. From Browning.

Price: 12 ga., 3 in. **$950.00**
Price: 3 1/2 in. **$1,030.00**

BROWNING BPS MICRO MIDAS

Gauges: 12 ga, 20 ga., 28 ga. or .410 bore. **Barrels:** 24 or 26 in. Three Invector choke tubes for 12 and 20 ga., standard tubes for 28 ga. and .410. **Stock:** Walnut with pistol grip and recoil pad. Satin finished and scaled down to fit smaller statured shooters. Length of pull is 13.25 in. Two spacers included for stock length adjustments. **Weights:** 7–7.8 lbs.

Price: .... **$700.00–$740.00**

BROWING BPS HIGH CAPACITY

Gauge: .410 bore. 3 in. **Capacity:** 5-round magazine. **Barrel:** 20 in. fixed Cylinder choke; stainless Steel; Matte finish. **Weight:** 6 lbs. **Length:** 40.75 in. **Stock:** Black composite on All Weather with matte finish. **Features:** Forged and machined steel; satin nickel finish. Bottom ejection; dual steel action bars; top tang safety. HiViz Tactical fiber-optic front sight; stainless internal mechanism; swivel studs installed.

Price: Synthetic **$800.00**

CHARLES DALY 300 SERIES

Gauges: 12 ga., 20 ga. or 28 ga. 3 in. and 2 3/4-in. shells (12 ga. and 20 ga.), 2 3/4 in. (28 ga.). Model 335 Master Mag is chambered for 12-ga. 3 1/2-inch shells. **Barrels:** 24 in., 26 in., 28 in. and 30 in., depending upon specific model. Ventilated rib. Three choke tubes (REM-Choke pattern) are provided. **Stock:** Synthetic, walnut or camo. **Weights:** 7–8 lbs. Left-hand models available. Imported from Turkey.

Price: Field .... **$365.00–$495.00**
Price: Tactical .... **$423.00–$503.00**
Price: Turkey **$553.00**

CZ 612

Gauge: 12 ga. Chambered for all shells up to 3 1/2 in. **Capacity:** 5+1, magazine plug included with Wildfowl Magnum. **Barrels:** 18.5 in. (Home Defense), 20 in. (HC-P), 26 in. (Wildfowl Mag). **Weights:** 6–6.8 pounds. **Stock:** Polymer. **Finish:** Matte black or full camo (Wildfowl Mag.) HC-P model has pistol grip stock, fiber optic front sight and ghost-ring rear. Home Defense Combo comes with extra 26-in. barrel.

Price: Wildfowl Magnum **$428.00**
Price: Home Defense .... **$304.00–$409.00**

CZ MODEL 620/628 Field Select

Gauges: 20 ga. or 28 ga. **Barrel:** 28 inches. **Weight:** 5.4 lbs. Features: Similar to Model 612 except for chambering. Introduced in 2017.

Price: **$429.00**

ESCORT PUMP SERIES

Gauges: 12 ga., 20 ga.; 3 in. **Barrels:** 18 in. (AimGuard, Home Defense and MarineGuard), 22 in. (Youth Pump), 26 in., and 28 in. lengths. **Weight:** 6.7-7.0 lbs. **Stock:** Polymer in black, Shadow Grass camo or Obsession camo finish. Two adjusting spacers included. Youth model has Trio recoil pad. **Sights:** Bead or Spark front sights, depending on model. AimGuard and MarineGuard models have blade front sights. **Features:** Black-chrome or dipped camo metal parts, top of receiver dovetailed for sight mounts, gold plated trigger, trigger guard safety, magazine cutoff. Three choke tubes (IC, M, F) except AimGuard/MarineGuard which are cylinder bore. Models include: FH, FH Youth, AimGuard and Marine Guard. Introduced in 2003. Imported from Turkey by Legacy Sports International.

Price: **$379.00**
Price: Youth model **$393.00**
Price: Model 87 w/wood stock........ **$350.00**
Price: Home Defense (18-in. bbl.) **$400.00**

HARRINGTON & RICHARDSON (H&R) PARDNER PUMP

Gauges: 12 ga., 20 ga. 3 in. **Barrels:** 21–28 in. **Weight:** 6.5–7.5 lbs. **Stock:** Synthetic or hardwood. Ventilated recoil pad and grooved fore-end. **Features:** Steel receiver, double action bars, cross-bolt safety, easy takedown, ventilated rib, screw-in choke tubes.

Price: From........ **$231.00–$259.00**

IAC MODEL 97T TRENCH GUN

Gauge: 12 ga., 2 3/4 in. **Barrel:** 20 in. with cylinder choke. **Stock:** Hand rubbed American walnut. **Features:** Replica of Winchester Model 1897 Trench Gun. Metal handguard, bayonet lug. Imported from China by Interstate Arms Corp.

Price: **$465.00**

IAC HAWK SERIES

Gauge: 12, 2 3/4 in. **Barrel:** 18.5 in. with cylinder choke. **Stock:** Synthetic. **Features:** This series of tactical/home defense shotguns is based on the Remington 870 design. 981 model has top Picatinny rail and bead front sight. 982 has adjustable ghost ring sight with post front. 982T has same sights as 982 plus a pistol grip stock. Imported from China by Interstate Arms Corporation.

Price: 981 .... **$275.00**
Price: 982 .... **$285.00**
Price: 982T **$300.00**

ITHACA MODEL 37 FEATHERWEIGHT

Gauges: 12 ga., 20 ga., 16 ga., 28 ga. **Capacity:** 4+1. **Barrels:** 26 in., 28 in. or 30 in. with 3-in. chambers (12 and 20 ga.), plain or ventilated rib. **Weights:** 6.1–7.6 lbs. **Stock:** Fancy-grade black walnut with Pachmayr Decelerator recoil pad. Checkered fore-end made of matching walnut. **Features:** Receiver machined from a single block of steel or aluminum. Barrel is steel shot compatible. Three Briley choke tubes provided. Available in several variations including turkey, home defense, tactical and high-grade.

Price: 12 ga., 16 ga. or 20 ga. From **$895.00**
Price: 28 ga. From **$1,149.00**
Price: Turkey Slayer w/synthetic stock, From **$925.00**
Price: Trap Series 12 ga **$999.00**
Price: Waterfowl **$885.00**
Price: Home Defense 18- or 20-in. bbl **$784.00**

ITHACA DEERSLAYER III SLUG

Gauges: 12 ga., 20 ga. 3 in. **Barrel:** 26 in. fully rifled, heavy fluted with 1:28 twist for 12 ga. 1:24 for 20 ga. **Weights:** 8.14–9.5 lbs. with scope mounted. **Length:** 45.625 in. overall. **Stock:** Fancy black walnut stock and fore-end. **Sights:** NA. **Features:** Updated, slug-only version of the classic Model 37. Bottom ejection, blued barrel and receiver.

Price: **$1,350.00**

MAVERICK ARMS MODEL 88

Gauges: 12 ga., 20 ga. 3 in. **Barrels:** 26 in. or 28 in., Accu-Mag choke tubes for steel or lead shot. **Weight:** 7.25 lbs. **Stock:** Black synthetic with recoil pad. **Features:** Crossbolt safety, aluminum alloy receiver. Economy model of Mossberg Model 500 series. Available in several variations including Youth, Slug and Special Purpose (home defense) models.

Price: **$298.00**

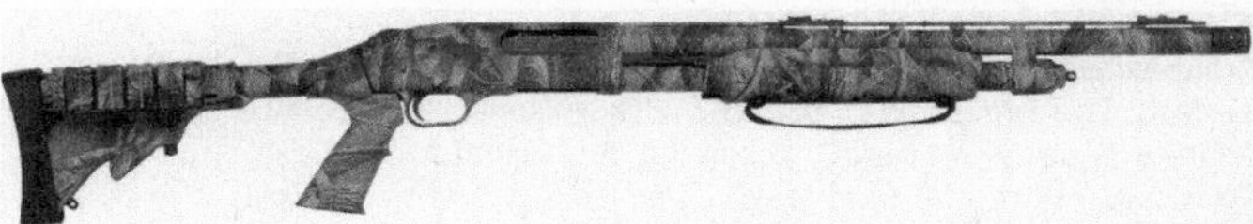

MOSSBERG MODEL 835 ULTI-MAG

Gauge: 12 ga., 3 1/2 in. **Barrels:** Ported 24 in. rifled bore, 24 in., 28 in., Accu-Mag choke tubes for steel or lead shot. Combo models come with interchangeable second barrel. **Weight:** 7.75 lbs. **Length:** 48.5 in. overall. **Stock:** 14 in. x 1.5 in. x 2.5 in. Dual Comb. Cut-checkered hardwood or camo synthetic; both have recoil pad. **Sights:** White bead front, brass mid-bead; fiber-optic rear. Turkey Thug has red dot sight. **Features:** Shoots 2 3/4-, 3- or 3 1/2-in. shells. Back-bored and ported barrel to reduce recoil, improve patterns. Ambidextrous thumb safety, twin extractors, dual slide bars. Mossberg Cablelock included. Introduced 1988.

Price: Turkey .... **$601.00–$617.00**
Price: Waterfowl .... **$518.00–$603.00**
Price: Turkey/Deer combo........ **$661.00–$701.00**
Price: Turkey/Waterfowl combo **$661.00**

MOSSBERG MODEL 500 SPORTING SERIES

Gauges: 12 ga., 20 ga., .410 bore, 3 in. **Barrels:** 18.5 in. to 28 in. with fixed or Accu-Choke, plain or vent rib. Combo models come with interchangeable second barrel. **Weight:** 6.25 lbs. (.410), 7.25 lbs. (12). Length: 48 in. overall (28-in. barrel). **Stock:** 14 in. x 1.5 in. x 2.5 in. Walnut-stained hardwood, black synthetic, Mossy Oak Advantage camouflage. Cut-checkered grip and fore-end. **Sights:** White bead front, brass mid-bead; fiber-optic. **Features:** Ambidextrous thumb safety, twin extractors, disconnecting safety, dual action bars. Quiet Carry fore-end. Many barrels are ported. FLEX series has many modular options and accessories including barrels and stocks. From Mossberg. Left-hand versions (L-series) available in most models.

Price: Turkey, From **$486.00**
Price: Waterfowl, From **$537.00**
Price: Combo, From **$593.00**
Price: FLEX Hunting........ **$702.00**
Price: FLEX All Purpose **$561.00**
Price: Field, From **$419.00**
Price: Slugster, From **$447.00**
Price: FLEX Deer/Security combo........ **$787.00**

Prices given are believed to be accurate at time of publication however, many factors affect retail pricing so exact prices are not possible.

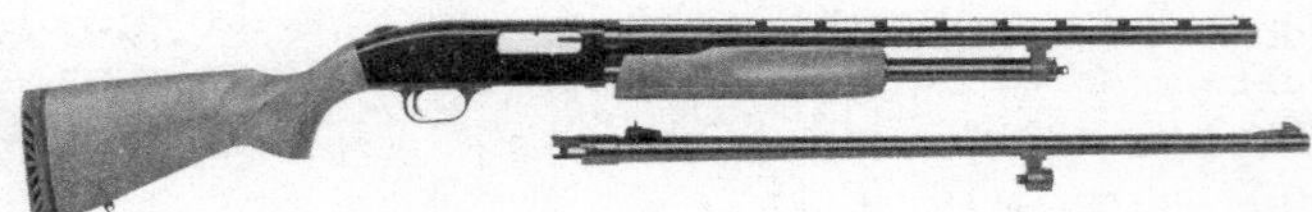

MOSSBERG MODEL 500 SUPER BANTAM PUMP
Same as the Model 500 Sporting Pump except 12 or 20 ga., 22-in. vent rib Accu-Choke barrel with choke tube set; has 1 in. shorter stock, reduced length from pistol grip to trigger, reduced fore-end reach. Introduced 1992.
Price: **$419.00**
Price: Combo with extra slug barrel, camo finish **$549.00**

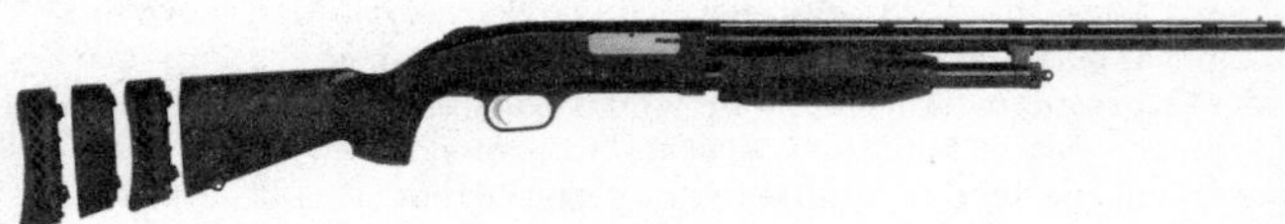

MOSSBERG 510 MINI BANTAM
Gauges: 20 ga., .410 bore, 3 in. **Barrel:** 18.5 in. vent-rib. **Weight:** 5 lbs. Length: 34.75 in. **Stock:** Synthetic with optional Mossy Oak Break-Up Infinity, Muddy Girl pink/black camo. **Features:** Available in either 20 ga. or .410 bore, the Mini features an 18.5-in. vent-rib barrel with dual bead sights. Parents don't have to worry about their young shooter growing out of this gun too quick, the adjustable classic stock can be adjusted from 10.5 to 11.5-in. length of pull so the Mini can grow with your youngster. This adjustability also helps provide a proper fit for young shooters and allowing for a more safe and enjoyable shooting experience.
Price: From .... **$419.00–$466.00**

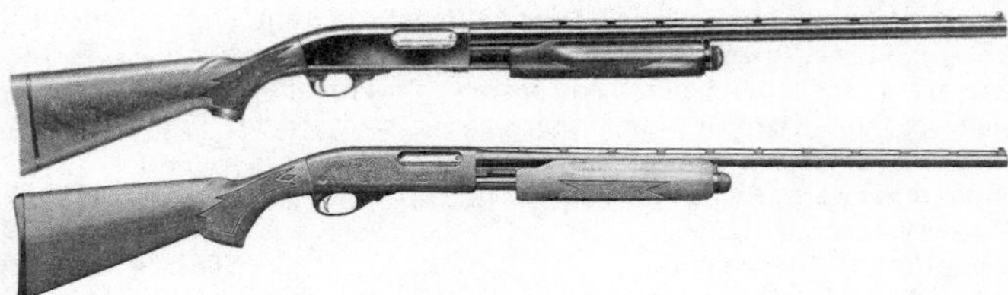

REMINGTON MODEL 870 WINGMASTER
Gauge: 12 ga., 20 ga., 28 ga., .410 bore. **Barrel:** 25 in., 26 in., 28 in., 30 in. (RemChokes). **Weight:** 7.25 lbs. **Lengths:** 46–48 in. **Stock:** Walnut, hardwood. **Sights:** Single bead (Twin bead Wingmaster). **Features:** Light contour barrel. Double action bars, cross-bolt safety, blue finish. LW is 28 ga. and .410 bore only, 25-in. vent rib barrel with RemChoke tubes, high-gloss wood finish. Gold-plated trigger, American B Grade walnut stock and fore-end, high-gloss finish, *fleur-de-lis* checkering. A classic American shotgun first introduced in 1950.
Price: **$847.00**

REMINGTON MODEL 870 MARINE MAGNUM
Similar to 870 Wingmaster except all metal plated with electroless nickel, black synthetic stock and fore-end. Has 18-in. plain barrel (cyl.), bead front sight, 7-round magazine. Introduced 1992. XCS version with TriNyte corrosion control introduced 2007.
Price: **$841.00**

REMINGTON MODEL 870 CLASSIC TRAP
Similar to Model 870 Wingmaster except has 30-in. vent rib, light contour barrel, singles, mid- and long-handicap choke tubes, semi-fancy American walnut stock, high-polish blued receiver with engraving. Chamber 2.75 in. From Remington Arms Co.
Price: **$1,120.00**

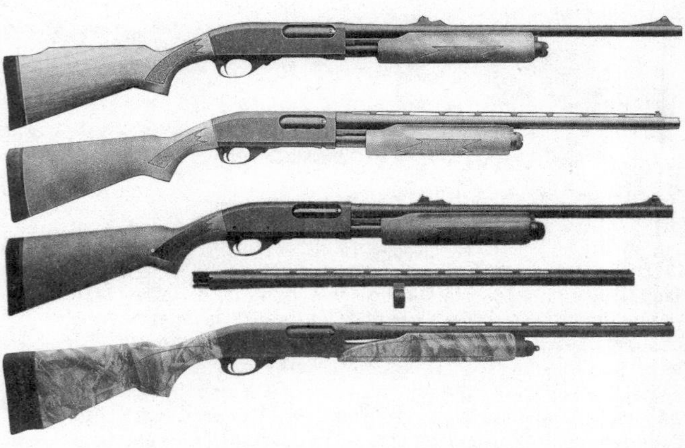

REMINGTON MODEL 870 EXPRESS
Similar to Model 870 Wingmaster except laminate, synthetic black, or camo stock with solid, black recoil pad and pressed checkering on grip and fore-end. Outside metal surfaces have black oxide finish. Comes with 26- or 28-in. vent rib barrel with mod. RemChoke tube. ShurShot Turkey (2008) has ShurShot synthetic pistol-grip thumbhole design, extended fore-end, Mossy Oak Obsession camouflage, matte black metal finish, 21-in. vent rib barrel, twin beads, Turkey Extra Full Rem Choke tube. Receiver drilled and tapped for mounting optics. ShurShot FR CL (Fully Rifled Cantilever, 2008) includes compact 23-in. fully rifled barrel with integrated cantilever scope mount.
Price: .... **$417.00–$629.00**

REMINGTON MODEL 870 EXPRESS SUPER MAGNUM
Similar to Model 870 Express except 28-in. vent rib barrel with 3 1/2-in. chamber, vented recoil pad. Introduced 1998. Model 870 Express Super Magnum Waterfowl (2008) is fully camouflaged with Mossy Oak Duck Blind pattern, 28-inch vent rib Rem Choke barrel, "Over Decoys" Choke tube (.007 in.) fiber-optic HiViz single bead front sight; front and rear sling swivel studs, padded black sling.
Price: **$469.00**

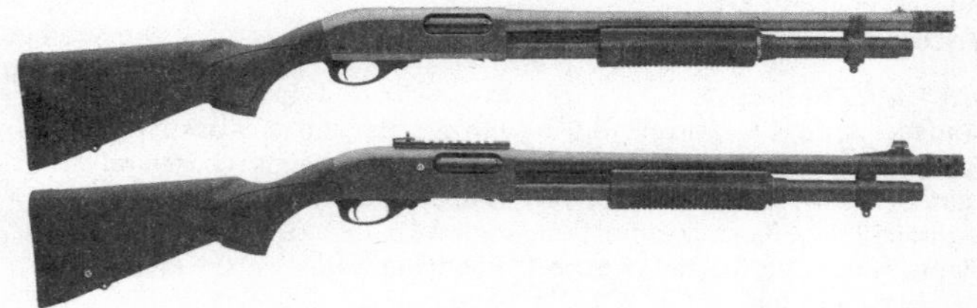

REMINGTON MODEL 870 EXPRESS TACTICAL
Similar to Model 870 but in 12 ga. only (2 3/4 in. and 3 in. interchangeably) with 18.5-in. barrel, Tactical RemChoke extended/ported choke tube, black synthetic buttstock and fore-end, extended magazine tube, gray powder coat finish overall. 38.5 in. overall length. Weighs 7.5 lbs.
Price: **$601.00**
Price: Model 870 TAC Desert Recon; desert camo stock and sand-toned metal surfaces **$692.00**
Price: Tactical Magpul **$898.00**

Prices given are believed to be accurate at time of publication however, many factors affect retail pricing so exact prices are not possible.

REMINGTON 870 DM SERIES
Gauge: 12 ga. (2 3/4 in. and 3 in. interchangeably). **Capacity:** Detachable 6-round magazine. **Barrel:** 18.5-in. cylinder bore. **Stock:** Hardwood or black synthetic with textured gripping surfaces. Tac-14 DM model features short pistol grip buttstock and 14-inch barrel.
Price: **$559.00**

REMINGTON MODEL 870 SPS SHURSHOT SYNTHETIC SUPER SLUG
Gauge: 12 ga.; 2 3/4 in. and 3 in. interchangeable. **Barrel:** 25.5-in. extra-heavy, fully rifled pinned to receiver. **Weight:** 7.875 lbs. **Length:** 47 in. overall. **Features:** Pump-action model based on 870 platform. SuperCell recoil pad. Drilled and tapped for scope mounts with Weaver rail included. Matte black metal surfaces, ShurShot pistol grip buttstock with Mossy Oak Treestand camo.
Price: **$829.00**
Price: 870 SPS ShurShot Synthetic Turkey; adjustable sights and APG HD camo buttstock and fore-end **$681.00**

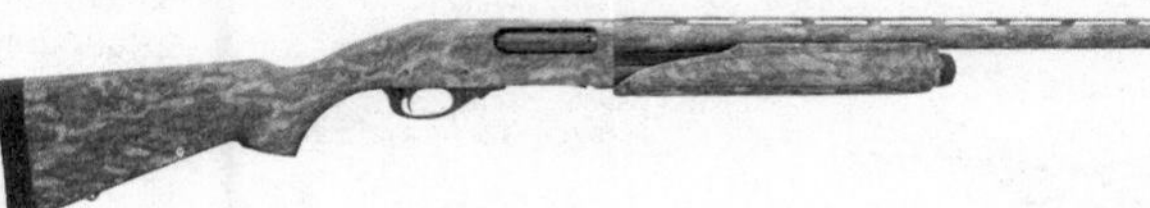

REMINGTON 870 EXPRESS SYNTHETIC SUPER MAG TURKEY-WATERFOWL CAMO
Gauge: 12 ga., 2 3/4 to 3 1/2 in. **Features:** Pump-action shotgun. Full Mossy Oak Bottomland camo coverage; 26-inch barrel with HiViz fiber-optics sights; Wingmaster HD Waterfowl and Turkey Extra Full RemChokes; SuperCell recoil pad; drilled and tapped receiver.
Price: **$629.00**

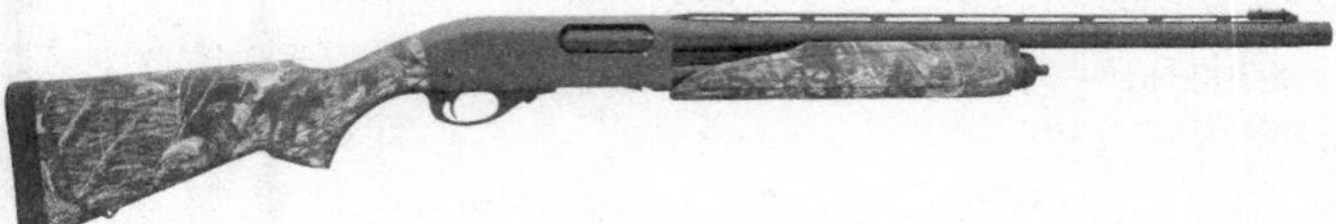

REMINGTON 870 EXPRESS SYNTHETIC TURKEY CAMO
Gauge: 12 ga., 2 3/4 and 3 in. **Features:** Pump-action shotgun. 21-inch vent rib bead-sighted barrel; standard Express finish on barrel and receiver; Turkey Extra Full RemChoke; synthetic stock with integrated sling swivel attachment.
Price: **$492.00**

REMINGTON 870 SUPER MAG TURKEY-PREDATOR CAMO WITH SCOPE
Gauge: 12 ga., 2 3/4 to 3 1/2 in. **Features:** Pump-action shotgun. 20-in. barrel; TruGlo red/green selectable illuminated sight mounted on pre-installed Weaver-style rail; black padded sling; Wingmaster HDTurkey/Predator RemChoke; full Mossy Oak Obsession camo coverage; ShurShot pistol grip stock with black overmolded grip panels; TruGlo 30mm Red/Green Dot Scope pre-mounted.
Price: **$710.00**

STEVENS MODEL 320
Gauges: 12 ga., or 20 ga. with 3-in. chamber. **Capacity:** 5+1. **Barrels:** 18.25 in., 20 in., 22 in., 26 in. or 28 in. with interchangeable choke tubes. Features include all-steel barrel and receiver; bottom-load and ejection design; black synthetic stock.
Price: Security Model **$276.00**
Price: Field Model 320 with 28-inch barrel **$251.00**
Price: Combo Model with Field and Security barrels **$307.00**

STOEGER P3000
Gauge: 12 ga. 3-in. **Barrels:** 18.5 in., 26 in., 28 in., with ventilated rib. **Weight:** 6.5–7 lbs. **Stock:** Black synthetic. Camo finish available. Defense Model available with or without pistol grip.
Price: **$299.00**
Price: Camo finish **$399.00**
Price: Defense model w/pistol grip **$349.00**

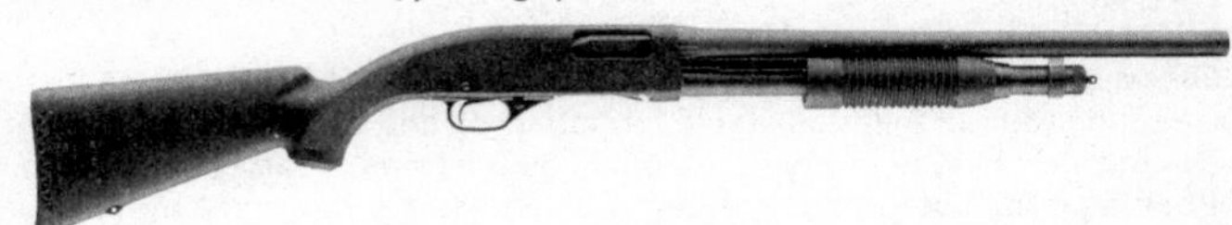

WINCHESTER SUPER X (SXP)
Gauges: 12 ga., 3 in. or 3 1/2 in. chambers; 20 ga., 3 in. **Barrels:** 18 in., 26 in., 28 in. Barrels .742-in. back-bored, chrome plated; Invector Plus choke tubes. **Weights:** 6.5–7 lbs. **Stocks:** Walnut or composite. **Features:** Rotary bolt, four lugs, dual steel action bars. Walnut Field has gloss-finished walnut stock and forearm, cut checkering. Black Shadow Field has composite stock and forearm, non-glare matte finish barrel and receiver. SXP Defender has composite stock and forearm, chromed plated, 18-in. cylinder choked barrel, non-glare metal surfaces, five-shot magazine, grooved forearm. Some models offered in left-hand versions. Reintroduced 2009. Made in USA by Winchester Repeating Arms Co.
Price: Black Shadow Field, 3 in. **$380.00**
Price: Black Shadow Field, 3 1/2 in. **$430.00**
Price: SXP Defender .... **$350.00–$400.00**
Price: Waterfowl Hunter 3 in. **$460.00**
Price: Waterfowl Hunter 3 1/2 in. **$500.00**
Price: Turkey Hunter 3 1/2 in. **$520.00**
Price: Black Shadow Deer **$520.00**
Price: Trap **$480.00**
Price: Field, walnut stock .... **$400.00–$430.00**

BARRETT SOVEREIGN ALBANY
Gauges: 12 ga., 20 ga., 28 ga. 3 in. (2 3/4 for 28 ga.) **Barrels:** 26 in., 28 in. or 30 in. **Stock:** Checkered grade AAA Turkish walnut with rounded Prince of Wales pistol grip. **Features:** Receiver scaled to individual gauges. Round body boxlock design, ornamental sideplates, coin-finished receiver. Introduced in 2016. Imported from Italy by Barrett Firearms.
Price: 12 or 20 ga. **$5,700.00**
Price: 28 ga. **$6,150.00**

BARRET SOVEREIGN BX-PRO
Gauge: 12 ga. **Barrels:** 30 in., 32 in. with 6 extended choke tubes. Ventilated rib tapered from 10mm to 7mm. **Stock:** A+ grade walnut with rounded Prince of Wales pistol grip. Cast-off comb and toe for right-handed shooters Length of pull: 14.5 inches. Adjustable comb. Right-hand palm swell. **Features:** Automatic ejectors, single selective trigger, coin finished and engraved receiver. Imported from Fausti of Italy by Barrett Firearms.
Price: **$3,075.00**

BARRET SOVEREIGN RUTHERFORD
Gauges: 12 ga., 16 ga., 20 ga., 28 ga. **Barrels**: 26 in., 28 in. with 5 choke tubes. Chamber lengths are 3-in. for 12 and 20 ga., 2 ¾ in. for 16 ga. and 28 ga. **Stock:** A+ grade with cut checkering, red recoil pad, and rounded Prince of Wales pistol grip. **Features:** Receivers are sized to individual gauge, automatic ejectors, single selective trigger, coin finished receiver. Imported from Fausti of Italy by Barrett Firearms.
Price: 12, 20 ga.......... **$2,200.00**
Price: 16, 28 ga.......... **$2,520.00**

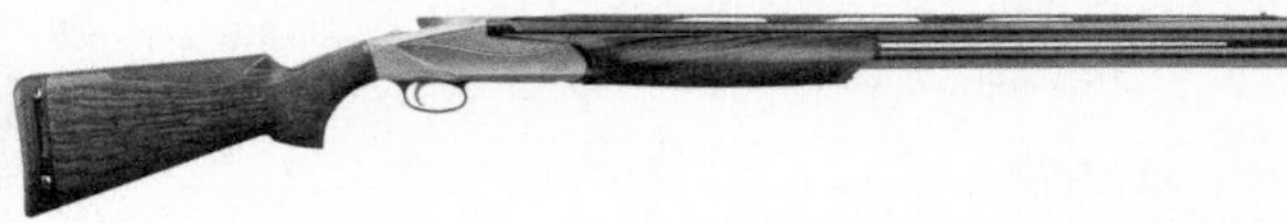

BENELLI 828U
Gauges: 12 ga. 3 in. **Barrels:** 26 in., 28 in. **Weights:** 6.5–7 lbs. **Stock:** AA-grade satin walnut, fully adjustable for both drop and cast. **Features:** New patented locking system allows use of aluminum frame. Features include carbon fiber rib, fiber-optic sight, removable trigger group, and Benelli's Progressive Comfort recoil reduction system.
Price: Matte black.......... **$2,499.00**
Price: Nickel **$2,999.00**

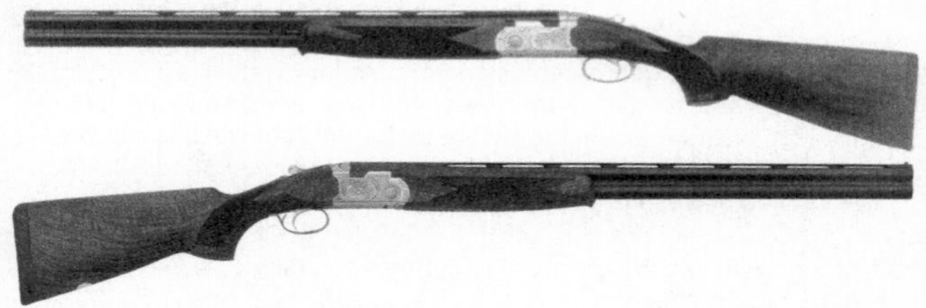

BERETTA 686/687 SILVER PIGEON SERIES
Gauges: 12 ga., 20 ga., 28 ga., 3 in. (2 3/4 in. 28 ga.). .410 bore, 3 in. **Barrels:** 26 in., 28 in. **Weight:** 6.8 lbs. **Stock:** Checkered walnut. **Features:** Interchangeable barrels (20 ga. and 28 ga.), single selective gold-plated trigger, boxlock action, auto safety, Schnabel fore-end.
Price: 686 Silver Pigeon Grade I **$2,350.00**
Price: 686 Silver Pigeon Grade I, Sporting **$2,400.00**
Price: 687 Silver Pigeon Grade III **$3,430.00**
Price: 687 Silver Pigeon Grade V **$4,075.00**

BERETTA MODEL 687 EELL
Gauges: 12 ga., 20 ga., 28 ga., 410 bore. **Features:** Premium-grade model with decorative sideplates featuring lavish hand-chased engraving with a classic game scene enhanced by detailed leaves and flowers that also cover the trigger guard, trigger plate and fore-end lever. Stock has high-grade, specially selected European walnut with fine-line checkering. Offered in three action sizes with scaled-down 28 ga. and .410 receivers. Combo models are available with extra barrel sets in 20/28 or 28/.410.
Price: **$8,450.00**
Price: Combo model **$9,995.00**

BERETTA MODEL 690
Gauge: 12 ga. 3 in. **Barrels:** 26 in., 28 in., 30 in. with OptimaChoke HP system. Features: Similar to the 686/687 series with minor improvements. Stock has higher grade oil-finished walnut. Re-designed barrel/fore-end attachment reduces weight.
Price: .... **$2,650.00–$3,100.00**

BERETTA MODEL 692 SPORTING
Gauge: 12 ga., 3 in. **Barrels:** 30 in. with long forcing cones of approximately 14 in.. Skeet model available with 28- or 30-in. barrel, Trap model with 30 in or 32 in. Receiver is .50-in. wider than 682 model for improved handling. **Stock:** Hand rubbed oil finished select walnut with Schnabel fore-end. Features include selective single adjustable trigger, manual safety, tapered 8mm to 10mm rib.
Price: **$4,800.00**
Price: Skeet **$5,275.00**
Price: Trap **$5,600.00**

BERETTA DT11
Gauge: 12 ga. 3 in. **Barrels:** 30 in., 32 in., 34 in. Top rib has hollowed bridges. **Stock:** Hand-checkered buttstock and fore-end. Hand-rubbed oil, Tru-Oil or wax finish. Adjustable comb on skeet and trap models. **Features:** Competition model offered in Sporting, Skeet and Trap models. Newly designed receiver, top lever, safety/selector button.
Price: Sporting, From.......... **$8,650.00**
Price: Skeet, From.......... **$8,650.00**
Price: Trap, From **$8,999.00**

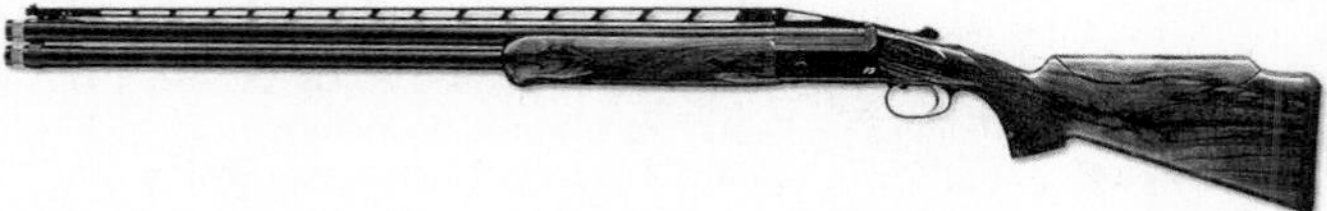

BLASER F3 SUPERSPORT
Gauge: 12 ga., 3 in. **Barrel:** 32 in. **Weight:** 9 lbs. **Stock:** Adjustable semi-custom, Turkish walnut wood grade: 4. **Features:** The latest addition to the F3 family is the F3 SuperSport. The perfect blend of overall weight, balance and weight distribution make the F3 SuperSport the ideal competitor. Briley Spectrum-5 chokes, free-floating barrels, adjustable barrel hanger system on o/u, chrome plated barrels full length, revolutionary ejector ball system, barrels finished in a powder coated nitride, selectable competition trigger.
Price: SuperSport, From **$9,076.00**
Price: Competition Sporting.......... **$7,951.00**
Price: Superskeet American Super Trap.......... **$9,076.00**

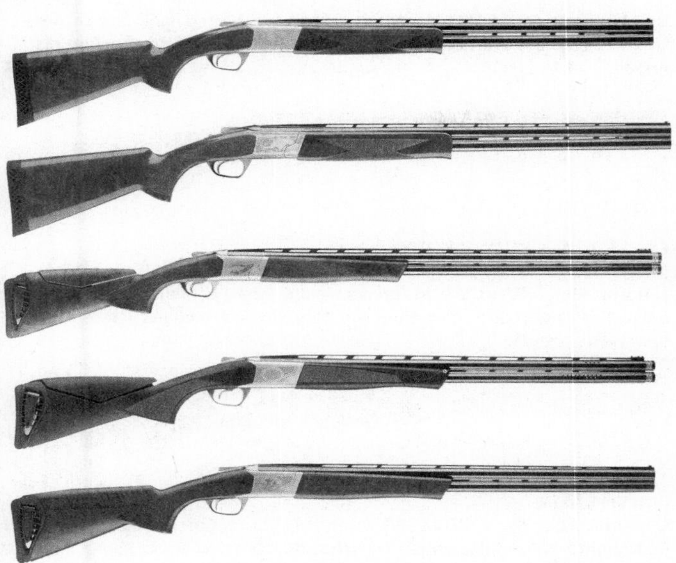

BROWNING CYNERGY

Gauges: .410 bore, 12 ga., 20 ga., 28 ga. **Barrels:** 26 in., 28 in., 30 in., 32 in. **Stocks:** Walnut or composite. **Sights:** White bead front most models; HiViz Pro-Comp sight on some models; mid bead. **Features:** Mono-Lock hinge, recoil-reducing interchangeable Inflex recoil pad, silver nitride receiver; striker-based trigger, ported barrel option. Imported from Japan by Browning.

Price: Field Grade Model, 12 ga. **$1,870.00**
Price: CX composite **$1,670.00**
Price: CX walnut stock **$1,740.00**
Price: Field, small gauges **$1,940.00**
Price: Feather model, From **$2,140.00**
Price: Sporting, From **$2,400.00**
Price: Sporting w/adjustable comb **$2,670.00**
Price: Camo, Mossy Oak Shadow Grass or Realtree Max 5 .... **$2,000.00**
Price: Ultimate Turkey, Mossy Oak Breakup camo **$2,340.00**

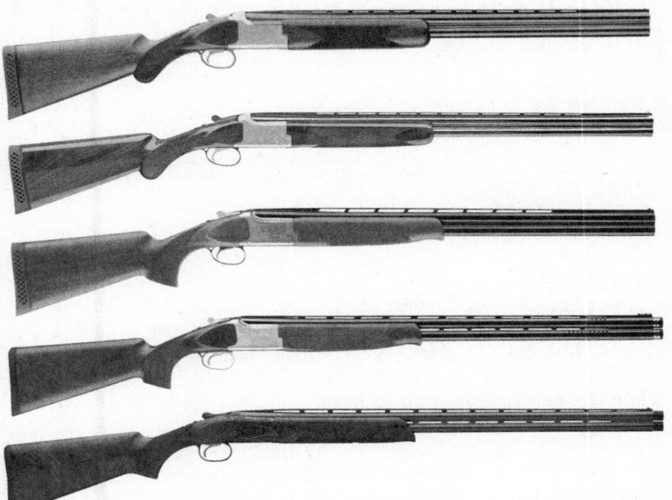

BROWNING CITORI SERIES

Gauges: 12 ga., 20 ga., 28 ga., .410 bore. **Barrels:** 26 in., 28 in. in 28 ga. and .410 bore. Offered with Invector choke tubes. All 12- and 20-ga. models have back-bored barrels and Invector Plus choke system. **Weights:** 6 lbs., 8 oz. (26 in. .410) to 7 lbs., 13 oz. (30 in. 12 ga.). Length: 43 in. overall (26-in. bbl.). **Stock:** Dense walnut, hand checkered, full pistol grip, beavertail fore-end. Field-type recoil pad on 12 ga. field guns and trap and skeet models. **Sights:** Medium-raised beads, German nickel silver. **Features:** Barrel selector integral with safety, automatic ejectors, three-piece takedown. Imported from Japan by Browning.

Price: Lightning, From **$1,990.00**
Price: White Lightning, From **$2,070.00**
Price: Superlight Feather **$2,390.00**
Price: Lightning Feather, combo 20 and 28 ga. **$3,580.00**
Price: Crossover Target (CXT) **$2,200.00**
Price: Crossover (CXS) **$2,140.00**
Price: Micro Midas Satin Hunter w/13 in. stock **$1,650.00**

BROWNING 725 CITORI

Gauges: 12 ga., 20 ga., 28 ga. or .410 bore. **Barrels:** 26 in., 28 in., 30 in. **Weights:** 5.7–7.6 lbs. **Length:** 43.75–50 in. **Stock:** Gloss oil finish, grade II/III walnut. Features: New receiver that is significantly lower in profile than other 12-gauge Citori models. Mechanical trigger, Vector Pro lengthened forcing cones, three Invector-DS choke tubes, silver nitride finish with high relief engraving.

Price: 725 Field (12 ga. or 20 ga.) **$2,470.00**
Price: 725 Field (28 ga. or .410 bore) **$2,540.00**
Price: 725 Feather (12 ga. or 20 ga.) **$2,550.00**
Price: 725 Sporting, From **$3,070.00**
Price: 725 Sporting w/adjustable comb **$3,530.00**
Price: 725 Skeet, From **$3,140.00**
Price: 725 Trap, From **$3,340.00**

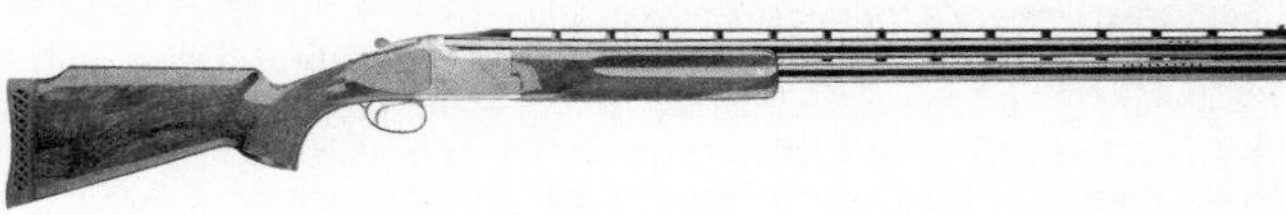

BROWNING CITORI XT TRAP

Gauge: 12 ga. **Barrels:** 30 in., 32 in. Invector-Plus choke tubes, adjustable comb and buttplate. **Features:** Engraved silver nitride receiver with gold highlights, vented side barrel rib. Introduced 1999. Imported by Browning.

Price: XT Trap **$2,650.00**
Price: XT Trap w/adjustable comb **$3,000.00**

CAESAR GUERINI

Gauges: 12 ga., 20 ga., 28 ga., also 20/28 gauge combo. Some models are available in .410 bore. **Barrels:** All standard lengths from 26–32 inches. **Weights:** 5.5–8.8 lbs. **Stock:** High-grade walnut with hand-rubbed oil finish. **Features:** A wide range of over/under models designed for the field, sporting clays, skeet and trap shooting. The models listed below are representative of some of the different models and variants. Many optional features are offered including high-grade wood and engraving, and extra sets of barrels. Made it Italy and imported by Caesar Guerini USA.

Price: Summit Sporting **$3,995.00**
Price: Tempio **$4,195.00**
Price: Ellipse **$4,650.00**
Price: Ellipse Curve **$7,295.00**
Price: Ellipse EVO Sporting **$6,950.00**
Price: Magnus **$4,925.00**
Price: Maxum **$6,650.00**
Price: Forum **$11,120.00**
Price: Woodlander **$3,700.00**
Price: Invictus Sporting **$7,200.00**
Price: Maxum Trap **$8,995.00**
Price: Maxum Sporting **$7,150.00**

Prices given are believed to be accurate at time of publication however, many factors affect retail pricing so exact prices are not possible.

CONNECTICUT SHOTGUN A10 AMERICAN
Gauges: 12 ga., 20 ga., 28 ga., .410 bore. 2 3/4, 3 in. Sidelock design. **Barrels:** 26 in., 28 in., 30 in. or 32 in. with choice of fixed or interchangeable chokes. **Weight:** 6.3 lbs. **Stock:** Hand rubbed oil finish, hand checkered at 24 LPI. Black, English or Turkish walnut offered in numerous grades. Pistol or Prince of Wales grip, short or long tang. **Features:** Low-profile, shallow frame full sidelock. Single-selective trigger, automatic ejectors. Engraved models available. Made in the USA by Connecticut Shotgun Mfg. Co.
Price: 12 ga., From **$7,995.00**
Price: Smaller ga., From **$9,045.00**
Price: Sporting Clays **$13,500.00**

CONNECTICUT SHOTGUN MODEL 21 O/U
Gauge: 20 ga., 3 in. **Barrels:** 26–32 in. chrome-lined, back-bored with extended forcing cones. **Weight:** 6.3 lbs. **Stock:** A Fancy (2X) American walnut, standard point checkering, choice of straight or pistol grip. Higher grade walnut is optional. **Features:** The over/under version of Conn. Shotgun's replica of the Winchester Model 21 side-by-side, built using the same machining, tooling, techniques and finishes. Low-profile shallow frame with blued receiver. Pigeon and Grand American grades are available. Made in the USA by Connecticut Shotgun Mfg. Co.
Price: From **$3,995.00**

CZ SPORTER
Gauge: 12 ga., 3 in. **Barrels:** 30 in., 32 in. chrome-lined, back-bored with extended forcing cones. **Weight:** 8.5 lbs. **Length:** NA. **Stock:** Neutral cast stock with an adjustable comb, trap style fore-end, pistol grip and ambidextrous palm swells. No. 3 grade Circassian walnut. At lowest position, drop at comb: 1.625 in.; drop at heel: 2.375 in.; length of pull: 14.5 in. **Features:** Designed for Sporting Clays and FITASC competition. Hand engraving, satin black-finished receiver. Tapered adjustable rib with center bead and a red fiber-optic front bead, 10 choke tubes with wrench, single selective trigger, automatic ejectors, thin rubber pad with slick plastic top. Introduced 2008. Made in the Czech Republic and imported by CZ-USA.
Price: G2 grade **$2,497.00**
Price: Standard grade **$1,899.00**

CZ REDHEAD PREMIER
Gauges: 12 ga., 20 ga., 28 ga., .410 bore (3 in. chambers), 28 ga. (2 3/4 in.). **Barrel:** 28 in. **Weight:** 7.4 lbs. **Length:** NA. **Stock:** Round-knob pistol grip, Schnabel fore-end, Turkish walnut. **Features:** Single selective triggers and extractors (12 & 20 ga.), screw-in chokes (12 ga., 20 ga., 28 ga.) choked IC and Mod (.410), coin-finished receiver, multi chokes. From CZ-USA.
Price: Deluxe **$953.00**
Price: Mini (28 ga., .410 bore) **$1,057.00**
Price: Target **$1,389.00**

CZ SUPER SCROLL COMBO
Gauges: 20 and 28 combo. **Barrels:** 30 in. for both gauges with five choke tubes for each set. **Stock:** Grave V Turkish walnut with Schnabel fore-end, rounded grip. **Weight:** 6.7 pounds. **Features:** Ornate hand-engraved scrollwork on receiver, faux sideplates, trigger guard and mono-block. Comes in a custom-fitted aluminum case.
Price: **$3,899.00**

CZ UPLAND STERLING
Gauge: 12 ga., 3 in. **Barrels:** 28 in. with ventilated rib, fiber optic sight, five choke tubes. **Stock:** Turkish walnut with stippled gripping surfaces. **Weight:** 7.5 pounds. Lady Sterling has smaller stock dimensions.
Price: **$999.00**
Price: Lady Sterling **$1,321.00**

CZ WINGSHOOTER ELITE
Gauge: 12 ga., 20 ga., 2 3/4 in. **Barrel:** 28 in. flat ventilated rib. **Weight:** 6.3 lbs. **Length:** 45.5 in. **Stock:** Turkish walnut. **Features:** This colorful Over/Under shotgun has old world craftsmanship but with a new stylish look. This elegant hand engraved work of art is available in four gauges and its eye-catching engraving will stand alone in the field or range. 12- and 20-ga. models have auto ejectors, while the 28 ga. and .410 have extractors only. Heavily engraved scroll work with special side plate design, mechanical selective triggers, box Lock frame design, 18 LPI checkering, coil spring operated hammers, chrome lined, 5 interchangeable choke tubes and special engraved skeleton butt plate.
Price: 12 ga. or 20 ga. **$1,059.00**

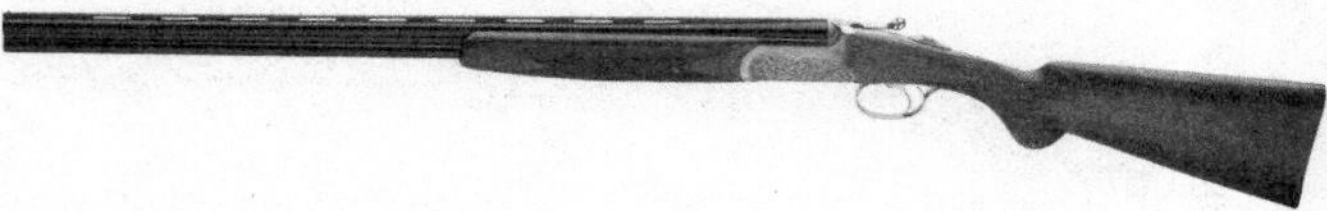

FAUSTI CLASS ROUND BODY
Gauges: 16 ga., 20 ga., 28 ga.. **Barrels:** 28 or 30 in. **Weights:** 5.8–6.3 lbs. **Lengths:** 45.5–47.5 in. **Stock:** Turkish walnut Prince of Wales style with oil finish. Features include automatic ejectors, single selective trigger, laser-engraved receiver.
Price: From **$4,199.00**

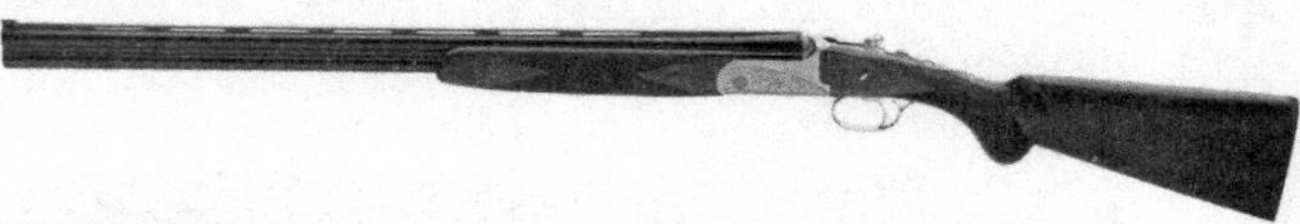

FAUSTI CALEDON
Gauges: 12 ga., 16 ga., 20 ga., 28 ga. and .410 bore. **Barrels:** 26 in., 28 in., 30 in. **Weights:** 5.8–7.3 lbs. **Stock:** Turkish walnut with oil finish, round pistol grip. **Features:** Automatic ejectors, single selective trigger, laser-engraved receiver. Coin finish receiver with gold inlays.
Price: 12 ga. or 20 ga. **$1,999.00**
Price: 16 ga., 28 ga., .410 bore **$2,569.00**

FAUSTI MAGNIFICENT
Gauges: 12 ga., 16 ga., 20 ga., 28 ga., .410 bore. **Barrels:** 26 in., 28 in., 30 in. **Stock:** AAA-Grade oil finished walnut. **Features:** Frame size scaled to gauge. Laser deep sculpted engraving coin finished receiver with gold inlays. Automatic ejectors, single selective trigger.
Price: 12 ga. **$4,999.00**
Price: Smaller ga. **$5,559.00**

FRANCHI INSTINCT SERIES
Gauges: 12 ga., 20 ga., 3 in. **Barrels:** 26 in., 28 in. **Weight:** 5.3–6.4 lbs. **Lengths:** 42.5–44.5 in. **Stock:** AA-grade satin walnut (LS), A-grade (L) with rounded pistol grip and recoil pad. Single trigger, automatic ejectors, tang safety, choke tubes. L model has steel receiver, SL has aluminum alloy receiver. Sporting model has higher grade wood, extended choke tubes. Catalyst model is designed for women, including stock dimensions for cast, drop, pitch, grip and length of pull.
Price: L **$1,349.00**
Price: SL **$1,699.00**
Price: Sporting **$1,899.00**
Price: Catalyst **$1,599.00**

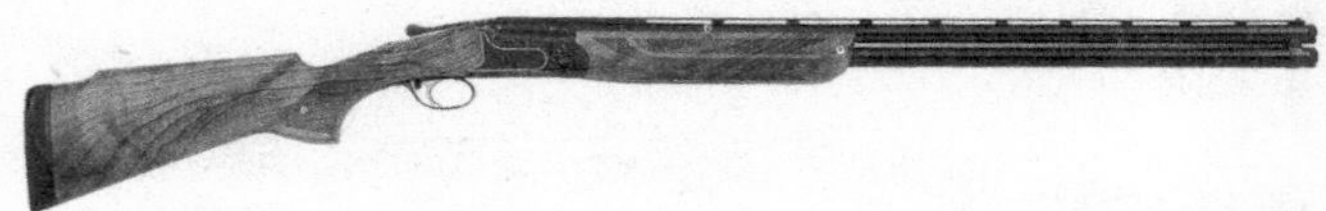

KOLAR SPORTING CLAYS
Gauge: 12 ga., 2 3/4 in. **Barrels:** 30 in., 32 in., 34 in.; extended choke tubes. **Stock:** 14.625 in. x 2.5 in. x 1.875 in. x 1.375 in. French walnut. Four stock versions available. **Features:** Single selective trigger, detachable, adjustable for length; overbored barrels with long forcing cones; flat tramline rib; matte blue finish. Made in U.S. by Kolar.
Price: Standard **$11,995.00**
Price: Prestige **$14,190.00**
Price: Elite Gold **$16,590.00**
Price: Legend **$17,090.00**
Price: Select **$22,590.00**
Price: Custom .... **Price on request**

KOLAR AAA COMPETITION TRAP
Gauge: 12 ga. Similar to the Sporting Clays gun except has 32 in. O/U 34 in. Unsingle or 30 in. O/U 34 in. Unsingle barrels as an over/under, unsingle, or combination set. Stock dimensions are 14.5 in. x 2.5 in. x 1.5 in.; American or French walnut; step parallel rib standard. Contact maker for full listings. Made in USA by Kolar.
Price: Single bbl., From **$8,495.00**
Price: O/U, From **$11,695.00**

Prices given are believed to be accurate at time of publication however, many factors affect retail pricing so exact prices are not possible.

KOLAR AAA COMPETITION SKEET
Similar to the Sporting Clays gun except has 28 in. or 30 in. barrels with Kolarite AAA sub-gauge tubes; stock of American or French walnut with matte finish; flat tramline rib; under barrel adjustable for point of impact. Many options available. Contact maker for complete listing. Made in USA by Kolar.
Price: Max Lite, From **$13,995.00**

KRIEGHOFF K-80 SPORTING CLAYS
Gauge: 12 ga. **Barrels:** 28 in., 30 in., 32 in., 34 in. with choke tubes. **Weight:** About 8 lbs. **Stock:** #3 Sporting stock designed for gun-down shooting. **Features:** Standard receiver with satin nickel finish and classic scroll engraving. Selective mechanical trigger adjustable for position. Choice of tapered flat or 8mm parallel flat barrel rib. Free-floating barrels. Aluminum case. Imported from Germany by Krieghoff International, Inc.
Price: Standard grade with five choke tubes, From **$11,395.00**

KRIEGHOFF K-80 SKEET
Gauge: 12 ga., 2 3/4 in. **Barrels:** 28 in., 30 in., 32 in., (skeet & skeet), optional choke tubes. **Weight:** About 7.75 lbs. **Stock:** American skeet or straight skeet stocks, with palm-swell grips. Walnut. **Features:** Satin gray receiver finish. Selective mechanical trigger adjustable for position. Choice of ventilated 8mm parallel flat rib or ventilated 8–12mm tapered flat rib. Introduced 1980. Imported from Germany by Krieghoff International, Inc.
Price: Standard, skeet chokes **$11,295.00**

KRIEGHOFF K-80 TRAP
Gauge: 12 ga., 2 3/4 in. **Barrels:** 30 in., 32 in. (Imp. Mod. & Full or choke tubes). **Weight:** About 8.5 lbs. **Stock:** Four stock dimensions or adjustable stock available; all have palm-swell grips. Checkered European walnut. **Features:** Satin nickel receiver. Selective mechanical trigger, adjustable for position. Ventilated step rib. Introduced 1980. Imported from Germany by Krieghoff International, Inc.
Price: K-80 O/U (30 in., 32 in., Imp. Mod. & Full), From **$11,295.00**
Price: K-80 Unsingle (32 in., 34 in., Full), standard, From **$12,995.00**
Price: K-80 Combo (two-barrel set), standard, From **$16,295.00**

KRIEGHOFF K-20
Similar to the K-80 except built on a 20-ga. frame. Designed for skeet, sporting clays and field use. Offered in 20 ga., 28 ga. and .410; **Barrels:** 28 in., 30 in. and 32 in. Imported from Germany by Krieghoff International Inc.
Price: K-20, 20 ga., From **$11,695.00**
Price: K-20, 28 ga., From **$12,395.00**
Price: K-20, .410, From **$12,395.00**

LEBEAU-COURALLY BOSS-VEREES
Gauges: 12 ga., 20 ga., 2 3/4 in. **Barrels:** 25–32 in. **Weight:** To customer specifications. **Stock:** Exhibition-quality French walnut. **Features:** Boss-type sidelock with automatic ejectors; single or double triggers; chopper lump barrels. A custom gun built to customer specifications. Imported from Belgium by Wm. Larkin Moore.
Price: From **$96,000.00**

MERKEL MODEL 2001EL O/U
Gauges: 12 ga., 20 ga., 3 in., 28 ga. 2-3/4 in. chambers. **Barrels:** 12 ga. 28 in.; 20 ga., 28 ga. 26.75 in. **Weight:** About 7 lbs. (12 ga.). **Stock:** Oil-finished walnut; English or pistol grip. **Features:** Self-cocking Blitz boxlock action with cocking indicators; Kersten double cross-bolt lock; silver-grayed receiver with engraved hunting scenes; coil spring ejectors; single selective or double triggers. Imported from Germany by Merkel USA.
Price: **$9,995.00**
Price: Model 2001EL Sporter; full pistol grip stock **$9,995.00**

MERKEL MODEL 2000CL
Similar to Model 2001EL except scroll-engraved casehardened receiver; 12 ga., 20 ga., 28 ga. Imported from Germany by Merkel USA.
Price: **$12,235.00**

MOSSBERG SILVER RESERVE II
Gauge: 12 ga., 3 in. **Barrels:** 28 in. with ventilated rib, choke tubes. **Stock:** Select black walnut with satin finish. **Sights:** Metal bead. Available with extractors or automatic ejectors. Also offered in Sport model with ported barrels with wide rib, fiber optic front and middle bead sights. Super Sport has extra wide high rib, optional adjustable comb.
Price: Field **$773.00**
Price: Sport **$950.00**
Price: Sport w/ejectors **$1,070.00**
Price: Super Sport w/ejectors **$1,163.00**
Price: Super Sport w/ejectors, adj. comb **$1,273.00**

PERAZZI MX8/MX8 TRAP/SKEET
Gauge: 12 ga., 20 ga. 2 3/4 in. **Barrels:** Trap: 29.5 in. (Imp. Mod. & Extra Full), 31.5 in. (Full & Extra Full). Choke tubes optional. Skeet: 27.625 in. (skeet & skeet). **Weights:** About 8.5 lbs. (trap); 7 lbs., 15 oz. (skeet). **Stock:** Interchangeable and custom made to customer specs. **Features:** Has detachable and interchangeable trigger group with flat V springs. Flat .4375 in. vent rib. Many options available. Imported from Italy by Perazzi USA, Inc.
Price: Trap, From **$11,760.00**
Price: Skeet, From **$11,760.00**

PERAZZI MX8
Gauge: 12 ga., 20 ga. 2 3/4 in. **Barrels:** 28.375 in. (Imp. Mod. & Extra Full), 29.50 in. (choke tubes). **Weight:** 7 lbs., 12 oz. **Stock:** Special specifications. **Features:** Has single selective trigger; flat .4375 in. x .3125 in. vent rib. Many options available. Imported from Italy by Perazzi USA, Inc.
Price: Standard, From **$11,760.00**
Price: Sporting, From **$11,760.00**
Price: SC3 Grade (variety of engraving patterns), From **$21,000.00**
Price: SCO Grade (more intricate engraving/inlays), From **$36,000.00**

PERAZZI MX12 HUNTING
Gauge: 12 ga., 2 3/4 in. **Barrels:** 26.75 in., 27.5 in., 28.375 in., 29.5 in. (Mod. & Full); choke tubes available in 27.625 in., 29.5 in. only (MX12C). **Weight:** 7 lbs., 4 oz. **Stock:** To customer specs; interchangeable. **Features:** Single selective trigger; coil springs used in action; Schnabel fore-end tip. Imported from Italy by Perazzi USA, Inc.
Price: From **$12,700.00**
Price: MX12C (with choke tubes), From **$12,700.00**

PERAZZI MX20 HUNTING
Gauges: 20 ga., 28 ga., .410 with 2 3/4 in. or 3 in. chambers. **Barrel:** 26 in. standard barrel choked Mod. & Full. **Weight:** 6 lbs., 6 oz. Features: Similar to the MX12 except 20 ga. frame size. Non-removable trigger group. Imported from Italy by Perazzi USA, Inc.
Price: From **$12,700.00**
Price: MX20C (with choke tubes), From **$13,700.00**

PERAZZI MX2000S
Gauges: 12 ga., 20 ga. **Barrels:** 29.5 in., 30.75 in., 31.5 in. with fixed I/M and Full chokes, or interchangeable. Competition model with features similar to MX8.
Price: **$13,200.00**

PERAZZI MX15 UNSINGLE TRAP
Gauge: 12 ga. **Barrel:** 34 in. with fixed Full choke. **Features:** Bottom single barrel with 6-notch adjustable rib, adjustable stock, drop-out trigger or interchangeable. Competition model with features similar to MX8.
Price: **$9,175.00**

PIOTTI BOSS
Gauges: 12 ga., 16 ga., 20 ga., 28 ga., .410 bore. **Barrels:** 26–32 in., chokes as specified. **Weight:** 6.5–8 lbs. **Stock:** Dimensions to customer specs. Best quality figured walnut. **Features:** Essentially a custom-made gun with many options. Introduced 1993. Imported from Italy by Wm. Larkin Moore.
Price: From **$75,000.00**

SHOTGUNS Over/Unders

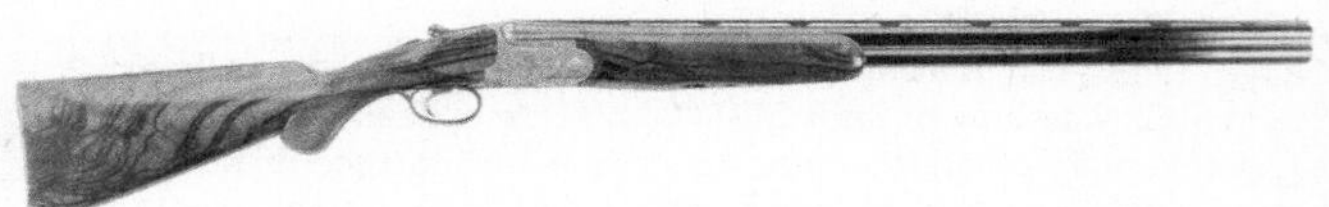

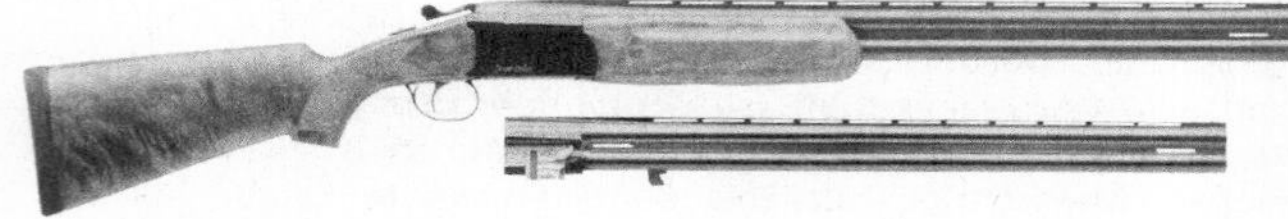

RIZZINI S790 EMEL
Gauges: 20 ga., 28 ga., .410 bore. **Barrels:** 26 in., 27.5 in. (Imp. Cyl. & Imp. Mod.). **Weight:** About 6 lbs. **Stock:** 14 in. x 1.5 in. x 2.125 in. Extra fancy select walnut. **Features:** Boxlock action with profuse engraving; automatic ejectors; single selective trigger; silvered receiver. Comes with Nizzoli leather case. Introduced 1996. Made in Italy by Battista Rizzini and distributed by Wm. Larkin Moore & Co.
Price: From.......... **$14,600.00**

RIZZINI S792 EMEL
Similar to S790 EMEL except dummy sideplates with extensive engraving coverage. Nizzoli leather case. Introduced 1996. Made in Italy by Battista Rizzini and distributed by Wm. Larkin Moore & Co.
Price: From.......... **$15,500.00**

RIZZINI UPLAND EL
Gauges: 12 ga., 16 ga., 20 ga., 28 ga., .410 bore. **Barrels:** 26 in., 27.5 in., Mod. & Full, Imp. Cyl. & Imp. Mod. choke tubes. **Weight:** About 6.6 lbs. **Stock:** 14.5 in. x 1.5 in. x 2.25 in. **Features:** Boxlock action; single selective trigger; ejectors; profuse engraving on silvered receiver. Comes with fitted case. Introduced 1996. Made in Italy by Battista Rizzini and distributed by Wm. Larkin Moore & Co.
Price: From.......... **$6,595.00**

RIZZINI ARTEMIS
Gauges: 12 ga., 16 ga., 20 ga., 28 ga., .410 bore. Same as Upland EL model except dummy sideplates with extensive game scene engraving. Fancy European walnut stock. Fitted case. Introduced 1996. Imported from Italy by Fierce Products and by Wm. Larkin Moore & Co.
Price: From.......... **$4,250.00**
Price: Artemis Light.......... **$4,395.00**

RIZZINI S782 EMEL
Gauge: 12 ga., 2 3/4 in. **Barrels:** 26 in., 27.5 in. (Imp. Cyl. & Imp. Mod.). **Weight:** About 6.75 lbs. **Stock:** 14.5 in. x 1.5 in. x 2.25 in. Extra fancy select walnut. **Features:** Boxlock action with dummy sideplates, extensive engraving with gold inlaid game birds, silvered receiver, automatic ejectors, single selective trigger. Nizzoli leather case. Introduced 1996. Made in Italy by Battista Rizzini and distributed by Wm. Larkin Moore & Co.
Price: From.......... **$18,800.00**

SKB 590 FIELD
Gauges: 12 ga., 20 ga., 3 in. **Barrels:** 26 in., 28 in., 30 in. Three SKB Competition choke tubes (IC, M, F). Lengthened forcing cones. **Stock:** Oil finished walnut with Pachmayr recoil pad. **Weight:** 7.1–7.9 lbs. **Sights:** NA. **Features:** Boxlock action, bright blue finish with laser engraved receiver. Automatic ejectors, single trigger with selector switch incorporated in thumb-operated tang safety. Youth Model has 13 in. length of pull. Imported from Turkey by GU, Inc.
Price: **$1,300.00**

SKB 90TSS
Gauges: 12 ga., 20 ga., 2 3/4 in. **Barrels:** 28 in., 30 in., 32 in. Three SKB Competition choke tubes (SK, IC, M for Skeet and Sporting Models; IM, M, F for Trap). Lengthened forcing cones. **Stock:** Oil finished walnut with Pachmayr recoil pad. **Weight:** 7.1–7.9 lbs. **Sights:** Ventilated rib with target sights. **Features:** Boxlock action, bright blue finish with laser engraved receiver. Automatic ejectors, single trigger with selector switch incorporated in thumb-operated tang safety. Sporting and Trap models have adjustable comb and buttpad system. Imported from Turkey by GU, Inc.
Price: Skeet.......... **$1,470.00**
Price: Sporting Clays, Trap.......... **$1,720.00**

STEVENS MODEL 555
Gauges: 12 ga., 20 ga., 28 ga., .410; 2 3/4 and 3 in. **Barrels:** 26 in., 28 in. **Weights:** 5.5–6 lbs. **Features:** Five screw-in choke tubes with 12 ga., 20 ga., and 28 ga.; .410 has fixed M/IC chokes. Turkish walnut stock and Schnabel fore-end. Single selective mechanical trigger with extractors.
Price: **$694.00**

STOEGER CONDOR
Gauge: 12 ga., 20 ga., 2 3/4 in., 3 in.; 16 ga., .410. **Barrels:** 22 in., 24 in., 26 in., 28 in., 30 in. **Weights:** 5.5–7.8 lbs. **Sights:** Brass bead. **Features:** IC, M, or F screw-in choke tubes with each gun. Oil finished hardwood with pistol grip and fore-end. Auto safety, single trigger, automatic extractors.
Price: From.......... **$449.00–$669.00**
Price: Combo with 12 and 20 ga. barrel sets.......... **$899.00**
Price: Competition.......... **$669.00**

TRISTAR HUNTER EX
Gauge: 12 ga., 20 ga., 28 ga., .410. **Barrels:** 26 in., 28 in. **Weights:** 5.7 lbs. (.410); 6.0 lbs. (20, 28), 7.2–7.4 lbs. (12). Chrome-lined steel mono-block barrel, five Beretta-style choke tubes (SK, IC, M, IM, F). Length: NA. **Stock:** Walnut, cut checkering. 14.25 in. x 1.5 in. x 2.375 in. **Sights:** Brass front sight. **Features:** All have extractors, engraved receiver, sealed actions, self-adjusting locking bolts, single selective trigger, ventilated rib. 28 ga. and .410 built on true frames. Five-year warranty. Imported from Italy by Tristar Sporting Arms Ltd.
Price: From.......... **$630.00**

TRISTAR SETTER
Gauge: 12 ga., 20 ga., 3-in. **Barrels:** 28 in. (12 ga.), 26 in. (20 ga.) with ventilated rib, three Beretta-style choke tubes. **Weights:** 6.3–7.2 pounds. **Stock:** High gloss wood. Single selective trigger, extractors.
Price: **$559.00**
Price: Sporting Model.......... **$824.00**

WEBLEY & SCOTT O/U SERIES
Gauge: 12 ga., 20 ga., 28 ga., .410. **Barrels:** 26 in., 28 in., 30 in., five interchangeable choke tubes. **Weights:** 5.5–7.5 lbs. **Stock:** Checkered Turkish walnut with recoil pad. **Features:** Automatic ejectors, single selective trigger, ventilated rib, tang selector/safety. 2000 Premium Model has higher-grade select walnut stock, color casehardening. 3000 Sidelock Model is a high-grade gun with 7-pin sidelocks, oil-finished premium-grade walnut stock with checkered butt, jeweled monobloc walls, and comes with high quality, fleeced line lockable case. Made in Turkey and imported by Centurion International.
Price: 900 Sporting.......... **$1,250.00**
Price: 2000 Premium.......... **$2,500.00**
Price: 3000 Sidelock.......... **$6,000.00**

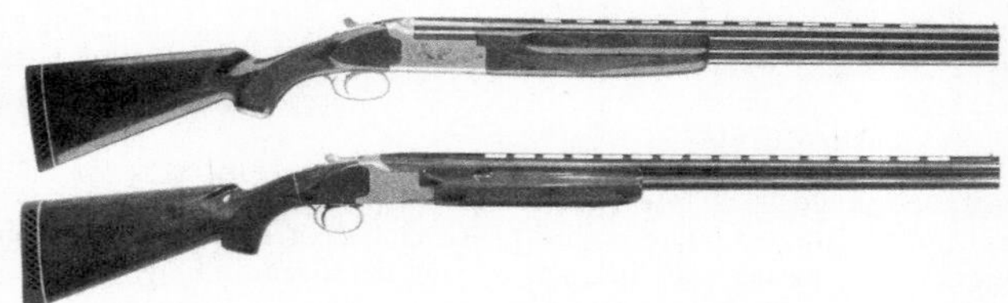

WINCHESTER MODEL 101
Gauge: 12 ga., 2 3/4 in., 3 in. **Barrels:** 28 in., 30 in., 32 in., ported, Invector Plus choke system. **Weights:** 7 lbs. 6 oz.–7 lbs. 12. oz. **Stock:** Checkered high-gloss grade II/III walnut stock, Pachmayr Decelerator sporting pad. **Features:** Chrome-plated chambers; back-bored barrels; tang barrel selector/safety; Signature extended choke tubes. Model 101 Field comes with solid brass bead front sight, three tubes, engraved receiver. Model 101 Sporting has adjustable trigger, 10mm runway rib, white mid-bead, Tru-Glo front sight, 30 in. and 32 in. barrels. Camo version of Model 101 Field comes with full-coverage Mossy Oak Duck Blind pattern. Model 101 Pigeon Grade Trap has 10mm steel runway rib, mid-bead sight, interchangeable fiber-optic front sight, porting and vented side ribs, adjustable trigger shoe, fixed raised comb or adjustable comb, Grade III/IV walnut, 30 in. or 32 in. barrels, molded ABS hard case. Reintroduced 2008. Made in Belgium by FN. Winchester 150th Anniversary Commemorative model has grade IV/V stock, deep relief scrolling on a silver nitride finish receiver.
Price: Field.......... **$1,900.00**
Price: Sporting.......... **$2,300.00**
Price: Pigeon Grade Trap.......... **$2,520.00**
Price: Pigeon Grade Trap w/adj. comb.......... **$2,680.00**
Price: 150th Anniversary Commemorative.......... **$3,070.00**

Prices given are believed to be accurate at time of publication however, many factors affect retail pricing so exact prices are not possible.

ARRIETA SIDELOCK DOUBLE

Gauges: 12 ga., 16 ga., 20 ga., 28 ga., .410 bore. **Barrels:** Length and chokes to customer specs. **Weight:** To customer specs. **Stock:** To customer specs. Straight English with checkered butt (standard), or pistol grip. Select European walnut with oil finish. **Features:** Essentially custom gun with myriad options. H&H pattern hand-detachable sidelocks, selective automatic ejectors, double triggers (hinged front) standard. Some have self-opening action. Finish and engraving to customer specs. Imported from Spain by Quality Arms, Wm. Larking Moore and others.

Price: Model 557 .... **$6,970.00**
Price: Model 570 .... **$7,350.00**
Price: Model 578 .... **$12,200.00**
Price: Model 600 Imperial **$14,125.00**
Price: Model 803 .... **$17,000.00**
Price: Model 931 .... **$40,000.00**

AYA MODEL 4/53

Gauges: 12 ga., 16 ga., 20 ga., 28 ga., 410 bore. **Barrels:** 26 in., 27 in., 28 in., 30 in. **Weights:** To customer specifications. **Length:** To customer specifications. **Features:** Hammerless boxlock action; double triggers; light scroll engraving; automatic safety; straight grip oil finished walnut stock; checkered butt. Made in Spain. Imported by New England Custom Gun Service.

Price: **$5,500.00**
Price: No. 2 .... **$7,000.00**
Price: No. 2 Rounded Action **$7,400.00**

AYA MODEL ADARRA

Gauges: 12 ga., 16 ga., 20 ga., 28 ga., 410 bore. **Barrel:** 26 in., 28 in. **Weight:** Approx. 6.7 lbs. **Features:** Hammerless boxlock action; double triggers; light scroll engraving; automatic safety; straight grip oil finished walnut stock; checkered butt. Made in Spain. Imported by New England Custom Gun Service.

Price: **$6,000.00**

BARRETT SOVEREIGN BELTRAMI

Gauges: 12 ga., 20 ga. or 28 ga. 3 in. (2 3/4 for 28 ga.). **Barrels:** 26 in., 28 in. or 30 in. **Stock:** Checkered grade AAA Turkish walnut with straight grip. **Features:** Boxlock design, ornamental sideplates, coin-finished receiver. Receiver scaled to individual gauges. Imported from Italy by Barrett Firearms.

Price: 12 ga. or 20 ga. **$6,150.00**
Price: 28 ga. **$6,550.00**

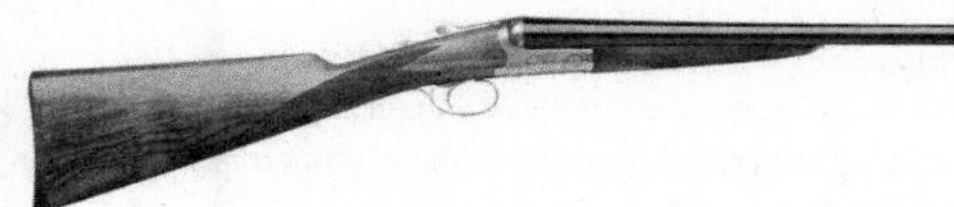

BERETTA 486 PARALELLO

Gauges: 12 ga., 20 ga., 3 in., or 28 ga. 2 3/4 in. **Barrels:** 26 in., 28 in., 30 in. **Weight:** 7.1 lbs. **Stock:** English-style straight grip, splinter fore-end. Select European walnut, checkered, oil finish. **Features:** Round action, Optima-Choke Tubes. Automatic ejection or mechanical extraction. Firing-pin block safety, manual or automatic, open top-lever safety. Imported from Italy by Beretta USA

Price: From **$5,350.00**

CIMARRON 1878 COACH GUN

Gauge: 12 ga. 3 in. **Barrels:** 20 in., 26 in. **Weights:** 8–9 lbs. **Stock:** Hardwood. External hammers, double triggers. **Finish:** Blue, Cimarron "USA", Cimarron "Original."

Price: Blue .... **$575.00 (20 in.)–$594.00 (26 in.)**
Price: Original .... **$675.00–$694.00**
Price: USA .... **$832.00–$851.00**

CIMARRON DOC HOLLIDAY MODEL

Gauge: 12 ga. **Barrels:** 20 in., cylinder bore. **Stock:** Hardwood with rounded pistol grip. **Features:** Double triggers, hammers, false sideplates.

Price: **$1,715.00**

CONNECTICUT SHOTGUN MANUFACTURING CO. RBL

Gauges: 12 ga., 16 ga., 20 ga.. **Barrels:** 26 in., 28 in., 30 in., 32 in. **Weight:** NA. **Length:** NA. **Stock:** NA. **Features:** Round-action SxS shotguns made in the USA. Scaled frames, five TruLock choke tubes. Deluxe fancy grade walnut buttstock and fore-end. Quick Change recoil pad in two lengths. Various dimensions and options available depending on gauge.

Price: 12 ga. **$3,795.00**
Price: 16 ga. **$3,795.00**
Price: 20 ga. Special Custom Model **$7,995.00**

CONNECTICUT SHOTGUN MANUFACTURING CO. MODEL 21

Gauges: 12 ga., 16 ga., 20 ga., 28 ga., .410 bore. Features: A faithful re-creation of the famous Winchester Model 21. Many options and upgrades are available. Each frame is machined from specially produced proof steel. The 28 ga. and .410 guns are available on the standard frame or on a newly engineered small frame. These are custom guns and are made to order to the buyer's individual specifications, wood, stock dimensions, barrel lengths, chokes, finishes and engraving.

Price: 12 ga., 16 ga. or 20 ga., From **$15,000.00**
Price: 28 ga. or .410, From **$18,000.00**

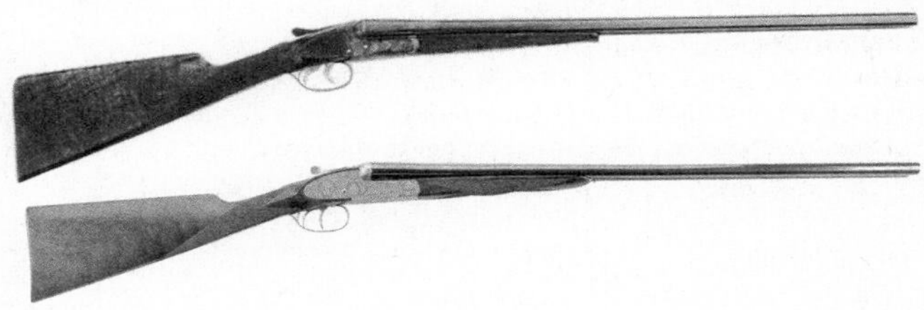

CZ SHARP-TAIL

Gauges: 12 ga., 20 ga., 28 ga., .410. (5 screw-in chokes in 12 and 20 ga. and fixed chokes in IC and Mod in .410). **Barrels:** 26 in. or 28 in. **Weight:** 6.5 lbs. **Stock:** Hand-checkered Turkish walnut with straight English-style grip and single selective trigger.

Price: Sharp-Tail **$1,022.00**
Price: Sharp-Tail Target **$1,298.00**

CZ HAMMER COACH

Gauge: 12 ga., 3 in. **Barrel:** 20 in. **Weight:** 6.7 lbs. **Features:** Following in the tradition of the guns used by the stagecoach guards of the 1880s, this cowboy gun features double triggers, 19th-century color casehardening and fully functional external hammers.

Price: **$922.00**
Price: Classic model w/30-in. bbls. **$963.00**

EMF MODEL 1878 WYATT EARP
Gauge: 12. **Barrel:** 20 in.. **Weight:** 8 lbs. **Length:** 37 in. overall. **Stock:** Smooth walnut with steel butt place. **Sights:** Large brass bead. **Features:** Colt-style exposed hammers rebounding type; blued receiver and barrels; cylinder bore. Based on design of Colt Model 1878 shotgun. Made in Italy by Pedersoli.
Price: **$1,590.00**

FAUSTI DEA SERIES
Gauges: 12 ga., 16 ga., 20 ga., 28 ga., .410. **Barrels:** 26 in., 28 in., 30 in. **Weight:** 6–6.8 lbs. **Stock:** AAA walnut, oil finished. Straight grip, checkered butt, classic fore-end. **Features:** Automatic ejectors, single non-selective trigger. Duetto model is in 28 ga. with extra set of .410 barrels. Made in Italy and imported by Fausti, USA.
Price: 12 ga. or 20 ga. **$3,518.00**
Price: 16 ga., 28 ga., .410 .... **$4,190.00**
Price: Duetto **$5,790.00**

FOX, A.H.
Gauges: 16 ga., 20 ga., 28 ga., .410. **Barrels:** Length and chokes to customer specifications. Rust-blued Chromox or Krupp steel. **Weight:** 5.5–6.75 lbs. **Stock:** Dimensions to customer specifications. Hand-checkered Turkish Circassian walnut with hand-rubbed oil finish. Straight, semi or full pistol grip; splinter, Schnabel or beavertail fore-end; traditional pad, hard rubber buttplate or skeleton butt. **Features:** Boxlock action with automatic ejectors; double or Fox single selective trigger. Scalloped, rebated and color case-hardened receiver; hand finished and hand-engraved. Grades differ in engraving, inlays, grade of wood, amount of hand finishing. Introduced 1993. Made in U.S. by Connecticut Shotgun Mfg.
Price: CE Grade **$19,500.00**
Price: XE Grade **$22,000.00**
Price: DE Grade **$25,000.00**
Price: FE Grade **$30,000.00**
Price: 28 ga./.410 CE Grade **$21,500.00**
Price: 28 ga./.410 XE Grade **$24,000.00**
Price: 28 ga./.410 DE Grade **$27,000.00**
Price: 28 ga./.410 FE Grade **$32,000.00**

GARBI MODEL 101
Gauges: 12 ga., 16 ga., 20 ga., 28 ga. **Barrels:** 26 in., 28 in., choked to customer specs. **Weights:** 5.5–7.5 lbs. **Stock:** 14.5 in. x 2.25 in. x 1.5 in. Select European walnut. Straight grip, checkered butt, classic fore-end. **Features:** Sidelock action, automatic ejectors, double triggers standard. Color casehardened action, coin finish optional. Single trigger; beavertail fore-end, etc. optional. Hand engraved with scroll engraving. Imported from Spain by Wm. Larkin Moore.
Price: From **$15,950.00**

GARBI MODEL 103A, 103B
Similar to the Garbi Model 101 except has Purdey-type fine scroll and rosette engraving. Model 103B has nickel-chrome steel barrels, H&H-type easy opening mechanism; other mechanical details remain the same. Imported from Spain by Wm. Larkin Moore.
Price: Model 103A, From **$21,000.00**
Price: Model 103B, From **$28,000.00**

GARBI MODEL 200
Similar to the Garbi Model 101 except has heavy-duty locks, magnum proofed. Very fine Continental-style floral and scroll engraving, well figured walnut stock. Other mechanical features remain the same. Imported from Spain by Wm. Larkin Moore.
Price: **$24,000.00**

MERKEL MODEL 47SL, 147SL
Similar to Model 47E except H&H style sidelock action with cocking indicators, ejectors. Silver-grayed receiver and sideplates have arabesque engraving, engraved border and screws (Model 47SL), or fine hunting scene engraving (Model 147SL). Limited edition. Imported from Germany by Merkel USA.
Price: Model 47SL **$8,995.00**
Price: Model 147SL **$13,255.00**

MERKEL MODEL 280EL, 360EL
Similar to Model 47E except smaller frame. Greener crossbolt with double under-barrel locking lugs, fine engraved hunting scenes on silver-grayed receiver, luxury-grade wood, Anson and Deeley boxlock action. H&H ejectors, single-selective or double triggers. Introduced 2000. Imported from Germany by Merkel USA.
Price: Model 280EL (28 ga., 28 in. barrel, Imp. Cyl. and Mod. chokes) **$8,870.00**
Price: Model 360EL (.410, 28 in. barrel, Mod. and Full chokes) **$8,870.00**

MERKEL MODEL 280SL AND 360SL
Similar to Model 280EL and 360EL except has sidelock action, double triggers, English-style arabesque engraving. Introduced 2000. Imported from Germany by Merkel USA.
Price: Model 280SL (28 ga., 28 in. barrel, Imp. Cyl. and Mod. chokes) **$12,995.00**
Price: Model 360SL (.410, 28 in. barrel, Mod. and Full chokes) **$12,995.00**

MERKEL MODEL 1620
Gauge: 16 ga. **Features:** Greener crossbolt with double under-barrel locking lugs, scroll-engraved casehardened receiver, Anson and Deeley boxlock action, Holland & Holland ejectors, English-style stock, single selective or double triggers, or pistol grip stock with single selective trigger. Imported from Germany by Merkel USA.
Price: Model 1620EL **$8,870.00**
Price: Model 1620EL Combo; 16- and 20-ga. two-barrel set **$13,255.00**

MERKEL MODEL 40E
Gauges: 12 ga., 20 ga. **Barrels:** 28 in. (12 ga.), 26.75 in. (20 ga.). **Weight:** 6.2 lbs. **Features:** Anson & Deeley locks, Greener-style crossbolt, automatic ejectors, choice of double or single trigger, blue finish, checkered walnut stock with cheekpiece.
Price: **$4,795.00**

PIOTTI KING NO. 1
Gauges: 12 ga., 16 ga., 20 ga., 28 ga., .410. **Barrels:** 25–30 in. (12 ga.), 25–28 in. (16 ga., 20 ga., 28 ga., .410). To customer specs. Chokes as specified. **Weight:** 6.5–8 lbs. (12 ga. to customer specs.). **Stock:** Dimensions to customer specs. Finely figured walnut; straight grip with checkered butt with classic splinter fore-end and hand-rubbed oil finish standard. Pistol grip, beavertail fore-end. **Features:** Holland & Holland pattern sidelock action, automatic ejectors. Double trigger; non-selective single trigger optional. Coin finish standard; color case-hardened optional. Top rib; level, file-cut; concave, ventilated optional. Very fine, full coverage scroll engraving with small floral bouquets. Imported from Italy by Wm. Larkin Moore.
Price: From **$42,800.00**

Prices given are believed to be accurate at time of publication however, many factors affect retail pricing so exact prices are not possible.

PIOTTI LUNIK SIDE-BY-SIDE SHOTGUN
Similar to the Piotti King No. 1 in overall quality. Has Renaissance-style large scroll engraving in relief. Best quality Holland & Holland-pattern sidelock ejector double with chopper lump (demi-bloc) barrels. Other mechanical specifications remain the same. Imported from Italy by Wm. Larkin Moore.
Price: From **$46,000.00**

PIOTTI PIUMA
Gauges: 12 ga., 16 ga., 20 ga., 28 ga., .410. **Barrels:** 25–30 in. (12 ga.), 25–28 in. (16 ga., 20 ga., 28 ga., .410). **Weights:** 5.5–6.25 lbs. (20 ga.). **Stock:** Dimensions to customer specs. Straight grip stock with walnut checkered butt, classic splinter fore-end, hand-rubbed oil finish are standard; pistol grip, beavertail fore-end, satin luster finish optional. **Features:** Anson & Deeley boxlock ejector double with chopper lump barrels. Level, file-cut rib, light scroll and rosette engraving, scalloped frame. Double triggers; single non-selective optional. Coin finish standard, color case-hardened optional. Imported from Italy by Wm. Larkin Moore.
Price: From **$25,000.00**

SKB 200 SERIES
Gauges: 12 ga., 20 ga., .410, 3 in.; 28 ga., 2 3/4 in. **Barrels:** 26 in., 28 in. Five choke tubes provided (F, IM, M, IC, SK). **Stock:** Hand checkered and oil finished Turkish walnut. Prince of Wales grip and beavertail fore-end. **Weight:** 6–7 lbs. **Sights:** Brass bead. **Features:** Boxlock with platform lump barrel design. Polished bright blue finish with charcoal color case hardening on receiver. Manual safety, automatic ejectors, single selective trigger. 200 HR target model has high ventilated rib, full pistol grip. 250 model has decorative color casehardened sideplates. Imported from Turkey by GU, Inc.
Price: 12 ga., 20 ga. **$2,100.00**
Price: 28 ga., .410 .... **$2,250.00**
Price: 200 28 ga./.410 Combo **$3,300.00**
Price: 200 HR 12 ga., 20 ga. **$2,500.00**
Price: 200 HR 28 ga., .410 .... **$2,625.00**
Price: 200 HR 28 ga./.410 combo **$3,600.00**
Price: 250 12 ga., 20 ga. **$2,600.00**
Price: 250 28 ga., .410 .... **$2,725.00**
Price: 250 28 ga./.410 Combo **$3,700.00**

SKB 7000SL SIDELOCK
Gauges: 12 ga., 20 ga. **Barrels:** 28 in., 30 in. Five choke tubes provided (F, IM, M, IC, SK). **Stock:** Premium Turkish walnut with hand-rubbed oil finish, fine-line hand checkering, Prince of Wales grip and beavertail fore-end. **Weights:** 6–7 lbs. **Sights:** Brass bead. **Features:** Sidelock design with Holland & Holland style seven-pin removable locks with safety sears. Bison Bone Charcoal casehardening, hand engraved sculpted sidelock receiver. Manual safety, automatic ejectors, single selective trigger. Available by special order only. Imported from Turkey by GU, Inc.
Price: From **$6,700.00**

STOEGER UPLANDER
Gauges: 12 ga., 20 ga., .410, 3 in.; 28 ga., 2 3/4. **Barrels:** 22 in., 24 in., 26 in., 28 in. **Weights:** 6.5–7.3 lbs. **Sights:** Brass bead. **Features:** Double trigger, IC & M choke tubes included with gun. Other choke tubes available. Tang auto safety, extractors, black plastic buttplate. Imported by Benelli USA.
Price: Standard **$499.00**
Price: Supreme (single trigger, AA-grade wood) **$539.00**
Price: Longfowler (12 ga., 30-in. bbl.) **$499.00**
Price: Home Defense (20 or 12 ga., 20-in. bbl., tactical sights) **$499.00**
Price: Double Defense (20 ga.) fiber-optic sight, accessory rail **$499.00**

STOEGER COACH GUN
Gauges: 12 ga., 20 ga., 2 3/4 in., 3 in. **Barrel:** 20 in. **Weight:** 6.5 lbs. **Stock:** Brown hardwood, classic beavertail fore-end. **Sights:** Brass bead. **Features:** Double or single trigger, IC & M choke tubes included, others available. Tang auto safety, extractors, black plastic buttplate. Imported by Benelli USA.
Price: .... **$449.00–$499.00**

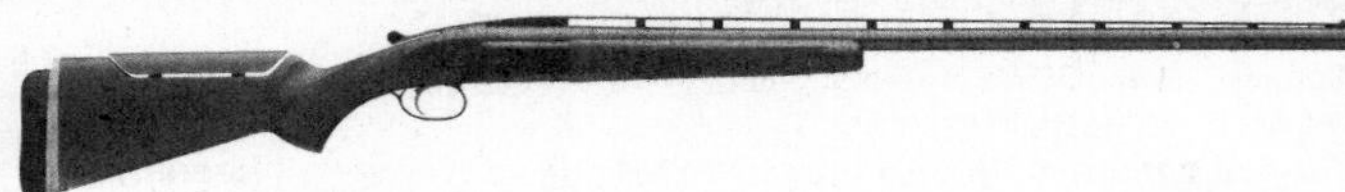

BROWNING BT-99 TRAP

Gauge: 12 ga. **Barrels:** 30 in., 32 in., 34 in. **Stock:** Walnut; standard or adjustable. **Weights:** 7 lbs. 11 oz.–9 lbs. **Features:** Back-bored single barrel; interchangeable chokes; beavertail forearm; extractor only; high rib.

Price: BT-99 w/conventional comb, 32- or 34-in. barrels **$1,430.00**
Price: BT-99 w/adjustable comb, 32- or 34-in. barrels **$1,680.00**
Price: BT-99 Golden Clays w/adjustable comb, 32- or 34-in. barrels **$4,340.00**
Price: BT-99 Grade III .... **$2,540.00–$2,840.00**

HENRY .410 LEVER-ACTION SHOTGUN

Gauge: .410, 2 1/2 in. **Capacity:** 5. **Barrels:** 20 or 24 in. with either no choke (20 in.) or full choke (24 in.). **Stock:** American walnut. **Sights:** Gold bead front only. **Finish:** Blued. Introduced in 2017. **Features:** Design is based on the Henry .45-70 rifle.

Price: 20-in. bbl.. **$893.00**
Price: 24-in. bbl.. **$947.00**

HENRY SINGLE-SHOT SHOTGUN

Gauges: 12 ga., 20 ga. or .410 bore, 3 1/2 in. (12 ga.), 3 in. (20 ga. and 410). **Barrels:** 26 or 28 in. with either modified choke tube (12 ga., 20 ga., compatible with Rem-Choke tubes) or fixed full choke (.410). **Stock:** American walnut, straight or pistol grip. **Sights:** Gold bead front only. **Weight:** 6.33 lbs. **Finish:** Blued or brass receiver. **Features:** Break-open single-shot design. Introduced in 2017.

Price: **$448.00**
Price: Brass receiver, straight grip... **$576.00**

KRIEGHOFF K-80 SINGLE BARREL TRAP GUN

Gauge: 12 ga., 2 3/4 in. **Barrel:** 32 in., 34 in. Unsingle. Fixed Full or choke tubes. **Weight:** About 8.75 lbs. **Stock:** Four stock dimensions or adjustable stock available. All hand-checkered European walnut. **Features:** Satin nickel finish. Selective mechanical trigger adjustable for finger position. Tapered step vent rib. Adjustable point of impact.

Price: Standard Grade Full Unsingle, From **$12,995.00**

KRIEGHOFF KX-6 SPECIAL TRAP GUN

Gauge: 12 ga., 2 3/4 in. **Barrel:** 32 in., 34 in.; choke tubes. **Weight:** About 8.5 lbs. **Stock:** Factory adjustable stock. European walnut. **Features:** Ventilated tapered step rib. Adjustable position trigger, optional release trigger. Fully adjustable rib. Satin gray electroless nickel receiver. Fitted aluminum case. Imported from Germany by Krieghoff International, Inc.

Price: **$5,995.00**

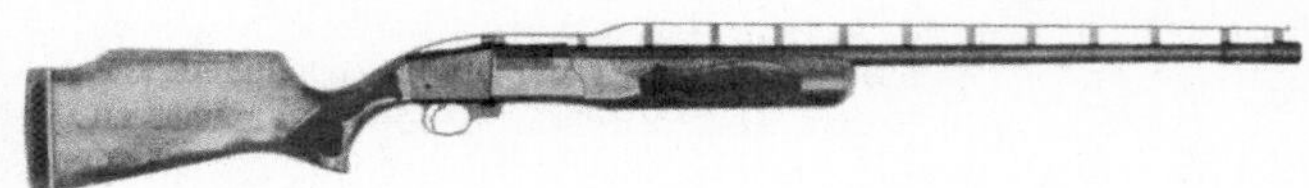

LJUTIC MONO GUN SINGLE BARREL

Gauge: 12 ga. **Barrel:** 34 in., choked to customer specs; hollow-milled rib, 35.5-in. sight plane. **Weight:** Approx. 9 lbs. **Stock:** To customer specs. Oil finish, hand checkered. **Features:** Custom gun. Pull or release trigger; removable trigger guard contains trigger and hammer mechanism; Ljutic pushbutton opener on front of trigger guard. From Ljutic Industries.

Price: Std., med. or Olympic rib, custom bbls., fixed choke. **$7,495.00**
Price: Stainless steel mono gun.. **$8,495.00**

LJUTIC LTX PRO 3 DELUXE MONO GUN

Deluxe, lightweight version of the Mono gun with high-quality wood, upgrade checkering, special rib height, screw-in chokes, ported and cased.

Price: **$8,995.00**
Price: Stainless steel model... **$9,995.00**

ROSSI CIRCUIT JUDGE

Revolving shotgun chambered in .410 (2 1/2- or 3-in./.45 Colt. Based on Taurus Judge handgun. Features include 18.5-in. barrel; fiber-optic front sight; 5-round cylinder; hardwood Monte Carlo stock.

Price: From.. **$689.00**

TAR-HUNT RSG-12 PROFESSIONAL RIFLED SLUG GUN

Gauge: 12 ga., 2 3/4 in., 3 in., **Capacity:** 1-round magazine. **Barrel:** 23 in., fully rifled with muzzle brake. **Weight:** 7.75 lbs. **Length:** 41.5 in. overall. **Stock:** Matte black McMillan fiberglass with Pachmayr Decelerator pad. **Sights:** None furnished; comes with Leupold windage or Weaver bases. **Features:** Uses rifle-style action with two locking lugs; two-position safety; Shaw barrel; single-stage, trigger; muzzle brake. Many options available. All models have area-controlled feed action. Introduced 1991. Made in U.S. by Tar-Hunt Custom Rifles, Inc.

Price: 12 ga. Professional model **$2,895.00**
Price: Left-hand model **$3,000.00**

TAR-HUNT RSG-16 ELITE

Similar to RSG-12 Professional except 16 ga.; right- or left-hand versions.

Price: **$2,895.00**

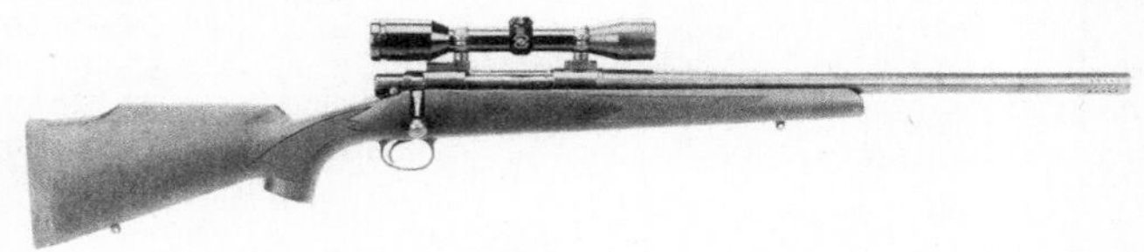

TAR-HUNT RSG-20 MOUNTAINEER SLUG GUN

Similar to the RSG-12 Professional except chambered for 20 ga. (2 3/4 in. and 3 in. shells); 23 in. Shaw rifled barrel, with muzzle brake; two-lug bolt; one-shot blind magazine; matte black finish; McMillan fiberglass stock with Pachmayr Decelerator pad; receiver drilled and tapped for Rem. 700 bases. Right- or left-hand versions. Weighs 6.5 lbs. Introduced 1997. Made in USA by Tar-Hunt Custom Rifles, Inc.

Price: **$3,495.00**

BENELLI M2 TACTICAL

Gauge: 12 ga., 2 3/4 in., 3 in. **Capacity:** 5-round magazine. **Barrel:** 18.5 in. IC, M, F choke tubes. **Weight:** 6.7 lbs. **Length:** 39.75 in. overall. **Stock:** Black polymer. **Sights:** Rifle type ghost ring system, tritium night sights optional. **Features:** Semi-auto inertia recoil action. Cross-bolt safety; bolt release button; matte-finish metal. Introduced 1993. Imported from Italy by Benelli USA.

Price: From .... **$1,239.00–$1,359.00**

BENELLI M3 TACTICAL

Gauge: 12 ga., 3 in. **Barrel:** 20 in. **Stock:** Black synthetic w/pistol grip. **Sights:** Ghost ring rear, ramp front. Convertible dual-action operation (semi-auto or pump).

Price: **$1,599.00**

BENELLI M4 TACTICAL

Gauge: 12 ga., 3 in. **Barrel:** 18.5 in. **Weight:** 7.8 lbs. **Length:** 40 in. overall. **Stock:** Synthetic. **Sights:** Ghost Ring rear, fixed blade front. **Features:** Auto-regulating gas-operated (ARGO) action, choke tube, Picatinny rail, standard and collapsible stocks available, optional LE tactical gun case. Introduced 2006. Imported from Italy by Benelli USA.

Price: From **$1,999.00**

KEL-TEC KSG BULL-PUP TWIN-TUBE

Gauge: 12 ga. **Capacity:** 13+1. **Barrel:** 18.5 in. **Overall Length:** 26.1 in. **Weight:** 8.5 lbs. (loaded). **Features:** Pump-action shotgun with two magazine tubes. The shotgun bears a resemblance to the South African designed Neostead pump-action gun. The operator is able to move a switch located near the top of the grip to select the right or left tube, or move the switch to the center to eject a shell without chambering another round. Optional accessories include a factory installed Picatinny rail with flip-up sights and a pistol grip. KSG-25 has 30-in. barrel and 20-round capacity magazine tubes.

Price: **$990.00**
Price: KSG-25 .... **$1400.00**

MOSSBERG MODEL 500 SPECIAL PURPOSE

Gauges: 12 ga., 20 ga., .410, 3 in. **Barrels:** 18.5 in., 20 in. (Cyl.). **Weight:** 7 lbs. **Stock:** Walnut-finished hardwood or black synthetic. **Sights:** Metal bead front. **Features:** Slide-action operation. Available in 6- or 8-round models. Top-mounted safety, double action slide bars, swivel studs, rubber recoil pad. Blue, Parkerized, Marinecote finishes. Mossberg Cablelock included. The HS410 Home Security model chambered for .410 with 3 in. chamber; has pistol grip fore-end, thick recoil pad, muzzle brake and has special spreader choke on the 18.5-in. barrel. Overall length is 37.5 in. Blued finish; synthetic field stock. Mossberg Cablelock and video included. Mariner model has Marinecote metal finish to resist rust and corrosion. Synthetic field stock; pistol grip kit included. 500 Tactical 6-shot has black synthetic tactical stock. Introduced 1990.

Price: 500 Mariner **$636.00**
Price: HS410 Home Security **$477.00**
Price: Home Security 20 ga. **$631.00**
Price: FLEX Tactical .... **$583.00–$630.00**
Price: 500 Chainsaw pistol grip only; removable top handle **$547.00**
Price: JIC (Just In Case) **$500.00**
Price: Thunder Ranch **$514.00**

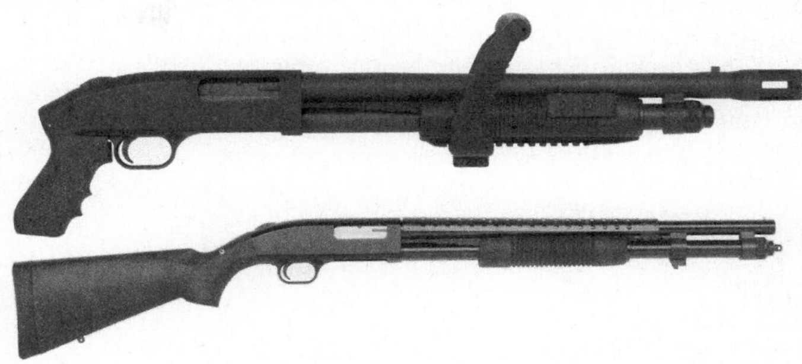

MOSSBERG MODEL 590 SPECIAL PURPOSE

Gauges: 12 ga., 20 ga., .410 3 in. **Capacity:** 9-round magazine. **Barrel:** 20 in. (Cyl.). **Weight:** 7.25 lbs. **Stock:** Synthetic field or Speedfeed. **Sights:** Metal bead front or Ghost Ring. **Features:** Slide action. Top-mounted safety, double slide action bars. Comes with heat shield, bayonet lug, swivel studs, rubber recoil pad. Blue, Parkerized or Marinecote finish. Shockwave has 14-inch heavy walled barrel, Raptor pistol grip, wrapped fore-end and is fully BATFE compliant. Magpul model has Magpul SGA stock with adjustable comb and length of pull. Mossberg Cablelock included. From Mossberg.

Price: From **$559.00**
Price: Flex Tactical **$672.00**
Price: Tactical Tri-Rail Adjustable **$879.00**
Price: Mariner **$756.00**
Price: Shockwave **$455.00**
Price: MagPul 9-shot **$836.00**

MOSSBERG 930 SPECIAL PURPOSE SERIES

Gauge: 12 ga., 3 in. **Barrel:** 28 in. flat ventilated rib. **Weight:** 7.3 lbs. **Length:** 49 in.. **Stock:** Composite stock with close radius pistol grip; Speed Lock forearm; textured gripping surfaces; shim adjustable for length of pull, cast and drop; Mossy Oak Bottomland camo finish; Dura-Touch Armor Coating. **Features:** 930 Special Purpose shotguns feature a self-regulating gas system that vents excess gas to aid in recoil reduction and eliminate stress on critical components. All 930 autoloaders chamber both 2 3/4 inch and 3-in. 12-ga. shotshells with ease — from target loads, to non-toxic magnum loads, to the latest sabot slug ammo. Magazine capacity is 7+1 on models with extended magazine tube, 4+1 on models without. To complete the package, each Mossberg 930 includes a set of specially designed spacers for quick adjustment of the horizontal and vertical angle of the stock, bringing a custom-feel fit to every shooter. All 930 Special Purpose models feature a drilled and tapped receiver, factory-ready for Picatinny rail, scope base or optics installation. 930 SPX models conveniently come with a factory-mounted Picatinny rail and LPA/M16-Style Ghost Ring combination sight right out of the box. Other sighting options include a basic front bead, or white-dot front sights. Mossberg 930 Special Purpose shotguns are available in a variety of configurations; 5-round tactical barrel, 5-round with muzzle brake, 8-round pistol-grip, and even a 5-round security/field combo.

Price: Tactical 5-Round **$714.00**
Price: Home Security **$662.00**
Price: Standard Stock **$787.00**
Price: Pistol Grip 8-Round **$883.00**
Price: 5-Round Combo w/extra 18.5-in. barrel **$679.00**

SHOTGUNS Military & Police

REMINGTON 870 DM SERIES
Gauge: 12 ga. (2 3/4 in., 3 in. interchangeably) **Barrel:** 18.5-in. cylinder bore. Detachable 6-round magazine. **Stock:** Hardwood or black synthetic with textured gripping surfaces. Tac-14 DM model features short pistol grip buttstock and 14-in. barrel.
Price: **$559.00**

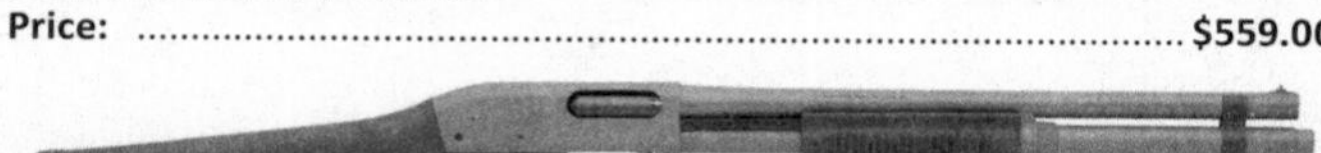

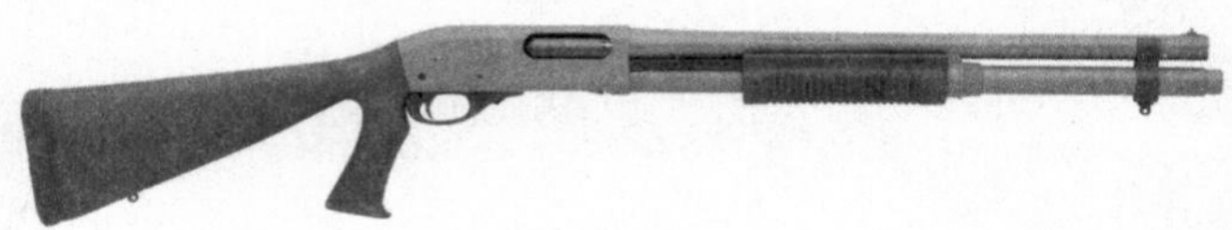

REMINGTON MODEL 870 PUMP AND MODEL 1100 AUTOLOADER TACTICAL SHOTGUNS
Gauges: 870: 12 ga., 2 3/4 or 3 in.; 1100: 2 3/4 in. **Barrels:** 18 in., 20 in., 22 in. (Cyl or IC). **Weight:** 7.5–7.75 lbs. **Length:** 38.5–42.5 in. overall. **Stock:** Black synthetic, synthetic Speedfeed IV full pistol-grip stock, or Knoxx Industries SpecOps stock w/recoil-absorbing spring-loaded cam and adjustable length of pull (12 in. to 16 in., 870 only). **Sights:** Front post w/dot only on 870; rib and front dot on 1100. **Features:** R3 recoil pads, LimbSaver technology to reduce felt recoil, 2-, 3- or 4-round extensions based on barrel length; matte-olive-drab barrels and receivers. Model 1100 Tactical is available with Speedfeed IV pistol grip stock or standard black synthetic stock and fore-end. Speedfeed IV model has an 18-in. barrel with two-shot extension. Standard synthetic-stocked version is equipped with 22-in. barrel and four-round extension. Introduced 2006. From Remington Arms Co.
Price: 870 Express Tactical Knoxx 20 ga. **$555.00**
Price: 870 Express Magpul **$898.00**
Price: 870 Special Purpose Marine (nickel)... **$841.00**
Price: 1100 TAC-4 .... **$1,015.00**

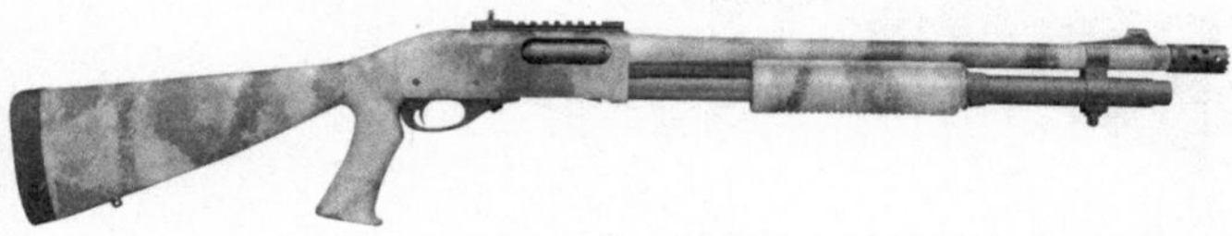

REMINGTON 870 EXPRESS TACTICAL A-TACS CAMO
Gauge: 12 ga., 2 3/4 and 3 in. **Features:** Pump-action shotgun. Full A-TACS digitized camo; 18.5-in. barrel; extended ported Tactical RemChoke; SpeedFeed IV pistol-grip stock with SuperCell recoil pad; fully adjustable XS Ghost Ring Sight rail with removable white bead front sight; 7-round capacity with factory-installed 2-shot extension; drilled and tapped receiver; sling swivel stud.
Price: **$720.00**

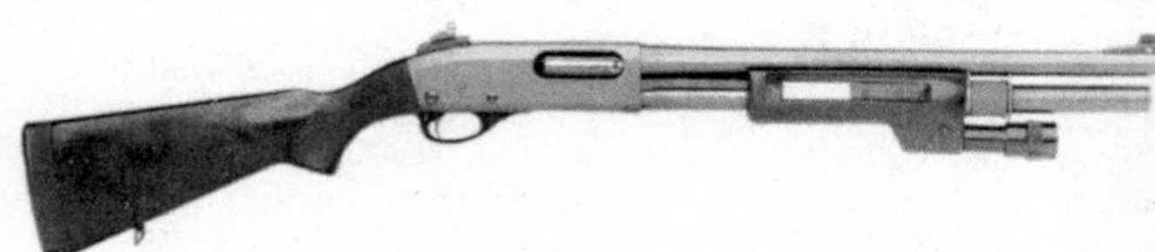

REMINGTON 887 NITRO MAG TACTICAL
Gauge: 12 ga., 2 3/4 to 3 1/2 in. **Features:** Pump-action shotgun,18.5-in. barrel with ported, extended tactical RemChoke; 2-shot magazine extension; barrel clamp with integral Picatinny rails; ArmorLokt coating; synthetic stock and fore-end with specially contour grip panels.
Price: **$534.00**

TACTICAL RESPONSE STANDARD MODEL
Gauge: 12 ga., 3 in. **Capacity:** 7-round magazine. **Barrel:** 18 in. (Cyl.). **Weight:** 9 lbs. **Length:** 38 in. overall. **Stock:** Fiberglass-filled polypropylene with non-snag recoil absorbing butt pad. Nylon tactical fore-end houses flashlight. **Sights:** Trak-Lock ghost ring sight system. Front sight has Tritium insert. **Features:** Highly modified Remington 870P with Parkerized finish. Comes with nylon three-way adjustable sling, high visibility non-binding follower, high-performance magazine spring, Jumbo Head safety, and Side Saddle extended 6-shotshell carrier on left side of receiver. Introduced 1991. From Scattergun Technologies, Inc.
Price: Standard model, From... **$1,540.00**
Price: Border Patrol model, From **$1,135.00**
Price: Professional Model 13-in. bbl. (Law enf., military only)........ **$1,550.00**

TRISTAR COBRA
Gauge: 12 ga., 3 in. **Barrel:** 28 in. **Weight:** 6.7 lbs. Three Beretta-style choke tubes (IC, M, F). **Length:** NA. **Stock:** Matte black synthetic stock and forearm. **Sights:** Vent rib with matted sight plane. **Features:** Five-year warranty. Cobra Tactical Pump Shotgun magazine holds 7, return spring in forearm, 20-in. barrel, Cylinder choke. Introduced 2008. Imported by Tristar Sporting Arms Ltd.
Price: Tactical.. **$319.00–$429.00**

TRISTAR TEC12 AUTO/PUMP
Gauge: 12 ga. 3 in. **Barrel:** 20-in. ported barrel with fixed cylinder choke. Capable of operating in pump-action or semi-auto model with the turn of a dial. **Stock:** Pistol-grip synthetic with matte black finish. **Weight:** 7.4 lbs. **Sights:** Ghost-ring rear, raised bridge fiber-optic front. Picatinny rail.
Price: **$689.00**

CARLETON UNDERHAMMER MATCH PERCUSSION PISTOL
Caliber: .36. **Barrel:** 9.5 in., browned octagonal, rifled. **Weight:** 2.25 lbs. **Length:** 16.75 in. overall. Stocks: Walnut grip. **Sights:** Blade front, open rear, adjustable for elevation. **Features:** Percussion, under-hammer ignition, adjustable trigger, no half cock. No ramrod. Made by Pedersoli. Imported by Dixie Gun Works.
Price: Dixie, FH0332 .... **$915.00**

CONTINENTAL TARGET PISTOL
Caliber: .44 smoothbore, .45 rifled. **Barrel:** 11 in. **Weight:** 2.2 lbs. **Length:** 16 in. **Stocks:** Walnut. **Sights:** Adjustable for windage. **Features:** Percussion ignition, casehardened lock, single-set trigger, no ramrod. Made by Pedersoli. Introduced 2017.
Price: .45 rifled barrel S.373-450, Pedersoli... .... **$549.00**
Price: .44 smooth barrel S.373-450, Pedersoli... .... **$549.00**

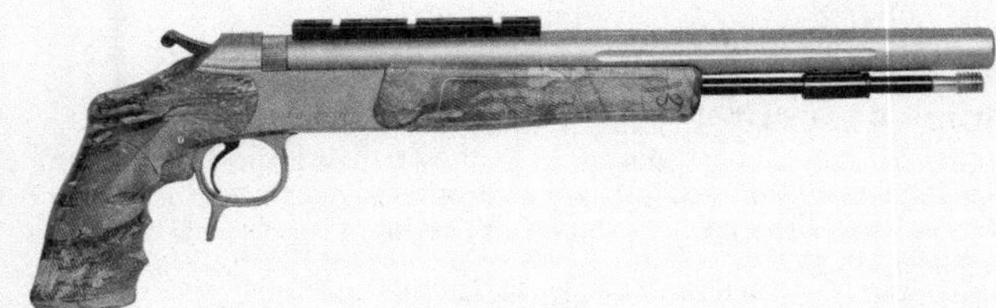

CVA OPTIMA V2 PISTOL Caliber: .50. **Barrel:** 14 in., 1:28-in. twist, Cerakote finish. **Weight:** 3.7 lbs. **Length:** 19 in. Stocks: Black synthetic, Realtree Xtra Green. Ramrod: Aluminum. **Sights:** Scope base mounted. **Features:** Break-open action, all stainless construction, quick-removal breech plug for 209 primer. From CVA. Production discontinued in 2018 some remain in dealer's hands.
Price: PP222SM Stainless/Realtree Xtra, rail mount **$354.00**
Price: PP221SM Stainless/black, rail mount **$307.00**

FRENCH AN IX, AN XIII, AND GENDARMERIE NAPOLEONIC PISTOLS
Caliber: .69. **Barrel:** 8.25 in. **Weight:** 3 lbs. **Length:** 14 in. overall. Stocks: Walnut. **Sights:** None. **Features:** Flintlock, casehardened lock, brass furniture, buttcap, lock marked "Imperiale de S. Etienne." Steel ramrod. Other Napoleonic pistols include half-stocked "AN XIII" and Gendarmerie with 5.25-inch barrel. Made by Pedersoli. Imported by Dixie Gun Works.
Price: Dixie Gun Works FH0890 .... **$740.00**
Price: Dixie Gun Works AN XIII FHO895 .... **$710.00**
Price: Dixie Gun Works Gendarmerie FHO954 .... **$725.00**

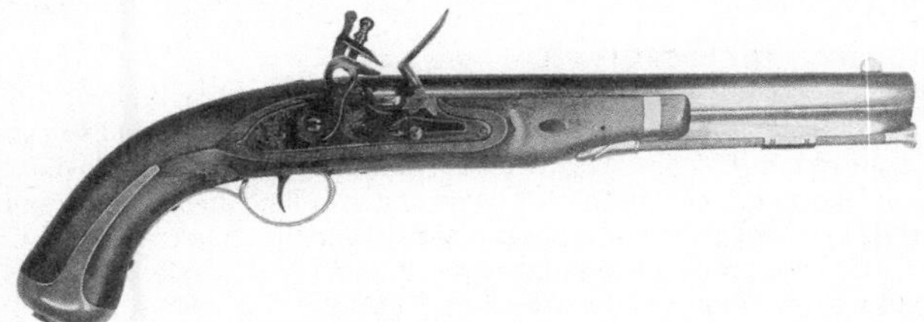

HARPER'S FERRY 1805 PISTOL
Caliber: .58. **Barrel:** 10 in. **Weight:** 2.5 lbs. **Length:** 16 in. overall. Stocks: Walnut. **Sights:** Fixed. **Features:** Flintlock. Casehardened lock, brass-mounted German silver-colored barrel. Wooden ramrod. Replica of the first U.S. government made flintlock pistol. Made by Pedersoli. Imported by Dixie Gun Works.
Price: Dixie Gun Works RH0225 Flintlock **$565.00**
Price: Dixie Gun Works Kit FH0411 Flintlock **$433.00**
Price: Dixie Gun Works PH0951 Caplock **$550.00**
Price: Dixie Gun Works Kit PK0937 Caplock **$395.00**

HOWDAH HUNTER PISTOLS
Caliber: .50, 20 ga., .58 **Barrels:** 11.25 in., blued, rifled in .50 and .58 calibers **Weight:** 4.25–5 lbs. **Length:** 17.25 in. **Stocks:** American walnut with checkered grip. **Sights:** Brass bead front sight. **Features:** Blued barrels, swamped barrel rib, engraved, color casehardened locks and hammers, captive steel ramrod. Available with detachable shoulder stock, case, holster and mold. Made by Pedersoli. Imported by Dixie Gun Works, and individual models by Cabela's, Taylor's and others.
Price: Dixie, 50X50, PH0572 .... **$850.00**
Price: Dixie, 58XD58, PH09024 .... **$875.00**
Price: Dixie, 20X20 ga., PH0581 .... **$815.00**
Price: Dixie, 50X20 ga., PH0581 .... **$850.00**
Price: Dixie, 50X50, Kit, PK0952 .... **$640.00**
Price: Dixie, 50X20, Kit, PK1410 .... **$675.00**
Price: Dixie, 20X20, Kit, PK0954 .... **$640.00**

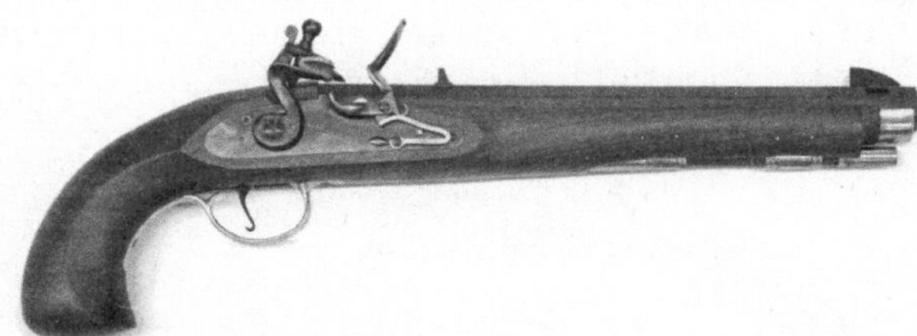

KENTUCKY PISTOL
Caliber: .45, .50, .54 **Barrel:** 10.25 in. **Weight:** 2.5 lbs. **Length:** 15.4 in. overall. **Stocks:** Walnut with smooth rounded birds-head grip. **Sights:** Fixed. **Features:** Available in flint or percussion ignition in various calibers. Casehardened lock, blued barrel, drift-adjustable rear sights, blade front. Wooden ramrod. Kit guns of all models available from Dixie Gun Works. Made by Pedersoli. Imported by Dixie Gun Works, EMF and others.
Price: Dixie, .45 Percussion, PH0440 .... **$395.00**
Price: Dixie, .45 Flint, FH0430 .... **$410.00**
Price: Dixie, .45 Flint, Kit FH0320 .... **$299.00**
Price: Dixie, .50 Flint, FH0935 .... **$475.00**
Price: Dixie, .50 Percussion, PH0930 .... **$450.00**
Price: Dixie, .54 Flint, FH0080 .... **$440.00**
Price: Dixie, .54 Percussion, PH0330 .... **$395.00**
Price: Dixie, .54 Percussion, Kit PK0436 .... **$283.00**
Price: Dixie, .45 Percussion, Navy Moll, brass buttcap, PK0903 .... **$565.00**

LE PAGE PERCUSSION DUELING PISTOL
Caliber: .44 (Pedersoli), .45 (Armi, Chiappa). **Barrel:** 10.25 in. browned octagon, rifled. **Weight:** 2.5 lbs. **Length:** 16.6 in. overall. Stocks: Walnut, rounded checkered butt (Pedersoli), fluted butt (Armi). **Sights:** Blade front, open-style rear. **Features:** Single set trigger (Pedersoli), double set (Armi) trigger. Browned barrel (Dixie International). Bright barrel, silver-plated brass furniture (Armi). External ramrod. Made by Pedersoli, Armi, Chiappa. Imported by Dixie Gun Works.
Price: Dixie, Pedersoli, PH0431 .... **$925.00**
Price: Dixie, International, Flintlock,Pedersoli, FH0231 .... **$1,250.00**
Price: Dixie, Armi, PH0310 .... **$627.00**
Out of production, some dealer stock remains

LYMAN PLAINS PISTOL
Caliber: .50 or .54. **Barrel:** 8 in.; 1:30-in. twist, both calibers. **Weight:** 50 oz. **Length:** 15 in. overall. **Stocks:** Walnut. **Sights:** Blade front, square-notch rear adjustable for windage. **Features:** Polished brass trigger guard and ramrod tip, color casehardened coil spring lock, spring-loaded trigger, stainless steel nipple, blackened iron furniture. Hooked patent breech, detachable belt hook. Introduced 1981. From Lyman, Dixie Gun Works.
Price: Dixie PH0940 .50-cal. **$345.00**
Price: Dixie PH0943 .54-cal **$345.00**
Price: Dixie PK0945 .50-cal Kit **$285.00**
Price: Dixie PK0945 .54-cal. Kit **$285.00**

MAMELOUK
Caliber: .54. **Barrel:** 7.625 in., bright. **Weight:** 1.61 lbs. **Length:** 13 in. overall. **Stocks:** Walnut, with brass end cap and medallion. **Sights:** Blade front. **Features:** Flint, lanyard ring, wooden ramrod. Made by Davide Pedersoli. Available on order from IFG (Italian Firearms Group).
Price: **$445.00**

MORTIMER TARGET PISTOL
Caliber: .44. **Barrel:** 10 in., bright octagonal on Standard, browned on Deluxe, rifled. **Weight:** 2.25 lbs. **Length:** 16 in. overall. **Stocks:** Walnut, checkered saw-handle grip on Deluxe. **Sights:** Blade front, open-style rear. **Features:** Percussion or flint, single set trigger, sliding hammer safety, engraved lock on Deluxe. Wooden ramrod. Made by Pedersoli. Imported by Dixie Gun Works.
Price: Dixie, Flint, FH0316........ **$1,175.00**
Price: Dixie, Percussion, PH0311........ **$1,095.00**
Price: Dixie, Deluxe, FH0950........ **$2,200.00**

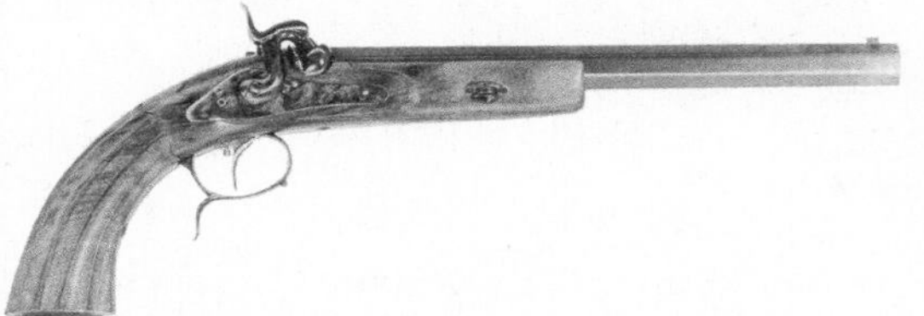

PEDERSOLI MANG TARGET PISTOL
Caliber: .38. **Barrel:** 10.5 in., octagonal; 1:15-in. twist. **Weight:** 2.5 lbs. **Length:** 17.25 in. overall. Stocks: Walnut with fluted grip. **Sights:** Blade front, open rear adjustable for windage. **Features:** Browned barrel, polished breech plug, remainder color casehardened. Made by Pedersoli. Imported by Dixie Gun Works.
Price: PH0503........ **$1,750.00**

PEDERSOLI REMINGTON 1858 PATTERN CUSTOM
Caliber: .44 **Barrel:** 8 in., tapered octagon, 1:18 right-hand twist. **Weight:** 2.71 lbs. **Length:** 13.75 in. overall. **Grips:** One-piece hardwood. **Sights:** V-notch on top strap, steel blade front. **Features:** Special metal treatment with hardening and smoothing of internal parts, dulled chrome finish, brass trigger guard. A higher grade gun for U.S. and international match shooting.
Price: V.349-44........ **$NA**

PHILADELPHIA DERRINGER
Caliber: .45. **Barrel:** 3.1 in., browned, rifled. **Weight:** .5 lbs. **Length:** 6.215 in. Grips: European walnut. **Sights:** V-notch rear, blade front. **Features:** Back-hammer percussion lock with engraving, single trigger. From Pedersoli. Sold by Dixie Gun Works.
Price: Dixie, PH0913........ **$550.00**
Price: Dixie, Kit PK0863........ **$385.00**

QUEEN ANNE FLINTLOCK PISTOL
Caliber: .50. **Barrel:** 7.5 in., smoothbore. Stocks: Walnut. **Sights:** None. **Features:** Flintlock, German silver-colored steel barrel, fluted brass trigger guard, brass mask on butt. Lockplate left in the white. No ramrod. Introduced 1983. Made by Pedersoli. Imported by Dixie Gun Works.
Price: Dixie, RH0211........ **$495.00**
Price: Dixie, Kit, FH0421........ **$375.00**

REMINGTON RIDER DERRINGER
Caliber: 4.3 mm (BB lead balls only). **Barrel:** 2.1 in., blued, rifled. **Weight:** .25 lbs. **Length:** 4.75 in. Grips: All-steel construction. **Sights:** V-notch rear, bead front. **Features:** Fires percussion cap only — no powder. Available as casehardened frame or polished white. From Pedersoli. Sold by Dixie Gun Works.
Price: Dixie, Casehardened PH0923........ **$210.00**

SCREW BARREL PISTOL
Caliber: .44. **Barrel:** 2.35 in., blued, rifled. **Weight:** .5 lbs. **Length:** 6.5 in. **Grips:** European walnut. **Sights:** None. **Features:** Percussion, boxlock with center hammer, barrel unscrews for loading from rear, folding trigger, external hammer, combination barrel and nipple wrench furnished. From Pedersoli. Sold by Dixie Gun Works.
Price: Dixie, PH0530........ **$210.00**
Price: Dixie, PH0545........ **$165.00**

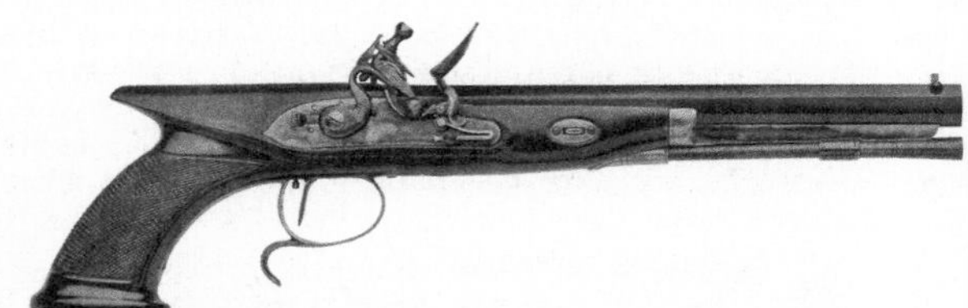

TATHUM & EGG PISTOL
Caliber: .45 smoothbore. **Barrel:** 11 in. browned. **Weight:** 2.42 lbs. **Length:** 16.5 in. **Stocks:** Walnut. **Sights:** Adjustable for windage. **Features:** Flintlock ignition, casehardened lock, single-set trigger, ramrod. Made by Pedersoli. Introduced 2017.
Price: .45 smooth barrel S.372-450, Pedersoli........ **$NA**

TRADITIONS KENTUCKY PISTOL
Caliber: .50. **Barrel:** 10 in., 1:20 in. twist. **Weight:** 2.75 lbs. **Length:** 15 in. Stocks: Hardwood full stock. **Sights:** Brass blade front, square notch rear adjustable for windage. **Features:** Polished brass finger spur-style trigger guard, stock cap and ramrod tip, color casehardened leaf spring lock, spring-loaded trigger, No. 11 percussion nipple, brass furniture. From Traditions, and as kit from Bass Pro and others.
Price: P1060 Finished........ **$244.00**
Price: KPC50602 Kit........ **$209.00**

TRADITIONS TRAPPER PISTOL
Caliber: .50. **Barrel:** 9.75 in., octagonal, blued, hooked patent breech, 1:20 in. twist. **Weight:** 2.75 lbs. **Length:** 15.5 in. **Stocks:** Hardwood, modified saw-handle style grip, half-stock. **Sights:** Brass blade front, rear sight adjustable for windage and elevation. **Features:** Percussion or flint, double set triggers, polished brass trigger guard, stock cap and ramrod tip, color casehardened leaf spring lock, spring-loaded trigger, No. 11 percussion nipple, brass furniture. From Traditions and as a kit from Bass Pro and others.
Price: P1100 Finished, percussion........ **$329.00**
Price: P1090 Finished, flint........ **$369.00**
Price: KPC51002 Kit, percussion........ **$299.00**
Price: KPC50902 Kit, flint........ **$359.00**

TRADITIONS VEST POCKET DERRINGER
Caliber: .31. **Barrel:** 2.35 in., round brass, smoothbore. **Weight:** .75 lbs. **Length:** 4.75 in. **Grips:** Simulated ivory. **Sights:** Front bead. **Features:** Replica of riverboat gambler's derringer. No. 11 percussion cap nipple, brass frame and barrel, spur trigger, external hammer. From Traditions.
Price: P1381, Brass........ **$194.00**

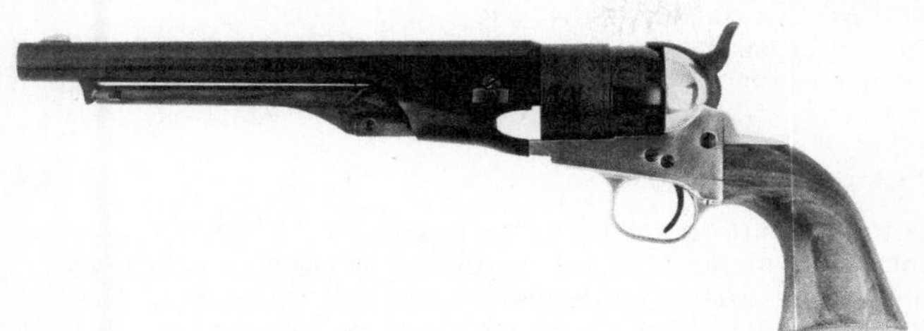

COLT ARMY 1860 PERCUSSION REVOLVER

Caliber: .44. **Barrel:** 8 in. **Weight:** 2.75 lbs. **Length:** 13.25 in. overall. **Grips:** One-piece walnut. **Sights:** Brass blade front, hammer notch rear. **Features:** Steel or casehardened frame, brass trigger guard, casehardened creeping loading lever. Many models and finishes are available for this pistol. Made by Pietta and Uberti. Imported by Cabela's, Cimarron, Dixie Gun Works, EMF, Taylor's, Uberti USA and others.

Price: Dixie, standard model with brass trigger guard RH0705 .... **$260.00**
Price: Dixie, standard model kit RK0965 .... **$250.00**
Price: Dixie, half-fluted cylinder cut for shoulder stock RH0125 ...... **$295.00**
Price: Dixie, 5.5 in. Sheriff's model RH0975 .... **$325.00**

COLT ARMY 1862 POLICE SNUBNOSE (THUNDERER) PERCUSSION REVOLVER

Caliber: .44, Capacity: 6-round cylinder. **Barrel:** 3 in. **Weight:** 1.5 lbs. **Length:** 9.2 in. overall. Grips: Varnished birds-head walnut. **Sights:** Brass pin front, hammer notch rear. **Features:** Steel or casehardened frame, steel trigger guard, no loading. Ramrod: Brass loading rod. Made by Uberti. Imported by EMF, Taylor's, Uberti USA

Price: Pietta CPPSNB44MYLC **$398.00**

COLT BABY DRAGOON 1848, 1849 POCKET, WELLS FARGO PERCUSSION REVOLVER

Caliber: .31. **Barrel:** 3 in., 4 in., 5 in., 6 in.; seven-groove; RH twist. **Weight:** About 21 oz. **Grips:** Varnished walnut. **Sights:** Brass pin front, hammer notch rear. **Features:** No loading lever on Baby Dragoon or Wells Fargo models. Unfluted cylinder with stagecoach holdup scene, cupped cylinder pin, no grease grooves, one safety pin on cylinder and slot in hammer face, straight (flat) mainspring. Made by Uberti. Imported by Cimarron, Dixie Gun Works, EMF, Uberti USA and others.

Price: From .... **$310.00–$346.00**

COLT 1847 WALKER PERCUSSION REVOLVER

Caliber: .44 **Barrel:** 9 in. **Weight:** 4.5 lbs. **Length:** 15.7 in. overall. **Grips:** One-piece hardwood. **Sights:** Brass blade front, hammer notch rear. **Features:** Copy of Sam Colt's first U.S. contract revolver. Engraved cylinder, casehardened hammer and loading lever. Blued finish. Made by Uberti, imported by Cabela's, Cimarron, Dixie Gun Works, EMF, Taylor's, Uberti USA and others.

Price: Dixie, standard model, blued steel RH0450 .... **$410.00**
Price: Dixie, standard model, blued steel kit RK0447 .... **$355.00**

COLT 1848 DRAGOON PERCUSSION REVOLVERS

Caliber: .44 **Barrel:** 7.5 in. **Weight:** 4.1 lbs. **Grips:** One-piece walnut. **Sights:** Brass blade front, hammer notch rear. **Features:** Copy of Eli Whitney's design for Colt using Walker parts and improved loading lever latch. Blued barrel, backstrap and trigger guard. Made in Italy by Uberti. Imported by Dixie Gun Works, Taylor's, Uberti USA and others.

Price: 1848 Dragoon, 1st-3rd models, RH0230 .... **$385.00**
Price: 1848 Dragoon, 3rd. model, cut for stock RH0234 .... **$410.00**

COLT TEXAS PATTERSON PERCUSSION REVOLVER

Caliber: .36 **Barrel:** 9 in. tapered octagon. **Weight:** 2.75 lbs. **Length:** 13.75 in. Grips: One-piece walnut. **Sights:** Brass pin front, hammer notch rear. **Features:** Folding trigger, blued steel furniture, frame and barrel; engraved scene on cylinder. Ramrod: Loading tool provided. Made by Pietta. Imported by Dixie Gun Works.

Price: Dixie RH0600 .... **$595.00**

COLT NAVY MODEL 1851 PERCUSSION REVOLVER

Caliber: .36, .44. **Capacity:** 6-round cylinder **Barrel:** 7.5 in. **Weight:** 44 oz. **Length:** 13 in. overall. **Grips:** Walnut. **Sights:** Post front, hammer notch rear. **Features:** Many authentic and non-authentic variations are offered that include, brass backstrap and trigger guard, steel or brass frame options, some have 1st Model square-back trigger guard, engraved cylinder with navy battle scene; casehardened hammer, loading lever. Cartridge conversion pistols and cylinders are also available from Cimarron and Taylor's. Made by Uberti and Pietta. Imported by Cabela's, Cimarron, EMF, Dixie Gun Works, Taylor's, Traditions (.44 only), Uberti USA and others.

Price: Brass frame (Dixie Gun Works RH0100) **$240.00**
Price: Steel frame (Dixie Gun Works RH844) **$285.00**
Price: Confederate Navy (Cabela's) **$200.00**
Price: Cartridge conversion cylinders .38 Spl. and .45 LC .... **$240.00–$300.00**

COLT SHERIFF MODEL 1851 PERCUSSION REVOLVER

Caliber: .44. **Capacity:** 6-round cylinder. **Barrel:** 5.5 in. **Weight:** 40 oz. **Length:** 10.5 in. overall. **Grips:** Walnut. **Sights:** Fixed. **Features:** Steel frame, brass backstrap and trigger guard; engraved navy scene; casehardened frame, hammer, loading lever. Made by Uberti. Imported by EMF.

Price: PF51CH44512 Steel frame **$235.00**
Price: PF51BR44512 Brass frame **$200.00**

COLT NAVY 1861 PERCUSSION REVOLVER

Caliber: .36 **Barrel:** 8 in. **Weight:** 2.75 lbs. **Length:** 13.25 in. overall. **Grips:** One-piece walnut. **Sights:** Brass blade front, hammer notch rear. **Features:** Steel or casehardened frame, brass trigger guard, casehardened creeping loading lever. Many models and finishes are available for this pistol. Made by Pietta and Uberti. Imported by Cabela's, Cimarron, Dixie Gun Works, EMF, Taylor's, Uberti USA and others.

Price: Dixie, standard model with brass trigger guard RH0841 .... **$325.00**
Price: Dixie, Sheriff's 5.5 in. barrel RK0975 .... **$325.00**

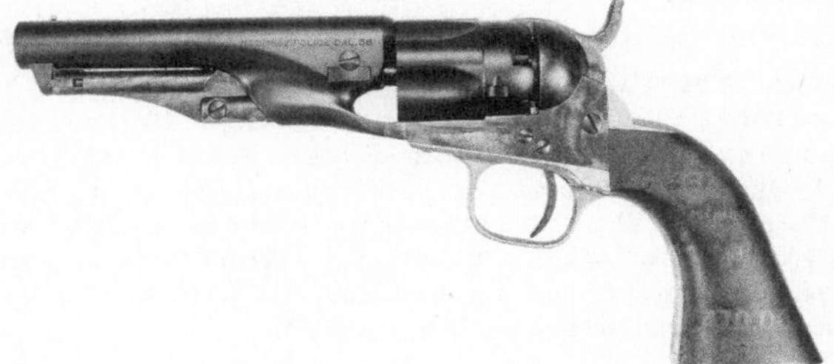

COLT POCKET POLICE 1862 PERCUSSION REVOLVER

Caliber: .36. **Capacity:** 5-round cylinder. **Barrels:** 4.5 in., 5.5 in., 6.5 in., 7.5 in. **Weight:** 26 oz. **Length:** 12 in. overall (6.5-in. bbl.). **Stocks:** Walnut. **Sights:** Fixed. **Features:** Round tapered barrel; half-fluted and rebated cylinder; casehardened frame, loading lever and hammer; silver or brass trigger guard and backstrap. Made by Uberti. Imported by Cimarron, Dixie Gun Works, Taylor's, Uberti USA and others.

Price: Dixie Gun Works RH0422 .... **$340.00**

NAVY YANK PEPPERBOX
Caliber: .36. **Capacity:** 6-round cylinder. **Barrel:** 3.1 in. **Weight:** 2.2 lbs. **Length:** 7 in. overall. **Grips:** European walnut. **Sights:** Hammer notch rear. **Features:** Casehardened frame, brass trigger guard, no loading lever or ramrod. Made by Pietta. Imported by Dixie, Taylor's.
Price: Pietta YAN36PP **$225.00**

DRAGOON PISTOL U.S. MODEL OF 1858 WITH DETACHABLE SHOULDER STOCK
Caliber: .58. **Barrel:** 12 in. **Weight:** 3.75 lbs., with shoulder stock 5.5 lbs. **Length:** 18.25 in. overall pistol. **Stocks:** Walnut pistol and shoulder stock. **Sights:** Flip-up blued steel rear, blade steel front. **Features:** Percussion, musket-cap nipple, casehardened lock, brass furniture. Captive steel ramrod. Shoulder stock included. Made by Palmetto. Imported by Dixie Gun Works.
Price: Dixie Gun Works, with shoulder stock PH1000 .... **$650.00**

DANCE AND BROTHERS PERCUSSION REVOLVER
Caliber: .44 **Barrel:** 7.4 in., round. **Weight:** 2.5 lbs. **Length:** 13 in. overall. **Grips:** Two-piece walnut. **Sights:** Fixed. **Features:** Reproduction of the C.S.A. revolver. Brass frame and trigger guard. Made by Pietta. From Dixie Gun Works, Cabela's and others.
Price: Dixie Gun Works RH0344 .... **$343.00**

DIXIE REMINGTON ARMY SHOOTERS REVOLVER
Caliber: .44 **Barrel:** 8 in., tapered octagon progressive twist. **Weight:** 2.75 lbs. **Length:** 13-3/4 in. overall. **Grips:** One-piece hardwood. **Sights:** V-notch on topstrap, blued steel blade front. **Features:** Silver plated brass trigger guard, blued steel backstrap and frame, casehardened hammer, trigger and loading lever. Navy size shoulder stock requires minor fitting. A higher grade gun for international match shooting. Won gold medals in 1987 and 1989. Made by Pietta. From Dixie Gun Works.
Price: RH0135 .... **$950.00**

DIXIE TEXAS OR BUFFALO PERCUSSION REVOLVER
Caliber: .44 **Barrel:** 12 in., octagon. **Weight:** 46 oz. **Length:** 18 in. overall. **Grips:** One-piece hardwood. **Sights:** Rear adjustable. **Features:** Highly polished Remington-style brass frame, backstrap and trigger guard; blued barrel and cylinder; casehardened hammer, trigger and loading lever. Made by Pietta. From Dixie Gun Works, EMF. After being carried for many years this gun has apparently been discontinued. Not listed in current catalog. A similar Bison revolver is still being sold by Traditions.
Price: SS1039 .... **$275.00**

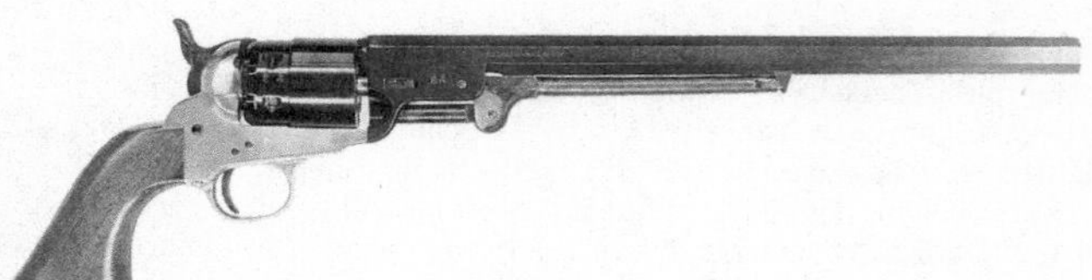

DIXIE WYATT EARP PERCUSSION REVOLVER
Caliber: .44 **Barrel:** 12 in., octagon. **Weight:** 46 oz. **Length:** 18 in. overall. **Grips:** One-piece hardwood. **Sights:** Fixed. **Features:** Highly polished brass frame, backstrap and trigger guard; blued barrel and cylinder; casehardened hammer, trigger and loading lever. Navy size shoulder stock requires minor fitting. Made by Pietta. From Dixie Gun Works, EMF.
Price: RH0130 .... **$225.00**

GRISWOLD AND GUNNISON PERCUSSION REVOLVER
Caliber: .36 **Barrel:** 7.5 in., round. **Weight:** 2.5 lbs. **Length:** 13.25 in. **Grip:** One-piece walnut. **Sights:** Fixed. **Features:** Reproduction of the C.S.A. revolver. Brass frame and trigger guard. Made by Pietta. From Cabela's and others.
Price: Cabelas JC-21-7650 .... **$209.99**

LEACH AND RIGDON PERCUSSION REVOLVER
Caliber: .36. **Barrel:** 7.5 in., octagon to round. **Weight:** 2.75 lbs. **Length:** 13 in. **Grip:** One-piece walnut. **Sights:** Hammer notch and pin front. **Features:** Steel frame. Reproduction of the C.S.A. revolver. Brass backstrap and trigger guard. Made by Uberti. From Dixie Gun Works and others.
Price: Dixie Gun Works RH0611 .... **$340.00**

LEMAT PERCUSSION REVOLVER
Caliber: .44/20 ga. **Barrel:** 6.75 in. (revolver); 4.875 in. (single shot). **Weight:** 3 lbs., 7 oz. **Length:** 14 in. overall. **Grips:** Hand-checkered walnut. **Sights:** Post front, hammer notch rear. **Features:** Exact reproduction with all-steel construction; 44-cal. 9-round cylinder, 20-ga. single barrel; color casehardened hammer with selector; spur trigger guard; ring at butt; lever-type barrel release. Made by Pietta. From Dixie Gun Works, and Navy from Cabela's. **Price:** LeMat Navy with knurled pin barrel release **$1,095.00**
Price: LeMat Calvary with trigger spur and lanyard ring **$1,095.00**
Price: LeMat Army with cross pin barrel selector **$1,095.00**

NEW MODEL 1858 REMINGTON ARMY PERCUSSION REVOLVER
Calibers: .36 or .44. **Capacity:** 6-round cylinder. **Barrels:** Standard 8 in., and 5.5–12 in. **Weight:** Standard 2 lbs. **Length:** Standard 13.5 in. **Grips:** Walnut, two-piece. **Sights:** Standard blade front, groove-in-frame rear; adjustable on some models. **Features:** Many variations of this gun are available. Also available as the Army Model Belt Revolver in .36 cal., a shortened and lightened version of the .44 model. Target Model (Uberti USA) has fully adjustable target rear sight, target front, .36 or .44. Imported by Cabela's, Cimarron F.A. Co., EMF, Taylor's, Traditions (.44 only), Uberti USA and others.
Price: Steel frame, Dixie RH0140 .... **$295.00**
Price: Steel frame kit, Dixie, oversized grips and frame RV0440 .... **$260.00**
Price: Stainless steel Model 1858, Cabela's, Traditions **$400.00**
Price: Target Model, adj. rear sight Dixie RH0710 .... **$435.00**
Price: Brass frame Traditions, ... **$289.00**
Price: Bison model, brass frame, 12-in. .44-cal. (Cabela's) **$324.00**
Price: New Model Army Target adj. sights blued Dixie **$325.00**
Price: Dixie New Model Army Shooters Prog. Rif. Dixie RH0135 .... **$950.00**
Price: Buffalo, blued, .44-cal., 12-in. (Old South FR185822) **$365.00**
Price: Traditions Redi-Pak, steel frame, accessories .... **$294.00–$319.00**
Price: 1858 Target Carbine 18-in. barrel Dixie PR0338 .... **$525.00**

NEW MODEL REMINGTON POCKET PERCUSSION REVOLVER
Caliber: .31. **Capacity:** 5-round cylinder. **Barrel:** 3.5 in. **Weight:** 1 lb. **Length:** 7.6 in. **Grips:** Walnut, two-piece. **Sights:** Pin front, groove-in-frame rear. **Features:** Spur trigger; iron, brass or nickel-plated frame. Made by Pietta. Imported by Dixie Gun Works, EMF, Taylor's and others.
Price: Brass frame, Dixie PH0407 .... **$260.00**
Price: Steel frame, Dixie PH0370 .... **$295.00**
Price: Nickel-plated, Dixie PH0409 .... **$305.00**

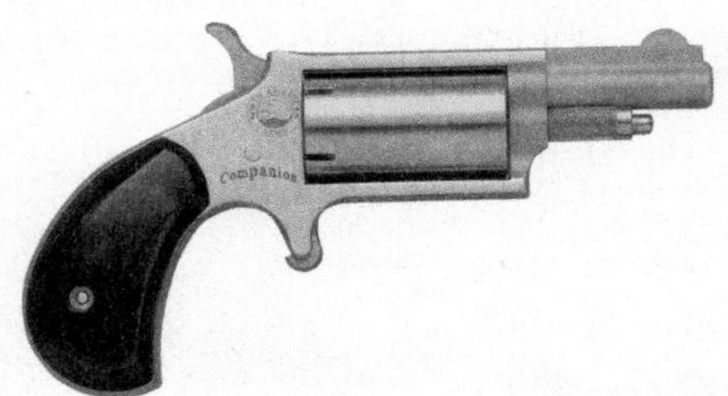

NORTH AMERICAN COMPANION PERCUSSION REVOLVER
Caliber: .22 **Barrel:** 1.125 in. **Weight:** 5.1 oz. **Length:** 4 in. overall. **Grips:** Laminated wood. **Sights:** Blade front, notch rear. **Features:** All stainless steel construction. Uses No. 11 percussion caps. Comes with bullets, powder measure, bullet seater, leather clip holster, gun rag. Long Rifle frame. Introduced 1996. Made in U.S. by North American Arms.
Price: NAA-22LR-CB Long Rifle frame **$251.00**

NORTH AMERICAN EARL PERCUSSION REVOLVER
Caliber: .22 **Barrel:** 4 in. **Weight:** 9.4 oz. **Length:** 7.75 in. **Sights:** Post front, notch rear. **Features:** All stainless steel construction. No. 11 percussion caps. Nonfunctional loading lever. Comes with bullets, powder measure, bullet seater, leather clip holster, gun rag. Introduced 1996. Magnum frame. Introduced 2012. Made in U.S. by North American Arms.
Price: NAA-1860-4-CB Magnum frame **$316.00**

NORTH AMERICAN SUPER COMPANION PERCUSSION REVOLVER
Caliber: .22 **Barrel:** 1.625 in. **Weight:** 7.2 oz. **Length:** 5.125 in. **Grips:** Laminated wood. **Sights:** Blade front, notched rear. **Features:** All stainless steel construction. No. 11 percussion caps. Comes with bullets, powder measure, bullet seater, leather clip holster, gun rag. Introduced 1996. Larger "Magnum" frame. Made in U.S. by North American Arms.
Price: NAA-Mag-CB Magnum frame **$306.00**

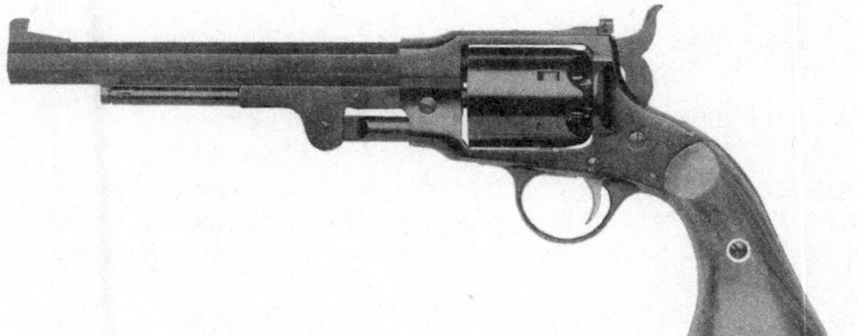

ROGERS & SPENCER PERCUSSION REVOLVER
Caliber: .44 **Barrel:** 7.5 in. **Weight:** 47 oz. **Length:** 13.75 in. overall. **Stocks:** Walnut. **Sights:** Cone front, integral groove-in-frame for rear. **Features:** Accurate reproduction of a Civil War design. Solid frame, extra-large nipple cut-out on rear of cylinder; loading lever and cylinder easily removed for cleaning. From Dixie Gun Works and others.
Price: **$500.00**

SPILLER & BURR PERCUSSION REVOLVER
Caliber: .36 **Barrel:** 7-in., octagon. **Weight:** 2.5 lbs. **Length:** 12.5 in. overall. **Grips:** Two-piece walnut. **Sights:** Fixed. **Features:** Reproduction of the C.S.A. revolver. Brass frame and trigger guard. Also available as a kit. Made by Pietta. From Dixie Gun Works, Traditions and others.
Price: Dixie RH0120 .... **$275.00**
Price: Dixie kit RH0300 .... **$235.00**

STARR DOUBLE-ACTION 1858 ARMY REVOLVER
Caliber: .44 **Barrel:** 6-in. tapered round. **Weight:** 3 lbs. **Length:** 11.75 in. **Stocks:** Walnut one-piece. **Sights:** Hammer notch rear, dovetailed front. **Features:** Double-action mechanism, round tapered barrel, all blued frame and barrel. Made by Pietta. Imported by Dixie Gun Works and others.
Price: Dixie RH0460 .... **$565.00**

STARR SINGLE-ACTION ARMY REVOLVER
Caliber: .44 **Barrel:** 8-in. tapered round. **Weight:** 3 lbs. **Length:** 13.5 in. Stocks: Walnut one-piece. **Sights:** Hammer notch rear, dovetailed front. **Features:** Single-action mechanism, round tapered barrel, all blued frame and barrel. Made by Pietta. Imported by Cabela's, Dixie Gun Works and others.
Price: Dixie RH0462 .... **$550.00**

TRADITIONS ENGRAVED CIVIL WAR REVOLVERS
Caliber: .44 **Barrels:** 7.5–8 in. **Weights:** 2.65–2.75 lbs. depending on model. **Lengths:** 13.5–13.75 in. overall. **Grips:** Walnut or simulated ivory. **Sights:** Fixed. **Features:** Blued or nickel finishes, brass backstrap and trigger guard; casehardened hammer, trigger and loading lever.
Price: FR186012 Colt 1860 Engraved Brass Frame **$329.00**
Price: FR185821 Remington 1858 Engraved Steel Frame.......... **$399.00**
Price: FR185117 Colt 1851 Engraved Steel Frame, Sim Ivory **$399.00**

TRADITIONS JOSEY WALES NAVY
Caliber: .36 **Barrel:** 7.5 in. **Weight:** 2.75 lbs. **Length:** 13.75 in. overall. **Grips:** Walnut **Sights:** Fixed. **Features:** Antique finish on steel, brass backstrap and trigger guard; casehardened hammer, trigger and loading lever.
Price: FR186126 Antiqued steel frame.......... **$519.00**

TRADITIONS 1858 REMINGTON BLUED AND BRASS-FRAMED PERCUSSION REVOLVER
Caliber: .44 **Barrel:** 8 in., octagon. **Weight:** 2.7 lbs. **Length:** 14.5 in. overall. **Grips:** Black laminate **Sights:** Fixed. **Features:** Highly polished Remington-style brass frame, backstrap and trigger guard; casehardened hammer, trigger and loading lever.
Price: FR18582 Blued steel frame **$359.00**
Price: FR18581 Brass frame.......... **$289.00**

TRADITIONS 1858 REMINGTON BISON PERCUSSION REVOLVER
Caliber: .44 **Barrel:** 12 in., octagon. **Weight:** 2.7 lbs. **Length:** 17 in. overall. **Grips:** One-piece hardwood. **Sights:** Adjustable sights **Features:** Highly polished Remington-style brass frame, backstrap and trigger guard; blued barrel and cylinder; casehardened hammer, trigger and loading lever. Made by Pietta.
Price: FR185812 .... **$324.00**

TRADITIONS 1858 REMINGTON NICKEL PERCUSSION REVOLVER
Caliber: .44 **Barrel:** 8 in., octagon. **Weight:** 2.7 lbs. **Length:** 14.5 in. overall. **Grips:** Black laminate **Sights:** Fixed. **Features:** Highly polished Remington-style brass frame, backstrap and trigger guard; nickel-plated barrel and cylinder; casehardened hammer, trigger and loading lever.
Price: FR185836 .... **$439.00**

TRADITIONS SPILLER & BURR PERCUSSION REVOLVER
Caliber: .36 **Barrel:** 6.5 in. blued. **Weight:** 2.75 lbs. **Length:** 12.5 in. overall. **Grips:** Walnut **Sights:** Fixed. **Features:** Polished brass frame, backstrap and trigger guard; hardened hammer, trigger and loading lever. One of the more authentic replicas of a Confederate revolver.
Price: FR18625 .... **$324.00**

Prices given are believed to be accurate at time of publication however, many factors affect retail pricing so exact prices are not possible.

BROWN BESS MUSKET, SECOND MODEL
Caliber: .75. **Barrel:** 42 in., round, smoothbore. **Weight:** 9 lbs. **Length:** 57.75 in. **Stock:** European walnut, full stock. **Sights:** Steel stud on front serves as bayonet lug. **Features:** Flintlock using 1-inch flint with optional brass flash guard (SCO203), steel parts all polished armory bright, brass furniture. Lock marked Grice, 1762 with crown and GR. Made by Pedersoli. Imported by Cabela's, Dixie Gun Works, others.
Price: Dixie Complete gun FR0810 .... **$1,350.00**
Price: Dixie Kit Gun FR0825 .... **$1,050.00**
Price: Cabela's Complete Gun **$1,100.00**
Price: Dixie Trade Gun, 30.5-in. barrel, browned FR0665 .... **$1,495.00**
Price: Dixie Trade Gun Kit FR0600 .... **$950.00**
Price: Dixie Trade Musket, 30.5-in. barrel, browned FR0665 .... **$1,495.00**
Price: Dixie Trade Musket Kit FR3370 .... **$995.00**

CABELA'S BLUE RIDGE RIFLE
Calibers: .32, .36, .45, .50, .54. **Barrel:** 39 in., octagon. **Weight:** 7.75 lbs. **Length:** 55 in. overall. **Stock:** American black walnut. **Sights:** Blade front, rear drift adjustable for windage. **Features:** Color casehardened lockplate and cock/hammer, brass trigger guard and buttplate; double set, double-phased triggers. From Cabela's.
Price: Percussion **$600.00**
Price: Flintlock **$650.00**

CABELA'S KODIAK EXPRESS DOUBLE RIFLE
Calibers: .50, .54, .58, .72. **Barrel:** 1:48 in. twist. **Weight:** 9.3 lbs. **Length:** 45.25 in. overall. **Stock:** European walnut, oil finish. **Sights:** Fully adjustable double folding-leaf rear, ramp front. **Features:** Percussion. Barrels regulated to point of aim at 75 yards; polished and engraved lock, top tang and trigger guard. From Cabela's.
Price: .54-cal **$1,299.99**

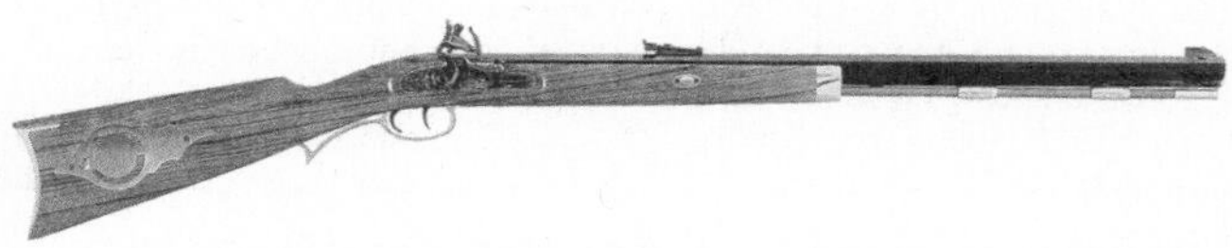

CABELA'S TRADITIONAL HAWKEN
Calibers: .50, 54. **Barrel:** 29 in. **Weight:** 9 lbs. **Stock:** Walnut. **Sights:** Blade front, open adjustable rear. **Features:** Flintlock or percussion. Adjustable double-set triggers. Polished brass furniture, color casehardened lock. Imported by Cabela's.
Price: Percussion, right hand or left hand **$600.00**
Price: Flintlock, right hand **$650.00**

CVA ACCURA V2 LR
Caliber: .50 **Barrels:** 27 in. or 30 in. **Weight:** 7.3 lbs. **Lengths:** 42 in. or 45 in. **Stock:** Synthetic. **Features:** Ambidextrous stock, quick release breech plug, crush-zone recoil pad, reversible hammer spur quake claw sling, lifetime warranty. Also available with exposed ignition as a Northwest model.
Price: PR3124NM (.50-cal, Nitride stainless/Realtree Max-1 thumbhole, scope mount) **$573.00**
Price: PR3122SNM (.50-cal., stainless/Realtree APG thumbhole) ... **$563.00**
Price: PR3116SM (.50-cal., stainless/Realtree HD .... thumbhole, scope mount) **$525.00**
Price: PR3125N (.50-cal., Nitride, stainless/Realtree HD, fib. opt. sight) **$538.00**
Price: PR3125NM (.50-cal., Nitride,stainless/black/Realtree HD, scope mount) **$544.00**
Price: PR3112SM (.50-cal., stainless/Realtree APG, scope mount) **$487.00**
Price: PR3112S (.50-cal, stainless/Realtree APG. fib. opt. sights) **$482.00**
Price: PR3110S (.50-cal, stainless/black, fib. opt. sights) **$421.00**

CVA ACCURA MOUNTAIN RIFLE
Caliber: .50. **Barrel:** 25 in. **Weight:** 6.35 lbs. **Length:** 40 in. **Stock:** Synthetic. **Features:** Ambidextrous stock, quick release breech plug, crush-zone recoil pad, reversible hammer spur quake claw sling, lifetime warranty.
Price: PR3121SNM (.50-cal, Nitride stainless/Realtree .... Max-1, scope mount) **$546.00**
Price: PR3120SM (.50-cal., stainless/black) **$494.00**

CVA ACCURA PLAINS RIFLE
Caliber: .50. **Barrel:** 28 in. **Weight:** 6.35 lbs. **Length:** 43-in. **Stock:** Synthetic. **Features:** Ambidextrous stock, quick release breech plug, crush-zone recoil pad, reversible hammer spur quake claw sling, lifetime warranty.
Price: PR3131NM (.50-cal, Nitride stainless/Realtree Max-1, scope mount) **$551.00**
Price: PR3120NM (.50-cal., stainless/black) **$494.00**

CVA APEX
Caliber: .45, .50. **Barrel:** 27 in., 1:28 in. twist. **Weight:** 8 lbs. **Length:** 42 in. **Stock:** Synthetic. **Features:** Interchangeable centerfire barrels, ambidextrous with rubber grip panels in black or Realtree APG camo, crush-zone recoil pad, reversible hammer spur, quake claw sling, lifetime warranty. Discontinued.
Price: CR4013s (.45-cal., stainless/Realtree APG) **$738.00**
Price: CR4012S (.50-cal., stainless/Realtree APG) **$695.00**
Price: CR4011S (.45-cal., stainless/black) **$615.00**
Price: CR4010S (.50-cal., stainless/black) **$615.00**

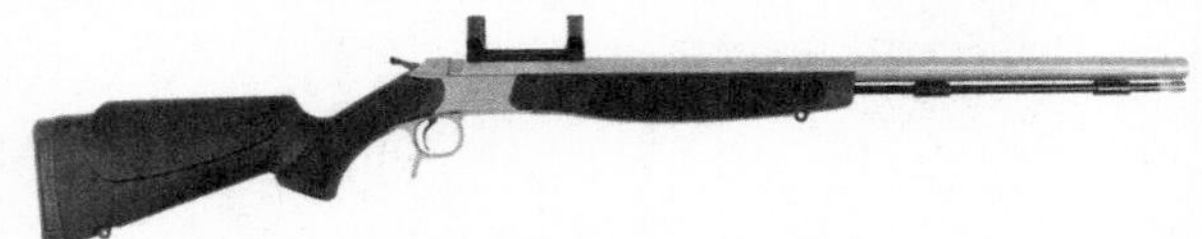

CVA OPTIMA V2 STAINLESS BREAK-ACTION RIFLE
Caliber: .50. **Barrel:** 28 in. fluted. **Weight:** 8.8 lbs. **Stock:** Ambidextrous solid composite in standard or thumbhole. **Sights:** Adj. fiber-optic. **Features:** Break-action, quick release breech plug, aluminum loading rod, cocking spur, lifetime warranty. Also available with exposed ignition as a Northwest Model.
Price: PR2029NM (.50-cal., Nitride stainless/Realtree Xtra, thumbhole, scope mount) **$420.00**
Price: PR2023N (.50-cal., Nitride stainless/Realtree Xtra, fib. opt. sight) **$383.00**
Price: PR2023NM (.50-cal., Nitride stainless/Realtree Xtra, thumbhole, scope mount) **$389.00**
Price: PR2028SM (.50-cal, stainless/ Realtree Xtra, scope mount) **$375.00**
Price: PR2022SM (.50-cal, stainless/Realtree Xtra, scope mount sight) **$351.00**
Price: PR2022S (.50-cal., stainless/Realtree Xtra, fib opt) **$368.00**
Price: PR2020SM (.50-cal., stainless/black, scope mount) **$309.00**
Price: PR2020S (.50-cal., stainless/black, fib. opt. sight) **$303.00**

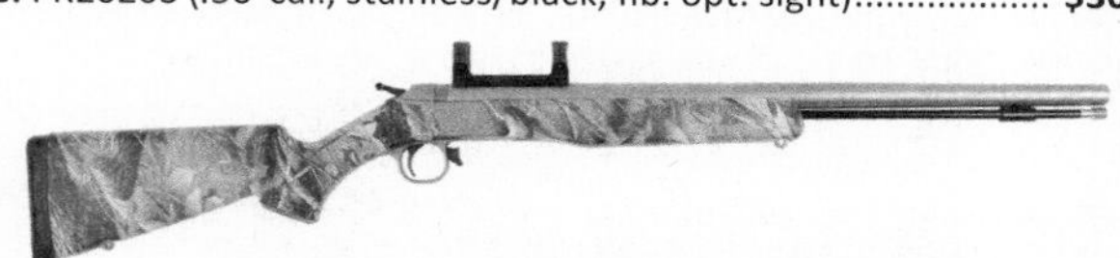

CVA WOLF 209 MAGNUM BREAK-ACTION RIFLE
Caliber: .50 **Barrel:** 24 in. **Weight:** 6.23 lbs. **Stock:** Ambidextrous composite. **Sights:** Dead-On Scope Mounts or Fiber Optic. **Features:** Break-Action, quick detachable breech plug for 209 primer, aluminum loading rod, cocking spur, lifetime warranty. Also available with exposed ignition as a Northwest model.
Price: PR2115SM (.50-cal, stainless/Realtree Hardwoods HD, scope mount) **$290.00**
Price: PR2110SM (.50-cal, stainless/black, scope mount) **$241.00**
Price: PR2110S (.50-cal, stainless/black, fib. opt. sight) **$253.00**
Price: PR2113S Northwest (.50-cal, stainless/Realtree Hardwoods HD, fib. opt sight) **$237.00**
Price: PR2110M (.50-cal, blued/black, scope mount) **$203.00**
Price: PR2110 (.50-cal, blued/black, fib. opt. sight) **$203.00**

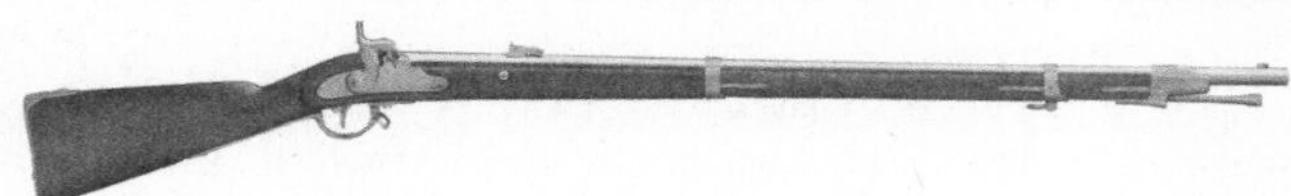

DIXIE AUSTRIAN LORENZ
Caliber: .54. **Barrel:** 28 in., rifled four lands .538 **Weight:** 9.75 lbs. **Length:** 39 in. overall. **Stock:** European walnut w/oil finish. **Sights:** Open adjustable for elevation to 1,000 yards. **Features:** Armory bright finish. Made by Arms-Moravia, Czech Republic. Imported by Dixie Gun Works.
Price: FR0171 .... **$650.00**

Prices given are believed to be accurate at time of publication however, many factors affect retail pricing so exact prices are not possible.

DIXIE 1803 HARPERS FERRY FLINTLOCK RIFLE
Caliber: .54. **Barrel:** 35.5 in., smoothbore. **Weight:** 9.5 lbs. **Length:** 29.5 in. overall. **Stock:** Halfstock, walnut w/oil finish. **Sights:** Blade front, notched rear. **Features:** Color casehardened lock, browned barrel, with barrel key. Made by Euro Arms. Imported by Dixie Gun Works. Discontinued. Some still in dealer stocks.
Price: FR0171 .... **$795.00**

DIXIE 1816 FLINTLOCK MUSKET
Caliber: .69. **Barrel:** 42 in., smoothbore. **Weight:** 9.75 lbs. **Length:** 56.975 in. overall. **Stock:** Walnut w/oil finish. **Sights:** Blade front. **Features:** All metal finished in "National Armory Bright," three barrel bands w/springs, steel ramrod w/button-shaped head. Made by Pedersoli. Imported by Dixie Gun Works.
Price: FR0305, Flintlock **$1,495.00**
Price: PR0257, Percussion conversion **$1,425.00**

DIXIE DELUXE CUB RIFLE
Caliber: .32, .36, .45. **Barrel:** 28 in. octagonal. **Weight:** 6.5 lbs. **Length:** 44 in. overall. **Stock:** Walnut. **Sights:** Fixed. **Features:** Each gun available in either flint or percussion ignition. Short rifle for small game and beginning shooters. Brass patchbox and furniture. Kit guns available in .32 or .36 calibers in percussion ($690) or flint ($710). From Dixie Gun Works.
Price: Deluxe Cub (.32-cal. flint) PR3130 .... **$890.00**
Price: Deluxe Cub (.36-cal. flint) FR3135 .... **$890.00**
Price: Deluxe Cub kit (.32-cal. percussion) PK3360 .... **$690.00**
Price: Deluxe Cub kit (.36-cal. percussion) PK3365 .... **$690.00**
Price: Deluxe Cub kit (.32-cal. flint) FK3350 .... **$710.00**
Price: Deluxe Cub kit (.36-cal. flint) FK3355 .... **$710.00**
Price: Deluxe Cub (.32-cal. percussion) PR3140 .... **$850.00**
Price: Deluxe Cub (.36-cal. percussion) PR3145 .... **$850.00**

DIXIE EARLY AMERICAN JAEGER RIFLE
Caliber: .54. **Barrel:** 27.5 in. octagon, 1:24 in. twist. **Weight:** 8.25 lbs. **Length:** 43.5 in. overall. **Stock:** American walnut; sliding wooden patchbox on butt. **Sights:** Notch rear, blade front. **Features:** Flintlock or percussion. Conversion kits available, and recommended converting percussion guns to flintlocks using kit LO1102 at $209.00. Browned steel furniture. Made by Pedersoli. Imported by Dixie Gun Works.
Price: Percussion, PR0835 .... **$1,295.00**
Price: Flint, PR0835 .... **$1,375.00**
Price: Percussion, kit gun, PK0146 .... **$1,075.00**
Price: Flint, kit gun, PKO143 .... **$1,075.00**

DIXIE HAWKEN RIFLE
Calibers: .50 and .54. **Barrel:** 29.5 in. octagonal, 1:48 in. twist. **Weight:** 9 or 8.5 lbs. **Length:** 45.5 in. overall. **Stock:** European walnut, half-stock. **Sights:** Rear click adjustable for windage and elevation, blade front. **Features:** Percussion and flintlock, brass patchbox, double-set triggers, one barrel key. Flint gun available for left-handed shooters. Both flint and percussion guns available as kit guns. Made by Pedersoli. Imported by Dixie Gun Works.
Price: Percussion, .50 PR0502 .... **$495.00**
Price: Percussion, .54 PR0507 .... **$495.00**
Price: Flint, .50 FR1332 .... **$525.00**
Price: Flint, .50 left hand, FR1336 .... **$525.00**
Price: Percussion, .50 kit PK0516 .... **$425.00**
Price: Percussion, .54 kit PK0519 .... **$425.00**
Price: Flint, .50 kit FK1340 .... **$475.00**
Price: Flint, .50 left hand, kit, Fk1345 .... **$475.00**

DIXIE JAPANESE TANEGASHIMA MATCHLOCK
Caliber: .50. **Barrel:** 53 in. **Weight:** 8.75 lbs. **Length:** 53 in. overall. **Stock:** Japanese cherry with drilled hole on bottom for wooden ramrod. **Sights:** Post front, block rear. **Features:** A replica of the snapping matchlock guns used in Japan from the 17th to 19th centuries. Brass lock with ball trigger, and brass lockplate and hammer. Pan has pivoting cover. Browned barrel. Casehardened lock. Made by Miroku. Discontinued. Imported by Dixie Gun Works. The same or a very similar gun is being produced by Davide Pedersoli.
Price: Dixie MM0005 .... **$1,100.00**

DIXIE J.P. MURRAY ARTILLERY CARBINE
Caliber: .58. **Barrel:** 23.5 in. **Weight:** 8 lbs. **Length:** 39.5 in. **Stock:** European walnut. **Sights:** Blade front, fixed notch rear. **Features:** Percussion musket-cap ignition. Reproduction of the original Confederate carbine. Lock marked "J.P. Murray, Columbus, Georgia." Blued barrel. Made Euro Arms. Imported by Dixie Gun Works and others.
Price: Dixie, PRO173 .... **$1,100.00**

DIXIE PEDERSOLI 1857 MAUSER RIFLE
Caliber: .54. **Barrel:** 39.375 in. **Weight:** 9.5 lbs. **Length:** 52 in. overall. **Stock:** European walnut. **Sights:** Blade front, rear steel adjustable for windage and elevation. **Features:** Percussion musket-cap ignition. Color casehardened lockplate marked "Konigi.Wurt Fabrik." Armory bright steel barrel. Made by Pedersoli. Imported by Dixie Gun Works.
Price: Dixie PR1330 .... **$1,650.00**

DIXIE PENNSYLVANIA RIFLE & KIT
Calibers: .45 and .50. **Barrels:** 41.5 in. octagonal, .45/1:48, .50/1:56 in. twist. **Weights:** 8.5, 8.75 lbs. **Length:** 56 in. overall. **Stock:** European walnut, full-length stock. **Sights:** Notch rear, blade front. **Features:** Flintlock or percussion, brass patchbox, double-set triggers. Also available as kit guns for both calibers and ignition systems. Made by Pedersoli. Imported by Dixie Gun Works.
Price: Percussion, .45, PF1070 .... **$995.00**
Price: Flint, .45, FR1060 .... **$999.95**
Price: Percussion, .50, PR3205 .... **$999.95**
Price: Flint, .50, FR3200 .... **$999.95**
Price: Percussion, .45, PR1075 .... **$910.00**
Price: Flint, .45, FR1065 .... **$910.00**
Price: Percussion, .50, PK3425 .... **$910.00**
Price: Flint, .50, FK3420 .... **$910.00**

DIXIE POTSDAM 1809 PRUSSIAN MUSKET
Caliber: .75 **Barrel:** 41.2 in. round, smoothbore. **Weight:** 9 lbs. **Length:** 56 in. **Stock:** European walnut, fullstock. **Sights:** Brass lung on upper barrel band. **Features:** Flintlock using 1-inch flint. Steel parts all polished armory bright, brass furniture. Lock marked "Potsdam over G.S." Made by Pedersoli. Imported by Dixie Gun Works.
Price: Dixie FR3175 .... **$1,495.00**

DIXIE SHARPS NEW MODEL 1859 MILITARY CARBINE
Caliber: .54. **Barrel:** 22 in., 6-groove, 1:48 in. twist. **Weight:** 8 lbs. **Length:** 39.25 in. overall. **Stock:** Oiled walnut. **Sights:** Blade front, ladder-style rear. **Features:** Blued barrel, color casehardened barrel bands, receiver, hammer, nose cap, lever, patchbox cover and buttplate. Introduced 1995. Made by Pedersoli.
Price: Carbine (22-in. barrel, 39-1/4 in. long, 8 lbs.) PR0982 .... **$1,400.00**

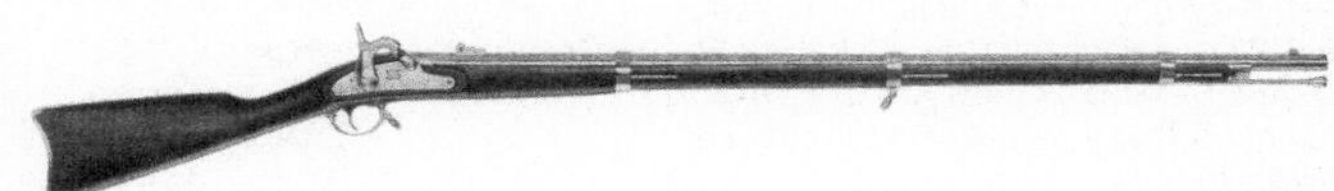

DIXIE SHARPS NEW MODEL 1859 MILITARY RIFLE
Caliber: .54. **Barrel:** 30 in., 7-groove, 1:48 in. twist. **Weight:** 9.25 lbs. **Length:** 39.25 in. overall. **Stock:** Oiled walnut. **Sights:** Blade front, ladder-style rear. **Features:** Percussion ignition, Blued barrel, color casehardened barrel bands, receiver, hammer, nose cap, lever, patchbox cover and buttplate. Made by Pedersoli.
Price: Dixie PR0862 .... **$1,550.00**

DIXIE SHARPS NEW MODEL 1863 SPORTING RIFLE
Caliber: .45. **Barrel:** 32 in., 6-groove, 1:48 in. twist. **Weight:** 10.75 lbs. **Length:** 39.25 in. overall. **Stock:** Oiled, checkered walnut. **Sights:** Blade front, ladder-style rear. **Features:** Percussion ignition, Blued barrel, color casehardened barrel bands, receiver, hammer, nose cap, lever, and buttplate. Made by Pedersoli.
Price: Dixie PR5001 .... **$1,400.00**

DIXIE SMITH CARBINE
Caliber: .50. **Barrel:** 21.5 in., 3-groove, 1:66 in. twist. **Weight:** 7.75 lbs. **Length:** 39 in. **Stock:** Oiled walnut. **Sights:** Blade front, ladder-style rear. **Features:** Hinged breech that drops barrel to allow loading of pre-loaded brass or plastic cartridges fired by a musket cap. Blued barrel, color casehardened receiver and hammer. Cavalry Carbine has saddle bar and ring, Artillery Carbine has sling swivel on buttstock and barrel band. Rifle made by Pietta. Imported from Italy by Dixie Gun Works.
Price: Dixie Cavalry Carbine PR0220 .... **$1,050.00**
Price: Dixie Artillery Carbine PR0223 .... **$1,050.00**

DIXIE TRYON RIFLE

Caliber: .50. **Barrel:** 32 in. octagonal, 1:48 in. twist. **Weight:** 9.5 lbs. **Length:** 49 in. overall. **Stock:** European walnut, half-stock. **Sights:** Elevation-adjustable rear with stair-step notches, blade front. **Features:** Percussion, brass patchbox, double-set triggers, two barrel keys. Made by Pedersoli. Imported by Dixie Gun Works.

Price: Percussion, PR0860 .... **$1,075.00**
Price: Percussion, kit, PR0255 .... **$890.00**
Price: Creedmore with adjustable sights PR0180 .... **$1,395.00**

DIXIE MODEL 1863 ZOUAVE RIFLE

Caliber: .58. **Barrel:** 33 in. **Weight:** 9.5 lbs. **Length:** 49 in. **Stock:** European walnut. **Sights:** Blade front, three-leaf military rear. **Features:** Percussion musket-cap ignition. Casehardened lock and blued barrel. One-piece solid barrel and bolster. Made in Italy by Armi Sport. Imported by Dixie Gun Works, others.

Price: PF0340 .... **$975.00**

ENFIELD MUSKETOON P1861

Caliber: .58. **Barrel:** 33 in. **Weight:** 9 lbs. **Length:** 35 in. overall. **Stock:** European walnut. **Sights:** Blade front, flip-up rear with elevator marked to 700 yards. **Features:** Reproduction of the original cavalry version of the Enfield rifle. Percussion musket-cap ignition. Blued barrel with steel barrel bands, brass furniture. Casehardened lock. Euro Arms version marked London Armory with crown. Pedersoli version has Birmingham stamp on stock and Enfield and Crown on lockplate. Made by Euro Arms, Pedersoli. Imported by Cabela's, Dixie Gun Works and others.

Price: Dixie Euro Arms PR0343 .... **$1,050.00**

ENFIELD THREE-BAND P1853 RIFLE

Caliber: .58. **Barrel:** 39 in. **Weight:** 10.25 lbs. **Length:** 52 in. overall. **Stock:** European walnut. **Sights:** Blade front, flip-up rear with elevator marked to 800 yards. **Features:** Reproduction of the original three-band rifle. Percussion musket-cap ignition. Blued barrel with steel barrel bands, brass furniture. Casehardened lock. Lockplate marked "London Armory Co. and Crown." Made by Euro Arms, Armi Sport (Chiappa), Pedersoli. Imported by Cabela's, Dixie Gun Works and others.

Price: Cabela's, Pedersoli **$949.99**
Price: Dixie Armi Sport/Chiappa PR1130 .... **$895.00**
Price: Dixie Smoothbore PR1052 .... **$750.00**

ENFIELD TWO-BAND P1858 RIFLE

Caliber: .58. **Barrel:** 33 in. **Weight:** 7.75 lbs. **Length:** 43.25 in. overall. **Stock:** European walnut. **Sights:** Blade front, flip-up rear with elevator marked to 1,000 yards. **Features:** Reproduction of the original two-band rifle. Percussion musket-cap ignition. Blued barrel with steel barrel bands, brass furniture. Casehardened lock. Lockplate marked "1858 Enfield and Crown." Made by Euro Arms, Pedersoli, Chiappa. Imported by Cabela's, Dixie Gun Works and others.

Price: Cabela's, Pedersoli PR1135 .... **$930.00**
Price: Dixie/Pedersoli PR3460 .... **$995.00**
Price: Dixie Chiappa 150th Aniv. Mod. PR0106 .... **$750.00**

KNIGHT BIGHORN

Caliber: .50. **Barrel:** 26 in., 1:28 in. twist. **Weight:** 7 lbs. 3 oz. **Length:** 44.5 in. overall. **Stock:** G2 straight or thumbhole, Carbon Knight straight or thumbhole or black composite thumbhole with recoil pad, sling swivel studs. Ramrod: Carbon core with solid brass extendable jag. **Sights:** Fully adjustable metallic fiber optic. **Features:** Uses four different ignition systems (included): #11 nipple, musket nipple, bare 208 shotgun primer and 209 Extreme shotgun primer system (Extreme weatherproof full plastic jacket system); vented breech plug, striker fired with one-piece removable hammer assembly. With recommended loads, guaranteed to have 4-inch, three-shot groups at 200 yards. Also available as Western gun with exposed ignition. Made in U.S. by Knight Rifles.

Price: Standard stock **$664.00**
Price: With maximum available options, scope **$1,324.00**

KNIGHT DISC EXTREME

Caliber: .50, .52. **Barrel:** 26 in., fluted stainless, 1:28 in. twist. **Weight:** 7 lbs. 14 oz.–8 lbs. **Length:** 45 in. overall. **Stock:** Carbon Knight straight or thumbhole with blued or SS; G2 thumbhole; left-handed Nutmeg thumbhole. Ramrod: Solid brass extendable jag. **Sights:** Fully adjustable metallic fiber optics. **Features:** Bolt-action rifle, full plastic jacket ignition system, #11 nipple, musket nipple, bare 208 shotgun primer. With recommended loads, guaranteed to have 4-inch, three-shot groups at 200 yards. Also available as Western gun with exposed ignition. Made in U.S. by Knight Rifles.

Price: Standard **$722.00**
Price: With maximum available options, scope **$1,485.00**

KNIGHT LITTLEHORN

Caliber: .50. **Barrel:** 22 in., 1:28 in. twist. **Weight:** 6.7 lbs. **Length:** 39 in. overall. **Stock:** 12.5 in. length of pull, G2 straight or pink Realtree AP HD. Ramrod: Carbon core with solid brass extendable jag. **Sights:** Fully adjustable Williams fiber optic. **Features:** Uses four different ignition systems (included): Full Plastic Jacket, #11 nipple, musket nipple or bare 209 shotgun primer; vented breech plug, striker-fired with one-piece removable hammer assembly. Finish: Stainless steel. With recommended loads, guaranteed to have 4-inch, three-shot groups at 200 yards. Also available as Western gun with exposed ignition. Made in U.S. by Knight Rifles.

Price: Standard **$400.00**
Price: With maximum available options, scope **$1,060.00**

KNIGHT MOUNTAINEER FOREST GREEN

Calibers: .45, .50, .52. **Barrel:** 27 in. fluted stainless steel, free-floated. **Weights:** 8 lbs. (thumbhole stock), 8.3 lbs. (straight stock). **Length:** 45.5 inches. **Sights:** Fully adjustable metallic fiber optic. **Features:** Bolt-action rifle, adjustable match-grade trigger, aluminum ramrod with carbon core, solid brass extendable jag, vented breech plug. Ignition: Full plastic jacket, #11 nipple, musket nipple, bare 208 shotgun primer. With recommended loads, guaranteed to have 4-inch, three-shot groups at 200 yards. Also available as Western gun with exposed ignition. Made in U.S. by Knight Rifles.

Price: Standard **$1,017.00**
Price: Maximum available options, scope **$1,681.00**

KNIGHT ULTRA-LITE

Caliber: .50. **Barrel:** 24 in. Ignition: 209 Primer with Full Plastic Jacket, musket cap or #11 nipple, bare 208 shotgun primer; vented breech plug. **Stock:** Black, tan or olive green Kevlar spider web. **Weight:** 6 lbs. **Features:** Bolt-action rifle. Ramrod: Carbon core with solid brass extendable jag. **Sights:** With or without Williams fiber-optic sights, drilled and tapped for scope mounts. Finish: Stainless steel. With recommended loads, guaranteed to have 4-inch, three-shot groups at 200 yards. Also available as Western version with exposed ignition. Made in U.S. by Knight Rifles.

Price: Standard **$1,117.00**
Price: Maximum available options, scope **$1,752.00**

LYMAN DEERSTALKER RIFLE

Calibers: .50, .54. **Barrel:** 24 in., octagonal, 1:48 in. rifling. **Weight:** 10.4 lbs. **Stock:** Walnut with black rubber buttpad. **Sights:** Lyman #37MA beaded front, fully adjustable fold-down Lyman #16A rear. **Features:** Percussion and flintlock ignition. Stock has less drop for quick sighting. All metal parts are blackened, with color casehardened lock, single trigger. Comes with sling and swivels. Available in flint or percussion. Made by Investarms, Italy, Introduced 1990. From Lyman.

Price: Dixie .50-cal. percussion PR0670 .... **$475.00**

Prices given are believed to be accurate at time of publication however, many factors affect retail pricing so exact prices are not possible.

Price: Dixie .54-cal. percussion PR0673 .... **$475.00**
Price: Lyman 6033185 .50-cal. percussion stainless **$590.00**
Price: Lyman 6033146 .50-cal. flintlock blue **$640.00**
Price: Lyman 6033147 .54-cal. flintlock blue **$640.00**
Price: Lyman 6033148 .50-cal. flintlock left hand **$640.00**

LYMAN GREAT PLAINS RIFLE
Calibers: .50, .54. **Barrel:** 32 in., 1:60 in. twist. **Weight:** 11.6 lbs. **Stock:** Walnut. **Sights:** Steel blade front, buckhorn rear adjustable for windage and elevation, and fixed notch primitive sight included. **Features:** Percussion or flint ignition. Blued steel furniture. Stainless steel nipple. Coil spring lock, Hawken-style trigger guard and double-set triggers. Round thimbles recessed and sweated into rib. Steel wedge plates and toe plate. Introduced 1979. From Lyman.
Price: Dixie: .50-cal./.54-cal percussion PR0102 .... **$640.00**
Price: Dixie: .50-cal./.54-cal flintlock FR0106 .... **$685.00**
Price: Dixie .50-ca./.54-cal left-hand percussion PR0122 .... **$670.00**
Price: Dixie 50/.54-cal. percussion kit PK0682 .... **$520.00**
Price: Lyman 6031114/5 .50/.54-cal. flintlock kit **$715.00**

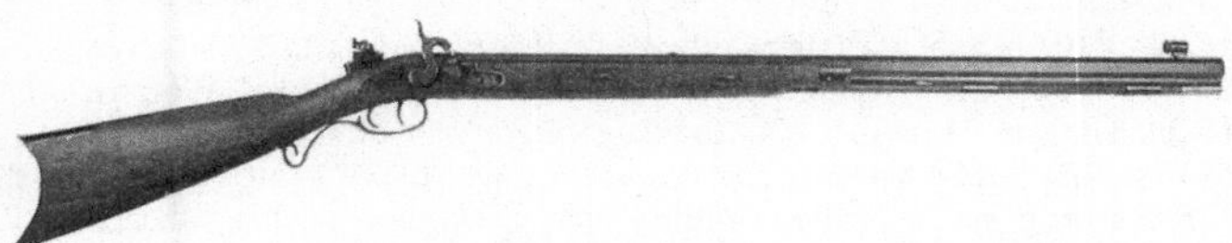

LYMAN GREAT PLAINS HUNTER MODEL
Similar to Great Plains model except 1:32 in. twist, shallow-groove barrel and comes drilled and tapped for Lyman 57GPR peep sight.
Price: Dixie .50-cal./.54-cal percussion PR0688 .... **$635.00**
Price: Dixie: .50-cal/.54-cal flintlock PR0690 .... **$635.00**
Price: Lyman 6031142 .50-cal left-hand percussion **$800.00**

LYMAN MUSTANG BREAKAWAY 209
Caliber: .50. **Barrel:** 26 in., 1:28 twist. Ignition: 209 primer. **Weight:** 7 lbs. **Stock:** Ultra-Grade wood finish, checkered, rubber recoil pad. Ramrod: Solid aluminum. **Sights:** Fiber-optic front and rear. **Features:** Hammerless break-open action for 209 shotshell primer and up to 150-grain charges. Imported by Lyman.
Price: Dixie: PR0306 .... **$464.00**

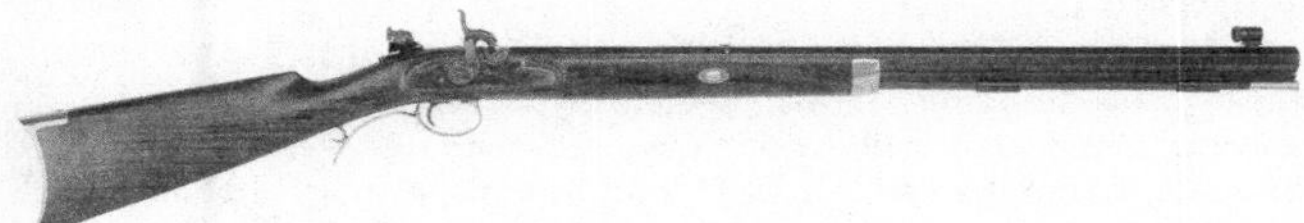

LYMAN TRADE RIFLE
Calibers: .50, .54. **Barrel:** 28 in. octagon, 1:48 in. twist. **Weight:** 10.8 lbs. **Length:** 45 in. overall. **Stock:** European walnut. **Sights:** Blade front, open rear adjustable for windage, or optional fixed sights. **Features:** Fast-twist rifling for conical bullets. Polished brass furniture with blue steel parts, stainless steel nipple. Hook breech, single trigger, coil spring percussion lock. Steel barrel rib and ramrod ferrules. Introduced 1980. From Lyman.
Price: Dixie: .50-cal./.54-cal. percussion PR0652 .... **$470.00**
Price: Dixie .50-cal./.54-cal. flintlock FR0703 .... **$515.00**

NAVY ARMS PARKER-HALE VOLUNTEER RIFLE
Caliber: .451. **Barrel:** 32 in., round interior bore 1:20 in. twist. **Weight:** 9.5 lbs. **Length:** 49 in. **Stock:** Oiled Grade 1 American walnut. **Sights:** Blade front, ladder-style rear. **Features:** Checkered stock wrist and fore end. Blued barrel, steel ramrod, bone charcoal casehardened receiver and hammer. Designed for .451 conical bullet. Compare to hexagonal-bored Whitworth Rifle below. Hand fitted and finished in U.S. with Parker Hale stock cartouche.
Price: Dixie PR1375 .... **$1,395.00**

NAVY ARMS PARKER-HALE WHITWORTH RIFLE
Caliber: .451. **Barrel:** 36 in., hexagonal interior bore 1:20 in. twist. **Weight:** 9.6 lbs. **Length:** 52.5 in. **Stock:** Oiled Grade 1 American walnut. **Sights:** Blade front, ladder-style rear. **Features:** Checkered stock wrist and fore end. . Blued barrel, steel ramrod, bone charcoal casehardened receiver and hammer. Designed for .451 conical hexagonal bullet. Compare to round-bored Volunteer Rifle above. Hand finished in the U.S. with Parker Hale stock cartouche.
Price: **$1,500.00**

NAVY ARMS SMITH CARBINE (DISCONTINUED)
Caliber: .50. **Barrel:** 21.5 in., 3-groove, 1:66 in. twist. **Weight:** 7.75 lbs. **Length:** 39 in. **Stock:** Oiled Grade 1 American walnut. **Sights:** Blade front, ladder-style rear. **Features:** Hinged breech that drops barrel to allow loading of pre-loaded brass or plastic cartridges fired by a musket cap. Blued U.S.-made barrel, bone charcoal casehardened receiver and hammer. Cavalry Carbine has saddle bar and ring, Artillery Carbine has sling swivel on buttstock and barrel band. Hand fitted and finished.
Price: Cavalry Carbine **$1,499.95**
Price: Artillery Model **$1,499.95**

PEDERSOLI 1766 CHARLEVILLE MUSKET
Caliber: .69. **Barrel:** 44.75 in. round, smoothbore. **Weight:** 10.5 lbs. **Length:** 60 in. **Stock:** European walnut, full-stock. **Sights:** Steel stud on upper barrel band. **Features:** Flintlock using one-inch flint. Steel parts all polished armory bright, brass furniture. Lock marked Charleville. Made by Pedersoli. Imported by Cabela's, Dixie Gun Works, others.
Price: Dixie Complete gun FR1045 .... **$1,425.00**
Price: Dixie Kit Gun FK3440 .... **$1,140.00**
Price: Dixie French Model 1777 Complete gun FR0930 .... **$1,450.00**
Price: Dixie French Currige An IX Charleville FR0157 .... **$1,450.00**

PEDERSOLI 1795 SPRINGFIELD MUSKET
Caliber: .69. **Barrel:** 44.75 in., round, smoothbore. **Weight:** 10.5 lbs. **Length:** 57.25 in. **Stock:** European walnut, full-stock. **Sights:** Brass stud on upper barrel band. **Features:** Flintlock using one-inch flint. Steel parts all polished armory bright, brass furniture. Lock marked US Springfield. Made by Pedersoli. Imported by Cabela's, Dixie Gun Works, others.
Price: Dixie Complete gun FR3210 .... **$1,495.00**

PEDERSOLI 1841 MISSISSIPPI RIFLE
Caliber: .58. **Barrel:** 33 in. **Weight:** 9.5 lbs. **Length:** 48.75 in. overall. **Stock:** European walnut. **Sights:** Blade front, notched rear. **Features:** Percussion musket-cap ignition. Reproduction of the original one-band rifle with large brass patchbox. Color casehardened lockplate with browned barrel. Made by Pedersoli. Imported by Dixie, Cabela's.
Price Dixie: PR3470 .... **$1,075.00**

PEDERSOLI 1861 SPRINGFIELD RIFLE
Caliber: .58. **Barrel:** 40 inches. **Weight:** 10 lbs. **Length:** 55.5 in. overall. **Stock:** European walnut. **Sights:** Blade front, three-leaf military rear. **Features:** Reproduction of the original three-band rifle. Percussion musket-cap ignition. Lockplate marked 1861 with eagle and U.S. Springfield. Armory bright steel. Made by Armi Sport/Chiappa, Pedersoli. Imported by Cabela's, Dixie Gun Works, others.
Price: Cabela's, Pedersoli **$1,000.00**
Price: Dixie Armi Sport/Chiappa PR3180 .... **$1,150.00**

PEDERSOLI BRISTLEN MORGES AND WAADTLANDER TARGET RIFLES
Calibers: .44, .45. **Barrel:** 29.5 in. tapered octagonal, hooked breech. **Weight:** 15.5 lbs. **Length:** 48.5 in. overall. **Stock:** European walnut, half-stock with hooked buttplate and detachable palm rest. **Sights:** Creedmoor rear on Morges, Swiss Diopter on Waadtlander, hooded front sight notch. **Features:** Percussion back-action lock, double-set, double-phase triggers, one barrel key, muzzle protector. Specialized bullet molds for each gun. Made by Pedersoli. Imported by Dixie Gun Works.
Price: Percussion, .44 Bristlen Morges PR0165 .... **$2,995.00**
Price: Percussion, .45 Waadtlander PR0183 .... **$2,995.00**

PEDERSOLI COOK & BROTHER CONFEDERATE CARBINE /ARTILLERY/RIFLE
Caliber: .58 **Barrels:** 24 in., 33 in., 39 in. **Weights:** 7.5 lbs., 8.4 lbs., 8.6 lbs. **Lengths:** 40.5 in., 48 in., 54.5 in. **Stock:** Select oil-finished walnut. **Features:** Percussion musket-cap ignition. Color casehardened lock, browned barrel. Buttplate, trigger guard, barrel bands, sling swivels and nose cap of polished brass. Lock marked with stars and bars flag on tail and Athens, Georgia. Made by Pedersoli. Imported by Dixie Gun Works, others.
Price: Carbine PR3495 .... **$925.00**
Price: Dixie Artillery Carbine PR0223 .... **$925.00**

PEDERSOLI COUNTRY HUNTER
Caliber: .50. **Barrel:** 26 in. octagonal. **Weight:** 6 lbs. **Length:** 41.75 in. overall. **Stock:** European walnut, half-stock. **Sights:** Rear notch, blade front. **Features:** Percussion, one barrel key. Made by Pedersoli. Imported by Dixie Gun Works.
Price: Percussion, .50 PR3155 .... **$625.00**

PEDERSOLI KENTUCKY RIFLE
Calibers: .32, .45 and .50. **Barrel:** 35.5 in. octagonal. **Weights:** 7.5 (.50 cal.)–7.75 lbs. (.32 cal.) **Length:** 51 in. overall. **Stock:** European walnut, full-length stock. **Sights:** Notch rear, blade front. **Features:** Flintlock or percussion, brass patchbox, double-set triggers. Also available as kit guns for all calibers and ignition systems. Made by Pedersoli. Imported by Dixie Gun Works.
Price: Percussion, .32, PR3115 .... **$695.00**
Price: Flint, .32, FR3100 .... **$750.00**
Price: Percussion, .45, FR3120.......... **$695.00**
Price: Flint, .45, FR3105 .... **$750.00**
Price: Percussion, .50, FR3125 .... **$625.00**
Price: Flint, .50, FR3110 .... **$650.00**

PEDERSOLI KODIAK DOUBLE RIFLES AND COMBINATION GUN
Calibers: .50, .54 and .58 **Barrels:** 28.5 in.; 1:24/1:24/1:48 in. twist. **Weights:** 11.25 lbs., 10.75 lbs., 10 lbs. **Stock:** Straight grip European walnut. **Sights:** Two adjustable rear, steel ramp with brass bead front. **Features:** Percussion ignition, double triggers, sling swivels. A .72-caliber express rifle and .50-caliber/12-gauge shotgun combination gun are also available. Blued steel furniture. Stainless steel nipple. Made by Pedersoli. Imported by Dixie Gun Works and some models by Cabela's and others.
Price: Rifle 50X50 PR0970 .... **$1,495.00**
Price: Rifle 54X54 PR0975 .... **$1,495.00**
Price: Rifle 58X58 PR0980 .... **$1,495.00**
Price: Combo 50X12 gauge PR0990 .... **$1,350.00**
Price: Express Rifle .72 caliber PR0916 .... **$1,525.00**

PEDERSOLI AUSTRIAN 1854 LORENZ TYPE II
Caliber: 13.9mm **Barrel:** 37 in., 1:79 in. twist. **Weight:** 9 lbs. **Length:** 53 in. **Stock:** Walnut. **Sights:** Bright steel rear elevation adjustments. **Features:** Percussion ignition. Bright steel furniture. Single trigger. Made by Pedersoli. Newly introduced to be first available through Dixie Gun Works.
Price: Type II.......... **$1,965.00**

PEDERSOLI MORTIMER RIFLE & SHOTGUN
Caliber: .54, 12 ga. **Barrel:** 36 in., 1:66 in. twist, and cylinder bore. **Weights:** 10 lbs. rifle, 9 lbs. shotgun. **Length:** 52.25 in. **Stock:** Half-stock walnut. **Sights:** Blued steel rear with flip-up leaf, blade front. **Features:** Percussion and flint ignition. Blued steel furniture. Single trigger. Lock with hammer safety and "waterproof pan" marked Mortimer. A percussion .45-caliber target version of this gun is available with a peep sight on the wrist, and a percussion shotgun version is also offered. Made by Pedersoli. Imported by Dixie.
Price: Flint Rifle, FR0151 .... **$1,525.00**
Price: Flint Shotgun FS0155 .... **$1,495.00**
Price: Percussion Shotgun PS3160 .... **$1,350.00**
Price: Mortimer-Whitworth Target Rifle PR0175 .... **$1,595.00**

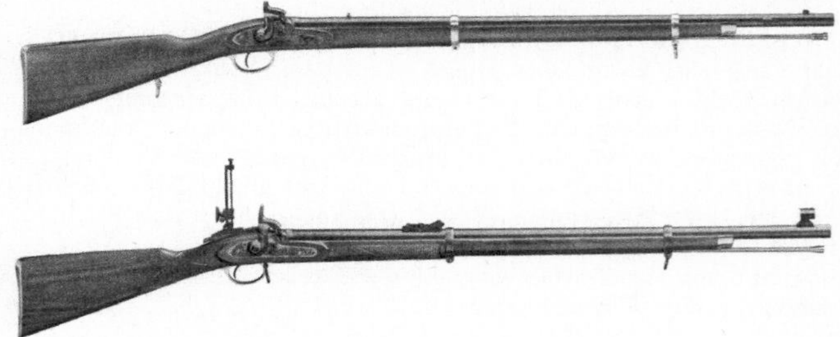

PEDERSOLI VOLUNTEER RIFLE
Caliber: .451. **Barrel:** 32 in., round interior bore 1:20 in. twist. **Weight:** 9.5 lbs. **Length:** 49 in. **Stock:** Oiled Grade 1 American walnut. **Sights:** Blade front, ladder-style rear. **Features:** Checkered stock wrist and fore end. Blued barrel, steel ramrod, bone charcoal casehardened receiver and hammer. Designed for .451 conical bullet. Compare to hexagonal-bored Whitworth Rifle below.
Price: **$1295.00**

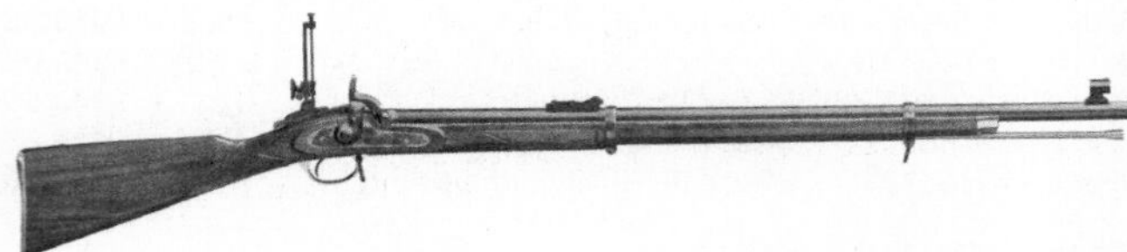

PEDERSOLI WHITWORTH RIFLE
Caliber: .451. **Barrel:** 36 in., hexagonal interior bore 1:20 in. twist. **Weight:** 9.6 lbs. **Length:** 52.5 in. **Stock:** Oiled Grade 1 American walnut. **Sights:** Blade front, ladder-style rear. **Features:** Checkered stock wrist and fore end. Blued barrel, steel ramrod, bone charcoal casehardened receiver and hammer. Designed for .451 conical hexagonal bullet. Compare to round-bored Volunteer Rifle above.
Price: Dixie, PR0175 .... **$1695.00**

PEDERSOLI ROCKY MOUNTAIN & MISSOURI RIVER HAWKEN RIFLES
Calibers: .54 (Rocky Mountain), .45 and .50 in Missouri River. **Barrels:** 34.75 in. octagonal with hooked breech; Rocky Mountain 1:65 in. twist; Missouri River 1:47 twist in .45 cal., and 1:24 twist in .50 cal. **Weight:** 10 lbs. **Length:** 52 in. overall. **Stock:** Maple or walnut, half-stock. **Sights:** Rear buckhorn with push elevator, silver blade front. **Features:** Percussion, brass furniture, double triggers, two barrel keys. Made by Pedersoli. Imported by Dixie Gun Works, others.
Price: Rocky Mountain, Maple PR3430 .... **$1,395.00**
Price: Rocky Mountain, Walnut PR3435 .... **$1,175.00**
Price: Missouri River, .50 Walnut PR3415 .... **$1,275.00**
Price: Missouri River, .50 Maple PR3410 .... **$1,525.00**
Price: Missouri River, .45 Walnut PR3405 .... **$1,275.00**
Price: Missouri River, .45 Maple PR3080 .... **$1,575.00**

PEDERSOLI ZOUAVE RIFLE **Caliber:** .58 percussion. **Barrel:** 33 inches. **Weight:** 9.5 lbs. **Length:** 49 in. **Stock:** European walnut. **Sights:** Blade front, three-leaf military rear. **Features:** Percussion musket-cap ignition. One-piece solid barrel and bolster. Brass-plated patchbox. Made in Italy by Pedersoli. Imported by Cabela's, others.
Price: **$1,050.00**

RICHMOND 1861 RIFLE
Caliber: .58. **Barrel:** 40 inches. **Weight:** 9.5 lbs. **Length:** 55.5 in. overall. **Stock:** European walnut. **Sights:** Blade front, three-leaf military rear. **Features:** Reproduction of the original three-band rifle. Percussion musket-cap ignition. Lock marked C. S. Richmond, Virginia. Armory bright. Made by Pedersoli, Euro Arms. Imported by Dixie Gun Works and others.
Price: From Dixie Gun Works, Made by Euro Arms PR0846 .... **$1,150.00**

REMINGTON MODEL 700 ULTIMATE MUZZLELOADER
Caliber: .50 percussion. **Barrel:** 26 in., 1:26-in twist, satin stainless steel, fluted. **Length:** 47 in. **Stock:** Bell & Carlson black synthetic or laminated wood. **Sights:** None on synthetic stocked model, Williams peep and blade front on laminated-wood model. **Ramrod:** Stainless steel. **Weight:** 8.5 lbs. **Features:** Remington single shot Model 700 bolt action, Reprimable cartridge-case ignition using Remington Magnum Large Rifle primer, sling studs.
Price: 86960 .50-cal. synthetic black, no sights **$1,015.00**
Price: 86950 .50-cal. laminated wood, Williams peep sights **$949.00**

THOMPSON/CENTER ENCORE PRO HUNTER FX
Caliber: .50 as muzzleloading barrel. **Barrel:** 26 in., Weather Shield with relieved muzzle on muzzleloader; interchangeable with 14 centerfire calibers. **Weight:** 7 lbs. **Length:** 40.5 in. overall. **Stock:** Interchangeable American walnut butt and fore-end, black composite, FlexTech recoil-reducing camo stock as thumbhole or straight, rubber over-molded stock and fore-end. Ramrod: Solid aluminum. **Sights:** TruGlo fiber optic front and rear. **Features:** Blue or stainless steel. Uses the frame of the Encore centerfire pistol; break-open design using trigger guard spur; stainless steel universal breech plug; uses #209 shotshell primers. Made in U.S. by Thompson/Center Arms.
Price: .50-cal. Stainless/Black FlexTech Stock Model 5800 .... **$649.00**
Price: .50-cal. Stainless/Engraved frame FlexTech RT-AP camo **$709.00**

Prices given are believed to be accurate at time of publication however, many factors affect retail pricing so exact prices are not possible.

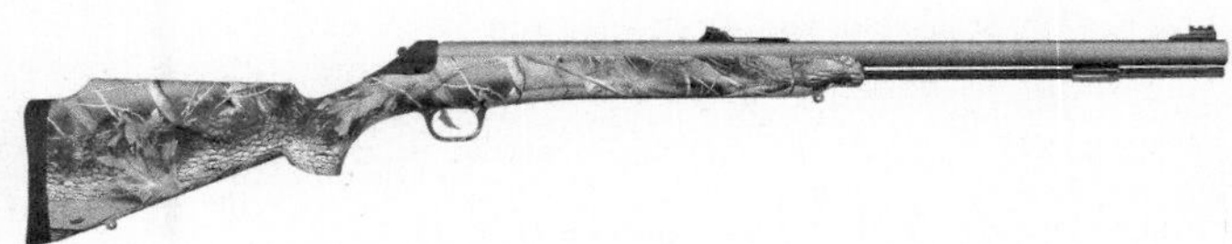

THOMPSON/CENTER IMPACT MUZZLELOADING RIFLE
Caliber: .50 cal. **Barrel:** 26 in., 1:28 twist, Weather Shield finish. **Weight:** 6.5 lbs. **Length:** 41.5 in. **Stock:** Straight Realtree Hardwoods HD or black composite. **Features:** Sliding-hood, break-open action, #209 primer ignition, removable breech plug, synthetic stock adjustable from 12.5 to 13.5 in., adjustable fiber-optic sights, aluminum ramrod, camo, QLA relieved muzzle system.
Price: .50-cal Stainless/Realtree Hardwoods, Weather Shield **$324.00**
Price: .50-cal Blued/Black/scope, case **$264.00**

THOMPSON/CENTER TRIUMPH MUZZLELOADER
Caliber: .50. **Barrel:** 28 in. Weather Shield coated. **Weight:** 6.5 lbs. **Stock:** FlexTech recoil-reducing. Black composite or Realtree AP HD camo straight, rubber over-molded stock and fore-end. **Sights:** Fiber optic. **Ramrod:** Solid aluminum. **Features:** Break-open action. Quick Detachable Speed Breech XT plug, #209 shotshell primer ignition, easy loading QLA relieved muzzle, Cabela's, Bass Pro. Made in U.S. by Thompson/Center Arms.
Price: .50 cal. Blued/Black composite **$456.00**
Price: .50 cal. Weather Shield/Black composite **$517.00**
Price: .50 cal. Weather Shield/AP Camo stock **$578.00**

THOMPSON/CENTER TRIUMPH BONE COLLECTOR
Similar to the Triumph but with added FlexTech technology and Energy Burners to a shorter stock. Also added is Thompson/Center's premium fluted barrel with Weather Shield and their patented Power Rod.
Price: .50-cal Synthetic Realtree AP, fiber optics **$720.00**
Price: .50-cal Synthetic/Weather Shield Black **$638.00**
Price: .50-cal. Weather Shield/AP Camo **$679.00**
Price: .50 cal. Silver Weather Shield/AP Camo **$689.00**

THOMPSON/CENTER STRIKE
Caliber: .50. **Barrels:** 24 in. or 20 in. nitride finished, tapered barrel. **Weights:** 6.75 or 6.25 lbs. **Lengths:** 44 in. or 40 in. **Stocks:** Walnut, black synthetic, G2-Vista Camo. **Finish:** Armornite nitride. **Features:** Break-open action, sliding hammerless cocking mechanism, optional pellet or loose powder primer holders, easy removable breech plugs retained by external collar, aluminum frame with steel mono-block to retain barrel, recoil pad. **Sights:** Williams fiber-optic sights furnished, drilled and tapped for scope. Made in the U.S. Introduced by Thompson/Center in 2015.
Price: .50 cal. 24-in. barrel, black synthetic stock **$499.00**
Price: .50 cal. 24-in. barrel, walnut stock **$599.00**
Price: .50 cal. 24-in. barrel, G2 camo stock **$549.00**

TRADITIONS BUCKSTALKER
Caliber: .50. **Barrel:** 24 in., Cerakote finished, Accelerator Breech Plug. **Weight:** 6 lbs. **Length:** 40 in. **Stock:** Synthetic, G2 Vista camo or black. **Sights:** Fiber-optic rear. **Features:** Break-open action, matte-finished action and barrel. Ramrod: Solid aluminum.
Price: R72003540 .50-cal. Synthetic stock /blued **$219.00**
Price: R72103540 .50-cal. Synthetic stock/Cerakote **$254.00**
Price: R72103547 .50-cal. Synthetic stock/G2-Vista **$294.00**
Price: R5-72003540 .50-cal. Synthetic stock/blued, scope **$294.00**
Price: R5-72103547 .50-cal. Synthetic stock/Cerakote, scope **$369.00**
Price: RY7223540 .50-cal. 13-in. pull, synthetic stock/blued.. .... **$219.00**

TRADITIONS CROCKETT RIFLE
Caliber: .32. **Barrel:** 32 in., 1:48 in. twist. **Weight:** 6.75 lbs. **Length:** 49 in. overall. **Stock:** Beech, inletted toe plate. **Sights:** Blade front, fixed rear. **Features:** Set triggers, hardwood half-stock, brass furniture, color casehardened lock. Percussion. From Traditions.
Price: Dixie .32-cal. Percussion, finished PR0642 .... **$468.00**
Price: Dixie .32-cal. Kit, percussion, hardwood, Armory bright, unfinished brass P0919 .... **$401.00**

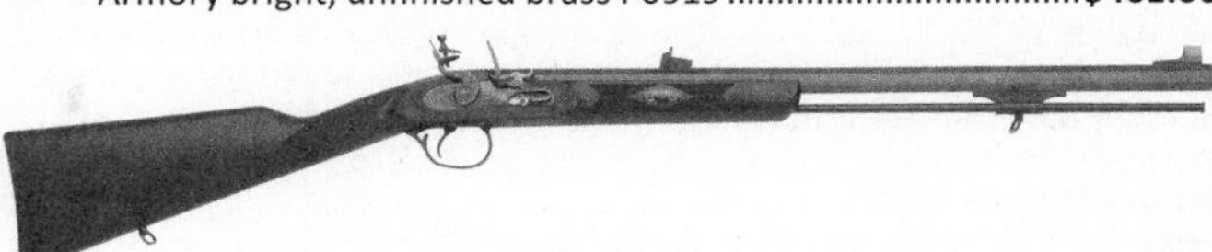

TRADITIONS DEERHUNTER RIFLE SERIES
Caliber: .50. **Barrel:** 24 in., Cerakote finish, octagonal, .9375-in. flats, 1:48 in. twist. **Weight:** 6 lbs. **Length:** 40 in. overall. **Stock:** Stained hardwood or All-Weather composite with rubber buttpad, sling swivels. Ramrod: Synthetic polymer. **Sights:** Fiber Optic blade front, adjustable rear fiber optics, offset hammer spur. **Features:** Flint or percussion with color casehardened lock. Hooked breech, oversized trigger guard, blackened furniture, PVC ramrod. Drilled and tapped for scope mounting. Imported by Traditions, Inc.
Price: R36128101 .50-cal. Percussion hardwood, fib.opt **$324.00**
Price: R3590801 .50-cal. Flintlock, hardwood/blued, fib.opt. **$384.00**
Price: R3690801 .50-cal. Flintlock, hardwood/blued, fiber optic L.H **$389.00**
Price: R36108101 .50-cal. Percussion, hardwood/ blued fiber optic **$269.00**
Price: R3500850 .50-cal. Flintlock, synthetic Cerakote fiber optic **$351.00**
Price: R3670856 .50-cal. Flintlock, synthetic Realtree, fiber optic **$384.00**
Price: R35108150 .50-cal. Percussion, blued, synthetic black fiber optic. **$269.00**

TRADITIONS 1853 ENFIELD
Caliber: .58 percussion. **Barrel:** 39 in. **Length:** 52 in. **Sights:** Rear blued steel flip-up elevator, blade front **Weight:** 10 lbs. **Features:** Blued steel barrel, brass furniture, walnut stock, musket cap ignition, Made by Chiappa, Italy.
Price: R185303 .... **$999.00**
Price: KR6185303 .... **$793.00**

TRADITIONS EVOLUTION BOLT-ACTION BLACKPOWDER RIFLE
Caliber: .50 percussion. **Barrel:** 26 in., 1:28 in. twist, Cerakote finished barrel and action. **Length:** 39 in. **Sights:** Steel Williams fiber-optic sights. **Weight:** 7–7.25 lbs. **Length:** 45 in. overall. **Features:** Bolt action, cocking indicator, thumb safety, shipped with adaptors for No. 11 caps, musket caps and 209 shotgun primer ignition, sling swivels. Ramrod: Aluminum, sling studs. Available with exposed ignition as a Northwest Gun.
Price: R67113350 .50-cal. synthetic black, Cerakote **$314.00**
Price: R67113353 .50-cal. synthetic Realtree AP camo **$374.00**

TRADITIONS HAWKEN MOUNTAIN RIFLE
Caliber: .50. **Barrel:** 32 in., browned CeraKote, 1/48 twist. **Weight:** 8.25 lbs. **Length:** 49 in. overall. **Stock:** Walnut stained hardwood. **Sights:** Beaded blade front, hunting-style open rear adjustable for windage and elevation. **Features:** Brass patchbox and furniture. Double-set triggers. Flint or percussion. From Traditions.
Price: R9250801 .50-cal. Flintlock **$609.00**
Price: R9305801 .50-cal. Percussion **$549.00**
Price KR59208 .50-cal. Kit, flintlock, hardwood/ Armory bright, unfinished brass **$525.00**
Price: KR59308 .50-cal. Kit, Percussion, .50 cal., hardwood/blued **$459.00**

TRADITIONS MOUNTAIN RIFLE
Caliber: .50. **Barrel:** 32 in. octagon, browned CeraKote, 1/48 twist. **Weight:** 8.25 lbs. **Length:** 49 in. overall. **Stock:** Walnut stained hardwood. **Sights:** Blued steel base silver blade front dovetail blued steel base w/ elev. adj. **Features:** Brass buttplate, toeplate, nosecap w/brown oxide coating. Double-set triggers. Flint or percussion. From Traditions.
Price: PR0655.50-cal. Mountain Rifle Percussion **$499.95**
Price: FR0657 .50-cal. Mountain Rifle Flintlock **$555.00**
Price: PK0410 ,50-cal. Mountain Rifle Kit, Percussion, .50 cal. **$425.00**
Price: FK0643 .50-cal. Mountain Rifle Kit, Flintlock **$475.00**

TRADITIONS PRAIRIE HAWKEN

Caliber: .50. **Barrel:** 28 in., blued, 1/48 twist. **Weight:** 8.5 lbs. **Length:** 44 in. overall. **Stock:** Walnut stained hardwood, two barrel keys, **Sights:** Beaded blade front, hunting-style open rear adjustable for windage and elevation. **Features:** Silver barrel keys. Double-set triggers. Flint or percussion. From Traditions.

Price: R2190 .50-cal. Flintlock **$659.00**
Price: R2170 .50-cal. Percussion **$609.00**
Price: KR5190 .50-cal. Kit, flintlock, hardwood/ Armory bright, unfinished brass **$529.00**
Price: KR5170 .50-cal. Kit, Percussion, .50 cal., hardwood/blued ... **$478.00**

TRADITIONS HAWKEN WOODSMAN RIFLE

Caliber: .50. **Barrel:** 28 in., blued, .9375-in. flats. 1:48 twist **Weight:** 7 lbs., 11 oz. **Length:** 44.5 in. overall. **Stock:** Walnut stained hardwood. **Sights:** Fixed blade. **Features:** Brass patchbox and furniture. Double-set triggers. Flint or percussion. From Traditions.

Price: R2390801 .50-cal. Flintlock **$519.00**
Price: R24008 .50-cal. Percussion **$479.00**
Price: KRC5208 .50-cal. Kit, percussion, hardwood/ Armory bright, unfinished brass **$374.00**
Price: R3300801 ,50-cal. Percussion, .50 cal., hardwood/blued **$324.00**
Price: R3200850 .50-cal. Flintlock,synthetic/blued, fib.opt **$329.00**
Price: RKC53008 .50-cal. Percussion Kit, hardwood, Armory bright, Unfinished Brass **$299.00**

TRADITIONS KENTUCKY RIFLE

Caliber: .50. **Barrels:** 33.5 in., .875-in. flats, 1:66 in. twist. **Weight:** 7 lbs. **Length:** 49 in. overall. **Stock:** Beech, inletted toe plate. **Sights:** Blade front, fixed rear. **Features:** Full-length, two-piece stock; brass furniture; color casehardened lock. Flint or percussion. From Traditions, Bass Pro and others.

Price: R2010 .50-cal. Flintlock, 1:66 twist **$489.00**
Price: R2020 .50-cal. Percussion, 1:66 twist **$429.00**
Price: KRC52206 .50-cal. Kit, percussion, hardwood/Armory bright, unfinished brass **$355.00**

TRADITIONS PA PELLET ULTRALIGHT FLINTLOCK

Caliber: .50. **Barrel:** 26 in., Chromoly steel, Nitride finished, 1:48 in. twist.,. **Weight:** 7 lbs. **Length:** 45 in. **Stock:** Hardwood, synthetic and synthetic break-up, sling swivels. **Sights:** Fiber optic. **Features:** New flintlock action, removable breech plug, available as left-hand model with hardwood stock.

Price: R389001 .50-cal. Hardwood, blued, fib.opt **$426.00**
Price: R389091 L. .50-cal. Hardwood, left-hand, blued **$426.00**
Price: R389050 .50-cal. Synthetic/blued, fib. opt **$492.00**
Price: R3890516 .50-cal. Hardwood/MO Break up fib.opt **$506.00**

TRADITIONS PENNSYLVANIA RIFLE

Caliber: .50. **Barrel:** 40.25 in., .875-in. flats, 1:66 in. twist, octagon. **Weight:** 9 lbs. **Length:** 57.5 in. overall. **Stock:** Walnut. **Sights:** Blade front, adjustable rear. **Features:** Single-piece walnut stock, brass patchbox and ornamentation. Double-set triggers. Flint or percussion. From Traditions.

Price: R2090 .50-cal. Flintlock, 1:66 twist **$824.00**
Price: R2100 .50-cal. Percussion, 1:66 twist **$794.00**

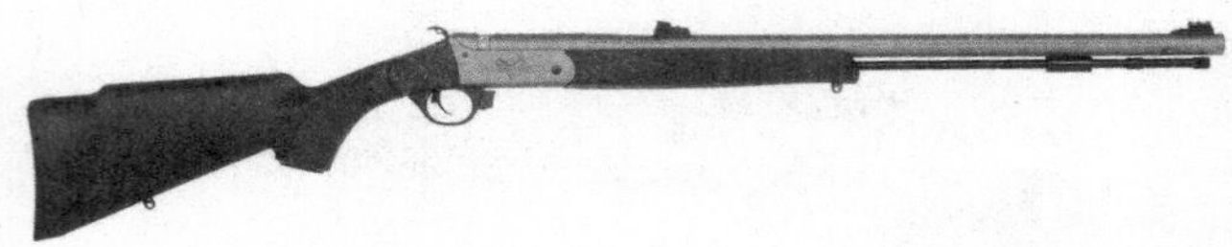

TRADITIONS PURSUIT G4 ULTRALIGHT MUZZLELOADER

Caliber: .50. **Barrel:** 26 in., Chromoly tapered, fluted barrel with premium Cerakote or Nitride finishes, Accelerator Breech Plug. **Weight:** 5.5 lbs. **Length:** 42 in. **Stock:** Rubber over-molded Soft Touch, Mossy Oak or Realtree camouflage at same price, straight and thumbhole stock options. **Sights:** 3-9x40 scope with medium rings and bases, mounted and bore sighted by a factory trained technician. **Features:** Break-open action, Williams fiber-optic sights.

Price: R7492416NS .50-cal. 26-in. Synthetic/Nitride fib.opt MO. **$389.00**
Price: R741140 .50-cal. Synthetic/CeraKote **$344.00**
Price: R5-749246 .50-cal. Synthetic/Nitride, Realtree Camo, 3x9 scope **$461.00**
Price: Rs-741140 .50-cal. Synthetic/Nitride, Black stock finish, 3x9 scope **$404.00**
Price: R74446NS .50-cal. Synthetic/Realtree Xtra stock and barrel, 3x9 range-finding scope **$515.00**

TRADITIONS SPRINGFIELD 1842

Caliber: .69 percussion. **Barrel:** 42 in. **Length:** 57 in. **Sights:** Blade front **Weight:** 10 lbs. **Features:** Bright steel barrel, steel furniture, walnut stock, musket cap ignition. Made by Chiappa, Italy.

Price: R184200 .... **$1119.00**
Price: KR184200 .... **$883.00**

TRADITIONS SPRINGFIELD 1861

Caliber: .58 percussion. **Barrel:** 40 in. **Length:** 53 in. **Sights:** Rear with two steel flip-ups, blade front **Weight:** 10 lbs. **Features:** Bright steel barrel, steel furniture, walnut stock, musket cap ignition. Made by Chiappa, Italy. **Price:** R186100 .... **$1059.00**
Price: KR18600 .... **$839.00**

TRADITIONS TENNESSEE RIFLE

Caliber: .50. **Barrel:** 24 in., octagon, .9375-in. flats, 1:66 in. twist. **Weight:** 6 lbs. **Length:** 40.5 in. overall. **Stock:** Stained beech. **Sights:** Blade front, fixed rear. **Features:** One-piece stock has brass furniture, cheekpiece, double-set trigger, V-type mainspring. Flint or percussion. From Traditions. Discontinued.

Price: R2310 .50-cal. Flintlock/hardwood stock **$539.00**
Price: R2320 .50-cal. Percussion/hardwood stock **$479.00**

TRADITIONS TRACKER 209 IN-LINE RIFLE

Caliber: .50. **Barrel:** 24 in., blued or Cerakote, 1:28 in. twist. **Weight:** 6 lbs., 4 oz. **Length:** 43 in. **Stock:** Black synthetic. Ramrod: Synthetic, high-impact polymer. **Sights:** Lite Optic blade front, adjustable rear. **Features:** Striker-fired action, thumb safety, adjustable trigger, rubber buttpad, sling swivel studs. Takes 150 grains of Pyrodex pellets, one-piece musket cap and 209 ignition systems. Drilled and tapped for scope. Legal for use in Northwest. From Traditions.

Price: R44003470 .50-cal. Synthetic/blued **$184.00**

TRADITIONS VORTEK STRIKERFIRE BACK COUNTRY

Caliber: .50 **Barrel:** 26 in., Chromoly, nitride finished, tapered, fluted barrel. **Weight:** 5.8 lbs. **Length:** 42 in. **Stock:** Over-molded soft-touch straight stock, removable buttplate for in-stock storage. Finish: Premium Cerakote and Realtree Xtra. **Features:** Break-open action, sliding hammerless cocking mechanism, drop-out trigger assembly, speed load system, accelerator breech plug, recoil pad. **Sights:** Optional 3-9x40 muzzleloader scope.

Price: R549246NS .50-cal. Synthetic/black Hogue Over-mold, RT EXtra **$566.00**

Price: R5-549241 .50-cal. Synthetic Highlander camo stock and barrel, 3X9 scope **$649.00**

TRADITIONS VORTEK STRIKERFIRE

Caliber: .50 **Barrel:** 28 in., Chromoly, tapered, fluted barrel. **Weight:** 6.25 lbs. **Length:** 44 in. **Stock:** Over-molded soft-touch straight stock, removable buttplate for in-stock storage. Finish: Premium Cerakote and Realtree Xtra. **Features:** Break-open action, sliding hammerless cocking mechanism, drop-out trigger assembly, speed load system, accelerator breech plug, recoil pad. **Sights:** Optional 3-9x40 muzzleloader scope.

Price: R561140NS .50-cal. Synthetic/black Hogue Over-mold, Cerakote barrel **$493.00**

Price: R561146NS .50-cal. Synthetic/Realtree Xtra camo, Cerakote barrel **$569.00**

Price: R29564446 .50-cal. Synthetic Realtree Xtra camo stock and barrel, 3X9 scope **$649.00**

TRADITIONS VORTEK STRIKERFIRE LDR

Caliber: .50 **Barrel:** 30 in., Chromoly, tapered, fluted barrel. **Weight:** 6.8 lbs. **Length:** 46 in. **Stock:** Over-molded soft-touch straight stock, removable buttplate for in-stock storage. **Finish:** Premium Cerakote and Realtree Xtra. **Features:** Break-open action, sliding hammerless cocking mechanism, drop-out trigger assembly, speed load system, accelerator breech plug, recoil pad. **Sights:** Optional 3-9x40 muzzleloader scope.

Price: R591120NS .50-cal, Synthetic/black Hogue Over-mold, Cerakote barrel, no sights **$524.00**

Price: R599246NS .50-cal Synthetic/Realtree Xtra camo, Cerakote barrel 3-9 scope **$685.00**

Price: R29-594446 .50-cal Synthetic/Realtree Xtra camo, Cerakote barrel 3-9 range-finding scope **$693.00**

TRADITIONS VORTEK STRIKERFIRE LDR NORTHWEST MODEL

Caliber: .50. **Barrels:** 28 in. or 30 in. chromoly tapered, fluted barrel. **Weights:** 6.25 or 6.8 lbs. **Lengths:** 46 or 48 in. **Stock:** Synthetic black, over-molded soft-touch straight stock, removable buttplate for in-stock storage. **Finish:** Premium Cerakote. **Features:** Break-open action, sliding hammerless cocking mechanism, drop-out trigger assembly, speed load system, accelerator breech plug, recoil pad. **Sights:** Williams fiber-optic sights.

Price: R599246WA .50-cal. Northwest, synthetic/black, LDR Model, 30-in. nitride barrel **$524.00**

Price: R591146WA .50-cal. Northwest, synthetic/Realtree Xtra Camo, soft touch Hogue overmold, 30-in. Cerakote barrel **$619.00**

TRADITIONS VORTEK ULTRALIGHT

Caliber: .50. **Barrel:** 28 in., Chromoly, tapered, fluted barrel. **Weight:** 6.25 lbs. **Length:** 44 in. **Stock:** Over-molded soft-touch straight stock. **Finish:** Premium Cerakote, Realtree AP, Reaper Buck. **Features:** Break-open action, hammer cocking mechanism, drop-out trigger assembly, speed load system, accelerator breech plug, recoil pad. **Sights:** Optional 3-9x40 muzzleloader scope.

Price: R461143 .50-cal. Synthetic/black Hogue Over-mold, Cerakote barrel, fib. opt **$534.00**

Price: R461140NS .50-cal Synthetic/Realtree AP camo Hogue, Cerakote barrel, fib. opt **$449.00**

Price: R461128 .50-cal Synthetic/Reaper Buck camo, Hogue Over-Mold, 3X9 scope **$634.00**

TRADITIONS VORTEK ULTRALIGHT NORTHWEST MAGNUM

Caliber: .50. **Barrels:** 28 in. or 30 in. chromoly tapered, fluted barrel. **Weights:** 6.25 lbs. or 6.8 lbs. **Length:** 44 in. or 46 in. **Stock:** Over-molded, soft-touch, straight or thumbhole stock. **Finish:** Premium Cerakote and Realtree AP. **Features:** Break-open action, hammer cocking mechanism, musket-cap ignition, drop-out trigger assembly, speed load system, accelerator breech plug, recoil pad. **Sights:** Williams fiber-optic sights.

Price: R461140WA .50-cal. Synthetic/black Hogue Over-mold, Cerakote barrel, fib. opt. **$469.00**

Price: R461146WA .50-cal. Synthetic/Realtree AP, Hogue, Cerakote barrel, fib. opt... .... **$529.00**

Price: R481146WA .50-cal. Synthetic Thumbhole/ Realtree Xtra camo, Cerakote barrel, fib. opt. **$529.00**

Price: R491140WA (LDR) , Synthetic/Black, Hogue, 30-in. barrel, Cerakote barrel, fib. opt **$499.00**

TRADITIONS ZOUAVE 1863

Caliber: .58 percussion. **Barrel:** 33 in. **Length:** 44 in. **Sights:** Rear with two steel flip-ups, blade front **Weight:** 9.5 lbs. **Features:** Brass patchbox, furniture, walnut stock, musket cap ignition. Made by Chiappa, Italy.

Price: R186306 .... **$1175.00**

Price: KR186306 .... **$939.00**

WOODMAN ARMS PATRIOT

Caliber: .45, .50. **Barrel:** 24 in., nitride coated 416 stainless, 1:24 twist in .45, 1:28 twist in .50. **Weight:** 5.75 lbs. **Length:** 43-in. **Stocks:** Laminated, walnut or hydrographic dipped. Synthetic black, over-molded soft-touch straight stock. **Finish:** Nitride black and black anodized. **Features:** Break-open action, hammerless cocking mechanism, match-grade patented trigger assembly, speed load system, recoil pad. **Sights:** Picatinny rail with built-in rear and 1-inch or 30 mm scope mounts, red fiber-optic front bead. Production has apparently been discontinued.

Price: Patriot .45 or .50-cal **$899.00**

BAKER CAVALRY SHOTGUN
Gauge: 20 ga.. **Barrels:** 11.25 in. **Weight:** 5.75 lbs. **Length:** 27.5 in. overall. **Stock:** American walnut. **Sights:** Bead front. **Features:** Reproduction of shotguns carried by Confederate cavalry. Single non-selective trigger, back-action locks. No. 11 percussion musket-cap ignition. Blued barrel with steel furniture. Casehardened lock. Pedersoli also makes a 12-gauge coach-length version of this back-action-lock shotgun with 20-inch barrels, and a full-length version in 10, 12 and 20 ga. Made by Pedersoli. Imported by Cabela's and others.
Price: Cabela's, Pedersoli **$995.00**

DIXIE SCOUT SHOTGUN
Gauge: 12 ga. **Barrel:** 11.25 in. **Weight:** 5.75 lbs. **Length:** 27.5 in. overall. **Stock:** American walnut. **Sights:** Bead front. **Features:** Available in right and left-hand percussion and right-hand flintlock. Reproduction of shotguns carried by Confederate cavalry. Single non-selective trigger, back-action locks. No. 11 percussion musket-cap ignition. Plum brown barrel with steel furniture. Casehardened lock. Pedersoli also makes a 12-gauge coach-length version of this back-action-lock shotgun with 20-inch barrels, and a full-length version in 10, 12 and 20 ga. Made by Pedersoli. Imported by Cabela's and others.
Price: Cabela's, Pedersoli **$995.00**

DIXIE/PEDERSOLI SCOUT
Gauge: 12 ga. **Barrel:** Blued 30.25 in. Octagon to round w/two wedding bands at transition **Weight:** 5.5 lbs. **Length:** 46.25 in. overall. **Stock:** Half-stock, walnut 2.5 in drop, 14.25-in. pull, rubber recoil pad. **Sights:** Blade front, rear steel adjustable for windage and elevation. **Features:** Brass nosecap, wedge plate inlays, blued trigger and guard, color casehardened lock and hammer. Made by Pedersoli. Imported by Dixie Gun Works.
Price: Dixie PS3021 12 ga. Perc **$675.00**
Price: Dixie PS3031 12 ga. Flint **$699.95**
Price: Dixie PS3021 12 ga. Perc LH **$665.00**

HOWDAH HUNTER 20-GAUGE PISTOL
Gauge: 20 ga. **Barrels:** Cylinder bored, 11.25 in. **Weight:** 4.5 lbs. **Length:** 17.25 in. **Stock:** American walnut with checkered grip. **Sights:** Brass bead front sight. **Features:** Blued barrels, swamped barrel rib, engraved, color casehardened locks and hammers, captive steel ramrod. Available with detachable shoulder stock, case, holster and mold. Made by Pedersoli. Imported by Cabela's, Dixie Gun Works, Taylor's and others.
Price: Dixie, 20X20 PH0581 .... **$815.00**
Price: Dixie 20X20 PK0945.......... **$640.00**

KNIGHT TK-2000 TURKEY SHOTGUN
Gauge: 12 ga. Ignition: #209 primer with Full Plastic Jacket, musket cap or No. 11. Striker-fired with one-piece removable hammer assembly. **Barrel:** 26 in. Choke: Extra-full and improved cylinder available. **Stock:** Realtree Xtra Green straight or thumbhole. **Weight:** 7.7 lbs. **Sights:** Williams fully adjustable rear, fiber-optic front. **Features:** Striker-fired action, receiver is drilled and tapped for scope, adjustable trigger, removable breech plug, double-safety system. Made in U.S. by Knight Rifles.
Price: Standard **$743.00**
Price: Thumbhole stock.......... **$739.00**

PEDERSOLI BACK-ACTION DOUBLE-BARREL COACH GUN
Gauge: .50 caliber/12 gauge. **Barrels:** 20 in. browned **Weight:** 6.75 lbs. **Stock:** Straight grip, European walnut. **Sights:** Brass bead. **Features:** Percussion ignition, single trigger, cylinder bore barrel. Blued steel furniture. Stainless steel nipple. Made by Pedersoli. Imported by Dixie Gun Works and others.
Price: Dixie PS34500 .... **$895.00**

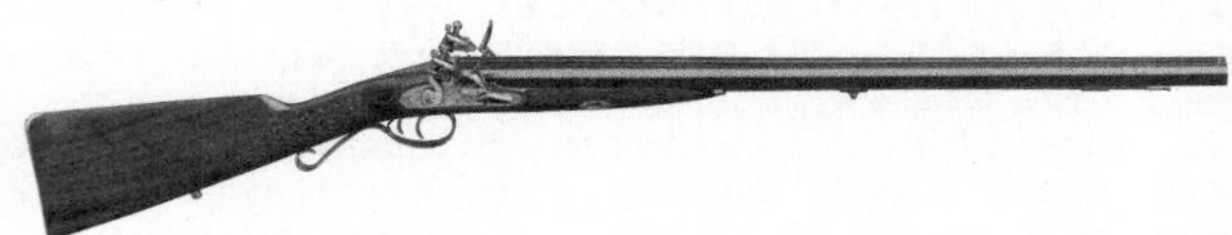

PEDERSOLI FLINTLOCK DOUBLE BARREL SHOTGUN
Gauge: 20 ga. **Barrels:** 28 in. browned **Weight:** 7.5 lbs. **Stock:** Pistol grip, Select walnut. **Sights:** Brass bead. **Features:** Heavily engraved flintlocks, double triggers, cylinder/modified bored barrels. chrome lined, Floral engraved steel furniture. Made by Pedersoli. Newly announced gun with production to start in September. To be imported by Dixie Gun Works.
Price: **$1,965.00**

PEDERSOLI INDIAN TRADE MUSKET
Gauge: 20 **Barrels:** Browned, 1-inch at breech, 36 in. Octagon to round. **Weight:** 7.25 lbs. **Length:** 51.5 in. overall. **Stock:** American walnut, 14-in. pull. **Features:** Flintlock for 1-inch flint, large trigger guard bow, serpent sideplate, casehardened lock and trigger. Patterned after Hudson Bay Co. trade guns. Made by Pedersoli. From Dixie Gun Works, others.
Price: FR 3170 .... **$1,050.00**
Price: FK 3370 Trade Musket Kit protective bluing on barrel **$995.00**

PEDERSOLI KODIAK MK III RIFLE-SHOTGUN COMBINATION GUN
Gauge: .50 cal./12 ga. **Barrels:** 28.5 in. **Weight:** 10.75 lbs. **Stock:** Straight grip, European walnut. **Sights:** Two adjustable rear, steel ramp with brass bead. **Features:** Percussion ignition, double triggers, sling swivels, 12-ga. cylinder bored barrel. Blued steel furniture. Stainless steel nipple. Made by Pedersoli. Imported by Dixie Gun Works, and some models by Cabela's and others.
Price: Dixie Combo 50X12 gauge PR0990 .... **$1,350.00**
Price: Dixie Combo .58X12 gauge PR0995 .... **$1,350.00**

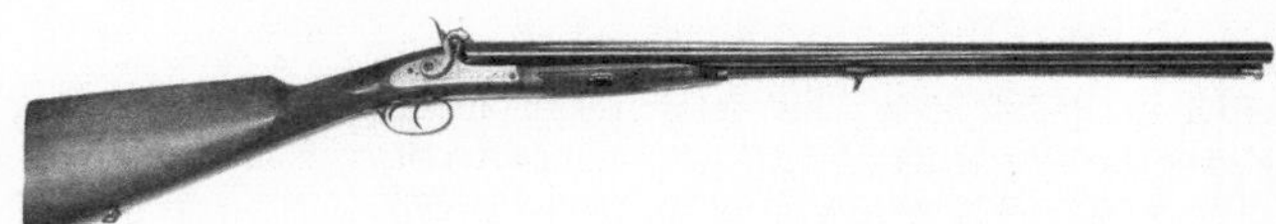

PEDERSOLI MAGNUM PERCUSSION SHOTGUN & COACH GUN
Gauges: 10 ga., 12 ga., 20 ga. **Barrels:** Chrome-lined blued barrels, 25.5 in. Imp. cyl. and Mod. **Weight:** 7.25 lbs., 7 lbs., 6.75 lbs. **Length:** 45 in. overall. **Stock:** Hand-checkered walnut, 14-in. pull. **Features:** Double triggers, light hand engraving, casehardened locks, sling swivels. Made by Pedersoli. From Dixie Gun Works, others.
Price: 10-ga. PS1030 .... **$1,195.00**
Price: 10-ga. kit PS1040 .... **$975.00**
Price: 12-ga. PS0930.......... **$1,175.00**
Price: 12-ga. Kit PS0940 .... **$875.00**
Price: 12-ga. Coach gun, 25.5-in. barrels, Cyl, XCyl. PS0914 .... **$1,050.00**
Price: 20-ga. PS0334.......... **$1,175.00**

PEDERSOLI MORTIMER SHOTGUN
Gauge: 12 ga. **Barrel:** 36 in., 1:66 in., cylinder bore. **Weight:** 9 pounds. **Length:** 52.25 in. **Stock:** Halfstock walnut. **Sights:** Bead front. **Features:** Percussion and flint ignition. Blued steel furniture. Single trigger. Lock with hammer safety and "waterproof pan" on flintlock gun. Lock marked Mortimer. Rifle versions of this gun are also available. Made by Pedersoli. Imported by Dixie.
Price: Flint Shotgun FS0155.......... **$1,495.00**
Price: Percussion Shotgun PS3160 .... **$1,350.00**

PEDERSOLI OLD ENGLISH SHOTGUN
Gauge: 12 ga. **Barrels:** Browned, 28.5 in. Cyl. and Mod. **Weight:** 7.5 lbs. **Length:** 45 in. overall. **Stock:** Hand-checkered American maple, cap box, 14-in. pull. **Features:** Double triggers, light hand engraving on lock, cap box and tang, swivel studs for sling attachment. Made by Pedersoli. From Dixie Gun Works, others.
Price: PR4090 .... **$1,750.00**

Prices given are believed to be accurate at time of publication however, many factors affect retail pricing so exact prices are not possible.

AIR ARMS ALFA PROJ COMPETITION PCP PISTOL
Caliber: .177 pellets. **Barrel:** Rifled. **Weight:** 1.94 lbs. **Length:** 15.5 inches. **Power:** Pre-charged pneumatic. **Sights:** Front post, fully adjustable rear blade, **Features:** 10-Meter competition class pistol, highly adjustable trigger, Velocity: 500 fps.
Price: **$850.00**

AIRFORCE TALON P

AIRFORCE TALON P PCP AIR PISTOL, SPIN-LOC TANK
Caliber: .25. **Barrel:** Rifled 12.0 in. **Weight:** 3.5 lbs. **Length:** 23.25 in. **Sights:** None, grooved for scope. **Features:** Quick-detachable air tank with adjustable power. Match-grade Lothar Walther, massive power output in a highly compact size **Velocity:** 900 fps.
Price: **$479.95**

AIR VENTURI V10 MATCH AIR PISTOL
Caliber: .177 pellets. **Barrel:** Rifled. **Weight:** 1.95 lbs. **Length:** 12.6 in. **Power:** Single stroke pneumatic. **Sights:** Front post, fully adjustable rear blade, **Features:** 10-Meter competition class pistol, fully adjustable trigger, 1.5-lb. trigger pull **Velocity:** 400 fps.
Price: **$300.00**

ASG CZ P-09 DUTY CO2 PISTOL
Caliber: .177 pellets and steel BBs. **Barrel:** Rifled. **Power:** CO2. **Weight:** 1.6 lbs. **Length:** 8.2 in. **Sights:** Fixed. **Features:** Polymer frame, blowback **Velocity:** 412 fps.
Price: **$104.95**

ASG CZ 75 SP-01 SHADOW CO2 BB PISTOL KIT
Caliber: .177 steel BBs. **Barrel:** Smoothbore threaded for barrel extension. **Power:** CO2. **Weight:** 1.3 lbs. **Length:** 8.27 in. **Sights:** Fiber optics front and rear. **Features:** Replica based on the CZ 75 series pistols. Velocity: 380 fps.
Price: **$89.95**

ASG CZ 75 P-07 DUTY BLOWBACK AIR PISTOL

ASG CZ 75 BLOWBACK PISTOL
Caliber: .177 BBs. **Barrel:** Smoothbore. **Weight:** 2.09 lbs. **Length:** 8.27 in. **Power:** CO2. **Sights:** Fixed. **Features:** Full metal construction, blowback. **Velocity:** 312 fps.
Price: **$159.95**

ASG CZ 75 P-07 DUTY BLOWBACK AIR PISTOL
Caliber: .177 steel BBs. **Barrel:** Smoothbore. **Weight:** 1.81 lbs. **Length:** 7.32 in. **Power:** CO2. **Sights:** Fixed. **Features:** Full metal construction, weaver rail, blowback. **Velocity:** 320 fps.
Price: **$120.95**

ASG CZ 75 P-07 DUTY CO2 BB PISTOL
Caliber: .177 steel BBs. **Barrel:** Smoothbore. **Weight:** 1.8 lbs. **Length:** 7.5 in. **Power:** CO2. **Sights:** Fixed. **Features:** Realistic look and feel **Velocity:** 377 fps.
Price: **$79.95**

ASG CZ 75 P-07 DUTY DUAL-TONE CO2 PISTOL
Caliber: .177 steel BBs. **Barrel:** Smoothbore. **Weight:** 1.81 lbs. **Length:** 7.32 in. **Power:** CO2 **Sights:** Fixed. **Features:** Metal slide, front rail. **Velocity:** 320 fps.
Price: **$119.95**

ASG CZ 75D COMPACT CO2 BB PISTOL
Caliber: .177 steel BBs. **Barrel:** Smoothbore. **Weight:** 1.46 lbs. **Length:** 7.28 in. **Power:** CO2. **Sights:** Adjustable rear sight and blade front sight. **Features:** Compact design. **Velocity:** 380 fps.
Price: **$90.00**

BERSA THUNDER 9 PRO BB PISTOL
Caliber: .177 steel BBs. **Barrel:** Smoothbore **Weight:** 1.17 lbs. **Length:** 7.56 in. **Power:** CO2. **Sights:** Fixed, 3 white dot system. **Features:** Highly realistic replica action pistol, 19-shot semi-automatic, composite/synthetic construction **Velocity:** To 400 fps.
Price: **$79.95**

ASG BERSA BP9CC

ASG BERSA BP9CC DUAL TONE BLOWBACK AIR PISTOL
Caliber: .177 steel BBs. **Barrel:** Smoothbore **Weight:** 1.35 lbs. **Length:** 6.61 in. **Power:** CO2. **Sights:** Fixed 3-dot system. **Features:** Blowback, metal slide, weaver accessory rail. **Velocity:** 350 fps.
Price: **$119.95**

ASG STI DUTY ONE CO2 BB PISTOL
Caliber: .177 steel BBs. **Barrel:** Smoothbore **Weight:** 1.82 lbs. **Length:** 8.66 in. **Power:** CO2. **Sights:** Fixed. **Features:** Blowback, accessory rail, and metal slide. **Velocity:** 383 fps.
Price: **$120.00**

ATAMAN AP16 REGULATED COMPACT AIR PISTOL, SILVER
Caliber: .22 pellets. **Barrel:** Rifled Match Barrel **Weight:** 1.76 lbs. **Length:** 12.0 in. **Power:** Pre-Charged Pneumatic. **Sights:** Fixed Front Ramp, Adjustable Rear Notch. **Features:** 7-round Rotary Magazine, 300 Bar Max Fill, Regulated for hunting power, exceptional build quality, available in satin and blued finishes **Velocity:** 590 fps.
Price: **$1,049.99**

ATAMAN AP16 REGULATED STANDARD AIR PISTOL
Caliber: .22 pellets. **Barrel:** Rifled Match Barrel **Weight:** 2.2 lbs. **Length:** 14.37 in. **Power:** Pre-Charged Pneumatic. **Sights:** Fixed Front Ramp, Adjustable Rear Notch. **Features:** 7-round Rotary Magazine, 300 Bar Max Fill, Regulated for hunting power, exceptional build quality, **Velocity:** 656 fps.
Price: **$1,049.99**

BEEMAN P17 MAGNUM AIR PISTOL
Caliber: .177 pellets. **Barrel:** Rifled. **Weight:** 1.7 lbs. **Length:** 9.6 in. **Power:** Single stroke pneumatic. **Sights:** Front and rear fiber-optic sights, rear sight fully adjustable. **Features:** Exceptional trigger, Grooved for scope mounting with dry-fire feature for practice. **Velocity:** 410 fps.
Price: **$44.99**

BEEMAN P1 MAGNUM AIR PISTOL
Caliber: .177, .20, .22. pellets. **Barrel:** Rifled. **Weight:** 2.5 lbs. **Length:** 11 in. **Power:** Single stroke, spring-piston. **Grips:** Checkered walnut. **Sights:** Blade front, square notch rear with click micrometer adjustments for windage and elevation. Grooved for scope mounting. **Features:** Dual power for .177 and 20 cal.; Compatible with all Colt 45 auto grips. Dry-firing feature for practice. Velocity: varies by caliber and power setting.
Price: .... **$529.95–$564.95**

BEEMAN P3 PNEUMATIC AIR PISTOL
Caliber: .177. pellets. **Barrel:** Rifled **Weight:** 1.7 lbs. **Length:** 9.6 in. **Power:** Single-stroke pneumatic. **Sights:** Front and rear fiber-optic sights, rear sight fully adjustable. **Features:** Grooved for scope mounting, exceptional trigger, automatic safety. **Velocity:** 410 fps.
Price: **$289.95**

BEEMAN P11 AIR PISTOL
Caliber: .177, .22. **Barrel:** Rifled. **Weight:** 2.6 lbs. **Length**: 10.75 in. **Power:** Single-stroke pneumatic with high and low settings. **Sights:** Front ramp sight, fully adjustable rear sight. **Features:** 2-stage adjustable trigger and automatic safety. **Velocity:** Up to 600 fps in .177 caliber and Up to 460 fps in .22 caliber.
Price: .... **$614.95–$634.95**

BEEMAN HW70A AIR PISTOL
Caliber: .177. pellets **Barrel:** Rifled. **Weight:** 2.4 lbs. **Length:** 12.8 in. **Power:** Single stroke, spring-piston. **Sights:** Hooded post front, square notch rear adjustable for windage and elevation. **Features:** Adjustable trigger, 31-lbs. cocking effort, automatic barrel safety. **Velocity:** 440 fps.
Price: **$334.95**

BENJAMIN MARAUDER PCP PISTOL
Caliber: .22 **Barrel:** Rifled. **Weight:** 2.7 lbs. **Length:** Pistol length 18 in./ Carbine length 29.75 in. **Power:** Pre-charged pneumatic **Sights:** None. Grooved for optics. **Features:** Multi-shot (8-round rotary magazine) bolt action, shrouded steel barrel, two-stage adjustable trigger, includes both pistol grips and a carbine stock and is built in America. **Velocity:** 700 fps.
Price: **$500.00**

BENJAMIN MARAUDER WOODS WALKER PCP PISTOL
Caliber: .22 **Barrel:** Rifled. **Weight:** 2.7 lbs. **Length:** Pistol length 18 in./ Carbine length 29.75 in. **Power:** Pre-charged pneumatic **Sights:** Includes CenterPoint Multi-TAC Quick Aim Sight. **Features:** Multi-shot (8-round rotary magazine) bolt action, shrouded steel barrel, two-stage adjustable trigger, includes both pistol grips and a carbine stock and is built in America. **Velocity:** 700 fps.
Price: **$550.00**

BENJAMIN MARAUDER AIR PISTOL, AR15 STOCK
Caliber: .22 **Barrel:** Rifled. **Weight:** 2.7–3 lbs. **Length:** Pistol length 18 in./ Carbine length 27.88–31.68 in. **Power:** Pre-charged pneumatic **Sights:** None. **Features:** Multi-shot (8-round rotary magazine) bolt action, shrouded steel barrel, two-stage adjustable trigger, includes both pistol grips and AR-15 adjustable stock and is built in America. **Velocity:** 700 fps.
Price: **$700.00**

BENJAMIN TRAIL NP AIR PISTOL
Caliber: .177 pellets. **Barrel:** Rifled. **Weight:** 3.43 lbs. **Length:** 16 in. **Power:** Single cock, nitro piston. **Sights:** Fiber-optic front, fully adjustable rear. **Features:** Grooved for scope, **Velocity:** To 625 fps.
Price: **$80.00**

BERETTA APX BLOWBACK AIR PISTOL
Caliber: .177 steel BBs. **Barrel:** Smoothbore. **Weight:** 1.47 lbs. **Length:** 7.48 in. **Power:** CO2. **Sights:** Fixed. **Features:** Highly accurate replica action pistol, 19-shot capacity, front accessory rail, metal and ABS plastic construction. **Velocity:** 400 fps.
Price: **$69.95**

Prices given are believed to be accurate at time of publication however, many factors affect retail pricing so exact prices are not possible.

BERETTA MODEL 84FS

BERETTA M84FS AIR PISTOL
Caliber: .177 steel BBs. **Barrel:** Smoothbore **Weight:** 1.4 lbs. **Length:** 7 in. **Power:** CO2. **Sights:** Fixed. **Features:** Highly realistic replica action pistol, blowback operation, full metal construction. **Velocity:** To 360 fps.
Price: **$119.95**

BERETTA PX4 CO2 PISTOL
Caliber: .177 pellet /.177 steel BBs. **Barrel:** Rifled **Weight:** 1.6 lbs. **Length:** 7.6 in. **Power:** CO2. **Sights:** Blade front sight and fixed rear sight. **Features:** Semi-automatic, 16-shot capacity with maximum of 40-shots per fill, dual ammo capable. **Velocity:** To 380 fps.
Price: **$119.99**

BERETTA ELITE II CO2 PISTOL
Caliber: .177 steel BBs. **Barrel:** Smoothbore **Weight:** 1.5 lbs. **Length:** 8.5 in. **Power:** CO2. **Sights:** Blade front sight and fixed rear sight. **Features:** Semi-automatic, 19-shot capacity. **Velocity:** Up to 410 fps.
Price: **$49.99**

BERETTA 90TWO CO2 BB PISTOL & LASER
Caliber: .177 steel BBs. **Barrel:** Smoothbore. **Weight:** 1.99 lbs. **Length:** 8.5 in. **Power:** CO2. **Sights:** Blade front sight and fixed rear sight. **Features:** Includes rail-mounted tactical laser, semi-automatic, 21-shot capacity. **Velocity:** To 375 fps.
Price: **$69.90**

BERETTA 92A1 CO2 FULL AUTO BB PISTOL
Caliber: .177 steel BBs. **Barrel:** Smoothbore **Weight:** 2.4 lbs. **Length:** 8.5 in. **Power:** CO2. **Sights:** Fixed. **Features:** Highly realistic replica action pistol, 18-shot semi-automatic, full metal construction, selectable fire semi-automatic & full-automatic. **Velocity:** To 330 fps.
Price: **$149.99**

BERETTA 92FS CO2 PELLET GUN
Caliber: .177 pellets. **Barrel:** Rifled **Weight:** 2.75 lbs. **Length:** 8.0 in. **Power:** CO2. **Sights:** Fixed front sight, rear adjustable for windage. **Features:** Highly realistic replica-action pistol, 8-shot semi-automatic, full metal construction, available in various finishes and grips. **Velocity:** To 425 fps.
Price: **$329.00**

BLACK OPS 1911 FULL METAL CO2 BLOWBACK AIR
Caliber: .177 steel BBs. **Barrel:** Smoothbore **Weight:** 1.80 lbs. **Length:** 8.6 in. **Power:** CO2. **Sights:** Fixed blade and ramp. **Features:** Highly realistic replica-action pistol, 17-shot semi-automatic, full metal construction **Velocity:** To 320 fps.
Price: **$119.99**

BROWNING 800 EXPRESS AIR PISTOL BROWNING 800 EXPRESS
Caliber: .177 pellets. **Barrel:** Rifled **Weight:** 3.9 lbs. **Length:** 18 in. **Power:** Single cock, spring-piston. **Sights:** Fiber-optic front sight and adjustable fiber-optic rear sight. **Features:** Automatic safety, 11mm dovetail rail scope mounting possible. **Velocity:** 700 fps.
Price: **$168.00**

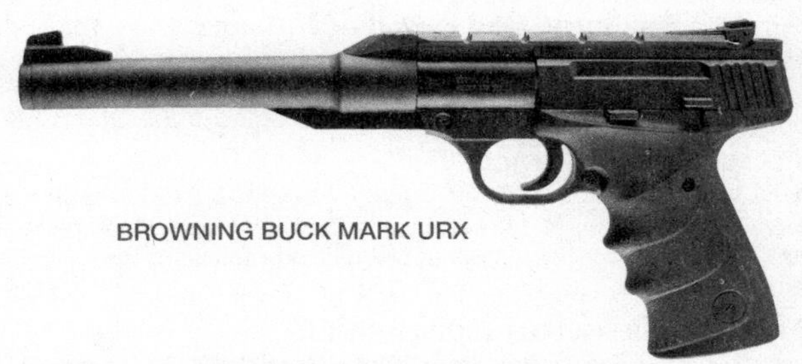
BROWNING BUCK MARK URX

BROWNING BUCK MARK URX AIR PISTOL BROWNING BUCK MARK AIR PISTOL
Caliber: .177 pellets. **Barrel:** Rifled **Weight:** 1.5 lbs. **Length:** 12.0 in. **Power:** Single cock, spring-piston. **Sights:** Front ramp sight, fully adjustable rear notch sight. **Features:** Weaver rail for scope mounting, light cocking force. **Velocity:** 360 fps.
Price: **$50.00**

COLT PYTHON

COLT PYTHON CO2 PISTOL
Caliber: .177 steel BBs. **Barrel:** Smoothbore **Weight:** 2.6 lbs. **Length:** 11.25 in. **Power:** CO2. **Sights:** Fixed. **Features:** High-quality replica, swing-out cylinder, removable casings and functioning ejector, multiple finishes other options. **Velocity:** To 400 fps.
Price: **$149.99**

COLT PYTHON 2.5-INCH CO2 PISTOL
Caliber: .177 steel BBs/.177 pellets. **Barrel:** Rifled **Weight:** 1.24 lbs. **Length:** 8.0 in. **Power:** CO2. **Sights:** Fixed front sight, rear sight adjustable for windage and elevation. **Features:** High-quality replica, 10-round magazine, swing-out cylinder. **Velocity:** To 375 fps.
Price: **$59.95**

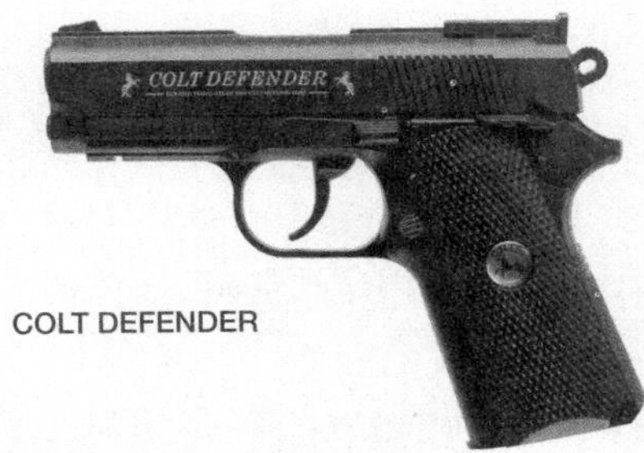

COLT DEFENDER

COLT DEFENDER BB PISTOL
Caliber: .177 steel BBs. **Barrel:** Smoothbore **Weight:** 1.6 lbs. **Length:** 6.75 in. **Power:** CO2. **Sights:** Fixed with blade ramp front sight. **Features:** Semi-automatic, 16-shot capacity, all metal construction, realistic weight and feel. **Velocity:** 410 fps.
Price: **$75.00**

COLT 1911 SPECIAL COMBAT CLASSIC BB PISTOL
Caliber: .177 steel BBs. **Barrel:** Smoothbore. **Weight:** 2.05 lbs. **Length:** 8.58 in. **Power:** CO2. **Sights:** Blade front sight and adjustable rear sight. **Features:** Semi-automatic, 20-shot capacity, realistic action, weight and feel. **Velocity:** 400 fps.
Price: **$120.00**

COLT 1911 A1 CO2 PELLET PISTOL
Caliber: .177 pellets. **Barrel:** Rifled **Weight:** 2.4 lbs. **Length:** 9.0 in. **Power:** CO2. **Sights:** Blade ramp front sight and adjustable rear sight. **Features:** Semi-automatic, 8-shot capacity, all metal construction, realistic weight and feel. **Velocity:** 425 fps.
Price: **$259.99**

COLT COMMANDER CO2 PISTOL
Caliber: .177 steel BBs. **Barrel:** Smoothbore. **Weight:** 2.1 lbs. **Length:** 8.5 in. **Power:** CO2. **Sights:** Blade front sight and fixed rear sight. **Features:** Semi-automatic, 18-shot capacity, highly realistic replica pistol. **Velocity**: 325 fps.
Price: **$119.99**

COLT PEACEMAKER SAA CO2 REVOLVER, NICKEL
Caliber: .177 steel BBs. **Barrel:** Smoothbore. **Weight:** 2.1 lbs. **Length:** 11 in. **Power:** CO2. **Sights:** Blade front sight and fixed rear sight. **Features:** Full metal revolver with manual safety, realistic loading, 6 individual shells, highly accurate, full metal replica pistol, multiple finishes, grips and custom engraved, special editions available. **Velocity:** 410 fps.
Price: **$149.99**

COLT SAA CO2 PELLET REVOLVER, NICKEL
Caliber: .177 pellets. **Barrel:** Rifled. **Weight:** 2.1 lbs. **Length:** 11 in. **Power:** CO2. **Sights:** Blade front sight and fixed rear sight. **Features:** Full metal revolver with manual safety, realistic loading, 6 individual shells, highly accurate, full metal replica pistol, multiple finishes and grips available. **Velocity:** 380 fps.
Price: **$179.99**

JOHN WAYNE "DUKE" COLT SINGLE ACTION ARMY CO2 PELLET REVOLVER
Caliber: .177 steel BBs. **Barrel:** Smoothbore. **Weight:** 2.1 lbs. **Length:** 11 in. **Power:** CO2. **Sights:** Blade front sight and fixed rear sight. **Features:** Officially licensed "John Wayne Duke" imagery and signature, full metal revolver with manual safety, realistic loading, 6 individual shells, highly accurate, full metal replica pistol, multiple finishes and grips available. **Velocity:** 380 fps.
Price: **$159.99**

COMETA INDIAN AIR PISTOL, NICKEL/BLACK
Caliber: .177 pellets. **Barrel:** Rifled. **Weight:** 2.43 lbs. **Length:** 10.43 in. **Power:**

Spring Powered. **Sights:** Blade front sight and adjustable rear sight. **Features:** Single shot, cold-hammered forged barrel, textured grips. **Velocity:** 492 fps.
Price: .... **$189.95–$219.95**

CROSMAN 2240
Caliber: .22. **Barrel:** Rifled. **Weight:** 1.8 lbs. **Length:** 11.13 in. **Power:** CO2. **Sights:** Blade front, rear adjustable. **Features:** Single shot bolt action, ambidextrous grip, all metal construction. **Velocity:** 460 fps.
Price: **$79.95**

CROSMAN 2300S TARGET PISTOL
Caliber: .177 pellets. **Barrel:** Rifled. **Weight:** 2.66 lbs. **Length:** 16 in. **Power:** CO2. **Sights:** Front fixed sight and Williams notched rear sight. **Features:** Meets IHMSA rules for Production Class Silhouette Competitions. Lothar Walter match-grade barrel, adjustable trigger, adjustable hammer, stainless steel bolt, 60 shots per CO2 cartridge. **Velocity:** 520 fps.
Price: **$320.00**

CROSMAN 2300T
Caliber: .177 pellets. **Barrel:** Rifled. **Weight:** 2.66 lbs. **Length:** 13.25 in. **Power:** CO2. **Sights:** fixed front sight and LPA rear sight. **Features:** Single-shot, bolt action, adjustable trigger, designed for shooting clubs and organizations that teach pistol shooting and capable of firing 40 shots per CO2 cartridge. **Velocity:** 420 fps.
Price: **$190.00**

CROSMAN SILHOUETTE PCP AIR PISTOL
Caliber: .177 pellets. **Barrel:** Rifled Lothar Walther Match. **Weight:** 2.5 lbs. **Length:** 14.75 in. **Power:** Pre-charged Pneumatic. **Sights:** fixed front sight rear sight not included Features: Adjustable trigger, designed for shooting silhouette competition, 50 shots per fill. **Velocity:** 450 fps.
Price: **$429.95**

CROSMAN 1720T PCP TARGET PISTOL
Caliber: .177 pellets. **Barrel:** Rifled Lothar Walther Match. **Weight:** 2.96 lbs. **Length:** 18.00 in. **Power:** Pre-charged Pneumatic. **Sights:** Not included **Features:** Adjustable trigger, designed for shooting silhouettes, fully shrouded barrel, 50 shots per fill. **Velocity:** 750 fps.
Price: **$500.00**

CROSMAN SR .357 Revolver
Caliber: .177 steel BBs. **Barrel:** Smoothbore. **Weight:** 2 lbs. **Length:** 11.5 in. **Power:** CO2. **Sights:** Blade front, rear adjustable. **Features:** Semi-auto 6-round revolver styling and finger-molded grip design. Multiple finishes and configurations available. **Velocity:** 450 fps.
Price: .... **$99.99–$129.99**

CROSMAN SR.357S DUAL AMMO CO2 REVOLVER
Caliber: .177 steel BBs/.177 pellets. **Barrel:** Smoothbore **Weight:** 2.00 lbs. **Length:** 11.73 in. **Power:** CO2. **Sights:** Adjustable rear sight, Fixed Front Blade. **Features:** Full metal revolver in "stainless steel" finish. Comes with shells for BBs and .177 lead pellets **Velocity:** up to 426 fps. with steel BBs.
Price: **$149.99**

CROSMAN C11 CO2 BB GUN
Caliber: .177 steel BBs. **Barrel:** Smoothbore **Weight:** 1.4 lbs. **Length:** 7.0 in. **Power:** CO2. **Sights:** Fixed. **Features:** Compact semi-automatic BB pistol, front accessory rail. **Velocity:** 480 fps.
Price: **$49.99**

CROSMAN C41 CO2 BB PISTOL
Caliber: .177 steel BBs. **Barrel:** Smoothbore **Weight:** 2 lbs. **Length:** 6.75 in. **Power:** CO2. **Sights:** Fixed. **Features:** Compact, realistic weight and feel. **Velocity**: To 450 fps.
Price: **$90.00**

CROSMAN PFM16 FULL METAL CO2 BB PISTOL
Caliber: .177 steel BBs. **Barrel:** Smoothbore **Weight:** 1.6 lbs. **Length:** 6.5 in. **Power:** CO2. **Sights:** Fixed. **Features:** Compact semi-automatic BB pistol, full metal construction, 20-shot capacity, kit includes: co2, BBs, and holster. **Velocity:** 400 fps.
Price: **$49.99**

CROSMAN 1377C / PC77, BLACK
Caliber: .177 pellets. **Barrel:** Rifled **Weight:** 2 lbs. **Length:** 13.63 in. **Power:** Multi-pump pneumatic. **Sights:** Front fixed sight and adjustable rear sight. **Features:** Single shot, bolt action. **Velocity:** 600 fps.
Price: **$76.95**

CROSMAN 1322 AIR PISTOL, BLACK
Caliber: .22. **Barrel:** Rifled **Weight:** 2 lbs. **Length:** 13.63 in. **Power:** Multi-pump pneumatic. **Sights:** Front Blade & Ramp. **Features:** Single shot, bolt action. **Velocity:** To 460 fps.
Price: **$76.95**

Prices given are believed to be accurate at time of publication however, many factors affect retail pricing so exact prices are not possible.

CROSMAN VIGILANTE CO2 REVOLVER
Caliber: .177 steel BBs/.177 pellets. **Barrel:** Rifled. **Weight:** 2 lbs. **Length:** 11.38 in. **Power:** CO2. **Sights:** Blade front, rear adjustable. **Features:** Single- and double-action revolver (10-shot pellet/6-shot BBs) synthetic frame and finger-molded grip design. **Velocity:** 465 fps.
Price: **$79.95**

CROSMAN GI MODEL 1911 CO2 BLOWBACK BB PISTOL
Caliber: .177 steel BBs. **Barrel:** Smoothbore. **Weight:** 1.88 lbs. **Length:** 8.63 in. **Power:** CO2. **Sights: Rear** Fixed sights **Front Blade. Features:** Full metal replica with realistic blowback, 20-round capacity, double-action only. **Velocity:** 450 fps.
Price: **$99.99**

DAISY POWERLINE 340 AIR PISTOL
Caliber: .177 steel BBs. **Barrel:** Smoothbore. **Weight:** 1.0 lbs. **Length:** 8.5 in. **Power:** Single cock, spring-piston. **Sights: Rear sight** Fixed **Front blade. Features:** Spring-air action, 200-shot BB reservoir with a 13-shot Speed-load Clip located in the grip. **Velocity:** 240 fps.
Price: **$23.99**

DAISY POWERLINE 415 CO2 BB PISTOL
Caliber: .177 steel BBs. **Barrel:** Smoothbore. **Weight:** 1.0 lbs. **Length:** 8.6 in. **Power:** CO2. **Sights:** Front blade, Rear fixed open rear. **Features:** Semi-automatic 21-shot BB pistol. **Velocity:** 500 fps.
Price: **$35.99**

DAISY POWERLINE 5170

DAISY POWERLINE 5170 AIRSTRIKE
Caliber: .177 steel BBs. **Barrel:** Smoothbore. **Weight:** 1.0 lbs. **Length:** 9.5 in. **Power:** CO2. **Sights:** Blade and ramp front, Fixed rear. **Features:** Semi-automatic, 21-shot capacity, upper and lower weaver rails for mounting sights and other accessories. **Velocity:** 520 fps.
Price: **$47.99**

DAISY POWERLINE 5501
Caliber: .177 steel BBs. **Barrel:** Smoothbore. **Weight:** 1.0 lbs. **Length:** 6.8 in. **Power:** CO2. **Sights:** Blade and ramp front, Fixed rear. **Features:** CO2 semi-automatic blowback action. 15-shot clip. **Velocity:** 430 fps.
Price: **$79.99**

DAN WESSON 2.5 in./4 in./6 in./8 in. PELLET REVOLVER
Caliber: .177 pellets. **Barrel:** Rifled. **Weights:** 1.65–2.29 lbs. **Lengths:** 8.3–13.3 in. **Power:** CO2. **Sights:** Blade front and adjustable rear sight. **Features:** Highly realistic replica revolver, multiple finishes and grip configurations, 6 realistic cartridges, includes a speed loader. **Velocities:** 318–426 fps.
Price: .... **$159.95–$199.95**

DAN WESSON 2.5 in./4 in./6 in./ 8 in. BB REVOLVER
Caliber: .177 steel pellets. **Barrel:** Smoothbore **Weights:** 1.65–2.29 lbs. **Lengths:** 8.27–13.3 in. **Power:** CO2. **Sights:** Blade front and adjustable rear sight. **Features:** Highly realistic replica revolver, multiple finishes and grip configurations, 6 realistic cartridges, includes a speed loader. **Velocities:** 318–426 fps.
Price: .... **$150.00–$199.95**

EVANIX HUNTING MASTER AR6 AIR PISTOL
Caliber: .22. **Barrel:** Rifled. **Weight:** 3.05 lbs. **Length:** 17.3 in. overall. **Power:** Pre-charged Pneumatic. **Sights:** Adjustable rear, blade front. **Features:** Checkered hardwood grips, 6-shot repeater with rotary magazine, single or double action, receiver grooved for scope **Velocity:** .22 cal. with 3,000 psi charge: 922 fps–685 fps.
Price: **$659.99**

EVANIX REX P AIR PISTOL
Calibers: .22, .22, .35 (9mm), .45. **Barrel:** Rifled. **Weight:** 4.00 lbs. **Length:** 20.7 in. overall. **Power:** Pre-charged Pneumatic. **Sights:** None. **Features:** Extremely compact and massively powerful, capable of putting out well over 120 ft-lbs at the muzzle in .45 caliber, truly effective hunting power in a tiny package **Velocity:** .22, 900 fps/.25, 810 fps/.35, 700 fps/.45, 635 fps.
Price: .... **$699.99–$799.99**

FWB P11 PICCOLO AIR PISTOL (LONG)
Caliber: .177 pellets. **Barrel:** Rifled. **Weight:** 1.6 lbs. **Length:** 13.58 in. **Power:** Pre-charged pneumatic. **Sights:** Front post, fully adjustable rear blade, **Features:** 10-Meter competition class pistol, meets ISSF requirements, highly adjustable match trigger, **Velocity:** 492 fps.
Price: **$1,600.00**

FWB P8X PCP 10-METER AIR PISTOL
Caliber: .177 pellets. **Barrel:** Rifled. **Weight:** 2.09 lbs. **Length:** 16.33 in. **Power:** Pre-charged pneumatic. **Sights:** Front post, fully adjustable rear blade. **Features:** 10-Meter competition class pistol with highly customizable grip system, meets ISSF requirements, highly adjustable match trigger. **Velocity:** 508 fps.
Price: **$2,073.89**

GAMO P-900 IGT AIR PISTOL
Caliber: .177 pellets. **Barrel:** Rifled. **Weight:** 1.3 lbs. **Length:** 12.6 in. **Power:** Single cock, gas-pistol. **Sights:** Fiber-optic front and fully adjustable fiber-optic rear sight. Features: Break-barrel single-shot, ergonomic design, rubberized grip. **Velocity:** 508 fps.
Price: **$79.95**

GAMO P-25 AIR PISTOL
Caliber: .177 pellets. **Barrel:** Rifled. **Weight:** 1.5 lbs. **Length:** 7.75 in. **Power:** CO2. **Sights:** Fixed. **Features:** Semi-automatic, 16-shot capacity, realistic blowback action. **Velocity:** 450 fps.
Price: **$109.95**

GAMO P-27 DUAL PELLET/BB AIR PISTOL

Caliber: .177 steel BBs, .177 pellets. **Barrel:** Smoothbore. **Weight:** 1.5 lbs. **Length:** 7.0 in. **Power:** CO2. **Sights:** Fixed. **Features:** Semi-automatic, 16-shot capacity, front accessory rail. **Velocity:** 430 fps.
Price: **$69.99**

GAMO PR-776 CO2 REVOLVER

Caliber: .177 pellets. **Barrel:** Rifled. **Weight:** 2.29 lbs. **Length:** 11.5 in. **Power:** CO2. **Sights:** Fixed front sight with fully adjustable rear sight. **Features:** All metal frame, comes with two 8-shot clips, double- and single-action **Velocity:** 438 fps.
Price: **$120.00**

GAMO PT-85 CO2 PISTOL

Caliber: .177 pellets. **Barrel:** Rifled. **Weight:** 1.5 lbs. **Length:** 7.8 in. **Power:** CO2. **Sights:** Fixed. **Features:** Semi-automatic, 16-shot capacity, realistic blowback action **Velocity:** 450 fps.
Price: **$119.95**

GAMO PT-85 BLOWBACK TACTICAL CO2 AIR PISTOL

Caliber: .177 pellets. **Barrel:** Rifled. **Weight:** 3.3 lbs. **Length:** 14.93 in. **Power:** CO2. **Sights:** Fixed/Red-dot optical sight included. **Features:** Semi-automatic design, compensator, rifled steel barrel, manual safety, 16-shot double magazine, quad rail, laser and light included. **Velocity:** 560 fps.
Price: **$159.99**

GLETCHER STECHKIN APS BLOWBACK CO2 BB PISTOL

Caliber: .177 steel BBs. **Barrel:** Smoothbore. **Weight:** 2.3 lbs. **Length:** 8.88 in. **Power:** CO2. **Sights:** Fixed **Features:** Full metal frame, highly realistic replica, 22-round magazine, double action and single action. **Velocities:** 361–410 fps.
Price: **$129.95**

GLETCHER GRACH NBB CO2 BB PISTOL

Caliber: .177 steel BBs. **Barrel:** Smoothbore. **Weight:** 2.12 lbs. **Length:** 7.75 in. **Power:** CO2. **Sights:** Fixed **Features:** Full metal frame, highly realistic replica, 18-round magazine, double action and single action. **Velocity:** 361 fps.
Price: **$129.95**

GLETCHER NGT F CO2 BB REVOLVER

Caliber: .177 steel BBs. **Barrel:** Smoothbore. **Weight:** 1.54 lbs. **Length:** 9.00 in. **Power:** CO2. **Sights:** Fixed **Features:** Full metal frame, highly realistic replica, 7-shot cylinder with realistic "shells," double action and single action, available in blued and polished silver finishes. **Velocity:** 403 fps.
Price: .... **$107.99–$124.99**

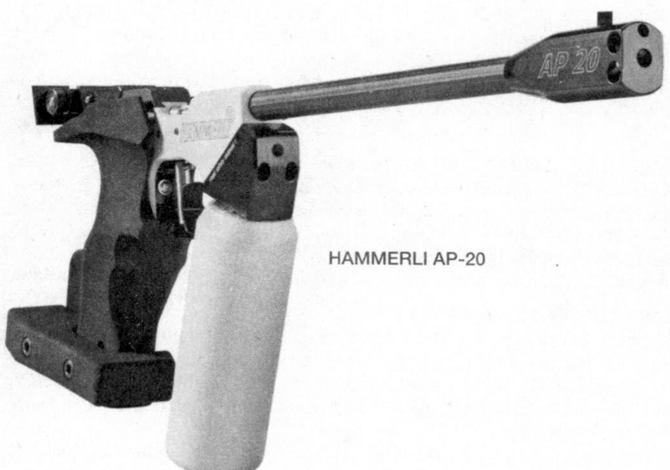

HAMMERLI AP-20

HAMMERLI AP-20 AIR PISTOL

Caliber: .177 pellets. **Barrel:** Rifled. **Weight:** 1.92 lbs. **Length:** 16.34 in. **Power:** Pre-charged pneumatic. **Sights:** Fully adjustable micrometer. **Features:** 2-stage adjustable trigger factory set to 500 grams pull weight, single shot, bolt action, up to 120 shots per fill. **Velocity:** 492 fps.
Price: **$999.99**

HATSAN USA MOD 25 SUPERCHARGER VORTEX PISTOL

HATSAN MODEL 25 SUPERCHARGER VORTEX AIR PISTOL

Caliber: .177 pellets. **Barrel:** Rifled. **Weight:** 3.9 lbs. **Length:** 11.2 in. **Power:** Single cock, air-piston **Sights:** Fiber-optic front and fully adjustable fiber-optic rear Sight. Features: Molded right-handed grips, left-handed grips available, fully adjustable "Quattro," integrated anti-recoil system. **Velocity:** 700 fps with lead pellets.
Price: **$189.99**

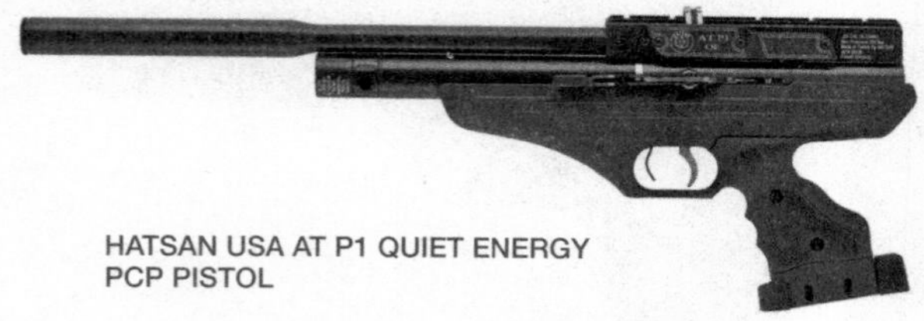

HATSAN USA AT P1 QUIET ENERGY PCP PISTOL

HATSAN USA AT P1 QUIET ENERGY PCP PISTOL

Calibers: .177, .22, .25. **Barrel:** Rifled. **Weight:** 4.7 lbs. **Length:** 23.2 in. **Power:** Pre-charged pneumatic. **Sights:** N/A. Grooved for scope mounting. **Features:** Multi-shot magazine feed, integrated suppressor, muzzle energy suitable for pest control and small game hunting. **Velocity:** .177, 870 fps/.22, 780 fps/.25, 710 fps.
Price: **$479.99**

H&K USP CO2 BB PISTOL

Caliber: .177 steel BBs. **Barrel:** Smoothbore. **Weight:** 1.35 lbs. **Length:** 7.5 in. **Power:** CO2. **Sights:** Fixed **Features:** Highly realistic replica, integrated front weaver accessory rail, 22-round magazine, double action only. **Velocity:** 360 fps.
Price: **$60.00**

HK45 CO2 BB

Caliber: .177 steel BBs. **Barrel:** Smoothbore. **Weight:** 1.4 lbs. **Length:** 8.0 in. **Power:** CO2. **Sights:** Fixed. **Features:** Highly realistic replica, integrated front weaver accessory rail, 20-shot capacity, double-action only. **Velocity:** 400 fps.
Price: **$54.99**

Prices given are believed to be accurate at time of publication however, many factors affect retail pricing so exact prices are not possible.

ISSC M-22 CO2 AIR PISTOL
Caliber: .177 steel BBs. **Barrel:** Smoothbore. **Weight:** 1.3 lbs. **Length:** 6.75 in. **Power:** CO2. **Sights:** Fixed front sight and adjustable rear sight. **Features:** Realistic replica, integrated front weaver accessory rail, 18-shot capacity, metal slide with blowback action. **Velocity:** 400 fps.
Price: **$110.00**

MARKSMAN 1010 Classic
Caliber: .177 steel BBs, .177 darts. **Barrel:** Smoothbore. **Weight:** 1.0 lbs. **Length:** (not provided). **Power:** Spring-piston. **Sights:** Blade front, adjustable rear. **Features:** 18-shot BB reservoir. **Velocity:** 200 fps.
Price: **$29.75**

MORINI MOR-162EL AIR PISTOL
Caliber: .177 pellets. **Barrel:** Rifled. **Weight:** 2.25 lbs. **Length:** 16.14 in. **Power:** Pre-charged pneumatic. **Sights:** Front post, rear adjustable for windage. **Features:** Adjustable electronic trigger, single-shot bolt action, extreme match grade accuracy, over 200 regulated shots per 200 bar fill. **Velocity:** 500 fps.
Price: **$2,200.00**

RED ALERT RD-1911 BLOWBACK CO2 BB PISTOL
Caliber: .177 steel BBs. **Barrel:** Smoothbore. **Weight:** 2.00 lbs. **Length:** 8.5 in. **Power:** CO2. **Sights:** Fixed. **Features:** Realistic replica action pistol modeled after the 1911, 20-round capacity, metal slide with blowback action. **Velocity:** 430 fps.
Price: **$79.99**

REMINGTON 1911 RAC
CO2 BB PISTOL

REMINGTON 1911 RAC CO2 BB PISTOL
Caliber: .177 steel BBs. **Barrel:** Smoothbore. **Weight:** 2.0 lbs. **Length:** 8.0 in. **Power:** CO2. **Sights:** Fixed. **Features:** All metal, blowback, extremely realistic replica pistol, bottom weaver/picatinny accessory rail. **Velocity:** 320 fps.
Price: **$111.98**

DIANA RWS LP8
Caliber: .177 pellets. **Barrel:** Rifled. **Weight:** 3.20 lbs. **Length:** 7.00 in. **Power:** Spring powered. **Sights:** Fixed front sight with fully adjustable rear sight. **Features:** Powerful spring powered air pistol, single cock delivers full power, exceptional design and build quality. **Velocity:** 700 fps.
Price: **$329.95**

SCHOFIELD NO. 3 BB REVOLVER, FULL METAL
Caliber: .177 steel BBs. **Barrel:** Smoothbore. **Weight:** 2.4 lbs. **Length:** 12.5 in. **Power:** CO2. **Sights:** Fixed. **Features:** Highly detailed replica revolver, 6-shot capacity, realistic reusable cartridges, available in black and nickel finishes. **Velocity:** 445 fps.
Price: .... **$99.95–$129.95**

SIG SAUER P226 X-FIVE .177 CO2 PISTOL, SILVER WITH WOOD GRIPS
Caliber: .177 steel BBs. **Barrel:** Smoothbore. **Weight:** 2.75 lbs. **Length:** 9.75 in. **Power:** CO2. **Sights:** Fixed. **Features:** Realistic replica action pistol, 18-shot capacity, front accessory rail, full metal construction, metal slide with blowback action. **Velocity:** 300 fps.
Price: **$159.95**

SIG SAUER 1911 METAL BLOWBACK CO2 BB PISTOL
Caliber: .177 steel BBs. **Barrel:** Smoothbore. **Weight:** 2.0 lbs. **Length:** (not provided) **Power:** CO2. **Sights:** Fixed. **Features:** Extremely Realistic replica action pistol, 18-shot capacity, front accessory rail, full metal construction, metal slide with blowback action. **Velocity:** 330 fps.
Price: **$149.95**

SIG SAUER P226 CO2 PELLET PISTOL, BLACK
Caliber: .177 pellets. **Barrel:** Rifled. **Weight:** 2.35 lbs. **Length:** 8.25 in. **Power:** CO2. **Sights:** Fixed. **Features:** Highly detailed replica action pistol, 16-shot capacity, front accessory rail, full metal construction, metal slide with blowback action, available in dark earth and black. **Velocity:** 450 fps.
Price: **$109.99**

SIG SAUER P250 CO2 PISTOL, METAL SLIDE, OD GREEN
Caliber: .177 pellets. **Barrel:** Rifled. **Weight:** (not provided) **Length:** (not provided) **Power:** CO2. **Sights:** Fixed. **Features:** Replica action pistol, 16-shot capacity, front accessory rail, polymer frame construction, metal slide with blowback action available in two tone OD green/black slide and all black. **Velocity:** 430 fps.
Price: **$88.95**

SIG SAUER MAX MICHEL 1911 FULL METAL CO2 BB PISTOL
Caliber: .177 steel BBs. **Barrel:** Smoothbore. **Weight:** 2.06 lbs. **Length:** 8.7 in. **Power:** CO2. **Sights:** Fixed. **Features:** Replica action pistol, 16-shot capacity, front accessory rail, all metal construction, metal slide with blowback action. **Velocity:** 410 fps.
Price: **$109.95**

SMITH & WESSON 586 & 686
Caliber: .177 pellets. **Barrel:** Rifled. **Weights:** Model 586 4 in. 2.50 lbs. / Model 586 & 686 6 in. 2.8 lbs. **Length:** Model 586 4-in. barrel - 9.5 in. - Model 586, 6 in. barrel - 11.50 in. / Model 686 6 in. barrel - 11.5 in. Power: CO2. **Sights:** Fixed front, adjustable rear **Features:** Extremely accurate, full metal, replica revolvers.
Price: 586 4-in. barrel. Velocity - 400 fps **$300.00**
Price: 586 6-in. barrel. Velocity - 425 fps **$295.95**
Price: 686 6-in. barrel. Velocity - 425 fps **$329.95**

Prices given are believed to be accurate at time of publication however, many factors affect retail pricing so exact prices are not possible.

SMITH & WESSON M&P 45 CO2 PISTOL
Caliber: .177 steel BBs. **Barrel:** Smoothbore. **Weight:** 1.35–1.61 lbs. **Lengths:** 7.5–8.10 in. **Power:** CO2. **Sights:** Blade front and ramp rear fiber optic. **Features:** Integrated accessory rail, drop-free 8- to 19-shot BB magazine, double-action only, synthetic frame available in dark earth brown or black color. Velocity: 300–480 fps.
Price: ....$39.99–$99.99

SMITH & WESSON M&P 40 CO2 BB PISTOL

SMITH & WESSON M&P 40 CO2 BB PISTOL
Caliber: .177 steel BBs. **Barrel:** Smoothbore. **Weight:** 1.61 lbs. **Length:** 7.75 in. **Power:** CO2. **Sights:** Fixed. **Features:** All-metal replica action pistol, blowback, 15-shot semi-automatic. **Velocity:** 300 fps.
Price: **$119.99**

SMITH & WESSON M&P 45 CO2 PISTOL
Caliber: .177 steel BBs, .177 pellets. **Barrel:** Rifled. **Weight:** 1.35 lbs. **Length:** 8.1 in. **Power:** CO2. **Sights:** Fixed front sight, fully adjustable rear sight. **Features:** Double and single action, 8-shot semi-automatic. **Velocity:** 370 fps.
Price: **$80.00**

SMITH & WESSON 327 TRR8 CO2 BB PISTOL
Caliber: .177 steel BBs. **Barrel:** Smoothbore. **Weight:** 2.0 lbs. **Length:** 12 in. **Power:** CO2. **Sights:** Fiber-optic front sight, fully adjustable fiber-optic rear sight. **Features:** High-quality replica, top-mounted weaver scope rail, weaver accessory rail under the barrel, swing-out cylinder, removable casings and functioning ejector. **Velocity:** 400 fps.
Price: **$120.00**

SMITH & WESSON DOMINANT TRAIT (TRR8) CO2 BB PISTOL
Caliber: .177 steel BBs. **Barrel:** Smoothbore. **Weight:** 2.0 lbs. **Length:** 12 in. **Power:** CO2. **Sights:** Fiber-optic front sight, fully adjustable fiber-optic rear sight. **Features:** High-quality replica, top-mounted weaver scope rail, weaver accessory rail under the barrel, swing-out cylinder, removable casings and functioning ejector, Includes speedloader, 6 shells, 12 Walther 12-gram CO2 cartridges & 1500 Walther steel BBs. **Velocity:** 400 fps.
Price: **$170.00**

TANFOGLIO WITNESS 1911 CO2 BB PISTOL, BROWN GRIPS
Caliber: .177 steel BBs. **Barrel:** Smoothbore. **Weight:** 1.98 lbs. **Length:** 8.6 in. **Power:** CO2. **Sights:** Fixed. **Features:** Often recognized as the "standard" for 1911 replica action pistols, 18-shot capacity, full metal construction with metal slide with blowback action. **Velocity:** 320 fps.
Price: **$119.99**

TANFOGLIO GOLD CUSTOM CO2 BLOWBACK BB PISTOL
Caliber: .177 steel BBs. **Barrel:** Smoothbore. **Weight:** 3.05 lbs. **Length:** 9.84 in. **Power:** CO2. **Sights:** None, weaver rail for optics. **Features:** Officially licensed, highly detailed replica action pistol, 20-shot capacity, custom accessory rail for dot sights and other optics, full metal construction with metal slide with blowback action, single action only. **Velocity:** 330 fps.
Price: **$189.95**

UMAREX LEGENDS MAKAROV ULTRA BLOWBACK CO2 BB PISTOL
Caliber: .177 steel BBs. **Barrel:** Smoothbore. **Weight:** 1.40 lbs. **Length:** 6.38 in. **Power:** CO2. **Sights:** Fixed. **Features:** Highly realistic replica, all-metal construction with blowback action, semi-automatic and fully-automatic capable, 16-round capacity. **Velocity:** 350 fps.
Price: **$119.95**

UMAREX LEGENDS M712 FULL-AUTO CO2 BB PISTOL
Caliber: .177 steel BBs. **Barrel:** Smoothbore. **Weight:** 3.10 lbs. **Length:** 12.00 in. **Power:** CO2. **Sights:** Fixed front sight with rear sight adjustable for elevation. **Features:** Highly realistic replica that functions as the original, all-metal construction with blowback action, semi-automatic and fully-automatic capable, 18-round capacity. **Velocity:** 360 fps.
Price: **$149.99**

UMAREX LEGENDS P08 BLOWBACK CO2 BB PISTOL
Caliber: .177 steel BBs. **Barrel:** Smoothbore. **Weight:** 1.90 lbs. **Length:** 8.75 in. **Power:** CO2. **Sights:** Fixed. **Features:** Highly realistic replica that functions as the original, all-metal construction with blowback action, 21-round capacity. **Velocity:** 300 fps.
Price: **$149.99**

Prices given are believed to be accurate at time of publication however, many factors affect retail pricing so exact prices are not possible.

UMAREX 9XP/40XP CO2 BB PISTOL METAL SLIDE

Caliber: .177 steel BBs. **Barrel:** Smoothbore. **Weight:** 1.5 lbs. **Length:** 7.5 in. **Power:** CO2. **Sights:** Fixed. **Features:** Realistic action pistol, 20-shot capacity, front accessory rail, metal/ABS construction. **Velocity:** 400 fps.

Price: **$69.99**

UMAREX BRODAX BB

Caliber: .177 steel BBs. **Barrel:** Smoothbore. **Weight:** 1.52 lbs. **Length:** 10.0 in. **Power:** CO2. **Sights:** Fixed. **Features:** Aggressively styled BB revolver, 10-shot capacity, top accessory rail, front accessory rail, synthetic construction. **Velocity:** 375 fps.

Price: **$42.99**

UMAREX MORPH 3X CO2 BB PISTOL/RIFLE

Caliber: .177 steel BBs. **Barrel:** Smoothbore. **Weight:** 2.5 lbs. **Length:** Up to 38.5 in. **Power:** CO2. **Sights:** Fixed fiber optic. **Features:** Convertible from pistol to short carbine to full rifle, 30-shot capacity, semi-automatic repeater, weaver top rail for optics. **Velocity:** 380 fps as pistol/600 fps as rifle.

Price: **$90.00**

UMAREX STRIKE POINT PELLET MULTI-PUMP AIR PISTOL

Caliber: .177 pellets. **Barrel:** Rifled. **Weight:** 2.6 lbs. **Length:** 14.00 in. **Power:** Multi-pump pneumatic. **Sights:** Adjustable rear sight, fixed fiber-optic front sight. **Features:** Variable power based on number of pumps, bolt action, includes integrated "silenceair" moderator for quite shooting. **Velocity:** Up to 650 fps.

Price: **$59.99**

UMAREX TREVOX AIR PISTOL

Caliber: .177 pellets. **Barrel:** Rifled. **Weight:** 3.5 lbs. **Length:** 18.25 in. **Power:** Gas Piston. **Sights:** Adjustable rear sight, fixed fiber-optic front sight. **Features:** full power from a single cock, suitable for target practice and plinking, includes integrated "silenceair" moderator for quite shooting. **Velocity:** 540 fps.

Price: **$89.95**

MINI UZI CARBINE

Caliber: .177 steel BBs. **Barrel:** Smoothbore. **Weight:** 2.45 lbs. **Length:** 23.5 in. **Power:** CO2. **Sights:** Fixed. **Features:** Realistic replica airgun, 28-shot capacity, foldable stock, semi-automatic with realistic blowback system, heavy bolt provides realistic "kick" when firing. **Velocity:** 390 fps.

Price: **$120.95**

UZI CO2 BB SUBMACHINE GUN

Caliber: .177 steel BBs. **Barrel:** Smoothbore. **Weight:** 4.85 lbs. **Length:** 23.5 in. **Power:** CO2. **Sights:** Fixed. **Features:** Realistic replica airgun, 25-shot capacity, foldable stock, semi-automatic and fully-automatic selectable fire, realistic blowback system. **Velocity:** 360 fps.

Price: **$199.99**

WALTHER CP88, BLUED, 4-INCH BARREL

Caliber: .177 pellets. **Barrel:** Rifled. **Weight:** 2.3 lbs. **Length:** 7 in. **Power:** CO2. **Sights:** Blade ramp front sight and adjustable rear sight. **Features:** Manual safety, semi-auto repeater, single or double action, available in multiple finishes and grip materials, 8-shot capacity. **Velocity:** 400 fps.

Price: .... **$229.99–$300.00**

WALTHER CP88, BLUED, 6-INCH BARREL

Caliber: .177 pellets. **Barrel:** Rifled. **Weight:** 2.5 lbs. **Length:** 9 in. **Power:** CO2. **Sights:** Blade ramp front sight and adjustable rear sight. **Features:** Manual safety, Semi-auto repeater, single or double action, available in multiple finishes and grip materials, 8-shot capacity. **Velocity:** 450 fps.

Price: .... **$229.95–$329.99**

WALTHER CP99 CO2 GUN, BLACK

Caliber: .177 pellets. **Barrel:** Rifled **Weight:** 1.6 lbs. **Length:** 7.1 in. **Power:** CO2. **Sights:** Fixed front and fully adjustable rear sight. **Features:** Extremely realistic replica pistol, single and double action, 8-shot rotary magazine. **Velocity:** 360 fps.

Price: **$200.00**

WALTHER CP99 COMPACT

WALTHER CP99 COMPACT & COMPACT NICKEL

Caliber: .177 steel BBs. **Barrel:** Smoothbore. **Weight:** 1.7 lbs. **Length:** 6.6 in. **Power:** CO2. **Sights:** Fixed front and rear. **Features:** Extremely realistic replica pistol, semi-automatic 18-shot capacity, available in various configurations including a nickel slide. **Velocity:** 345 fps.

Price: .... **$100.00–$105.99**

Prices given are believed to be accurate at time of publication however, many factors affect retail pricing so exact prices are not possible.

WALTHER PPQ

WALTHER PPQ / P99 Q CO2 PISTOL
Caliber: .177 steel BBs, .177 pellets. **Barrel:** Rifled **Weight:** 1.37 lbs. **Length:** 7.0 in. **Power:** CO2. **Sights:** Fixed front and fully adjustable rear sight. **Features:** Extremely realistic replica pistol, semi-automatic 8-shot rotary magazine. **Velocity:** 360 fps.
Price: **$70.00**

WALTHER P38 CO2 BB PISTOL
Caliber: .177 steel BBs. **Barrel:** Smoothbore. **Weight:** 1.9 lbs. **Length:** 8.5 in. **Power:** CO2. **Sights:** Fixed. **Features:** Authentic replica action pistol, blowback action, semi-automatic 20-shot magazine. **Velocity:** 400 fps.
Price: **$120.00**

WALTHER PPS

WALTHER PPS CO2 PISTOL
Caliber: .177 steel BBs. **Barrel:** Smoothbore. **Weight:** 1.2 lbs. **Length:** 6.38 in. **Power:** CO2. **Sights:** Fixed. **Features:** Authentic replica action pistol, blowback action, semi-automatic 18-shot capacity. **Velocity:** 350 fps.
Price: **$89.99**

WEIHRAUCH HW 75
Caliber: .177 pellets. **Barrel:** Rifled. **Weight:** 2.34 lbs. **Length:** 11.0 in. **Power:** Spring-powered. **Sights:** Fixed front sight with fully adjustable rear sight. **Features:** Single shot, designed precision shooting, beautifully crafted German airgun, two-stage adjustable trigger. **Velocity:** 410 fps.
Price: **$516.99**

WINCHESTER MODEL 11

WINCHESTER MODEL 11 BB PISTOL
Caliber: .177 steel BBs. **Barrel:** Smoothbore. **Weight:** 1.9 lbs. **Length:** 8.5 in. **Power:** CO2. **Sights:** Fixed. **Features:** All-metal replica action pistol, blowback action, 4-lb. 2-stage trigger, semi-automatic 15-shot capacity. **Velocity:** 410 fps.
Price: **$110.00**

AIR ARMS TX200 MKIII AIR RIFLE
Calibers: .177, .22. **Barrel:** Rifled, Lothar Walter match-grade, 13.19 in. **Weight:** 9.3 lbs. **Length:** 41.34 in. **Power:** Single cock, spring-piston **Stock:** Various; right- and left-handed versions, multiple wood options. Sights: 11mm dovetail. **Features:** Fixed barrel, heirloom quality craftsmanship, holds the record for the most winning spring powered airgun in international field target competitions. **Velocities:** .177, 930 fps/.22, 755 fps.
Price: .... **$699.99–$829.99**

AIR ARMS PRO-SPORT
Calibers: .177, .22. **Barrel:** Rifled, Lothar Walter match-grade, 9.5 in. **Weight:** 9.03 lbs. **Length:** 40.5 in. **Power:** Single cock, spring-piston **Stock:** Various; right-and left-handed versions, multiple wood options. Sights: 11mm dovetail. **Features:** Fixed barrel, Heirloom quality craftsmanship, unique inset cocking arm. **Velocities:** .177, 950 fps/.22, 750 fps.
Price: **$824.99–879.99**

AIR ARMS S510 XTRA FAC PCP AIR RIFLE
Calibers: .177, .22, .25. **Barrel:** Rifled, Lothar Walter match-grade, 19.45 in. **Weight:** 7.55 lbs. **Length:** 43.75 in. **Power:** Pre-charged pneumatic **Stock:** Right-handed, multiple wood options. Sights: 11mm dovetail. **Features:** Side-lever action, 10-round magazine, shrouded barrel, variable power, Heirloom quality craftsmanship **Velocities:** .177, 1,050 fps/.22, 920 fps/.25, 850 fps.
Price: **$1,199.99**

AIR ARMS S510 ULTIMATE SPORTER
Calibers: .177, .22, .25. **Barrel:** Rifled, Lothar Walter match-grade, 19.5 in. **Weight:** 8.6 lbs. **Length:** 44.25 in. **Power:** Pre-charged pneumatic **Stock:** Fully adjustable, ambidextrous laminate stock. Sights: 11mm dovetail. **Features:** Side-lever action, 10-shot magazine, integrated suppressor, variable power, Heirloom quality craftsmanship. **Velocities:** .177, 1,050 fps/.22, 920 fps/.25, 850 fps.
Price: **$1,699.99**

AIR ARMS S200 FT
Caliber: .177 pellets. **Barrel:** Rifled, match-grade, 19.09 in. **Weight:** 6.17 lbs. **Length:** 35.7 in. **Power:** Pre-charged pneumatic **Stock:** Ambidextrous hardwood stock. **Sights:** 11mm dovetail. **Features:** Single-shot, designed for international field target competition. **Velocity:** 800 fps.
Price: **$850.00**

AIR ARMS FTP 900 FIELD TARGET PCP AIR RIFLE
Caliber: .177. **Barrel:** Rifled, Lothar Walter match-grade, 19.0 in. **Weight:** 11.00 lbs. **Length:** 42.50 in. **Power:** Pre-charged pneumatic **Stock:** Fully adjustable competition style, available in right- or left-handed laminate stock. **Sights:** 11mm dovetail. **Features:** Side-lever action, single shot for maximum accuracy, integrated muzzle break, heirloom quality craftsmanship, regulated for supreme shot consistency, delivers up to 100 shots per fill. **Velocity:** 800 fps.
Price: **$2,799.99**

AIR ARMS GALAHAD RIFLE REG FAC
Calibers: .22, .25. **Barrel:** Rifled, Lothar Walter match-grade, 19.4 in. **Weight:** 8.6 lbs. **Length:** 35.5 in. **Power:** Pre-charged pneumatic. **Stock:** Ambidextrous bullpup stock available in "soft touch" synthetic over beech or walnut. Sights: 11mm dovetail. **Features:** Moveable side-lever action, 10-shot magazine, available with integrated moderator, variable power with integrated regulator, Heirloom quality craftsmanship. **Velocity:** .22, 900 fps/.25, 800 fps.
Price: .... **$1699.99–$1849.00**

AIR VENTURI WING SHOT AIR SHOTGUN
Caliber: .50. **Barrel:** Smoothbore 22.5 in. **Weight:** 7.4 lbs. **Length:** 43.0 in. **Power:** Pre-charged pneumatic. **Stock:** Ambidextrous wood stock. **Sights:** Fixed bead shotgun-style sight. **Features:** 244cc reservoir delivers several powerful shots, shoots shot cartridges and round ball, exceptionally reliable. **Velocity:** 1,130 fps.
Price: **$849.99**

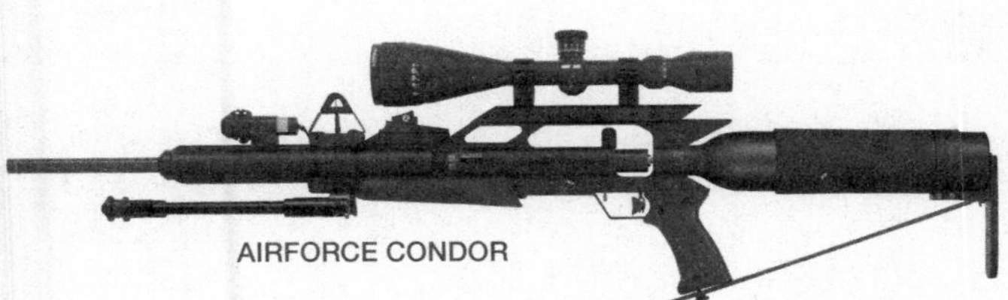
AIRFORCE CONDOR

AIRFORCE CONDOR RIFLE
Calibers: .177, .20, .22, .25. **Barrel:** Rifled, Lothar Walther match-grade, 24 in. **Weight:** 6.1 lbs. **Length:** 38.75 in. **Power:** Pre-charged pneumatic. **Stock:** Synthetic pistol grip, tank acts as buttstock. Sights: Grooved for scope mounting. **Features:** Single shot, adjustable power, automatic safety, large 490cc tank volume, extended scope rail allows easy mounting of the largest air-gun scopes, optional CO2 power system available, manufactured in the USA by AirForce Airguns. **Velocities:** .177, 1,450 fps/.20, 1,150 fps/.22, 1,250 fps/.25, 1,100 fps.
Price: **$744.95**

AIRFORCE CONDOR SS AIR RIFLE
Calibers: .177, .20, .22, .25. **Barrel:** Rifled, Lothar Walther match-grade, 18 in. **Weight:** 6.1 lbs. **Length:** 38.13 in. **Power:** Pre-charged pneumatic. **Stock:** Synthetic pistol grip, tank acts as buttstock. Sights: Grooved for scope mounting. **Features:** Fully shrouded barrel with integrated suppressor, single shot, adjustable power, automatic safety, large 490cc tank volume, extended scope rail allows easy mounting of the largest air-gun scopes, multiple color options available, optional CO2 power system available, manufactured in the USA by AirForce Airguns. **Velocities:** .177, 1,300 fps/.20, 1,000 fps/.22, 1,100 fps/.25, 950 fps.
Price: **$774.95**

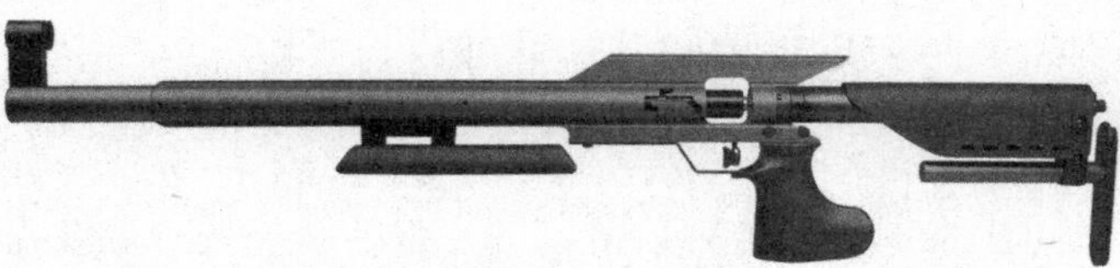

AIRFORCE EDGE 10-METER AIR RIFLE
Caliber: .177. **Barrel:** Rifled, Lothar Walther match-grade, 12 in. **Weight:** 6.1 lbs. **Length:** 40.00 in. **Power:** Pre-charged pneumatic. **Stock:** Synthetic pistol grip, tank acts as buttstock. Sights: Match front globe and rear micrometer adjustable diopter sight. **Features:** Single shot, automatic safety, two-stage adjustable trigger, accepted by CMP for completive shooting, available in multiple colors and configurations, manufactured in the USA by AirForce Airguns. **Velocity:** .530 fps.
Price: **$694.95**

AIRFORCE ESCAPE AIR RIFLE
Calibers: .22, .25. **Barrel:** Rifled, Lothar Walther match-grade, 24 in. **Weight:** 5.3 lbs. **Length:** 39.00 in. **Power:** Pre-charged pneumatic. **Stock:** Synthetic pistol grip, tank acts as buttstock. Sights: Grooved for scope mounting. **Features:** Single shot, adjustable power, automatic safety, extended scope rail allows easy mounting of the largest airgun scopes, manufactured in the USA by AirForce Airguns. **Velocities:** .22, 1,300 fps/.25, 1,145 fps.
Price: **$694.95**

AIRFORCE ESCAPE ss AIR RIFLE
Calibers: .22, .25. **Barrel:** Rifled, Lothar Walther match-grade, 12 in. **Weight:** 4.3 lbs. **Length:** 32.25 in. **Power:** Pre-charged pneumatic. **Stock:** Synthetic pistol grip, tank acts as buttstock. Sights: Grooved for scope mounting. **Features:** Fully shrouded barrel with integrated suppressor, single shot, adjustable power, automatic safety, extended scope rail allows easy mounting of the largest airgun scopes, manufactured in the USA by AirForce Airguns. **Velocities:** .22, 1,054 fps/.25, 900 fps.
Price: **$684.95**

AIRFORCE ESCAPE UL AIR RIFLE
Calibers: .22, .25. **Barrel:** Rifled, Lothar Walther match-grade, 18 in. **Weight:** 4.25 lbs. **Length:** 33.0 in. **Power:** Pre-charged pneumatic. **Stock:** Synthetic pistol grip, tank acts as buttstock. Sights: Grooved for scope mounting. **Features:** Single-shot, adjustable power, automatic safety, extended scope rail allows easy mounting of the largest airgun scopes, manufactured in the USA by AirForce Airguns. **Velocities:** .22, 1,200 fps/.25, 1,041 fps.
Price: **$642.95**

AIRFORCE TALON PCP AIR RIFLE
Calibers: .177, .22, .25. **Barrel:** Rifled, Lothar Walther match-grade, 18 in. **Weight:** 5.5 lbs. **Length:** 32.6 in. **Power:** Pre-charged pneumatic, **Stock:** Synthetic pistol grip, tank acts as buttstock. Sights: Grooved for scope mounting. **Features:** Single shot, adjustable power, automatic safety, large 490cc tank volume, extended scope rail allows easy mounting of the largest airgun scopes, optional CO2 power system available, manufactured in the USA by AirForce Airguns. **Velocities:** .177, 1,100 fps/.22, 950 fps/.25, 850 fps.
Price: **$609.95**

AIRGUNS Long Guns

AIRFORCE TALON SS PCP AIR RIFLE

Calibers: .177, .20, .22, .25. **Barrel:** Rifled, Lothar Walther match-grade, 12 in. **Weight:** 5.25 lbs. **Length:** 32.75 in. **Power:** Pre-charged pneumatic. **Stock:** Synthetic pistol grip, tank acts as buttstock. Sights: Grooved for scope mounting. **Features:** Fully shrouded barrel with integrated suppressor, single shot, adjustable power, automatic safety, large 490cc tank volume, extended scope rail allows easy mounting of the largest airgun scopes, multiple color options available, optional CO2 power system available, manufactured in the USA by AirForce Airguns. **Velocities:** .177, 1,000 fps/.20, 800 fps/.22, 800 fps/.25, 665 fps.

Price: **$652.95**

AIRFORCE TEXAN / TEXAN SS AIR RIFLE

Calibers: .30, .35, .45. **Barrel:** Rifled, 34.00 in. **Weight:** 7.65 lbs. **Length:** 48.00 in. **Power:** Pre-charged pneumatic. **Stock:** Synthetic pistol grip, tank acts as buttstock. Sights: Grooved for scope mounting. **Features:** Delivers massive energy and long-range accuracy, two-stage non-adjustable trigger, very easy to cock, open receiver accepts a vast selection of off the shelf or custom cast ammunition, available in a fully shrouded suppressed model, manufactured in the USA by AirForce Airguns. **Velocities:** .30, 1,100 fps, 300 ft-lbs/.35, 1,000 fps, 350 ft-lbs/.45, 1,000 fps 500 ft-lbs.

Price: .... **$1,054.95–$1210.95**

AIRFORCE INTERNATIONAL ORION AIR RIFLE

Calibers: .177, .22, .25. **Barrel:** Hammer forged barrel, 18.5 in. **Weight:** 7.25 lbs. **Length:** 41.00 in. **Power:** Pre-charged pneumatic. **Stock:** Right-handed hardwood stock with adjustable cheek riser. Sights: 11mm dovetail for scope mounting. **Features:** Multi-shot magazine varies on caliber, side-lever action, adjustable power and adjustable trigger. **Velocities:** .177, 1,000 fps/.22, 800 fps/.25, 600 fps.

Price: **$629.95**

ASG TAC-4.5 CO2 BB RIFLE

Caliber: .177 steel BBs. **Barrel:** Smoothbore. **Weight:** 3.5 lbs. **Length:** 36.0 in. **Power:** CO2 **Stock:** Synthetic thumbhole stock. **Sights:** Fixed fiber-optic front sight and fully adjustable fiber-optic rear sight/weaver rail for optics. **Features:** Semi-automatic action, includes bi-pod, 21-shot capacity. **Velocity:** 417 fps.

Price: **$119.99**

ATAMAN M2R CARBINE AIR RIFLE

Calibers: .177, .22, .25, .30, .35. **Barrel:** Lothar Walther rifled match-grade, 20.47 in. **Weight:** 8.82 lbs. **Length:** 43.31 in. **Power:** Pre-charged pneumatic. **Stock:** Ambidextrous stock available in various configurations and finishes. Sights: weaver rails for scope mounting. **Features:** Multi-shot side-lever action, shot capacity varies on caliber, adjustable match trigger, finely tuned regulator matched to optimal velocity in each caliber for maximum accuracy. **Velocities:** .177, 980 fps/.22, 980 fps/.25, 980 fps/.30, 984 fps/.35, 900 fps.

Price: .... **$1429.99–$1649.99**

ATAMAN M2R BULLPUP TYPE 1 & 2 AIR RIFLE

Calibers: .22, .25, .35. **Barrel:** Lothar Walther rifled match-grade, 20.47 in. **Weight:** 8.81 lbs. **Length:** 32.38 in. **Power:** Pre-charged pneumatic. **Stock:** Ambidextrous bullpup stock available in walnut or "soft touch" synthetic. Sights: Weaver rails for scope mounting. **Features:** Multi-shot side level action, shot capacity varies on caliber, adjustable match trigger, side-lever action, finely tuned regulator matched to optimal velocity in each caliber for maximum accuracy. **Velocities:** .22, 980 fps/.25, 980 fps/.35, 900 fps.

Price: **$1429.99–1649.99**

ATAMAN M2R CARBINE ULTRA COMPACT AIR RIFLE

Caliber: .22. **Barrel:** Lothar Walther rifled match-grade, 15.39 in. **Weight:** 6.17 lbs. **Length:** 36.48 in. **Power:** Pre-charged pneumatic. **Stock:** Ambidextrous adjustable/foldable stock available in walnut or "soft touch" synthetic. Sights: Weaver rails for scope mounting. **Features:** Multi-shot side-lever action, 10-shot capacity, adjustable match trigger, finely tuned regulator matched to optimal velocity. **Velocity:** 850 fps.

Price: **$1,319.99**

BEEMAN AR2079 CO2 TARGET AIR RIFLE

Calibers: .177, .22. **Barrel:** Rifled, 21.5 in. **Weight:** 7.80 lbs. **Length:** 39.5 in. **Power:** CO2. **Stock:** Biathlon-style beech, right-handed stock. **Sights:** Front globe with aperture inserts and diopter micrometer adjustable rear sight. Features: Single-shot bolt action, two-stage adjustable trigger, outstanding accuracy and performance to price point. **Velocities:** .177, 650 fps/.22, 450 fps.

Price: **$229.99**

BEEMAN HW100 s FSB PRECHARGE PNEUMATIC AIR RIFLE

Caliber: .177. **Barrel:** Rifled 23.63 in. **Weight:** 8.6 lbs. **Length:** 42.13 in. **Power:** Pre-charged pneumatic. **Stock:** Right-handed hardwood stock. **Sights:** Grooved for scope mounting. Features: Multi-shot side lever, 14 round magazine, shrouded barrel. **Velocity:** 1,135 fps.

Price: **$1,769.95**

BEEMAN RS-2 DUAL-CALIBER GAS RAM AIR RIFLE COMBO

Calibers: .177, .22. **Barrel:** Rifled. **Weight:** 6.9 lbs. **Length:** 45.5 in. **Power:** Break-barrel, gas-piston. **Stock:** Ambidextrous hardwood stock. **Sights:** Fiber-optic front and rear, includes 4x32 scope and rings. Features: Single-shot, easily exchangeable .177 and .22 cal. barrels, two-stage trigger. **Velocities:** .177, 1,000 fps/.22, 830 fps.

Price: **$179.99**

BEEMAN QUIET TEK DC DUAL CALIBER GAS RAM AIR RIFLE COMBO

Calibers: .177, .22. **Barrel:** Rifled. **Weight:** 6.7 lbs. **Length:** 47 in. **Power:** Break-barrel, spring-piston. **Stock:** Ambidextrous synthetic stock. **Sights:** None, grooved for scope mounting, includes 4x32 scope and rings. **Features:** Integrated suppressor, single shot, easily exchangeable .177- and .22-cal. barrels, two-stage trigger. **Velocities:** .177, 1,000 fps/.22, 830 fps.

Price: **$179.99**

BEEMAN MACH 12.5 AIR RIFLE, RS3 Trigger

Calibers: .177, .22. **Barrel:** Rifled **Weight:** 10 lbs. **Length:** 49 in. **Power:** Break-barrel, spring-piston. **Stock:** Ambidextrous hardwood stock. **Sights:** None, grooved for scope mounting, includes 3-9x40AO scope and rings. **Features:** Single shot, adjustable two-stage trigger. **Velocity:** .177, 1,250 fps/.22, 1,000 fps.

Price: **$269.99**

BEEMAN R7 AIR RIFLE

Calibers: .177, .20. **Barrel:** Rifled 13.5 in. **Weight:** 6.1 lbs. **Length:** 37 in. **Power:** Break-barrel, spring-piston. **Stock:** Ambidextrous walnut-stained beech, cut-checkered pistol grip, Monte Carlo comb and rubber buttpad. Sights: None, grooved for scope. **Features:** German quality, limited lifetime warranty, highly adjustable match-grade trigger, very easy to cock and shoot, extremely accurate. **Velocities:** .177, 700 fps/.20, 620 fps.

Price: .... **$329.99–$379.99**

BEEMAN R9 AIR RIFLE

Calibers: .177, .20, .22. **Barrel:** Rifled 16.33 in. **Weight:** 7.3 lbs. **Length:** 43 in. **Power:** Break-barrel, spring-piston. **Stock:** Ambidextrous walnut-stained beech, cut-checkered pistol grip, Monte Carlo comb and rubber buttpad. Sights: None, grooved for scope. **Features:** German quality, limited lifetime warranty, highly adjustable match-grade trigger, extremely accurate. **Velocities:** .177, 935 fps/.20, 800 fps/.22, 740 fps.

Price: .... **$439.99–$479.99**

BEEMAN RAM AIR RIFLE COMBO, RS2 TRIGGER

Calibers: .177, .22. **Barrel:** Rifled 20 in. **Weight:** 7.9 lbs. **Length:** 46.5 in. **Power:** Break-barrel, spring-piston. **Stock:** Ambidextrous hardwood stock. **Sights:** None, grooved for scope mounting, includes 3-9x32 scope and rings. **Features:** Muzzle brake for extra cocking leverage, single-shot, adjustable two-stage trigger. **Velocities:** .177, 1,000 fps/.22, 850 fps.

Price: **$220.00**

BEEMAN WOLVERINE CARBINE COMBO AIR RIFLE

Caliber: .177 pellets. **Barrel:** Rifled. **Weight:** 8.5 lbs. **Length:** 45.5 in. **Power:** Break-barrel, spring-piston. **Stock:** Ambidextrous synthetic stock. **Sights:** Fiber-optic front sight, fully adjustable fiber-optic rear sight, grooved for scope, includes 4x32 scope and mounts. **Features:** Single-shot, two-stage trigger. **Velocity:** 1,000 fps.

Price: **$129.99**

BEEMAN GUARDIAN COMBO AIR RIFLE

Caliber: .177 pellets. **Barrel:** Rifled. **Weight:** 5.85 lbs. **Length:** 37 in. **Power:** Break-barrel, spring-piston. **Stock:** Monte Carlo-style synthetic stock. **Sights:** None, grooved for scope, includes mounted 4x20 scope and mounts. **Features:** Lightweight youth airgun. **Velocity:** 550 fps.

Price: **$59.99**

Prices given are believed to be accurate at time of publication however, many factors affect retail pricing so exact prices are not possible.

BEEMAN SPORTSMAN RANGER COMBO AIR RIFLE
Caliber: .177 pellets. **Barrel:** Rifled. **Weight:** 4.15 lbs. **Length:** 40 in. **Power:** Break-barrel, spring-piston. **Stock:** Lightweight skeleton, synthetic stock. **Sights:** None, grooved for scope, includes 4x20 scope and mounts. Features: Lightweight youth airgun. **Velocity:** 480 fps.
Price: **$79.99**

BEEMAN SILVER KODIAK X2 COMBO AIR RIFLE
Calibers: .177, .22. **Barrel:** Rifled. **Weight:** 8.75 lbs. **Length:** 47.75 in. **Power:** Break-barrel, spring-piston. **Stock:** Ambidextrous synthetic stock. **Sights:** None includes 4x32 scope and rings. **Features:** Satin finish nickel plated receiver and barrels, single-shot, easily exchangeable .177 and .22 cal barrels, two-stage trigger. **Velocities:** .177, 1,000 fps/.22, 830 fps.
Price: **$169.99**

BEEMAN HW97K AIR RIFLE
Caliber: .20. **Barrel:** Rifled 11.81 in. **Weight:** 9.2 lbs. **Length:** 40.25 in. **Power:** Under-lever, spring-piston. **Stock:** Ambidextrous beech stock with checkering on the forearm and grip. **Sights:** None, grooved for scope. **Features:** German quality, limited lifetime warranty, highly adjustable match-grade trigger. Extremely accurate fixed barrel design. **Velocity:** 820 fps.
Price: **$749.95**

BEEMAN HW97K THUMBHOLE STOCK AIR RIFLE
Caliber: .20. **Barrel:** Rifled 11.81 in. **Weight:** 9.37 lbs. **Length:** 40.35 in. **Power:** Under-lever, spring-piston. **Stock:** Ambidextrous thumbhole beech stock with checkering on the fore-end and grip. **Sights:** None, grooved for scope. **Features:** German quality, limited lifetime warranty, highly adjustable match-grade trigger. Extremely accurate fixed barrel design. **Velocity:** 820 fps.
Price: **$890.00**

BEEMAN HW97K BLUE AIR RIFLE
Caliber: .20. **Barrel:** Rifled 11.81 in. **Weight:** 9.2 lbs. **Length:** 40.25 in. **Power:** Under-lever, spring-piston. **Stock:** Right-handed blue laminate stock with checkering on the fore-end and grip. Sights: None, grooved for scope. **Features:** German quality, limited lifetime warranty, highly adjustable match-grade trigger. Extremely accurate fixed barrel design. **Velocity:** 820 fps.
Price: **$869.95**

BENJAMIN 329 / 397 AIR RIFLE
Calibers: .177, .22. **Barrel:** Rifled 19.25 in. **Weight:** 5.5 lbs. **Length:** 36.25 in. **Power:** Multi-pump Pneumatic. **Stock:** Ambidextrous wood stock. **Sights:** Front ramp and adjustable rear sight. **Features:** Multi-pump system provides variable power, single-shot bolt action. **Velocities:** .177, 800 fps/.20, 685 fps.
Price: **$200.00**

BENJAMIN ARMADA, BASE, TACTICAL, & MAGPUL EDITION AIR RIFLE

BENJAMIN ARMADA
Calibers: .177, .22, .25. **Barrel:** Rifled, 20 in. **Weight:** 7.3 lbs. (10.3 lbs. with scope and bipod). **Length:** 42.8 in. **Power:** Pre-charged pneumatic. **Stock:** Adjustable mil-spec AR-15-style buttstock, all metal M-LOK compatible handguard with 15 in. of picatinny rail space. **Sights:** None, weaver/Picatinny rail for scope mounting. **Features:** Fully shrouded barrel with integrated suppressor, depinger device, bolt action, multi shot, choked barrel for maximum accuracy. **Velocities:** .177, 1,100 fps/.22, 1,000 fps/.25, 900 fps.
Price: **$750.00**

BENJAMIN BULLDOG .357 BULLPUP

BENJAMIN BULLDOG .357 BULLPUP
Caliber: .357. **Barrel:** Rifled 28 in. **Weight:** 7.7 lbs. **Length:** 36 in. **Power:** Pre-charged pneumatic. **Stock:** Synthetic bullpup stock with pistol grip. **Sights:** Full top Picatinny rail. **Features:** Innovative bullpup design, massive power output of up to 180 ft-lbs, 5-shot magazine, shrouded barrel for noise reduction, large cylinder delivers up to 10 usable shots, available in multiple bundled configurations and stock finishes. **Velocity:** Up to 900 fps based on the weight of the projectile.
Price: **$1,099.99**

BENJAMIN DISCOVERY PCP AIR RIFLE AND PUMP
Calibers: .177, .22. **Barrel:** Rifled 24.25 in. **Weight:** 5.2 lbs. **Length:** 39.0 in. **Power:** Pre-Charged Pneumatic/CO2. **Stock:** Ambidextrous hardwood stock. **Sights:** Front fiber-optic and adjustable rear fiber-optic sight/grooved 11mm dovetail for scope mounting. **Features:** Dual fuel allows this to run on HPA or bulk fill CO2, turn-key PCP package with included 3-stage hand pump, built in pressure gauge. **Velocities:** .177, 1,000 fps/.22, 900 fps.
Price: **$479.99**

BENJAMIN EVA SHOCKEY GOLDEN EAGLE (NP2) AIR RIFLE
Caliber: .177. **Barrel:** Rifled. **Weight:** 8 lbs. **Length:** 45.8 in. **Power:** Break-barrel, 2nd generation gas-piston. **Stock:** Ambidextrous synthetic stock. **Sights:** None, Weaver/Picatinny rail for scope mounting, includes Crosman CenterPoint 4x32 scope and mounts. **Features:** Very quiet due to the shrouded barrel with integrated suppressor, extremely easy cocking, single-shot, advanced adjustable two-stage trigger, innovative sling mounts for optional Benjamin break-barrel rifle sling. **Velocity:** 1,400 fps.
Price: **$249.99**

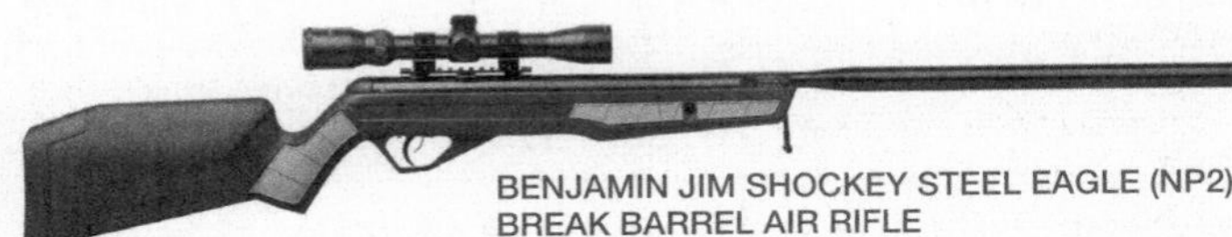
BENJAMIN JIM SHOCKEY STEEL EAGLE (NP2) BREAK BARREL AIR RIFLE

BENJAMIN JIM SHOCKEY STEEL EAGLE (NP2) BREAK BARREL AIR RIFLE
Caliber: .22. **Barrel:** Rifled. **Weight:** 8 lbs. **Length:** 45.8 in. **Power:** Break-barrel, 2nd generation gas-piston. **Stock:** Ambidextrous synthetic stock **Sights:** None, Weaver/Picatinny rail for scope mounting, includes Crosman CenterPoint 3-9x32 scope and mounts. **Features:** Very quiet due to the shrouded barrel with integrated suppressor, extremely easy cocking, single shot, advanced adjustable two stage trigger, innovative sling mounts for optional Benjamin break-barrel rifle sling. **Velocity:** 1,100 fps.
Price: **$279.99**

BENJAMIN MARAUDER PCP AIR RIFLE
Caliber: .177, .22, .25. **Barrel:** Rifled 20 in. **Weight:** Synthetic 7.3 lbs./Hardwood 8.2 lbs. **Length:** 42.8 in. **Power:** Pre-charged pneumatic. **Stock:** Ambidextrous stock available in hardwood or synthetic, adjustable cheek riser. **Sights:** None, grooved for scope mounting. **Features:** Multi-shot bolt action, 10-shot in .177 and .22, 8-shot in .25, user-adjustable performance settings for power and shot count. **Velocities:** .177, 1,100 fps/.22, 1,000 fps/.25, 900 fps.
Price: .... **$579.99–$599.99**

BENJAMIN PIONEER AIRBOW
Caliber: Requires Special Arrows. **Barrel:** Smoothbore. **Weight:** 7.00 lbs. **Length:** 33.5 in. **Power:** Pre-charged pneumatic. **Stock:** Synthetic bullpup stock with pistol grip. **Sights:** Full top Picatinny rail. **Features:** Highly innovative arrow system fires broadhead equipped arrows at up to 450 fps generating 168 ft-lbs of energy. **Velocity:** 450 fps.
Price: **$999.99**

AIRGUNS Long Guns

BENJAMIN TITAN GP BREAK BARREL AIR RIFLE
Calibers: .177, .22. **Barrel:** Rifled 15 in. **Weight:** 6.75 lbs. **Length:** 43.5 in. **Power:** Break-barrel, gas-piston. **Stock:** Ambidextrous thumbhole wood stock with dual raised cheekpieces. Sights: none, grooved for scope mounting, includes 4x32 scope and rings. **Features:** Muzzle brake for extra cocking leverage, single-shot, adjustable two-stage trigger. **Velocities:** .177, 1,200 fps/.22, 950 fps.
Price: **$199.99**

BENJAMIN TRAIL NITRO PISTON 2 (NP2) BREAK BARREL AIR RIFLE
Calibers: .177, .22. **Barrel:** Rifled 15.75 in. **Weight:** 8.3 lbs. **Length:** 46.25 in. **Power:** Break-barrel, 2nd generation gas-piston. **Stock:** Ambidextrous thumbhole stock available in wood and synthetic options as well as multiple finishes and patterns. **Sights:** None, picatinny rail for scope mounting, multiple Crosman CenterPoint scope options available as factory bundles. **Features:** Very quiet due to the shrouded barrel with integrated suppressor, extremely easy cocking, single-shot, advanced adjustable two-stage trigger, innovative sling mounts for optional Benjamin break-barrel rifle sling. **Velocities:** .177, 1,400 fps/.22, 1,100 fps.
Price: .... **$295.95–$349.95**

BENJAMIN TRAIL NITRO PISTON 2 (NP2) SBD BREAK BARREL AIR RIFLE
Calibers: .177, .22. **Barrel:** Rifled 15.75 in. **Weight:** 8.3 lbs. **Length:** 45.6 in. **Power:** Break-barrel, 2nd generation gas-piston. **Stock:** Ambidextrous thumbhole stock available in wood and synthetic options as well as multiple finishes and patterns. **Sights:** None, Picatinny rail for scope mounting, multiple Crosman CenterPoint scope options available as factory bundles. **Features:** Newly introduced SBD integrated suppressor does not interfere with scope sight picture, extremely easy cocking, single-shot, advanced adjustable two-stage trigger, innovative sling mounts for optional Benjamin break-barrel rifle sling. **Velocities:** .177, 1,400 fps/.22, 1,100 fps.
Price: .... **$299.95–$339.99**

BENJAMIN MAXIMUS PCP AIR RIFLE
Calibers: .177, .22. **Barrel:** Rifled 26.25 in. **Weight:** 5.0 lbs. **Length:** 41.7 in. **Power:** Pre-Charged Pneumatic. **Stock:** Ambidextrous synthetic stock. **Sights:** Front Fiber-optic and adjustable rear fiber-optic sight/grooved 11mm dovetail for scope mounting. **Features:** HPA required only 2000 psi to operate, built in pressure gauge. **Velocities:** .177, 1,000 fps/.22, 850 fps.
Price: **$249.99**

BENJAMIN VARMINT POWER PACK
Caliber: .22. **Barrel:** Rifled. **Weight:** 7.38 lbs. **Length:** 44.5 in. **Power:** Break-barrel, gas-piston. **Stock:** Ambidextrous synthetic stock. **Sights:** none, Weaver rail for scope mounting, includes a Crosman CenterPoint 4x32 scope with laser and light attachments complete with intermittent pressure switches. **Features:** Shrouded barrel, easy cocking, single-shot, adjustable two-stage trigger. **Velocity:** 950 fps.
Price: **$249.95**

BENJAMIN WILDFIRE SEMI-AUTOMATIC PCP AIR RIFLE
Caliber: .177. **Barrel:** Rifled 20.39 in. **Weight:** 3.69 lbs. **Length:** 36.88 in. **Power:** Pre-Charged Pneumatic. **Stock:** Ambidextrous synthetic stock. **Sights:** Front fiber- optic and adjustable rear sight/grooved 11mm dovetail for scope mounting. **Features:** HPA required only 2000 psi to operate, built in pressure gauge, 12-shot semi-automatic system, double-action only. **Velocity:** .177, 800 fps.
Price: **$199.99**

BERETTA CX4 STORM

BERETTA CX4 STORM
Caliber: .177 pellets. **Barrel:** Rifled 17.5 in. **Weight:** 5.25 lbs. **Length:** 30.75 in. **Power:** CO2. **Stock:** Synthetic thumbole. **Sights:** Adjustable front and rear. **Features:** Multi-shot semi-automatic with 30-round belt-fed magazine, highly realistic replica, utilizes large 88/90 gram disposable CO2 canisters for high shot count and uninterrupted shooting sessions. Available bundled with a Walther red-dot optics. **Velocity:** 600 fps.
Price: .... **$375.95–$400.00**

BLACK OPS TACTICAL SNIPER GAS-PISTON AIR RIFLE
Calibers: .177, .22. **Barrel:** Rifled. **Weight:** 9.6 lbs. **Length:** 44.0 in. **Power:** Break-barrel, gas-piston. **Stock:** Ambidextrous pistol grip synthetic stock. **Sights:** none, Weaver rail for scope mounting, includes a 4x32 scope. **Features:** Muzzle break helps with cocking force, single-shot, single cock delivers maximum power, adjustable single-stage trigger. **Velocity:** .177, 1,250 fps/.22, 1,000 fps.
Price: .... **$179.99–$199.99**

BLACK OPS JUNIOR SNIPER AIR RIFLE COMBO
Caliber: .177 steel BBs, .117 pellets. **Barrel:** Rifled. **Weight:** 4.41 lbs. **Length:** 39.37 in. **Power:** Multi-pump pneumatic. **Stock:** Ambidextrous pistol grip synthetic stock. **Sights:** Fiber-optic front and rear fiber-optic sights, 11mm rail for scope mounting, includes a 4-15 scope. **Features:** Multi-pump system delivers variable power, single-shot, single cock delivers maximum power, adjustable single-stage trigger. **Velocity:** 675 fps.
Price: **$69.99**

BROWNING LEVERAGE AIR RIFLE
Calibers: .177, .22. **Barrel:** Rifled 18.9 in. **Weight:** 8.6 lbs. **Length:** 44.8 in. **Power:** Under-lever cock, spring-piston **Stock:** Hardwood right handed with raised cheekpiece. **Sights:** Front fiber-optic sight and fully adjustable rear fiber-optic sight, Weaver/Picatinny rail for scope mounting, includes 3-9x40 scope. **Features:** Fixed barrel accuracy, easy cocking, two-stage trigger. **Velocities:** .177, 1,000 fps/.22, 800 fps.
Price: **$230.00**

BSA METEOR EVO AIR RIFLE
Calibers: .177, .22. **Barrel:** Rifled 17.5 in. **Weight:** 6.1 lbs. **Length:** 43.5 in. **Power:** Break-barrel, spring-piston. **Stock:** Ambidextrous beech stock. **Sights:** Front fiber-optic sight and fully adjustable rear fiber-optic sight grooved for scope mounting. **Features:** European quality, fitted with BSA-Made cold hammer forged barrel known for precision and accuracy, adjustable two-stage trigger, single-shot, manufactured to stringent quality control and testing. **Velocities:** .177, 950 fps/.22, 722 fps.
Price: **$199.99**

BSA R-10 MK2 PCP AIR RIFLE

BSA R-10 MK2 PCP AIR RIFLE
Calibers: .177, .22. **Barrel:** Rifled, BSA-made cold hammer forged precision barrel, 18 in. **Weight:** 7.3 lbs. **Length:** 43 in. **Power:** Pre-charged pneumatic. **Stock:** Right-hand, walnut stock or right-hand soft-touch coated beech. **Sights:** None, grooved for scope mounting. **Features:** Multi-shot bolt action, 10-shot magazine, fully regulated valve for maximum accuracy and shot consistency, free-floating, shrouded barrel. **Velocities:** .177, 1,000 fps/.22, 900 fps.
Price: **$1,299.99**

Prices given are believed to be accurate at time of publication however, many factors affect retail pricing so exact prices are not possible.

BSA BUCCANEER SE AIR RIFLE

Calibers: .177, .22. **Barrel:** Rifled, BSA-made cold hammer forged precision barrel, 24 in. **Weight:** 7.7 lbs. **Length:** 42.5 in. **Power:** Pre-charged pneumatic. **Stock:** Ambidextrous beech stock or hardwood stock wrapped in innovative black soft-touch. **Sights:** None, grooved for scope mounting. **Features:** Multi-shot bolt action, 10-shot magazine, enhanced valve system for maximum shot count and consistency, integrated suppressor, adjustable two-stage trigger. **Velocities:** .177, 1,000 fps/.22, 800 fps.

Price: .... $649.99–$749.99

BSA GOLD STAR SE HUNTER FIELD TARGET PCP AIR RIFLE

Caliber: .177. **Barrel:** Rifled, BSA-made enhanced cold hammer forged precision barrel, 15.2 in. **Weight:** 7 lbs. **Length:** 35.8 in. **Power:** Pre-charged pneumatic. **Stock:** Highly adjustable gray laminate field target competition stock. **Sights:** None, grooved for scope mounting. **Features:** Multi-shot bolt action, 10-shot magazine, fully regulated valve for maximum accuracy and shot consistency, 70 consistent shots per charge, free-floating barrel with 1/2 UNF threaded muzzle, includes adjustable air stripper, adjustable match-grade trigger. **Velocity:** 800 fps.

Price: $1,949.95

BSA SCORPION 1200 SE AIR RIFLE

BSA SCORPION 1200 SE AIR RIFLE

Calibers: .177, .22. **Barrel:** Rifled, BSA-made cold hammer forged free-floating shrouded recision barrel, 24 in. **Weight:** 87.5 lbs. **Length:** 44.5 in. **Power:** Pre-charged pneumatic. Stock: Ambidextrous synthetic. **Sights:** None, grooved for scope mounting. **Features:** Multi-shot bolt action, 10-shot magazine, enhanced valve system for maximum shot count and consistency up to 80 shots in .177, 45 in .22, adjustable two-stage trigger. **Velocities:** .177, 1,200 fps/.22, 1000 fps.

Price: $979.95

CROSMAN CHALLENGER PCP COMPETITION

CROSMAN CHALLENGER PCP COMPETITION AIR RIFLE

Caliber: .177. **Barrel:** Match-grade Lothar Walther rifled barrel. **Weight:** 7.3 lbs. **Length:** 41.75 in. **Power:** Pre-charged pneumatic/CO2. **Stock:** Highly adjustable synthetic competition stock. **Sights:** Globe front sight and Precision Diopter rear sight. **Features:** Innovative dual fuel design allows this rifle to run on HPA or CO2, single-shot, adjustable match-grade trigger, approved by the Civilian Marksmanship Program (CMP) for 3-position air rifle Sporter Class competition. **Velocity:** 530 fps.

Price: $600.00

CROSMAN GENESIS NP AIR RIFLE

Caliber: .22. **Barrel:** Rifled. **Weight:** 7.44 lbs. **Length:** 44.5 in. **Power:** Break-barrel, gas-piston. **Stock:** Ambidextrous wood stock with dual raised cheekpieces and checkered grip and forearm. **Sights:** None, Weaver/Picatinny rail for scope mounting, includes 4x32 scope and rings. **Features:** Shrouded barrel with integrated suppressor, extremely easy cocking, single-shot, adjustable two-stage trigger, innovative sling mounts for optional Benjamin break-barrel rifle sling. **Velocity:** 950 fps.

Price: $229.99

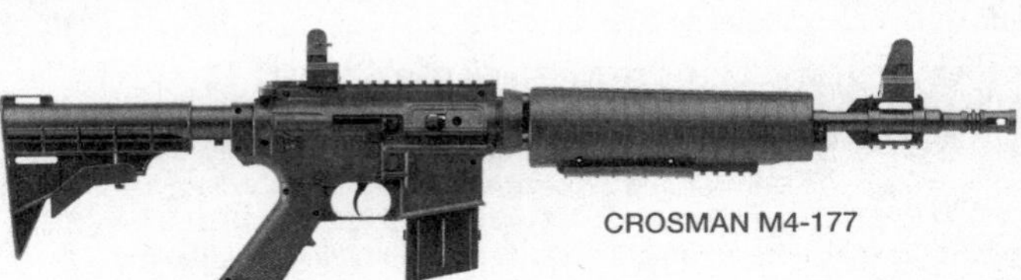

CROSMAN M4-177

CROSMAN M4-177 (various styles and kits available)

Caliber: .177 steel BBs, .177 pellets. **Barrel:** Rifled 17.25 in. **Weight:** 3.75 lbs. **Length:** 33.75 in. **Power:** Multi-pump pneumatic. **Stock:** M4-style adjustable plastic stock. **Sights:** Weaver/Picatinny rail for scope mounting and flip-up sights. Bundled packages include various included sighting options. **Features:** Single-shot bolt action, lightweight and very accurate, multiple colors available. "Ready to go" kits available complete with ammo, safety glasses, targets and extra 5-shot pellet magazines. **Velocity:** 660 fps.

Price: .... $110.00–$149.95

CROSMAN MODEL 760 PUMPMASTER AIR RIFLE

Caliber: .177 steel BBs, .177 pellets. **Barrel:** Rifled 16.75 in. **Weight:** 2.75 lbs. **Length:** 33.5 in. **Power:** Multi-pump pneumatic. **Stock:** Ambidextrous plastic stock. **Sights:** Blade and ramp, rear sight adjustable for elevation, grooved for scope mounting. **Features:** Single-shot pellet, BB repeater, bolt action, lightweight, accurate and easy to shoot. Multiple colors available and configurations available. "Ready to go" kits available complete with ammo, safety glasses, targets and extra 5-shot pellet magazines. **Velocity:** 625 fps.

Price: .... $50.00–$60.00

CROSMAN 1077 AIR RIFLE

Caliber: .177 pellets. **Barrel:** Rifled 20.38 in. **Weight:** 3.75 lbs. **Length:** 36.88 in. **Power:** CO2. **Stock:** Ambidextrous plastic stock. **Sights:** Blade and ramp, rear sight adjustable for windage and elevation, grooved for scope mounting. **Features:** Multi-shot, semi-automatic, 12-shot magazine, lightweight, fun and easy to shoot. "Ready to go" kits available complete with ammo, CO2, targets, target trap, etc. **Velocity:** 625 fps.

Price: .... $94.95–$120.00

CROSMAN 2100B CLASSIC AIR RIFLE

Caliber: .177 steel BBs, .177 pellets. **Barrel:** Rifled 20.84 in. **Weight:** 4.81 lbs. **Length:** 39.75 in. **Power:** Multi-pump pneumatic. **Stock:** Ambidextrous plastic stock with simulated wood grain. Sights: Blade and ramp, rear sight adjustable for windage and elevation, grooved for scope mounting. **Features:** Adult-size inexpensive airgun, single-shot, bolt action, lightweight, accurate and easy to shoot. **Velocity:** 755 fps.

Price: $79.95

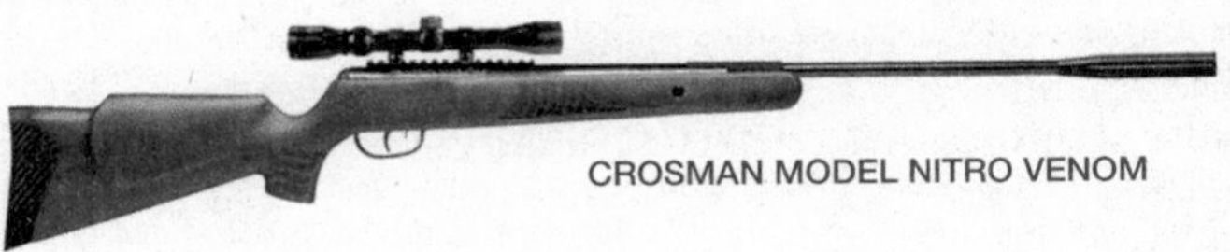

CROSMAN MODEL NITRO VENOM

CROSMAN NITRO VENOM AIR RIFLE

Caliber: .177, .22. **Barrel:** Rifled 18.63 in. **Weight:** 7.4 lbs. **Length:** 44.25 in. **Power:** Break-barrel, gas-piston. **Stock:** Ambidextrous wood stock with dual raised cheekpieces and checkered grip and forearm. Sights: None, Weaver/Picatinny rail for scope mounting, includes 3-9x32 scope and rings. **Features:** Muzzle break action for extra cocking leverage, single-shot, adjustable two-stage trigger. **Velocities:** .177, 1,200 fps/.22, 950 fps.

Price: $220.00

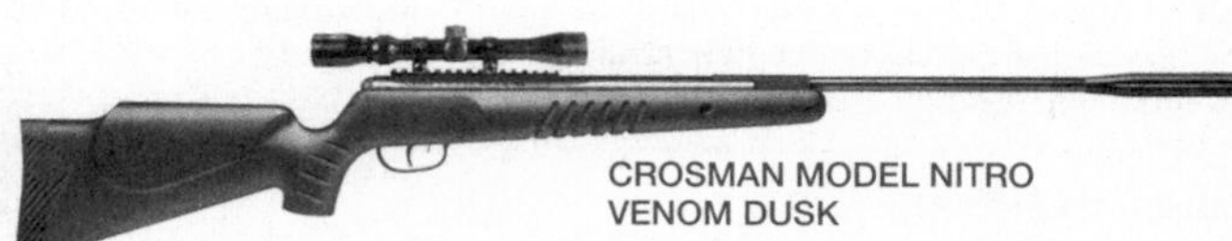
CROSMAN MODEL NITRO VENOM DUSK

CROSMAN NITRO VENOM DUSK AIR RIFLE
Calibers: .177, .22. **Barrel:** Rifled 18.63 in. **Weight:** 7.4 lbs. **Length:** 44.75 in. **Power:** Break-barrel, gas-piston. **Stock:** Ambidextrous synthetic stock with dual raised cheekpieces and grooved grip and forearm. **Sights:** None, Weaver/Picatinny rail for scope mounting, includes 3-9x32 scope and rings. **Features:** Muzzle break for extra cocking leverage, single-shot, adjustable two-stage trigger. **Velocity:** .177, 1,200 fps/.22, 950 fps.
Price: **$220.00**

CROSMAN DPMS CLASSIC A4 NITRO PISTON AIR RIFLE
Caliber: .177 pellets. **Barrel:** Rifled 15 in. **Weight:** 7 lbs. **Length:** 40 in. **Power:** Break-barrel, gas-piston. **Stock:** Ambidextrous AR-15-styled stock. **Sights:** none, Weaver/Picatinny rail for flip-up sights and scope mounting, includes 4x32 scope and rings. **Features:** Aggressive and realistic AR-15 styling. Sling mounts, single-shot, adjustable two-stage trigger. **Velocity:** 1,200 fps.
Price: **$229.95**

CROSMAN REDTAIL AIR RIFLE
Calibers: .177, .22. **Barrel:** Rifled. **Weight:** 6.25 lbs. **Length:** 45.5 in. **Power:** Break-barrel, gas-piston. **Stock:** Ambidextrous synthetic with dual raised cheekpieces. Sights: 11mm grooved dovetail for scope mounting, includes 4x32 scope and rings. **Features:** Single-shot, integrated suppressor, adjustable two-stage trigger. **Velocities:** .177, 1,200 fps/.22, 950 fps.
Price: **$179.99**

CROSMAN SHOCKWAVE NP AIR RIFLE
Calibers: .177, .22. **Barrel:** Rifled 15.00 in. **Weight:** 6.0 lbs. **Length:** 43.5 in. **Power:** Break-barrel, gas-piston. **Stock:** Ambidextrous synthetic with dual raised cheekpieces. **Sights:** Front fiber-optic sight and fully adjustable fiber-optic rear sight, Weaver/Picatinny rail for scope mounting, includes 4x32 scope and rings. **Features:** Single-shot, includes bipod, adjustable two-stage trigger. **Velocities:** .177, 1,200 fps/.22, 950 fps.
Price: **$179.99**

CROSMAN TR77 NPS AIR RIFLE COMBO
Caliber: .177 pellets. **Barrel:** Rifled 12 in. **Weight:** 5.8 lbs. **Length:** 40 in. **Power:** Break-barrel, gas-piston. **Stock:** Ambidextrous synthetic skeleton stock. **Sights:** None, grooved for scope mounting, includes 4x32 scope and rings. Features: Aggressive styling, single-shot, adjustable two-stage trigger. **Velocity:** 1200 fps.
Price: **$179.99**

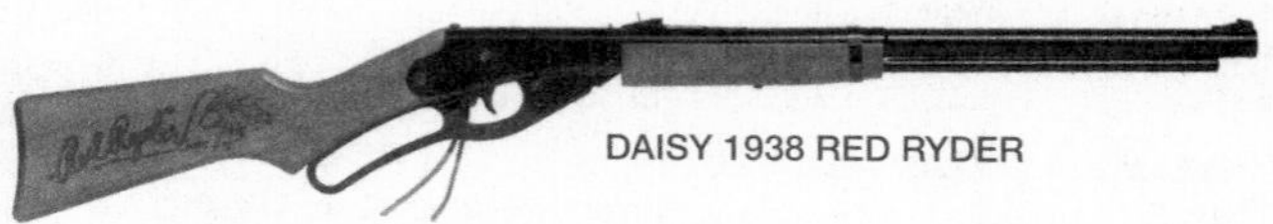
DAISY 1938 RED RYDER

DAISY 1938 RED RYDER air rifle
Caliber: .177 steel BBs. **Barrel:** Smoothbore 10.85 in. **Weight:** 2.2 lbs. **Length:** 35.4 in. **Power:** Single-cock, lever action, spring-piston. **Stock:** Solid wood stock and fore-end. **Sights:** Blade front sight, adjustable rear sight. **Features:** 650 BB reservoir, single-stage trigger, designed for all day fun and backyard plinking, exceptional first airgun for young shooters. **Velocity:** 350 fps.
Price: **$56.99**

DAISY RED RYDER LASSO SCOPED BB RIFLE
Caliber: .177 steel BBs. **Barrel:** Smoothbore 10.85 in. **Weight:** 3.0 lbs. **Length:** 35.4 in. **Power:** Single-cock, lever action, spring-piston. **Stock:** Solid wood stock and fore-end. **Sights:** Blade front sight, adjustable rear sight, includes 4x15 Daisy Scope and mount. **Features:** 650 BB reservoir, single-stage trigger, designed for all day fun and backyard plinking, exceptional first airgun for young shooters. **Velocity:** 350 fps.
Price: **$99.99**

DAISY AVANTI MODEL 887 GOLD MEDALIST COMPETITION
Caliber: .177 pellets. **Barrel:** Rifled, match-grade Lothar Walther barrel, 20.88 in. **Weight:** 6.9 lbs. **Length:** 38.5 in. **Power:** CO2. **Stock:** Ambidextrous laminated wood stock. Sights: Globe front sight and Precision Diopter rear sight. **Features:** Precision bored and crowned barrel for match accuracy, bulk fill CO2 is capable of up to 300 shots, additional inserts available for front sight, ideal entry level rifle for all 10-meter shooting disciplines. **Velocity:** 500 fps.
Price: **$563.99**

DAISY MODEL 105 BUCK AIR RIFLE
Caliber: .177 steel BBs. **Barrel:** Smoothbore 7.97 in. **Weight:** 1.6 lbs. **Length:** 29.8 in. **Power:** Single-cock, lever action, spring-piston. **Stock:** Solid wood buttstock. **Sights:** Fixed front and rear sights. **Features:** 400 BB reservoir, single-stage trigger, designed for all day fun and backyard plinking. **Velocity:** 275 fps.
Price: **$35.99**

DAISY MODEL 753 ELITE

DAISY MODEL 753S MATCH GRADE AVANTI
Caliber: .177 pellets. **Barrel:** Rifled, Lothar Walther, 19.5 in. **Weight:** 7.3 lbs. **Length:** 38.5 in. **Power:** Single-stroke pneumatic. **Stock:** Ambidextrous wood stock & Synthetic stock available **Sights:** Globe front sight and Precision Diopter rear sight. **Features:** Full-size wood stock, additional inserts available for front sight, fully self-contained power system, excellent "first" rifle for all 10-meter shooting disciplines. **Velocity:** 495 fps.
Price: .... **$300.00–$469.99**

DAISY MODEL 4841 GRIZZLY AIR RIFLE
Caliber: .177 steel BBs, .177 pellets. **Barrel:** Smoothbore 19.07 in. **Weight:** 2.25 lbs. **Length:** 36.8 in. **Power:** Single-stroke pneumatic. **Stock:** Ambidextrous plastic stock, Mossy Oak Break-Up pattern. **Sights:** Blade and ramp, rear sight adjustable for elevation, grooved for scope mounting, includes 4x15 scope and mounts. **Features:** Single-shot, lightweight, easy to shoot. **Velocity:** 350 fps.
Price: **$59.99**

DAISY MODEL 10 BB Carbine
Caliber: .177, steel BBs. **Barrel:** Smoothbore. **Weight:** 1.6 lbs. **Length:** 29.8 in. **Power:** Single-cock, lever action, spring-piston. **Stock:** Solid wood stock and forearm. **Sights:** Fixed rear, blade and ramp front and rear sights. **Features:** 400 BB reservoir, single-stage trigger, designed for all day fun and backyard plinking, lightweight youth airgun. **Velocity:** 350 fps.
Price: **$41.99**

DAISY PINK 1998 BB GUN
Caliber: .177, steel BBs. **Barrel:** Smoothbore 10.85 in. **Weight:** 2.2 lbs. **Length:** 35.4 in. **Power:** Single-cock, lever action, spring-piston. **Stock:** Solid wood stock and forearm painted pink. **Sights:** Blade front sight, adjustable rear sight. **Features:** 650 BB reservoir, single-stage trigger, designed for all day fun and backyard plinking, great option for young ladies just starting out. **Velocity:** 350 fps.
Price: **$47.99**

DAISY POWERLINE MODEL 35 AIR RIFLE
Caliber: .177 steel BBs, .177 pellets. **Barrel:** Smoothbore. **Weight:** 2.25 lbs. **Length:** 34.5 in. **Power:** Multi-pump pneumatic. **Stock:** Ambidextrous plastic stock, available in black and pink camo. **Sights:** Blade and ramp, rear sight adjustable for elevation, grooved for scope mounting. **Features:** Single-shot pellet, BB rep, lightweight, accurate and easy to shoot. **Velocity:** 625 fps.
Price: .... **$41.99-$69.95**

DAISY POWERLINE 901
Caliber: .177 steel BBs, .177 pellets. **Barrel:** Rifled 20.8 in. **Weight:** 3.2 lbs. **Length:** 37.75 in. **Power:** Multi-pump pneumatic **Stock:** Ambidextrous black wood grain plastic stock. **Sights:** Front fiber-optic sight, rear blade sight adjustable for elevation, grooved for scope mounting. **Features:** Full-size adult airgun, single-shot pellet, BB repeater, bolt action, lightweight, accurate and easy to shoot. "Ready to go" kit available complete with ammo, safety glasses, shatterblast targets, 4x15 scope and mounts. **Velocity:** 750 fps.
Price: .... **$71.99–$95.99**

DAYSTATE HUNTSMAN REGAL XL AIR RIFLE
Calibers: .177, .22, .25. **Barrel:** Rifled 17 in. **Weight:** 6.17 lbs. **Length:** 40.0 in. **Power:** Pre-charged pneumatic. **Stock:** Right-handed Monte Carlo hardwood. **Sights:** None, 11mm grooved dovetail for scope mounting. **Features:** Features the

Prices given are believed to be accurate at time of publication however, many factors affect retail pricing so exact prices are not possible.

exceptional pedigree of the finest European airguns, 10-shot rotary magazine, rear bolt action, adjustable trigger, fully moderated barrel. **Velocity:** (not provided).
Price: **$1,208.90**

DIANA AR8 N-TEC AIR RIFLE
Calibers: .177, .22. **Barrel:** Rifled 19.5 in. **Weight:** 8.45 lbs. **Length:** 48.0 in. **Power:** Break-barrel, German gas-piston. **Stock:** Ambidextrous synthetic thumbhole stock. **Sights:** Front post and fully adjustable rear sight, grooved for scope mounting. **Features:** European quality, exceptional two-stage adjustable match trigger, single-shot, German manufactured to stringent quality control and testing, limited lifetime warranty. The new N-TEC gas-piston power plant boasts smoother cocking and shooting, making the N-TEC line of Diana guns the most refined Diana airguns to date. **Velocities:** .177, 1,320 fps/.22, 975 fps.
Price: **$399.99**

DIANA 240 CLASSIC AIR RIFLE
Caliber: .177. **Barrel:** Rifled 16.5 in. **Weight:** 5.0 lbs. **Length:** 40 in. **Power:** Break-barrel, spring-piston. **Stock:** Ambidextrous beech stock. **Sights:** Front fiber-optic sight and fully adjustable rear fiber-optic sight, grooved for scope mounting. **Features:** European quality, exceptional two-stage adjustable trigger, single-shot, German manufactured to stringent quality control and testing, limited lifetime warranty. Various bundled configurations available. **Velocity:** .177, 580 fps.
Price: **$219.99**

DIANA Mauser K98 AIR RIFLE
Calibers: .177, .22. **Barrel:** Rifled 18.0 in. **Weight:** 9.5 lbs. **Length:** 44 in. **Power:** Break-barrel, spring-piston. **Stock:** Authentic Mauser K98 hardwood stock. **Sights:** Front post and fully adjustable rear sight, 11mm dovetail grooved for scope mounting. **Features:** European quality, fixed barrel with underlever cocking, exceptional two-stage adjustable match trigger, single-shot, German manufactured to stringent quality control and testing, limited lifetime warranty. **Velocities:** .177, 1,150 fps/.22, 850 fps.
Price: **$469.99**

DIANA RWS 34P STRIKER COMBO
Calibers: .177, .22. **Barrel:** Rifled 19.0 in. **Weight:** 7.75 lbs. **Length:** 46 in. **Power:** Break-barrel, spring-piston. **Stock:** Ambidextrous beech or synthetic stock. **Sights:** Front fiber-optic sight and fully adjustable rear fiber-optic sight, grooved for scope mounting. **Features:** European quality, exceptional two-stage adjustable match trigger, single-shot, German manufactured to stringent quality control and testing, limited lifetime warranty. Various bundled configurations available. **Velocity:** .177, 1,000 fps/.22, 800 fps.
Price: **$399.99**

DIANA MODEL 340 AIR RIFLE

DIANA 340 N-TEC PREMIUM AIR RIFLE
Calibers: .177, .22. **Barrel:** Rifled 19.5 in. **Weight:** 7.9 lbs. **Length:** 46 in. **Power:** Break-barrel, German gas-piston. **Stock:** Ambidextrous beech stock. **Sights:** Front fiber-optic sight and fully adjustable rear fiber-optic sight, grooved for scope mounting. **Features:** European quality, exceptional two-stage adjustable match trigger, single-shot, German manufactured to stringent quality control and testing, limited lifetime warranty. The new N-TEC gas-piston power plant boasts smoother cocking and shooting, making the N-TEC line of Diana guns the most refined Diana airguns to date. Various bundled configurations available. **Velocities:** .177, 1,000 fps/.22, 800 fps.
Price: **$449.99**

DIANA RWS 350 MAGNUM
Calibers: .177, .22. **Barrel:** Rifled 19.25 in. **Weight:** 8.2 lbs. **Length:** 48 in. **Power:** Break-barrel, spring-piston. **Stock:** Right handed beech stock with grip and forearm checkering. **Sights:** Post and globe front sight and fully adjustable rear sight, grooved for scope mounting. **Features:** European quality, exceptional two-stage adjustable match trigger, single-shot, German manufactured to stringent quality control and testing, limited lifetime warranty. Various bundled configurations available. **Velocities:** .177, 1,250 fps/.22, 1,000 fps.
Price: **$499.95**

DIANA 350 N-TEC MAGNUM PREMIUM AIR RIFLE
Calibers: .177, .22. **Barrel:** Rifled 19.5 in. **Weight:** 6.7 lbs. **Length:** 48.5 in. **Power:** Break-barrel, German gas-piston. **Stock:** Ambidextrous stock, available in beech and synthetic options. **Sights:** Front post and fully adjustable rear sight, grooved for scope mounting. **Features:** European quality, exceptional two-stage adjustable match trigger, single-shot, German manufactured to stringent quality control and testing, limited lifetime warranty. The new N-TEC gas-piston power plant boasts smoother cocking and shooting, making the N-TEC line of Diana guns the most refined Diana airguns to date. **Velocities:** .177, 1,250 fps/.22, 1,000 fps.
Price: **$499.99**

DIANA MODEL 48 AIR RIFLE

DIANA MODEL RWS 48 AIR RIFLE, T06 TRIGGER
Calibers: .177, .22. **Barrel:** Rifled 17 in. **Weight:** 8.5 lbs. **Length:** 42.13 in. **Power:** Single-cock, side-lever, spring-piston. **Stock:** Ambidextrous beech thumbhole stock. **Sights:** Blade front sight, fully adjustable rear sight, grooved for scope mounting. **Features:** European quality, exceptional two-stage match trigger, single-shot, German manufactured to stringent quality control and testing, limited lifetime warranty. **Velocities:** .177, 1,100 fps/.22, 900 fps.
Price: **$529.95**

DIANA 460 MAGNUM
Calibers: .177, .22. **Barrel:** Rifled 18.44 in. **Weight:** 8.3 lbs. **Length:** 45 in. **Power:** Under-lever, spring-piston. **Stock:** Right-hand hardwood stock with grip and fore-end checkering. **Sights:** Post front sight and fully adjustable rear sight, grooved for scope mounting. **Features:** European quality, exceptional two-stage adjustable match trigger, single-shot, German manufactured to stringent quality control and testing, limited lifetime warranty. Various bundled configurations available. **Velocity:** .177, 1,200 fps/.22, 1,000 fps.
Price: **$599.95**

DIANA MODEL 470 TARGET HUNTER AIR RIFLE
Calibers: .177, .22. **Barrel:** 18 in. **Weight:** 7.8 lbs. **Length:** 47 in. overall. **Power:** Break-barrel, single-shot. **Stock:** Ambidextrous thumbhole hardwood, adjustable buttplate for elevation. **Features:** Upgraded two-stage adjustable trigger assembly with all-metal parts, rifled barrel. **Velocities:** .177, 1,120 fps/.22, 1,000 fps.
Price: **$699.99**

DIANA 56 TARGET HUNTER AIR RIFLE
Calibers: .177, .22. **Barrel:** Rifled 17.3 in. **Weight:** 11.1 lbs. **Length:** 44 in. **Power:** Single-cock, side-lever, spring-piston. **Stock:** Ambidextrous beech thumbhole stock. **Sights:** None, grooved for scope mounting. **Features:** European quality, exceptional two-stage match trigger, single-shot, German manufactured to stringent quality control and testing. **Velocities:** .177, 1,100 fps/.22, 890 fps.
Price: **$809.99**

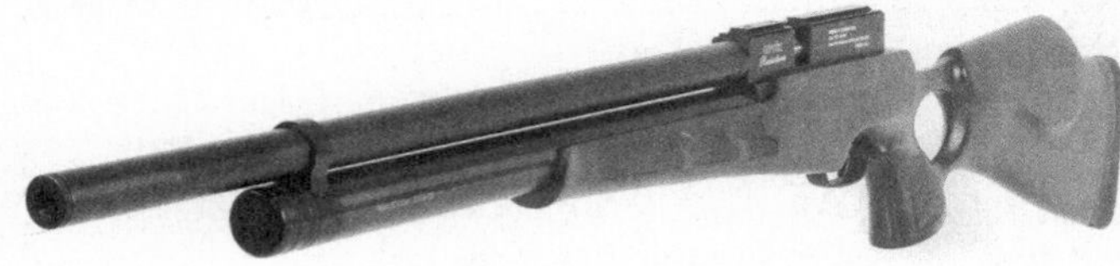

EVANIX RAINSTORM II PCP AIR RIFLE
Calibers: .22, .25, .30, .35 (9mm). **Barrel:** Rifled, 17.00 in. **Weight:** 7.2 lbs. **Length:** 39.00 in. overall. **Power:** Pre-charged Pneumatic. **Stock:** Ambidextrous beech thumbhole stock. **Sights:** None, grooved 11mm dovetail for scope mounting **Features:** Multi-shot side-lever action, shot count varies based on caliber, very well made and versatile hunting airgun. **Velocities:** .22, 1,176 fps/.25, 910 fps/.30, 910 fps/.35, 800 fps.
Price: **$1,150.00**

EVANIX REX AIR RIFLE
Calibers: .22, .25, .35 (9mm), .45. **Barrel:** Rifled, 19.68 in. **Weight:** 5.51 lbs. **Length:** 35.82 in. overall. **Power:** Pre-charged Pneumatic. **Sights:** weaver rail for scope mounting **Features:** Lightweight, compact and massively powerful, single shot, capable of putting out well over 200 foot pounds at the muzzle in .45 caliber, truly effective hunting power in a compact package **Velocities:** .22, 1,080 fps/.25, 970 fps/.35, 860 fps/.45, 700 fps.
Price: **$699.99-799.99**

FEINWERKBAU 800X FIELD TARGET AIR RIFLE
Caliber: .177. **Barrel:** Rifled 16.73 in. **Weight:** 11.7–15.05 lbs. **Length:** 49.76 in. **Power:** Pre-charged pneumatic. **Stock:** Highly adaptable field target competition stock **Sights:** None, 11mm grooved for scope mounting. **Features:** Designed from airguns featuring Olympic accuracy, this field target variant is designed to win., 5-way adjustable match trigger, bolt action, competition grade airgun **Velocity:** 825 fps.
Price: **$3,799.99**

FEINWERKBAU P75 BIATHLON AIR RIFLE
Caliber: .177. **Barrel:** Rifled 16.73 in. **Weight:** 9.26 lbs. **Length:** 42.91 in. **Power:** Pre-charged pneumatic. **Stock:** Highly adaptable laminate wood competition stock Sights: Front globe with aperture inserts and diopter micrometer rear. **Features:** 5-shot bolt action, competition grade airgun, inspired from airguns featuring Olympic accuracy, 5-way adjustable match trigger. **Velocity:** 564 fps.
Price: **$3,254.95**

FEINWERKBAU SPORT AIR RIFLE
Caliber: .177. **Barrel:** Rifled 18.31 in. **Weight:** 8.27 lbs. **Length:** 44.84 in. **Power:** Spring-piston break barrel. **Stock:** Ambidextrous wood stock with dual raised cheekpieces. **Sights:** Front globe, fully adjustable rear sight, grooved for scope mounting. **Features:** Lightweight, single-shot, easy cocking, adjustable two-stage trigger. **Velocity:** .177, 850 fps.
Price: **$999.99**

FX IMPACT AIR RIFLE
Calibers: .25, .30. **Barrel:** Rifled 24.4 in. **Weight:** 7.0 lbs. **Length:** 34.0 in. **Power:** Pre-charged pneumatic. **Stock:** Compact bullpup stock in various materials and finishes **Sights:** None, 11mm grooved for scope mounting. **Features:** Premium airgun brand known for exceptional build quality and accuracy, regulated for consistent shots, adjustable two-stage trigger, FX smooth twist barrel, multi-shot side lever action, fully moderated barrel, highly adjustable and adaptable air rifle system. **Velocities:** .25, 900 fps/.30, 870 fps.
Price: **$2,099.99**

FX WILDCAT AIR RIFLE
Calibers: .22, .25. **Barrel:** Rifled 19.7 in. **Weight:** 6.1 lbs. **Length:** 26.5 in. **Power:** Pre-charged pneumatic. **Stock:** Compact bullpup stock in various materials and finishes. **Sights:** None, 11mm grooved for scope mounting. **Features:** Premium airgun brand known for exceptional build quality and accuracy, regulated for consistent shots, adjustable two-stage trigger, FX smooth twist barrel, multi-shot side lever action, fully moderated barrel. **Velocity:** .22, 1,200 fps/.25, 900 fps.
Price: **$1,499.99–1,849.99**

FX .30 BOSS AIR RIFLE
Caliber: .30. **Barrel:** Rifled 24.4 in. **Weight:** 7.0 lbs. **Length:** 47.5 in. **Power:** Pre-charged pneumatic. **Stock:** Right-handed Monte Carlo Stock available in various materials and finishes. **Sights:** None. 11mm grooved for scope mounting. **Features:** Premium airgun brand known for exceptional build quality and accuracy, regulated for consistent shots, adjustable two-stage trigger, FX smooth twist barrel, multi-shot side lever action, fully moderated barrel. **Velocities:** .22, 1,200 fps/.25, 900 fps.
Price: .... **$1949.99–$2399.99**

GAMO CAMO ROCKET IGT AIR RIFLE
Caliber: .177 pellets. **Barrel:** Rifled 18 in. **Weight:** 6.6 lbs. **Length:** 43 in. **Power:** Break-barrel, gas-piston. **Stock:** Ambidextrous lightweight composite camo stock. **Sights:** None, grooved for scope mounting, includes 4x32 scope and mounts. **Features:** Very lightweight, single-shot, easy cocking, adjustable two-stage trigger, all-weather fluted barrel. **Velocity:** 1,300 fps.
Price: **$249.95**

GAMO COYOTE SE PCP AIR RIFLE
Calibers: .177, .22. **Barrel:** Cold hammer-forged match-grade rifled barrel, 24.5 in. **Weight:** 6.6 lbs. **Length:** 42.9 in. **Power:** Pre-charged pneumatic. **Stock:** Ambidextrous hardwood stock. Sights: None, grooved for scope mounting, **Features:** European class airgun, highly accurate and powerful, adjustable two-stage trigger, integrated moderator, 10-shot bolt action. **Velocities:** .177, 1,200 fps/.22, 1,000 fps.
Price: **$559.99**

GAMO MAGNUM AIR RIFLE
Calibers: .177, .22. **Barrel:** Rifled 21.3 in. **Weight:** 6.88 lbs. **Length:** 48.0 in. **Power:** Break-barrel, gas-piston. **Stock:** Ambidextrous composite thumbhole stock. Sights: Fiber-optic front sight and fully adjustable fiber-optic rear sight, grooved for scope mounting, includes 3-9x40AO scope and mounts. **Features:** Most powerful break barrel from Gamo USA, single-shot, adjustable two-stage trigger. **Velocity:** .177, 1,650 fps/.22, 1,300 fps.
Price: **$329.99**

GAMO SWARM MAXXIM MULTI-SHOT AIR RIFLE
Calibers: .177, .22. **Barrel:** Rifled 19.9 in. **Weight:** 5.64 lbs. **Length:** 45.3 in. **Power:** Break-barrel, gas-piston. **Stock:** Ambidextrous lightweight composite stock. **Sights:** None, grooved for scope mounting, includes recoil-reducing rail, 3-9x32 scope and mounts. **Features:** New for 2017, loaded with patented features including an ingenious 10-shot multi-shot system allows for automatic loading with each cock of the barrel, easy cocking, adjustable two-stage trigger, all-weather fluted barrel, features integrated suppressor technology. **Velocities:** .177, 1,300 fps/.22, 975 fps.
Price: **$249.99**

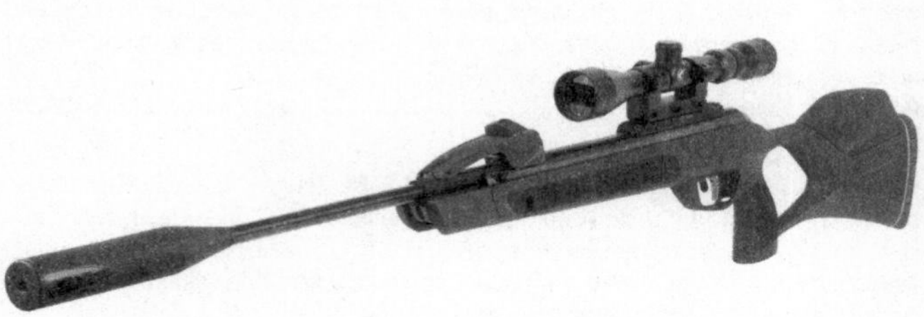

GAMO SWARM MAGNUM MULTI-SHOT AIR RIFLE
Caliber: .22. **Barrel:** Rifled 21.3 in. **Weight:** 6.88 lbs. **Length:** 49.2 in. **Power:** Break-barrel, gas-piston. **Stock:** Ambidextrous lightweight composite stock. **Sights:** None, grooved for scope mounting, includes recoil-reducing rail, 3-9x32 scope and mounts. **Features:** New for 2018, loaded with patented features including an ingenious 10-shot multi-shot system allows for automatic loading with each cock of the barrel, easy cocking, adjustable two-stage trigger, steel barrel, features integrated suppressor technology. **Velocity:** 1,300 fps.
Price: **$329.99**

GAMO URBAN PCP AIR RIFLE
Caliber: .22. **Barrel:** Cold hammer forged match grade rifled barrel. **Weight:** 6.7 lbs. **Length:** 42.0 in. **Power:** Pre-charged pneumatic. **Stock:** Ambidextrous composite thumbhole stock. Sights: None, grooved for scope mounting, **Features:** European class airgun, highly accurate and powerful, adjustable two-stage trigger, integrated moderator, 10-shot bolt action. **Velocity:** 800 fps.
Price: **$450.00**

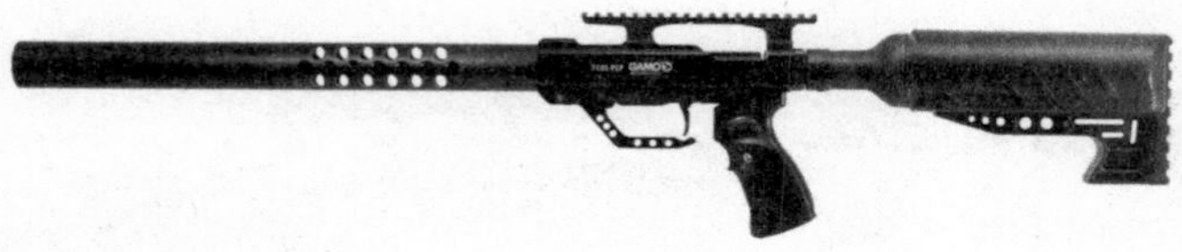

GAMO TC35 AIR RIFLE
Caliber: .35. **Barrel:** rifled, 14.96 in. **Weight:** 6.0 lbs. **Length:** 35.88 in. **Power:** Pre-charged pneumatic. **Stock:** Ambidextrous. **Sights:** None, weaver rail for scope mounting, **Features:** Very light and yet very powerful producing up to 170 ft-lbs of muzzle energy, adjustable trigger, two power settings, shrouded barrel, single-shot action allows for an extremely wide range of ammo choices.
Price: **$1,099.99**

GAMO TC45 AIR RIFLE
Caliber: .45. **Barrel:** rifled, 24.24 in. **Weight:** 8.0 lbs. **Length:** 47.13 in. **Power:** Pre-charged pneumatic. **Stock:** Ambidextrous. **Sights:** None, weaver rail for scope mounting. **Features:** Very light and yet very powerful producing over 400 ft-lbs of muzzle energy shooting 350-grain cast slugs, adjustable trigger, two power settings, shrouded barrel, single shot action allows for an extremely wide range of ammo choices.
Price: **$1,099.99**

Prices given are believed to be accurate at time of publication however, many factors affect retail pricing so exact prices are not possible.

GAMO VARMINT HUNTER HP AIR RIFLE

Caliber: .177 pellets. **Barrel:** Rifled 18 in. **Weight:** 6.61 lbs. **Length:** 43.78 in. **Power:** Break-barrel, spring-piston. **Stock:** Ambidextrous lightweight composite with dual raised cheekpieces. **Sights:** None, grooved for scope mounting, includes recoil-reducing rail, 4x32 scope and mounts, laser and light with intermittent pressure switches included. **Features:** Lightweight, single-shot, easy cocking, adjustable two-stage trigger, all-weather fluted barrel. **Velocity:** 1,400 fps.

Price: **$309.99**

GAMO WHISPER FUSION AIR RIFLE, IGT

Calibers: .177, .22. **Barrel:** Rifled 18 in. **Weight:** 8 lbs. **Length:** 43 in. **Power:** Break-barrel, gas-piston. **Stock:** Ambidextrous lightweight composite stock with adjustable cheekpiece. Sights: Globe fiber-optic front sight and fully adjustable fiber-optic rear sight, grooved for scope mounting, includes recoil reducing rail, 3-9x40 scope and heavy-duty mount. **Features:** Integrated Gamo "Whisper" noise dampening system and bull barrel noise suppression system for maximum stealth, lightweight, single-shot, easy cocking, adjustable two-stage trigger. **Velocities:** .177, 1,300 fps/.22, 975 fps.

Price: **$329.99**

HAMMERLI 850 AIR MAGNUM

Calibers: .177, .22. **Barrel:** Rifled 23.62 in. **Weight:** 5.65 lbs. **Length:** 41 in. **Power:** CO2. **Stock:** Ambidextrous lightweight composite stock with dual raised cheekpieces. **Sights:** Globe fiber-optic front sight and fully adjustable fiber-optic rear sight, grooved for scope mounting. **Features:** Multi-shot bolt action, 8-shot rotary magazine, utilizes 88-gram disposable CO2 canisters delivering up to 200 shots per cartridge. Extremely accurate, very easy to shoot. German manufacturing. **Velocities:** .177, 760 fps/.22, 655 fps.

Price: **$349.99**

HATSAN USA EDGE CLASS AIRGUNS

Calibers: .177, .22, .25. **Barrel:** Rifled 17.7 in. **Weight:** 6.4–6.6 lbs. **Length:** 43 in. **Power:** Break-barrel, spring-piston and gas-spring variations. **Stock:** Multiple synthetic and synthetic skeleton stock options. Available in different colors such as black, muddy girl camo, moon camo, etc. **Sights:** Fiber-optic front sight and fully adjustable fiber-optic rear sight, grooved for scope mounting, includes 3-9x32 scope and mounts. Features: European manufacturing with German steel, single-shot, adjustable two-stage trigger, performance tested at the factory with lead pellets for accurate velocity specifications. **Velocities:** .177, 1,000 fps/.22, 800 fps/.25, 650 fps.

Price: .... **$150.00–$180.00**

HATSAN USA BULLBOSS QE AIR RIFLE

Calibers: .177, .22, .25. **Barrel:** Rifled 23.0 in. **Weight:** 8.6 lbs. **Length:** 36.8 in. **Power:** Pre-charged pneumatic. **Stock:** Ambidextrous synthetic bullpup stock **Sights:** None, innovative dual rail 11mm dovetail and Weaver compatible for scope mounting. **Features:** Multi-shot side-lever action, 10-shot .177 and .22 magazines/9-shot .25 magazine, "Quiet Energy" barrel shroud with integrated suppressor, European manufacturing with German steel, removable air cylinder, fully adjustable two-stage "Quattro" trigger, performance tested at the factory with lead pellets for accurate velocity specifications. **Velocities:** .177, 1,170 fps/.22, 1,070 fps/.25, 970 fps.

Price: **$899.99**

HATSAN USA BARRAGE SEMI-AUTOMATIC PCP AIR RIFLE

Calibers: .177, .22 .25. **Barrel:** Rifled, 19.7 in. **Weight:** 10.1 lbs. **Length:** 40.9 in. **Power:** Pre-charged pneumatic. **Stock:** Ambidextrous adjustable synthetic thumbhole stock with integrated magazine storage. **Sights:** None, innovative dual rail 11mm dovetail and Weaver compatible for scope mounting. **Features:** Air-driven true semi-automatic action, 14 shots in .177 and 12 shots in .22, "Quiet Energy" barrel shroud with integrated suppressor, 500 cc cylinder with 250BAR capacity, European manufacturing with German steel, performance tested at the factory with lead pellets for accurate velocity specifications. **Velocities:** .177, 1,100 fps/.22, 1,000 fps/.25, 900 fps.

Price: .... **$1,099.99–$1,199.99**

HATSAN USA BULLMASTER SEMI-AUTOMATIC PCP AIR RIFLE

Calibers: .177, .22, .25. **Barrel:** Rifled, 19.7 in. **Weight:** 10.3 lbs. **Length:** 30.9 in. **Power:** Pre-charged pneumatic. **Stock:** Ambidextrous adjustable synthetic bullpup stock with integrated magazine storage. **Sights:** None, innovative dual rail 11mm dovetail and Weaver compatible for scope mounting. **Features:** Air-driven true semi-automatic action, 14 shots in .177 and 12 shots in .22, "Quiet Energy" barrel shroud with integrated suppressor, 500 cc cylinder with 250BAR capacity, European manufacturing with German steel, performance tested at the factory with lead pellets for accurate velocity specifications. **Velocities:** .177, 1,100 fps/.22, 1,000 fps/.25 900 fps.

Price: **$1,099.99–1,199.99**

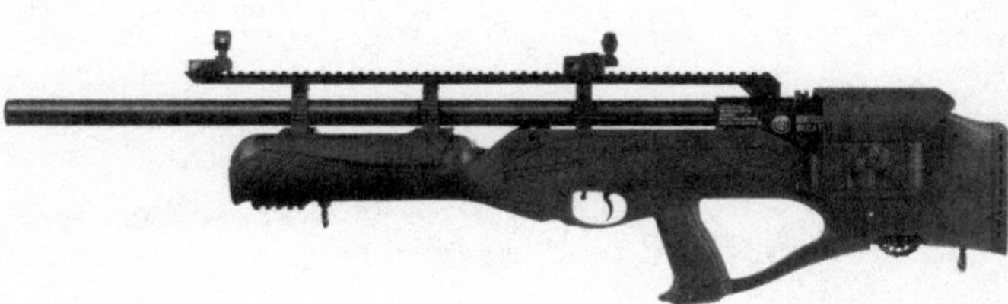

HATSAN USA BULLY (BULLPUP) PCP AIR RIFLE

Calibers: .177, .22, .25, .30, .35, .45. **Barrel:** Rifled 23 in. **Weight:** 13 lbs. **Length:** 48.4 in. **Power:** Pre-charged pneumatic. **Stock:** Adjustable synthetic all-weather bullpup stock with, sling mounts. **Sights:** None, innovative dual rail 11mm dovetail and Weaver compatible for scope mounting. **Features:** Available in 6 calibers, 500cc of air via carbon fiber reservoir, multi-shot side-lever action, 17-shot .177 magazine, 14-shot .22 magazine, 13-shot .25 magazine, 10-shot .30 magazine, 9-shot .35 magazine, 7-shot .45 magazine. "Quiet Energy" barrel shroud with integrated suppressor, European manufacturing with German steel, fully adjustable two-stage "Quattro" trigger, performance tested at the factory with lead pellets for accurate velocity specifications. **Velocities:** .177, 1,450 fps/.22, 1,300 fps/.25, 1,200 fps/.30, 1,070 fps/.35, 910 fps/.45, 850 fps.

Price: **$999.99**

HATSAN USA FLASH QE PCP

Calibers: .177, .22, .25. **Barrel:** Rifled, 17.7 in. **Weight:** 5.9 lbs. **Length:** 42.3 in. **Power:** Pre-charged pneumatic. **Stock:** Ambidextrous synthetic thumbhole stock **Sights:** None, innovative dual rail 11mm dovetail and Weaver compatible for scope mounting. **Features:** Very lightweight, multi-shot side-lever action, multi-shot magazine (shot count varies by caliber). "Quiet Energy" barrel shroud with integrated suppressor, European manufacturing with German steel, fully adjustable two-stage "Quattro" trigger, performance tested at the factory with lead pellets for accurate velocity specifications. **Velocities:** .177, 1,250 fps/.22, 1,100 fps/.25, 900 fps.

Price: **$329.99**

HATSAN USA FLASHPUP QE PCP

Calibers: .177, .22, .25. **Barrel:** Rifled, 19.4 in. **Weight:** 6.1 lbs. **Length:** 32.0 in. **Power:** Pre-charged pneumatic. **Stock:** Ambidextrous hardwood bullpup stock **Sights:** None, innovative dual rail 11mm dovetail and Weaver compatible for scope mounting. **Features:** Very lightweight, multi-shot side-lever action, multi-shot magazine (shot count varies by caliber). "Quiet Energy" barrel shroud with integrated suppressor, European manufacturing with German steel, fully adjustable two-stage "Quattro" trigger, performance tested at the factory with lead pellets for accurate velocity specifications. **Velocity:** .177, 1,250 fps/.22, 1,100 fps/.25, 900 fps.

Price: **$439.99**

HATSAN USA GLADIUS AIRGUN (LONG VERSION)

Calibers: .177, .22, .25. **Barrel:** Rifled, 23.0 in. **Weight:** 10.6 lbs. **Length:** 38 in. **Power:** Pre-charged pneumatic. **Stock:** Ambidextrous adjustable synthetic bullpup stock with integrated magazine storage **Sights:** None, innovative dual rail 11mm dovetail and Weaver compatible for scope mounting. **Features:** 6 way variable power, multi-shot side-lever action, 10-shot .177 and .22 magazines / 9-shot .25 magazine, "Quiet Energy" barrel shroud with integrated suppressor, European manufacturing with German steel, removable air cylinder, fully adjustable two-stage "Quattro" trigger, performance tested at the factory with lead pellets for accurate velocity specifications. **Velocities:** .177, 1,070 fps/.22, 970 fps/.25, 870 fps.
Price: **$999.99**

HATSAN USA MOD 87 QE VORTEX AIRGUN

HATSAN USA MOD 87 QE VORTEX AIR RIFLE

Calibers: .177, .22, .25. **Barrel:** Rifled 10.6 in. **Weight:** 7.4 lbs. **Length:** 44.5 in. **Power:** Break-barrel, gas-spring. **Stock:** Synthetic all-weather stock with adjustable cheekpiece. Sights: Fiber-optic front sight and fully adjustable fiber-optic rear sight, grooved for scope mounting, includes 3-9x32 scope and mounts. **Features:** "Quiet Energy" barrel shroud with integrated suppressor, European manufacturing with German steel, single-shot, fully adjustable two-stage "Quattro" trigger, performance tested at the factory with lead pellets for accurate velocity specifications. **Velocities:** .177, 1,000 fps/.22, 800 fps/.25, 650 fps.
Price: **$219.99**

HATSAN USA MOD 125 SNIPER VORTEX AIRGUN

HATSAN USA MOD 125 SNIPER VORTEX AIR RIFLE

Calibers: .177, .22, .25. **Barrel:** Rifled 19.6 in. **Weight:** 9 lbs. **Length:** 48.8 in. **Power:** Break-barrel, gas-spring. **Stock:** Synthetic all-weather stock with adjustable cheekpiece, available in black or camo options. **Sights:** Fiber-optic front sight and fully adjustable fiber-optic rear sight, grooved for scope mounting, includes 3-9x32 scope and mounts. **Features:** Integrated suppressor, European manufacturing with German steel, single-shot, fully adjustable two-stage "Quattro" trigger, performance tested at the factory with lead pellets for accurate velocity specifications. **Velocities:** .177, 1,250 fps/.22, 1,000 fps/.25, 750 fps.
Price: .... **$319.99-$379.99**

HATSAN USA MOD 135 QE VORTEX AIRGUN

HATSAN USA MOD 135 QE VORTEX AIR RIFLE

Calibers: .177, .22, .25, .30. **Barrel:** Rifled 10.6 in. **Weight:** 9.9 lbs. **Length:** 47.2 in. **Power:** Break-barrel, gas-spring. **Stock:** Turkish walnut stock with grip and fore-end checkering, adjustable buttplate and cheekpiece. **Sights:** Fiber-optic front sight and fully adjustable fiber-optic rear sight, innovative dual rail 11mm dovetail and Weaver compatible for scope mounting. **Features:** The most powerful break barrel in the world. Worlds first "big-bore" break-barrel airgun, "Quiet Energy" barrel shroud with integrated suppressor, European manufacturing with German steel, single-shot, fully adjustable two-stage "Quattro" trigger, performance tested at the factory with lead pellets for accurate velocity specifications. **Velocities:** .177, 1,250 fps/.22, 1,000 fps/.25, 750 fps/.30, 550 fps.
Price: **$299.99-329.99**

HATSAN USA MOD "TORPEDO" 150 SNIPER VORTEX AIRGUN

Calibers: .177, .22, .25. **Barrel:** Rifled 13 in. **Weight:** 9.4 lbs. **Length:** 48.4 in. **Power:** Under-lever, gas-spring. **Stock:** Synthetic all-weather stock with adjustable cheekpiece. **Sights:** Fiber-optic front sight and fully adjustable fiber-optic rear sight, innovative dual rail 11mm dovetail and Weaver compatible for scope mounting. **Features:** Integrated suppressor, enhanced fixed barrel accuracy, European manufacturing with German steel, single-shot, fully adjustable two-stage "Quattro" trigger, performance tested at the factory with lead pellets for accurate velocity specifications. **Velocities:** .177, 1,250 fps/.22, 1,000 fps/.25, 750 fps.
Price: **$359.99**

HATSAN USA AT44 QE PCP AIRGUN

HATSAN USA AT44 QE PCP AIRGUN

Calibers: .177, .22, .25. **Barrel:** Rifled 19.5 in. **Weight:** 8 lbs. **Length:** 45.4 in. **Power:** Pre-charged pneumatic. **Stock:** Various configurations, synthetic all-weather stock with front accessory rail and sling mounts. Turkish hardwood with sling mounts, full tactical stock with soft rubber grip inserts, adjustable buttstock and cheek riser. **Sights:** None, innovative dual rail 11mm dovetail and Weaver compatible for scope mounting. **Features:** Multi-shot side-lever action, 10-shot .177 and .22 magazines / 9-shot .25 magazine. "Quiet Energy" barrel shroud with integrated suppressor, European manufacturing with German steel, removable air cylinder, fully adjustable two-stage "Quattro" trigger, performance tested at the factory with lead pellets for accurate velocity specifications. **Velocities:** .177, 1,070 fps/.22, 970 fps/.25, 870 fps.
Price: **$599.00**

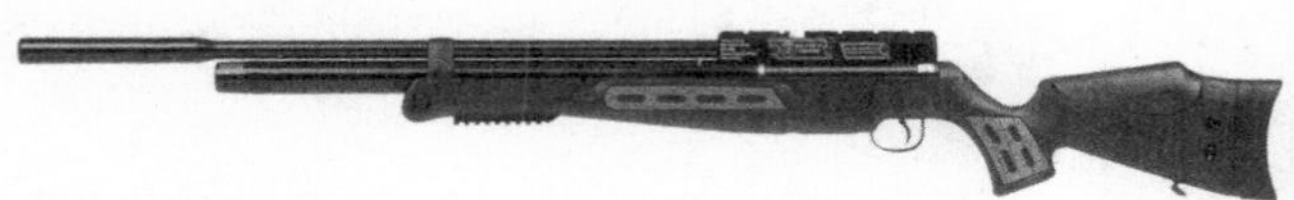

HATSAN USA BT BIG BORE CARNIVORE BIG BORE QE AIR RIFLE

Calibers: .30, .35. **Barrel:** Rifled 23 in. **Weight:** 9.3 lbs. **Length:** 48.9 in. **Power:** Pre-charged pneumatic. **Stock:** Synthetic all-weather stock with sling mounts, front accessory rail, adjustable cheekpiece and buttpad. **Sights:** None, innovative dual rail 11mm dovetail and Weaver compatible for scope mounting. **Features:** Multi-shot bolt action, 6-shot .35 magazine / 7-shot .30 magazine. "Quiet Energy" barrel shroud with integrated suppressor, European manufacturing with German steel, removable air cylinder, fully adjustable two-stage "Quattro" trigger, performance tested at the factory with lead pellets for accurate velocity specifications. **Velocities:** .30, 860 fps/.35, 730 fps.
Price: **$800.00**

HATSAN USA GALATIAN QE AIR RIFLE

Calibers: .177, .22, .25. **Barrel:** Rifled 17.7 in. **Weight:** 8.6 lbs. **Length:** 43.3 in. **Power:** Pre-charged pneumatic. **Stock:** Synthetic all-weather stock with extra mag storage, sling mounts, tri-rail front accessory rails, adjustable cheek riser and buttstock. **Sights:** None, innovative dual rail 11mm dovetail and Weaver compatible for scope mounting. **Features:** Multi-shot side-lever action, 17-shot .177 magazine, 14-shot .22 magazine, 13-shot .25 magazine. "Quiet Energy" barrel shroud with integrated suppressor, European manufacturing with German steel, removable air cylinder, fully adjustable two-stage "Quattro" trigger, performance tested at the factory with lead pellets for accurate velocity specifications. **Velocities:** .177, 1,130 fps/.22, 1,050 fps/.25, 950 fps.
Price: **$999.99**

HATSAN USA HERCULES QE AIR RIFLE

Calibers: .177, .22, .25, .30, .35, .45. **Barrel:** Rifled 23 in. **Weight:** 13 lbs. **Length:** 48.4 in. **Power:** Pre-charged pneumatic. **Stock:** Fully adjustable synthetic all-weather stock with, sling mounts. **Sights:** None, innovative dual rail 11mm dovetail and Weaver compatible for scope mounting. **Features:** Available in 6 calibers, 1000cc of air on board provides industry leading shot count and energy on target. Multi-shot side-lever action, 17-shot .177 magazine, 14-shot .22 magazine, 13-shot .25 magazine, 10-shot .30 magazine, 9-shot .35 magazine, 7-shot .45 magazine. "Quiet Energy" barrel shroud with integrated suppressor, European manufacturing with German steel, fully adjustable two-stage "Quattro" trigger, performance tested at the factory with lead pellets for accurate velocity specifications. **Velocities:** .177, 1,300 fps/.22, 1,230 fps/.25, 1,200 fps/.30, 1,070 fps/.35, 930 fps/.45, 810 fps.
Price: **$1,399.99**

Prices given are believed to be accurate at time of publication however, many factors affect retail pricing so exact prices are not possible.

KALIBR CRICKET BULLPUP PCP AIR RIFLE
Caliber: .22. **Barrel:** Rifled 17.5 in. **Weight:** 6.95 lbs. **Length:** 27.0 in. **Power:** Pre-charged pneumatic. **Stock:** Ambidextrous bullpup stock available in various materials. Sights: None, weaver rail for scope mounting. **Features:** Multi-shot side-lever action, 14-shot magazine, shrouded barrel with integrated suppression technology, adjustable two-stage trigger. **Velocity:** .22, 925 fps.
Price: .... **$1,629.00–$1,835.00**

KRAL ARMS PUNCHER MEGA WALNUT SIDELEVER PCP AIR RIFLE
Calibers: .177, .22, .25. **Barrel:** Rifled 21.0 in. **Weight:** 8.35 lbs. **Length:** 42.0 in. **Power:** Pre-charged pneumatic. **Stock:** Ambidextrous stock available in synthetic with adjustable cheek piece, and Turkish walnut. **Sights:** None, 11mm grooved dovetail for scope mounting. **Features:** Multi-shot side-lever action, 14-shot .177 magazine, 12-shot .22 magazine, 10-shot .25 magazine, half shrouded barrel with integrated suppression technology, available in blue and satin marine finish, adjustable two-stage trigger. **Velocities:** .177, 1,070 fps/.22, 975 fps/.25, 825 fps.
Price: **$599.99**

KRAL ARMS PUNCHER PRO PCP AIR RIFLE
Calibers: .177, .22, .25. **Barrel:** Rifled 22.8 in. **Weight:** 8.6 lbs. **Length:** 41.3 in. **Power:** Pre-charged pneumatic. **Stock:** Monte Carlo hardwood right-handed stock. **Sights:** None, 11mm grooved dovetail for scope mounting. **Features:** Multi-shot rear bolt action, 14-shot .177 magazine, 12-shot .22 magazine, 10-shot .25 magazine, half shrouded barrel with integrated suppression technology, two-stage adjustable trigger. **Velocities:** .177, 1,070 fps/.22, 975 fps/.25, 825 fps.
Price: **$599.99**

KRAL ARMS PUNCHER BREAKER SILENT SYNTHETIC SIDELEVER PCP AIR RIFLE
Calibers: .177, .22, .25. **Barrel:** Rifled 21.0 in. **Weight:** 7.4 lbs. **Length:** 29.0 in. **Power:** Pre-charged pneumatic. **Stock:** Ambidextrous bullpup stock available in synthetic and Turkish walnut. **Sights:** None, 11mm grooved dovetail for scope mounting. **Features:** Multi-shot side-lever action, 14-shot .177 magazine, 12-shot .22 magazine, 10-shot .25 magazine, half shrouded barrel with integrated suppression technology, available in blue and satin marine finish, adjustable two-stage trigger. **Velocities:** .177, 1,100 fps/.22, 975 fps/.25, 825 fps.
Price: **$549.99**

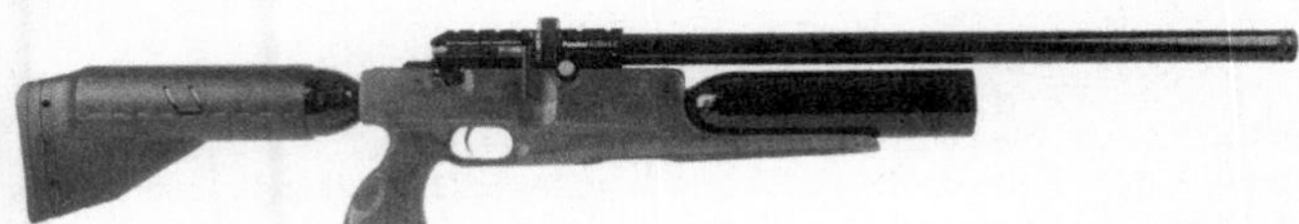

KRAL ARMS PUNCHER BIG MAX PCP AIR RIFLE
Calibers: .177, .22, .25. **Barrel:** Rifled 22.0 in. **Weight:** 9.5 lbs. **Length:** 42.1 in. **Power:** Pre-charged pneumatic. **Stock:** Ambidextrous Turkish walnut pistol grip. **Sights:** None, 11mm grooved dovetail for scope mounting. **Features:** Multi-shot side-lever action, 14-shot .177 magazine, 12-shot .22 magazine, 10-shot .25 magazine, shrouded barrel, adjustable two-stage trigger, massive dual air reservoirs with total of 850 CC. **Velocities:** .177, 1,070 fps/.22, 975 fps/.25, 825 fps.
Price: **$779.99**

KRAL ARMS PUNCHER PITBULL PCP AIR RIFLE
Calibers: .177, .22, .25. **Barrel:** Rifled 23.0 in. **Weight:** 8.65 lbs. **Length:** 42.3 in. **Power:** Pre-charged pneumatic. **Stock:** Ambidextrous Turkish walnut pistol grip. **Sights:** None, 11mm grooved dovetail for scope mounting. **Features:** Multi-shot side-lever action, 14-shot .177 magazine, 12-shot .22 magazine, 10-shot .25 magazine, shrouded barrel, adjustable two-stage trigger, massive dual air reservoirs with total of 755 CC. **Velocities:** .177, 1,070 fps/.22, 975 fps/.25, 825 fps.
Price: **$749.99**

KRAL ARMS N-07 BREAKBARREL AIR RIFLE, WOOD OR SKULL
Calibers: .177, .22, .25. **Barrel:** Rifled, 17.9 in. **Weight:** 7.49–7.85 lbs. **Length:** 47.6 in. **Power:** Break-barrel, spring-piston **Stock:** Available in ambidextrous wood and various synthetic options. **Sights:** Fiber-optic front sight and fully adjustable fiber-optic rear sight, 11mm grooved dovetail for scope mounting. **Features:** Single-shot, full power with just one cock of the barrel, two-stage trigger. Velocities: .177, 1,200 fps/.22, 1,000 fps/.25, 750 fps.
Price: .... **$179.99–$199.99**

KRAL ARMS N-11 BREAKBARREL AIR RIFLE, BLACK
Calibers: .177, .22, .25. **Barrel:** Rifled, 15.7 in. **Weight:** 7.82 lbs. **Length:** 49.0 in. **Power:** Break-barrel, spring-piston **Stock:** Available in ambidextrous thumbhole synthetic options. **Sights:** Fiber-optic front sight and fully adjustable fiber-optic rear sight, 11mm grooved dovetail for scope mounting. **Features:** Muzzle break suppressor for quite shooting and easier cocking, single-shot, full power with just one cock of the barrel, two-stage trigger. **Velocities:** .177, 1,200 fps/.22, 950 fps./.25, 750 fps.
Price: **$179.99**

MARKSMAN 2040
Caliber: .177 steel BBs. **Barrel:** Smoothbore 10.5 in. **Weight:** 4 lbs. **Length:** 33.5 in. **Power:** Single-cock, spring-piston **Stock:** Ambidextrous plastic stock. **Sights:** Blade and ramp, adjustable rear sight adjustable for elevation, grooved for scope mounting, includes 4x20 scope and mounts. **Features:** BB repeater, lightweight, easy to shoot. **Velocity:** 300 fps.
Price: **$59.50**

REMINGTON EXPRESS

REMINGTON EXPRESS AIR RIFLE W/SCOPE COMBOS
Caliber: .22. **Barrel:** Rifled, 19 in. **Weight:** 8 lbs. **Length:** 45 in. **Power:** Break-barrel, spring-piston **Stock:** Available in ambidextrous wood with grip and fore-end checkering and textured synthetic options. **Sights:** Fiber-optic front sight and fully adjustable fiber-optic rear sight, grooved for scope mounting, includes 4x32 scope and mounts. Features: Single-shot, two-stage trigger. **Velocity:** 800 fps.
Price: **$179.99**

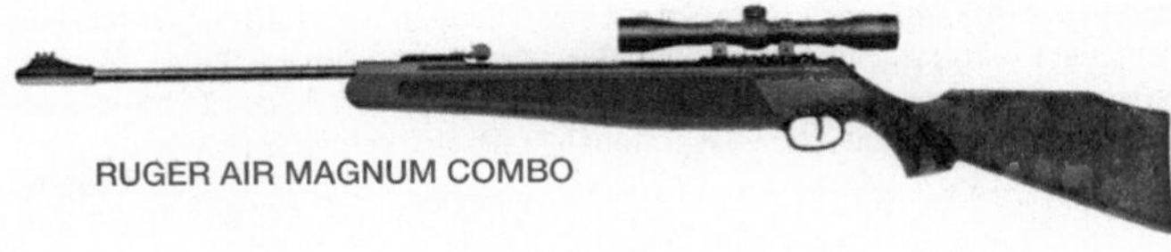

RUGER AIR MAGNUM COMBO

RUGER AIR MAGNUM COMBO
Calibers: .177, .22. **Barrel:** Rifled 19.5 in. **Weight:** 9.5 lbs. **Length:** 48.5 in. **Power:** Break-barrel, spring-piston. **Stock:** Ambidextrous Monte Carlo synthetic stock with textured grip and fore-end. **Sights:** Fiber-optic front sight and fully adjustable fiber-optic rear sight, Weaver scope rail, includes 4x32 scope and mounts. **Features:** Single-shot, two-stage trigger. **Velocities:** .177, 1,400 fps/.22, 1,200 fps.
Price: **$220.00**

RUGER BLACKHAWK COMBO
Caliber: .177 pellets. **Barrel:** Rifled 18.7 in. **Weight:** 6.95 lbs. **Length:** 44.8 in. **Power:** Break-barrel, spring-piston. **Stock:** Ambidextrous synthetic stock with checkering on the grip and fore-end. **Sights:** Fiber-optic front sight and fully adjustable fiber-optic rear sight, grooved for scope mounting, includes 4x32 scope and mounts. Features: Single-shot, two-stage trigger. **Velocity:** 1,000 fps.
Price: **$130.00**

Prices given are believed to be accurate at time of publication however, many factors affect retail pricing so exact prices are not possible.

RUGER EXPLORER
Caliber: .177 pellets. **Barrel:** Rifled 15 in. **Weight:** 4.45 lbs. **Length:** 37.12 in. **Power:** Break-barrel, spring-piston **Stock:** Ambidextrous synthetic skeleton stock. **Sights:** Fiber-optic front sight and fully adjustable fiber-optic rear sight, grooved for scope mounting. **Features:** Designed as an entry level youth break-barrel rifle, easy to shoot and accurate, single-shot, two-stage trigger. **Velocity:** 495 fps.
Price: **$79.99**

RUGER TARGIS HUNTER AIR RIFLE COMBO
Caliber: .22. **Barrel:** Rifled 18.7 in. **Weight:** 9.85 lbs. **Length:** 44.85 in. **Power:** Break-barrel, spring-piston. **Stock:** Ambidextrous synthetic stock with texture grip and fore-end, includes rifle sling. **Sights:** Fiber-optic front sight and fully adjustable fiber-optic rear sight, picatinny optics rail, includes 3-9x40AO scope and mounts. Features: Integrated "SilencAIR" suppressor, single-shot, two-stage trigger. **Velocity:** 1,000 fps.
Price: **$210.00**

RUGER TARGIS AIR RIFLE
Caliber: .177. **Barrel:** Rifled 18.7 in. **Weight:** 9.85 lbs. **Length:** 44.85 in. **Power:** Break-barrel, spring-piston, single-shot. **Stock:** Black colored synthetic with ventilated comb. **Sights:** Fiber-optic front sight and adjustable rear sight with Weaver/Picatinny rail system. **Features:** Two-stage trigger with 3.3-lb. trigger pull weight and rubber buttplate. Velocities: 1,200 fps with alloy pellets and 1,000 fps with lead pellets.
Price: **$175.95**

SENECA BIG BORE 44 909 LIGHT HUNTER 500CC TANK
Caliber: .45. **Barrel:** Rifled 21.65 in. **Weight:** 8.5 **Length:** 42.1 in. **Power:** Pre-charged pneumatic. **Stock:** Right-handed wood stock. **Sights:** Fixed front sight with fully adjustable rear sight. **Features:** Massive 500cc reservoir delivers several powerful shots, delivers well over 200 ft-lbs at the muzzle, long-range hunting accuracy, exceptionally reliable. **Velocity:** 730 fps.
Price: **$729.99**

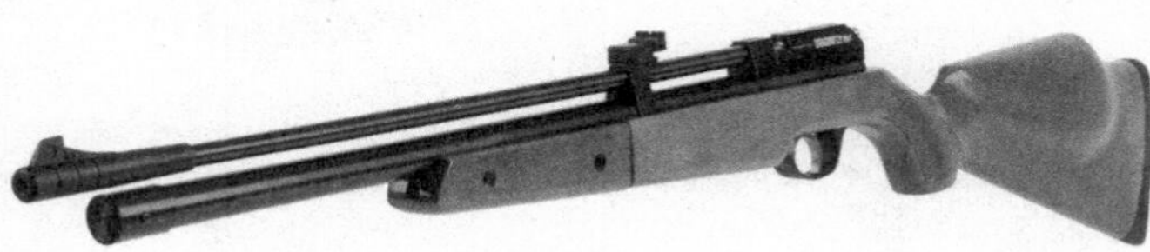

SENECA DRAGON FLY MULTI-PUMP AIR RIFLE
Calibers: .177, .22. **Barrel:** Rifled 21.7 in. **Weight:** 6.65 lbs. **Length:** 38.5 in. **Power:** Multi-Pump pneumatic. **Stock:** Ambidextrous wood stock. **Sights:** Fixed front sight with fully adjustable rear sight. **Features:** No recoil for maximum precision, variable power based on number of pumps, bolt action, single shot and multi-shot capability. **Velocities:** .177, 800 fps/.22 630 fps.
Price: **$219.99**

SENECA RECLUSE AIR RIFLE
Caliber: .35 (9mm). **Barrel:** Rifled 21.60 in. **Weight:** 7.5 lbs. **Length:** 42.1 in. **Power:** Pre-charged pneumatic. **Stock:** Right-handed wood stock. **Sights:** Fixed front sight with fully adjustable rear sight. **Features:** Massive 500cc reservoir delivers several powerful shots, delivers well over 150 ft-lbs at the muzzle, long-range hunting accuracy, exceptionally reliable. **Velocity:** 983 fps.
Price: **$699.95**

SIG SAUER MCX CO2 RIFLE & SCOPE, BLACK
Caliber: .177. **Barrel:** Rifled 17.7 in. **Length:** 34.7 in. **Power:** CO2. **Stock:** Synthetic stock, various color options. **Sights:** Varies with model, weaver rail system for iron sight systems, red dot systems, and traditional scope mounting. **Features:** 30-round semi-auto, reliable belt fed magazine system, available in various colors and sighting combination, very realistic replica. **Velocity:** 700 fps.
Price: **$269.99**

SIG SAUER MPX CO2 RIFLE, DOT SIGHT, BLACK
Caliber: .177. **Barrel:** Rifled 8 in. **Length:** 25.8 in. **Power:** CO2. **Stock:** Synthetic stock, various color options. **Sights:** Varies with model, weaver rail system for iron sight systems, red dot systems, and traditional scope mounting. **Features:** 30-round semi-auto, reliable belt fed magazine system, available in various colors and sighting combination, very realistic replica. **Velocity:** 575 fps.
Price: **$245.95**

STOEGER ARMS A30 S2 AIR RIFLE COMBO
Calibers: .177, .22. **Barrel:** Rifled 16.5 in. **Weight:** 8.2 lbs. **Length:** 42.5 in. **Power:** Break-barrel, gas-piston **Stock:** Ambidextrous synthetic stock with textured grip and fore-end. **Sights:** None, picatinny optics rail, includes 4x32 scope and mounts. **Features:** Single-shot, two-stage trigger. **Velocities:** .177, 1,200 fps/.22, 1,000 fps.
Price: **$220.00**

STOEGER ARMS X20S2 SUPPRESSOR AIR RIFLE
Calibers: .177, .22. **Barrel:** Rifled 16.5 in. **Weight:** 7 lbs. **Length:** 43 in. **Power:** Break-barrel, spring-piston. **Stock:** Ambidextrous Monte Carlo synthetic stock. **Sights:** None, grooved for scope mounting, includes compact 4x32 scope and mounts. **Features:** Industry leading dual-stage noise reduction technology makes the X20s perhaps the quietest spring-powered magnum airgun on the market. Single-shot, two-stage trigger. **Velocity:** .177, 1,200 fps/.22, 1,000 fps.
Price: **$300.00**

STOEGER X3-TAC AIR RIFLO
Caliber: .177. **Barrel:** Rifled 14.5 in. **Weight:** 5.6 lbs. **Length:** 36.25 in. **Power:** Break-barrel, spring-piston. **Stock:** Ambidextrous synthetic skeleton stock. **Sights:** Fiber-optic front sight and fully adjustable fiber-optic rear sight, grooved for scope mounting. **Features:** Easy cocking, designed for younger shooters, single-shot. **Velocity:** 550 fps.
Price: **$99.99**

UMAREX FUSION CO2 AIR RIFLE
Caliber: .177. **Barrel:** Rifled 17.13 in. **Weight:** 5.71 **Length:** 40.1 in. **Power:** CO2 **Stock:** Ambidextrous synthetic. **Sights:** None, grooved 11mm dovetail for scope mounting, includes 4x32 and mounts. **Features:** Single-shot bolt action, includes integrated suppressor. **Velocity:** .177, 750 fps.
Price: **$195.99**

UMAREX GAUNTLET PCP AIR RIFLE, SYNTHETIC STOCK
Caliber: .177, .22. **Barrel:** Rifled 23.5 in. **Weight:** 8.5 **Length:** 46 in. **Power:** Pre-charged pneumatic. **Stock:** Ambidextrous synthetic. **Sights:** None, grooved 11mm dovetail for scope mounting. **Features:** Removable regulated bottle, multi-shot bolt action, fully shrouded and moderated, adjustable two-stage trigger, first production PCP with these high-end features at this low price point. **Velocities:** .177, 1,000 fps/.22, 900 fps.
Price: **$329.95**

UMAREX THROTTLE AIR RIFLE COMBO, GAS PISTON
Calibers: .177, .22. **Barrel:** Rifled 15.9 in. **Weight:** 8.3 lbs. **Length:** 45.3 in. **Power:** Break-barrel, gas-piston. **Stock:** Ambidextrous synthetic. **Sights:** None, Weaver rail for scope mounting, includes 3-9x32 AO scope and mounts. **Features:** Single shot, includes integrated suppressor, features new "STOPSHOX" anti-recoil feature. **Velocities:** .177, 1,200 fps/.22, 1,000 fps.
Price: **$229.95**

WALTHER LG400 UNIVERSAL AIR RIFLE, AMBI GRIP
Caliber: .177. **Barrel:** Advanced match-grade rifled barrel 16.53 in. **Weight:** 8.6 lbs. **Length:** 43.7 in. **Power:** Pre-charged pneumatic. **Stock:** Ambidextrous competition, highly adjustable wood stock. **Sights:** Olympic-grade, match Diopter/Micrometer adjustable sights. **Features:** True professional class 10-meter target rifle, meets ISSF requirements. **Velocity:** 557 fps.
Price: **$2,500.00**

WALTHER MAXIMATHOR AIR RIFLE
Calibers: .22, .25. **Barrel:** Advanced match-grade rifled barrel, 23.5 in. **Weight:** 9.6 lbs. **Length:** 41.75 in. **Power:** Pre-charged pneumatic. **Stock:** Ambidextrous wood stock. **Sights:** None, grooved 11mm dovetail for scope mounting. **Features:** Bolt action 8-shot magazine, pure hunting PCP with range and accuracy. **Velocities:** .22, 1,260 fps/.25, 1,000 fps.
Price: .... **$799.99–$829.99**

Prices given are believed to be accurate at time of publication however, many factors affect retail pricing so exact prices are not possible.

WALTHER LEVER ACTION

WALTHER LEVER ACTION CO2 RIFLE, BLACK
Caliber: .177. **Barrel:** Rifled 18.9 in. **Weight:** 6.2 lbs. **Length:** 39.2 in. **Power:** CO2 **Stock:** Ambidextrous wood stock. **Sights:** Blade front sight, adjustable rear sight. **Features:** Lever-action repeater, 8-shot rotary magazine, great wild west replica airgun. **Velocity:** 600 fps.
Price: **$500.00**

WALTHER 1250 DOMINATOR COMBO AIR RIFLE
Calibers: .177, .22. **Barrel:** Rifled 23.62 in. **Weight:** 8 lbs. **Length:** 40.94 in. **Power:** Pre-charged pneumatic. **Stock:** Ambidextrous synthetic stock with dual raised cheekpieces. **Sights:** None, grooved for scope mounting, includes 8-32x56 side focus mil-dot scope and mounts. **Features:** German-engineered and manufactured, bolt-action repeater, 8-shot rotary magazine, adjustable two-stage trigger. Ships with hard case, bipod and muzzle brake. **Velocities:** .177, 1,200 fps/.22, 1,000 fps.
Price: **$949.99**

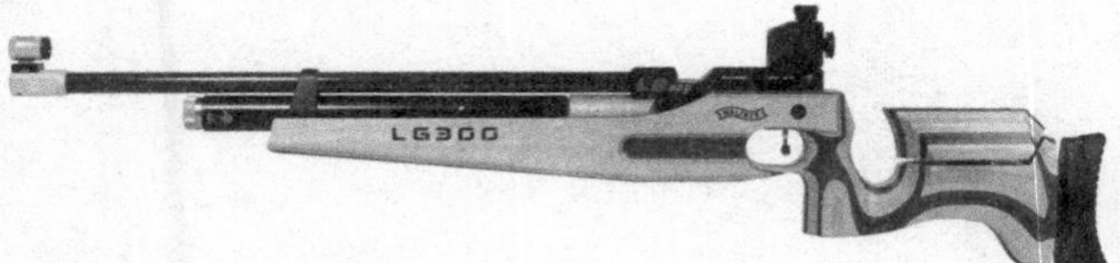

WALTHER LG300-XT JUNIOR AIR RIFLE, LAMINATED STOCK
Caliber: .177. **Barrel:** Advanced match-grade rifled barrel, 16.54 in. **Weight:** 7.72 lbs. **Length:** 39.76 in. **Power:** Pre-charged pneumatic. **Stock:** Ambidextrous highly adjustable competition laminate wood stock. **Sights:** Olympic-grade, match Diopter/Micrometer adjustable sights. **Features:** 10-meter competition target rifle, meets ISSF requirements, removable air cylinder delivers up to 400 shots per fill. **Velocity:** 570 fps.
Price: **$1,725.95**

***WALTHER PARRUS AIR RIFLE**
Caliber: .177, .22. **Barrel:** Rifled 19.25 in. **Weight:** 8.8 lbs. **Length:** 48.00 in. **Power:** Single-cock, spring-piston. **Stock:** Ambidextrous beech and synthetic stock options available. **Sights:** Front fiber-optic sight and fully adjustable rear fiber-optic sight, grooved for scope mounting. **Features:** German-engineered and manufactured, very easy cocking and shooting, 1/2 UNF threaded muzzle, single-shot, adjustable trigger, limited lifetime warranty. **Velocities:** .177, 1,300 fps/.22, 1,000 fps.
Price: .... **$339.95–$349.95**

WALTHER TERRUS AIR RIFLE
Calibers: .177, .22. **Barrel:** Rifled 17.75 in. **Weight:** 7.52 lbs. **Length:** 44.25 in. **Power:** Single-cock, spring-piston. **Stock:** Ambidextrous beech and synthetic stock options available. **Sights:** Front fiber-optic sight and fully adjustable rear fiber-optic sight, grooved for scope mounting. **Features:** German engineered and manufactured, very easy cocking and shooting, 1/2 UNF threaded muzzle, single-shot, two-stage target trigger, limited lifetime warranty. **Velocities:** .177, 1,050 fps /.22, 800 fps.
Price: .... **$279.95–$329.95**

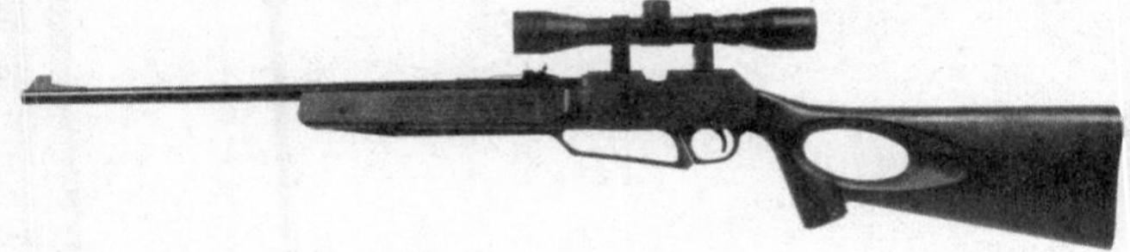

WINCHESTER 77XS MULTI-PUMP AIR RIFLE
Caliber: .177 steel BBs, .177 Pellet. **Barrel:** Rifled 20.8 in. **Weight:** 3.1 lbs. **Length:** 37.6 in. **Power:** Multi-pump pneumatic. **Stock:** Ambidextrous synthetic thumbhole stock. **Sights:** Blade front sight, adjustable rear sight, grooved for scope mounting, includes 4x32 scope and mounts. **Features:** Single-shot pellet, 50-round BB repeater, bolt action, lightweight, accurate and easy to shoot. **Velocity:** 800 fps.
Price: **$95.45**

WINCHESTER 500S AIR RIFLE
Caliber: .177. **Barrel:** Rifled. **Weight:** 6 lbs. **Length:** 39.38 in. **Power:** Break-barrel, spring-piston. **Stock:** Ambidextrous synthetic stock with textured grip and fore-end. **Sights:** Fiber-optic front sight and fully adjustable fiber-optic rear sight, grooved for scope mounting. **Features:** Easy cocking, designed for younger shooters, single-shot. **Velocity:** 490 fps.
Price: **$119.99**

WINCHESTER 1100WS AIR RIFLE
Caliber: .177. **Barrel:** Rifled. **Weight:** 8.5 lbs. **Length:** 46.25 in. **Power:** Break-barrel, spring-piston. **Stock:** Ambidextrous synthetic stock and wood stock options, textured grip and fore-end on both stock types. **Sights:** Fixed front sight and fully adjustable rear sight, grooved for scope mounting, includes 4x32 scope and mounts. **Features:** Single-shot, aggressive pricing. **Velocity:** 1,100 fps.
Price: .... **$131.99–$143.99**

WINCHESTER 1250CS AIR RIFLE, MOSSY OAK CAMO MODEL 1250 CS
Caliber: .177. **Barrel:** Rifled. **Weight:** 8.7 lbs. **Length:** 46.5 in. **Power:** Break-barrel, spring-piston. **Stock:** Ambidextrous synthetic thumbhole camo pattern stock. **Sights:** Fixed fiber-optic front sight and fully adjustable fiber-optic rear sight, grooved for scope mounting, includes 3-9x32 scope and mounts. **Features:** Integrated suppressor, single-shot, includes web sling, integrated bipod. **Velocity:** 1,250 fps.
Price: **$215.99**

WINCHESTER 1400CS AIR RIFLE, MOSSY OAK CAMO
Caliber: .177. **Barrel:** Rifled. **Weight:** 9 lbs. **Length:** 51.2 in. **Power:** Break-barrel, spring-piston. **Stock:** Ambidextrous synthetic thumbhole Mossy Oak camo pattern stock. **Sights:** None, grooved for scope mounting, includes 3-9x32 scope and mounts. **Features:** Single-shot, includes web sling, integrated bipod. **Velocity:** 1,400 fps.
Price: **$239.99**

WINCHESTER 1052SS AIR RIFLE COMBO
Caliber: .22. **Barrel:** Rifled. **Weight:** 8.2 lbs. **Length:** 46.25 in. **Power:** Break-barrel, spring-piston. **Stock:** Ambidextrous synthetic thumbhole stock. **Sights:** None, grooved for scope mounting, includes 3-9x32 scope and mounts. **Features:** Single-shot, includes web sling, all-weather fluted barrel jacket. **Velocity:** 1,000 fps.
Price: **$219.99**

WINCHESTER MODEL 70
Calibers: .35, .45. **Barrel:** Rifled, 20.87 in. **Weight:** 9.0 lbs. **Length:** 41.75 in. **Power:** Pre-charged pneumatic. **Stock:** Right handed hardwood. **Sights:** None, grooved for scope mounting. **Features:** Multi-Shot big bore (6 shots .35 / 5 shots .45), highly stable shot strings for maximum accuracy, traditional Winchester styling, .35 produces up to 134 ft-lbs, .45 produces over 200 ft-lbs. **Velocities:** .35, 865 fps/.45, 803 fps.
Price: **$849.99**

THE 2019 GUN DIGEST

Web directory

AMMUNITION AND COMPONENTS

2 Monkey Trading **www.2monkey.com**
2nd Amendment Ammunition **www.secondammo.com**
Accurate Reloading Powders **www.accuratepowder.com**
Advanced Tactical **www.advancedtactical.com**
Aguila Ammunition **www.aguilaammo.com**
Alexander Arms **www.alexanderarms.com**
Alliant Powder **www.alliantpowder.com**
American Derringer Co. **www.amderringer.com**
American Eagle **www.federalpremium.com**
American Pioneer Powder **www.americanpioneerpowder.com**
American Specialty Ammunition **www.americanspecialityammo.com**
Ammo Depot **www.ammodepot.com**
Ammo Importers **www.ammoimporters.com**
Ammo-Up **www.ammoupusa.com**
Applied Ballistics Munitions **www.buyabmammo.com**
Arizona Ammunition, Inc. **www.arizonaammunition.net**
Armscor **www.us.armscor.com**
ASYM Precision Ammunition **www.asymammo.com**
Atesci **www.atesci.com**
Australian Munitions **www.australian-munitions.com**
B&T (USA) **www.bt-ag.ch**
Ballistic Products Inc. **www.ballisticproducts.com**
Barnes Bullets **www.barnesbullets.com**
Baschieri & Pellagri **www.baschieri-pellagri.com**
Berger Bullets, Ltd. **www.bergerbullets.com**
Berry's Mfg., Inc. **www.berrysmfg.com**
Big Bore Express **www.powerbeltbullets.com**
Black Hills Ammunition, Inc. **www.black-hills.com**
BlackHorn209 **www.blackhorn209.com**
Brenneke of America Ltd. **www.brennekeusa.com**
Browning **www.browning.com**
Buffalo Arms **www.buffaloarms.com**
Buffalo Bore Ammunition **www.buffalobore.com**
Buffalo Cartridge Co. **www.buffalocartridge.com**
Calhoon, James, Bullets **www.jamescalhoon.com**
Cartuchos Saga **www.saga.es**
Cast Performance Bullet **www.grizzlycartridge.com**
CCI **www.cci-ammunition.com**
Century International Arms **www.centuryarms.com**
Cheaper Than Dirt **www.cheaperthandirt.com**
Cheddite France **www.cheddite.com**
Claybuster Wads **www.claybusterwads.com**
Combined Tactical Systems **www.combinedsystems.com**
Cor-Bon/Glaser **www.corbon.com**
Creedmoor Sports **www.creedmoorsports.com**
Custom Cartridge **www.customcartridge.com**
Cutting Edge Bullets **www.cuttingedgebullets.com**
Dakota Arms **www.dakotaarms.com**
DDupleks, Ltd. **www.ddupleks.com**
Dead Nuts Manufacturing **www.deadnutsmfg.us**
Defense Technology Corp. **www.defense-technology.com**
Denver Bullets **www.denverbullets.com**
Desperado Cowboy Bullets **www.cowboybullets.com**
Dillon Precision **www.dillonprecision.com**
Double Tap Ammunition **www.doubletapammo.net**
Down Range Mfg. **www.downrangemfg.com**
Dynamic Research Technologies **www.drtammo.com**
E. Arthur Brown Co. **www.wabco.com**
EcoSlug **www.eco-slug.com**
Eley Ammunition **www.eley.co.uk**
Environ-Metal **www.hevishot.com**
Estate Cartridge **www.estatecartridge.com**
Federal Cartridge Co. **www.federalpremium.com**
Fiocchi of America **www.fiocchiusa.com**
G2 Research **www.g2rammo.com**
Gamebore Cartridge **www.gamebore.com**
GaugeMate **www.gaugemate.com**
Glaser Safety Slug, Inc. **www.corbon.com**
GOEX Inc. **www.goexpowder.com**
Graf & Sons **www.grafs.com**
Grizzly Cartridge Co. **www.grizzlycartridge.com**
Haendler & Natermann **www.hn-sport.de**
Hawk Bullets **www.hawkbullets.com**
Herter's Ammunition **www.cabelas.com**
Hevi.Shot **www.hevishot.com**
High Precision Down Range **www.hprammo.com**
Hodgdon Powder **www.hodgdon.com**
Hornady **www.hornady.com**
HSM Ammunition **www.thehuntingshack.com**
Huntington Reloading Products **www.huntingtons.com**

IMR Smokeless Powders **www.imrpowder.com**
International Cartridge Corp **www.iccammo.com**
J&G Sales **www.jgsales.com**
James Calhoon **www.jamescalhoon.com**
Kent Cartridge America **www.kentgamebore.com**
Knight Bullets **www.benchrest.com/knight/**
Lapua **www.lapua.com**
Lawrence Brand Shot **www.lawrencebrandshot.com**
Lazzeroni Arms **www.lazzeroni.com**
Leadheads Bullets **www.proshootpro.com**
Lehigh Defense **www.lehighdefense.com**
Lightfield Ammunition Corp **www.litfld.com**
Lyman **www.lymanproducts.com**
Magnum Muzzleloading Products **www.mmpsabots.com**
Magnus Bullets **www.magnusbullets.com**
MagSafe Ammo **www.magsafeonline.com**
Magtech **www.magtechammunition.com**
Meister Bullets **www.meisterbullets.com**
Midway USA **www.midwayusa.com**
Mitchell's Mausers **www.mauser.org**
National Bullet Co. **www.nationalbullet.com**
Navy Arms **www.navyarms.com**
Nobel Sport **www.nobelsportammo.com**
Norma **www.norma.cc**
North Fork Technologies **www.northforkbullets.com**
Nosler Bullets, Inc. **www.nosler.com**
Old Western Scrounger **www.ows-ammo.com**
Pattern Control **www.patterncontrol.com**
PCP Ammunition **www.pcpammo.com**
Piney Mountain Ammunition
www.pineymountainammunitionco.com
PMC **www.pmcammo.com**
PolyCase Ammunition **www.polycaseammo.com**
Polywad **www.polywad.com**
PowerBelt Bullets **www.powerbeltbullets.com**
PPU Ammunition **www.prvipartizan.com**
PR Bullets **www.prbullet.com**
Precision Delta **www.precisiondelta.com**
Precision Reloading **www.precisionreloading.com**
Pro Load Ammunition **www.proload.com**
Prvi Partizan Ammunition **www.prvipartizan.com**
Rainier Ballistics **www.rainierballistics.com**
Ram Shot Powder **www.ramshot.com**
Rare Ammunition **www.rareammo.com**
Reloading Specialties Inc. **www.reloadingspecialtiesinc.com**
Remington **www.remington.com**
Rio Ammunition **www.rioammo.com**
Rocky Mountain Cartridge **www.rockymountaincartride.com**
Sauvestre Ammunition **www.centuryarms.com**
SBR Ammunition **www.sbrammunition.com**
Schuetzen Powder **www.schuetzenpowder.com**
Sellier & Bellot **www.sellier-bellot.cz**
Shilen **www.shilen.com**
Sierra **www.sierrabullets.com**
SIG Sauer **www.sigammo.com**
Silver State Armory **www.ssarmory.com**
Simunition **www.simunition.com**
SinterFire, Inc. **www.sinterfire.com**
Spectra Shot **www.spectrashot.com**
Speer Ammunition **www.speer-ammo.com**
Speer Bullets **www.speer-bullets.com**
Sporting Supplies Int'l Inc. **www.wolfammo.com**
Starline **www.starlinebrass.com**
Stealth Gunpowder **www.stealthgunpowder.com**
Swift Bullets Co. **www.swiftbullets.com**
Tannerite **www.tannerite.com**
Tascosa Cartridge Co. **www.tascosacartridge.com**
Ted Nugent Ammunition **www.americantactical.us**
Ten-X Ammunition **www.tenxammo.com**
Top Brass **www.topbrass-inc.com**
TulAmmo **www.tulammousa.com**
Velocity Tactics **www.velocitytactics.com**
Vihtavuori **www.vihtavuori.com**
Weatherby **www.weatherby.com**
Western Powders Inc. **www.westernpowders.com**
Widener's Reloading & Shooters Supply **www.wideners.com**
Winchester Ammunition **www.winchester.com**
Windjammer Tournament Wads **www.windjammer-wads.com**
Wolf Ammunition **www.wolfammo.com**
Woodleigh Bullets **www.woodleighbullets.com.au**
Xtreme Bullets **www.xtremebullets.com**
Zanders Sporting Goods **www.gzanders.com**

CASES, SAFES, GUN LOCKS AND CABINETS

Ace Case Co. **www.acecase.com**
AG English Sales Co. **www.agenglish.com**
Dee Zee **www.deezee.com**
American Security Products **www.amsecusa.com**
Americase **www.americase.com**
Assault Systems **www.elitesurvival.com**
Avery Outdoors, Inc. **www.averyoutdoors.com**
Birchwood Casey **www.birchwoodcasey.com**
Bore-Stores **www.borestores.com**
Boyt Harness Co. **www.boytharness.com**
Gardall Safes **www.gardall.com**
Campbell Industrial Supply **www.gun-racks.com**
Cannon Safe Co. **www.cannonsafe.com**
Fort Knox Safes **www.ftknox.com**
Franzen Security Products **www.securecase.com**
Goldenrod Dehumidifiers **www.goldenroddehumidifiers.com**
Gunlocker Phoenix USA Inc. **www.gunlocker.com**

Gun Storage Solutions **www.storemoreguns.com**
GunVault **www.gunvault.com**
Hakuba USA Inc. **www.hakubausa.com**
Heritage Safe Co. **www.heritagesafe.com**
Homak Safes **www.homak.com**
Hunter Company **www.huntercompany.com**
Liberty Safe & Security **www.libertysafe.com**
Morton Enterprises **www.uniquecases.com**
New Innovative Products **www.starlightcases.com**
Pelican Products **www.pelican.com**
Phoenix USA Inc. **www.gunlocker.com**
Plano Molding Co. **www.planomolding.com**
Plasticase, Inc. **www.nanuk.com**
Rhino Safe **www.rhinosafe.com**
Rotary Gun Racks **www.gun-racks.com**
Sack-Ups **www.sackups.com**
Safe Tech, Inc. **www.safrgun.com**
Securecase **www.securecase.com**
Sentry Safe **www.sentrysafe.com**
Shot Lock Corp. **www.shotlock.com**
SKB Cases **www.skbcases.com**
Smart Lock Technology Inc. **www.smartlock.com**
Snap Safe **www.snapsafe.com**
Sportsmans Steel Safe Co. **www.sportsmansteelsafes.com**
Stack-On Safes **www.stackon.com**
Starlight Cases **www.starlightcases.com**
Strong Case **www.strongcasebytnb.com**
Technoframes **www.technoframes.com**
Titan Gun Safes **www.titangunsafes.com**
Tracker Safe **www.trackersafe.com**
T.Z. Case Int'l **www.tzcase.com**
U.S. Explosive Storage **www.usexplosivestorage.com**
Vanguard World **www.vanguardworld.com**
Versatile Rack Co. **www.versatilegunrack.com**
V-Line Industries **www.vlineind.com**
Winchester Safes **www.winchestersafes.com**
Ziegel Engineering **www.ziegeleng.com**

CHOKE DEVICES, RECOIL REDUCERS, SUPPRESSORS AND ACCURACY DEVICES

ACT Tactical **www.blackwidowshooters.com**
Advanced Armament Corp. **www.advanced-armament.com**
Alpha Dog Silencers **www.alphadogsilencers.com**
100 Straight Products **www.100straight.com**
Briley Mfg. **www.briley.com**
Carlson's **www.choketube.com**
Colonial Arms **www.colonialarms.com**
Comp-N-Choke **www.comp-n-choke.com**
Elite Iron **www.eliteiron.net**
Gemtech **www.gem-tech.com**
Great Lakes Tactical **www.gltactical.com**
KDF, Inc. **www.kdfguns.com**
Kick's Industries **www.kicks-ind.com**
LimbSaver **www.limbsaver.com**
Lyman Products **www.lymanproducts.com**
Mag-Na-Port Int'l Inc. **www.magnaport.com**
Metro Gun **www.metrogun.com**
Operators Suppressor Systems **www.osssuppressors.com**
Patternmaster Chokes **www.patternmaster.com**
Poly-Choke **www.polychoke.com**
SilencerCo **www.silencerco.com**
Silencer Shop **www.silencershop.com**
Sims Vibration Laboratory **www.limbsaver.com**
SRT Arms **www.srtarms.com**
SureFire **www.surefire.com**
Teague Precision Chokes **www.teaguechokes.com**
Truglo **www.truglo.com**
Trulock Tool **www.trulockchokes.com**
Vais Arms, Inc. **www.muzzlebrakes.com**

CHRONOGRAPHS AND BALLISTIC SOFTWARE

Barnes Ballistic Program **www.barnesbullets.com**
Ballisticard Systems **www.ballisticards.com**
Competition Electronics **www.competitionelectronics.com**
Competitive Edge Dynamics **www.cedhk.com**
Hodgdon Shotshell Program **www.hodgdon.com**
Lee Shooter Program **www.leeprecision.com**
NECO **www.neconos.com**
Oehler Research Inc. **www.oehler-research.com**
PACT **www.pact.com**
ProChrony **www.competitionelectronics.com**
Quickload **www.neconos.com**
RCBS Load **www.rcbs.com**
Shooting Chrony **www.shootingchrony.com**
Sierra Infinity Ballistics Program **www.sierrabullets.com**
Winchester Ballistics Calculator **www.winchester.com**

CLEANING PRODUCTS

Accupro **www.accupro.com**
Ballistol USA **www.ballistol.com**
Birchwood Casey **www.birchwoodcasey.com**
Bore Tech **www.boretech.com**
Break-Free, Inc. **www.break-free.com**
Bruno Shooters Supply **www.brunoshooters.com**
Butch's Bore Shine **www.butchsboreshine.com**
C.J. Weapons Accessories **www.cjweapons.com**
Clenzoil **www.clenzoil.com**
Corrosion Technologies **www.corrosionx.com**

Dewey Mfg. **www.deweyrods.com**
DuraCoat **www.lauerweaponry.com**
Emby Enterprises **www.alltemptacticallube.com**
Extreme Gun Care **www.extremeguncare.com**
G96 **www.g96.com**
Gun Butter **www.gunbutter.com**
Gun Cleaners **www.guncleaners.com**
Gunslick Gun Care **www.gunslick.com**
Gunzilla **www.topduckproducts.com**
Hoppes **www.hoppes.com**
Hydrosorbent Products **www.dehumidify.com**
Inhibitor VCI Products **www.theinhibitor.com**
Jag Brush **www.jagbrush.com**
KG Industries **www.kgcoatings.com**
L&R Ultrasonics **www.ultrasonics.com**
Lyman **www.lymanproducts.com**
Mil-Comm Products **www.mil-comm.com**
Montana X-Treme **www.montanaxtreme.com**
MPT Industries **www.mptindustries.com**
Mpro7 Gun Care **www.mp7.com**
Old West Snake Oil **www.oldwestsnakeoil.com**
Otis Technology, Inc. **www.otisgun.com**
Outers **www.outers-guncare.com**
Prolix Lubricant **www.prolixlubricant.com**
ProShot Products **www.proshotproducts.com**
ProTec Lubricants **www.proteclubricants.com**
Rigel Products **www.rigelproducts.com**
Sagebrush Products **www.sagebrushproducts.com**
Sentry Solutions Ltd. **www.sentrysolutions.com**
Shooters Choice Gun Care **www.shooters-choice.com**
Slip 2000 **www.slip2000.com**
Southern Bloomer Mfg. **www.southernbloomer.com**
Stony Point Products **www.unclemikes.com**
Top Duck Products, LLC **www.topduckproducts.com**
Triangle Patch **www.trianglepatch.com**
Wipe-Out **www.sharpshootr.com**
World's Fastest Gun Bore Cleaner **www.michaels-oregon.com**

FIREARM AUCTION SITES

Alderfer Auction **www.alderferauction.com**
Amoskeag Auction Co. **www.amoskeagauction.com**
Antique Guns **www.antiqueguns.com**
Auction Arms **www.auctionarms.com**
Batterman's Auctions **www.battermans.com**
Bonhams & Butterfields **www.bonhams.com/usarms**
Cowan's **www.cowans.com**
Fontaine's Auction Gallery **www.fontainesauction.net**
Guns America **www.gunsamerica.com**
Gun Broker **www.gunbroker.com**
Guns International **www.gunsinternational.com**
Heritage Auction Galleries **www.ha.com**
James D. Julia, Inc. **www.jamesdjulia.com**
Little John's Auction Service **www.littlejohnsauctionservice.net**
Lock, Stock & Barrel Investments **www.lsbauctions.com**
Morphy Auctions **www.morphyauctions.com**
Poulin Auction Co. **www.poulinantiques.com**
Rock Island Auction Co. **www.rockislandauction.com**
Wallis & Wallis **www.wallisandwallis.org**

FIREARM MANUFACTURERS AND IMPORTERS

Accu-Tek **www.accu-tekfirearms.com**
Accuracy Int'l North America **www.accuracyinternational.com**
Adcor Defense **www.adcorindustries.com**
AGP Arms In. **www.agparms.com**
AIM **www.aimsurplus.com**
AirForce Airguns **www.airforceairguns.com**
Air Gun Inc. **www.airrifle-china.com**
Air Ordnance/Tippmann Armory **www.tippmannarmory.com**
Airguns of Arizona **www.airgunsofarizona.com**
Alexander Arms **www.alexanderarms.com**
America Remembers **www.americaremembers.com**
American Classic **www.americanclassic1911.com**
American Derringer Corp. **www.amderringer.com**
American Spirit Arms **www.americanspirtarms.com**
American Tactical Imports **www.americantactical.us**
American Classic **www.eagleimportsinc.com**
American Western Arms **www.awaguns.com**
Angstadt Arms **www.angstadtarms.com**
Anschutz **www.anschutz-sporters.com**
AR-7 Industries **www.ar-7.com**
Ares Defense Systems **www.aresdefense.com**
Armalite **www.armalite.com**
Armi Sport **www.armisport.com**
Armscor Precision Internationl **www.armscor.com**
Armscorp USA Inc. **www.armscorpusa.com**
Arrieta **www.arrietashotguns.com**
Arsenal Inc. **www.arsenalinc.com**
Atlanta Cutlery Corp. **www.atlantacutlery.com**
Atlas Gun Works **www.atlas-gunworks.com**
ATA Arms **www.ataarms.com**
Auto-Ordnance Corp. **www.tommygun.com**
AYA **www.aya-fineguns.com**
B&T (USA) **www.bt-ag.ch**
Ballard Rifles **www.ballardrifles.com**
Barrett Firearms Mfg. **www.barrettrifles.com**
Bat Machine Co. **www.batmachine.com**
Battle Arms Development **www.battlearmsdevelopment.com**
Beeman Precision Airguns **www.beeman.com**
Benelli USA Corp. **www.benelliusa.com**

Benjamin Sheridan **www.crosman.com**
Beretta U.S.A. **www.berettausa.com**
Bergara Rifles **www.bergararifles.com**
Bernardelli **www.bernardelli.com**
Bersa **www.bersa.com**
Bighorn Arms **www.bighornarms.com**
Big Horn Armory **www.bighornarmory.com**
Blaser Jagdwaffen Gmbh **www.blaser.de**
Bleiker **www.bleiker.ch**
Bond Arms **www.bondarms.com**
Borden Rifles, Inc. **www.bordenrifles.com**
Boss & Co. **www.bossguns.co.uk**
Bowen Classic Arms **www.bowenclassicarms.com**
Breda **www.bredafucili.com**
Briley Mfg. **www.briley.com**
BRNO Arms **www.cz-usa.com**
Brown, E. Arthur **www.eabco.com**
Brown, Ed Products **www.edbrown.com**
Brown, McKay **www.mckaybrown.com**
Browning **www.browning.com**
BRP Corp. **www.brpguns.com**
BUL Ltd. **www.bultransmark.com**
Bushmaster Firearms **www.bushmaster.com**
BWE Firearms **www.bwefirearms.com**
Cabot Guns **www.cabotguns.com**
Caesar Guerini USA **www.gueriniusa.com**
Calico **www.calicoweaponsystems.com**
Caracal **www.caracal-usa.com**
Carolina Arms Group **www.carolinaarmsgroup.com**
Caspian Arms, Ltd. **www.caspianarmsltd.com**
CDNN Sports **www.cdnnsports.com**
Century Arms **www.centuryarms.com**
Champlin Firearms **www.champlinarms.com**
Charles Daly **www.charlesdaly.com**
Charter Arms **www.charterfirearms.com**
CheyTac USA **www.cheytac.com**
Chiappa Firearms **www.chiappafirearms.com**
Christensen Arms **www.christensenarms.com**
Cimarron Firearms Co. **www.cimarron-firearms.com**
CK Arms/Freedom Gunworks **www.ckarms.com**
Clark Custom Guns **www.clarkcustomguns.com**
CMMG **www.cmmginc.com**
Cobalt Kinetics **www.cobaltarms.com**
Cobra Enterprises **www.cobrapistols.net**
Cogswell & Harrison **www.cogswellandharrison.com**
Collector's Armory, Ltd. **www.collectorsarmory.com**
Colt's Mfg Co. **www.colt.com**
Comanche **www.eagleimportsinc.com**
Connecticut Shotgun Mfg. Co. **www.connecticutshotgun.com**
Connecticut Valley Arms **www.cva.com**
Coonan, Inc. **www.coonaninc.com**
Cooper Firearms **www.cooperfirearms.com**
Core Rifle Systems **www.core15.com**
Corner Shot **www.cornershot.com**
CPA Rifles **www.singleshotrifles.com**
Crickett Rifles **www.crickett.com**
Crosman **www.crosman.com**
CVA **www.cva.com**
Cylinder & Slide Shop **www.cylinder-slide.com**
Czechp Int'l **www.czechpoint-usa.com**
CZ USA **www.cz-usa.com**
Daisy Mfg Co. **www.daisy.com**
Daniel Defense **www.danieldefense.com**
Dan Wesson **www.danwessonfirearms.com**
Dakota Arms Inc. **www.dakotaarms.com**
Desert Eagle **www.magnumresearch.com**
Detonics USA **www.detonicsdefense.com**
Devil Dog Arms **www.devildogarms.com**
Diamondback **www.diamondbackamerica.com**
Diana **www.diana-airguns.de**
Dixie Gun Works **www.dixiegunworks.com**
Double D Armory **www.ddarmory.com**
DoubleStar **www.star15.com**
Downsizer Corp. **www.downsizer.com**
DPMS, Inc. **www.dpmsinc.com**
DSA Inc. **www.dsarms.com**
Dumoulin **www.dumoulin-herstal.com**
EAA Corp. **www.eaacorp.com**
Eagle Imports, Inc. **www.eagleimportsinc.com**
Ed Brown Products **www.edbrown.com**
EMF Co. **www.emf-company.com**
Empty Shell **www.emptyshell.com**
E.R. Shaw **www.ershawbarrels.com**
European American Armory Corp. **www.eaacorp.com**
Evans, William **www.williamevans.com**
Excel Arms **www.excelarms.com**
Fabarm **www.fabarm.com**
Fausti USA **www.faustiusa.com**
FightLite Industries **www.fightlite.com**
Flint River Armory **www.flintriverarmory.com**
Flodman Guns **www.flodman.com**
FMK **www.fmkfirearms.com**
FN Herstal **www.fnherstal.com**
FN America **www.fnamerica.com**
FNH USA **www.fnhusa.com**
Franchi **www.franchiusa.com**
Franklin Armory **www.franklinarmory.com**
Freedom Arms **www.freedomarms.com**
Freedom Group, Inc. **www.freedom-group.com**
Galazan **www.connecticutshotgun.com**
Gambo Renato **www.renatogamba.it**
Gamo **www.gamo.com**
GA Precision **www.gaprecision.net**
Gary Reeder Custom Guns **www.reedercustomguns.com**

German Sport Guns **www.german-sport-guns.com**
Gibbs Rifle Company **www.gibbsrifle.com**
Glock **www.glock.com**
Griffin & Howe **www.griffinhowe.com**
Gunbroker.com **www.gunbroker.com**
Guncrafter Industries **www.guncrafterindustries.com**
Gun Room Co. **www.onlylongrange.com**
Hammerli **www.carl-walther.com**
Hardened Arms **www.hardenedarms.com**
Hatsan Arms Co. **www.hatsan.com.tr**
Heckler and Koch **www.hk-usa.com**
Heizer Defense **www.heizerdefense.com**
Henry Repeating Arms Co. **www.henryrepeating.com**
Heritage Mfg. **www.heritagemfg.com**
High Standard Mfg. **www.highstandard.com**
Hi-Point Firearms **www.hi-pointfirearms.com**
Holland & Holland **www.hollandandholland.com**
Honor Defense **www.honordefense.com**
Horizon Firearms **www.horizonfirearms.com**
Howa **www.howausa.com**
H&R 1871 Firearms **www.hr1871.com**
H-S Precision **www.hsprecision.com**
Hunters Lodge Corp. **www.hunterslodge.com**
Hudson Manufacturing **www.hudsonmfg.com**
Inland Arms **www.inland-mfg.com**
International Military Antiques, Inc. **www.ima-usa.com**
Inter Ordnance **www.interordnance.com**
ISSC, LLC **www.issc-austria.com**
Ithaca Gun Co. **www.ithacagun.com**
Iver Johnson Arms **www.iverjohnsonarms.com**
IWI US Inc. **www.iwi.us**
Izhevsky Mekhanichesky Zavod **www.baikalinc.ru**
James River Armory **www.jamesriverarmory.com**
Jarrett Rifles, Inc. **www.jarrettrifles.com**
Jesse James Firearms **www.jjfu.com**
J&G Sales, Ltd. **www.jgsales.com**
Johannsen Express Rifle **www.johannsen-jagd.de**
JP Enterprises, Inc. **www.jprifles.com**
Kahr Arms/Auto-Ordnance **www.kahr.com**
Kalashnikov USA **www.kalashnikov-usa.com**
KDF, Inc. **www.kdfguns.com**
KE Arms **www.kearms.com**
Keystone Sporting Arms **www.keystonesportingarmsllc.com**
Kifaru **www.kifaru.net**
Kimber **www.kimberamerica.com**
Kingston Armory **www.kingstonarmory.com**
Knight's Armament Co. **www.knightarmco.com**
Knight Rifles **www.knightrifles.com**
Kolar **www.kolararms.com**
Korth **www.korthwaffen.de**
Krebs Custom Guns **www.krebscustom.com**
Kriss **www.kriss-usa.com**
Krieghoff Int'l **www.krieghoff.com**
KY Imports, Inc. **www.kyimports.com**
K-VAR **www.k-var.com**
Larue **www.laruetactical.com**
Layke Tactical **www.layketactical.com**
Lazzeroni Arms Co. **www.lazzeroni.com**
Legacy Sports International **www.legacysports.com**
Legendary Arms Works **www.legendaryarmsworks.com**
Les Baer Custom, Inc. **www.lesbaer.com**
Lewis Machine & Tool Co. **www.lewismachine.net**
Linebaugh Custom Sixguns **www.customsixguns.com**
Lionheart **www.lionheartindustries.com**
Ljutic **www.ljuticgun.com**
Llama **www.eagleimportsinc.com**
LMT Defense **www.lmtdefense.com**
Lyman **www.lymanproducts.com**
LWRC Int'l **www.lwrci.com**
MAC **www.eagleimportsinc.com**
Magnum Research **www.magnumresearch.com**
Majestic Arms **www.majesticarms.com**
Marksman Products **www.marksman.com**
Marlin **www.marlinfirearms.com**
MasterPiece Arms **www.masterpiecearms.com**
Mauser **www.mauser.com**
McMillan Firearms **www.mcmillanfirearms.com**
Meacham Rifles **www.meachamrifles.com**
Merkel USA **www-die-jagd.de**
Milkor USA **www.milkorusainc.com**
Miltech **www.miltecharms.com**
MOA Maximum **www.moaguns.com**
MOA Precision **www.moaprecision.com**
Modern Weapon Systems **www.modernweaponsystems.com**
Montana Rifle Co. **www.montanarifleco.com**
Mossberg **www.mossberg.com**
Navy Arms **www.navyarms.com**
New England Arms Corp. **www.newenglandarms.com**
New England Custom Gun **www.newenglandcustomgun.com**
New Ultra Light Arms **www.newultralight.com**
Nighthawk Custom **www.nighthawkcustom.com**
North American Arms **www.northamericanarms.com**
Nosler **www.nosler.com**
O.F. Mossberg & Sons **www.mossberg.com**
Ohio Ordnance Works **www.ohioordnanceworks.com**
Olympic Arms **www.olyarms.com**
Osprey Defense **www.gaspiston.com**
Panther Arms **www.dpmsinc.com**
Pedersoli Davide & Co. **www.davide-pedersoli.com**
Perazzi **www.perazzi.com**
Pietta **www.pietta.it**
Piotti **www.piotti.com/en**
Pistol Dynamics **www.pistoldynamics.com**
PKP Knife-Pistol **www.sanjuanenterprise.com**

Pointer Shotguns **www.legacysports.com/catalog/pointer**
Power Custom **www.powercustom.com**
Precision Small Arm Inc. **www.precisionsmallarms.com**
Primary Weapons Systems **www.primaryweapons.com**
Proof Research **www.proofresearch.com**
PTR 91,Inc. **www.ptr91.com**
Purdey & Sons **www.purdey.com**
Pyramyd Air **www.pyramydair.com**
Quarter Minute Magnums **www.quarterminutemagnums.com**
Remington **www.remington.com**
Republic Forge **www.republicforge.com**
Rifles, Inc. **www.riflesinc.com**
Rigby **www.johnrigbyandco.com**
Ritter & Stark **www.ritterstark.com**
Riverman Gun Works **www.rivermangunworks.com**
Rizzini USA **www.rizziniusa.com**
RM Equipment, Inc. **www.40mm.com**
Robar Companies, Inc. **www.robarguns.com**
Roberts Defense **www.robertsdefense.com**
Robinson Armament Co. **www.robarm.com**
Rock Island Armory **www.armscor.com**
Rock River Arms, Inc. **www.rockriverarms.com**
Rossi Arms **www.rossiusa.com**
RUAG Ammotec **www.ruag.com**
Ruger **www.ruger.com**
Safety Harbor Firearms **www.safetyharborfirearms.com**
Sarco **www.sarcoinc.com**
Sarsilmaz Silah San **www.sarsilmaz.com**
Sauer & Sohn **www.sauer.de**
Savage Arms Inc. **www.savagearms.com**
Scattergun Technologies Inc. **www.wilsoncombat.com**
SCCY Firearms **www.sccy.com**
Schmeisser Gmbh **www.schmeisser-germany.de**
SD Tactical Arms **www.sdtacticalarms.com**
Searcy Enterprises **www.searcyent.com**
Seecamp **www.seecamp.com**
Shaw **www.ershawbarrels.com**
Shilen Rifles **www.shilen.com**
Shiloh Rifle Mfg. **www.shilohrifle.com**
Sig Sauer, Inc. **www.sigsauer.com**
Simpson Ltd. **www.simpsonltd.com**
SKB Shotguns **www.skbshotguns.com**
Smith & Wesson **www.smith-wesson.com**
Southeast Arms, Inc. **www.southeastarms.net**
Sovereign Shotguns **www.barrettrifles.com**
Springfield Armory **www.springfield-armory.com**
SPS **www.eagleimportsinc.com**
SSK Industries **www.sskindustries.com**
Stag Arms **www.stagarms.com**
Stevens **www.savagearms.com**
Steyr Arms, Inc. **www.steyrarms.com**
STI International **www.stiguns.com**
Stoeger Industries **www.stoegerindustries.com**
Strayer-Voigt Inc. **www.sviguns.com**
Sturm, Ruger & Company **www.ruger.com**
Surgeon Rifles **www.surgeonrifles.com**
Tactical Solutions **www.tacticalsol.com**
Tar-Hunt Slug Guns, Inc. **www.tarhunt.com**
Taser Int'l **www.taser.com**
Taurus **www.taurususa.com**
Tempco Mfg. Co. **www.tempcomfg.com**
Thompson/Center Arms **www.tcarms.com**
Tikka **www.tikka.fi**
Time Precision **www.benchrest.com/timeprecision**
TNW, Inc. **www.tnwfirearms.com**
Traditions **www.traditionsfirearms.com**
Tristar Sporting Arms **www.tristarsportingarms.com**
Turnbull Mfg. Co. **www.turnbullmfg.com**
Uberti **www.ubertireplicas.com**
Ultra Light Arms **www.newultralight.com**
Umarex **www.umarex.com**
U.S. Armament Corp. **www.usarmamentcorp.com**
Uselton Arms, Inc. **www.useltonarmsinc.com**
Valkyrie Arms **www.valkyriearms.com**
Vektor Arms **www.vektorarms.com**
Verney-Carron **www.verney-carron.com**
Volquartsen Custom Ltd. **www.volquartsen.com**
Warrior **www.warrior.co**
Walther USA **www.waltherarms.com**
Weapon Depot **www.weapondepot.com**
Weatherby **www.weatherby.com**
Webley and Scott Ltd. **www.webley.co.uk**
Westley Richards **www.westleyrichards.com**
Wild West Guns **www.wildwestguns.com**
William Larkin Moore & Co. **www.williamlarkinmoore.com**
Wilson Combat **www.wilsoncombat.com**
Winchester Rifles and Shotguns **www.winchesterguns.com**

GUN PARTS, BARRELS, AFTERMARKET ACCESSORIES

300 Below **www.300below.com**
Accuracy International of North America
www.accuracyinternational.us
Accuracy Speaks, Inc. **www.accuracyspeaks.com**
Accuracy Systems **www.accuracysystemsinc.com**
Accurate Airguns **www.accurateairguns.com**
Advantage Arms **www.advantagearms.com**
AG Composites **www.agcomposites.com**
Aim Surplus **www.aimsurplus.com**
American Spirit Arms Corp. **www.americanspiritarms.com**
Amhurst-Depot **www.amherst-depot.com**

Apex Gun Parts **www.apexgunparts.com**
Armaspec **www.armaspec.com**
Armatac Industries **www.armatac.com**
Arthur Brown Co. **www.eabco.com**
Asia Sourcing Corp. **www.asiasourcing.com**
Barnes Precision Machine **www.barnesprecision.com**
Bar-Sto Precision Machine **www.barsto.com**
Bellm TC's **www.bellmtcs.com**
Belt Mountain Enterprises **www.beltmountain.com**
Bergara Barrels **www.bergarabarrels.com**
Beyer Barrels **www.beyerbarrels.com**
Bighorn Arms **www.bighornarms.com**
Bill Wiseman & Co. **www.wisemanballistics.com**
Bluegrass Gun Works **www.rocksolidind.com**
Bravo Company USA **www.bravocompanyusa.com**
Briley **www.briley.com**
Brownells **www.brownells.com**
B-Square **www.b-square.com**
Buffer Tech **www.buffer-tech.com**
Bullberry Barrel Works **www.bullberry.com**
Bulldog Barrels **www.bulldogbarrels.com**
Bullet Central **www.bulletcentral.com**
Bushmaster Firearms/Quality Parts **www.bushmaster.com**
Butler Creek Corp **www.butlercreek.com**
Cape Outfitters Inc. **www.capeoutfitters.com**
Cavalry Arms **www.cavalryarms.com**
Caspian Arms Ltd. **www.caspianarms.com**
CDNN Sports **www.cdnnsports.com**
Cheaper Than Dirt **www.cheaperthandirt.com**
Chesnut Ridge **www.chestnutridge.com/**
Choate Machine & Tool Co. **www.riflestock.com**
Christie's Products **www.1022cental.com**
CJ Weapons Accessories **www.cjweapons.com**
Colonial Arms **www.colonialarms.com**
Comp-N-Choke **www.comp-n-choke.com**
Criterion Barrels **www.criterionbarrels.com**
Custom Gun Rails **www.customgunrails.com**
Cylinder & Slide Shop **www.cylinder-slide.com**
Dave Manson Precision Reamers **www.mansonreamers.com**
DC Machine **www.dcmachine.net**
Digi-Twist **www.fmtcorp.com**
Dixie Gun Works **www.dixiegun.com**
DPMS **www.dpmsinc.com**
D.S. Arms **www.dsarms.com**
E. Arthur Brown Co. **www.eabco.com**
Ed Brown Products **www.edbrown.com**
EFK/Fire Dragon **www.efkfiredragon.com**
E.R. Shaw **www.ershawbarrels.com**
FJ Fedderson Rifle Barrels **www.gunbarrels.net**
FTF Industries **www.ftfindustries.com**
Fulton Armory **www.fulton-armory.com**

Galazan **www.connecticutshotgun.com**
Gemtech **www.gem-tech.com**
Gentry, David **www.gentrycustom.com**
GG&G **www.gggaz.com**
Great Lakes Tactical **www.gltactical.com**
Green Mountain Rifle Barrels **www.gmriflebarrel.com**
Gun Parts Corp. **www.gunpartscorp.com**
Guntec USA **www.guntecusa.com**
Harris Engineering **www.harrisbipods.com**
Hart Rifle Barrels **www.hartbarrels.com**
Hastings Barrels **www.hastingsbarrels.com**
Heinie Specialty Products **www.heinie.com**
High Performance Firearms/Hiperfire **www.hiperfire.com**
HKS Products **www.hksspeedloaders.com**
Holland Shooters Supply **www.hollandguns.com**
H-S Precision **www.hsprecision.com**
100 Straight Products **www.100straight.c**
I.M.A. **www.ima-usa.com**
Jarvis, Inc. **www.jarvis-custom.com**
J&T Distributing **www.jtdistributing.com**
JP Enterprises **www.jprifles.com**
Keng's Firearms Specialties **www.versapod.com**
KG Industries **www.kgcoatings.com**
Kick Eez **www.kickeezproducts.com**
Kidd Triggers **www.coolguyguns.com**
KM Tactical **www.kmtactical.net**
Knoxx Industries **www.impactguns.com**
Krieger Barrels **www.kriegerbarrels.com**
K-VAR Corp. **www.k-var.com**
LaRue Tactical **www.laruetactical.com**
Les Baer Custom, Inc. **www.lesbaer.com**
Lilja Barrels **www.riflebarrels.com**
Lone Wolf Dist. **www.lonewolfdist.com**
Lothar Walther Precision Tools **www.lothar-walther.de**
M&A Parts, Inc. **www.mapartsinc.com**
Magna-Matic Defense **www.magna-matic-defense.com**
Magpul Industries Corp. **www.magpul.com**
Majestic Arms **www.majesticarms.com**
MEC-GAR USA **www.mec-gar.com**
Mech Tech Systems **www.mechtechsys.com**
Mesa Tactical **www.mesatactical.com**
Midway USA **www.midwayusa.com**
Model 1 Sales **www.model1sales.com**
New England Custom Gun Service **www.newenglandcustomgun.com**
NIC Industries **www.nicindustries.com**
North Mfg. Co. **www.rifle-barrels.com**
Numrich Gun Parts Corp. **www.e-gunparts.com**
Osprey Defense LLC **www.gaspiston.com**
Pac-Nor Barrels **www.pac-nor.com**
Power Custom, Inc. **www.powercustom.com**

Precision Reflex **www.pri-mounts.com**
Promag Industries **www.promagindustries.com**
RCI-XRAIL **www.xrailbyrci.com**
Red Star Arms **www.redstararms.com**
River Bank Armory **www.riverbankarmory.com**
Riverman Gun Works **www.rivermangunworks.com**
Rock Creek Barrels **www.rockcreekbarrels.com**
Royal Arms Int'l **www.royalarms.com**
R.W. Hart **www.rwhart.com**
Sage Control Ordnance **www.sageinternationalltd.com**
Sarco Inc. **www.sarcoinc.com**
Scattergun Technologies Inc. **www.wilsoncombat.com**
Schuemann Barrels **www.schuemann.com**
Score High Gunsmithing **www.scorehi.com**
Shaw Barrels **www.ershawbarrels.com**
Shilen **www.shilen.com**
SilencerCo **www.silencerco.com**
Sims Vibration Laboratory **www.limbsaver.com**
Slide Fire **www.slidefire.com**
Smith & Alexander Inc. **www.smithandalexander.com**
Sprinco USA **www.sprinco.com**
Springfield Sporters, Inc. **www.ssporters.com**
STI Int'l **www.stiguns.com**
S&S Firearms **www.ssfirearms.com**
SSK Industries **www.sskindustries.com**
Sun Devil Mfg. **www.sundevilmfg.com**
Sunny Hill Enterprises **www.sunny-hill.com**
Tac Star **www.lymanproducts.com**
Tactical Innovations **www.tacticalinc.com**
Tactical Solutions **www.tacticalsol.com**
Tapco **www.tapco.com**
Triple K Manufacturing Co. Inc. **www.triplek.com**
Ultimak **www.ultimak.com**
Verney-Carron SA **www.verney-carron.com**
Vintage Ordnance **www.vintageordnance.com**
VItor Weapon Systems **www.vltor.com**
Volquartsen Custom Ltd. **www.volquartsen.com**
W.C. Wolff Co. **www.gunsprings.com**
Weigand Combat Handguns **www.jackweigand.com**
Western Gun Parts **www.westerngunparts.com**
Wilson Arms **www.wilsonarms.com**
Wilson Combat **www.wilsoncombat.com**
XLR Industries **www.xlrindustries.com**

GUNSMITHING SUPPLIES AND INSTRUCTION

4-D Products **www.4-dproducts.com**
American Gunsmithing Institute
www.americangunsmith.com
Baron Technology **www.baronengraving.com**
Battenfeld Technologies **www.btibrands.com**
Bellm TC's **www.bellmtcs.com**
Blue Ridge Machinery & Tools
www.blueridgemachinery.com
Brownells, Inc. **www.brownells.com**
B-Square Co. **www.b-square.com**
Cerakote Firearm Coatings **www.ncindustries.com**
Clymer Mfg. Co. **www.clymertool.com**
Dem-Bart **www.dembartco.com**
Doug Turnbull Restoration **www.turnbullrestoration.com**
Du-Lite Corp. **www.dulite.com**
DuraCoat Firearm Finishes **www.lauerweaponry.com**
Dvorak Instruments **www.dvorakinstruments.com**
Gradiant Lens Corp. **www.gradientlens.com**
Grizzly Industrial **www.grizzly.com**
Gunline Tools **www.gunline.com**
Harbor Freight **www.harborfreight.com**
JGS Precision Tool Mfg. LLC **www.jgstools.com**
Mag-Na-Port International **www.magnaport.com**
Manson Precision Reamers **www.mansonreamers.com**
Midway USA **www.midwayusa.com**
Murray State College **www.mscok.edu**
New England Custom Gun Service
www.newenglandcustomgun.com
Olympus America Inc. **www.olympus.com**
Pacific Tool & Gauge **www.pacifictoolandgauge.com**
Penn Foster Career School **www.pennfoster.edu**
Pennsylvania Gunsmith School **www.pagunsmith.edu**
Piedmont Community College **www.piedmontcc.edu**
Precision Metalsmiths, Inc.
www.precisionmetalsmiths.com
Sonoran Desert Institute **www.sdi.edu**
Trinidad State Junior College **www.trinidadstate.edu**

HANDGUN GRIPS

Ajax Custom Grips, Inc. **www.ajaxgrips.com**
Altamont Co. **www.altamontco.com**
Aluma Grips **www.alumagrips.com**
Barami Corp. **www.hipgrip.com**
Crimson Trace Corp. **www.crimsontrace.com**
Decal Grip **www.decalgrip.com**
Eagle Grips **www.eaglegrips.com**
Falcon Industries **www.ergogrips.net**
Handgun Grips **www.handgungrips.com**
Herrett's Stocks **www.herrettstocks.com**
Hogue Grips **www.hogueinc.com**
Kirk Ratajesak **www.kgratajesak.com**
N.C. Ordnance **www.gungrip.com**
Nill-Grips USA **www.nill-grips.com**
Pachmayr **www.pachmayr.com**

Pearce Grips **www.pearcegrip.com**
Rio Grande Custom Grips **www.riograndecustomgrips.com**
Talon Grips **www.talongrips.com**
Uncle Mike's **www.unclemikes.com**

HOLSTERS AND LEATHER PRODUCTS

Active Pro Gear **www.activeprogear.com**
Akah **www.akah.de**
Aker Leather Products **www.akerleather.com**
Alessi Distributor R&F Inc. **www.alessigunholsters.com**
Alien Gear Holsters **www.aliengearholsters.com**
Armor Holdings **www.holsters.com**
Bagmaster **www.bagmaster.com**
Barranti Leather **www.barrantileather.com**
Bianchi International **www.safariland.com/our-brands/bianchi**
Black Dog Machine **www.blackdogmachinellc.net**
Blackhawk Outdoors **www.blackhawk.com**
Blackhills Leather **www.blackhillsleather.com**
Boyt Harness Co. **www.boytharness.com**
Bravo Concealment **www.bravoconcealment.com**
Brigade Gun Leather **www.brigadegunleather.com**
Clipdraw **www.clipdraw.com**
Comp-Tac Victory Gear **www.comp-tac.com**
Concealed Carrie **www.concealedcarrie.com**
Concealment Shop Inc. **www.theconcealmentshop.com**
Coronado Leather Co. **www.coronadoleather.com**
Creedmoor Sports, Inc. **www.creedmoorsports.com**
Cross Breed Holsters **www.crossbreedholsters.com**
Deep Conceal **www.deepconceal.com**
Defense Security Products **www.thunderwear.com**
DeSantis Holster **www.desantisholster.com**
Dillon Precision **www.dillonprecision.com**
Don Hume Leathergoods, Inc. **www.donhume.com**
DSG Holsters **www.dssgarms.com**
Duty Smith **www.dutysmith.com**
Elite Survival **www.elitesurvival.com**
El Paso Saddlery **www.epsaddlery.com**
Fobus USA **www.fobusholster.com**
Frontier Gun Leather **www.frontiergunleather.com**
Galco **www.usgalco.com**
Gilmore's Sports Concepts **www.gilmoresports.com**
Gould & Goodrich **www.gouldusa.com**
High Noon Holsters **www.highnoonholsters.com**
Holsters.com **www.holsters.com**
Houston Gun Holsters **www.houstongunholsters.com**
Hunter Co. **www.huntercompany.com**
JBP/Master's Holsters **www.jbpholsters.com**
KJ Leather **www.kbarjleather.com**
KNJ **www.knjmfg.com**
Kramer Leather **www.kramerleather.com**
K-Rounds Holsters **www.krounds.com**
Mernickle Holsters **www.mernickleholsters.com**
Milt Sparks Leather **www.miltsparks.com**
Mitch Rosen Extraordinary Gunleather **www.mitchrosen.com**
N82 Tactical **www.n82tactical.com**
Pacific Canvas & Leather Co. **www.pacificcanvasandleather.com**
Pager Pal **www.pagerpal.com**
Phalanx Corp. **www.smartholster.com**
Purdy Gear **www.purdygear.com**
Safariland Ltd. Inc. **www.safariland.com**
Shooting Systems Group Inc. **www.shootingsystems.com**
Simply Rugged Holsters **www.simplyrugged.com**
Snagmag Magazine Holster **www.snagmag.com**
Sneaky Pete Holsters **www.sneakypete.com**
Skyline Tool Works **www.clipdraw.com**
Stellar Rigs **www.stellarrigs.com**
Talon Holsters **www.talonholsters.com**
Tex Shoemaker & Sons **www.texshoemaker.com**
The Outdoor Connection **www.outdoorconnection.com**
Tuff Products **www.tuffproducts.com**
Triple K Manufacturing Co. **www.triplek.com**
Urban Carry Holsters **www.urbancarryholsters.com**
Wilson Combat **www.wilsoncombat.com**
Wright Leatherworks **www.wrightleatherworks.com**

MISCELLANEOUS SHOOTING PRODUCTS

ADCO Sales **www.adcosales.com**
American Body Armor **www.americanbodyarmor.com**
AMI Defense **www.amidefense.com**
Ammo-Up **www.ammoupusa.com**
Battenfeld Technologies **www.btibrands.com**
Beartooth **www.beartoothproducts.com**
Burnham Brothers **www.burnhambrothers.com**
Collectors Armory **www.collectorsarmory.com**
Dead Ringer Hunting **www.deadringerhunting.com**
Deben Group Industries Inc. **www.deben.com**
E.A.R., Inc. **www.earinc.com**
ESP **www.espamerica.com**
Global Gun Safety **www.globalgunsafety.com**
GunSkins **www.gunskins.com**
Gunstands **www.gunstands.com**
Howard Leight Hearing Protectors **www.howardleight.com**
Hunters Specialities **www.hunterspec.com**
Johnny Stewart Wildlife Calls **www.hunterspec.com**
Joseph Chiarello Gun Insurance **www.guninsurance.com**
Mec-Gar USA **www.mec-gar.com**
Merit Corporation **www.meritcorporation.com**
Michaels of Oregon Co. **www.michaels-oregon.com**
Midway USA **www.midwayusa.com**
MT2, LLC **www.mt2.com**

MTM Case-Gard **www.mtmcase-gard.com**
Natchez Shooters Supplies **www.natchezss.com**
Oakley, Inc. **www.usstandardissue.com**
Plano Molding **www.planomolding.com**
Practical Air Rifle Training Systems **www.smallarms.com**
Pro-Ears **www.pro-ears.com**
Quantico Tactical **www.quanticotactical.com**
Santa Cruz Gunlocks **www.santacruzgunlocks.com**
Sergeants Gun Cleaner **www.sergeantsguncleaner.com**
Second Chance Body Armor Inc. **www.secondchance.com**
SilencerCo **www.silencerco.com**
Smart Lock Technologies **www.smartlock.com**
SportEAR **www.sportear.com**
Surefire **www.surefire.com**
Taser Int'l **www.taser.com**
Walker's Game Ear Inc. **www.walkersgameear.com**

MUZZLELOADING FIREARMS AND PRODUCTS

American Pioneer Powder **www.americanpioneerpowder.com**
Armi Sport **www.armisport.com**
Barnes Bullets **www.barnesbullets.com**
Black Powder Products **www.bpiguns.com**
Buckeye Barrels **www.buckeyebarrels.com**
Cabin Creek Muzzleloading **www.cabincreek.net**
CVA **www.cva.com**
Caywood Gunmakers **www.caywoodguns.com**
Davide Perdsoli & Co. **www.davide-pedersoli.com**
Dixie Gun Works, Inc. **www.dixiegun.com**
Goex Black Powder **www.goexpowder.com**
Green Mountain Rifle Barrel Co. **www.gmriflebarrel.com**
Gunstocks Plus **www.gunstocksplus.com**
Gun Works **www.thegunworks.com**
Honorable Company of Horners **www.hornguild.org**
Hornady **www.hornady.com**
Jedediah Starr Trading Co. **www.jedediah-starr.com**
Jim Chambers Flintlocks **www.flintlocks.com**
Knight Rifles **www.knightrifles.com**
Knob Mountain **www.knobmountainmuzzleloading.com**
The Leatherman **www.blackpowderbags.com**
Log Cabin Shop **www.logcabinshop.com**
L&R Lock Co. **www.lr-rpl.com**
Lyman **www.lymanproducts.com**
Muzzleload Magnum Products **www.mmpsabots.com**
Navy Arms **www.navyarms.com**
Nosler, Inc. **www.nosler.com**
Palmetto Arms **www.palmetto.it**
Parker Productions **www.parkerproductionsinc.com**
Pecatonica River **www.longrifles-pr.com**
Pietta **www.pietta.it**
Powerbelt Bullets **www.powerbeltbullets.com**
Precision Rifle Dead Center Bullets **www.prbullet.com**
R.E. Davis Co. **www.redaviscompany.com**
Rightnour Mfg. Co. Inc. **www.rmcsports.com**
Savage Arms, Inc. **www.savagearms.com**
Schuetzen Powder **www.schuetzenpowder.com**
TDC **www.tdcmfg.com**
Tennessee Valley Muzzleloading
www.tennesseevalleymuzzleloading.com
Thompson Center Arms **www.tcarms.com**
Tiger Hunt Stocks **www.gunstockwood.com**
Track of the Wolf **www.trackofthewolf.com**
Traditions Performance Muzzleloading **www.traditionsfirearms. com**
Turnbull Restoration & Mfg. **www.turnbullmfg.com**
Vernon C. Davis & Co. **www.stonewallcreekoutfitters.com**

PUBLICATIONS, VIDEOS AND CDs

Arms and Military Press **www.skennerton.com**
A&J Arms Booksellers **www.ajarmsbooksellers.com**
American Cop **www.americancopmagazine.com**
American Gunsmithing Institute **www.americangunsmith.com**
American Handgunner **www.americanhandgunner.com**
American Hunter **www.nrapublications.org**
American Pioneer Video **www.americanpioneervideo.com**
American Rifleman **www.nrapublications.org**
Athlon Outdoors **www.athlonoptics.com**
Backwoodsman **www.backwoodsmanmag.com**
BLADE Magazine **www.blademag.com**
Blue Book Publications **www.bluebookinc.com**
Combat Handguns **www.combathandguns.com**
Concealed Carry **www.uscca.us**
Cornell Publications **www.cornellpubs.com**
Deer & Deer Hunting **www.deeranddeerhunting.com**
Field & Stream **www.fieldandstream.com**
Firearms News **www.firearmsnews.com**
FMG Publications **www.fmgpubs.com**
Fouling Shot **www.castbulletassoc.org**
Fur-Fish-Game **www.furfishgame.com**
George Shumway Publisher **www.shumwaypublisher.com**
Grays Sporting Journal **www.grayssportingjournal.com**
Gun Digest, The Magazine **www.gundigest.com**
Gun Digest Books **www.gundigeststore.com**
Gun Dog **www.gundogmag.com**
Gun Mag **www.thegunmag.com**
Gun Tests **www.gun-tests.com**
Gun Video **www.gunvideo.com**
Gun World **www.gunworld.com**
Guns & Ammo **www.gunsandammo.com**
GUNS Magazine **www.gunsmagazine.com**
Guns of the Old West **www.gunsoftheoldwest.com**

Handloader **www.riflemagazine.com**
Handguns **www.handguns.com**
Hendon Publishing Co. **www.hendonpub.com**
Heritage Gun Books **www.gunbooks.com**
Krause Publications **www.krause.com**
Law and Order **www.hendonpub.com**
Man at Arms **www.manatarmsbooks.com**
Muzzle Blasts **www.nmlra.org**
Muzzleloader **www.muzzleloadermag.com**
North American Whitetail **www.northamericanwhitetail.com**
On-Target Productions **www.ontargetdvds.com**
Outdoor Channel **www.outdoorchannel.com**
Outdoor Life **www.outdoorlife.com**
Petersen's Hunting **www.petersenshunting.com**
Police and Security News **www.policeandsecuritynews.com**
Police Magazine **www.policemag.com**
Primitive Arts Video **www.primitiveartsvideo.com**
Pursuit Channel **www.pursuitchannel.com**
Recoil Gun Magazine **www.recoilweb.com**
Rifle Magazine **www.riflemagazine.com**
Rifle Shooter Magazine **www.rifleshootermag.com**
Safari Press Inc. **www.safaripress.com**
Shoot! Magazine **www.shootmagazine.com**
Shooting Illustrated **www.nrapublications.org**
Shooting Industry **www.shootingindustry.com**
Shooting Times Magazine **www.shootingtimes.com**
Shooting Sports Retailer **www.shootingsportsretailer.com**
Shooting Sports USA **www.nrapublications.org**
Shop Deer Hunting **www.shopdeerhunting.com**
Shotgun Report **www.shotgunreport.com**
Shotgun Sports Magazine **www.shotgunsportsmagazine.com**
Single Shot Exchange **www.singleshotexchange.com**
Single Shot Rifle Journal **www.assra.com**
Skyhorse Publishing **www.skyhorsepublishing.com**
Small Arms Review **www.smallarmsreview.com**
Sporting Classics **www.sportingclassics.com**
Sports Afield **www.sportsafield.com**
Sportsman Channel **www.thesportsmanchannel.com**
Sportsmen on Film **www.sportsmenonfilm.com**
Standard Catalog of Firearms **www.gundigeststore.com**
Successful Hunter **www.riflemagazine.com**
SWAT Magazine **www.swatmag.com**
Trapper & Predator Caller **www.trapperpredatorcaller.com**
Turkey & Turkey Hunting **www.turkeyandturkeyhunting.com**
Varmint Hunter **www.varminthunter.com**
VSP Publications **www.gunbooks.com**
Wildfowl **www.wildfowlmag.com**

RELOADING TOOLS

21st Century Shooting **www.xxicsi.com**
Ballisti-Cast Mfg. **www.ballisti-cast.com**
Battenfeld Technologies **www.btibrands.com**
Black Hills Shooters Supply **www.bhshooters.com**
Bruno Shooters Supply **www.brunoshooters.com**
Buffalo Arms **www.buffaloarms.com**
CabineTree **www.castingstuff.com**
Camdex, Inc. **www.camdexloader.com**
CH/4D Custom Die **www.ch4d.com**
Corbin Mfg & Supply Co. **www.corbins.com**
Dillon Precision **www.dillonprecision.com**
Forster Precision Products **www.forsterproducts.com**
Gracey Trimmer **www.matchprep.com**
Harrell's Precision **www.harrellsprec.com**
Hornady **www.hornady.com**
Hunter's Supply, Inc. **wwwhunters-supply.com**
Huntington Reloading Products **www.huntingtons.com**
J & J Products Co. **www.jandjproducts.com**
Lead Bullet Technology **www.lbtmoulds.com**
Lee Precision, Inc. **www.leeprecision.com**
L.E. Wilson **www.lewilson.com**
Little Crow Gun Works **www.littlecrowgunworks.com**
Littleton Shotmaker **www.littletonshotmaker.com**
Load Data **www.loaddata.com**
Lyman **www.lymanproducts.com**
Mayville Engineering Co. (MEC) **www.mecreloaders.com**
Midway USA **www.midwayusa.com**
Montana Bullet Works **www.montanabulletworks.com**
NECO **www.neconos.com**
NEI **www.neihandtools.com**
Neil Jones Custom Products **www.neiljones.com**
New Lachaussee SA **www.lachaussee.com**
Ponsness/Warren **www.reloaders.com**
Precision Reloading **www.precisionreloading.com**
Quinetics Corp. **www.quineticscorp.com**
RCBS **www.rcbs.com**
Redding Reloading Equipment **www.redding-reloading.com**
Sinclair Int'l Inc. **www.sinclairintl.com**
Stealth Gunpowder **www.stealthgunpowder.com**
Stoney Point Products Inc. **www.stoneypoint.com**
Vickerman Seating Die **www.castingstuff.com**

RESTS— BENCH, PORTABLE, ATTACHABLE

Accu-Shot **www.accu-shot.com**
Battenfeld Technologies **www.btibrands.com**
Bench Master **www.bench-master.com**
B-Square **www.b-square.com**
Center Mass, Inc. **www.centermassinc.com**
Desert Mountain Mfg. **www.benchmasterusa.com**
DOA Tactical **www.doatactical.com**

Harris Engineering Inc. **www.harrisbipods**
KFS Industries **www.versapod.com**
Level-Lok **www.levellok.com**
Midway **www.midwayusa.com**
Rotary Gun Racks **www.gun-racks.com**
R.W. Hart **www.rwhart.com**
Sinclair Intl, Inc. **www.sinclairintl.com**
Shooting Bench USA **www.shootingbenchusa.com**
Stoney Point Products **www.stoneypoint.com**
Target Shooting **www.targetshooting.com**

SCOPES, SIGHTS, MOUNTS AND ACCESSORIES

Accumount **www.accumounts.com**
Accusight **www.accusight.com**
Advantage Tactical Sight **www.advantagetactical.com**
Aimpoint **www.aimpoint.com**
Aim Shot, Inc. **www.aimshot.com**
Aimtech Mount Systems **www.aimtech-mounts.com**
Alaska Arms, LLC **https://alaskaarmsllc.com**
Alpen Outdoor Corp. **www.alpenoutdoor.com**
American Technologies Network, Corp. **www.atncorp.com**
AmeriGlo, LLC **www.ameriglo.net**
ArmaLaser **www.armalaser.com**
Amerigun USA **www.amerigunusa.com**
Armament Technology, Inc. **www.armament.com**
ARMS **www.armsmounts.com**
Athlon Optics **www.athlonoptics.com**
ATN **www.atncorp.com**
Badger Ordnance **www.badgerordnance.com**
Barrett **www.barrettrifles.com**
Beamshot-Quarton **www.beamshot.com**
BKL Technologies, Inc. **www.bkltech.com**
BSA Optics **www.bsaoptics.com**
B-Square **www.b-square.com**
Burris **www.burrisoptics.com**
Bushnell Performance Optics **www.bushnell.com**
Carl Zeiss Optical Inc. **www.zeiss.com**
CenterPoint Precision Optics **www.centerpointoptics.com**
Centurion Arms **www.centurionarms.com**
C-More Systems **www.cmore.com**
Conetrol Scope Mounts **www.conetrol.com**
Crimson Trace Corp. **www.crimsontrace.com**
D&L Sports **www.disports.com**
DuraSight Scope Mounting Systems **www.durasight.com**
EasyHit, Inc. **www.easyhit.com**
EAW **www.eaw.de**
Elcan Optical Technologies **www.elcan. com**
Electro-Optics Technologies **www.eotech.com**
Elusive Technologies **www.elusivetechnologies.com**
EoTech **www.eotechinc.com**
Eurooptik Ltd. **www.eurooptik.com**
Field Sport Inc. **www.fieldsportinc.com**
GG&G **www.gggaz.com**
Gilmore Sports **www.gilmoresports.com**
Gradient Lens Corp. **www.gradientlens.com**
Guangzhou Bosma Corp. **www.bosmaoptics.com**
Hahn Precision **www.hahn-precision.com**
Hi-Lux Optics **www.hi-luxoptics.com**
HIVIZ **www.hivizsights.com**
Horus Vision **www.horusvision.com**
Huskemaw Optics **www.huskemawoptics.com**
Insight **www.insighttechnology.com**
Ironsighter Co. **www.ironsighter.com**
Kahles **www.kahlesusa.com**
KenSight **www.kensight.com**
Knight's Armament **www.knightarmco.com**
Konus **www.konus.com**
LaRue Tactical **www.laruetactical.com**
Lasergrips **www.crimsontrace.com**
LaserLyte **www.laserlytesights.com**
LaserMax Inc. **www.lasermax.com**
Laser Products **www.surefire.com**
Leapers, Inc. **www.leapers.com**
Leatherwood **www.hi-luxoptics.com**
Leica Camera Inc. **www.leica-camera.com**
Leupold **www.leupold.com**
Lewis Machine and Tool **www.lmtdefense.com**
Lewis Machine & Tool **www.lewismachine.net**
LightForce/NightForce USA **www.nightforceoptics.com**
LUCID LLC **www.mylucidgear.com**
Lyman **www.lymanproducts.com**
Lynx **www.b-square.com**
Matech **www.matech.net**
Marble's Gunsights **www.marblearms.com**
Meopta **www.meopta.com**
Meprolight **www.meprolight.com**
Mini-Scout-Mount **www.amegaranges.com**
Minox USA **www.minox.com**
Montana Vintage Arms **www.montanavintagearms.com**
Mounting Solutions Plus **www.mountsplus.com**
NAIT **www.nait.com**
Newcon International Ltd. **www.newcon-optik.com**
NG2 Defense **www.ng2defense.com**
Night Force Optics **www.nightforceoptics.com**
Night Ops Tactical **www.nightopstactical.com**
Night Optics USA, Inc. **www.nightoptics.com**
Night Owl Optics **www.nightowloptics.com**
Nikon Inc. **www.nikonhunting.com**
Nitehog **www.nitehog.com**
Nite Site LLC **www.darkwidowgear.com**

North American Integrated Technologies **www.nait.com**
Novak Sights **www.novaksights.com**
O.K. Weber, Inc. **www.okweber.com**
Optolyth-Optic **www.optolyth.de**
Precision Reflex **www.pri-mounts.com**
Pride Fowler, Inc. **www.rapidreticle.com**
Redfield **www.redfield.com**
Schmidt & Bender **www.schmidtundbender.de**
Scopecoat **www.scopecoat.com**
Scopelevel **www.scopelevel.com**
SIG Sauer **www.sigsauer.com**
Sightmark **www.sightmark.com**
Simmons **www.simmonsoptics.com**
S&K **www.scopemounts.com**
Springfield Armory **www.springfield-armory.com**
Steiner Optik **www.steiner-optics.com**
Sun Optics USA **www.sunopticsusa.com**
Sure-Fire **www.surefire.com**
SWATSCOPE **www.swatscope.com**
Talley Mfg. Co. **www.talleyrings.com**
Steve Earle Scope Blocks **www.steveearleproducts.com**
Swarovski Optik **www.swarovskioptik.com**
Tacomhq **www.tacomhq.com**
Tasco **www.tasco.com**
Tech Sights **www.tech-sights.com**
Trijicon Inc. **www.trijicon.com**
Trinity Force **www.trinityforce.com**
Troy Industries **www.troyind.com**
Truglo Inc. **www.truglo.com**
Ultimak **www.ultimak.com**
UltraDot **www.ultradotusa.com**
U.S. Night Vision **www.usnightvision.com**
U.S. Optics Technologies Inc. **www.usoptics.com**
Valdada-IOR Optics **www.valdada.com**
Viridian Green Laser Sights **www.viridiangreenlaser.com**
Vortex Optics **www.vortexoptics.com**
Warne **www.warnescopemounts.com**
Weaver Scopes **www.weaveroptics.com**
Wilcox Industries Corp **www.wilcoxind.com**
Williams Gun Sight Co. **www.williamsgunsight.com**
Wilson Combat **www.wilsoncombat.com**
XS Sight Systems **www.xssights.com**
Zeiss **www.zeiss.com**

SHOOTING ORGANIZATIONS, SCHOOLS AND MUSEUMS

Accuracy 1st, Inc. **www.accuracy1st.com**
Amateur Trapshooting Assoc. **www.shootata.com**
American Custom Gunmakers Guild **www.acgg.org**
American Gunsmithing Institute **www.americangunsmith.com**
American Pistolsmiths Guild **www.americanpistol.com**
American Single Shot Rifle Assoc. **www.assra.com**
American Snipers **www.americansnipers.org**
Assoc. of Firearm & Tool Mark Examiners **www.afte.org**
Autry National Center of the American West **www.theautry.org**
BATFE **www.atf.gov**
Boone and Crockett Club **www.boone-crockett.org**
Browning Collectors Association **www.browningcollectors.com**
Buffalo Bill Center of the West **www.centerofthewest.org**
Buckmasters, Ltd. **www.buckmasters.com**
Cast Bullet Assoc. **www.castbulletassoc.org**
Citizens Committee for the Right to Keep & Bear Arms **www. ccrkba.org**
Civilian Marksmanship Program **www.odcmp.com**
Colorado School of Trades **www.schooloftrades.edu**
Contemporary Longrifle Assoc. **www.longrifle.com**
Colt Collectors Assoc. **www.coltcollectors.com**
Cylinder & Slide Pistolsmithing Schools **www.cylinder-slide. com**
Ducks Unlimited **www.ducks.org**
4-H Shooting Sports Program **www.4-hshootingsports.org**
Fifty Caliber Shooters Assoc. **www.fcsa.org**
Firearms Coalition **www.nealknox.com**
Fox Collectors Association **www.foxcollectors.com**
Front Sight Firearms Training Institute **www.frontsight.com**
Garand Collectors Assoc. **www.thegca.org**
German Gun Collectors Assoc. **www.germanguns.com**
Gibbs Military Collectors Club **www.gibbsrifle.com**
Gun Clubs **www.associatedgunclubs.org**
Gun Owners Action League **www.goal.org**
Gun Owners of America **www.gunowners.org**
Gun Trade Asssoc. Ltd. **www.gtaltd.co.uk**
Gunsite Training Center, Inc. **www.gunsite.com**
Hunting and Shooting Sports Heritage Fund **www.hsshf.org**
I.C.E. Training **www.icetraining.us**
International Ammunition Assoc. **www.cartridgecollectors.org**
IWA **www.iwa.info**
International Defensive Pistol Assoc. **www.idpa.com**
International Handgun Metallic Silhouette Assoc. **www.ihmsa.org**
International Hunter Education Assoc. **www.ihea.com**
International Single Shot Assoc. **www.issa-schuetzen.org**
Ithaca Owners **www.ithacaowners.com**
Jews for the Preservation of Firearms Ownership **www.jpfo.org**
L.C. Smith Collectors Assoc. **www.lcsmith.org**
Lefever Arms Collectors Assoc. **www.lefevercollectors.com**
Mannlicher Collectors Assoc. **www.mannlicher.org**
Marlin Firearms Collectors Assoc. **www.marlin-collectors.com**
Mule Deer Foundation **www.muledeer.org**
Muzzle Loaders Assoc. of Great Britain **www.mlagb.com**
National 4-H Shooting Sports **www.4-hshootingsports.org**
National Association of Sporting Goods Wholesalers **www.nasgw.org**

National Benchrest Shooters Assoc. **www.nbrsa.com**
National Defense Industrial Assoc. **www.ndia.org**
National Cowboy & Western Heritage Museum
www.nationalcowboymuseum.org
National Firearms Museum **www.nramuseum.org**
National Mossberg Collectors Assoc.
www.mossbergcollectors.org
National Muzzle Loading Rifle Assoc. **www.nmlra.org**
National Rifle Association **www.nra.org**
National Rifle Association ILA **www.nraila.org**
National Shooting Sports Foundation **www.nssf.org**
National Tactical Officers Assoc. **www.ntoa.org**
National Wild Turkey Federation **www.nwtf.com**
NICS/FBI **www.fbi.gov**
North American Hunting Club **www.huntingclub.com**
Order of Edwardian Gunners (Vintagers) **www.vintagers.org**
Outdoor Industry Foundation
www.outdoorindustryfoundation.org
Parker Gun Collectors Assoc. **www.parkerguns.org**
Pennsylvania Gunsmith School **www.pagunsmith.com**
Pheasants Forever **www.pheasantsforever.org**
Piedmont Community College **www.piedmontcc.edu**
Quail & Upland Wildlife Federation **www.quwf.net**
Quail Forever **www.quailforever.org**
Remington Society of America **www.remingtonsociety.com**
Right To Keep and Bear Arms **www.rkba.org**
Rocky Mountain Elk Foundation **www.rmef.org**
Ruffed Grouse Society **www.ruffedgrousesociety.org**
Ruger Collectors Assoc. **www.rugercollectorsassociation.com**
Ruger Owners & Collectors Society **www.rugersociety.com**
SAAMI **www.saami.org**
Safari Club International **www.scifirstforhunters.org**
Sako Collectors Club **www.sakocollectors.com**
Scholastic Clay Target Program
www.sssfonline.org/scholasti-clay-target-program
Scholastic Shooting Sports Foundation **www.sssfonline.org**
Second Amendment Foundation **www.saf.org**
Shooting for Women Alliance
www.shootingforwomenalliance. com
Sig Sauer Academy **www.sigsauer.com**
Single Action Shooting Society **www.sassnet.com**
Smith & Wesson Collectors Assoc. **www.theswca.org**
L.C. Smith Collectors Assoc. **www.lcsmith.org**
Steel Challenge Pistol Tournament **www.steelchallenge.com**
Students for Second Amendment **www.sf2a.org**
Sturgis Economic Development Corp.
www.sturgisdevelopment.com
Suarez Training **www.warriortalk.com**
Tactical Defense Institute **www.tdiohio.com**
Tactical Life **www.tactical-life.com**
Thompson/Center Assoc.
www.thompsoncenterassociation.org
Thunder Ranch **www.thunderranchinc.com**
Trapshooters Homepage **www.trapshooters.com**
Trinidad State Junior College **www.trinidadstate.edu**
United Sportsmen's Youth Foundation **www.usyf.com**
Universal Shooting Academy
www.universalshootingacademy.com
U.S. Concealed Carry Association **www.uscca.us**
U.S. Fish and Wildlife Service **www.fws.gov**
U.S. Practical Shooting Assoc. **www.uspsa.org**
U.S. Sportsmen's Alliance **www.ussportsmen.org**
USA Shooting **www.usashooting.com**
Weatherby Collectors Assoc. **www.weatherbycollectors.com**
Wild Sheep Foundation **www.wildsheepfoundation.org**
Winchester Arms Collectors Assoc.
www.winchestercollector.com

STOCKS, GRIPS, FORE-ENDS

10/22 Fun Gun **www.1022fungun.com**
Advanced Technology **www.atigunstocks.com**
AG Composites **www.agcomposites.com**
Battenfeld Technologies **www.btibrands.com**
Bell & Carlson, Inc. **www.bellandcarlson.com**
Butler Creek Corp **www.butlercreek.com**
Cadex **www.vikingtactics.com**
Calico Hardwoods, Inc. **www.calicohardwoods.com**
Choate Machine **www.riflestock.com**
Command Arms **www.commandarms.com**
C-More Systems **www.cmore.com**
D&L Sports **www.dlsports.com**
E. Arthur Brown Co. **www.eabco.com**
Fajen **www.battenfeldtechnologies.com**
Grip Pod **www.grippod.com**
Gun Stock Blanks **www.gunstockblanks.com**
Herrett's Stocks **www.herrettstocks.com**
High Tech Specialties **www.hightech-specialties.com**
Hogue Grips **www.getgrip.com**
Knight's Mfg. Co. **wwwknightarmco.com**
Knoxx Industries **www.blackhawk.com**
KZ Tactical **www.kleyzion.com**
LaRue Tactical **www.laruetactical.com**
Lewis Machine & Tool **www.lewismachine.net**
Magpul **www.magpul.com**
Manners Composite Stocks **www.mannersstocks.com**
McMillan Fiberglass Stocks **www.mcmfamily.com**
Phoenix Technology/Kicklite **www.kicklitestocks.com**
Precision Gun Works **www.precisiongunstocks.com**
Ram-Line **www.outers-guncare.com**
Richards Microfit Stocks **www.rifle-stocks.com**
Rimrock Rifle Stock **www.bordenrifles.com**

Royal Arms Gunstocks **www.royalarmsgunstocks.com**
Speedfeed **www.safariland.com**
Tango Down **www.tangodown.com**
TAPCO **www.tapco.com**
Slide Fire **www.slidefire.com**
Stocky's **www.stockysstocks.com**
Surefire **www.surefire.com**
Tiger-Hunt Curly Maple Gunstocks **www.gunstockwood.com**
UTG Pro **www.leapers.com**
Wenig Custom Gunstocks Inc. **www.wenig.com**
Wilcox Industries **www.wilcoxind.com**
Yankee Hill **www.yhm.net**

TARGETS AND RANGE EQUIPMENT

Action Target Co. **www.actiontarget.com**
Advanced Training Systems **www.atsusa.biz**
Alco Target **www.alcotarget.com**
Arntzen Targets **www.arntzentargets.com**
Birchwood Casey **www.birchwoodcasey.com**
Caswell Meggitt Defense Systems **www.mds-caswell.com**
Champion Traps & Targets **www.championtarget.com**
Custom Metal Products **www.custommetalprod.com**
Laser Shot **www.lasershot.com**
MGM Targets **www.mgmtargets.com**
MTM Products **www.mtmcase-gard.com**
National Muzzleloading Rifle Assoc. **www.nmlra.org**
National Target Co. **www.nationaltarget.com**
Newbold Target Systems **www.newboldtargets.com**
Paragon Tactical **www.paragontactical.com**
PJL Targets **www.pjltargets.com**
Savage Range Systems **www.savagerangesystems.com**
ShatterBlast Targets **www.daisy.com**
Super Trap Bullet Containment Systems **www.supertrap.com**
Thompson Target Technology **www.thompsontarget.com**
Thundershot Exploding Targets **www.gryphonenergetics.com**
Unique Tek **www.uniquetek.com**
Visible Impact Targets **www.crosman.com**
White Flyer **www.whiteflyer.com**

TRAP AND SKEET SHOOTING EQUIPMENT AND ACCESSORIES

Atlas Trap Co **www.atlastraps.com**
Auto-Sporter Industries **www.auto-sporter.com**
Do-All Traps, Inc. **www.doalloutdoors.com**
Gamaliel Shooting Supply **www.gamaliel.com**
Howell Shooting Supplies **www.howellshootingsupplies.com**
Promatic, Inc. **www.promatic.biz**
White Flyer **www.whiteflyer.com**

TRIGGERS

American Trigger Corp. **www.americantrigger.com**
Brownells **www.brownells.com**
Geissele Automatics **https://geissele.com**
Huber Concepts **www.huberconcepts.com**
Jard, Inc. **www.jardinc.com**
Kidd Triggers **www.coolguyguns.com**
Shilen **www.shilen.com**
Spec-Tech Industries, Inc. **www.spec-tech-industries.com**
Timney Triggers **www.timneytriggers.com**
Williams Trigger Specialties **www.williamstriggers.com**

MAJOR SHOOTING WEBSITES AND LINKS

24 Hour Campfire **www.24hourcampfire.com**
Accurate Shooter **www.6mmbr.com**
Alphabetic Index of Links **www.gunsgunsguns.com**
Ammo Guide **www.ammoguide.com**
Auction Arms **www.auctionarms.com**
Benchrest Central **www.benchrest.com**
Big Game Hunt **www.biggamehunt.net**
Bullseye Pistol **www.bullseyepistol.com**
Firearms History **www.researchpress.co.uk**
Glock Talk **www.glocktalk.com**
Gun Broker Auctions **www.gunbroker.com**
Gun Blast **www.gunblast.com**
Gun Boards **www.gunboards.com**
Gun Digest **www. gundigest.com**
Gun Digest Gun Values **https://gunvalues.gundigest.com**
Guns & Ammo Forum **www.gunsandammo.com**
GunsAmerica **www.gunsamerica.com**
Gun Shop Finder **www.gunshopfinder.com**
Guns and Hunting **www.gunsandhunting.com**
Hunt and Shoot (NSSF) **www.huntandshoot.org**
Keep and Bear Arms **www.keepandbeararms.com**
Leverguns **www.leverguns.com**
Load Swap **www.loadswap.com**
Long Range Hunting **www.longrangehunting.com**
Real Guns **www.realguns.com**
Ruger Forum **www.rugerforum.com**
Savage Shooters **www.savageshooters.com**
Shooters Forum **www.shootersforum.com**
Shotgun Sports Resource Guide **www.shotgunsports.com**
Shotgun World **www.shotgunworld.com**
Sniper's Hide **www.snipershide.com**
Sportsman's Web **www.sportsmansweb.com**
Tactical-Life **www.tactical-life.com**